CW00542040

Rock'n'Roll Unravelled

Rock'n'Roll Unravelled

A unique three part take on the history of Rock 'n' Roll
From rock'n'roll's roots to mid-1970s punk

Timeline

What Happened Today?

Pocket Histories

With the world events that shaped the sounds ...
Vietnam War – Civil Rights Movement – Cold War +++

The music ...The people ...The Events ...The Influences

Derek Shelmerdine

Published by DCA Rock'n'Roll Ltd

www.rocknrollunravelled.com

A CIP catalogue record for this book is available from the British Library.

ISBN 978-0-9935894-0-9

Book layout and cover design by Clare Brayshaw

Cover image © Ba-mi | Dreamstime.com

Prepared and printed by:

York Publishing Services Ltd
64 Hallfield Road
Layerthorpe
York YO31 7ZQ

Tel: 01904 431213

Website: www.yps-publishing.co.uk

Contents

Introduction

Rock'n'Roll Unravelled tells the story of rock'n'roll, from its roots in blues, jazz, folk, rockabilly, country music and R&B, up until the mid-1970s when punk rock turned the music full circle and returned to simple songs played in small, intimate venues. The music scene is presented in juxtaposition with social and political events, showing how music was influenced by events of the day. The Civil Rights Movement and the Vietnam War helped to shape the music of the 1950s and '60s. In addition to those landmarks, there are many other events that provide a flavour of the times, including the *Berlin Airlift* (25 June 1948), the *Bay of Pigs* invasion of Cuba (15 April 1961), the *Cuban Missile Crisis* (17 October 1962), Mods and Rockers battling it out on England's beaches (28 March 1964), the march to mourn the "death of Hippie" (6 October 1967), Enoch Powell's "rivers of blood" speech (20 April 1968), and many, many more.

Rock'n'Roll emerged in the mid-1950s and continued to develop across the 1960s and '70s. By the mid-1970s not all of rock'n'roll's diversity was welcomed by the fans. Prog-rock bands were turning out albums with a single track taking up a whole side and delivering live guitar solos that went on for twenty minutes or more. Big business was taking over the industry and popular bands were playing in larger and larger venues. This all combined to herald rock'n'roll's counter-revolution – punk rock. The nature of the music had also changed. In the 1950s songs were mostly about young love, whereas twenty years on, punk was far more concerned with political anarchy. The punk bands took their frenetically paced rock'n'roll back to small clubs and three-chord, two-minute songs that captured the very essence of early rock'n'roll.

The Sex Pistols were the poster boys for the genre and epitomised punk's cynical and anarchic philosophy. Hence, their last concert is taken as my end-point for introducing new artists into *Rock'n'Roll Unravelled*. Events are listed after that date but only for people and bands that were active before the Pistols' swan song on 14 January 1978.

Rock'n'Roll Unravelled is divided into three sections:

Part 1: Timeline

Presents the *What Happened Today?* stories in chronological order.

Part 2: What Happened Today?

A day-by-day look at the story of rock'n'roll and the events that shaped it.

Part 3: Pocket Histories

Cross-references people, bands and events in *What Happened Today?*

Part 1: Timeline

The *Timeline* gives a chronological perspective for all of the events in Part 2, *What Happened Today?* The *Timeline* also makes it possible to read between rock'n'roll's lines, to see how the music was developing and how it was being influenced.

Shows musical trends

It can be seen how the music scene was dominated by America in the 1950s and how this shifted towards the prominence of British beat groups in the early 1960s. This reached its peak with the British Invasion in the mid-1960s. A time when American bands even took to adopting British sounding names in order to try and get a look in. Before finding fame as "The Byrds" the group tried their hand as "The Beefeaters".

Few events can signify the passing of one genre to the next better than two festivals held in New York in 1975. The *War Is Over* rally, on 11 May, signified the end of the Vietnam War. One of the last of the baby-boomer events. Just two months later, on 16 July, the *Top 40 New York Unrecorded Rock Bands* festival at the CBGB club heralded punk rock and the new Generation X.

Provides a soundtrack to the era

Many of the most significant albums and singles are included, with additional information about writers, covers and originals. It also shows record releases in the context of their times and other artists' output. With the ease of access to music nowadays, there has never been a better time to listen to old favourites or discover new songs. Having read the background to these recordings, the well-known ones might well be heard with a new appreciation of their significance and the new songs listened to with the knowledge of how they helped to shape the story of rock'n'roll.

Answers the question – What else was happening when...?

The Beatles released *Love Me Do* on 5 October 1962. The three months following this British release date saw some interesting events: Little Richard's rock'n'roll comeback (12 October); a one-brother Everly Brothers tour of the UK (13 October); the *Cuban Missile Crisis*, which very nearly started World War III and the prospect of nuclear annihilation (17 October); Bill Wyman auditioned for the Rolling Stones (7 December); and Bob Dylan released his debut single in America (14 December).

Part 2: What Happened Today?

Set in a day-by-day, January to December, format, this section recounts gigs, record releases, recording sessions, band backgrounds, birthdays, deaths, festivals, movies, 'lost' albums, failed auditions, famous rock'n'roll events, such as Led Zeppelin's notorious *Mud Shark Incident* (28 July 1969), and much more.

The music of the 1960s continued to build on the influences that had preceded it. Of the many examples of cover versions and originals, *Dust My Broom* shows how the music was evolving. Recorded by Robert Johnson as *I Believe I'll Dust My Broom* on 23 November 1936, it was reworked by Elmore James as *Dust My Broom* in 1951 and went on to become the staple diet of 1960s R&B groups. These music stories are augmented by other events, such as assassinations, wars, demonstrations and social changes, all helping to mould the sound of rock'n'roll.

Part 3: Pocket Histories

The information in *What Happened Today?* is comprehensively cross-referenced to provide a history for individuals, bands and events.

As well as the original story, *Pocket Histories* elaborates to provide additional information around the event. For instance, the lineup information is often augmented with an insight as to where a musician came from or went to. For some of the titans of the music industry, the Beatles, Stones, Doors and others, their histories start with a look at how the various band members came together. *Pocket Histories* contains a wealth of additional information, about people, bands and music. Recordings and releases are often garnished with extra background about writers, covers and original versions.

Events which are not concerned with the music of the era are grouped together under topic headings such as: *Vietnam War*, *Civil Rights Movement* and *What's Going On*. Some of the more weird and wonderful musical activities have also been brought together, with topics including: *Rock'n'Roll High Jinks and Mayhem*, *Failed Auditions and 'Lost' Albums*, and *Plagiarism, Litigation, Murder and Suicide*.

Author's Note

Rock'n'Roll Unravelled has been a labour of love and is the culmination of over seven years of extensive research. I should like to take this opportunity to thank my wife, Jo, for her patience and understanding whilst I have been closeted away listening to rock'n'roll music and transcribing this tome.

PART ONE

Timeline

The Events in What Happened Today?

This *Timeline* provides a chronological perspective for the people, bands and events in the day-by-day stories of Part 2: *What Happened Today?*

Key

Record Releases

(UK) British record release (US) American record release

In most cases UK release dates have been chosen for British artists and US release dates for American artists.

Highlighting in bold type

This has been used to make it easier to identify people, bands, songs and albums.

Beatles Discography

The Beatles is the only act listed with complete British and American discographies for singles and albums.

As well as music related people and events, the *Timeline* includes social and political influences that were shaping the development of rock'n'roll, including the Cold War, the American struggle for Civil Rights and the Vietnam War. This *Timeline* gives a fascinating insight into rock'n'roll's development, with the juxtaposition of artists and bands, politics, movies, venues, concerts, TV, radio and many other factors. Artists' and bands' careers can be seen to wax and wane as the music continued to develop.

The singles and albums included here create a soundtrack for the era. Original versions, covers, classic recordings and landmark songs provide the reader with a plethora of material to discover and listen to in the context of its place in rock'n'roll history.

Rock'n'Roll Unravelled chronicles rock'n'roll's highlights and influences from the early part of the 20th century, up until it turned full circle with the advent of punk rock in the mid-1970s. Punk took the music back to its roots, with two-minute songs, played (mostly) by non-virtuoso musicians in small intimate venues.

1927 Aug 4 **Jimmie Rodgers'** 1st recording session – known as the "Father of Country Music"

1936 Nov 23 **Robert Johnson** began his 1st recording session – recorded 16 songs

1937 Jun 19 **Robert Johnson**'s 2nd and final recording session – recorded 13 songs
Sep 26 **Bessie Smith died** – automobile accident

1938 Aug 16 **Robert Johnson died** at the age of 27 – murdered...

...an early member of the 27 *Club*

1941 Jul 7 Almanac Singers recorded ***Sod Buster Ballads***

...paved the way for the 1960s protest singers

1947 Aug 11 **Chet Atkins**'s 1st recording session for RCA

Dec 28 Wynonie Harris recorded ***Good Rockin' Tonight*** – written and originally by Roy Brown

1948 Jan 1 RECORDING BAN: 2nd *Petrillo Recording Ban* came into effect across America

Jun 1 **Sonny Boy Williamson (I) died** – murdered

Jun 25 COLD WAR: Berlin Airlift began...

...dawn of the Cold War

Sep 4 Orioles 1st single, ***It's Too Soon to Know***, was reviewed...

...dawn of doo wop

1949 Jan 21 **Miles Davis**'s 1st recording session for *Birth of the Cool* – released in 1957

Apr 20 **Phil Spector**'s father committed suicide

Jun 25 HIT RECORDS: *Billboard* magazine started to refer to "rhythm and blues"...

..."Race Music" charts became "Rhythm & Blues"

Nov 19 **Jerry Lee Lewis**'s 1st public performance

Dec 10 Fats Domino recorded ***The Fat Man***

1950 Feb 20 COMMUNIST WITCH HUNTS: **Senator Joe McCarthy**'s speech to the Senate...

...heralded the communist witch hunts in America

Jun 3 RECORD LABELS: Aristocrat changed its name to "Chess Records"

Aug 30 poor sales for the only release on **Sam Phillips**'s 1st record label, It's The Phillips

Sep 1 **Jerry Lee Lewis** enrolled in Bible school

Dec 30 Dominoes recorded ***Sixty Minute Man***

1951 Mar 5 Jackie Brenston recorded ***Rocket 88***...

...often cited as the "1st rock'n'roll record"

Jun 14 Bill Haley and the Saddlemen recorded their cover version *of* ***Rocket 88***...

...contender for 1st rock'n'roll record by a white artist

Jul 11 **Alan Freed** used the name "Moondog" – later sued by **Louis "Moondog" Hardin**

Aug 5 Elmore James recorded ***Dust My Broom***

Oct 16 **Little Richard**'s 1st-ever recording session – giving him his 1st single for RCA

1952 Mar 1 Sam Phillips recorded Johnny London's ***Drivin' Slow***...

...RECORD LABELS: this became the 1st single released on Sun Records

Mar 13 Lloyd Price recorded ***Lawdy Miss Clawdy*** – became his 1st single...
...one of rock'n'roll's most covered songs

Mar 21 **Alan Freed** organised the 1st-ever rock'n'roll concert...
...it ended prematurely in a near riot

Aug 13 Willie Mae "Big Mama" Thornton recorded the original version of ***Hound Dog***

Aug 18 Little Willie Littlefield recorded ***KC Loving*** – later re-titled "***Kansas City***"

Sep 8 **Ray Charles**'s 1st recording session for Atlantic Records

Nov 14 HIT RECORDS: *New Musical Express* published the 1st list of hit records...
...1st British singles chart

1953 Jan 1 **Hank Williams died** at the age of 29 – alcohol related

Feb 10 Crows recorded ***Gee***

May 5 **Spaniels** 1st recording session...
...RECORD LABELS: the birth of Vee-Jay Records

May 7 **Clyde McPhatter** signed to Atlantic Records – created **The Drifters** shortly afterwards

Jul 18 Elvis Presley's 1st visit to Sam Phillips's studio, for the private recording of ***My Happiness***

Aug 9 Drifters recorded ***Money Honey*** – their 1st R&B hit

Sep 2 Ken Colyer's Jazzmen recorded ***New Orleans to London...***
...from trad jazz to rock'n'roll

Sep 23 Spaniels recorded the doo wop classic ***Goodnite Sweetheart Goodnite***

Oct 27 Guitar Slim recorded ***Things That I Used to Do***

Nov 12 Drifters recorded ***Such a Night*** – their 2nd single

Dec 29 Jimmy Reed recorded ***You Don't Have to Go***

Dec 30 MOVIES: **Marlon Brando**'s *The Wild One* opened, New York – banned in the UK until '68

1954 Jan 4 **Elvis Presley**'s 2nd private recording with **Sam Phillips** at Memphis Recording Service

Jan 7 Muddy Waters recorded the original version of ***(I'm Your) Hoochie Coochie Man***

Feb 1 Johnny "Guitar" Watson recorded ***Space Guitar...***
...with pioneering feedback and reverb

Feb 15 Big Joe Turner recorded the original version of ***Shake, Rattle and Roll***

Mar 15 Chords recorded ***Sh-Boom***

Apr 10 Midnighters released ***Work with Me Annie*** (US)

Apr 12 Bill Haley and His Comets recorded ***(We're Gonna) Rock Around the Clock***

Apr 24 Midnighters' ***Work with Me Annie*** entered the R&B charts – from the Royals to *The Twist*

May 7 VIETNAM WAR: French defeat at Dien Bien Phu...
...start of America's war in Vietnam

May 17 CIVIL RIGHTS: landmark judgement in the case of *Brown v Board of Education...*
...dawn of the modern Civil Rights Movement

Jul 10 Bill Haley and His Comets released cover of ***Shake, Rattle and Roll*** (US) – 1st hit record

Jul 13 Chris Barber's Jazz Band recorded **New Orleans Joys...**
...included Lonnie Donegan's *Rock Island Line*
...dawn of British skiffle when released as single in 1955

Jul 19 Elvis Presley released ***That's All Right*** (US) – Elvis's 1st Sun single

Aug 13 **Chuck Berry**'s 1st-ever recording session – as a part of **Jo Alexander and the Cubans**

Sep 10 Ken Colyer's Jazzmen recorded ***Back to the Delta*** – with Alexis Korner on skiffle tracks

Sep 22 Elvis Presley released ***Good Rockin' Tonight*** (US) – his 2nd Sun single

Oct 2 **Elvis Presley**'s only performance at the Grand Ole Opry

Oct 16 Richard Berry released the self-penned ***The Big Break*** (US)

Nov 6 **Elvis Presley**'s only radio commercial aired on the *Louisiana Hayride*

Dec 25 **Johnny Ace died** at the age of 25 – Russian roulette

1955 Jan 8 Elvis Presley released ***Milkcow Blues Boogie*** (US) – his 3rd Sun single

Jan 25 Little Walter recorded ***My Babe***

Feb 13 **Buddy Holly**, as **Buddy and Bob**, opened for **Elvis** in Lubbock, Texas

Feb 26 RECORDING LANDMARKS: in America 45s outsold 78s for the 1st time

Mar 2 Bo Diddley recorded ***Bo Diddley*** and ***I'm a Man*** – released as his 1st single

Mar 19 Carl Perkins released his 1st single, ***Movie Magg*** (US) – on Sam Phillips's Flip label

Mar 21 Big Maybelle recorded the original version of ***Whole Lotta Shakin' Goin' On***

Mar 25 MOVIES: *Blackboard Jungle* released – opening credits used **Rock Around the Clock...**
...the movie kick-started rock'n'roll around the world

Apr 25 Elvis Presley released ***Baby Let's Play House*** (US) – his 4th Sun single

May 6 Platters released the re-recorded Mercury version of ***Only You (And You Alone)*** (US)

May 21 Chuck Berry recorded ***Maybellene*** – 1st session at Chess

May 23 Smiley Lewis recorded ***I Hear You Knocking***

Aug 1 Carl Perkins released ***Let the Juke Box Keep on Playing*** (US) – 1st single on Sun

Aug 1 Elvis Presley released ***I Forgot to Remember to Forget*** (US) – 5th and final Sun single

Aug 12 Sonny Boy Williamson (II) recorded ***Don't Start Me Talkin'***

Aug 15 **Elvis Presley** signed with **Colonel Tom Parker** – now two managers, **Bob Neal** and CTP

Sep 14 Little Richard recorded ***Tutti-Frutti*** – his 1st single on the Speciality label

Sep 15 **Chuck Berry**'s "duck-walk" started around the time of this **Alan Freed** concert

Sep 30 **James Dean** died at the age of 24 – automobile accident

Oct 7 BEAT WRITERS: **Allen Ginsberg** gave the 1st reading of his beat poem *Howl*

Oct 27 MOVIES: *Rebel Without a Cause* opened in America – 2nd of three **James Dean** movies...
...heralded the 1st generation of teenagers

Oct 29 US RADIO: **Sam Phillips** opened the 1st all-female radio station, WHER

Nov 20 **Elvis Presley** left Sun – signed with RCA the following day

Nov 20 **Bo Diddley** went off script on the *Ed Sullivan Show* – he was never invited back

Dec 1 CIVIL RIGHTS: **Rosa Parks** arrested for not giving up her seat for a white passenger...
...the flashpoint that ignited the Civil Rights Movement

Dec 5 Teenagers featuring Frankie Lymon recorded ***Why Do Fools Fall in Love...***
...Lymon became the 1st black teenage idol

Dec 12 Bill Haley and His Comets recorded ***See You Later Alligator***

Dec 19 Carl Perkins recorded ***Honey Don't*** – one of three Perkins songs covered by the Beatles

Dec 24 **Weavers** reunion concert at Carnegie Hall...
...paved the way for the 1960s protest singers

1956 Jan 1 Carl Perkins released ***Blue Suede Shoes*** (US)

Jan 10 Elvis Presley recorded ***Heartbreak Hotel*** – 1st recording session for RCA

Jan 11 **Coasters'** 1st recording session

Jan 24 CIVIL RIGHTS: *Look* magazine article, confession by **Emmett Till**'s murderers...
...the murder was committed in August 1955

Jan 26 **Buddy Holly**'s 1st recording session at Decca

Jan 28 **Elvis Presley**'s 1st appearance on national TV

Feb 6 Everly Brothers released ***Keep a Lovin' Me*** (US) – debut single, on Columbia

Feb 8 **Buddy Holly** signed his 1st recording contract, with Decca

Mar 3 James Brown and the Famous Flames released 1st single, ***Please, Please, Please*** (US)

Mar 21 MOVIES: *Rock Around the Clock* opened in America...
...1st rock'n'roll movie

Mar 22 **Carl Perkins** had a near-fatal car accident

Mar 23 Elvis released his debut album, ***Elvis Presley***

Mar 27 Roy Orbison re-recorded ***Ooby Dooby*** at Sun Records

Mar 31 eleven-year-old **Brenda Lee** made her 1st national TV appearance

Apr 16 Buddy Holly released ***Blue Days - Black Nights*** (US) – 1st single, on Decca

Apr 22 UK VENUES: 2i's coffee bar opened...
...the spiritual home of British skiffle music

Apr 23 **Elvis Presley**'s 1st concert performance in Las Vegas

May 4 Gene Vincent recorded ***Be-Bop-A-Lula*** – his 1st recording session for Capitol

Jul 2 Johnny Burnette and the Rock 'n Roll Trio recorded ***The Train Kept A-Rollin'***

Jul 14 **Vipers Skiffle Group** played at London's 2i's coffee bar for the 1st time

Aug 22 MOVIES: seminal rock'n'roll movie *The Girl Can't Help It* opened in America

Sep 9 **Elvis Presley** made his 1st appearance on the *Ed Sullivan Show*

Sep 17 Brenda Lee released ***Jambalaya*** (US) – 1st single

Sep 24 Tommy Steele's 1st recording session, ***Rock with the Caveman...***
...1st British rock'n'roll hit

Oct 15 Little Richard recorded ***Good Golly, Miss Molly***

Oct 23 COLD WAR: Hungarian uprising began – crushed by the Russians just two weeks later

Nov 15 MOVIES: **Elvis Presley**'s *Love Me Tender* opened in New York – his 1st movie

Nov 16 **Conway Twitty** failed his audition with **Sam Phillips** at Sun Records

Dec 1 Jerry Lee Lewis released ***Crazy Arms*** (US) – his 1st Sun single

Dec 4 ***Million Dollar Quartet*** session – Elvis, Jerry Lee Lewis, Carl Perkins and Johnny Cash

Dec 15 **Horace Logan** was the 1st person to announce that "**Elvis** has left the building"

Dec 29 **Elvis Presley** had ten singles on the *Billboard Top 100*

1957 Jan 6 **Elvis Presley**'s censored 'no hips' performance on the *Ed Sullivan Show*

Jan 16 UK VENUES: Liverpool's Cavern Club opened – as a jazz club

Jan 23 Carl Perkins released ***Matchbox*** (US)

Jan 23 Billy Riley and His Little Green Men released ***Flyin' Saucers Rock & Roll*** (US)

Jan 31 Bill Haley's ***Rock Around the Clock*** became the...

...UK's 1st million selling single

Feb 5 **Bill Haley** arrived in London...

...1st American rock'n'roll star to play the UK

Feb 8 Diamonds released their cover of the Gladiolas' ***Little Darlin'*** (US)

Feb 13 Alexis Korner recorded ***Blues from the Roundhouse...***

...early British blues milestone

Feb 16 UK TV: 1st episode of the BBC's *Six-Five Special...*

...UK's 1st TV pop music show

Feb 19 CIVIL RIGHTS: dynamite was thrown at the stage during at a **Louis Armstrong** gig

Feb 25 Buddy Holly and the Crickets recorded ***That'll Be the Day***

Mar 7 Mose Allison recorded ***Blues*** – famously covered by the Who as ***Young Man*** in 1970

Mar 15 Jerry Lee Lewis released ***Whole Lot of Shakin' Going On*** (US)

Mar 26 COMMUNIST WITCH HUNTS: **Pete Seeger** was indicted for Contempt of Congress...

...protest singers targeted by McCarthy's witch hunts

Apr 10 Ricky Nelson sang ***I'm Walkin'*** on TV – released his cover version shortly afterwards

Apr 20 Everly Brothers released **Bye Bye Love** (US) – 1st Cadence single – start of their success

May 3 MOVIES: *The Tommy Steele Story* premiered in London...

...Britain's 1st rock'n'roll movie

...1st UK artist with a #1 album

May 16 **Buddy Holly** signed to Coral

May 27 ***That'll Be the Day*** was released as "The Crickets" (US)

May 29 Crickets' drummer Jerry Allison used his knees rather than his drum kit for ***Everyday***

Jul 6 **John Lennon** met **Paul McCartney** at a **Quarry Men** gig – birth of the **Beatles**

Jul 19 outrage when **Frankie Lymon** danced with a white girl on **Alan Freed**'s *The Big Beat*

Aug 5 US TV: national TV debut of *American Bandstand* – with host **Dick Clark**

Aug 7 **John Lennon**'s Cavern Club debut – as a member of the **Quarry Men**

	Aug 12	Decca released their earlier, solo Buddy Holly, version of ***That'll Be the Day*** (US)
	Aug 31	**Elvis Presley** gave his last concert outside the USA – in Canada
	Sep 8	Jackie Wilson released ***Reet Petite*** (US) – 1st solo single
	Sep 20	Buddy Holly and the Crickets released ***Peggy Sue*** (US) – Jerry Allison's girlfriend
	Sep 25	CIVIL RIGHTS: *Little Rock Nine* attended school... ...protected by the 101st Airborne, with bayonets fixed
	Oct 2	Connie Francis recorded ***Who's Sorry Now*** – 1st international hit
	Oct 3	1st episode of **Pat Boone**'s own TV show, *The Pat Boone Chevy Showroom*
	Oct 4	John Barry and the Seven recorded ***Zip Zip*** – released as their 1st UK single
	Oct 12	whilst on tour in Australia **Little Richard** found God and renounced rock'n'roll... ...end of Little Richard's rock'n'roll career
	Oct 18	**Paul McCartney**'s debut performance with the **Quarry Men**
	Oct 18	**Little Richard**'s final rock'n'roll recording session of the 1950s
	Nov 3	Jerry Lee Lewis released ***Great Balls of Fire*** (US)
	Nov 8	MOVIES: **Elvis Presley**'s 3rd movie, *Jailhouse Rock*, opened... ...end of Elvis's rock'n'roll years
	Nov 10	**Elvis Presley**'s final concert appearances before joining the Army
	Nov 22	**Tom & Jerry** performed debut single on *American Bandstand* – early **Simon & Garfunkel**
	Nov 25	Ray Charles scored his 1st crossover hit with ***Swanee River Rock***
	Nov 27	Buddy Holly and the Crickets released ***The Chirping Crickets*** (US) – 1st album
	Nov 28	**Chris Barber** gig with **Sister Rosetta Tharpe** – Barber, the unsung hero of UK rock'n'roll
1958	Jan 15	Champs released ***Tequila*** as the B-side of *Train to Nowhere* (US)
	Jan 20	US RADIO: St Louis radio station KWK smashed rock'n'roll records on-air
	Jan 24	Elvis Presley's ***Jailhouse Rock*** was the... ...1st single to enter the UK charts at #1
	Feb 18	**Terry Dean** arrested for being drunk and disorderly – beginning of the end of his career
	Feb 19	Larry Williams recorded ***Dizzy Miss Lizzy***
	Feb 22	RECORDING LANDMARKS: Roy Hamilton's ***Don't Let Go*** was the... ...1st stereo single to appear on the American charts
	Feb 28	Chuck Berry recorded ***Johnny B Goode*** and ***Around and Around***
	Mar 1	opening night of the **Buddy Holly and the Crickets** UK tour
	Mar 17	Coasters recorded ***Yakety Yak***
	Mar 24	**Elvis Presley** was inducted into the US Army – he was discharged on 5 March 1960
	Mar 28	Eddie Cochran recorded ***Summertime Blues***
	Mar 28	**Jerry Lee Lewis** tour opened – featured the piano burning rivalry with **Chuck Berry**
	Apr 3	Johnny Otis Show recorded ***Willie and the Hand Jive***
	Apr 9	Jerry Lee Lewis released ***High School Confidential*** (US) – his last rock'n'roll hit
	May 3	**Alan Freed** was charged with incitement to riot, after the Boston *Big Beat* show

May 17 ***Jerry Lee Lewis Day*** in Ferriday – this marked the high point of his career

May 20 Phil Spector's 1st-ever recording session, ***Don't You Worry My Little Pet***

May 22 **Jerry Lee Lewis** arrived in London for his ill-fated UK tour...
...end of Jerry Lee Lewis's rock'n'roll career

May 30 whole **Drifters** group was fired and replaced by the **Crowns** – renamed to "The Drifters"

May 30 Jerry Lee Lewis recorded ***The Return of Jerry Lee*** – 1st attempt at damage limitation

Jun 2 **Kingston Trio** released their eponymous 1st album...
...American folk music revival came of age

Jun 7 **Cliff Richard and the Drifters** made their 1st private demo recording

Jun 9 **Jerry Lee Lewis**'s open letter in *Billboard* magazine – damage limitation after his UK tour

Jun 9 Ritchie Valens released ***Come on, Let's Go*** (US) – 1st single

Jun 18 Connie Francis cut ***Stupid Cupid*** – 1st hit for Aldon Music, mainstay of the Brill Building

Jul 5 Johnny O'Keefe and the Dee Jays released ***The Wild One*** in Australia...
...birth of Australian rock'n'roll

Jul 22 Crickets' drummer **Jerry Allison** married his girlfriend, Peggy Sue

Aug 10 Jerry Lee Lewis released ***Break Up*** (US) – poor sales following his disastrous British tour

Aug 29 Cliff Richard and the Drifters released their 1st single, ***Move It!*** (UK) – originally the B-side

Sep 8 Boots Randolph recorded ***Yakety Sax***

Sep 11 Lloyd Price recorded ***Stagger Lee*** for the 1st time

Oct 1 **Billy Fury** made an impromptu appearance at a **Marty Wilde** concert

Oct 5 **Kalin Twins** tour – **Cliff Richard and the Drifters** also on the bill...
...debut with **Hank Marvin** and **Bruce Welch**

Oct 6 **Marty Wilde** and **Nancy Whiskey** appeared at Chatham's Empire Theatre...
...British music scene in the 2nd half of the 1950s

Oct 14 Ritchie Valens released ***Donna*** c/w ***La Bamba*** (US) – 2nd and final single

Oct 19 Brenda Lee recorded ***Rockin' Around the Christmas Tree*** – it did not chart until 1960

Oct 21 **Buddy Holly**'s final recording session – famous string recordings

Oct 26 riot at 1st **Bill Haley** gig in Germany – rock'n'roll made youth "ripe for atomic war"

Oct 26 **Muddy Waters'** historic 1st UK tour

Oct 27 **Tommy Steele** appeared on the British TV show *This Is Your Life*

Oct 28 one of **Buddy Holly and The Crickets'** last performances together

Nov 5 Buddy Holly and the Crickets released ***Heartbeat*** (US) – their final single together

Nov 11 Hank Ballard and the Midnighters recorded ***The Twist***...
...released as the B-side of *Teardrops on Your Letter*

Nov 26 Billy Fury recorded the self-penned ***Maybe Tomorrow*** – 1st single

Dec 11 Coasters recorded ***Charlie Brown***

Dec 27 UK TV: last episode of the 1st pop music show, *Six-Five Special*

1959 Jan 5 Buddy Holly released ***It Doesn't Matter Anymore*** (US) – 1st single since Crickets split

Jan 9 Drifters (later became the Shadows) recorded ***Feelin' Fine*** – 1st single

Jan 10 debut of the lineup that became the **Shadows** – still called "**The Drifters**"

Jan 12 RECORD LABELS: **Berry Gordy Jr** formed his 1st record label, Tamla

Jan 23 **Buddy Holly**'s ill-fated *Winter Dance Party* tour opened in Milwaukee

Feb 3 **Buddy Holly died**, 22, along with **Big Bopper,** 28, and **Ritchie Valens,** 17 – plane crash

Feb 5 Eddie Cochran recorded the Buddy Holly tribute song ***Three Stars***

Feb 7 **Guitar Slim died** at the age of 32 – pneumonia

Feb 9 Cliff Richard's 1st of two days of recording for his 1st album, ***Cliff***

Feb 18 Ray Charles recorded his cross-over hit ***What'd I Say***

Feb 29 **Little Richard, Elvis Presley, Jerry Lee Lewis** and **Buddy Holly** – had 'left the stage'...
...passing of the golden-age of rock'n'roll

Mar 6 ex-Crowns lineup of the Drifters recorded ***There Goes My Baby*** – Ben E King lead vocal

Apr 18 Johnny Kidd and the Pirates' 1st recording session – cut 1st single, ***Please Don't Touch***

May 14 MOVIES: **Cliff Richard**'s 1st movie, *Serious Charge,* opened in London

May 18 Crickets recorded ***I Fought the Law***

Jun 8 Clovers recorded the original version of ***Love Potion #9***

Jun 12 **Moonglows** concert – with a new lineup that included **Marvin Gay(e)**

Jul 9 VIETNAM WAR: 1st American personnel died in Vietnam...
...Americans were only there in an advisory capacity

Jul 15 Sandy Nelson recorded his 1st single, ***Teen Beat*** – rock'n'roll's 1st drum-hero

Jul 16 Coasters recorded ***Poison Ivy***

Aug 10 all four of the **Platters'** male singers were arrested for lewd behaviour in Cincinnati

Sep 26 **Rory Storm and the Hurricanes** appeared at Lathom Hall – with drummer **Ringo Starr**...
...Liverpool scene before the Beatles

Oct 26 **Johnny and the Moondogs** qualified for the final of the *Carroll Levis* talent contest

Nov 2 Cliff Richard's 1st appearance on the US charts, ***Living Doll*** – still as "CR and the Drifters"

Nov 17 **Stuart Sutcliffe** financed his bass guitar and joined **Johnny and the Moondogs**

Nov 21 **Alan Freed** was sacked by ABC...
...payola scandal took hold

Dec 14 RECORD LABELS: **Berry Gordy Jr** founded the Motown recording company

1960 Jan 8 **Eddie Cochran**'s final recording session

Jan 24 **Eddie Cochran**'s last tour opened in the UK

Jan 25 Sam Cooke recorded ***Chain Gang*** – 1st recording session at RCA

Feb 6 **Jesse Belvin died at the age of 27** – automobile accident

Mar 3 **Elvis Presley** stopped off in Scotland – only time (officially) that he set foot on British soil

Mar 18 Everly Brothers recorded ***Cathy's Clown*** – $1m deal from Warner Brothers

Mar 20 **Elvis Presley**'s 1st recording session since leaving the Army...

...heralded Elvis's second era: Elvis the Hollywood movie idol

Mar 22 Ventures recorded the original Blue Horizon version of ***Walk–Don't Run***

Mar 23 Elvis Presley released ***Stuck on You*** (US) – 1st single since leaving the US Army

Apr 8 Elvis Presley released ***Elvis Is Back!*** (US) – 1st album since leaving the US Army

Apr 17 **Eddie Cochran died** at the age of 21 – automobile accident

May 10 **Silver Beetles** failed their audition to become Billy Fury's backing band

May 13 Johnny Kidd and the Pirates recorded ***Shakin' All Over***

May 21 Billy Fury released his 1st album, ***The Sound of Fury*** (UK)

May 25 UK VENUES: 1st "Beat Night" at Liverpool's Cavern Club

Jul 9 **Tony Sheridan and the Jets** led the way to Hamburg...

...dawn of the British beat groups

Jul 27 end-of-the-pier show, with a host of British rock'n'roll stars managed by **Larry Parnes**

Aug 1 Chubby Checker released his cover of ***The Twist*** (US)...

...beginning of the twist dance craze

Aug 8 Roy Orbison recorded ***Blue Angel*** – as his follow-up to ***Only the Lonely***

Aug 17 **Beatles**' debut on their 1st Hamburg trip – arranged by 1st manager **Allan Williams...**

...Pete Best joined as drummer

...they renamed to "The Beatles"

Oct 15 **John, Paul, George** and **Ringo**'s 1st recording together – with bassist **Wally Walters**

Oct 20 UK EVENTS: *Lady Chatterley's Lover* trial in UK...

...end of literary censorship in the UK

...in the US it came with *Naked Lunch* in 1966

Nov 3 with ***Now or Never***, Elvis Presley became the...

...1st act ever to have five #1s in the UK

Nov 5 **Johnny Horton died** at the age of 35 – automobile accident

Dec 1 **Paul McCartney** and **Pete Best** deported from Germany – **George** was deported earlier

Dec 5 Crickets released ***In Style with the Crickets*** – 1st post-Buddy Holly album

Dec 16 end of road for **Cass and the Cassanovas** – without Brian Casser became the **Big Three**

Dec 17 1st of four gigs for **Chas Newby** as the **Beatles**' temporary bass player

1961 Jan 5 **Paul McCartney**'s debut as the **Beatles**' bass guitarist

Jan 16 Helen Shapiro recorded ***Don't Treat Me Like a Child*** – 1st single

Jan 24 Del Shannon recorded ***Runaway*** – 1st single

Feb 9 1st Cavern appearance as **"The Beatles"** – also Cavern debut for **George Harrison**

Feb 23 Top Notes recorded original version of ***Twist and Shout*** – co-produced by Phil Spector...

...six months later Spector launched his own label and the "wall of sound"

Mar 1 **Fourmost** debuted at the Cavern Club – as the **"Four Jays"**

Mar 23 VIETNAM WAR: **President Kennedy** expressed concern about the "domino effect"

Mar 25 **Elvis Presley**'s last live performance for seven years
Apr 3 Billy Fury released his cover of ***Halfway to Paradise*** (UK)
Apr 11 **Bob Dylan** played his 1st major gig – Gerde's Folk City in New York's Greenwich Village
Apr 15 COLD WAR: **President Kennedy** launched the ill-fated *Bay of Pigs* invasion of Cuba
May 4 CIVIL RIGHTS: 1st *Freedom Riders* set out by bus from Washington DC
May 31 **Jimi Hendrix** enlisted into the US Army
Jun 22 Beatles recorded ***My Bonnie*** – released as Tony Sheridan and the Beat Brothers
Jul 21 **Jimmy Page** accompanied beat poet **Royston Ellis** in a fusion of music and poetry
Jul 24 Temptations released ***Oh, Mother of Mine*** (US) – 1st single
Jul 29 Chuck Berry recorded ***Come On***
Aug 21 Marvelettes released 1st single, ***Please Mr. Postman*** (US)...
...Motown's 1st American #1
Aug 23 Dick Dale and the Del-Tones recording session for the surf classic ***Let's Go Trippin'***
Sep 30 **Bob Dylan**'s 1st studio recording session – provided harmonica for **Carolyn Hester**
Oct 1 **John** and **Paul** met Hamburg friend **Jürgen Vollmer** – adopted famous Beatles hairstyle
Oct 3 Beach Boys recorded ***Surfin*** at their 1st-ever recording session
Oct 19 **Beatles** combined with **Gerry and the Pacemakers** to form the **Beatmakers**
Oct 28 Raymond Jones walked into Brian Epstein's shop and asked for a copy of ***My Bonnie***
Nov 4 **Bob Dylan**'s 1st paid-attendance gig
Nov 9 **Brian Epstein** visited the Cavern to see the **Beatles** for the 1st time
Nov 20 Bob Dylan's 1st recording session for one of his own recordings, 1st album, ***Bob Dylan***
Nov 24 **Howlin' Wolf** arrived in the UK for his 1st British tour
Nov 25 **Everly Brothers** joined the US Marine Corps
Dec 2 **Billy Fury** toured the UK with the newly-formed **Blue Flames**
Dec 9 **Beatles'** 1st gig in the south of England – attended by just a handful of people
Dec 10 MOVIES: premiere of **Cliff Richard**'s *The Young Ones...*
...British rockers were morphing into entertainers
Dec 31 early gig as **"The Beach Boys"** – recently changed their name from **"The Pendletones"**

1962 Jan 1 **Beatles** failed their Decca audition
Jan 2 WITCH HUNTS: **Weavers** were banned from performing on *The Jack Parr Show*
Jan 5 Tony Sheridan and the Beatles released ***My Bonnie*** (UK)
Jan 12 VIETNAM WAR: American involvement escalated...
...1st participation of American forces in direct combat
Feb 2 Bob Dylan recorded harmonica for Harry Belafonte's version of ***The Midnight Special***
Feb 2 **Ronnie Hawkins** recording session – including all five future members of **The Band**
Feb 19 **Chuck Berry** started a three-year jail stretch for violating the *Mann Act*
Mar 17 **Alexis Korner's Blues Incorporated** gig...
...billed as "Britain's First Rhythm & Blues Band"

Mar 19 Bob Dylan released his 1st album, ***Bob Dylan*** (US)

Apr 6 **Alexis Korner** performed at the Marquee in **Chris Barber's Jazz Band**'s interval group

Apr 7 **Mick Jagger** and **Keith Richard** met **Brian Jones** and **Charlie Watts**

Apr 10 **Stuart Sutcliffe died** at the age of 21 – brain haemorrhage

Apr 13 RECORDING LANDMARKS: 1st British group to be awarded a Gold Disc...
...Shadows for ***Apache***

Apr 23 Beatles released 1st US single, ***My Bonnie*** – as "Tony Sheridan and the Beat Brothers"

Apr 29 opening night of **Jerry Lee Lewis**'s 1st UK tour since his disastrous 1958 visit

May 19 Brian Poole and the Tremeloes on TV to promote their 1st single, ***Twist Little Sister***

Jun 4 Beach Boys released ***Surfin' Safari*** (US) – 1st single on Capitol

Jun 5 Elvis Presley released **Pot Luck** – his last album of new rock material for seven years

Jun 6 Beatles' 1st ***Love Me Do*** recording session at Abbey Road – with drummer Pete Best

Jun 8 Alexis Korner's Blues Incorporated recorded ***R&B from the Marquee***

Jun 23 **Brian Epstein** formed NEMS Enterprises Ltd...
...from the **Quarry Men** to the **Beatles**

Jun 25 **Keith Moon** asked **Screaming Lord Sutch**'s drummer, **Carlo Little**, for lessons

Jun 27 Muddy Waters recorded the lyrics to Earl Hookers' *Blue Guitar* to produce ***You Shook Me***

Jun 29 Contours released the original version of ***Do You Love Me*** (US)

Jul 12 Rolling Stones 1st-ever gig – as the **Rollin' Stones**

Jul 13 Phil Spector recorded ***He's a Rebel*** with Darlene Love – but issued it as "The Crystals"

Jul 21 Crystals' ***He Hit Me (And It Felt Like a Kiss)*** reviewed – withdrawn shortly afterwards

Aug 16 Stevie Wonder released 1st single, ***I Call It Pretty Music...***(US) – Marvin Gaye on drums

Aug 17 Tornados released ***Telstar*** (UK)...
...later became the 1st American #1 by a British group

Aug 18 **Ringo Starr**'s 1st gig as an official Beatle – after leaving **Rory Storm and the Hurricanes**

Sep 4 Beatles' 2nd ***Love Me Do*** recording session at Abbey Road – 1st session with Ringo Starr

Sep 5 **Mark Twain and the Strangers** with **Keith Moon** auditioned for BBC Radio – they failed

Sep 11 Beatles' 3rd ***Love Me Do*** recording session – Andy White drums and Ringo tambourine

Oct 5 Beatles released their British debut single, ***Love Me Do*** c/w *P.S. I Love You* (UK-1)

Oct 12 **Little Richard**'s UK rock'n'roll comeback tour – supported by the **Beatles**

Oct 13 single brother, **Everly Brothers** tour of the UK

Oct 17 COLD WAR: the *Cuban Missile Crisis* started to unfold...
...the world stood on the brink of World War III

Oct 27 **Rolling Stones'** 1st recording session – demo recording at Curly Clayton's studio

Oct 30 **Beatles'** 4th Hamburg trip – same bill as **Little Richard** – met **Billy Preston**

Oct 31 **Joni Mitchell**'s 1st paid gig

Nov 26 Beatles recorded ***Please Please Me*** – 1st 'true' Beatles recording session

Dec 7 **Bill Wyman** auditioned as bass player for the **Rolling Stones**

Dec 14 Bob Dylan released 1st single, ***Mixed-Up Confusion*** (US) – withdrawn shortly afterwards

1963 Jan 11 Beatles released their 2nd UK single, ***Please Please Me*** c/w *Ask Me Why* (UK-2)

Jan 11 last outing for **Tony Chapman** as the **Rolling Stones**' drummer...
...Stones that kept right on rolling

Jan 13 **Bob Dylan**'s 1st UK visit – for an appearance in BBC TV's *The Madhouse on Castle Street*

Jan 14 CIVIL RIGHTS: **George Wallace**'s inaugural speech as Governor of Alabama...
..."segregation forever"

Jan 16 early gig for the newly formed **Cyril Davies and His Rhythm and Blues All Stars**

Jan 26 **Wayne Fontana and the Jets** gig – became **WF and the Mindbenders** soon afterwards

Jan 31 Beach Boys recorded ***Surfin' USA***...
...Chuck Berry later sued for plagiarism

Feb 2 opening night of the **Beatles'** 1st UK package tour – supporting **Helen Shapiro**

Feb 2 debut of the classic five members of the **Rolling Stones** – plus pianist **Ian Stewart**

Feb 20 Penguins released ***Memories of El Monte*** (US) – co-writer and producer, Frank Zappa

Feb 20 Duffy Power recorded ***I Saw Her Standing There*** – with the Graham Bond Quartet

Feb 25 Beatles released 1st US single, ***Please Please Me*** c/w *Ask Me Why* (US-1) – on Vee-Jay

Feb 27 **Searchers** supported **Gene Vincent** in Hamburg

Mar 11 **Rolling Stones** demo session at IBC Studios – they were still looking for a recording deal

Mar 14 **Gerry and the Pacemakers** were in the vanguard of beat groups...
...1st beat group to have a British #1

Mar 22 Beatles released their UK debut album, ***Please Please Me*** (UK-1)

Mar 27 Frank Zappa performed his ***Concerto for Two Bicycles*** on TV's *The Steve Allen Show*

Apr 11 Beatles released ***From Me to You*** c/w *Thank You Girl* (UK-3) – 1st Beatles UK #1...
...started a run of 11 consecutive #1s

Apr 14 **Rolling Stones** met the **Beatles** for the 1st time

Apr 18 Del Shannon decided to record ***From Me to You*** – 1st Lennon/McCartney hit in the US

Apr 21 Four Tops recording session for the 'lost' ***Breaking Through*** album

Apr 28 **Rolling Stones** met manager **Andrew Loog Oldham** – he moulded their 'bad-boy' image

Apr 30 Billy Fury recorded 'live' album, ***We Want Billy*** – with his backing band the Tornados

May 11 **Carter Lewis and the Southerners** appeared on BBC Radio's *Saturday Club*

May 12 **Bob Dylan** pulled out of the *Ed Sullivan Show* because of censorship issues

May 27 Beatles released ***From Me to You*** c/w *Thank You Girl* (US-2) – 2nd single on Vee-Jay

May 27 Bob Dylan released his 2nd album, ***The Freewheelin' Bob Dylan*** (US)...
...dawn of the 1960s protest songs

Jun 7 Rolling Stones released their UK debut single, ***Come On***

Jun 11 CIVIL RIGHTS: Governor **George Wallace**'s *Schoolhouse Door* stand

Jun 11 CIVIL RIGHTS: **President Kennedy** announced his *Civil Rights Bill*...
...direct result of Wallace's *Schoolhouse Door* stand

Jun 12 CIVIL RIGHTS: Civil Rights leader **Medgar Evers** was murdered in Jackson, Mississippi

Jun 30 package tour concert starring **Jet Harris and Tony Meehan**

Jun 30 **Rolling Stones** were the house band when the Crawdaddy Club moved to a new location

Jul 9 Rolling Stones recorded ***Fortune Teller*** – released as 2nd UK single but was withdrawn

Jul 22 Beatles released their US debut album, ***Introducing the Beatles*** (US-1) – on Vee-Jay

Jul 26 Billy J Kramer released ***Bad to Me*** (UK) – 1st Lennon/McCartney #1 not by the Beatles

Aug 3 last **Beatles** appearance at Liverpool's Cavern Club

Aug 7 **Rolling Stones** performed at Eel Pie Island...
...British R&B groups revitalised US blues singers

Aug 9 UK TV: debut of *Ready Steady Go!* – with the Surfaris' ***Wipe Out*** as the theme music

Aug 23 Beatles released ***She Loves You*** c/w *I'll Get You* (UK-4) – Beatles' 1st million-seller

Aug 23 Jerry Lee Lewis's last recording session for Sun, ***Carry Me Back to Old Virginny***

Aug 28 CIVIL RIGHTS: *March on Washington* Civil Rights demonstration...
...**Martin Luther King Jr**'s *I Have a Dream* speech

Aug 30 **David Bowie**'s 1st-ever recording session – as a member of the Konrads

Aug 30 Fourmost released their 1st single, ***Hello Little Girl***

Sep 6 **Jerry Lee Lewis** left Sun Records...
...the last rock'n'roll star to leave the label

Sep 7 1st performance of the lineup that became the **Animals**

Sep 15 CIVIL RIGHTS: four young girls murdered by the Ku Klux Klan...
...in a church bombing in Birmingham, Alabama

Sep 15 **Animals**' 1st-ever recording session – at Graphic Sound Studios in Newcastle

Sep 16 Beatles released ***She Loves You*** c/w *I'll Get You* on Swan (US-3) – charted February 1964

Oct 4 **Rod Stewart** gig with his 1st band, **Jimmy Powell and the Five Dimensions**

Oct 10 **Gerry and the Pacemakers'** 3rd single entered the UK charts at #1...
...1st act to have their 1st three singles chart at #1

Oct 19 **Top Topham**'s final gig as the **Yardbirds**' lead guitarist – replaced by **Eric Clapton**

Oct 31 **Ed Sullivan** experienced Beatlemania at Heathrow airport

Nov 1 Rolling Stones released their cover of the Beatles' ***I Wanna Be Your Man*** (UK)

Nov 4 **Beatles** appeared on the prestigious *Royal Command Performance* TV show

Nov 13 **Vance Arnold and the Avengers**, singer **Joe Cocker**, supported the **Rolling Stones**

Nov 22 ASSASSINATIONS: **President Kennedy** was assassinated in Dallas, Texas

Nov 22 Beatles released ***With the Beatles*** (UK-2)...
...1st British album to sell a million copies

Nov 23 Gene Pitney's ***That Girl Belongs to Yesterday*** was the 1st hit for Jagger and Richard

Nov 25 Beatles' 1st North American Capitol LP was in Canada, ***Beatlemania! With The Beatles***

Nov 29 Beatles released ***I Want to Hold Your Hand*** c/w *This Boy* (UK-5)...
...1st British single with 1m advance orders

Nov 30 Kingsmen's version of ***Louie Louie*** hit the American charts – and a legend was born

Dec 2 **Beatles** appeared on UK TV's uber-popular *Morecambe and Wise Show*

Dec 7 all four **Beatles** appeared on the UK version of *Juke Box Jury*

Dec 8 **Sonny Boy Williamson and The Yardbirds** recorded a live album at the Crawdaddy
Dec 13 **Cleo's Mood**, a typical early 1960s semi-pro group, formed by **Shelley**, **Bone** and **Bunz**
Dec 14 Beatles' ***I Want to Hold Your Hand*** knocked ***She Loves You*** off the UK #1 spot
Dec 22 **Detours** opened for the **Rolling Stones** – four months before becoming "The Who"
Dec 26 Beatles released ***I Want to Hold Your Hand*** (US-4) – 1st US single on Capitol

1964 Jan 1 UK TV: debut of *Top of the Pops*
Jan 2 **Cyril Davies**'s last performance at the Marquee
Jan 7 **Cyril Davies died** at the age of 31 – natural causes
Jan 10 Manfred Mann's ***5-4-3-2-1*** replaced the Surfaris' ***Wipe Out*** as the theme tune for *RSG!*
Jan 13 Dylan released ***The Times They Are A-Changin'*** (US) – 1st album with all original songs
Jan 17 **Holy Modal Rounders** recording session for their eponymous 1st album
Jan 20 Capitol released their 1st American Beatles album, ***Meet the Beatles*** (US-2)
Jan 27 Beatles re-released their Vee-Jay album ***Introducing the Beatles*** – track listing changed
Jan 30 Beatles released ***Please Please Me*** c/w *From Me to You* (US-5) – 3rd Vee-Jay single
Feb 1 Beatles' 1st US #1, ***I Want to Hold Your Hand...***
...beginning of the British Invasion
Feb 9 **Beatles'** 1st appearance on the *Ed Sullivan Show*
Feb 9 **Lovin' Spoonful** met, watching the Beatles on the *Ed Sullivan Show*
Feb 11 **Beatles** made their American concert debut
Feb 21 **Dave Clark Five** on *Ready Steady Go!* – but was it DC or **Bobby Graham** on the singles?
Feb 21 Rolling Stones released ***Not Fade Away*** (UK)
Mar 2 Beatles released ***Twist and Shout*** c/w *There's a Place* (US-6) – on Tollie
Mar 8 Dave Clark Five achieved international success with ***Glad All Over***
Mar 10 Simon & Garfunkel recorded the original acoustic version of ***The Sounds of Silence***
Mar 16 Beatles released ***Can't Buy Me Love*** c/w *You Can't Do That* (US-7) – 2nd on Capitol
Mar 20 Beatles released ***Can't Buy Me Love*** c/w *You Can't Do That* (UK-6)
Mar 23 Beatles released ***Do You Want to Know a Secret*** c/w *Thank You Girl* (US-8)...
...4th and final single on the Vee-Jay label
Mar 28 UK EVENTS: Mods and Rockers chose Margate to battle it out for the 1st time
Mar 29 UK RADIO: Radio Caroline made its 1st radio broadcast...
...pirate radio had arrived, playing non-stop pop music
Apr 4 **Beatles** dominated the American charts with 12 songs in the Top 100
Apr 9 **Who** failed their audition for Fontana
Apr 10 Beatles released ***The Beatles' Second Album*** (US-3)
Apr 13 **Doug Sandom**'s last gig as the **Who**'s drummer
Apr 14 **Van Morrison** and the birth of **Them**
Apr 17 Rolling Stones released their UK debut album, ***The Rolling Stones***

Apr 27 Beatles released ***Love Me Do*** c/w *PS I Love You* (US-9) – 2nd single on Tollie...
...Andy White on drums

Apr 30 **Keith Moon**'s audition as drummer for the **Who**

May 2 **Moody Blues'** 1st gig

May 5 **Who**'s 2nd audition for Fontana – **Keith Moon** was now the drummer

May 9 **Chuck Berry** opened his 1st British tour

May 17 **Bob Dylan**'s 1st formal concert in the UK

May 18 Animals recorded ***House of the Rising Sun***

May 20 **Rudy Lewis died at the age of 27** – various causes cited

May 21 Drifters recorded ***Under the Boardwalk*** – lead singer Johnny Moore

May 21 Beatles released ***Sie Liebt Dich*** c/w *I'll Get You* (US-10) – 2nd Swan single

May 24 **Dave Clark Five** arrived in America...
...1st tour by a British Invasion group

May 27 UK RADIO: **Screaming Lord Sutch** launched his own pirate radio station, Radio Sutch

May 31 **Hollies** and the **Rolling Stones** supported **Adam Faith** in a star-studded bill at Wembley

Jun 4 **Jimmy Nicol** stood in for **Ringo Starr** for a week on the **Beatles'** 1st world tour

Jun 5 1st-ever single from David Bowie, ***Liza Jane*** – as Davie Jones with The King Bees

Jun 9 Bob Dylan recorded his 4th album, ***Another Side of Bob Dylan*** – last all-acoustic album

Jun 20 last night of the **Rolling Stones'** 1st American tour

Jun 26 Rolling Stones cover of the Valentinos' ***It's All Over Now*** gave them their 1st UK #1

Jun 26 Beatles released ***A Hard Day's Night*** (US-4) – different track listing to the UK

Jul 2 CIVIL RIGHTS: *Civil Rights Act* became law...
...initiated by **Kennedy**, passed by **Johnson**

Jul 3 High Numbers (shortly to rename to "The Who") released their only single, ***Zoot Suit***...
...promoted as the 1st Mod record

Jul 5 **Them**'s 1st Decca recording session

Jul 10 Beatles released ***A Hard Day's Night*** c/w *Things We Said Today* (UK-7)...
...and the British version of ***A Hard Day's Night*** movie soundtrack (UK-3)

Jul 10 Four Tops released ***Baby I Need Your Loving*** (US) – their debut on Motown

Jul 13 Beatles released ***A Hard Day's Night*** c/w *I Should Have Known Better* (US-11)...
...3rd single on Capitol – all Capitol releases from here

Jul 17 Billy J Kramer with The Dakotas released ***From a Window*** (UK)

Jul 20 Beatles released ***Something New*** (US-5)...
...and, ***I'll Cry Instead*** c/w *I'm Happy Just to Dance with You* (US-12)
...and, ***And I Love Her*** c/w *If I Fell* (US-13)

Jul 25 Rolling Stones released their 4th American single, ***It's All Over Now***

Aug 1 **Frank Zappa** opened his Studio Z in Cucamonga

Aug 4 VIETNAM WAR: *Gulf of Tonkin Incident*...
...led to American military action, without a declaration of war

Aug 4 Kinks released ***You Really Got Me*** (UK)

Aug 5 VIETNAM WAR: 1st American bombing raid on North Vietnam

Aug 14 **Johnny Burnette died** at the age of 30 – drowned

Aug 16 **High Numbers** and the **Kinks** supported the **Beatles** in concert

Aug 19 **Beatles** opened their 1st American tour

Aug 24 Beatles released ***Matchbox*** c/w *Slowdown* (US-14)

Aug 28 **Beatles** met **Bob Dylan** – he introduced them to pot

Sep 10 Rod Stewart recorded his 1st single, ***Good Morning Little Schoolgirl***

Sep 16 US TV: 1st edition of the rock'n'roll music show, *Shindig!*

Oct 7 **Bill Haley and His Comets** in Sheffield, with **Manfred Mann** and **Nashville Teens**...
...from American rock'n'roll to the British Invasion

Oct 13 early **Pretty Things** gig at London's 100 Club

Nov 1 VIETNAM WAR: one of the 1st Viet Cong attacks against an American military base

Nov 13 Moody Blues released their 1st single, ***Go Now!*** (UK)

Nov 13 Rolling Stones released their cover of Willie Dixon's ***Little Red Rooster*** – 2nd UK #1

Nov 23 Beatles released ***I Feel Fine*** c/w *She's a Woman* (US-15)...
...and ***The Beatles' Story*** (US-6) – an album of words and music

Nov 24 **Who** began their Marquee residency

Nov 27 Beatles released ***I Feel Fine*** c/w *She's a Woman* (UK-8)

Dec 2 Frank Zappa's ***I Was a Teen-age Malt Shop*** was...
...nearly the 1st-ever rock opera

Dec 4 Beatles released ***Beatles for Sale*** (UK-4)

Dec 11 **Sam Cooke died** at the age of 33 – shot dead

Dec 15 Beatles released ***Beatles '65*** (US-7)

Dec 23 Beach Boys' **Brian Wilson** had a nervous breakdown – replaced by **Glen Campbell**

Dec 25 **Zombies'** 1st US concert appearance – on *Murray the K's Christmas Show*

Dec 26 **Rolling Stones'** tongue-in-cheek Christmas greeting to British hairdressers

1965 Jan 15 Bob Dylan recorded ***If You Gotta Go, Go Now*** – released in Benelux as a single in 1967

Jan 15 Who released their 1st single, ***I Can't Explain*** (UK)

Jan 20 **Alan Freed died** at the age of 43 – natural causes – he coined the phrase "rock'n'roll"

Jan 29 **PJ Proby**'s notorious trouser splitting UK tour with Cilla Black

Feb 12 **Donovan**'s career started with three consecutive appearances on *Ready Steady Go!*

Feb 15 Beatles released ***Eight Days a Week*** c/w *I Don't Want to Spoil the Party* (US-16)

Feb 26 Rolling Stones released ***The Last Time*** – 1st Jagger and Richard penned A-side in the UK

Mar 2 VIETNAM WAR: *Operation Rolling Thunder* began...
...bombing campaign that lasted until late 1968

Mar 3 **Eric Clapton**'s final gig with the **Yardbirds** – he was replaced by **Jeff Beck**

Mar 5 Yardbirds released ***For Your Love*** (UK) – last single with guitarist Eric Clapton

Mar 8 VIETNAM WAR: 1st American combat troops arrived in Vietnam...
...start of America's ground-war

Mar 8 **David Bowie** made his UK TV debut – with **The Manish Boys**

Mar 14 **Paramounts** supported **Sandie Shaw**

Mar 15 CIVIL RIGHTS: march from Selma to Montgomery, Alabama

Mar 15 Jerry Lee Lewis released his final Sun single, ***Carry Me Back to Old Virginia*** (US)

Mar 18 **Mick Jagger**, **Brian Jones** and **Bill Wyman** were charged with "insulting behaviour"

Mar 22 Beatles released ***The Early Beatles*** (US-8)

Mar 22 Bob Dylan released ***Bringing It All Back Home*** (US) – 1st album with electric songs

Mar 26 **Frank Zappa** arrested in Cucamonga on pornography charges

Apr 2 **Artwoods** appeared on the 1st live edition of *Ready Steady Go!*

Apr 7 VIETNAM WAR: **President Johnson** delivered his speech, *Peace Without Conquest*

Apr 9 **Bruce Johnston** joined **Beach Boys** to become **Brian Wilson**'s permanent replacement

Apr 9 Beatles released ***Ticket to Ride*** c/w *Yes It Is* (UK-9)

Apr 12 Byrds released their 1st single, ***Mr. Tambourine Man*** (US)

Apr 19 Beatles released ***Ticket to Ride*** c/w *Yes It Is* (US-17)

May 10 **Frank Zappa** joined the **Soul Giants** – became the **Mothers**, moved to original material

May 28 MOVIES: premiere of **Elvis**'s 18th movie, *Tickle Me*...
...soundtrack of previously released songs

Jun 14 Beatles released ***Beatles VI*** (US-9)

Jun 15 Bob Dylan recorded ***Like a Rolling Stone***

Jun 19 **Kinks** opened their ill-fated US debut tour – did not perform in America again until 1969

Jun 21 **Charlatans** played at the opening night of the Red Dog Saloon in Virginia City

Jun 29 VIETNAM WAR: 1st "search and destroy" offensive carried out...
...America escalated its activities

Jul 8 UK EVENTS: *Great Train Robber* **Ronnie Biggs** escaped from prison...
...Biggs recorded with the **Sex Pistols** in 1978

Jul 11 **Rising Sons** played an early gig at the Ash Grove in Los Angeles

Jul 19 Beatles released ***Help*** c/w *I'm Down* (US-18)

Jul 23 Beatles released ***Help*** c/w *I'm Down* (UK-10)

Jul 23 Neil Young recorded his 1st single, ***The Sultan*** – as a member of the Squires

Jul 25 **Bob Dylan** performed his infamous electric set at the Newport Folk Festival

Jul 29 Bob Dylan recording session for ***Highway 61 Revisited***

Aug 2 **The Birds** issued **The Byrds** with a writ for using a similar sounding name

Aug 6 Small Faces released their 1st single, ***Whatcha Gonna Do About It***

Aug 6 Beatles released their movie soundtrack album, ***Help*** (UK-5)

Aug 11 US EVENTS: 1st day of the Watts riots in Los Angeles

Aug 13 **Jefferson Airplane**'s 1st gig

Aug 13 Beatles released their movie soundtrack album, ***Help*** (US-10)

Aug 15 **Beatles**' Shea Stadium concert...
...1st stadium gig for a rock'n'roll band

Aug 20 Rolling Stones released ***(I Can't Get No) Satisfaction*** (UK) – different B-side in the US

Aug 20 RECORD LABELS: **Andrew Loog Oldham** formed his own record label, Immediate...
...launch was marked with three singles

Aug 27 **Beatles** met **Elvis Presley** at his Bel Air home

Aug 31 VIETNAM WAR: legislation was passed to criminalise the burning of draft cards...
...the War was becoming increasingly unpopular

Sep 2 **Rick & the Ravens** demo recording session – **Jim Morrison**'s 1st-ever studio time

Sep 8 casting ads appeared looking for "4 insane boys", to appear in the ***Monkees*** TV show

Sep 12 Yardbirds recorded ***The Train Kept A-Rollin'*** at Sun studios in Memphis

Sep 13 Beatles released ***Yesterday*** c/w *Act Naturally* (US-19)

Sep 15 a goose-stepping **Mick Jagger** caused a riot at a Rolling Stones concert in Berlin

Sep 16 David/Davie Jones changed his name to "**David Bowie**"

Oct 10 US EVENTS: **Lenny Bruce** lodged a harassment complaint with the FBI

Oct 15 **Jimi Hendrix** signed a management contract with **Ed Chalpin**

Oct 16 US VENUES: 1st **Family Dog** dance concert held at Longshoreman's Hall

Oct 21 **Bill Black died** at the age of 39 – brain tumour

Oct 29 Who released ***My Generation*** c/w *Shout and Shimmy* (UK)

Nov 1 keyboardist **Ian McLagan** joined **Small Faces** – classic lineup was now in place

Nov 3 1st-ever **Grateful Dead** recording session – still called "**Warlocks**"

Nov 6 **Eric Clapton** was back with **John Mayall** – after his Greek jaunt with the **Glands**

Nov 11 **Velvet Underground**'s 1st gig – supporting **Myddle Class,** featuring singer **David Palmer**

Nov 12 Marc Bolan's 1st TV appearance – performed his 1st single, ***The Wizard***

Nov 19 early appearance as **"David Bowie"** – as **David Bowie with The Lower Third**

Nov 19 **Roger Daltrey** stormed off the stage when the **Who** played the *Glad Rag Ball* at Wembley

Nov 27 **Warlocks** performed at the 1st of **Ken Kesey**'s *Acid Tests...*
...birth of psychedelic rock

Dec 3 Beatles released ***We Can Work it Out*** c/w *Day Tripper* (UK-11)...
...and ***Rubber Soul*** (UK-6) – 1st Beatles album with all original material

Dec 6 **Viv Prince** began a 10-day stint as the **Who**'s drummer – substituting for **Keith Moon**

Dec 6 Beatles released ***We Can Work it Out*** c/w *Day Tripper* (US-20)...
...and ***Rubber Soul*** (US-11)

Dec 10 **Warlocks** debuted as the "**Grateful Dead**"

Dec 12 **Beatles**' last-ever UK concert

1966 Jan 13 **Velvet Underground**'s 1st gig with vocalist **Nico**

Jan 14 ***Thinking About Me,*** 1st single released as "David Bowie" (UK) – with the Lower Third

Jan 17 **Move** formed from three other Birmingham groups

Jan 23 FESTIVALS: psychedelic multimedia *Trips Festival* in San Francisco...
...one of the 1st multimedia events

Jan 28 Small Faces released ***Sha-La-La-La-Lee*** (UK) – 1st single with Ian McLagan

Feb 4 **Bob Dylan**'s infamous electric world tour opened

Feb 4 Rolling Stones released ***19th Nervous Breakdown*** c/w *As Tears Go By* (UK)

Feb 10 review of a **13th Floor Elevators** gig...
...one of the 1st references to "psychedelic rock"

Feb 17 Beach Boys started to record their epic ***Good Vibrations***

Feb 21 Beatles released ***Nowhere Man*** c/w *What Goes On* (US-21)

Mar 4 original **John Lennon** "More Popular Than Jesus" interview, London's *Evening Standard*

Mar 7 Phil Spector recording session for ***River Deep–Mountain High***...
...heralded the end of his "wall of sound" era

Mar 7 **Mike Millward died** at the age of 23 – leukaemia

Mar 14 Who released the 3rd version of ***Substitute*** (UK) – with ***Waltz for a Pig*** on the B-side

Apr 1 David Bowie released ***Do Anything You Say*** (UK) – 1st single as just "David Bowie"

Apr 1 **Noddy Holder** joined the **'N Betweens** – future **Slade** lineup was then in place

Apr 6 legendary accidental encounter of the people who would soon form **Buffalo Springfield**

Apr 12 **Jan Berry** was badly injured when he crashed his Stingray near Dead Man's Curve

Apr 15 Manfred Mann released ***Pretty Flamingo*** (UK) – last single to feature singer Paul Jones

Apr 15 Rolling Stones released ***Aftermath*** (UK) – 1st album with all Jagger and Richard songs

Apr 22 Troggs released ***Wild Thing*** (UK)

Apr 26 **Neil Christian and the Crusaders** gig – with final lead guitarist **Ritchie Blackmore**

May 9 **Doors** auditioned at LA's Whisky a Go Go club

May 16 Jeff Beck recorded ***Beck's Bolero*** – with Keith Moon and Jimmy Page

May 16 Beach Boys released ***Pet Sounds*** (US)

May 16 Bob Dylan released ***Blonde on Blonde*** (US)

May 17 Bob Dylan recorded the legendary ***Live at the Albert Hall*** bootleg album

May 19 **Grateful Dead**'s Avalon concert was bootlegged...
...Grateful Dead encouraged fans to record gigs

May 20 **Keith Moon** and **John Entwistle** quit the **Who** – Moon returned with double bass drum kit

May 25 **Elvis Presley**'s 1st recording session for a non-movie-soundtrack album, since *Pot Luck*

May 30 Beatles released ***Paperback Writer*** c/w *Rain* (US-22)

Jun 1 Eric Clapton and the Powerhouse released three tracks on ***What's Shakin'*** (US)

Jun 6 **Roy Orbison's wife died** – two of his children died in a house fire two years later

Jun 10 Beatles released ***Paperback Writer*** c/w *Rain* (UK-12)

Jun 10 **Janis Joplin**'s 1st gig as lead vocalist with **Big Brother and the Holding Company**

Jun 20 Beatles released ***Yesterday...And Today*** (US-12) – notorious "butcher" cover

Jun 21 **Jimmy Page**'s 1st gig with the **Yardbirds** – joined as bassist, before moving to lead guitar

Jun 21 **Reg Calvert died** at the age of 38 – shot dead

Jun 24 **Beatles'** ill-fated last world tour opened in Germany – on to Japan and the Philippines

Jun 24 **Lenny Bruce** opened what would be his last concerts – supported by the **Mothers**

Jun 27 Mothers of Invention released their 1st album, ***Freak Out*** (US)

Jul 1 goodbye **Mama Michelle** ...hello **Mama Jill** – although, not for very long

Jul 4 Frank Zappa arranged two of the songs on the Animals' American album ***Animalism***

Jul 10 Cat Stevens recorded ***I Love My Dog***

Jul 18 **Bobby Fuller died** at the age of 23 – inhalation of gasoline

Jul 22 John Mayall released ***Bluesbreakers with Eric Clapton*** (UK)

Jul 23 UK VENUES: Liverpool's Cavern Club reopened following a financial crisis

Jul 28 Rolling Stones' founder and guitarist **Brian Jones** played his last-ever concert in America

Jul 29 **Bob Dylan**'s motorcycle accident – followed by nearly 18 months out of the limelight

Jul 31 **Cream**'s official debut gig

Aug 3 **Lenny Bruce** died at the age of 40 – drug overdose

Aug 5 Beatles released ***Yellow Submarine*** c/w *Eleanor Rigby* (UK-13)...

...and ***Revolver*** (UK-7) – different track listing to the US album of the same name

Aug 6 early **Cream** gig...

...heralded the end of beat music

...and the dawn of virtuoso and prog rock

Aug 6 Miracles recorded the original version of ***I Heard It Through the Grapevine***

Aug 8 Beatles released ***Eleanor Rigby*** c/w *Yellow Submarine* (US-23)...

...and ***Revolver*** (US-13) – different track listing to the UK version

...transition from the Brill Building songwriters to songwriting bands

Aug 18 **Doors** signed to Elektra

Aug 29 **Beatles'** last-ever concert performance, at San Francisco's Candlestick Park

Sep 5 **Animals'** final performance before splitting up

Sep 12 US TV: 1st ***Monkees*** TV show aired in America

Oct 1 **Jimi Hendrix** jammed on stage with **Cream** – shortly after he arrived in London

Oct 7 **Johnny Kidd died** at the age of 30 – automobile accident

Oct 10 penultimate recording session for ***The Psychedelic Sounds of the 13th Floor Elevators***

Oct 11 UK EVENTS: counterculture newspaper *it* held its launch party at the Roundhouse

Oct 13 1st **Jimmy Hendrix Experience** performance – backing **Johnny Hallyday** in France

Oct 14 early **Pink Floyd** concert

Oct 16 vocalist **Grace Slick**'s debut with **Jefferson Airplane**

Oct 22 **Chain Reaction** supported the **Yardbirds**, Connecticut – **Steven Tyler** in Chain Reaction

Oct 23 **Jimi Hendrix Experience**'s 1st recording session

Oct 25 **Jimi Hendrix Experience**'s British debut concert, at London's Scotch of St James club

Nov 3 Jefferson Airplane recorded ***White Rabbit***

Nov 4 **Incredible String Band**'s 1st gig outside Scotland

Nov 24 Beatles recorded ***Strawberry Fields Forever***

Nov 25 **Moby Grape**'s 1st major gig

Nov 25 **Jimi Hendrix Experience** was introduced to the UK press at the Bag O' Nails club

Dec 3 **Monkees'** 1st-ever live concert performance

Dec 5 Buffalo Springfield recorded ***For What It's Worth***

Dec 9 Beatles released ***A Collection of Beatles Oldies*** (UK-8) – ***Bad Boy*** was the only new song

Dec 16 Jimi Hendrix Experience released their 1st single, ***Hey Joe*** (UK)

Dec 18 MOVIES: *Blow-Up* opened (US) – featured dual lead guitars, **Jeff Beck** and **Jimmy Page**

Dec 23 UK TV: final edition of *Ready Steady Go!*

1967 Jan 4 Doors released their 1st single, ***Break on Through (to the Other Side)*** (US)...

...and their debut album ***The Doors*** (US)

Jan 6 Paul McCartney and George Martin released ***The Family Way*** movie soundtrack album

Jan 7 early denial of the **"Paul [McCartney] is dead"** myth

Jan 8 VIETNAM WAR: *Operation Cedar Falls*, America's war was nearing its peak...

...largest ground operation of the Vietnam War

...also the 1st use "tunnel rats"

Jan 9 Buffalo Springfield recording session for their 'lost' 2nd album, ***Stampede***

Jan 13 Rolling Stones released ***Let's Spend the Night Together*** (UK)

Jan 14 FESTIVALS: *A Gathering of the Tribes for a Human Be-In...*

...in Haight-Ashbury – centre of the hippie universe

Jan 15 **Stones** censored on the *Ed Sullivan Show* – to stop them spending the "night" together

Jan 21 Monkees recorded ***A Little Bit Me, A Little Bit You*** – the end of Don Kirshner's reign

Jan 22 last gig on the **Monkees'** 1st American tour

Jan 22 **Rolling Stones** refused to wave from the revolving stage at the end of *Palladium* TV show

Feb 3 **Joe Meek died** at the age of 37 – suicide

Feb 13 Beatles released ***Strawberry Fields Forever*** c/w *Penny Lane* (US-24)

Feb 17 Beatles released ***Strawberry Fields Forever*** c/w *Penny Lane* (UK-14)

Feb 17 Soft Machine released their 1st single, ***Love Makes Sweet Music*** (UK)

Feb 27 Pink Floyd recorded their 1st single, ***Arnold Layne***

Mar 3 early gig for the **Jeff Beck Group** – lineup included **Rod Stewart** and **Ron Wood**

Mar 6 Buffalo Springfield re-released 1st album, ***Buffalo Springfield***, with track changes (US)

Mar 12 Velvet Underground released their 1st album, ***The Velvet Underground and Nico*** (US)

Mar 13 **Spencer Davis Group**'s final tour with the lineup that included **Steve** and **Muff Winwood**

Mar 17 Jimi Hendrix Experience released their 2nd single, ***Purple Haze*** (UK)...

...RECORD LABELS: this was Track Records' 1st single

Mar 25 **Cream**'s American concert debut

Mar 28 **Van Morrison** started to record his 1st solo album – after recently splitting from Them

Mar 31 1st time that **Jimi Hendrix** set fire to his guitar on stage

Apr 2 **Steve Winwood** left the **Spencer Davis Group** to form **Traffic**

Apr 3 Cream began to record ***Disraeli Gears***

Apr 4 CIVIL RIGHTS and VIETNAM WAR: **Martin Luther King Jr**'s *Beyond Vietnam* speech...

...protests were blending together

Apr 8 Engelbert Humperdinck's ***Release Me*** broke the Beatles' run of 11 consecutive UK #1s...

...*Penny Lane* c/w *Strawberry Fields* only reached #2

Apr 12 end of the road for **John's Children** as the **Who**'s support band on infamous German tour

Apr 28 VIETNAM WAR: boxer **Mohammad Ali** was arrested for refusing to join the US Army

Apr 29 FESTIVALS: *14-Hour Technicolor Dream* was held at London's Alexandra Palace

May 2 Beach Boy Brian Wilson abandoned his magnum opus, ***Smile***

May 12 Procol Harum released ***A Whiter Shade of Pale*** (UK)

May 12 Jimi Hendrix Experience released their 1st album, ***Are You Experienced*** (UK)

May 23 Pink Floyd recorded their 2nd single, ***See Emily Play***

May 24 John's Children released ***Desdemona*** (UK) – 1st single to feature Marc Bolan

May 29 Moby Grape released their 1st album, ***Moby Grape*** (US)

May 29 **Who**'s drummer **Keith Moon** was substituted by **Julian Covey**

Jun 1 Beatles released ***Sgt Pepper's Lonely Hearts Club Band*** (UK-9)...

...topped "best album of all-time" lists decades later

Jun 1 David Bowie released his 1st album, ***David Bowie*** (UK)

Jun 2 Small Faces released ***Here Comes the Nice*** (UK) – 1st single on Immediate...

Jun 2 ...and despite the band having left Decca, the label released ***From the Beginning*** (UK)

Jun 2 Beatles released ***Sgt Pepper*** (US-14) – 1st US and UK album to be the same

Jun 10 FESTIVALS: *Fantasy Fair and Magic Mountain Music Festival* in San Francisco...

...1st rock festival

Jun 10 **Chris Townson** deputised for the **Who**'s drummer **Keith Moon**

Jun 16 FESTIVALS: 1st *Monterey International Pop Festival*

Jun 17 **Elton John** was introduced to **Bernie Taupin**, after replying to an ad in the *NME*

Jun 21 US EVENTS: *Summer of Love* began on a hilltop above Haight-Ashbury

Jun 25 **Beatles** appeared on the *Our World* live global TV broadcast – to 400 million viewers

Jun 28 Who recorded ***The Last Time*** and ***Under My Thumb*** – without John Entwistle

Jul 7 Beatles released ***All You Need is Love*** c/w *Baby You're a Rich Man* (UK-15)

Jul 8 **Jimi Hendrix Experience** joined the **Monkees'** American tour as the opening act

Jul 14 John's Children released ***Come and Play with Me in the Garden*** (UK)

Jul 17 Beatles released ***All You Need Is Love*** c/w *Baby You're a Rich Man* (US-25)

Jul 24 UK EVENTS: advert in *The Times* newspaper called for the legalization of marijuana

Jul 27 UK EVENTS: *The Sexual Offences Act 1967* received the Royal Assent...

...decriminalized homosexuality in England and Wales

Jul 31 **Mick Jagger** and **Keith Richard** successfully appealed against their drugs convictions

Aug 5 Pink Floyd released their 1st album, ***Piper at the Gates of Dawn*** (UK)

Aug 13 Fleetwood Mac's 1st concert – as **Peter Green's Fleetwood Mac**

Aug 14 disconcerting plane flight inspired Pete Townshend to write ***Glow Girl*** – led to **Tommy**

Aug 18 Stones released ***We Love You*** (UK) – last single produced by Andrew Loog Oldham

Aug 24 **Daevid Allen** left **Soft Machine** – end of the band's 1st era

Aug 27 **Brian Epstein died** at the age of 32 – accidental overdose

Sep 1 1st **Steve Miller Band** appearance with **Boz Scaggs**

Sep 10 Pete Seeger's ***Waist Deep in the Big Muddy*** censored on Smothers Brothers TV show... ...political music censorship still existed on US TV

Sep 11 Beach Boys released ***Smiley Smile*** (US) – from the ashes of the 'lost' ***Smile*** album... ...RECORD LABELS: 1st album released on their Brother label

Sep 17 Doors refused to change the lyrics for ***Light My Fire*** on the *Ed Sullivan Show*

Sep 17 **Who**'s exploding bass drum performance, on the *Smothers Brothers Comedy Hour*

Sep 21 **Tomorrow** appeared on the 1st *John Peel Sessions* BBC Radio show

Sep 29 UK VENUES: final gig at London's 1st psychedelic club, the UFO – opened 23 Dec. 1966

Sep 30 UK RADIO: Radio 1 made its 1st broadcast... ...1st official rock and pop radio station in the UK

Oct 6 US EVENTS: *Death of Hippie* march in Haight-Ashbury, San Francisco

Oct 9 REVOLUTIONARY ICON: **Che Guevara died** at the age of 39 – executed... ...an icon for the revolutionary ideals of the 1960s

Oct 11 Move's ***Flowers in the Rain*** libel suit with Harold Wilson settled

Oct 17 THEATRE: hippie musical *Hair* opened off-Broadway

Oct 18 MOVIES: **John Lennon**'s *How I Won the War* premiered in London

Oct 21 VIETNAM WAR: anti-War demonstration to levitate the Pentagon

Oct 22 **Castiles'** drummer KIA in Vietnam – **Bruce Springsteen**'s 1st band, 1965 to '68

Oct 30 **Brian Jones** pleaded guilty to drugs offences

Nov 4 **Pink Floyd**'s opening concert for their disastrous 1st American tour

Nov 9 **Spirit** recording session for their eponymous 1st album

Nov 9 ROCK PRESS: 1st issue of *Rolling Stone* magazine

Nov 11 **Van Morrison**'s 1st solo appearance on *American Bandstand*

Nov 14 UK tour opened, headlined by **Jimi Hendrix** – support included **Pink Floyd** and the **Nice**

Nov 18 Pink Floyd released ***Apples and Oranges*** (UK) – 3rd and last Syd Barrett penned single

Nov 24 Beatles released ***Hello Goodbye*** c/w *I Am the Walrus* (UK-16)

Nov 27 Beatles released ***Hello Goodbye*** c/w *I Am the Walrus* (US-26)... ...and ***Magical Mystery Tour*** – album format in America (US-15)

Nov 29 VIETNAM WAR: **Robert McNamara** resigned as America's Secretary of Defense... ...America's politicians were turning against the War

Dec 8 Beatles released ***Magical Mystery Tour*** – double-EP format in the UK

Dec 9 **Jim Morrison** was arrested on stage in New Haven

Dec 9 Rolling Stones released ***Their Satanic Majesties Request*** (US) – to mixed reviews

Dec 20 VIETNAM WAR: **Joan Baez** received a 45-day jail sentence for anti-War activities

Dec 22 FESTIVALS: *Christmas on Earth Continued* concert in London

Dec 22 VIETNAM WAR: last days of positive spin from America's politicians and military...
...the tide was about to turn for America in Vietnam

Dec 26 UK TV: premiere of the **Beatles'** *Magical Mystery Tour* – panned by the critics

Dec 27 Leonard Cohen released his 1st album, ***Songs of Leonard Cohen*** (US)

Dec 27 Bob Dylan released ***John Wesley Harding*** (US) – 1st album since his motorcycle accident

1968 Jan 3 Byrds released ***The Notorious Byrd Brothers*** (US)

Jan 21 VIETNAM WAR: siege of Khe Sanh began...
...prelude to the devastating *Tet Offensive*

Jan 25 early Steppenwolf gig – recorded **Born to Be Wild** around this time...
...term "heavy metal" was coined in this song

Jan 31 VIETNAM WAR: *Tet Offensive* began...
...beginning of the end for America in Vietnam

Jan 31 end of the **Who**'s ill-fated Australian tour – Townshend vowed never to play there again

Feb 15 **Little Walter died** at the age of 37 – street fight

Feb 22 Genesis released their 1st single, ***The Silent Sun*** (UK)

Feb 23 **Band of Joy** gig at the Marquee – split up shortly afterwards

Feb 25 **Jimi Hendrix** had a stimulating encounter with legendary groupie **Cynthia Plaster Caster**

Feb 27 **Frankie Lymon died** at the age of 25 – drug overdose

Mar 5 **Jerry Lee Lewis** played Iago in *Catch My Soul* – an adaptation of Shakespeare's *Othello*

Mar 6 Rascals recorded ***A Beautiful Morning*** – 1st single as "The Rascals"

Mar 7 Ginger Baker recorded his epic drum solo ***Toad***...
...the rock drum solo came of age

Mar 8 US VENUES: **Bill Graham** opened the Fillmore East in New York

Mar 9 Love were on tour to support ***Forever Changes*** – band imploded at the end of the tour

Mar 15 Beatles released ***Lady Madonna*** c/w *The Inner Light* (UK-17)

Mar 16 VIETNAM WAR: infamous My Lai massacre...
...America's darkest hour in the Vietnam War

Mar 16 US VENUES: **Grateful Dead/Jefferson Airplane**'s ill-fated Carousel Ballroom venture

Mar 17 VIETNAM WAR: riot in London's Grosvenor Square
...violent anti-War demonstrations spread to Europe

Mar 18 Beatles released ***Lady Madonna*** c/w *The Inner Light* (US-27)

Mar 29 a faux **Moby Grape** played a gig in Santa Monica

Mar 31 VIETNAM WAR: **President Johnson** announced "Vietnamization"...
...also that he would not be seeking re-election

Apr 3 Moby Grape released ***Wow/Grape Jam*** (US) – last album to feature Skip Spence

Apr 4 ASSASSINATIONS: **Martin Luther King Jr**, in Memphis, Tennessee

Apr 6 **David Gilmour** replaced **Syd Barrett** in **Pink Floyd**

Apr 11 **Al Kooper** left **Blood, Sweat & Tears** after their four-day stint in New York

Apr 19 **Free**'s 1st-ever gig

Apr 19 Marc Bolan released ***Debora*** (UK) – 1st single as Tyrannosaurus Rex

Apr 20 UK EVENTS: politician **Enoch Powell** delivered his infamous "rivers of blood" speech...
...concerns about immigration were growing in the UK

Apr 20 **Deep Purple**'s 1st gig – as "Roundabout"

May 5 **Buffalo Springfield**'s final gig

May 10 VIETNAM WAR: start of the peace negotiations...
...Paris Peace Talks began – ended on 27 January 1973

May 24 Rolling Stones released ***Jumping Jack Flash*** (UK) – 1st single produced by Jimmy Miller

May 24 Small Faces released ***Ogden's Nut Gone Flake*** (UK)

May 26 **Little Willie John died** at the age of 30 – in prison

May 28 Mike Bloomfield walked out after recording half of the ***Supersession*** album

May 29 recording session for songs that might have been on Who's 'lost' album ***Who's for Tennis***

May 31 **Skip Spence**'s final performances with **Moby Grape** – just before the axe incident

Jun 5 ASSASSINATIONS: **Robert Kennedy**, in Los Angeles, California

Jun 11 Beatles recording session for ***Revolution 9*** – cited as an inspiration by Charles Manson

Jun 14 Iron Butterfly released the album ***In-A-Gadda-Da-Vida*** (US)

Jun 15 **Jeff Beck Group** performed at New York's Fillmore East – upstaged **Grateful Dead**

Jun 26 **Nice** banned for life from the Albert Hall – after a flag-burning performance of *America*...
...1st instrumental protest song

Jun 29 Pink Floyd released ***A Saucerful of Secrets*** (UK) – input from Barrett and Gilmour

Jul 1 Band released their 1st album, ***Music from the Big Pink*** (US)

Jul 7 **Yardbirds**' last performance

Jul 8 **Gram Parsons** quit the **Byrds** – formed the **Flying Burrito Brothers** shortly afterwards

Jul 15 VIETNAM WAR: Yippies applied for a youth festival permit...
...for the Chicago Democratic Convention

Jul 18 Grateful Dead released 2nd album, ***Anthem of the Sun*** – 1st album with two drummers

Jul 30 end of the **Beatles**' Apple Boutique

Aug 4 1st **Yes** gig

Aug 25 VIETNAM WAR: 1st day of the violence at the Democratic Party Convention in Chicago...
...public opinion was turning firmly against the War

Aug 26 Beatles released ***Hey Jude*** c/w *Revolution* (US-28)

Aug 30 Beatles released ***Hey Jude*** c/w *Revolution* (UK-18)

Sep 6 Eric Clapton recorded the solo for George Harrison's ***While My Guitar Gently Weeps***

Sep 7 1st gig for the **Led Zeppelin** lineup – but billed as **"The Yardbirds"**

Sep 18 **Rush**'s 1st paid gig

Sep 27 UK EVENTS: *Hair* opened in London – with full-frontal nude scenes...
...end of formal censorship in live British theatre

Sep 27 **Led Zeppelin**'s 1st recording session
Oct 5 Muddy Waters released his psychedelic blues album ***Electric Mud*** (US)
Oct 8 disastrous beginning to **Cass Elliot**'s solo career
Oct 24 Joe Cocker promoted ***With a Little Help from My Friends*** on *Top of the Pops*
Oct 24 US EVENTS: LSD (Acid) became illegal in America...
...after starting out as a CIA experimental drug
Oct 25 Jethro Tull released their 1st album, ***This Was*** (UK)
Oct 25 Jimi Hendrix Experience released their 3rd album, ***Electric Ladyland*** (UK)
Oct 30 MC5 recorded their 1st album, ***Kick Out the Jams*** – live in Detroit
Oct 31 VIETNAM WAR: **President Johnson** ended *Operation Rolling Thunder...*
...intensive bombing campaign, started on 2 March 1965
Nov 1 George Harrison released ***Wonderwall Music*** (UK) – 1st solo album by a Beatle
Nov 4 **Cream**'s final concert in America
Nov 6 MOVIES: world premiere of the **Monkees**' *Head*
Nov 9 **Led Zeppelin** performed under that name for the 1st time
Nov 13 MOVIES: **Beatles**' animated movie *Yellow Submarine* opened in America
Nov 16 end of the road together for **Cliff Richard** and **The Shadows**
Nov 21 **Stooges** concert – Psychedelic Stooges formed 1967 – Stooges' debut album mid-1969
Nov 22 Beatles released the ***White Album*** (UK-10)
Nov 22 Kinks released ***Village Green Preservation Society*** (UK) – last album with Pete Quaife
Nov 23 **John and Yoko** appeared naked on the cover of *Rolling Stone* magazine
Nov 25 Beatles released ***White Album*** (US-16) – beginning of the end for the Beatles
Nov 26 **Cream**'s farewell concert at the Royal Albert Hall
Nov 29 John Lennon released ***Unfinished Music No.1: Two Virgins*** – 1st solo album
Dec 1 **Janis Joplin**'s last performance with **Big Brother and the Holding Company**
Dec 3 **Elvis Presley**'s *Comeback Special* TV show
Dec 7 **Eric Burdon** said goodbye to the music business – **New Animals** split up shortly before
Dec 8 **Graham Nash** left the **Hollies** to form **Crosby, Stills & Nash**
Dec 11 **Rolling Stones** recorded their TV special *Rock and Roll Circus* – not seen until 1996
Dec 26 **Led Zeppelin**'s debut concert in America
Dec 29 early **Poco** gig – still calling themselves "Pogo" – changed to "Poco" shortly afterwards
Dec 30 **Popcorn Blizzard** supported the **Fugs** in Detroit – Blizzard's lead singer was **Meat Loaf**
Dec 31 **Steve Marriott** stormed off during a **Small Faces** gig – formed **Humble Pie** soon after

1969 Jan 2 work started on the Beatles' ill-fated ***Get Back*** project
Jan 3 early **Colosseum** gig – supported by **Earth** at the Marquee club
Jan 4 unscheduled performance of ***Sunshine of Your Love*** by Jimi Hendrix on Lulu's TV show
Jan 12 eponymous debut album ***Led Zeppelin*** released in America – ten weeks before the UK
Jan 13 Beatles released the movie soundtrack album ***Yellow Submarine*** (US-17)

Jan 17 Beatles released **Yellow Submarine** album (UK-11)

Jan 18 **Pete Best** won his lawsuit against the **Beatles**

Jan 18 John McLaughlin recorded his 1st solo album, ***Extrapolation***

Jan 22 VIETNAM WAR: beginning of *Operation Dewey Canyon*...

...nearing the end of the US Marines' time in Vietnam

Jan 27 Beach Boys released **20/20** (US) – contained a song written by Charles Manson

Jan 30 **Beatles'** swan song rooftop performance

Feb 1 **Rascals** announced that they would only perform if the concert bill was 50% black

Feb 17 **James Taylor** released his eponymous 1st album (US)

Feb 22 **Fugs** final gig – re-formed in 1984

Feb 27 Grateful Dead opened four nights at Fillmore West – recordings used for ***Live Dead***

Mar 1 Cream released ***Goodbye*** (UK)

Mar 2 Doors frontman **Jim Morrison** faced obscenity charges after a concert in Miami

Mar 7 Genesis released their 1st album, ***From Genesis to Revelation*** (UK)

Mar 10 Led Zeppelin released ***Good Times Bad Times*** – 1st American single

Mar 20 VIETNAM WAR: *Chicago 8* indicted...

...result of the riots at the 1968 Democratic Convention

Mar 28 **Led Zeppelin** released their eponymous 1st album (UK) – ten weeks after its US release

Mar 30 1st **Allman Brothers Band** gig

Apr 8 PJ Proby released ***Three Week Hero*** (UK) – 1st time "Led Zeppelin" recorded together

Apr 11 Beatles released ***Get Back*** c/w *Don't Let Me Down* (UK-19) – early lyrics deemed racist

Apr 16 **MC5** were dropped by Elektra after running ads deemed to be offensive

Apr 17 debut concert as "**The Band**"

May 2 Ambrose Slade released their only single, ***Genesis*** (UK)

May 5 Beatles released ***Get Back*** c/w *Don't Let Me Down* (US-29)

May 8 MOVIES: premiere of *Easy Rider* at the Cannes Film Festival

May 12 **Martin Lamble** and **Jeannie Franklyn died** – automobile accident

May 15 VIETNAM WAR: battle for Hill 937 – *Hamburger Hill*...

...**Nixon** started troop withdrawals shortly afterwards

May 19 Alice Cooper released their 1st single, ***Reflected*** (US) – the name still referred to the band

May 23 Who released ***Tommy*** (UK)

May 30 Beatles released ***Ballad of John and Yoko*** c/w *Old Brown Shoe* (UK-20)...

...A-side had no input from either Ringo or George

...B-side was one of George's compositions

...this was to be their last UK #1

Jun 4 Beatles released ***Ballad of John and Yoko*** c/w *Old Brown Shoe* (US-30)

Jun 4 end of the line for **Episode Six, Ian Gillan** and **Roger Glover** left to join **Deep Purple**

Jun 7 **Blind Faith**'s debut performance at a free concert in London's Hyde Park

Jun 8 guitarist and founder **Brian Jones** left the Rolling Stones

Jun 8 VIETNAM WAR: **President Nixon** announced that American troops were coming home...
...1st American troop withdrawals from Vietnam

Jun 13 **Atomic Rooster** formed by **Vincent Crane** and **Carl Palmer**

Jun 16 Captain Beefheart released ***Trout Mask Replica*** (US)

Jun 17 Elvis Presley released ***From Elvis in Memphis*** (US) – 1st new rock album since 1962

Jun 18 recording session for Colosseum's 2nd album, ***Valentyne Suite***...
...RECORD LABELS: Vertigo's 1st album release

Jun 29 last gig for classic **Jimi Hendrix Experience** lineup – Noel Redding left shortly afterwards

Jul 1 RECORD LABELS: **Sam Phillips** sold Sun Records/back catalogue to **Shelby Singleton**

Jul 3 **Brian Jones died at the age of 27** – drowned in his own swimming pool

Jul 4 Rolling Stones released ***Honky Tonk Women*** (UK) – 1st single to feature Mick Taylor

Jul 5 **Rolling Stones'** free concert in London's Hyde Park – 1st gig with guitarist **Mick Taylor**

Jul 6 **Procol Harum** performed with a full symphony orchestra and chorus

Jul 11 David Bowie released his break-through single ***Space Oddity*** (UK)

Jul 25 **Crosby, Stills & Nash**'s 1st performance

Jul 26 FESTIVALS: **Flying Burrito Brothers** played the *Seattle Pop Festival*

Jul 28 **Led Zeppelin** participated in one of rock'n'roll's most notorious après-rock moments...
...*Edgewater Inn Mud Shark Incident*

Jul 31 **Elvis Presley**'s 1st performance at the Las Vegas International Hotel...
...heralded Elvis's 3rd career stage – the cabaret years

Aug 10 US EVENTS: Charles Manson murders...
...Leno and Rosemary LaBianca, and Sharon Tate

Aug 15 FESTIVALS: 1st day of the legendary *Woodstock* festival...
...most famous festival of them all – "3 days of peace and music"

Aug 19 Miles Davies started recording ***Bitches Brew***...
...dawn of jazz rock fusion

Aug 20 final recording session with all four **Beatles**

Aug 20 **Frank Zappa** disbanded the original **Mothers of Invention**

Aug 22 Radha Krishna Temple (London) released ***Hare Krishna Mantra*** (US)

Aug 24 final **Blind Faith** concert

Aug 26 Elvis Presley released ***Suspicious Minds*** (US) – last American chart topper in his lifetime

Aug 29 Jack Bruce released his solo album ***Songs for a Tailor*** (UK)

Aug 29 **Hawkwind** played their 1st gig – as "Band X"

Sep 1 Hollies released ***He Ain't Heavy....He's My Brother*** (UK)

Sep 3 VIETNAM WAR: announcement of the death of **Ho Chi Minh** – he actually died on 2 Sep.

Sep 5 early **Mott the Hoople** gig

Sep 9 1st time **Freddie Mercury, Brian May** and **Roger Taylor** performed on stage together

Sep 13 FESTIVALS: **Plastic Ono Band**'s debut at the *Toronto Rock and Roll Revival*

Sep 13 **Alice Cooper**'s notorious *Chicken Incident* at the *Toronto Rock and Roll Revival* festival

Sep 24 Deep Purple recorded ***Concerto for Group and Orchestra***

Sep 24 Fairport Convention's Albert Hall concert to promote upcoming album, ***Liege & Lief***...
...dawn of British folk rock

Sep 25 recording session for the studio portion of Alexis Korner's New Church's ***Both Sides***

Sep 26 Beatles released ***Abbey Road*** (UK-12) – last album to be recorded

Sep 27 1st date as "**Black Sabbath**"

Sep 29 G.T.O.'s released ***Circular Circulation*** (US)

Oct 1 Beatles released ***Abbey Road*** (US-18)

Oct 6 Beatles released ***Something*** c/w *Come Together* (US-31)

Oct 10 King Crimson released their 1st album, ***In the Court of the Crimson King*** (UK)

Oct 11 VIETNAM WAR: Weathermen's *Days of Rage* protest in Chicago...
...demos moved from peaceful protest to direct action

Oct 15 VIETNAM WAR: the North's **Pham Van Dong** encouraged US anti-War protestors

Oct 20 Who performed ***Tommy*** for the 1st of six nights at the Fillmore East

Oct 25 Pink Floyd released their 4th album, ***Ummagumma***

Oct 31 Beatles released ***Something*** c/w *Come Together* (UK-21) – George's 1st A-side

Oct 31 Led Zeppelin released ***Led Zeppelin II*** (UK)

Nov 1 *Rolling Stone* magazine's hoax review for the **Masked Marauders** led to a spoof album

Nov 7 **Rolling Stones** opened their 1st American tour for three years

Nov 7 Led Zeppelin released ***Whole Lotta Love*** single (US) – released but withdrawn in the UK

Nov 7 John and Yoko released ***Wedding Album*** (UK)

Nov 8 **Allman Brothers Band** released their eponymous 1st album (US)

Nov 10 MOVIES: **Elvis Presley**'s *Change of Habit* opened (US) – 31st and final movie as an actor

Nov 11 **Jim Morrison** was arrested after becoming obnoxious on a plane

Nov 14 early **Faces** gig

Nov 14 early outing for **Skid Row** as a power trio

Nov 15 VIETNAM WAR: *March Against Death*, mass march on the White House...
...one of the biggest anti-War protests of the 1960s

Nov 16 **Janis Joplin** was arrested at a gig for using "vulgar and indecent language"

Nov 27 Rolling Stones' Madison Square Garden gig – recorded for ***Get Yer Ya-Ya's Out!***

Nov 30 **3-Monkee** tour, penultimate gig – **Davy Jones** and **Micky Dolenz** continued as a duo

Dec 2 **George Harrison** joined **Delaney & Bonnie** on stage in Bristol – and rest of the tour

Dec 3 Tim Rice and Andrew Lloyd Webber reputedly asked **John Lennon** to play Jesus Christ

Dec 6 FESTIVALS: ill-fated Altamont festival – fatal stabbing by a Hells Angel...
...spiritual end of the 1960s

Dec 7 live LP recorded, ***Delaney & Bonnie & Friends: on Tour with Eric Clapton***

Dec 8 **Jimi Hendrix** was found not guilty of drug possession in Canada

Dec 15 start of **John Lennon** and **Yoko Ono**'s international peace campaign, *War is Over*

Dec 17 **Tiny Tim** married Miss Vicki live on TV's *Johnny Carson Show*

1970	Jan 3	Syd Barrett released his 1st solo album, ***The Madcap Laughs*** (UK)
	Jan 11	Free recorded ***All Right Now***
	Jan 17	Procol Harum recorded ***Ain't Nothing to Get Excited About*** – as "Liquorice John Death"
	Jan 26	**Elvis Presley** wore a jumpsuit on stage for the 1st time
	Jan 27	John Lennon wrote and recorded ***Instant Karma*** – 1st collaboration with Phil Spector
	Jan 28	demise of **Jimi Hendrix**'s short-lived **Band of Gypsys**
	Feb 4	**Flaming Youth** gig – with drummer **Phil Collins**
	Feb 10	**ZZ Top**'s 1st gig
	Feb 13	**Black Sabbath** released their eponymous 1st album (UK)
	Feb 14	Who's legendary ***Live at Leeds*** concert
	Feb 26	Beatles released the album ***Hey Jude*** in America (US-19) – not released in the UK
	Feb 28	**Led Zeppelin** performed in Denmark, billed as "The Nobs"
	Mar 6	Beatles released their final UK single ***Let It Be*** c/w *You Know My Name...*(UK-22)
	Mar 11	penultimate Beatles US release ***Let It Be*** c/w *You Know My Name...*(US-32)
	Mar 23	Phil Spector began work on the Beatles' album ***Get Back*** – to turn it into ***Let It Be***
	Mar 27	Joe Cocker recorded the live album ***Mad Dogs & Englishmen***
	Apr 3	**Brinsley Schwarz**'s over-hyped attempt to impress – flew UK rock journalists to US gig
	Apr 10	*Daily Mirror* (UK) headline, **"Paul Is Quitting The Beatles"**
	Apr 17	Paul McCartney released his 1st solo album, ***McCartney*** (UK)
	Apr 21	**Elton John** embarked on his solo career – supporting T.Rex
	Apr 24	Ringo Starr released his 1st solo album, ***Sentimental Journey*** (US)
	Apr 25	**Jimi Hendrix** opened his last American tour
	May 1	VIETNAM WAR: 1st day of the Kent State University protests... ...four students were shot dead on 4 May
	May 8	Beatles released their final album ***Let It Be*** (UK-13) – produced by Phil Spector
	May 11	Beatles released ***Long and Winding Road*** c/w *For You Blue* (US-33) – last US single
	May 15	orchestral premiere of Frank Zappa's ***200 Motels***
	May 16	**Cactus**'s 1st gig
	May 18	Beatles released the album ***Let It Be*** (US-20)
	May 20	MOVIES: *Let It Be* premiered in Britain – none of the Beatles attended... ...end of the line for the **Beatles**
	May 28	original guitarist **Peter Green**'s final gig with **Fleetwood Mac**
	Jun 3	Deep Purple released ***In Rock*** (UK)
	Jun 7	**Who** performed *Tommy* at New York's Metropolitan Opera House
	Jun 14	**Derek and the Dominos'** 1st concert
	Jun 27	1st **Queen** concert – bassist John Deacon joined a year later
	Jun 28	FESTIVALS: *Festival Express* played Toronto, then on to Winnipeg and Calgary
	Jul 11	early **Kraftwerk** concert... ...dawn of "Krautrock" – a name coined by the UK press

Aug 3 MOVIES: **Mick Jagger**'s 1st movie, *Performance*, was released – filmed in 1968
Aug 7 FESTIVALS: opening day of Michigan's 3-day *Goose Lake International Music Festival*
Aug 14 **Hawkwind** released their eponymous 1st album (UK)
Aug 23 last **Velvet Underground** concert with Lou Reed
Aug 25 **Emerson, Lake & Palmer** played their 1st gig
Aug 28 FESTIVALS: *Isle of Wight Festival* was attended by over 500,000 people
Sep 3 **Alan "Blind Owl" Wilson died at the age of 27** – drug overdose
Sep 5 VIETNAM WAR: US troops began their last major ground action...
...America's war in Vietnam was drawing to a close
Sep 9 Eric Clapton recorded ***Layla*** – his ode to Pattie Boyd
Sep 12 **Eric Burdon and War** performed at Hyde Park
Sep 14 **Elvis Presley** was back on the road again – for the 1st time since 1957
Sep 18 Black Sabbath released ***Paranoid*** (UK)
Sep 18 Fleetwood Mac released **Kiln House** (US) – 1st post-Pete Green and last Jeremy Spencer
Sep 18 **Jimi Hendrix died at the age of 27 –** inhalation of vomit: open verdict
Sep 19 FESTIVALS: 1st Glastonbury festival
Oct 2 T.Rex released their 1st single, ***Ride a White Swan*** (UK)...
...dawn of British glam rock
Oct 3 Janis Joplin's final recording session for ***Pearl***
Oct 4 **Janis Joplin died at the age of 27** – drug overdose
Oct 23 Led Zeppelin released their 3rd album, ***Led Zeppelin III*** (UK)
Oct 30 **Jim Morrison** was sentenced, following events at the notorious Miami concert in 1969
Nov 6 **Aerosmith**'s 1st concert
Nov 12 **Jim Morrison**'s final concert performance with the **Doors**
Nov 27 George Harrison released ***All Things Must Pass*** (UK)
Dec 5 **Derek and the Dominos'** penultimate gig – Eric Clapton became a recluse
Dec 9 **Jerry Lee Lewis** divorced his 3rd wife, Myra Gale
Dec 11 John Lennon released his 1st 'true' solo album, ***Plastic Ono Band*** (UK)
Dec 11 **T.Rex** released their eponymous 1st album (UK)
Dec 21 **Elvis Presley** met President Nixon and became a drugs enforcement officer
Dec 25 **Little Feat**'s debut concert

1971 Jan 18 CANADIAN RADIO: introduced a minimum playlist of 30% home-grown music
Jan 19 **Amazing Blondel** supported **Mott the Hoople** at London's Marquee club
Jan 30 **Eric Burdon** collapsed on stage – parted company with **War** shortly afterwards
Feb 6 founding member **Richard Thompson** parted company with **Fairport Convention**
Feb 10 George Harrison received a plagiarism lawsuit for ***My Sweet Lord***
Feb 10 **Patti Smiths'** 1st performance with guitarist **Lenny Kaye**
Feb 15 guitarist **Jeremy Spencer** found God and quit **Fleetwood Mac**

Feb 16 recording started on Weather Report's 1st album, ***Weather Report***

Mar 4 **Rolling Stones** opened their *Goodbye to Great Britain* tour...

...1st British rock'n'roll tax exiles

...UK tax rates were in the region of 90%

Mar 5 Led Zeppelin's 1st-ever performance of ***Stairway to Heaven***

Mar 11 **Allman Brothers Band** recorded their acclaimed live album at the Fillmore East

Mar 18 Colosseum concert recorded for the ***Live*** album – band split up at the end of the year

Mar 26 Emerson, Lake & Palmer recorded Mussorgsky's ***Pictures at an Exhibition***...

...prog rock embraced the classics

Apr 15 **Masked Marauders** were dropped from Warner Brothers' catalogue – the hoax was over

Apr 16 Rolling Stones released ***Brown Sugar*** (UK)...

...RECORD LABELS: 1st single on their own Rolling Stones Records label

Apr 23 Rolling Stones released ***Sticky Fingers*** (UK) – album sleeve designed by Andy Warhol

Apr 26 Pete Townshend abandoned his ***Lifehouse*** project

Apr 27 **Grateful Dead** performed together with the **Beach Boys** at the Fillmore East

May 6 US VENUES: **Bill Graham** announced the closure of the Fillmore East and Fillmore West

May 9 Free supported **Deep Purple** in Australia – **Free** split up for the 1st time shortly afterwards

May 14 Who's John Entwistle released his solo album, ***Smash Your Head Against the Wall***

Jun 6 **John Lennon** performed with **Frank Zappa** at the Fillmore East

Jun 13 VIETNAM WAR: publication of the *Pentagon Papers* – chronicled US involvement...

...successive US governments misled the people

Jun 27 VIETNAM WAR: last US Marine combat unit left Vietnam...

...US military involvement was drawing to a close

Jun 30 early **Lynyrd Skynyrd** recording session at Muscle Shoals

Jul 2 debut concert by the classic **Queen** lineup

Jul 3 **Jim Morrison died at the age of 27** – heart failure

Jul 5 riot at a **Led Zeppelin** concert in Italy

Jul 12 **Eagles** played together for the 1st time – as **Linda Ronstadt**'s backing band

Jul 16 Elastic Oz Band released ***God Save Us***...

...in support of the defendants in the *OZ* obscenity trial

Jul 20 **Elvis Presley**'s 1st stage entrance to *Also Sprach Zarathustra*

Aug 1 ***Concert for Bangladesh*** organised by ex-Beatle George Harrison and Ravi Shankar

Aug 13 **King Curtis died** at the age of 37 – murdered by a junkie

Aug 27 Who released ***Who's Next*** (UK) – some tracks salvaged from the *Lifehouse* project

Aug 30 Beach Boys released ***Surf's Up*** (US)

Sep 1 **Rolling Stones** issued a lawsuit against their ex-manager **Allen Klein**

Sep 17 T.Rex released ***Electric Warrior*** (UK)

Sep 21 UK TV: 1st edition of *The Old Grey Whistle Test*

Oct 8 John Lennon released his album ***Imagine*** (UK) – featured guitarist George Harrison

Oct 9 VIETNAM WAR: "combat refusal" by the 1st Air Cavalry Division...

...anti-War feeling was growing amongst US troops

Oct 12 **Gene Vincent died** at the age of 36 – natural causes

Oct 29 **Duane Allman died** at the age of 24 – motorcycle accident

Nov 4 UK VENUES: **Who** performed on the opening night of London's Rainbow Theatre

Nov 12 Led Zeppelin released their untitled 4th album (UK) – included ***Stairway to Heaven***

Nov 17 **Bob Dylan** and beat poet **Allen Ginsberg** recorded together

Dec 4 fire at Zappa's Montreux Casino concert – inspired Deep Purple's ***Smoke on the Water***

Dec 10 Trevor Howell pushed **Frank Zappa** off the stage and seriously injured him

Dec 13 US EVENTS: **John Sinclair** freed from prison...

...after receiving a ten-year sentence for two joints

1972 Feb 11 **King Crimson** opened US tour – all except **Fripp** joined **Alexis Korner** at the tour's end

Feb 12 Allman Brothers released ***Eat a Peach*** (US) – last album with Duane Allman

Feb 13 Man, Hawkwind and Brinsley Schwarz recorded the live album ***Greasy Truckers Party***

Feb 17 press debut concert of Floyd's ***Dark Side of the Moon*** – a year before album's release

Feb 18 **Roxy Music**'s 1st gig after **Manzanera** joined – 1st gig for lineup that recorded 1st album

Feb 25 Wings released their protest single ***Give Ireland Back to the Irish*** (UK)

Mar 24 **David Bowie** rescued a disillusioned **Mott the Hoople** from splitting up

Mar 30 VIETNAM WAR: *Easter Offensive* began...

...full-scale attack on the South by Northern forces

Apr 16 **Electric Light Orchestra**'s 1st gig – as they transitioned from the **Move**

Apr 28 Brinsley Schwarz included on the ***Greasy Truckers Party*** album...

...dawn of British pub rock

May 3 **Les Harvey died** at the age of 25 – electrocuted on stage

May 12 Rolling Stones released ***Exile on Main Street*** (US)

May 14 Mott the Hoople recorded ***All the Young Dudes***

May 22 **Creedence Clearwater Revival**'s final concert

Jun 1 **Eagles** released their eponymous 1st album (US)

Jun 3 **Rolling Stones** opened their legendary North American *Exile on Main Street* tour

Jun 6 Bowie released ***The Rise and Fall of Ziggy Stardust and the Spiders from Mars*** (UK)

Jun 13 **Clyde McPhatter died** at the age of 39 – alcohol related

Jun 14 early **Eagles** gig supporting **Jethro Tull** – lineup came from **Linda Ronstadt**'s band

Jun 16 British glam-rockers Roxy Music released their 1st album, ***Roxy Music*** (UK)

Jun 17 US EVENTS: five men were arrested in the Watergate building...

...Watergate scandal began

...led to President Nixon's resignation in August 1974

Jul 21 **Doors** opened their last-ever tour

Aug 21 riot at a **Jefferson Airplane** concert in Akron, Ohio – **Grace Slick** was arrested

Aug 22 early **New York Dolls** gig...

...pioneers of US punk rock

Sep 21 **Jefferson Airplane**'s final performances – 1st of two nights at the Winterland

Sep 22 1st David Bowie concert in America – **Ziggy Stardust and the Spiders from Mars**

Sep 28 **Rory Storm died** at the age of 33 – sleeping tablet overdose

Sep 29 Pete Townshend released ***Who Came First*** (UK) – 1st solo LP, dedicated to Meher Baba

Oct 6 David Bowie recorded ***The Jean Genie*** – as Ziggy Stardust and the Spiders from Mars

Nov 6 **Billy Murcia died** at the age of 21 – choked after drink and drugs

Nov 8 UK EVENTS: **Detective Sergeant Norman Pilcher** was arrested for perjury...

...drug-busting policeman who arrested numerous rock luminaries in the 1960s

Nov 11 **Berry Oakley died** at the age of 24 – motorcycle accident

Nov 18 **Danny Whitten died** at the age of 29 – drug overdose

Dec 9 Who's orchestral performance of ***Tommy*** at London's Rainbow Theatre

Dec 11 **Genesis**'s US concert debut

Dec 14 MOVIES: London premiere of **Mark Bolan**'s *Born to Boogie* – directed by **Ringo Starr**

Dec 18 VIETNAM WAR: **President Nixon** initiated the *Christmas Bombing* of Hanoi...

...America's final act of aggression – finished 29 December

Dec 23 **Grand Funk Railroad**'s ex-manager **Terry Knight** seized band's equipment at a concert

Dec 31 **MC5**'s last-ever gig...

...US VENUES: also the last-ever concert at Detroit's Grande Ballroom

1973 Jan 5 Bruce Springsteen released his 1st album, ***Greetings from Asbury Park N.J.*** (US)

Jan 13 Aerosmith released their 1st album, ***Aerosmith*** (US)

Jan 13 **Eric Clapton**'s Rainbow Theatre comeback concert

Jan 14 Elvis Presley's ***Aloha from Hawaii*** concert played to over a billion people

Jan 20 **Jerry Lee Lewis** made his debut at Nashville's Grand Ole Opry

Jan 23 VIETNAM WAR: **President Nixon**'s *Peace with Honor* speech

Jan 27 VIETNAM WAR: *Paris Peace Accords* were signed...

...America's war in Vietnam was over BUT the fighting continued

...Statistics:

Peak troop strength in Vietnam (30 April 1969):	543,482
Troops on active duty during the Vietnam era:	9,078,000
Deaths:	58,272

Jan 30 **Kiss**'s 1st gig

Feb 12 VIETNAM WAR: *Operation Homecoming* began...

...American prisoners of war began to return home

Feb 24 **Byrds**' last gig – the only 'classic' Byrd remaining was **Roger McGuinn**

Mar 23 King Crimson released ***Larks' Tongues in Aspic*** (UK) – Robert Fripp plus a new lineup

Mar 24 Pink Floyd released ***Dark Side of the Moon*** (UK)

Mar 29 **Dr Hook and the Medicine Show** made the cover of *Rolling Stone* magazine

Apr 13 David Bowie released ***Aladdin Sane*** (UK)

May 25 Mike Oldfield released ***Tubular Bells*** (UK)...

...RECORD LABELS: 1st release on **Richard Branson**'s Virgin label

Jun 28 FESTIVALS: *British Re-Invasion Show* at Madison Square Garden...

...early days of nostalgia rock

Jul 3 **David Bowie**'s last outing as Ziggy Stardust and the Spiders from Mars

Jul 13 **Queen** released their eponymous 1st album (UK)

Jul 14 **Everly Brothers'** on stage bust up – parting of the ways

Jul 28 FESTIVALS: *Summer Jam* in New York – bigger than Woodstock

Aug 4 Fripp and Eno recording session for ***No Pussyfooting***...

...early example of ambient music

Aug 13 Lynyrd Skynyrd released their 1st album ***(pronounced 'lĕh-'nérd 'skin-'nérd)*** (US)

Sep 19 **Gram Parsons died** at the age of 26 – drug overdose

Oct 4 Pink Floyd recording session for the 'lost' album, ***Household Objects***

Oct 16 VIETNAM WAR: *Nobel Peace Prizes* awarded to **Henry Kissinger** and **Le Duc Tho**...

...refused by Le Duc Tho because he believed that the War was not over

Oct 26 **Bob Weston** was sacked from Fleetwood Mac...

...**bogus Fleetwood Mac** created shortly afterwards

Oct 28 Who's shambolic debut performance of ***Quadrophenia***

Oct 29 Who's ***Quadrophenia*** tour lumbered on – three songs removed

Nov 2 Who released ***Quadrophenia*** (UK)

Nov 5 Pete Townshend stormed off stage during a performance of ***Quadrophenia***

Nov 20 **Keith Moon** collapsed on stage – replaced by audience member Scott Halpin

Dec 2 **Who** were arrested for hotel-wrecking high jinks after a concert in Montreal

Dec 31 **AC/DC**'s 1st official gig – Sydney, Australia, with guitarists **Angus** and **Malcolm Young**

1974 Jan 26 **Beck, Bogert & Appice** live performance – recorded shortly before they split up

Feb 14 **Roy Harper** concert at the Rainbow – backed by **Keith Moon** and **Jimmy Page**

Mar 8 **Bad Company**'s 1st gig

Mar 8 Badfinger released ***Apple of My Eye*** (UK)...

...RECORD LABELS: last single to be issued on the Apple label

Mar 12 **John Lennon** was ejected from the Troubadour – halfway through his "lost weekend"

Mar 19 **Jefferson Starship**'s 1st gig – Jefferson Airplane had split up in September 1972

Mar 30 1st performance of punk pioneers **Ramones** – as a trio...

...US punk rock was coming of age

Mar 31 last time that **John Lennon** and **Paul McCartney** ever played together

Apr 5 early **Van Halen** gig

May 8 **Graham Bond died** at the age of 36 – coroner recorded an open verdict

May 9 **Jon Landau**'s premonition that he saw "rock'n'roll future" – **Bruce Springsteen**

Jun 16 **Butts Band** supported the **Kinks** – nearing the end of the Butts Band's 1st incarnation

Jun 19 Eric Clapton was back from his drug-fuelled isolation – with ***461 Ocean Boulevard*** tour

Jun 24 Lynyrd Skynyrd released ***Sweet Home Alabama*** (US)

Jul 4 final **Steely Dan** concert – they became a studio group

Jul 17 **Moody Blues** opened their own recording studio...

...RECORDING LANDMARKS: reputed to be the 1st with quadraphonic capabilities

Jul 22 AC/DC's 1st single ***Can I Sit Next to You Girl*** – released in Australia and New Zealand

Jul 29 **"Mama" Cass Elliot died** at the age of 32 – heart attack

Aug 11 **Iggy Pop**'s infamous chest-slashing gig

Aug 26 **Rush**'s Agora Ballroom gig – classic trio was in place

Sep 7 1st **101'ers** gig – featured future **Clash** founding member **Joe Strummer**

Sep 11 **Stranglers** formed in Guildford, Surrey – as the Guildford Stranglers

Sep 20 Splinter released ***The Place I Love*** (UK)...

...RECORD LABELS: 1st album on **George Harrison**'s Dark Horse Records

Nov 2 **George Harrison** opened his ill-fated solo tour – 1st tour by a Beatle

Nov 8 **Connie Francis** was raped in her hotel room

Nov 13 **Ritchie Blackmore** imposter wrecked a Porsche and conned hapless fans for food

Nov 15 Elton John released ***Lucy in the Sky with Diamonds*** – featured John Lennon

Nov 15 final single from the Faces, ***You Can Make Me Dance, Sing or Anything (Even Take the Dog for a Walk, Mend a Fuse, Fold Away the Ironing Board, or Any Other Domestic Shortcomings)*** – released as "Faces/Rod Stewart"

Nov 28 **John Lennon**'s final concert appearance – on stage with **Elton John**

Dec 12 guitarist **Mick Taylor** left the **Rolling Stones**

Dec 24 **Elvis Presley** abandoned his karate movie

1975 Jan 9 dissolution of **The Beatles** – Paul McCartney dissolved the partnership

Feb 21 John Lennon released his album ***Rock'n'Roll*** (UK)

Mar 10 VIETNAM WAR: final invasion of South Vietnam began...

...beginning of the end of the war in Vietnam

Apr 7 original guitarist **Ritchie Blackmore**'s final gig with **Deep Purple**

Apr 14 **Ron Wood** joined the **Rolling Stones** for their US tour – stayed to become 2nd guitarist

Apr 24 **Pete Ham died** at the age of 27 – suicide

Apr 30 VIETNAM WAR: last Americans left Vietnam – the War was over...

...Vietnam was unified under communist rule

May 11 **Phil Ochs** arranged and also performed at the *War is Over* rally in New York

May 18 **Lemmy** was sacked from **Hawkwind** – formed **Motörhead** shortly afterwards

Jun 5 **Pink Floyd**'s last contact with **Syd Barrett**

Jun 8 **Talking Heads**' debut concert – at CBGB supporting the **Ramones**

Jun 26 Bob Dylan released ***The Basement Tapes*** – it was recorded back in 1967

Jul 16 FESTIVALS: *Top 40 New York Unrecorded Rock Bands festival*, New York's CBGB club...

...host of acts in America's new wave and punk scene

Jul 20 **Motörhead**'s 1st concert

Aug 17 **Bruce Springsteen** closed at New York's Bottom Line club – the hype changed to legend

Aug 25 Bruce Springsteen released his breakthrough 3rd album, ***Born to Run*** (US)

Sep 4 1st day of live recording by Bob Seger and the Silver Bullet Band for ***Live Bullet***

Sep 12 **Runaways'** 1st gig – a private party at rock writer Phast Phreddie Patterson's home

Sep 15 Pink Floyd released ***Wish You Were Here*** (UK)

Oct 17 **New York Dolls**: post-Johnny Thunders, no record deal, Malcolm McLaren as manager

Oct 30 **Bob Dylan**'s *Rolling Thunder Review* tour opened

Oct 31 Queen released ***Bohemian Rhapsody*** (UK)

Nov 6 **Sex Pistols'** 1st gig...

...British punk rock was coming of age

Nov 18 **Bruce Springsteen** opened his 1st European tour – to mixed reviews

Nov 28 end of the road for **Rod Stewart and the Faces**

Dec 8 **Dylan**'s *Night of the Hurricane* concert, in support of jailed boxer Rubin "Hurricane" Carter

Dec 20 **Cat Stevens**'s final British concert performance

1976 Jan 5 **Mal Evans died** at the age of 40 – shot dead by the Los Angeles police

Jan 19 promoter Bill Sargent offered the **Beatles** $30m for a single reunion concert

Feb 13 Peter Frampton released ***Frampton Comes Alive!*** (UK)

Feb 29 beginning of the **Stranglers**' rise to fame

Mar 15 **Deep Purple**'s last gig

Mar 19 **Paul Kossoff died** at the age of 25 – drug related heart problems

Mar 26 **Phil Collins**'s 1st gig as vocalist for Genesis

Apr 9 **Phil Ochs died** at the age of 35 – suicide

Apr 16 **Ramones** released their eponymous 1st album (US)

Apr 23 Rolling Stones released ***Black and Blue*** (UK) – featured Ron Wood and Harvey Mandel

Apr 29 **Bruce Springsteen** was removed from Graceland, after an attempt to meet Elvis

May 4 last gig before the **Allman Brothers Band**'s acrimonious split

May 14 **Keith Relf died** at the age of 33 – electrocuted by his guitar in his own home

Jun 1 Runaways released their 1st album, ***Runaways*** (US)

Jul 4 1st gig as "**The Clash**" – recently renamed from "**London SS**"

Jul 4 **Ramones'** UK debut concert

Aug 9 Grand Funk Railroad released ***Good Singin' Good Playin'*** (US) – folded after the album

Aug 14 Nick Lowe released ***So It Goes*** (UK)...

...RECORD LABELS: 1st single released on Stiff Records

Aug 27 early **Boston** gig...

...AOR (album oriented rock) emerged in the mid 1970s

Sep 20 FESTIVALS: 1st British punk festival – held at London's 100 Cub

Sep 29 **Jerry Lee Lewis** accidentally shot his bass player, Norman Owens, in the chest

Oct 8 **Sex Pistols** signed their 1st record deal, with EMI – on their way from **Swankers** to Virgin

Oct 18 **Throbbing Gristle**'s notorious *Prostitution* gig

Oct 20 MOVIES: premiere of **Led Zeppelin**'s *The Song Remains the Same*

Oct 21 **Keith Moon**'s last-ever concert performance – at the end of their North American tour

Oct 22 Damned released ***New Rose*** (UK)...

...1st single released by a UK punk band

Oct 29 **Elvis Presley**'s final studio recording session – held at Graceland

Nov 23 **Jerry Lee Lewis** arrested for brandishing a gun outside Elvis's Graceland home

Nov 25 **Band**'s swan song concert, *The Last Waltz*

Nov 26 Sex Pistols released their 1st single, ***Anarchy in the UK*** (UK)

Dec 1 **Sex Pistols**' notorious appearance on the UK TV show, *Today*...

...British punk rock had arrived

Dec 3 **Pink Floyd**, with pigs on the wing over Battersea Power Station

Dec 4 **Tommy Bolin died** at the age of 25 – drug overdose

Dec 6 **Sex Pistols** opened their ill-fated *Anarchy in the UK* tour – most dates were cancelled

Dec 8 Eagles released ***Hotel California*** (US) – 1st album to feature guitarist Joe Walsh

Dec 12 **Elvis Presley**'s last-ever performance at the Las Vegas Hilton Hotel

Dec 21 UK VENUES: Roxy Club opened in London...

...1st UK venue specifically for punk bands

Dec 28 Buzzcocks recorded their ***Spinal Scratch*** EP...

...early UK punk record on an independent label

1977 Jan 26 **Peter Green** was institutionalised for threatening his accountant with an air rifle

Feb 12 Police recorded their 1st single, ***Fall Out*** – with original guitarist Henri Padovani

Feb 18 Damned released their 1st album, ***Damned Damned Damned*** (UK)...

...1st UK punk rock album

Mar 10 **Damned** supported **Marc Bolan** on his last UK tour...

...1st major tour by a UK punk band

Mar 12 early **Police** gig – with guitarist **Henri Padovani**

Mar 18 Clash released their 1st single, ***White Riot*** (UK)

Mar 18 Iggy Pop released his 1st solo album, ***The Idiot*** (US)

Apr 1 **Led Zeppelin**'s ill-fated 11th US tour opened – it proved to be their last outing in the US

Apr 7 **Damned** opened at New York's CBGB club...

...1st UK punk band to play in America

Apr 8 **Clash** released their eponymous 1st album (UK)...

...track changes for the US release two years later

	Apr 15	Stranglers released their 1st album, ***IV Rattus Norvegicus*** (UK)
	Apr 26	US VENUES: Club 54 discotheque opened in New York...
		...disco-music came of age
	May 1	**Clash**'s British *White Riot* tour opened
	May 6	Jam released their 1st album, ***In the City*** (UK)
	May 22	**Blondie** began their 1st tour of the UK – supporting **Television**
	May 27	Sex Pistols released ***God Save the Queen*** (UK) – their 1st single on Virgin
	May 31	**Pavlov's Dog**'s final concert
	Jun 6	Elvis Presley released ***Way Down*** (US) – last single to be released in his lifetime
	Jun 23	Who's **Keith Moon** joined **Led Zeppelin**'s drummer **John Bonham** on stage
	Jun 26	**Elvis Presley** gave his last-ever concert performance – in Indianapolis
	Jul 6	Pink Floyd's **Roger Waters** spat in a fan's face at a gig in Montreal – roots of *The Wall*
	Jul 19	Elvis Presley released ***Moody Blue*** (US) – last album to be released in his lifetime
	Jul 24	**Led Zeppelin**'s last-ever American concert
	Aug 2	early **Elvis Costello and the Attractions** concert
	Aug 2	early **Dire Straits** gig
	Aug 16	**Elvis Presley died** at the age of 42 – heart failure...
		...Elvis had "left the building" for the very last time
	Aug 17	**Rush**'s *A Farewell to Kings* tour opened – dawn of their international success
	Sep 3	end of Eagles' ***Hotel California*** tour – Randy Meisner left, replaced by Timothy B Schmit
	Sep 16	**Marc Bolan died** at the age of 29 – automobile accident
	Oct 14	**Johnny Thunders and the Heartbreakers** UK tour – split up at the end of the tour
	Oct 17	Lynyrd Skynyrd released ***Street Survivors*** (US) – cover changed after plane crash
	Oct 20	plane crash that killed three **Lynyrd Skynyrd** band members
	Oct 21	Meat Loaf released ***Bat Out of Hell*** (US)
	Oct 28	Sex Pistols released their only LP, ***Never Mind the Bollocks Here's the Sex Pistols*** (UK)
1978	Jan 6	**Black Sabbath** made a rare appearance with singer **Dave Walker**
	Jan 14	final **Sex Pistols** gig, Winterland, San Francisco

The Sex Pistols were the poster boys for punk rock and their demise on 14 January 1978 marks this book's end-point for the inclusion of new artists and bands. Rock'n'Roll Unravelled *chronicles highlights from rock'n'roll's roots in the early 20th century, up until the advent of punk rock in the mid-1970s. This was when the music turned full circle and returned to simple music played in small venues, although the nature of the music had changed dramatically. The love songs of the 1950s had been replaced by the angst ridden anarchy of the punk bands.*

From this point on, the events in Rock'n'Roll Unravelled *are no longer concerned with the development of rock'n'roll but are highlights for artists and bands whose careers were already underway. But, as always, rock'n'roll was still a very interesting place.*

And the Story Continued...

1978	Jan 23	**Terry Kath died** at the age of 31 – accidentally shot himself
	Feb 10	Judas Priest released ***Stained Glass*** (UK) – subject of a suicide lawsuit in 1985
	Apr 21	**Sandy Denny died** at the age of 31 – fell down a stairway
	May 25	**Keith Moon**'s final performance with the **Who**
	Aug 18	Who released ***Who Are You*** (UK)
	Sep 7	**Keith Moon died** at the age of 32 – accidental overdose
	Oct 1	Black Sabbath released ***Never Say Die*** (UK) – last album with vocalist Ozzy Osbourne
	Oct 12	**Nancy Spungen died** at the age of 20 – stabbed by Sid Vicious (accident or murder?)
	Oct 23	**Police** played to an audience of just three people on their US tour
	Nov 10	Clash released their 2nd album, ***Give 'Em Enough Rope*** (UK) – 1st with Topper Headon
	Nov 27	**Def Leppard** drummer **Tony Kenning** was replaced by **Rick Allen**
	Dec 11	**Ozzy Osbourne**'s final performance with **Black Sabbath**
	Dec 31	**Runaways**' final performance
1979	Jan 29	US EVENTS: "I don't like Mondays", shootings in San Diego... ...immortalised by the **Boomtown Rats**
	Feb 2	**Sid Vicious died** at the age of 21 – drug overdose
	Mar 27	**Eric Clapton** married **George Harrison**'s ex-wife, Pattie Boyd
	May 1	Phil Spector's recording sessions began for the Ramones' album ***End of the Century***
	May 11	Clash released their EP, ***The Cost of Living*** (UK) – contained the track ***I Fought the Law***
	May 13	**Who** began a new era – with drummer **Kenny Jones**
	Jun 29	**Lowell George died** at the age of 34 – heart attack
	Aug 3	AC/DC released their breakthrough album ***Highway to Hell*** (US)
	Oct 19	Tom Petty and the Heartbreakers released ***Damn the Torpedoes*** (US)
	Nov 12	Marty Balin's rock opera ***Rock Justice*** opened
	Nov 17	**John Glascock died** at the age of 28 – heart problems
	Nov 19	**Chuck Berry** was released from prison – for the 3rd time!
	Nov 26	last-ever British appearance of **Bill Haley and His Comets**
	Dec 3	11 fans died in a rush for seating at a **Who** concert in Cincinnati
	Dec 14	Clash released ***London Calling*** (UK)
1980	Feb 7	Pink Floyd gave their 1st concert performance of ***The Wall***
	Feb 19	**Bon Scott died** at the age of 33 – acute alcoholic poisoning
	Mar 17	Beach Boys issued ***Keepin' the Summer Alive*** (US) – last LP with three Wilson brothers
	Apr 5	Ozzy Osbourne recording session for ***Blizzard of Ozz*** – 1st post-Black Sabbath album
	Apr 17	**Ronnie Dio**'s debut as **Black Sabbath**'s lead singer – replaced Ozzy Osbourne
	Jun 27	**Led Zeppelin**'s drummer **John Bonham** collapsed on stage in Germany

	Jul 7	**Led Zeppelin**'s final performance with **John Bonham**
	Jul 25	AC/DC released ***Back in Black*** (US) – 1st album with singer Brian Johnson
	Jul 30	day before the **Eagles'** notorious Long Beach gig – end of the band
	Sep 25	**John Bonham died** at the age of 32 – alcohol related
	Oct 27	**Steve Peregrin Took died** at the age of 31 – choked on a cocktail cherry
	Nov 17	John Lennon released his final album, ***Double Fantasy*** (US)
	Dec 8	**John Lennon died** at the age of 40 – shot dead outside his New York apartment
1981	Feb 15	**Mike Bloomfield died** at the age of 37 – drug overdose
	May 28	**Clash** opened a 15-day residency in New York – 10 June, **Ginsberg** joined them on stage
	Jun 17	**Roger Waters'** last concert with **Pink Floyd** – a performance of *The Wall*
1982	Jan 20	**Ozzy Osbourne** bit off a bat's head during a concert in Iowa… …legendary rock'n'roll high jinks
	Mar 19	**Randy Rhoads died** at the age of 25 – plane crash
	May 29	**Clash** opened *Casbah Club* tour – **Terry Chimes** replaced **Topper Headon** just before
1983	Jan 28	**Billy Fury died** at the age of 42 – natural causes
	Feb 24	**Screaming Lord Sutch,** 1st election as candidate for Official Monster Raving Loony Party
	Mar 21	Pink Floyd released ***The Final Cut*** – last Floyd album to include Roger Waters
	Apr 17	**Felix Pappalardi died** at the age of 43 – shot dead by his wife
	Jul 27	Neil Young released ***Everybody's Rockin'*** – it brought on a lawsuit from David Geffen
	Sep 20	ARMS charity concert – with **Eric Clapton, Jeff Beck** and **Jimmy Page** on stage together
	Nov 19	**Tom Evans died** at the age of 36 – suicide
	Dec 23	lawsuit against Judas Priest, claiming that their album ***Stained Glass*** led to suicide
	Dec 28	**Dennis Wilson died** at the age of 39 – drowned
1984	Jan 21	**Jackie Wilson died** at the age of 49 – he had collapsed on stage ten years earlier
	Apr 27	announcement that **Deep Purple** was back
	Jun 22	**Aerosmith** reunited for the *Back in the Saddle* tour
	Dec 31	**Def Leppard**'s drummer **Rick Allen** lost his arm in a car crash
	Dec 31	Aerosmith recorded ***Classic Live II*** (mostly) in Boston
1985	Jan 7	John Fogerty released ***Centerfield*** (US) – sued over ***Old Man Down the Road***
	Sep 19	**Frank Zappa** addressed Congress – spoke out against censorship
	Dec 12	**Ian Stewart died** at the age of 47 – heart attack
	Dec 23	lawsuit following suicide pact, citing Judas Priest's album ***Stained Glass***

1986	Jan 23	inaugural inductions into America's Rock and Roll Hall of Fame
	Mar 4	**Richard Manuel died** at the age of 42 – suicide
1987	Jan 6	opening night of the 1st **Eric Clapton** residency at London's Royal Albert Hall
	Jul 4	**Bob Dylan** and the **Grateful Dead** tour opened – to very mixed reviews
	Aug 3	Def Leppard released ***Hysteria*** (UK) – 1st album recorded after Rick Allen lost his arm
	Sep 23	**Lynyrd Skynyrd** tribute tour opened – ten years after the plane crash
1988	Jan 20	**The Beatles** was the 1st British act to be inducted into the Rock and Roll Hall of Fame
	Nov 5	22 years between US Beach Boys #1s – *Good Vibrations* in 1966 and ***Kokomo*** in 1988
1989	Feb 14	**Vincent Crane died** at the age of 45 – overdose of pain killers

The 1990s and on...

1990	Feb 8	**Del Shannon died** at the age of 55 – suicide
1991	Apr 20	**Steve Marriott died** at the age of 44 – house fire
1994	May 26	eve of the **Eagles'** *Hell Freezes Over* tour – 1st Eagles concert for 14 years
	Nov 18	**Rolling Stones** were the 1st major band with a live internet broadcast of a concert
1995	Mar 5	**Viv Stanshall died** at the age of 51 – house fire
	Jul 9	**Grateful Dead**'s last-ever concert
	Nov 19	***The Beatles Anthology*** arrived – with the 1st new single for 25 years, ***Free as a Bird***
1997	Jun 20	end of rock'n'soul's longest running lineup when Lawrence Payton died... ...Four Tops originally came together in 1954
1999	Jun 16	**Screaming Lord Sutch died** at the age of 58 – suicide
	Jun 27	**Brian O'Hara died** at the age of 57 – suicide
	Nov 10	RIAA announced its *Artists of the Century*
	Dec 14	**Paul McCartney** appeared at the Cavern – backed by **Ian Paice** and **David Gilmour**
2000	Mar 6	**Eric Clapton** was inducted into the Rock and Roll Hall of Fame – for the 3rd time
2003	Feb 3	actress Lana Clarkson was found dead in **Phil Spector**'s mansion... ...he was found guilty at his 2nd trial in 2009
2004	Sep 28	Brian Wilson finally released his album ***Smile*** (US) – abandoned in 1967

2005 Jul 2 Pigs did fly! **Pink Floyd** and **Roger Waters** were reunited on stage – for the last time

2007 Dec 10 **Led Zeppelin** reunion concert – with drummer **Jason Bonham**

2008 Feb 27 Eric Burdon's ***Mirage*** album was finally released (US) – recorded in 1973 and 1974
Apr 21 revealed that British rock'n'roll star **Tommy Steele** showed **Elvis** around London in 1958

PART TWO

What Happened Today?

Key:

Record Releases

(UK) British record release (US) American record release

In most cases UK release dates have been chosen for British artists and US release dates for American artists

Date*

An asterisk denotes an associated date which provides more information about events mentioned in the item.

Take for example this Jefferson Airplane concert on 21 August 1972:

1972 Jefferson Airplane riot at a concert in Ohio

A Jefferson Airplane concert at Akron's Rubber Bowl in Ohio descended into a riot, resulting in singer Grace Slick and road manager Chick Casady being arrested. Commander Cody and His Lost Planet Airmen supported the Airplane that night.

Riots at rock concerts were not unusual in the late 1960s and early 1970s. This one was similar in nature to a lot of the others, with over-enthusiastic policemen using tear gas to clear over-excited fans from the venue. The Rolling Stones' 1972 American tour, which kicked off on 3 June*, was blighted by unrest. Led Zeppelin hit problems in Italy on 5 July* 1971 and the Doors' New Haven concert on 9 December* 1969 ended with fighting on the streets.

From the beginning, the writing was on the wall for the relationship between concertgoers and the authorities. Alan Freed organised the first-ever rock'n'roll concert, *Moondog's Coronation Ball* on 21 March* 1952, only for it to be closed down early by the local authorities after thousands of fans tried to gatecrash the show.

The * indicates that more information can be found at the following dates regarding:

3 June*	The Rolling Stones 1972 tour
5 July*	Led Zeppelin concert
9 December*	Doors concert
21 March*	the first-ever rock'n'roll concert, organised by Alan Freed

January

Events today

1948 Rock'n'Roll Developments *Petrillo Recording Ban* came into effect

Three days after Wynonie Harris recorded his classic version of *Good Rockin' Tonight*, the *Petrillo Recording Ban* came into force across America. Introduced by James Petrillo, leader of the American Federation of Musicians, it prevented its 225,000 members from participating in recording sessions. He objected to the lack of royalties for musicians, following the displacement of live performances by "canned" music. The ban lasted for the whole year and came to an end in December.

This was the second recording ban introduced by Petrillo. In 1942 the musicians' boycott of recording sessions lasted for nearly two years.

1962 The Beatles failed their Decca audition

On New Year's Day the Beatles famously failed their audition at Decca records.

It had been organised by Decca's A&R man Mike Smith, who had travelled up to Liverpool a couple of weeks earlier to see them perform at the Cavern Club. At the audition they cut fifteen songs, including three original compositions later covered by others: *Hello Little Girl* (The Fourmost, 1963), *Love of the Loved* (Cilla Black, 1963) and *Like Dreamers Do* (The Applejacks, 1964). The remainder were covers and included Barrett Strong's *Money*, Chuck Berry's *Memphis Tennessee* and the Teddy Bears' *To Know Her Is to Love Her*. The final decision as to whether or not to add the Beatles to Decca's artist roster was down to Dick Rowe. Sadly for the Liverpool lads, he opted for the other group auditioning that day, London's Brian Poole and the Tremeloes.

This decision gave Dick Rowe eternal fame as the man who turned down the Beatles.

1964 Landmark TV *Top of the Pops* debuted in the UK

The first-ever *Top of the Pops* opened with the Stones' cover of the Beatles' *I Wanna Be Your Man*. Presented by DJ Jimmy Saville, the show featured studio performances from: Dusty Springfield, The Dave Clark Five, The Hollies and The Swinging Blue Jeans.

Single released today

1956 Carl Perkins *Blue Suede Shoes c/w Honey Don't* (US)

Written by Carl Perkins, this release gave Sun Records its first million-seller. It was also the first rock'n'roll record to make Top 3 on all three *Billboard*[37] charts: Pop, R&B and Country. Elvis Presley achieved a similar feat with *Heartbreak Hotel* three months later.

Elvis Presley covered the A-side, and the B-side was covered by the Beatles.

Births and deaths today

1942 Country Joe McDonald singer: Country Joe and the Fish; solo

Country Joe and the Fish formed in San Francisco in the mid-1960s and were one of America's most overtly political bands. Their repertoire included *Super Bird*, a satire on President Johnson and the anti-Vietnam War anthem, *I Feel Like I'm Fixin' to Die Rag*.

The extension to Joe McDonald's name reputedly came about as a tip of the cap to the Russian communist leader Joe Stalin's nickname, "Country Joe".

1953 Hank Williams iconic singer-songwriter, died at the age of twenty-nine

After a short but spectacular career the booze finally caught up with Hank Williams. He died in the back of his chauffer driven Cadillac on the way to a gig in Canton, Ohio.

Events today

2

1962 The Weavers banned from the *Jack Paar Show*

The Weavers were banned from appearing on the *Jack Paar Show*. NBC insisted that each member of the group signed a loyalty oath before the network would allow them to perform on the show. They refused and were excluded.

Founding member Pete Seeger had a history of run-ins with the American authorities for refusing to answer questions about his political beliefs, including an indictment for Contempt of Congress on 26 March* 1957. Seeger and his peers sang songs of universal freedom and supported pro-union activities. The sixties generation of folk and protest singers owed a large debt of gratitude to Seeger, Woody Guthrie, The Weavers, The Almanac Singers and a host of others who paved the way for their protestations.

This was a part of the communist witch hunt of musicians. To see this banning in the context of the period, it happened exactly a year after Bob Dylan had arrived in New York. He had recorded his first album just six weeks before the Weaver's television ban.

1964 Cyril Davies and His R&B All Stars final Marquee performance

Cyril Davies and His Rhythm and Blues All Stars played their Thursday night residency spot for the last time at London's Marquee club.

Davies died less than a week later, on 7 January*. The band continued to play at the Marquee under Davies's name for the next four gigs. After that, singer and new leader Long John Baldry rebranded the group as "Long John Baldry's Hoochie Coochie Men".

When Cyril Davies split from Alexis Korner's Blues Incorporated in November 1962, his new band also took over the Thursday night residency at London's Marquee club. This spot had previously been a regular night for Korner's Blues Incorporated, who then moved on to a new residency at the Flamingo.

1969 The Beatles start of the *Get Back* project

Paul McCartney came up with the idea of taking some new songs, rehearsing them for a concert and an album, whilst filming the whole thing as an integrated project. The Beatles met at London's Twickenham Studios to make a start on their new venture.

By this time Beatle relationships were at an all-time low. On 10 January George Harrison stormed out of the session, saying that he was quitting the Beatles. Filming and recording lumbered on throughout the month, with the legendary rooftop performance taking place on 30 January*. Work continued on the project, including a book to accompany the album. Glyn Johns was responsible for turning the sessions into an album, with little involvement from the Beatles. He produced an album called *Get Back* but scheduled release dates came and went. In the meantime the Beatles returned to the studio to record their next album, *Abbey Road*. *Get Back* remained unreleased but the saga continued. Phil Spector entered the picture and started work on 23 March* 1970. He took the existing material and transformed it into what would become the Beatles' final album, *Let It Be*.

Keyboardist Billy Preston also worked on the *Get Back* project with the Beatles. The Fab Four had previously been introduced to Preston when they were opening for Little Richard on their fourth Hamburg trip in November 1962. The sixteen-year-old Preston was in Little Richard's backing band. This was also the first time that Ringo Starr had been the Beatles' official drummer in Germany. The previous trips had featured his predecessor Pete Best.

Event today

1969 Colosseum the early days

The recently formed Colosseum gave one of their earliest performances at London's Marquee club. The band was highly respected for its fusion of progressive rock, jazz and blues. They were supported that night by Earth, who later became Black Sabbath.

Drummer Jon Hiseman put the band together with saxophonist Dick Heckstall-Smith and bassist Tony Reeves, after all three had decamped from John Mayall's Bluesbreakers. The lineup was completed by keyboardist Dave Greenslade and guitarist Jim Roche. By the time of their first album, *Those Who Are About to Die Salute You*, guitarist Jim Roche had been replaced by James Litherland. More changes followed after the second album, *Valentyne Suite*, Litherland left and went on to form Mogul Thrash, and Reeves departed to move into production and session work. They were replaced by guitarist Dave "Clem" Clempson and bassist Mark Clarke. Yet more changes were to come and by their third album, *Daughter of Time*, the lineup was extended to include veteran British R&B singer Chris Farlowe.

Albums released today

1968 The Byrds *The Notorious Byrd Brothers* (US)

Despite being a founding member of the Byrds, David Crosby was fired from the band in the autumn of 1967. They were reunited briefly in 1973 to record the album *Byrds*.

The sleeve for *The Notorious Byrd Brothers* album famously depicted a stable, with just three of the band members looking out of the four windows. The four window frames showed Jim (soon to be Roger) McGuinn, Chris Hillman and Michael Clarke looking out but instead of Crosby, a horse can be seen framed in the fourth window. The jury's out as to whether this was a deliberate pop at Crosby.

This album marked the end of the classic Byrds period. By the time of their next offering, *Sweetheart of the Rodeo*, fellow founding member Michael Clarke had also moved on.

1970 Syd Barrett *The Madcap Laughs* (UK)

Nearly two years after leaving Pink Floyd, on 6 April* 1968, Syd Barrett released his first solo album. Barrett's debut album featured old Floyd cohorts Roger Waters and David Gilmour. They both played on the album and also assisted as co-producers.

Birthdays today

1926 George Martin producer: The Beatles and others; composer

George Martin signed the Beatles to EMI's Parlophone label after they had been turned down by Decca. This was quite a departure for Martin, as previously his production expertise had been focussed on classical music, jazz and comedy.

1945 Stephen Stills guitar, singer-songwriter: Buffalo Springfield, CSN(&Y)

1946 John Paul Jones bass: Led Zeppelin; arranger and sessions

John Baldwin was working as an arranger for Rolling Stones' manager Andrew Loog Oldham, when he suggested that Baldwin should choose a more appropriate stage name. Oldham suggested John Paul Jones, inspired by the movie starring Robert Stack as the American revolutionary hero. Before joining Led Zeppelin, Jones was a busy session musician and also featured as a backing musician with Jet Harris and Tony Meehan.

Event today

1969 Jimi Hendrix Experience anarchy on Lulu's TV show

4

One of the UK TV highlights of the 1960s was the Jimi Hendrix Experience's appearance on BBC's *Happening for Lulu* show. It started off as planned with *Voodoo Chile.* At the end of the song the camera cut to Lulu and she announced that they would now play *Hey Joe.* This started with an extended introduction of drum rolls and screaming guitar before Hendrix broke into the vocals. During the guitar solo he paused and proclaimed that they were going to stop playing this "rubbish" and proceeded to dedicate a song to Cream. *Hey Joe* stopped and they launched into a storming introduction to *Sunshine of Your Love.* The programme went out live and Lulu's planned duet with Hendrix fell by the wayside. This impromptu change of plan ran the programme late and just before finishing, Hendrix can be heard to say that they were being put off the air.

Recording session today

1954 Elvis Presley second private recording with Sam Phillips

Elvis Presley made his second visit to Sam Phillips's Memphis Recording Service and recorded two songs, *I'll Never Stand in Your Way* and *It Wouldn't Be the Same Without You.* Both songs were co-written by Fred Rose, who founded the Acuff-Rose music publishing company in Nashville in 1942.

Some sources list *Casual Love Affair* as the second song recorded that day but according to *Master and Session: Elvis Presley Studio Recordings*' website, "When this acetate was discovered a few years ago it turned out that the second song was *It Wouldn't Be the Same Without You,* instead of *Casual Love Affair*".[63]

It was on the strength of this private recording that Sam Phillips invited Elvis back six months later to see how he sounded with the song *Without You.* That did not quite work out but it did lead to Elvis releasing his first Sun single, *That's All Right*, on 19 July*.

Single released today

1967 The Doors *Break on Through (To the Other Side)* c/w *End of the Night* (US)

Album released today

1967 The Doors *The Doors* (US)

The Doors' landmark debut album and debut single were released on the same day.

A shortened version of *Light My Fire* was also taken from the album as their second single. It gave them an American #1 but only graced the bottom of the British charts for a solitary week. The album also contained the epic track *The End*, clocking in at nearly twelve minutes. All three songs were written by the Doors.

Birthday today

1942 John McLaughlin guitar: Graham Bond, Mahavishnu Orchestra

John McLaughlin was considered to be one of the most accomplished British guitarists of the time. In the 1960s he worked with well-respected artists such as Georgie Fame, Graham Bond and Miles Davies, featuring on the latter's landmark album *Bitches Brew.* In the early 1970s he led the seminal jazz-rock fusion band Mahavishnu Orchestra. McLaughlin also worked with a number of other rock luminaries, including Jack Bruce, Ginger Baker and Carlos Santana.

Event today

5

1961 The Beatles Paul moved from six to four strings

Stuart Sutcliffe had been the bass player since John introduced him into the group a year earlier. When the rest of the Beatles returned from their first Hamburg trip in December, Sutcliffe stayed behind with his fiancée, professional photographer Astrid Kirchherr. Chas Newby took the bass spot for four gigs but when he returned to college the Beatles were once again a bass player light. Lennon initially asked Harrison to move to bass but after his refusal McCartney stepped up and swapped six strings for four. McCartney's debut as the group's new bass player took place at Litherland Town Hall.

Although Sutcliffe had not yet officially left the group, this effectively marked their move to a quartet. When they returned to Hamburg in April for their second residency, he occasionally joined them on stage but Sutcliffe's days as a Beatle were all but over.

Singles released today

1959 Buddy Holly *It Doesn't Matter Anymore c/w Raining in My Heart* (US)

Written by Paul Anka, this was Buddy Holly's first solo recording since parting company with the Crickets. It also proved to be the final single released during his lifetime.

1962 Tony Sheridan and the Beatles *My Bonnie c/w The Saints* (UK)

This was the first recording to be issued as "The Beatles".

It was originally released in Germany as Tony Sheridan and the Beat Brothers. The name change was deemed necessary because it was felt that "Beatles" sounded too much like "peedles", the German slang word for penis.

Album released today

1973 Bruce Springsteen *Greetings from Asbury Park N.J.* (US)

Manfred Mann's Earth Band scored a major hit on both sides of the Atlantic in 1976 with their cover of Bruce Springsteen's *Blinded by the Light*, taken from this debut album.

Births and deaths today

1923 Sam Phillips record producer and founder of Sun Records

DJ Alan Freed may have coined the phrase "rock'n'roll" but Sam Phillips can certainly claim to have helped to set the ball rolling. He recorded and released, through Chess Records, Jackie Brenston's *Rocket 88*, often accredited as the first rock'n'roll record. The careers of three of rock'n'roll's finest were also launched by Phillips. Elvis Presley's first five singles were Sun releases. Wild man Jerry Lee Lewis's rock'n'roll career was with Sun and Carl Perkins gave the label its first million seller with *Blue Suede Shoes*.

1976 Mal Evans Beatles' road manager, died at the age of forty

On the night in question Mal Evans was in his Los Angeles apartment, agitated and waving a gun around. Reports varied but the weapon was often referred to as an air-gun. Concerned for his safety his live-in girlfriend, Fran Hughes, called the police. When Evans refused to put the gun down, the police shot him.

Evans had joined the Beatles in 1963 and was with them throughout their career. He was a bouncer at Liverpool's Cavern Club when the offer came for the job as a roadie. With the end of the Beatles' touring days this role came to an end but he went on to work on the Apple project. After the Beatles split up he moved to Los Angeles.

Events today

6

1957 Elvis Presley censored on the *Ed Sullivan Show*

Elvis's third and final appearance on the prestigious *Ed Sullivan Show* found him falling foul of the CBS censors. After Elvis's gyrating performances on the previous shows, his TV audience this time was only shown Elvis from the waist up. He delivered a number of songs, including *Hound Dog* and the Otis Blackwell penned *Don't Be Cruel*.

At the end of Elvis's set, despite the censorship decision, Ed Sullivan had nothing but praise for the young singer, "I wanted to say to Elvis Presley and the country that this is a real decent, fine boy, and wherever you go, Elvis, we want to say we've never had a pleasanter experience on our show with a big name than we've had with you."[20]

1978 Black Sabbath rare appearance with singer Dave Walker

Dave Walker, previously with Savoy Brown and Fleetwood Mac, made a rare appearance as vocalist for Black Sabbath, on the BBC Midlands TV show *See Hear*.

The band were working on their new album, *Never Say Die* and performed an early version of *Junior's Eyes*, written by the band. This was a different version to the one found later on the completed album. Singer Ozzy Osbourne had parted company with the group a couple of months earlier but rejoined shortly after this TV show.

1987 Eric Clapton first Royal Albert Hall residency

Eric Clapton opened a six-night residency at London's Royal Albert Hall. For this first gig Mark Knopfler provided the second guitar presence and drummer Phil Collins joined the backing musicians for the shows on the 11th and 12th.

This was so successful that it became a much anticipated annual event and in 1991 the duration was extended to twenty-four nights.

Album released today

1967 Paul McCartney *The Family Way* (UK)

The first solo Beatle project was Paul McCartney's composition for the movie soundtrack *The Family Way*. George Martin handled the arrangements for this Boulting Brothers production, starring Hywel Bennett, Hayley Mills and her father John Mills.

Birthdays today

1946 Syd Barrett original guitarist, singer and songwriter: Pink Floyd, Stars

Syd Barrett was not just a founding member of Pink Floyd he was their inspiration and guiding light. He was the main songwriter of their early singles and first album. Sadly, mind enhancing drugs took their toll and by the time of Pink Floyd's British tour with Jimi Hendrix in late 1967, Barrett's stage performances had become increasingly erratic. By the spring of 1968 he had been replaced by guitarist David Gilmour and the Floyd moved progressively from psychedelic to stadium rock.

1947 Sandy Denny singer: Strawbs, Fairport Convention, Fotheringay; solo

As well as being one of the leading singers on the 1960s British folk-rock scene, Sandy Denny was the only singer to gain a Led Zeppelin credit. This came about on their fourth album, when she sang a duet with Robert Plant on *The Battle of Evermore*.

1953 Malcolm Young rhythm guitarist and founding member of AC/DC

Event today

7

1967 Paul McCartney official denial that Macca was dead

The February issue of the *Beatles Monthly Book* ran a short report to suggest that there was absolutely no truth in the rumour that Paul McCartney had been killed in a car crash on the M1 motorway on 7 January.

Rock'n'Roll's greatest conspiracy theory concerned Paul McCartney's death in a motor accident, followed by his replacement with a double for the remainder of the Beatles' career. The *Beatles Monthly* suggested that the supposed crash had been on 7 January, other theories put the date of the automobile accident as 9 November 1966. This "Paul is dead" theory took on a life of its own, with McCartney even appearing on the cover of *Life* magazine on 7 November 1969, with the suggestion that Paul was still "with us".

Recording session today

1954 Muddy Waters *(I'm Your) Hoochie Coochie Man*

Muddy Waters recorded the original version of Willie Dixon's classic *(I'm Your) Hoochie Coochie Man*, destined to become the staple diet of a generation of up and coming 1960s R&B groups. Waters, who provided vocals and electric guitar, was backed by some of his regular musicians: Little Walter on harmonica, guitarist Jimmy Rogers, pianist Otis Spann, drummer Fred Bellow and Dixon on electric bass.

When British blues pioneer Cyril Davies died, ten years later to the day, the Cyril Davies All Stars' vocalist Long John Baldry took over the leadership of the band and renamed it "Long John Baldry's Hoochie Coochie Men".

Album released today

1985 John Fogerty *Centerfield* (US)

When John Fogerty released *Centerfield*, his first album in ten years, he received not only his first platinum album in his own right – but also a lawsuit for plagiarism.

In one of rock'n'roll's more bizarre instances of two songs sounding a little too similar, Fogerty himself was the victim of his own alleged song theft. During his days with swamp-rockers Creedence Clearwater Revival he wrote the song *Run Through the Jungle*, used as the B-side to *Up Around the Bend*. Both sides found chart success in 1970. Creedence Clearwater Revival had been signed to the Fantasy label, which owned the copyright to the song. When *Old Man Down the Road* was included on John Fogerty's Warner Brothers album *Centerfield*, Fantasy owner Saul Zaentz considered that it infringed his copyright on *Run Through the Jungle*. The court case was eventually settled in Fogerty's favour and he was found not guilty of ripping himself off.

On the *Centerfield* album John Fogerty played all of the instruments himself.

Births and deaths today

1938 Paul Revere keyboards: Paul Revere and the Raiders

1945 Dave Cousins guitar and vocals: Strawbs; solo

1964 Cyril Davies British blues harp player, died at the age of thirty-one

A little over a year after he left Alexis Korner's Blues Incorporated and formed his own Rhythm and Blues All Stars, Cyril Davies's health deteriorated and he died.

Along with Alexis Korner, Cyril Davis was responsible for pioneering British rhythm and blues in the late 1950s and early 1960s.

Event today

1967 Vietnam War introduction of "tunnel-rats"

The first use of "tunnel rats" by US forces was in *Operation Cedar Falls*, which started on 8 January and lasted just over two weeks. This was the largest ground operation of the war. 30,000 American and South Vietnamese troops used search-and-destroy tactics to remove the Viet Cong from their stronghold in the *Iron Triangle*, an area near Saigon.

The Viet Cong used vast networks of tunnels to store supplies and evade US troops. "Tunnel rats" were the guys who descended into these tunnels to look for enemy soldiers, supplies and to destroy the tunnel. The dangers were immense, not just from booby traps and ambushes but also natural hazards such as snakes and scorpions.

Recording session today

1960 Eddie Cochran final recording session

The night before he flew to England for his ill-fated British tour, Eddie Cochran stepped into Gold Star studios in Los Angeles for what was to become his final recording session. He cut three songs, *Three Steps to Heaven, Cut Across Shorty* and the Sharon Sheeley penned *Cherished Memories.* He was backed on these recordings by the Crickets' guitarist Sonny Curtis and drummer Jerry Allison.

Single released today

1955 Elvis Presley *Milkcow Blues Boogie* c/w *You're a Heartbreaker* (Sun-3)

Milkcow Blues Boogie was recorded by Kokomo Arnold in the mid-1930s.

Birthdays today

1931 Bill Graham concert promoter

As well as promoting countless concerts, Bill Graham opened the legendary rock venues Fillmore West in San Francisco and Fillmore East in New York.

1935 Elvis Presley the "King of Rock and Roll"

Elvis Presley was born to Gladys Love and Vernon Presley in their home at 306 Old Saltillo Road, East Tupelo, Mississippi. His twin brother Jesse Garon was stillborn. When Elvis was just three years old Vernon was sentenced to serve three years imprisonment for forging a cheque. On 3 October 1945 Elvis gave his first public performance, singing Red Foley's *Old Shep* in a talent competition at the *Mississippi-Alabama Fair and Dairy Show*. Elvis famously bought his first guitar at the Tupelo Hardware Company on his eleventh birthday. He was served that day by Forrest L Bobo, who remembered the incident well: "He wanted to buy a .22cal rifle and his mother wanted him to buy a guitar".[34] The Presley family relocated to Memphis in 1948 and moved into federal-funded accommodation at 185 Winchester Avenue, Lauderdale Courts. His confidence was growing and he performed at school events and elsewhere. Elvis graduated from Humes High School on 3 June 1953 as a part of Class 202 and found employment as a truck driver for the Crown Electric Company.

On 18 July* 1953 he visited Sam Phillips's Memphis Recording Service, made a private recording of *My Happiness* for $3.98 and the rest, as they say, is history.

1946 Robbie Krieger guitar: Psychedelic Rangers, The Doors, Butts Band

1947 David Bowie aka Ziggy Stardust and Aladdin Sane

9

Events today

1967 Buffalo Springfield the 'lost' second album ...*Stampede*

Buffalo Springfield were back in the recording studio, cutting versions of Neil Young's *Mr. Soul*, Richie Furay's *My Kind of Love* and Steve Stills's *We'll See.*

Their eponymous debut album had been released but between that and their second official release *Buffalo Springfield Again*, their studio sessions were destined to be mostly confined to the speculation of their might-have-been 'lost' album *Stampede*. The band became unstable after the release of the first album. Bassist Bruce Palmer was deported back to Canada after a drugs bust and Neil Young was in and out of the band, failing to play at the Monterey gig on 16 June*. A number of bass players stepped into the breach. Palmer did return for a while but was replaced on a permanent basis by Jim Messina. All that survived of the *Stampede* project was the album sleeve, with an Atco logo, depicting the five band members on the porch of an old wooden building. And of course, the inevitable bootlegs of the songs that were destined for the never-to-be-released second album. The cover showed one of the band seated with his head bowed and his identity obscured by a hat. It probably wasn't Bruce Palmer.

1975 The Beatles dissolution of The Beatles

Five years after the Beatles went their separate ways, their story officially came to an end when a judge agreed to Paul McCartney's request to dissolve the partnership.

The writing had been on the wall for the Beatles demise even before they had released their last two albums, *Abbey Road* and *Let It Be*. On 18 April 1969 John Lennon, George Harrison and Ringo Starr signed a letter addressed to Eastman and Eastman informing them that their organisation was no longer authorised to act for The Beatles. The Fab Three recognised that the Eastman organisation still represented Paul McCartney but they informed the American attorneys that the other three Beatles' interests were now being handled by Allen Klein's ABKCO Industries Co. Paul McCartney had originally introduced the other Beatles to his future father-in-law's attorney business after he met Linda Eastman.

In 1971 McCartney instigated a lawsuit to dissolve the Beatles Partnership.

Recording session today

1959 The Drifters *Feelin' Fine and Don't Be a Fool (With Love)*

This was the British group called "The Drifters", who backed singer Cliff Richard and changed their name shortly afterwards to "The Shadows". They became Britain's most successful instrumental combo but this recording session for their debut single comprised two vocal numbers, with the A-side written by ex-Drifter Ian Samwell.

Birthday today

1944 Jimmy Page guitar: Yardbirds, Led Zeppelin; session; solo

Before finding success with the Yardbirds and legend with Led Zeppelin, Jimmy Page was already a well-respected guitarist. In his early career he recorded with Neil Christian and the Crusaders, and Carter Lewis and the Southerners. He was also one of the busiest session guitarists in London, appearing on the Nashville Teens' *Tobacco Road* and Them's *Here Comes the Night,* written by *Bert Berns.* The jury's still out as to whether he played on the Who's *I Can't Explain* or the Kinks' *You Really Got Me.*

Event today

1959 Cliff Richard and the Drifters debut of the lineup that became the Shadows

Cliff Richard's backing group the Drifters was now the lineup that would soon change its name to become "The Shadows". Lead guitarist Hank Marvin, rhythm guitarist Bruce Welch, bassist Jet Harris and drummer Tony Meehan made their debut in the north of England at Manchester's Free Trade Hall.

Half of the group, Marvin and Welch, were in place when Cliff kicked off his British tour supporting the Kalin Twins on 5 October* 1958. Also supporting the Twins on that tour were the Most Brothers, backed by bass guitarist Jet Harris. During the tour Harris also played with the Drifters, backing Cliff. Bassist Ian Samwell left the group at the end of the tour and Harris was the obvious choice to replace him. Meehan had previously played with both Marvin and Harris in Wally Whyton's Vipers Skiffle Group. He joined shortly afterwards when the last of the original Drifters, Terry Smart, left to join the Navy.

Recording session today

1956 Elvis Presley *Heartbreak Hotel*

For the first time since leaving Sam Phillips and Sun Records Elvis was back in the recording studio, this time for his new record company RCA. He was accompanied by his old Sun buddies, guitarist Scottie Moore and upright-bass player Bill Black. By now he had also acquired a regular drummer DJ Fontana and added the services of legendary Nashville session musicians, guitarist Chet Atkins and pianist Floyd Cramer.

The song was written by Tommy Durden and Mae Boren Axton after spotting a newspaper article headed "Do You Know This Man?" The paper wanted to identify a man who had killed himself and left a note simply saying, "I walk a lonely street".

Single released today

1964 Manfred Mann *5-4-3-2-1* c/w *Without You* (UK)

Manfred Mann's first chart success came with their third single, *5-4-3-2-1*. It was written specifically for the British TV music show *Ready Steady Go!* by band members: singer Paul Jones, drummer Mike Hugg and keyboard player Manfred Mann. The bluesy *5-4-3-2-1* replaced the original *Ready Steady Go!* theme, the surf-sounds of *Wipe Out* by the Surfaris.

Birthdays today

1935 Ronnie Hawkins rockabilly singer: Ronnie Hawkins and the Hawks

Ronnie Hawkins was born in America but found fame as a rockabilly star after making Canada his home in the late 1950s. His band, The Hawks, moved on and after backing Bob Dylan on his notorious 1966 world tour, found fame in their own right as "The Band".

1945 Rod Stewart singer: Hoochie Coochie Men, Jeff Beck Group, Faces

1946 Aynsley Dunbar drums: Mojos, John Mayall, Jeff Beck, Journey

One of rock's most talented drummers, Aynsley Dunbar has played with a host of the genre's luminaries. In between playing with the Jeff Beck Group and Frank Zappa he formed his own band,

Aynsley Dunbar's Retaliation. Urban legend has it that the band's name came about after Dunbar auditioned against Mitch Mitchell for a place in the Jimi Hendrix Experience but lost out on the flip of a coin.

Event today

11

1963 The Rolling Stones — Stones that kept right on rolling

Drummer Tony Chapman played his final gig with the Rolling Stones at the Ricky Tick Club, in the Star and Garter pub in Windsor. He was replaced by Charlie Watts.

The Rolling Stones evolved from guitarist Brian Jones's groups. Thunder Odin and the Big Secret's lineup boasted Paul Pond, who later changed his name to Paul Jones and found fame as Manfred Mann's original vocalist. Other people to play in Jones's pre-Jagger and Richard lineups included Brian Knight and Geoff Bradford. Knight left to form Blues By Six, poaching future Stones drummer Charlie Watts from Alexis Korner's Blues Incorporated. Guitarist Geoff Bradford moved on to join Brian Knight's Blues By Six. The only future Rolling Stone with Jones from the beginning was pianist Ian Stewart, although he was relegated to road manager after Andrew Loog Oldham took over the Stones' management, following their first meeting on 28 April* 1963.

Brian Jones and Ian Stewart rebuilt a new lineup with singer Mick Jagger, guitarist Keith Richard and Dick Taylor, all from Little Boy Blue and the Blue Boys; Taylor moved from guitar to bass. Drummer Tony Chapman had joined from the Cliftons (which would soon provide the Stones with bassist Bill Wyman). This was the lineup that debuted at the Marquee club on 12 July* 1962 as "The Rollin' Stones". Dick Taylor left soon after the gig and formed the Pretty Things. A number of bass players, including Ricky Fenson, and drummers also filled in, including Screaming Lord Sutch's drummer Carlo Little.

Recording sessions today

1956 The Coasters — first studio session

When the Robins split up, Carl Gardner and Bobby Nunn joined Leon Hughes and Billy Guy to form the Coasters. Leiber and Stoller produced their first recording session, where they cut three of their songs: *Down in Mexico, Turtle Dovin'* and *One Kiss Led to Another*. With *Brazil*, they had their first two singles and immediate R&B chart success.

Their third single, Leiber and Stoller's *Searchin'*, gave them their first hit on both sides of the Atlantic and heralded them as one of the most successful vocal groups of all time.

1970 Free — *All Right Now*

Free's first taste of chart success came with their third single, the anthemic *All Right Now*, written by bassist Andy Fraser and singer Paul Rodgers.

Re-releases of *All Right Now* gave Free more UK chart success. It charted again in 1973 and its inclusion on the EP *Free* produced further chart appearances in 1978 and 1982. In America, *All Right Now* provided them with their only chart appearance.

Single released today

1963 The Beatles — *Please Please Me c/w Ask Me Why* (UK)

Please Please Me was originally recorded during the Beatles third Abbey Road session on 11 September*. This was when they recorded the third version of *Love Me Do* with drummer Andy White. When John Lennon wrote *Please Please Me* he envisioned it as a Roy Orbison-esque ballad. The Beatles returned to the studio to record *Please Please Me* again on 26 November* but by then the ideas had changed and the new, faster version became their second single. Sadly, none of the original Orbison-esque takes survived for posterity.

When *Please Please Me* was released in the UK it failed to make #1 on every chart.

Events today

1959 Berry Gordy Jr launched his first record label

With the aid of an $800 loan Berry Gordy Jr started his first record label, Tamla.

The first record released on his new label was Marv Johnson's *Come to Me*, written by Johnson and Gordy. The Tamla release of the single was only regional but the song was given a national release on the United Artists label. This issue made it onto the lower regions of the American charts.

Before setting up Tamla, Gordy had already worked as a record producer; a songwriter, co-writing Jackie Wilson's *Reet Petite*; and formed his own music publishing company Jobete, named after his children. At the end of the year he formed the legendary Motown company and label.

For his British releases Gordy combined the two label names to form Tamla Motown.

1962 Vietnam War first US involvement in direct combat

Operation Chopper marked the first direct American combat role in the Vietnam War. American pilots manned the helicopters which transported over 1,000 South Vietnamese paratroopers for an assault on a Viet Cong stronghold, ten miles west of Saigon.

To put this into perspective, John F Kennedy was President and Joan Baez was singing about love and murder on the *Banks of the Ohio*.

Album released today

1969 Led Zeppelin *Led Zeppelin* (US)

Shortly after morphing from the New Yardbirds into Led Zeppelin, the band entered Olympic Studios on 27 September* 1968 to record material for their first album. At this stage they were still without a recording deal, a situation rectified in November, when manager Peter Grant flew to America and signed a deal with Atlantic Records.

The band embarked on a series of American gigs. Their eponymous album was released stateside, two and a half months before it found its way into British shops.

Muddy Waters' *You Shook Me* was included as one of the covers on the album. The song started out as the Earl Hooker penned instrumental *Blue Guitar*, which he recorded as a single in 1961. Willie Dixon added lyrics and it became *You Shook Me* and a single for Muddy Waters in 1962.

Birthday today

1941 Long John Baldry singer: Alexis Korner, Cyril Davies, Hoochie Coochie Men

Long John Baldry's career started in the first flush of the British blues boom. He was the vocalist with Britain's first blues band, Alexis Korner's Blues Incorporated, who also boasted future rock luminaries such as Mick Jagger, Charlie Watts and Jack Bruce.

In late 1962 Cyril Davies left Blues Incorporated to form a more traditional blues group, the Rhythm and Blues All Stars. Baldry was with the Horace Silver Quintet at the time, on a sabbatical from Blues Incorporated. When he returned he opted to join Cyril Davies in his new venture. After Davies died on 7 January* 1964, Baldry became the band's leader and rebranded as "Long John Baldry's Hoochie Coochie Men". To augment the band's vocal capabilities he recruited a young Rod Stewart into its ranks as an additional singer.

In 1966 Baldry joined Bluesology alongside pianist Reg Dwight, who later changed his name to Elton John. Long John Baldry had the distinction of being the inspiration for the "John" of Elton John.

Events today

13

1963 Bob Dylan — first UK visit ...*The Madhouse on Castle Street*

BBC TV broadcast *The Madhouse on Castle Street*, featuring an unknown Bob Dylan in his first appearance outside America.

Dylan's first visit to Britain was at the invitation of BBC director Philip Saville, to appear in the TV play *The Madhouse on Castle Street*. Saville had previously seen Dylan performing in New York's Greenwich Village. The play, written by Evan Jones, centred on a man in a boarding house who locked himself in his room in order to retire from the world. Dylan played Bobby, an itinerant guitar player whose songs punctuated the action; the songs were: *Blowing in the Wind, Ballad of the Gliding Swan, Hang Me, Oh Hang Me* and *The Cuckoo*. This was the first-ever broadcast of *Blowing in the Wind*.

Sadly, the BBC wiped the tape and Dylan's debut performance has been lost.

1966 The Velvet Underground — first gig with vocalist Nico

Pop artist Andy Warhol was invited to address the Annual Dinner of the New York Society for Clinical Psychiatry, at New York's Delmonico Hotel. Various members of his "Factory" entourage accompanied him, including his newly discovered rock prodigies the Velvet Underground.

The Velvet Underground, including singer Nico performing for the first time, was a part of Warhol's multi-media experience, the *Exploding Plastic Inevitable*.

1973 Eric Clapton — Rainbow Theatre comeback concert

After a two-year drug induced wilderness for Eric Clapton, the Who's Pete Townshend enticed him back to performing with a comeback concert at London's Rainbow Theatre.

Clapton and his wife Alice arrived at the theatre just as the show was due to start. The delay was apparently due to Clapton's trousers being let out in order to accommodate his increased size since his last performance. Introduced as "Eric and the Palpitations", Clapton took to the stage with guitarists Pete Townshend and Ron Wood, drummers Jim Capaldi and Jimmy Karstein, bassist Rick Grech, keyboard player Steve Winwood, and percussionist Reebop Kwaku Baah.

The evening was captured on the album *Eric Clapton's Rainbow Concert*.

Single released today

1967 The Rolling Stones *Let's Spend the Night Together* c/w *Ruby Tuesday* (UK)

When the Stones appeared on the *Ed Sullivan Show* on 15 January* the lyrics were a tad too suggestive for the show's producers. The B-side was one of the Stones' earliest ventures into psychedelia and also gave Melanie a British hit in 1970.

Albums released today

1964 Bob Dylan *The Times They Are A-Changin'* (US)

Produced by Tom Wilson, this was the first album with all original Dylan songs.

1969 The Beatles *Yellow Submarine* (US)

1973 Aerosmith *Aerosmith* 1st album (US)

Birthday today

1938 Daevid Allen guitar and vocals: Soft Machine, Gong

Daevid Allen was a founding member of both Soft Machine and Gong.

Events today

1963 Civil Rights Movement George Wallace "segregation forever"

In his *Inaugural Address* as Governor of Alabama, George Wallace left no doubt as to where he stood on the issue of the integration of black and white Americans. During the course of his speech the newly appointed Governor of Alabama told his audience that he believed in segregation today, tomorrow and indeed, "segregation forever".

He certainly did everything in his power to maintain this stance but he was thwarted by the White House on several occasions. Just six months later, on 11 June*, he made his famous *Schoolhouse Door* stand at the University of Alabama, in an attempt to prevent two black students from enrolling. In 1965 he strongly opposed the *Voting Rights* march from Selma to Montgomery, prompting President Johnson to address Congress on 15 March* on the *Right To Vote*.

1967 Landmark Festivals *A Gathering of the Tribes for a Human Be-In*

Billed as *A Gathering of the Tribes for a Human Be-In*, the event was held in Golden Gate Park. It set the scene for San Francisco's Haight-Ashbury district to become the centre of the hippy universe. The festival was inspired by a new law banning the use of the psychedelic drug LSD, effective from 6 October* 1966.

This was an occasion that brought the beat generation and hippie culture together. The *Be-In* had poets, speakers and rock bands, including beat poet Allen Ginsberg, LSD guru Timothy Leary, counter-culture figure Jerry Rubin, and music courtesy of Quicksilver Messenger Service, Jefferson Airplane and The Grateful Dead.

1973 Elvis Presley *Aloha from Hawaii* concert

With his show at the Honolulu International Center Arena, Elvis played to the largest audience of his career. The TV special was transmitted live via satellite to Australasia, Japan and the Far East, and on a delayed basis to around thirty European countries.

When the show was aired in America, on 4 April, it was seen by over 50 per cent[45] of the viewing population. An estimated 1-1.5 billion people in 40 countries[54] tuned in. Just in case the satellite failed, the rehearsal show on 12 January was taped and ready to roll.

1978 Sex Pistols final concert

From their debut performance on 6 November* 1975, to this last-ever gig at San Francisco's Winterland Ballroom, British punk pioneers the Sex Pistols' energy and controversy left an indelible mark on the world of rock'n'roll. But what made them great also tore them apart and by the time that they reached the Winterland the band was at the end of its journey. This final performance came at the end of a short seven-venue American tour. The band was falling apart and the day after the concert, it was all over.

Their farewell came after the band had encored with *No Fun*. Johnny Rotten, who clearly wasn't having any fun, turned to the audience and asked them if they got the feeling that they'd been cheated. *No Fun* was released in mid-1977 as the B-side of *Pretty Vacant* and was a cover of the Stooges penned song released by them in 1969.

Single released today

1966 David Bowie with The Lower Third *Can't Help Thinking About Me* (UK)

Having changed his name from Davie Jones, to avoid confusion with the Monkee, he released his self-penned debut single as "David Bowie", albeit still with the Lower Third.

Event today

15

1967 The Rolling Stones censorship on the *Ed Sullivan Show*

The Rolling Stones appeared on American TV's *Ed Sullivan Show*, performing *Ruby Tuesday* and *Let's Spend the Night Together*. As the producers were unhappy about the lyrics, Mick Jagger sang of spending "some time" rather than "the night" together.

Jim Morrison was not so accommodating on 17 September*, when the Doors performed *Light My Fire* on the show.

Recording session today

1965 Bob Dylan *If You Gotta Go, Go Now*

Written by Bob Dylan and recorded during the *Bringing It All Back Home* sessions.

In September 1965 Manfred Mann took the song to the #2 spot on the British charts but this was not the first recording to see the light of day. British Invasion group, the Liverpool Five released it as a single in America two months earlier. It proved popular in the Pacific North West but failed to chart nationally.

In 1967 one of the takes was released as a single by Dylan but only in the Benelux.

Singles released today

1958 The Champs *Train to Nowhere c/w Tequila* (US)

Tequila was originally issued as a B-side on Gene Autry's Challenge record label.

Gene Autry was a country and western TV and movie star. Known as the "Singing Cowboy", he had a string of country hits in the 1940s and early 1950s.

The group's moniker was inspired by the name of Gene Autry's horse, *Champion*.

1965 The Who *I Can't Explain c/w Bald Headed Woman* (UK)

This was their Townsend penned debut single. Background vocals were provided by the Ivy League but the jury is out as to whether guitarist Jimmy Page played on the record.

Birthdays today

1929 Martin Luther King Jr leader of the American Civil Rights Movement

Church Leader, orator and civil rights activist, Martin Luther King Jr was a pivotal figure in championing black civil rights in America, from the Montgomery Bus Boycott in 1955 until his assassination in Memphis on 4 April* 1968. He delivered his most famous speech, *I Have a Dream*, at the *March on Washington* rally on 28 August* 1963.

1941 Captain Beefheart singer and multi-instrumentalist

Captain Beefheart and His Magic Band were responsible for some of the late 1960s and early 1970s most cutting edge rock'n'roll, including the 1969 album *Trout Mask Replica*. Beefheart often worked with Frank Zappa in the mid-1960s, when Zappa had his own recording studio in Cucamonga, California. Beefheart's name came from an early collaboration, *Captain Beefheart vs The Grunt People*.

1948 Ronnie Van Zant singer: My Backyard, Noble Five, Lynyrd Skynyrd

Ronnie Van Zant was one of the six people killed when Lynyrd Skynyrd's plane crashed on 20 October* 1977.

The name of the band, "Lynyrd Skynyrd", was inspired by the name of their gym teacher, Leonard Skinner, at the Robert E Lee High School in Jacksonville, Florida.

Events today

1957 Landmark Venues Liverpool's Cavern Club opened

Liverpool's Cavern Club opened its doors in 1957 as a jazz club, named after the Parisian jazz club, Le Caveau. Owner Alan Sytner welcomed skiffle but was not a fan of rock'n'roll. John Lennon famously made his debut at the club on 7 August* 1957 with his skiffle group the Quarry Men. After opening with skiffle songs they gave an unappreciative Sytner a taste of Elvis Presley. This only served to prompt the club's outraged owner to send them a note on stage, reputedly telling Lennon to "cut out the bloody rock".

In 1959 Ray McFall took over the ownership of the club. He slowly moved it away from being a 1950s jazz venue and ushered in the 1960s beat music that the Cavern became famous for. The club's first "Beat Night" was held on 25 May* 1960.

1963 Cyril Davies R&B All Stars goodbye Blues Incorporated

Shortly after parting company with Alexis Korner's Blues Incorporated, Cyril Davies and his new band the Rhythm and Blues All Stars performed at London's Piccadilly Jazz Club.

After playing the blues together for nearly a decade, Davies and Korner's approach diverged. Korner favoured a more jazz based direction, whilst Davies wanted to play in the style of Chicago blues. In November 1962 Davies left Korner's Blues Incorporated and set up his own band, the Rhythm and Blues All Stars. The lineup featured drummer Carlo Little, bassist Rick Brown (aka Ricky Fenson) and pianist Nicky Hopkins, all hailing from Screaming Lord Sutch's band the Savages. Led Zeppelin's future guitarist Jimmy Page was, albeit very briefly, the band's first guitarist. He was soon replaced in the All Stars by Bernie Watson, another ex-Savage.

Singer Long John Baldry had also been a Blues Incorporated regular but left to perform with the jazz based Horace Silver Quintet. When they returned from their tour of Germany in early January, Baldry opted not to rejoin Blues Incorporated but instead decided to throw in his lot with Cyril Davies's new venture.

When Davies began his residency at London's Marquee club at the beginning of January he was supported for the first four weeks by the Rolling Stones. Before the Stones settled on Charlie Watts as their permanent drummer, Davies's drummer Carlo Little regularly performed with them. British blues in the early 1960s was pretty incestuous, as can be seen by the fact that Watts was yet another ex-Blues Incorporated musician.

Recording session today

1961 Helen Shapiro *Don't Treat Me Like a Child*

Fourteen-year-old Helen Shapiro recorded her first single at the famous Abbey Road studios. This started a string of hits that lasted into the mid-1960s.

Before becoming one of Britain's earliest female pop stars, Shapiro performed in the school band Susie and the Hula Hoops in the late 1950s. The group also featured an even younger Mark Feld, who later changed his name to Marc Bolan and became an international superstar. Helen Shapiro headlined the package tour that opened on 2 February* 1963 and featured the Beatles on their debut tour of the UK.

Birthday today

1934 Bob Bogle bass and guitar: founding member of the Ventures

Event today

1966 The Move formed from three Birmingham groups

17

The Move was formed in Birmingham's Cedar Club, when five local musicians from three different Midlands groups decided to get together and form a new band.

Carl Wayne and the Vikings provided lead singer Carl Wayne, along with their rhythm section, drummer Bev Bevan and bassist Chris "Ace the Face" Kefford. Multi-instrumentalist Roy Wood had been with Mike Sheridan and the Nightriders, latterly renamed to "Mike Sheridan's Lot". The Move was completed by guitarist Trevor Burton from Danny King and the Mayfair Set. The three bands had strong reputations locally and the Move was created as a Birmingham supergroup.

The remaining Nightriders, including guitarist and vocalist Jeff Lynne, morphed into the Idle Race. In 1970 when the Move was nearing the end of its life and transforming into the Electric Light Orchestra, Lynne joined Roy Wood for this new venture.

Recording sessions today

1964 The Holy Modal Rounders *The Holy Modal Rounders*

The Holy Modal Rounders spent their second and final day in the studio recording their eponymous debut album.

The duo, violinist and vocalist Peter Stampfel, and guitarist and vocalist Steve Weber, came together in the early 1960s in New York. They played a unique blend of folk and country music tinged with beat poetry. After their second album, *The Holy Modal Rounders 2*, the duo joined poets Tuli Kupferberg and Ed Sanders in 1965 to become the Village Fugs, later shortening their name to "The Fugs".

1970 Procol Harum back to the Paramounts

Procol Harum grew out of the British mid-1960s R&B group the Paramounts. By 1970 Procol's lineup once again comprised all ex-Paramounts people. During the rehearsals for their fourth album, *Home*, they decided to rent time at Abbey Road Studios and lay down some of their old Paramounts repertoire. The result was the album *Ain't Nothin' to Get Excited About*, released as "Liquorice John Death" – but not issued until 1997!

Album released today

1969 The Beatles *Yellow Submarine* (UK)

This was the only Beatles movie album to have the same listings in Britain and the US.

Birthday today

1948 Mick Taylor guitar: Gods, John Mayall's Bluesbreakers, Rolling Stones

Mick Taylor was best known for replacing Brian Jones, guitarist and founder of the Rolling Stones. Taylor's first performance with the Stones was at their free Hyde Park concert on 5 July* 1969, just two days after Jones had been found dead in the swimming pool of his Sussex home. Before his days as a Rolling Stone, Taylor was one of the founding members of the Gods with Ken Hensley in 1965. Hensley later went on to join Spice, who found fame after they changed their name to "Uriah Heep". In mid-1967 Taylor and the Gods parted company when he left to replace guitarist Peter Green in John Mayall's Bluesbreakers. Green had moved on to form Peter Green's Fleetwood Mac. Taylor's final album with the Stones was *It's Only Rock'n'Roll*, after which he was replaced by Ronnie Wood.

Events today

1969 Pete Best settled his lawsuit against the Beatles

Pete Best, Ringo Starr's predecessor in the Beatles, finally settled his three-year-old lawsuit against his old band.

In February 1965 *Playboy* magazine published an interview with the Beatles, in which his old band mates made comments of which Best took rather a dim view. As a result, Best initiated an $8m lawsuit against his old buddies. After more than three years of legal wrangling Best settled out of court, reputedly for less than the $8m he was seeking.

Pete Best left his group the Blackjacks to become the Beatles' first regular drummer. He joined them for the opening night of their first Hamburg trip on 17 August* 1960 and stayed through to their first EMI recording session on 6 June* 1962. His demise came when producer George Martin told manager Brian Epstein that the drummer was not right for the group. Very shortly afterwards Best was replaced by Ringo Starr.

1971 Landmark Radio 30 per cent quota for Canadian music

The Canadian Radio and Telecommunications Commission (CRTC) regulations took effect to force Canadian radio stations into a quota system, which ensured that they played at least 30 per cent of Canadian music content between the hours of 6am and midnight. The CanCon regulations were designed to ensure that homegrown music had an assured place on Canadian radio.

The definition of "Canadian" was taken from the MAPL[60] formula. A song was considered "Canadian" if two of four key characteristics were met. A Canadian: composed the music, wrote the lyrics, or performed the piece. In the case of a live performance, it must be recorded in Canada, or performed and broadcast live in Canada.

Recording session today

1969 John McLaughlin *Extrapolation*

Extrapolation marked John McLaughlin's debut as a solo performer and established him as one of Britain's premier jazz-rock guitarists. The album was produced by Giorgio Gomelsky and released on his short-lived label, Marmalade Records.

Gomelsky was one of the pioneers of the British blues scene. He founded London's Crawdaddy Club and managed both the Rolling Stones and the Yardbirds.

Six months later McLaughlin joined Miles Davis on his landmark *Bitches Brew* album.

Birthdays today

1941 David Ruffin singer: Soul Stirrers, The Temptations; solo

David Ruffin came to fame as one of the lead singers with the Temptations. He was in the lineup that became known as the "classic five" and provided the lead vocal on their first American #1, *My Girl*. In 1968 he left and signed to Motown for a solo career.

My Girl was written by two of the founding members of the Miracles, Smokey Robinson and Ronald White.

1943 Dave Greenslade keyboards: Chris Farlowe, Colosseum, Greenslade

In the mid-1960s Dave Greenslade was a part of the British R&B group Chris Farlowe and the Thunderbirds, before joining the cult UK soul band Gino Washington and the Ram Jam Band. In 1968 he moved to the newly formed jazz-rock band Colosseum, before founding his own band Greenslade in 1972.

Events today

1971 Amazing Blondel performed at the Marquee club

One of Britain's more esoteric rock bands, Amazing Blondel, supported Mott the Hoople at London's Marquee club.

Amazing Blondel came together in 1969 as a trio of multi-instrumentalists, playing acoustic music with renaissance and baroque influences. The group took its name from the 12th-century minstrel Blondel de Nesle, who found the imprisoned King Richard I.

1976 The Beatles $30m offered for a reunion concert

Nearly six years after the Beatles parted company, promoter Bill Sargent offered the Fab Four $30m to perform a one-off reunion concert. Sargent's offer was declined.

The opportunity to earn $30m to play together might have been spurned on this occasion but Sargent's desire to bring the Liverpool lads together again was not necessarily over-optimistic. Since going their separate ways, various permutations of the world's most famous group had indeed performed together. Since the famous headline "Paul Is Quitting The Beatles" on 10 April* 1970, Ringo Starr and George Harrison had shared the same stage at the *Concert for Bangladesh* on 1 August* 1971. George Harrison had accompanied John Lennon on the latter's *Imagine* album, released on 8 October* 1971. The most unlikely coupling came when John Lennon and Paul McCartney jammed together for the very last time on 31 March* 1974, an event that was captured on the bootleg album *A Toot and a Snore in '74*.

Hopes of a reunion ended with John Lennon's murder on 8 December* 1980.

Birthdays today

1935 Johnny O'Keefe singer: Australia's first rock'n'roll star

Inspired in 1955 by hearing *Rock Around the Clock* playing over the opening credits of the movie *Blackboard Jungle*, Johnny O'Keefe became a singer and Australia's first rock'n'roll hero. O'Keefe formed Australia's first rock'n'roll band, the Dee Jays. In 1957 they secured a recording deal with Festival Records. The band's breakthrough came with their third single, *The Wild One*, co-written by O'Keefe. The single was released on 5 July* 1958 and is generally considered to mark the birth of Australian rock'n'roll.

1939 Phil Everly younger of the two Everly Brothers

The Everly Brothers' career started when they joined their parents on the radio in the *Everly Family Show*. Chet Atkins was a fan of the show and introduced the Brothers to Columbia. This proved to be a short-lived experience. They moved to Cadence and found success on both sides of the Atlantic in 1957 with *Bye Bye Love*. This was the first of a string of hits written by the wife and husband team Felice and Boudleaux Bryant.

1943 Janis Joplin singer: The Waller Creek Boys, Big Brother; solo

In 1962 Janis Joplin left her hometown of Port Arthur to pursue a degree at the University of Texas. She started singing around the Austin coffee bars and performed with the Waller Creek Boys. In early 1963 she headed for San Francisco and after a couple of years in California, went on to New York in a bid to kick-start her singing career. Joplin returned to Texas where she turned down an offer of lead singer with the psychedelic group the 13th Floor Elevators. Success finally beckoned in mid-1966 after Joplin returned to San Francisco to front Big Brother and the Holding Company.

Events today

20

1958 Landmark Radio — Radio KWK's on air record smashing

St Louis radio station KWK came to the end of its "Record Breaking Week".

Radio station manager Robert Convey decided that rock'n'roll music was undesirable and for the week his DJ's weeded out rock'n'roll records, played them one last time and smashed them on air. One of the station's DJs famously announced, just before shattering yet another disc, that "Rock and Roll has Got to Go and Go It Does Here on KWK".[21]

1973 Jerry Lee Lewis — debuted at the Grand Ole Opry

Sixteen years after releasing his first record, *Crazy Arms*, Lewis made his belated debut at the Grand Ole Opry. In case any of the audience doubted his credentials he reputedly declared from the stage that he was "a rock'n'rollin', country and western, rhythm'n'blues singin' motherfucker."

1982 Ozzy Osbourne — bit off a bat's head on stage

Ozzy Osbourne bit off the head of a bat on stage during a concert at the Veterans Memorial Auditorium in Des Moines, Iowa. During the concert a fan threw a bat on stage and thinking that it was made of rubber, Osbourne picked it up and bit off its head. Legend has it that the bat took a dim view of this and bit him back, though it's hard to see quite how if it had already been decapitated. A trip to hospital followed for the intrepid ex-Black Sabbath front man, where he was given the first in a series of rabies injections.

1988 The Beatles — inducted into the Rock and Roll Hall of Fame

In its third year of inductions, the Beatles was the first British act to be elected to the hallowed halls of the Rock and Roll Hall of Fame.

All four of the Beatles were also inducted individually later, John in 1994, Paul in 1999, George in 2004 and finally Ringo in 2015. Producer George Martin was inducted in 1999 but manager Brian Epstein had to wait until 2014 for his entry, although he did beat Ringo.

Album released today

1964 The Beatles — *Meet the Beatles* (US)

By the time that Capitol deigned to release the Beatles' first US album it had already been preceded by two other albums, Vee-Jay's *Introducing the Beatles* on 22 July* and *Beatlemania! With the Beatles*, from the Canadian arm of Capitol on 25 November*.

Meet the Beatles contained ten Lennon and McCartney compositions and one from George Harrison, *Don't Bother Me*. The only cover, *Till There Was You*, was written for the 1957 musical *The Music Man* and provided Peggy Lee with a minor UK hit in 1961.

Births and deaths today

1945 Eric Stewart guitar and vocals: Wayne Fontana and the Mindbenders, 10cc

Stewart joined Wayne Fontana when his backing group the Jets became the Mindbenders.

1952 Paul Stanley guitar and vocals: Wicked Lester, Kiss

1965 Alan Freed iconic DJ and concert promoter, died aged forty-three

Alan Freed is the DJ generally given the credit for coining the phrase "rock'n'roll". The payola scandal brought him crashing down to earth in the early 1960s. His fall was complete and he died of kidney failure at the age of just 43, a penniless and broken man.

Event today

21

1968 Vietnam War siege of Khe Sanh

Just prior to the *Tet Offensive* on 31 January*, a force of 20,000 North Vietnamese troops launched the first of their attacks on the 6,000 US Marines based at Khe Sanh.

This was an important US Marine base located near the Laotian border, just south of the Demilitarized Zone. The besieged Marines were supplied from the air and assisted in their defence by an intensive bombing campaign. They were finally relieved at the beginning of April by the forces of *Operation Pegasus*.

The 26th Marines and the USAF 834th Air Division both received Presidential Unit Citations for their parts in the siege.

Recording sessions today

1949 Miles Davis *Birth of the Cool*

Miles Davis went into the studio for the first of three recording sessions, which were eventually released in 1957 as the landmark album *Birth of the Cool*. Davis might have been a jazz artist but he exerted considerable influence on many rock musicians.

1967 The Monkees *A Little Bit Me, A Little Bit You*

Since the inception of the *Monkees* TV show, Don Kirshner had been responsible for the musical content and the record releases on the Colgems record label. The band members, particularly Mike Nesmith, were becoming increasingly frustrated with not being allowed to play their own instruments and not having their own compositions considered for future releases. The Monkees were coming to the end of their first live tour and this had given them a considerable boost in confidence. As their TV show increased in popularity so did the Monkees' clout with producers Bob Rafelson and Bert Schneider.

Don Kirshner was determined to keep control of the Monkees' musical output and without their permission issued the Neil Diamond penned *A Little Bit Me, A Little Bit You*, coupled with another Brill Building B-side *She Hangs Out*, written by Jeff Barry and Ellie Greenwich. The Monkees took their grievances to the producers, who backed them against Kirshner. The single had only been issued in Canada and was quickly withdrawn. It was replaced by Michael Nesmith's B-side *The Girl I Knew Somewhere*. Don Kirshner was fired and the Monkees took more control of their output.

Births and deaths today

1938 Wolfman Jack legendary American disc jockey

The gravel-voiced DJ started out as Daddy Jules on Virginia radio station WYOU. He came to fame in the mid-1960s after moving to Mexico and transmitting across the USA on super-transmitters. In 1973 he appeared as himself in the movie *American Graffiti*.

1941 Richie Havens singer, guitarist and songwriter

1947 Pye Hastings guitar and vocals: Wilde Flowers, Caravan

1984 Jackie Wilson seminal R&B singer, died at the age of forty-nine

Jackie Wilson suffered a massive heart attack during a live show in New Jersey, on 29 September 1975. The attack resulted in severe brain damage and he lapsed into a coma. Despite making a slight recovery he remained semi-comatose until his death a decade later.

Events today

22

1966 Landmark Festivals *Trips Festival*

This was the middle day of the three-day, psychedelic, multimedia *Trips Festival,* held at the Longshoreman's Hall in San Francisco. The festival's handbill proclaimed that "this is the FIRST gathering of its kind anywhere. The TRIP – or electronic performance – is a new medium of communication & entertainment".

The event was held over three evenings and featured music, lights, poetry, dancing, and "The Acid Test" with Ken Kesey's Merry Band of Pranksters and their Psychedelic Symphony. There was music from the Grateful Dead, and Big Brother and the Holding Company, and poetry courtesy of beat icon Allen Ginsberg.

LSD was still legal and was widely available. It was not outlawed until 24 October* 1968. Big Brother and the Holding Company had only just formed and this was one of their earliest appearances. They had not yet signed up lead singer Janis Joplin, who made her debut with the band on 10 June*.

1967 The Monkees final concert of their first tour

The Monkees played the final concert of their first American tour at the Cow Palace, San Francisco.

1967 The Rolling Stones snubbed the Palladium's revolving stage

The Rolling Stones appeared on UK TV's prestigious *Sunday Night at the London Palladium*. They famously refused to stand on the revolving stage for the show's traditional finale, a goodbye wave from the assembled performers.

The reason for the Stones' reluctance to join the others on the revolving stage was probably an attempt to regain some street credibility, after succumbing to censorship on the *Ed Sullivan Show* just a week earlier. The show's producers had insisted on a lyric change to *Let's Spend the Night Together*. They wanted the Stones to spend "some time", rather than the more racy "night" together.

1969 Vietnam War — US Marines' combat role drew to a close

Operation Dewey Canyon opened. This lasted until 18 March and was one of the last major operations by US Marines in the Vietnam War. The A Shau Valley, located on the Laos border, was a stronghold for the North Vietnamese Army. This operation pushed the communist troops back, as well as successfully locating enemy supplies and weapons.

Birthdays today

1931 Sam Cooke — singer: Highway QCs, The Soul Stirrers; solo

Sam Cooke's singing career started with his family's gospel group the Singing Children, before joining the Highway QCs gospel group. In early 1951 he famously replaced Robert "RH" Harris as lead singer with the Soul Stirrers. In 1957 Cooke recorded *Forever* c/w *Lovable* but the single was released under the name of "Dale Cook" so as not to offend his gospel fans. Cooke and his producer Bumps Blackwell both moved to Keen, where he had his first crossover hit *You Send Me* in late 1957.

1940 Addie "Micki" Harris — singer and founding member of the Shirelles

1949 Steve Perry — singer: Journey

Events today

23

1959 Buddy Holly — final tour opened in Milwaukee

Buddy Holly's last tour, the ill-fated *Winter Dance Party*, kicked off at George Devine's Ballroom in Milwaukee, Wisconsin. Holly had recently split with the Crickets and was backed by guitarist Tommy Allsup, drummer Carl Bunch and bassist Waylon Jennings.

Bunch suffered from frostbite on the poorly heated tour-bus and was hospitalised after the concert at Duluth, Minnesota on 31 January. This meant that he missed the concert at Clearlake, Iowa two days later. It was there that Holly decided that he could not cope with the tour-bus conditions any longer. Instead, he hired a light aircraft to take some of the artists to the next gig in Moorhead, Minnesota. The plane never arrived but the tour continued. Bunch rejoined the tour a couple of days after the crash.

1973 Vietnam War — Nixon's *Peace with Honor* speech

In a TV broadcast President Nixon told the nation that, "...we today have concluded an agreement to end the war and bring peace with honor in Vietnam ...America did not settle for a peace that would have betrayed our allies ...that would have ended the war for us but would have continued the war for the 50 million people of Indochina."[108]

That night singer Neil Young was handed a note on stage, whereupon he stopped his concert at New York's Madison Square Garden to announce that "peace has come".

1986 Rock'n'Roll Developments — Rock and Roll Hall of Fame inaugural inductions

New York's Waldorf Astoria Hotel played host to the inaugural inductions into the Rock and Roll Hall of Fame. The "Performers" inducted were Chuck Berry, James Brown, Ray Charles, Sam Cooke, Fats Domino, The Everly Brothers, Buddy Holly, Jerry Lee Lewis, Elvis Presley and Little Richard.

The "Father of Country Music" Jimmie Rodgers, blues icon Robert Johnson and boogie-woogie pioneering pianist Jimmy Yancey all qualified as an "Early Influence".

"Non-Performers" were: Alan Freed, generally considered to have coined the phrase "rock'n'roll" and Sam Phillips, the man who discovered Elvis Presley, Jerry Lee Lewis and Carl Perkins.

The "Lifetime Achievement" place went to talent scout and producer John Hammond. He famously signed Bob Dylan to Columbia but his faith in Dylan was not shared by his colleagues and the signing was referred to as "Hammond's folly".

Singles released today

1957 Carl Perkins *Matchbox* c/w *Your True Love* (US)

Matchbox was inspired by Blind Lemon Jefferson's 1927 song *Matchbox Blues* and featured Jerry Lee Lewis on piano.

1957 Billy Riley and His Little Green Men *Flyin' Saucers Rock & Roll* (US)

Jerry Lee Lewis played piano on this rockabilly classic.

Births and deaths today

1932 Cyril Davies harmonica and guitar: Blues Incorporated, R&B All Stars

1978 Terry Kath founding member of Chicago, died aged thirty-one

Terry Kath died when he accidentally shot himself after putting the gun to his head and pulling the trigger. He believed that the gun was unloaded.

Events today

24

1956 Civil Rights Movement Emmett Till's murder

Look magazine published the article *The Shocking Story of Approved Killing in Mississippi*, by William Bradford Huie. It was based on interviews with Roy Bryant and JW Milam and described in detail how they carried out the kidnap and brutal murder of fourteen-year-old black youth Emmett Till on 28 August 1955.

Till was from Chicago, Illinois but at the time of his death he was staying with his great-uncle in the small Delta town of Money, Mississippi. There are various accounts as to what actually happened but what is known is that there was a trivial encounter between Till and Carolyn Bryant, the white female owner of the local store, Bryant's Grocery and Meat Market. Till was later abducted from his great-uncle's house. His battered body was found in the Tallahatchie River three days later. Carolyn's husband Roy Bryant and his half-brother JW Milam stood trial for murder but the jury acquitted them after deliberating for just over an hour.

Bob Dylan immortalised the story in his song *The Ballad of Emmett Till*, released under the pseudonym "Blind Boy Grunt".

1958 Elvis Presley first-ever single to enter the UK charts at #1

Just before Elvis was inducted into the US Army his latest single, *Jailhouse Rock*, entered the British charts at the #1 position. This was the first time that a single had leapt into the top-spot on its release. *Jailhouse Rock* and its B-side, *Treat Me Nice*, were both Leiber and Stoller penned songs taken from Elvis's third movie, *Jailhouse Rock*.

1960 Eddie Cochran final tour opened

Eddie Cochran's final tour opened at the Gaumont Theatre in Ipswich. On 17 April* he died in a car crash whilst travelling to Heathrow Airport from his final gig, in Bristol.

The tour was co-headlined with Gene Vincent, who was already in Britain and had been touring throughout January with support from British rocker Wee Willie Harris. The Cochran and Vincent tour was promoted by Larry Parnes and featured an array of his own British acts to support the two Americans. The support acts varied at different shows but included Vince Eager, Billy Fury, Joe Brown, Georgie Fame and The Tony Sheridan Trio.

Both Cochran and Vincent were backed by Marty Wilde's Wildcats. The Wildcats included lead guitarist "Big" Jim Sullivan, and future Shadows, drummer Brian Bennett and bassist Brian "Licorice" Locking.

Recording session today

1961 Del Shannon *Runaway*

When *Runaway* was coupled with *Jody* as Del Shannon's first single it gave him a #1 on both sides of the Atlantic. Both songs were co-written by Shannon. His career took off with this release, beginning a run of hit singles that lasted into the mid-1960s.

In 1986 the song received a new lease of life when Shannon re-recorded it as the theme to NBC-TV's *Crime Story*.

Birthday today

1947 Warren Zevon keyboardist, guitarist, singer and songwriter

Best known for his 1978 hit *Werewolves of London*. But there was so much more...

Event today

25

1968 Steppenwolf "heavy metal" arrived

Shortly after rising from the ashes of Canadian group The Sparrow, Steppenwolf played one of their earliest gigs at the Whisky a Go Go club in Los Angeles.

Around this time Steppenwolf were in the studio recording their first album. One of the tracks was to become the heavy metal anthem *Born to Be Wild*, accredited with coining the phrase "heavy metal". This song was chosen to play behind the opening credits of the quintessential 1960s movie *Easy* Rider, which premiered on 8 May* 1969. The song was written by Jack London and the Sparrows founding member Mars Bonfire.

The name "Steppenwolf" was inspired by the title of a Herman Hesse novel.

Recording sessions today

1955 Little Walter *My Babe*

Blues harmonica player Little Walter recorded the classic *My Babe*, written by Willie Dixon and featuring him on bass.

The song was originally inspired by the traditional gospel song *This Train (Is Bound for Glory)*. Early recorded versions of the song included the Florida Normal Industrial Institute Quartet (as *Dis Train*) in 1922 and Sister Rosetta Tharpe in 1939.

Little Walter pioneered the electric harmonica and influenced many of the blues harp players in the 1960's blues revival.

1960 Sam Cooke *Chain Gang*

Having recently parted company with the Keen record label and signed with RCA, Sam Cooke was back in the studio to record his own song *Chain Gang*.

Cooke was lead singer for the gospel group Soul Stirrers when producer Bumps Blackwell suggested that he should record a secular song. After recording *Forever* and releasing it as "Dale Cook", to avoid upsetting his gospel fans, he moved to the Keen record label and began a run of hits, starting with *You Send Me* in late 1957.

With *Chain Gang* the hits continued on both sides of the Atlantic, until his untimely death on 11 December* 1964.

Birthdays today

1938 Etta James blues singer

Etta James's first success came with *The Wallflower* in 1955, an answer song to Hank Ballard's classic *Work with Me Annie*. The song, written by Etta James and Johnny Otis, was also known as *Roll with Me Henry* and featured vocals from Richard Berry.

This was followed by a string of R&B hits into the early 1970s.

1945 Dave Walker singer: Redcaps, Idle Race, Savoy Brown, Fleetwood Mac

Dave Walker's singing career started with the Redcaps in the early 1960s. The second half of the decade was spent with Beckett, before replacing Jeff Lynne in Idle Race after he moved on to join Roy Wood in the Move and Electric Light Orchestra. Walker went on to join Savoy Brown, after their core lineup departed to form Foghat. He stayed with the group for three albums, *Street Corner Talking*, *Hellbound Train* and *Lion's Share*, before splitting to join Fleetwood Mac for their 1973 album *Penguin*. Following his brief stint with Fleetwood Mac, Walker performed with several bands, including a very short stay in late 1977 to early 1978 as Ozzy Osbourne's replacement in Black Sabbath.

Events today

1963 Wayne Fontana and the Jets from the Jets to the Mindbenders

Wayne Fontana and the Jets supported the Beatles at Macclesfield's El Rio Club.

Shortly after this gig the group had an audition for Fontana records. The Jets' drummer and guitarist both failed to show up and Wayne Fontana invited guitarist Eric Stewart and drummer Ric Rothwell to stand in for them. Fontana passed the audition, with the proviso that he recorded with the same musicians.

Wayne Fontana's new backing band took their name, "The Mindbenders", from a contemporaneous Dirk Bogarde movie *The Mind Benders*.

1970 Elvis Presley wore a jumpsuit on stage for the first time

The world was treated to the sartorial elegance of Elvis Presley performing in a jumpsuit for the first time. The jumpsuit was known as the "Cossack Suit" and the concert was the opening night of a one-month residency at the Las Vegas International Hotel.

Two-thirds of Elvis's *On Stage* album featured songs recorded at concerts on the 17 and 18 February.

1974 Jeff Beck final recording of Beck, Bogert & Appice

Beck, Bogert & Appice recorded their live performance at London's Rainbow Theatre shortly before splitting up. The performance was broadcast on radio but never officially released as an album.

The power trio formed in mid-1972, after the demise of the second version of the Jeff Beck Group. Beck originally planned to hook up with Vanilla Fudge's rhythm section in 1969 but an automobile accident meant that the duo formed Cactus in the meantime.

1977 Peter Green institutionalised for threatening his accountant

Original guitarist and founding member of Fleetwood Mac, Peter Green was institutionalised after threatening his accountant with an air rifle. The hapless messenger was trying to present Green with a royalty cheque for £30,000. Green was adamant that he did not want the money and his behaviour resulted in a trip to the Horton psychiatric hospital in Epsom, Surrey.

Green had parted company with Fleetwood Mac after a final gig at London's Roundhouse club on 28 May* 1970.

Recording session today

1956 Buddy Holly first recording session for Decca

Buddy Holly's first recording session for Decca took place at Owen Bradley's recording studio in Nashville, with guitarist Sonny Curtis and bassist Don Guess. He recorded *Love Me, Don't Come Back Knocking, Midnight Shift* and *Blue Days - Black Nights.*

Decca coupled *Blue Days - Black Nights* with *Love Me* and Buddy Holly's first single was released on 16 April*. It generated very little interest. Success was still fourteen months away, when his rock'n'roll classic *That'll Be the Day* topped the charts.

Birthdays today

1934 Huey "Piano" Smith R&B pianist: Huey Smith and the Clowns; sessions; solo

1955 Eddie Van Halen guitar: Mammoth, Van Halen

Event today

1973 Vietnam War America's war in Vietnam was over

The *Paris Peace Accords* were signed and an immediate ceasefire came into effect. America agreed that 150,000 North Vietnamese soldiers already in South Vietnam could remain there after the ceasefire.

It had been nineteen years since America picked up the baton from the French, after their defeat at Dien Bien Phu on 7 May* 1954. This negotiated peace agreement was tenuous at best. Skirmishes continued until the North launched its full-scale invasion of South Vietnam and took control of the whole country on 30 April* 1975.

To commemorate the American casualties the Vietnam Veterans Memorial Wall was completed in 1984. This lists the names of the 58,272[59] American military personnel who lost their lives in the conflict. The peak troop strength in Vietnam was 543,482 on 30 April 1969[105] and the troops on active duty during the era numbered 9,078,000.[105]

Recording session today

1970 John Lennon *Instant Karma*

John Lennon wrote, recorded and mixed *Instant Karma* in a single day. The Plastic Ono Band lineup for the recording included: guitarist George Harrison, keyboardist Billy Preston, bassist Klaus Voormann and drummer Alan White.

This was Lennon's first collaboration with producer Phil Spector.

Albums released today

1964 The Beatles *Introducing the Beatles* ...re-issued by Vee-Jay (US)

The first Beatles album released in America was from Vee-Jay on 22 July* 1963. This re-release, with some track changes, was aimed to capitalise on the 20 January* release of Capitol Records' first Beatles album, *Meet the Beatles*. (There is much speculation amongst Beatles chroniclers as to the dates of these Vee-Jay releases.)

This album contained six Lennon and McCartney originals and six covers. *Baby It's You* was a US hit for the Shirelles in 1962. *Boys* was another Shirelles song, issued as the B-side to the 1960 classic *Will You Love Me Tomorrow*. The Cookies scored a 1962 US hit with the Goffin and King composition *Chains*. *Twist and Shout* is usually attributed to the Isley Brothers but the Top Notes recorded the original version in 1961. *Anna (Go to Him)* was written and originally recorded by Arthur Alexander in 1962. A *Taste of Honey* started out as an instrumental piece; Lenny Welch recorded a vocal version in 1961.

In 1963 *Do You Want to Know a Secret* had provided Billy J Kramer with his first hit.

1969 The Beach Boys *20/20* (US)

20/20 contained the song *Never Learn Not to Love*, which was a reworked version of Charles Manson's *Cease to Exist*.

Beach Boys' drummer Dennis Wilson befriended Manson after being introduced to him by two female hitchhikers. Manson and his "Family" even lived with Dennis for a while and made some recordings in Brian's home studio. The relationship ended after the mass murders committed by Manson on 9 and 10 January* 1969.

28

Birthdays today

1918 Elmore James — influential blues guitarist, singer and songwriter

1944 Nick Mason — drums: Sigma 6, Abdabs, Meggadeaths, Pink Floyd

Events today

1956 Elvis Presley — first-ever national TV appearance

Elvis made his national TV debut on the *Dorsey Brothers' Stage Show*. He appeared with Scotty Moore, Bill Black and DJ Fontana. Introduced by disc jockey Bill Randle, he opened with a medley of Big Joe Turner songs *Shake, Rattle and Roll*, and *Flip Flop and Fly*, both Jesse Stone songs. Elvis's short set ended with Ray Charles's *I've Got a Woman.*

1970 Jimi Hendrix — demise of the Band of Gypsys

The Band of Gypsys lineup was short-lived and only managed to perform two gigs. The second appearance came less than a month after their debut and was an ignominious performance at the *Winter Festival for Peace*, an anti-Vietnam War benefit gig held at Madison Square Garden. The band played just two songs, *Who Knows* and *Earth Blues*, before an altercation between Hendrix and a lady in the audience resulted in our guitar hero cutting the performance short and storming off the stage.

Jimi Hendrix's Band of Gypsys, with drummer Buddy Miles and bassist Billy Cox, made their debut at New York's Fillmore East on 31 December. The performance was released as the live album *Band of Gypsys*. The royalties from the album went to former manager Ed Chalpin, in part settlement of a deal signed on 15 October* 1965.

Single released today

1966 Small Faces — *Sha-La-La-La-Lee* c/w *Grow Your Own* (UK)

This was the first single released by the classic lineup: singer Steve Marriott, bassist Ronnie Lane, drummer Kenny Jones and keyboardist Ian McLagan.

Births and deaths today

1943 Dick Taylor — bass: The Rollin' Stones; guitar: The Pretty Things

Before co-founding British R&B legends the Pretty Things, Dick Taylor was very nearly a founding member of the Rolling Stones. Taylor played guitar with Mick Jagger and Keith Richard in their first band, Little Boy Blue and the Blue Boys. The road to the Rolling Stones continued when they met Brian Jones at an Alexis Korner's Blues Incorporated gig. Drummer Charlie Watts was also in the lineup. The three Blue Boys joined Jones's band, which already included pianist Ian Stewart. Taylor had switched to bass when the Rollin' Stones made their debut at London's Marquee club on 12 July* 1962. He left the group to go to art college around the time of their first recording on 27 October*.

Taylor went on to form one of the UK's premier R&B bands, the Pretty Things. One of the reasons he left the Rollin' Stones was to return to guitar after playing bass.

1945 Robert Wyatt drums and vocals: Wilde Flowers, Soft Machine; solo

Robert Wyatt was a member of the influential Wilde Flowers before going on to become a founding member of Soft Machine. He left after their fourth album. In 1970 he recorded his first solo album, *The End of an Ear*, before forming Matching Mole. In 1973 Wyatt fell from a third floor window, leaving him paralysed from the waist down.

1983 Billy Fury British rock'n'roll singer, died at the age of forty-two

One of England's greatest rock'n'roll stars, Fury was plagued with health problems throughout his life. A bout of rheumatic fever as a child weakened his heart and led to recurrent ill-health. Despite extensive surgery he finally succumbed to his ailments.

Events today

1965 PJ Proby trouser-splitting performances

The *Cilla Black-PJ Proby Show* package tour had reached Croydon's ABC Theatre in south London, when Proby's gyrations on stage famously caused his skin-tight velvet bell-bottom trousers to split.

He explained it away as a wardrobe malfunction but when it happened again two days later retribution was swift and decisive. Proby was removed from the show and replaced by Tom Jones. He was banned from theatres across the UK and the BBC removed him from their playlists. At the end of February he released a new single, *I Apologise*. In a demonstration of Proby's popularity, the song still managed a showing on the UK Top 20 despite his inability to promote it.

The package tour was co-promoted by Brian Epstein. As well as the two headlining acts, Cilla Black and PJ Proby, the bill was made up mostly of other acts from the Epstein stable: The Fourmost, Tommy Quickly, The Remo Four and Sounds Incorporated.

Tommy Quickly replaced Johnny Sandon as the Remo Four's front man in late 1963.

1979 The Boomtown Rats "I don't like Mondays."

Sixteen-year-old Barbara Spencer went on a shooting spree from the window of her home in San Diego, California. Her target was the Grover Cleveland Elementary School situated across the road from her home.

Before surrendering to the police she had killed two men and wounded a police officer and eight children. When asked why she did it, Spencer reputedly told a reporter that she didn't like Mondays, the shooting livened up her day and that she did it simply for the fun of it. This dislike for Mondays resulted in a prison term of twenty-five years to life.

Six months later Bob Geldof's band, The Boomtown Rats, took inspiration from the incident and *I Don't Like Mondays* gave them their second British #1.

Birthdays today

1944 Andrew Loog Oldham managed the Rolling Stones; founded Immediate

Andrew Loog Oldham took over the management of the Rolling Stones from Giorgio Gomelsky shortly after meeting them on 28 April* 1963. He wanted a different image to that of the clean-cut, suited Beatles. His approach was more to pose the question, would you want your daughter going out with a Rolling Stone? He also made other changes to the fundamental nature of the Stones. Mick Jagger and Keith Richard were encouraged to become the band's main songwriters. He also shifted the group's focal point away from guitarist and founder Brian Jones to singer Mick Jagger. When Oldham met the Stones they were a sextet. Pianist Ian Stewart had been the first Rolling Stone to join Brian Jones's group but Oldham felt that he had the wrong image for the Stones. Stewart was sidelined from performer to road manager but he continued to play keyboards on many of their recordings. Oldham managed and produced the band until 1967, when he cut a deal with future Beatles manager Allan Klein to take over the Stones' business affairs.

In August 1965 he launched his own record label, Immediate. This label produced some of the greatest sounds of the 1960s, including Chris Farlowe, Small Faces and The Nice. It folded in 1970.

1947 David Byron singer: Spice, Uriah Heep, Rough Diamond; solo

Events today

30

1969 The Beatles final gig ...a rooftop performance

As part of the *Get Back* project, which had started on 2 January*, the Beatles gave their last ever 'public' performance, from the London rooftop of their Apple building at 3 Savile Row. Unbelievably there were complaints about the noise. The set even brought the traffic below to a standstill. The police intervened and eventually, after deliberating for half an hour, stopped the performance. With Billy Preston on keyboards they performed: *Get Back, Don't Let Me Down, I've Got a Feeling, The One After 909* and *Dig a Pony*.

When they finished John quipped that he hoped that they had passed the audition. This was possibly a reference to their previous audition failures, Billy Fury's backing band on 10 May* 1960 and a Decca recording contract on 1 January* 1962.

1971 Eric Burdon collapsed on stage ...that was just the beginning

Eric Burdon collapsed on stage in Sutton Coldfield, during a concert with his band War.

This was a low period in Eric Burdon's life. The ex-Animals lead singer was still depressed by the death of his friend Jimi Hendrix on 18 September* 1970. At another concert a week later he was unable to make it through the show. His poor health, asthma and pneumonia all caught up with him and in the middle of this European tour he parted company with his backing band. War went on to finish the tour without him.

Things went from bad to worse and he found himself in dispute with both his management company and his record label, MGM.

All this and the IRS was also chasing him for unpaid taxes.

1973 Kiss debut gig

Wicked Lester changed their name to "Kiss" and played their debut gig with the new moniker at New York's Popcorn Club in Queens. The performance went virtually unnoticed and was witnessed by just a handful of punters.

Singer and guitarist Paul Stanley and bassist Gene Simmons parted company with the other members of Wicked Lester after Epic rejected an album recorded by the group. They hooked up with drummer

Peter Criss and lead guitarist Ace Frehley, adopted the name Kiss and went on to sell more than 100 million albums[65] worldwide.

Single released today

1964 The Beatles *Please Please Me c/w From Me to You* (US)

Following the Beatles' American chart success on Capitol and Swan in early 1964, Vee-Jay took the A-sides of their first two singles, both released in 1963, and reissued them as this single. Vee-Jay was rewarded with the first of two hit singles. The other being *Do You Want to Know a Secret c/w Thank You Girl* three months later.

Birthdays today

1942 Marty Balin singer: Jefferson Airplane/Starship; solo

1947 Steve Marriott vocals and guitar: Small Faces, Humble Pie

1951 Phil Collins drums and vocals: Flaming Youth, Genesis, Brand X; solo

Drummer Phil Collins joined Genesis in 1971, in time for their third album *Nursery Cryme*. In 1975 he became the band's lead singer, after the departure of Peter Gabriel following the album and tour for *The Lamb Lies Down on Broadway*.

Events today

1957 Bill Haley first British million seller

Decca announced that Bill Haley and His Comets' recording of *Rock Around the Clock* had become the first million selling single in Britain.

The road to the song's appearance in the record books was by no means a smooth one. It was originally released by Sonny Dae and His Knights in early 1954 but sank without trace. Bill Haley recorded the song during his first Decca session on 12 April* 1954 but once again the song failed to trouble the best-selling lists. It was only after it was reissued that it hit the American charts in mid-1955, following its soundtrack appearance behind the opening credits of the movie *Blackboard Jungle*. It caught the world's imagination and kick-started rock'n'roll.

In Britain it charted initially for a couple of weeks at the lower end of the Top 20 in January 1955. The song became a UK #1 after its chart re-entry in October.

1968 The Who ill-fated Australian tour ended

Supported by ex-Manfred Mann singer Paul Jones and the Small Faces, the Who's ill-fated antipodean tour came to an end at the Town Hall in Wellington, New Zealand.

The tour started badly with the band receiving negative press after a less-than-friendly press conference when they arrived in Sydney. A contretemps with one of the cabin crew on the flight from Sydney to Melbourne led to the entourage being questioned by the police on landing at Melbourne. At the end of the tour Pete Townshend vowed that he would never set foot in Australia again.

1968 Vietnam War *Tet Offensive* began ...the tide turned

The devastating *Tet Offensive* was launched by 80,000 Viet Cong, South Vietnamese guerrilla fighters, aided by North Vietnamese regular troops. This was a daring simultaneous attack on over a hundred towns and cities across South Vietnam. It took the Americans by surprise and marked the first time that street fighting had taken place in the cities. Some of the attacks were repulsed within hours, others in days but some targets, such as the battle for Hue, saw fierce fighting which lasted for months. By early March the *Tet Offensive* had been halted but public opinion turned firmly against the war. It was the beginning of the end of the American adventure in Vietnam.

The false optimism being expressed by the likes of General Westmoreland was over. President Johnson announced on 31 March* that he was stepping down from the Presidential race. The *Paris Peace Talks* opened on 10 May* and newly elected President Nixon announced US troop withdrawals on 8 June* 1969.

Recording session today

1963 The Beach Boys *Surfin' USA*

The second American hit single from the Beach Boys, *Surfin' USA*, originally gave Brian Wilson the credit for writing the song. Chuck Berry took a dim view of this because he considered it to be a tad too similar to his song *Sweet Little Sixteen*. A threatened lawsuit resulted in Berry's name being added to the writing credits.

Birthdays today

1944 Charlie Musselwhite seminal white blues harmonica player

1956 Johnny Rotten singer: Swankers, Sex Pistols, PIL

February

Events today

1964 Rock'n'Roll Developments beginning of the "British Invasion"

The Beatles first single to enter the Billboard Top 40, *I Want to Hold Your Hand*, was also their first American #1. This marked the beginning of two years of major American success for British artists and it became known as the "British Invasion".

Small independent label Vee-Jay had released the Beatles' first American single, *Please Please Me*, a year earlier on 25 February* but it took the marketing clout of Capitol Records to get the Beatles into the American charts. The British Invasion was consolidated a week later, when an estimated seventy-three million people watched the Beatles for the first time on the *Ed Sullivan Show* on 9 February*. By 4 April* the Beatles accounted for a staggering twelve of the Top 100 singles, including all of the Top 5 slots!

Before the Beatles hit the American #1 spot only two other British acts had preceded them, Mr Acker Bilk with *Stranger on the Shore* and the Tornados with *Telstar*. The previous generation of 1950s British rock'n'roll stars, such as Cliff Richard, Billy Fury and Marty Wilde, had achieved very limited success across the Atlantic. Interestingly, their fortunes didn't change much with the British Invasion. In the wake of the Beatles' success a whole raft of British groups and individual artists found fame in America. The boot was very much on the other foot now, with some American acts adopting English sounding names. You can't get much more "English" than the Beefeaters, although they did achieve a certain degree of success after morphing into the Byrds.

The Dave Clark Five were the first British act to tour America. Herman's Hermits, particularly lead singer Peter Noone, went on to achieve considerable recognition there. The Rolling Stones followed the Beatles into the American charts six months later with *Tell Me*, although it would be June 1965 before they scored their first #1 with *(I Can't Get No) Satisfaction*. British acts continued to find success but the ability to make the American charts on the strength of an English accent eventually petered out. In 1967 Lulu's *To Sir with Love* was the last British #1 (not by the Beatles or Stones) for four years, until Rod Stewart's *Maggie May* in the autumn of 1971.

1969 The Rascals only performed if 50 per cent of the acts were black

The Rascals announced[56] their concert policy was going to be one of only performing when half of the acts on the bill were black. This political statement extended to not appearing on what they considered to be establishment television programmes.

The blue-eyed soul group came together as "The Rascals" in 1965. They added the "Young" to avoid confusion with the Harmonica Rascals but later reverted to "The Rascals". The first single as "The Rascals" was *A Beautiful Morning*, released in 1968.

Recording session today

1954 Johnny "Guitar" Watson *Space Guitar*

Shortly after switching from piano to guitar, Johnny "Guitar" Watson recorded the instrumental *Space Guitar* for Federal records. This guitar work pioneered feedback and reverb. The self-penned instrumental was recorded as "Young John Watson".

Birthdays today

1937 Don Everly — elder of the two Everly Brothers

1937 Ray Sawyer — singer: Dr Hook and the Medicine Show; solo

Events today

2

1963 The Beatles — first UK tour

The Beatles opened their first British tour at Bradford's Gaumont Cinema.

The package tour was headlined by British teenage singing sensation Helen Shapiro. By the time of the tour she had already topped the British charts twice, with *You Don't Know* and *Walkin' Back to Happiness*. The Beatles' second single, *Please Please Me*, had just entered the charts and their increasing popularity meant that by the end of the tour a month later, they had moved up the billing to close the first half of the show.

1963 The Rolling Stones — debut of all five of the classic lineup

In researching this book the date of the debut performance of Brian Jones, Mick Jagger, Keith Richard, Bill Wyman and Charlie Watts proved to be one of the most disputed dates I encountered amongst rock historians and sources. I have opted for 2 February[52] because this is the final date suggested. It is also the date by which the sources would all be agreed that bass player Bill Wyman and drummer Charlie Watts were permanent members of the Rolling Stones.

This gig on 2 February was at west London's Ealing Jazz Club. At this stage the Rolling Stones was still a sextet. Piano player Ian Stewart had been with Brian Jones's band since the beginning, preceding both Jagger and Richard.

Recording sessions today

1962 Bob Dylan — recorded with Harry Belafonte

In between the recording session on 20 November* 1961 for his own eponymous debut album and its release on 19 March*, Bob Dylan made a rare appearance in the studio in support of an established artist. This time he provided harmonica for the title track on Harry Belafonte's upcoming album *The Midnight Special*, a song popularised by Lead Belly, who made a recording of it in Louisiana State Penitentiary in the summer of 1934.

1962 Ronnie Hawkins — *Mojo Man*

The Billy Lee Riley penned *Mojo Man* appeared on the 1964 Roulette album, *The Best of Ronnie Hawkins*. His backing band, The Hawks, became Bob Dylan's backing band and in 1967 renamed to "The Band". All five of the future Band members performed that day: guitarist Robbie Robertson, bassist Rick Danko, drummer Levon Helm, organist Garth Hudson and pianist Richard Manuel. The session also featured blues harmonica player Sonny Terry and was produced by Jerry Leiber and Mike Stoller.

Births and deaths today

1942 Graham Nash — guitarist, singer-songwriter: Deltas, The Hollies, CS&N

1979 Sid Vicious notorious Sex Pistols bassist, died aged twenty-one

Just over a year after the Sex Pistols' swan song performance on 14 January* 1978, bassist Sid Vicious died from a drugs overdose.

At the time of his death he was on bail in New York accused of murdering his girlfriend Nancy Spungen. Vicious died before coming to trial, so whether the knifing of Spungen was accidental or deliberate will always be the stuff of rock'n'roll mythology.

Births and deaths today

3

1935 Johnny "Guitar" Watson guitar: Shields; solo

Johnny "Guitar" Watson was a member of the Shields, in a lineup that included *Earth Angel* co-author Jesse Belvin. As well as pioneering guitar feedback and reverb, he was one of Frank Zappa's influences and made guest appearances on his albums and at live shows.

1959 Buddy Holly the day the music died

The *Winter Dance Party* had reached the Surf Ballroom in Clear Lake, Iowa. It was a short tour of the Midwest which had started out on 23 January* in Milwaukee. The tour bus had been breaking down regularly in the sub-zero temperatures and to make the journey more comfortable Holly had chartered a light aircraft to fly to Fargo, North Dakota for the next concert at Moorhead, Minnesota. Holly's backing musicians Waylon Jennings and Tommy Allsup were originally planning to accompany him on the flight to Fargo. Fate took a hand and Jennings gave up his seat for the Big Bopper. Ritchie Valens 'won' the flip of a coin and he took Allsup's seat. The plane took off shortly after midnight but crashed a few miles out of Clear Lake, killing the pilot Roger Peterson and his three passengers, Buddy Holly, aged twenty-two, the Big Bopper, twenty-eight, and Ritchie Valens, who was only seventeen.

It's an ill wind...and the tragedy launched the career of Fargo's own Bobby Vee. As news of the fatal air crash spread around Fargo, the search for local talent began. Fifteen-year-old Bobby Vee with his backing group the Shadows stepped up to perform at the Moorhead concert that very same evening.

The tour continued and gave its final performance on 15 February at Springfield's Illinois State Armory. Frankie Sardo and Dion continued with the tour and were joined by new headliners Jimmy Clanton and teen idols Fabian and Frankie Avalon.

1967 Joe Meek pioneering British producer, died aged thirty-seven

On the eighth anniversary of the death of Buddy Holly, Joe Meek killed himself.

Meek was a groundbreaking British record producer who was often compared to Phil Spector. He died at 304 Holloway Road, Islington, London, famous as both his home and recording studio. On that fateful anniversary of Buddy Holly's death he argued with his landlady, Violet Shenton, shot her dead and then turned the shotgun on himself. The gun was owned by former Tornados bass player and solo star Heinz.

In 1962 Meek produced the Tornados instrumental *Telstar*, which was the first American #1 by a British group. This feat was achieved a full year before the British Invasion.

Heinz was born Heinz Burt in Germany. He was the Tornados' bass player before Meek turned him into a solo singer with his first British hit, *Just Like Eddie*.

2003 Phil Spector Lana Clarkson found dead

Actress Lana Clarkson was found dead at the home of "wall of sound" producer Phil Spector. Adriano De Souza, Spector's driver, discovered the body slumped in a chair in the foyer of the record producer's mansion in Alhambra, Los Angeles. Clarkson had a gunshot wound through the roof of her mouth.

Spector was charged with murder but it took a little over six years for justice to run its course. The first trial ended in September 2007 when the jury failed to reach agreement, with ten jurors voting guilty and the other two opting for not guilty. Following a second trial Spector was found guilty and in May 2009 he was given a sentence of nineteen years to life.

Events today

4

1966 Bob Dylan infamous electric world tour

Backed by the group (well, almost) that was destined to become the Band, Bob Dylan continued his world tour with a gig in Kentucky, at Louisville's Convention Centre.

When this leg of the tour opened, the Hawks' lineup comprised guitarist Robbie Robertson, bassist Rick Danko, pianist Richard Manuel, organist Garth Hudson and drummer Mickey Jones. The tour had started its American leg the previous autumn with the Hawks' original drummer Levon Helm but he quit after becoming tired of playing to jeering audiences night after night. Dylan's first electric set was delivered to a mixed response at the Newport Folk Festival on 25 July* 1965. This 1966 tour rolled on to Australia in mid-April, before rounding off in Europe at the end of May. The most infamous gig of the tour came in England on 17 May* when one of the audience taunted Dylan with shouts of "Judas". This concert was captured on the bootleg album *Royal Albert Hall 1966*, a slightly misleading title since the gig was in Manchester and not London.

In July, Dylan had a motorcycle accident which kept him out of action until June 1967, when he ensconced himself with the Band for three months of recording at the *Big Pink*.

1970 Phil Collins the early days

In his pre-Genesis days, drummer Phil Collins played a gig with his band Flaming Youth at the New Joints Club in Wimbledon, south-west London.

Collins started out as a child actor, including a part as the Artful Dodger in a West End production of Lionel Bart's musical *Oliver*. He also had a cameo role in the Beatles' first movie *A Hard Day's Night*. His drumming career took shape in the spring of 1968, after he was reputedly the only respondent to an ad placed by the group Freehold in the music magazine *Melody Maker*. During this time he made his first recording, when Freehold visited Regent Sound studios and cut the Collins-penned *Lying Crying Dying*.

Freehold and Collins parted company in the autumn of 1968. Before the split he recorded *Green Light* and *Key*, released by CBS as "Hickory" in early 1969. This single was Phil Collins' first record release. The band backed singer John Walker on tour, before morphing into Flaming Youth and recording the concept album *Ark II*.

In the summer of 1970 Genesis was looking for yet another drummer. In their short lifetime of just two albums the band was looking for its fourth drummer, following Chris Stewart, John Silver and John Mayhew; Collins auditioned in early August. Genesis not only found a permanent sticksman but unbeknown to them at the time, they also had a singer-in-waiting, ready to fill Peter Gabriel's shoes when he decided to move on in 1976.

Single released today

1966 The Rolling Stones *19th Nervous Breakdown c/w As Tears Go By* (UK)

As Tears Go By was one of the earliest Jagger and Richard songs to find chart success on both sides of the Atlantic. The song was originally released as a single by Marianne Faithfull in 1964. She was later connected romantically to Mick Jagger.

Birthday today

1948 Alice Cooper highly theatrical rock singer

As Vincent Furnier he started out in a school band, The Earwigs, where he first played alongside guitarist Glen Buxton. They became the Spiders, then Nazz and finally Alice Cooper, which he later adopted as his own name.

Event today

1957 Bill Haley and His Comets American rock'n'roll came to Britain

American rock'n'roll music finally came to Britain. Bill Haley and His Comets arrived in England on the cruise liner *Queen Elizabeth*, to become the first of the true rock'n'roll greats from across the water to embark on a tour of the UK. Haley and his band landed in Southampton and journeyed by train to London's Waterloo station, where they were mobbed by thousands of fans.

The tour was organised by light entertainment promoters Leslie and Lew Grade. The other acts on the bill were surprisingly lacking in rock'n'roll credentials. Haley was supported on this historic first rock'n'roll tour by: The Vic Lewis Orchestra, the comedy duo Kenneth Earle and Malcolm Vaughan, and the tin whistle playing Desmond Lane.

The drummer with the Vic Lewis Orchestra was none other than Andy White. On 11 September* 1962, at the invitation of producer George Martin, White substituted for Ringo Starr when the Beatles made their third journey to EMI's Abbey Road studios to record the third version of their first British single, *Love Me Do*.

Recording session today

1959 Eddie Cochran *Three Stars*

Two days after Buddy Holly, the Big Bopper and Ritchie Valens died in a plane crash on 3 February*, Eddie Cochran recorded his tribute, *Three Stars*. It was not released at the time. In Britain it appeared in 1966 as a single, coupled with *Somethin' Else*. American fans had to wait until 1972 for the album release on *Legendary Masters Series #4*.

The song was written by Tommy Donaldson, a disc jockey at radio station KFXM in San Bernardino, California. He became a one-hit wonder a couple of months after the Eddie Cochran recording session, when he recorded the song himself as Tommy Dee with Carol Kay and the Teen-Aires.

Birthdays today

1929 Hal Blaine drums: session musician, The Wrecking Crew

As a member of the Wrecking Crew, Hal Blaine was one of the busiest session drummers on the West Coast. Phil Spector's "wall of sound" used his talents, along with some of rock'n'roll's finest, ncluding

Elvis Presley, The Beach Boys and The Byrds. Blaine's tally of hit records was staggering, with estimates that he played on over 5,000[66] records, film scores and TV jingles.

The Wrecking Crew was a highly successful group of Californian session musicians who played with the crème de la crème of performers in the 1960s and '70s.

1944 Al Kooper keyboards and vocals: Blues Project; Blood, Sweat & Tears

One of the 1960s most influential keyboard players, Al Kooper was responsible for the signature organ riff on Bob Dylan's classic *Like a Rolling Stone*. Kooper also backed Dylan at his notorious appearance at the *Newport Folk Festival* on 25 July* 1965. Following a stint as an original member of the Blues Project, Kooper left in 1967 to form Blood, Sweat & Tears. Despite founding the group he left after their first album, *Child Is Father to the Man*. The multi-talented Kooper was also: a songwriter, *This Diamond Ring* for Gary Lewis and the Playboys; a producer, Lynyrd Skynyrd's first three albums; and musician, collaborating with Mike Bloomfield and Stephen Stills on *Super Session*. He'd come a long way from his start in 1958, as guitarist with the Royal Teens.

Event today

1971 Fairport Convention Richard Thompson moved on

Founding member of Fairport Convention, Richard Thompson left the group to pursue a solo career. He went on to release a string of critically acclaimed albums, including several with his wife Linda.

Singer, guitarist and songwriter, Thompson was one of the founding members, in mid-1967, of the seminal British folk-rock band Fairport Convention, along with: singers Judy Dyble and Iain Matthews, guitarist Simon Nicol, bassist Ashley Hutchings and drummer Martin Lamble. Technically Lamble was not the original drummer; he had replaced the first drummer Shaun Frater after just one gig. Lamble died on 12 May* 1969 when the group's van crashed following a gig in Birmingham. He was replaced by drummer Dave Mattacks. When Thompson left the group, only Nicol remained from the original lineup.

Several original members of Fairport Convention left to form other successful bands. In 1969 singer Iain Matthews moved on and formed Matthews' Southern Comfort and bassist Ashley Hutchings also created pastures green with Steeleye Span.

Single released today

1956 The Everly Brothers *Keep a Lovin' Me* c/w *The Sun Keeps Shining* (US)

The Everly Brothers released their self-penned, debut single on the Columbia label.

Before finding international success with the Cadence record label, the Everly Brothers had a brief recording career with Columbia. They started out with their parents on the radio, as a part of the *Everly Family Show*. Chet Atkins was a big fan of the show and introduced the brothers to Columbia. They signed in early November 1955 and cut four songs on 9 November, in what would be their only recording session for the label. This first single was released but it sank without trace, resulting in their swift removal from Columbia's roster of artists.

Births and deaths today

1943 Fabian — American teen singing idol

Fabian was one of the clean-cut teen idols to emerge in America after the demise of the first wave of rock'n'roll in the late 1950s. He had a string of American hits in 1959 and 1960 before moving into a successful movie career.

After Elvis joined the US Army, Little Richard found religion and Jerry Lee Lewis's career imploded when he married his cousin's thirteen-year-old daughter, the rock'n'roll mantle was carried by a new breed of clean-cut, good-looking, all-American teen idols. As if to act as a bridge between the two generations, Fabian and fellow teen idol Frankie Avalon were replacement acts for Buddy Holly, the Big Bopper and Ritchie Valens when the *Winter Dance Party* continued after their plane crashed on 3 February* 1959.

1960 Jesse Belvin — R&B singer and songwriter, died aged twenty-seven

Jesse Belvin, his wife and chauffer died when their car was involved in a head-on collision. He had just finished performing in Little Rock, Arkansas, sharing a bill with Sam Cooke, Jackie Wilson and Marv Johnson.

At the time of his death Belvin was a successful R&B singer and songwriter, with co-authorship of the Penguins' classic *Earth Angel* amongst his songwriting credits.

He died when he was twenty-seven years of age, qualifying him for the macabre *27 Club*, along with Jimi Hendrix, Brian Jones, Janis Joplin and Jim Morrison.

Event today

1980 Pink Floyd — first concert performance of *The Wall*

The first concert performance of Pink Floyd's epic album *The Wall* took place in America, at the Sports Arena in Los Angeles. The opening night's performance had to be stopped briefly to extinguish a fire started by the show's pyrotechnics.

The concept for *The Wall* grew out of an incident at a concert in Montreal on 6 July* 1977, when Roger Waters spat at a fan after an increasingly frustrating evening of firecrackers and crowd noise. That 1977 tour was called *In the Flesh*. The tour name was used as the title of the opening song on *The Wall* album. It was also the name of a track on side four of the original double album. The second *In the Flesh* song was a conversation with the audience and finished with Waters screaming that he would like to have them "all shot".

In the concert performance of *The Wall* a thirty-foot-high barrier was constructed brick by brick during the first half of the show. The Pink Floyd remained hidden from the audience until the wall was torn down at the end of the performance. One of the night's highlights was seeing David Gilmour lifted on a platform to tower above the wall for his signature solo in *Comfortably Numb*.

Original keyboard player Rick Wright had been fired during the recording of the album and was now simply on the payroll for the tour. Guitarist Snowy White and bass player Andy Bown performed in the "surrogate band" in the 1980 performances. Andy Bown reprised his role in the 1981 shows but Snowy White was replaced by guitarist Andy Roberts. White joined Irish rockers Thin Lizzy after completing the *Wall* concerts.

The Wall was only performed in three countries and at four different venues. After the opening in Los Angeles it moved to the east coast to be staged at New York's Nassau Coliseum. In August British fans had a chance to see the show at London's Earls Court. In 1981 *The Wall* was seen in Germany at the Westfalenhalle in Dortmund, before the final performances once again at Earls Court. The last London performance on 17 June* was Roger Waters' swan song concert-length performance with Pink Floyd.

Births and deaths today

1934 King Curtis session saxophonist; solo

King Curtis was one of the prominent session saxophonists of the 1950s and '60s. He performed on such classics as the Coasters' *Yakety Yak* and *Charlie Brown*, Buddy Holly's *Reminiscing* and Sam Cooke's album *Live at the Harlem Square Club 1963*. As well as his session work and live appearances he also had a number of American hit singles, the best known being his self-penned instrumental *Soul Twist* in 1962.

Buddy Holly's *Reminiscing* was written by Curtis and released posthumously in 1962.

1959 Guitar Slim flamboyant blues guitarist, died at the age of thirty-two

The highly influential blues guitarist Guitar Slim died of pneumonia, complicated by a lifetime of hard living and heavy drinking.

He was one of the first guitarists to deliver a flamboyant stage show. Using a guitar lead around three hundred feet long he would often perform his guitar solos whilst wandering around the audience, sometimes as far as the theatre entrance. As well as being a very visual artist, he also experimented with distortion a decade before Pete Townshend and Jimi Hendrix. The self-penned *The Things That I Used to Do* was his best known song and gave him an R&B #1 in 1954.

Event today

1956 Buddy Holly "Holley" became "Holly"

Buddy Holley signed his first recording deal with Decca. When he came to put his name to the contract he found that the record company had omitted the "e" from his surname, Holley. He famously signed with the new spelling and adopted it as his stage name, "Buddy Holly".

This first recording venture proved short lived. His two Decca singles, *Blue Days - Black Nights*, and *Modern Don Juan* both sank without trace and Decca dropped him.

On 16 May* 1957 Holly once again signed a recording contract with Decca but this time to its subsidiary Coral. The Crickets had already signed a separate deal, which resulted in the American recordings by Buddy Holly and the Crickets being released as either "Buddy Holly" on the Coral label or "The Crickets" on the Brunswick label. The duality of this contract arrangement plagued Holly's royalty payments and contributed to his split with the Crickets and his manager Norman Petty, shortly before his tragic death on 3 February* 1959 on the *Winter Dance Party* tour.

Single released today

1957 The Diamonds *Little Darlin'* c/w *Faithful and True* (US)

White, Canadian vocal group the Diamonds specialised in covering songs by black, R&B artists. They had a string of American hits in the second half of the 1950s, starting with their cover of Frankie Lymon and the Teenagers' *Why Do Fools Fall in Love*.

Little Darlin' was a rare example of a white cover of a black vocal group being generally considered to be superior to the original. The song was written by Maurice Williams and originally recorded by his group the Gladiolas. Even in the R&B charts the Diamonds achieved more success and it gave the group their only British hit.

The Gladiolas later became Maurice Williams and the Zodiacs and scored a hit on both sides of the Atlantic in late 1960 with the Williams penned *Stay*.

Births and deaths today

1937 Ben Palmer piano: Roosters, Glands, Powerhouse; roadie: Cream

Pianist Ben Palmer was one of rock'n'roll's lesser known heroes. His musical career started out alongside a young Eric Clapton in the Roosters. His association with Clapton continued when they teamed up in the Glands. In the summer of 1965 Clapton took a break from his role as guitarist with John Mayall's Bluesbreakers to embark on a tour of Europe and beyond. The Glands' experience proved to be a little more eventful than expected and by 6 November* Clapton was back with the Bluesbreakers. Palmer joined Clapton once again as pianist with his studio group Eric Clapton and the Powerhouse. The group had three tracks included on the compilation album *What's Shakin'*, released on 1 June* 1966. Around this time Clapton teamed up with drummer Ginger Baker and bassist Jack Bruce to form Cream. Palmer joined them as their roadie.

1990 Del Shannon singer in rock'n'roll's second wave, died aged fifty-five

Despite rumours that he might have replaced Roy Orbison in the Traveling Wilburys, Del Shannon chose to commit suicide by shooting himself in his Californian home in Santa Clarita.

Events today

9

1961 The Beatles first Cavern appearance as "The Beatles"

This lunchtime session was the first time that the black leather clad Liverpudlians had performed there as "The Beatles". It also gave George Harrison his Cavern debut. Pete Best occupied the drumming stool for this performance.

John Lennon and Paul McCartney had both performed on stage at the Cavern as a part the Quarry Men. Sources vary for drummer Ringo Starr's Cavern debut but the Cavern's own website gives the date as 31 July 1957, when he played there with the Eddie Clayton Skiffle Group. This would have been just before the Quarry Men's debut on 7 August* 1957. Ringo's first Cavern visit as a Beatle was five years later, on 19 August 1962.

1964 The Beatles first appearance on the *Ed Sullivan Show*

Ed Sullivan had been aware of the Beatles since 31 October* 1963, when he had experienced Beatlemania first hand at London's Heathrow airport. For their legendary debut appearance on the *Ed Sullivan Show* they performed five songs live: *All My Loving, Till There Was You, She Loves You, I Saw Her Standing There* and *I Want to Hold Your Hand*. This first Beatles outing was watched by seventy-three million[67] people.

Singer Davy Jones was also on the show, two years before his Monkees TV debut.

1964 The Lovin' Spoonful road to the Lovin' Spoonful

The glint in the eye came when guitarist, vocalist and songwriter John Sebastian and guitarist and singer Zal Yanovsky were both invited by future-Mama Cass Elliot over to her place to watch the Beatles debut on the *Ed Sullivan Show*.

Yanovsky was in the Canadian folk group the Halifax Three with Denny Doherty. When it folded they formed the Mugwumps with Cass Elliot. John Sebastian was well known on the Greenwich Village folk scene. He had played with the Even Dozen Jug Band and also sat in on occasions with the Mugwumps. In late 1964 the Mugwumps split. Yanovsky and Sebastian went on to form the Lovin' Spoonful and Doherty and Elliot became the Mamas & the Papas (via John Phillips's group the New Journeymen).

Bassist Steve Boone and drummer Joe Butler were members of Steve's brother Skip's band the Kingsmen, before joining the Lovin' Spoonful. (The Long Island Kingsmen, not to be confused with the *Louie Louie* boys from Portland, Oregon.)

The band's name was inspired by Mississippi John Hurt's reference to his need for a "lovin' spoonful" of his favourite coffee, in his song *Coffee Blues*.

Album recorded today

1959 Cliff Richard *Cliff*

Performing in front of a couple of hundred fans, Cliff Richard and the Drifters were in the studios at EMI's Abbey Road for the first of two days of 'live' recording for their first album.

His classic backing band of lead guitarist Hank Marvin, rhythm guitarist Bruce Welch, bassist Jet Harris and drummer Tony Meehan had only played their first concert together a month earlier, in Manchester on 10 January*.

They were still calling themselves "The Drifters" but that would soon change to "The Shadows", to avoid confusion with the American vocal group of the same name.

Birthday today

1942 Carole King songwriter and singer: Goffin and King; solo

Events today

1966 The 13th Floor Elevators early review as "psychedelic rock"

The day after the 13th Floor Elevators played Austin's New Orleans Club in Texas, the local newspaper, *The Austin Statesman*, reviewed the gig under the headline "Unique Elevators Shine With 'Psychedelic Rock'". This was one of the earliest press references to a band being described as "psychedelic".

The 13th Floor Elevators were one of the pioneers of psychedelic rock, titling their debut album *The Psychedelic Sounds of the 13th Floor Elevators*. In the summer of 1966 they offered Janis Joplin the opportunity to join them as lead vocalist. She declined the offer and opted to move to San Francisco to front Big Brother and the Holding Company.

1970 ZZ Top debut gig

ZZ Top made their performing debut at a gig in Columbus Hall in Beaumont, Texas.

They would have to wait another decade for their greatest commercial success, which came in the first half of the 1980s with a string of hits on both sides of the Atlantic.

1971 George Harrison accused of plagiarism

George Harrison's debut single, *My Sweet Lord*, was still riding high in the charts on both sides of the Atlantic, when Bright Tunes Music filed a lawsuit claiming that the song was too similar to the Chiffons' 1963 hit *He's So Fine*, written by Ronnie Mack.

The case finally reached the courts in 1976. Harrison was found guilty of subconscious plagiarism and it cost him a reputed $587,000.

1971 Patti Smith first performance with Lenny Kaye

Singer and poet Patti Smith's first performance with guitarist Lenny Kaye was at the *Poetry Project* in St Mark's Church-in-the-Bowery on New York's Lower East Side. The half hour performance included Bertolt Brecht's *Mack the Knife* and her own poem *Ballad of a Bad Boy*.

Smith later formed the Patti Smith Group with Lenny Kaye. The group went on to become one of the leading lights in New York's mid-1970s new wave music scene.

Recording session today

1953 The Crows *Gee*

Gee was one of the first R&B crossover hits and a contender for the first rock'n'roll record.

Album released today

1978 Judas Priest *Stained Glass* (UK)

Almost seven years after the release of their album *Stained Glass*, Judas Priest and their record company Columbia were sued by the parents of two American fans who claimed that subliminal messages contained in the songs had triggered a suicide pact.

The suicide happened on 23 December* 1985 but it took another five years for the courts to settle in favour of the band and its record company.

Birthday today

1933 Don Wilson guitarist and founding member of the Ventures

At the time of writing Don Wilson was still performing with the Ventures, fifty-six years after the formation of the world's most successful instrumental combo.

Events today

1964 The Beatles concert debut in America

Two days after their triumphant appearance on the *Ed Sullivan Show*, the Beatles gave their first-ever American concert performance at the Washington Coliseum. The Liverpool lads headlined the show and were supported by Tommy Roe, The Chiffons, Jay and the Americans, The Caravelles and The Righteous Brothers, although some reports suggest that not all of these artists actually performed on the night.

The following night the Beatles performed two sets at New York's Carnegie Hall. These two gigs were their only concert performances on this trip. The Fab Four would not embark on their first full American tour until 19 August*.

The Beatles initiated the onslaught of the British Invasion with their first #1, *I Want to Hold Your Hand*, on 1 February*. Their debut on the *Ed Sullivan Show* followed on 9 February*, watched by a staggering 73 million viewers. This was consolidated by their unparalleled chart listings on 4 April*, when they took 12 of the Top 100 spots, including all of the top five places. However, it was the Dave Clark Five who started the Invasion when they landed on America's shores on 24 May*, to undertake the first tour of America by a British beat group. This domination of the American music scene by British artists became known as the "British Invasion" and lasted about two years.

1972 King Crimson American tour opened

King Crimson opened their six-week American tour with a concert at the Armoury in Wilmington, Delaware.

Despite having been the most stable King Crimson lineup to date, saxophonist Mel Collins, drummer Ian Wallace and bass playing vocalist Boz Burrell parted company with founding member Robert Fripp at the end of this American tour. They left in order to join Alexis Korner and Peter Thorup in Korner's latest venture, Snape (Something Nasty 'Appens Practically Everyday).

This King Crimson lineup was responsible for the group's fourth studio album, *Islands*, which was the last album to feature the work of lyricist Pete Sinfield.

The American tour was captured on the live album *Earthbound*.

Birthdays today

1935 Gene Vincent seminal rock'n'roll singer

Gene Vincent was one of the earliest rock'n'roll stars, scoring a hit on both sides of the Atlantic in 1956 with his self-penned *Be-Bop-A-Lula*. In their Hamburg days the Beatles were influenced by his leather attire, before Brian Epstein transformed their image to smart suits. His life was blighted by two road accidents. A motorcycle crash in 1955 nearly cost him his leg and in 1960 he survived the car crash that killed Eddie Cochran.

1939 Gerry Goffin songwriter: partnership with his wife Carole King; solo

With his wife, Carole King, they were one of the most successful songwriting partnerships of the era. Their hits included the Drifters' *Up on the Roof*, the Monkees' *Pleasant Valley Sunday* and Little Eva's *Locomotion*.

They also wrote the controversial song, *He Hit Me (And It Felt Like a Kiss)*. The single was released by the Crystals as the follow-up to their second hit *Uptown* but it was quickly withdrawn in favour of *He's a Rebel*. Despite being released as a Crystals single, *He's a Rebel* was actually recorded by their Philles stablemate Darlene Love.

12

Events today

1965 Donovan early days

Donovan's career was just starting out when he made the second of three consecutive appearances on TV's *Ready Steady Go!* Six weeks later his self-penned debut single, *Catch the Wind*, was in the British charts and by mid-June he was also on the American best-selling lists.

Donovan's early career was guided by Peter Eden and Jeff Stephens. His singing style, acoustic guitar and harmonica brought constant (usually unfavourable) comparison with Bob Dylan. Like Dylan, he was a great admirer of American folk icon Woody Guthrie. This admiration extended to his guitar, carrying the slogan "This machine kills". Guthrie's guitar was a little more specific and was emblazoned with "This machine kills fascists". In late 1966 after his first two albums, *What's Bin Did and What's Bin Hid*, and *Fairytale*, Donovan parted company with Eden and Stephens. He moved to a more pop-orientated sound with the aid of producer Mickie Most, recording such 1960s classics as *Sunshine Superman* and *Mellow Yellow*.

1973 Vietnam War American POWs returned home

Operation Homecoming, the repatriation of American prisoners of war (POWs), started as the first POWs left Hanoi. The last of approximately 600 POWs returned home six weeks later. There were a number of prisons used in Hanoi to house American prisoners but the best known was the old French prison nicknamed the "Hanoi Hilton".

Recording session today

1977 The Police *Fall Out* and *Nothing Achieving*

The Police recorded their debut single, *Fall Out*, with original guitarist Henri Padovani. Stuart Copeland wrote both sides, with a little help from his brother, Ian, on the B-side.

Album released today

1972 The Allman Brothers Band *Eat a Peach* (US)

Urban legend has it that the album's title came about because Duane Allman died after his motorcycle collided with a peach truck. This was not the case. The origin of the title was explained in a Duane Allman interview with Ellen Mandel in *Good Times* magazine in 1971. When asked, "How are you helping the revolution?" He replied, "...every time I'm in Georgia, I eat a peach for peace."[74]

This album contained the last three studio tracks ever recorded by Duane Allman.

Birthday today

1939 Ray Manzarek keyboards and vocals: The Doors; solo

The Doors famously delivered their live performances without a bass guitarist, with keyboard player Ray Manzarek covering the bass lines. In the studio they used various session musicians to fill the gap. After the death of singer Jim Morrison on 3 July* 1971, the three remaining musicians recorded two more albums, *Other Voices* and *Full Circle*, with Manzarek taking the lead vocals. In mid-1973 they travelled to England in search of a new lead vocalist. Manzarek decided to call it a day and returned to America in order to embark on a solo career. Guitarist Robbie Krieger and drummer John Densmore stayed on and formed the Butts Band.

Event today

1955 Buddy Holly — Buddy and Bob opened for Elvis

Buddy Holly, as one half of the duo Buddy and Bob, opened for Elvis Presley at Fair Park Coliseum in Lubbock, Texas.

Buddy and Bob described themselves on their business card as "WESTERN AND BOP". Bob Montgomery accompanied Holly on many of his early recordings and in 1977 MCA Coral released *Western and Bop* by Buddy Holly and Bob Montgomery.

Recording session today

1957 Alexis Korner's Breakdown Group — *Blues from the Roundhouse*

Released as a limited edition of 99[75] copies, this 10 inch album was guitarist Alexis Korner and harmonica player Cyril Davies's first recording together as a group. The album was one of the early milestones of British blues. Korner and Davies had previously recorded together in late 1956 as members of Beryl Bryden's Backroom Skiffle Group.

Single released today

1967 The Beatles — *Strawberry Fields Forever c/w Penny Lane* (US)

Strawberry Fields Forever was the first recording for their new album *Sgt Pepper*. However, it was released as a single before the album was completed.

Album recorded live today

1972 Man/Hawkwind/Brinsley Schwarz — *Greasy Truckers Party*

The Greasy Truckers' benefit concert with prog-rockers Man, space-rockers Hawkwind and emerging pub-rockers Brinsley Schwarz was recorded at London's Roundhouse. Hawkwind's debut performance of *Silver Machine* had vocals from Robert Calvert.

Albums released today

1970 Black Sabbath — *Black Sabbath* (UK)

This eponymous Black Sabbath debut album was reputedly recorded in a single day.

1976 Peter Frampton — *Frampton Comes Alive!* (UK)

Ex-Herd and Humble Pie guitarist Peter Frampton released his live magnum opus *Frampton Comes Alive*! The album was mostly recorded at San Francisco's Winterland in 1975 and went on to sell over sixteen million[15] copies, making it one of the best selling live albums of all time.

Frampton became one of the biggest stadium attractions of the 1970s.

Birthdays today

1942 Peter Tork — vocals, bass, keyboards: Monkees

1950 Peter Gabriel vocals, flute and keyboards: Genesis; solo

Peter Gabriel was one of the founding members of Genesis and lead singer until his departure after the *Lamb Lies Down on Broadway* tour in 1975. During his time with the group Gabriel's stage performances became increasingly theatrical, including donning a fox's head and becoming a flower. After leaving Genesis he embarked on a very successful solo career.

Event today

1974 Roy Harper concert with Keith Moon and Jimmy Page

Roy Harper was backed by some of rock's finest when he took to the stage at London's Rainbow Theatre. Performing as the Intergalactic Elephant Band, Harper was backed by the Who's drummer Keith Moon, Led Zeppelin's guitarist Jimmy Page and drummer John Bonham, ex-Small Faces bassist Ronnie Lane and the Jeff Beck Group's keyboardist Max Middleton. Led Zeppelin's singer Robert Plant acted as Master of Ceremonies on that memorable night.

The gig was recorded and can be heard on the album *Flashes from the Archives of Oblivion*, along with other Roy Harper concert performances.

Album recorded live today

1970 The Who *Live at Leeds* concert

On St Valentine's Day the Who recorded their performance at Leeds University, in the north of England. The resulting album, *Live at Leeds*, proved to be one of the greatest live albums of all time.

The set was a mixture of original material and covers, including Mose Alison's 1957 *Blues*, covered by the Who as *Young Man*, Eddie Cochran's 1958 *Summertime Blues* and Johnny Kidd and the Pirates' 1960 *Shakin' All Over*. The original vinyl album only contained six songs: the three covers above and three Who classics, *My Generation*, *Substitute* and *Magic Bus*. The performance of *Tommy* recorded that night had to wait until 2001 for a release date, when the 2xCD *Deluxe Edition* devoted one of the CDs to the rock opera.

The album was very nearly *Live at Hull*. The Hull concert at the City Hall the following night was also recorded but problems with the bass guitar sound made much of the material unusable.

The *Live at Leeds* album was released with memorabilia inserts in a mock-bootleg sleeve, very similar to the Rolling Stones' cover for *Live R Than You'll Ever Be*.

This live performance received a rare accolade in the form of a wall-mounted blue plaque, awarded by the Leeds Civic Trust to represent the event's historical significance. The inscription on the plaque reads, "LIVE AT LEEDS: The University Refectory is a legendary concert venue. The Who's performance here on 14 February 1970 was recorded and released as 'Live at Leeds', the most celebrated live album of its generation."

Births and deaths today

1941 Big Jim Sullivan guitar: Marty Wilde and the Wildcats; sessions

As a member of Marty Wilde's backing group the Wildcats, he backed Eddie Cochran on his ill-fated final British tour. In the 1960s and '70s Sullivan was a much sought after session guitarist and is reputed to have played on around 1,000[72] hit records.

1989 Vincent Crane founding member of Atomic Rooster, died aged forty-five

Keyboardist Vincent Crane, born Vincent Cheesman, died after taking an overdose of painkillers.

Crane was a mainstay of the Crazy World of Arthur Brown, co-writing the memorable *Fire* with Brown. He parted company with the Crazy World in 1969 to set up Atomic Rooster with drummer Carl Palmer.

Event today

1971 Fleetwood Mac Jeremy Spencer found God and quit the band

During the stop-over in Los Angeles on Fleetwood Mac's American tour, guitarist and founding member Jeremy Spencer left the band's hotel to visit a bookshop on Hollywood Boulevard. He never returned. A member of the evangelic Church of God encountered Spencer and this chance meeting led to a new spiritual direction.

Without realising it, he had played his final gig with Fleetwood Mac the night before at San Francisco's Fillmore West. Several days later they managed to track him down but by then his mind was made up to leave the band for a life with the Church of God.

The tour continued with guitarist and founding member Peter Green flying out as a temporary replacement for Spencer.

Recording session today

1954 Big Joe Turner *Shake, Rattle and Roll*

Big Joe Turner recorded a string of R&B hits from the mid-1940s up until the late 1950s. As well as giving Turner an R&B #1, *Shake, Rattle and Roll* launched rock'n'roll's first superstar Bill Haley. It was written by Jesse Stone under the pseudonym "Calhoun".

Bill Haley and His Comets' cover of *Shake, Rattle and Roll* gave them their first taste of chart success, making Top 10 on both sides of the Atlantic. In America Haley would go on to score three more Top 20 chart appearances before the movie *Blackboard Jungle* projected *(We're Gonna) Rock Around the Clock* to international success and kick-started rock'n'roll.

Single released today

1965 The Beatles *Eight Days a Week* c/w *I Don't Want To Spoil the Party* (US)

In Britain both songs were released on the *Beatles for Sale* album.

Births and deaths today

1942 Glyn Johns engineer, producer: Led Zeppelin, Eagles, Who, Beatles

Glyn Johns's career started at IBC Studios shortly after leaving school in 1959. He worked with a plethora of rock'n'roll royalty throughout his career. On 11 March* 1963 he recorded the Rolling Stones at IBC, prior to their recording contract with Decca. When the Beatles started work on their ill-fated *Get Back* project on 2 January* 1969, Johns worked with them and delivered the *Get Back* album. This was rejected by the Beatles and remained in the vaults until Phil Spector turned the recordings into the *Let It Be* album. Johns also worked with Eric Clapton on *Slowhand*, the Who on *Who's Next* and *Quadrophenia*, and Led Zeppelin on their debut album.

1968 Little Walter blues harmonica player, died at the age of thirty-seven

Blues harmonica legend Little Walter died from injuries received in a street fight in Chicago, Illinois.

1981 Mike Bloomfield guitarist, died at the age of thirty-seven

Guitarist Mike Bloomfield died of a drug overdose. His body was found in a car parked on a San Francisco side street.

Event today

1957 Landmark TV first episode of the UK's first pop music show

BBC Television debuted Britain's first-ever pop music TV show, *Six-Five Special*. After the opening credits showed a steam train zooming along, co-presenter Pete Murray informed his live audience that it was "time to jive on the old six five".

The show was originally produced by Jack Good, who later moved across to ITV to produce *Oh Boy!* *Six-Five Special* became a showpiece for skiffle and homegrown rock'n'rollers but this inaugural programme was dominated by jazz from Kenny Baker and His Dozen and the gentle sounds of Michael Holliday and the King Brothers. The theme tune was provided by resident house band Don Lang and His Frantic Five.

Six-Five Special ran for nearly two years, before its final airing on 27 December* 1958.

At this time Britain only had one TV channel, the BBC. Broadcasts from the BBC started in the early 1930s. The British public had to wait until the mid-1950s for a choice of TV programmes. This alternative was provided by ITV, a network of regional, commercial TV channels. Each region of the UK had a different independent broadcaster, giving the viewer a choice of two TV channels. It would be nearly a decade before a third channel appeared in the form of BBC2 in the mid-1960s. BBC2 was designed to be a cut above the other two channels and provided a more intellectual approach to programming.

Recording session today

1971 Weather Report first recording session

The recently formed jazz-rock fusion band went into the studio for the first time to record tracks that would comprise their eponymous debut album.

The group was formed by saxophonist Wayne Shorter and keyboardist Joe Zawinul at the end of 1970. Both had previously played with Miles Davis and featured on Davis's seminal jazz-rock album *Bitches Brew*, which began recording on 19 August* 1969. Weather Report was one of the bands in the vanguard of jazz rock, along with Chick Corea's Return to Forever and John McLaughlin's Mahavishnu Orchestra.

It was one of the longest-lived bands of this genre, with a number of notable musicians passing through its ranks, including bassist Jaco Pastorius who joined the band in time for their 1976 album *Black Market*. Founding members Shorter and Zawinul were the one constant throughout the life of the band.

Birthday today

1935 Sonny Bono singer: Wrecking Crew, Sonny and Cher; solo

Before finding fame as a singing duo with his wife Cher, Sonny Bono was a member of the famous Wrecking Crew collection of session musicians. He often worked with "wall of sound" producer Phil Spector and received a sleeve credit for providing percussion on his legendary album *A Christmas Gift for You*. His solo career included the self-penned singles *Laugh at Me* and *The Revolution Kind*, before he opted for the political life and became Mayor of Palm Springs, California. Along the way he also wrote hit songs, including co-authorship with Jack Nitzsche of the Searchers' *Needles and Pins*.

When he teamed up with Cher they initially tried for fame as Caesar & Cleo. They released a handful of singles but fame was still out on the horizon. Whilst Sonny was working in the Wrecking Crew he introduced Cher to Phil Spector and this resulted in Cher providing backing vocals on some of Spector's biggest hits, including the Ronettes' *Be My Baby* and the Righteous Brothers' *You've Lost That Lovin' Feelin'*.

Event today

1972 Pink Floyd early performance of *Dark Side of the Moon*

Before an audience of press and fans at London's Rainbow Theatre, Pink Floyd gave an early glimpse of their magnum opus *Dark Side of the Moon*.

This performance preceded the recording of the album and was a full year before its release. The original title was intended to be *Eclipse (A Piece for Assorted Lunatics)*. The first public outing for the piece had been at the Brighton Dome on 20 January.

Recording session today

1966 The Beach Boys *Good Vibrations*

Brian Wilson rolled the tapes for the first time on his masterpiece *Good Vibrations*.

The song was written by Brian Wilson and Mike Love and was originally intended to be included on the *Pet Sounds* album but the recording process was so extensive that the album was released before the track was completed. Wilson's vision was for a musical collage, with the various layers being recorded in four different studios. One of his innovations was the use of the electro-theremin, played by Paul Tanner, to obtain the distinctive "woo-woo" sound. The recording was not completed until September and cost over $50,000,[73] making it one of the most expensive singles ever recorded at that time.

Wilson also planned to use the same "layering" concept for his next album *Smile* but that project failed to come to fruition and it became his legendary 'lost' album.

Singles released today

1967 The Beatles *Strawberry Fields Forever c/w Penny Lane* (UK)

Sadly, this single only made #2 and ended the Beatles' run of 11 consecutive UK #1s, which had started in 1963 with their third single, *From Me to You*.

It was also a rare homage to British rather than American landmarks. Penny Lane was a street in Liverpool. Strawberry Field was a Salvation Army Children's Home near Lennon's childhood home in Menlove Avenue.

1967 Soft Machine *Love Makes Sweet Music* c/w *Feelin' Reelin' Squeelin'* (UK)

This debut single, written by Kevin Ayres, was the only release to feature guitarist and founder Daevid Allen, with Ayres, Robert Wyatt and Mike Ratledge.

Album released today

1969 James Taylor *James Taylor* (US)

James Taylor was the first non-Beatle to release an album on the Beatles' Apple label. When his eponymous debut album was released in Britain it became the third album to be released on Apple, after Harrison's *Wonderwall Music* and Lennon's *Two Virgins*.

Birthday today

1940 Gene Pitney singer and songwriter

As well as having a string of hits on both sides of the Atlantic in the 1960s, Gene Pitney was also a successful songwriter, penning the Crystals' *He's a Rebel*. On 23 November* 1963 he appeared on TV with the Rolling Stones. Pitney heard the Jagger and Richard composition *My Only Girl*, changed the melody, renamed it *That Girl Belongs to Yesterday*, and gave the songwriting Stones their first hit record by another artist.

Events today

18

1958 Terry Dene beginning of the end

British rock'n'roll singer Terry Dean was arrested for being drunk and disorderly after a concert in Gloucester.

Dean was riding high after scoring two hits with *A White Sports Coat* and *Start Movin'*. Sadly, this drunken rampage in Bristol marked the downturn in his career. He was removed from the package tour and later that summer was conscripted into the British Army, only to be discharged shortly afterwards for psychological ill-health.

1972 Roxy Music first album's lineup took shape

After a few changes to their original lineup, the Roxy Music musicians who would record their eponymous debut album played their first gig, at the Hand and Flower in London's Hammersmith.

Roxy Music came together in early 1971. Original guitarist Roger Bunn was the first to leave, replaced by ex-Nice axeman David O'List. The next departure was percussionist Dexter Lloyd, who made way for Paul Thompson. The final change was yet another new guitarist. O'List and Roxy Music had different musical ambitions and his place was taken by the band's soundman Philip Targett-Adams. He adopted the stage name "Phil Manzanera" and Roxy Music was ready to record its first album. The lineup was completed by founding members: vocalist Brian Ferry, bassist Graham Simpson, saxophonist and oboe player Andy MacKay and synthesizer wizard Brian Eno.

Recording session today

1959 Ray Charles *What'd I Say (parts 1 & 2)*

This classic song had its origins in a live performance a couple of months earlier. It was late one evening, Ray Charles and his band had exhausted their repertoire but still had time to go until the end of the set. Charles told the others to follow his lead and they performed an improvised first version of *What'd I Say*. When he recorded the song it proved to be too long for one side but rather than edit it, Charles insisted that it was split across both sides of the single.

Charles had scored a succession of R&B hits since the early 1950s but this was his first big crossover success. The record began a string of hits that lasted into the 1970s.

The song has inspired a multitude of covers. It gave Jerry Lee Lewis a hit on both sides of the Atlantic in 1961 and Bobby Darin a US hit in 1962. Elvis scored American chart success after using the song in his fifteenth movie, *Viva Las Vegas* in 1964.

Album released today

1977 The Damned *Damned Damned Damned* (UK)

Punk rock arrived in the UK. The Damned delivered the first album by a British punk band.

The Clash's eponymous debut album was released nearly two months later, on 8 April*. It would take another eight months for the Sex Pistols' debut, *Never Mind the Bollocks Here's the Sex Pistols*, to hit the streets on 28 October*.

Birthday today

1933 Yoko Ono avant-garde artist, performer, Lennon's second wife

Events today

1957 Louis Armstrong dynamite thrown at a concert stage

A single stick of dynamite was thrown at the stage during a Louis Armstrong concert in Knoxville, Tennessee.

Armstrong was performing in front of a segregated audience with a band containing both black and white musicians, when a stick of dynamite was thrown at the stage from a car driving by. He was widely reported at the time to have told the segregated audience of 2,000 white people on one side and 1,000 black people on the other, that it was "just the phone".

The incident was in protest at Armstrong's mixed-race band. Racial integration was a major issue in the American Deep South. Integration legislation for schools came on 17 May* 1954 with *Brown v Board of Education* but the *Civil Rights Act* took another decade to come into force on 2 July* 1964.

1962 Chuck Berry began his second term of jail time

Chuck Berry started his second prison sentence after being found guilty of contravening the *Mann Act*, taking a minor across the state line for immoral purposes.

Berry had met Janice Escalante, a fourteen-year-old Native American girl, in an El Paso bar in Texas, in December 1959. She then accompanied him on the rest of his tour and was invited by Berry to work in his St Louis nightclub, *Club Bandstand*. The girl became known to the St Louis police, leading to Berry being charged with violation of the *Mann Act*. Berry had two trials before being found guilty and was sentenced to three years in jail with a fine of $10,000.

This was not Berry's first taste of prison life. In 1947 he was freed after serving nearly three years for armed robbery. Jail time was to visit Berry yet again in 1979 when he was convicted of tax evasion.

Recording session today

1958 Larry Williams *Dizzy Miss Lizzy*

Larry Williams released *Dizzy Miss Lizzy* coupled with *Slow Down* as a single, both his own compositions and both rock'n'roll classics. The Beatles covered three of Williams's songs, both sides of this single and *Bad Boy*.

Births and deaths today

1948 Tony Iommi guitar: Earth, Jethro Tull, Black Sabbath

The founding members of Black Sabbath were originally called Earth. During this period guitarist Tony Iommi left Earth for a short stay in Jethro Tull. It might have been a brief encounter but it included Jethro Tull's performance on the Rolling Stones' *Rock'n'Roll Circus* on 11 December* 1968. Iommi was disenchanted with Jethro Tull and returned to Earth shortly before they changed their name to "Black Sabbath".

1980 Bon Scott AC/DC's lead singer, died at the age of thirty-three

AC/DC's vocalist Bon Scott was found dead in his friend's car, after being left to sleep off a heavy drinking session. The death certificate gave the cause of death as "acute alcoholic poisoning".

The first AC/DC album after his death was *Back in Black*, featuring new vocalist Brian Johnson. With a touch of gallows humour it included the track *Have a Drink on Me*.

Event today

1950 America's war on Communism McCarthy's communist witch hunts began

Senator Joe McCarthy delivered a six-hour speech to the Senate, based on his list of more than 200 people in the State Department that he believed to be members of the Communist Party and traitors to America.

Thus began an era of witch hunts to identify communist sympathisers. After World War II the world polarized into the communist East and the capitalist West, separated by the "Iron Curtain". This became known as the "Cold War", creating a world where the threat of nuclear war was a real possibility. East and West came to the very brink of nuclear annihilation with the events surrounding the Cuban Missile Crisis on 22 October* 1962. McCarthyism fuelled America's paranoia about communism. Pete Seeger was famously indicted for Contempt of Congress on 26 March* 1957, for refusing to divulge his political views.

Recording session today

1963 Duffy Power *I Saw Her Standing There*

For his cover of Lennon and McCartney's *I Saw Her Standing There*, the British blues singer Duffy Power was backed by the Graham Bond Quartet. As well as leader Bond, the Quartet consisted of future Cream rhythm section Jack Bruce and Ginger Baker, and future Mahavishnu Orchestra guitarist and founding member John McLaughlin.

I Saw Her Standing There was recorded again at a session on 20 March but McLaughlin was unavailable and his place was taken by session guitarist Big Jim Sullivan. The song was coupled with the Graham

Bond composition *Farewell Baby* and released in May as Power's eighth British single. Sadly, even this Beatles cover failed to bring Power the commercial success he so richly deserved.

Single released today

1963 The Penguins *Memories of El Monte c/w Be Mine* (US)

The Penguins released *Memories of El Monte* with lead singer Cleveland Duncan, the same lead singer as on their 1954 doo wop classic *Earth Angel*. He was backed by a new Penguins lineup which included Walter Saulsberry and studio vocal group the Viceroys.

The song was written by Frank Zappa and future Mothers of Invention vocalist Ray Collins, produced by Zappa and recorded at the Pal Studios in Cucamonga. On 1 August* 1964 Zappa bought that same studio and renamed it "Studio Z".

Birthdays today

1898 Jimmy Yancey piano: boogie-woogie pioneer

Pioneering boogie-woogie piano player Jimmy Yancey started playing the piano around 1915 but did not record until the 1930s. His influence on the genre can be seen from the fact that he was inducted into the Rock and Roll Hall of Fame in its inaugural ceremony on 23 January* 1986.

1951 Randy California guitar and vocals: Spirit; solo

Before founding Spirit, Randy California played with Jimi Hendrix in his band Jimmy James and the Blue Flames, founded by Hendrix before he moved to the UK with Chas Chandler. He was one of two Randys in the band. In order to avoid any confusion Hendrix designated him as "Randy California", after his home State. The nickname stuck.

Event today

21

1964 The Dave Clark Five but was Dave Clark the drummer?

The Dave Clark Five appeared on the British TV rock show *Ready Steady Go!* and with drummer and leader Dave Clark performed their latest hit *Bits and Pieces*.

One of rock'n'roll's great controversies is whether or not it was the sound of Dave Clark's drumming on those Dave Clark Five hit singles. On his website[40] session drummer Bobby Graham claims to have kept the beat for all of the hit singles, from their first chart success with a cover of the Contour's *Do You Love Me* in 1963, to *You Got What It Takes* in 1967. This claim has been supported by some and refuted by others.

Singles released today

1964 The Rolling Stones *Not Fade Away c/w Little by Little* (UK)

The A-side was a cover of Buddy Holly's 1957 B-side of *Oh, Boy!* released as "The Crickets". The B-side was written by Phelge and Phil Spector. When the writing credit went to the whole band, the Stones used the pseudonym "Phelge".

1966 The Beatles *Nowhere Man c/w What Goes On* (US)

Nowhere Man was originally released in the UK on *Rubber Soul* and not issued as a single. Written mostly by John, it was the first Lennon and McCartney composition not to be about the trials and tribulations of love and romance.

Ringo took his first writing credit for a Beatles song with *What Goes On*, credited as Lennon, McCartney and Starkey.

Album released today

1975 John Lennon *Rock'n'Roll* (UK)

Made during John Lennon's "lost weekend", this was an eventful time resulting in disputes with both producer Phil Spector and Chuck Berry's publisher Morris Levy.

Having worked with Spector on a number of occasions, Lennon enlisted his help once again to produce an album of some of his favourite rock'n'roll songs. The sessions proved to be highly volatile and eventually fell apart. Spector had paid for the studio time and believing that he was entitled to the results, absconded with the tapes. Lennon eventually retrieved the recordings but only used four of the tracks produced by Spector. This was the last time that Lennon and Spector ever worked together.

Chuck Berry's publisher, Morris Levy, had previously brought a lawsuit against Lennon because he had used some of Berry's lyrics from *You Can't Catch Me* in his Beatles song *Come Together*. To placate the situation Lennon agreed to include Berry compositions on his forthcoming album. When Lennon gave Levy the tapes from some of the early Spector sessions, Levy released these songs as the album *Roots: John Lennon Sings the Great Rock & Roll Hits*, claiming that it was an official album sanctioned by Lennon. Suit and countersuit followed. These resulted in the withdrawal of the *Roots* album and the early release of the official *Rock'n'Roll* album. *Rock'n'Roll* included two Chuck Berry songs, *You Can't Catch Me* and *Sweet Little Sixteen*.

Birthday today

1943 David Geffen music industry executive; record label owner: Geffen

David Geffen sued Neil Young after his 1983 album *Everybody's Rockin'*, his second album on the Geffen label. The owner did not believe that Young was trying hard enough.

Events today

1958 Roy Hamilton stereo singles arrived

Written by Jesse Stone and often quoted as the first stereo single to make an impact on the American charts, Roy Hamilton's *Don't Let Go* bubbled just under the Top 10.

Hamilton had previously scored an American Top 10 hit in the spring of 1955 with his cover of Al Hibbler's *Unchained Melody*, also a big hit for the Righteous Brothers in 1965.

1969 The Fugs final performance

After five years the Fugs decided to call it a day with a final performance at the Vulcan Gas Company in Austin, Texas. A steady stream of musicians passed through the Fugs' ranks over the years but three of the original members, Tuli Kupferberg, Ed Sanders and Ken Weaver were on stage for this swan song performance.

The Fugs came about when founding members and poets, Kupferberg and Sanders recruited drummer Ken Weaver and then the Holy Model Rounders duo Peter Stampfel and Steve Weber. The band performed on 24 February 1965 at the official opening of the Peace Eye Bookstore on New York's Lower East Side.

Deeply rooted in the beat generation, the band's name was taken from Norman Mailer's euphemism for fornication in his book *The Naked and the Dead*. The Fugs became stalwarts of the counterculture and were prominent in the anti-Vietnam War protestations.

It would be fifteen years before Kupferberg and Sanders re-formed the Fugs.

Single released today

1968 Genesis *The Silent Sun* c/w *That's Me* (UK)

Genesis released their debut single, *The Silent Sun*.

The band started as a middle class ensemble of schoolboys who met at Charterhouse, one of England's most prestigious Public Schools. The school was founded in London in 1611, before relocating to a 250-acre site near Godalming, Surrey, in 1872.

The school band was formed by vocalist and flautist Peter Gabriel, keyboardist Tony Banks, bassist Mike Rutherford, guitarist Anthony Phillips and drummer Chris Stewart. When Charterhouse old boy Jonathan King visited the school they managed to give him a demo tape to listen to. He liked it, suggested that the group changed their name to "Genesis" and signed them to a one year contract with Decca.

Banks and Gabriel wrote *The Silent Sun*. King produced three singles and their first album, *From Genesis to Revelation*. Before their debut album was even recorded, Stewart had been replaced on drums by John Silver. The singles and album failed to attract much interest and Decca dropped the band from its roster.

Birthday today

1923 Norman Smith engineer, producer and singer

Working as the engineer, Norman Smith assisted producer George Martin on all of the Beatles recordings up to and including *Rubber Soul*. He then went on to work as a producer, with an impressive portfolio that included Pink Floyd's *Piper at the Gates of Dawn* and the Pretty Things' *SF Sorrow*, a recording often cited as the first concept album. As the singer Hurricane Smith, he achieved chart success on both sides of the Atlantic in 1972 with *Oh Babe, What Would You Say*.

Event today

23

1968 Band of Joy road to Led Zeppelin

Band of Joy played London's Marquee club shortly before splitting up. The lineup that night included future Led Zeppelin members, singer Robert Plant and drummer John Bonham. Advertised as a "*Blues Night*" and billed as "Robert Plant and the Band of Joy", the evening's entertainment was headlined by Tim Rose and also featured the Aynsley Dunbar Retaliation.

Plant was fired from the original Band of Joy but responded by forming his own group and calling it – "Band of Joy". This second Band of Joy included drummer John Bonham, who had previously played alongside Plant in the Crawling King Snakes.

Band of Joy went their separate ways soon after this gig. Bonham had impressed Tim Rose so much that he was invited to join Rose's touring band. Despite being at a loose end and working as a labourer, Plant's rock'n'roll ambitions lived on. This included a stint with the Godfather of British blues Alexis Korner, where he recorded *Steal Away* and *Operator*. It was Plant's next group Hobbstweedle that proved to be his final stop before finding international fame with Led Zeppelin.

The Yardbirds played their last gig on 7 July*. Singer Terry Reid was approached by the Yardbirds' guitarist Jimmy Page to front his new band but Reid declined and recommended Robert Plant. Page, Yardbirds' bassist Chris Dreja and manager Peter Grant went to watch a Hobbstweedle gig to see Plant in action. The Yardbirds were still contracted for a Scandinavian tour but by then Dreja had moved on to become a professional photographer. Page had worked with bassist John Paul Jones on numerous session recordings and invited him to join his new group. Robert Plant recommended his old drumming buddy John Bonham and with Peter Grant at the helm as manager, Led Zeppelin played their first gig under that name on 9 November*.

Band of Joy also counted other rock luminaries amongst its members. Future Slade frontman Noddy Holder was a roadie; drummer Pete Robinson and guitarist Kevyn Gammond went on to join Jess Roden in Bronco; and future Fairport Convention and Jethro Tull bassist Dave Pegg briefly adorned the lineup.

Recording session today

1961 The Top Notes *Twist and Shout*

The original version of *Twist and Shout* was recorded in New York by the Top Notes.

The song was released by Atlantic Records as the B-side of another song recorded that day, *Always Late (Why Lead Me On)*. Phil Spector had recently joined the Atlantic Records team and in a joint effort with Jerry Wexler took this on as one of his earliest productions. The record label credited his involvement as "Supervised by Phil Spector".

Spector was still learning his craft and was yet to develop his "wall of sound" concept. Bert Berns co-wrote the song and was very disappointed with the final version by the Top Notes. When this single failed to make any impression on the charts he took the song to the Isley Brothers at Wand. This time Berns handled the production personally, giving the Isley Brothers their first hit on both sides of the Atlantic.

The song is probably best known for the cover version by the Beatles, released in the UK on their debut album, *Please Please Me*. In America the song was included on their first-ever American album, *Introducing the Beatles*, released on the small, independent Vee-Jay label.

Events today

1973 The Byrds last gig

The Byrds gave their swan song performance at Passaic's Capitol Theatre in New Jersey. The lineup that recorded their final album had fallen apart and the ad hoc group for this final gig consisted of Roger McGuinn, the only constant member throughout the life of the band, guitarist Clarence White, bassist Chris Hillman and drummer Joe Lala.

Their final album *Farther Along* had been issued over a year earlier, at the end of 1971. The lineup on that album comprised guitarist Roger McGuinn, guitarist and mandolin player Clarence White, drummer Gene Parsons and bassist Skip Battin.

1983 Screaming Lord Sutch Official Monster Raving Loony Party

In the 1983 British by-election, Bermondsey was the first seat to be contested by a candidate from the Official Monster Raving Loony Party, a political party to represent teenage interests set up by seminal British rock'n'roll singer Screaming Lord Sutch.

Sutch had been campaigning since the early 1960s. The first political party he formed was the Sod 'Em All Party, although he never actually fought any campaigns under that name. His first election campaign was in 1963, when he stood in the Stratford-upon-Avon by-election as the member for the Teenage Party. His next outing, again as the Teenage Party candidate, was against Prime Minister Harold Wilson when he fought Huyton in the 1966 General Election: Harold Wilson 41,122 votes, David Sutch 585 votes[16]. After this the Party's name changed to the Young Ideas Party, then the Go to Blazes Party, before finally settling on the Official Monster Raving Loony Party.

He went on to fight numerous constituency seats as an Official Monster Raving Loony candidate until his suicide in 1999.

Birthdays today

1942 Paul Jones vocals, harmonica: Manfred Mann, Blues Band; solo

Before Brian Jones hooked up with Mick Jagger and Keith Richard he played with Paul Pond in Thunder Odin and the Big Secret. The two Joneses (no relation) also played together with British blues pioneer Alexis Korner's Blues Incorporated. Paul Pond changed his name to Paul Jones and became the front man for Manfred Mann.

1943 George Harrison road to the Beatles

George Harrison met Paul McCartney and they became firm friends, with a common interest in music. He formed the short-lived Rebels with his brother Peter and friend Arthur Kelly. McCartney introduced Harrison to John Lennon as a potential new guitarist but Lennon had misgivings that Harrison was too young to join the Quarry Men. This initial apprehension was overcome after Lennon heard Harrison play the Bill Justis guitar classic *Raunchy* and in early 1958 Harrison became a Quarry Man.

1944 Nicky Hopkins keyboards: Lord Sutch, Cyril Davies; sessions; solo

In the early 1960s keyboard wizard Nicky Hopkins started his career with some of Britain's finest R&B pioneers, including Screaming Lord Sutch's Savages, Cliff Bennett's Rebel Rousers and Cyril Davies's Rhythm and Blues All Stars. Hopkins also developed a reputation as one of the most respected session keyboard players around, with album credits that included the Who's *My Generation*, the Rolling Stones' *Their Satanic Majesties Request* and *Let It Bleed*, and Jeff Beck's *Truth* and *Beck-Ola*.

Event today

1968 Jimi Hendrix met the *Plaster Casters of Chicago*

The Plaster Casters of Chicago had a stimulating meeting with Jimi Hendrix in his hotel room at the Chicago Hilton and added #00004 to their collection of rock stars' anatomical appendages. At the time of writing, this particular piece of art was on sale, in an edition of 30, for $2,000.[3]

Hendrix's encounter was one of the early outings for Cynthia Plaster Caster. Similar plaster casts were obtained[103] for a host of rock stars, including the Young Rascals' Eddie Brigati, Canned Heat's Harvey Mandel and the Lovin' Spoonful's Zal Yanovsky.

Recording session today

1957 Buddy Holly and the Crickets *That'll Be the Day*

Buddy Holly's backing band was now settling down to drummer Jerry Allison, guitarist Niki Sullivan and bass player Joe B Mauldin, although Larry Welborn played bass on the Holly and Allison penned *That'll Be the Day*.

After Holly's failure at Decca, Norman Petty became his and the Crickets' manager. They travelled to his Clovis Studios in New Mexico and recorded *That'll Be the Day*. Shortly afterwards, on 16 March*, the Crickets signed to Coral Records. Buddy Holly signed a separate recording contract, resulting in *That'll Be the Day* being credited as a "Crickets" release. It became an immediate smash hit. This inspired Decca to also release their Buddy Holly version of *That'll Be the Day*, recorded at their studios the previous July.

An early-Holly collaborator, Welborn also played with the Crickets after Holly's death.

The song title was taken from a line in John Wayne's movie *The Searchers*.

Singles released today

1963 The Beatles *Please Please Me* c/w *Ask Me Why* (US)

Following the Beatles' success in the UK, producer George Martin tried to interest EMI's American sister company, Capitol Records, to take up their option on the Beatles. Capitol was not convinced that the Liverpudlians would sell in America so passed up on the opportunity to release their material. Seizing the moment, the small independent label Vee-Jay jumped at the chance to market the Beatles and this single became the Fab Four's first-ever release in America. It failed to chart, as did their second single *From Me to You*. Vee-Jay's first taste of chart success came with their third release in January 1964, which coupled the first two A-sides, *Please Please Me* and *From Me to You*.

1972 Wings *Give Ireland Back to the Irish* c/w *(Version)* (UK)

Paul McCartney's band Wings made a rare excursion into politics with the release of his protest song *Give Ireland Back to the Irish*, backed by an instrumental of the same name. Following his recent departure from the Grease Band, guitarist Henry McCullough joined the McCartneys, along with long-time Wings member Denny Laine.

This song was written by Paul and his wife Linda as a response to the events of *Bloody Sunday*, just three weeks earlier on 30 January. Thirteen people died on the streets of Londonderry (aka Derry) when British troops from the Parachute Regiment opened fire on civil rights protestors.

McCartney's old songwriting partner John Lennon also wrote his own tribute to the thirteen people who died that day. His song was *Sunday Bloody Sunday* and was released on his *Some Time in New York City* album.

Event today

1955 Rock'n'Roll Developments 45s outsold 78s for the first time

The 26 February edition of *Billboard* magazine reported[77] that, for the first time (in America) the 45-rpm format was selling more copies than the older 78-rpm version.

The recording industry was born in 1877 with Thomas Edison's invention of the phonograph. In the 1890s recorded cylinders were updated to flat discs by Emile Berliner. The gramophone, with its needle, turntable and platter with a single groove, had arrived. The speed of early recordings varied from company to company but by the mid-1920s the industry had pretty much standardised on the shellac based 78-rpm platter. RCA introduced the more durable vinyl based 45-rpm discs in 1949.

Single released today

1965 The Rolling Stones *The Last Time* c/w *Play with Fire* (UK)

The Stones' third consecutive British #1 was the first Jagger and Richard penned A-side released in the UK. The B-side featured Jack Nitzsche on harpsichord and Phil Spector on tuned-down guitar.

More than thirty years later Allen Klein, infamous as the business manager for the Stones and the Beatles, sued the Verve for misusing a sampling agreement on their song *Bitter Sweet Symphony*. Klein's company ABKCO owned the rights to *The Last Time* and he agreed that the Verve could sample the version recorded by the Andrew Oldham Orchestra. After its release Klein sued for misuse of the agreement but settled after *Bitter Sweet Symphony* credited Jagger and Richard as the songwriters.

Album released today

1970 The Beatles *Hey Jude* (US)

This was the Beatles' penultimate American album. It was not released in Britain but slipped onto the American record racks between *Abbey Road* and *Let It Be*. The album contained a mishmash of previously released material, from *Can't Buy Me Love* to *The Ballad of John and Yoko*.

Birthdays today

1928 Fats Domino seminal rock'n'roll piano player, singer and songwriter

Fats Domino was one of the most successful rock'n'roll singers of all time. His first release, *The Fat Man* in 1950, is often cited as one of the contenders for the title of "the first rock'n'roll record". *Ain't It a Shame* gave him his first crossover hit five years later. The hits, mostly on the Imperial label, continued until the British Invasion in 1964. As well as being a talented singer and piano player he also co-wrote many of his hits with Dave Bartholomew, a producer and arranger at Imperial. This collaboration included both *The Fat Man* and *Ain't It a Shame*. With sales estimated at over sixty-five million[76] he sold more records than any other 1950s rock'n'roller except Elvis Presley.

1932 Johnny Cash country and rockabilly singer and songwriter

Johnny Cash was best remembered as a country singer who achieved success across six decades. He was also one of the four artists, along with Elvis Presley, Carl Perkins and Jerry Lee Lewis, who helped to establish Sam Phillips's Sun Records as a major force during the emergence of rock'n'roll in the mid-1950s. On 4 December* 1956 they recorded the legendary jam session known as "The Million Dollar Quartet".

Events today

1963 The Searchers supported Gene Vincent in Hamburg

Like many of the British groups in the early 1960s, the Searchers served their time in Germany and were supporting Gene Vincent at Hamburg's Star Club. Also on the bill that night were the Dakotas from Manchester, who later became the backing band for Liverpool singer Billy J Kramer. Plus the German group the Rattles, who scored a British hit in 1970 with their single *The Witch*.

The Searchers had previously been Johnny Sandon and the Searchers but lead singer Johnny Sandon left to front another popular Liverpool group, the Remo Four. After the split, guitarists Mike Pender and John McNally, bassist Tony Jackson and drummer Chris Curtis continued as a quartet. They all shared the role of lead singer.

The Remo Four saga continued. Johnny Sandon moved on again and with a new singer they became Tommy Quickly and the Remo Four. In 1965 Quickly called it a day, after becoming disillusioned with the music business. The Remo Four went on to become Billy J Kramer's backing band and changed their name to the New Dakotas.

The band's name was inspired by John Ford's *The Searchers*, starring John Wayne.

1969 Grateful Dead legendary appearance at the Fillmore West

The Grateful Dead opened a four-night residency at San Francisco's Fillmore West, supported by the Pentangle and Sir Douglas Quintet

The bulk of the Grateful Dead's highly acclaimed album *Live Dead* came from performances taped on those Fillmore nights. Two tracks, *Dark Star* and *St Stephen*, were generated from the opening night's show. Both tracks were written by Jerry Garcia and lyricist Robert Hunter, with additional credit given to Phil Lesh on *St Stephen*.

Recording session today

1967 Pink Floyd *Arnold Layne*

The Pink Floyd's debut single was written by Syd Barrett and produced by Joe Boyd.

Album released today

2008 Eric Burdon *Mirage* (US)

Another one of the great 'lost' albums finally received a belated release.

Mirage was recorded by the Eric Burdon Band back in 1973 and '74. It was intended to be a concept album and movie. The story was set around three people, "an American Indian in the 1860s; ...a black trooper in the 1960s; and ...a rock star on tour in the 60s. They all died under violent, perverse circumstances, and they meet in the afterworld, to discuss what we can do to change the world."[44]

The title track was credited to both Burdon and his friend Jimi Hendrix and incorporated lyrics from *The Story of Life*, written by Hendrix on the night that he died.

Died today

1968 Frankie Lymon — first black teenage idol, died at the age of twenty-five

Why Do Fools Fall in Love propelled Frankie Lymon and the Teenagers into stardom and made Frankie Lymon the first black teenage idol. After a handful of hit singles Lymon split for a solo career but he never managed to recapture his earlier success. Since the late 1950s he had been experimenting with drugs and his lifestyle finally caught up with him when he died from a heroin overdose.

Event today

1970 Led Zeppelin — performed as "The Nobs"

A descendant of the airship dynasty, Eva von Zeppelin threatened to sue Led Zeppelin if they performed in her home country using her family's name without permission. In order to avoid complications they performed as "The Nobs" at Copenhagen's KB Hallen concert hall in Denmark.

Recording session today

1958 Chuck Berry — *Johnny B Goode,* and *Around and Around*

These two Chuck Berry penned songs were coupled and released as a single on Chess Records, with both songs becoming the staple diet of beat and R&B groups in the early 1960s. *Johnny B Goode* was inspired by his pianist Johnnie Johnson but became more autobiographical of Berry's life. Ironically, Johnson did not play on the song. The pianist that day was Lafayette Leake. The rhythm section for this session comprised the iconic blues songwriter Willie Dixon on bass and the highly respected blues session drummer Fred Bellow.

Pianist Jonnie Johnson was a long-time associate of Berry's, playing on many of his 1950s and '60s classics. However, in late 2000 he sued Berry for unpaid royalties, claiming that he had co-written 52 of Berry's songs. The lawsuit was dismissed because of the considerable elapsed time since the songs had been written.

Johnny B Goode featured in several more Berry songs, including the 1960 A-side *Bye Bye Johnny* and the 1961 B-side *Go-Go-Go*. The latter's A-side was Berry's *Come On*, which gave the Rolling Stones their first British hit single in the summer of 1963.

Birthdays today

1934 Giorgio Gomelsky — manager: early Rolling Stones, Yardbirds; club owner

Before Andrew Loog Oldham appeared on the scene, the Rolling Stones were managed by Giorgio Gomelsky, a very influential figure in the development of the early 1960s London R&B scene. His Crawdaddy Club was a springboard for up and coming groups, the Rolling Stones and the Yardbirds both had spells as house bands and were managed by Gomelsky. His empire included Marmalade Records, founded in the mid-late 1960s.

1942 Brian Jones — guitar: founder of the Rolling Stones

Multi-instrumentalist and founder of the Rolling Stones, Brian Jones started his musical career playing saxophone in local jazz bands in his hometown Cheltenham. His focus moved to guitar and he joined future Manfred Mann singer Paul Jones in the blues-orientated Thunder Odin and the Big Secret. After moving to London he formed his own group, which included British blues pioneer Brian Knight and the pianist who became known as the "Sixth Stone", Ian Stuart. After playing with Alexis Korner's Blues Incorporated, Jones formed a second lineup, with future Stones Mick Jagger and Keith Richard, and future Pretty Things founder Dick Taylor. By then Paul Jones and Brian Knight had moved on, with Knight forming his own band Blues By Six. Brian Jones's second lineup called itself "The Rollin' Stones" and gave their debut performance on 12 July* 1962, when they stood in for Blues Incorporated at London's Marquee club.

When he started playing with Blues Incorporated Jones took to calling himself "Elmo Lewis". Elmo after his blues guitar hero Elmore James and Lewis from his own first name, he was born Lewis Brian Hopkin Jones.

Events today

29

1959 Rock'n'Roll Developments — end of the golden age of rock'n'roll

Unsurprisingly February 29 was a very quiet date in rock'n'roll history, only being available one year in four. That makes it an ideal opportunity to note the significance of the ending of the decade and to mourn the passing of the golden age of American rock'n'roll, as it transitioned into the new age of British beat and R&B groups.

Rock'n'Roll developed from the music of the blues, gospel, country and R&B vocal groups. It emerged in its own right in the mid-1950s. Bill Haley's first hit, *Shake, Rattle and Roll*, and Elvis Presley's first Sun single, *That's Alright*, both appeared in the summer of 1954. The breakthrough came in the spring of 1956 with the movie *Blackboard Jungle* and its main title music of Bill Haley's *Rock Around the Clock*. This, coupled with Elvis's first hit single *Heartbreak Hotel*, kick-started the rock'n'roll phenomenon. From that point the genre went from strength to strength. American artists dominated the British charts but very few British offerings were leaving their mark on the American hits listings. By the end of the 1950s the first age of rock'n'roll was all but over. The titans of rock'n'roll were all out of the picture. Elvis was in the US Army. Jerry Lee Lewis's career imploded after he married his cousin's thirteen-year-old daughter. Little Richard found God in Australia and abandoned secular music. The bespectacled Buddy Holly died in a plane crash on 3 February* 1959. The man who arguably started it all, Bill Haley, was still performing but by 1959 the hits had dried up.

The first British beat groups started to play in the Hamburg clubs in Germany in the summer of 1960. From that time until to the end of 1962 there was a sort of rock'n'roll limbo. The existing 1950s American artists were mostly experiencing their final days of success. There were some innovations. Elvis was back. Chubby Checker was introducing a host of new dance crazes. Phil Spector was building his "wall of sound". But by and large it was not until the Beatles burst on the national British scene at the beginning of 1963 that rock'n'roll gained the impetus it needed to reignite the excitement of those mid-1950s days. Multitudes of British beat and R&B groups sprang up and in 1964 this new British-based rock'n'roll crossed the Atlantic as the "British Invasion". For the first time in rock'n'roll history British artists were finding real success in America.

By 1966 the times were indeed a-changin' – again. Harder edged sounds were emerging from the likes of Cream, Pink Floyd, Jimi Hendrix and The Doors. San Francisco became the epicenter of hippiedom. And another new era of rock'n'roll dawned...

1976 The Stranglers — began their rise to fame

The Stranglers moved up a notch from playing pubs and small clubs to a gig as the support act for Deaf School, Nasty Pop and Jive Bombers, at the *Special Leap Year Concert* at London's Roundhouse.

February

No one could ever accuse the Stranglers of being an overnight success. They formed as the Guildford Stranglers in early 1974, with a lineup of guitarist and vocalist Hugh Cornwell, bassist Jean Jacques Burnel, drummer Jet Black, and Swedish guitarist and keyboard player Hans Wärmling. Later that autumn they shortened the band's name to "The Stranglers". In mid-1975 keyboardist Dave Greenfield replaced Wärmling and the classic lineup was in place.

The *Leap Year Concert* at the Roundhouse was certainly a landmark gig for the band but they would not secure a recording deal with a major label until they signed with United Artists in December 1976.

March

Events today

1

1952 Sam Phillips first single on Sun Records

Two years after his first attempt to release his productions on his own record label, It's The Phillips, Sam Phillips launched Sun Records.

Phillips recorded sixteen-year-old saxophonist Johnny London playing *Drivin' Slow* and *Flat Tyre* and the first Sun single hit the shops in April 1952, both sides were written by London. It achieved only limited local success but Phillips was on his way into rock'n'roll history.

1958 Buddy Holly and the Crickets opening night of their UK tour

Buddy Holly and the Crickets opened their headlining British tour at the Trocadero in London's Elephant and Castle. They were performing as a trio with Holly backed by drummer Jerry Allison and bassist Joe B Mauldin.

This was an influential tour, with British fans having a rare opportunity to see one of the greatest American rock'n'roll stars in person.

1961 The Fourmost debuted at the Cavern Club

The Four Jays made their debut at Liverpool's Cavern Club, three weeks before the Beatles gave their first evening performance there.

The Fab Four made their evening debut at the Cavern on 21 March but gave their first performance as "The Beatles" in an afternoon performance on 9 February*.

The Fourmost formed as the Blue Jays in Liverpool in 1958. Shortly before their Cavern debut they changed their name to the "Four Jays", then the "Four Mosts" before settling on "The Fourmost". The group had a number of links to the Beatles: they were managed by Brian Epstein, signed to Parlophone and produced by George Martin. Their first two singles, *Hello Little Girl* and *I'm in Love*, were both UK hits and Lennon and McCartney compositions. The Beatles never recorded the latter song. In 1969, as Format, they released their version of the Beatles' *Maxwell's Silver Hammer*.

Album released today

1969 Cream *Goodbye* (UK)

By the time that *Goodbye* hit the shops the trio had already parted company, Clapton and Baker to form Blind Faith and Bruce to record his solo album *Songs for a Tailor*.

Goodbye was originally envisioned as a double album, another *Wheels of Fire* with half live and half studio tracks. This never came to fruition and the album ended up with three tracks recorded live at the Forum in Los Angeles on 19 October 1968 and three tracks recorded shortly afterwards at IBC studios in London.

The studio track *Badge* was written by Eric Clapton and George Harrison, with Harrison also performing on the recording under the pseudonym "L'Angelo Misterioso".

Birthdays today

1944 Mike d'Abo — singer and songwriter: A Band of Angels, Manfred Mann

In 1966 Mike d'Abo replaced Paul Jones as the vocalist in Manfred Mann, staying until the band dissolved in 1969. He wrote *Handbags and Gladrags*, originally recorded by Chris Farlowe in 1967 and covered by Rod Stewart in 1970.

1944 Roger Daltrey — singer: The Detours, The High Numbers, The Who; solo

Events today

2

1965 Vietnam War — *Operation Rolling Thunder* ...the bombing began

North Vietnam was pounded by a hundred American fighter bombers, heralding the beginning of *Operation Rolling Thunder*.

The newly elected President Johnson had initiated this sustained bombing campaign to destroy supplies and supply routes in North Vietnam, in an attempt to prevent aid reaching the Viet Cong, the South Vietnamese guerrilla fighters. The bombing was also aimed at the territories in South Vietnam controlled by the Viet Cong. *Operation Rolling Thunder* was initially planned to last for just eight weeks but continued for the next three and a half years. On 31 October* 1968 President Johnson appeared on national television to announce an end to this unrelenting bombing campaign.

1969 The Doors — Jim Morrison's arrest in Miami

At a Doors concert in Miami, Florida, front man Jim Morrison's behaviour led to charges of lewd and lascivious behaviour, profanity, drunkenness and indecent exposure. These charges were to haunt him for the rest of his life. On 30 October* 1970 he was sentenced but his appeal was still outstanding when he died on 3 July* 1971.

Recording session today

1955 Bo Diddley — *Bo Diddley* and *I'm a Man*

In his first recording session for Chess's subsidiary Checker, Bo Diddley recorded two of his own songs. These were then coupled to give him his first single.

Bo Diddley had previously recorded *Uncle John* and *I'm a Man*, in order to hawk them around the local record labels in search of a recording deal. After several rejections he played the tracks to the Chess brothers. They liked the songs but suggested that when he re-recorded them he should personalise the name "Uncle John". This gave rise to his signature song *Bo Diddley*.

His backing band at this session included pianist Otis Span and harmonica player Billy Boy Arnold.

Single released today

1964 The Beatles — *Twist and Shout* c/w *There's a Place* (US)

Twist and Shout is usually associated with the Isley Brothers but was originally recorded by the Top Notes on 23 February* 1961. This was not released as a single in the UK.

Birthdays today

1942 Lou Reed guitar and vocals: Primitives, Velvet Underground; solo

As the beat groups were coming to the end of the trail in 1966, the music scene was evolving towards greater sophistication. Virtuoso groups such as Cream, prog-rock bands and the likes of Doors and Jefferson Airplane were on the rise. The sounds of peace and love were on the horizon, as San Francisco's Haight-Ashbury became the centre of the hippie universe. Meanwhile in New York, the Velvet Underground led by guitarist, vocalist and songwriter Lou Reed was making its own mark. Theirs was a much darker view of the world of drugs, sex and hedonism. They came to fame as prodigies of Pop artist Andy Warhol and his multi-media experience, the *Exploding Plastic Inevitable*.

1948 Rory Gallagher guitar and vocals: The Impact, Taste; solo

Events today

3

1960 Elvis Presley only time he set foot in Britain (officially!)

On completion of his military service, Sergeant Elvis Presley flew back to America from his German assignment in Hamburg. On the journey home the plane stopped briefly to refuel at the Prestwick American Airbase in Scotland. Elvis took a stroll around the facility, making this the one and only time that he was officially reported as having set foot on British soil. A couple of hundred fans managed to make it to the airport and a relaxed Elvis chatted to them before the two-hour stopover was ended and Elvis continued his journey home.

Author Allan Morrison has traced Elvis's ancestry back to the 1700s in Lonmay near Aberdeen in Scotland. Elvis even had his own tartan design, *Presley of Lonmay Tartan*.

A less well documented visit to Britain's shores was revealed on 21 April* 2008 by Tommy Steele's friend Bill Kenwright, when he divulged in a radio interview that Steele had actually given Elvis a guided tour of London in 1958.

1965 The Yardbirds Eric Clapton's final gig

Eric Clapton's final outing as the Yardbirds' lead guitarist was at Bristol's Corn Exchange in south-west England. He had become increasingly frustrated by the group's pop- orientated direction and particularly their third British single, *For Your Love*.

Clapton's next move was to join John Mayall's Bluesbreakers. His role as the Yardbirds' lead guitarist was taken by Jeff Beck.

1967 Jeff Beck Group Roy Orbison's UK package tour kicked off

The newly formed Jeff Beck Group supported Roy Orbison when his tour opened at the Astoria in London's Finsbury Park. The Small Faces were also on the bill and closed the first half of the show.

Soon after leaving the Yardbirds, guitarist Jeff Beck formed the Jeff Beck Group with guitarist Ron Wood and singer Rod Stewart. Initially, there was a fast turnover of rhythm section musicians, involving very brief stays for ex-Shadows bassist Jet Harris and ex-Pretty Things drummer Viv Prince. Ron Wood switched to bass. The drummers came and went until Aynsley Dunbar joined a month or so later, staying long enough to feature on the group's first album, *Truth*.

In a glimpse of the future, the people that would become the Faces were all on stage that night – but in different bands. The Small Faces, minus Steve Marriott, joined up with the Jeff Beck Group's Rod Stewart and Ron Wood and became the Faces.

Single released today

1956 James Brown with The Famous Flames *Please, Please, Please* (US)

Written by James Brown and Johnny Terry this debut single gave Brown an R&B hit. It would be another four years before he scored a mainstream American hit with *Think* and nine years before *Papa's Got a Brand New Bag* gave him his first UK chart success.

Please, Please, Please became a pivotal part of Brown's stage act. He used it to feign collapse and the need for assistance to leave the stage at the climax of his act.

Birthday today

1942 Mike Pender guitar and vocals: Searchers

In late 1985 Mike Pender broke away and formed his own Mike Pender's Searchers.

Events today

4

1966 The Beatles "more popular than Jesus"

One of the Beatles' darkest times resulted from a John Lennon interview with journalist Maureen Cleave, titled *How Does a Beatle Live? John Lennon Lives Like This* and originally published in London's *Evening Standard* newspaper.

In the original article Lennon was quoted as saying:

"Christianity will go. It will vanish and shrink. I needn't argue about that; I'm right and I will be proved right. We're more popular than Jesus now; I don't know which will go first – rock'n'roll or Christianity. Jesus was all right but his disciples were thick and ordinary. It's them twisting it that ruins it for me."[80]

When it was originally published in Britain there was no adverse reaction whatsoever. In America it was a very different story. *Datebook* magazine's issue on 29 July published extracts from the interview, including Lennon's comments on religion. It came out just before the Beatles' tour of America and caused an outrage.

Fearful of having to cancel the entire American tour, Brian Epstein flew out in advance to try and calm the waters. When the Beatles arrived in America they held a press conference, where Lennon made what he considered to be an apology. His 'apology' was more of an explanation of his comments. Unfortunately, America's Bible Belt wanted a more unequivocal apology. The tour was beset by a multitude of protests, including demonstrations, death threats, radio stations boycotting Beatles records and even organised sites for the burning of Beatles records and books. The level of outrage can be seen by the fact that the Ku Klux Klan took it upon themselves to picket a concert being held at the Mid-South Coliseum in Memphis.

The Beatles' greatest fear was that someone would be shot whilst they were performing on stage. When the Beatles arrived home they made the decision to quit touring altogether.

1971 The Rolling Stones became tax exiles

In their first British tour since 1966, the Rolling Stones opened their short *Goodbye to Great Britain* tour at Newcastle's City Hall in the north of England. They announced that they were becoming tax exiles and moving to France. Keyboard player Nicky Hopkins augmented the tour lineup.

The tax rates in Britain at that time were in the region of 90 per cent, encouraging the Stones to become the UK's first self-imposed, rock'n'roll tax exiles. The first album recorded after their new tax status was the aptly titled *Exile on Main Street.*

George Harrison had already bemoaned this sad state of affairs with his song *Taxman*, on the Beatles' 1966 album *Revolver.*

Died today

1986 Richard Manuel musician, died at the age of forty-two

Keyboardist, drummer and singer, Richard Manuel was a member of Ronnie Hawkins's Hawks before co-founding the highly respected American group the Band.

After the Band's farewell performance at the Winterland on 25 November* 1976 the members went their separate ways in pursuit of solo projects. In 1983 four members of the Band reunited as a touring group, Robbie Robertson was replaced on guitar by Earl Cate. Manuel had battled drink and drug addiction for some years and after a gig at the Cheek to Cheek lounge he hanged himself in his motel room in Winter Park, Florida.

Events today

5

1968 Jerry Lee Lewis trod the boards playing the Bard

Rock'n'roll wild man Jerry Lee Lewis opened at the Ahmanson Theatre in downtown Los Angeles in *Catch My Soul*, a rhythm and blues adaptation of Shakespeare's *Othello*.

Lewis played the part of Othello's treacherous friend Iago. In a review in the 30 March edition of *Billboard*, the magazine described Lewis's performance as "first rate" and that his presence added "impact to the score".[49]

The musical was the brainchild of Jack Good, producer of TV shows *Six-Five Special* and *Oh Boy!* in the UK, and *Shindig!* in America. Darlene Love's vocal group the Blossoms also appeared in the production.

1971 Led Zeppelin *Stairway to Heaven*'s debut

The first-ever live performance of *Stairway to Heaven*, written by Jimmy Page and Robert Plant, was performed at Belfast's Ulster Hall in Northern Ireland. The song can be found on their fourth album and is one of the most played songs on radio.

Recording session today

1951 Jackie Brenston and His Delta Cats *Rocket 88*

Written by Jackie Brenston and often cited as the first rock'n'roll record, *Rocket 88* was an early recording by Sam Phillips at his Memphis Recording Service studio.

The session was arranged to record Ike Turner and His Kings of Rhythm. Turner's band cut four tracks that day. Piano player Turner took the lead vocal on *Heartbroken and Worried*, and *I'm Lonesome Baby*. This was released as Ike Turner and His Kings of Rhythm. Sax player Jackie Brenston took lead vocal on *Rocket 88*, a song that was to go down in rock'n'roll history. This was coupled with *Come Back Where You Belong* and released as Jackie Brenston and His Delta Cats. Willie Kizart played the fuzz guitar and provided one of rock'n'roll's first examples of deliberate distortion. The two singles were released on the Chess label.

Bill Haley and His Saddle Men covered *Rocket 88* shortly afterwards, four years before rock'n'roll burst onto the scene with his version of *Rock Around the Clock*.

Single released today

1965 The Yardbirds *For Your Love c/w Got to Hurry* (UK)

The Yardbirds' third British single, written by Graham Gouldman and produced by Giorgio Gomelsky, proved to be too pop orientated for guitarist Eric Clapton. In order to satisfy his desire to stay with his blues roots, he left shortly after the single's release to join John Mayall's Bluesbreakers. Jeff Beck stepped in to take over as lead guitarist.

The B-side, *Got to Hurry*, was Clapton's first recorded composition.

Died today

1995 Viv Stanshall singer Bonzo Dog Doo-Dah Band, died aged fifty-one

Viv Stanshall died in a house fire at his Muswell Hill apartment in London.

He was the front man and one of the founding members of the unique, Dadaist, Bonzo Dog Doo-Dah Band. They came together in the mid-1960s and split in 1970. Their music incorporated the theatre of the absurd with all genres of music, parody and satire. Bonzo Dog was a quintessentially British group, in a similar groove to Frank Zappa's take on America (but much less sophisticated musically).

Events today

6

1968 The Rascals from the Starliters to the Rascals

Having recently dropped the "Young" from their name, the Rascals recorded *A Beautiful Morning*. Written by Felix Cavaliere and Eddie Brigati, this was the first single to be released with the new shortened name.

The Young Rascals formed in New Jersey in early 1965, after keyboard player Felix Cavaliere, percussionist Eddie Brigati and guitarist Gene Cornish left Joey Dee and the Starliters. They hooked up with jazz drummer Dino Danelli and soon acquired a reputation as a top class blue-eyed soul band. They signed to Atlantic Records and generated a string of American hit singles. Their success started with a cover of the Olympics' *Good Lovin'* as "The Young Rascals" in 1966 and continued after the name change to "The Rascals" until the late 1960s. Brigati and Cornish left in the early 1970s. The band continued but never managed to regain its former glory.

2000 Eric Clapton third induction into the Rock and Roll Hall of Fame

Eric Clapton was the first person to be inducted into the Rock and Roll Hall of Fame for the third time, this time as recognition of him as a solo artist. At the time of writing he was the only person to have received this honour on three separate occasions. The first induction was in 1992 with the Yardbirds and the second with Cream in 1993.

Recording session today

1959 The Drifters *There Goes My Baby*

The new Drifters lineup recorded their first single *There Goes My Baby*, co-written by lead singer Ben E King. It gave the group their first crossover hit.

All of the Drifters singers were sacked en masse at the end of a week at the Apollo, having opened there on 30 May* 1958. The old Drifters were replaced by the Crowns, which included lead singer Ben E King. After being renamed "The Drifters" they hit the road to fulfil the performance obligations already in place. It would be nearly a year before the new lineup arrived in the studio for this debut recording session.

Single released today

1970 The Beatles *Let It Be* c/w *You Know My Name (Look Up the Number)* (UK)

Let It Be was the Beatles' final British single. The lyric "mother Mary" was a reference to Paul's mother. The B-side featured the Rolling Stones' Brian Jones on saxophone.

Album released today

1967 Buffalo Springfield *Buffalo Springfield* (US)

Buffalo Springfield re-released their debut album with the track *Baby Don't Scold Me* replaced by their first hit single, *For What It's Worth*. Both songs were written by Steve Stills. The original release had been in mono but this reissue was remixed into stereo.

In between the original release of the album in December 1966 and this re-release, Buffalo Springfield started recording songs for their second album. One of the sessions was on 9 January* but work on the album was aborted and *Stampede* became one of the great 'lost' albums of the 1960s.

Birthday today

1946 David Gilmour guitar: Jokers Wild, Flowers, Bullitt, Pink Floyd; solo

Events today

7

1966 Phil Spector end of the "wall of sound" era

Tina Turner started to lay down her vocal part for the monumental *River Deep Mountain High*, written by Jeff Barry and Ellie Greenwich, and Phil Spector. Sadly, the single received a mixed reception and it heralded the end of Spector's "wall of sound" era.

Despite making #3 in Britain, the single devastated producer Phil Spector when it hardly troubled the American charts, crawling to just #88. A handful of releases followed on the Philles label before Spector withdrew from the music world. The "wall of sound" era was over but Spector did return to producing. In 1970 he resuscitated the Beatles' *Get Back* and transformed it into the *Let It Be* album. The Ramones also had a memorable experience with Spector whilst recording their 1980 album *End of the Century*.

Although Spector released a number of singles prior to launching the Philles label, his hallmark "wall of sound" developed from the freedom he achieved from setting up his own label with Lester Sill. Philles was launched in late 1961 with the Crystals' *There's No Other (Like My Baby)*. With the Crystals, the Ronettes and Darlene Love hit followed hit, until his most successful song, the Righteous Brothers' 1965 hit *You've Lost That Lovin' Feelin'* written by Spector with Barry Mann and Cynthia Weil. By 1966 relations with the Righteous Brothers had soured and Tina Turner's *River Deep Mountain High* was intended to be Phil Spector's next big thing.

1968 Ginger Baker the rock drum solo came of age

Cream performed Ginger Baker's epic drum solo *Toad* at San Francisco's Fillmore West, captured for posterity on the live portion of Cream's *Wheels of Fire* double album.

Drum solos had been a standard feature of jazz and big band music, with stunning percussion displays from the likes of Louie Bellson, Elvin Jones, Gene Krupa and Buddy Rich. Sandy Nelson had a hit with *Teen Beat* in 1959. The Who's Keith Moon and Jimi Hendrix's Mitch Mitchell established the prominence of drummers in rock bands. But Baker led the way to the extended drum solo, much loved by prog and hard rock bands.

Recording session today

1957 Mose Allison *Blues*

Recorded as *Blues* and released on his album *Back Country Suite*, the song was famously covered by the Who as *Young Man* on their legendary 1970 LP *Live at Leeds*.

Album released today

1969 Genesis *From Genesis to Revelation* (UK)

One of the most successful of the British prog-rock bands, Genesis released their debut album to an indifferent reception from the great British public. Their album and three singles failed to make any impact and Decca opted not to renew their contract.

By the time that this album came to be recorded, original drummer Chris Stewart had been replaced by John Silver. Silver was then replaced by John Mayhew for the second album, *Trespass*. Drummer and future lead singer Phil Collins joined in 1970.

Died today

1966 Mike Millward singer, guitarist, The Fourmost, died aged twenty-three

Two years earlier Mike Millward had been diagnosed with throat cancer. He had beaten that only to succumb to leukaemia. He was previously with the Undertakers.

Events today

1964 The Dave Clark Five international fame with *Glad All Over*

The Dave Clark Five had existed since 1958. The hit making combo came together in 1962 but it took *Glad All Over* to launch them to international fame. This first outing on the *Ed Sullivan Show* was a major stepping stone to their success in America.

Written by Dave Cark and Mike Smith, *Glad All Over* paved the way for a string of American hits lasting into the summer of 1967. In fact, they were the second most successful British Invasion group.

1965 The Manish Boys David Bowie's UK TV debut

Singer David Bowie made his British TV debut with the Manish Boys on BBC2's *Gadzooks! It's All Happening*.

Urban myth has it that the BBC told the band that they would not be allowed to go on unless they had a haircut! Auntie Beeb obviously relented and the Boys performed what turned out to be their only single, a cover of Bobby "Blue" Bland's *I Pity the Fool*.

1965 Vietnam War first American combat troops arrived in Vietnam

The first American combat troops, 3,500 United States Marines landed in Vietnam. Their mission was to defend the US air bases in the Da Nang area.

1968 Landmark Venues Fillmore East opened

Bill Graham's Fillmore East opened on Second Avenue in New York's Greenwich Village, at a venue previously known as the Village Theatre. The opening acts were Big Brother and the Holding Company, Tim Buckley and Albert King. It closed in June 1971.

1974 Bad Company debut gig

Bad Company gave their debut performance at Newcastle upon Tyne's City Hall.

When Free disbanded, singer Paul Rodgers and drummer Simon Kirke teamed up with ex-Mott the Hoople guitarist Mick Ralphs and former King Crimson bassist Boz Burrell and Bad Company was born. The group's name was inspired by Robert Benton's American civil war movie of the same name, starring Jeff Bridges and Barry Brown. Management was provided by Led Zeppelin's Peter Grant and keeping it in the family, Bad Company was the first band to sign to Zeppelin's new Swan Song record label.

Single released today

1974 Badfinger *Apple of My Eye c/w Blind Owl* (UK)

Pete Ham's *Apple of My Eye,* Apple-49, was the last single released on the Apple label.

Birthdays today

1944 Keef Hartley drums: The Artwoods, John Mayall, Keef Hartley Band

After Ringo left in mid-1962 to join the Beatles, Keef Hartley had his first taste of fame when he took the vacant drumming stool for Rory Storm and the Hurricanes in mid-1963.

1945 Micky Dolenz vocals and drums: The Monkees; actor

1946 Randy Meisner bass and vocals: Poco, The Stone Canyon Band, Eagles

Event today

1968 Love 'lost' *Gethsemane* album

Love played San Francisco's Avalon Ballroom, shortly after embarking on the tour to promote their third album, *Forever Changes*. The headliners were supported by Congress of Wonders and Sons of Champlin.

The band was still essentially the same as the one that recorded the eponymous first album: guitarists and vocalists Arthur Lee and Bryan MacLean, guitarist John Echols and bassist Ken Forssi, plus drummer Michael Stuart who joined in time for Love's second album, *Da Capo*.

By now the band was falling apart and at the end of the tour Arthur Lee replaced the entire band before recording their fourth album, *Four Sail*.

Urban legend has it that before the original band disintegrated there was a fourth album, *Gethsemane*, in the pipeline. In January the band recorded two Arthur Lee penned songs *Laughing Stock*, and *Your Mind and We Belong Together*. These were later coupled as a single but speculation persists that the two songs might have been contributions towards another one of rock'n'roll's great 'lost' albums.

Birthdays today

1933 Lloyd Price seminal R&B singer and songwriter

Lloyd Price was one of the 1950s most successful R&B singers with a string of hits into the early 1960s. Unlike many of his contemporaries he wrote most of his own material and was one of the most covered songwriters in rock'n'roll history. Two of his biggest American hits, *Lawdy Miss Clawdy* and *Stagger Lee* were the staple diet of many of the groups in the early 1960s blues boom. He took his nickname, "Mr Personality", from his 1959 crossover hit *Personality*. As well as his success as a singer he was also a songwriter, producer and founder of the record labels Kent Records and Double-L.

1942 John Cale viola, bass, keyboards, vocals: Velvet Underground; solo

Classically trained and with a leaning towards the avant-garde, John Cale was one of the founding members of the hugely influential Velvet Underground. He was with the band for their first two albums, before internal differences drove a wedge between Cale and the others. After leaving the Velvets, Cale extended his experience as a producer and worked with a number of cutting edge artists including Iggy Pop, Nico and Patti Smith. He has also recorded a raft of solo albums, including collaborations with Little Feat guitarist Lowell George, Genesis drummer Phil Collins and keyboard player Brian Eno. In 1990 he reunited with Lou Reed to write, record and produce *Songs for Drella*, a fictional tribute to Andy Warhol. The iconic 1960s Pop artist was their mentor and a major influence behind the early Velvet Underground.

1945 Robin Trower guitar: The Paramounts, Procol Harum, Jude; solo

In 1959 school friends guitarist Robin Trower and pianist Gary Brooker formed a group that became the Paramounts, one of the early 1960s most respected British R&B bands. Sadly, by the mid-1960s they had become little more than pop-singer Sandie Shaw's backing group and they disbanded. Brooker met lyricist Keith Reid and recorded *A Whiter Shade of Pale* as Procol Harum, a band that comprised mostly of session musicians. Trower rejoined Brooker in the ranks of Procol Harum in time to promote one of the most successful singles of all time.

Events today

1975 Vietnam War final invasion of South Vietnam began

The beginning of the end of the Vietnam War came when the North launched an attack on Ban Me Thuot in South Vietnam's Central Highlands.

When the Paris Peace Accords were signed on 27 January* 1973, it enabled America to withdraw from the conflict but it failed to find a solution for a peaceful coexistence between North and South Vietnam. In planning the attack the North Vietnamese Army strategists had anticipated a two-year campaign but the rapid progress made by the invaders resulted in the fall of South Vietnam's capital city, Saigon, in just fifty-five days.

In a speech made by President Ford at Tulane University on 23 April 1975, he distanced America from the conflict and said, "Today, America can regain the sense of pride that existed before Vietnam. But it cannot be achieved by refighting a war that is finished as far as America is concerned."[19] The last Americans were airlifted out of Saigon around breakfast time on 30 April* and by lunchtime the Viet Cong flag was flying over the Presidential Palace.

The Vietnam War was finally over. North and South were both under communist control.

1977 The Damned the first punks past the post

As well as having the first punk single, *New Rose* written by guitarist Brian James, and the first album by a British punk band, *Damned Damned Damned.* When they opened at Newcastle's City Hall as support for glam-rock legend Marc Bolan on 10 March, they became the first punks to embark on a major UK tour. The Damned also became the first British punk band to play in America, when they opened at New York's CBGB on 7 April*.

This proved to be Marc Bolan's last tour. He died in a car accident on 16 September*.

Recording session today

1964 Simon & Garfunkel *The Sounds of Silence*

After recording separately and together as Tom & Jerry, Paul Simon and Art Garfunkel reunited under their own names to record the folk-based album *Wednesday Morning, 3am.* Paul Simon's *The Sounds of Silence* was recorded as an acoustic piece for the album. Released in October, the album sank without trace and the duo split up. All was not lost: the song started to receive airplay and the album's producer, Tom Wilson, overdubbed an electric backing band to the song and released it as a single in September 1965.

Single released today

1969 Led Zeppelin *Good Times Bad Times c/w Communication Breakdown* (US)

Despite have a "no singles" policy, the first single was released in America. It was written by Jimmy Page, John Paul Jones and John Bonham.

In Britain the singles only appeared as promos, with the exception of *Whole Lotta Love* which did receive an official release but was immediately withdrawn, all making for some very sought after Led Zeppelin collectables.

Birthday today

1940 Dean Torrence — half of surf duo Jan and Dean

In the early days of Jan and Dean, the duo's backing band included drummer Sandy Nelson and future Beach Boy Bruce Johnston.

Event today

1971 The Allman Brothers Band — opened their historic performance at Fillmore East

Just six months before founding member Duane Allman died in a tragic motorcycle accident, the Allman Brothers Band opened for a three-night stint at New York's Fillmore East. The band was still the classic lineup of dual lead guitarists Duane Allman and Dickey Betts, Gregg Allman on keyboards, bassist Berry Oakley and drummers Butch Trucks and Jaimoe Johanson.

The occasion was captured on *The Allman Brothers at Fillmore East*, produced by Tom Dowd. Written by Gregg Allman, *Whipping Post* occupied the whole of side four of the double album. The song was also a firm favourite at Frank Zappa concerts.

Recording session today

1963 The Rolling Stones — demo recordings made at IBC Studios

In an attempt to attract interest from a record label, the Stones' classic lineup made its first demo recordings at London's IBC Studios. As well as the five Stones, pianist Ian Stewart was still performing with the band. Produced by Glyn Johns, they recorded five songs: Bo Diddley's *Diddley Daddy* and *Road Runner*, Jimmy Reed's *Baby What's Wrong* and *Bright Lights Big City*, and Willie Dixon's *I Want to Be Loved*.

I Want to Be Loved was also chosen as the B-side of their first UK single, *Come On*.

Single released today

1970 The Beatles — *Let It Be* c/w *You Know My Name (Look Up the Number)* (US)

Their last single in the UK but the Beatles' penultimate American 45.

Birthdays today

1940 Bobby Graham — drums: Outlaws, Joe Brown; sessions

Bobby Graham was one of the most prolific British session drummers of the 1960s, claiming to have played on 15,000 titles[22]. He featured on scores of hits, including the Kinks' *You Really Got Me*, Them's *Gloria* and reputedly most of the Dave Clark Five singles. He was also an original member of Joe Meek's house band, the Outlaws. Urban legend has it that he was almost Pete Best's replacement in the Beatles. As the story goes, the Beatles were supporting Joe Brown and the Bruvvers at a gig, when Beatles' manager Brian Epstein approached Graham and asked him if he would like to join the soon-to-be Fab Four.

1945 Harvey Mandel — guitar: Canned Heat, John Mayall

Harvey Mandel has played guitar with some of the most respected blues-based rock bands. In his early days he was lead guitarist for legendary blues harmonica player Charlie Musselwhite and he later replaced Henry Vestine for a couple of years in Canned Heat. With Canned Heat's bassist Larry Taylor, Mandel joined John Mayall's first all American lineup, captured on the album *USA Union*. In the mid-1970s he was a contender to replace Mick Taylor in the Rolling Stones. Ron Wood secured that gig but Mandel did appear on two *Black and Blue* album tracks, *Hot Stuff* and *Memory Motel*.

Mandel had a stimulating encounter, #28, with the legendary *Plaster Casters of Chicago*, famed for their meeting with Jimi Hendrix on 25 February* 1968.

1947 Blue Weaver keyboards: Amen Corner, Strawbs, Mott the Hoople

Events today

1974 John Lennon his "lost weekend"

John Lennon and his drinking buddy, singer and songwriter Harry Nilsson, were famously ejected from West Hollywood's Troubadour club for heckling the Smothers Brothers.

In October 1973 Yoko Ono decided that it was time for a break from Lennon. She told him to move out of their New York home and to take her secretary, May Pang, with him. Lennon and Pang became lovers during the eighteen months that Lennon referred to as his "lost weekend". From New York they moved across to Los Angeles where he began a party lifestyle, drinking heavily with fellow boozers Harry Nilsson, Keith Moon and Ringo Starr.

Lennon continued to make music, delivering the albums *Walls and Bridges*, and *Rock'n'Roll* with Phil Spector. He also produced the album *Pussy Cats* for Harry Nilsson and the Willie Dixon song *Too Many Cooks (Spoil the Soup)* for Mick Jagger.

His "lost weekend" effectively came to an end on 28 November* when Yoko Ono met Lennon backstage at Elton John's Madison Square Garden concert. Lennon was there to join Elton John on stage for a duet on Lennon's *Whatever Gets You Thru the Night*.

1977 The Police the road to the Police

The recently formed Police supported groupie turned punk rocker Cherry Vanilla at a gig in Middlesbrough's Rock Garden. Bassist Sting and drummer Stuart Copeland also played as the rhythm section for Cherry Vanilla's backing band that night. Johnny Thunders and the Heartbreakers shared the bill.

The Police had already visited the recording studio a month earlier to record their debut single, *Fall Out*. Henri Padovani was the trio's guitarist but his tenure proved to be brief. In mid-1977 Sting and Copeland played together with guitarist Andy Summers in the short-lived Strontium 90. Summers joined the Police in late July but the quartet reverted to a trio in mid-August when original guitarist Padovani left.

Sting started out in a number of Newcastle bands, including the Phoenix Jazzmen and Last Exit. It was during his time with the Jazzmen that he picked up the nickname "Sting", a reference to his distinctive black and yellow striped sweater. Before joining the Police, Andy Summers was a member of several highly respected bands. His first professional gig was with Zoot Money's Big Roll Band in the early 1960s, they morphed into Dantalian's Chariot in 1967. This was followed by stints in Soft Machine and, Eric Burdon and the Animals. American born Stuart Copeland moved to England in the mid-1970s. He joined Curved Air as a roadie before becoming their drummer.

Album released today

1967 The Velvet Underground *The Velvet Underground and Nico* (US)

The Velvet underground released their groundbreaking debut album featuring German born vocalist Nico. The album cover was famously designed by American Pop artist Andy Warhol and comprised a banana with the invitation to "peel slowly and see".

Birthday today

1917 Leonard Chess co-founder of Chess Records

The Czyz family emigrated from Poland to America in the late 1920s, settled in Chicago and changed the family name to Chess. Leonard and his brother Philip moved into the nightclub business before becoming involved with Aristocrat Records. They took over control of the label and changed its name to "Chess Records".

Event today

1967 The Spencer Davis Group final UK tour with Steve and Muff Winwood

One of Britain's premier R&B bands, The Spencer Davis Group, played the Doncaster Gaumont Theatre on the final tour with its original members. Singer and keyboard player Steve Winwood and his bass playing brother Muff were moving on to pastures green. They shared the billing on that tour with the Hollies and ex-Manfred Mann singer Paul Jones.

The Winwood brothers came together with guitarist and singer Spencer Davis and drummer Pete York in the spring of 1963, calling themselves the "Rhythm and Blues Quartet". In early 1964 they met Island Records founder Chris Blackwell. He became their manager and suggested a name change to "The Spencer Davis Group". They went on to have hit records on both sides of the Atlantic.

After the tour Steve Winwood formed Traffic and brother Muff became A&R man for Blackwell's rapidly growing Island Records label. The Spencer Davis group continued, with the Winwood brothers' places being filled by organist Eddie Hardin and guitarist Phil Sawyer.

A youthful Reginald Dwight unsuccessfully auditioned for the band, although he later found fame as the solo artist Elton John. Guitarist Dave Mason spent some time with Spencer Davis as a roadie, before joining Steve Winwood as one of the founding members of Traffic.

Recording session today

1952 Lloyd Price *Lawdy Miss Clawdy*

Lloyd Price launched his singing career on the Speciality label with the self-penned *Lawdy Miss Clawdy*. The song was produced by Dave Bartholomew and featured Fats Domino on piano.

Price wrote much of his own material and was one of the most covered rock'n'roll artists in history. *Lawdy Miss Clawdy* was covered over a hundred times. It was released as a single by Elvis Presley in 1956. Little Richard covered the song on his 1964 Vee-Jay album *Little Richard Is Back* and in 1970 the Beatles included it in their movie version of *Let It Be*.

Little Richard's album *Little Richard Is Back* marked his return to rock'n'roll, after finding religion in Australia in 1957 and renouncing the Devil's music on 12 October*. This announcement was followed by a recording output of solely religious music. Little Richard might well have been back but he never again managed to recapture his old rock'n'roll magic.

Birthday today

1933 Mike Stoller producer and songwriter: Leiber and Stoller

With his partner Jerry Leiber, the writing and production partnership of Leiber and Stoller was one of the mainstays of rock'n'roll. An early songwriting success was *Hound Dog*, originally written for Big Mama Thornton in 1952. Although, it would be another four years before it found worldwide acclaim when it was covered by Elvis Presley in 1956. The duo also ventured into record label ownership in the early 1950s with Spark. The Robins were one of the label's most successful acts, recording *Riot in Cell Block No 9* and *Smokey Joe's Cafe*. When they sold Spark to Atlantic in 1956 half of the Robins stayed with Leiber and Stoller and became the Coasters.

Events today

1963 Gerry and the Pacemakers three singles straight in at #1

Gerry and the Pacemakers' debut single *How Do You Do It?* entered the British charts at #1. This was the first British #1 for a beat group.

This success meant that Gerry and the Pacemakers had beaten the Beatles to the top spot. The Beatles' second single, *Please Please Me*, had only made #1 on some of the charts and was generally considered to have peaked at #2. It took the Beatles three attempts to reach the top spot. They finally made #1 with *From Me to You* but that was not released until April 11*.

The Mitch Murray penned *How Do You Do It?* was originally offered to the Beatles. They recorded it during their second trip to Abbey Road on 4 September* 1962, their first session with Ringo Starr. That day they also recorded their own composition *Love Me Do* and opted for the self-penned song as their first single.

Gerry and the Pacemakers became the first act to have a run of three consecutive singles to enter the British charts straight in at #1 when their third single, *You'll Never Walk Alone*, hit the top on 10 October*.

1965 The Paramounts from Sandie Shaw to Procol Harum

Backed by the Paramounts and part-way through their British package tour, Adam Faith and Sandie Shaw headlined at Bradford's St George's Hall.

The Paramounts was formed at the turn of the decade by school friends, pianist Gary Brooker and guitarist Robin Trower. They developed into one of the most respected British R&B outfits and in late 1963 released their first single, a cover of the Coaster's *Poison Ivy*. This debut single did manage to graze the British charts but the band's critical success did not translate into any further chart appearances. By the mid-1960s the Paramounts had essentially become pop-singer Sandie Shaw's backing group. Despite signing with Brian Epstein in early 1965, frustration at their demise led to the group splitting up.

Along the way, drummer BJ Wilson joined the Paramounts and Brooker teamed up with lyricist Keith Reid. *A Whiter Shade of Pale* became an anthem for 1967's *Summer of Love* and Procol Harum was born out of the ashes of the Paramounts.

Single released today

1966 The Who *Substitute* c/w *Waltz for a Pig* (UK)

The Who's follow-up to their classic *My Generation* single was also their first release on the new Reaction label. Two versions of Townshend's *Substitute* were released, one with the B-side *Circles*, the other with *Instant Party*. In reality they were both the same song. The producer of their earlier Brunswick singles, Shel Talmy, had already recorded *Instant Party* and he took a dim view of the Who re-recording the song for their new label. He made his point by releasing his version of *Instant Party* as the B-side for *A Legal Matter*. To right the wrong, he obtained an injunction which stopped sales and prevented the Who from recording. They rescued the situation by changing the B-side to *Waltz for a Pig*, performed by the Who Orchestra with a writing credit for Harry Butcher.

This new B-side was actually performed by the Graham Bond Organisation. Drummer and future Cream sticksman Ginger Baker was the writer, credited as "Harry Butcher".

Birthday today

1943 Jim Pons bass and vocals: The Leaves, The Turtles, Frank Zappa

Events today

1965 Civil Rights Movement march from Selma to Montgomery ...Voting Rights

Despite the *Civil Rights Act* passing into American law on 2 July* 1964, black Americans were still encountering brutal opposition when they tried to register to vote. In order to draw attention to the problems, Martin Luther King Jr organised a march down Highway 80 from Selma to Montgomery, Alabama. There was considerable resistance to the protest from Alabama's Governor George Wallace and the local police. On 7 March a few hundred protestors approached the Edmund Pettus Bridge but were beaten back so violently by local police that ABC interrupted its Sunday night movie, *Judgement at Nuremberg,* to show news reporting of the events in Selma. As a result of the plight of the Civil Rights protestors, President Johnson addressed Congress on 15 March with a *Special Message to the Congress on the Right To Vote.*[26] Three thousand people finally left Selma on 21 March. They concluded four days later in Montgomery with a speech from Martin Luther King Jr.

This event marked the high point for the Civil Rights Movement. It also heralded the beginning of the end for non-violent protest. The *Voting Rights Act* became law on 6 August, just a week before one of the worst riots of the 1960s, in Watts, Los Angeles.

1976 Deep Purple last concert (well, until 1984 anyway!)

The Deep Purple lineup that formed after the gig on 7 April* 1975, played their swan song at Liverpool's Empire Theatre. David Coverdale went on to form Whitesnake.

Recording session today

1954 The Chords *Sh-Boom*

This rock'n'roll landmark was originally released as the B-side of their cover version of Patti Page's *Cross Over the Bridge,* until it was flipped by disc jockeys and became a big R&B hit. Despite *Sh-Boom* being cited as one of contenders for rock'n'roll's first record, the Chords were consigned to the annals of one-hit wonders.

Singles released today

1957 Jerry Lee Lewis *Whole Lot of Shakin' Going On c/w It'll Be Me* (US)

Jerry Lee Lewis's first hit came with his second Sun Records release, originally recorded by Big Maybelle as *Whole Lotta Shakin' Goin' On* on 21 March* 1955.

1965 Jerry Lee Lewis *Carry Me Back to Old Virginia c/w I Know What It Means* (US)

This was Jerry Lee's final single of his initial releases on the Sun label, 1957 to 1965.

1968 The Beatles *Lady Madonna c/w The Inner Light* (UK)

Jazz legend and club owner Ronnie Scott's sax was featured on *Lady Madonna*.

The Inner Light was George Harrison's first songwriting credit on a single. The lyrics drew on the Chinese Taoist philosophical work *Tao Te Ching*, attributed to Lao Tzu.

Birthdays today

1941 Mike Love vocals, sax and songwriter: Pendletones, The Beach Boys

Founding member of the Beach Boys, Mike Love was the Wilson brothers' first cousin.

1947 Ry Cooder guitar and vocals: Rising Sons; sessions; solo

Events today

1968 Vietnam War My Lai Massacre

A search-and-destroy mission into My Lai hamlet became one of the most notorious incidents of the whole Vietnam War.

Intelligence reports had indicated that enemy troops were taking refuge in villages in the area. My Lai was one of the hamlets and the ensuing assault was led by Charlie Company Commander Captain Ernest Medina and First Platoon Leader Lt William Calley. Despite not finding any Viet Cong in the village the American soldiers proceeded to massacre the villagers, mostly women, children and old men. Over 300 and possibly as many as 500 civilians were killed: estimates vary considerably. The total would have been higher if it had not been for the actions of some of the US military personnel there. One of those whose actions saved Vietnamese lives that day was helicopter pilot Hugh Thompson. He could see what was happening and managed to evacuate some of the villagers away from the slaughter.

The facts about the My Lai massacre did not emerge until a year later. Vietnam veteran Ron Ridenhour learned about the events from conversations with some of the men from Charlie Company who were involved in the incident. On leaving the Army in December 1968 Ridenhour was determined to bring the perpetrators to justice. In March 1969 he wrote to President Nixon, the Pentagon, the State Department and numerous members of Congress asking them to investigate the matter. By late April General Westmoreland had initiated an investigation. The American public first heard of the atrocity in November 1969 when journalist Seymour Hersh broke the story. This and later reports earned him a Pulitzer Prize in 1970. A number of people were brought to trial in 1970, including Medina and Calley but only Calley was found guilty. He received a life sentence but after a number of appeals was paroled in November 1974.

In 1998 three people were awarded the Soldier's Medal for stopping their comrades killing innocent civilians at My Lai. Helicopter pilot Hugh Thompson, door gunner Lawrence Colburn and crew chief Glenn Andreotta landed their helicopter between the rampaging troops and the local people. They stopped the killings and managed to evacuate a number of villagers. Thompson and Colburn were presented with their medals in person; Andreotta had been killed in action shortly afterwards.

1968 Grateful Dead Carousel Ballroom venture

The Grateful Dead and Jefferson Airplane played the second of a three-night gig at San Francisco's Carousel Ballroom.

In the spring of 1968 the Grateful Dead and Jefferson Airplane took out a lease on the Carousel Ballroom, a huge Irish ballroom in San Francisco's Market Street. The business side of the arrangement did not sit comfortably with the Dead and by the end of the summer the venue had been taken over by promoter Bill Graham and became the Fillmore West.

Single released today

1964 The Beatles *Can't Buy Me Love* c/w *You Can't Do That* (US)

Can't Buy Me Love was recorded at EMI's Pathé Marconi Studios in Paris, along with German language songs *Komm Gib Mir Deine Hand* and *Sie Liebt Dich.*

Can't Buy Me Love was the only previously released song to be included on the American version of the *Hard Day's Night* album.

Events today

1962 Alexis Korner's Blues Incorporated the early days

One of the pioneers of the British blues scene, Alexis Korner's Blues Incorporated played for the first time at the Ealing Club in west London, billed as "Britain's First Rhythm & Blues Band".[27] That night the musicians included: harmonica player Cyril Davies, saxophonist Dick Heckstall-Smith, future Rolling Stones drummer Charlie Watts and vocalist Art Wood, who would put together the mid-1960s cult band the Artwoods.

Korner started his career with Chris Barber's amateur jazz band in 1949. He also played on Ken Colyer's Skiffle Group's *Back to the Delta*, recorded on 10 September* 1954. During his time with Barber and Colyer he met singer, harmonica player and guitarist Cyril Davies. In early 1957 Davies was running a skiffle club when he asked Korner to come in with him to change it into a blues club. The resulting Barrelhouse Club was one of the earliest blues clubs in Britain. In the late 1950s Korner formed Blues Incorporated as a loose ensemble of musicians interested in the blues. Cyril Davis was one of the most consistent members, until he left to form his own band in November 1962.

Blues Incorporated was a breeding ground for upcoming musicians. As well as Watts and Wood, early Blues Incorporated lineups included: future Rolling Stones Brian Jones (as Elmo Lewis), Mick Jagger and Keith Richard, the future Cream rhythm section Ginger Baker and Jack Bruce, and future Manfred Mann front man Paul Jones.

1968 Vietnam War anti-Vietnam War demonstration in London

London's Grosvenor Square was the scene of one of the most violent anti-Vietnam War demonstrations seen in Britain.

Recording session today

1958 The Coasters *Yakety Yak*

Written and produced by Leiber and Stoller, and featuring the legendary sax solo from session musician King Curtis.

Single released today

1967 Jimi Hendrix Experience *Purple Haze* c/w *51st Anniversary* (UK)

Following the release of their first single *Hey Joe* on the Polydor label, their second single *Purple Haze* was the first to be released on the newly formed Track Records.

Track was the brainchild of Kit Lambert and Chris Stamp. The Hendrix penned *Purple Haze* was followed by *Pictures of Lily* from the Who and John's Children's *Desdemona.*

Album released today

1980 The Beach Boys *Keepin' the Summer Alive* (US)

Keepin' the Summer Alive marked the end of an era for the Beach Boys. This album was the last to feature all three Wilson brothers. By the end of the 1970s the Beach Boys were hardly recognisable as the band that had delivered *Pet Sounds.*

Carl Wilson split from the band for a solo career shortly after this album was released.

Birthdays today

1941 Paul Kantner guitar and vocals: Jefferson Airplane, Jefferson Starship

1944 John Sebastian guitarist, singer and songwriter: Lovin' Spoonful; solo

Event today

18

1965 The Rolling Stones that was a relief!

Rolling Stones Mick Jagger, Brian Jones and Bill Wyman, together with several friends, were on the way home in their chauffeur-driven car when a call of nature forced them to pull into an all-night garage in Stratford, East London. Wyman asked the owner, Charles Keeley, if they could partake of the facilities but Keeley refused, reputedly describing Wyman as a shaggy-haired monster. The car's occupants leapt out and relieved themselves against the forecourt wall. Urban legend has it that they informed the hapless garage owner that "we piss anywhere, man".

A court hearing four months later fined the three Stones for insulting behaviour.

Recording session today

1960 The Everly Brothers *Cathy's Clown*

Having sensationally moved from producing hit records on the Cadence label, the Everly Brothers recorded *Cathy's Clown* at Warner Brothers. This Don and Phil penned song delivered their first hit for the new label.

Warner Brothers enticed the Everly Brothers away from Cadence with a deal which gave the Brothers a guaranteed $100,000 a year, for ten years. At the time this was touted as the music industry's first $1m deal, although it proved to be a tad optimistic for the record company. Like many of the American artists who started out in the 1950s, the hits dried up in America after the British Invasion in 1964. Also, like some other American rock'n'roll artists of this era, such as the Drifters and Eddie Cochran, the Everly Brothers continued to be successful in Britain after they dropped out of sight in their homeland.

Singles released today

1968 The Beatles *Lady Madonna* c/w *The Inner Light* (US)

1977 The Clash *White Riot* c/w *1977* (UK)

The Joe Strummer and Mick Jones penned *White Riot* was the Clash's UK debut single.

Live album recorded today

1971 Colosseum *Live*

The first concert for Colosseum's *Live* album was recorded at Manchester University.

The next session was recorded at a concert at Brighton's Big Apple a week or so later. This album marked the end of the road for Colosseum. In an interview in 2004 Jon Hiseman told rock journalist Dmitry M Epstein, "I think with the 'Live' album we were finished, we could only repeat after that, which is why I stopped it."[38] Colosseum did soldier on, until finally parting company at the end of the year.

Drummer Jon Hiseman and bassist Mark Clarke formed Tempest, Clarke via a short stint in Uriah Heep. Dave Greenslade formed Greenslade with original Colosseum bassist Tony Reeves. Guitarist Clem Clempson replaced Peter Frampton in Humble Pie. Singer Chris Farlowe joined Atomic Rooster and saxophonist Dick Heckstall-Smith opted for a solo career.

Album released today

1977 Iggy Pop *The Idiot* (US)

David Bowie produced and performed on Iggy Pop's debut solo album.

Event today

1974 Jefferson Starship first gig as the Starship

Nine years after their debut concert at the Matrix, the seminal San Francisco psychedelic rock band Jefferson Airplane morphed into Jefferson Starship. It played its first gig with the new name at Chicago's Auditorium Theatre. Five core members of Airplane took to the stage that night as Jefferson Starship: guitarist and vocalist Paul Kantner, singer Grace Slick, drummer John Barbata, vocalist and keyboardist David Freiberg and violinist Papa John Creach. They were joined by guitarist Craig Chaquico and bassist Peter Kaukonen, Airplane founding member and lead guitarist Jorma's brother.

Jefferson Airplane bowed out from live performances with two nights at San Francisco's Winterland on 21* and 22 September 1972. The group splintered into various solo projects and collaborations. Bassist Jack Casady formed the blues-based Hot Tuna with guitarist and vocalist Jorma Kaukonen.

When Jefferson Airplane re-formed to tour again, Kaukonen and Casady were unwilling to return. The band had joint ownership of the old name so they called the new group "Jefferson Starship".

Single released today

1955 Carl Perkins *Movie Magg c/w Turn Around* (US)

Rockabilly pioneer Carl Perkins's self-penned debut single was recorded by Sam Phillips and released on his subsidiary Flip record label. Perkins described rockabilly as "a country man's song with a black man's rhythm".[17] Flip was another short-lived label from Sam Phillips. After a handful of releases it was discontinued, following threats of a lawsuit from the owner of an existing record label of the same name.

Album released today

1962 Bob Dylan *Bob Dylan* (US)

After playing harmonica at the recording of Carolyn Hester's album on 30 September* 1961, producer John Hammond was so impressed with Bob Dylan that he signed him to Columbia shortly afterwards. Dylan's debut album contained two original songs, *Talkin' New York* and *Song to Woody*, the latter being a homage to his hero, the itinerant folk singer Woody Guthrie. The rest of the album contained a mixture of traditional folk and blues songs, some of which were credited with Dylan's own arrangements.

Album sales were disappointing at first and Dylan's signing to the label became known as "Hammond's folly".

Died today

1976 Paul Kossoff Free's guitarist, died at the age of twenty-five

Guitarist and a founding member of Free, died from drug related heart problems.

1982 Randy Rhoads Ozzy Osbourne's guitarist, died at the age of twenty-five

Guitarist Randy Rhodes was on tour in America with Ozzy Osbourne's band, when a high jinks escapade went tragically wrong and Rhodes was killed. The band was parked up calling on a friend when Rhodes was persuaded to go for a spin in a light aeroplane. As a prank they decided to buzz the band's tour bus but the plane clipped the vehicle and crashed.

Before joining Osbourne's post-Black Sabbath band, Rhodes had been a founding member of Quiet Riot.

Event today

1969 Vietnam War *Chicago 8* indicted

A Grand Jury indicted the *Chicago 8* as a result of street riots outside the 1968 Democratic Convention in Chicago. The eight people indicted were all well-known political activists: Jerry Rubin, Abbie Hoffman, David Dellinger, Lee Weiner, Rennie Davis, John Froines, Tom Hayden and Black Panther leader Bobby

Seale. The *Chicago 8* were the first people to be charged under the rioting provisions of the *1968 Civil Rights Act*, which made it a federal offence to cross state lines in order to incite a riot.

The trial started on 24 September and famously saw Bobby Seale ordered by Judge Julius Hoffman to be bound and gagged, after his constant outbursts in the courtroom. Hoffman severed Seale from the case and sentenced him to four years for contempt.

The trial continued and became known as the *Chicago 7*, finally going to the jury on 14 February. The following day, Judge Hoffman convicted all seven AND their two defence lawyers for contempt of court. The jury returned on 18 February acquitting Froines and Weiner. The others each received a $5,000 fine and five years in jail.

All the convictions were overturned on appeal.

Recording session today

1960 Elvis Presley first recording session since leaving the Army

Having finished his spell in the US Army, Elvis arrived back in America on 3 March. A little over a couple of weeks later he was back in a Memphis studio to begin a two-day recording session.

He was accompanied by some of his pre-Army buddies: guitarist Scotty Moore, drummer DJ Fontana and vocal group the Jordanaires, plus Nashville session musicians, including pianist Floyd Cramer and saxophonist "Boots" Randolph. He recorded six songs over the two days. Both sides of his new single, *Stuck on You*, and *Fame and Fortune*. Three tracks for his first post-Army album, *Elvis Is Back!*: *Make Me Know It*, *Soldier Boy* and *It Feels So Right*. Plus *A Mess of Blues*, destined for the B-side of his follow-up single, *It's Now or Never*.

Bass player Bill Black had played with Elvis in his pre-Army days but was conspicuous by his absence from these Nashville sessions. He had been credited on all five of Elvis's Sun releases, as Elvis Presley Scotty and Bill. Following Elvis's return from the Army Black opted for a solo career with his own group, the Bill Black Combo.

Single released today

1964 The Beatles *Can't Buy Me Love* c/w *You Can't Do That* (UK)

Both songs were given a second outing on the UK version of the album *Hard Day's Night*.

The different guitar sound on *You Can't Do That* was attributed to John Lennon playing lead guitar and George Harrison using his new twelve-string Rickenbacker for the first time.

Birthday today

1950 Carl Palmer drums: Chris Farlowe, Arthur Brown, Atomic Rooster, ELP

In mid-1970 Carl Palmer teamed up with ex-Nice keyboardist Keith Emerson and ex-King Crimson bassist Greg Lake, to form the prog-rock supergroup Emerson, Lake & Palmer.

Events today

1952 Alan Freed first rock'n'roll concert

Having established a strong R&B following since he started his show on Cleveland's Radio WJW on 11 July* 1951, Alan Freed, calling himself "Moondog", organised what is generally considered to be the first-ever rock'n'roll concert.

The *Moondog Coronation Ball* at the Cleveland Arena advertised the "sensational stars": Paul Williams Hucklebuckers (that's the sax playing band leader, not the Temptations singer), Tiny Grimes Rockin' Highlanders, The Dominoes, Danny Cobb and Varetta Dillard. Freed also broadcasted his *Moondog Radio Show* over WJW, directly from the *Ball*. The 10,000 capacity Arena was sold out. Thousands more fans tried to gatecrash their way into the concert, causing the authorities to close the show down long before the advertised finishing time of 2.00am.

1956 Landmark Movies *Rock Around the Clock*

Rock Around the Clock, as well as being the first international rock'n'roll hit, was also the title of the first movie to be based around a rock'n'roll storyline. The group that made the song famous, Bill Haley and His Comets, starred in the movie alongside vocal groups, The Platters, and Freddie Bell and His Bell Boys. Disc jockey Alan Freed, the man who coined the phrase "rock'n'roll", completed the film's credentials.

The song *Rock Around the Clock* owed its success to an earlier screen gem. It was propelled to fame as the music behind the opening credits for the delinquent teen-movie *Blackboard Jungle,* which had opened a year earlier on 25 March* 1955.

In a taste of rock'n'roll things to come, cinema audiences across America and Europe ripped up the seating and danced in the aisles.

Recording session today

1955 Big Maybelle *Whole Lotta Shakin' Goin' On*

Big Maybelle recorded the original version of *Whole Lotta Shakin' Goin' On.*

The song was co-written and also released as a single in 1955 by rockabilly star and boogie-woogie pianist Roy Hall but it took the 1957 cover by Jerry Lee Lewis for the song to become one of rock'n'roll's anthems.

Album released today

1983 Pink Floyd *The Final Cut* (UK)

The Final Cut was the last Pink Floyd album to include Roger Waters. It was released as a Pink Floyd album but was more of a Waters solo project. It was described on the original packaging as "a requiem for the post war dream" by Waters, with credits for guitarist David Gilmour and drummer Nick Mason.

By the time that their swan song album was released the band had disintegrated in a cloud of acrimony. Keyboard player Rick Wright had ceased to be a member of the band and was relegated to the payroll. They did not take *The Final Cut* on the road. Their last-ever concert performance had been given nearly two years earlier on 17 June* 1981.

This was the end of the road for the Pink Floyd. Solo albums and litigation ensued until Gilmour, Mason and Wright arose phoenix-like to present a new Pink Floyd to the world. Despite previously being the Floyd's main songwriter, Waters' solo career was surprisingly eclipsed by his former colleagues.

Event today

1956 Carl Perkins car accident slowed down *Blue Suede Shoes*

Shortly after releasing *Blue Suede Shoes* tragedy struck rockabilly singer Carl Perkins when he was seriously injured in an automobile accident, on his way to make a television appearance on the *Perry Como Show* in New York.

The accident kept Perkins laid up and despite his own commercial success with *Blue Suede Shoes*, he had to watch Elvis Presley make the song his own. Perkins saw his moment of glory slip away and *Blue Suede Shoes* was to be his only major appearance on the American charts. It was also his only British hit single.

Perkins's version gave Sam Phillips and Sun Records its first million seller and made Top 3[37] on the Billboard Pop, R&B and Country charts

Recording session today

1960 The Ventures *Walk–Don't Run*

The Ventures recorded their first version of *Walk–Don't Run* and achieved local Pacific West Coast success when it was originally released on Blue Horizon.

The executives at Dolton Records became aware of the instrumental and invited the Ventures to re-record the track. It was then issued again, this time on the Dolton label. The new version gave them a Top 10 hit on both sides of the Atlantic.

The Ventures went on to become one of the world's top instrumental bands, although they did not start out that way. Their first single for Blue Horizon coupled *The Real McCoy* with *Cookies and Cream*, both sides written by Bob Bogle and Don Wilson. *The Real McCoy* was an instrumental, with Wilson's spoken voice remonstrating about the difficulty of dancing to the music. *Cookies and Cream* had lyrics credited to Jo Wilson. At this stage they were a trio, Bob Bogle, Don Wilson and drummer George Babbitt. After the success of *Walk–Don't Run*, they needed to find a permanent drummer.

Albums released today

1963 The Beatles *Please Please Me* (UK)

All ten of the new songs for the album were recorded at a single recording session on 11 February. The four remaining songs on the album were the A and B-sides of the first two British singles.

1965 The Beatles *The Early Beatles* (US)

Released two years to the day later, this album contained eleven of the fourteen songs found on the Beatles' first British album, *Please Please Me*. The three tracks omitted from the album were, *I Saw Her Standing There*, *Misery* and *There's a Place.*

1965 Bob Dylan *Bringing It All Back Home* (US)

This was the first Dylan album to contain electric songs.

Birthday today

1943 Keith Relf — vocals, harmonica and guitar: Yardbirds, Renaissance

Keith Relf was a member of the Metropolis Blues Quartet when they changed their name to "The Yardbirds". With the demise of the Yardbirds, Relf stayed with drummer Jim McCarty and formed the acoustic duo Together. After recording a couple of singles they extended the lineup to become Renaissance, with Relf providing vocals and guitar.

Events today

1961 Vietnam War — JFK speech: the "domino effect"

American President John F Kennedy was very concerned about the "domino effect" of communism in South East Asia. (The theory that if one country became communist, then the whole region might follow.) In a news conference he stated his concerns, "The security of all South East Asia is in danger if Laos loses its neutral independence."[36]

The CIA provided weapons and training for the Hmong guerrilla tribesmen who were fighting the Pathet Lao and North Vietnam's Viet Minh in the Laotian mountains.

1970 The Beatles — *Get Back* morphed into *Let It Be*

Phil Spector started work on the *Get Back* project and just over a week later it became the Beatles' final album, *Let It Be.*

The *Get Back* project started on 2 January* 1969. The Beatles were dissatisfied with the results for the *Get Back* album from producer Glyn Johns and called in Phil Spector.

On 27 January* John Lennon, assisted on guitar by George Harrison, recorded his third solo single, *Instant Karma.* This was produced by Phil Spector and the two Beatles were sufficiently impressed that they invited him to take the *Get Back* recordings and produce a new album. Paul McCartney was very unhappy with the final product, so much so that he reworked it over thirty years later as *Let It Be – Naked.*

Singles released today

1960 Elvis Presley — *Stuck on You* c/w *Fame and Fortune* (US)

This was the first single released by Elvis Presley after he came out of the Army. RCA rushed this one out just two days after it was recorded. It came in a company sleeve with two small photos of Elvis and a slogan proclaiming that this was for his 50,000,000 fans. The King had returned to the studio in Nashville on 20 March*, the two songs were cut on the second and final day of recording. Both sides charted in America, with *Stuck on You* making #1. In Britain it did not quite make the top spot.

1964 The Beatles — *Do You Want to Know a Secret* c/w *Thank You Girl* (US)

This was to be their fourth and final American release on the Vee-Jay label.

The Beatles never released *Do You Want to Know a Secret* as a single in Britain, it started life on their debut album, *Please Please Me.* They did, however, give the song to Billy J Kramer and the Dakotas. Their version made #2 in Britain and gave Lennon and McCartney their first major hit by another artist.

Albums released today

1956 Elvis Presley *Elvis Presley* (US)

Elvis Presley released his debut album in America. In Britain it had the same cover but five different tracks. The British album was also the first of three albums to be issued on the HMV label, the other two being *Rock'n'Roll N°2* and the 10 inch *The Best of Elvis*.

1973 King Crimson *Larks' Tongues in Aspic* (UK)

After the 1972 American tour, the group members split from Robert Fripp to join Alexis Korner in Snape. Fripp rebuilt the group with new members, including ex-Family bassist and vocalist John Wetton and drummer Bill Bruford, a founding member of Yes in 1968. Lyricist Pete Sinfield was replaced by Richard Palmer-James.

Events today

24

1958 Elvis Presley US Army time

The US Army greeted 53310761, Elvis Presley, into its family when he was inducted at the Memphis Draft Board.

He received his Army haircut the following day and proceeded to Fort Hood, Texas for basic training. He was there for six months.

Whilst on leave on 10 and 11 June he made what would be his last recordings for nearly two years. He recorded five songs: *I Need Your Love Tonight, Ain't That Loving You Baby, I Got Stung, A Fool Such As I* and *A Big Hunk O' Love*. Session artists included regular drummer DJ Fontana, guitarist Chet Atkins and pianist Floyd Cramer.

In October Elvis arrived at his German base in Friedberg, near Frankfurt, where he spent the next year and a half. In mid-September 1959 he met his future wife, the fourteen-year-old Priscilla Beaulieu. He was promoted to Sergeant in January 1960. Elvis's two years of service life came to an end on 2 March when he flew out of Germany and headed for home. He was officially discharged on 5 March 1960.

Three weeks later Elvis returned to being the "King of Rock'n'Roll". On 20 March* he was back in the studio working on his new album, *Elvis Is Back!* and cutting his first post-Army single, *Stuck on You*. Filming for his fifth movie, *G.I. Blues*, started shortly afterwards and heralded the next phase of Elvis's career – the 1960s Hollywood screen idol.

1972 Mott the Hoople disillusioned and about to split up

Mott the Hoople played in Switzerland at Zurich's Volkshaus, supported by Duffy. Two nights later after a disastrous gig, also in Zurich, the band decided to split up. In fact they had become so disenchanted that the band even wrote a song called *Ballad of Mott (March 26th '72, Zurich)*.

By the time that the band reached Zurich they had become increasingly disappointed with their lack of any real success. When they returned to England they decided that enough was enough and it was time for a change. Fellow glam-rocker David Bowie, whose star was in the ascendency, was a fan of the band and persuaded them to carry on. He offered them his song *Suffragette City* but they turned it down. He also offered them another one of his songs, *All the Young Dudes*, which gave the band a huge hit and the break that they needed. Bowie went on to produce their next album, named after the hit single. Mott the Hoople was back...

Album released today

1973 Pink Floyd *Dark Side of the Moon* (UK)

Pink Floyd's magnum opus, *Dark Side of the Moon*, was released in Britain. When it was released in America it became the most successful US chart album of all time. It entered the Billboard album chart on 17 March 1973 and stayed on the charts for a staggering 736[7] consecutive weeks.

The vocal gymnastics on *The Great Gig in the Sky* were courtesy of Clare Torry. This was the first Pink Floyd album with all of the lyrics written by Roger Waters.

Birthday today

1949 Nick Lowe musician, singer, songwriter: Brinsley Schwartz, Rockpile

Nick Lowe was one of the seminal figures, as a musician, songwriter and producer, in the British pub rock and new wave music scenes of the mid-1970s.

Events today

1955 Landmark Movies *Blackboard Jungle* ...kick-started rock'n'roll

The movie *Blackboard Jungle* was released in America.

Based on the novel by Evan Hunter, it was set in an inner-city New York school against a backdrop of teenage delinquency. The movie opened with a written preamble about the problems of juvenile delinquency, with the opening credits rolling to the strains of Bill Haley and His Comets playing *Rock Around the Clock*. Reaction to the movie was immediate and it kick-started rock'n'roll around the world.

The song was originally recorded by Sonny Dae and His Knights in early 1954. Bill Haley then recorded it during his first session for Decca on 12 April*. It was released as the B-side of *Thirteen Women* but failed to attract much interest. The film caused a sensation in the cinemas and it was following this reaction to *Blackboard Jungle* that *Rock Around the Clock* was re-released and became an international hit.

Rock'n'roll had arrived!

1961 Elvis Presley last live performance for seven years

Elvis gave a benefit performance at the Bloch Arena at Pearl Harbor to raise money for the building of the USS Arizona Memorial.

This would be his last live performance until the *TV Special* on 3 December* 1968 and his last concert performance until his appearance at the Las Vegas International Hotel on 31 July* 1969.

1967 Cream American concert debut

Billed as "direct from England", America was introduced to Cream as part of disc jockey Murray the "K"'s *Live in Person, Music in the Fifth Dimension* package show.

It ran for nine consecutive days, with five shows a day at New York's RKO Theatre. Multiple acts were billed, including The Who, Wilson Pickett, Smokey Robinson and the Miracles, Mitch Ryder, The Blues Project and Murray the "K"'s wife, with her dance troop Jackie and the "K" Girls. The poorly attended shows were chaotic, with short performances and a number of acts not even turning up. The Who gave storming performances, with a crowd-pleasing demolition of their equipment five times a day.

The run of shows ended on 2 April. The following day Cream were in Atlantic Records' New York studios to begin recording their second album, *Disraeli Gears*.

Birthdays today

1933 Wee Willie Harris — seminal British rock'n'roll singer

1934 Johnny Burnette — guitar and vocals: Johnny Burnette Rock'n Roll Trio; solo

1947 Brinsley Schwarz — guitar and vocals: Kippington Lodge, Brinsley Schwarz

1947 Elton John — singer and pianist: Bluesology, solo

Reginald Dwight's music career started in earnest when he joined Bluesology in the early 1960s. In 1966 they became British R&B singer Long John Baldry's backing band. Elton John took his stage name from Bluesology's sax player Elton Dean and front man Long John Baldry. He was introduced to lyricist Bernie Taupin in 1967 and they became house-songwriters for Dick James's fledgling DJM record label.

Before finding international success as a solo artist he worked as a session musician and can be heard playing piano on the Hollies' hit *He Ain't Heavy....He's My Brother*.

Events today

26

1957 Pete Seeger — hunted as a communist

Folk singer Pete Seeger was indicted for Contempt of Congress.

A resolute union man, Pete Seeger was a natural target for the reds-under-the-beds brigade and was subpoenaed to appear before the House Un-American Activities Committee on 18 August 1955. Addressing the committee Seeger claimed his First Amendment rights and refused to answer any questions regarding his philosophical, religious or political beliefs, how he voted in any election, or anything concerning his private affairs. After his indictment in 1957, a guilty verdict was returned by the jury at his trial in March 1961 and he was sentenced to a one-year jail term. In May 1962 an appeals court overturned the conviction.

In the early 1950s America was in the grip of anti-communist paranoia, with witch hunts led by the Republican Senator for Wisconsin, Joe McCarthy. As the senator's grasp reached ever wider, actors and musicians found themselves being denounced as communists alongside union activists and government officials.

1965 Frank Zappa — arrested on pornography charges

Seven months after opening his recording studio in Cucamonga, California, Frank Zappa and his girlfriend, Lorraine Belcher, were arrested on pornography charges.

He had been trapped by an undercover police officer who wanted Zappa to make a sexy recording for him. Zappa and Belcher recorded the desired sound effects by jumping on the bed and making

appropriate grunts and moans but with no sex taking place. When the officer came to collect his tape Zappa and his girlfriend were arrested. The case against Belcher was dropped but Zappa was convicted. This experience had a marked effect on Zappa and he became far more cynical about the 'real' America.

He moved away from Cucamonga shortly afterwards and joined the Soul Giants.

1976 Genesis Phil Collins' first gig as vocalist

The band kicked off their 1976 *A Trick of the Tail* tour in London, Ontario, Canada. In order to facilitate Collins' move to the front of the stage, the tour band was augmented by ex-Yes and King Crimson drummer Bill Bruford.

The first era of Genesis came to an end when lead vocalist Peter Gabriel left after the epic *The Lamb Lies Down on Broadway* tour. After an unsuccessful search for a new vocalist, drummer Phil Collins stepped up to take on the role. Genesis completed their next album, *A Trick of the Tail*, with Collins providing both the drums and vocals.

Live album recorded today

1971 Emerson, Lake & Palmer *Pictures at an Exhibition*

A live performance of Mussorgsky's *Pictures at an Exhibition* was recorded at Newcastle's City Hall by prog-rockers Emerson, Lake & Palmer, giving a clear indication that progressive rock was headed in a symphonic direction.

Russian composer Modest Mussorgsky wrote *Pictures at an Exhibition* as a piano suite in 1874, inspired by a memorial exhibition of drawings and watercolours by his friend Victor Hartmann. It was orchestrated by French composer Maurice Ravel in 1922.

Birthday today

1948 Steven Tyler singer: Chain Reaction, Aerosmith

Events today

27

1963 Frank Zappa *Concerto for Two Bicycles*

Frank Zappa's TV performance of his *Concerto for Two Bicycles* on the *Steve Allen Show* gave the audience an early glimpse of the avant-garde nature of things to come.

When host Steve Allen asked Zappa how long he had been playing the bicycle, he replied, "two weeks". Zappa then proceeded to demonstrate the various sounds that could be extracted from the bicycles. He blew through the handlebars and played the spokes using a variety of techniques. These included plucking them like a harp, bowing them with a violin bow and using drumsticks to treat the spokes as a percussion instrument. For maximum effect he played the wheel both stationary and in motion. He was aided with some pre-recorded sounds, played at the discretion of the sound engineer. The house band joined in but was instructed by Zappa to refrain from musical tones. Zappa and Allen both took part in the improvisation, with one bicycle upright and the other upside down with the wheels free to spin.

1979 Eric Clapton love triangle ended in marriage

One of rock's greatest love triangles came to its logical conclusion when Eric Clapton married George Harrison's ex-wife and model Pattie Boyd.

Clapton became infatuated with Boyd in 1970 when he was working closely with Harrison on his first solo album since the Beatles split, *All Things Must Pass.* Despite cracks in the Harrisons' marriage the affair was slow to ignite. It was not until the summer of 1974 that Boyd finally left Harrison and Clapton's dreams came true.

Both rock heroes wrote a number of songs expressing their love for the blonde model. Clapton's songs included: *Wonderful Tonight* and *Layla,* inspired by the twelfth century epic Persian poem of unrequited love, *The Story of Layla and Majnun.* Harrison's songs included: *I Need You* and *Something,* one of the Beatles' most covered songs.

Sadly, the great love affair faded and divorce ensued a decade later.

Recording session today

1956 Roy Orbison *Ooby Dooby* (Sun)

In Roy Orbison's first recording session at Sun he re-recorded *Ooby Dooby* with the Teen Kings.

Three weeks earlier they had recorded the song in Norman Petty's studio in Clovis, New Mexico. It was released on Je-Wel as the B-side of *Trying to Get to You,* with the recording credited to the Teen Kings vocal Roy Orbison. Sam Phillips liked *Ooby Dooby* and invited them into his Sun studio to re-record the song. It was released on Sun with the Orbison penned B-side *Go! Go! Go!* This time the performance was credited to Roy Orbison and Teen Kings.

Unlike Elvis Presley, Jerry Lee Lewis and Carl Perkins, Orbison's stay at Sun records was brief and unspectacular. He did not find commercial success until he moved to Monument. His 1960 recording of *Only the Lonely (Know the Way I Feel)* began a string of hits which lasted until the mid-1960s.

Live album recorded today

1970 Joe Cocker *Mad Dogs & Englishmen*

This classic live album was recorded at New York's Fillmore East on 27 and 28 March. Leon Russell acted as musical director as well as contributing guitar and keyboards.

Events today

1958 Jerry Lee Lewis set alight to his piano

Alan Freed's *Big Beat* package tour opened at New York's Brooklyn Paramount.

The tour entered the realms of rock'n'roll mythology for the rivalry between Jerry Lee Lewis and Chuck Berry, as to which of them should close the show. Berry was the more seasoned performer but Lewis had recently scored two massive hits with *Whole Lot of Shakin' Going On* and Otis Blackwell's *Great Balls of Fire.* In his wisdom, Freed decided that the show should be closed by Chuck Berry. Lewis took a dim view of this and delivered a storming performance which included setting fire to his piano. Urban legend has it that when he left the stage he said to Berry words to the effect of, "Follow that!!"

The package show played across America, visited the Canadian cities of Ontario and Montreal and featured a galaxy of stars, including Buddy Holly and the Crickets, Frankie Lymon and Larry Williams.

1964 Landmark Events Mods and Rockers clashed

Mid-1960s British Bank Holiday weekends were popular times for Mods and Rockers to meet at various seaside holiday towns and battle it out on the beaches. The first of these confrontations took place at Margate over the 1964 Easter weekend and resulted in a hundred arrests. Three months later 1,000 teenagers skirmished on the beaches at Brighton.

Mods were clean-cut, wore suits and parkers, rode scooters fitted with a dozen mirrors and listened to R&B, soul, ska and beat groups like the Who and the Small Faces. Rockers believed Mods were effeminate. They wore black leather, rode motor cycles and listened to white American rock'n'rollers like Eddie Cochran and Gene Vincent.

The Who captured the mood of the time with their album and movie *Quadrophenia*. The clashes continued until the short-lived Mod culture mutated and diversified. Some went down the hippie trail, following the new musical trends of the mid-1960s.

Recording sessions today

1967 Van Morrison *Blowin' Your Mind!*

Having recently parted company with Them and signed with Bert Berns's Bang label, Van Morrison entered the studio for the first of two days of recordings for his debut solo album, *Blowin' Your Mind!* Produced by Berns, the album opened with the self-penned song that was used as his first solo single, *Brown Eyed Girl*.

The Bang label was formed in 1965 by Bert Berns, along with Atlantic Records luminaries Ahmet Ertegun, his brother Neshui and Jerry Wexler.

1958 Eddie Cochran *Summertime Blues*

Summertime Blues gave Eddie Cochran his only American Top 10 single. Surprisingly, he only scored two other major US hits,[94] *Sittin' in the Balcony* and *C'mon Everybody*, before he died on 17 April* 1960. He fared better in Britain with six posthumous hits,[94] starting with *Three Steps to Heaven*, prophetically cut at his last session on 8 January*.

Written by Eddie Cochran and his manager Jerry Capehart, *Summertime Blues* was a much covered rock'n'roll favourite. The Beach Boys included it on their debut album *Surfin' Safari* and the Who delivered a storming version on *Live at Leeds*.

Album released today

1969 Led Zeppelin *Led Zeppelin* 1st album (UK)

Events today

1964 Landmark Radio pirate radio arrived

British music radio was turned on its head with the arrival of the first pirate radio broadcast from Radio Caroline. The new era was heralded with an announcement from Chris Moore and Simon Dee, "This is Radio Caroline on 199, your all-day music station." The Rolling Stones' *Not Fade Away* was dedicated to the station's founder, Ronan O'Rahilly and pop and rock music in Britain would never be the same again.

America was blessed with a multitude of music-based radio stations, often specialising in R&B, country or rock. Britain just had the BBC Light Programme, which devoted the occasional spot, such as *Saturday Club*, to pop music. Radio Luxembourg was beamed across from mainland Europe on Medium Wave frequency 208, with broadcasts from the likes of Jimmy Saville and Alan Freeman. The signal famously faded in and out as fans across the country strained to hear the latest from their rock and pop favourites.

Other pirate stations, such as Radio London, sprang up and offered a completely new type of radio. They operated out of international waters and were not illegal but the authorities soon managed to make life difficult for these pop-broadcasting pioneers. The BBC was forced to completely change its format. Out went the Light Programme, the Home Service and the Third Network and in came Radios 1, 2, 3 and 4.

1968 Moby Grape gig given by a fake Moby Grape

A bunch of Seattle musicians played at Santa Monica's Cheetah club under the name of Moby Grape. The real Moby Grape were in dispute with their ex-manager, Matthew Katz, who believed that he had the rights to the group's name. He sent out a faux Moby Grape to perform in less mainstream venues where the audiences were less likely to recognise the real thing. For a time there were two Moby Grapes playing rock'n'roll.

This was not unheard of in the music industry. Fleetwood Mac's manager did exactly the same thing after Bob Weston's sacking from the band on 26 October* 1973.

1973 Dr Hook and the Medicine Show made the cover of *Rolling Stone*

Dr Hook and the Medicine Show achieved their ambition and appeared on the cover of issue 131 of *Rolling Stone* magazine.

Their 1972 single, *The Cover of "Rolling Stone"*, bemoaned the fact that they could not get their picture on the cover of *Rolling Stone* magazine. When they did appear on the cover it was not a photograph but a caricature drawing. Just three of the band made it onto the front page, Dennis Locorriere, Ray Sawyer (the one with the eyepatch) and Bill Francis, under the heading "What's-Their-Names Made The Cover".

In Britain the BBC refused to play the record because it referred to a commercial product, *Rolling Stone*. The band also recorded a version called *On the Cover of the Radio Times*, which the Beeb seemed to find acceptable to its censorship sensibilities. After all, the *Radio Times* was only a commercial magazine for BBC listings.

Birthday today

1909 Moon Mullican country and rockabilly singer and pianist

Moon Mullican was one of the seminal country and rockabilly influences on rock'n'roll. He was a singer, songwriter, piano player and often cited as a major influence on Jerry Lee Lewis. Reputedly, he co-wrote *Jambalaya (On the Bayou)* with Hank Williams but was not credited on the record.

Events today

1969 The Allman Brothers debut gig

Just four days after forming at the legendary Jacksonville Jam, the Allman Brothers Band performed their first gig at the Jacksonville Armory in Florida.

All of the Allman Brothers Band performed at the Jam: dual lead guitarists Duane Allman and Dickey Betts, keyboardist Gregg Allman, bassist Berry Oakley and drummers Jai Johanny "Jaimoe" Johanson and Butch Trucks. For this first gig however, Gregg Allman was replaced on keyboards by Reese Wynans.

1972 Vietnam War *Easter Offensive* began

The *Easter Offensive*, also known as the *Nguyen Hue Offensive*, was an attempt by Hanoi to mount a full-scale invasion of South Vietnam. The invasion was focussed on three South Vietnamese targets, Quang Tri Province in the north, Kontum in central Vietnam and An Loc in the south. The 200,000 North Vietnamese troops were led by General Vo Nguyen Giap, who had defeated the French at Dien Bien Phu on 7 May* 1954. The first attack was made on 30 March at Quang Tri.

The South Vietnamese Army mounted a counter-offensive at the end of June to re-take Quang Tri, finally recapturing the city in mid-September. Following the failure of the offensive, General Giap was replaced by General Van Tien Dung. The operation was one of the bloodiest conflicts of the whole war, resulting in 100,000 casualties for the North and 40,000 for South Vietnam (casualty rates vary from source to source).

The ground war was waged by South Vietnamese troops with massive support from American air and naval bombardment. As a result of Hanoi's attack, America and South Vietnam withdrew from the Paris peace talks on 4 May. Resumption of the talks did not take place until 13 July.

1974 Ramones debut performance ...as a trio

The Ramones made their debut at New York's Performance Studio.

Guitarist Johnny Ramone, bassist Dee Dee Ramone and drummer Joey Ramone formed the band as a trio in New York's Queens, with Tom Erdelyi as their manager.

A couple of months after this gig Joey switched to lead singer and Erdelyi became sticksman, adopting the name Tommy Ramone. The classic quartet of punk pioneers was then in place.

Birthday today

1945 Eric Clapton guitarist, singer: The Roosters, The Yardbirds, Cream; solo

In early 1963 Eric Clapton joined his first group the Roosters, formed by fellow guitarist Tom McGuinness. The band lasted until the late summer of the same year and with its demise they both joined the pop-orientated Casey Jones and the Engineers. Casey Jones was actually Liverpool's Brian Casser, who had achieved considerable local success with Cass and the Cassanovas before moving to London and forming Casey Jones and the Engineers. Clapton soon became disenchanted with the lightweight pop music performed by the group and longed to join a blues based band. After only half a dozen gigs with the Engineers he accepted an invitation in October 1963 to join the Yardbirds, to replace the original guitarist Top Topham.

Tom McGuinness switched from guitar to bass and joined Manfred Mann, just as they were achieving success with their single 5-4-3-2-1.

Events today

1956 Brenda Lee — first TV performance

At the age of just eleven, Brenda Lee made her first national TV appearance on Red Foley's *Ozark Jubilee*, singing the Hank Williams classic *Jambalaya*.

Six months later Lee released the song as her first single, although she didn't achieve chart success until her third single, *One Step at a Time*, in January 1957.

1967 Jimi Hendrix Experience — first time he set fire to his guitar

The Jimi Hendrix Experience kicked off their first British package tour at the Finsbury Park Astoria, on a bill supporting headliners the Walker Brothers.

The audience that night witnessed a piece of rock history when Hendrix set fire to his guitar for the first time. His inexperience with pyrotechnics led to him needing treatment for burns to his hands but this still became a trademark of his stage performances.

The Fender Stratocaster Hendrix set fire to that night was sold at auction by the Fame Bureau in 2008 for £280,000.

Cat Stevens and Engelbert Humperdinck were also on that tour.

1968 Vietnam War — "Vietnamization" and standing down

Initiated on 31 January*, the *Tet Offensive* fundamentally changed America's view of the Vietnam War. President Johnson used his televised *Address to the Nation* to announce a reducing American commitment to the war and an end to his presidency.

He began, "Good evening, my fellow Americans: Tonight I want to speak to you of peace in Vietnam and Southeast Asia."[13] He explained that American involvement would be reduced, with South Vietnam taking over responsibility for the direct combat role. This transfer of responsibility became known as "Vietnamization". The 525,000 American troops already deployed in Vietnam would only be augmented by an additional 13,500 personnel. (Following the *Tet Offensive* General Westmoreland had requested an extra 206,000 troops.) The speech ended with his decision not to stand for re-election. "I have concluded that I should not permit the presidency to become involved in the partisan divisions that are developing in this political year. ...Accordingly, I shall not seek, and I will not accept, the nomination of my party for another term as your President."[13] American personnel deployed peaked at 543,482[105] in April 1969.

1974 John Lennon and Paul McCartney — last time they ever played together

Accompanied by Stevie Wonder, Harry Nilsson, Jesse Ed Davis and Bobby Keys, John Lennon and Paul McCartney were together in a jam session. This would prove to be the last time that Lennon and McCartney ever played together.

Lennon was in Los Angeles at the time working with Harry Nilsson on his *Pussy Cats* album, during his so-called "lost weekend" which effectively came to an end with his on stage performance with Elton John on 28 November*. The jam session surfaced some years later as the bootleg album *A Toot and a Snore in '74*.

Birthdays today

1944 Mick Ralphs guitar: Buddies, Mott the Hoople, Bad Company

1955 Angus Young lead guitarist and founding member of AC/DC

Angus Young was famed for appearing on stage wearing his trademark school uniform.

April

Events today

1966 Slade came together as the 'N Betweens

On or around 1 April singer Noddy Holder joined the 'N Betweens, completing the lineup that would become British glam-rockers Slade.

The future Slade lineup of Holder, guitarist Dave Hill, drummer Don Powell and bassist Jim Lea was in place but they still had to transition through their Ambrose Slade phase.

1977 Led Zeppelin ill-fated 11th US tour kicked off

It had been two years since the previous Led Zeppelin concert performance, given at London's Earls Court Stadium on 25 May 1975. The last time that the foursome had performed on American soil was even earlier, Los Angeles on the 27 March. Anticipation was running high for the eleventh American tour but the trouble-laden visit proved to be the last time American audiences would see Led Zeppelin in action.

The ill-fated 11th US tour kicked off ominously on All Fools' Day, 1 April, at the Memorial Auditorium in Dallas, Texas.

9 April: Chicago, Illinois: After an hour and six songs, finishing with the Jimmy Page and Robert Plant penned *Ten Years Gone*, the show was halted. The abrupt end to the show was blamed on a case of food poisoning for guitarist Jimmy Page.

19 April: Cincinnati, Ohio: The gig went ahead as scheduled but 70 people who had failed to secure tickets were arrested as they tried to gatecrash the concert, in a near riot outside the Riverfront Coliseum.

20 April: Cincinnati: For the second night at Cincinnati, police battled Led Zeppelin fans.

3 June: Tampa, Florida: Despite concertgoers holding "rain or shine" tickets, a rainstorm caused the concert to be cancelled after just three songs. A riot ensued and over 200 policemen in riot gear forced the irate fans out of the stadium, leaving dozens of concertgoers injured. The rescheduled "rain date" performance, initially announced for the following night, was cancelled by the police because of the riot.

23 July: Oakland, California: In what turned out to be the penultimate show of the tour, drummer John Bonham, manager Peter Grant and Zeppelin bodyguard John Bindon were arrested for beating up one of promoter Bill Graham's staff. The incident was provoked after John Bonham witnessed one of Graham's staff members thumping Peter Grant's son for removing a nameplate from a backstage door.

24 July: Oakland: The following night the foursome were back on stage at Oakland's Alameda County Coliseum, unaware that they were giving what would turn out to be their last-ever concert performance in America. A couple of days later, singer Robert Plant received information that his son Karac had been taken seriously ill. Sadly, he died shortly afterwards. The tour was due to run until the middle of August but the remaining shows were cancelled.

Single released today

1966 David Bowie *Do Anything You Say c/w Good Morning Girl* (UK)

This self-penned single was the first to be credited simply as "David Bowie", although Bowie was backed by his band at that time, the Buzz.

Birthday today

1946 Ronnie "Plonk" Lane bass: Small Faces, Faces, Slim Chance

Events today

2

1965 The Artwoods appeared on the first live *Ready Steady Go!*

Highly respected London R&B group the Artwoods appeared on the first live edition of the British TV rock show *Ready Steady Go!* The band performed their first single, Lead Belly's *Sweet Mary*. Other guests on that first edition of *Ready Steady Goes Live!* included: Donovan, The Roulettes, The Kinks, Manfred Mann and Tom Jones, although despite the new format, Jones reputedly mimed.

The Artwoods was one of the British R&B groups from the mid-1960s that never quite managed to turn critical acclaim into commercial success. Singer Art Wood, brother of Rolling Stone Ronnie Wood, formed the Art Wood Combo after leaving Alexis Korner's Blues Incorporated. Deep Purple's future keyboard player, Jon Lord, had been playing with Don Wilson's group when they combined with Art Wood to become the New Art Wood Combo. The group shortened its name to "The Artwoods" in the summer of 1964.

One player who almost made it into the Artwoods was future Jimi Hendrix drummer Mitch Mitchell but unfortunately for him it was felt that Keef Hartley's style was more appropriate. Previously, Hartley had followed in Ringo Starr's footsteps as sticksman for Rory Storm and the Hurricanes, after Starr sought out pastures green as a Beatle.

1967 Steve Winwood goodbye Spencer Davis Group ...hello Traffic

Keyboard player and vocalist Steve Winwood announced that he was leaving the Spencer Davis Group.

Despite the fact that the Spencer Davis Group had enjoyed four British Top 10 hits from their previous five releases, Winwood felt that it was time to move on. He did so in spectacular style by forming Traffic, one of the premier rock bands of its time.

The initial Traffic lineup alongside Winwood consisted of: ex-Spencer Davis roadie, guitarist and vocalist Dave Mason, who had also been a member of the Hellions with drummer and vocalist Jim Capaldi; and ex-Locomotive flautist and saxophonist Chris Wood. By June they were in the British charts with their first single *Paper Sun*, produced by Jimmy Miller and with the writing credit initially going to all four group members.

Birthdays today

1939 Marvin Gaye singer and songwriter

Before finding international fame as a singer at the Motown record label, Marvin Gaye was lead singer with doo wop group the Marquees. Leader of the Moonglows, Harvey Fuqua, replaced the existing Moonglows with Gaye's group the Marquees and they made one of their earliest appearances together on 12 June* 1959. At Motown in the summer of 1971 Gaye delivered his pièce-de-résistance album *What's Going On.*

1942 Leon Russell keyboards and vocals: Wrecking Crew; solo

Keyboardist, session musician, producer and songwriter, Leon Russell worked with rock's alumni and played on numerous 1960s and '70s classics. With the legendary group of session musicians who made up the Wrecking Crew, he played on many of Phil Spector's "wall of sound" classics, including *He's a Rebel* in 1962. He was one of the "Byrds" playing on *Mr. Tambourine Man* in 1965 and as an honorary "Englishman" he played a major part in Joe Cockers's acclaimed *Mad Dogs* tour in 1970. Russell also released work as a solo artist, achieving chart success on both sides of the Atlantic. As if all that was not enough, he formed his own record label, Shelter, in the late 1960s.

Event today

1970 Brinsley Schwarz overhyped press debut gig

In one of the most overhyped British press debut gigs ever, Brinsley Schwarz flew rock journalists over to America to see the band in concert at New York's Fillmore East. Supporting headliners Quicksilver Messenger Service, Brinsley Schwarz were in a lineup which included Van Morrison and folk singer Tom Paxton. Sadly, the British journalists were deeply unimpressed. The pub-rock band never really recovered from the experience, becoming synonymous with rock hype.

Named after its lead guitarist Brinsley Schwarz, it evolved from Kippington Lodge to become one of the pioneers of the early 1970s British pub-rock scene. The lineup also included bassist, vocalist and songwriter Nick Lowe.

Recording sessions today

1958 The Johnny Otis Show *Willie and the Hand Jive*

This self-penned song was Johnny Otis's biggest hit. It was also the B-side for Cliff Richard's Ian Samwell penned 1960 British hit *Fall in Love with You* and Eric Clapton's American hit in 1974.

1967 Cream *Disraeli Gears*

Cream began work on their second album, *Disraeli Gears*, at New York's Atlantic studios. It was produced by Felix Pappalardi, with assistance from engineer Tom Dowd.

Cream had just completed their run of American debut concerts as a part of disc jockey Murray the "K"'s *Live in Person, Music in the Fifth Dimension* package show.

Single released today

1961 Billy Fury *Halfway to Paradise* c/w *Cross My Heart* (UK)

Goffin and King's *Halfway to Paradise* was originally recorded by American singer Tony Orlando but Billy Fury achieved relatively more success with the song in his home country than Orlando did in his. Peaking at #3 in Britain, this was Fury's biggest hit to date.

Album released today

1968 Moby Grape *Wow/Grape Jam* (US)

Grape Jam was a bonus album featuring Al Kooper and Mike Bloomfield.

Wow proved to be founding member Skip Spence's final outing on vinyl, making his swan song appearance with the band on 31 May* 1968. An incident with an axe and a hotel door led to him spending time in New York's Bellevue psychiatric hospital, where he wrote his solo album *Oar*.

Birthdays today

1943 Richard Manuel keyboards, drums and vocals: The Hawks, The Band

After splitting from rockabilly star Ronnie Hawkins, the Hawks backed Bob Dylan on his groundbreaking electric tour of 1965/1966.

1949 Richard Thompson guitarist, singer, songwriter: Fairport Convention; solo

In 1967 Richard Thompson was one of the founding members of the seminal British folk-rock group Fairport Convention. After their fifth album, *Full House* in early 1971, Thompson left to embark on what would be an acclaimed solo career.

Events today

4

1964 The Beatles dominated the American charts

In both the *Billboard* and *Cash Box Top 100* charts issued on 4 April, the Beatles held all of the top five positions: *Can't Buy Me Love, Twist and Shout, She Loves You, I Want to Hold Your Hand* and *Please Please Me*. Both charts also included: *From Me to You, Do You Want to Know a Secret, All My Loving, You Can't Do That, Roll Over Beethoven* and *Thank You Girl*. In addition, *Billboard* listed *I Saw Her Standing There* as a hit but *Cashbox* included *Love Me Do*. Amazingly the top five songs were on four different record labels: Capitol, Tollie, Swan and Vee-Jay.

1967 Vietnam War Martin Luther King Jr's speech *Beyond Vietnam*

By the time of the *Summer of Love* American public opinion was turning firmly against the Vietnam War. Demonstrations against the war and for Civil Rights were increasingly overlapping when Martin Luther King Jr spoke out against the Vietnam War in his speech *Beyond Vietnam*, made to an audience at the Riverside Church in New York.

He talked of his concern that the war was drawing resources away from the issues of the poor at home. Black soldiers were fighting in Vietnam for freedoms for Asian people that were not afforded to the same young black men when they were at home. King pointed out the bitter irony of black and white soldiers fighting and dying side by side, when, back at home they were not even allowed to sit together in parts of the Deep South.

1968 Martin Luther King Jr assassinated

At 6.01pm Martin Luther King Jr was assassinated as he stood on the balcony of his room at the Lorraine Hotel in Memphis, Tennessee. He had leaned over the balcony to speak to his chauffer and was killed by a single shot fired by James Earl Ray. The Rev. Jessie Jackson was by his side when the shot rang out.

Ray was later arrested in England. After pleading guilty in March 1969 he was sentenced to ninety-nine years' imprisonment. He died in 1998.

As a result of the assassination racial unrest erupted in over a hundred cities across America.

Birthdays today

1915 Muddy Waters blues singer, guitarist and songwriter

The Rolling Stones took their name from the Muddy Waters song *Rollin' Stone*. In fact, at their debut concert at London's Marquee club on 12 July* 1962 they were billed as "The Rollin' Stones".

1940 Sharon Sheeley songwriter

Sharon Sheeley was one of the first female rock'n'roll songwriters to work solo. Many of her contemporaries were in partnerships with a man. One of her earliest successes was Ricky Nelson's 1958 American #1 *Poor Little Fool*, which also went Top 5 in Britain. Sheeley wrote a number of songs in partnership with Jackie De Shannon.

Sheeley became romantically attached to rock'n'roll legend Eddie Cochran and survived the car crash that killed him 17 April* 1960. Cochran recorded a number of Sheeley's compositions, including *Cherished Memories* and the classic *Somethin' Else*, co-written with Eddie Cochran's brother Bob.

1952 Gary Moore guitar, vocals: Skid Row, Colosseum II, Thin Lizzy; solo

Event today

5

1974 Van Halen early gig with the new name

Having opened their residency the previous night, Van Halen gave their second performance at Gazzarri's on Hollywood's Sunset Boulevard.

Van Halen had recently renamed from "Mammoth", with soon-to-be guitar hero Eddie Van Halen, his brother Alex on drums, David Lee Roth providing the vocals and bassist Michael Anthony completing the lineup. Van Halen became established as one of the world's leading rock bands. David Lee Roth left in 1985 and was replaced by former Montrose vocalist Sammy Hagar.

Recording session today

1980 Ozzy Osbourne *Blizzard of Ozz*

Ozzy Osbourne was about halfway through the four weeks of recording sessions for *Blizzard of Ozz*, his first album since leaving Black Sabbath. Osbourne's new band included guitarist Randy Rhoads and bassist Bob Daisley.

The track *Suicide Solution*, written by Osbourne, Rhoads and Daisley, led to a lawsuit after Californian teenager John McCollum shot and killed himself in October 1984, whilst listening to the bat-muncher's music. McCollum had listened to a number of albums but it was the song *Suicide Solution* that was singled out when McCollum's parents brought the action against Osbourne and his record label CBS. The parents' action failed. The court decided that Osbourne's music was not responsible for the young man's death.

Birthdays today

1928 Tony Williams singer: The Platters; solo

The Platters, with lead singer Tony Williams, were one of the 1950s most successful vocal groups. Their fortunes changed after all four male singers were arrested for aiding and abetting prostitution on 10 August* 1959. Williams left shortly afterwards to embark on a solo career.

1929 Joe Meek groundbreaking 1960s British producer

Working from his London home studio in Holloway Road, Islington, Joe Meek was a true pioneer of British rock'n'roll. One of the first independent record producers, he also launched one of Britain's first independent record labels, Triumph. After a handful of releases Meek opted to become an independent producer and deliver his recordings through mainstream labels. One of his early singles was *Tell Laura I Love Her* on Top Rank, by actor-turned-singer John Leyton. It was a cover of Ray Peterson's original but it was Ricky Valance who scored the UK hit. Other recordings followed on various labels, including Pye, HMV and Decca. In 1962 the Tornados' *Telstar* gave Meek a #1 on both sides of the Atlantic. This American achievement gave him the accolade of having the first #1 by a British group, an advance guard for the British Invasion in 1964.

1941 Dave Swarbrick violin: Ian Campbell Folk Group, Fairport Convention

Dave Swarbrick was one of the most influential of the folk-rock fiddle players. As well as his long association with Fairport Convention, he also released a number of albums in collaboration with another folk hero, guitarist and singer Martin Carthy.

1942 Allan Clarke lead singer: The Two Teens, The Deltas, The Hollies

Events today

1962 Alexis Korner R&B interval act at the Marquee club

6

The Chris Barber Jazz Band had been appearing regularly at London's Marquee club since the beginning of the year. Alexis Korner and Cyril Davies provided an R&B set as Barber's interval group.

Chris Barber formed the group in order to give his wife, Ottilie Patterson, an opportunity to sing a blues set during the interval, when the Jazz Band players were taking a break. Guitarist Alexis Korner was joined in the band by harmonica and 12-string guitar player Cyril Davies. A month later Korner and Davies started their own Thursday night residency at the Marquee, with Alexis Korner's Blues Incorporated.

Barber's interval group in 1954 had been the Lonnie Donegan Skiffle Group, which kick-started British rock'n'roll when *Rock Island Line* hit the charts in January 1956.

1966 Buffalo Springfield chance meeting led to the band's formation

The origin of Buffalo Springfield is the stuff of rock'n'roll legend. Details of the meeting vary but in essence, Neil Young and Bruce Palmer were driving through Los Angeles in Young's hearse, when they were spotted by Stephen Stills and Richie Furay who were driving a van in the opposite direction. Some accounts suggest that they were in a traffic jam, others that the van did a U-turn. Either way, the occupants of the two vehicles made contact. At the time Stills was putting a band together and now

80 per cent of what would soon be Buffalo Springfield were talking to each other. Drummer Dewey Martin was recruited shortly afterwards and the highly rated Buffalo Springfield was born.

Young and Palmer had been playing together in the Canadian band the Mynah Birds. Stills and Furay were together in the Au Go-Go Singers. Stills and Furay had previously met Young when they saw him playing in Canada.

The band took its name from a steamroller manufactured by the Buffalo-Springfield Roller Company.

1968 Pink Floyd goodbye Syd Barrett ...hello David Gilmour

By the end of 1967 Syd Barrett had succumbed to a drug induced parallel universe. His behaviour had become increasingly erratic on the Jimi Hendrix tour, which had kicked off on 14 November*. By the end of the year guitarist David Gilmour had been invited to join the band and in early 1968 the group briefly became a quintet. The end came with a press release on 6 April announcing Barrett's departure from the group.

Syd Barrett and David Gilmour were childhood friends in Cambridge and played guitar together when they both attended the Cambridge College of Arts and Technology. In 1965 Gilmour and Barrett spent the summer busking together around the South of France. The parting of the ways came when Barrett joined Pink Floyd, playing their first underground concert on 14 October* 1966.

In the early 1960s Gilmour joined Jokers Wild. The group produced just one single and album, both private pressings. In the mid-1960s he toured Europe with Flowers and later Bullitt. Gilmour joined his childhood friend in Pink Floyd in January 1967 but sadly, it was as his replacement. The Pink Floyd played just four gigs as a quintet with both Barrett and Gilmour. The post-Barrett lineup performed for the first time at the Southampton University concert on 26 January. Roger Waters took over the role as the band's main songwriter. Pink Floyd then moved away from the whimsical Barrett pop songs towards the soundscapes that would take them into rock's premier league.

Events today

1962 The Rolling Stones Mick and Keith met Brian and Charlie

Alexis Korner's Blues Incorporated performed at London's Ealing Club, with a lineup that included drummer Charlie Watts and guitarist Elmo Lewis, Brian Jones's stage name at that time. Mick Jagger and Keith Richard were at the club that night and were treated to Jones's guitar work on Elmore James's *Dust My Blues*, written by James and a follow-on to his earlier *Dust My Broom*.

Blues Incorporated's vocalist was a young Paul Pond, later to change his name to Paul Jones and find international fame as the lead singer with Manfred Mann. Not only did Jagger and Richard meet Brian Jones but they both went on to perform with Blues Incorporated. It was as substitutes for that legendary band that they performed for the first time as the Rollin' Stones on 12 July* 1962.

1965 Vietnam War LBJ's *Peace Without Conquest* speech

President Johnson delivered his *Peace Without Conquest* speech at the Johns Hopkins University in Baltimore, Maryland.

The speech gave an insight into Johnson's thinking about the war. In it he said, "Since 1954 every American President has offered support to the people of South Vietnam. ...I intend to keep that promise. ...Our objective is the independence of South Vietnam ... We will do everything necessary to reach that objective. ...And we will do only what is absolutely necessary. ...we do this [the bombing campaigns] to convince the leaders of North Vietnam ...We will not be defeated. ...We will not withdraw, either openly or under the cloak of a meaningless agreement."[41]

1975 Deep Purple final gig with Ritchie Blackmore

Original guitarist Ritchie Blackmore played his swan song with Deep Purple in France at the Paris Palais des Sports.

As well as Blackmore, the lineup now consisted of original members, keyboardist Jon Lord and drummer Ian Paice, with bassist and vocalist Glenn Hughes, and lead singer David Coverdale, who had both joined the band in mid-1973.

When he left to form Rainbow, Blackmore was replaced by guitarist Tommy Bolin. This lineup went on to play their final gig on 15 March* 1976.

1977 The Damned first British punk band to play in America

When the Damned opened at New York's CBGB club they became the first British punk band to perform in America. The lineup comprised: drummer Rat Scabies, bassist Captain Sensible, guitarist Brian James and vocalist David Vanian.

Captain Sensible had previously been with Johnny Moped, Rat Scabies and Brian James had both been members of London SS. This was Vanian's first band, having previously earned a crust digging graves. Ironically they were supported that night by the Dead Boys.

Birthday today

1943 Mick Abrahams guitar and vocals: Jethro Tull, Blodwyn Pig

In 1965 Mick Abrahams joined Neil Christian and the Crusaders, a group whose original guitarist had been Led Zeppelin's Jimmy Page. He became a founding member of Jethro Tull in late 1967 but left to form Blodwyn Pig after their first album, *This Was*.

Event today

1967 Engelbert Humperdinck *Release Me* swam against the tide

Engelbert Humperdinck's cover of *Release Me* began the last week of its six-week run[4] at the top of the British charts. It spent a total of 56[9] consecutive weeks on the charts.

This sickly-sweet Humperdinck ballad was a complete contrast to the new music emerging in one of the most exciting years of the 1960s. Ironically, despite the Beatles being at the peak of their career, with the release of *Sgt Pepper's Lonely Hearts Club Band* just a couple of months later, the Fab Four's new single, *Penny Lane* and *Strawberry Fields Forever,* could only manage two weeks at #2 before falling from view. It was kept from the top spot by this most unlikely of competitors. Humperdinck's debut chart entry broke the Beatles' run of eleven consecutive #1 singles. If this Beatles #2 had been a #1, they would have achieved a consecutive run of eighteen #1 singles.

The song *Release Me* was no stranger to the charts, having been an American country hit for Jimmy Heap in 1954 and a pop and R&B hit for Esther Phillips in 1962.

Humperdinck was born Arnold George (Gerry) Dorsey, taking his stage name from the German composer born in the mid-19th century and best known for his opera *Hänsel and Gretel.*

Albums released today

1960 Elvis Presley *Elvis Is Back!* (US)

Elvis's first album since returning from the Army was released just four days after the final recording session on 4 April.

1969 PJ Proby *Three Week Hero* (UK)

PJ Proby's album *Three Week Hero* is best remembered for being the first time that the 'Led Zeppelin' members recorded together. Proby had recorded the album the previous September, around the time that the band formed.

PJ Proby's career was also punctuated by other memorable events. He released his self-penned first single, *Go, Girl, Go*, as far back as 1957, when he was calling himself "Jett Powers". Commercial success came in the mid-1960s with a string of hits starting with *Hold Me*. Notoriety followed his famous trouser-splitting performance on 29 January* 1965, when he was on a package tour with Cilla Black. In the 1960s he recorded demos for Elvis Presley to listen to, for possible inclusion in his movies. Some of these demos are still in existence, including the title track for *Fun in Acapulco*.

Three Week Hero also featured session drummer Clem Cattini.

1977 The Clash *The Clash* (UK)

The American version of the album was released with track changes two years after this British release. The US version also featured both the original drummer Terry Chimes (aka Tory Crimes) and his replacement Topper Headon. Whereas, the original British release preceded Headon's band membership.

This British debut album from the Clash was released nearly two months after the Damned's first album, *Damned Damned Damned* but six months before the Sex Pistols released their only album, *Never Mind the Bollocks Here's the Sex Pistols*.

Birthdays today

1942 Roger Chapman singer: Farinas, Family, Streetwalkers; solo

1947 Steve Howe guitar and vocals: The In Crowd, Tomorrow, Yes

Events today

9

1964 The Who failed auditions for Fontana and BBC Radio

The Who, Pete Townshend, Roger Daltrey, John Entwistle and drummer Doug Sandom, auditioned for Fontana A&R man Chris Parmenter. The session met with a mixed reception, with Sandom being identified as the weak link. Later that same day they auditioned again, this time for BBC Radio. They failed that audition as well.

Sandom left and after trying out several drummers, the band settled on Keith Moon. All was not lost. After a second audition for Parmenter, this time with Keith Moon, they were offered a record deal that lead to their first single, *Zoot Suit* c/w *I'm the Face*.

What's in a name? The Who's name was fluid at this time. They auditioned for Fontana as "The Who" but by the time that their single came out they were "The High Numbers". When Pete Townshend applied to the BBC for an audition he did so as "The Detours" but on the day, they auditioned as "The Who".

1965 The Beach Boys Bruce Johnston replaced Glen Campbell

Bruce Johnston replaced Glen Campbell and made his debut concert performance in New Orleans.

After his nervous breakdown on 23 December* 1964, Brian Wilson stopped touring to concentrate on his writing and studio activities. His initial touring replacement was Glen Campbell but he left after a few months to concentrate on his own solo activities. Johnston's contribution to the Beach Boys extended beyond simply standing in for Brian on stage and he became a full band member, making his album debut with *Summer Days (And Summer Nights)*.

Singles released today

1958 Jerry Lee Lewis *High School Confidential* c/w *Fools Like Me* (US)

This proved to be his fourth and final major rock'n'roll hit, although it failed to make the Top 20. Shortly after its release Lewis's rock'n'roll career imploded. When he arrived in England on 22 May* for the start his UK tour, news broke that he had recently married his cousin's thirteen-year-old daughter. Disapproval of his marital status was mirrored in America and sales of his single stalled. Interest in his subsequent rock'n'roll records never recovered. With his rock'n'roll career firmly behind him, Lewis reinvented himself as a country artist and scored a string of country hits from the late 1960s and into the early 1980s.

1965 The Beatles *Ticket to Ride* c/w *Yes It Is* (UK)

Births and deaths today

1932 Carl Perkins guitarist, singer, songwriter and rockabilly legend

Carl Perkins's version of his most famous song, the rockabilly anthem *Blue Suede Shoes* gave Sun Records its first million seller, as well as helping to establish Elvis Presley as the King of Rock'n'Roll. His stay at Sun lasted until 1958 and included the jam session recording as the "Millionaire Dollar Quartet" on 4 December* 1956. By the mid-1960s Perkins had joined Johnny Cash's touring troupe and regularly appeared with him until the mid-1970s. He wrote the Johnny Cash favourite *Daddy Sang Bass*.

1976 Phil Ochs 1960s protest singer, died at the age of thirty-five

Folk singer and songwriter Phil Ochs committed suicide by hanging himself.

Events today

1957 Rick Nelson first song performed on the family's TV show

Sixteen-year-old Ricky Nelson sang for the first time on the Nelson family's TV show, *The Adventures of Ozzie and Harriet*. He performed *I'm Walkin'*, written by Fats Domino and Dave Bartholomew. It had been an American hit for Domino a month earlier.

In his early days Rick Nelson was known as "Ricky" and played himself, alongside his mother, father and elder brother, in the family's long-running TV show. The programme started out on the radio in the mid-1940s. *I'm Walkin'* and its B-side *A Teenager's Romance* were both smash hits. This single launched Nelson's singing career and started a string of hits on both sides of the Atlantic that continued until the mid-1960s.

1970 The Beatles "Paul Is Quitting The Beatles"

A press release planned to accompany Paul's debut solo album, *McCartney*, found its way prematurely into the press. Britain's *Daily Mirror* newspaper read between the lines and led with the front page headline, "Paul Is Quitting The Beatles".

McCartney never actually said that he was parting company with the band but the writing had been on the wall for so long that the inevitable became reality. Ringo quit the group back in August 1968. The *Get Back* project, which began on 2 January* 1969, was fraught to say the least but the polarization between McCartney and the others came with John Lennon's insistence on using business manager Allen Klein.

Single released today

1954 The Midnighters *Work with Me Annie* c/w *Until I Die* (US)

This seminal rock'n'roll classic was written by lead singer Hank Ballard and was one of the first R&B songs by a black group to be very popular with white teenagers.

Album released today

1964 The Beatles *The Beatles' Second Album* (US)

The second Capitol album released in America contained five Lennon and McCartney originals and six covers: Chuck Berry's *Roll Over Beethoven*; the Smokey Robinson penned *You Really Got a Hold on Me*, a hit for the Miracles in 1963; *Devil in Her Heart,* originally a 1962 single by the Donays; *Money*, co-written by Motown founder Berry Gordy Jr and an R&B hit for Barrett Strong in 1960; *Long Tall Sally*, a 1956 hit for Little Richard, co-written with Bumps Blackwell and Enortis Johnson; and *Please Mr. Postman*, recorded by the Marvelettes and giving Motown its first-ever #1 single in 1961.

The story of the origins of *Long Tall Sally* is recounted in the entry for Bumps Blackwell's birthday on 23 May* 1918.

Died today

1962 Stuart Sutcliffe Beatles' original bassist, died at the age of twenty-one

The Beatles' arrival in Hamburg for their third residency was bitter sweet, as they learned of the death of their friend Stuart Sutcliffe from a brain haemorrhage.

Sutcliffe was a painter, introduced into the group by his art college friend John Lennon. He had never been comfortable playing bass on stage and often stood with his back to the audience. When the others returned home to Liverpool after their first trip to Hamburg in December 1960, Sutcliffe stayed behind with his fiancée Astrid Kirchherr. He had effectively ceased to be a Beatle and Paul McCartney switched to bass in January 1961.

Events today

1961 Bob Dylan first major gig

After arriving in New York at the end of January, Bob Dylan joined the folk community and played the coffee houses around Greenwich Village. He played his first major gig at Gerde's Folk City, supporting bluesman John Lee Hooker.

On 3 September* Dylan took part in his first recording session, providing the harmonica for three tracks on Carolyn Hester's first album for Columbia. This led producer John Hammond to sign Dylan to the label. By the end of November he was back in the studio but this time it was to begin recording his own eponymous debut album.

1968 Blood, Sweat & Tears goodbye Al Kooper

Blood, Sweat & Tears opened a four-night stint at New York's Garrick Theatre. At the end of this short run keyboard player, vocalist and founding member, Al Kooper parted company with the band.

In 1967 Al Kooper left the Blues Project and with fellow band member Steve Katz formed the jazz-rock combo Blood, Sweat & Tears in New York. Despite being the band's founding member, he left a year later after the release of their first album, *Child Is Father to the Man*. Kooper's next step was to work as a producer with Columbia. One of his first projects was a collaboration with Mike Bloomfield and Stephen Stills on the album *Super Session*. Existing Blood, Sweat & Tears trombonist Dick Halligan moved across to replace Kooper on keyboards and David Clayton-Thomas joined the band as their new lead vocalist.

The group's name "Blood, Sweat & Tears" was Al Kooper's inspiration, after a jam session when he played with a cut on his hand which left the keyboard covered in blood.

Singles released today

1963 The Beatles *From Me to You* c/w *Thank You Girl* (UK)

This was their first British #1 and began a run of eleven consecutive #1s.

1969 The Beatles *Get Back* c/w *Don't Let Me Down* (UK)

This was the only Beatles song to credit another artist, "The Beatles with Billy Preston".

Early versions of *Get Back* caused quite a stir when bootlegs of the *Get Back Sessions* emerged. The lyrics were seen as racist, with references to Pakistanis taking the people's jobs. Paul McCartney suggested that his lyrics were satirical, not racist.

Immigration was a hot topic in Britain in the late 1960s. Enoch Powell, Member of Parliament for Wolverhampton South West, had delivered his notorious "rivers of blood" speech in Birmingham on 20 April* 1968, calling for a reduction in immigration.

Many a good quote was never actually spoken. Cagney never admonished anyone with, "You dirty rat". Bogart never requested his piano player in *Rick's Bar* to, "Play it again Sam" and Powell never talked of "rivers of blood" in his speech. He was a classics scholar and was quoting from Virgil's *The Aeneid* which included the line, "the River Tiber foaming with much blood".

Birthday today

1935 Richard Berry singer, songwriter: Flamingos, Debonairs, Flairs; solo

As the writer and original performer of the rock'n'roll classic *Louie Louie*, Richard Berry's place in rock'n'roll history is assured. In his early days he was a member of the Los Angeles based vocal group the Flamingos, not to be confused with the Chicago based doo wop giants of the same name.

Events today

1966 Jan Berry — hurt in a car crash near Dead Man's Curve

Half of surf duo Jan and Dean, Jan Berry was badly injured when he crashed his Chevrolet Corvette Stingray into the back of a stationery truck, just a few blocks away from Dead Man's Curve.

Two years earlier Jan and Dean had been riding high in the American charts with *Dead Man's Curve*, co-written by a number of songwriters, including Berry and head Beach Boy Brian Wilson. The song told the story of a Stingray and Jaguar XKE racing from Sunset and Vine, with the inevitable death and destruction at Dead Man's Curve.

1967 John's Children — infamous German tour

Shortly after future T.Rex front man Marc Bolan joined John's Children they embarked on their infamous tour of Germany, as the opening act for the Who. John's Children were well known for their outrageous stage show but by the time they reached Friedrich-Ebert-Halle in Ludwigshafen on 12 April, the concert had descended into a full-blown riot. The Who kicked them off their tour and John's Children returned home to England.

John's Children's drummer Chris Townson stood in for an incapacitated Keith Moon just six weeks later, ending his stint with the Who on 10 June*.

Recording session today

1954 Bill Haley and His Comets — *(We're Gonna) Rock Around the Clock*

Bill Haley recorded this rock'n'roll classic at New York's Pythian Temple studios during his first session for Decca. It might not have been the first rock'n'roll record but it was definitely the spark that ignited the rock'n'roll explosion.

The song was written by James Myers and Max C Freedman, and originally recorded by Sonny Dae and His Knights in early 1954. That version sank without trace. Haley released his version in May as the flipside of *Thirteen Women (And Only One Man in Town)*, recorded at the same session. This initial release met with limited enthusiasm. The song's meteoric rise came after it was used as the soundtrack behind the opening credits of the 1955 movie *Blackboard Jungle. Rock around the Clock* went on to top the charts around the world and has sold an estimated twenty-five[79] million copies.

Single released today

1965 The Byrds — *Mr. Tambourine Man c/w I Knew I'd Want You* (US)

The only member of the Byrds to play his instrument on their Bob Dylan penned debut single was Roger McGuinn, the rest of the band were session musicians. He played his trademark twelve-string guitar and the fledgling Byrds provided the vocals. Producer Terry Melcher called on the services of legendary session musicians from the Wrecking Crew to provide the music, including keyboardist Leon Russell and drummer Hal Blaine.

The other Byrds at that first recording session were (guitarist) David Crosby, vocalist Gene Clark, (bassist) Chris Hillman and (drummer) Michael Clarke.

Birthday today

1944 John Kay guitar and vocals: Sparrow, Steppenwolf

The term "heavy metal" was first coined in Steppenwolf's *Born to Be Wild*, recorded around 25 January* 1968.

Events today

13

1962 The Shadows first British group to receive a Gold single

The Shadows were awarded a Gold Disc for *Apache* on the TV show *Thank Your Lucky Stars*. This made them the first British group to receive such an accolade for a hit single.

Released in mid-1960, *Apache* was the Shadows second single, the first being *Saturday Dance*. As "The Drifters", the group had previously issued two other singles, *Feelin' Fine* and Hank Marvin's *Driftin'*. They changed their name to "The Shadows" to avoid confusion with the American vocal group. *Apache* was written by Jerry Lordan and originally recorded by Britain's first guitar hero Bert Weedon. Lordan later provided the post-Shadows combo of Jet Harris and Tony Meehan more chart success with *Diamonds*.

The latter-day Drifters and original Shadows lineup that recorded *Apache* was the classic quartet of lead guitarist Hank Marvin, rhythm guitarist Bruce Welch, bassist Jet Harris and drummer Tony Meehan.

At the time of this presentation, Silver and Gold Discs were awarded by the British music paper *Disc*: Silver for sales of 250,000 and Gold for sales exceeding 1,000,000 units (in Britain). In 1973 the awards were brought under the auspices of the British Phonographic Industry (BPI).

1964 The Who drummer Doug Sandom's last gig

After nearly two years with the Detours and the first two months as the Who, drummer Doug Sandom took to the stage for the last time in a concert at London's 100 Club.

The end came a week earlier, on 9 April*, when the group auditioned for Fontana's A&R man Chris Parmenter. He liked the band but did not take to Sandom. Rather than lose the opportunity for a recording contract Sandom was persuaded to stand down. The flamboyant Keith Moon replaced him a couple of weeks later.

Sandom's demise from the Who bore an uncanny similarity with Pete Best's departure from the Beatles. Best had also been with the band for about two years, when he too was given his marching orders after a record company executive decided that he was unsuitable for the group. Both drummers went just before the band cut their first record.

Album released today

1973 David Bowie *Aladdin Sane* (UK)

After Ziggy Stardust, David Bowie adopted the new alter ego Aladdin Sane. The name was a play on words for "a lad insane". For this album he was once again backed by the Spiders from Mars, including guitarist Mick Ronson.

Birthdays today

1944 Jack Casady — bass: Jefferson Airplane, Hot Tuna

Jack Casady replaced original bassist Bob Harvey in Jefferson Airplane shortly after their debut gig on 13 August* 1965. By 1970 Casady and Jefferson Airplane's lead guitarist Jorma Kaukonen had formed the blues-based Hot Tuna. The band was set up during the latter days of Jefferson Airplane's life but they still continued to play in the Airplane. Jefferson Airplane folded in the early 1970s. Casady and Kaukonen opted to continue with Hot Tuna when their former band mates re-formed in the mid-1970s and launched Jefferson Starship.

1945 Lowell George — guitar, vocals: The Factory, Frank Zappa, Little Feat; solo

Events today

14

1963 The Rolling Stones — met the Beatles for the first time

The Rolling Stones played the Crawdaddy Club in Richmond's Station Hotel in Surrey.

The Beatles were in nearby Teddington recording an episode of the TV pop show *Thank Your Lucky Stars*. At the invitation of the club's owner and Rolling Stones' manager Giorgio Gomelsky, they travelled to Richmond to see this new London group that was taking R&B clubs by storm. After the show they all partied back at the flat in London's Edith Grove that was home to Mick Jagger, Keith Richard and Brian Jones.

Giorgio Gomelsky regularly booked the Stones into his club and acted as their first manager, before Andrew Loog Oldham appeared on the scene. When the Stones' fame outgrew the Crawdaddy, Gomelsky filled the hole they left with another one of the groups that he managed, the Yardbirds.

1964 Them — Van Morrison and the birth of Them

An advertisement in a Belfast newspaper on the 14 April asked, "Who Are? What Are? THEM". This was followed by similar ads, until Friday 17th when the final ad announced that Them were playing that evening at the Rhythm & Blues Club in the Maritime Hotel.

After the Monarchs split up and following short stints with a couple of other Belfast groups, singer Van Morrison joined the Gamblers. Shortly after he joined they renamed to "Them" and played this first gig at the Maritime Hotel. Them became regulars at the Maritime and soon attracted interest from Decca Records. The group entered the recording studios for the first time on 5 July*.

1964 The Gamblers — one name ...three different groups

There were three different groups from three different locations, all called "The Gamblers" and each with their own piece of rock'n'roll history.

The Belfast, Northern Ireland Gamblers were the group that changed their name to "Them" soon after being joined by Van Morrison. Above is the account of the advertising campaign that started it all on 14 April and led up to their first gig as "Them".

The Newcastle, Northern England Gamblers were a highly respected beat group. As well as a combo in their own right, they replaced the Tornados, of *Telstar* fame, as Billy Fury's backing band in 1964.

The Los Angeles, California based Gamblers released Derry Weaver's seminal surf rock classic *Moon Dawg* in 1960, covered by the Beach boys on their 1962 debut album *Surfin' Safari*. This was coupled with the B-side *LSD-25*, the first song title to make reference to the drug. Elliot Ingber, later with the Mothers of Invention, future Beach Boy Bruce Johnston, and future Canned Heat's Larry Taylor all played on *Moon Dawg*. Other people to play with the band included drummer Sandy Nelson.

1975 Rolling Stones Ron Wood joined for the American tour

A press release announced that guitarist Ron Wood was joining the Rolling Stones for their upcoming American tour. At this stage Wood was still in the Faces and was on loan to the Stones. However, this remained a permanent arrangement and he became the third second-guitarist, following in the footsteps of Brian Jones and Mick Taylor.

Birthday today

1945 Ritchie Blackmore guitar: Lord Sutch, Roundabout, Deep Purple, Rainbow

Events today

15

1961 America's war on Communism Cuba: *Bay of Pigs* invasion

America opened its attack with the bombing of Cuba's airfields, destroying half of President Fidel Castro's air force. Two days later 1,400 CIA trained Cuban exiles landed on the beaches at the Bahia de Cochinos (Bay of Pigs), 95 miles south-east of Havana. The Americans had expected this attack to cause a popular uprising which would sweep Castro from power. That local support never materialised. President Kennedy could see that the mission had failed and cancelled follow-up bombing raids and reinforcements. The attack faltered and the invading forces surrendered three days after the assault began.

The exiles were tried and sentenced to thirty years' imprisonment. American negotiations with Castro followed but it would be nearly two years before the captured rebels were released in exchange for $53m[81] of food and medicine.

Castro's defeat of Cuba's President Batista in 1959 meant that a communist state existed in the northern Caribbean, a little too close to Florida for America's comfort. In March 1960 America's President Eisenhower authorised *A Program of Covert Action Against the Castro Regime*. Newly elected President Kennedy continued with this policy.

1971 The Masked Marauders the hoax was over

Rolling Stone magazine announced[61] that Warner Brothers had dropped the Masked Marauders from their catalogue, bringing their super-session hoax to an end.

It all came about after *Rolling Stone* ran a hoax album review, with a follow-up on 1 November* 1969. Instead of Jagger, Dylan, Lennon et al, the album was actually cut by the Cleanliness and Godliness Skiffle Band. But it still reputedly sold 65,000 copies.

Single released today

1966 Manfred Mann *Pretty Flamingo* c/w *You're Standing By* (UK)

This was the final single from original vocalist Paul Jones. He was replaced by Mike D'Abo. It featured Jack Bruce on bass, just before he left to set up Cream. There is some speculation as to whether Manfred Mann or Gene Pitney had the original version.

Albums released today

1966 The Rolling Stones *Aftermath* (UK)

The Rolling Stones released their fourth British album *Aftermath*, the first to contain all Jagger and Richard compositions.

Initially the album was to be called "*Could YOU Walk on Water*" but their record company, Decca, baulked at the idea of such a title. A few song changes later and the album was released as *Aftermath*.

1977 The Stranglers *IV Rattus Norvegicus* (UK)

The Stranglers' debut album was released a couple of weeks after the Clash's debut album but six months before the first album from the Sex Pistols.

Birthday today

1939 Marty Wilde seminal British rock'n'roll singing star

Reginald Smith's stage name "Marty Wilde", came courtesy of his manager Larry Parnes. Billy Fury's career took off when he made an impromptu appearance at a Marty Wilde concert on 1 October* 1958.

Events today

1969 MC5 dropped by their record label Elektra

Detroit rockers MC5 were dropped by their record label Elektra, after running ads in the Ann Arbor Angus proclaiming, "Fuck Hudson's!"

The problem stemmed from the reaction of record retailers to the opening line of the title track on the band's debut album, *Kick Out the Jams*. The song opened with the title line, followed by the expletive "motherfuckers". One of the retailers in their hometown which refused to sell the album was the mighty JL Hudson's. The group took a dim view of this and ran ads in the Ann Arbor Angus repeating the controversial first line of the song and added the suggestion to kick in the door if the store refused to sell the album. At the bottom of the ad it became more specific with "Fuck Hudson's!" This proved too much for the sensibilities of their record label Elektra: their next album was on Atlantic.

1972 Electric Light Orchestra first gig

Having already released their eponymous first album, the Electric Light Orchestra finally gave their debut performance at Croydon's Fox and Greyhound pub in London.

The Electric Light Orchestra evolved out of the Move, with Roy Wood's vision of carrying on where the Beatles' *Sgt Pepper* left off. When Carl Wayne left the Move in early January 1970, Jeff Lynne joined from the acclaimed but only mildly successful, Idle Race. The intention was to transition the two bands, The Move and Electric Light Orchestra, side by side with core members Roy Wood, Jeff Lynne and drummer Bev Bevan. This happened but was slowed down by the Move's continued success.

ELO's debut album was released in the UK at the end of 1971. When it came out in America it carried the intriguing new title, *No Answer*. This was reputedly due to a mix-up over a telephone conversation between the American record company and the band.

Singles released today

1956 Buddy Holly *Blue Days - Black Nights c/w Love Me* (US)

Buddy Holly's first release (pre-Crickets) on the Decca label. It was poorly received.

1971 The Rolling Stones *Brown Sugar c/w Bitch* and *Let It Rock* (UK)

Decca became history for the Rolling Stones with this first single released on their own label, Rolling Stones Records.

The B-side included Chuck Berry's 1960 B-side *Let It Rock*, recorded by the Stones live at Leeds University on their 1971 British tour. Chuck Berry used the pseudonym "E Anderson" for the writing credit, taken from his full name Chuck Edward Anderson Berry.

Album released today

1976 Ramones *Ramones* (US)

Punk rock had arrived. Ramones' eponymous debut album was recorded for just $6,000.[82] Punk was about to turn corporate based stadium rock on its head. Some argue that punk was the last great innovation in rock'n'roll. In many ways punk took rock'n'roll full circle, with a return to simple, energetic music, small record labels and intimate venues.

Birthday today

1939 Dusty Springfield singer: The Springfields; solo

Events today

17

1969 The Band debut concert

Canadian musicians Robbie Robertson, Richard Manuel, Garth Hudson, Rick Danko and American Levon Helm had performed together many times. They opened for the first time as "The Band" at a three-night gig at San Francisco's Winterland ballroom.

The members of the Band originally came together in the early 1960s as rockabilly legend Ronnie Hawkins's Toronto based backing group, the Hawks. The future Band members and Hawkins had parted company by 1964 and after a few of their own recordings hooked up with Bob Dylan. Still known as "The Hawks" they become Dylan's backing band for his notorious first electric tour in 1965 and 1966.

In 1968 they released their debut album, *Music from the Big Pink*, as "The Band".

1980 Black Sabbath Ronnie James Dio's debut performance

Ozzy Osbourne made his final appearance with Black Sabbath in Albuquerque on 11 December* 1978. He was replaced by vocalist Ronnie James Dio from Rainbow. Dio debuted on the *Heaven and Hell* tour, which opened in Germany at Aurich's Stadthalle.

Dio was with Sabbath for three albums *Heaven and Hell*, *Mob Rules* and *Live Evil*.

Albums released today

1964 The Rolling Stones *The Rolling Stones* 1st album (UK)

1970 Paul McCartney *McCartney* 1st album (UK)

Births and deaths today

1930 Chris Barber trombonist, jazz band leader: UK skiffle pioneer

1940 Billy Fury seminal British rock'n'roll singer

1943 Roy Estrada bass: Frank Zappa, Little Feat, Captain Beefheart

1960 Eddie Cochran rock'n'roll singer, died at the age of twenty-one

Gene Vincent and Eddie Cochran had just completed their British tour with a week-long residency at the Bristol Hippodrome. Anxious to return to America as soon as possible, a taxi was arranged to collect them after the concert and drive to Heathrow Airport for the flight home the following afternoon. The journey of a little over a hundred miles would never be completed. Just after midnight, near Chippenham with three-quarters of the journey still to go, the driver lost control of his Ford Consul and skidded into a lamp post. Gene Vincent, songwriter and Cochran's girlfriend Sharon Sheeley, and tour manager Pat Thompkins were also travelling in car on that fateful night. They were all taken to St Martin's Hospital in Bath, where Cochran died later that afternoon.

The driver George Martin was later convicted of causing Cochran's death by dangerous driving. He received a six-month prison sentence and was banned from driving for fifteen years. Attending the accident that night was a young Police Cadet named Dave Harman, who later found fame as Dave Dee, fronting Dozy, Beaky, Mick and Tich.

1983 Felix Pappalardi bassist and producer, died at the age of forty-three

Cream producer and founding member of Mountain, Felix Pappalardi was shot dead in their Manhattan apartment by his wife, Gail. Claiming that the incident was an accident, she was convicted of criminally negligent homicide and given a four-year prison sentence.

Event today

1963 Del Shannon Lennon and McCartney's first US hit

Del Shannon appeared at London's Royal Albert Hall supporting the Beatles in a concert that was broadcast live by the BBC. The Beatles performed *From Me to You* and Shannon was so taken with the song that he decided to record it for release in America.

This became the first Lennon and McCartney song to chart in America, albeit at the less glamorous end of the Top 100.

Recording session today

1959 Johnny Kidd and the Pirates *Please Don't Touch* and *Growl*

Abbey Road played host to Johnny Kidd and the Pirates' first recording session, where they cut two of Kidd's songs *Please Don't Touch* and *Growl*.

It was at this session that they adopted the name "Johnny Kidd and the Pirates", having previously performed under various names, including "The Five Nutters". Lead singer Fred Heath, now Johnny Kidd, had previously given his song *Please Don't Touch* to the Bachelors, so when he recorded it he was technically making a cover version of his own song. It gave Kidd a minor British hit but real success followed a year later with *Shakin' All Over*.

The Bachelors was a British duo, not to be confused with the Irish trio which found chart success on both sides of the Atlantic in the mid-1960s.

Birthdays today

1928 Ken Colyer — trumpeter, jazz band leader and seminal skiffle figure

Ken Colyer was one of the pivotal British figures in the transition from late 1940s trad jazz to mid-1950s rock'n'roll. He formed the Crane River Jazz Band in the late 1940s but became disillusioned with British jazz in the early 1950s and travelled to America to play with his jazz heroes in New Orleans. He returned to England in 1953 and formed Ken Colyer's Jazzmen with two other key figures from the British jazz scene, Chris Barber and Lonnie Donegan. After the split with Barber and Donegan he introduced skiffle into his performances with the aid of Alexis Korner.

Donegan went on to kick-start British rock'n'roll with *Rock Island Line*. Barber supported Muddy Waters on his 1960 UK tour and was responsible for bringing many of the American blues giants to British shores. Alexis Korner became the godfather of British rhythm and blues and with his band Blues Incorporated inspired a generation of British blues musicians. Blues Incorporated was the first British electric blues band and is often cited as the first white electric blues band in the world.

1946 Skip Spence — drums: Jefferson Airplane; guitar and vocals: Moby Grape

Guitarist Skip Spence featured in the early days of Quicksilver Messenger Service but in October 1965 he was persuaded to switch to drums and move to another fledgling San Francisco band, Jefferson Airplane. He stayed there long enough to record their debut album, *Takes Off*, before leaving to return to guitar and form Moby Grape. The second Moby Grape album *Wow/Grape Jam* marked the parting of the ways for Spence and the band. This came about after an escapade with an axe and a hotel room door at New York's Albert Hotel. The axe-through-the-door incident, shortly after 31 May* 1968, led to Spence's admission to the Psychiatric Ward of New York's Bellevue Hospital. His acclaimed solo album *Oar* was conceived there and recorded soon after his release.

Event today

1968 Free — first gig

One of the 1960s premier rock bands, Free came together and played their first gig-come-rehearsal at the Nag's Head pub in Battersea, London.

With a little help from British blues godfather Alexis Korner, drummer Simon Kirke and guitarist Paul Kossoff from Black Cat Bones, singer Paul Rodgers from the recently formed Brown Sugar and bassist Andy Fraser recently exited from John Mayall's Bluesbreakers, came together to form Free. As well as making some of the introductions, Korner helped them to arrange the Nag's Head gig. This was to be a memorable event for Korner, since he was celebrating his birthday that night.

Korner suggested the band's name "Free", taken from one of his previous bands, Free at Last.

The group Black Cat Bones took their name from the Hoodoo use of a black cat's bone as a good luck charm. Willie Dixon mentions that he has a black cat bone in his song *(I'm Your) Hoochie Coochie Man.*

Singles released today

1965 The Beatles *Ticket to Ride c/w Yes It Is* (US)

This was the Beatles' 17th single to be released in America. In Britain this same coupling was the group's 9th single.

1968 Tyrannosaurus Rex *Debora c/w Child Star* (UK)

Marc Bolan released the self-penned *Debora* for his first single as Tyrannosaurus Rex.

In the summer of 1967, after his brief sortie as a guitarist with John's Children, Marc Bolan formed the psychedelic-folk duo Tyrannosaurus Rex with percussionist Steve Peregrine Took. Initially the duo was not well received but found a champion in DJ John Peel. With his help they soon gained a strong following on the underground scene.

Birthdays today

1928 Alexis Korner guitar and vocals: Alexis Korner's Blues Incorporated, CCS

One of the founding fathers of British blues, Alexis Korner played and recorded R&B and skiffle in the 1950s and formed the highly influential Blues Incorporated. Korner started his career with Chris Barber's amateur jazz band in 1949, played in Ken Colyer's Skiffle group and formed the Barrelhouse Club with harmonica player Cyril Davies. Blues Incorporated was as a loose ensemble of musicians interested in the blues and became a breeding ground for upcoming musicians. Early lineups of Blues Incorporated included: future Rolling Stones Charlie Watts, Brian Jones, Mick Jagger and Keith Richard; the future Cream rhythm section Ginger Baker (who replaced Charlie Watts) and Jack Bruce; and future Manfred Mann front man Paul Jones.

Blues Incorporated is often cited as the first white electric blues band in the world.

1942 Alan Price keyboards and vocals: The Animals, Alan Price Set

Vocalist Eric Burdon joined the Alan Price Rhythm and Blues Combo shortly before they changed their name to "The Animals" and became one of Britain's top R&B combos.

1947 Mark Volman singer: The Turtles, Mothers of Invention, Flo & Eddie

Events today

1949 Phil Spector "To Know Him Was To Love Him"

Phil Spector's father, Ben, committed suicide by channelling exhaust fumes into his car. The future production icon was just nine years old at the time.

Ben Spector's headstone bore the inscription "To Know Him Was To Love Him". Phil launched his career in 1958 by taking this sentiment, changing the tense, forming the Teddy Bears, and writing and producing his first hit, *To Know Him Is to Love Him.*

1968 Enoch Powell "rivers of blood" speech

The Conservative Member of Parliament for Wolverhampton South West, Enoch Powell delivered his notorious "rivers of blood" speech in Birmingham in the West Midlands.

When Powell delivered his historic speech in the late 1960s, immigration issues were running high in Britain. His speech never actually referred to "rivers of blood".

He was a classics scholar and used his speech to quote Virgil's *The Aeneid*. What he actually said was, "Here is the means of showing that the immigrant communities can organise to consolidate their members, to agitate and campaign against their fellow citizens, and to overawe and dominate the rest with the legal weapons which the ignorant and the ill-informed have provided. As I look ahead, I am filled with foreboding. Like the Roman, I seem to see 'the River Tiber foaming with much blood'."[78]

1968 Deep Purple from Roundabout to Deep Purple

Deep Purple gave their first ever performance, at the Vestpoppen Parkskolen club in Tastrup, Denmark.

When the group embarked on their short Scandinavian tour they were still called "Roundabout". It was during this first jaunt that they became "Deep Purple". Initially the idea for Roundabout came from ex-Searchers drummer and vocalist Chris Curtis. He started to put the group together but was out of the picture before the project was completed. Keyboardist Jon Lord had previously been with the Artwoods and the Flower Pot Men's touring band, where he met bassist Nick Simper. Simper's background included Johnny Kidd and the Pirates and he was in the same car crash that killed Kidd. Guitarist Richie Blackmore's heritage included Screaming Lord Sutch and Neil Christian. They merged with vocalist Rod Evans and drummer Ian Paice from the Maze and Deep Purple was born.

Single released today

1957 The Everly Brothers *Bye Bye Love* c/w *I Wonder If I Care as Much* (US)

After releasing their unsuccessful debut single *Keep a Lovin' Me* on Columbia, the brothers moved to Cadence and released the first of a string of hits that would take them to international stardom.

Bye Bye Love was the first of many of the Everly Brothers' hits to be penned by wife and husband team Felice and Boudleaux Bryant.

Died today

1991 Steve Marriott Small Faces singer, died at the age of forty-four

Founding member of the Mod band Small Faces, Steve Marriott died in a house fire at his home. The cause of the fire was not established but some sources attributed the cause to a cigarette.

Events today

1970 Elton John embarked on his solo career

After establishing himself as a member of Bluesology and as a session musician, Elton John finally ventured out on a solo career. He opened for Tyrannosaurus Rex (at the time transitioning to T.Rex), Spooky Tooth and Jackie Lomax at London's Roundhouse.

On his 23rd birthday, 25 March, he made his debut at the Revolution Club in a promotional event for his new album, *Elton John*.

2008 Tommy Steele showed Elvis around London in 1958

Show business impresario Bill Kenwright, Tommy Steel's friend, revealed that Steele had given the King of Rock'n'Roll a one-day guided tour of London back in 1958. Kenwright divulged the information to BBC Radio 2 DJ Ken Bruce, during his interview for the *Tracks of My Years* section of Bruce's morning radio show.

In an article in the British newspaper the *Daily Mail* the following day, Steele confirmed in a note to the newspaper that he had been Presley's London tour guide and that it had been "secret and memorable".

This must qualify as one of rock'n'roll's best kept secrets. The only reported instance of Presley setting foot on British soil was when he touched down at Prestwick American Airbase on 3 March* 1960, on his return home from military service in Germany.

Recording session today

1963 The Four Tops the 'lost' *Breaking Through* album

After performing together for nearly a decade, the Four Tops signed to Motown's Workshop Jazz label. On 21 April they were in the Hitsville USA studios to record the song *Young and Foolish*, for possible inclusion on their first album, *Breaking Through*.

The album was described contemporaneously on the inner sleeves of other albums as, the Four Tops singing jazz versions of songs such as *I Left My Heart in San Francisco* and *Stranger on the Shore*. The album failed to be released at the time and languished in Motown's vaults until its appearance in the *Lost and Found* series in 1999.

Births and deaths today

1947 Iggy Pop singer: The Iguanas, The Stooges; solo

Iggy Pop joined his first band as the drummer of the Iguanas in the early 1960s. By the end of the decade his band the Stooges, formally the Psychedelic Stooges, had a recording contract with Elektra and an eponymous debut album produced by the Velvet Underground's John Cale. Pop was one of the architects of punk rock, before the name was even coined. His debut solo album, *The Idiot*, was produced by David Bowie and released in 1977, a time when punk rock was bringing rock'n'roll back full circle.

1978 Sandy Denny folk-rock singer, died at the age of thirty-one

Seminal British folk-rock singer and songwriter Sandy Denny died of a brain haemorrhage, following her fall down a staircase a few days earlier.

Denny was a part of British folk-rock royalty, appearing on the Strawbs' first album *All Our Own Work*. She left the Strawbs to replace Judy Dyble in Fairport Convention in time for their second album, *What We Did on Our Holidays*. After recording two further Fairport albums, *Unhalfbricking* and *Liege & Lief*, Denny left to form Fotheringay.

22

Event today

1956 Landmark Venues 2i's coffee bar opened

The 2i's coffee bar, located in London's red-light district of Soho, was the launching pad for many of Britain's new skiffle groups. It was bought by Australian wrestlers Paul Lincoln and Ray Hunter and urban legend holds that it was named after the previous owners, two brothers named Irani.

Shortly after the antipodeans took over they introduced live skiffle music. Wally Whyton's Vipers Skiffle Group was one of the first to appear there, sometimes with Tommy Hicks, later to become Britain's first rock'n'roll star Tommy Steele. Other regular performers included Terry Dene and Wee Willie Harris. In November 1957 Britain's first rock'n'roll TV show, *Six-Five Special*, hosted a live show from the 2i's. By then the Worried Men were the house band. The show's producer, Jack Good, liked their lead singer Terry Nelhams; he changed his name to Adam Faith and a star was born.

Single released today

1966 The Troggs *Wild Thing c/w From Home* (UK)

Penned by Chip Taylor, the Troggs' second single, *Wild Thing*, gave them a smash hit on both sides of the Atlantic.

Although heavily associated with the Troggs and later Jimi Hendrix, the song was originally released by the Wild Ones in late 1965. The Troggs version was reputed to have been recorded in a single take during a very short recording session.

The Troggs debut single, *Lost Girl* written by lead singer Reg Presley under his birth name of Reginald Ball, had been issued on CBS. *Wild Thing* was produced by manager Larry Page and released on Fontana. Their fourth single, *I Can't Control Myself* also written by Presley, was the first release on Page's newly formed Page One label.

Birthdays today

1924 George "Harmonica" Smith harmonica: Muddy Waters' band, Bacon Fat

George "Harmonica" Smith was one of the pioneers of the amplified harmonica. He formed a relationship with fellow blues-harp player Rod Piazza and in the late 1960s this developed into the dual-harmonica band Bacon Fat.

1937 Jack Nitzsche keyboardist, arranger, producer and songwriter

The multi-talented Jack Nitzsche worked with many of the 1960s rock'n'roll luminaries. He co-wrote *Needles and Pins* with Sonny Bono for Jackie DeShannon; the Searchers 1964 cover of the song went on to give the band a British #1. Phil Spector's "wall of sound" regularly featured arrangements by Nitzsche. Other credits included: Buffalo Springfield's *Expecting to Fly*; Mick Jagger's song *Memo from Turner*, from the movie *Performance*; and the vocal arrangement for the Rolling Stones' *You Can't Always Get What You Want*.

1950 Peter Frampton guitar and vocals: The Herd, Humble Pie; solo

After finding success with the Herd, Peter Frampton formed Humble Pie in 1969 with ex-Small Faces front man Steve Marriott. He went on to become a star in his own right and in 1976 recorded *Frampton Comes Alive!*, one of the biggest selling live albums of all time.

Event today

1956 Elvis Presley first appearance in Las Vegas

Elvis, billed as "The Atomic Powered Singer", played a two-week stint at the New Frontier Hotel in what was his first-ever appearance in Las Vegas. He was ably assisted by guitarist Scotty Moore, bassist Bill Black and drummer DJ Fontana. Unfortunately, the Vegas crowd was not ready for Elvis yet and his reception was decidedly lukewarm.

Elvis would not play Vegas again until 1969. That would be a very different Elvis and without Scotty, DJ and Bill.

Single released today

1962 Tony Sheridan and the Beat Brothers *My Bonnie* c/w *The Saints* (US)

The Beat Brothers were in fact the pre-Ringo Beatles. Pete Best was the drummer when this Decca release became the group's first appearance on vinyl in America.

The song was recorded on 22 June* 1961, during the group's second trip to Hamburg. It was originally released in October 1961 on Polydor in Germany, before receiving a British release the following January. This was a full nine months before their own debut single, *Love Me Do*, hit the shops.

Ironically, Decca allowed the Beatles to slip through its fingers on both sides of the Atlantic. It was the first American record company to release a "Beatles" record, *My Bonnie*, but it sank without trace. When it did chart in early 1964, it was a reissue on the MGM label. The American branch of Decca can be forgiven for not spotting the Beatles' potential but its British counterpart actually auditioned the same quartet in London on 1 January* 1962 but turned them down in favour of the London based Brian Poole and the Tremeloes.

Albums released today

1971 The Rolling Stones *Sticky Fingers* (UK)

This album featured guitarist Mick Taylor and a zipper cover designed by Pop artist Andy Warhol.

1976 The Rolling Stones *Black and Blue* (UK)

Black and Blue was the first Stones album to be recorded after the departure of guitarist Mick Taylor.

The album featured Ron Wood and Harvey Mandel, who were both contenders for the gig to replace Taylor. Ron Wood won the day, he had previously played with the Birds, Jeff Beck and the Faces. Harvey Mandel had an impressive blues pedigree, including Charlie Musselwhite, Canned Heat and John Mayall.

Birthday today

1936 Roy Orbison guitarist, singer and songwriter

Roy Orbison's recording of *Ooby Dooby* as the Teen Kings on the small Je-Wel record label, may not have set the world on fire but it did bring him to the attention of Sun Records' owner Sam Phillips. Orbison signed to Sun, re-recorded the song and released it again in early 1956. Unlike his contemporaries Carl Perkins and Jerry Lee Lewis, he did not achieve much success with the label. His fortunes changed when he moved to Monument and released *Only the Lonely* in mid-1960, his third single on the new label. This also heralded the beginning of his songwriting collaboration with Joe Melson.

Event today

1954 The Midnighters from The Royals to *The Twist*

The controversial *Work with Me Annie*, entered the *Billboard* R&B chart and marked the group's transition from the Royals to the Midnighters.

R&B vocal group the Royals had their first taste of success in November 1951, when they won a talent contest at Detroit's Paradise Theater. They were spotted and signed to Federal by Johnny Otis, who was a talent scout for Federal as well as an influential R&B artist. Their first few singles sold well locally but it was not until their 1953 release *Get It*, co-written by Hank Ballard, that they scored their first national R&B hit. Between that talent night and *Get It*, singer and songwriter Hank Ballard had joined the lineup.

Work with Me Annie was one of the early R&B songs by a black act to become very popular with white teenagers. This rock'n'roll classic, with its racy lyrics, also marked a name change for the group. The original Federal blue label copies were credited to "The Royals", later reissues bore the lengthier moniker "The Midnighters (Formally known as the Royals)". The name change reputedly came about to avoid confusion with Lowman Pauling's group the Five Royales but it might be just coincidental that the Five Royales moved from their label Apollo, to Federal's parent label King shortly afterwards.

On 8 November* 1958 Ballard was responsible for another piece of rock'n'roll history when he recorded his own composition *The Twist*, as Hank Ballard and the Midnighters. This gave the group a moderate hit in 1959 but started a worldwide dance craze when Chubby Checker covered the song in the summer of 1960.

Album released today

1970 Ringo Starr *Sentimental Journey* (US)

Released in America nearly a month after it hit the British record racks, Ringo's debut album was the last of the Beatles' solo efforts to reach their American fans.

Births and deaths today

1954 Captain Sensible bass, guitar, keyboards, vocals: Damned; solo

Before becoming bassist and founding member of the Damned, Captain Sensible was with covers band Oasis (a name revived by the Gallagher brothers for their band formed in the early 1990s) and punk-rockers Johnny Moped.

1975 Pete Ham Badfinger vocalist, died at the age of twenty-seven

Pete Ham hanged himself in his garage. The band had been in dispute with their manager, Stan Polley, over the handling of the group's finances. These problems weighed heavily on Ham and his depression eventually led to suicide. He died when he was twenty-seven years of age, qualifying him for the macabre *27 Club*, with other performers, such as Jimi Hendrix and Janis Joplin, who died at the same age.

Despite recording on Apple and having singles written by Paul McCartney and produced by George Harrison, the British group Badfinger had its problems. Two of its founding members, vocalist Pete Ham and bass player Tom Evans both committed suicide.

Eight years later, on 19 November* 1983, fellow Badfinger songwriter Tom Evans also took his own life.

Events today

1966 Neil Christian and the Crusaders from Jimmy Page to Ritchie Blackmore

Neil Christian and the Crusaders performed at High Wycombe Town Hall, with a lineup that included guitarist and future Deep Purple founding member Ritchie Blackmore.

Back in the late 1950s the London based group Red E Lewis and the Red Caps was carving out a niche in the Gene Vincent vein, when it recruited a young guitarist named Jimmy Page, later to join the Yardbirds and form Led Zeppelin. The group morphed into Neil Christian and the Crusaders at the turn of the decade. Despite releasing a steady stream of singles up until their demise in 1967, they never achieved much commercial success. But they did boast two other accomplished guitarists amongst their ranks in the many lineups across the years. Guitarist Albert Lee followed in Jimmy Page's footsteps, before moving on to join Chris Farlowe. Mick Abrahams replaced him and went on to become a founding member of Jethro Tull. Ritchie Blackmore joined the band in early 1966 and was their lead guitarist until the end came in mid-1967.

1970 Jimi Hendrix the final concerts

Following the demise of Band of Gypsys on 28 January* 1970, Jimi Hendrix went back to a power trio lineup, with original drummer Mitch Mitchell and his old Army buddy, bassist Billy Cox. As "The Jimi Hendrix Experience" the trio embarked on the *Cry of Love* tour, with the opening concert at the Forum in Inglewood, California.

The tour closed in Hawaii three months later on 1 August at the Honolulu International Centre. This was to be Hendrix's final appearance in America. At the end of August he officially opened his Electric Lady Studios in New York's Greenwich Village.

His final concert in Britain was on 30 August at the three-day Isle of Wight festival, alongside Joan Baez, the Who and the Doors. From there he headed off to Europe for concerts in Sweden, Denmark and Germany. He played his last-ever concert on 6 September at the *Love and Peace Festival* on the Isle of Fehmarn in Germany. On his return to Britain Hendrix made his last-ever appearance on 16 September, when he jammed with Eric Burdon and War at London's Ronnie Scott's club. In this swan song appearance they played *Blues for Memphis Slim*, *Mother Earth* and *Tobacco Road*.

He died less than two days later on 18 September*.

Single released today

1955 Elvis Presley *Baby Let's Play House c/w I'm Left, You're Right, She's Gone* (US)

Baby Let's Play House was written and originally recorded by Arthur Gunter. This was Elvis's fourth Sun single and it gave him his first national hit, albeit in the Country charts.

Birthday today

1933 Jerry Leiber producer and songwriter: Leiber and Stoller

With his partner Mike Stoller, he wrote and produced many of rock'n'roll's early classics. Their songs were regularly covered by the early 1960s R&B and beat groups. They were one of rock'n'roll's most successful writers with credits that included: Elvis Presley's *Hound Dog*, *Jailhouse Rock* and *King Creole*;

the Coasters' *Charley Brown, I'm A Hog For You (Baby)* and *Poison Ivy*; Wilbert Harrison's *Kansas City* (originally released as *KC Loving* by Little Willie Littlefield); the Clovers' *Love Potion #9*; and Richie Barrett's *Some Other Guy*.

Jerry Leiber co-wrote Ben E King's *Spanish Harlem* with Phil Spector.

Events today

1971 The Who — *Lifehouse,* Townshend's lost magnum opus

This proved to be the last *Lifehouse* concert performance at London's Young Vic theatre.

Townshend's magnum opus had a very short life. Rehearsals started at the Young Vic in early January, with a press announcement on the thirteenth. Following a handful of performances and a New York recording session, Townshend abandoned the project shortly after this show was recorded.

Lifehouse was Pete Townshend's complex follow-up to his acclaimed rock opera *Tommy*. Universal Studios was behind the project. The end result was to be a movie, incorporating live footage and audience participation filmed at the Young Vic. The futuristic storyline was set in a post-apocalyptic, polluted, mind-controlled world, where the hero attempted to provide freedom through rock'n'roll. The climax came with a freedom concert thwarted by the state. The concertgoers and some of the mind-controlled people who had tuned in, simply vanished into thin air.

The project never really gathered a head of steam and eventually fell apart. Some studio recordings involving organist Al Kooper and guitarist Leslie West were made at the Record Plant in New York. A single album of material was salvaged from the wreckage of *Lifehouse* and released as the superb *Who's Next*. But it was not over, *Lifehouse* would continue to occupy Townshend's mind for many years to come. The *Lifehouse* recordings were released in 2003, as a bonus disc with the *Who's Next* deluxe reissue CD.

1977 Landmark Venues — Club 54 opened

With the disco craze in full swing, the most famous discothèque in the world, Club 54, opened its doors at 254 West 54th Street, New York. The club was opened by Steve Rubell and Ian Schrager and was a favourite haunt of the rich and famous.

Sadly, all good things come to an end and Club 54's demise came at the hands of the tax scrutinizers at the IRS. The legendary discothèque closed its doors for the last time under its original management in early 1980.

Birthdays today

1938 Duane Eddy — King of the "twang" guitar

Duane Eddy was one of rock'n'roll's earliest guitar heroes. His distinctive "twang" sound gave him a string of hits in the late 1950s and early 1960s.

1943 Gary Wright — keyboards and vocals: Spooky Tooth, sessions; solo

When American keyboardist Gary Wright came to London in mid-1967 he joined the British group Art, which had previously covered Buffalo Springfield's *For What It's Worth*. When Wright joined their ranks the band changed their name to "Spooky Tooth". They were together on and off until 1974.

Wright took a break from the band after their third album, *Ceremony*. Amongst other things, he formed another band, Wonderwheel and worked with George Harrison on his debut solo album *All Things Must Pass*. After Spooky Tooth went their separate ways, Wright released his acclaimed solo album *The Dream Weaver*, an early example of the new synthesiser based albums.

One of the songs he wrote for Spooky Tooth, *Better By You, Better Than Me*, was covered by Judas Priest on their 1978 album *Stained Glass*. Their version was the subject of a lawsuit, after it was claimed that the song had inspired two American youths to form a suicide pact on 23 December* 1985.

Events today

1971 Grateful Dead and The Beach Boys — played together at the Fillmore

The Grateful Dead were joined on stage by the Beach Boys at New York's Fillmore East.

When the Beach Boys joined the Dead on stage they opened with the Coaster's *Searchin'*, followed by the Robins' *Riot in Cell Block #9*, complete with screaming police sirens. The Beach Boys then had the stage to themselves for two of their biggest hits, *I Get Around* and *Good Vibrations*. A third Beach Boys number, *Help Me Rhonda*, saw the return of the Grateful Dead to the stage, before the two bands wrapped up with, rather ironically for the Dead, Merle Haggard's *Okie from Muskogee* and Chuck Berry's *Johnny B Goode*. The Grateful Dead's lineup consisted of: guitarist and vocalist Jerry Garcia, guitarist Bob Weir, organist and percussionist Pigpen McKernan, bassist Phil Lesh and drummer Bill Kreutzmann. Guitarist Carl Wilson was the only one of the brothers to take to the stage that night, along with Mike Love, Bruce Johnson and Al Jardine.

Supported by the New Riders of the Purple Sage, the Grateful Dead were playing their final residency, from April 25 to 29, before the world famous rock venue closed its doors for the last time just two months later.

All three Beach Boys songs were written by Brian Wilson, with a little help from Mike Love on *Good Vibrations*. Merle Haggard's 1969 single *Okie from Muskogee* was co-written with Eddie Burris and attacked the liberal, hippie values of the late 1960s. It celebrated mid-America's desire for conservatism, short hair and a lack of marijuana.

1984 Deep Purple — after a gap of eight years, they were back

London's *Evening Standard* newspaper carried the news that Deep Purple was back. Their previous public outing had been a concert in Liverpool on 15 March* 1976.

Of that 1976 lineup, only keyboardist Jon Lord and drummer Ian Paice were in the re-formed group. They were joined by original guitarist Ritchie Blackmore, bassist Roger Glover and vocalist Ian Gillan. This was a re-forming of the classic second lineup, which lasted from mid-1969 to mid-1973 and recorded the *In Rock* and *Machine Head* albums. Their first studio album, *Perfect Strangers*, was in the British charts in November and was followed by the band's debut performance in Perth, Australia.

The other members of the 1976 group had also moved on. Vocalist David Coverdale formed Whitesnake, whereas bassist Glen Hughes opted for a solo career. Sadly, guitarist Tommy Bolin had died of a drugs overdose.

Single released today

1964 The Beatles *Love Me Do c/w P.S. I Love You* (US)

The ninth Beatles single to be released in America had the same coupling as the Fab Four's British debut, released on 5 October* 1962. This American release, their second on the Tollie label, was taken from the third *Love Me Do* recording session at Abbey Road, on 11 September* 1962. It featured session drummer Andy White, with Ringo sidelined to tambourine.

Birthday today

1951 Ace Frehley guitar and vocals: Kiss; solo

Gene Simmons and Paul Stanley parted company with the other members of Wicked Lester and teamed up with drummer Peter Criss. When they enlisted lead guitarist Ace Frehley, Kiss was born. They played their first gig on 30 January* 1973. Frehley moved on in 1982 to pursue a solo career.

Events today

1963 The Rolling Stones the birth of the Stones

Andrew Loog Oldham and Eric Easton travelled to Richmond's Crawdaddy Club in west London for their first glimpse of the club's house band, the Rolling Stones.

The road to the Rolling Stones began with guitarist Brian Jones and his early lineups, which included pianist Ian Stewart, future Manfred Mann singer Paul Jones and Brian Knight, who left to form his own band Blues By Six. Meanwhile singer Mick Jagger, guitarist Keith Richard and future Pretty Thing Dick Taylor had their own group, Little Boy Blue and the Blue Boys. Jagger and Richard met Brian Jones through Alexis Korner, the godfather of British blues. They all made appearances with Korner's Blues Incorporated. After Brian Knight left, the Blue Boys joined Brian Jones's band and made their debut as "The Rollin' Stones" at London's Marquee club on 12 July* 1962.

Dick Taylor originally played guitar with the Blue Boys but moved to bass when they joined Brian Jones. The desire to return to guitar was one of the reasons why he left and formed the Pretty Things. Various rhythm sections came and went, until 2 February* 1963 when the posts were permanently filled by drummer Charlie Watts and bassist Bill Wyman.

Watts had been with Alexis Korner's Blues Incorporated and Brian Knight's Blues By Six, before being enticed to give up his day job as a graphic designer to join the Stones. Wyman played with the Cliftons before auditioning as bass player and famously being taken on because of his Vox AC30 amplifiers.

When Oldham saw the Rolling Stones at the Crawdaddy the band was being managed by the club's owner Giorgio Gomelsky. Shortly after this performance the Stones signed a management contract with Oldham. He made four crucial decisions that moulded their future. Having seen the Beatles' success with their own material, he wanted Jagger and Richard to follow suit. In contrast, Oldham wanted a 'bad-boy' image for the Stones, rather than Epstein's clean-cut look for the Beatles. He also changed the focus of the group from founder Brian Jones to singer Mick Jagger. Sadly for pianist Ian Stewart, Oldham decided that his image was wrong for concert appearances. He was relegated to road manager and his piano playing was mostly limited to recording sessions.

1967 Vietnam War "No Viet Cong ever called me nigger."

Boxing champion Mohammad Ali was arrested for refusing to be conscripted into the US Army. He had previously been denied conscientious objector status and was subsequently sentenced to five years' imprisonment. Almost immediately after his arrest he was stripped of his World Heavyweight boxing title. He was often quoted as saying that "no Viet Cong ever called me nigger" but this may have been a tad apocryphal.

Album released today

1972 Brinsley Schwarz/Man/Hawkwind *Greasy Truckers Party* (UK)

Recorded at London's Roundhouse on 13 February*, this live album was an indication of how Britain's rock scene was developing.

Since the late 1960's, rock music had become more virtuoso and graduated to stadium venues. Brinsley Schwarz was one of a new breed of back-to-basics groups that heralded an era of pub rock. Bands like Dr Feelgood and Bees Make Honey went back to short, good-time rock'n'roll songs, played in small, intimate venues. Times changed again in 1976 with the emergence of punk, when both pub rock and prog rock were consigned to the annals of rock'n'roll history.

Events today

1962 Jerry Lee Lewis back in the UK

29

Four years after Jerry Lee Lewis's career-ending British tour, he made a triumphant return when he opened in the north of England at Newcastle's City Hall. Lewis headlined the tour and was supported by Johnny Kidd and the Pirates, Vince Eager, and The Viscounts.

Jerry Lee Lewis's rock'n'roll career imploded after it became common knowledge that he had married his bass-playing cousin's thirteen-year-old daughter, Myra Gale Brown. The British press broke the story shortly after his British tour opened on 22 May* 1958. Following the news stories, British audiences became hostile to Lewis and he had to withdraw from his own headlining tour after just three performances. This time around he was well received but he never managed to recapture his old status as a challenger to Elvis Presley for the title of "King of Rock'n'Roll".

1967 Landmark Festivals *14-Hour Technicolor Dream*

The Summer of Love's most infamous British freak-out was held at North London's Alexandra Palace and according to some reports 10,000 people joined in the happening.

The UK's counterculture mouthpiece, *International Times*, was facing prosecution and needed money for its defence. As a flier at the time put it, "London's Own Hip Newspaper The International Times Presents Giant Benefit 14-Hour Technicolor Dream, 30 Top Groups, Kaleidoscopic Colour, Beautiful People ...Followed by Free BE-IN on Sunday ...Tickets £1". The two-stage mixed media happening delivered a mind-blowing mixture of light shows, music and poetry. The drug fuelled event meant that facts are a little hazy about who actually performed, although most reports include: Pink Floyd (with Syd Barrett), The Crazy World of Arthur Brown, The Move, Alexis Korner, Graham Bond, Yoko Ono, The Pretty Things, Soft Machine, John's Children (featuring guitarist Marc Bolan) and The Creation. Pink Floyd delivered their set as dawn broke.

1976 Bruce Springsteen almost knocked on Elvis's Graceland door

After finishing a gig at the Ellis Auditorium in Memphis, Bruce Springsteen and E Street Band guitarist Steve Van Zant jumped into a cab and sped off to Graceland in an attempt to meet Elvis Presley. When they arrived Springsteen climbed over the wall but before he could knock on Elvis's door he was apprehended by security guards. His explanations fell on deaf ears and he was escorted from the premises. The guards failed to recognise Springsteen and considered him to be just another over-enthusiastic Elvis fan. As it happened, his trip had been in vain because the King was in Lake Tahoe, Nevada, about to start a ten-day residency at the Sahara Tahoe Hotel.

Springsteen had been joined on stage that evening by Eddie Floyd. They performed a number of songs together, including Floyd's hit *Knock on Wood*.

Birthdays today

1928 Carl Gardner — singer: The Robins, founding member of the Coasters

1931 Lonnie Donegan — vocals, guitar and banjo: skiffle pioneer

Lonnie Donegan's cover of Lead Belly's *Rock Island Line*, released in late 1955, heralded the skiffle boom and the dawn of British rock'n'roll. His name came about when his Tony Donegan Jazz Band was backing American bluesman Lonnie Johnson and the MC mixed up their first names, mistakenly introducing him as "Lonnie Donegan".

Events today

30

1964 The Who — Keith Moon's audition

The Who were regulars at the Oldfield Hotel in London's Greenford but it was probably[47] on this night that the concert goers were treated to the first glimpse of drummer Keith Moon, when he sat in with the band for a rendition of Bo Diddley's *Road Runner*.

Despite being the Who's drummer for the previous two years, Doug Sandom was sacked after their unsuccessful audition for Fontana on 9 April*. Session drummer Dave Golding filled in whilst the band sought a new permanent stickman. Urban legend has it that there was a sign of things to come with Moon's drumming style, after he managed to destroy the bass pedal during his brief time on stage.

1975 Vietnam War — last Americans left Vietnam

The last Americans and South Vietnamese dignitaries rallied to the American Embassy, amid scenes of panic and desperation of those South Vietnamese who were desperate not to be left behind. These last evacuees made their way up to the roof of the Embassy and were airlifted by helicopter to ships waiting nearby.

The Americans entered the war after the French were defeated at Dien Bien Phu on 7 May* 1954. Since then each successive American President, Eisenhower, Kennedy and Johnson, had escalated America's involvement in the war, fearful that the "domino effect" would cause the whole of South-East Asia to fall into communist hands. The war reached its peak with the North's launch of the *Tet Offensive* on 31 January* 1968. This full-scale invasion of the South was eventually beaten back but it marked the turning point in the war. Public opinion against the war hardened. President Johnson refused to run for a second term and Nixon spent the next five years extricating America from the conflict.

The twin strategies of "Vietnamization", handing over the responsibility for fighting the war to South Vietnam, and the winning of "hearts and minds" both failed. Massive bombing campaigns on Vietnam and its neighbours also had little impact on the communists' effectiveness.

In 1973 America signed a peace treaty with the North and withdrew from the conflict. America's Henry Kissinger accepted the *1973 Nobel Peace Prize*. North Vietnam's Le Duc Tho was also offered the *Nobel Peace Prize* but refused to accept it because he did not believe that the war was over. The beginning of the end came on 10 March* 1975 when North Vietnam launched its final invasion of the South. Just fifty-five days later South Vietnam's capital city, Saigon, fell to the communist forces. The war was over.

'Live' album recorded today

1963 Billy Fury and The Tornados *We Want Billy*

Backed by the Tornados, Billy Fury recorded the album *We Want Billy*, in front of a live audience of screaming fans in Decca's recording studio #3.

The Tornados had become Fury's backing band after they replaced the Blue Flames in early 1962. The Blue Flames' piano player became their new front man and Georgie Fame and the Blue Flames was born. The Tornados was one of the most successful instrumental combos of the time. In the summer of 1962 their second single, *Telstar*, was a British #1. By the beginning of 1963 it was also #1 in America; the first American #1 by a British group. Billy Fury and the Tornados parted company at the end of the year.

In January 1964 Fury began working with his new backing band the Gamblers, who hailed from Newcastle in the north-east of England.

May

Events today

1970 Vietnam War four students shot dead

The protests started on 1 May with an anti-war demonstration on the grassy Commons area in the middle of Kent State University campus. In a symbolic gesture a copy of the American Constitution was buried. That evening the protest moved to downtown Kent and escalated to a violent confrontation between the demonstrators and the police. This prompted Kent's mayor, LeRoy Satrom, to declare a state of emergency. The following day Ohio's governor, James Rhodes, sent the Ohio National Guard to Kent. By Sunday there were 1,000 members of the Guard on campus. That evening at another rally on the campus the National Guard used tear gas to disperse the crowd.

A demonstration was scheduled for Monday 4 May. The University authorities tried to ban the event but by midday 3,000 people had gathered on the University's Commons. When the crowd refused to disperse, the Guard once again resorted to the use of tear gas but this time it failed to break up the anti-war demonstration. The students yelled and threw stones at the National Guard and a small number of Guardsmen responded by firing directly into the crowd. When the shooting stopped four students were dead and another nine wounded. The four students who died were Allison Krause, Jeffrey Miller, Sandra Scheuer and William Schroeder

John Filo, a Kent State photography major in 1970, won a Pulitzer Prize for his iconic photograph showing a distraught Mary Ann Vecchio kneeling over the dead body of Jeffrey Miller.

A number of songs were inspired by the events of 4 May, the most famous being the Neil Young penned *Ohio*, performed by Crosby, Stills, Nash & Young.

1977 The Clash *White Riot* UK tour

The *White Riot* tour kicked off at Guildford's Civic Hall, in the affluent south-east of England.

This was the first major British Clash tour to feature drummer Topper Headon, who had replaced Terry Chimes six weeks earlier. The hectic tour finished just thirty days later at the California Ballroom in Dunstable. The Slits provided support at some of the gigs.

The entourage rolled into London on 9 May for a performance at the Rainbow Theatre. The crowd took a distinct dislike to the fixed seating arrangements and the offending seats were torn up and thrown onto the stage. The Clash were supported that night by The Buzzcocks, Subway Sect, The Prefects and The Jam. Following their experience at the Rainbow the Jam decided to quit the tour.

Recording session today

1979 Ramones *End of the Century*

The Ramones and Phil Spector began work on the new album at Gold Star Studios.

Birthday today

1930 Little Walter harmonica, vocals: Muddy Waters; solo

Little Walter's distinctive harmonica playing featured on a host of classic Muddy Waters Chess recordings, including *(I'm Your) Hoochie Coochie Man*. He pioneered the electric harmonica and influenced a generation of 1960s harmonica players with his solo recordings such as Willie Dixon's *My Babe* and the self-penned *Juke*.

Event today

1964 The Moody Blues road to their first gig

The Moody Blues played their debut gig at Erdington's Carlton Ballroom in Birmingham.

The lineup had only recently come together from some of Birmingham's most respected groups. Guitarist and vocalist Denny Laine had recently left his own band Denny Laine and the Diplomats. Vocalist, flautist and harmonica player Ray Thomas, and keyboardist and vocalist Mike Pinder hailed from the Krew Cats, which they joined after the demise of El Riot and the Rebels. Drummer Graeme Edge had been with Gerry Levene and the Avengers, and bassist and singer Clint Warwick was from Danny King and the Dukes.

This lineup recorded the first album, *The Magnificent Moodies* and their first hit single *Go Now!*, a cover of Bessie Banks's R&B hit. Changes followed in 1966, with Lane leaving to set up Denny Laine's Electric String Band and Warwick quitting the music business to become a carpenter, in order to spend more time with his family.

The group originally planned to use the moniker "The M&B Five". At the time they were hoping to obtain sponsorship from the local M&B Brewery. When this support failed to materialise they stayed with "M" and "B" and became "The Moody Blues".

Recording session today

1967 Beach Boys *Smile*, the greatest 'lost' album of the 1960s

Following this last day of recording, Brian Wilson abandoned his magnum opus *Smile*.

The album was originally planned by Wilson as the follow-up to his 1966 masterpiece *Pet Sounds* but it would be another thirty-eight years before the most famous 'lost' album of the 1960s was released. Wilson's vision for the album was to take the layered musical collage techniques that he had used so successfully on *Good Vibrations* and apply the same concept to this new album. Sadly, ill-health, stress and a mixed reception from some of the other Beach Boys to this departure from their normal output, forced Wilson to abandon the project. This also marked the end of Brian Wilson's creative peak with the Beach Boys.

With the help of his original collaborator, lyricist Van Dyke Parks, the album was finally recorded and released in 2004.

Single released today

1969 Ambrose Slade *Genesis* c/w *Roach Daddy* (UK)

After a change of name from the "'N Betweens", Ambrose Slade released just one album, *Beginnings*, using two band-penned tracks to give them their only single.

Their record label Fontana introduced them to Chas Chandler, who became their new manager. Chandler had previously been the bass player with Newcastle's R&B giants the Animals, before discovering and managing Jimi Hendrix. He shortened their name to Slade and with his guidance they became one of the 1970s biggest glam-rock bands.

Birthday today

1929 Link Wray — early guitar hero and father of the power chord

Link Wray started playing in a group with his two brothers in the 1940s. He was a pioneer of guitar distortion and is credited as the father of the power chord. In 1958 he released his most famous recording, *Rumble*. Despite being an instrumental, it was banned by many radio stations because the title was slang for a gang fight.

Events today

1957 Landmark Movies — *The Tommy Steele Story*

Britain's first rock'n'roll movie, *The Tommy Steele Story*, opened in London. It was based on the life story of Britain's first rock'n'roll superstar, the twenty-year-old Tommy Steele.

With his collaborators Lionel Bart and Mike Pratt, Steele co-wrote the songs that featured in the movie, including *A Handful of Songs*. Pratt later starred as the living half, in the original 1960s British TV series *Randall and Hopkirk (Deceased)*.

When *The Tommy Steele Story* was released in America it was retitled *Rock Around the World* because Tommy Steele's personal fame had not yet spread across the Atlantic. The ten inch format album of the movie soundtrack became the first album by a British artist to top the British album charts.

1958 Alan Freed — "Boston Riot" concert

Alan Freed's *Big Beat* concert tour featured some of the biggest names of the day, including Chuck Berry, Jerry Lee Lewis and Buddy Holly. It caused a riot when it reached Boston, Massachusetts. During the show the houselights were brought up, in an attempt to stop the rowdiness and the kids dancing in the aisles. Freed took to the stage to appeal to the police to turn off the house lights. This was when he was alleged to have said, "It looks like the police in Boston don't want you kids to have fun." The violence continued outside the theatre, resulting in at least one person being stabbed.

As a result of the violence, rock'n'roll concerts in Boston were banned. Freed was charged with inciting a riot but the charges were eventually dropped.

Births and deaths today

1919 Pete Seeger — influential banjo player, folk singer and songwriter

Without Pete Seeger and Woody Guthrie there might not have been a 1960s folk-protest movement with Bob Dylan, Phil Ochs, Joan Baez, et al. Seeger formed the Almanac Singers in the early 1940s, singing songs of inequality and workers' solidarity. He continued this theme of political protest with the Weavers, formed with Lee Hays in the late 1940s. Seeger and the Weavers were both blacklisted as communists. In 1955 he was subpoenaed to appear before the House Un-American Activities Committee and on 26 March* 1957 Seeger was indicted for Contempt of Congress. Many of his songs, such as *Where Have All the Flowers Gone* (inspired by Mikhail Sholokhov's *And Quiet Flows the Don*) and *We Shall Overcome*, became 1960s anthems.

In keeping with his outspoken views the slogan on his banjo read, "This Machine Surrounds Hate and Forces it to Surrender".

1933 James Brown singer: "Godfather of Soul"

Before becoming the "Godfather of Soul", James Brown's rock'n'roll credentials were sufficient for him to be one of artists inducted into the Rock and Roll Hall of Fame in its inaugural membership ceremony in 1986.

1934 Frankie Valli singer: Four Lovers, The Four Seasons

1972 Les Harvey Stone the Crows guitarist, died at the age of twenty-five

Guitarist and Stone the Crows founding member Les Harvey died on stage at the Top Rank in Swansea when he was electrocuted after touching an unearthed microphone.

Events today

1961 Civil Rights Movement CORE *Freedom Riders*

The first *Freedom Riders* set out from Washington DC on two interstate busses. Their objective was to test out the new equality laws banning segregation on transport and in waiting rooms and refreshment areas. CORE (Congress of Racial Equality) organised the event, with thirteen black and white *Freedom Riders* and two black journalists. The black *Freedom Riders* would use the white waiting and dining areas, whilst their white colleagues would avail themselves of the facilities available for black travellers.

The *Riders* encountered considerable violence on the journey. White segregationists and Ku Klux Klan members attacked and beat them, both on and off the busses. Very little protection was forthcoming from the local police forces. Outside Anniston, Alabama one of the busses was set on fire. The beatings intensified when they arrived in Birmingham, Alabama. When the time came to leave Birmingham for Montgomery on 15 May, the bus driver refused to take the *Freedom Riders* any further. The journey was originally planned to end in New Orleans and the *Riders* decided to complete the journey by air.

Undeterred, more *Freedom Riders* stepped up to the mark and despite the violence the rides continued.

1976 The Allman Brothers Band last gig before their acrimonious split

Just before the Allman Brothers Band went their separate ways they gave their final performance in Virginia, at the Roanoke Civic Centre. The lineup at that time was Gregg Allman vocals and keyboards, Dickey Betts guitar and vocals, keyboardist Chuck Leavell, bassist Lamar Williams, with drums and percussion from Butch Trucks and Jaimoe.

When the end came, the parting of the ways was less than amicable. Band relationships had been souring, with Allman and Betts both releasing solo albums. The band's demise followed Allman's testimony against road manager Scooter Herring, made in order to extricate himself from a drugs bust. The others vowed never to work with Allman again.

Three years later the Allman Brothers Band was back on the road, with Greg once again playing alongside Betts, Trucks and Jaimoe.

Recording session today

1956 Gene Vincent *Be-Bop-A-Lula*

Following his recent signing to Capitol Records, Gene Vincent travelled to Owen Bradley's studio in Nashville for his first recording session. The first single, *Woman Love*, was released with his co-written classic, *Be-Bop-A-Lula* as the B-side. It was thanks to radio DJs flipping the record that *Be-Bop-A-Lula* became a rock'n'roll classic.

Birthday today

1937 Dick Dale guitar: "King of the Surf Guitar"

Dick Dale was one of rock'n'roll's pioneering guitarists. He worked with the manufacturer Fender to develop amplification and to optimise the sound of the electric guitar. Dale also had a unique playing style. He played the guitar left handed without restringing it, effectively playing it upside down. A keen surfer, he looked to recreate the sound of the waves, gaining the title of "King of the Surf Guitar".

With his band the Del-Tones he recorded his self-penned classic *Let's Go Trippin'* in 1961. This is often cited as the first surf-rock instrumental.

Events today

5

1964 The Who the classic lineup was in place

The Who met Fontana's A&R man, Chris Parmenter, for their second audition but this time they had replaced drummer Doug Sandom with Keith Moon.

This second audition went well and led to the first single from guitarist Pete Townshend, singer Roger Daltrey, bassist John Entwistle and drummer Keith Moon. The single was *Zoot Suit* c/w *I'm the Face* but by the time it was released they had renamed to "The High Numbers".

Sandom had departed after two years as the group's drummer, following the first audition with Parmenter on 9 April*. A number of drummers were in the frame to replace Sandom, including future Jimi Hendrix Experience sticksman Mitch Mitchell. At the time of this audition ex-Fourmost drummer Brian Redman was still in the running but Keith Moon won the day and was established as the final piece of the Who jigsaw.

1968 Buffalo Springfield final gig

Musical differences finally caused Buffalo Springfield to implode. They played their final gig at Long Beach Arena in Long Beach, California.

Neil Young opted for a solo career, Jim Messina and Richie Furay stayed together and formed Poco, Dewey Martin went on to form a New Buffalo Springfield and Stephen Stills linked up with David Crosby and Graham Nash.

Recording session today

1953 The Spaniels first recording session ...birth of Vee-Jay Records

Doo wop vocal group the Spaniels held their first recording session with the newly formed Vee-Jay Records. *Baby, It's You* and *Bounce* were coupled and released as their first single. This sold well locally but needed to be licensed to Chance for the national release that took it into the R&B charts. Both sides of their debut single were written by the Spaniels. *Baby, It's You* should not be confused with the Williams, David and Bacharach song of the same name, made famous by the Shirelles and the Beatles.

Vee-Jay Records was founded in Gary, Indiana by wife and husband team Vivian Carter and James Bracken, after they heard the Spaniels sing for them in their record store. Vee-Jay became a well-respected independent label, with artists including Jimmy Reed and John Lee Hooker. It also produced rock'n'roll classics such as Gene Chandler's *Duke of Earl*. In 1962 the label started a run of hits after signing the Four Seasons as its first white vocal group.

The Beatles famously signed to Vee-Jay after their British label Parlophone failed to persuade its American sister company, Capitol Records, to release the Fab Four's records in America.

Single released today

1969 The Beatles *Get Back* c/w *Don't Let Me Down* (US)

Birthday today

1948 Bill Ward drums: Mythology, Polka Tulk, Earth, Black Sabbath

Bill Ward played in Mythology, before joining the band that eventually became Black Sabbath. When the various members of the future Black Sabbath came together in 1968, the band was initially called "The Polka Tulk Blues Band", then "Earth".

Event today

1971 Landmark Venues end of the road for both Fillmores

New York's *Village Voice* published a letter from Bill Graham, dated 29 April, informing concert-going rock fans on both coasts that he was closing his Fillmore East in New York and its sister venue the Fillmore West in San Francisco.

The lengthy letter outlined Graham's disillusionment with the industry and his intended withdrawal from concert promotion. He listed seven reasons for his decision to close the Fillmores. In essence, Graham felt that the music world had changed and he no longer wanted to be a part of it. Instead of dealing with musicians, he found that he was now negotiating with corporations and agents more interested in money than music. He also felt that it was becoming increasing difficult to provide bands of the right quality. The top bands were playing much bigger venues and agents often wanted to sell a package, with an inferior second or third band to accompany the main act. Even the audiences seemed less sophisticated to Graham. All in all, he felt that now was the right time to go back to having a personal life.

In the letter he announced that 27 June would be the final day for the Fillmore East. The acts billed for the last three days, 25-27 June, were: The Allman Brothers, J Geils Band and Albert King. The last night also featured guest performances from: Country Joe McDonald, Edgar Winter's White Trash, Mountain and The Beach Boys. The show was broadcast live by radio stations WNEW-FM and WPLJ.

The Fillmore West was set to close with five days of concerts, starting 29 June and finishing with a star studded jam on 4 July. Those final concerts included performances from: Grateful Dead, Santana, Jefferson Airplane, Hot Tuna and Quicksilver Messenger Service. The final night was broadcast live by radio stations KSAN and KSFX.

Single released today

1955 The Platters *Only You (And You Alone)* c/w *Bark, Battle & Boil* (US)

After gaining only limited success at the Federal record label, the Platters moved to Mercury and re-recorded *Only You (And You Alone)*, originally released on Federal.

The Mercury version was a smash hit on both sides of the Atlantic and started a run of hits which lasted into the early 1960s. The Platters were one of the most successful and durable of the doo wop vocal groups, with many of their singles scoring on both the R&B and pop charts. The song was written by the Platters' manager Buck Ram, who wrote and produced many of their hits.

Only You (And You Alone) was originally released by Mercury with a purple label, to denote it as an R&B release. At the time Mercury used different label colours for different genres, Country and Western releases sported a green label. Shortly after this Platters release, Mercury dropped the colour coding and standardised its releases onto black labels.

Album released today

1977 The Jam *In the City* (UK)

British punk rock was reaching the end of its time and morphing into new wave.

The Jam formed in 1972. By the time that they released their debut album, *In the City*, they had settled into the power trio of: guitarist and vocalist Paul Weller, bassist Bruce Foxton and drummer Rick Buckler. Weller wrote most of the material on this album.

Events today

7

1954 Vietnam War Dien Bien Phu ...goodbye France – hello America

Vietnam became a French Colony in the late 19th century. In 1940 France lost control to Japan, after surrendering to Germany in the Second World War. In 1941 the communist revolutionary Ho Chi Minh organised the Viet Minh as a nationalist force to fight the Japanese for Vietnam's independence. After Japan and Germany were defeated in 1945, France tried to re-establish its colonial control of Vietnam. Ho Chi Minh simply saw the French as the new army of occupation and continued his struggle. Thus began nearly a decade of conflict between French troops and the revolutionary forces of the Viet Minh.

This struggle culminated in the final battle at Dien Bien Phu. The Vietnamese attack on the French position started on 13 March. Fierce fighting continued, until the French were forced to surrender on 7 May.

Shortly after Ho Chi Minh's victory, the *Geneva Agreement* divided Vietnam at the 17th Parallel, creating North and South Vietnam as two separate entities.

At the time of Dien Bien Phu, America was bankrolling France's attempt to subdue the forces of Ho Chi Minh. When France withdrew from Vietnam, America stepped up its involvement by sending in military advisers and funding South Vietnam's war against the North. America's motivation was its fear of the "domino effect". This was the belief that if Vietnam fell to communism, then the rest of South-East Asia would surely follow suit.

1953 The Drifters the rocky road to two different "Drifters" groups

Clyde McPhatter, the first in a long line of lead singers, signed to Ahmet Ertegun's Atlantic record label – and The Drifters was born.

McPhatter had just parted company with Billy Ward and His Dominoes. His remit at Atlantic was to recruit a new vocal group. His first attempt was to select a lineup from the Mount Lebanon Gospel Singers. The record company was very disappointed with their first recording session and he found himself going back to the drawing board. McPhatter formed a new lineup with Bill Pinkney, the brothers Andrew and Gerhart Thrasher and Willie Ferbie. They recorded *Money Honey* and the Drifters went on to become one of the most successful vocal groups of all time. McPhatter stayed with the group until he was inducted into the US Army in mid-1954. Bill Pinkney occasionally sang lead vocal but David Baughan was brought in as lead vocalist to replace McPhatter. Baughan's tenure was short-lived and he was soon replaced by Johnny Moore (not the Johnny Moore of the Three Blazers fame). When Uncle Sam called on Moore to do his duty, Bobby Hendricks joined the group as their new lead singer.

On leaving the Drifters, McPhatter sold his share in the group to manager George Treadwell, giving him the rights to the name, "The Drifters". The end of the first era came after a disagreement, when Treadwell fired the whole group following an appearance at Harlem's Apollo theatre on 30 May* 1958. In their place he hired the Crowns vocal group with lead singer Ben E King – and renamed them "The Drifters". The Drifters' history really starts to get complicated now. With the demise of the first Drifters group, Bill Pinkney decided to pull some of the other original members together to form the "Original Drifters". He recruited David Baughan as lead singer along with the Thrasher brothers and began to perform as the "Original Drifters". Meanwhile, the old Crowns group, with lead singer Ben E King, toured as "The Drifters".

The group's name was taken from a type of bird. This was a very popular source of names at the time, with the Ravens, the Penguins and the Crows, to name but three.

Event today

1969 Landmark Movies *Easy Rider*

The counterculture classic *Easy Rider* was premiered at the Cannes Film Festival. Dennis Hopper won the award for the *Best Film from a New Director*.

The story followed the journey of two young men, Peter Fonda and Dennis Hopper, on a motorcycle odyssey in search of America. Their adventure took them from LA to the New Orleans Mardi Gras. The movie featured a young Jack Nicholson as an alcoholic lawyer and gave a fleeting glimpse of Phil Spector as a drug dealer. Fonda, Hopper and Terry Southern wrote the Oscar-nominated screenplay. Small independent studio BBS Productions produced the movie for a budget reputed to be around $400,000. Nicholson was also nominated for an Oscar as *Best Supporting Actor*.

Album released today

1970 The Beatles *Let It Be* (UK)

With the provisional title of "*Get Back*", work started on 2 January* 1969 for this follow-up to *The Beatles* (aka *The White Album*). Paul McCartney envisioned this as an album and a concert, with the process being filmed to provide a movie of the whole thing. By now two of the Fab Four had already released solo albums, *Wonderwall Music* from George Harrison and *Unfinished Music No.1: Two Virgins* by John and Yoko. After a turbulent series of recording sessions, Glyn Johns produced a finished version of the *Get Back* album but the relationships between the group members were deteriorating and it was never released. In the autumn of 1969 a completely different Beatles album, *Abbey Road*, was released. John Lennon and George Harrison had worked with legendary "wall of sound" producer

Phil Spector on Lennon's single *Instant Karma*. He was invited to rework the existing recordings and on 23 March* 1970 he started work to complete the *Get Back* album. Nearly a year and a half after that first session and retitled "*Let It Be*", this Spector produced album became the Beatles swan song.

Births and deaths today

1911 Robert Johnson iconic blues guitarist, singer and songwriter

He was one of the most influential of the original bluesmen. Legend has it that, "at the crossroads", he sold his soul to the devil as the price for becoming a brilliant guitarist.

1940 Rick(y) Nelson singer: 1950s teenage idol

Ricky Nelson came to fame in the mid-1950s in his parents' TV show, *The Adventures of Ozzie and Harriet*. In 1957 he scored a massive American hit with both sides of his first single, *A Teenager's Romance* and a cover of Fats Domino's *I'm Walkin'*. This began a run of hits on both sides of the Atlantic, which lasted until the British Invasion in 1964. He then reinvented himself as a country artist and in 1966 released the acclaimed album *Bright Lights and Country Music*. He went on to form the Stone Canyon Band, which included bassist Randy Meisner in his period between stints in Poco and the Eagles.

1974 Graham Bond British blues band-leader, died at the age of thirty-six

One of the pioneers of the early 1960s British blues boom, Graham Bond died under the wheels of a tube train at London's Finsbury Park underground (metro) station. The coroner recorded an open verdict.

Events today

1964 Chuck Berry opened his first UK tour

Maybellene hit the streets in 1955 but British fans had to wait until the mid-1960s to see Chuck Berry live in concert. He opened his first UK tour at the Astoria in London's Finsbury Park, with support acts The Animals, The Swinging Blue Jeans and Carl Perkins.

1966 The Doors appeared on the scene

The Doors' audition at LA's Whisky a Go Go on Sunset Strip marked the beginning of their rise to fame.

Club owner Elmer Valentine liked them and they were hired as the house band. In the coming months they opened for a host of rock luminaries, including Captain Beefheart, Them and Love. It was at the Whisky that Jac Holzman first saw the Doors and was sufficiently impressed to sign them to his Elektra label on 18 August*.

The Doors came together from two LA groups, Rick & the Ravens, and the Psychedelic Rangers. Jim Morrison joined Ray Manzarek's band Rick & the Ravens, which also included Manzarek's brothers Rick and Jim. At that time John Densmore and Robbie Krieger were with the Psychedelic Rangers. Densmore joined Rick & the Ravens in time to make the demo recording on 2 September* 1965. Shortly after that, Rick and Jim Manczarek left and Densmore's friend Robbie Krieger joined the band. The Doors lineup was then in place.

The band's name was taken from Aldous Huxley's novel *The Doors of Perception*. This in turn had its roots in William Blake's *The Marriage of Heaven and Hell*, "If the doors of perception were cleansed every thing would appear to man as it is, infinite. For man has closed himself up, till he sees all things thro' narrow chinks of his cavern."

1971 Free split for the first time

Disappointed with their achievements since forming in 1968, Free went their separate ways after the final gig of their Australian tour, at Sydney's Randwick Race Course. Free, together with Manfred Mann and local band Pirana, were supporting Deep Purple.

The individual members focussed on solo projects but were reunited as Free and gigging again the following January. They finally called it a day in the summer of 1973.

1974 Bruce Springsteen I have seen "rock'n'roll future"

Bruce Springsteen and the E Street Band opened for Bonnie Raitt at the Harvard Square theatre in Cambridge, Massachusetts.

In the audience that night was rock critic and writer Jon Landau. He wrote up his account of the show for the 22 May edition of Boston's counterculture weekly, *The Real Paper*. His review held one of the most famous rock predictions of all time. He proclaimed that the previous night he had seen "rock'n'roll future" ... and that future was – Bruce Springsteen.

Bruce Springsteen was certainly Jon Landau's future. Shortly after the review, Landau became involved with Springsteen in both management and record production.

Birthdays today

1937	Sonny Curtis	guitarist, songwriter: Crickets, pre and post-Buddy Holly
1944	Richie Furay	guitar and vocals: Buffalo Springfield, Poco
1945	Steve Katz	guitar, vocals: The Blues Project; Blood, Sweat & Tears

Events today

1960 The Beatles failed their audition to back Billy Fury

At this stage our heroes were called "The Silver Beetles", with John, Paul and George on guitar and Stu Sutcliff on bass. London rock impresario Larry Parnes was looking for a backing band for British rock'n'roll star Billy Fury's upcoming British tour. Manager Allan Williams arranged an audition at his Wyvern Social Club in Liverpool. Things started badly. Their current drummer, Tommy Moore, was late and they performed most of their set with Johnny Hutchinson of Cass and the Cassanovas, another popular Liverpool combo. The performance failed to secure the gig with Billy Fury but Parnes used them to back another one of his acts, Johnny Gentle, who was about to embark on a Scottish tour.

Drummer Tommy Moore quit the group at the end of that tour.

1965 Frank Zappa Soul Giants became the Mothers

It was Mother's Day 1965 when the Soul Giants' name was officially changed to "The Mothers"[32]. When they signed to MGM, their new record company found the name a tad risqué and insisted on a change to the more innocuous "Mothers of Invention".

The Soul Giants lineup that became the Mothers was singer Ray Collins, drummer Jimmy Carl Black, bassist Roy Estrada and the recently enlisted guitarist Frank Zappa. The Soul Giants had been a typical bar covers band, with Zappa's arrival they moved on to perform their own (Frank Zappa's) material.

1968 Vietnam War Paris peace talks began

Five years of on-off official peace talks between America and North Vietnam began in Paris, with chief negotiators Xuan Thuy for Hanoi and Averell Harriman for the US.

The first five months of the talks were deadlocked. America insisted that North Vietnamese troops were withdrawn from the South and Hanoi required a complete secession of American bombing campaigns. There were also disagreements about the attendance of the National Liberation Front, the political arm of the Viet Cong. Even the shape of the negotiating table was contentious.

Agreement eluded the negotiators until the *Peace Accords* were signed on 27 January* 1973. Henry Kissinger also conducted clandestine meetings alongside these official peace negotiations. The last Americans left Vietnam on 30 April* 1975, after the invasion by the North resulted in Hanoi's complete control of North and South Vietnam.

Birthdays today

1920 Bert Weedon Britain's first guitar hero

Bert Weedon was a major influence on British skiffle and rock'n'roll guitarists. His book *Play in a Day* inspired a generation of seminal British axmen.

1935 Larry Williams rock'n'roll singer and songwriter

The Beatles covered three of his songs, *Dizzy Miss Lizzy*, *Slow Down* and *Bad Boy*.

1957 Sid Vicious drums: The Banshees; bass: Sex Pistols

Before finding notoriety with the Sex Pistols, Sid Vicious was the drummer with another punk band, Siouxsie and the Banshees. He played with them when they performed at the 100 Club's punk festival on 20 September* 1976. The following February he replaced the original bass player Glen Matlock in the Sex Pistols.

Events today

11

1963 Carter Lewis and the Southerners on BBC Radio's *Saturday Club*

In the UK in 1963 there were no commercial radio stations and very few dedicated pop music programmes on the pre-Radio 1 BBC. The Light Programme was the only channel to play pop and *Saturday Club* was a rare oasis in a desert of Mantovani on *Housewives' Choice* and *Sing Something Simple*. At that time BBC radio was subject to "needle time". This guideline had a limit of only five hours of recorded music, the rest of the output had to be from live performances. This allowed bands such as Carter Lewis and the Southerners to appear on highly prestigious pop and rock radio programmes, without ever having troubled the British charts.

Carter Lewis and the Southerners was formed in 1961 by songwriters John Carter and Ken Lewis. They started out as a close harmony duo, before extending to include a backing band. As "Carter Lewis and the Southerners" they released a handful of singles between 1961 and 1964, with some of their early recordings being engineered by legendary producer Joe Meek. In 1963 The Southerners lineup included pre-Led Zeppelin guitarist Jimmy Page and pre-Pretty Things drummer Viv Prince. This lineup released the single *Your Momma's Out of Town*, written by Mitch Murray.

Carter and Lewis went on to find chart success after reinventing themselves as the Ivy League, releasing their first, self-penned, British hit *Funny How Love Can Be* in early 1965.

1975 Phil Ochs *War Is Over* rally

Phil Ochs gave one of his last live performances at the *War Is Over* rally in New York's Central Park.

The war in Vietnam finally came to an end on 30 April* 1975. The last Americans to leave the country were airlifted by helicopter from the American Embassy rooftop at breakfast time. By lunch, the North Vietnamese Army had taken over Saigon. To mark this historic moment Phil Ochs helped to organise the *War Is Over* rally, with performances from an array of artists, including Joan Baez, Richie Havens, Odetta, Tom Paxton, Patti Smith, Paul Simon and Pete Seeger. The event attracted over 100,000 people.

Ochs and Baez duetted on *There but for Fortune*. It was written by Ochs and released on *New Folks* 2 in 1964; it was also a UK hit for Baez in 1965. Ochs closed with a rendition of his song *The War Is Over*, first released on his 1968 album *Tape from California*.

Single released today

1970 The Beatles *Long and Winding Road c/w For You Blue* (US)

Lifted off the Beatles' final album *Let it Be*, this was the Fab Four's swan song single in America but was not released in Britain.

EP released today

1979 The Clash *The Cost of Living* (UK)

This EP included the song *I Fought the Law*. It was written by Sonny Curtis of the Crickets and first appeared on their 1960 album *In Style with the Crickets*.

The song was also famously covered by the Bobby Fuller Four and a hit for them on both sides of the Atlantic in 1966.

Birthday today

1941 Eric Burdon vocals: The Animals, The New Animals, War; solo

Events today

1963 Bob Dylan censorship on the *Ed Sullivan Show*

The *Ed Sullivan Show* might well have helped to launch the careers of Elvis Presley and the Beatles but this held little sway with the rising star Bob Dylan. He was booked to appear on the prestigious TV show and planned to perform *Talkin' John Birch Paranoid Blues*. At rehearsals the show's producers took exception to the song and told Dylan that he would have to perform something else. Dylan declined to change his song choice and pulled out of the show.

The song satirised the right-wing *John Birch Society* and its tendency to see communist conspiracies around every corner.

1969 Fairport Convention fatal auto accident

On the way home from a gig at Birmingham's Mothers club, Fairport Convention's van crashed on the M1 near Mill Hill. Drummer Martin Lamble and passenger Jeannie Franklyn were killed and bassist Ashley Hutchings was seriously injured. The group had recently completed their third album, *Unhalfbricking*.

Nineteen-year-old Martin Lamble had replaced original drummer Shaun Frater, who only managed to play a single gig with the band. At the end of that Church Hall gig in May 1967, Lamble was hired after he approached the group and told them that he could play better than their existing drummer.

The passenger who died that night was guitarist Richard Thompson's American girlfriend Jeannie Franklyn. She was protest singer Phil Ochs's cousin and a prominent clothes designer, who was also known as "Genie the Tailor". One of the bands that Franklyn designed clothes for was Cream. As a tribute, she was the "Tailor" in the title of ex-Cream bassist Jack Bruce's 1969 solo album, *Songs for a Tailor*.

Single released today

1967 Procol Harum *A Whiter Shade of Pale* c/w *Lime Street Blues* (UK)

This British #1 became the subject of a lawsuit forty years later. The song was originally credited to the group's piano playing vocalist and founding member Gary Brooker and lyricist Keith Reid. In May 2005 Procol Harum's organist, Matthew Fisher, launched a lawsuit claiming that he had co-written the music to the rock classic with Brooker. The action was finally settled in Fisher's favour in 2009. There was also a third contributor to the music. The German composer Johann Sebastian Bach's *Suite No.3 in D Major* was another influence on the music behind Keith Reid's enigmatic lyrics.

In 2009 a BBC chart compiled for radio 2, declared *A Whiter Shade of Pale* to be the "most played song in public places in the past seventy-five years".[106]

Albums released today

1967 Jimi Hendrix Experience *Are You Experienced* (UK)

This debut LP was the first album to be released on the newly founded Track Records.

1972 The Rolling Stones *Exile on Main Street* (US)

The album featured Mick Taylor, with Nicky Hopkins, Ian Stewart and Billy Preston.

Birthday today

1948 Steve Winwood keyboards and vocals: Spencer Davis, Traffic, Blind Faith

Event today

1979 The Who dawn of the Kenny Jones era

The Who played at the Arenes Des Frejus for the second gig of a short four-date French tour. They had already made their debut with new drummer Kenny Jones a couple of weeks earlier, at London's Rainbow Theatre on 2 May.

The Who's original drummer, Keith Moon, died on 7 September* 1978. The group picked up the pieces and began the second phase of their career with Jones, who had been a founding member of the Small Faces and then the Faces.

Recording session today

1960 Johnny Kidd and the Pirates *Shakin' All Over* and *Yes Sir, That's My Baby*

Shortly before this recording session the group's lineup went through some changes. Guitarist Mike West moved on. Johnny Kidd and guitarist Alan Caddy were joined by bassist Brian Gregg and drummer Clem Cattini.

Johnny Kidd was one of the most respected British rock'n'rollers of the 1950s and the self-penned *Shakin All Over* was the height of his success. The B-side, *Yes Sir, That's My Baby*, had already been recorded in the summer of 1959 as a possible follow up to Kidd's first single *Please Don't Touch* but it was this re-recorded version that was coupled with Kidd's most successful A-side.

The Who covered the A-side on their legendary 1970 live album, *Live at Leeds*.

In the summer of 1961 Kidd's backing trio Caddy, Gregg and Cattini, decamped en masse to become Colin Hicks's backing band, The Cabin Boys, for a two month tour of Italy. Colin Hicks was the brother of Britain's first rock'n'roll star Tommy Steele. After their Italian sojourn Cattini and Caddy joined producer Joe Meek, who was in the process of forming the Tornados. Gregg joined the group later, after bassist Heinz left to go solo in early 1963.

Birthdays today

1941 Joe Brown guitar and vocals: The Spacemen, JB and the Bruvvers

Joe Brown was one of the pioneers of British skiffle and rock'n'roll in the 1950s. He was a part of Larry Parnes's stable of artists but unlike the others he did not adopt a new 'emotional' surname such as (Billy) Fury, (Marty) Wilde or (Vince) Eager. Brown joined the Spacemen skiffle group in 1957 as lead guitarist. They became the house band for other Larry Parnes artists, as well as backing visiting Americans such as Gene Vincent. Along the way the band renamed to "Joe Brown and the Bruvvers". When Brown was invited by Jack Good to be a regular on his new *Boy Meets Girl* TV show, the Bruvvers found themselves at a loose end and renamed to "The Echoes".

1941 Ritchie Valens guitar and vocals: Silhouettes; solo

Ritchie Valens's career was short but spectacular. He started as a guitarist with a local group, the Silhouettes. Record label Del-Fi signed him up and released the self-penned *Come on, Let's Go*. His second single, *Donna*, was written for his girlfriend Donna Ludwig-Fox. This was coupled with *La Bamba* and both became American hits. Sadly, before Valens could capitalise on his new-found stardom, he tragically died in the same plane crash that took the lives of Buddy Holly and the Big Bopper on 3 February* 1959.

Event today

1959 Cliff Richard debut movie opened

Britain's biggest rock'n'roll star followed Elvis onto the silver screen, when his first movie, *Serious Charge*, had its premiere in London. Directed by Terence Young, it starred Anthony Quayle and Sarah Churchill but is mostly remembered for providing Cliff Richard with his movie debut.

Serious Charge spawned an eponymous EP, with the tracks: *Living Doll, No Turning Back, Mad About You* and the Drifters instrumental *Chinchilla.* Written by Lionel Bart, *Living Doll* gave Richard his first British #1. It also gave him his first American hit but it would be nearly five years before he achieved his second stateside chart appearance.

Recording session today

1972 Mott the Hoople *All the Young Dudes*

When Mott the Hoople threatened to disband, two days after their Swiss concert on 24 March*, David Bowie proclaimed himself to be a huge fan of the band and persuaded them to stay together. He initially offered them his song *Suffragette City* but that was declined in favour of another one of his songs, *All the Young Dudes.* Bowie produced their version of the song as a single and also their next album, which used the song as its title. This proved to be a turning point for the group's fortunes. *All the Young Dudes* gave the band their first hit, the only one on both sides of the Atlantic. It also marked a change of record labels from Island to CBS.

Up until this point commercial success had eluded the band. Mott the Hoople were phenomenal in live performance but the magic failed to transfer to their recordings. Some bands just do not seem to be able capture their live energy in a recording studio. In the early 1960s Liverpool's Big Three were one of the most popular live acts on the circuit but delivered lacklustre recordings.

Album released today

1971 John Entwistle *Smash Your Head Against the Wall* (UK)

John Entwistle was the Who's bass player and the first one in the band to release a solo album. Percussion was provided by the Who's drummer Keith Moon and Bonzo Dog Doo-Dah Band's Viv Stanshall and Neil Innes. The Who's roadie Dave "Cyrano" Langston featured on lead guitar.

Births and deaths today

1943 Jack Bruce bass: Alexis Korner, Graham Bond, Manfred Mann, Cream

Jack Bruce was one of the most respected bass players of his generation. In his early career he played with all three of the influential seminal British blues bands: Alexis Korner's Blues Incorporated, The Graham Bond Organisation and John Mayall's Bluesbreakers. On his way to immortality with Cream, he featured on Manfred Mann's 1966 hit *Pretty Flamingo.* At the other end of the music spectrum, Bruce can be heard providing the bass lines on Frank Zappa's album *Apostrophe'.*

1976 Keith Relf Yardbirds founding member, died at the age of thirty-three

Keith Relf was the vocalist, guitarist and founding member of both the Yardbirds and Renaissance. He died after being electrocuted by his guitar at home.

Events today

1969 Vietnam War battle for Hill 937 ...*Hamburger Hill*

The ten-day battle for *Hill 937* in the A Shau Valley was halfway through. It became one of battles that hardened American public opinion against the war.

Operation *Apache Snow* started on 10 May and resulted in multiple assaults on *Hill 937*. By the time that the North Vietnamese had been defeated on 20 May, the high profile reporting in America had significantly shifted public opinion. It was already an unpopular war but now there was no longer the stomach for such a high cost in American lives, particularly when the position was abandoned on 5 June.

This marked an end to search-and-destroy tactics, with General Creighton Abrams altering his strategy from "maximum pressure" to "protective reaction" (only fighting when an enemy attack is anticipated). On 19 June President Nixon talked of his strategy in Vietnam, "As far as the orders to General Abrams are concerned, they are very simply this: He is to conduct this war with a minimum of American casualties".[2] On 8 June* Nixon announced that the first troop withdrawals would repatriate 25,000 soldiers.

This bloody battle became known as *Hamburger Hill* and was immortalised in John Irvin's 1987 Hollywood movie.

1970 Frank Zappa orchestral premiere of *200 Motels*

Frank Zappa had been writing away on the road and in hotels for three years, when his efforts finally surfaced as *200 Motels*. It received its premiere at UCLA's Pauley Pavilion, with the Los Angeles Philharmonic Orchestra conducted by Zubin Mehta.

The Mothers of Invention had been disbanded. Zappa needed an electric band for the night's performance so he recruited vocalist Ray Collins, keyboardist Don Preston, sax players Ian Underwood on alto and Motorhead Sherwood on baritone, bassist and vocalist Jeff Simmons, and drummers Billy Mundi and Aynsley Dunbar.

Fans had to wait until late 1971 for the official *200 Motels* movie and album.

Birthdays today

1948 Brian Eno keyboards: Roxy Music; solo; producer

Innovative synthesiser player Brian Eno came to fame as a founding member of Roxy Music, although musical differences with Brian Ferry led to his departure in the summer of 1973. His first project was a collaboration with King Crimson's Robert Fripp on the album *No Pussyfooting*, an early example of ambient music.

1953 Mike Oldfield composer and multi-instrumentalist: Whole World; solo

At the age of fifteen Mike Oldfield formed his first group with his sister Sally, a folk duo called the Sallyangie. This venture generated two singles and an album. In 1969 he joined Kevin Ayres and the Whole World. Solo activities followed, with his 1973 composition *Tubular Bells* catapulting him to international fame.

Tubular Bells was also the catalyst for entrepreneur Richard Branson's global empire. Until then he had been a record dealer but with the album's success, as V2001 on his newly formed Virgin label, Branson was on his way to becoming one of the most high profile businessmen in the world. The album was released on 25 May* 1973.

In 1974 Oldfield won a Best Instrumental Composition Grammy award, as composer for *Tubular Bells – Theme from the Exorcist.*

16

Events today

1957 Buddy Holly and the Crickets the Coral/Brunswick thing (in America)

Norman Petty, who had recorded *That'll Be the Day* at his Clovis Studios in New Mexico on 25 February*, was now the manager of both Buddy Holly and The Crickets. On 19 March Petty arranged for the Crickets to sign with Coral Records, a subsidiary of Decca Records. The Crickets recordings were released on the Brunswick label.

Holly had previously been signed to Decca but was dropped after the lack of interest in his first single, *Blue Days - Black Nights*. As a result, he was prohibited from recording any songs that he had previously cut for Decca. The first single Holly and the Crickets released together was the Allison and Holly penned *That'll Be the Day*, a song which he had already recorded during his short signing to Decca. In order to avoid potential problems with Decca, it was credited to "The Crickets" and released on Brunswick.

On 16 May Petty arranged for Holly to sign a separate contract. This was also with Coral Records but his recordings would be released on the Coral label. In America, despite the fact that all of the recordings were made by both Holly and the Crickets, some were released on Coral as "Buddy Holly" and others on Brunswick as "The Crickets".

In Britain the songs were all released on the Coral label.

1970 Cactus debut gig

When Vanilla Fudge folded, the rhythm section of drummer Carmine Appice and bassist Tim Bogert formed Cactus. Their first concert performance was at Philadelphia's Temple Stadium, with The Steve Miller Band, Grateful Dead and headliner Jimi Hendrix.

The Jeff Beck Group was history at that time and Bogert and Appice had intended to hook up with Beck. But fate intervened. Jeff Beck was out of action following an automobile accident. As a result, Bogert and Appice formed Cactus and Beck put a new lineup of the Jeff Beck Group together, which included drummer Cozy Powell.

After the demise of both bands in mid-1972, the three musicians finally came together as Beck, Bogert & Appice.

Recording session today

1966 Jeff Beck *Beck's Bolero*

Still a Yardbird, Jeff Beck went into London's IBC Studios and recorded his rock interpretation of Ravel's *Bolero*. He called it *Beck's Bolero*, although the writing credit went to guitarist Jimmy Page. He was ably assisted by fellow Yardbird Page, the Who's drummer Keith Moon, future Led Zeppelin bassist John Paul Jones and keyboardist Nicky Hopkins. When Jeff Beck left the Yardbirds in late 1966 to launch his solo career, the track was issued as the B-side of *Hi Ho Silver Lining*.

Albums released today

1966 The Beach Boys *Pet Sounds* (US)

Pet Sounds is often referred to as a major inspiration for the Beatles' *Sgt Pepper*. The album featured Wrecking Crew drummer Hal Blaine and saxophonist Steve Douglas.

1966 Bob Dylan *Blonde on Blonde* (US)

Birthday today

1946 Robert Fripp guitarist, composer and producer: King Crimson; solo

Events today

1954 Civil Rights Movement integration in public schools

Since the late 19th century the *Jim Crow* laws had maintained a "separate but equal" segregation of white and black Americans.

The first change to this philosophy came in education. The landmark judgment by the US Supreme Court in the case of *Brown v Board of Education*, marked a change from the policy of segregation and paved the way for integration and the coming of the modern Civil Rights Movement. The decision to end segregation meant that previous rulings were overturned and it was declared that separate public schools for black and white students deprived black students of an equal opportunity for education.

This ruling did not end segregation in other areas nor was the road to an integrated education a smooth one. However, it was a giant step in the direction of equal rights for black Americans and marked the beginning of the modern Civil Rights Movement.

1958 Jerry Lee Lewis peak of his success

Ferriday, Louisiana celebrated its most famous citizen with the *Jerry Lee Lewis Day*. The town held a parade in the afternoon, with a concert in the High School that evening.

This marked the high point of Lee's success. Less than a week later, on 22 May*, he arrived in London for his British tour, where news of the marriage to his cousin's thirteen-year-old daughter emerged and brought his career crashing down around him.

1964 Bob Dylan first formal concert in the UK

Bob Dylan gave his first formal British concert at London's Royal Festival Hall. John Lennon sent a note to Dylan requesting a meeting but that never materialised. The Beatles did famously meet Dylan three months later on 28 August*.

This was not technically his British debut, on 13 January* 1963 he had appeared in the BBC Radio play *The Madhouse on Castle Street*. During that brief stay in London he also made the occasional impromptu appearance at a London folk club or two.

Album recorded live today

1966 Bob Dylan (Not-quite-the) *Royal Albert Hall 1966*

One of the most famous concert bootleg albums of all time, Bob Dylan's *Royal Albert Hall 1966*, turned out to have been recorded at Manchester's Free Trade Hall a week earlier! Both concerts were recorded by Columbia but the bootleggers following the tour mistakenly accredited this gig to the Royal Albert Hall in London.

Dylan's historic 1966 tour marked his move to working with an electric band and was greeted with a mixed reception from his fans. This recording was famous for the heckling Dylan received for moving away from his acoustic folk roots. The album culminated in a particularly vitriolic exchange at the end of *Ballad of a Thin Man*, when someone in the audience shouted out, "Judas!" and Dylan replied, "I don't believe you. You're a liar!" He then turned to the band and could be heard to say, "play fucking loud" as they went into a blistering version of *Like a Rolling Stone*.

With the exception of drummer Mickey Jones, his backing group the Hawks became the Band.

Birthday today

1949 Bill Bruford drums: Yes, King Crimson, Genesis

Event today

1975 Hawkwind end of the road for Lemmy

Hawkwind were halfway through the North American leg of their *Warrior on the Edge of Time* tour, when they played Toronto's Convocation Hall in Canada. This gig proved to be the end of the road for bass guitarist and singer Lemmy.

The tour took the band over the border from America into Canada. During the crossing Lemmy was stopped for carrying drugs, believed to be cocaine. When they were tested it transpired that the substance was amphetamine, a much less serious offence in Canada. There was good news and bad news for Lemmy. On the upside, the Canadian authorities took no further action but the band sacked him mid-tour and he found himself on a plane back to Blighty. Maybe that was not such bad news for him after all, before long he had formed his own band Motörhead.

Recording sessions today

1959 The Crickets *I Fought the Law*

I Fought the Law was one of the first songs to be recorded by the Crickets after Buddy Holly's death in a plane crash on 3 February*. Buddy Holly and the Crickets had parted company before the tragedy and he was accompanied by other musicians, including country star Waylon Jennings, on that fateful *Winter Dance Party* tour of America's cold and snowy mid-West.

By the time of this recording session, the Crickets were lead guitarist Sonny Curtis, who also wrote *I Fought the Law*, bassist Joe Mauldin, drummer Jerry Allison, and rhythm guitarist and singer Earl Sinks. The song was first released on the album *In Style with the Crickets*. In Britain it was released as a single, coupled with another track from the album, *A Sweet Love* but it failed to chart.

Bobby Fuller recorded the song in 1964 and then again as the Bobby Fuller Four, generating an international hit in 1966. British punk-rockers the Clash also included the song on the American version of their eponymous debut album, released in 1979.

1964 The Animals *House of the Rising Sun*

This was a traditional folk-blues song but despite Hilton Valentine's haunting guitar work, the songwriting credit on the single was only for Alan Price, "Trad. Arr. A. Price". Produced by Mickie Most, it was the first British Invasion single not associated with the Beatles to make the American #1 spot.

Nearly a quarter of a century earlier, on 7 July* 1941, the song was recorded by the Almanac Singers, with a lineup that included Pete Seeger and Woody Guthrie.

Album released today

1970 The Beatles *Let It Be* (US)

In Britain the album was originally released in a deluxe package with a glossy book.

Birthday today

1949 Rick Wakeman keyboards: Spinning Wheel, Strawbs, Yes; session; solo

Flamboyant keyboard player Rick Wakeman studied at London's Royal College of Music in 1968. He left in 1969 and started session work, which included David Bowie's *Space Oddity*. After a spell with the Strawbs he joined Yes in mid-1971, before launching his solo career in 1973 with *The Six Wives Of Henry VIII*.

Events today

1962 Brian Poole and the Tremeloes beat the Beatles to a debut single

Having secured their recording deal with Decca, Brian Poole and the Tremeloes promoted their debut single, *Twist Little Sister*, on TV's *Thank Your Lucky Stars*.

Brain Poole and the Tremeloes were chosen over the Beatles when they both auditioned at Decca on 1 January*. The soon-to-be Fab Four were still three weeks away from securing their own record contract, with their first visit to EMI's recording studios on 6 June*. It might have taken the Beatles six months longer to secure a recording deal but they hit the singles charts in October with their first single *Love Me Do*. It was not until Poole and his London-based chums' fifth attempt, with their cover of the Top Notes' *Twist and Shout*, that they secured their first British hit single in July 1963.

1966 Grateful Dead probably the most bootlegged band in history

The Grateful Dead played at San Francisco's Avalon Ballroom. Naturally, the performance was illegally recorded and became available as a bootleg.

There are very few artists in the music industry who advocate the illicit recording of live performances. The Grateful Dead are a rare exception. Not only did the band invite the audience to capture the moment, they sometimes had special areas where Deadheads could gather to record the concert. This approach has meant that the Grateful Dead are probably the most recorded band of all time.

Single released today

1969 Alice Cooper *Reflected* c/w *Living* (US)

When this debut single was released, "Alice Cooper" referred to the name of the band not just the lead singer. Both songs were credited to Alice Cooper for writing and production.

Frank Zappa had recently created his own record label Straight and *Reflected* was Straight's first single.

Alice Cooper's first album *Pretties for You* was Straight's debut album release.

Birthdays today

1938 Herbie Flowers bass: Blue Mink, Sky; sessions

Respected session musician Herbie Flowers has played with rock royalty such as Lou Reed, Elton John, Marc Bolan and David Bowie. At the end of the 1960s he co-founded Blue Mink and a decade later formed Sky with classical guitarist John Williams. At the two ends of the music spectrum, he wrote Clive Dunn's novelty hit *Grandad* (with Kenny Pickett) and provided the signature bass riff on Lou Reed's *Walk on the Wild Side.*

1945 Pete Townshend guitarist, singer, songwriter: The Detours, The Who; solo

1951 Joey Ramone drums and vocals: Ramones

The band formed as a trio with Joey, Johnny and Dee Dee Ramone, in this lineup Joey played drums. He switched to lead singer when their manager, Tom Erdelyi, became Tommy Ramone and took over as sticksman.

Each member of the Ramones took the band's name as a surname. This was inspired by an early Beatles decision to adopt stage names, when Paul McCartney became "Paul Ramon", John Lennon "Long John" and George Harrison "Carl Harrison".

Events today

20

1966 The Who Keith Moon and John Entwistle quit

Drummer Keith Moon and bass player John Entwistle arrived late for the Who's gig at Newbury's *Ricky Tick Club*, having stayed a little longer than planned at a *Ready Steady Go!* party. By the time that the errant pair arrived at the gig, singer Roger Daltrey and guitarist Pete Townshend had already started the set using the support band's rhythm section. Feelings ran high and an on stage altercation took place during the equipment smashing *My Generation* finale, leaving Moon with a black eye and injured leg. Moon and Entwistle quit the band that night.

Entwistle returned to the fold shortly afterwards but Moon was absent for all of the following week's gigs. His place was filled by a local drummer each night. When he did return, it was with his new Premier double bass drum kit.

1970 The Beatles THE END

The Beatles' last movie, apply titled *Let It Be*, premiered simultaneously in London and their home-town Liverpool. None of the Beatles showed up to see it.

The group split up acrimoniously with Paul McCartney in splendid isolation. The end was triggered by worldwide press headlines on 10 April* proclaiming that, "Paul Is Quitting The Beatles". Relationships within the band had been deteriorating for a while, with all three of the other Beatles having previously walked out. Ringo took flight back in August 1968, George left during the *Get Back* sessions in January 1969 and John had announced to the others in September that he was quitting.

Recording session today

1958 Phil Spector *Don't You Worry My Little Pet*

Phil Spector was in Gold Star studios in Los Angeles to record his first song, *Don't You Worry My Little Pet*. Spector wrote, produced and performed on the recording, along with his three friends, Annette Kleinbard (later Carol Connors), Marshall Leib and Harvey Goldstein. This was three years before the dawn of his "wall of sound" and the first Philles release in 1961, the Crystals' *There's No Other (Like My Baby)*, co-written with Leroy Bates.

When they returned to the studio to record the B-side, they were minus Harvey Goldstein and called themselves "The Teddy Bears". They originally planned to record the Spector penned *Wonderful Lovable You* as the B-side but instead opted for *To Know Him, Is to Love Him*. DJs flipped the songs and *To Know Him, Is to Love Him* gave Spector his first hit record. *Wonderful Lovable You* became the Teddy Bears second release on Dore.

Births and deaths today

1944 Joe Cocker — singer: Joe Cocker's Big Blues, Grease Band; solo

In the early days Jo Cocker also used the moniker "Vance Arnold", in Vance Arnold and the Avengers. His Grease Band featured guitarist Henry McCullough, who left in 1972 to join Paul McCartney's Wings.

1964 Rudy Lewis — Drifters' lead singer, died at the age of twenty-seven

Rudy Lewis died at his home on the evening before he was due in the studio with his fellow Drifters to record *Under the Boardwalk*. Sources differ as to the cause of his death. Lewis had replaced Ben E King as lead singer in 1960.

Recording sessions today

1955 Chuck Berry — *Maybellene*

When Chuck Berry travelled to Chicago he was introduced to Chess Records by the great bluesman Muddy Waters. At his first recording session for Chess he recorded *Maybellene*, a new title given to his reworking of an old Bob Wills country song, *Ida Red*.

When the single was released the songwriting credit went to Chuck Berry and DJs Alan Freed and Russ Fratto.

1964 The Drifters — *Under the Boardwalk*

Drifters' lead singer Rudy Lewis died at his home on the evening before the recording session for *Under the Boardwalk*, scheduled with producer Bert Berns.

At the time the Drifters had two lead vocalists, Rudy Lewis and Johnny Moore. They shared lead vocals and *Boardwalk* was slated for Lewis but with his untimely demise Moore stepped into the breach and provided the lead on this Drifters classic.

Single released today

1964 The Beatles — *Sie Liebt Dich* c/w *I'll Get You* (US)

The German language version of *She Loves You* was recorded at EMI Pathé Marconi studio in Paris on 29 January 1964. This coupling was the second single on the Swan label but was never released in Britain.

Album released today

1960 Billy Fury *The Sound of Fury* (UK)

Billy Fury's debut album, released on a 10 inch format, is often hailed as the best British rock'n'roll album of the time. Fury wrote all of the songs on the album. The backing musicians included another British skiffle and rock'n'roll pioneer Joe Brown on guitar, along with session drummer Andy White.

White stood in for Ringo Starr at the Beatles' third EMI studio session on 11 September* 1962. His version *of Love Me Do* is the one with the tambourine, played by Ringo.

Birthdays today

1926 Albert Grossman artist manager and record label owner

Grossman managed Bob Dylan and Janis Joplin. He also founded Bearsville Records.

1940 Tony Sheridan guitar and vocals: Vince Taylor, TS and the Jets

Before finding rock immortality by having the Beatles as his backing band in Hamburg in the early 1960s, Tony Sheridan was a member of seminal British rockers Vince Taylor and the Playboys. The Playboys also featured two future Shadows, Brian Bennett and Brian "Licorice" Locking. He was also one of only two people to share a record label credit with the Beatles. The other recording credit went to Billy Preston on *Get Back*.

1943 John Dalton bass: Mark Four, The Kinks

John Dalton replaced original Kinks bassist Pete Quaife. He joined from the Mark Four in 1966 but became a permanent member of the band in 1969.

Events today

1958 Jerry Lee Lewis career-ending British tour

At the height of his success as a rock'n'roll performer, Jerry Lee Lewis arrived in London for the beginning of his first British tour. He was supported by The Treniers and The Hedley Ward Trio.

Myra Gale was identified as Lewis's child bride when responding to a reporter's question about her age. Lewis told the British press that she was fifteen. It soon transpired that Myra Gale was only thirteen years old and the daughter of his bass-playing cousin, JW Brown. His relationship might well have been legal in Louisiana but Lewis soon discovered that in the eyes of his British fans it was totally unacceptable. He played just three poorly received concerts before pulling out of the tour and returning to America. The tour continued with British skiffle legend Chas McDevitt brought in as Lewis's replacement.

As a result of the scandal American audiences also deserted Lewis in their droves and his record sales plummeted. His rock'n'roll career never recovered, despite previously being a real contender for Elvis Presley's title of the "King of Rock'n'Roll".

He left Sun records in 1963 and moved to Mercury's subsidiary label Smash. Reinventing himself as a country artist, Lewis began a string of American country hits in the late 1960s and continued with his new found success into the early 1980s.

1972 Creedence Clearwater Revival end of the road

In support of what would prove to be their final album *Mardi Gras*, Creedence Clearwater Revival embarked on their American tour in mid-April. It concluded in Denver, Colorado with their swan song performance at the Denver Coliseum.

Tom Fogerty had already left the band in 1971 to pursue a solo career. Both the *Mardi Gras* album and tour were poorly received and the band decided to call it a day.

John Fogerty formed the high school band the Blue Velvets in the late 1950s and was later joined by his older brother Tom. In 1964 the band was signed by Fantasy, who changed their name to "The Golliwogs" in order to sound more English and compete with the British Invasion bands. They continued to evolve and in 1967 they rebranded again, this time to "Creedence Clearwater Revival".

After thirteen years and several name changes, Creedence Clearwater Revival and their record label Fantasy announced on the 16 October that the band was splitting up.

1977 Blondie and Television American new wave arrived in Britain

For their second gig of a short tour of the UK, Blondie supported Television at Glasgow's Apollo.

Founded by guitarist and singer Tom Verlaine, and bassist and singer Richard Hell, the band started out as the Neon Boys. By late 1973 they had become Television and were one of the leading lights on New York's new wave scene. By the time that Television reached the UK for this tour, Richard Hell had already moved on to pastures green.

In the summer of 1974, singer Debbie Harry formed Blondie out of her previous group the Stillettos. They also became firm favourites of the New York community and were regular performers at CBGB.

Recording sessions today

1955 Smiley Lewis *I Hear You Knocking*

Written by Dave Bartholomew, *I Hear You Knocking* was an answer song to the 1920s blues classic *Keep a Knockin' an You Can't Get In*. The session musicians that day included Huey "Piano" Smith.

The original version of *Keep a Knockin' an You Can't Get In* was recorded on Paramount in 1928 by James "Boodle It" Wiggins, accompanied by Bob Call on piano. It became a blues standard, attracting a cover from Louis Jordan in 1939. Little Richard released his classic rock'n'roll cover as *Keep a Knockin'* in 1957, taking the songwriting credit for himself.

1967 Pink Floyd *See Emily Play*

This second Floyd single was written by Syd Barrett and produced by ex-Beatles engineer Norman Smith, who also achieved his own chart success as Hurricane Smith.

Album released today

1969 The Who *Tommy* (UK)

The Who's *Tommy* is often cited as the first rock opera but the Pretty Things' *SF Sorrow* was released in Britain six months before Townshend's magnum opus.

In the autumn of 1967 the art director for the British counterculture periodical *International Times*, Mike McInnerney, introduced the Who's guitarist and principle songwriter Pete Townshend to the works of the Indian Avatar, Meher Baba. Townshend became a keen follower of Baba and *Tommy* was inspired by his teachings. On 10 July 1925 Meher Baba took a vow of silence, which he maintained until his death in 1969.

Seeds for *Tommy* can also be found in the song *Glow Girl*, written after the traumatic plane journey to Chattanooga on 14 August* 1967 but it was not released until the *Odds and Sods* album in 1974. The song finished with a line that tells Mrs Walker that, "It's a girl", whereas, *Tommy*'s Mrs Walker had a boy.

The distinctive album sleeve was designed by Mike McInnerney.

Birthday today

1918 Bumps Blackwell producer, songwriter and arranger

Bumps Blackwell was one of the pivotal non-performing figures of the early days of rock'n'roll. As house-producer with Speciality records, he was responsible for Little Richard's debut single *Tutti-Frutti*, recorded on 14 September* 1955. As well as producing many of Little Richard's hits, he also co-wrote a number of his songs, including the classics *Good Golly, Miss Molly* and *Long Tall Sally*. The idea for *Long Tall Sally* was brought to Blackwell by Enortis Johnson, with her tale of Aunt Mary and the philandering Uncle John. Blackwell and Richard deliberately set the song to a frenetic pace in an attempt to discourage yet another cover version from Pat Boone. Far from discouraged, Boone took the song into the Top 20 on both sides of the Atlantic.

Blackwell was also a major influence on Sam Cooke. The relationship started when Cooke was lead singer with the Soul Stirrers. The gospel group was also on the Speciality label and produced by Blackwell. He could see Cooke's potential beyond the gospel marketplace and in 1957 they both moved to Keen to launch Cooke's solo career, with *You Send Me* as his first solo hit.

Event today

1964 The Dave Clark Five led the British Invasion ashore

The Dave Clark Five arrived in America to begin the first tour by a British beat group, in what would become known as the "British Invasion". They opened in Newark, New York at the Mosque Theatre the following night.

The Beatles had played their first American concert at the Washington Coliseum on 11 February* but it would be another three months before they began their first American tour on 19 August*.

Singles released today

1967 John's Children *Desdemona c/w Remember Thomas A-Beckett* (UK)

The third single from John's Children, *Desdemona*, was the first to feature guitarist Marc Bolan, who also wrote the song.

This was the first single by John's Children on the fledgling Track Records label, following in the illustrious footsteps of Tracks' first two releases, *Purple Haze* by the Jimi Hendrix Experience and *Pictures of Lily* from the Who.

1968 The Rolling Stones *Jumping Jack Flash c/w Child of the Moon* (UK)

This was the first of a run of singles produced by Jimmy Miller. The previous singles had mostly been produced by the Stones' manager Andrew Loog Oldham.

Album released today

1968 Small Faces *Ogdens' Nut Gone Flake* (UK)

The album featured spoken links from Stanley Unwin, made in Unwin's own unique language. The original releases came in an ornate fold-out round sleeve.

Birthdays today

1941 Bob Dylan iconic singer and songwriter

At an early age Bob Dylan's family moved from his birthplace in Duluth to Hibbing, Minnesota. He taught himself to play the piano, harmonica and guitar and performed with a number of high school bands. In the 1959 Hibbing High School graduation *Yearbook* he famously gave his teenage ambition as "to join Little Richard". By the time that he arrived in Minneapolis to enrol at the University of Minnesota he was calling himself "Bob Dylan". During this time he began performing as a folk singer in the local coffee houses and became very interested in folk legend Woody Guthrie. Dylan arrived in New York in January 1961 and quickly established a reputation amongst the folkies in the Greenwich Village coffee houses. His first major appearance came on 4 November* 1961, on one of the smaller stages at Carnegie Hall.

1947 Cynthia Plaster Caster groupie

The *Plaster Casters of Chicago* were groupies who were infamous for taking plaster casts of rock stars' intimate protuberances. Jimi Hendrix was famously sampled on 25 February* 1968. At the time of writing, his cast was available, in an edition of 30, for $2,000.[3]

In 2011 Caster stood for public office as the Mayor of Chicago. At the time the post was held by Richard M Daley, son of the notorious 1960s Mayor of Chicago, Richard J Daley.

Cynthia and her companions were immortalised by Kiss in their song *Plaster Casters*, written by Gene Simmons and included on their 1977 album *Love Gun*.

Events today

1960 Landmark Concerts first "Beat Night" at the Cavern

The opening set on the first "Beat Night" at Liverpool's Cavern Club was performed by Rory Storm and the Hurricanes, featuring future Beatles drummer Ringo Starr. The Beatles debuted there on 9 February* 1961 with Pete Best on drums.

When Alan Sytner opened the Cavern Club's doors on 16 January* 1957 it was firmly rooted as a jazz club, with just a nodding acquaintance to the skiffle boom. In 1959 when Ray McFall took the helm it was still a jazz club but the growing interest in rock'n'roll meant that he was forced commercially to introduce the new beat bands to the Cavern's stage.

1978 The Who Keith Moon's final performance

The Who's final concert performance with drummer Keith Moon had been nearly two years earlier, in Canada on 21 October* 1976. Although, Moon did perform with the Who again, twice. Both appearances were for closed audiences during the filming of the movie *The Kids Are Alright*. The first time was on 15 December 1977 at the Kilburn State Theatre in north London. This final outing with the Who came six months later when more concert footage was required and he gave his swan song performance before another invited audience at Shepperton Studios.

Sadly, Keith Moon died shortly afterwards on 7 September* 1978.

Recording session today

1966 Elvis Presley first non-movie recording session in four years

Elvis entered RCA's Nashville studio for the first time since his 1962 album *Pot Luck*. In a change to his usual visits, this one was to record material that was not destined for a movie soundtrack album. This was the first of four days of recording, where the bulk of the output was for his album of religious recordings, *How Great Thou Art*. He was backed by his old stalwarts, guitarist Scotty Moore, drummer DJ Fontana, keyboard player Floyd Cramer and saxophonist Boots Randle. His regular vocal backing group the Jordanaires was augmented by the Imperials. Elvis was particularly looking forward to working with his hero, gospel singer Jake Hess, who had formed the Imperials in 1963.

Soon after Elvis's post-Army film career began, his manager Colonel Parker took the decision to only release singles, EPs and albums of songs taken from his movies. Songs not actually featured in the film were sometimes added to the soundtrack albums as bonus songs.

Album released today

1973 Mike Oldfield *Tubular Bells* (UK)

Richard Branson's recently formed Virgin record label used Mike Oldfield's *Tubular Bells* as its inaugural album release. It was a huge success and marked the beginning of Branson's Virgin empire, which went on to encompass businesses internationally in industries as diverse as trains, planes, finance and radio stations.

Bonzo Dog's Viv Stanshall took the part of Master of Ceremonies on the album.

Birthday today

1958 Paul Weller guitar, vocals and songwriter: The Jam; solo

Event today

1994 Eagles Hell froze over

The Eagles had re-formed and were poised to perform their first concert in nearly fourteen years.

When they parted company in 1980, not exactly as the best of friends, they famously said that they would not play together again until, "Hell freezes over". Well, the ice age came on 27 May when Glen Frey, Don Henley, Don Felder, Joe Walsh and Timothy B Schmit opened their tour at Irvine Meadows Amphitheater in Laguna Hills, California.

The *Hell Freezes Over* tour rolled on around the world, finishing up in Scotland in the summer of 1996. The Eagles set a new record for being the first rock'n'roll act to charge more than $100[83] for a ticket.

Births and deaths today

1916 Moondog New York street performer

A blind, avant-garde composer, musician and poet, Moondog made his home on the streets of New York in the mid-1940s. Resplendent in a Viking cape and helmet, and brandishing a spear, he performed at the corner of 54th Street and Sixth Avenue. He entertained the passers-by there until the mid-1970s, when he left to make his home in Germany.

The name "Moondog"[57] came from a pet dog and a fond childhood memory of when they used to howl at the moon together.

Legendary American disc jockey Alan Freed, the man who coined the phrase rock'n'roll, started his radio career by referring to himself as "Moondog". The New York street performer took a dim view of having his named purloined by a rock'n'roll DJ and successfully sued Freed in the early 1950s, forcing him to drop the use of the name.

1940 Levon Helm drums, mandolin and vocals: The Hawks, The Band

The only non-Canadian member of the Band, Levon Helm was born in Elaine, Arkansas. After splitting from rockabilly star Ronnie Hawkins, the Hawks backed Bob Dylan on his groundbreaking electric tour of 1965/1966. Dylan's move to electric folk led to a mixed reaction from audiences and attracted jeers at many of his concerts. Helm was unhappy about this reception and pulled out of the tour. He was replaced by Mickey Jones. Helm rejoined the band for the legendary *Big Pink* recordings. These resulted in their debut album *Music from the Big Pink,* and Dylan's *Basement Tapes* released on 26 June* 1975.

1946 Mick Ronson guitar: David Bowie, Mott the Hoople, Hunter-Ronson

1968 Little Willie John R&B singer, died at the age of thirty

R&B singer Little Willie John died in Washington State Penitentiary. He had been convicted of manslaughter two years earlier after knifing a man during a fight in Seattle. The exact circumstances of John's death are the subject of much speculation. Pneumonia and heart attack have been cited officially but some suspected foul play.

John had a string of R&B hits in the mid-1950s and into the early 1960s. These included the crossover hit *Fever* in 1956, which was also an international hit for Peggy Lee in 1958. The Beatles recorded John's 1959 R&B hit *Leave My Kitten Alone,* for inclusion on their 1964 album *Beatles for Sale.* The song never made the album and gathered dust in EMI's vaults until its release thirty years later on *Anthology 1.* In 1968 James Brown released his tribute album, *Thinking about Little Willie John and a Few Nice Things.*

Event today

1964 Screaming Lord Sutch launched his own pirate radio station

Britain's first pirate radio station, Radio Caroline, took to the airwaves on 29 March*. Flamboyant British rock'n'roll singer Screaming Lord Sutch followed hot on the heels of this new phenomenon, with the launch of his own radio station, Radio Sutch.

After sailing around in the fishing trawler *Cornucopia,* emblazoned with the banner Radio Sutch, he took over the disused *Shivering Sands* army fort in the Thames Estuary as his base for this new venture. Listeners to the new station were treated to Sutch's own, Joe Meek produced, *Jack the Ripper* as the opening song to herald the short era of Radio Sutch, billed as "Britains [sic] First Teenage Radio Station".

By September Sutch had grown tired of radio ownership and sold it to his manager and co-founder Reg Calvert, who changed its name to "Radio City". Two years later, on 21 June*, Calvert was shot dead by a rival pirate radio operator.

Singles released today

1957 The Crickets *That'll Be the Day* c/w *I'm Looking for Someone to Love* (US)

This was Buddy Holly and the Crickets' debut single. Buddy Holly signed a solo contract with Coral on 16 May*, thereafter for contractual reasons, Buddy Holly and the Crickets recordings were released either as "Buddy Holly" on Coral or "The Crickets" on Brunswick.

1963 The Beatles *From Me to You* c/w *Thank You Girl* (US)

From Me to You gave the Beatles their first British #1 but this Vee-Jay release did little to trouble the American charts.

On 18 April* Del Shannon was appearing with the Beatles in London when he heard them perform *From Me to You*. He liked the song, recorded it, and gave Lennon and McCartney their first, albeit minor, hit in America.

1977 Sex Pistols *God Save the Queen* c/w *Did You No Wrong* (UK)

After their short stay at EMI, signing up on 8 October*, the Sex Pistols spent two weeks at A&M, where they originally recorded the self-penned *God Save The Queen*. In mid-May they found their final recording home at Virgin and released *God Save the Queen* as their debut single there. It was their homage to Queen Elizabeth's Silver Jubilee.

Album released today

1963 Bob Dylan *The Freewheelin' Bob Dylan* (US)

The Freewheelin' Bob Dylan's original track listing generated one of the most sought after albums ever released. Four tracks, *Rocks and Gravel, Let Me Die in My Footsteps, Ramblin', Gamblin' Willie* and *Talkin' John Birch Society Blues*, were replaced on the second version of the album by: *Girl of the North Country, Masters of War, Bob Dylan's Dream* and *Talking World War III Blues*.

This second album from Dylan contained the track *Blowin' in the Wind*, an early anthem for the age of 1960s protest songs.

Birthday today

1957 Siouxsie Sioux singer: Siouxsie and the Banshees

An early lineup of the Banshees featured drummer Sid Vicious, before he switched to bass and replaced Glen Matlock in the Sex Pistols in early 1977.

Events today

1965 Elvis Presley *Tickle Me* ...Elvis's recycled movie soundtrack

Elvis Presley's eighteenth movie, *Tickle Me*, received its premiere in Atlanta, Georgia.

When Elvis made *Tickle Me* for Allied Artists, the studio was experiencing financial difficulties. One of the cost cutting actions taken was to use songs already released, rather than to pay for musicians and songwriters to deliver a custom made movie soundtrack. Of the nine songs used for the movie: four had previously appeared on the 1962 album *Pot Luck with Elvis*; two were taken from *Elvis is Back!* released in 1960; and a song was lifted from 1961's *Something for Everybody*. Two tracks were even recycled from previous soundtrack albums. Neither of the soundtrack songs had actually been used in the movies but they had both appeared as bonus tracks on the soundtrack albums: *(It's a) Long Lonely Highway* from *Kissin' Cousins*, written by Pomus and Shuman; and *Slowly but Surely* from *Fun in Acapulco*.

In Britain the nine songs were spread across two EPs, *Tickle Me* and *Tickle Me Vol 2*. The American release consisted of an EP and two singles. The EP had the same tracks as the first British EP. The two singles both made the American charts, *I'm Yours* and Otis Blackwell's *(Such an) Easy Question*.

1970 Fleetwood Mac Peter Green's final gig

Having announced his intension to leave Fleetwood Mac a few weeks earlier, founding member and seminal British blues guitarist Peter Green gave his swan song performance with the band at London's Roundhouse club.

The group was originally called "Peter Green's Fleetwood Mac". After leaving the band Green embarked on a solo career but did play with Fleetwood Mac again. Sadly, the drugs took their toll on Green and his career became increasingly spasmodic.

1981 The Clash fifteen-day residency in New York

The Clash opened a residency at New York's Bond International Casino on Times Square. The concerts were due to finish on 5 June but enthusiastic ticket selling meant that they were over-subscribed and the run had to be extended until 13 June.

The support acts varied across the residency and included Grandmaster Flash and the Furious Five, and The Dead Kennedys. On 10 June the audience was treated to an impromptu performance from beat poet legend Allen Ginsberg, when he joined the Clash on stage and performed his poem/song, *Capitol Air*.

Recording session today

1968 Mike Bloomfield left after recording half of *Supersession*

Al Kooper arranged a recording session with Electric Flag's guitarist Mike Bloomfield. When Bloomfield was unable to complete the session, Buffalo Springfield's guitarist Stephen Stills stepped into the breach.

The album was released as *Supersession*, with one side by each guitarist.

Birthday today

1945 John Fogerty guitar, vocals, songwriter: Creedence Clearwater Revival

John and his brother Tom were both members of the Blue Velvets and Golliwogs, before the band morphed into successful swamp-rockers Creedence Clearwater Revival.

Events today

1967 The Who Keith Moon was substituted by Julian Covey

Keith Moon was replaced for five gigs after an incident at Oxford University's *May Ball* when he "threw the drums so hard he gave himself a hernia ...[it] required an operation at St George's Hospital in Central London, and caused the cancellation of a major show in Paris".[1]

Before forming Julian Covey and the Machine, Covey was a member of Brian Auger's original Trinity, when it was a jazz trio. He deputised for Moon for one gig at Glasgow's Locarno Ballroom. Covey was unavailable to cover again and John's Children's drummer Chris Townson stepped into the breach on 3 June* for the next four gigs.

1982 The Clash *Casbah Club* tour opened

The *Casbah Club* tour opened at Asbury Park's Convention Hall in New Jersey. The American leg ended in Canada at Edmonton's Kinsmen Fieldhouse on 29 June. After a short break, the UK leg opened in London and wound up in Bristol on 3 August.

This outing marked a major change for the Clash. The relationship between drummer Topper Headon and the rest of the group had reached a low point. After recording the album *Combat Rock* and shortly before the *Casbah Club* tour, Headon and the Clash parted company. The band had now moved full circle and Headon's replacement was the band's original drummer, Terry Chimes (aka Tory Crimes).

Recording sessions today

1957 Buddy Holly and the Crickets *Everyday*

Drummer Jerry Allison replaced his drum kit with some knee-slapping percussion when he provided backing for the Buddy Holly penned *Everyday*. The song was used as the B-side of *Peggy Sue*, released on 20 September*.

By contrast the drumming for the A-side, *Peggy Sue*, used a rudiment not often found in rock drumming, the paradiddle (L-R-L-L R-L-R-R).

1968 The Who their 'lost' album ...*Who's for Tennis*

The Who spent time at Advision studios recording tracks that might well have been destined for the album *Who's for Tennis*, planned as the follow-up to *The Who Sell Out*.

The idea behind the album's title was that it would be released during the famous tennis tournament at London's Wimbledon. The album, possibly a double, was reputed to have *Glow Girl* as its lead song with a mixture of old and new songs. Amongst the tracks recorded that day was a cover of Benny Spellman's 1962 B-side, *Fortune Teller*.

Album released today

1967 Moby Grape *Moby Grape* (US)

This eponymous debut album from Moby Grape was greeted with critical acclaim.

In a marketing ploy to promote the album, record label Columbia took five singles from the album and released them simultaneously.

Birthday today

1945 Gary Brooker vocals, keyboards: The Paramounts, Procol Harum; solo

Event today

1958 The Drifters whole band sacked in one night

The Drifters began a one-week run at the Apollo in New York's Harlem. At the end of the week George Treadwell sacked the entire band and replaced them with the Crowns. Treadwell was the Drifters' manager and owned the rights to "The Drifters" name.

Dr Jive and His Rhythm 'n' Blues Review were headlining, with other acts on the bill including Ray Charles and The Crowns.

The Crowns had formerly been the Five Crowns and had released a string of singles dating back to 1952. By the night of this Apollo gig, the Crowns' lineup had become Charlie Thomas, Benjamin Earl Nelson (Ben E King), Dock Green, Elsbeary Hobbs and James "Papa" Clark.

After a string of R&B hits, stretching back to *Money Honey* in 1953, the current version of the Drifters had not seen chart action since Leiber and Stoller's *Fools Fall in Love*, nine months before this Apollo gig. To make matters worse, the Drifters' lead singer Bobby Hendricks had parted company with the group and headed off for a solo career. Treadwell had a number of outstanding commitments for the group. Faced with the problem of having bookings for "The Drifters" and a group of that name with no lead singer and no hit records, Treadwell's solution was to take over the management of the Crowns and rebrand them as "The Drifters". James "Papa" Clark was the only Crown not to be invited to become a Drifter. After confirming that the Crowns were up for it, he sacked all of the existing Drifters backstage at the Apollo at the end of their week-long residency.

The new Drifters took to the road to fulfil the obligations booked for the old Drifters. It would be the 6 March* 1959 before they were able to record their first single, *There Goes My Baby*. Along the way Benjamin Earl Nelson changed his name to "Ben E King".

Recording session today

1958 Jerry Lee Lewis *The Return of Jerry Lee*

This attempt at a humorous single was Sun Records' first attempt at damage limitation following Jerry Lee Lewis's disastrous British tour. He had played only a handful of dates after arriving on 22 May*, before British outrage at the marriage to his child bride forced Lewis to withdraw from his own headlining tour and return to America.

The Return of Jerry Lee was written as a mock interview, where Lewis was supposedly interviewed as he stepped off the plane on his return from London. On the recording the reporter's questions were answered by snippets of Lewis's songs. Radio stations failed to see the humour and it received minimal airplay. Lewis's American fans also deserted him in their droves, prompting a full-page apology in *Billboard* magazine on 9 June*.

Neither the single nor the apology placated the fans and this marked the end of Jerry Lee Lewis as a rock'n'roll star.

Singles released today

1966 The Beatles *Paperback Writer c/w Rain* (US)

1969 The Beatles *The Ballad of John and Yoko c/w Old Brown Shoe* (UK)

On the A-side John took lead vocal and played guitars and percussion, with Paul providing vocal backing, bass, piano, maracas and drums. George and Ringo were not involved in the recording. This was the Beatles' last British #1.

The B-side, *Old Brown Shoe*, was a George Harrison composition.

Events today

31

1961 Jimi Hendrix enlisted into the US Army

Jimi Hendrix enlisted into the US Army and after initial training joined the "Band of Brothers", the 101st Airborne Division.

Whilst stationed at Fort Campbell in Kentucky, he met bass player Billy Cox and they formed the King Casuals. His Army career came to an abrupt end just over a year later, when he broke his ankle in a parachute jump.

1964 The Hollies road to the Hollies

The Hollies appeared in a star-studded bill at Wembley's Empire Pool in London almost a year-to-the-day that their first single, a cover of the Coaster's *(Ain't That) Just Like Me*, hit the British charts. Singer Adam Faith topped the bill, with a lineup that included: The Rolling Stones, Wayne Fontana and the Mindbenders, and The Swinging Blue Jeans.

The road to the Hollies began in the mid-1950s when school friends, guitarist and singer Graham Nash, and singer Allan Clarke formed the Two Teens. By 1960 they had teamed up with bassist Eric Haydock in the Deltas. Nash parted company with the Hollies on 8 December* 1968, to form Crosby Stills and Nash.

(Ain't That) Just Like Me was written by two of the Coasters, Earl Carroll and Billy Guy.

1968 Moby Grape Skip Spence ...an axe, a drummer and a hotel door

Guitarist, singer and founding member, Skip Spence's swan song performance with Moby Grape came when they opened for three nights at New York's Fillmore East.

Spence famously had a psychotic incident at this time and went to New York's Albert Hotel in search of the band's drummer Don Stevenson, whom he reputedly believed to be possessed by the Devil. In his search for Stevenson, Spence chopped down the drummer's hotel room door. Discovering that he was not there, Spence's next step was to take his axe over to the CBS building and to wreak havoc on the 58th floor, where he was eventually overpowered. The incident culminated in Spence's committal to the Psychiatric Ward of New York's Bellevue Hospital.

In mid-1969 Spence released his acclaimed solo album *Oar*, which was conceived in Bellevue and recorded on his return to society.

1977 Pavlov's Dog farewell gig

When Pavlov's Dog decided to call it a day, they gave their final concert in their St Louis hometown, on the riverboat *The Admiral*. The lineup that night included original members, vocalist David Surkamp, violinist Siegfried Carver, guitarist Steve Scorfina, bassist Rick Stockton and keyboard player Doug Rayburn.

The group grew out of the more exotically named "Pavlov's Dog and the Condition Reflex Soul Revue and Concert Choir". In 1974 Pavlov's Dog was signed up by ABC Dunhill for a reputed $650,000, a very high fee in the mid-1970s for a new band. By the time that their debut album, *Pampered Menial*, was ready to be released the band and record company had parted company. Pavlov's Dog signed to Columbia for another reputed $600,000. This led to *Pampered Menial* being availably simultaneously from both ABC Dunhill and Columbia, albeit in different sleeves.

Birthday today

1948 John Bonham drums: Band of Joy, Tim Rose, Led Zeppelin

June

Albums released today

1966 Eric Clapton *What's Shakin'* (US)

1

Before Cream came into existence, guitarist Eric Clapton played in another 'supergroup', Powerhouse. Clapton was a member of John Mayall's Bluesbreakers at the time and this was a one-off studio project.

As "Eric Clapton and the Powerhouse" they contributed three tracks to the Elektra compilation album *What's Shakin'*. Two of the Powerhouse musicians were with Manfred Mann, harmonica player Paul Jones and bassist Jack Bruce. Clapton and Bruce formed Cream shortly afterwards. The Spencer Davis Group also contributed two players, vocalist Stevie Winwood, billed as "Steve Anglo" for contractual reasons, and drummer Pete York. Clapton also invited his old friend Ben Palmer to join them on piano. He had played with Clapton in his first group the Roosters and also accompanied old Slowhand in his ill-fated Greek 'holiday' band the Glands. The three tracks were *I Want to Know*, Memphis Slim's *Steppin' Out*, and Robert Johnson's *Crossroads*.

The album also included tracks from The Lovin' Spoonful, Paul Butterfield Blues Band, Al Kooper and Tom Rush.

The album was called *Good Time Music* when it was released in Britain.

1967 The Beatles *Sgt Pepper's Lonely Hearts Club Band* (UK)

The cover was designed by Peter Blake. The album took a reputed 700 hours to record.

1967 David Bowie *David Bowie* 1st album (UK)

David Bowie's debut album, all fourteen songs were written by Bowie.

1972 Eagles *Eagles* 1st album (US)

The Eagles' eponymous debut album spawned their first three American hit singles, *Take It Easy*, *Witchy Woman* and *Peaceful Easy Feeling*. It would be another three years before their first British hit, *One of These Nights*, in 1975.

1976 The Runaways *The Runaways* 1st album (US)

Between playing their first gig as a trio on 12 September* and releasing their debut album, the band had broadened out to become a quintet. The founding members Joan Jett and Sandy West were still in place but the original bass player Mickie Steel had been replaced by Jackie Fox. The lineup now also included lead guitarist Lita Ford and lead singer Cherie Currie, who often performed resplendent in waspie, suspender belt and stockings.

Births and deaths today

1947 Ron Wood guitar: Birds, Jeff Beck Group, Creation, Faces, Stones

1948 Sonny Boy Williamson (I) the original Sonny Boy, died at the age of thirty-four

John Lee Williamson, better known as Sonny Boy Williamson (I) died after a violent beating during a robbery on the streets of Chicago. He was one of the most influential of the blues harp players of the 1930s and '40s.

Sonny Boy Williamson's name was adopted by Aleck Ford, also known as Rice Miller. As "Sonny Boy Williamson (II)", he too was a very influential harmonica player and recorded a live album with the Yardbirds on 8 December* 1963.

Event today

1958 The Kingston Trio American folk revival came of age

The American folk music revival movement came of age with the release of the Kingston Trio's eponymous debut album.

The folk music revival movement had begun in the 1940s with pioneers like Pete Seeger, the Weavers, Lead Belly and Woody Guthrie. These politically motivated artists often performed at union events. The social nature of many of the songs meant that they and others fell foul of the McCarthy communist witch hunts of the 1950s. The Kingston Trio took a far more pop based approach and was one of the first groups to establish folk as a popular music genre. The Trio's debut album included *Tom Dooley*, a traditional song with an arrangement by founding member Dave Guard. The song was one of the landmarks in folk music. The Kingston Trio were a vital part of the development towards the 1960s folk-protest singers like Bob Dylan, Phil Ochs and Joan Baez.

Single released today

1967 Small Faces *Here Comes the Nice c/w Talk to You* (UK)

Three months after signing to Immediate, the Small Faces released their first single on their new label. Both sides were written by Steve Marriott and Ronnie Lane.

Their old record label Decca chose the same day to release their second Small Faces album *From the Beginning*, a mishmash of old material and outtakes.

Albums released today

1967 The Beatles *Sgt Pepper's Lonely Hearts Club Band* (US)

This was the first American Beatles album to have the same title and track listing as its British counterpart.

1967 Small Faces *From the Beginning* (UK)

Decca released their second Small Faces album on the same day that the band released their debut single on their new label, Immediate.

By the time that Decca released this album the Small Faces had moved on and signed with Andrew Loog Oldham's Immediate label. This Decca album was a mixed bag of re-releases and unissued material. The Small Faces were unimpressed by Decca's decision to release the album and advised their fans to ignore it.

Their debut Immediate album used the band's name as its title, just as Decca had done previously. Different versions of two Steve Marriott and Ronnie Lane songs ended up on both albums, *(Tell Me) Have You Ever Seen Me* and *My Way of Giving*.

Birthday today

1941 Charlie Watts drums: Blues Incorporated, Blues By Six, Rolling Stones

Drummer Charlie Watts started his career with one of England's seminal blues bands, Alexis Korner's Blues Incorporated. Brian Jones, Mick Jagger and Keith Richard also performed with the band and it provided them all with their introduction to Watts. Alongside Ian Stewart in Brian Jones's first group, was another seminal British blues pioneer, Brian Knight. When Knight left Jones to form Blues By Six, Watts left Blues Incorporated and joined Knight in his new venture. Watts was replaced in Blues Incorporated by future Cream sticksman Ginger Baker. In January 1963 Charlie Watts played his first gig as a full-time Rolling Stone.

Events today

1950 Music Milestones Aristocrat became Chess Records

One of the most influential record labels of the 1950s came into being when the Chess brothers, Leonard and Phil, took complete control of the Aristocrat label and renamed it "Chess Records". The first Chess release, *Bless You c/w My Foolish Heart* by Gene Ammons, was given the number 1425, taken from the childhood address of the Chess family home at 1425 South Karlov Street in Chicago.

The second release, Chess 1426, was Muddy Waters' self-penned *Rollin' Stone*, Brian Jones's inspiration for the name of his new lineup after he was joined by Mick Jagger and Keith Richard. They debuted as the "Rollin' Stones" on 12 July* 1962.

1972 The Rolling Stones fabled 1972 North American tour

The 1972 North American tour kicked off on Canada's Pacific West Coast, with a performance at the Canadian Pacific Coliseum in Vancouver.

The tour was to promote the Stones' new album *Exile on Main Street*. It was the first time that the Stones had performed in America since their ill-fated Altamont concert on 6 December* 1969. Folklore has it that this sojourn was the epitome of the Rolling Stones' sex, drugs and rock'n'roll times. The legend-making *Stones Touring Party* winged its way from the west coast, to finish on 26 July with three nights at New York's Madison Square Garden. Mayhem followed the tour as it rolled across America. There were several clashes between police and fans, including an incident in Arizona when the police resorted to tear gas at a concert in Tucson on 14 June. During their stay in Chicago the Stones' entourage partied at Hugh Heffner's *Playboy* mansion. On 17 July they were back in Canada for a concert in Montreal, where someone put a bomb under one of the trucks and blew it up. The following day Mick and Keith were arrested for an alleged attack on a local photographer. This tour was certainly the stuff of rock'n'roll legend! Mick Taylor was the Stones' guitarist and Stevie Wonder opened most of the shows. The tour spawned the concert-movie, *Ladies and Gentlemen: The Rolling Stones*.

Album released today

1970 Deep Purple *In Rock* (UK)

This was the first rock album from the classic lineup of singer Ian Gillan, drummer Ian Paice, guitarist Ritchie Blackmore, bassist Roger Glover and keyboardist Jon Lord.

Birthdays today

1926 Allen Ginsberg pivotal beat generation poet

Poet Allen Ginsberg was one of the leading lights of the beat generation. His seminal 1955 poem *Howl* was a cornerstone of beat literature. In the 1960s he was involved with the counterculture and participated in numerous rock-associated events.

1939 Ian Hunter vocals, piano, songwriter: Silence, Mott the Hoople; solo

He formed the Hunter-Ronson band after Mott the Hoople folded in late 1974.

1946 Michael Clarke drums: The Byrds, The Flying Burrito Brothers

A Beefeater and founding member of the Byrds, drummer Michael Clarke left after their fifth album, *The Notorious Byrd Brothers*. He joined the Flying Burrito Brothers before they recorded their second album, *Burrito Deluxe*.

Events today

1964 The Beatles Jimmy Nicol ...Beatle for a week

On the eve of their first world tour Ringo was taken ill with tonsillitis and Jimmy Nicol stepped in to occupy the vacant drumming stool. After a brief rehearsal the day before, Nicol played his first gig as a Beatle on 4 June at the KB Hallen in Copenhagen, Denmark. He went on to play dates in the Netherlands and Hong Kong, before making his final appearance on 13 June in Australia, at Adelaide's Centennial Hall. Ringo rejoined the Fab Three in Melbourne on the 17th and Jimmy Nicol's fifteen minutes of fame were over.

Jimmy (sometimes Jimmie) Nicol emerged out of the 2i's scene and was a member of Colin Hicks and the Cabin Boys in 1957 and '58. Shortly before his stint with the Beatles he had formed the Shubdubs and also played with Georgie Fame and the Blue Flames.

1969 Episode Six Ian Gillan invited to join Deep Purple

Episode Six came to the end of its journey when Ritchie Blackmore and Jon Lord travelled to the Ivy Club in Woodford, Essex, to see the singer Ian Gillan in action. The frontman was about to be extended an invitation to join them in Deep Purple.

Roger Glover was one of the original members of Episode Six when it formed in 1963. Ian Gillan joined in 1965, just before they recorded their first single, *Put Yourself in My Place*. The song was credited to "L Ransford", a pseudonym used by the Hollies' songwriting team of Graham Nash, Allan Clarke and Tony Hicks.

Deep Purple gave their debut performance in Denmark on 20 April* 1968. Following the group's third album their original singer Rod Evans and bassist Nick Simper moved on. The gaps were filled when guitarist Ritchie Blackmore contacted his old Outlaws buddy Mick Underwood, who was Episode Six's drummer, to ask him if he knew any good singers. Underwood recommended his own frontman Ian Gillan. Gillan accepted the offer to become Deep Purple's vocalist and was followed shortly afterwards by Episode Six's bassist Roger Glover. The classic Deep Purple lineup was now in place.

Singles released today

1962 The Beach Boys *Surfin' Safari* c/w *409* (US)

This was the first Beach Boys single released on the Capitol label. They had previously recorded both sides as part of a demo recording that they were hawking around in search of a record deal. After refusals from several record companies, Capitol Records released the Brian Wilson and Mike Love penned *Surfin' Safari*.

By this time Al Jardine had left the group to return to college. He was replaced by David Marks but he did return in mid-1963.

1969 The Beatles *Ballad of John and Yoko* c/w *Old Brown Shoe* (US)

Old Brown Shoe was Harrison's second and final composition for a Beatles B-side.

Birthday today

1940 Cliff Bennett singer: Cliff Bennett and the Rebel Rousers, Toe Fat

Cliff Bennett was one of Britain's pioneering R&B singers. Despite working with producer Joe Meek and manager Brian Epstein, he only achieved limited commercial success. One of his high points came with the Lennon and McCartney song, *Got to Get You into My Life*. It was produced by Paul McCartney and released by Bennett as a single around the time that the Beatles' version appeared on *Revolver*.

Events today

5

1968 Robert Kennedy assassinated

Five years after his brother, President John F Kennedy, was assassinated in Dallas on 22 November* 1963, Robert Kennedy also died at the hands of an assassin's bullet. The senator from New York State had just finished addressing his Democratic Party supporters in the Ambassador Hotel in Los Angeles. He was making his way through the kitchens when he was shot by Palestinian immigrant Sirhan Sirhan. The attacker was overpowered and arrested on the spot.

Sirhan was found guilty of murdering Robert Kennedy and sentenced to death. This was commuted to life imprisonment in 1972, when the State of California abolished the death penalty. As with President John F Kennedy's assassination, conspiracy theories abound. Did Sirhan act alone? Was he in a hypnotic state when he carried out the shooting?

1975 Pink Floyd last contact with Syd Barrett

The members of Pink Floyd were taken by surprise when original guitarist, singer and songwriter Syd Barrett dropped by the Abbey Road recording studios, where they were working on their next album, *Wish You Were Here*. As fate would have it, they were recording *Shine on You Crazy Diamond*, a song about Barrett. When he wandered into their studio no one recognised him. He had put on weight, was balding and had shaved his eyebrows. This was to be the group's last contact with their former leader.

Syd Barrett had been the Pink Floyd's guiding light but hallucinogenic drugs took their toll and a press announcement on 6 April* 1968 told of his replacement in the band by David Gilmour. He retired into seclusion in his hometown, Cambridge.

Single released today

1964 Davie Jones and the King Bees *Liza Jane c/w Louie, Louie Go Home* (UK)

This was Bowie's first-ever single. The A-side was based on *Li'l Liza Jane*, written by Countess Ada DeLachau and used in the 1916 comedy *Come Out of the Kitchen.* His debut B-side was a cover of Paul Revere and the Raiders' 1964 single, *Louie - Go Home.*

On 16 September* 1965 Davie Jones changed his name to David Bowie.

Album released today

1962 Elvis Presley *Pot Luck with Elvis* (US)

Following manager Colonel Tom Parker's decision to release only movie soundtrack recordings, *Pot Luck with Elvis* would prove to be his last studio album of new rock material for seven years. As well as Elvis's regular backing musicians Scotty Moore, DJ Fontana, Floyd Cramer, "Boots" Randolph and the Jordanaires, he was also accompanied by Wrecking Crew session drummer Hal Blaine on some tracks.

After *Pot Luck with Elvis*, fans would have to be content with albums which were movie soundtracks, big hits, old material, religious or a TV special. His next non-soundtrack album of new material was a collection of religious songs on the 1967 album *How Great Thou Art.* It would take until the summer of 1969 for Elvis to release a studio album of new rock material, *From Elvis in Memphis.*

Four of the songs from *Pot Luck with Elvis* were used for the soundtrack of Elvis's movie *Tickle Me*, premiered on 28 May* 1965. To save production costs it was decided not to record any new songs for this, Elvis's eighteenth movie.

Events today

6

1962 The Beatles first recording session at Abbey Road

Shortly after returning from their third Hamburg trip, Brian Epstein attended the first recording session with George Martin, at EMI's famous Abbey Road studios.

This was the only Beatles recording session with drummer Pete Best. They recorded four songs: *Love Me Do, P.S. I Love You, Ask Me Why* and *Besame Mucho*, the latter was written by Consuelo Velazquez. This Pete Best version of *Love Me Do* did not see the light of day until the release of *Anthology 1* in 1995.

1966 Roy Orbison double family tragedy

Roy Orbison's wife Claudette died in a motorcycle accident. They were riding their motorcycles in Gallatin, Tennessee when Claudette's motorcycle was hit by a truck.

The song *Claudette* was used by the Everly Brothers as the B-side of their 1958 hit single *All I Have to Do Is Dream.* Orbison had written the song as a tribute to his wife shortly after they started married life in 1957. Sadly, the marriage did not work out and they divorced in late 1964, only to re-marry less than a year later.

Family tragedy struck Roy Orbison once again in September 1968, when two of his three sons died in a fire at his home at Old Hickory Lake in Henderson, Tennessee.

1971 John Lennon performed with Frank Zappa

Frank Zappa and the Mothers were appearing at New York's Fillmore East, where they captured the concert as the live album *Fillmore East, June 1971*. John and Yoko joined them on stage and performed four numbers: *Well (Baby Please Don't Go)*, *Jamrag*, *Scumbag* and *Au*.

John Lennon released the jam as a live bonus album, packaged with *Some Time in New York City*. Zappa was unimpressed with Lennon's release of this live album. In his excellent book *Frank Zappa*, Barry Miles summed up Zappa's feelings on the matter, "John and Yoko claimed copyright on the entire jam, giving 'King Kong' the new title 'Jam Rag' (British slang for a tampon). Frank was exceedingly annoyed".[6]

Single released today

1977 Elvis Presley *Way Down c/w Pledging My Love* (US)

Way Down was to be the last single issued in Elvis's lifetime. Both songs were recorded during his last recording session, at his Graceland home on 29 October*.

The B-side, *Pledging My Love*, had been a posthumous crossover hit for R&B singer Johnny Ace in early 1955. Ace's career had also been cut short but for him it was as the result of a game of Russian roulette, backstage at a gig in Texas on 25 December* 1954.

Album released today

1972 David Bowie *The Rise and Fall of Ziggy Stardust and the Spiders from Mars* (UK)

The Spiders were guitarist Mick Ronson, bassist Trevor Bolder and drummer Mick Woodmansey.

Birthday today

1936 Levi Stubbs lead singer: The Four Aims, The Four Tops

The Four Tops scored their first hit in 1964 with *Baby I Need Your Loving*, by which time they had been together for a decade. The original lineup stayed together until 1997.

Events today

1958 Cliff Richard and the Drifters private recording demo

Still to secure a record deal, Cliff Richard and the Drifters invested £10 in a private recording session at the HMV record store in London's Oxford Street. They chose two cover songs, Jerry Lee Lewis's *Breathless* and Lloyd Price's *Lawdy Miss Clawdy*.

EMI's Norrie Paramour heard the recordings and invited them in for an audition. On 29 August* they released their first single, the Paramour produced *Move It!*

1969 Blind Faith debut performance

Over-hyped and with the accolade of being referred to as a 'supergroup', Blind Faith gave their debut performance at a free festival in London's Hyde Park. Other performers that day included Donovan, Third Ear Band, Edgar Broughton and Richie Havens. This turned out to be their only British appearance.

The hype accompanying the arrival of Blind Faith was not surprising, the band was formed in the wake of Cream splitting up. Each of the four members came with a very impressive pedigree. Guitarist and singer Eric Clapton had previously been with the Yardbirds, John Mayall's Bluesbreakers and Cream. Ginger Baker was a jazz drummer who had played with two of Britain's foremost R&B bands, Alexis Korner's Blues Incorporated and the Graham Bond Organisation, before forming Cream. Keyboardist and singer Steve Winwood was with the Spencer Davis Group before leaving to form Traffic. Bassist Rick Grech was a founding member of Family. Sadly, the whole never managed to achieve the sum of its parts and the band burnt out before the summer was over. Blind Faith's final gig was in Hawaii on 24 August*.

1970 The Who *Tommy* took a bow at the New York Met

The Who kicked off their American tour with two shows at New York's prestigious Metropolitan Opera House. The posters billed the event as "The Who in the final performance of their rock opera 'Tommy'."

The shows received standing ovations at both performances but when fans demanded an encore, Pete Townshend told the audience that they were too tired after two two-hour performances. This elicited a boo or two from the crowd, to which Townshend retorted, "After two fucking hours, boo to you, too!"[25]

Single released today

1963 The Rolling Stones *Come On c/w I Want to Be Loved* (UK)

For their British debut single the Rolling Stones chose to cover Chuck Berry's *Come On* for the A-side and to couple it with Willie Dixon's *I Want to Be Loved*. Both sides were produced by their new manager Andrew Loog Oldham.

Things had moved quickly for the Stones since they met Oldham on the 28 April*. He had secured them a recording contract with Decca and trimmed them down from a sextet to a quintet. Pianist Ian Stewart had been the first of the Stones to join Brian Jones's group in early 1962 but Oldham decided that he had the wrong image for the Rolling Stones. Stewart was relegated from the stage to road manager, although he often played his piano with the band when they were in the studio. They debuted as "The Rollin' Stones" on 12 July* 1962 but now the classic lineup of Brian Jones, Mick Jagger, Keith Richard, Bill Wyman and Charlie Watts was finally in place.

Events today

1969 The Rolling Stones Brian Jones left the Rolling Stones

When Brian Jones left the Rolling Stones he talked to Alexis Korner about joining him in his new venture, New Church, but Korner suggested that he should form his own group.

Jones had originally formed the Rollin' Stones but his relationship with the others had deteriorated as their music moved progressively away from the blues that he loved. Sadly, less than a month later, on 3 July*, he was found dead in the swimming pool of his home, Cotchford Farm in Sussex. This sixteenth century property had previously been owned by writer AA Milne and was used as the setting for his *Winnie the Pooh* stories.

He was replaced in the group by ex-John Mayall guitarist Mick Taylor. The new lineup played their first gig at the free Hyde Park concert on 5 July*.

1969 Vietnam War American troop withdrawals began

America's President Nixon met with South Vietnam's President Thieu on Midway Island.

In an ensuing statement both Nixon and Thieu commented on their plans for American troop withdrawals and the increasing Vietnamization of the war. This meant that South Vietnam would progressively carry more and more of the burden for waging the war. With regard to American troop withdrawals, Nixon said, "I have decided to order the immediate redeployment from Vietnam of a division equivalent of approximately 25,000 men."[84]

1975 Talking Heads debut concert

Talking Heads gave their first concert, as the Ramones' support act at New York's CBGB club.

At this stage Talking Heads was a trio, guitarist and vocalist David Byrne, drummer Chris Franz and bassist Tina Weymouth. It would be another year before they became a quartet, with the addition of guitarist and keyboard player Jerry Harrison.

Recording sessions today

1959 The Clovers *Love Potion #9*

The Clovers recorded the original version of Leiber and Stoller's *Love Potion #9*. They recorded two versions of the song, with the album track containing a final verse pondering on the possibilities of *Love Potion #10*.

The vocal group had been one of Atlantic Records' more successful acts, generating a string of R&B hits in the first half of the 1950s. This recording session was their first time in the studio for United Artists. *Love Potion #9* gave the Clovers their biggest hit but it was also their final chart appearance.

The Liverpudlian beat group the Searchers took the song back to America in the British Invasion of 1964 and scored their biggest stateside hit.

1962 Alexis Korner's Blues Incorporated *R&B from the Marquee*

Billed as Britain's "first rhythm and blues band" at their Ealing Club debut on 17 March*, Alexis Korner's Blues Incorporated recorded their debut album, *R&B from the Marquee*.

Korner had recently started his Thursday night residency at London's Marquee club but despite the album's title it was recorded at Decca's studios in West Hampstead. The band included harmonica player Cyril Davies, vocalist Long John Baldry, the tenor saxophone of Dick Heckstall-Smith and background vocals from Big Jim Sullivan.

Event today

1958 Jerry Lee Lewis damage limitation after his disastrous UK tour

The scene was set for Jerry Lee Lewis's downfall the moment he arrived in London for the beginning of his British tour on 22 May*. It was then that the British press broke the story that he was married to his cousin's thirteen-year-old daughter, Myra Gale. The backlash that followed forced Lewis to pull out of his own headlining tour after just three poorly received concerts. He returned to America only to find that his fans there were also deserting him in their droves. Sales of his latest single *High School Confidential* stalled. In an attempt at reconciliation he released another single, *The Return of Jerry Lee* but this failed to gain airplay. His next ruse to win back the record buying public was to publish an *Open Letter to the Industry.*[92] To get his message across, Lewis took the whole of page eleven in the 9 June edition of *Billboard* magazine. In it he acknowledged the strength of negative feeling against him but was dismayed that it all started out because he told the truth. The final paragraph included a prophetic comment, where he hoped that if he was "washed up" it was not because of this bad publicity.

Sadly, he was "washed up" as a rock'n'roll star. Despite continued attempts by Sam Phillips to push his Sun recordings, he never again managed to regain his former glory. Lewis left Sun Records in 1963 and moved to the Mercury subsidiary Smash. He reinvented himself as a country artist and scored a string of hits into the early 1980s.

Recording session today

1964 Bob Dylan *Another Side of Bob Dylan*

This fourth album from Dylan was recorded in a single day. It was to be his last album made up entirely of acoustic folk music.

Single released today

1958 Ritchie Valens *Come on, Let's Go c/w Framed* (US)

Ritchie Valens released the first of only two singles, the self-penned *Come on, Let's Go.*

Birthdays today

1915 Les Paul guitar player and designer; recording innovator

1934 Jackie Wilson singer: The Dominos; solo

In his early days Jackie Wilson was a successful amateur boxer and gospel singer. In 1953 he replaced Clyde McPhatter as lead singer with Billy Ward and the Dominos, after he left to form the Drifters. In 1957 Wilson left the Dominoes for a successful solo career. He notched up a string of R&B hits, many of which crossed over into the pop charts.

1941 Jon Lord keyboards: The Artwoods, Deep Purple, Whitesnake

Jon Lord studied classical piano as a child but his interests moved to jazz and R&B. In 1963 he was with the Don Wilson Combo when it joined up with Art Wood's group and morphed into the Artwoods. Lord then joined Art's brother and future Rolling Stone, Ron Wood, in his recently formed Santa Barbara Machine Head. The group had a lineup that included future Pink Fairies drummer Twink. After this short-lived group Lord joined the Flower Pot Men's touring band, along with bassist Nick Simper. They both moved on to join guitarist Ritchie Blackmore in Roundabout. Deep Purple was born when the trio combined with drummer Ian Paice and vocalist Rod Evans from the Maze.

10

Events today

1966 Janis Joplin first gig with Big Brother and the Holding Company

Big Brother and the Holding Company's first gig with new vocalist Janis Joplin was at San Francisco's Avalon Ballroom.

Joplin's first venture into performing was in 1962 with the Austin based folk trio the Waller Creek Boys. This embryonic music career was short-lived and she dropped out of the music scene for a while. After passing up the opportunity to join the 13th Floor Elevators she moved to San Francisco and become the lead singer with Big Brother and the Holding Company.

1967 Landmark Festivals *Fantasy Fair and Magic Mountain Music Festival*

The two-day *Fantasy Fair and Magic Mountain Music Festival* opened on Mount Tamalpais, just north of San Francisco. With an entrance fee of $2 and presented by radio station KFRC, the event was a benefit for the Hunter's Point Child Care Centre. It was originally scheduled for 3 and 4 June but inclement weather pushed the event back.

Preceding Monterey by a week, the *Magic Mountain Music Festival* is generally considered to be the first rock'n'roll festival. The *Summer of Love* was heralded by an array of some of the top rock bands of the day, including The Doors, Jefferson Airplane, Country Joe and the Fish, Canned Heat, Captain Beefheart and the Magic Band, The 13th Floor Elevators, Moby Grape and The Byrds.

1967 The Who Keith Moon substituted by Chris Townson

With Keith Moon's sudden incapacitation following a hernia operation, Julian Covey stepped in for one gig as the Who's drummer on 29 May*. Covey's lack of availability meant that the remaining four dates were covered by John's Children's drummer Chris Townson. He kicked off at Southampton's Floral Hall and finished on the 10 June at the Palace Ballroom, Douglas on the Isle of Man.

The Who had recently completed an eventful German tour with John's Children as the opening act. The support band's outrageous stage behaviour culminated in them being thrown off the tour halfway through, after causing a riot at Friedrich-Ebert-Halle in Ludwigshafen on 12 April*. To get their own back, the Who used flash-powder to make sure that Townson's last gig with them at Douglas went off with a bang!

Single released today

1966 The Beatles *Paperback Writer c/w Rain* (UK)

Rain was the first Beatles song to feature the use of backwards tapes. This was attributed to John Lennon listening to a playback but threading the tape incorrectly. He loved the result of hearing the tape playing backwards and built the sound into the song.

Beat poet Royston Ellis was the inspiration for *Paperback Writer*.

Birthday today

1910 Howlin' Wolf blues harmonica, guitarist and singer

Howlin' Wolf was taught harmonica by Sonny Boy Williamson (II), aka Rice Miller. He recorded one of the most influential catalogues of blues songs, many of which were written for him by Willie Dixon. His output included the self-penned classics *Smokestack Lightning*, *Back Door Man* and *Killing Floor*, and *Willie Dixon's The Red Rooster*, a hit for the Rolling Stones as *Little Red Rooster*.

Events today

1963 Civil Rights Movement George Wallace's *Schoolhouse Door* stand

Two black students, Vivian Malone and James Hood, attempted to enrol into the University of Alabama in Tuscaloosa. George Wallace, the Governor of Alabama and a staunch segregationist, physically placed himself in the entrance doorway to prevent them from taking their lawful place at the University.

President Kennedy responded by federalizing the Alabama National Guard and providing an escort for the students. George Wallace was ordered to step aside and the two students registered for their university courses.

Wallace had made his position clear in his 1963 *Inaugural Address* on 14 January*, when he said that he believed in "segregation forever".

1963 Civil Rights Movement JFK announced his *Civil Rights Bill*

On the evening of the same day that Alabama's Governor George Wallace made his defiant *Schoolhouse Door* stand at the University of Alabama, President Kennedy delivered a radio and television broadcast[86] announcing his intention to introduce a *Civil Rights Bill.*

Sadly, Kennedy was assassinated before the Bill could be introduced. It was passed into law as the *Civil Rights Act* by President Lyndon Johnson on 2 July* 1964.

1968 Charles Manson songs supposedly bearing messages of death

The Beatles' *White Album* was in production, with work being carried out on the track *Revolution 9*. In the not too-distant future, this and other tracks from the album would be claimed as the inspiration for one of America's most notorious murder sprees.

On 9 August* 1969 members of Charles Manson's "Family" murdered the actress Sharon Tate and everyone with her. The following day Manson and other "Family" members murdered Leno and Rosemary LaBianca, leaving messages written in blood around the scene of the crime. A number of songs from the *White Album*, including *Revolution 9*, *Piggies* and *Helter Skelter*, have been tied to this atrocity.

Several other rock songs have also been linked to deaths. Judas Priest faced a lawsuit after a suicide on 23 December* 1985 was linked to their version of *Better By You, Better Than Me*. Ozzy Osbourne faced a similar prosecution after a suicide in 1984 by a youth who had been listening to *Suicide Solution*, recorded around 5 April* 1980. In the mid-1980s AC/DC's song *Night Prowler* was linked to serial killer Richard Ramirez. The track had featured on their album *Highway to Hell*, released on 3 August* 1979.

Sometimes it works the other way around; the shootings by sixteen-year-old Barbara Spencer on 29 January* 1979 inspired the Boomtown Rats' *I Don't Like Mondays*.

Birthday today

1940 Joey Dee singer: Joey Dee and the Starliters

The Peppermint Lounge house band, Joey Dee and the Starliters, were famous for their 1961 hit *Peppermint Twist*. The Starliters also had some famous names pass through its ranks. Sisters Veronica (aka Ronnie Spector) and Estelle Bennett and their cousin Nedra Talley sang backing vocals, they later became the Ronettes. Felix Cavaliere, Eddie Brigati and Gene Cornish left to form the Young Rascals. And, oh yes, one of the Starliters' guitarists was Jimmy James, who changed his name to Jimi Hendrix.

Events today

1959 The Moonglows now featuring Marvin Gay

12

The Moonglows appeared at Chicago's Tivoli Theatre. This revamped lineup now included a young Marvin Gaye, who was still spelling his surname "Gay".

Co-founded by Harvey Fuqua, doo wop vocal group the Moonglows started life as the Crazy Sounds. In 1952 the group, based in Cleveland Ohio, came to the attention of a local radio DJ at WJW. The disc jockey was the legendary Alan Freed, accredited with coining the term "rock'n'roll". At the time Freed was calling himself "Moondog". He liked them, signed the group to his own Champagne label, changed their name to "The Moonglows" and released *I Just Can't Tell No Lie*. Freed took the writing credit for the song under his pen name "Al Lance", derived from his children's names. The pseudonym was used as a way of obtaining income from record promotions, aka payola. Freed's use of the name "Moondog" also caused him a problem. The original Moondog, New York street performer Louis Thomas Hardin, sued Freed and he dropped the nickname.

By the time that the Moonglows had released *Ten Commandments of Love*, their final hit in 1958, the band was coming to the end of the road and this single was released as "Harvey and the Moonglows". Shortly after this hit Marvin Gay and his group the Marquees came to Fuqua's attention. He recruited them as his new Moonglows but they never achieved the same level of success as the original group.

Fuqua moved on to became a producer and writer for Berry Gordy's newly formed Motown company. He signed Gay to the new label as "Marvin Gaye" and he went on to become one of the label's biggest stars.

1963 Civil Rights Movement Medgar Evers was murdered

In the early 1960s during the dark days of racial civil unrest in America's Deep South, one of the highest profile murders was that of Civil Rights campaigner Medgar Evers. He was the field secretary in Mississippi for the NAACP (National Association for the Advancement of Coloured People). Evers was shot in the back on his own driveway, by an assassin hiding in the bushes outside his home in Jackson, Mississippi.

Evers was an active Civil Rights campaigner petitioning, amongst other things, to ensure that schools and colleges complied with new laws requiring schools to move from segregation to integration. He actively promoted voter registration and organised a much publicised boycott of retail shops in Jackson.

Ku Klux Klan member Byron De La Beckwith was tried for the murder twice, both times resulting in a hung verdict from the all-white juries. He was finally convicted in 1994 after evidence surfaced that the original juries had been tampered with. Beckwith died in prison in 2001.

Bob Dylan immortalised the death of Medgar Evers in his song *Only a Pawn in Their Game*, on his album *The Times They Are A-Changin'*.

Birthday today

1941 Roy Harper guitarist singer and songwriter

An influential songwriter, Roy Harper often appeared on the same bill as the likes of Pink Floyd and Fairport Convention. He was the only guest singer to take lead vocal on a Pink Floyd song, with his rendition of *Have a Cigar* on the album *Wish You Were Here*. Led Zeppelin also tipped their caps to Harper, with their song *Hats Off To (Roy) Harper* on *Led Zeppelin III*.

Events today

1969 Atomic Rooster goodbye to the Crazy World of Arthur Brown

On the Crazy World of Arthur Brown's third American visit, the tour was cut short when keyboard player Vincent Crane and drummer Carl Palmer quit the group and flew back to Britain together. The date was Friday 13th and on the journey home they decided to form a band. Crane and Palmer recruited bass playing vocalist Nick Graham and Atomic Rooster was born.

Crane had been an integral part of Brown's band, co-writing with Brown his memorable hit *Fire*. Palmer had only joined Brown's Crazy World just before the group embarked on their American jaunt. Before that he had been with Chris Farlowe's Thunderbirds. Palmer parted company with Atomic Rooster in the early summer of 1970 to form Emerson, Lake & Palmer.

1971 Vietnam War damning *Pentagon Papers* published

The *Pentagon Papers* was the popular name for the archive of secret Defense Department papers which documented the decisions taken by successive White House administrations regarding the Vietnam War. The *Papers* were leaked by Daniel Ellsberg, assisted by Anthony Russo and were first published by *The New York Times* on 13 June. On 18 June the *Washington Post* started to publish its own articles based on the *Papers*.

The *Pentagon Papers* report was commissioned in 1967 by the Secretary of Defense Robert McNamara and covered the period from 1945 to 1967. They were intended as a history of the war in Vietnam but they also detailed how successive administrations had misled the American public.

On 28 June *Time* magazine ran the front page story, *Pentagon Papers: The Secret War*. In the article it outlined some of the deceptions, under the headings: Concealment of Air Strikes, Concealment at Tonkin, Concealment About Troops and Provocation Plans. The leaks caused great embarrassment to the Nixon administration and the President set up a team called the "Plumbers" to stop the leaks.

Both Ellsberg and Russo faced prosecution under the Espionage Act but the charges were eventually dismissed against them. On 12 May 1973, *The New York Times* announced that the *Pentagon Papers* charges had been dismissed. Its front page headline ended by quoting the judge's suggestion that there had been "improper Government conduct".

Births and deaths today

1949 Dennis Locorriere vocals and guitar: Dr Hook and the Medicine Show; solo

Dennis Locorriere was the lead singer (the one without the eyepatch).

1972 Clyde McPhatter singer and Drifters founder, died at the age of thirty-nine

Singer Clyde McPhatter died of alcohol-related heart failure.

In the 1950s he achieved considerable success as a founding member of both the Dominoes and the Drifters, and also as a solo artist. Sadly, his career lost momentum in the early 1960s. He tried to rekindle his fortunes in the late 1960s by relocating to England but this failed to stem the tide of his ebbing career.

Events today

1970 Eric Clapton Derek and the Dominos debut

Derek and the Dominos played their debut concert at London's Lyceum Ballroom.

After the demise of the short-lived Blind Faith, Eric Clapton joined Delaney & Bonnie who had been their support band on the American tour. During this new venture they recorded *Delaney & Bonnie & Friends: On Tour with Eric Clapton*. After the tour Clapton returned to England and put together a new band, Derek and the Dominos. It consisted of three of Delaney & Bonnie's Friends: keyboards player Bobby Whitlock, bassist Carl Randle and drummer Jim Gordon. Dave Mason, ex-Traffic co-founder and ex-Friends guitarist, also played at this gig but his time as a Domino was brief.

Duane Allman joined the band for the *Layla and Other Love Songs* album.

1972 Eagles early gig supporting Jethro Tull

Shortly after releasing their eponymous debut album on 1 June*, the Eagles supported Jethro Tull at the Fair Grounds Pavilion in Oklahoma City.

This first Eagles lineup came together in the summer of 1971 and consisted of guitarists Glenn Frey and Bernie Leadon, drummer Don Henley and bassist Randy Meisner. They had all previously been a part of Linda Ronstadt's backing band.

Recording session today

1951 Bill Haley and the Saddlemen *Rocket 88*

Bill Haley's cover of *Rocket 88*, on the Holiday record label, is often cited as the first rock'n'roll record by a white artist. By the time that they had signed to Decca and recorded the historic *(We're Gonna) Rock Around the Clock* on 12 April* 1954, his backing group the Saddlemen had morphed into His Comets.

The original version of *Rocket 88* was recorded just three months earlier, at Sun Records on 5 March*. It was credited to Jackie Brenston and His Delta Cats but the song could just as easily have been released as Ike Turner and His Kings of Rhythm. It was Turner's studio session that day but he chose to put his name to two other songs recorded there.

Albums released today

1965 The Beatles *Beatles VI* (US)

Beatles VI contained six Lennon and McCartney songs, *You Like Me Too Much* by George Harrison and four covers. The first cover, *Kansas City*, was in fact a medley of Leiber and Stoller's *Kansas City*, a US #1 for Wilbert Harrison in 1959, and Little Richard's *Hey-Hey-Hey-Hey*. Little Richard often performed these two songs as a medley himself. Two of the covers were written and originally recorded by Larry Williams, *Bad Boy* and *Dizzy Miss Lizzy*. The fourth cover, *Words of Love*, was written by Buddy Holly and was the first single released on the Coral label and credited to him.

This was actually the seventh album from Capitol but the record label chose not to include 1964's album of talk and music, *The Beatles Story*, in its numbering sequence.

1968 Iron Butterfly *In-A-Gadda-Da-Vida* (US)

Urban legend has it that the name for their colossal 17-minute title track came about when its writer Doug Ingle, the band's vocalist and keyboard player, was stoned and incapable of pronouncing the intended title of his new song, *In the Garden of Eden*.

Event today

1968 Jeff Beck Group storming gig at the Fillmore East

The Jeff Beck Group played the second of two nights at New York's Fillmore East. Singer Rod Stewart fronted the group and was backed by guitarist Jeff Beck, bassist Ron Wood who was later guitarist with the Faces and the Rolling Stones, and drummer Mickey Waller who had played with both John Mayall and Cyril Davies.

Beck was supporting the Grateful Dead and their storming performance that night was described by *Rolling Stone* magazine as leaving the Dead as "upstaged and dispirited".[62]

Recording session today

1965 Bob Dylan *Like a Rolling Stone*

Like a Rolling Stone was a pivotal song for Bob Dylan. He was transitioning from an acoustic to an electric artist and this was his first song with an electric band to be released as a single in America. *Maggie's Farm* had preceded *Like a Rolling Stone* as a single in Britain. The musicians working with Dylan that day included guitarist Mike Bloomfield and the organist responsible for the song's memorable riff, Al Kooper.

Dylan's journey to an electric backing band would not be looked on favourably by some folk purists. Six weeks later, on 25 July*, he performed at the Newport Folk Festival to a very mixed reception. This hostility was still present on his 1966 European tour, when he was famously heckled on 17 May* at a gig widely bootlegged as *Live at the Royal Albert Hall* (in London) but was actually recorded in Manchester.

Like a Rolling Stone was also remarkable for its six minutes duration, at a time when three minutes was the norm for a single. His record company, Columbia, was nervous about DJs not playing the song because it was too long. Accordingly, they issued it with the full version as the A-side, coupled with *Gates of Eden*. It was also released as a DJ copy *Like a Rolling Stone Parts 1 & 2*, with the song spread across both the A and B-sides. Dylan's fans loved the song and it was a big hit on both sides of the Atlantic.

Birthdays today

1941 Harry Nilsson singer and songwriter

In a strange twist of fate, Keith Moon and Mama Cass Elliott were both found dead in Nilsson's London apartment.

1943 Johnny Hallyday French rock'n'roll singer

French rock'n'roll singer Johnny Hallyday may not have scored any hits in Britain or America but he was France's greatest rock'n'roll hero. He was relatively unknown in Britain but was involved in the beginning and the end of the careers of two major acts. On 13 October* 1966 a newly formed Jimi Hendrix Experience played their first-ever gig opening for Hallyday in Paris. At the other end of the spectrum, the Small Faces played together in the studio for the very last time on Hallyday's album *Rivière ...Ouvre ton Lit*, produced by Glyn Johns. The album also featured guitarist Peter Frampton, who was about to set up Humble Pie with ex-Small Face's singer Steve Marriott. Hallyday's own band featured guitarist Mick Jones, who went on to form Foreigner in 1976.

1946 Noddy Holder singer: 'N Betweens, Ambrose Slade, Slade

Before he joined the 'N Betweens, Noddy Holder was a roadie with Roger Plant's group Band of Joy. Slade was initially managed by ex-Jimi Hendrix manager, Chas Chandler.

Events today

16

1967 Landmark Festivals *Monterey International Pop Festival*

The first of the great rock festivals opened at the 7,500 seat, out-door arena at Monterey County Fairgrounds in California. It was run as a non-profit event by Alan Pariser, Lou Adler and the Mamas & the Papas' John Phillips.

The Who and Jimi Hendrix appeared on the third day and famously both refused to follow the other on stage. The toss of a coin put the Who on first. This was the Jimi Hendrix Experience's American debut and it led to their invitation to support the Monkees tour. Not quite in keeping with the general feeling of peace, love and flower power, the Who smashed up their equipment at the end of *My Generation* and in a feedback laden version of *Wild Thing*, Hendrix set fire to his guitar, smashed it into the stage until it snapped and then threw the neck into the audience. Now there's a collector's item!

The Grateful Dead refused to allow their set to be included on any subsequent albums or movies about the event. Janis Joplin's performance with Big Brother and the Holding Company established her reputation and was so well received that she was invited back to repeat the set. Guitarist Mike Bloomfield's new band, the Electric Flag, gave its debut performance. In a sign of things to come, Byrd's guitarist David Crosby stood in for an absent Neil Young in Buffalo Springfield. A host of other rock luminaries also appeared, including Quicksilver Messenger Service, Country Joe and the Fish, The Mamas & The Papas, Jefferson Airplane and The Byrds, plus blues from Paul Butterfield, soul music from Otis Redding and a standing ovation for Ravi Shankar's Indian sitar music.

1974 Butts Band nearing the end of its first incarnation

The Butts Band supported the Kinks at the world-famous London Palladium.

In mid-1973 the three remaining members of the Doors travelled to England in search of a vocalist to replace Jim Morrison. Ex-Audience singer Howard Werth rehearsed with the remaining Doors but before the new lineup even started, Ray Manzarek decided to leave and rode off into the sunset for a solo career. John Densmore and Robbie Krieger stayed in Britain and formed the Butts Band with ex-Bronco vocalist Jess Roden. They recorded one eponymous album before falling apart. The two ex-Doors returned home and recruited an American lineup, which also managed just one album, *Hear & Now*.

The band's name was inspired by a British street, The Butts, in Kidderminster, Worcestershire.

Albums released today

1969 Captain Beefheart and His Magic Band *Trout Mask Replica* (US)

Captain Beefheart's third album was produced by Frank Zappa and originally released on Zappa's new Straight record label.

1972 Roxy Music *Roxy Music* (UK)

British glam-rockers Roxy Music released their eponymous debut album.

Died today

1999 Screaming Lord Sutch flamboyant British rocker, died aged fifty-eight

Seminal British rock'n'roll singer and founder of the Official Monster Raving Loony Party, Screaming Lord Sutch committed suicide. He was found by partner Yvonne Elwood hanged in his late mother's house in Harrow, London; he had suffered from depression.

Events today

17

1967 Elton John met Bernie Taupin

Liberty Records' Ray Williams placed an ad in the British music weekly *New Musical Express*, proclaiming that Liberty was looking for new talent to form a group. It attracted poet and lyricist Bernie Taupin, and singer and musician Reg Dwight (soon to be Elton John), at the time a member of Long John Baldry's backing band Bluesology. Williams felt that there might be a connection and introduced the two hopefuls to each other, thereby creating one of the most successful songwriting teams in rock'n'roll history.

1972 President Nixon start of the *Watergate* scandal

The arrest of five men inside the Democratic National Committee's office in the Watergate building led to political scandal and the resignation of the nation's President.

The gravity of the affair progressively increased until it forced President Richard Nixon to announce his resignation on national television on 8 August 1974. Nixon's resignation also sealed the fate of South Vietnam. He had assured his old ally, South Vietnam's President Thieu, that he would come to his assistance if Hanoi contravened the *Paris Peace Accords*. However, when the North did launch its final invasion of South Vietnam on 10 March* 1975, Nixon was no longer in a position to honour any such promises. America remained on the sidelines and watched as South Vietnam finally succumbed to the communist invaders.

1981 Pink Floyd last concert with Roger Waters

After fifteen years in the vanguard of progressive rock music, the classic post-Barratt lineup gave its swan song performance. With the final outing of *The Wall* at London's Earl's Court, Roger Waters, David Gilmore, Nick Mason and Rick Wright played together on stage for their last-ever, concert-length performance.

By now relationships were at breaking point. Wright had been sacked and Waters and Gilmore were at serious odds. The band stayed together for one aptly titled album, *The Final Cut* in 1983. This was followed by solo albums and litigation, before Gilmore, Mason and Wright re-emerged as "Pink Floyd" and Waters embarked on a solo career.

Album released today

1969 Elvis Presley *From Elvis in Memphis*

From Elvis in Memphis was Elvis Presley's first album of new rock material since *Pot Luck with Elvis* in 1962. For the rest of the 1960s fans had to be content with movie soundtrack albums, with the occasional morsel of big hits, old material, religious songs or TV special. Elvis's regular backing musicians, guitarist Scotty Moore, drummer DJ Fontana, pianist Floyd Cramer, saxophonist Boots Randolph and vocal group the Jordanaires were all conspicuous by their absence.

This album marked a distinct change of direction for Elvis as he transitioned from the Hollywood movie dominated 1960s into the Las Vegas driven 1970s. When it was released, Elvis was just six weeks away from the first of his concerts at the Vegas Hilton Hotel on 31 July*. By the end of the year his Hollywood acting career was behind him with the release of his thirty-first and final movie, *Change of Habit*.

Birthday today

1944 Chris Spedding guitar: Battered Ornaments; solo; session

Event today

1958 Rock'n'Roll Developments the Brill Building

Connie Francis recorded the Neil Sedaka and Howard Greenfield penned *Stupid Cupid* and gave the newly formed Aldon Music its first major hit record. The business had been set up some weeks earlier by Al Nevins and Don Kirshner, to publish music aimed at the rapidly growing teenage marketplace.

Nevins and Kirshner's Aldon Music operated out of their New York office at 1650 Broadway, directly opposite the famous Brill Building at 1619 Broadway. The Brill Building was named after the Brill Brothers clothing store operating on the ground floor but it become famous as an office block dominated by music writers and producers. Since the 1930s it had been home to writers such as Cole Porter and Irving Berlin. By the 1950s it had become the heart of Tin Pan Alley. Aldon Music signed up some of the most talented writers of the time and became one of the most successful elements of the 'Brill Building' music factory. As well as Sedaka and Greenfield, writers on the Aldon Music team included Gerry Goffin and Carole King, Doc Pomus and Mort Shuman, Jeff Barry and Ellie Greenwich, and Barry Mann and Cynthia Weil. These and other Brill Building writers dominated the marketplace until the Beatles came along in the early 1960s, heralding a new generation of rock artists who wrote their own material.

Recording session today

1969 Colosseum *Valentyne Suite*

This was the third and final day of recording for Colosseum's second album, *Valentyne Suite*, destined to be the final album by the original lineup. By the time that they came to record the third album, *Daughter of Time*, guitarist James Litherland had been replaced by Dave "Clem" Clempson and bassist Tony Reeves by Mark Clarke. Veteran British R&B singer Chris Farlowe had also joined the band by then as well.

Valentyne Suite was the first album to be released by the new Vertigo label, original copies had the distinctive "swirl" label design.

James Litherland left around the time that *Valentyne Suite* was released. He formed his own band and after John Wetton came on board it morphed into Mogul Thrash.

Birthday today

1942 Paul McCartney bassist, singer and songwriter: The Beatles, Wings

Paul McCartney was born in Liverpool, England. His father, Jim, was a pianist who also played the trumpet in the Jimmy Mac Jazz Band. Paul initially learnt to play the piano and trumpet but with the skiffle boom changing the face of British music, he decided that the guitar was the way forward. On 6 July* 1957 McCartney's friend Ivan Vaughan took him along to the Woolton Village Fête. Vaughan wanted to introduce McCartney to John Lennon, who was performing there with his skiffle group the Quarry Men. McCartney joined the Quarry Men on guitar and vocals shortly afterwards, after impressing Lennon with his rendition of Eddie Cochran's *Twenty Flight Rock*. By the time of their Hamburg debut on 17 August* 1960, Stuart Sutcliffe was the group's bass player. When Sutcliffe left the group McCartney switched to bass. He played the instrument on stage for the first time on 5 January* 1961.

Ringo was yet to join the group but from the time that they arrived in Germany for the first of their Hamburg gigs, they were performing as "The Beatles".

Events today

19

1965 The Kinks ill-fated first American tour

The Kinks opened their first, ill-fated American tour at New York's Academy of Music.

This American debut tour was to be their only visit to America until late 1969. During the tour they found themselves in dispute with the American Federation of Musicians. Urban legend provides a number of reasons for the contretemps, including Ray Davies thumping a union representative, disputes over money but mostly the use of non-union labour. The upshot was that the Kinks were delisted and effectively banned from performing in America. Their next American concert would not be until their appearance at New York's Fillmore East in October 1969.

The Moody Blues were originally scheduled to accompany the Kinks on this tour but they had to pull out at the last minute due to problems in obtaining the appropriate visas.

1974 Eric Clapton old Slowhand was back

Eric Clapton opened his *461 Ocean Boulevard* tour in Stockholm, the first of a couple of warm-up gigs in Scandinavia before America, Japan and Europe.

This was Clapton's first tour since Derek and the Dominos and his isolation soon after their gig on 5 December* 1970. Since then he had battled drugs and alcohol, before being coaxed out of his self-imposed exile by the Who's guitarist Pete Townshend. He arranged Clapton's comeback performance at London's Rainbow Theatre on 13 January* 1973.

Clapton's 1960s career was spent as an iconic blues guitarist. He started with the Yardbirds but when they become too commercial he joined John Mayall's Bluesbreakers. He left Mayall to form his own band Cream, with Ginger Baker and Jack Bruce. Band tensions led to its demise and Clapton's next venture was the short-lived Blind Faith. By now Clapton no longer sought the limelight and just wanted to be one of the band, which he found with Delaney and Bonnie. It was there that he was encouraged to do more singing. At the turn of the decade he formed his last band, Derek and the Dominos and also released his eponymous debut solo album, before drifting into a drug-fuelled exile.

The Rainbow performance marked the first tentative steps of Clapton's return but this time as a solo performer with a backing band. His second solo album, *461 Ocean Boulevard*, provided the basis for his first tour since Derek and the Dominos. From then on his career went from strength to strength. He performed his first residency at London's Royal Albert Hall in 1987, with a twenty-four-night stint there in 1991.

In 2000 he became the first artist to be inducted into the Rock and Roll Hall of Fame three times, his solo induction, the Yardbirds and Cream.

Recording session today

1937 Robert Johnson second and final recording session

Robert Johnson began his second and final recording session, at the Brunswick Records Building in Dallas, Texas. All of the songs were Johnson's own compositions.

He only ever recorded twenty-nine songs. The first sixteen were recorded over three days at the Gunter Hotel in San Antonio, starting on 23 November*. This second recording session in Dallas spanned two days, 19 and 20 June, when he recorded a further thirteen songs:

Stones in My Passway – I'm a Steady Rollin' Man – From Four Till Late – Malted Milk

Little Queen of Spades – Me and the Devil Blues – Traveling Riverside Blues

Honeymoon Blues – Love in Vain – Milkcow's Calf Blues – Hellhound on My Trail

Drunken Hearted Man – Stop Breakin' Down Blues

Events today

20

1964 The Rolling Stones American debut

The Stones played their first-ever concert in America on 5 June, opening on the West Coast in San Bernardino's Swing Auditorium in California. This American debut tour ended on the East Coast on 20 June at New York's Carnegie Hall.

1997 The Four Tops death ended rock'n'soul's longest serving lineup

The Four Tops lineup of Levi Stubbs, Abdul Fakir, Renaldo Benson and Lawrence Payton formed in 1954 as the Four Aims. Their big break came in 1964 with *Baby I Need Your Loving*. The quartet were together for over forty years, until Payton's death in 1997.

Album released today

1966 The Beatles *Yesterday...And Today* (US)

The Beatles' tenth Capitol album, *Yesterday...And Today*, was originally released on 15 June with the notorious "butcher" cover. This depicted the Beatles dressed in butcher's aprons and draped with cuts of raw meat, false teeth, and nude decapitated toy dolls. There was an outcry from fans and DJs alike, with major stores refusing to stock the album. It was quickly withdrawn and replaced on 20 June with a 'nice' cover. The new sleeve depicted the Beatles leaning on a steamer trunk. However, when the album found its way back into the shops many of the original sleeves had simply been re-covered by pasting the "trunk" cover on top of the original "butcher" cover. These new covers could be steamed off to reveal the original "butcher" cover underneath.

There was only one cover song on the album, *Act Naturally*, a country #1 for Buck Owens in 1963. With the exception of the traditional song *Maggie Mae* on the *Let It Be* album, this was the last cover song that the Beatles released in America.

The last cover song released in Britain was Larry Williams's *Bad Boy*, on the 1966 album *A Collection of Beatles Oldies.*

Birthdays today

1924 Chet Atkins guitar: architect of the "Nashville sound"

1938 Mickie Most singer: Most Brothers, Gear; producer

In the late 1950s Mickie Most formed the vocal duo the Most Brothers, with Alex Murray. In the 1960s he changed his focus to become a producer, with a string of credits including The Animals' *House of the Rising Sun*, Donovan's *Mellow Yellow* and Jeff Beck's album *Truth.* Moving more towards pop, Most became one of Britain's most successful producers and in 1976 set up RAK Recording Studios in London.

1942 Brian Wilson bass, keyboards, vocals and songwriter: The Beach Boys

The creative genius behind the Beach Boys was undoubtedly musician, singer, songwriter, producer and arranger, Brian Wilson. He co-wrote and produced one of the 1960s greatest albums *Pet Sounds*, said by Paul McCartney to have been an inspiration for the iconic *Sgt Pepper*. Intended as the follow-up to *Pet Sounds*, he was responsible for the great 1960s 'lost' album *Smile*, which did not see the light of day for nearly forty years. *Pet Sounds*, *Good Vibrations* and the demise of *Smile*, marked the high-point of Brain Wilson's creative period with the Beach Boys. Following this, ill health and stress meant that he took more of a back seat, particularly in live performances.

Events today

1965 The Charlatans opened at the Red Dog Saloon

San Francisco band the Charlatans played at the opening night of Virginia City's Red Dog Saloon in Nevada and were the venue's first house band.

The Charlatans were one of the proto-hippie bands and trailblazers for what became the San Francisco scene. The Red Dog Saloon was one of the first psychedelic dancehalls.

In 1966 Big Brother and the Holding Company became the house band.

1966 The Yardbirds Jimmy Page's first gig

When Jimmy Page joined the Yardbirds it was to replace the recently departed bass guitarist Paul Samwell-Smith. His first gig with the band was at the Marquee club in London's Soho. This was to be the group's last outing there.

Page continued on bass whilst rhythm guitarist Chris Dreja brought himself up to speed with the new instrument. For a short while after Dreja switched from six to four strings, the Yardbirds sported the dual lead guitars of Jeff Beck and Jimmy Page.

1967 Rock'n'Roll Developments *Summer of Love*

On a hilltop overlooking San Francisco's Haight-Ashbury district, a group of hippies celebrated the Summer Solstice and officially welcomed in the *Summer of Love*.

Concert promoter and founder of Fillmores East and West, Bill Graham trademarked the phrase "Summer of Love", despite Chet Helms being known as the "Father of the Summer of Love". This was a beautiful irony from one of the most successful promoters of 1960s psychedelic and hippie bands. Graham took the very name of the era mourned by the *Death of Hippie* march in Haight-Ashbury on 6 October* and turned it into a trademark. American idealism meets American capitalism.

Births and deaths today

1944 Jon Hiseman drums: Graham Bond, Georgie Fame, Colosseum I and II

When Ginger Baker left the Graham Bond Organisation to form Cream he was replaced by Jon Hiseman. Later Hiseman went on to co-found UK jazz-prog-rockers Colosseum.

1944 Ray Davies singer, songwriter and guitarist: The Kinks, solo

1966 Reg Calvert Screaming Lord Sutch's manager, died aged thirty-eight

Seminal British rock'n'roll singer Screaming Lord Sutch's manager and owner of Radio City pirate radio station, Reg Calvert was shot dead by Major Oliver Smedley.

Calvert and Sutch set up the pirate radio station Radio Sutch, launched on 27 May* 1964. Calvert bought Sutch out four months later and changed its name to Radio City. In the summer of 1965 Calvert was in discussions to merge with Radio Caroline. As a part of these discussions Radio City received enhanced transmitting equipment from Smedley. These talks came to nothing but Calvert retained the apparatus. In June 1966 Calvert was once again in merger discussions, this time with Radio London. Smedley wanted his transmitter back, boarded Radio City and repossessed the equipment. That evening Calvert went to see Smedley at his Saffron Walden home. A scuffle ensued and Smedley shot Calvert with a shotgun. Charges were brought against Smedley but he was acquitted on grounds of self-defence.

Smedley founded Radio Atlanta which ultimately became Radio Caroline South.

Event today

1984 Aerosmith reunited

The Aerosmith reunion was marked by the *Back in the Saddle* North American tour, kicking off at the Capitol Theatre in Concord, New Hampshire. This marked Aerosmith's return to success.

By the end of the 1970s Aerosmith had fallen apart. Guitarists Joe Perry and Brad Whitford had both left and been replaced by Jimmy Crespo and Rick Dufay. In the early 1980s Aerosmith faded away from playing stadia and were reduced to headlining theatres. By mid-1984 the rifts had healed and the two guitarists were reunited with the other original members: vocalist Steven Tyler, drummer Joey Kramer and bassist Tom Hamilton.

Recording session today

1961 The Beatles — Hamburg recording session with Tony Sheridan

During their second Hamburg trip in 1961, the Beatles took time out to record with another British star of the time, Tony Sheridan. John, Paul, George and drummer Pete Best backed Sheridan on *My Bonnie* and *The Saints*, both traditional songs arranged by Sheridan. The recording session was held at the Friedrich Ebert Halle in Hamburg, under the auspices of producer Bert Kaempfert.

This coupling was originally released by Polydor in Germany and credited to Tony Sheridan and the Beat Brothers. The name change was deemed necessary because it was felt that "Beatles" sounded too much like "peedles", the German slang word for penis. This single was issued in Britain in January 1962. Their own debut single *Love Me Do* was not available until 5 October* that same year.

The soon-to-be Fab Four (well, Fab Three, Pete Best never quite made the transition from Beatle to Fab Four) also backed him on some other tracks, later released as the album *The Beatles First*. The recordings included two Beatles songs performed without Sheridan, *Ain't She Sweet* with John taking the lead vocal and the Harrison and Lennon penned instrumental *Cry for a Shadow*, released as an American B-side by MGM in 1964.

Ain't She Sweet was written in 1927 and became a Tin Pan Alley standard.

Birthdays today

1937 Chris Blackwell — founder of Island Records

Island Records was one of the most successful British independent labels in rock history. Chris Blackwell started his operation in Jamaica in 1959, specialising in reggae and ska music. The company's name was inspired by Alec Waugh's novel *Island in the Sun*. He transferred his operation to London in 1962, initially continuing along the same vein with artists such as Jimmy Cliff and Derrick Morgan. When rock started to become more sophisticated in the mid-1960s, Island records moved into the vanguard of the new rock sound with bands like Jethro Tull, Traffic, Fairport Convention and Free.

1947 Howard Kaylan — singer: Turtles, Frank Zappa, Flo & Eddie

When the Turtles folded in 1970 Howard Kaylan and Mark Volman joined Frank Zappa. In order to overcome the ongoing contractual wrangling that prevented them from using their own names or "The Turtles", they became "The Phlorescent Leech & Eddie".

1948 Todd Rundgren — guitar and vocals: Nazz, Utopia; solo; producer

Events today

1962 Brian Epstein — the road to the Beatles

Having signed the Beatles to a management contract at the beginning of the year, Brian Epstein set up his management company NEMS Enterprises Ltd.

John Lennon and his washboard playing friend Pete Shotton formed the Black Jacks skiffle group in early 1957, renamed to "The Quarry Men" shortly afterwards. Paul McCartney famously met John at a Quarry Men gig at Woolton Garden Fete on 6 July*. McCartney's friend, George Harrison joined in early 1958. On 14 July the Quarry Men, John, Paul and George, with drummer Colin Hanton and pianist John Lowe, made a personal recording at Percy Phillips's studio in Liverpool. Guitarist Ken Brown joined the core trio briefly for the final Quarry Men gigs, before they changed their name to "Johnny and the Moondogs" in late 1959. In January 1960 they were joined on bass by John's art college friend Stuart Sutcliffe and changed their name to "The Silver Beetles". Drummer Tommy Moore came on board in early May. On 10 May* they failed an audition to support singer Billy Fury on his upcoming UK tour. Moore moved on and in July drummer Norman Chapman had a very brief spell in the band. Pete Best joined as the group's first permanent drummer. On 17 August* 1960 and finally called "The Beatles", Best played his debut gig when they opened in Hamburg for the first time. After Chas Newby's brief stint as bass player, with the first of four gigs starting on 17 December* 1960, Sutcliffe left and Paul moved to bass guitar. The final piece of the jigsaw came when Ringo Starr played his first gig as drummer on 18 August* 1962.

Epstein changed their image from leather to smart suits and after their failed audition at Decca, on 1 January* 1962, he secured them one with EMI.

1977 Led Zeppelin Keith Moon joined them on stage

One of the highlights of Led Zeppelin's ill-fated 1977 American tour, which had kicked off on 1 April*, was the concert at LA's Forum when the Who's Keith Moon joined the band on stage. Moon accompanied Bonham on his *Moby Dick* drum solo, giving Bonham's tympani drums an enthusiastic beating.

Keith Moon and John Entwistle inadvertently inspired the band's name, when they suggested that their proposed new group would go down like a "lead zeppelin".

Birthday today

1940 Stuart Sutcliffe artist and original Beatles bass player

In January 1960, John Lennon persuaded his Liverpool Art College friend Stuart Sutcliffe to spend his winnings from an art competition on a bass guitar and join him in his group Johnny and the Moondogs. (This was the group's name after the Quarry Men but before the Silver Beetles). Sutcliffe never really mastered the instrument and spent much of his time on stage with his back to the audience. During the trips to Hamburg, Sutcliffe fell in with an arty crowd who called themselves the "Exis". The group included his future girlfriend, the photographer Astrid Kirchherr. Sutcliffe was more interested in his art than the Beatles' music and when the others returned from the first trip to Hamburg in December 1960, he stayed behind with Kirchherr. It was at this time that Paul McCartney switched to bass guitar. Sutcliffe did occasionally appear on stage with the Beatles on subsequent Hamburg trips but his days as a Beatle were over.

Events today

1966 The Beatles final world tour

The Beatles began their ill-fated final world tour, taking in Germany, Japan and the Philippines. To be followed by their final American tour. Having played in Munich and Essen, the Beatles gave their last-ever Hamburg performance on 26 June. From there the tour was all downhill.

Their next port of call was Japan, to give five shows at Tokyo's Nippon Budokan Hall. This was the first time that the hallowed halls of the Budokan had been used by a rock'n'roll band. To many of Japan's martial arts followers the Budokan held a great spiritual significance. Protests against the Beatles included death threats and resulted in a strong police presence at the concerts. These death threats also kept the Fab Four virtual prisoners in their hotel room. In order to alleviate the boredom they collaborated on the painting *Images of a Woman*.

When the Beatles flew on to the Philippines things went from bad to worse. On 4 July they played two shows at the Rizal Memorial Football Stadium. The problems arose when the President's wife, Imelda Marcos, arranged a party at the Palace and invited the Fab Four to attend. Brian Epstein had respectfully refused the invitation but it was more of a summons than a request. Imelda Marcos took the refusal as a personal snub and the group had a very uncomfortable exit from Manila.

If they thought that things couldn't get any worse, the American tour was on the horizon and the teen magazine *Datebook* was about to publish the infamous John Lennon quote about being "more popular than Jesus", first seen in London's *Evening Standard* newspaper on 4 March*.

1966 Lenny Bruce last gig

Iconoclastic comedian Lenny Bruce opened what would prove to be his final concerts, with the first of two nights at San Francisco's Fillmore Auditorium. Frank Zappa's Mothers, which now included guitarist Elliott Ingber, provided the support. The event was promoted by Bill Graham, who would later open the Fillmore West in San Francisco.

This was the end of the line for Bruce. He died six weeks later from a morphine overdose. But for the Mothers of Invention it was just the beginning. Their debut album *Freak Out* was released a couple of days later. For the Lenny Bruce concert they were billed as "The Mothers" but this name proved to be a tad too risqué for their record company MGM, who insisted on a change to "The Mothers of Invention".

Single released today

1974 Lynyrd Skynyrd *Sweet Home Alabama* c/w *Take Your Time* (US)

This classic Lynyrd Skynyrd song was written by Ronnie Van Zant, Ed King and Gary Rossington, and produced by Al Kooper. The song was written as an answer to Neil Young's songs *Southern Man* and *Alabama*.

Birthday today

1944 Jeff Beck guitar: Yardbirds, Jeff Beck Group, Beck, Bogert & Appice

Jeff Beck replaced Eric Clapton in the Yardbirds in 1965. He formed the Jeff Beck Group in 1967, with singer Rod Stewart and bassist Ron Wood, who switched to guitar in the Faces and Stones. In 1972 he joined former Vanilla Fudge and Cactus rhythm section Carmine Appice and Tim Bogert, in Beck, Bogert & Appice.

Events today

1948 Cold War Berlin Airlift started

The Second World War had ended with the final battle for the German capital, Berlin. On 2 May 1945 the city fell, leaving Germany occupied by Russia, America and Britain. After the war Berlin was divided into sectors, each occupied by one of the allied countries, including France. The German territory occupied by Russia became the separate country of East Germany, with Berlin enclosed within its boundaries.

Two economic and political philosophies dominated the world at that time, single party communism in the East, championed by Russia (USSR) and democratic capitalism in the West, championed by

America. Relations between the two sides quickly deteriorated, with Winston Churchill referring to an "Iron Curtain" in a speech on 5 March 1946 and Bernard Baruch coining the expression "Cold War" in 1947.

One of the first major standoffs in the *Cold War* came about when Russia closed the land access to Berlin. Rather than desert their territories, the Western allies flew in supplies for the people of West Berlin. The blockade lasted until 12 May 1949. During that time more than a quarter of a million flights delivered over two million tons of supplies.[91]

1949 Rock'n'Roll Developments "Race Music" became "Rhythm & Blues"

American music magazine *The Billboard* changed the name of its best-sellers charts from "Race Music" to "Rhythm & Blues".

In a heavily segregated America even the charts differentiated between black and white artists. In 1948 record company RCA Victor started to market its "race music" as "blues and rhythm". *Billboard* magazine followed suit in 1949 and its *Best Selling Retail Race Records* chart became *Best-Selling Retail Rhythm & Blues Records*, and *Most-Played Juke Box Race Records* chart became *Most-Played Juke Box Rhythm & Blues Records*.

1962 Screaming Lord Sutch Keith Moon, Ritchie Blackmore and Nicky Hopkins

Screaming Lord Sutch and the Savages were headlining at London's Wembley Town Hall. After the show a fifteen-year-old Keith Moon went backstage and asked Savages' drummer Carlo Little if he would give him some drumming lessons. On 5 May* 1964 Moon was embarking on his career with the Who, at an audition for Fontana.

On stage with the Savages that night was future Deep Purple and Rainbow guitarist Ritchie Blackmore. He had joined the group in May. In October Blackmore left to join the Outlaws, who provided the backing for many of Joe Meek's artists.

Just before Blackmore joined the Savages, another stalwart of British rock music Nicky Hopkins had parted company with the band. Hopkins had been a member of the original Savages but left and rejoined, only to leave again a month or so before this gig, to join Cliff Bennett and the Rebel Rousers for their residency in Hamburg.

1967 The Beatles *Our World* TV broadcast

Our World was the first global, satellite TV show. It was transmitted to five continents and watched by an audience estimated between three and five million people. The British segment consisted of the Beatles performing *All You Need Is Love*. The studio audience was filled with a host of rock luminaries, including Eric Clapton, Mick Jagger and Keith Moon, who all sang along with the refrain.

The Beatles wrote *All You Need Is Love* especially for the show, an apt song that became an anthem for the *Summer of Love*.

Events today

1968 The Nice protest song as an instrumental

The Nice managed to achieve a lifetime ban after a flag-burning performance at London's Royal Albert Hall.

The problems arose over their rendition of *America*, loosely based on Leonard Bernstein's song from *West Side Story*. Their version had a much darker edge, including an opening that incorporated gunshots and screams. Conceived as an instrumental protest song after the assassination of Robert Kennedy on 5 June*, it had been released as a single shortly before this performance at the Royal Albert Hall. The lifetime ban from the venue resulted from the burning of the American flag at the end of the song, when the only spoken line bemoaned that America's "promise and anticipation" had been murdered by the "inevitable". Interestingly, the line was taken from a previous song *Dawn*, from *The Thoughts of Emerlist Davjack*, where the name "Dawn" was swapped for "America".

1977 Elvis Presley last-ever concert performance

Elvis gave his last-ever concert performance, at Indiana's Market Square Arena, Indianapolis. Seven weeks later the King of Rock'n'Roll was dead.

Single released today

1964 The Rolling Stones *It's All Over Now* c/w *Good Times Bad Times* (UK)

The Stones first British #1 came with *It's All Over Now*, penned by Bobby and Shirley Womack and originally released by the Valentinos in 1964.

Albums released today

1964 The Beatles *A Hard Day's Night* (US)

The content varied considerably from the British album. The UK tracks *Any Time at All*, *Things We Said Today*, *When I Get Home*, *You Can't Do That* and *I'll Be Back* were replaced by four soundtrack instrumental cuts by George Martin and His Orchestra.

1975 Bob Dylan *The Basement Tapes* (US)

Recorded between June and October 1967, the plethora of bootlegs of the sessions finally persuaded CBS to put 24 of the tracks out on this official double album release.

After his motorcycle accident on 29 July* 1966, Dylan sought a self-imposed solitude. A year later, with his previous backing band the Hawks, he took over the house known as *Big Pink* in Woodstock, New York and recorded over a hundred songs.

Shortly afterwards, the Hawks renamed to "The Band" and the nickname for the house became the title of their debut album, *Music from the Big Pink*.

Birthdays today

1909 Colonel Tom Parker Elvis Presley's manager

Dutch-born Parker emigrated to America in the late 1920s. Some sources suggest that he was fleeing from a crime committed in the Netherlands. Louisiana Governor Jimmie Davies bestowed Parker with the rank of honorary Colonel in the late 1940s. He managed Hank Snow and Eddy Arnold before signing Elvis Presley on 15 August* 1955.

1943 Georgie Fame keyboards and vocals: The Blue Flames; solo

1955 Mick Jones guitar and vocals: The Delinquents, London SS, The Clash

Events today

1970 Queen debut concert

Freddie Mercury had recently left his band Sour Milk Sea and joined Brian May and Roger Taylor in Smile. They changed the band's name to "Queen" and played their first gig together at Truro's City Hall in Cornwall.

The concert was arranged by the British Red Cross Society and a local advertisement for the event enticingly suggested that "We invite YOU to come and DANCE". The booking was taken as Smile, resulting in Queen's first appearance being billed as "Smile". In this first Queen lineup Mike Grose filled the spot as bass player. It would be another year before bassist John Deacon joined and the classic Queen lineup was in place.

1971 Vietnam War the US Marine Corps went home

The bulk of the remaining US Marines left Vietnam. A small number of Marines remained but for the United States Marine Corps the war was over.

1980 Led Zeppelin John Bonham collapsed on stage

During what turned out to be their final tour, drummer John Bonham collapsed on stage during the gig in Nuremberg's Messehalle in Germany. From the beginning of the show Bonham audibly missed some rhythms and by the time of their third number, *Black Dog*, the concert came to an end. There was press speculation about drink and drugs but the band insisted that he had simply overeaten earlier in the day. The tour ended in Berlin on 7 July. Bonham died three months later on 25 September*.

Recording session today

1962 Muddy Waters *You Shook Me*

You Shook Me started life as the instrumental *Blue Guitar*, written and recorded by Earl Hooker in 1961. Muddy Waters recorded the Willie Dixon penned vocals over the track and released it on Chess as *You Shook Me*.

The song was covered by Led Zeppelin on their eponymous debut album in 1969.

Album released today

1966 The Mothers of Invention *Freak Out* (US)

Frank Zappa's debut was released as a double album in America but was pruned down to a single platter for British consumption.

The band on this groundbreaking album consisted of guitarist Frank Zappa, vocalist Ray Collins, drummer Jimmy Carl Black, bassist Roy Estrada and guitarist Elliot Ingber.

Died today

1999 Brian O'Hara Fourmost guitarist, died at the age of fifty-seven

Lead guitarist, singer and founding member of the Fourmost, Brian O'Hara was found hanged at his home in the Waverley area of Liverpool.

O'Hara was one of the original Two Jays formed in the late 1950s. They became a quartet and by the early 1960s had morphed into the Fourmost. The group was managed by Brian Epstein and played at Liverpool's legendary Cavern Club on 1 March* 1961, before the Beatles made their evening debut there. The Fourmost scored their first British hit in 1963 with the Lennon and McCartney penned *Hello Little Girl.*

Events today

1970 Landmark Festivals *Festival Express*

One of the more ambitious festivals of the late 1960s and early '70s was the *Festival Express*, which used a train to carry the performers from Toronto to gigs in Winnipeg and Calgary. The trilogy of festivals opened with two days at Toronto's CNE Stadium on 27 and 28 June. Rock stars rubbing shoulders on the coaches included Janis Joplin, Grateful Dead, The Band, Delaney & Bonnie, Ten Years After, Traffic, Mountain, Buddy Guy and The Flying Burrito Brothers.

All had not gone smoothly in the run-up to the opening of the festival in Toronto. But a group of locals believed that they were being ripped off and that this should be a free festival. One of the organisations leading the discontent was the M4M, May 4th Movement, a group set up to commemorate the four students shot dead at Kent State University. The shootings were the tragic conclusion to events that began to unfold on 1 May*, 1970. To placate the demonstrators the Grateful Dead held a free concert nearby.

The musicians boarded the train after the Toronto gig and spent five days partying, with a stop-off for the Winnipeg concert. The troubadours arrived in Calgary for the final concert on 4 July. The whole event was captured by a film crew but problems at the time meant that it would be nearly thirty-five years before the tour movie saw the light of day.

1973 Landmark Concerts *British Re-Invasion Show*

Not necessarily a landmark as a show but following on the heels of 1950s revival shows it heralded an increasing interest in nostalgia for live gigs by beat groups from the early 1960s. Almost a decade after the original British Invasion of 1964 to 1966, Richard Nader staged this concert at New York's Madison Square Garden as a part of an eighteen-city tour. The bill was headlined by Herman's Hermits, ably supported by Wayne Fontana and the Mindbenders, Gerry and the Pacemakers, The Searchers and Billy J Kramer.

The British Invasion started around 1 February* 1964 but by the end of 1966 beat groups were giving way to the harder-edged rock of bands like Pink Floyd, Cream and the Doors. With the exception of Herman's Hermits, none of the other groups appearing in the *Re-Invasion Show* had progressed beyond the beat genre.

Herman's Hermits developed into a pop group, lead singer Peter Noone went on to have a successful solo career in America. Wayne Fontana and the Mindbenders parted company in 1965, with both finding UK chart success as independent acts. By the end of 1966 the original Gerry and the Pacemakers was history. The Searchers continued on with a number of lineup changes. Original drummer Chris Curtis left in 1966 for a solo career. In 1967 he started to put together a new group, Roundabout but he had moved on before it morphed into Deep Purple. Original Searchers lead singer and bass player Tony Jackson left in 1964 to form his own group the Vibrations and was replaced by Frank Allen. Billy J Kramer and The Dakotas parted company in 1967.

Recording session today

1967 The Who *The Last Time* and *Under My Thumb*

The Who recorded two Jagger and Richard compositions to show solidarity with Mick Jagger and Keith Richard, both facing jail sentences for drug possession. Jagger had been found guilty and Richard was up in court the following day. Only three of the Who appeared on the record. John Entwistle was away on his honeymoon at the time, Pete Townshend covered for him on bass. The single was released in Britain two days later.

Events today

1965 Vietnam War "search-and-destroy" tactic launched

American forces completed their first search-and-destroy mission in Vietnam.

General William C Westmorland had been head of the American forces in Vietnam since replacing General Paul Harkins in June 1964. In order to counter the growing number of attacks by both the Viet Cong and the North Vietnamese Army, he requested additional American combat troops and introduced a "search-and-destroy" tactic. In his book *How We Lost the Vietnam War*, Nguyen Cao Ky, South Vietnam's prime minister at the time, tells of the first "search-and-destroy" mission. This was a three day operation starting on 27 June and targeting a Viet Cong force north of Saigon. It was carried out by a combination of American, Australian and South Vietnamese troops. Ky suggests that Westmoreland believed that his "search and destroy" methods would defeat the communists by the end of 1967.

Westmoreland was *Time* magazine's "Man of the Year" in 1965.

1969 The Jimi Hendrix Experience curtain call for the Experience

The final outing for the classic lineup of Jimi Hendrix, Mitch Mitchell and Noel Redding as the Jimi Hendrix Experience, came when the trio headlined the final day of the three-day *Denver Pop Festival* at the Mile High Stadium in Denver, Colorado.

Noel Redding left the group after this performance. He had already formed his own band Fat Mattress, where he moved back to guitar and took a larger share of the vocals. Redding played in both bands when he opened on the Jimi Hendrix Experience tour.

Single released today

1962 The Contours *Do You Love Me c/w Move Mr. Man* (US)

The Berry Gordy Jr penned *Do You Love Me* gave the Contours their biggest American hit. The British cover by the Dave Clark Five gave them their first, albeit minor, UK hit but they lost out to the Brian Poole and the Tremeloes' cover which scored a UK #1.

Album released today

1968 Pink Floyd *A Saucerful of Secrets* (UK)

A Saucerful of Secrets was Pink Floyd's second album but the first to feature guitarist David Gilmour. It also contained contributions from former frontman Syd Barrett.

Births and deaths today

1943 Bob Brunning bass: Fleetwood Mac, Savoy Brown, Brunning Sunflower

Before the "Mac" (John McVie) of Fleetwood Mac joined the group, Bob Brunning was the bass player. When McVie finally left John Mayall's Bluesbreakers to join Peter Green's Fleetwood Mac, Brunning moved on to Savoy Brown.

1948 Ian Paice drums: The Maze, Deep Purple

1979 Lowell George guitarist and singer, died at the age of thirty-four

Little Feat founder Lowell George died of a heart attack whilst on tour promoting his solo album *Thanks I'll Eat It Here.*

Events today

1963 The Rolling Stones opened the resited Crawdaddy Club

The Rolling Stones performed at the reopening of London's Crawdaddy Club. It relocated from the Station Hotel in Richmond, west London, to a larger venue a short distance away at the grounds of the Richmond Athletic Association, home to London Scottish rugby club.

The Crawdaddy Club was a breeding ground for London R&B bands. At the time of the relocation the Rolling Stones were the club's house band. They had taken over from the original house band, the Dave Hunt R&B Band, four months earlier. The Stones were replaced by the Yardbirds, when they moved on at the end of September following the success of their first single, a cover of Chuck Berry's *Come On.*

The club was owned by Giorgio Gomelsky, who managed the Rolling Stones at this time before they signed a deal with Andrew Loog Oldham. Gomelsky also managed the Yardbirds until Peter Grant took them over and helped them to morph into Led Zeppelin.

The original Crawdaddy house band, the Dave Hunt R&B Band, had boasted amongst its ranks the future founder of the Kinks, Ray Davies on guitar and, on occasions, future Rolling Stones drummer Charlie Watts.

1963 Jet Harris and Tony Meehan package tour concert in Torquay

This was a time of package tour one-night stands, with multiple artists playing every night at different theatres and concert halls across the UK. In 1963 Jet Harris and Tony Meehan could be seen on different package tours with Gene Vincent and John Leyton, Paul Anka and Jimmy Justice, and Del Shannon and Duffy Power. On this particular night, they were playing at Torquay's Princess Theatre, sharing a bill with Shane Fenton.

Bassist Jet Harris and drummer Tony Meehan had both been founding members of the Shadows. Meehan had been the first to leave the group in late 1961 to join Decca. Harris left six months later for a solo career. He scored a couple of hits with *Besame Mucho* and Elmer Bernstein's *The Man with the Golden Arm*, before teaming up with Meehan in late 1962. Their first single, *Diamonds*, featured the young session guitarist Jimmy Page, who later joined the Yardbirds and morphed them into Led Zeppelin. The duo's backing group also included future Led Zeppelin bassist John Paul Jones.

His fellow performer that night, Shane Fenton, reinvented himself as Alvin Stardust and had a string of British hits in the 1970s and '80s.

Recording session today

1971 Lynyrd Skynyrd nearly their first album

Lynyrd Skynyrd were in the Muscle Shoals recording studio laying down tracks for an intended first album.

In 1971 and 1972 Southern-rockers Lynyrd Skynyrd recorded enough material for their debut album but at the time it was not deemed to be suitable for release. It eventually saw the light of day as the original band's final release six years later as *Skynyrd's First and ...Last*. The album's release was prompted by the plane crash on 20 October* 1977 which killed three band members. The band's personnel changed during the sessions but included Lynyrd Skynyrd founding members, vocalist Ronnie Van Zant, and guitarists Gary Rossington and Allen Collins. Billy Powell joined as a roadie but became the band's keyboard player.

Lynyrd Skynyrd's debut album finally appeared in the form of *pronounced ('lĕh-'nérd 'skin-'nérd)* in August 1973.

July

Events today

1966 The Mamas & The Papas goodbye Mama Michelle and hello Mama Jill

The Mamas & The Papas opened a short American tour at the Dallas Memorial Auditorium. This was Jill Gibson's debut performance, having recently replaced Michelle Phillips after she was sacked by the rest of the group.

Michelle was the wife of Papa John Phillips, the group's main songwriter and guiding light. The last straw in their relationship came after her affair with the Byrds' Gene Clark. Phillips and the other two group members, Cass Elliot and Denny Docherty, famously wrote Mama Michelle a letter informing her that they no longer wanted to record or perform with her.[43] Michelle's replacement Mama Jill was the girlfriend of the group's producer Lou Adler. Gibson's tenure as a Mama was short lived. Mama Michelle was reinstated after constant chants at live performances for her return.

1969 Sam Phillips sold Sun Records

The end of an era came when founder Sam Phillips sold the pioneering Sun Records label and back catalogue to former Mercury executive Shelby Singleton.

Phillips had founded his Memphis recording studio in the early 1950s and initially licensed his recordings to established labels. One of his earliest recordings released on the Chess label was Jackie Brenston's *Rocket 88*, recorded on 5 March* 1951 and hailed by many as the first rock'n'roll record. In the spring of 1952 Sun Records released its first single, Johnny London's *Drivin' Slow*. The label's fortunes changed when Phillips discovered Elvis Presley and released his first single, *That's All Right* on 19 July* 1954. Rockabilly pioneer Carl Perkins became one of Sun's brightest stars, giving the label its first million selling single with *Blue Suede Shoes* in 1956. In the summer of 1957 Jerry Lee Lewis was in the Top 10 on both sides of the Atlantic with *Whole Lot of Shakin' Going On*. A little after this Johnny Cash scored a handful of hits before moving on to Columbia and international success. Over the same period, Roy Orbison released a clutch of singles without troubling the charts. He too moved on to find international success after a change of label to Monument. The artist Sam Phillips really missed out on was Conway Twitty. He auditioned in 1956 but was not signed to the label. Twitty went on to become one of the biggest selling country artists of all time.

The 1950s was Sun's golden era. Phillips never managed to replicate this success but will always be remembered as one of rock'n'roll's true pioneers.

Album released today

1968 The Band *Music from the Big Pink* 1st album (US)

Birthdays today

1915 Willie Dixon Chicago blues guitarist, singer and songwriter

One of the most influential and prolific blues songwriters of his generation, Willie Dixon wrote many of the blues classics, including *I Just Want to Make Love to You*, *Spoonful* and *I'm Your Hoochie Coochie Man*. His song *You Need Love* was used by Led Zeppelin as the basis for their *Whole Lotta Love* and after legal action Dixon was included on the songwriting credits. Dixon also played bass guitar on a number of Muddy Waters' songs as well as Chuck Berry's early Chess recordings.

1945 Debbie Harry singer: Wind in the Willows, Stillettos, Blondie

Events today

1964 Civil Rights Movement *Civil Rights Act* passed

2

This was a landmark act which outlawed racial segregation in schools, public places and employment. The *Civil Rights Bill* was initiated by President Kennedy in a television broadcast on 11 June* 1963, as a response to Alabama Governor George Wallace's defiant *Schoolhouse Door* stand at the University of Alabama. Wallace's actions were an attempt to stop two black youths from registering to become students.

The Bill was still being debated when President Kennedy was assassinated in Dallas on 23 November* 1963. The *Civil Rights Act* was finally signed into law by President Johnson.

1971 Queen classic lineup's debut concert

With bassist John Deacon in place, the classic Queen lineup played its debut gig at a Surrey College just outside London.

Freddie Mercury, Brian May and Roger Taylor came together in Smile and soon changed their name to "Queen". They played their first gig, albeit billed as "Smile", on 27 June* 1970. It took them another year to find a permanent bass player.

2005 Pink Floyd pigs did fly! Pink Floyd and Roger Waters reunited

After a gap of twenty-four years, David Gilmour, Nick Mason, Rick Wright and Roger Waters reunited for the last-ever stage performance of the post-Syd Barrett Pink Floyd lineup.

The occasion was prompted by the worldwide concerts to raise poverty awareness ahead of the upcoming G8 conference in Scotland. The 20-minute set at London's Wembley Stadium comprised the songs *Speak to Me, Breathe/Breathe Reprise, Money, Wish You Were Here* and *Comfortably Numb.* The set reached its climax with a stunning guitar solo from David Gilmour at the end of *Comfortably Numb.*

The four musicians had not played together since performing *The Wall* for the last time at London's Earls Court on 17 June* 1981. After that *Wall* gig the group imploded. One more album, *The Final Cut,* followed but solo albums and litigation ensued. Until, in 1987 Gilmour, Mason and Wright emerged with the album and tour for *A Momentary Lapse of Reason.* Thus began the third era of Pink Floyd. There was an occasional collaboration but with the deaths of Syd Barrett on 7 July 2006 and Rick Wright on 15 September 2008, the classic Pink Floyd lineups would never again grace the concert stage.

Recording session today

1956 The Johnny Burnette Trio *The Train Kept A-Rollin'*

The Trio, guitarist and singer Johnny Burnette, his brother Dorsey on upright bass and guitarist Paul Burlison, recorded *The Train Kept A-Rollin'* for inclusion on their debut album, *Johnny Burnette and the Rock 'n Roll Trio.*

The song was co-written and originally recorded by Tiny Bradshaw in 1951. The Trio also released *The Train Kept A-Rollin'* as a single, coupled with a cover of Big Joe Turner's *Honey Hush*, recorded the following day. Sadly, this rock'n'roll classic failed to bother the charts. The Yardbirds, featuring guitarist Jeff Beck, gave the song a whole new lease of life when they included it on their mid-1960s album *Having a Rave Up*.

When Screaming Lord Sutch released his cover in the UK in 1965, he also chose to couple it with *Honey Hush* – the same B-side as Johnny Burnett. Sutch's version was produced by Joe Meek.

Event today

1973 David Bowie Ziggy Stardust's final appearance

After nearly 18 months of concerts in America, Japan and Britain, Ziggy Stardust and the Spiders from Mars gave their last performance, at London's Hammersmith Odeon.

The Spiders were guitarist Mick Ronson, bassist Trevor Bolder and drummer Mick Woodmansey, who was later replaced in Bowie's backing band by Aynsley Dunbar.

Single released today

1964 The High Numbers *Zoot Suit c/w I'm the Face* (UK)

Drummer Keith Moon had joined the Who a couple of months earlier and by the time that their first single, *Zoot Suit*, was released they had renamed to "The High Numbers".

The group performed for about eighteen months as "The Detours", with Moon joining just after the group had renamed to "The Who". Around this time they met publicist Peter Meaden who set about creating the group's Mod image and changed their name to "The High Numbers". That summer they signed a management contract with Kit Lambert and Chris Stamp who changed their name back to "The Who".

Both sides of the single were written by Meaden and it was promoted as the first authentic Mod record.

Births and deaths today

1947 Anthony "Top" Topham guitar: Metropolis Blues Quartet, Yardbirds; solo

Top Topham was lead guitarist in the Metropolis Blues Quartet (sometime referred to as the Metropolitan Blues Quartet). When ex-Country Gentlemen lead guitarist Paul Samwell-Smith and drummer Jim McCarty joined, Samwell-Smith moved to bass. The Quartet morphed into the Yardbirds, with Topham as the first lead guitarist in a group to boast three of rock's greatest guitarists: Eric Clapton, Jeff Beck and Jimmy Page.

Eric Clapton replaced Top Topham in October 1963 when, with increasing group commitments, the sixteen-year-old Topham opted to leave in order to continue his education.

1969 Brian Jones Rolling Stones founder, died at the age of twenty-seven

Around midnight on 2/3 July, Brian Jones was found dead in the swimming pool of Cotchford Farm, his home in rural Sussex, previously owned by the author AA Milne. The events surrounding Jones's death have always been shrouded in controversy. The British *Daily Mail* national newspaper ran an article on 30 August 2009 to say that police were reviewing Jones's death because new evidence had come to light. The death certificate gave the cause of death as, "Drowning ...Severe liver dysfunction due to fatty degeneration and the ingestion of alcohol and drugs: Swimming whilst under the influence of alcohol and drugs: MISADVENTURE."[50] [their underlines and upper case]

1971 Jim Morrison the Lizard King, died at the age of twenty-seven

On 30 October* 1970 Jim Morrison was sentenced for indecency offences committed at a Miami concert on 2 March* 1969 and was freed on a $50,000 bond. He made his final concert appearance with the Doors in New Orleans on 12 November*. Whilst awaiting the appeal against his sentence Morrison and his girlfriend, Pamela Courson, moved to Paris. They lived together at 17 rue Beautreillis and it was there that Courson found Morrison dead in his bathtub. No post mortem was carried out and the cause of death was given as "heart failure".[11] He was buried in Paris in the Père Lachaise Cemetery.

Events today

1974 Steely Dan final concert

Steely Dan gave their final performance at the Santa Monica Centre in California.

Songwriters and musicians Donald Fagen and Walter Becker formed the group in 1972, taking their name from a reference to a dildo in William Burroughs' beat generation novel *Naked Lunch*. After this gig they quit live performances to become a studio band, with session musicians augmenting Fagen and Becker. Original guitarist Jeff "Skunk" Baxter left to join the Doobie Brothers. It would be nearly twenty years before Fagen and Becker took to the road again with an all-new Steely Dan.

1976 The Clash debut gig

In mid-1976 punk was just breaking in the UK. The Sex Pistols were still three months away from signing their first record deal, clinched on 8 October*. The London SS had recently renamed to "The Clash" and travelled up to the north of England to give their debut performance, supporting the Sex Pistols at Sheffield's Black Swan.

This lineup consisted of Clash stalwarts Joe Strummer, Mick Jones and Paul Simonon, with original drummer Terry Chimes, aka Tory Crimes, and third guitarist Keith Levene.

Levene left after a handful of gigs to join Sid Vicious in Flowers of Romance.

1976 Ramones UK debut gig

A couple of months after the American release of their eponymous debut album, the Ramones opened their first British tour with a concert at London's Roundhouse.

The Sex Pistols had played their first gig on 6 November* 1975. The Clash's debut was on this very same day, when they opened for the Sex Pistols 160 miles away in Sheffield. Both the Pistols and the Clash acknowledged the Ramones as being a major influence and recognised their importance in paving the way for British punk bands.

1987 Bob Dylan and Grateful Dead toured together

The unlikely combination of Bob Dylan backed by the Grateful Dead played the opening night of their tour at Sullivan Stadium in Foxboro, Massachusetts.

Five more dates followed across five American states, finishing on 26 July at California's Anaheim Stadium. The Grateful Dead lineup for the tour was Jerry Garcia guitar, Bob Weir guitar and vocals, bassist Phil Lesh, keyboard player Brent Mydland and drummers Bill Kreutzmann and Mickey Hart. The liaison spawned the album *Dylan and the Dead*. The album met with a mixed reaction, *Rolling Stone's* reviewer was unimpressed and suggested that you probably had to be there.

Recording session today

1966 The Animals *Animalism* session with Frank Zappa

Frank Zappa arranged two of the tracks for the American *Animalism* album, recorded at the TTG Studios in Los Angeles. The tracks were, the Zappa composition *All Night Long* and the Fred Neil song *The Other Side of This Life*, released by him in 1965.

Zappa probably also played guitar on the first track and bass on the second.

Single released today

1969 The Rolling Stones *Honky Tonk Women* c/w *You Can't Always Get What You Want* (UK)

This was the first Rolling Stones single to feature new guitarist Mick Taylor.

Events today

5

1958 Johnny O'Keefe and the Dee Jays birth of Australian rock'n'roll

Australia's first rock'n'roll band, Johnny O'Keefe and the Dee Jays released their fourth single, *The Wild One* and entered rock history – the birth of Australian rock'n'roll.

The song is sometimes known as *Real Wild Child* and has been widely covered. Jerry Lee Lewis recorded it shortly before his career imploded after he landed in England on 22 May* 1958. The Crickets' Jerry Allison released his 1958 cover using his middle name, "Ivan". Jet Harris included it on an EP in 1962 and Iggy Pop on an album in 1986.

1969 The Rolling Stones free concert in Hyde Park

An estimated quarter of a million people turned up for the free concert in central London's Hyde Park, headlined by the Rolling Stones.

Brian Jones was asked to leave the Rolling Stones on 8 June*. He was replaced by ex-John Mayall guitarist Mick Taylor. This was his first appearance but the debut was eclipsed by Jones's sudden death on 3 July*. To mark the passing of the Rolling Stones' founder, Mick Jagger opened their set by reading a poem. He chose an extract from Shelley's *Adonais*, an elegy on the death of his friend John Keats.

Also appearing that day were Family, King Crimson, Roy Harper, Alexis Korner's New Church and Battered Ornaments (without Pete Brown who had been sacked by his own band the day before). The event was policed by Hell's Angels, a decision repeated with tragic consequences at the notorious Altamont concert on 6 December*.

1971 Led Zeppelin riot at a concert in Italy

The end of Led Zeppelin's 1971 European tour was marred by a riot at their notorious final concert at Milan's Vigorelli Velodrome.

The gig was a day-long festival attended by 15,000 fans. Disruption built up throughout the day, with escalating confrontations between the police and concertgoers. By the time that Led Zeppelin opened their performance with the *Immigrant Song*, the situation was spiralling out of control. Missiles were thrown and the police responded by firing tear gas into the audience. Led Zeppelin played on but when tear gas started to waft across the stage the band decided that discretion was the better part of valour. They abandoned the set and barricaded themselves in a room backstage. The situation had become a full-blown riot.

Recording session today

1964 Them first recording session

Them were in the studio for their first Decca recording session.

The band recorded seven songs that day, including both sides of their debut single. The A-side was a cover of Slim Harpo's self-penned 1961 single *Don't Start Crying Now*, coupled with Van Morrison's *One Two Brown Eyes*. Another Morrison song *Gloria*, also cut at the session, provided the B-side for their second single. The A-side was a cover of Big Joe Williams's blues classic *Baby Please Don't Go*, recorded in 1935.

Birthday today

1943 Robbie Robertson guitar: The Hawks, The Band

After splitting from rockabilly star Ronnie Hawkins, the Hawks backed Bob Dylan on his groundbreaking electric tour of 1965/1966, before renaming to "The Band".

Events today

6

1957 Quarry Men John met Paul

The Beatles' story really started on 6 July 1957, the day that Paul McCartney went to see John Lennon's skiffle group the Quarry Men perform at St Peter's Church fete in Woolton, a leafy suburb of Liverpool.

Paul had been taken to see John and the boys by his friend Ivan Vaughan. After the Quarry Men's set Paul auditioned for them. He played the guitar left handed and impressed them by knowing all of the words to Eddie Cochran's *Twenty Flight Rock*. A couple of weeks later Paul was a Quarry Man.

1969 Procol Harum prog rock became orchestral

Procol Harum performed at the *Stratford Festival* in Ontario, Canada, with the Stratford Festival Orchestra and Festival Rock Chorus, conducted by Lawrence Smith. Following on from two pieces by JS Bach, the programme listed the items to be premiered by Procol Harum and Orchestra as: *A Salty Dog, In Held 'Twas in I, Repent Walpurgis, A Whiter Shade of Pale, Stoke Poges* and *Skip Softly My Moonbeams.*

This fusion of rock and classical music was a continuing development of prog rock and Procol Harum was by no means the only exponent of the genre. Three months later, on 24 September*, Deep Purple recorded their *Concerto for Group and Orchestra* at London's Royal Albert Hall. On 13 August 1970 underground favourites Soft Machine performed three pieces at the BBC Proms, *Out-Bloody-Rageous, Facelift* and *Esther's Nose Job*. Later on that same year, the newly formed Emerson, Lake & Palmer treated the Isle of Wight festivalgoers to their rendition of Mussorgsky's *Pictures at an Exhibition*, recorded live seven months later on 26 March*.

1977 Pink Floyd notorious spitting incident

One of rock's most notorious incidents took place at the end of the *In the Flesh* tour, when Roger Waters spat in the face of a fan during the concert at Montreal's Olympic Stadium in Canada.

This was the last concert of the tour and was attended by nearly 80,000 people. Waters became increasingly frustrated with the rowdiness of the fans and the constant sound of firecrackers. The situation culminated in his infamous act of spitting in the face of a concertgoer. Guitarist David Gilmour had also had enough and failed to return to the stage for the encore. This left Snowy White, second guitarist and temporary Pink Floyder, to handle the guitar part for the blues jam used to close the show.

It was from this experience that the seeds for *The Wall* album and concert were planted in Roger Waters' mind.

Birthdays today

1925 Bill Haley vocals, guitar: The Saddlemen, His Comets

Bill Haley was rock'n'roll's first superstar. After his version of *Rock Around the Clock* was released for the second time, it became a worldwide smash hit and kick-started rock'n'roll. The impetus for the song's success came after it was played over the opening credits of the 1955 movie *Blackboard Jungle*.

1939 Jet Harris bass: Vipers, Shadows, Jet Harris and Tony Meehan

After starting out on the skiffle circuit, Jet Harris became the Shadows first bass player.

Events today

7

1968 The Yardbirds last gig

The final lineup of the Yardbirds, vocalist Keith Relf, drummer Jim McCarty, guitarist Jimmy Page and bassist Chris Dreja, gave their swan song performance at Luton Technical College in Bedfordshire.

Relf and McCarty formed the acoustic duo Together. After a couple of singles, they recruited pianist John Hawken from the Nashville Teens, bassist Louis Cennamo previously with the Herd, and with Keith's sister Jane as vocalist they morphed into Renaissance. Chris Dreja sought pastures green as a professional photographer. Jimmy Page and manager Peter Grant put a new lineup together – and became Led Zeppelin.

1980 Led Zeppelin final performance with John Bonham

The end came unexpectedly for Led Zeppelin. As their European tour drew to a close with the final performance in Berlin's Eissporthalle, Jimmy Page, Roger Plant, John Paul Jones and drummer John Bonham had unknowingly played their last gig together. The set finished with *Whole Lotta Love*, written by the four group members. It was all over for Led Zeppelin.

John Bonham had collapsed on stage a week earlier on 27 June* and on 25 September* he died following a heavy drinking session.

Recording session today

1941 The Almanac Singers *Sod Buster Ballads*

The lineup that recorded *Sod Buster Ballads* was Pete Seeger, Woody Guthrie, Lee Hays, Millard Lampell and Peter Hawes. The album contained the song *House of the Rising Sun*, twenty years before the Animals' arrangement made #1 on both sides of the Atlantic.

Co-founded by Pete Seeger, and counting Woody Guthrie amongst its ranks, the Almanac Singers were a group of left-wing musicians who sang songs of political protest. They laid the foundations for 1960s protest singers such as Bob Dylan and Phil Ochs.

After Woody Guthrie left, Pete Seeger and Lee Hayes stayed together and formed the Weavers. Pete Seeger's political commentaries drew the wrath of the American government and on 26 March* 1957 he was indicted for Contempt of Congress.

Single released today

1967 The Beatles *All You Need Is Love c/w Baby, You're a Rich Man* (UK)

All You Need Is Love was written especially for *Our World*, the first-ever live global TV link-up of over twenty countries, broadcast on 25 June* 1967.

Birthday today

1940 Ringo Starr drums: Rory Storm, The Beatles; solo

Ringo was the final piece of the Beatles jigsaw. He played with a number of Liverpool groups, including The Eddie Clayton Skiffle Group, The Darktown Skiffle Group and The Raving Texans, which morphed into Rory Storm and the Hurricanes. It was when he was with the Hurricanes that he first met and sometimes sat in with the Beatles. Shortly after the Beatles first EMI recording session on 6 June* 1962, drummer Pete Best was sacked and on 18 August* Starr played his first date as their official drummer.

Ringo adopted his stage name when Rory Storm and the Hurricanes played at Butlin's holiday camp; Ringo from his penchant for wearing rings and Starr from his surname.

Events today

1965 Ronnie Biggs escaped from prison

Ronnie Biggs escaped from Wandsworth Prison and eventually settled in Brazil. There was no extradition treaty but he returned voluntarily in 2001.

Biggs gained notoriety for his involvement in one of the most high profile crimes of the 1960s, the *Great Train Robbery*. The crime took place in the summer of 1963, with the gang making off with £2.6m. The perpetrators were caught and received some of the heaviest sentences in British legal history: Biggs got thirty years.

After the Sex Pistols split up following their concert at San Francisco's Winterland on 14 January* 1978, manager Malcolm McLaren, guitarist Steve Jones and drummer Paul Cook headed off to Brazil. There they hooked up with Biggs and recorded *No One is Innocent (A Punk Prayer by Ronald Biggs)*. It was released as a single in June 1978.

1967 The Jimi Hendrix Experience joined the Monkees' American tour

After their stunning debut performance at the *Monterey Pop Festival*, the Jimi Hendrix Experience were invited by the Monkees to join them on their American tour. This unlikely support act joined mid-tour and opened for the Monkees for the first time at Florida's Jacksonville Coliseum.

The audiences for the two acts could not have been more different, with the typical Monkees fan being a young teenage girl. Hendrix's performances were greeted with chants of, "We want the Monkees." For Jimi and the lads the tour came to a premature end at New York's Forest Hills Stadium on 16 July. Urban legend has it that the conservative *Daughters of the American Revolution* put pressure on the promoter to tone down Hendrix's stage act. This myth came about from an article by Australian journalist Lillian Roxon, who was accompanying the tour. Her tongue-in-cheek piece was written to explain the Experience's sudden departure from the tour. In reality, Hendrix had simply had enough of the "we want the Monkees" chants and had quit the tour but remained on friendly terms with the TV musicians.

1968 Gram Parsons quit the Byrds

Guitarist and singer Gram Parsons announced that he was quitting the Byrds because he did not want to go on their upcoming tour of South Africa, a country steeped in apartheid. At the end of the tour Chris Hillman also left the Byrds and joined Parsons.

The previous evening Parsons had given his last performance with the Byrds at a charity bash at London's Royal Albert Hall. The evening's entertainment, *Sounds 68*, was in aid of Boys' Clubs and featured performances from The Move, The Easybeats, Alan Bown, Joe Cocker and Grapefruit.

Before joining the Byrds, Parsons had been a member of the International Submarine Band. When some of the group split to form the original Flying Burrito Brothers, Parsons stayed on with the Submarine Band. He recorded the album *Safe at Home* with them before leaving to join the Byrds. His stay with the Byrds was short and sweet, producing the seminal country-rock album *Sweetheart of the Rodeo*.

After quitting the Byrds he formed his version of the Flying Burrito Brothers.

Birthday today

1940 Joe B Mauldin bass: original Crickets and post-Holly Crickets

Events today

9

1959 Vietnam War first American casualties

Two military advisors, Major Dale Buis and Master Sgt Chester Ovnand were the first US personnel to die in Vietnam, after they were attacked by the Viet Minh at Bien Hoa.

1960 Tony Sheridan dawn of the British beat groups

When they opened at the Kaiserkeller club at the beginning of June, Tony Sheridan and the Jets were the first British group to play in Hamburg. A month later they were enticed to change venue and opened at the neighbouring Top Ten club.

Skiffle and trad jazz had changed the face of British music in the second half of the 1950s. By 1960, skiffle had developed into beat music. The makeshift tea-chest bass and washboard percussion gave way to the typical beat group lineup of two guitars, electric bass guitar, drums and vocals. The German port-town of Hamburg, with its insatiable desire for British groups, provided an opportunity for aspiring bands to hone their skills. Shortly after Tony Sheridan's debut, the Beatles famously arrived in Hamburg on 17 August* for their first visit. By the middle of 1963 Merseybeat groups were leading the way into the British charts. In early 1964 the beat groups launched the "British Invasion" and for the first time British acts were finding real success on the American charts.

By 1966 the harder-edged sounds of Cream, Pink Floyd and the Doors were taking over and for the beat groups, it was all over ...until the nostalgia marketplace arrived.

1995 Grateful Dead last-ever concert

After thirty years on the road, Grateful Dead gave their final concert, for Illinois Deadheads at Chicago's Soldier Field. The lineup at the end consisted of guitarists Jerry Garcia and Bob Weir, keyboards player Vince Welnick, bassist Phil Lesh and the two drummers Bill Kreutzmann and Mickey Hart. They bowed out with an encore of *Black Muddy River* and *Box of Rain*, both songs with lyrics from Robert Hunter.

This was not a planned farewell concert. Jerry Garcia died of a heart attack a month later and before the end of the year the group had announced that it was disbanding.

Recording session today

1963 The Rolling Stones *Fortune Teller*

In Britain, *Fortune Teller* was coupled with *Poison Ivy* and released as the Stones' second single. It was quickly withdrawn and is now a highly prized collector's item.

Birthdays today

1946 Bon Scott singer: The Valentines, Fraternity, AC/DC

Bon Scott's career started out as a drummer and vocalist. In 1974 he was between gigs and accepted an offer to become AC/DC's driver. Shortly afterwards, he replaced their original singer Dave Evans as AC/DC's frontman.

1947 Mitch Mitchell drums: Riot Squad, Georgie Fame, Jimi Hendrix

Before finding international fame as the drummer with the Jimi Hendrix Experience, Mitch Mitchell unsuccessfully auditioned for both the Who and the Artwoods. He was a founding member of the Riot Squad in the mid-1960s, before moving on to join Georgie Fame's Blue Flames after they had split from Billy Fury.

Event today

10

1964 The Four Tops from doo wop to Motown

After performing for a decade and releasing a handful of singles along the way, the Four Tops finally found fame with their first Motown single, *Baby I Need Your Loving*.

Lead singer Levi Stubbs, Abdul "Duke" Fakir, Lawrence Payton and Renaldo "Obie" Benson formed the Four Aims in 1954, whilst they were still High School students in Detroit. In 1956 they released a single on the Grady label, *If Only I Had Known*. Later that year they moved to Chess and changed their name to "The Four Tops" to avoid confusion with the Ames Brothers. Their Chess single, the Billy Davis penned *Could It Be You*, also failed to trouble the charts. The Four Tops continued to develop their stage act and from their doo wop and R&B roots extended to jazz tinged standards and show songs. They released another single *Ain't That Love*, for Columbia in 1960 and a move in 1962 to the Riverside label resulted in *Pennies from Heaven*.

In the spring of 1963 the Four Tops came to the notice of Motown, where they were signed to the subsidiary label, Workshop Jazz. Recording sessions followed for the album *Breaking Through*, described contemporaneously on the inner sleeves of other albums as singing jazz versions of songs such as *I Left My Heart in San Francisco* and *Stranger on the Shore*. The album failed to find a release at the time and the Tops found themselves in the recording studio providing background vocals for other Motown artists' hits. Their big break came when they were transferred to the Motown label and were given the Holland-Dozier-Holland song *Baby I Need Your Loving*.

The Four Tops went on to become one of the most successful male vocal groups of the era. Unlike their Motown stablemate the Temptations which had numerous singers, the original 1954 quartet continued until the death of Lawrence Payton in 1997.

Recording session today

1966 Cat Stevens *I Love My Dog*

The song was credited to Cat Stevens but it used a melody borrowed from jazz saxophonist and composer Yusef Lateef's *The Plum Blossom*, recorded in 1961.

Singles released today

1954 Bill Haley and His Comets *Shake, Rattle and Roll c/w ABC Boogie* (US)

Having missed the mark with his first Decca single, *Thirteen Women c/w Rock Around the Clock*, Bill Haley's cover of *Shake, Rattle and Roll* scored a Top 10 hit on both sides of the Atlantic.

Big Joe Turner's original version of *Shake, Rattle and Roll* had been released shortly before Haley's cover and gave him an R&B #1. Like many of the white covers of black R&B songs, Haley's sanitised version watered down Turner's raunchier lyrics.

1964 The Beatles *A Hard Day's Night c/w Things We Said Today* (UK)

Album released today

1964 The Beatles *A Hard Day's Night* (UK)

Birthdays today

1942 Ronnie James Dio singer: Rainbow, Black Sabbath

1959 Sandy West drums: The Runaways; solo

Events today

1951 Alan Freed "Moondog" opened his R&B show on WJW

Alan Freed was one of the first American disc jockeys to popularise music by black R&B artists and introduce it to a new white audience. He was also widely credited with coining the term "rock'n'roll". Throughout the 1940s he appeared on radio and television as a sports presenter and DJ. Encouraged by local record store owner Leo Mintz, he joined Radio WJW in Cleveland, called himself "Moondog" and began presenting an R&B show. As the popularity of rock'n'roll music increased he became one of the most influential 1950s DJs on radio and television. His activities soon expanded to include concert promotions and movies.

Freed had to drop the name "Moondog" after a threatened lawsuit from Louis Thomas "Moondog" Hardin, a well-known street performer who had moved to New York in the early 1940s. Resplendent in Viking cape and helmet and brandishing a spear, he could be found plying his art at the corner of 54th Street and Sixth Avenue.

1965 The Rising Sons early gig at the Ash Grove

The Rising Sons played the last night of a two-week residency at the Ash Grove club in Los Angeles.

Formed in early 1965 the Rising Sons managed to release just one single, *Candy Man* c/w *The Devil's Got My Woman*, before going their separate ways eighteen months later. An album was recorded but did not see the light of day until the early 1990s.

They might well have been described as a "supergroup". The drummer at the Ash Grove gig was Ed Cassidy, who went on to become one of the founding members of Spirit in mid-1967. Shortly after this gig Cassidy was replaced by Kevin Kelly, who later joined the Byrds in time for their seminal country-rock album *Sweetheart of the Rodeo*. Bassist Gary Marker worked with Captain Beefheart, both in the studio and on the road but was never a full member of the Magic Band. Guitarist Jesse Lee Kincaid later found success as a songwriter. The two other members of the group, Ry Cooder and Taj Mahal, both went on to become acclaimed solo performers.

1970 Kraftwerk dawn of "Krautrock"

The recently formed German band Kraftwerk played one of their earliest gigs at the *Tivoli Pop Festival*, held at the Reiterstadion in Aachen, Germany. Other bands performing at the festival included Pink Floyd, Caravan, Free, Deep Purple and Taste.

Following the demise of their first band Organisation, Ralf Hütter and Florian Schneider formed Kraftwerk. The band was one of the pioneers of electronic rock. Their international breakthrough came four years later with the album *Autobahn*.

Kraftwerk was one of the most commercially successful of the avant-garde, progressive rock bands to emerge from Germany in the early 1970s. The British music press coined the name "Krautrock" for this emerging experimental music genre, which included bands such as Faust, Tangerine Dream, Can and Amon Düül II.

Single released today

1969 David Bowie *Space Oddity* c/w *Wild Eyed Boy from Freecloud* (UK)

Six years after his first recording session as a member of the Konrads, David Bowie finally made his breakthrough with *Space Oddity*.

Keyboardist Rick Wakeman was one of the session musicians that day.

Events today

1962 The Rolling Stones first-ever gig ...as "The Rollin' Stones"

The Rollin' Stones made their debut when they substituted for Alexis Korner's Blues Incorporated at their Thursday night residency spot at London's Marquee club.

In mid-1962 Brian Jones formed his own band and in June the Rolling Stones started to take shape when he was joined by Mick Jagger and Keith Richard. All three had been playing at various times with the hugely influential Alexis Korner's Blues Incorporated. Jones's group's big opportunity came about because Korner had been offered the chance to perform live on BBC Radio's prestigious *Jazz Club* the same night. The lineup for that historic performance was Mick Jagger, Keith Richard and Brian Jones, with pianist Ian Stewart and bassist Dick Taylor. An urban myth puts future Kinks sticksman Mick Avory on the drumming stool (supported by the Stones' own website[71]) but other sources suggest that it was far more likely to have been Tony Chapman. In an interview with the website *Kast Off Kinks*, Avory confirmed that "I didn't actually play a gig with the Stones. I just rehearsed to do a gig with them, but it never happened."[70]

Jagger and Richard had already played together in their own group Little Boy Blue and the Blue Boys, along with their friend Dick Taylor. Taylor left shortly after this Marquee gig, moved back to playing the guitar and went on to form the Pretty Things.

Brian Jones's first lineup included pianist Ian Stewart, the first "Rolling Stone" to join Jones. Sadly for Stewart, when Andrew Loog Oldham took over their management, after meeting them on 28 April* 1963, he was relegated to road manager and only allowed to perform at recording sessions. Oldham felt that Stewart's image did not fit in with his plans for the band. Jones's original lineup also incorporated another seminal UK blues luminary Brian Knight, before the guitarist left to form Blues By Six. Blues Incorporated's original drummer Charlie Watts left Korner to join Knight in Blues By Six, before moving on to complete the Rolling Stones' classic lineup on 2 February* 1963.

The band took their name from the Muddy Waters song *Rollin' Stone*, the second single to be released on the Chess record label.

1971 The Eagles first time together

Linda Ronstadt opened her tour with a gig at Disneyland. The backing band that night included all four of the soon-to-be Eagles: Glenn Frey, Bernie Leadon, Don Henley and Randy Meisner.

This was the first time that all four of the future Eagles had played together. It was also the only time on the tour that they were all together. However, they were all involved as studio musicians on Linda Ronstadt's eponymous third album, released in early 1972.

Before joining Linda Ronstadt all four musicians had proven pedigrees. Bassist Randy Meisner joined the newly formed Poco after his band the Poor folded, before going on to become a member of Rick Nelson's Stone Canyon Band. Guitarist Bernie Leadon was a founding member of Dillard and Clark, before he joined a post-Gram Parsons version of the Flying Burrito Brothers. Drummer Don Henley's band Felicity was discovered by Kenny Rogers, who relocated them from Texas to Los Angeles. In

California they morphed into Shiloh. After finding local success with a number of bands in his Detroit hometown, guitarist Glenn Frey relocated to Los Angeles where he formed the duo Longbranch Pennywhistle with JD Souther. The duo had limited success but did release an eponymous album in 1969. However, this friendship developed into a long-term songwriting relationship, with Souther co-writing many of the Eagles' hits.

Recording sessions today

1954 Lonnie Donegan *New Orleans Joys* ...dawn of skiffle

13

Chris Barber's Jazz Band recorded the eight-track album *New Orleans Joys.*

Two of the songs, *Rock Island Line* and *John Henry*, were both popularised by folk-blues legend Lead Belly. These two tracks were credited separately on the album sleeve to "The Lonnie Donegan Skiffle Group". Donegan provided vocals and guitar, with Barber on bass and another British skiffle luminary Beryl Bryden on washboard.

Rock Island Line and *John Henry* were later coupled as a single and released in Britain in November 1955. The single made the Top 10 – skiffle had arrived and British rock'n'roll was on the horizon. This Donegan classic has been cited by a generation of musicians as one of their major inspirations to make music

Chris Barber's band played trad jazz and in the interval he would exchange his trombone for an upright bass to play a skiffle set with Lonnie Donegan. Eventually Donegan left to form his own skiffle group. By the end of the 1950s skiffle had morphed into rock'n'roll.

1962 Phil Spector *He's a Rebel*

Phil Spector was back in the studio to produce his next single, the Gene Pitney penned *He's a Rebel.* The song was released as the Crystals follow-up to *Uptown*, providing Spector's own Philles label with its first American #1.

At that time music fans would refer to "the latest Phil Spector single" rather than the name of the recording artist. *He's a Rebel* demonstrated the interchangeable nature of Spector's acts. He had recently relocated from New York to the West Coast and this was his first recording session in Hollywood's Gold Star Studios. The Crystals were not available at the time of recording but Spector was keen to push on because Vikki Carr was already in the process of recording the song. To fill the gap he used the talents of backing group the Blossoms, with lead singer Darlene Love. The first time that the Crystals knew about the record was when they heard it on the radio.

This song introduced arranger Jack Nitzsche to what would become a long recording relationship with Spector. Session musicians known as the "Wrecking Crew" provided the backing, including keyboard player Leon Russell, drummer Hal Blaine, guitarist Barney Kessel and with the sax solo courtesy of Steve Douglas.

He's a Rebel was not technically the follow-up to *Uptown.* The Crystals had released *He Hit Me (And It Felt Like a Kiss)* after *Uptown* but the general outcry at the title and content of the song resulted in the single being quickly withdrawn.

Single released today

1964 The Beatles *A Hard Day's Night c/w I Should Have Known Better* (US)

Album released today

1973 Queen *Queen* 1st album (UK)

Birthday today

1942 Roger (Jim) McGuinn guitar and vocals: Jet Set, The Beefeaters, The Byrds

One of the founding members, Roger (Jim) McGuinn was the only person to remain with the Byrds throughout its lifetime. Early recordings were credited to him with his birth name Jim McGuinn. He changed his name from "Jim" to "Roger" in 1967 after consulting an Indonesian guru.

Events today

1956 The Vipers Skiffle Group first performance at the 2i's

The procession for the second Soho festival was passing the 2i's coffee bar, newly reopened on 22 April*, when a sudden downpour of rain forced Wally Whyton and his Vipers Skiffle Group to abandon their flatbed truck and take shelter inside the café. The new owners invited the Vipers to continue playing their skiffle music in the café's basement. This attracted a crowd of jiving teenagers and the live music sessions that followed on at the 2i's became a cornerstone of British skiffle and rock'n'roll.

The Vipers was one of the most influential of the 1950s skiffle groups with three future Shadows, Jet Harris, Hank Marvin and Tony Meehan featuring in various lineups. Tommy Steele was also discovered singing with the Vipers at the 2i's.

1973 The Everly Brothers on stage bust up

The Everly Brothers gave their final performance at Knott's Berry Farm in Los Angeles.

Don and Phil's relationship had been deteriorating for some time, culminating in this on stage bust up. Midway through the performance Phil smashed his guitar into the stage and stormed off. Don announced that the Brothers had split and finished the set alone.

A decade passed before the Brothers performed together again.

Single released today

1967 John's Children *Come and Play with Me...*c/w *Sara Crazy Child* (UK)

The follow-up to *Desdemona* was intended to be another Marc Bolan composition *Midsummer Night's Scene* but Bolan was becoming increasingly dissatisfied with the group and the single was withdrawn, to be replaced by *Come and Play with Me in the Garden*. Although it never reached the shops, *Midsummer Night's Scene* was pressed up and a handful of copies did find their way to a very few, very lucky, John's Children fans.

Bolan left shortly afterwards and formed the psychedelic-folk duo Tyrannosaurus Rex with percussionist Steve Peregrine Took.

Birthdays today

1912 Woody Guthrie iconic American folk singer and songwriter

When Woody Guthrie was a child his Oklahoma hometown, Okemah, struck oil. By his early twenties the oil had run dry and the town's boom days were over. Guthrie took to the road and stepped into the history books as America's most famous itinerant troubadour. He joined Pete Seeger in the Almanac Singers, where they sang of social injustice, organised labour and corruption. Along with Seeger he popularised radical folk music and paved the way for the 1960s protest singers. He wrote hundreds of songs, including *This Land Is Your Land* and *Pretty Boy Floyd*. Bob Dylan was heavily influenced by Guthrie and paid tribute to him with *Song to Woody* on his 1962 debut album.

Guthrie's guitar bore the slogan "This Machine Kills Fascists".

1938 Jerry Rubin political activist and opponent of the establishment

Co-founder of the Yippie movement (Youth International Party), Jerry Rubin was one of the leading political activists and opponents of the Vietnam War.

1939 Vince Taylor singer: Vince Taylor and the Playboys; solo

Vince Taylor is best remembered as the inspiration for Bowie's character Ziggy Stardust.

Event today

15

1968 Vietnam War Yippies plan for the Democratic Convention

Members of the radical youth movement the Yippies (Youth International Party) applied for a permit to hold a youth convention in Chicago's Lincoln Park.

This youth convention, the *Festival of Life*, was one of a number of demonstrations being planned to coincide with the upcoming Democratic Party Convention in Chicago. The Yippies were not granted a permit and their attempts to organise a rock concert resulted in a lone performance from the Detroit-based MC5. During the convention the Yippies did manage to nominate a pig called "Pigasus" for President.

The tide of American public opinion had turned firmly against the Vietnam War after the disaster of the *Tet Offensive*, when North Vietnamese regulars and Viet Cong guerrilla fighters launched a massive attack on South Vietnam on 31 January*. Even though the communists were beaten back, it was the beginning of the end for America in Vietnam. The extraordinary levels of violence at the Democratic Party Convention started on 25 August* and escalated throughout the conference.

The Youth International Party was formed in late December 1967 by a group of political activists, including Abbie Hoffman and Jerry Rubin. In the September 1968 issue of *The Realist* counterculture magazine, Abbie Hoffman outlined the movement's four main objectives: the blending of pot and politics, linking together with other underground organisations, developing an alternative society and using action-theatre to make statements. Following the riots in Chicago, Rubin and Hoffman were both indicted by a Grand Jury on 20 March* 1969 as a part of the *Chicago 8* trial. The Yippies continued to make use of high profile political commentary and disruption, including famously taking over David Frost's British TV show in 1970.

Recording session today

1959 Sandy Nelson *Teen Beat*

Drummer Sandy Nelson's first single, *Teen Beat*, went Top 10 on both sides of the Atlantic and rock'n'roll had its first drum hero. Nelson was backed by future Beach Boy Bruce Johnston on piano and top session guitarist Barney Kessel. The song was jointly credited to Nelson and Art Laboe, the DJ who coined the phrase "Oldies but Goodies".

Nelson was a very active session musician and appeared on Phil Spector's Teddy Bears hit, *To Know Him Is to Love Him.*

Birthdays today

1947 Roky Erickson guitar and vocals: Spades, 13th Floor Elevators, Bleib Alien

Roky Erickson joined the Spades in 1965. They recorded his composition *You're Gonna Miss Me*, with the writing credit on the original Zero release as Erickson's alias "Emil Schwartze". At the end of the year he joined the seminal psychedelic band 13th Floor Elevators. They re-recorded the song as their debut single and ushered in rock's psychedelic era. In 1969 Erickson was busted for a drug offence and chose to be incarcerated in a mental hospital, rather than face a lengthy prison sentence. He spent the next three years in hospital. When he finally emerged he fronted Bleib Alien, Bleib being an anagram of Bible.

1952 Johnny Thunders New York Dolls, The Heartbreakers

Event today

16

1975 Landmark Festivals *Top 40 New York Unrecorded Rock Bands*

The first day of the *Top 40 New York Unrecorded Rock Bands* festival opened at New York's CBGB club.

The club opened in late 1973, taking its name "CBGB" from the music genres that founder Hilly Kristal planned to play there, namely country, bluegrass and blues. Things did not quite work out that way and the club became the heart of New York's punk and new wave scene. This can be seen from the as yet unsigned bands that appeared at the festival. An array of bands which found international success later, including Blondie, The Ramones, Talking Heads, Television, and Johnny Thunders and the Heartbreakers.

Recording session today

1959 The Coasters *Poison Ivy*

This Coasters original was written by Leiber and Stoller and was one of the songs that was much favoured by British beat groups in the mid-1960s. It was released as a single with another Leiber and Stoller song as the B-side, *I'm a Hog for You*, recorded the following day.

I'm a Hog for You was a Joe Meek production for the UK's Screaming Lord Sutch in 1963. It became one of Sutch's signature songs, along with *Jack the Ripper*.

Single released today

1971 Elastic Oz Band *God Save Us* c/w *Do the Oz* (UK)

The underground magazine *OZ* was in the British courts facing obscenity charges for its *School Kids Issue*. The single *God Save Us* was released to raise funds to support the magazine. The song was written by John Lennon and Yoko Ono and produced by Lennon, "wall-of-sound" producer Phil Spector and Beatles associate Mal Evans.

The A-side was credited to "Bill Elliot and the Electric Oz Band". Elliot was discovered by Evans singing with the Newcastle group Half Breed. After the demise of Apple, Elliot's band morphed into Splinter and was the first signing to George Harrison's newly-formed Dark Horse Records. Their first album *The Place I Love* was released in the autumn of 1974 and produced by Harrison.

OZ magazine fell foul of the British establishment with issue #28 in May 1970, *School Kids Issue*. Founded by Richard Neville in Sydney, Australia in 1963, *OZ* magazine arrived in London in 1967. The British counterculture magazine ran until the end of 1973. In June 1971 the *School Kids Issue* put the editors into the dock on obscenity charges. Ironically, the title of that particular issue meant that it had been edited by school kids, not that it was targeted at them. The magazine's editors were found guilty and received custodial sentences but these were overturned on appeal.

Birthday today

1952 Stuart Copeland drums: Curved Air, The Police

Born in America, Stuart Copeland was the son of a high ranking CIA officer and spent his early years in the Middle East. After a period back in America, Copeland moved to England in the mid-1970s where he worked as a roadie. His start with Curved Air was as a member of the road crew, before taking his place on stage as the band's drummer. In early 1977 he became a founding member of the Police.

Event today

17

1974 Moody Blues opened their own quadraphonic studio

The Moody Blues opened their own recording studio, one of the first with the capability to make quadraphonic recordings. The group bought Decca Studio One and changed its name to "Threshold Studios".

Rock'n'roll recordings started out in the 1950s as a relatively simple affair, with the artists essentially recording live in the studio. Records were produced in one-channel mono (monophonic), to be played through a gramophone with a single speaker. By the mid-1960s recordings had progressed to stereo (stereophonic), with the sound being mixed for two separated speakers. Two speakers simulated the sound of a concert, where the audience heard the sound as it was mixed for the two PA (public address) speaker stacks. "Wall of sound" producer Phil Spector was a big fan of mono recordings and after stereo replaced it, he was known to sport a badge emblazoned with the slogan "Back to Mono". In 1967 the Beatles recorded their iconic *Sgt Pepper* album on four-track recording machines. Recording technology continued to become more sophisticated and in the mid-1970s quadraphonic albums made an appearance. Quadraphonic systems required four speakers instead of just the two needed to reproduce stereo records. This was intended to take the listener from sitting in the audience, to hearing the sounds from a position in the middle of the orchestra. Quadraphonic surround-sound never really captured the public's imagination and stereo continued to be the preferred listening medium.

The quadraphonic sound concept had previously been explored by the Pink Floyd in their *Games for May* concert at London's Queen Elizabeth Hall in 1967. They had used an Azimuth Coordinator, a joystick device to move the sound around the theatre.

Singles released today

1964 Billy J Kramer with The Dakotas *From a Window* c/w *Second to None* (UK)

Four of the first five British singles released by Billy J Kramer with the Dakotas were written by John Lennon and Paul McCartney. The exception was their fourth offering, *Little Children*, written by Mort

Shuman and Leslie McFarland. *From a Window* was the final song from the pens of the Fab Two. It was never recorded by the Fab Four.

1967 The Beatles *All You Need Is Love c/w Baby You're a Rich Man* (US)

Birthdays today

1942 Zoot Money keyboards, vocals: ZM's Big Roll Band, Dantalian's Chariot

Zoot Money was one of Britain's best kept secrets. A highly respected musician and band leader, he never managed to turn his impressive stage performances into commercial success. He formed Zoot Money's Big Roll Band in the early 1960s, taking a brief break in 1963 to play with Alexis Korner's Blues Incorporated. In 1967 the Big Roll Band morphed into the more psychedelic sounds of Dantalian's Chariot. By mid-1968 Dantalian's Chariot had run its course and Money accepted an invitation to join Eric Burdon's Animals.

1949 Terry "Geezer" Butler bass: Polka Tulk Blues Band, Earth, Black Sabbath

Geezer Butler, along with Ozzy Osborne, came to Polka Tulk from Rare Breed in 1968.

Recording session today

1953 Elvis Presley 1st private recording

Elvis Presley called into Sam Phillips's Memphis Recording Service studio for the first time, paid his $3.98 and recorded *My Happiness* and *That's When Your Heartaches Begin*. When Sam Phillips's assistant Marion Keisker asked Elvis who he sounded like, he famously replied, "I don't sound like nobody".

Controversy surrounds whether Phillips or Keisker operated the tape that day. Doubt has also been cast on the idea that the recording was a birthday present for his mother Gladys. It would have been rather belated, given that her birthday was on 25 April.

Album released today

1968 Grateful Dead *Anthem of the Sun* (US)

This second album from the Grateful Dead used a collage of live and studio takes in an attempt to recreate the psychedelic experience of a live show.

It was the first of their albums to feature two drummers, with second drummer Mickey Hart.

Births and deaths today

1938 Ian Stewart keyboards: original member of the Rolling Stones

Pianist Ian Stewart was the first of the Rolling Stones to join Brian Jones's group and is often considered to be the "Sixth Stone". He played at the first-ever Rollin' Stones gig, at the Marquee club on 12 July* 1962. Unfortunately for Stewart, when Andrew Loog Oldham became the Stones' manager, he felt that Stewart's image was not right for the band. Oldham sidelined Stewart from the stage lineup but he stayed on as the Stones' tour manager. He occasionally played piano and keyboards in the wings at live shows and appeared on many of their albums.

1939 Dion (DiMucci) singer: Dion and the Belmonts, solo

Before embarking on a solo career, Dion found success with doo wop vocal group Dion and the Belmonts. He escaped death on the night of 3 February* 1959, when he declined to share the ill-fated flight with Buddy Holly on the *Winter Dance Party* tour.

1940 Johnny Hutchinson drums: Cass and the Cassanovas, The Big Three

In the days before Ringo Starr, Johnny Hutchinson was a stand-in drummer for the Beatles. On 10 May* 1960 he filled in for Tommy Moore, who was late for their audition as Billy Fury's backing band. (They failed the audition.) He also deputised for a couple of gigs between Pete Best leaving and Ringo joining the Beatles on 18 August* 1962.

1966 Bobby Fuller died in mysterious circumstances, aged twenty-three

Bobby Fuller was found dead in his car outside his Hollywood apartment. He was allegedly doused in petrol, bruised and had a broken finger. The LA police concluded that there had not been any foul play. The death certificate gave the cause of death as "ASPHYXIA" due to "INHALATION OF GASOLINE".[18] Since his death, there has been much speculation as to whether Fuller had been murdered.

The Bobby Fuller Four are best remembered for their 1966 cover version of the Crickets' *I Fought the Law*. It was originally issued by Buddy Holly's ex-backing group on their 1960 album *In Style with the Crickets*, released shortly after Holly's death.

Event today

1957 Frankie Lymon scandal when he danced with a white girl on TV

Frankie Lymon caused an outrage when, as a young black man, he danced with a white teenage girl whilst performing on Alan Freed's live ABC TV show *The Big Beat*. The resulting outcry, particularly from southern stations, resulted in the show's removal from the airwaves.

Singles released today

1954 Elvis Presley *That's All Right* c/w *Blue Moon of Kentucky* (Sun-1)

When Elvis made his second private recording at the Memphis Recording Service on 4 January*, owner Sam Phillips told him that he would give him a call if he found a song that he felt would suit Elvis. On a trip to Nashville, Phillips came across a song called *Without You* and duly called Elvis to come into the studio and try it out. The audition didn't go too well but rather than give up on the young singer, Phillips introduced him to guitarist Scotty Moore and bass player Bill Black. Phillips asked Elvis to perform some other songs that he knew. They tried out a few numbers and on 5 July, with Phillips at the controls, they recorded *That's All Right* as Elvis's first Sun single.

A couple of days later Phillips gave Memphis disk jockey Dewey "Daddy-O" Phillips (no relation) an acetate of the recording and he famously became the first DJ to play *That's All Right* on his *Red, Hot and Blue* show on Radio WHBQ.

The single credited the performance to Elvis Presley, Scotty and Bill and coupled two 1940s covers. The A-side was written and originally recorded by Arthur Crudup, with the B-side written and recorded by Bill Monroe and His Bluegrass Boys.

1965 The Beatles *Help c/w I'm Down* (US)

Album released today

1977 Elvis Presley *Moody Blue* (US)

A mixture of studio and live tracks, *Moody Blue* was to be the last album issued in Elvis's lifetime. The song *Let Me Be There*, penned by the Shadows' John Rostill, had already appeared on the 1974 album *Elvis: As Recorded Live on Stage in Memphis*.

Birthdays today

1947 Bernie Leadon guitar, banjo and vocals: Flying Burrito Brothers, Eagles

Bernie Leadon was a founding member of Dillard and Clark before joining a post-Gram Parsons version of the Flying Burrito Brothers. When the Burrito Brothers ended, he joined Linda Ronstadt's band with a lineup that morphed into the Eagles. He was the first Eagles founding member to leave, when personal differences took their toll at the end of 1975. He was replaced by guitarist Joe Walsh, before *Hotel California*.

1947 Brian May guitar: Smile, Queen

1952 Allen Collins guitar: My Backyard, Noble Five, Lynyrd Skynyrd

Allen Collins was a member of My Backyard when they renamed to the "Noble Five", before becoming Lynyrd Skynyrd. Although he was badly injured, Collins survived the plane crash on 20 October* 1977 that killed three of his band mates. After the crash he teamed up with fellow survivor Gary Rossington in the Rossington Collins Band.

Events today

1971 Elvis Presley first stage entrance to *Also Sprach Zarathustra*

Elvis made his first stage entrance to the dramatic tones of Richard Strauss's *Also Sprach Zarathustra*, on the opening night of his two-week residency at the Sahara Tahoe Hotel in Stateline, Nevada.

The music had been used to great effect three years earlier in Stanley Kubrick's sci-fi masterpiece *2001: A Space Odyssey*. It had not been written for the movie soundtrack but was an adaptation of German composer Richard Strauss's tone poem, *Also Sprach Zarathustra* op.30. The piece was written in 1896 and inspired by German philosopher Friedrich Nietzsche's philosophical treatise of the same name. Nietzsche's book was written in the mid-1880s and was the tale of a spiritual odyssey.

1975 Motörhead debut gig

Having been unceremoniously despatched from Hawkwind shortly after playing Toronto on 18 May*, Lemmy's new band Motörhead made its debut supporting Greenslade at London's Roundhouse.

Shortly after leaving Hawkwind, Lemmy recruited drummer Lucas Fox and Pink Fairies' guitarist Larry Wallis and with himself as bassist and singer, formed the trio Bastard. He was persuaded to change the name to "Motörhead", American slang for speed freak. *Motorhead* was also the title of the last song that he wrote with Hawkwind, issued as the B-side of Hawkwind's 1975 UK single *Kings of Speed*.

Singles and Album released today

1964 The Beatles — released two singles and an album in America

The British Invasion was now in full swing. On 4 April* the Beatles dominated the *Billboard Hot-100* with twelve singles on the chart, including all five top positions.

Mid-1964 was the height of Beatlemania in America and their record label, Capitol, took full advantage of this by releasing two singles and an album on the same day!

Singles: *I'll Cry Instead* c/w *I'm Happy Just to Dance with You*

And I Love Her c/w *If I Fell*

In America Capitol Records squeezed the last drop out of the Beatles' potential, by combining album tracks and releasing them as singles. Combinations were chosen, such as these two singles, which were never released in their British homeland.

Album: *Something New*

Well at least half of the album was new to American fans. This third album from Capitol contained nine Lennon and McCartney songs and two covers.

The first cover was a Larry Williams composition *Slow Down*, recorded by him as the B-side of his 1958 single *Dizzy Miss Lizzy*.

The other cover, *Matchbox*, was the first of three Beatles covers of songs associated with Carl Perkins. When Perkins released *Matchbox* as a single in 1957, he gave himself the writing credit. The song actually had a little more history than that. It was based on *Match Box Blues* recorded by Blind Lemon Jefferson in 1927, which itself was inspired by Ma Rainey's 1924 song, *Lost Wandering Blues*.

Birthdays today

1947 Carlos Santana — guitar and vocals: Santana

1956 Paul Cook — drums: Swankers, Sex Pistols

Events today

1961 Jimmy Page — fusion of music and beat poetry

Seventeen-year-old future Led Zeppelin guitarist Jimmy Page accompanied British beat poet Royston Ellis in a fusion of music and poetry, during the *Poetry at the Mermaid* festival at London's Mermaid Theatre.

Page joined his first group Red E Lewis and the Red Caps in the late 1950s, at the turn of the decade they morphed into Neil Christian and the Crusaders. Ellis had seen Page perform with the band on a number of occasions and invited him to appear at the poetry festival, to play guitar as an accompaniment to his reading of beat poetry.

Ellis was an accomplished beat poet and writer, who had also given poetry readings around this time accompanied by members of the pre-Hamburg Beatles and Cliff Richard's backing group the Shadows.

As part of the Dissenters, John Lennon and Stuart Sutcliff performed with Ellis at Liverpool's Jacaranda club in June 1960. It was after this gig that the group was inspired to change the spelling of their name from "The Silver Beetles" to "The Silver Beatles",[104] in line with the "beat" literature and poetry of the time. Ellis was an inspiration for the Beatles songs *Paperback Writer* and *Polythene Pam*.

1962 The Crystals short-lived *He Hit Me (And It Felt Like a Kiss)*

When producer Phil Spector was selecting the Crystals follow-up to their second American hit *Uptown*, he chose the Goffin and King composition *He Hit Me (And It Felt Like a Kiss)*. The title and content of the song proved a tad too much for the DJs and record-buying public alike and it was quickly withdrawn. It was around just long enough to be reviewed in the *Singles Reviews* of *Billboard Music Week*'s edition for 21 July. The review described the song as having a telling message and predicted that it could be a winner. There was no time to see if this was destined to be. Phil Spector's record company, Philles, withdrew the single in favour of a Gene Pitney composition, *He's a Rebel*. But that's another story. *He's a Rebel* might have been released as a Crystals single but the recording session on 13 July* was a little light on any input from the Crystals.

He Hit Me (And It Felt Like a Kiss) was inspired by Gerry Goffin and Carol King's babysitter Little "*Loco-Motion*" Eva, who was reputedly in an abusive relationship with her boyfriend. When Little Eva was asked about her bruises she apparently replied that he only hit her because he loved her.

1972 The Doors post-Morrison final tour's opening night

The three remaining Doors, keyboard player Ray Manzarek, drummer John Densmore and guitarist Robby Krieger kicked off their final Doors tour at Chicago's Aragon Ballroom. With the death of lead singer Jim Morrison on 3 July* 1971, Manzarek took over the responsibility for lead vocals. They were supported by Flo & Eddie and Dr John.

After Morrison's death the Doors released two studio albums, *Other Voices* and *Full Circle*. This final six-week tour was to support the recently released *Full Circle*.

The Doors finally came to the end of the road in the spring of 1973, after the three original members had travelled to England in search of a replacement for Morrison. They rehearsed briefly with ex-Audience singer Howard Werth but this new lineup was not to be. Manzarek decided to return to America for a solo career. Densmore and Krieger stayed on in England and put together a lineup for their new venture, Butts Band.

Event today

22

1958 The Crickets Peggy Sue got married

Crickets' drummer Jerry Allison married Peggy Sue Gerron in Honey Grove, Texas.

Allison and Peggy Sue met in Lubbock High School in Texas. He was keen to impress her and persuaded Buddy Holly to change the name of a song that they had just written together from *Cindy Lou* to *Peggy Sue*. The ruse worked and not only did Allison get his girl but the song gave Buddy Holly and the Crickets a Top 10 hit on both sides of the Atlantic. Sadly, the romance ended in divorce.

Single released today

1974 AC/DC *Can I Sit Next to You Girl c/w Rockin' in the Parlour* (AU & NZ)

AC/DC's first single was issued in Australia and New Zealand. It featured the original vocalist Dave Evans, who was replaced shortly afterwards by Bon Scott.

Albums released today

1963 The Beatles *Introducing the Beatles* (US)

The first Beatles album to be released in America was on the small, independent Vee-Jay label, founded in 1953 in Gary, Indiana. Vee-Jay had picked up the Beatles as an add-on when they signed up Frank Ifield.

After producer George Martin failed to persuade EMI's American subsidiary Capitol Records to pick up their option on the Beatles, Vee-Jay grabbed the opportunity with both hands. *Introducing the Beatles* was the Fab Four's first-ever American album, with two versions released by Vee-Jay. This first issue included *Love Me Do* and *P.S. I Love You*. The album was withdrawn and re-released on 27 January* 1964, with *Please Please Me* and *Ask Me Why* replacing those two tracks.

This release date of 22 July[93] is often quoted in discographies but is disputed by some Beatles historians. There is much speculation as to when the first copies of the album leaked into the marketplace, before it was reissued in early 1964.

When Capitol did finally wake up to the fact that the Beatles were taking the music world by storm, Vee-Jay came under severe pressure to bow out. Before finally giving in to Capitol they made the most of their fourteen Beatles songs. Vee-Jay produced four singles and five albums. The songs were recycled: on two versions of *Introducing the Beatles*, *The Beatles vs The Four Seasons*, *Jolly What! The Beatles & Frank Ifield on Stage*, and *Songs Pictures and Stories of the Fabulous Beatles*.

(This release and its reissue are the only Vee-Jay albums to be included in *Rock'n'Roll Unravelled* because the other Vee-Jay albums simply reused the same tracks.)

1966 John Mayall *Blues Breakers with Eric Clapton* (UK)

The album was released about that same time that Eric Clapton left the Bluesbreakers to form Cream. As well as Clapton and John Mayall, the lineup was completed by bassist John McVie and drummer Hughie Flint.

Birthday today

1947 Don Henley drums, singer and songwriter: Felicity, Shiloh, Eagles

Events today

1966 Landmark Venues Cavern Club reopened

Following a financial crisis Liverpool's Cavern Club was reopened by Britain's Prime Minister Harold Wilson, the local Member of Parliament for Huyton. The club had been reopened by popular demand but its best days were already behind it.

One of the acts performing that night was the Pete Best Combo. He had risen to personal fame at the club as the Beatles' drummer. When the Fab Four played at the Cavern following his sacking in the summer of 1962, they were greeted with chants of "Pete Best forever! Ringo never!"

By 1969 Best had hung up his drumsticks and become a Civil Servant.

The original Cavern Club closed its doors for the last time in May 1973 and was demolished to make way for Liverpool's underground railway. But the cellars remained. These were renovated and the club reopened in the mid-1980s.

1966 The Pete Best Combo from the Beatles to the Cavern Club

The Pete Best Combo was one of the bands to perform at the reopening of Liverpool's Cavern Club.

Drummer Pete Best had risen to personal fame locally as the Beatles' drummer, a role that he performed for two years, before he was unceremoniously fired in the summer of 1962. After leaving the soon-to-be Fab Four he joined Lee Curtis and the All Stars. Curtis went solo in 1964 and the remaining All Stars released their first British single *I'm Gonna Knock on Your Door* as the Pete Best Four. The lineup added a brass section and became the Pete Best Combo. They spent time in America releasing a number of singles and an album *Best of the Beatles*, which was a play on his surname and had nothing to do with his music in the world's most famous band.

By the time that he returned to Liverpool the Pete Best Combo was down to a trio. The group split up shortly afterwards and Best turned his back on the music business.

Recording session today

1965 Neil Young first-ever recording

As a part of his first group the Squires, Neil Young recorded *The Sultan* and *Aurora* at radio station CKRC in Winnipeg. Produced by Bob Bradburn, the writing credits for both instrumentals went to "The Squires".

The Squires was Neil Young's first serious group, formed whilst he was still attending Kelvin High School in Winnipeg. The Shadows-like instrumentals recorded at CKRC were coupled and released in Canada as a single on V-Records. Reputedly only 300 copies were pressed and sold at local gigs, making this one of the most sought after singles in the world.

It was in Young's next group, the Toronto based Mynah Birds, that he met Bruce Palmer, after Palmer had been swapped as bass guitarist from his previous group, Jack London and the Sparrows. After the Mynah Birds had flown their separate ways, a chance meeting in Los Angeles with Stephen Stills, on 6 April* 1966, led to the formation of Buffalo Springfield. Young had previously met Stills at a Squires gig in Canada.

Single released today

1965 The Beatles *Help* c/w *I'm Down* (UK)

Events today

24

1961 The Temptations from doo wop to Motown

Having recently signed to Berry Gordy's Miracle Records label, the newly formed Temptations released their first single *Oh, Mother of Mine*, co-written by Otis Williams.

The Temptations came about when two doo wop vocal groups, the Distants and the Primes, merged for an audition with Motown founder Berry Gordy. In the late 1950s Otis Williams and the Siberians came into existence and eventually morphed into the Distants, with a lineup that included Otis Williams, Elbridge "Al" Bryant and Melvin Franklin. The Primes was another vocal group playing the same Detroit clubs as the Distants and when Otis Williams was invited to audition for Motown, he asked Eddie Kendricks and Paul Williams (no relation) to join him. Calling themselves "The Elgins", Otis Williams, Elbridge "Al" Bryant, Melvin Franklin, Eddie Kendricks and Paul Williams passed the audition and were signed to Motown's short-lived label, Miracle Records. Another group was using the "Elgins" name so they became "The Temptations".

After a couple of singles on Miracle, their third release was *Dream Come True* on the Gordy label. It would take nearly three years and their fifth Gordy release, *The Way You Do the Things You Do*, before the Temptations found major success. The song was produced and co-written by Smokey Robinson and was the first single to feature the voice of David Ruffin, who had recently replaced Bryant.

1967 The Beatles advertisement to legalise marijuana

The Beatles funded a full-page advertisement calling for marijuana to be legalised, in the British newspaper *The Times*. It was in response to the jailing of John Hopkins, founder of both the counterculture periodical the *International Times* and London's first psychedelic venue the UFO Club.

The ad's heading suggested that the law against marijuana was immoral in principle and unworkable in practice. Following a lengthy justification, the petition suggested a plan for reform that included: the encouragement of research; allowing it to be smoked on private premises; its removal from the dangerous drugs list; and allowing possession to be permitted or, at worst, the subject of a small fine. The final point called for the commuting of the sentences of all persons currently in jail for possession. The petition was signed by sixty-four dignitaries, including all four Beatles, their manager Brian Epstein, editor of the Leninist periodical *Black Dwarf* Tariq Ali, broadcaster David Dimbleby, author Graham Greene, artist David Hockney, psychiatrist Dr RD Laing, jazz singer George Melly, photographer David Bailey and *Beyond the Fringe* member Dr Jonathan Miller.

1977 Led Zeppelin last-ever American concert

Led Zeppelin kicked off their ill-fated eleventh American tour in Dallas on 1 April*. It came to a premature end in California at Oakland's Alameda County Coliseum. The remaining tour dates were cancelled after Robert Plant received news that his son Karac had been taken seriously ill. He died shortly afterwards.

This proved to be their last-ever American concert. Their British swan song came at their second appearance at the Knebworth Park Festival on 11 August 1979.

Led Zeppelin gave their last-ever performance with drummer John Bonham in Berlin on 7 July* 1980. He died after a bout of heavy drinking on 25 September*, whilst rehearsing for their return to America.

Events today

1965 Bob Dylan first electric set ...*Newport Folk Festival*

Bob Dylan played his first electric set at the 1965 *Newport Folk Festival*. When he took to the stage for that historic performance he was backed by guitarist Mike Bloomfield, keyboardists Al Kooper and Barry Goldberg, and a rhythm section of bassist Jerome Arnold and drummer Sam Lay, who had both played previously with Howlin' Wolf's backing band. The set consisted of just three songs, *Maggie's Farm*, *Like a Rolling Stone* and *It Takes a Lot to Laugh, it Takes a Train to Cry*. The band left the stage to the accompaniment of a booing audience. Dylan returned with a borrowed acoustic guitar and played two more of his own compositions, *It's All Over Now, Baby Blue* and *Mr. Tambourine Man*.

There has been much debate about the booing. Folk diehards decried the use of an electric band. Others suggest that the trouble was poor sound quality and balance, which made it difficult to hear Dylan. His departure from the stage after just three numbers was probably a combination of these and other factors.

1969 Crosby, Stills & Nash debut performance

Crosby, Stills & Nash gave their first concert performance at New York's Fillmore East. At the end of the concert they were joined on stage by Neil Young. Shortly afterwards the trio became a quartet as Crosby, Stills, Nash & Young.

By the time of this performance they had already released their eponymous debut album, which spawned two American hit singles, Nash's *Marrakesh Express* and Stills's *Suite: Judy Blue Eyes*, the former also made the British Top 20.

The trio came together after David Crosby was fired from the Byrds and hooked up with Stephen Stills, who was on his own after Buffalo Springfield imploded. The two Americans were joined by Graham Nash after he left the British group the Hollies, following their concert on 8 December* 1968.

Single released today

1964 The Rolling Stones *It's All Over Now c/w Good Times Bad Times* (US)

The British Invasion was in full swing by the time that the Rolling Stones' fourth American single was released, a cover of the Valentinos' *It's All Over Now*.

The Stones' first American single, *Stoned* c/w *I Wanna Be Your Man*, was released in February but hastily withdrawn. Their second was a cover of Buddy Holly's *Not Fade Away* and this was followed by *Tell Me (You're Coming Back).* This third release was written by Mick Jagger and Keith Richard and was their first single to make an impact on the charts.

Tell Me was not released as a single in their British homeland.

Album released today

1980 AC/DC *Back in Black* (US)

Singer Bon Scott died six months after the release of their breakthrough album *Highway to Hell*. He was replaced by ex-Geordie vocalist Brian Johnson and the band recorded *Back in Black* as the follow-up album.

The RIAA (Record Industry Association of America) ranks *Back in Black* as one of the biggest selling albums of all time, awarding it 22xMulti-Platinum in December 2007.[55]

Event today

26

1969 The Flying Burrito Brothers two bands with one name

The Flying Burrito Brothers performed at the *Seattle Pop Festival*, held in Woodinville's Gold Creek Park. This was the second day of the three-day event, which saw performances from The Doors, Chuck Berry, The Byrds, Bo Diddley, Ike and Tina Turner, Santana, Spirit, Ten Years After, Alice Cooper, Vanilla Fudge and Led Zeppelin.

The original Flying Burrito Brothers was set up by bassist Ian Dunlop and drummer Mickey Gauvin, after they had parted company with the International Submarine Band. Gram Parsons remained in the Submarine Band but was an occasional contributor to the original Flying Burrito Brothers. He stayed with the Submarine Band long enough to record the album *Safe At Home*, before leaving to join the Byrds. Parsons' stay with the Byrds lasted about six months but included the seminal country-rock album *Sweetheart of the Rodeo*. Not wishing to tour South Africa with the Byrds he left them on 8 July* 1968.

After quitting the Byrds, Parsons formed a new version of the Flying Burrito Brothers. The original Dunlop and Gauvin band had been very loose, with musicians drifting in and out. In mid-1968 they relocated their band to New York, still performing under the name of "The Flying Burrito Brothers". Founding member Chris Hillman left the Byrds shortly after they returned from their South African jaunt. Hillman, together with some-time Byrd and steel guitarist Sneaky Pete Kleinow joined Parsons in the Flying Burrito Brothers. By the time that the Parsons version of the Burritos had recorded their first album, *The Gilded Palace of Sin*, the original Dunlop and Gauvin lineup had disbanded.

Two of the bands from the *Seattle Pop Festival*, Vanilla Fudge and Led Zeppelin, chose to stay at the Edgewater Inn and on 28 July* participated in the notorious *Mud Shark Incident*.

Single released today

1963 Billy J Kramer with The Dakotas *Bad to Me* c/w *I Call Your Name* (UK)

Both sides were Lennon and McCartney compositions. *Bad to Me* was the first Lennon and McCartney song to make #1 for a band other than the Beatles.

Birthdays today

1941 Darlene Love singer: The Blossoms, Bob B Soxx; solo

At just sixteen years of age Darlene Wright joined the Blossoms, one of rock'n'roll's most famous female vocal backing groups. Phil Spector changed Wright's name to Darlene Love and she became one of his most important singers. As well as solo hits, Love was also the lead singer for Bob B Soxx and the Blue Jeans. The Gene Pitney penned Crystals hit *He's a Rebel*, was recorded on 13 July* 1962 without a Crystal in sight. Despite its release as a Crystals single, the lead vocal was provided by Darlene Love.

1943 Mick Jagger singer, songwriter: Little Boy Blue, Rolling Stones

Mick Jagger's first band, Little Boy Blue and the Blue Boys, included Keith Richard and Dick Taylor, who went on to form the Pretty Things. In mid-1962 Jagger, sometimes accompanied by guitarist Keith Richard, was one of the vocalists with seminal British blues band Alexis Korner's Blues Incorporated. Shortly after this, Mick Jagger, Keith Richard and Dick Taylor joined Brian Jones's new lineup and performed at London's Marquee club on 12 July* 1962 – as the Rollin' Stones.

Events today

1960 Larry Parnes summer show of renamed acts

Great Yarmouth's end-of-the-pier show *Meet the Beat* opened, billed as "Larry Parnes presents: First Ever Anglo-American Summer Show". It consisted mostly of acts managed by Parnes. The show was headlined by Billy Fury, with Vince Eager, Dickie Pride and Johnny Gentle. Backing was provided by Parnes's own house band, the Beat Boys. The American element consisted of singer Davy Jones, although this was not the same "Davy Jones" who found fame as a future Monkee or the one who became David Bowie.

Larry Parnes was the first major British manager of rock'n'roll acts and one of the most influential non-performers in the development of British rock'n'roll. He groomed his protégés for stardom and liked to change the names of his acts, often to reflect the image he would like to project. His first signing

was Tommy Hicks, who became Britain's first rock'n'roll star Tommy Steele. Steele's name was derived from his Scandinavian grandfather Thomas Stil-Hicks, pronounced Steel-Hicks. His next singer was born Reginald Smith but became Marty Wilde. Parnes went on to sign a string of acts, including Roy Taylor who became Vince Eager; Ron Wycherley, Billy Fury; Richard Knellar, Dickie Pride; Ray Howard, Duffy Power; John Askew, Johnny Gentle; Terrence Williams, Terry Dene; and Clive Powell, who found fame as Georgie Fame. Parnes had less luck with singer Joe Brown, who was happy to stick with his original moniker.

1967 British Legislation homosexuality was no longer illegal

The Sexual Offences Act 1967 received the Royal Assent in England and Wales, meaning that it was no longer a criminal offence to commit a homosexual act.

Henry VIII introduced the first homosexuality legislation with the *Buggery Act* in 1533.

Album released today

1983 Neil Young *Everybody's Rockin'* (US)

Neil Young released his second album on the Geffen label, *Everybody's Rockin'* and attracted a $3m lawsuit from label owner David Geffen for not making his albums commercial enough.

In 1982 Neil Young moved from Reprise to the Geffen label. His first album released on the new label was the synth-based *Trans*. It received poor critical acclaim and achieved limited commercial success. His planned follow-up was a country based album, *Old Ways*. David Geffen rejected this choice, berating Young to write a rock'n'roll album. Young's response was *Everybody's Rockin'*, credited to Neil and the Shocking Pinks, and clocking in with a playing time of less than thirty minutes. Young's reaction to David Geffen's lawsuit was to issue his own multi-million dollar counter-suit.

Young followed *Everybody's Rockin'* with a reworked *Old Ways*. After a couple more albums and dropped lawsuits, Neil Young's Geffen days were behind him.

Birthday today

1929 Harvey Fuqua singer: The Moonglows; Motown executive

Harvey Fuqua was a founding member of the doo wop group the Moonglows. They started out as the Crazy Sounds and were renamed by legendary DJ Alan Freed. Fuqua left the Moonglows in the late 1950s and became a key figure in the development of the fledgling Motown Records. As well as signing up new artists such as Marvin Gaye, he was also a prolific songwriter and producer.

Events today

1966 The Rolling Stones Brian Jones's last American concert

When the Rolling Stones kicked off their North American tour in Massachusetts at Lynn's Manning Bowl on 24 June, guitarist Brian Jones could not have suspected that this would be his last tour on that continent. Four weeks later, when he walked off the stage at the end of the concert in Hawaii's Honolulu International Center, he had played his last-ever concert on American soil.

1969 Led Zeppelin *Edgewater Inn Mud Shark Incident*

One of après-rock's most notorious events followed a Led Zeppelin performance at the *Seattle Pop Festival*. It became known as the *Edgewater Inn Mud Shark Incident*.

Accounts of the precise circumstances vary but the incident took place at Led Zeppelin's hotel, during an after-show party with fellow musicians Vanilla Fudge. The Edgewater Inn was built on a pier looking directly onto Puget Sound and hotel guests were encouraged to fish out of their bedroom windows. Earlier in the day members of Zeppelin's road crew had been fishing out of their windows and had landed a number of mud sharks, which they hung up in the wardrobe. Urban legend has it that at the party that night members of Zeppelin's entourage frolicked with a groupie who was pleasured by using a mud shark as a makeshift sex-toy.

Some accounts suggest that the groupie was a redhead and that the fish involved was not a shark but a red snapper.

Frank Zappa immortalised the incident in his song *The Mud Shark*, on his album *Fillmore East, June 1971*. In it he suggests that Vanilla Fudge filmed the episode.

1973 Landmark Festivals *Summer Jam*

It may not have been as well remembered as the rock festivals at Woodstock, Altamont or the Isle of Wight but the one-day *Summer Jam* at New York's Watkins Glen Raceway was attended by more than 600,000 people. Estimates for the attendance at Woodstock vary between 400,000 and 500,000. There were just three bands playing at Watkins Glen that day: The Allman Brothers, Grateful Dead and The Band.

Birthdays today

1943 Mike Bloomfield guitar: Paul Butterfield Blues Band, The Electric Flag

One of the first guitar heroes, Mike Bloomfield left the Paul Butterfield Blues Band to form the Electric Flag. On 25 July* 1965 he was a part of Bob Dylan's backing band, when he made his notorious electric debut at the *Newport Folk Festival*.

1943 Rick Wright keyboards: Sigma 6, The Abdabs, Pink Floyd, Zee

After David Gilmour replaced Syd Barrett, Pink Floyd went on to become one of the most successful rock bands in the world. Sadly, inter-band relationships between bass player and main writer Roger Waters and the rest of the band deteriorated. Keyboards player Rick Wright was sacked from the band during the recording of *The Wall*. When they went on the road to perform the album, Wright was working on a salary basis. He did not participate in the last Pink Floyd album, *The Final Cut*.

1949 Steve Peregrin Took percussion: half of Tyrannosaurus Rex

In late 1969 Mickey Finn replaced Took in Tyrannosaurus Rex.

Event today

1966 Bob Dylan motorcycle accident

Bob Dylan was injured in a motorcycle accident near his home in Woodstock, New York. The circumstances and extent of Dylan's injuries have always been shrouded in mystery. Dylan himself has given various accounts of the incident.

At the time of the accident he had recently returned home from his notorious European tour, where he was backed by an electric band. This tour included the infamous jeers of "Judas" at a concert in England on 17 May*. Dylan had upset some of his traditional folk music fans by performing with an electric backing band. A couple of months before the accident, Dylan had released his acclaimed double album *Blond on Blond*. Considerable speculation followed Dylan's accident as to why he stayed out of the limelight for so long. Fans had to wait nearly 18 months for his next album *John Wesley Harding*, released in America in December 1967. His first concert appearance followed shortly afterwards, at the *Woody Guthrie Memorial Concert* at New York's Carnegie Hall on 20 January. He was backed that night by the Hawks, later to become the Band. Also appearing on the bill were Pete Seeger, Arlo Guthrie, Odetta, Richie Havens, Judy Collins and Ramblin' Jack Elliott.

Recording sessions today

1961 Chuck Berry *Come On*

In his last recording session before going to prison on 19 February* 1962 for violating the *Mann Act*, Chuck Berry recorded a number of songs, including the self-penned *Come On* and *Go-Go-Go*. These two songs were coupled as a single and released in America before his incarceration.

Neither side of the single troubled the American charts but both sides had an impact on the British best-selling lists. Shortly before he was released from prison, *Go-Go-Go* was a British hit for Berry in July 1963, giving him his first UK hit since *Sweet Little Sixteen* in 1958.

The other song, *Come On*, was famously covered by the Rolling Stones as their British debut single. It gave them their first hit, also in July 1963.

1965 Bob Dylan *Highway 61 Revisited*

Four days after his notorious electric performance at Newport, Bob Dylan was back in the studio working on his new album, *Highway 61 Revisited*. He was ably assisted in this new venture by guitarist Mike Bloomfield and keyboards player Al Kooper.

The album was available in American shops just a month later.

Died today

1974 Cass Elliot "Mama Cass", died at the age of thirty-two

Cass Elliot, who had been in the Mugwumps and found international fame with the Mamas & The Papas, was pursuing a solo career and in London for a two week engagement at the Palladium. An urban myth suggests that she choked to death on a ham sandwich but her Death Certificate gave the cause of death as "Fatty Myocardial Degeneration due to Obesity: Natural Causes".[109]

However there was an eerie element to her death. She was staying at an apartment in London's Curzon Place owned by Harry Nilsson. Four years later, on 7 September* 1978, the Who's drummer Keith Moon was found dead in that same apartment.

Events today

1968 The Beatles end of Apple Boutique

Just eight months after opening their Apple Boutique the Beatles closed the venture down. For the first of the two final days of trading, the merchandise was given away free of charge.

The Beatles had opened their Apple Boutique the previous December, at 94 Baker Street in central London. Dutch fashion designers known as *The Fool* were commissioned to create items for the Fab

Four's new venture into the fashion world. The shop was initially managed by former Quarry Man Pete Shotton but he was replaced by John Lyndon. The short-lived venture proved to be a financial disaster and was consigned to history.

1980 Eagles from Linda Ronstadt to the ice age

The Eagles were on the eve of their swan song concert, slated to take place the following night at Long Beach, California. This gig was the end of the *Long Run* tour and the end of the road for one of America's most successful 1970s bands.

The original lineup, guitarists Glenn Frey and Bernie Leadon, drummer Don Henley and bassist Randy Meisner, came together as Linda Ronstadt's backing band and performed for the first time at Disneyland on 12 July* 1971. They formed the Eagles shortly afterwards, with a lineup where each musician could perform lead vocals.

The original lineup recorded two albums, *Eagles* and *Desperado*, before recruiting a third guitarist, Don Felder, in early 1974. Two more albums followed, *On the Border* and *One of These Nights* but internal conflicts resulted in the departure of guitarist Bernie Leadon at the end of 1975. He was replaced by Joe Walsh, who gave the band a harder rock edge. This lineup delivered just one album and tour, *Hotel California*, before more disagreements, including a backstage fist fight, resulted in the departure of original bassist Randy Meisner and the arrival of Timothy B Schmit. The band's album and tour for the *Long Run* proved to be the end of the road for the original incarnation of the Eagles. The band disintegrated on stage during the final gig of the tour. That notorious night saw Frey and Felder exchanging insults between songs. It was so blatant that the mikes had to be turned down to prevent the audience from hearing the bickering musicians. The gig ended with the band swearing that they would never work together again – not until "Hell freezes over". Well, the ice age overcame Hades on 26 May* 1994.

Birthdays today

1941 Paul Anka singer and songwriter

Canada's first rock'n'roll star, Paul Anka was born in Ottawa. In the summer of 1957 he scored a smash international hit with his own composition *Diana*, reputedly written about a former babysitter. He followed this with a string of hits into the early 1960s, after which his chart appearances thinned out in America and dried up in the UK, with the exception of a solitary 1974 hit *(You're) Having My Baby*. He was also a prolific songwriter, penning Buddy Holly's *It Doesn't Matter Anymore* and the English lyrics to Frank Sinatra's *My Way*, based on the melody of the French song *Comme d'habitude*. This became one of the most covered songs of all time.

1957 Rat Scabies drums: London SS, The Damned

Events today

1966 Cream official debut concert

Cream made their official debut at the 6th *National Jazz and Blues Festival* at Windsor in the south of England. They appeared on the third and final day, alongside Georgie Fame, The Action and Alan Bown.

This gig followed a couple of days after a warm-up performance at Manchester's Twisted Wheel club. This virtuoso trio had an impeccable track record. Guitar legend Eric Clapton had previously played alongside bassist Jack Bruce in John Mayall's Bluesbreakers. Bruce had also worked with drummer Ginger Baker in both Alexis Korner's Blues Incorporated and the Graham Bond Organisation. It was always going to be a bumpy ride for Cream. Bruce and Baker were not the best of friends, particularly after Baker allegedly once pulled a knife on Bruce.

1967 The Rolling Stones victory in the Appeals Court

Mick Jagger and Keith Richard's drug conviction ordeals came to an end when the Appeals Court quashed Richard's guilty verdict and reduced Jagger's sentence to probation.

Richard's Redland home had been raided in February, resulting in drugs charges for Jagger, Richard and their friend Richard Fraser. Fraser subsequently pleaded guilty to heroin possession. After opting for a trial by jury, Jagger and Richard were found guilty and received prison sentences. An immediate appeal meant that they were bailed but not released before experiencing the joys of being held at Her Majesty's pleasure. They received support from an unexpected quarter: the *Times* newspaper published an editorial by William Rees-Mogg entitled, *Who Breaks a Butterfly on a Wheel?*

The Stones recounted their prison experiences with their next single, *We Love You*.

The Who provided moral support, by rush-releasing a cover version of *The Last Time*.

1969 Elvis Presley Las Vegas opening night

Elvis appeared at the Las Vegas International Hotel to give his first concert performance for eight years. This five-week residency ended on 28 August, generating Elvis's first live album, one half of the double-LP *From Memphis to Vegas/From Vegas to Memphis*. His first performance in Las Vegas was at the New Frontier Hotel on 23 April* 1956, though his reception then was a lot more subdued. He was not yet resplendent in a jumpsuit; that first sartorial pleasure was still six months away, on 26 January* 1970.

This performance marked the beginning of the third and final chapter of Elvis's career: the '50s rocker, the '60s movie star and now, the '70s ultimate cabaret act.

Birthday today

1923 Ahmet Ertegun producer and co-founder of Atlantic Records

Born in Istanbul, Turkey, Ahmet Ertegun went to live in America as a child. With his partner Herb Abrahamson he set up Atlantic Records in New York in 1947. This was to become a label with an impressive roster of artists, including The Drifters, The Young Rascals and Led Zeppelin. One of the early acts to record with Atlantic was the R&B group the Clovers. In order to secure royalty payments, a common practice at the time was for producers, managers and other assorted music industry dignitaries to attach their names to the writing credits. Ertegun was also a producer and an exception to this nefarious activity: he really did write many of the early Clovers songs under his pen name "Nugetre".

August

Events today

1964 Frank Zappa opened Studio Z

1

Frank Zappa purchased Pal Recording Studios from Paul Buff, renamed it to "Studio Z" and became the proud owner of his first recording studio, in Cucamonga, California.

Zappa had been working with Buff in his studio since the summer of 1962, often collaborating with Captain Beefheart and future-Mothers, singer Ray Collins and saxophonist Motorhead Sherwood. Many of his compositions from the period turned up on later Mothers of Invention albums. In Cucamonga Zappa worked on a lot of doo wop songs, including the Buff and Collins penned *Deseri*, and Collins and Zappa's *Love of My Life*, which featured on his doo wop tribute album *Cruising with Ruben and the Jets.*

1971 Landmark Concerts *Concert for Bangladesh*

Ravi Shankar and George Harrison organised a benefit concert to aid the plight of refugees from East Pakistan, recently renamed "Bangladesh". They had fled to neighbouring India to escape the violence following the political upheaval. The two concerts at New York's Madison Square Garden raised a quarter of a million dollars, to help UNICEF provide food and shelter for the refugees.

A host of rock luminaries performed at the concert, including ex-Beatles George Harrison and Ringo Starr, Eric Clapton, Bob Dylan, and keyboard players Billy Preston and Leon Russell. The backing musicians included Badfinger.

The matinee and evening performances spawned a triple album and a movie.

Singles released today

1955 Elvis Presley *I Forgot to Remember to Forget c/w Mystery Train* (Sun-5)

This was Elvis's fifth and final single to be released on Sam Phillips's Sun label. *Mystery Train* was a cover of the 1953 release from Sun stablemate Little Junior's Blue Flames' (Junior Parker).

Parker's version gave the songwriting credit to "Parker" but Elvis's version added Sam Phillips's name for a joint credit, "Parker – Phillips".

1955 Carl Perkins *Let the Juke Box Keep on Playing c/w Gone Gone Gone* (US)

Carl Perkins's self-penned debut Sun single was released on the same day as Presley's last. His debut for Sam Phillips, *Movie Magg*, was released on the subsidiary Flip label.

1960 Chubby Checker *The Twist c/w Toot* (US)

Although it had been released eighteen months earlier by the writer and his group, Hank Ballard and the Midnighters, it was Chubby Checker's cover version of *The Twist* that became a worldwide hit and inspired the dance sensation.

Birthdays today

1942 Jerry Garcia guitar and vocals: Warlocks, Grateful Dead

1951 Tommy Bolin guitar: Zephyr, James Gang, Deep Purple; solo

As well as playing with Zephyr and on Billy Cobham's *Spectrum* album, Tommy Bolin followed in the footsteps of two of rock's guitar greats. In 1973 he joined the James Gang as the second replacement for Joe Walsh, who left in 1971. Two years later he replaced Ritchie Blackmore to become the last of Deep Purple's lead guitarists.

Events today

1965 The Birds issued a writ against the Byrds

When the American group the Byrds arrived in England for their first tour of the UK, the British R&B group the Birds issued a writ against the US band, claiming that they were cashing in on the British group's established name.

The Birds formed in London in 1963, originally calling themselves "The Thunderbirds". The original lineup featured future Faces and Rolling Stones guitarist Ron Wood, and Kim Gardner, future bassist for the Creation, and Ashton Gardner and Dyke.

This homophonic writ was a little optimistic and failed to find favour with the establishment, since the Byrds had already scored a British #1 with their debut single *Mr. Tambourine Man*. Their follow-up, another Bob Dylan composition *All I Really Want to Do,* entered the UK charts a week later.

1977 Elvis Costello and the Attractions early gig together

With the recently formed Attractions, Elvis Costello performed at Eric's club in Liverpool. The concert was recorded and featured on the 3 December edition of the British TV show *So It Goes*.

Costello eventually found fame on both sides of the Atlantic but he was no overnight success. Still using his real name, Declan Patrick MacManus, he started performing in the late 1960s. In 1972 he formed the duo Rusty with Allan Mayes. By 1975 he was performing with Flip City, where he cut his first demo recordings. In early 1976 Costello became a solo artist. At the end of the year he submitted some of his demo recordings to the fledgling independent record label Stiff. He secured a recording contract and with Clover as his backing band cut his first album *My Aim Is True*. By now he had adopted the stage name "Elvis Costello". He recruited his backing band and as "Elvis Costello and the Attractions", proved to be one of the most successful bands to emerge out of the British new wave scene.

1977 Dire Straits AOR gathered a head of steam

One of the earliest gigs performed by the newly formed Dire Straits was given at the Tramshed in Woolwich.

When guitarist and singer Mark Knopfler formed Dire Straits in mid-1977, he bucked the trend of forming a punk band and laid the foundations for a band that would become one of the most successful next generation rock bands and stadium fillers. Mark Knopfler was in the group Café Racers with his brother and fellow guitarist David, before joining up with bassist John Illsley and drummer Pick Withers to form Dire Straits.

Dire Straits was one of the new breed of post-punk rock bands. Formed towards the end of the short-lived punk-rock era (the Sex Pistols gave their swan song performance five months later on 14 January*) they joined the ranks of the new era of rock, which became known as AOR (Album Oriented Rock).

Birthdays today

1937 Garth Hudson keyboards and horns: The Hawks, The Band

After splitting from rockabilly star Ronnie Hawkins, the Hawks backed Bob Dylan on his groundbreaking electric tour of 1965/1966. In 1968 The Hawks changed their name to "The Band" and released their debut album *Music from the Big Pink*.

1944 Jim Capaldi drums and vocals: The Hellions, Traffic; solo

Events today

3

1963 The Beatles last appearance at the Cavern

After nearly 300 appearances since their first performance on 9 February* 1961, the Beatles played Liverpool's Mathew Street Cavern Club for the last time.

1970 Mick Jagger first movie

Mick Jagger's first movie, *Performance*, was finally given a theatrical release in America.

Filmed in 1968 it starred James Fox and contained some controversial love scenes between Jagger and Keith Richard's girlfriend Anita Pallenberg (also the former girlfriend of Brian Jones). The original cinema trailer described the movie as being about, "madness...sanity...fantasy...reality...sensuality... death...life, vice and versa".[33] The finished movie shocked studio executives and it took many cuts and two years before it received a theatrical release in America. It opened to mixed reviews but over time has become a cult classic.

Mick Jagger's soundtrack single, the Jagger and Richard composition *Memo from Turner*, hardly grazed the charts when it was released in the UK.

Albums released today

1979 AC/DC *Highway to Hell* (US)

AC/DC had already released about half a dozen albums (it just depends how you count them) before their tour de force, *Highway to Heaven*, gave them their breakthrough and propelled them into the vanguard of hard-rock bands. Sadly, this was to be lead singer Bon Scott's final album. He died six months later on 19 February*, after a bout of heavy drinking.

The album contained the track *Night Prowler*. In the mid-1980s serial killer Richard "Night Stalker" Ramirez committed multiple murders across California. When he was finally brought to justice, AC/DC's song *Night Prowler* was cited as one of the influences behind Ramirez's actions.

Bon Scott was replaced by Brian Johnson and AC/DC returned with *Back in Black*.

1987 Def Leppard *Hysteria* (UK)

This was the band's fourth album and the follow-up to their 1983 offering *Pyromania*. The four year gap between albums was due to drummer Rick Allen losing his left arm in a car crash on 31 December* 1984. The group's perseverance and loyalty to their injured band mate certainly paid off. The album made #1 on both sides of the Atlantic and gained a certification as 12xPlatinum[31] in 1998.

Died today

1966 Lenny Bruce iconoclastic comedian, died at the age of forty

Controversial American comedian Lenny Bruce was found dead in his toilet by room-mate John Judnich. The death certificate gave the cause of death as "ACUTE MORPHINE POISONING due to INJECTION OF OVERDOSE".[35]

From the early 1960s Bruce continually crossed swords with the establishment. He was arrested on a number of occasions for both drug possession and stage performances which were considered to be obscene. Many American venues banned him from performing and he was officially banned from Australia. The British Home Office refused to allow him entry into the UK, considering him to be an undesirable alien.

Events today

4

1927 Jimmie Rodgers first recording session

Having recently signed to RCA Victor, Jimmie Rodgers made his first recordings, *Sleep Baby Sleep* and *The Soldier's Sweetheart*, one of his earliest compositions.

Rodgers's singing style drew on influences from across the spectrum of American music genres, including country, blues and hillbilly. He was one of the most influential singers of his generation, denoted by the fact that he was the first artist to be inducted into the Country Music Hall of Fame and one of the artists inducted by the Rock and Roll Hall of Fame in its inaugural year of 1986. In his next recording session on 30 November, he recorded the first of his *Blue Yodel* compositions, *T for Texas*, which gave him a huge hit. His working career started on the railroad and led to him being known as the "Singing Brakeman", as well as the "Father of Country Music". When he was just twenty-seven years old he contracted TB and died from the disease in 1933.

1964 Vietnam War *Gulf of Tonkin* incident

The *Gulf of Tonkin* incident marked the beginning of America's proactive war in Vietnam.

The destroyer *USS Maddox* was involved in electronic surveillance in the Gulf of Tonkin, on a mission to pinpoint North Vietnamese radar stations. On 2 August the destroyer was attacked by North Vietnamese torpedo boats but sustained only minor damage. The *Maddox* was joined by a second US destroyer *Turner Joy*. There was an alleged second attack on 4 August. Believing themselves to be under attack, the ships opened fire on the North Vietnamese radar stations. As a result of what was believed to be hostile action, Congress passed the *Gulf of Tonkin Resolution*. This authorised President Johnson to conduct military operations in South-East Asia without a declaration of war. It further allowed the President to take all necessary measures to repel any armed attack against the forces of the United States.

1968 Yes first gig

One of the mainstays of progressive rock, Yes, gave their debut performance at East Mercia Youth Camp in Essex.

Vocalist Jon Anderson, bassist Chris Squire, keyboard player Tony Kaye, guitarist Peter Banks and drummer Bill Bruford came together in Mabel Greer's Toyshop, before morphing into Yes.

Just over three months later, Yes supported Cream when they played their farewell concert at London's Royal Albert Hall on 26 November*. In 1972 Bill Bruford left Yes to join King Crimson, in time to perform on their album *Larks' Tongues in Aspic*.

Recording session today

1973 Fripp and Eno *Swastika Girls*

Shortly after parting company with Roxy Music, Brian Eno was in the studio with King Crimson's Robert Fripp to record the second side of their album *No Pussyfooting*. The album was an early example of the ambient music genre.

Single released today

1964 The Kinks *You Really Got Me* c/w *It's Alright* (UK)

This Ray Davies penned song was their breakthrough on both sides of the Atlantic. It featured future Deep Purple keyboardist Jon Lord and session drummer Bobby Graham.

Events today

1957 Landmark TV *American Bandstand* debut

Philadelphia TV station WFIL-TV launched the original programme on 7 October 1952 as *Bob Horn's Bandstand*. Five years later it made its debut on national television, on ABC-TV and renamed *American Bandstand*. Billy Williams and The Chordettes appeared on the first show.

Clean-cut Dick Clark had taken over from original *Bandstand* host Bob Horn on 9 July 1956, after Horn had been sacked for drink and morals related incidents. Clark continued as its host until 1989.

1964 Vietnam War first American bombing of North Vietnam

Following the *Gulf of Tonkin* affair on 4 August*, America's President Johnson ordered the first bombing of North Vietnam, targeting torpedo-boat bases and oil facilities.

The *Ho Chi Minh Trail* in Laos was also bombed for the first time in mid-December. The *Trail* ran through Vietnam's neighbours, Laos and Cambodia. It was used to great effect by the North to transport weapons and personnel into South Vietnam. Despite the *Trail* not actually being in Vietnam, it was bombed extensively throughout the war.

Recording session today

1951 Elmore James *Dust My Broom*

Elmore James recorded one of the blues standards that became a firm favourite with 1960s blues-based groups. Sonny Boy Williamson (II) featured on harmonica. This original recording on Trumpet was credited to Elmo James as both performer and writer, although the song was a reworking of Robert Johnson's *I Believe I'll Dust My Broom*.

Single released today

1966 The Beatles *Yellow Submarine c/w Eleanor Rigby* (UK)

Albums released today

1966 The Beatles *Revolver* (UK)

Friend from the Beatles' Hamburg days and future bassist with John Lennon's Plastic Ono Band, Klaus Voormann designed the cover for the *Revolver* album. He was also credited later on solo albums from Ringo Starr and George Harrison.

1967 Pink Floyd *Piper at the Gates of Dawn* (UK)

Pink Floyd's debut album heralded an era of British psychedelic rock. This pre-David Gilmour album was dominated by the group's leader Syd Barrett. He wrote ten of the tracks, including two in collaboration with the rest of the group. The only track without a Barrett writing credit was Roger Waters' song, *Take Up Thy Stethoscope and Walk*. The album was named after the title of Chapter 7 of one of Barrett's favourite books, *Wind in the Willows* by Kenneth Grahame. The song *Chapter 24* was inspired by the 5,000 year old Chinese tome, *I Ching: The Book of Changes*. Barrett was also responsible for the design of the back cover.

Producer Norman "Hurricane" Smith had recently parted company with George Martin, after a long association as engineer on all of the Beatles output since *Love Me Do*. He also enjoyed personal chart success on both sides of the Atlantic in 1972, with his own composition *Oh Babe, What Would You Say*.

Event today

1966 Cream rock'n'roll started to mature

Cream gave one of their earliest performances at Torquay's Town Hall in the picturesque south-west of England.

When Eric Clapton, Ginger Baker and Jack Bruce came together to form Cream they were described as the first "supergroup". All three were accomplished musicians in their own right and they epitomised the more sophisticated rock'n'roll music that was just around the corner. Since the emergence of the Beatles, British beat groups had dominated the music scene on both sides of the Atlantic. These British beat groups had taken 1950s American rock'n'roll and R&B, repackaged it and very successfully exported it back to America as the "British Invasion".

By 1966 the Invasion was all but over. A whole new music scene had developed independently on both sides of the Atlantic. In San Francisco the *Trips Festival* on 22 January* was one of the earliest psychedelic events and featured the music of Grateful Dead and a pre-Janis Joplin Big Brother and the Holding Company. Other West Coast bands such as the Doors and Jefferson Airplane were also making their presence felt. In the UK, Pink Floyd was in the vanguard of the emerging British underground scene and Jimi Hendrix had just arrived in London, jamming with Cream at a gig on 1 October*.

For the rest of the 1960s the music developed into prog rock (progressive rock), with accomplished musicians creating longer and longer solos. Some groups took to recording with an entire symphony orchestra. Albums appeared with a single song taking up an entire side. Groups also started to perform in much larger venues, with sports stadiums and arenas replacing the more intimate settings of clubs and theatres. In the early 1970s with the appearance of British glam rock, the tide started to turn. The likes of T.Rex and Slade created simpler music and marked the beginning of the end for virtuoso based rock'n'roll.

Recording session today

1966 The Miracles *I Heard It Through the Grapevine*

With Smokey Robinson, the Miracles recorded the original version of *I Heard It Through the Grapevine*. After hearing the Miracles recording of the Norman Whitfield and Barrett Strong song, Motown boss Berry Gordy Jr decided that it was not good enough to be released as a single. It remained in the vaults and the Miracles could only stand and watch as two of their stablemates achieved success with their versions of the song.

A little over a year later Gordy achieved chart success on both sides of the Atlantic, when he put the Gladys Knight and the Pips version of the song out as a single on his Soul label. Marvin Gaye had actually recorded a version of the song before Gladys Knight but his version was not released until the end of 1968.

Gaye's version was by far the most successful and has become a classic of the period.

Single released today

1965 Small Faces *Whatcha Gonna Do About It c/w What's a Matter Baby* (UK)

This debut single featured original organist Jimmy Winston. The A-side was co-written and produced by ex-Drifters (British) guitarist Ian Samwell.

Album released today

1965 The Beatles *Help* (UK)

Events today

7

1957 The Quarry Men John Lennon's Cavern debut

John Lennon and his band the Quarry Men made their first appearance at Liverpool's Cavern Club.

At the time it was a jazz club and owner Alan Sytner was not a fan of rock'n'roll. The Quarry Men were there as a skiffle group but John Lennon was rapidly moving their musical direction towards rock'n'roll. During their set the group broke away from skiffle and played *Hound Dog* and *Blue Suede Shoes*, prompting Sytner to famously send a note to Lennon on stage telling him to cut out the "bloody rock".

By now Paul McCartney was also a member of the Quarry Men but he missed this gig because he was away at camp with the Boy Scouts.

1963 The Rolling Stones British R&B groups revitalised American bluesmen

London group the Rolling Stones appeared at Twickenham's Eel Pie Island, promoting their recently released cover of Chuck Berry's *Come On*.

In the mid-1950s American rock'n'roll grew out of white country music and black blues and R&B. With more than a twist of irony, it was the British Invasion, starting on 1 February* 1964, that exported R&B back to America and as a consequence rekindled interest in the original blues and R&B artists such as Chuck Berry, BB King and Muddy Waters. Berry and King opened for the Stones on their legendary 1969 American tour.

1970 Landmark Festivals forgotten Michigan festival

Attended by over 200,000 people, the three-day *Goose Lake International Music Festival* opened in Jackson, Michigan.

Whereas Monterey, held on 16 June* 1967, was hailed as a groundbreaking rock event and Woodstock, on 15 August* 1969, epitomised the era, *Goose Lake* was largely unpublicised outside of Michigan at the time and the coverage was more focussed on drugs and discontented locals. Unlike Altamont, 6 December* 1969, no-one died. There were very few drug arrests inside the festival, no riots and no rain. In order to keep the concert on time the organisers constructed a large turntable stage, which enabled the road crews to set up behind the artist in performance. The festival's poster advertised a host of rock luminaries, including Savoy Brown, Jethro Tull, Joe Cocker, Ten Years After, Mountain, Chicago, Bob Seger, John Sebastian, Alice Cooper, James Gang, The Stooges and The Flying Burrito Brothers.

This proved to be the final outing for the original lineup of Iggy Pop's Stooges. Bass player Dave Alexander parted company with the band, after being fired for allegedly turning up at the festival too drunk to play.

Birthday today

1928 Herb Reed bass singer: The Platters

Co-founded by Herb Reed in 1953, the Platters became one of the most successful vocal groups of the doo wop era. The ever-changing lineup resulted in a number of groups performing under the name of "The Platters". Reed performed with the Platters and then his own version of the group, Herb Reed's Platters, until his death in 2012.

Event today

1966 Songwriting from the Brill Building to the bands

The Beatles released *Revolver* in America, their second album of all original songs.

The Fab Four led the transition from the Brill Building's ready-made rock'n'roll songs of the 1950s, to the mid-1960s groups who wrote their own material. In the 1950s songs were mostly written by professional songwriting teams, although some artists, notably Buddy Holly and Eddie Cochran, regularly wrote their own material. In the early 1960s the trend was moving away from solo artists with professionally written songs, towards groups that had their own songwriting capabilities. In fact, of the groups that started out in the early 1960s, the bands that were still around in the late 1960s were mostly the ones that did not rely on other people's songwriting skills. These notable songwriting bands included, obviously, Lennon and McCartney, and George Harrison for the Beatles; Jagger and Richard for the Rolling Stones; and Ray Davies for the Kinks. The new generation of bands that emerged on both sides of the Atlantic in the mid-1960s often used a combination of reworked blues songs and original material. Although once again, some bands mostly used the output of their own songwriters, such as Frank Zappa for the Mothers of Invention and Pete Townshend for the Who.

Recording session today

1960 Roy Orbison — *Blue Angel* and *Today's Teardrops*

Roy Orbison was back in the studio to record Gene Pitney's *Today's Teardrops*, and *Blue Angel*, another collaboration with Joe Melson. *Blue Angel* was the follow-up to his smash hit *Only the Lonely (Know How I Feel)* and gave him his second chart success.

Overnight success was not something that Roy Orbison could be accused of. He cut his first Sun single, *Ooby Dooby*, in Sam Phillips's studio on 27 March* 1956. That was followed by a handful of singles but the rockabilly style at Sun did not suit Orbison. Following his move from Sun a couple of years later, he recorded two singles for RCA Victor, before finally finding international success with his move to Monument in mid-1959. *Only the Lonely* was Orbison's third single for Monument but it started a run of hits that lasted until the mid-1960s in America and the late 1960s in Britain.

For the recording session that day Orbison was backed by saxophonist Boots Randolph and pianist Floyd Cramer.

Single released today

1966 The Beatles — *Eleanor Rigby* c/w *Yellow Submarine* (US)

Album released today

1966 The Beatles — *Revolver* (US)

This was to be the last American album to have a different track listing to its British counterpart. The three songs missed off the US edition of *Revolver* had previously been released on *Yesterday...and Today*, which was an additional American album issued between *Rubber Soul* and *Revolver*.

By the time of *Revolver*, the Beatles' songwriting had come of age. The previous album, *Rubber Soul*, was the first non-movie album to contain all original material. *Revolver* continued to increase the complexity of the songs, leading the way to the next album, *Sgt Pepper*, which took the rock world by storm and regularly topped the *Best Albums Ever* polls for decades to come.

Events today

9

1963 Landmark TV — *Ready Steady Go!* ...British TV debut

The show's catchphrase, "the weekend starts here!" was introduced and would be heard until the programme's final outing on 23 December* 1966. The Surfaris's *Wipe Out* provided the first theme tune but was replaced by Manfred Mann's *5-4-3-2-1* on 10 January* 1964. For this first edition, hosts Keith Fordyce and David Gell introduced performances from Billy Fury, and Brian Poole and the Tremeloes.

The Rolling Stones made their first appearance in episode 3 but the Beatles' debut was not until episode 9. It was 1964 before Cathy McGowan joined as co-presenter; her image as "Queen of the Mods" became an integral part of the show's appeal.

1963 The Surfaris — *Wipe Out* opened *Ready Steady Go!*

The Surfaris's self-penned instrumental *Wipe Out* had already been in the UK charts for two weeks when it was heard over the opening credits of Britain's latest music TV show *Ready Steady Go!*

By then *Wipe Out* had garnered a colourful history of different record releases. It was recorded in late 1962 at Pal Recording Studios in Cucamonga, California. Frank Zappa regularly worked at the studios at the time and become the proud owner of the enterprise when he bought it on 1 August* 1964, renaming it "Studio Z". *Wipe Out* was coupled with the saga of *Surfer Joe* and initially released on the small, local DFS label. It was then licensed and distributed on Princess, with releases of both the long and edited versions. The single came to the attention of major label Dot and it finally entered the American charts in mid-1963.

Dot released the associated album as *Wipe Out* by the Surfaris. The front cover of the first issue listed the platter's 12 tracks but failed to say that only *Wipe Out* and *Surfer Joe* were by the Surfaris, the rest were recorded by a different surf group, the Challengers.

Recording session today

1953 The Drifters *Money Honey*

With the lead vocals taken by founder Clyde McPhatter, the Drifters recorded the Jesse Stone penned *Money Honey*. This R&B hit heralded a run of pop hits that started in 1959/1960 and continued into the mid-1960s in America and the mid-1970s in Britain.

The Drifters were one of the most successful vocal groups of the era but they still suffered from a multitude of personnel changes. This included half a dozen lead singers and a complete personnel change overnight on 30 May* 1958. The group was formed by Clyde McPhatter after he left Billy Ward and His Dominoes. His first lineup recorded a number of songs, including the McPhatter penned *Lucille* but was disbanded after his record company, Atlantic, was unimpressed with the results. This *Money Honey* session had a new lineup of Bill Pinkney, who later ran his own version of the Drifters, Andrew "Bubba" Thrasher, his brother Gerhardt and bass singer Willie Ferbie.

Album released today

1976 Grand Funk Railroad *Good Singin' Good Playin'* (US)

Frank Zappa produced the album and featured as guitarist on *Out to Get You*.

The group had already disbanded at this stage but came back together to work with Zappa. They spit up again as soon as the album was completed.

Events today

1959 The Platters all four male singers were arrested

In Cincinnati, Ohio, all four of the male singers in the Platters were arrested and charged with aiding and abetting prostitution. The four Platters, Tony Williams, David Lynch, Paul Robi and Herb Reed, were discovered in their hotel room with four women, three of whom were white. They were acquitted in December but the publicity badly damaged the vocal group's reputation.

This marked the beginning of the end for the Platters. The Cincinnati escapade resulted in reduced airplay by radio DJs. Lead singer Tony Williams had already announced his intension to leave the group and planned to embark on a solo career with his first album, *a girl is a girl is a girl*. Musical tastes were changing and the Platters enjoyed their last British hit with *Harbour Lights* in early 1960. Their American chart appearances also dried up by the end of 1961.

1969 Charles Manson Sharon Tate and LaBianca murders

The actress Sharon Tate and four other people were murdered by members of Charles Manson's so-called "Family" at her Cielo Drive home in Los Angeles. They broke into the house in the early hours of 9 August and murdered everyone inside. One victim, Steven Parent, was shot to death whilst he was still in his car on the driveway. Tate was married to the film director Roman Polanski. At the time of the murders Sharon Tate was eight months pregnant and Polanski was away in Europe.

The following night Charles Manson, accompanied by a number of "Family" members, broke into the home of Leno LaBianca and his wife Rosemary in the Los Feliz area of Los Angeles. Both were viciously stabbed to death. The husband had the word "war" carved into his flesh. "Rise" and "Death To Pigs" were written in blood on the walls. "Healter Skelter" [sic] was written in blood on the refrigerator door.

The messages, written in blood, have all been tied to the tracks, *Piggies*, *Helter Skelter* and *Revolution* 9, on the Beatles' *White Album*. Manson perceived these and other songs to contain messages warning of an upcoming race war, by the name of "Helter Skelter". The *Revolution* 9 track was seen as a reference to the apocalyptic biblical references in Revelations, Chapter 9.

Single released today

1958 Jerry Lee Lewis *Break Up c/w I'll Make It All Up to You* (US)

Birthdays today

1909 Leo Fender solid electric guitar manufacturing pioneer

The electric guitar had been around since the 1930s. In the 1940s innovator Les Paul worked on his solid body guitar known as "the Log". Leo Fender was the first person to mass manufacture a solid body guitar. He started with the Broadcaster at the turn of the 1950s, soon to be renamed the "Telecaster". His tour de force the Stratocaster followed, becoming the guitar of choice for a generation of rock musicians. In the early 1950s he also introduced his electric bass, the Precision Bass.

1940 Bobby Hatfield singer: Variations, Paramours, Righteous Brothers; solo

1943 Ronnie Spector singer: Joey Dee, The Ronettes; solo

1947 Ian Anderson vocalist, multi-instrumentalist: John Evan Band, Jethro Tull

Events today

1965 Civil Rights first day of the Watts riot

One of the worst riots of the 1960s took place in the Watts neighbourhood of Los Angeles.

It started after a white police officer, California Highway Patrolman Lee W Minikus, pulled over a black motorist, Marquette Frye and arrested him for failing a sobriety test. The crowd of onlookers grew and the police radioed for more support. As the situation continued to deteriorate both Frye's mother and brother were arrested. Word of the incident spread and the local population took to the streets. Rioting and looting continued for the next five days. The situation was finally brought under control by the intervention of 14,000 National Guardsmen.

By the time that the dust had settled there had been thirty-four deaths, 1,032 people injured, 3,438 adults arrested and damage to property estimated at over $40m.[107] This was one of the landmarks in the transition from peaceful Civil Rights activities to a more violent approach to the resolution of grievances.

On his debut album, *Freak Out*, Frank Zappa immortalised the riots in his song *Trouble Every Day*.

1974 Iggy Pop infamous chest-slashing gig

Iggy Pop performed the improvised play *Murder of the Virgin* at Rodney Bingenheimer's English Disco in Los Angeles. This infamous performance included Pop being whipped by guitarist James Williamson, resplendent in Nazi uniform and climaxed with the singer repeatedly slashing himself across the chest with a knife.

Some reports even suggested that prior to the gig, rumours had circulated that Pop would kill himself on stage that night.

Recording session today

1947 Chet Atkins first session for RCA

In 1946 Chet Atkins recorded his first single, *Guitar Blues*, on the Bullet label. His appearances on various radio stations and activity as a sideman for Red Foley attracted the attention of RCA and he was signed to the label.

Atkins was one of the major influences on the early sound of rock'n'roll. He was credited as being one of the architects of the "Nashville sound". As well as continuing his solo career he was a prolific producer and session guitarist, including an appearance on Elvis Presley's *Heartbreak Hotel*. The Everly Brothers' career moved into first gear when Atkins introduced them to Columbia Records. Although the Brothers' tenure at the label was short, their subsequent move to Cadence established them as rock'n'roll's most successful duo.

Birthdays today

1942 Mike Hugg drums: Manfred Mann; keyboards: Chapter Three

Mike Hugg met Manfred Mann at Butlin's holiday camp in Clacton in 1962. They formed a jazz band which became the Mann-Hugg Blues Band and after teaming up with singer Paul Jones morphed into Manfred Mann. When the group folded in 1969 Mann and Hugg, who then moved to keyboards, formed Manfred Mann Chapter Three.

1949 Eric Carmen musician and songwriter: Cyrus Erie, Raspberries

Recording session today

12

1955 Sonny Boy Williamson (II) *Don't Start Me Talkin'*

In his first recording session for Chess's subsidiary Checker, Sonny Boy Williamson (II) recorded the self-penned *Don't Start Me Talkin'*. It was released shortly afterwards and became his most commercially successful single. He was backed by guitarists Muddy Waters and Jimmy Rogers, pianist Otis Span, bassist Willie Dixon and drummer Fred Below.

The background to Williamson's early life is a little vague. His birth name is open to speculation: Alex Miller is often suggested. The year of his birth is also shrouded in mystery, with dates varying from 1897 to 1912. He became known as "Rice Miller".

He initially found fame in the southern states as an accomplished blues harmonica player, sometimes using the name "Little Boy Blue". In the early 1940s he joined the *King Biscuit Time* show on Arkansas' radio station KFFA, one of the first live blues shows on radio. It was for these radio performances that he took the name of another established blues harp player, the Chicago-based John Lee Williamson known as "Sonny Boy Williamson". After the original Sonny Boy Williamson was killed on 1 June* 1948, he adopted his name on a permanent basis. Along the way, he married and divorced Howlin' Wolf's sister.

At the beginning of his career he played with legendary bluesman Robert Johnson. Williams reputedly tells of how he was with Johnson and cradled him in his arms on the night he died, 16 August* 1938. Towards the end of his career he played with an Eric Clapton version of the Yardbirds, when they supported him in the UK. They recorded a live performance together on 8 December* 1963.

In 1961 Mick Jagger, Keith Richard and Dick Taylor played together in a group called "Little Boy Blue and the Blue Boys". Jagger and Richard went on to form the Rolling Stones and Taylor became a founding member of the Pretty Things

Single released today

1957 Buddy Holly *That'll Be the Day c/w Rock Around With Ollie Vee* (US)

Buddy Holly was originally signed by Decca and recorded *That'll Be the Day* in July 1956. His two singles for the label attracted little attention and Decca let him go. Shortly afterwards, he signed to Coral/ Brunswick with the Crickets and recorded the song again.

When his version with the Crickets was released to great acclaim, Decca tried to cash in by releasing this version, recorded a year earlier.

Birthday today

1949 Mark Knopfler guitarist, singer, songwriter: Café Racers, Dire Straits; solo

Mark Knopfler formed Dire Straits in mid-1977, heralding a new generation of rock bands. Punk rock was peaking and the music industry was about to splinter into a number of new music genres, including the AOR (Album Oriented Rock) of bands like Dire Straits and Boston. Knopfler also achieved fame outside of Dire Straits. In 1979 he was the featured guitarist on Bob Dylan's album *Slow Train Coming*. Knopfler's guitar was once again called upon to assist another rock legend when he joined Eric Clapton to open the first of Clapton's residencies at London's Royal Albert Hall, on 6 January* 1987. Knopfler extended his composition skills into the movie world, with soundtrack credits including *Local Hero* and *Last Exit to Brooklyn*.

Events today

1965 Jefferson Airplane debut gig

Jefferson Airplane gave its debut performance at San Francisco's Matrix nightclub. Marty Balin was part-owner of the Matrix and this was the club's opening night. The lineup was lead guitarist Jorma Kaukonen, vocalists Signe Anderson and Marty Balin, Paul Kantner guitar and vocals, bassist Bob Harvey and drummer Jerry Peloquin.

Bassist Jack Casady and drummer Skip Spence joined a couple of months after this debut and Grace Slick replaced Anderson in October 1966.

1967 Fleetwood Mac debut gig

Peter Green's Fleetwood Mac gave its debut performance at the *Windsor Jazz and Blues Festival*, with a lineup of: guitarist Peter Green and drummer Mick Fleetwood, both previously with John Mayall, guitarist Jeremy Spencer and bassist Bob Brunning.

Although John McVie was the first choice for bass player, he was initially reluctant to leave the security of the prestigious John Mayall's Bluesbreakers. Brunning's stay with Fleetwood Mac was short but he did appear on some early recordings.

Recording sessions today

1952 Willie Mae "Big Mama" Thornton *Hound Dog*

Four years before Elvis Presley took *Hound Dog* into the international charts, "Big Mama" Thornton recorded the original version.

This was one of Leiber and Stoller's earliest compositions. Backing was provided by the Johnny Otis Band; Otis also produced the single. The original release gave the writing credits to Leiber, Stoller and Johnny Otis. Leiber and Stoller disputed this and by the time that Elvis's version hit the streets, Otis's name was no longer there.

1954 Chuck Berry recording debut

Chuck Berry made his recording debut with Jo Alexander and the Cubans, when they recorded two songs *Oh Maria* and *I Hope These Words Will Find You Well*. The single preceded his Chess offerings and was released on the American, Ballad label.

Albums released today

1965 The Beatles *Help* (US)

Once again the track selection for the movie album varied on both sides of the Atlantic. The British listing included *Act Naturally*, *It's Only Love*, *You Like Me Too Much*, *Tell Me What You See*, *I've Just Seen a Face*, *Yesterday* and *Dizzy Miss Lizzy*. The American version opted for six soundtrack instrumental cuts by George Martin.

1973 Lynyrd Skynyrd *(pronounced 'lĕh-'nérd 'skin-'nérd)* 1st album (US)

Died today

1971 King Curtis session saxophonist, died at the age of thirty-seven

King Curtis was carrying an air conditioning unit to a property he owned on New York's West 86th Street. Outside the building he became involved in an altercation with a junkie. This developed into a fight and Curtis was fatally stabbed.

14

Events today

1967 The Who bad flight inspired *Glow Girl* ...and led to *Tommy*

During their American tour, the Who's plane developed engine trouble on a flight from their Rhode Island gig to Chattanooga, Tennessee. This resulted in a nerve-wracking journey for the band and an emergency landing for the plane. The experience inspired Pete Townshend, the group's guitarist and main song writer, to write the plane-crash song *Glow Girl*.

Glow Girl was intended to be released as a single. It was also reputedly pegged as the opener for the 'lost' album *Who's for Tennis*, the planned follow-up to *The Who Sell Out*. The song was never released as a single and the *Who's for Tennis* album never materialised, replaced by *Direct Hits* in Britain and *Magic Bus: The Who on Tour* in America. *Glow Girl* also sowed the seeds of Pete Townshend's magnum opus, his rock opera *Tommy*. The song ends with a Mrs Walker being told repeatedly that it's a girl. *Tommy* opened with the *Overture* followed by *It's a Boy*, also for a Mrs Walker.

The song *Glow Girl* was finally released on the Who's 1974 album *Odds and Sods*.

1976 Nick Lowe debut single from Stiff Records

The first single released by Stiff Records was from the label's own house producer Nick Lowe, *So It Goes* c/w *Heart of the City*.

Times were once again a-changin' and punk was leaving the rest of the British music scene in its wake. Stiff was a new independent record label, founded by Jake Riviera and Dave Robinson. It paved the way for a host of other independent labels.

Album released today

1970 Hawkwind *Hawkwind* (UK)

Space-rockers Hawkwind released their eponymous debut album, which was produced by Dick Taylor who had recently parted company with the Pretty Things.

The band went through multiple lineup changes during its long journey into the 21st century. One constant on this epic musical voyage was founding member, guitarist, singer and songwriter Dave Brock. A shorter tenure was that of bassist and singer Lemmy, who joined them in 1971. He started with their third album, *Doremi Fasol Latido* and stayed until he was sacked on 18 May* 1975, after their sixth album *Warrior on the Edge of Time*. Lemmy went on to form Motörhead. With an even shorter stay in Hawkwind's lineup, ex-Cream and Blind Faith drummer Ginger Baker joined them for their 1980 album *Levitation*.

Births and deaths today

1941 David Crosby guitar and vocals: Jet Set, Beefeaters, Byrds, CSN, CSNY

Although he was a founding member of the Byrds, he was sacked from the band in the autumn of 1967. His fifth and final album, not counting the 1973 reunion album *The Byrds*, was *The Notorious Byrd Brothers* released on 3 January* 1968.

1964 Johnny Burnette rockabilly pioneer, died at the age of thirty

Rockabilly pioneer Johnny Burnette drowned in a fishing accident in Clear Lake, California.

Events today

1955 Elvis Presley now managed by Bob Neal and the Colonel

Despite still being under contract to his original manager Bob Neal, Elvis Presley signed a management deal with Colonel Tom Parker.

Presley signed his first management contract, with Bob Neal on 1 January 1955. Parker had heard Elvis perform on the *Louisiana Hayride* radio show on 15 January and made his first booking for the King of Rock'n'Roll a month later. Neal was providing gigs in the southern states and the Colonel came on board to broaden Presley's horizons. Neal was Presley's manager for a little over a year. Parker ensured Presley's future by arranging the deal to move him from Sun Records to RCA on 20 November*.

1965 The Beatles legendary Shea Stadium performance

The first-ever stadium gig in the history of rock'n'roll, was performed by the Beatles to a crowd of over 55,000 people at New York's Shea Stadium. This landmark performance was filmed for a TV documentary, *The Beatles at Shea Stadium*. The King Curtis Band, Cannibal and the Headhunters, Brenda Holloway and Sounds Incorporated provided the support. After being introduced on stage by Ed Sullivan, the Fab Four performed 12 songs, opening up with *Twist and Shout* and finishing with *I'm Down*.

By this stage of their touring career the level of screaming made it difficult for them to hear their own playing and their disenchantment with performing live was growing.

1969 Landmark Festival *Woodstock*

Billed as "3 days of peace & music", the most famous festival in rock'n'roll history, *Woodstock*, opened on Max Yasgur's dairy farm in upstate New York. Although history recalls the event as "Woodstock", Yasgur's farm was nearly fifty miles away in Bethel, Sullivan County. The festival was originally planned to be in Wallkill, Orange County, New York but concerns about the number of people likely to attend the festival, meant that the authorities declined to issue the appropriate licences. Despite the rain an estimated 400,000 to 500,000 people made their way to Yasgur's farm to experience rock'n'roll history in the making.

The roster of artists was a veritable who's who of rock luminaries, including Canned Heat, Grateful Dead, Janis Joplin, Jefferson Airplane, Country Joe and the Fish, The Band, Joe Cocker, Creedence Clearwater Revival, Jeff Beck Group, Crosby, Stills & Nash joined by Neil Young, Paul Butterfield Blues Band, Iron Butterfly, Ten Years After, Santana, The Who and Jimi Hendrix, performing as "Gypsy Sun and Rainbows".

Birthdays today

1930 Jackie Brenston sax and vocals: Ike Turner, Lowell Fulson

Jackie Brenston is best remembered for recording *Rocket 88* on 5 March* 1951, often cited as the first rock'n'roll record. As well as working in Ike Turner's Kings of Rhythm, he went on to play in Lowell Fulson's band.

1942 Eddie Phillips guitar: The Mark Four, The Creation

Jimmy Page is often cited as being the first person to play his guitar with a violin bow but this accolade belongs to Eddie Phillips, lead guitarist with Mod group, the Creation.

Events today

1938 Rock'n'Roll Legend *27 Club*

A surprising number of rock'n'roll luminaries have died at the age of twenty-seven, thus giving rise to the macabre *27 Club*. One of the earliest members of the club was the legendary bluesman Robert Johnson who was murdered on 16 August* 1938.

Johnson reputedly sold his soul to the devil, in exchange for genius and fame. Maybe this set a trend for future rock'n'roll stars. Rolling Stones founding member and guitarist Brian Jones drowned in his swimming pool on 3 July* 1969. Jimi Hendrix choked on his own vomit on 18 September* 1970. Janis Joplin died of a heroin overdose on 4 October* 1970. Doors frontman Jim Morrison died of heart failure on 3 July* 1971. Other Club members include: Jesse Belvin, Rudy Lewis and Pete Ham.

1964 The High Numbers supported the Beatles

Shortly before changing their name to "The Who", the High Numbers were one of the acts supporting the Beatles for two shows at *Harold Fielding's Sunday Night at the Blackpool Opera House*. The middle of the show was a veritable Mod-fest, with the Kinks closing the first half and the High Numbers opening up after the interval.

Single released today

1962 Stevie Wonder *I Call It Pretty Music (But Old People Call It the Blues)*

This was Stevie Wonder's first American single and featured Marvin Gaye on drums.

Births and deaths today

1938 Robert Johnson iconic bluesman, died at the age of twenty-seven

After writing and releasing just twenty-nine songs, Robert Johnson died prematurely at the age of just twenty-seven. He had been playing at a gig in Three Forks near Greenwood, Mississippi, where he was said to have been poisoned by a jealous husband.

Urban legend has it that Johnson's genius was gained as a result of selling his soul to the Devil. This meeting supposedly took place "at the crossroads", although there is still much speculation as to its location.

1944 Kevin Ayers guitar and vocals: The Wilde Flowers, Soft Machine; solo

1977 Elvis Presley has left the building (for the very last time!)

In the early hours of the morning, Elvis was found lying in the bathroom of his Graceland home by his girlfriend Ginger Alden. She called for help but all attempts to revive him failed. He was taken to the Baptist Memorial Hospital in Memphis, where he was pronounced dead later that afternoon. At the age of forty-two, rock'n'roll's greatest icon died of heart failure. There has been much speculation surrounding the King's untimely demise, even to the extent of the urban myth that Elvis is still alive.

Elvis's body was laid in an open casket in Graceland's entrance hallway and an estimated 25,000 fans filed past to pay their last respects. The funeral was held two days later in the same room, with a short service at the Forest Hill cemetery chapel. In October Elvis and his mother Gladys, who died on 14 August 1958, were reburied side by side in the grounds of his Graceland home.

Events today

1960 The Beatles opening night on the first Hamburg trip

Arranged by their first manager, Allan Williams, the Beatles made their German debut when they opened at the Indra Club in Hamburg's red light district. The band's lineup was a five piece, with John, George and Paul on guitar, bassist Stu Sutcliffe and newly recruited drummer Pete Best. The Silver had just been dropped from the name "Silver Beatles" and the Hamburg audience was treated to the first performance by "The Beatles".

This first visit to Hamburg ended in disarray in late November when three of the group were deported. George left first for working underage, followed shortly afterwards by Paul and Pete for alleged arson.

The origins of the band's name are steeped in Beatles mythology, with the inspiration accredited to Lennon and Sutcliffe. The name is often given a couple of derivations. Homage to Buddy Holly and his backing group the Crickets and the leather-clad motorcycle gang, the Beetles, in Marlon Brando's 1953 movie *The Wild One,* athough the movie was banned in the UK until 1968, so maybe not. John Lennon and Stuart Sutcliffe provided musical backing for beat poet Royston Ellis at a gig in June 1960[104] and were inspired to change the spelling of "The Silver Beetles" to "The Silver Beatles".

Pete Best joined the Beatles from his own band, the Blackjacks. (Not the same band as John Lennon and Pete Shotton's Black Jacks.) Best's band also featured future-Beatles stand-in bassist Chas Newby.

1975 Bruce Springsteen an end to the hype

After one of the most hyped beginnings in rock'n'roll, Bruce Springsteen had finally fulfilled his potential. By the time that he closed the final show, after five nights at New York's Bottom Line club, the New Jersey singer-songwriter had established himself as "The Boss". Jon Landau famously said that, in Springsteen, he had seen the future of rock'n'roll. This residency and the release of his third album *Born to Run* a week later, finally put Springsteen's over-hyped beginnings firmly behind him.

Springsteen may have taken American audiences by storm but when his first European tour opened in London on 18 November*, he received a very mixed reception.

1977 Rush international stardom blossomed

Canadian band Rush opened their tour in support of their fifth studio album *A Farewell to Kings*, at the Orpheum Theater in Davenport, Ohio.

It had been quite a journey since their first paid gig, in a church basement on 18 September* 1968. The classic trio of guitarist Alex Lifeson, bassist and vocalist Geddy Lee, and drummer Neil Peart came together a few weeks before their gig on 26 August* 1974. They had made their British concert debut a couple of months before this Ohio gig and *A Farewell to Kings* gave them their first UK chart album and Gold Record.

Single released today

1962 The Tornados *Telstar c/w Jungle Fever* (UK)

Written and produced by Joe Meek, *Telstar* was not only a British #1 but with the American release they achieved the first #1 on the US charts by a British group.

This was not the only occupation of the American #1 spot by a British artist. Trad jazz clarinettist Acker Bilk had secured the US #1 spot with *Stranger on the Shore* seven months earlier, making him the first British artist (in the pop era) with an American #1.

Events today

18

1962 The Beatles Ringo completed the lineup

Ringo's first gig as the official Beatles drummer was in Birkenhead, at the Port Sunlight Horticulture Society's *After Show Dance* at Hulme Hall. This was not the first time that Ringo had played with the Beatles. When he was with Rory Storm and the Hurricanes, he filled in for Pete Best when both groups were appearing in Hamburg.

There was a two-gig gap between Pete Best leaving and Ringo's arrival as the Beatles' new sticksman. For those couple of performances, the vacant drumming stool was occupied by Johnny Hutchinson of the popular Liverpool group the Big Three. He had previously acted as a surrogate drummer for the group when he helped them out at the ill-fated Billy Fury audition on 10 May* 1960.

1966 The Doors signed to Elektra

Three months after the Doors secured the gig as the house band at LA's Whisky a Go Go, Jac Holzman signed them to his Elektra label.

The Doors were opening at the Whisky for Love, another West Coast band already signed to Elektra. It was Love's guitarist, Arthur Lee, who encouraged Holzman to see the Doors. Ironically, the Doors would soon eclipse Love at Elektra.

Recording session today

1952 Little Willie Littlefield *KC Loving*

Shortly after providing Willie Mae "Big Mama" Thornton with *Hound Dog*, Leiber and Stoller were back in the studio. This time it was to produce Little Willie Littlefield's recording of another one of their compositions, *KC Loving*.

It made little impact at the time. Seven years later the song was rewritten as *Kansas City*, recorded by Wilbert Harrison and became a million-selling rock'n'roll classic.

Single released today

1967 The Rolling Stones *We Love You c/w Dandelion* (UK)

Following their victory in the appeals court for drug offences on 31 July*, Mick Jagger and Keith Richard expressed their feelings about spending time at Her Majesty's pleasure with the song *We Love You*. This was the last of their singles to be produced by Andrew Loog Oldham.

Showing solidarity with their rock'n'roll chums, John Lennon and Paul McCartney provided backing vocals on *We Love You*.

Album released today

1978 The Who *Who Are You* (UK)

Released shortly before Keith Moon's death on 7 September*, the album sleeve eerily showed Moon seated on a chair inscribed "NOT TO BE TAKEN AWAY".

Birthdays today

1928 Sonny Til lead singer: The Vibranaires, The Orioles

1943 Carl Wayne singer: Carl Wayne and the Vikings, The Move

After leaving the Move in early 1970 he pursued a career in cabaret and theatre, before taking over from Allen Clarke in early 2000 as lead singer for the Hollies.

Event today

19

1964 The Beatles first American tour opened

The Beatles' first full-blown American tour kicked off at San Francisco's Cow Palace.

The tour crossed North America, taking in three Canadian gigs in Vancouver, Toronto and Montreal, before finishing on 20 September with a charity night entitled *An Evening with the Beatles* at New York's Paramount Theatre. On the main tour the Fab Four were supported by: The Bill Black Combo, The Exciters, The Righteous Brothers and singer-songwriter Jackie DeShannon.

Tickets for the charity show on 20 September proclaimed that, "all proceeds to United Cerebral Palsy and retarded infants services".

Recording session today

1969 Miles Davis *Bitches Brew*

Miles Davis began recording his seminal jazz-rock fusion album, *Bitches Brew*.

Of the musicians who worked on this album: guitarist John McLaughlin and drummer Billy Cobham went on to form the Mahavishnu Orchestra; pianist Joe Zawinul and saxophonist Wayne Shorter set up Weather Report; and pianist Chick Corea founded Return to Forever. Ex-Electric Flag bassist Harvey Brooks also played on the album.

Birthdays today

1939 Ginger Baker drums: Alexis Korner, Graham Bond, Cream, Blind Faith

Starting out as a jazz drummer, Ginger Baker became one of rock's foremost sticksmen. In his early days he made his own drum kit by forming Perspex cylinders over a gas stove. Urban legend has it that the kit met its end during one of Baker's spectacular on stage bust-ups with bassist Jack Bruce. In another one of their contretemps Baker reputedly pulled a knife on Bruce. Baker pioneered the use of the double bass drum kit and also led the way to extended drum solos with his epic solo *Toad*. Following the short-lived Blind Faith, he formed Ginger Baker's Airforce. In 1980 he was back in the studio, recording *Levitation* with Hawkwind.

1943 Billy J Kramer singer: The Coasters, The Dakotas; solo

Billy J Kramer was one of a number of Liverpool artists managed by Brian Epstein. He started out with the semi-professional Billy Kramer and the Coasters. When opportunity knocked, the Liverpudlian Coasters weren't as keen as Kramer to abandon their apprenticeships and turn fully professional. In order to help the singer move forward, Epstein signed up the Manchester based Dakotas as his new backing band. They were essentially an instrumental group in their own right and signed a deal as "Billy J Kramer with The Dakotas" as well as a contract as "The Dakotas".

The Coasters later teamed up with Chick Graham and cut a couple of singles.

1945 Ian Gillan singer: Deep Purple, Ian Gillan Band, Black Sabbath

In the summer of 1969, after spending time with Episode Six, Ian Gillan was invited to replace original vocalist Rod Evans in Deep Purple. His album debut came with *Concerto for Group and Orchestra* and extended to *Who Do We Think We Are*, including *Machine Head* which sported the classic *Smoke on the Water*. In mid-1973 Gillan left and David Coverdale took over as Deep Purple's frontman. Gillan replaced vocalist Ronnie Dio in Black Sabbath in 1983, staying with them for just one album, *Born Again*.

Events today

20

1965 Andrew Loog Oldham launched Immediate Records

Rolling Stones' manager Andrew Loog Oldham and his partner Tony Calder released the first three singles on their new Immediate label. The McCoys' *Hang on Sloopy* was released under license from Bang Records. Fifth Avenue's *The Bells of Rhymney* was produced by Jimmy Page and first recorded by Pete Seeger in 1958, after he set the words of Idris Davies's 1938 poem to music. The final offering was a pre-Velvet Underground Nico's *I'm Not Sayin*, which was produced by Oldham.

1969 Frank Zappa disbanded the original Mothers of Invention

After completing a short tour of Canada, Frank Zappa disbanded the original Mothers of Invention. He felt that he did not need the expense of keeping a fulltime group on the road and would prefer to gather together musicians as and when he needed them.

The original Mothers of Invention gave their last performance in Ottawa on CJOH-TV.

With some lineup changes the original Mothers of Invention were responsible for the first five Zappa albums: the double album *Freak Out*; the satirical *Absolutely Free*; Zappa's *Sgt Pepper* parody *We're Only in It For the Money*; the instrumental *Lumpy Gravy*; and Zappa's homage to 1950s doo wop, *Cruising With Rubin and the Jets*.

Recording session today

1969 The Beatles last time they were in the studio together

In their last-ever studio session together, the four Beatles worked on the mix for John Lennon's *I Want You (She's So Heavy)*, destined for the *Abbey Road* album.

This might have been the last time that the Fab Four were in the studio together but there are a number of contenders for the title of "last Beatles studio session". They might have wrapped up the *Abbey Road* album but the work on the *Get Back* album lumbered on. Glyn Johns was driving the sessions and on 3 January 1970 Paul, George and Ringo recorded what would be the last-ever Beatles song, the Harrison penned *I Me Mine*. The following day the same three Beatles worked on *Let It Be*, which was the last time that the Beatles worked in the studio, or anywhere else, as a band. On 23 March* out went Glyn Johns and in came Phil Spector to complete the *Get Back* project. The last-ever recording session was with Ringo on 1 April.

Phil Spector finished the album and it became the Beatles' swan song, *Let It Be*.

Single released today

1965 The Rolling Stones *(I Can't Get No) Satisfaction* c/w *Spider and the Fly* (UK)

Jagger and Richard's *Satisfaction* gave the Rolling Stones their first American #1. It was released there with a different B-side, *The Under Assistant West Coast Promotion Man*.

When *Satisfaction* was initially released in Britain it was pressed up wrongly, using the American B-side rather than *Spider and the Fly*. Those pressings were used for export and not sold in the UK.

Birthdays today

1948 Robert Plant singer: Crawling King Snakes, Band of Joy, Led Zeppelin

1949 Phil Lynott bass and vocals: Skid Row, Orphanage, Thin Lizzy; solo

Event today

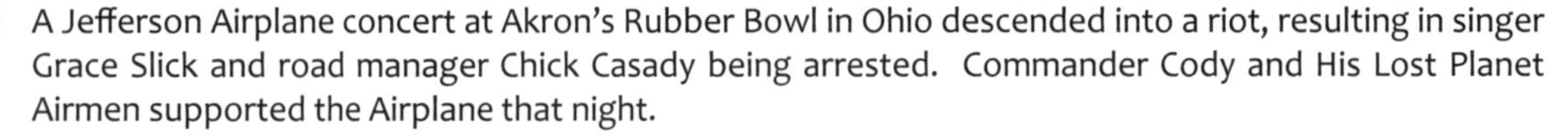

1972 Jefferson Airplane riot at a concert in Ohio

A Jefferson Airplane concert at Akron's Rubber Bowl in Ohio descended into a riot, resulting in singer Grace Slick and road manager Chick Casady being arrested. Commander Cody and His Lost Planet Airmen supported the Airplane that night.

Riots at rock concerts were not unusual in the late 1960s and early 1970s. This one was similar in nature to a lot of the others, with over-enthusiastic policemen using tear gas to clear over-excited fans from the venue. The Rolling Stones' 1972 American tour, which kicked off on 3 June*, was blighted by unrest. Led Zeppelin hit problems in Italy on 5 July* 1971 and the Doors' New Haven concert on 9 December* 1969 ended with fighting on the streets.

From the beginning, the writing was on the wall for the relationship between concertgoers and the authorities. Alan Freed organised the first-ever rock'n'roll concert, *Moondog's Coronation Ball* on 21 March* 1952, only for it to be closed down early by the local authorities after thousands of fans tried to gatecrash the show.

Single released today

1961 The Marvelettes *Please Mr. Postman* c/w *So Long Baby* (US)

The Marvelettes were the first of Motown's premier league girl groups. They signed to the label after coming fourth in a high school talent contest but still managed to convince the folks at their Motown audition that they had potential. When they released their debut single *Please Mr. Postman*, featuring Marvin Gaye on drums, their lead singer Gladys Horton was only fifteen years old. The single gave the Motown label its first American #1 and the Marvelettes their first of a run of hits that lasted across the 1960s.

The B-side should not to be confused with the Del Shannon hit of the same name.

Birthdays today

1939 James Burton — guitar: Dale Hawkins, Ricky Nelson, Elvis Presley; session

James Burton started playing guitar professionally when he was just fourteen years old. By the time that he was sixteen he was playing with rockabilly star Dale Hawkins. He played and reputedly wrote the music, albeit uncredited, for Hawkins's *Susie-Q*. Session work and a stint with Ricky Nelson followed, before he formed the Shindogs as one of the house bands on American TV's *Shindig!* When Elvis Presley returned to performing in 1969 he asked Burton to play guitar and to put together his backing band. Burton stayed with Presley until the King's death in 1977. Before, during and after Presley, Burton was a prolific session musician and played with some of rock'n'roll and country's finest, including Gram Parsons, The Everly Brothers and Jerry Lee Lewis.

1952 Joe Strummer — guitar, vocals: Vultures, 101'ers, Clash

In 1973 Joe Strummer moved to Newport, Wales and joined Flaming Youth, which changed its name to "The Vultures" shortly afterwards. He moved back to London in 1974 and joined the 101'ers, who played their first gig in Brixton on 7 September*. By mid-1976 the British punk scene was gathering a head of steam and urban legend has it that Strummer met guitarist Mick Jones in the Lisson Grove dole (unemployment) queue. Jones's seminal punk band the London SS was falling apart. He teamed up with Strummer and the Clash was born.

Events today

1956 Landmark Movies — *The Girl Can't Help It*

One of the most famous of the mid-1950s rock'n'roll movies opened in Hollywood but unlike most of the music movies that followed, this was essentially a light-hearted gangster romp with rock'n'roll as a backdrop.

The movie starred Jayne Mansfield and featured a host of rock'n'roll luminaries, including Fats Domino, Little Richard, Eddie Cochran and Gene Vincent. Urban legend has it that it was Eddie Cochran's *Twenty Flight Rock* that clinched McCartney's audition for Lennon on 6 July* 1957.

1972 New York Dolls — early gig

The New York Dolls made an early appearance, billed as "The Dolls of NY", at their Tuesday residency at New York's Mercer Art Center.

The band came together in late 1971 as Actress, with a lineup of guitarist and vocalist Johnny Thunders, drummer Billy Murcia, bassist Arthur Kane and guitarist Rick Rivets. By the time that they had become the New York Dolls, vocalist David Johansen had joined their ranks and guitarist Rick Rivets had been replaced by Sylvain Sylvain.

The New York Dolls was one of the first American punk bands and a major influence on the British punk bands that emerged in the mid-1970s. In October 1972 the New York Dolls undertook their first British tour, as the support act for British rock doyens the Faces and the Groundhogs. The tour was cut short when the Doll's drummer, Billy Mercia, was found dead in his hotel room on 6 November*.

Single released today

1969 Radha Krishna Temple *Hare Krishna Mantra c/w Prayer ...Spiritual Masters* (US)

The *Hare Krishna Mantra* was popularised by this George Harrison production, released on the Apple label. The full title of the B-side was *Prayer to the Spiritual Masters.*

A picture sleeve was designed for the single's American release but was not used. Some copies did find their way into the marketplace and are now very collectable items.

This was not the first the first rock recording of the *Mantra.* Beat poet Allen Ginsberg had been reciting the *Mantra* since the early 1960s. A version was also recorded by poets and rock band the Fugs, who included the song *Hare Krishna* on their album *Tenderness Junction*, released in America in early 1968 and featuring Allen Ginsberg.

Birthday today

1917 John Lee Hooker seminal blues guitarist, singer and songwriter

John Lee Hooker was one of the busiest blues recording artists of the late 1940s and '50s. As well as recording for some of the best known record labels of the time, such as Chess, King, Modern, Speciality and Vee-Jay, he also recorded for a bunch of independent labels. This was achieved by extending the names he recorded under from simply John Lee Hooker to John Lee Booker, Johnny Lee, John Lee Cooker, Texas Slim, Delta John, Birmingham Sam, Little Pork Chops and others.

He was also a prolific songwriter, with titles including the seminal *Boogie Chillun, Crawlin Kingsnake* (although this song had its roots in earlier versions) and *Boom Boom.* With the growth of the 1960s blues revival he was a major influence on both sides of the Atlantic. In a meeting of the two blues generations Hooker collaborated with Canned Heat on *Hooker 'n Heat* and recorded duets with Van Morrison.

Event today

1970 The Velvet Underground last concert with Lou Reed

Lou Reed's swan song with Velvet Underground came at Max's Kansas City, New York.

The only other member of the original lineup that night was guitarist Sterling Morrison. Original bassist John Cale had been replaced by Doug Yule in late 1968 and Yule's younger brother Bill was standing in as drummer for a pregnant Maureen Tucker.

The concert was recorded by Andy Warhol's associate Brigid Polk on a portable cassette recorder and later released as *Live at Max's Kansas City.*

Recording sessions today

1963 Jerry Lee Lewis final recording session at Sun

In his final recording session at Sun Records Jerry Lee Lewis recorded the James A Bland standard *Carry Me Back to Old Virginny.*

The song was written shortly after the American Civil War by the African American minstrel James A Bland. It became Virginia's State Song in 1940 but was declared "state song emeritus" in 1997 when the Virginia State Senate decided to look for a new state song. Lewis's recording did not see the light of day until 1965, when it was coupled with *I Know What It Means* and released as his final Sun single.

1961 Dick Dale and the Del-Tones *Let's Go Trippin'*

This Dick Dale penned classic instrumental is often cited as the first surf-rock record.

Single released today

1963 The Beatles *She Loves You c/w I'll Get You* (UK)

She Loves You gave the Fab Four their first million-selling British single.

Birthdays today

1936 Rudy Lewis replaced Ben E King as lead singer of the Drifters

The Drifters' manager George Treadwell famously sacked the entire group on 30 May* 1958 and replaced them with the Crowns. He renamed the group back to "The Drifters" and installed Ben E King as the new lead singer. Rudy Lewis replaced King in mid-1960 and was with the group until his untimely death on 20 May* 1964. During his tenure as lead singer Lewis recorded such Drifters classics as *On Broadway* and the Goffin and King songs *Some Kind of Wonderful* and *Up on the Roof.*

1946 Keith Moon drums: The Beachcombers, The High Numbers, The Who

Before finding fame as the Who's wild man drummer, Keith Moon played with Mark Twain and the Strangers, and the Beachcombers. In between playing with these two bands, Moon auditioned as sticksman for Shane Fenton (later to reinvent himself as Alvin Stardust) and the Fentones but lost out to future Hollies drummer Bobby Elliott. By the time that Moon auditioned for the Who on 30 April* 1964 they were already an established London band.

With eerie similarities to the Beatles, Moon replaced Doug Sandom after he was sacked following a two year stint with the group and their first audition for Fontana on 9 April* 1964. Ringo Starr replaced Beatles' drummer Pete Best after their recording studio debut with George Martin on 6 June* 1962. Best was also sacked after spending two years with the group and delivering an unsatisfactory performance at their first recording session.

Events today

1967 Soft Machine end of an era

Soft Machine came to the end of its first era when Australian born guitarist and founding member, Daevid Allen, was refused re-entry into the UK because his visa had expired.

Soft Machine had started out in 1963 as the Daevid Allen Trio, with drummer Robert Wyatt and bassist Hugh Hopper. After Allen moved to Paris in late 1963 Wyatt and Hopper formed Wilde Flowers, a stalwart of the Canterbury Scene. Wyatt hooked up with Allen again in 1966. Then, with bassist and vocalist Kevin Ayres, and keyboard player Mike Ratledge they formed Mister Head, renaming to "Soft Machine" shortly afterwards. Guitarist Larry Nolan was also in the original lineup but he only played at the first few gigs. After Allen was refused entry into the UK, Soft Machine continued as a trio. Allen went on to form Gong. In mid-1968 Kevin Ayres was replaced by Hugh Hopper in Soft Machine.

The band's name was inspired by the title of a 1961 novel by beat writer William S Burroughs.

1969 Blind Faith final concert

Blind Faith's high profile lineup seemed to offer so much when they played their debut concert in London's Hyde Park on 7 June*. After a short tour of Scandinavia they opened their ill-fated North American tour at New York's Madison Square Garden on 12 July. The stadium based tour proved very lucrative financially but was less satisfying musically. By the time that the quartet reached Hawaii for their final gig it was all but over.

Eric Clapton became very friendly with support act Delaney and Bonnie, often travelling with them between gigs and jamming with them on stage.

After the tour ended the band went their separate ways. Ginger Baker enlisted Steve Winwood and Rick Grech to form Airforce (along with ex-Moody Blues singer and guitarist Denny Laine). Eric Clapton played the *Toronto Rock'n'Roll Revival* festival with John Lennon's Plastic Ono Band on 13 September* and then toured with Delaney and Bonnie's band.

Single released today

1964 The Beatles *Matchbox* c/w *Slowdown* (US)

Matchbox was recorded by Carl Perkins in 1957. Although the writing credit went to Perkins, the song was inspired by Blind Lemon Jefferson's 1927 song *Matchbox Blues*. The B-side was a cover of Larry Williams's song recorded in 1958.

Birthdays today

1943 John Cipollina guitar: Quicksilver Messenger Service, Copperhead

1945 Ken Hensley keyboards: The Gods, Toe Fat, Spice, Uriah Heep; solo

Keyboard player, guitarist and singer Ken Hensley was best remembered as one of the stalwarts of heavy metal band Uriah Heep. Before his days with Heep, he was also a founding member of the respected British R&B outfit the Gods, co-founded with future Rolling Stones guitarist Mick Taylor. The Gods lineup also featured future King Crimson and Emerson, Lake & Palmer bassist and singer Greg Lake. After Taylor and Lake moved on to pastures green, British R&B pioneer Cliff Bennett joined Hensley and they renamed to "Toe Fat". Hensley moved on to join Spice, which morphed into Uriah Heep.

Events today

1968 Vietnam War riots at the Democratic Convention

Held at Chicago's International Amphitheatre, the Democratic National Convention became the focal point of a massive anti-war rally. Violence erupted on 25 August and escalated throughout the five days of the Convention, to produce some of the worst anti-war rioting of the 1960s.

With the election for President on the horizon, the Democratic candidate had to be chosen to compete with the Republican's Richard Nixon. Anti-war feeling was running high when 10,000 demonstrators converged on the Convention. As the rioting escalated Mayor Richard Daley brought in reinforcements. The Chicago History Museum puts the numbers as, "11,900 Chicago police, 7,500 Army regulars, 7,500 Illinois National Guardsmen and 1,000 FBI and Secret Service agents."[95] The authorities were determined to keep the demonstrators away from the convention area but the live TV coverage of the ensuing violence and brutal crackdown horrified the nation. The Museum's account of the events continues, "[by the end of the Convention] 589 persons had been arrested and more than 119 police and 100 demonstrators injured". Those arrested included Yippie leaders Abbie Hoffman and Jerry Rubin, and Bobby Seale, one of the founders of the Black Panther movement.

The *Chicago 8* were indicted on 20 March* 1969. This became the *Chicago 7* after Bobby Seale was tried separately.

The song *Chicago*, on Crosby, Stills, Nash & Young's live album *Four Way Street*, was introduced with the comment that it was a song for Mayor Daley.

Hubert Humphrey gained the nomination as the Democrat's man for the Presidency but in a close-run contest he lost out to Richard Nixon.

1970 Emerson, Lake & Palmer debut gig

Just four days before appearing in front of half a million rock fans at the *Isle of Wight Festival*, the prog rockers made their debut at Plymouth's Guildhall.

The trio came together after playing with some of rock's finest. Keyboard player Keith Emerson had come to prominence in the Nice. Bass player and vocalist Greg Lake was a member of the Gods and King Crimson. Carl Palmer's pedigree was equally impressive, including stints with Chris Farlowe and Arthur Brown, before co-founding Atomic Rooster.

Album released today

1975 Bruce Springsteen *Born to Run* (US)

This was Springsteen's breakthrough third album. Together with his recent five-day residency at New York's Bottom Line club, ending on 17 August*, it established his reputation as a world-class rock'n'roller.

Birthdays today

1949 Gene Simmons vocals and bass: Wicked Lester, Kiss

Paul Stanley and Gene Simmons parted company with the other members of Wicked Lester and formed Kiss. As well as selling more than 100 million albums[65] worldwide, he also found time to set up his own record label, Simmons Records, in a deal with RCA in the 1980s.

1951 Rob Halford singer: Hiroshima, Judas Priest

Event today

1974 Rush the classic trio was in place

26

The classic Rush trio was in place when the band played this gig at the Agora Ballroom in Cleveland, Ohio. The night's performance was captured by WMMS on an FM broadcast and by bootleggers on the album *Fifth Order of Angels*. This was the first recorded performance of Rush with new drummer Neil Peart.

Drummer John Rutsey and guitarist Alex Lifeson had formed the Projection in Toronto in the spring of 1968. From their first paid gig as "Rush", on 18 September*, the band started out on a career that would make them one of the most successful rock bands of all time. After various band names and personnel changes, they had solidified by mid-1971 into a trio with bassist and singer Geddy Lee. Still unable to secure a recording deal Rush decided to form their own label Moon Records. In 1973 they released a cover of the Buddy Holly penned *Not Fade Away* in Canada. This was followed by the Canadian release of their eponymous debut album, again on Moon. By 1974 the trio were starting to attract interest outside of their native Canada and on 18 May they played their first gig in America, in Lansing, Michigan. Their debut album came to the attention of Mercury and in the summer of 1974 it was released in America.

Sadly, just as their fortunes were on the up Rutsey had to leave the group because of ill-health. His place was taken by Neil Peart, who had joined the band at the end of July and played his first gig when Rush embarked on this American tour on 14 August.

Singles released today

1968 The Beatles *Hey Jude c/w Revolution* (US)

The song was written by Paul for John's son Julian. At the time, Lennon was getting together with Yoko Ono and had left his first wife Cynthia, Julian's mother. She had countersued Lennon for divorce a week earlier, citing his adultery with Yoko Ono.

1969 Elvis Presley *Suspicious Minds c/w You'll Think of Me* (US)

Suspicious Minds gave Elvis his biggest hit since quitting his movie career to return to live performance. It was a cover version of a song written by Mark James and released by him as a single in 1968.

Elvis returned to performing with his TV *Comeback Special* on 3 December* 1968. He began the third stage of his career when he opened at the Las Vegas Hilton International for the first time on 31 July* 1969. The King started out as a 1950s rocker. Then, following a stint in the US Army, he spent most of the 1960s with fans only able to access his presence through the silver screen, as a Hollywood film star. *Suspicious Minds* was released just before his first Las Vegas residency ended. It proved to be the last time that Elvis would achieve the #1 spot on the American charts.

Birthday today

1941 Chris Curtis drums, vocals: Searchers, Roundabout; solo

As well as being a founding member of the Searchers, one of Liverpool's most successful beat groups, he also set the wheels in motion for the formation of Deep Purple. In 1967 he decided to form a new group, Roundabout. Keyboard player Jon Lord, bassist Nick Simper and guitarist Ritchie Blackmore joined the band's ranks but Curtis had moved on before it morphed into Deep Purple and gave its debut performance on 20 April* 1968.

Events today

1965 The Beatles met Elvis Presley

The Beatles finally met their idol Elvis Presley after his manager Colonel Parker extended an invitation to come over to Elvis's home in Bel Air. By all accounts the meeting was a low key affair. They chatted and jammed a little, with Elvis choosing to play bass guitar. It was to be the only time that the Beatles and Elvis ever met.

1976 Boston early gig for the stalwarts of AOR

Shortly after releasing their eponymous debut album, Boston played one of their earliest concerts at the Armory in Manchester, New Hampshire.

The mid-1970s was a watershed in rock'n'roll music. Punk rock was sweeping all before it as fans rebelled against corporate rock and the excesses of progressive rock. Alongside this revolution there had also been a change in radio broadcasting. In the early 1970s high quality FM stations had begun to replace the older AM stations. The new FM stations were moving away from singles based music and by the mid-1970s these album based stations were in the ascendancy. One of the pioneers of this new radio programming was Mike Harrison, who was accredited with coining the expression AOR "album oriented rock". Boston was a mainstay of AOR and along with other bands formed in the mid-1970s went on to pioneer the stadium rock of the 1980s.

(AOR is sometimes referred to as "adult oriented rock".)

Album released today

1971 The Who *Who's Next* (UK)

When Pete Townshend abandoned his ambitious *Lifehouse* project shortly after a performance at London's Young Vic theatre on 26 April*, some of the songs were salvaged and used for their *Who's Next* album.

Births and deaths today

1944 Tim Bogert bass: Vanilla Fudge, Cactus; Beck, Bogert & Appice

Founding member of both Vanilla Fudge and Cactus, bassist Tim Bogert went on to join guitarist Jeff Beck in Beck, Bogert & Appice.

1953 Alex Lifeson guitarist and founding member of Rush

1956 Glen Matlock bass: Swankers, Sex Pistols, Rich Kids, Iggy Pop

In February 1977 Glen Matlock was replaced as bass player in the Sex Pistols by the infamous Sid Vicious. The Pistols signed to EMI on 8 October* 1976 and released *Anarchy in the UK*, the only single to feature Matlock. After their notorious TV appearance on 1 December*, EMI withdrew the single and cancelled their contract. By the time that the record deal with A&M materialised the following March, Matlock was history. After leaving the Sex Pistols he formed Rich Kids, which included a pre-Ultravox Midge Ure, before moving on to join Iggy Pop.

1967 Brian Epstein Beatles' manager, died at the age of thirty-two

Responsible for guiding the Beatles' career, Brian Epstein was found dead in his Belgravia home. He had accidentally taken an overdose of Carbatrol, a drug he had been taking to help him sleep.

Events today

1963 Martin Luther King Jr *I Have a Dream* speech

Martin Luther King Jr delivered the most famous of his speeches, *I Have a Dream*. The *March on Washington* demonstration also included performances from Peter Paul and Mary, Joan Baez, Odetta and Blind Boy Grunt, better known as Bob Dylan.

1964 The Beatles Bob Dylan introduced the Fab Four to pot

Bob Dylan met the Beatles for the first time and he famously introduced the Liverpool lads to the joys of herbal cigarettes. The Beatles were halfway through their first American tour when they met Dylan at their hotel, following a gig at the Forest Hills Tennis Stadium in New York.

1970 Landmark Festivals *Isle of Wight Festival*

Over half a million people witnessed what was probably the greatest British festival of all time. Billed as August 26-30, the main concert programme started on Friday 28th.

Jimi Hendrix gave one of his final performances. The Who still had drummer Keith Moon and the Doors were still fronted by Jim Morrison. When John Sebastian heard that Zal (Yanovsky) was in the crowd, he called out to his old Lovin' Spoonful chum to come up and join him on stage. On the Saturday night several thousand fans stayed in front of the stage and refused to move back to the camping area. Security threatened retribution but the crowd stayed put. When Jethro Tull came out on Sunday morning for the sound check, Ian Anderson shouted encouragement for not moving. Joan Baez followed Jimi Hendrix and exclaimed, "How can anyone follow Jimi!" Emerson, Lake & Palmer's performance included their arrangement of Mussorgsky's *Pictures at an Exhibition*. There were also performances from artists as diverse as Miles Davis, Tiny Tim, Ten Years After, The Moody Blues and Leonard Cohen.

Birthdays today

1937 Clem Cattini drums: Blue Flames, Johnny Kidd, Tornados; sessions

Before becoming one of Britain's most successful session drummers, Clem Cattini was with Johnny Kidd and the Pirates, performing on their British #1 *Shaking All Over*. He went on to join Larry Parnes's house band the Beat Boys, later to become the Blue Flames. They regularly backed other Parnes artists such as Billy Fury and Marty Wilde. Cattini's story continued with pioneering British producer Joe Meek, he backed many of Meek's artists and became a founding member of the Tornados. In 1965 his focus turned to session work, reputedly performing on more than 40 British #1 singles.

1949 Hugh Cornwell guitar and vocals: Johnny Sox, The Stranglers; solo

Hugh Cornwell's music career started as a bassist with Emil and the Detectives, a schoolboy band formed with Richard Thompson, who went on to become a founding member of seminal British folk-rockers Fairport Convention. After leaving university he took a job in Sweden, where he changed from bass to guitar and with Hans Wärmling formed Johnny Sox. Cornwell and Johnny Sox returned to England where they were joined by drummer Jet Black. By the mid-1970s they had morphed into the Guildford Stranglers, before dropping the town's name and becoming simply, the Stranglers.

Emil and the Detectives took its name from the title of Erich Kästner's 1929 children's novel.

Events today

1966 The Beatles last-ever concert

The last performance of this final North American tour was at San Francisco's Candlestick Park. The Beatles' concert days were over. One of the support acts that day was an American band The Cyrkle, also managed by Brian Epstein.

The Beatles' final American tour was set for a bumpy ride. Two weeks before their opening night, teen magazine *Datebook* had published the infamous John Lennon quote that they were "more popular than Jesus". The article had originally been published on 4 March* in London's *Evening Standard* newspaper. It received no adverse reaction in Britain but America was outraged. To try to placate the situation, Lennon offered an apology at a press conference held when they arrived in Chicago.

The Fab Four opened what would become their final American tour on 12 August, at Chicago's International Amphitheatre. The tour continued amid death threats, angry demonstrations and public burning of their records. Their final Canadian concert was held on 17 August at Toronto's Maple Leaf Gardens. At the Memphis concert held at the Mid-South Coliseum on 19 August, they had to contend with robed Ku Klux Klan members in the car park and also someone throwing a gunshot-sounding firecracker onto the stage. The adverse publicity took its toll on ticket sales and 11,000 seats went unsold at their return visit to New York's Shea Stadium on 23 August.

1969 Hawkwind gigging as "Group X"

With a lineup that included Dave Brock, an unknown group calling themselves "Group X" played a twenty minute jam at Notting Hill's All Saints Hall. Shortly afterwards they changed their name to "Hawkwind".

Single released today

1958 Cliff Richard and the Drifters *Schoolboy Crush* c/w *Move It!* (UK)

The original A-side was a cover of Bobby Helms's *Schoolboy Crush*. However, it didn't take long for the B-side to become the side of choice, Ian Samwell penned *Move It!* TV producer Jack Good helped it along by insisting that *Move It!* was played when they debuted on his show *Oh Boy!* Norrie Paramour produced it and Cliff's Drifters that day were guitarist Ian Samwell and drummer Terry Smart, augmented by session musicians.

Album released today

1969 Jack Bruce *Songs for a Tailor* (UK)

Jack Bruce released his first solo album after the dissolution of Cream. The musicians included: guitarist Chris Spedding, drummer Jon Hiseman, saxophonist Dick Heckstall-Smith and Cream's old producer Felix Pappalardi variously on guitar, percussion and vocals. As with his appearance on Cream's final album *Goodbye*, George Harrison made his contribution under the pseudonym "L'Angelo Misterioso".

A year earlier, whilst he was still with Cream, Bruce had recorded the album *Things We Like*, with guitarist John McLaughlin, drummer Jon Hiseman and saxophonist Dick Heckstall-Smith but this was not released until 1970, after *Songs for a Tailor*.

The "Tailor" referred to in the album's title was Jeannie Franklyn, aka "Genie the Tailor". She was the designer who made clothes for Cream but had tragically died in an automobile accident just three months earlier on 12 May*. The crash also killed Fairport Convention's drummer Martin Lamble.

Event today

1950 Sam Phillips first record label ...It's The Phillips

Two years before Sam Phillips founded the legendary Sun Records label and launched the King of Rock'n'Roll's career, he set up the short-lived, It's The Phillips record label.

This new venture was undertaken with Memphis DJ Dewey "Daddy-O" Phillips, no relation. The one and only release on the label was by one-man-band Joe Hill Louis, *Gotta Let You Go* c/w *Boogie in the Park*. Despite an "order for 300 copies ...on 30 August"[14] sales were poor and no further releases followed.

Recording session today

1963 David Bowie first-ever recording

As a member of his first professional group the Konrads, David Bowie made his first-ever recording at Decca's studios in London's west Hampstead. Performing as "David Jones", he provided vocals and saxophone for the only song recorded that day, *I Never Dreamed*. Bowie parted company with the Konrads shortly after this recording session.

Singles released today

1963 The Fourmost *Hello Little Girl* c/w *Just in Case* (UK)

Liverpool beat group the Fourmost released their first single, the Lennon and McCartney penned, George Martin produced, *Hello Little Girl*.

The song was John Lennon's first composition and a regular part of the Quarry Men's set list. On 1 January* 1962 the Beatles included the song in their Decca audition when they famously lost out to Brian Poole and the Tremeloes. The Beatles never recorded *Hello Little Girl* for EMI or Apple but fans did get to hear the Decca recording thirty years later on *Anthology 1*.

Gerry and the Pacemakers also recorded *Hello Little Girl* as a possible follow-up to their second #1 hit, *I Like It*. This was left unreleased at the time, in favour of their third #1, *You'll Never Walk Alone*, later adopted by Liverpool Football Club as their anthem.

1968 The Beatles *Hey Jude* c/w *Revolution* (UK)

Album released today

1971 The Beach Boys *Surf's Up* (US)

The highly acclaimed title song was written by Brian Wilson and Van Dyke Parks and intended for inclusion on the legendary 'lost' album *Smile*, abandoned on 2 May* 1967.

Birthdays today

1935 John Phillips singer, songwriter: Journeymen, The Mamas & The Papas

1939 John Peel influential British DJ

John Peel was one of the most influential British DJs of the 1960s, '70s and later. His radio career started in America, before he returned to Britain to work on the pirate station Radio London. Peel joined BBC Radio 1 around the time that it was launched on 30 September* 1967. From the beginning Peel was a champion of new musical innovations, he did much to popularise Marc Bolan and the fledgling Tyrannosaurus Rex. He formed his own label, Dandelion Records and had a series of live performances taken from his Radio 1 show and released in album form as *The Peel Sessions*.

Events today

1957 Elvis Presley last concert outside America

Elvis Presley gave his final concert outside America with a performance in neighbouring Canada at Vancouver's Empire Stadium. The concert posters billed Elvis's vocal backing group the Jordanaires and his bass player's group the Bill Black Combo separately. The gig was attended by over 20,000 excited fans. Soon after Elvis started his performance fans rushed the stage and the show was halted whilst they were urged to return to their seats. Elvis resumed his set but another stage rush shortly afterwards resulted in the show being cut short. Music critic for the *Vancouver Province*, Ida Halpern, described Elvis's performance as "an artificial and unhealthy exploitation of the enthusiasm of youth's body and mind ...One could call it subsidized sex".[30]

This was only the third performance Elvis had given outside the USA but it was also to be his last. Earlier in the year, on 2 and 3 April, he had given concerts in Toronto and Ottawa. With the exception of the US state of Hawaii, Elvis never again performed beyond the confines of Continental USA.

1965 Vietnam War anti-war protests gained momentum

In an attempt to clamp down on anti-war protestors, President Johnson signed into law the Bill criminalising the burning of draft cards.

The Vietnam War had never been a popular war. There was no declaration of war and it just crept up on the American people. From the defeat of the French at Dien Bien Phu on 7 May* 1954, successive Presidents had taken America deeper and deeper into the conflict, in an attempt to prop up an ineffective South Vietnamese regime.

The anti-war movement was galvanised into action by the *Rolling Thunder* bombing campaign, initiated on 2 March* 1965. The "teach-in" became a popular means of voicing opposition to the War. The first one was held at the University of Michigan on 24 March. These "teach-ins" soon spread across campuses throughout America. One of the first anti-war marches on Washington was organised by the Students for a Democratic Society (SDS) on 17 April. It attracted the support of some 25,000 people.

As well as spreading to other American cities, anti-war rallies were also being organised in Europe. One of the most violent demonstrations in the UK took place outside the American Embassy in London's Grosvenor Square in March 1968.

Birthdays today

1939 Jerry Ivan Allison drums: Buddy Holly and the Crickets, post-Holly Crickets

1945 Van Morrison singer and saxophonist: Monarchs, Them, solo

Van Morrison started his singing and saxophone playing career with Deanie Sands and the Javelins. This band morphed into the Monarchs. As with many of their early 1960s contemporaries, the Monarchs spent time learning their trade in Germany. The group broke up on its return to Belfast and after short spells in the Manhattan Showband and the Golden Eagles, Morrison joined local group the Gamblers. Shortly after he joined the band they renamed to "Them", taking the inspiration for their new moniker from the 1954 Sci-Fi movie. They played their first gig at the Maritime Hotel, following an advertising campaign that started on 14 April* 1964.

September

Events today

1

1950 Jerry Lee Lewis enrolled in Bible school

At the age of 15 Jerry Lee Lewis enrolled at the Southwestern Bible Institute in Waxahachie, Texas. He did not complete his studies: they came to a premature end when, reputedly, he was expelled for playing hymns to a boogie-woogie rhythm.

Religion ran in Lewis's family. One of his cousins was the TV evangelist Jimmy Swaggart.

1967 Steve Miller Band enter Boz Scaggs

Guitarist Boz Scaggs played his first concert with the Steve Miller Band at San Francisco's Avalon Ballroom. The group was billed as the "Miller Blues Band" and supported by Mother Earth and blues singer Bukka White.

In Texas at the end of the 1950s Scaggs had been the singer with a very young Steve Miller in his schoolboy band the Marksmen. After this they went their separate ways. Miller relocated to Chicago and in the mid-1960s teamed up with keyboardist Barry Goldberg in the Goldberg Miller Blues Band. By the turn of 1967 Miller had relocated again, this time to San Francisco where he was fronting his own Steve Miller Blues Band. That summer Scaggs joined him as rhythm guitarist and the band shortened its name to the "Steve Miller Band".

Capitol Records took an interest in the band and signed them for the colossal (at the time) sum of $50,000. Scaggs stayed around for the first two albums, *Children of the Future* and *Sailor*, before moving on for a solo career.

Mother Earth featured lead singer Tracy Nelson.

1971 The Rolling Stones dispute with Allen Klein

The Rolling Stones issued a lawsuit against their ex-manager Allen Klein.

Klein negotiated management rights for the Rolling Stones from Andrew Loog Oldham in the summer of 1965. He then managed the band until the end of the decade. One of the central issues in the dispute was the fact that the songs written by the Stones were owned by Klein and not by the band. In a newspaper article in the Alabama newspaper *The Gadsden Times* on 18 April 1984, Jagger related his famous account of the incident in 1974 when he chased Klein down a corridor at London's exclusive Savoy Hotel shouting at Klein that he owed the band $800,000. The Stones eventually settled, with Klein retaining the rights to the pre-1971 songs through his company ABKCO.

Allen Klein was also famously one of the catalysts for the demise of the Beatles. After Brian Epstein died, John Lennon, George Harrison and Ringo Starr wanted Klein to be their manager but Paul McCartney was adamant that this role should be filled by his father-in-law, Lee Eastman. The battle between the two sides led to lawsuits and the bitter feud between Lennon and McCartney.

Single released today

1969 The Hollies *He Ain't Heavy....He's My Brother c/w 'Cos You Like to Love Me* (UK)

The A-side was written by Bobby Russell and Bobby Scott and was inspired by the Boys Town community in Nebraska. The *Two Brothers* bronze statue that greeted visitors to the community depicted a boy carrying his younger brother on his back and was inscribed with the motto, "He Ain't Heavy Father.... He's M' Brother".

He Ain't Heavy....He's My Brother featured session pianist Elton John.

Recording sessions today

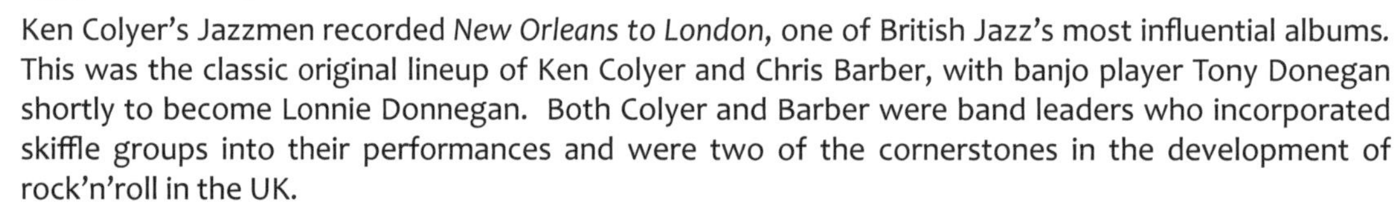

1953 Ken Colyer's Jazzmen *New Orleans to London*

Ken Colyer's Jazzmen recorded *New Orleans to London*, one of British Jazz's most influential albums. This was the classic original lineup of Ken Colyer and Chris Barber, with banjo player Tony Donegan shortly to become Lonnie Donnegan. Both Colyer and Barber were band leaders who incorporated skiffle groups into their performances and were two of the cornerstones in the development of rock'n'roll in the UK.

British rock'n'roll grew out of skiffle, which in turn grew out of trad jazz. In the early 1950s one of the most popular strains of British jazz was trad (traditional) jazz, which was rooted in New Orleans jazz. Two of the unsung heroes of British rock'n'roll had been leading their own trad jazz combos since the late 1940s. Chris Barber's Jazzmen started out as an amateur band and featured the future godfather of British blues, guitarist Alexis Korner. Ken Colyer had formed his first jazz band, the Crane River Jazz Band, in the late 1940s. By 1952 he had become disenchanted with the British jazz scene and took himself off to America to play with some of his music heroes in New Orleans. In March 1953 he returned to Britain, after being deported by the American authorities for not having a visa. Chris Barber welcomed him back with a readymade band and as "Ken Colyer's Jazzmen" they recorded the album *New Orleans to London*. They chose Colyer's name for the band, in order to capitalise on his fame for playing with New Orleans jazzmen during his short stay in America.

By mid-1954 Barber had parted company with Colyer. When he left, Barber took the rest of Colyer's band with him and became Chris Barber's Jazz Band. Colyer put together another band and recorded the album *Back to the Delta* on 10 September*. This album contained skiffle tracks featuring guitarist Alexis Korner. Meanwhile, Chris Barber recorded his own album *New Orleans Joys* on 13 July*; this included skiffle tracks featuring Lonnie Donegan. One of the Donegan skiffle tracks, a cover of Lead Belly's *Rock Island Line*, was released as a single in late 1955 and ignited the British skiffle scene – which soon morphed into rock'n'roll.

1965 The Doors it all started with Rick & the Ravens

Rick & the Ravens entered World Pacific Studios in Los Angeles and recorded six songs: *Moonlight Drive, My Eyes Have Seen You, Hello I Love You, Insane, End of the Night* and *Summer's Almost Gone*. This was Jim Morrison's first-ever recording session.

Before the Doors there was Rick & the Ravens. Jim Morrison joined Ray Manzarek and his two brothers Rick and Jim, in the LA band Rick & the Ravens. Drummer John Densmore had been playing with the Psychedelic Rangers before joining Manzarek and Morrison shortly before this recording session. The demo was poorly received when they hawked it around, leading to Ray's brothers and the bass player moving on. This paved the way for Densmore's band mate from the Psychedelic Rangers, guitarist Robbie Krieger – and the Doors was born.

September

Events today

3

1977 Eagles — Randy Meisner moved on

The Eagles ended their *Hotel California* tour in Wisconsin, with a concert at East Troy's Alpine Music Theatre. Bassist, singer, songwriter and founding member Randy Meisner moved on at the completion of the tour.

Meisner felt that he was being sidelined for singing and songwriting duties and by the time that the *Hotel California* tour had taken to the road his relationship with the rest of the band was at rock bottom. The others felt that his rock'n'roll lifestyle was a tad excessive. Things came to a head with a fist fight between Meisner and guitarist Glenn Frey on 28 June, backstage at a gig in Knoxville, Tennessee. The tour finished in September and Meisner moved on for a solo career.

He was replaced by Timothy B Schmit, who had also been Meisner's replacement when he quit Poco in 1969. Despite being a founding member of Poco, Meisner left after the band's debut album, *Pickin' Up the Pieces.*

Births and deaths today

1942 Al Jardine — guitar and vocals: The Pendletones, The Beach Boys

The Beach Boys consisted of the three Wilson brothers, their cousin Mike Love and the only non-family member, friend Al Jardine. He was a founding member but left in early 1962. David Marks filled the gap until mid-1963, when Jardine returned and continued touring with the Beach Boys until the late 1990s.

1942 Kenny Pickett — singer: The Mark Four, The Creation

As well as providing lead vocals for Mod group the Creation, Pickett was also a roadie for Led Zeppelin and co-wrote the novelty song *Grandad*, which gave Clive Dunn a British #1 in 1970.

1955 Steve Jones — guitar: Swankers, Sex Pistols

1969 Ho Chi Minh — North Vietnamese leader, died at the age of seventy-nine

North Vietnamese leader Ho Chi Minh died from heart failure. He had actually died on 2 September but the announcement was made the following day.

He formed the Viet Minh nationalist movement in 1941 to fight the Japanese invaders. After the end of World War II, he went on to lead the fight against the French in their attempt to re-establish colonialism. With their defeat at Dien Bien Phu on 7 May* 1954, Minh was a war hero to the people of both North and South Vietnam. After defeating the French he led the fight against the Americans, to once again establish a united Vietnam. On 19 May 1969 he wrote his *Testament*, which was read out by his successor, Le Duan, at his memorial ceremony in Hanoi on 9 September. In the *Testament* Ho Chi Minh urged his people to continue to "fight the US aggressors till total victory".[96]

1970 Alan "Blind Owl" Wilson — Canned Heat's guitarist, died aged twenty-seven

Canned Heat's guitarist, harmonica player, vocalist and co-founder, Alan "Blind Owl" Wilson was found dead on a hillside near fellow Canned Heat co-founder Bob Hite's home in Topanga Canyon, California. He died of a drug overdose.

Although Wilson had reputedly attempted suicide several times before, his death was recorded as an accident.

Event today

1948 The Orioles the dawn of doo-wop

Boston vocal group the Orioles' first single *It's Too Soon to Know*, was chosen by *The Billboard* music magazine as one of "The Billboard Picks", a new release most likely to gain airplay and show on the appropriate charts. An apt prediction indeed, hitting #1 on the R&B chart and becoming one of the first crossover singles to hit the pop charts. The brief review also singled out Sonny Til as a strong tenor lead.

The Orioles were not the first successful black vocal group: they were following in the footsteps of the Ink Spots and the Mills Brothers. By the end of the 1940s a new era of more earthy black vocal groups began to emerge. The Orioles and the Ravens were pioneers of this new doo wop style. They were followed by a multitude of street-corner vocal groups, some going on to international fame, but, sadly, the genre also generated a plethora of one-hit wonders. One of the more successful groups was Billy Ward and His Dominoes. In 1951 they scored a hit with their classic *Sixty Minute Man*, with lead singer Clyde McPhatter, who was later replaced by Jackie Wilson. The Penguins' British release of *Earth Angel* became one of the most sought after UK singles of all time.

As the 1950s became the 1960s, doo wop had run its course.

Recording session today

1962 The Beatles return to Abbey Road

By the time that the Beatles returned to Abbey Road for their second recording session, Ringo Starr had replaced Pete Best as the Fab Four's drummer. Just two songs were recorded that day, *Love Me Do* and *How Do You Do It*. Producer George Martin was very keen for the Beatles to release the Mitch Murray penned *How Do You Do It* as their first single but the Liverpudlians were adamant that they only wanted to release their own material as their debut single.

All was not lost for Murray, another popular Liverpool group Gerry and the Pacemakers released the song as their debut single and scored a British #1. It took the Beatles until May 1963 to hit the top spot, with their third single, *From Me to You*.

Live album recorded today

1975 Bob Seger and the Silver Bullet Band *Live Bullet*

This was the first of two days at Detroit's Cobo Hall in Michigan, when Bob Seger recorded his album *Live Bullet*. It was to be this live album and his next studio album, *Night Moves*, that established Seger as an international rock star.

Seger's career started in the early 1960s and continued with different bands throughout the decade. In 1968 he released *Ramblin' Gamblin' Man* as the Bob Seger System. He achieved some success with the System but by the early 1970s he had disbanded the group in favour of a solo approach. Success still eluded him, until 1974 when he started to work with the musicians who would become the Silver Bullet Band. They featured initially on his *Seven* album, although it was released simply as Bob Seger. This was followed by *Beautiful Loser*, still just credited to Seger. His fortunes changed with *Live Bullet*, which finally gave recognition to Bob Seger and the Silver Bullet Band.

5

Events today

1962 Keith Moon — Mark Twain and the Strangers audition

Before finding fame as the Who's drummer, Keith Moon was the sticksman for London group Mark Twain and the Strangers. The Who might have been a very different group if the outcome of a Strangers audition in 1962 had been successful. The audition in question was for the BBC Light Programme, the forerunner of Radio 1. Sadly for the Strangers, they lost out to fellow Londoners the Dave Clark Five.[12]

Keith Moon went on to join the Beachcombers before auditioning for the Who on 30 April* 1964. The group then changed their name to "The High Numbers" and recorded one single, *Zoot Suit* c/w *I'm the Face*, before changing their name back to "The Who" in late 1964.

1966 The Animals — end of the line

The Animals made their final appearance, at Atlantic City's Steel Pier resort.

By the time that the Animals undertook their final American tour the writing was already on the wall and at the end of the tour they all went their separate ways. Keyboard player Alan Price had already moved on a year earlier and drummer John Steel left shortly before the Animals embarked on this American summer tour, supporting teen-favourites Herman's Hermits. Vocalist Eric Burdon continued as Eric Burdon and the New Animals. Bass player Chas Chandler had a change of direction and moved into artist management. Whilst he was in New York he saw an unknown guitarist, Jimi Hendrix, in action. Chandler persuaded him to move to London, where they put together the Jimi Hendrix Experience.

1969 Mott the Hoople — early concert

In one of their earliest concerts as "Mott the Hoople" they supported King Crimson at Romford's Market Hall in Essex.

Drummer Dale Griffin, bassist Overend Watts and guitarist Mick Ralphs came together in the Doc Thomas Group. Keyboardist Verden Allen joined the group around the time that they changed their name to "Silence" in 1969. Silence became Mott the Hoople when existing singer Stan Tippins moved over to make way for Ian Hunter, although he did stay on to work as their road manager.

The group took its name from the 1966 Willard Manus novel *Mott the Hoople*.

1970 Vietnam War — an end for American ground forces

Operation Jefferson Glenn in Thau Thien Province was the last major operation in Vietnam to use American ground forces. It was a combined operation comprising the US 101st Airborne Division and South Vietnamese troops.

Birthdays today

1946	Freddie Mercury	singer: Ibex, Sour Milk Sea, Queen; solo
1947	Buddy Miles	drums: Electric Flag, Band of Gypsys; sessions and touring
1949	Dave "Clem" Clempson	guitar: Bakerloo, Colosseum, Humble Pie

Having started his musical career as guitarist in the power trio Bakerloo, Dave Clempson moved on in 1969 to replace guitarist James Litherland in Colosseum, in time for their third album *Daughter of Time*. He played on their 1971 *Live* album but left to replace Peter Frampton in Humble Pie, before Colosseum finally disbanded.

Event today

1963 Sam Phillips his last rock'n'roll star moved on

Jerry Lee Lewis's contract at Sun Records expired. This marked the end of an era for one of America's most influential small, independent record labels, which gave the world Elvis Presley, Carl Perkins and Jerry Lee Lewis.

Sam Phillips opened his Memphis Recording Service in early 1950. He focussed on blues artists and released his recordings under licence through other labels such as Chess Records. One of the most memorable Chess releases was Jackie Brenston's *Rocket 88*, released on 5 March* 1951 and often cited as the first rock'n'roll record.

When Elvis walked into Phillips's studio to cut a private recording on 4 January* 1954 the rock'n'roll age was just dawning. Six months later Presley released his first single, a cover of Arthur Crudup's *That's All Right*. In 1955 Johnny Cash joined Sun but Elvis left for RCA and became the King of Rock'n'Roll. Phillips signed up Carl Perkins in 1956 and was rewarded with his first million-seller, *Blue Suede Shoes*. In that same year Roy Orbison and Jerry Lee Lewis released their first singles. Cash and Orbison found international success but only after they had followed in Elvis's footsteps and moved from Sun to other labels, Columbia and Monument respectively.

Jerry Lee Lewis went on to become Sun's greatest rock'n'roll star, recording the anthems *Whole Lot of Shakin' Going On* and *Great Balls of Fire*. He looked as though he might usurp Presley as the new King of Rock'n'Roll when Elvis was drafted but Lewis's career came crashing down when he arrived in England for his UK tour on 22 May* 1958. The news broke of Lewis's marriage to his cousin's thirteen-year-old daughter. Lewis stayed with Sun until 1963 but never recaptured his former glory.

Phillips continued to release singles and the occasional album but his interest in the label ended when he sold out to Shelby Singleton on 1 July* 1969. He made some money from Sun Records but his main wealth came from a shrewd investment in the fledgling Holiday Inn hotel business.

Recording session today

1968 Eric Clapton *While My Guitar Gently Weeps*

One of the most famous unheralded guest appearances in rock music was recorded in EMI's Abbey Road Studio Two, when Eric Clapton took out his Les Paul guitar and started to play. George Harrison had invited him to perform the solo on his song *While My Guitar Gently Weeps*, destined for the Beatles' *White Album*.

Birthday today

1943 Roger Waters bass, vocals and songwriter: Abdabs, Pink Floyd; solo

Roger Waters took over the mantle of main songwriter in Pink Floyd after fellow founding member Syd Barrett left and was replaced by David Gilmour. Waters' relationship with the other musicians progressively deteriorated and by the time of the recording of *The Wall* keyboard player Rick Wright had been relegated from band member to salaried staff. The three remaining members of Pink Floyd, Waters, drummer Nick Mason and guitarist David Gilmour recorded *The Final Cut*, their last album together before an acrimonious parting of the ways. Waters became a solo act. A legal battle followed and resulted in the other band members gaining the right to continue to use the "Pink Floyd" brand.

There was a gap of twenty-four years before Waters was reunited with Pink Floyd on 2 July* 2005. This reunion was a one-off short set and their last-ever performance together.

Events today

1963 The Animals — still the Alan Price Rhythm and Blues Combo

Newcastle's Downbeat Club in the North of England played host to a performance by the latest lineup of the Alan Price Rhythm and Blues Combo – keyboards player Alan Price, guitarist Hilton Valentine, drummer John Steel, bassist Chas Chandler and vocalist Eric Burdon.

Shortly after this performance the group changed its name to "The Animals" and became one of England's premier R&B outfits. The name was inspired by the fans' description of their stage act.

1968 Led Zeppelin — debut gig ...billed as "Yardbirds"

The first concert performance for guitarist Jimmy Page, vocalist Robert Plant, drummer John Bonham and bass player John Paul Jones was at the Teen Clubs in Gladsaxe, Denmark – billed as "Yardbirds".

Keith Relf, Jim McCarty, Jimmy Page and Chris Dreja played their final gig together as the Yardbirds in Luton on 7 July*. Singer Relf and drummer McCarty left shortly afterwards to form Together. Guitarist Page and bassist Dreja then set about replacing them. They approached a number of people, including vocalist Terry Reid. He famously turned down the offer but recommended his friend Robert Plant. Plant in turn recommended John Bonham as their drummer. During this Yardbirds-to-Zeppelin transition Dreja also moved on to pastures green, embarking on a career as a professional photographer. The new lineup was completed by bass player and arranger John Paul Jones.

Manager Peter Grant was still committed, as "The Yardbirds", to a ten-day tour of Denmark and Sweden. After a short rehearsal they played their first gig. Following their return to the UK they continued as "The Yardbirds" or "New Yardbirds", before playing their first gig as "Led Zeppelin" on 9 November*.

1974 The 101'ers — first gig

Calling themselves "El Huaso and the 101 All Stars", the band made its debut at the Telegraph pub in London's Brixton. The guitarist that day was Joe Strummer, who went on to become a founding member of the Clash.

The band's name was not as Orwellian as it sounded. The group took its moniker from the address of the band members' house-squat at 101 Walterton Road, London W9.

Births and deaths today

1936 Buddy Holly — rock'n'roll singer and songwriter

Holly sometimes used the name "Charles Hardin" for his songwriting credits.

1978 Keith Moon flamboyant Who drummer, died at the age of thirty-two

On the evening of 6 September, Keith Moon attended a film preview of *The Buddy Holly Story* at the invitation of his friend Paul McCartney. After dining with Paul and Linda, Moon and his girlfriend, Annette Walter-Lax, uncharacteristically returned home early. The following day he died from an accidental overdose of tablets he was taking to combat alcoholism. The coroner returned an open verdict.

The London apartment he was staying in was owned by his friend Harry Nilsson. In a bizarre coincidence, Mama Cass Elliott had died in the same apartment on Curzon Place four years earlier, on 29 July* 1974.

Events today

1952 Ray Charles moved to Atlantic Records

Ray Charles was in Atlantic Records' studios after moving from Swing Time, where he found R&B chart success and was also the pianist for stablemate Lowell Fulson's touring band. Charles's style at Swing Time had been in the mould of Nat King Cole.

At Atlantic, Charles caused a degree of controversy when he fused gospel with R&B. He was with the label until 1960, when he moved over to ABC Paramount. During his time with Atlantic he scored a string of R&B hits, including *I've Got a Woman*, before making the crossover into the mainstream pop charts in 1959 with *What'd I Say*.

1965 The Monkees ads to find "4 insane boys"

The process of manufacturing the pop band started with casting ads in the *Daily Variety* and *Hollywood Reporter* trade papers, inviting hopefuls to try out for the parts of "4 insane boys". The ads proclaimed that they were looking for folk and roll musicians-singers, for acting roles in a new TV series. The applicants needed were "4 insane boys", who were "spirited Ben Frank's-types".

The TV show was being created as America's answer to the Beatles phenomenon and attracted over 400 would-be pop stars. Amongst those who auditioned but failed to make the grade, included future Beach Boys collaborator Van Dyke Parks, future Three Dog Night singer Danny Hutton, songwriter Paul Williams and John Lennon collaborator and singer-songwriter Harry Nilsson, although he did later contribute his songwriting talents to the show. Steven Stills failed the audition, apparently because of his teeth. Contrary to the persisting urban myth, mass murderer Charles Manson did not audition for a part.

The first episode aired almost a year later on 12 September*.

Recording session today

1958 Boots Randolph *Yakety Sax*

Highly respected saxophonist Boots Randolph recorded *Yakety Sax*, released shortly afterwards on the RCA label as the B-side to *Percolator*.

The quirky, self-penned *Yakety Sax* proved to be very popular and Randolph released it again on the Monument label, scoring an American hit in 1963. British comedian Benny Hill used *Yakety Sax* as the musical backdrop to the scenes in his TV show when he could be seen in pursuit of scantily-clad ladies.

As well as releasing material in his own right, Randolph was a very active session saxophonist. He worked extensively with Elvis Presley and featured on Roy Orbison's *Oh Pretty Woman* and Brenda Lee's *Rockin' Around the Christmas Tree*.

Single released today

1957 Jackie Wilson — *Reet Petite c/w By the Light of the Silvery Moon* (US)

In 1953 Jackie Wilson replaced Clyde McPhatter in Billy Ward and His Dominoes. Four years later he launched his own solo career with *Reet Petite.* The song made Top 10 in Britain but fared less favourably in his American homeland.

Co-written with songwriter Billy Davis, as "Tyran Carlo", *Reet Petite* helped to launch the career of Berry Gordy Jr, who went on to found the Motown record label.

Birthday today

1897 Jimmie Rodgers — singer and songwriter, aka "Father of Country Music"

Events today

1956 Elvis Presley — first appearance on the *Ed Sullivan Show*

When Elvis made his first appearance on the *Ed Sullivan Show* he attracted an audience of sixty million[42] viewers, representing an audience share of a staggering 82 per cent[42]. On the show he performed *Don't Be Cruel, Love Me Tender, Ready Teddy* and *Hound Dog.*

Sullivan was a bit slow off the mark in securing Presley for his TV show. The King's first TV appearance had been on the *Dorsey Brothers' Stage Show* on 28 January*.

1969 Queen — first time on stage together

Freddie Bulsara was playing at the Sink Club in Liverpool with his first band Ibex, soon to become Wreckage. For the encore they were joined on stage by Freddie's friends Brian May and Roger Taylor, both of whom were in the band Smile at the time.

Freddie Bulsara changed his second name to "Mercury" and joined May and Taylor in Smile. The band renamed to "Queen" and played their first gig together in Cornwall, at Truro's City Hall on 27 June* 1970.

They still needed to recruit John Deacon to complete the classic Queen lineup.

Recording session today

1970 Derek and the Dominos — *Layla*

The song was recorded for the album *Layla and Other Assorted Love Songs* and was later issued as a single.

Following the demise of the short-lived Blind Faith, Eric Clapton toured and recorded with Delaney & Bonney & Friends. When he decided to put a new band together he invited ex-Friends, keyboard player Bobby Whitlock, bassist Carl Randle and drummer Jim Gordon to join him. Duane Allman also joined Clapton as the second guitarist.

At the time Clapton was working closely with George Harrison on his album *All Things Must Pass*, Harrison's first solo project since the Beatles split. He had also fallen in love with Harrison's wife, the model Pattie Boyd. The song *Layla* was a personal account of the anguish he was feeling as he was torn between his friendship for Harrison and his love for another man's wife. His inspiration for the song came from the epic seventh century Arabic tale of unrequited love, retold in *The Story of Layla and Majnun* by the twelfth century Persian poet Nizami Ganjavi.

Birthdays today

1941 Duffy Power seminal British R&B singer

Duffy Power was one of the most respected early British R&B singers. Sadly, he never managed to find the same degree of commercial success as contemporaries like Eric Burdon and Chris Farlowe. He started out in a skiffle group after leaving school in the mid-1950s. Manager Larry Parnes signed him up and, true to form, changed his name to "Duffy Power". Changing his artists' names to something a little more descriptive was one of Parnes's trademarks, he also managed Billy Fury, Marty Wilde and Johnny Gentle. In mid-1963, backed by the Graham Bond Quartet, Power covered the Beatles' *I Saw Her Standing There*. He was given a "guest vocalist" credit on the front cover of Alexis Korner's Blues Incorporated's 1966 album *Sky High*. Despite releasing a string of singles he never quite managed to become more than a singer's singer.

1946 Bruce Palmer bass: Mynah Birds, Buffalo Springfield

Event today

1967 Pete Seeger censored on TV

As a part of his blacklisting for un-American activities, folk singer Pete Seeger was not allowed to perform on mainstream American TV. Comedy duo the Smothers Brothers were instrumental in ending this TV exile with an appearance on their *Smothers Brothers Comedy Hour*. The show was recorded on 1 September with Seeger performing a number of songs, including his anti-Vietnam War song *Waist Deep in the Big Muddy*. However, when the show was broadcast the following week CBS executives had cut the song from Seeger's performance.

To counter this injustice the Smothers Brothers enlisted the aid of the press to highlight the censorship. Seeger was invited back five months later and performed the song on the show which was broadcast on 25 February.

Recording sessions today

1954 Ken Colyer's Jazzmen *Back to the Delta*

Soon after splitting with Chris Barber and the rest of the original Jazzmen, Ken Colyer was back in the studio with an all-new Ken Colyer's Jazzmen to record the album *Back to the Delta*. This September session was the second one for the album.

Back to the Delta consisted of six tracks by Ken Colyer's Jazzmen and three songs by Ken Colyer's Skiffle Group. The Jazzmen included clarinettist Bernard Bilk, later to find success with his own trad jazz band as "Acker Bilk". *Stranger on the Shore* would give Bilk a smash hit on both sides of the Atlantic in the early 1960s. Alexis Korner provided guitar and mandolin on the three skiffle numbers. Korner went on to become one of the prime movers in the British rhythm and blues scene. His highly respected band Blues Incorporated, acted as a springboard for a host of future rock luminaries.

The six band tracks and three skiffle tracks were originally recorded on 25 June. The skiffle tracks were deemed to be fine but the band tracks were considered unsatisfactory. This led to the band numbers being re-recorded at this session. The new recordings used a different rhythm section, giving a noticeably different sound. Record collectors were treated to two different releases. In Britain the album had the June skiffle tracks and the September band numbers but in America the album was released with both the skiffle and band numbers from the June session.

1964 Rod Stewart *Good Morning Little Schoolgirl*

Rod Stewart chose to cover Sonny Boy Williamson (I)'s classic *Good Morning Schoolgirl* as his first British single.

Williamson recorded his version in 1937. The Yardbirds covered it shortly after Stewart's version reached the record stores. Both Stewart and the Yardbirds released the single as *Good Morning Little Schoolgirl*. One of the session musicians behind Stewart was future Led Zeppelin bassist John Paul Jones.

This was the Yardbirds second British single. They achieved their first chart success with their next release, *For Your Love*. It was a very different story for Rod Stewart, he had to wait until 1971 before his first solo effort graced the British charts, with a cover of Tim Hardin's *Reason to Believe*.

Birthday today

1950 Joe Perry lead guitar: The Jam Band, founding member of Aerosmith

Event today

11

1974 The Stranglers formed in Guildford, Surrey

Originally called "The Guildford Stranglers", they shortened their name to "The Stranglers" and found fame when punk rock changed the face of British rock music in 1976.

Recording sessions today

1958 Lloyd Price *Stagger Lee*

After his initial success at Speciality, Lloyd Price moved over to ABC-Paramount. This second single for the new label was his rock'n'roll classic *Stagger Lee*. The song was originally released as the B-side of *You Need Love* but like so many rock'n'roll classics, Cliff Richard's *Move It!* and Hank Ballard's *The Twist*, DJs preferred the flip-side – and that's the one they played.

The version Price recorded on 11 September was his take on the blues standard *Stack O'Lee Blues*, recorded by Ma Rainey in 1925 and Mississippi John Hurt in 1928. Price wrote different lyrics for the nineteenth century tale of the murder of Billy de Lyon by Stack O'Lee over a five-dollar Stetson. Price called his version *Stagger Lee*.

American Bandstand host Dick Clark considered Price's *Stagger Lee* lyrics to be too violent for the sensitivities of his TV audience. On 4 December Price was back in the studio to record a version with a happy ending. This 11 September version was the tale of Stagger Lee and Billy, where Stagger Lee shot Billy dead after accusing him of cheating at dice and taking his money and his Stetson. The new sanitised version, which became known as *Stagger Lee (Bandstand Version)*, had Stagger Lee accusing Billy of stealing his girlfriend but this time instead of shooting Billy, Stagger Lee gets his girl back and they all live happily ever after.

1962 The Beatles third visit to Abbey Road

Producer George Martin had not been satisfied with the second recording of *Love Me Do*, made on 4 September* with Ringo on drums. When the four Liverpudlians returned for their third trip to Abbey Road, Martin had secured the services of session drummer Andy White. A third version of *Love Me Do* was recorded, where Ringo took a backseat and played tambourine on *Love Me Do* and maracas on the UK B-side *P.S. I Love You*.

They also recorded several takes of another new Lennon and McCartney song, *Please Please Me*. This was a different arrangement to the one released as their second UK single. It was more in the style of a slow Orbison-esque ballad. Sadly, none of those takes survived for posterity.

Album released today

1967 The Beach Boys *Smiley Smile* (US)

The follow-up to the Beach Boys classic *Pet Sounds* was intended to be Brian Wilson's inspirational album *Smile*. Sadly, illness and adverse feedback from the others led to him abandoning the album and it became the legendary 'lost' album of the 1960s. The less complex *Smiley Smile* included re-recorded versions of several songs intended for *Smile*, plus the single *Good Vibrations* and additional new material. At the time of release it was received with mixed reviews. It also marked the beginning of the post-Brian Wilson era, with Brian exerting less creative influence over the band's output.

Smiley Smile was the first album released on the Beach Boys own label, Brother.

Events today

12

1966 The Monkees first TV show aired

The first episode of the Monkees TV show, *Royal Flush*, was broadcast on NBC. In this first outing the manufactured pop group saved the day for the Princess Bettina, Duchy of Harmonica.

The four Monkees who had successfully answered the press ads for "4 insane boys" a year earlier on 8 September*, were all entertainment veterans. Peter Tork and Mike Nesmith had both been folk performers. Micky Dolenz and Davy Jones, the only Englishman, had both found success as child actors.

1970 Eric Burdon and War from the Animals to War

Eric Burdon and War performed in Hyde Park, on a bill that included John Sebastian and Canned Heat.

The Animals, with frontman Eric Burdon, were one of the leading British R&B groups of the first half of the 1960s. When they all went their separate ways in the autumn of 1966, Burdon retained the brand name and performed as "Eric Burdon and the New Animals". Ex-Animals bassist Chas Chandler went off and discovered Jimi Hendrix. On 7 December* 1968 Burton announced that he was quitting the music business to seek his fortune as a Hollywood actor. When he discovered that there wasn't a vacancy for a Geordie matinee idol he returned to the music scene and teamed up with Los Angeles band War. The relationship with War lasted about a year and ended with Burdon collapsing on stage on 30 January* 1971.

Four days after this Hyde Park gig, Jimi Hendrix jammed with Eric Burdon and War on stage at Ronnie Scott's Club in London. This was to be Hendrix's final performance: he died on 18 September*.

1975 The Runaways first gig

The all-girl Runaways performed for the first time at a private party held at rock writer Phast Phreddie Patterson's home in Torrence, Los Angeles. This historic first outing was captured on tape and can reputedly be found on various bootleg albums.

The Runaways came into being when producer and writer Kim Fowley met drummer Sandy West and guitarist Joan Jett, all with the desire to form an all-girl rock band. It started out as a trio after recruiting bassist Micki Steele. A couple of weeks after their party debut, they gave their first public performance at Hollywood's Whiskey a Go Go.

Recording session today

1965 The Yardbirds *The Train Kept A-Rollin'*

The Yardbirds recorded the first takes of one of their trademark songs, *The Train Kept A-Rollin'*. This time they were in America at Sun Records' studio in Memphis, with Sam Phillips at the controls. Six months before this recording session, Eric Clapton had moved on to join John Mayall's Bluesbreakers and had been replaced by guitarist Jeff Beck. The other group members at the session were vocalist and harmonica player Keith Relf, rhythm guitarist Chris Dreja, bassist Paul Samwell-Smith and drummer Jim McCarty.

Co-written and originally recorded by Tiny Bradshaw in 1951, *The Train Kept A-Rollin'* was covered by Johnny Burnette in 1956.

Making the most of their time in America, the Yardbirds recorded Bo Diddley's *I'm a Man* at Chess Records' studio shortly afterwards.

Events today

1969 Landmark Concerts *Toronto Rock and Roll Revival*

Held at the Varsity Stadium, the *Toronto Rock and Roll Revival* show provided a rare opportunity to see performances from some of the 1950s and '60s rock'n'roll royalty. The Doors headlined the bill, which also included: Little Richard, Chuck Berry, Jerry Lee Lewis, Bo Diddley, Gene Vincent, Alice Cooper, Chicago Transit Authority and Screaming Lord Sutch.

This one-day festival also featured the debut performance of John Lennon's Plastic Ono Band, consisting of: Yoko Ono, guitarist Eric Clapton, bassist Klaus Voormann and future Yes drummer Alan White. Lennon put the band together at the last moment and they famously rehearsed their set on the plane journey over to the gig! Their performance was captured on the album *Live Peace in Toronto 1969*.

1969 Alice Cooper *Chicken Incident*

Alice Cooper's performance at the *Toronto Rock and Roll Revival* festival (see above) included the infamous *Chicken Incident*.

Rock'n'roll legend is full of apocryphal Alice Cooper stories but this one was right on the money. As part of Alice Cooper's normal act the band would explode some pillows on stage, showering the audience with feathers. In Toronto someone threw a live chicken to Cooper and rationalising that a bird with wings could fly, he threw the bird into the audience believing that it would simply fly away. Of course it didn't and the audience tore the bird to pieces. The following day it was reported that

Cooper had bitten the head off the live chicken and drunk its blood. Frank Zappa, who had recently signed Alice Cooper to his new Straight label, telephoned Cooper to ask if it was true about biting the head off. When Cooper replied that it wasn't, Zappa reputedly suggested that he should keep that information to himself – as the publicity was priceless.

Single released today

1965 The Beatles *Yesterday c/w Act Naturally* (US)

Yesterday was never issued as a single in Britain. Paul famously wrote the song and was the only Beatle to play on the recording. It was also the first Beatles song to feature a string quartet. *Yesterday* is the Beatles' most covered song and one of the most covered songs of all time. It was originally offered to another one of Brian Epstein's acts Billy J Kramer but he turned it down.

Act Naturally was a cover of the 1963 country hit for Capitol stablemate Buck Owens.

Birthdays today

1941 David Clayton-Thomas singer: Fabulous Shays; Blood, Sweat & Tears

Singer David Clayton-Thomas was born David Henry Thomsett in southern England but was brought up in Canada when his family emigrated there after the Second World War. He found fame with Blood, Sweat & Tears after replacing founding member Al Kooper in 1968. Kooper left after their first album, *Child is Father to the Man.*

1949 Fred "Sonic" Smith guitar and vocals: MC5, Sonic's Rendezvous Band

Fred "Sonic" Smith was born in West Virginia but moved to Detroit and founded MC5. He is accredited as one of the architects of the Detroit High Energy rock sound.

Event today

1970 Elvis Presley first tour since 1957

Elvis finished a short six-date tour in Mobile, Alabama. The tour had kicked off on 9 September in Phoenix, Arizona and was Elvis's first time on the road since his concerts in Hawaii on 10* and 11 November 1957.

This was a very different Elvis to the rock'n'roller of the 1950s. Gone were the three musicians who regularly backed him then, guitarist Scotty Moore, bass player Bill Black and drummer DJ Fontana. Some of his new Las Vegas musicians were with him for the tour, including guitarist James Burton, drummer Ronnie Tutt and musical director Joe Guercio but most of the orchestra behind him were pick-up musicians.

Some of the opening night's concert was used in Elvis's tour movie, *Elvis: That's the Way It Is.*

Recording session today

1955 Little Richard *Tutti-Frutti*

Although Little Richard's recording debut went back to a handful of singles on RCA in 1951 and 1952, it was this Bumps Blackwell produced song, his first single to be released on the Speciality label, that marked the beginning of his rise to becoming a rock'n'roll icon. The recording session featured Huey "Piano" Smith.

During a break in this first recording session, Little Richard started to sing one of the songs that he performed in the clubs. This lively song had a very catchy refrain in, "wop bop a loo bop". Blackwell could see the song's potential but the ribald lyrics were too much for the pop market. Dorothy LaBostrie was called in to clean them up and the result was *Tutti-Frutti*, with joint writing credits for LaBostrie and Little Richard.

Birthdays today

1949 Ed King and Steve Gaines — both guitarists with Lynyrd Skynyrd

In an eerie coincidence, two of Lynyrd Skynyrd's guitarists, Ed King and Steve Gaines, were both born on the same day. Each one took the other's place in the band.

Ed King joined Lynyrd Skynyrd in 1972 as the bass playing replacement for Leon Wilkeson. His departure from the band was temporary and when Wilkeson returned, King became Skynyrd's third-guitarist. King left in 1975 and was replaced by guitarist Steve Gaines in 1976. Gaines was killed in the plane crash that took the lives of three group members on 20 October* 1977. When the band returned to the road on 23 September* 1987, King rejoined the band with guitarist and crash survivor Gary Rossington.

Before King joined Lynyrd Skynyrd, he had made a name for himself as guitarist and one of the founding members of Strawberry Alarm Clock. An early Lynyrd Skynyrd often opened for them.

1950 Paul Kossoff — guitar: Black Cat Bones, Free, Back Street Crawler

Inspired by seeing Eric Clapton in concert, Paul Kossoff joined the British blues band Black Cat Bones in 1967. It was there that he first worked with drummer Simon Kirke. In 1968 the two of them moved on and teamed up with singer Paul Rodgers to form Free. When Free finally fell apart in 1973 Kossoff recorded a solo album, *Back Street Crawler*. He liked the result and decided to form a band of the same name.

Events today

15

1955 Chuck Berry — his "duck-walk" arrived

Chuck Berry appeared in *Alan Freed and his Rock'n Roll First Anniversary* concert at Brooklyn's Paramount Theatre. This was the final night of a two-week residency arranged by Alan Freed, the man who coined the expression "rock'n'roll". Amongst the artists Chuck Berry shared the stage with, were doo wop groups The Nutmegs, The Harptones and The Cardinals, gospel-turned-R&B singer Nappy Brown and rather incongruously, crooner Tony Bennett.

It was at the Paramount Theatre around this time that Chuck Berry started to include his famous "duck-walk" as part of his stage presentation.

1963 Civil Rights Movement — church bombing

Four young black girls were killed by a bomb planted at the Sixteenth Street Baptist Church in Birmingham, Alabama.

Four members of the white supremacy organisation the Ku Klux Klan were involved in the bombing. Klan member Robert Chambliss was seen placing a box underneath the church steps. He was arrested and charged with murder and possession of dynamite without a permit. A jury found him not guilty of murder but he received a $100 fine and six-month jail sentence for illegal possession of explosives.

Later, new evidence came to light and in 1977 Chambliss was retried, found guilty and sentenced to life imprisonment. In 2000 the FBI identified the other three men involved in the atrocity.

1965 The Rolling Stones goose-stepping Mick Jagger caused a riot

At a concert in West Berlin's Waldbühne, Mick Jagger literally caused a riot after goose-stepping around the stage in a manner reminiscent of Nazi soldiers in Hitler's Germany. The ensuing pitched battle between fans and police resulted in dozens of injuries and considerable damage to the venue.

The Waldbühne was built for the 1936 Olympic Games, in which Hitler intended to demonstrate to the world the supremacy of his Aryan race. His plans were thwarted by African-American athlete Jesse Owens who ran away with four Gold Medals.

Recording session today

1963 The Animals first-ever recording session

In their first-ever recording session, at Newcastle's Graphic Sound Studios, the Animals made a private recording of four blues covers: Muddy Waters' *I Just Wanna Make Love to You*, Jimmy Reed's *Big Boss Man*, John Lee Hooker's *Boom Boom* and Bo Diddley's *Pretty Thing*, written by Diddley and Willie Dixon.

Album released today

1975 Pink Floyd *Wish You Were Here* (UK)

The song *Have a Cigar* featured a lead vocal from Roy Harper, the only time that an outsider sang lead vocal on a Pink Floyd album. Reputedly, Roger Waters was unhappy with the way his vocal was going and invited Harper to sing the lead.

Dave Gilmour's guitar work featured on Harper's album *HQ*.

During the session on 5 June* founding member Syd Barrett wandered into the studio. This was the last time that any of the band would see their original guiding light.

Events today

1964 Landmark TV *Shindig!* debuted

ABC's new rock'n'roll music show *Shindig!* debuted, with performances from Sam Cooke, The Righteous Brothers and The Everly Brothers.

The show was produced by Jack Good, who was responsible for the groundbreaking British music shows *Six-Five Special* and *Oh Boy!*; *Shindig!* ran until 8 January 1966.

1965 David Bowie from David Jones to David Bowie

David Bowie announced to the press that he was changing his stage name from "Davie Jones" to "David Bowie", in order to avoid confusion with his namesake in the American group the Monkees. His new moniker was taken from the Bowie knife, created by American frontiersman and Alamo hero, Jim Bowie.

David Jones became Davie Jones and finally David Bowie. He recorded with a number of groups before finding international success as a solo artist. In 1962 he provided vocals and saxophone for his first professional group the Konrads. Other lineups to include Bowie, still performing as "David" or "Davie Jones", were the King Bees and the Manish Boys. As "Davie Jones and the King Bees" he released his first-ever single, *Liza Jane* c/w *Louie, Louie Go Home.*

In the spring of 1965 he joined the Lower Third. Initially they performed as "Davie Jones with The Lower Third" but on 16 September he changed his name to "David Bowie" and they became "David Bowie and the Lower Third".

His first release as "David Bowie", *Can't Help Thinking About Me* c/w *And I Say to Myself*, was in January 1966 as "David Bowie with The Lower Third". Bowie's first release as "David Bowie" followed on 1 April* 1966 with *Do Anything You Say* c/w *Good Morning Girl.* Amazingly he was still three years away from commercial success. In February 1966 he formed his own group, David Bowie and the Buzz. This was followed in the spring of 1967 by a short spell as frontman for the Riot Squad, which had boasted Mitch Mitchell, Graham Bonney and Jon Lord in previous lineups. In 1968 and 1969 he branched out into mixed media performances of music and mime with Turquoise, who morphed into Feathers.

In the summer of 1969 he finally hit the British charts with *Space Oddity*.

Single released today

1963 The Beatles *She Loves You* c/w *I'll Get You* (US)

Released on the Swan label, *She Loves You* was the Beatles' third American single. It gave the Fab Four their second American #1. Capitol Records had been slow off the mark, their first single *I Want to Hold Your Hand*, was the fourth Beatles single to be released in America. This Swan single then followed the Capitol release into the charts.

Births and deaths today

1925 BB King influential blues guitarist and singer

1948 Kenney Jones drums: Small Faces, Faces, The Who

1977 Marc Bolan British glam-rock pioneer, died at the age of twenty-nine

Gloria Jones and her boyfriend Marc Bolan were returning home from a night out, when Jones lost control of her Mini 1275GT and it crashed into a sycamore tree. The accident happened at the southern side of Barnes Common, in south-west London. Marc Bolan died at the scene.

Events today

1967 The Doors *Light My Fire* on the *Ed Sullivan Show*

17

The Doors' appearance on the *Ed Sullivan Show* followed the Rolling Stones' appearance back on 15 January*, when they acquiesced to Sullivan's desire to censor the lyrics of *Let's Spend the Night Together*, to simply spending "some time" together. When the Doors appeared on the show Jim Morrison was not so accommodating. Despite agreeing to changes during rehearsals, he performed the song *Light My Fire* with the contentious line suggesting that they "couldn't get much higher". They also performed a second song *People Are Strange* – but were never invited back.

1967 The Who TV show ends with a bang

The Who's legendary appearance on the *Smothers Brothers Comedy Hour* certainly ended with a bang. The act culminated with an equipment-smashing *My Generation* but no one was prepared for the huge explosion from the flash powder in Keith Moon's bass drum. Urban legend has it that Moon encouraged a stage hand to increase considerably the amount of flash powder stuffed into the bass drum. The resulting explosion showed that he succeeded. Townshend was smashing his guitar on the floor right in front of the bass drum, when it went off and he took the full force of the explosion.

Single released today

1956 Brenda Lee *Jambalaya c/w Bigelow 6-200* (US)

This cover of Hank Williams's *Jambalaya* was the debut single from the original "Little Miss Dynamite". Moon Mullican reputedly co-wrote the song with Williams but was not credited on the record.

Album released today

1971 T.Rex *Electric Warrior* (UK)

Marc Bolan came to fame with the psychedelic-folk sounds of Tyrannosaurus Rex. He shortened the name to T.Rex and released his eponymous debut album. This second album as T.Rex, *Electric Warrior*, signified a change of pace and was one of the seminal albums to herald the incoming British glam-rock scene.

The album featured ex-Turtles Mark Volman and Howard Kaylan on backing vocals.

Birthdays today

1923 Hank Williams enormously influential singer, guitarist and songwriter

1935 Ken Kesey writer, acid tests ...and His Merry Pranksters

Whilst at Stamford University in 1959, Ken Kesey took part in the CIA funded LSD experimental programme MKULTRA, set up to study the effects of psychoactive drugs. During this period he also worked part-time in the same Menlo Park Veterans Hospital where the experiments were being carried out. This background was put to good use in his acclaimed novel *One Flew Over the Cuckoo's Nest*. In 1964 Kesey and his Merry Pranksters set off in their bus, *Further*, on a journey across America from San Francisco to New York. The sojourn was documented for an intended movie, *The Merry Pranksters Search for a Cool Place*. The endeavour was one of Paul McCartney's inspirations for the Beatles' *Magical Mystery Tour*. Kesey's infamous "acid tests" followed, to a backdrop of music from the Grateful Dead.

Event today

1968 Rush first paid gig

Canadian group Rush played their first paid gig, at the Coff-In coffee house located in the unusual setting of the basement at St Theodore's of Canterbury Anglican Church in Toronto. The lineup for this debut consisted of guitarist Alex Lifeson, bassist Jeff Jones and drummer John Rutsey.

It would be nearly a decade, with both band name and personnel changes, before Rush managed to achieve international fame. Founding member Lifeson was the only one of this trio to remain with the group. A week after this gig Jones left, to be replaced by the second permanent member, bassist and singer Geddy Lee. More changes followed, including a spell in 1969 when the band was called "Hadrian". By mid-1971 the lineup had settled down to the trio of Lifeson, Lee and Rutsey. This lineup stayed in place until just before the gig at Cleveland's Agora Ballroom on 26 August* 1974.

Albums released today

1970 Black Sabbath *Paranoid* (UK)

1970 Fleetwood Mac *Kiln House* (US)

Kiln House was Fleetwood Mac's first post-Peter Green album, with drummer Mick Fleetwood, bassist John McVie and guitarists Jeremy Spencer and Danny Kirwan.

Founding member Green had played his last gig on 28 May* 1970 but returned briefly to play live with the band when Spencer walked out during the 1971 American tour, after a chance encounter on 15 February* with some evangelical Christians. This album proved to be the last vinyl outing for Spencer.

Christine McVie also made an appearance on the album, before joining the band as a full member. As "Christine Perfect", she had previously been a member of the highly respected British blues band Chicken Shack, providing the vocals and piano on their first two albums, *40 Blue Fingers Freshly Packed and Ready to Serve*, and *OK Ken?* During her time with Chicken Shack, Perfect met and married Fleetwood Mac's bass player John McVie. Having then retired to become a housewife, Christine McVie was enticed back to the music scene and joined Fleetwood Mac in the summer of 1970.

Births and deaths today

1945 PF Sloan singer, songwriter and producer

PF Sloan wrote the mid-1960s anthem *Eve of Destruction*, recorded by Barry McGuire.

1970 Jimi Hendrix iconic 1960s guitarist, died at the age of twenty-seven

Monika Dannemann, a German painter, found her boyfriend Jimi Hendrix unconscious and unable to wake him, called an ambulance to her London flat. The ambulance crew took Hendrix to hospital but the doctors failed to revive him. The death certificate gave the cause of death as "Inhalation of vomit: Barbiturate intoxication (quinalbarbitone): Insufficient evidence of circumstances: Open verdict."[48] Controversy has always surrounded Hendrix's death, with contradictory reports of the events and even claims that he was murdered.

He died at the age of twenty-seven, qualifying him for the macabre *27 Club*. Other club members include Brian Jones, Janis Joplin and Jim Morrison.

Events today

19

1970 Landmark Festivals first Glastonbury

Inspired by the Bath blues festival, farmer Michael Eavis decided to help with his farm's expenses by hosting his own *Pop Folk & Blues* festival in Somerset, at Worthy Farm in Pilton. The performers at that first event included Marc Bolan, Quintessence, Al Stewart, Keith Christmas, Stackridge, Amazing Blondel and Jethro Tull's Ian Anderson.

This first Glastonbury Festival was a modest affair, attended by 1,500 people at £1 a time. The poster promised "All food at fair prices! Ox roast! All farms [sic] milk free".

1985 Frank Zappa addressed Congress

Always an outspoken critic of censorship, Frank Zappa addressed Congress and spoke out against the drive by the PMRC for more censorship in pop music.

The PMRC (Parents' Music Resource Center) was a group of prominent Washington ladies, many of whom were married to politicians. They were seeking to clean up popular music by introducing a labelling system for records, similar to the one used by the movie industry.

On his 1985 album *Frank Zappa Meets the Mothers of Prevention*, the track *Porn Wars* included dialog from the hearing. Zappa attached his own lengthy *Warning Guarantee* to the album cover. It suggested that, contained within, there was material that "a truly free society would neither fear nor suppress".

Births and deaths today

1934 Brian Epstein Beatles' manager

On becoming the Beatles' manager, Brian Epstein changed their image from the Gene Vincent leather look to smart suits. After failing their Decca audition on 1 January* 1962, George Martin signed them to EMI's Parlophone label on 6 June*. Epstein guided the Beatles to become the most famous band in rock'n'roll history. He also had other successes, as the manager of Cilla Black, Gerry and the Pacemakers and Billy J Kramer but was less fortunate in the mid-1960s with The Paramounts and The Moody Blues.

1940 Bill Medley singer: The Paramours, The Righteous Brothers; solo

1941 Cass Elliot singer: Mugwumps, The Mamas & The Papas; solo

Before finding international fame as Mama Cass, Elliot was a member of the Big Three with singer-songwriter Tim Rose. This group morphed into the Mugwumps, with pre-Lovin' Spoonful's Zal Yanovsky and John Sebastian.

1973 Gram Parsons country-rock pioneer, died at the age of twenty-six

During a vacation in the Joshua Tree National Park, ex-Byrd and Flying Burrito Brother Gram Parsons died of a drug overdose in his room at the Joshua Tree Inn.

Whereas a drug death was not unusual in the rock world, the events following his demise assured Parsons a place in rock legend. He had fallen in love with Joshua Tree National Park and expressed a desire for this to be his last resting place. Parsons's road manager Phil Kaufman and a friend stole his body from Los Angeles airport and drove it out to the Joshua Tree desert. There, in line with Parsons's wishes, they poured petrol over the body and set fire to it. They could not be charged with stealing the body but were convicted of stealing the coffin.

Events today

1976 Sex Pistols Pistols and Sid Vicious ...same gig, different bands

In the autumn of 1976 London's 100 Club hosted the first-ever British punk festival. Most of the groups performing became household names but at that time they were still hunting down recording deals.

The two-day festival included the Sex Pistols on the first day. These punk pioneers were a couple of weeks away from signing to EMI, on 8 October*. The bill that night also included Siouxsie and the Banshees with Sid Vicious on drums. Five months later the Sex Pistol's bass player Glen Matlock was fired and replaced by Vicious.

Other punk bands appearing over the two days included The Clash, with original drummer Terry Chimes (aka Tory Crimes), The Damned and The Buzzcocks.

1983 Landmark Concert Clapton, Page and Beck together

The first of two epic charity concerts was staged at London's Royal Albert Hall. This opening night was in support of Ronnie Lane and ARMS (Action Research into Multiple Sclerosis). The following night's performance was for Prince Charles's charity, the Princes Trust.

The concerts were famous for being the first time that all three of the Yardbirds' guitarists, Eric Clapton, Jeff Beck and Jimmy Page (but not original guitarist Top Topham) appeared on stage together. Each guitarist performed an individual set, along with a set from Steve Winwood, before coming together for a guitar jousting performance of *Tulsa Time, Wee Wee Baby* and *Layla*. Ronnie Lane took the lead vocals to close the evening with *Bomber's Moon* and *Goodnight Irene*. The audience was treated to some of rock's finest that night, with musicians including drummers Charlie Watts and Kenny Jones, bassist Bill Wyman and guitarist Andy Fairweather-Low.

The success of the London concerts inspired the troupe to take the show on a short American tour. The three ex-Yardbirds made the trip but Steve Winwood was unable to accompany them. The tour may have been without Winwood but it did include Paul Rodgers and Joe Cocker.

Single released today

1957 Buddy Holly *Peggy Sue c/w Everyday* (US)

This was the first of the Buddy Holly and the Crickets' singles to be credited to "Buddy Holly" and released on Coral.

As a result of the two contracts, one for the Crickets and one for Buddy Holly (with Holly's signed on 16 May*), the American recordings by Buddy Holly and the Crickets were either credited to "Buddy Holly" and released on Coral or "The Crickets" and released on Brunswick.

Peggy Sue Gerron was Crickets' drummer Jerry Allison's girlfriend. The song was written by Allison and Holly. Holly's original name for the song was *Cindy Lou* but Allison persuaded him to change it to *Peggy Sue* in order to help him to impress his girlfriend. It worked. They were married, but, sadly, it ended in divorce.

Album released today

1974 Splinter *The Place I Love* (UK)

George Harrison was the only Beatle to create his own record label. Splinter's *The Place I Love* was the first album released on his newly formed Dark Horse Records.

Events today

21

1967 Tomorrow debut of the *John Peel Sessions*

John Peel had recently joined BBC Radio from the world of pirate radio. The first of his *John Peel Sessions* featured the British psychedelic band Tomorrow.

In the mid-1960s rock and pop music was mostly heard on pirate radio stations. Peel presented shows on the pirate station Radio London, before joining the BBC just before it launched its own pop music station Radio 1. Throughout his career with Radio 1 Peel continued to push new bands and his *Sessions* programme was often used to showcase new talent. The *John Peel Sessions* ran until his death in 2004.

Tomorrow performed a number of songs, including their recently released single *My White Bicycle*. The lineup had previously been known as the "In Crowd" and consisted of singer Keith West, guitarist Steve Howe, bassist John "Junior" Wood and drummer Twink. They changed their name to "Tomorrow" at the end of 1965 and became one of Britain's premier psychedelic bands. Steve Howe went on to join prog-rockers Yes. Twink hooked up with the Pretty Things in time to appear on their 1968 concept album *SF Sorrow*, before leaving in 1969 to become a founding member of the Pink Fairies.

1971 Landmark TV *Old Grey Whistle Test* debut

The *Old Grey Whistle Test* made its first appearance on the minority BBC 2 channel in a late-evening, mid-week slot, a fair indication that it was not aimed at the commercial, chart dominated end of the viewing public. This first show was hosted by Richard Williams and featured performances from the band America and the British singer-songwriter Lesley Duncan.

The show presented a thoughtful approach to rock, with a focus on album material and live performances from artists at the heavier end of the rock spectrum. "Whispering" Bob Harris was the show's presenter from 1972 to '78, during which time the music transitioned from progressive rock to punk. The programme's name came from an old Tin Pan Alley idea that, if a number of songs were played to the "old greys", doormen in grey suits, the likely hits were the ones that they could whistle after hearing just once or twice. Those songs had passed the "old grey whistle test".

The final episode was screened on 31 December 1987, by then the name had been shortened to the *Whistle Test*.

1972 Jefferson Airplane final concert performances

Formed in San Francisco in 1965, seminal psychedelic-rock band Jefferson Airplane gave its final performances with the first of two nights at San Francisco's Winterland.

Since their debut at the Matrix club on 13 August* 1965, the band had evolved to this final lineup of: guitarists and founding members Jorma Kaukonen and Paul Kantner; bassist Jack Casady, who joined a couple of months after the band's debut gig; and vocalist Grace Slick, who replaced original singer Signe Toly Anderson in 1966. Along the way they were joined by ex-Turtles drummer John Barbata, ex-Quicksilver Messenger Service bassist and vocalist David Freiberg, and violinist Papa John Creach.

The performance was captured on the live album *Thirty Seconds over Winterland.*

Birthday today

1934 Leonard Cohen Canadian poet and singer-songwriter

Events today

1954 Music Milestones first rock'n'roll record

When Elvis chose *Good Rockin' Tonight* as his second Sun single (see below), the King of Rock'n'Roll had chosen to cover one of the songs that was a strong contender for the title, "first rock'n'roll record". Elvis's version was strongly influenced by Wynonie Harris's very successful R&B hit in 1948.

Other songs that are often cited for the accolade include Fats Domino's *The Fat Man* 1950, the Dominoes' *Sixty Minute Man* 1951 and the Crows' *Gee* 1953. But *Rocket 88*, by Jackie Brenston and His Delta Cats, recorded on 5 March* 1951, is the song most often cited as the first rock'n'roll record.

Rock'n'Roll burst onto the scene when *Rock Around the Clock*, recorded by Bill Haley and His Comets on 12 April* 1954, was used behind the opening credits of the 1955 movie *Blackboard Jungle.*

1972 David Bowie first concert appearance in America

David Bowie finally made his American concert debut, at Cleveland's Music Hall in Ohio. The concert was part of the *Ziggy Stardust and the Spiders from Mars* tour, featuring guitarist Mick Ronson.

This had not been an overnight success for Bowie. His first recording, *Liza Jane* as "Davie Jones and the King Bees", was made way back in 1964.

Single released today

1954 Elvis Presley *Good Rockin' Tonight c/w I Don't Care if the Sun Don't Shine* (Sun-2)

Good Rockin' Tonight was written by Roy Brown and originally released by him in the autumn of 1947. This failed to make an impact but the cover by Wynonie Harris entered the R&B charts in the summer of 1948 and remained there until the end of the year. Elvis chose this song as the A-side for his second release on Sun Records.

The B-side, *I Don't Care if the Sun Don't Shine*, was another cover and had been a hit for Patti Page in 1950.

Birthdays today

1942 Mike Patto singer: Bo Street Runners, Timebox, Patto

After performing with a number of other bands, Mike Patto joined the respected R&B combo the Bo Street Runners as lead vocalist in mid-1965. The band was also famous for being one of drummer Mick Fleetwood's early ventures. Following the Runners, Patto played with a number of other bands before joining Timebox in the summer of 1967. At the turn of the decade the band changed its name to Patto and played a heavier sounding rock. In 1974 he replaced Gary Wright in the ailing Spooky Tooth. They disbanded shortly afterwards but Patto continued ever onwards, until his untimely death in 1979.

1951 David Coverdale singer: Deep Purple, Whitesnake; solo

Vocalist David Coverdale replaced Ian Gillan in a well-established Deep Purple in 1973. He made his album debut on *Burn*. When Deep Purple split up in the spring of 1976 he opted not to join another band. Instead, he released his first solo album *Whitesnake* in early 1977. His next step was to form another band, taking the name Whitesnake from his recent solo album. The group released their first album *Snakebite*, as David Coverdale and Whitesnake in the early summer of 1978.

Event today

1987 Lynyrd Skynyrd the second era

Lynyrd Skynyrd opened its first tour in a decade in Concord, California.

The Lynyrd Skynyrd band arose phoenix-like from the ashes of the plane crash on 20 October* 1977 which took the lives of three of the band and seriously injured others. In the intervening period the surviving members had undertaken various individual projects. The collaboration between the two guitarists in the Rossington Collins Band in the early 1980s also included two other Lynyrd Skynyrd members, Leon Wilkeson and Billy Powell. In 1987 the band regrouped for what was intended to be a single concert but became a tour to celebrate the passing of the original band. The lineup included crash survivors keyboardist Billy Powell, drummer Artimus Pyle, guitarist Gary Rossington and bassist Leon Wilkeson. They were joined by guitarist Ed King, who had left the band before the crash. Other musicians who had not been a part of the original band included fiddle player and vocalist Charlie Daniels. Original lead singer Ronnie Van Zant had died in the plane crash and his boots were filled by his younger brother Johnny Van Zant. The tour was captured on the live album *Southern By the Grace of God*.

Original guitarist Allen Collins survived the plane crash but an automobile accident in 1986 had confined him to a wheelchair. As a result of the car crash he was convicted of DUI (driving under the influence) manslaughter. Collins accompanied the tour as musical director and made a stage appearance every night to warn the audience of the perils of drinking and driving.

The band decided to continue on after the tour ended. Judy Van Zant and Teresa Gains, the widows of Ronnie van Zant and Steve Gains who had perished in the plane crash, filed a lawsuit because the surviving members of the band had pledged not to exploit the band's name. The lawsuit was settled and Lynyrd Skynyrd was back.

Recording session today

1953 The Spaniels *Goodnite Sweetheart Goodnite*

On 5 May* the Spaniels recorded *Baby It's You* and the record label Vee-Jay was born.

They were back in the recording studio to cut *Goodnite Sweetheart Goodnite*, *The Bells Ring Out* and *House Cleaning*. The latter two recordings were coupled as the Spaniels' second single but it was the release of *Goodnite Sweetheart Goodnite* as the group's third single that delivered one of the all-time classic doo wop songs.

Birthdays today

1930 Ray Charles singer, pianist: combined gospel, blues and country music

1940 Mike Sheridan singer: MS and the Nightriders, Mike Sheridan's Lot

Mike Sheridan was one of the pioneers of 1960s beat music in Birmingham. Mike Sheridan and the Nightriders went on to become Mike Sheridan's Lot. One of the later lineups boasted Roy Wood, who went on to form the Move, Electric Light Orchestra and Wizzard. After Wood left, Sheridan became disenchanted with the band and also moved on. Shortly afterwards he recruited a new lineup for Mike Sheridan's New Lot. In the meantime, his old band performed as the Nightriders, recruited Jeff Lyne and morphed into the highly respected Idle Race.

1949 Bruce Springsteen guitarist, singer, songwriter: Castiles, E Street Band; solo

Events today

1969 Deep Purple embraced a full orchestra

Deep Purple continued to develop the prog rock genre when they recorded their performance of *Concerto for Group and Orchestra* at London's Royal Albert Hall. The rock band was accompanied that night by the Royal Philharmonic Orchestra, conducted by Malcolm Arnold. The piece, in three movements, was composed by Deep Purple's keyboard player Jon Lord with lyrics by singer Ian Gillan.

This was the first Deep Purple album to feature Gillan and bassist Roger Glover, who had replaced Rod Evans and Nick Simper respectively. Gillan and Glover joined Deep Purple shortly after a performance with their previous band Episode Six, on 4 June*. This marked the beginning of the classic Deep Purple lineup.

Procol Harum had already laid the foundations for this genre three months earlier, when they performed with the Stratford Festival Orchestra in Canada on 6 July*.

1969 Fairport Convention dawn of British folk rock

This landmark concert by Fairport Convention at London's Royal Festival Hall was to premiere their fourth album, *Liege & Lief*, planned for released in December.

Tragedy had struck the band four months earlier, when drummer Martin Lamble was killed in a road accident returning home from a gig in Birmingham. With new drummer Dave Mattacks they recorded *Liege & Lief*, advertised at the time as the first British folk-rock album. Support that night came from Nick Drake, and John and Beverley Martyn.

Singer Sandy Denny left to form Fotheringay shortly after the album was released.

Recording session today

1956 Tommy Steele and the Steelmen *Rock with the Caveman*

Tommy Steele made his first visit to the recording studio, to record *Rock with the Caveman*. At that time the British charts were dominated by American acts, with the occasional oasis of British skiffle from Lonnie Donegan. *Rock with the Caveman* was the first British rock'n'roll hit single. It was written by the songwriting team Tommy Steele, Lionel Bart and Mike Pratt, who wrote much of Steele's material.

The trio had previously played in skiffle bars as the Cavemen. This changed when singer Tommy Hicks was signed up by Larry Parnes, who changed his name to "Tommy Steele". The song was recorded by the three Cavemen as "Tommy Steele and the Steelmen", with additional session musicians that included jazz saxophonist and club owner Ronnie Scott.

Birthdays today

1938 Steve Douglas saxophone: Wrecking Crew; session work

Steve Douglas was one of rock'n'roll's most accomplished session saxophonists. As a part of the Wrecking Crew, Phil Spector's regular group of session musicians, he played on many of the "wall of sound" hits and provided the sax solo on the Crystal's *He's a Rebel*. He also featured on the Beach Boys' classic *Pet Sounds* album.

1942 Gerry Marsden vocals and guitar: Gerry and the Pacemakers; solo

Gerry and the Pacemakers was the first British act to have their first three singles enter the charts at #1. The run started when their debut single *How Do You Do It* hit the top spot on 14 March* 1963. It was followed by *I Like It* and *You'll Never Walk Alone*. Their debut single was also the first British #1 by a beat group.

Events today

1957 Civil Rights Movement *Little Rock Nine* attended school

On 7 May* 1954 the United States Supreme Court ruled that racial segregation in schools was unconstitutional. In order to comply with this, the Little Rock Central High School board adopted a policy for gradual integration – starting in September 1957.

With enrolment due to begin on 3 September, Governor Orval Faubus ordered the National Guard to be at the school. When nine black students arrived to enrol the following day they were turned away by the National Guard, at the direction of Governor Faubus. Legal wrangling followed and the National Guard was withdrawn. The students eventually managed to enrol but when they entered the school on 23 September they encountered a violent reception, with only a handful of police officers to guard their safety. On 24 September President Eisenhower intervened and ordered that regular troops be deployed to protect the students.

The nine black students finally attended school on 25 September, defended by paratroopers of the elite 101st Airborne Division – with bayonets fixed.

1969 Alexis Korner's New Church almost Brian Jones's next step

Alexis Korner was midway through a week of recording sessions for the studio portion of his new album, *Both Sides*. As well as his new collaborator Peter Thorup, the musicians for the studio tracks included Free's singer Paul Rodgers and bassist Andy Fraser.

When Brian Jones was sacked from the Rolling Stones on 8 June*, he was keen to join Alexis Korner's latest venture, New Church. He wanted to get back on the road and join them on their planned trip to Germany. Jones knew Korner from way back. He had played with Alexis Korner's Blues Incorporated before forming the original Rollin' Stones. Sadly, the full circle back to his old mentor was not to be. Korner suggested to Jones that he should put his own band together. That never materialised. On 3 July*, before Jones had time to start work on his new project, he was found dead in the swimming pool of his Sussex home.

In another twist of rock'n'roll fate, Alexis Korner's New Church made their debut at the free Hyde Park concert headlined by the Rolling Stones on 5 July*, just two days after Jones's death.

Died today

1980 John Bonham Led Zeppelin's drummer, died at the age of thirty-two

John Bonham died following a heavy drinking session. He had returned to guitarist Jimmy Page's home in Windsor and was found dead in bed the following morning. He had died due to the inhalation of vomit during his sleep.

At the time Led Zeppelin were busy rehearsing for their forthcoming North American tour. A press release had already been issued just two week earlier with the proposed itinerary of dates and tour venues. This would have been the band's first visit to the continent since their ill-fated 1977 tour. That previous tour had kicked off in Dallas, Texas on 1 April* but had been cut short after the concert at Oakland, California on 24 July*. Robert Plant had to return unexpectedly to the UK after his son Karac was taken ill and died. This proved to be the last time that Led Zeppelin performed for an American audience.

Event today

1959 Music Milestones Liverpool music scene before the Beatles

Ringo Starr was on stage with Rory Storm and the Hurricanes at Seaforth's Lathom Hall. The band started out as the Raving Texans in early 1957. Ringo joined in 1959 after spells in the Darktown Skiffle Group and the Eddie Clayton Skiffle Group.

Liverpool had a thriving music scene long before the Beatles released *Love Me Do* on 5 October* 1962. Bob Evans and the Five Shillings were one of the first rock groups on Merseyside. They morphed into the Undertakers, famed for making their stage entrance carrying a coffin. Brian Casser formed Cass and the Cassanovas in mid-1959, until a parting of the ways came at the end of 1960. Casser headed south to London, the remaining band changed their name to "The Big Three" and became one of the most popular live acts in Liverpool. The first Liverpool group to release an album was Howie Casey and the Seniors, with *Twist at the Top* in early 1962.

Album released today

1969 The Beatles *Abbey Road* (UK)

Produced once again by George Martin, this was the Beatles' final album from a recording perspective. *Let It Be* was the last Beatles album to be released. *Get Back*, produced by Glyn Johns, was the intended follow-up to the *White Album* but it failed to materialise until producer Phil Spector reworked the recordings into *Let It Be*.

Abbey Road included two of George Harrison's best known Beatles-era songs, *Here Comes the Sun* and *Something*, the latter being released as Harrison's only Beatles A-side. The Ringo Starr penned song *Octopus's Garden* was his second and final composition to grace a Beatles record.

Births and deaths today

1934 Dick Heckstall-Smith saxophone: John Mayall, Colosseum

Dick Heckstall-Smith was a pioneering figure in the early 1960s British blues boom, playing in all three of the iconic British blues bands of the time: Alexis Korner's Blues Incorporated, Graham Bond Organisation and John Mayall's Bluesbreakers. In 1968 he parted with Mayall to join drummer Jon Hiseman and form prog-jazz-rockers Colosseum.

1945 Bryan Ferry singer: The Gas Board, Roxy Music; solo

1937 Bessie Smith blues singer, died at the age of forty-three

Blues singing legend Bessie Smith died after her car crashed into the back of a truck. When the crash occurred near Clarksdale, Mississippi, Smith's boyfriend, Richard Morgan, was at the wheel and was chauffeuring her to a gig near Memphis.

Urban legend had it that she was refused admission to a white hospital and died from blood loss by the time that the ambulance had reached a black hospital. This account was immortalised in Edward Lee's play *The Death of Bessie Smith*, premiered in West Berlin in 1960. These early accounts of racial discrimination have since been disputed.

Smith was buried in an unmarked grave in Mount Lawn Cemetery, Philadelphia. In 1970 rock singer Janis Joplin, who hailed Bessie Smith as one of her greatest inspirations, part-funded a headstone to mark the last resting place of one of the greatest female singers of all time. The inscription read, "The Greatest Blues Singer In The World Will Never Stop Singing".

Events today

1968 Landmark Theatre *Hair* ...marked the end of UK theatre censorship

When the hippie musical *Hair* opened at the Shaftsbury Theatre in London's West End it marked the end of formal censorship in British live theatre. The day before *Hair* opened, the Lord Chancellor's role as theatre censor was abolished. That role had been a part of the British way of life since 1737.

Hair originally opened in New York in an off-Broadway production on 17 October* 1967. When it came to London, this was the first theatre production in Britain to contain full-frontal nudity.

1969 Black Sabbath from the Polka Tulk Blues Band

In order to avoid confusion with another band called "Earth", the Midlands group changed their name to "Black Sabbath". The band played its first gig as "Black Sabbath" in Scotland at the Drill Hall in Dumfries.

In 1968 bass player Terry "Geezer" Butler, guitarist Tony Iommi, vocalist Ozzy Osbourne and drummer Bill Ward hooked up with a slide guitarist and keyboard player and formed the six-piece Polka Tulk Blues Band. The group went through some name changes, dropped the slide guitarist and keyboards player and became the quartet Earth. In late 1968 Iommi left Earth to join Jethro Tull. His stay there was very brief but was just long enough to include Tull's appearance on the Rolling Stones' TV special *Rock and Roll Circus*, recorded on 11 December* 1968.

The pioneers of heavy metal rock took their inspiration for the new name from the title of a 1963 Boris Karloff movie.

Recording session today

1968 Led Zeppelin first recording session

Three weeks after playing their first gig together, on 7 September*, Led Zeppelin entered Olympic Studios in London to record material for their debut album. Glyn Johns performed the engineering duties.

Very few bands morph from one Rock and Roll Hall of Fame inductee into another but the Yardbirds, through the New Yardbirds to Led Zeppelin managed just that. After the other members of the Yardbirds moved on, guitarist Jimmy Page and their final manager Peter Grant recruited singer Robert Plant, drummer John Bonham and bassist John Paul Jones to create Led Zeppelin. They were still contracted for a "Yardbirds" tour of Scandinavia and when they returned to Britain they transitioned through a number of gigs from the "Yardbirds" to "Led Zeppelin". Promoters often felt the need to explain the band's pedigree on the posters, with billing such as "New Yardbirds featuring Jimmy Page"[5] and "Yardbirds now known as Led Zeppelin".[10]

When they entered Olympic Studios the group was without a recording contract. Ahmet Ertegun signed them to Atlantic Records two months later, with an advance reputed to be in the region of $200,000. A fee considered to be colossal at that time. Initially work was scarce in Britain, inspiring the new band to head across the pond shortly after Christmas to see if they could build a reputation in America. They succeeded.

Birthdays today

1943	Randy Bachman	guitar and vocals: Guess Who, Bachman-Turner Overdrive
1947	Meat Loaf	singer: Meat Loaf Soul, Popcorn Blizzard; solo

Album released today

2004 Brian Wilson *Smile* (US)

Originally planned by Brian Wilson as the follow-up album to his 1966 masterpiece *Pet Sounds*, it would be another thirty-eight years before *Smile* was released. Written in collaboration with Van Dyke Parks, it became the most famous 'lost' album of the 1960s.

Brian Wilson had abandoned the *Smile* project on 2 May* 1967.

Births and deaths today

1901 Ed Sullivan presenter of the *Ed Sullivan Show*

Ed Sullivan's long running TV show was one of the most influential non-music TV shows in America. Some of rock'n'roll's most memorable TV appearances have been hosted by Sullivan. On 9 September* 1956 Elvis Presley attracted an audience of 60 million viewers with his first appearance on the show. Eight years later, on 9 February* 1964, the Beatles' first appearance was seen by 73 million people and signalled the beginning of the domination of American music by the British Invasion. The show also tried to censor rock'n'roll, sometimes succeeding, sometimes not. On 12 May* 1963 Bob Dylan was prevented from performing *Talkin' John Birch Paranoid Blues*. He declined to appear on the show. For their appearance on 15 January* 1967, the Rolling Stones complied with the producers' wishes to modify the words of their hit song from spending "the night" to "some time" together. Doors' frontman Jim Morrison was less accommodating later that year when, on 17 September*, he was asked to modify the lyrics to *Light My Fire*.

1923 Tuli Kupferberg poet, writer and performer: The Fugs

A pillar of the counterculture, Tuli Kupferberg was a founding member of the irreverent band, the Fugs. He was immortalized as the man who jumped off Brooklyn Bridge in Allen Ginsberg's classic beat poem *Howl*. Kupferberg did actually make a suicide attempt but it was Manhattan Bridge that he jumped off. The incident was mentioned in the prose poem *Memorial Day* by Ted Berrigan and Anne Waldman, published in 1971.

1938 Ben E King singer: Five Crowns, The Drifters; solo

Ben E King became the Drifters' lead singer when their manager, George Treadwell, sacked the entire group on 30 May* 1958. He replaced them with King's group, the Crowns. Since Treadwell owned the rights to the group's name, he simply rebranded the Crowns as "The Drifters".

Some members of the previous Drifters came together and toured as the "Original Drifters", causing legal wrangling for decades to come.

1972 Rory Storm Liverpool singer, died at the age of thirty-three

Rory Storm, born Alan Caldwell, had developed a chest infection and was taking sleeping tablets to help him rest. On the morning of 28 September, Storm and his mother were both found dead in their home. There was speculation of a joint suicide but a post mortem showed that he had not taken enough tablets to kill himself.

Rory Storm and the Hurricanes are mostly remembered as the group Ringo Starr left to join the Beatles. Ringo was not the only famous drummer to keep the beat for the Hurricanes: in mid-1963 Keef Hartley joined their ranks. Following his stint with the Hurricanes Hartley later went on to play with the Artwoods and John Mayall's Bluesbreakers.

Events today

1967 Landmark Venues last gig at the UFO club

London's first psychedelic venue, the UFO, hosted its final gig with performances from Jeff Beck and Ten Years After.

The UFO club was founded by Joe Boyd and John "Hoppy" Hopkins. It opened its doors for the first time on 23 December 1966 at the old Blarney Club, in the basement of 31 Tottenham Court Road. Pink Floyd performed that night and became the club's first house band. Sadly things didn't go too well, Hopkins was jailed in June for possession of marijuana and the UFO became a victim of its own success. In August they moved into larger premises at the Roundhouse in Chalk Farm Road. The move proved to be very expensive and the club closed after being open for less than a year.

1976 Jerry Lee Lewis accidentally shot his bass player

Jerry Lee Lewis nearly lived up to his nickname "The Killer", when he accidentally shot his bass player, Norman Owens, in the chest during his 41st birthday celebration.

Owens survived the shooting and sued his boss.

Single released today

1969 G.T.O.'s *Circular Circulation c/w Mercy's Tune* (US)

The notorious G.T.O.'s (Girls Together Outrageously) released their only single, produced by Lowell George and released on Frank Zappa's Straight record label.

The song can also be found on the G.T.O.'s' album *Permanent Damage*, produced by Frank Zappa and also released on Strait. The album featured a host of rock luminaries, including Mothers of Invention musicians, bassist Roy Estrada, drummer Jimmy Carl Black, keyboardist Ian Underwood and synthesizer player Don Preston; plus keyboardist Nicky Hopkins and two international superstars, guitarist Jeff Beck and singer Rod Stewart.

The G.T.O.'s was a collection of groupies who originally called themselves "The Cherry Sisters" before becoming "The Laurel Canyon Ballet Company". They were a performance art troupe who often opened shows for the Mothers of Invention. Zappa suggested that they should call themselves the G.T.O.'s. The most famous member of the group was Pamela Des Barres.

Album released today

1972 Pete Townshend *Who Came First* (UK)

The Who's guitarist Pete Townshend released his first solo album *Who Came First* and dedicated it to Indian Avatar Meher Baba.

Before releasing his debut solo album, Pete Townshend contributed to two other Meher Baba albums, *Happy Birthday* in 1970 and *I Am* in 1972. Both albums were pressed in small quantities and only available via mail order from Meher Baba organisations. The second Baba album, *I Am*, contained Townshend's demo version of *Baba O'Riley*. A third Meher Baba album, *With Love*, was released in 1976.

Ronnie Lane, Small Faces and Faces bassist and Meher Baba follower, contributed to Pete Townshend's *Who Came First* and the Meher Baba compilation *Happy Birthday*.

Birthdays today

1935 Jerry Lee Lewis vocals and piano: seminal rock'n'roll wild man

1948 Mark Farner guitar, vocals: The Pack; manager: Grand Funk Railroad

Event today

30

1967 Landmark Radio official pop-music radio finally reached the UK

BBC's Radio 1 arrived. Britain's first legal radio station dedicated to pop and rock music opened with DJ Tony Blackburn introducing the Move's *Flowers in the Rain*.

The BBC had a monopoly on radio broadcasting in the UK. Before Radio 1, pop music fans only had a handful of opportunities to hear their favourite songs. The BBC's Light Programme offered up a meagre serving of pop music shows, such as *Saturday Club* and *Pick of the Pops*. Radio Luxembourg began transmitting from mainland Europe, on frequency 208, long before rock'n'roll was even a glint in a record executive's eye. As the 1950s rolled into the '60s, the scant offerings on the Light Programme and the poor reception on Radio Luxembourg were the only ways to hear the latest pop songs. Many a teenager would lie in bed at night with a torch and a small transistor radio, straining to hear the latest sounds as the signal from 208 famously faded in and out.

Things looked up on 29 March* 1964, when the first pirate radio station, Radio Caroline, took to the airways playing non-stop rock and pop music. Other pirate radio stations soon followed. It took the British government three and a half years to determine that there was a demand for pop music. The result was to abolish the three existing BBC networks. The Light Programme was replaced by Radio 1 and Radio 2. The classical music based Third Network became Radio 3 and the Home Service's diet of current affairs and drama was satisfied by Radio 4.

Recording session today

1961 Bob Dylan first studio recording session

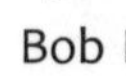

Bob Dylan made his first-ever visit to a recording studio, to provide harmonica on Carolyn Hester's first eponymous album on Columbia, released in 1962. Dylan provided harmonica for three tracks: *I'll Fly Away*, *Swing and Turn Jubilee*, and *Come Back Baby*. The session was produced by John Hammond.

Hammond was so impressed with Dylan that he signed him to Columbia shortly afterwards. The sales for Dylan's own eponymous debut album were very disappointing. Hammond's colleagues at the label were less than impressed by the new signee and Dylan became known as "Hammond's Folly".

Births and deaths today

1942 Frankie Lymon singer: Frankie Lymon and the Teenagers; solo

By the summer of 1956 Frankie Lymon and the Teenagers' *Why Do Fools Fall in Love* was a smash hit on both sides of the Atlantic. Lymon became the first black teenage idol.

1947 Marc Bolan guitar, singer, songwriter: John's Children, T.Rex

1955 James Dean iconic actor and the 'first' teenager, died aged twenty-four

Filming had just finished on James Dean's third movie *Giant*, when Dean and his mechanic, Rolf Wütherich, set off to drive to a race meeting in Salinas, California. At the junction of Highways 41 and 46 Dean's silver Porsche Spyder collided with a 1950 Ford Tudor, driven by Donald Turnupseed. The scene of the fatal accident has now been renamed as the "James Dean Memorial Junction".

James Dean only acted in three movies: *East of Eden*, *Rebel Without a Cause* and *Giant*. *Rebel* opened on 27 October*, a month after Dean's death.

October

Events today

1

1958 Billy Fury — impromptu appearance at a Marty Wilde concert

Billy Fury's career took off the night he made an impromptu appearance in the second half of Larry Parnes's *Extravaganza* show at Birkenhead's Essoldo Theatre. Marty Wilde was headlining, with support that included Vince Eager and The John Barry Seven.

Ronald Wycherley, still to become Billy Fury, had previously sent a demo recording to Larry Parnes, one of the most successful rock'n'roll managers in Britain with a stable of artists that included Marty Wilde, Tommy Steele and Joe Brown. Wycherley was invited to see Marty Wilde at the Essoldo. When Fury met them both backstage in the interval he was hoping to interest Wilde in recording one of his songs. To his surprise, he found himself on stage in the second half of the show, performing *Margo Don't Knock Upon My Door* and *Maybe Tomorrow*. Parnes signed him up and he appeared in the *Extravaganza* show the following night.

1961 The Beatles — iconic Beatle hairstyle arrived

To celebrate his upcoming 21st birthday, John Lennon set off with Paul McCartney on a hitchhiking holiday to Spain. They only made it as far as Paris, where they met their old Hamburg friend Jürgen Vollmer who had moved there to continue his photography studies. Vollmer wore his hair in the brushed forward Exi style and both Lennon and McCartney persuaded him to cut their hair the same way.

The Beatles' first trip to Hamburg opened on 17 August* 1960 and ended in disarray when George, Paul and Pete Best were deported. During this time bass player Stuart Sutcliffe met professional photographer Astrid Kirchherr. Sutcliffe's new girlfriend introduced the Beatles to her arty friends known as "The Exis", a name derived from their existentialist leanings. This circle of friends included Kirchherr's current boyfriend Klaus Voormann and fellow photographer Jürgen Vollmer. The Exis typically wore their hair in a fringe and Kirchherr cut Sutcliffe's hair in this style.

1966 Jimi Hendrix — jammed with Cream

Cream were playing at the Central London Polytechnic, supported by The Washington DC's. After an introduction to Eric Clapton from Hendrix's manager Chas Chandler, Jimi Hendrix joined them on stage and jammed on the Howlin' Wolf classic, *Killing Floor*.

Hendrix signed a recording contract with Ed Chalpin on 15 October* 1965 and continued to record and perform with Curtis Knight and the Squires. His other activities included session work for King Curtis and live performances backing the likes of Wilson Picket. In mid-1966 he formed his own group Jimmy James and the Blue Flames, which included future Spirit founder, guitarist and singer-songwriter Randy California.

Ex-Animals bassist Chas Chandler first saw Hendrix in a performance at the Cafe Wha? in New York's Greenwich Village. Moving from bassist to artist management, he persuaded Hendrix to: move to England, form a new band and change his name from "Jimmy" to "Jimi". They arrived in London in late September.

Albums released today

1969 The Beatles *Abbey Road* (US)

1978 Black Sabbath *Never Say Die* (UK)

This was the band's eighth album and Ozzie Osbourne's final appearance as vocalist.

Event today

1954 Elvis Presley only performance at the Grand Ole Opry

Elvis Presley made his first and last appearance on the hallowed boards of the Grand Ole Opry's stage. The country audience did not take to Elvis's style and his reception was decidedly lukewarm. The Opry's manager, Jim Denny, spoke to Elvis backstage after his performance and suggested that he should "consider giving up singing and return to truck driving".[8]

In an ironic twist of fate, Elvis's first showing on the national charts was in the country listings in 1955, with his Sun release *Baby Let's Play House*. It would take his RCA debut with *Heartbreak Hotel* in March 1956 before he managed to put in an appearance on the pop charts.

Recording session today

1957 Connie Francis *Who's Sorry Now*

After a string of unsuccessful singles Connie Francis entered the MGM studios for what was intended to be the last time. Ironically, the song that changed her life was one that she had been reluctant to record. *Who's Sorry Now* was a cover of Bob Thompson's 1923 song that had featured in the 1946 Marx Brothers movie, *A Night in Casablanca*. Francis reputedly recorded *Who's Sorry Now* in a single take at the end of the session.

The song gave Francis a major hit on both sides of the Atlantic and established her as one of the first female rock'n'roll stars. The hits continued to flow until the mid-1960s.

Single released today

1970 T.Rex *Ride a White Swan c/w Is It Summer/Summertime Blues* (UK)

Marc Bolan released his first single as T.Rex, the self-penned *Ride a White Swan.*

The acoustic, psychedelic-folk duo Tyrannosaurus Rex was morphing into an electric rock band. This was their first single as the new T.Rex and was one of the early markers for British glam rock.

Urban legend has it that when Eddie Cochran was in England for what proved to be his last tour in 1960, twelve-year-old Mark Feld (later to become Marc Bolan) carried the American rocker's guitar to the car waiting for him outside the Hackney Empire. In tribute, this single included one of Cochran's most famous releases, *Summertime Blues.*

Birthdays today

1938 Nick Gravenites singer and songwriter: The Electric Flag, Big Brother

One of the leading figures in the American blues boom of the early 1960s, Nick Gravenites wrote songs for Mike Bloomfield and Janis Joplin, and also wrote the score for Roger Corman's LSD movie, *The*

Trip. Gravenites was an original member of guitarist Mike Bloomfield's band the Electric Flag. His song *Buried Alive in the Blues* on Janis Joplin's final album *Pearl* was released as an instrumental because Joplin died the night before she was due in the studio to record the vocals.

1950 Mike Rutherford bass: founding member of Genesis; solo

1951 Sting singer, bassist and songwriter: Last Exit, Police; solo

The nickname "Sting" came about after he sported a bee-like black and yellow striped sweater during his early days with the Phoenix Jazzmen.

Event today

3

1957 Pat Boone first episode of his TV show

Just two and a half years after his first chart appearance Pat Boone was hosting his own ABC TV show, *The Pat Boone Chevy Showroom.*

Pat Boone was one of the clean-cut faces of 1950s rock'n'roll. Like Canadian vocal group the Crew Cuts, Boone initially built his fame with sanitised covers of R&B songs originally performed by black artists. His first American chart appearance came in early 1955 with a cover of the Charms' *Two Hearts.* He followed that with his version of Fats Domino's *Ain't It a Shame*, released as *Ain't That a Shame.* Other covers included: the Five Keys' *Gee Whittakers*, the Flamingo's *I'll Be Home*, two Little Richard songs *Tutti-Frutti* and *Long Tall Sally*, Big Joe Turner's *Chains of Love* and Lucky Millinder's *I'm Waiting Just for You.* All were hits prior to his TV show having its first airing.

Recording sessions today

1961 The Beach Boys *Surfin*

The Beach Boys first-ever recording session produced their first single *Surfin.* It brought them chart success and despite being released on a small record label, it still managed to reach the lower regions of the national charts.

This single has a very interesting release history. It had three separate releases, X Records 301, Candix 331 and Candix 301. The most valuable issue from a collector's point of view (at the time of writing) is the X Records release but the jury is still out as to whether this or Candix 331 was the first release. The jury is also still pondering on the question of the often reported date of 8 December as the actual release date of *Surfin.* Some Beach Boys chroniclers believe that this may well refer to another event associated with the song, such as the date when it was premiered on Los Angeles' Radio KFWB's *Battle of the Bands.*

This also marked the name change from "The Pendletones" to "The Beach Boys".

1970 Janis Joplin final recording session for *Pearl*

The album *Pearl* was nearing completion when Janis Joplin accidentally overdosed on heroin. The final day was spent on the instrumental backing for the Nick Gravenites penned song *Buried Alive in the Blues.* The album was released posthumously and the aptly titled track remained as an instrumental.

Pearl included a cover of Garnet Mimms' 1963 hit *Cry Baby*, written and produced by Bert Berns and Jerry Ragovoy, under the pseudonyms "B Russell" and "N Meade".

Birthdays today

1938 Eddie Cochran singer, songwriter, guitarist: seminal rock'n'roll hero

1941 Chubby Checker king of the twist dance craze

Ernest Evans worked at a produce market and used to entertain customers with his impressions of popular singers. Market owner Henry Colt heard the young man singing and introduced him to TV host Dick Clark. Evans made a private recording for Clark that he used as a Christmas card and this led to a recording contract with Cameo Parkway.

His stage name came about when Dick Clark's wife, Bobbie, suggested the name "Checker" to go with his existing nickname "Chubby". This new moniker was a tip of the cap to his hero Fats Domino.

Checker released *The Twist* on 1 August* 1960 and the dance craze was born.

Event today

1963 Rod Stewart/Jimmy Powell the early days

Rod Stewart appeared at London's Studio 51 with his first professional group Jimmy Powell and the Five Dimensions.

Rod Stewart's career started with a spot of busking around the bars of Spain and Italy, with his banjo and friend Wizz Jones. The sojourn ended when he was deported from Spain for vagrancy. The Dimensions formed in London in 1962, Stewart joined in 1963 as harmonica player and singer. Shortly afterwards, the group teamed up with singer Jimmy Powell and became Jimmy Powell and the Five Dimensions. By early 1964 Stewart had parted company with the group, taking a couple of the members with him. Stewart's next major career step was to join Long John Baldry's Hoochie Coochie Men.

Before teaming up with the Dimensions, Jimmy Powell had fronted an early lineup of the Rockin' Berries and had also released three solo singles. His first, *Sugar Babe* released in March 1962, is generally considered to be the first Brum Beat single.

Recording sessions today

1957 John Barry and the Seven *Zip Zip*

John Barry was one of the pioneers of British rock'n'roll. This recording of *Zip Zip* was coupled with *Three Little Fishes* and released as his debut single.

Barry had a number of hits in his own right, including UK TV's *Juke Box Jury* theme *Hit & Miss*, *Beat for Beatniks*, and his cover of the Ventures' *Walk Don't Run*. With his band the John Barry Seven, he toured with the likes of Tommy Steele and Adam Faith. He also worked as an arranger and wrote movie scores, including *Beat Girl* in 1959 and soundtracks to such classics as *Zulu* and *Born Free*. He became synonymous with the music for James Bond movies. He wrote the soundtrack music for the first Bond movie *Dr No* and went on to provide the music for eleven Bond movies in all. Guitarist Vic Flick worked with Barry on eight of the early James Bond movies and was responsible for the immortal *James Bond Theme*. He also provided the memorable riff on *Hit and Miss*.

1973 Pink Floyd 'lost' album ...*Household Objects*

Following the worldwide success of *Dark Side of the Moon*, Pink Floyd spent time in the studio between the beginning of October and early December to record their planned follow-up album,

Household Objects. One of those sessions was on 4 October. Even by Floyd standards this was a highly experimental project with, literally, household objects taking the place of traditional instruments. The sounds were recorded from an array of everyday items including mixers, elastic bands, wine glasses, bottles and aerosol cans.

The project was abandoned in early December in favour of *Wish You Were Here*. There was a slight link from the *Objects* sessions, some of the *Wine Glasses* sounds were featured on the track *Shine on You Crazy Diamond*.

Died today

1970 Janis Joplin iconic rock'n'roll singer, died at the age of twenty-seven

Janis Joplin was nearing the end of the recording sessions for her album *Pearl*. Alarmed by the fact that she had not turned up at the studio for the day's recording, road manager John Cook went to Joplin's hotel where he found her dead in her room at the Landmark Hotel, Hollywood, California. The Certificate of Death gave the cause of death as "Acute heroin-morphine intoxication. Injection of overdose".[51]

Joplin died at the age of twenty-seven, qualifying her for the macabre *27 Club* and putting her in good company with the likes of Jimi Hendrix, Brian Jones and Jim Morrison.

Event today

5

1958 Cliff Richard and the Drifters debut with Marvin and Welch

American singing stars the Kalin Twins opened their UK package tour at Hanley's Victoria Hall in Stoke-on-Trent.

One of the support acts that night was Cliff Richard and the Drifters, with debut performances from their new guitarists Hank Marvin and Bruce Welch. The other band members, drummer Terry Smart and Ian Samwell, were veterans from the Drifters' first single *Move It!* Samwell had moved to bass guitar but left at the end of this tour.

Bassist Jet Harris was also on the tour, as the bass player behind the Most Brothers. During the tour he sometimes stood in as one of Cliff's Drifters. He made his debut as a full-time Drifter in Manchester on 10 January* 1959.

Like the Righteous Brothers, the Most Brothers were not siblings, they were Alex Murray and Mickie Most. Murray went on to co-manage the Moody Blues and produced their first single *Go Now!* Mickie Most also left the stage to become one of Britain's top producers, with credits including Donovan, The Animals and Jeff Beck.

Single released today

1962 The Beatles *Love Me Do c/w P.S. I Love You* (UK)

Three versions of *Love Me Do* exist, with three different drummers. Pete Best was the sticksman for the Beatles' first Abbey Road recording session on 6 June*. By the time that they returned to the studio for the second visit on 4 September*, Best had been fired and replaced by Ringo Starr. Producer George Martin was unimpressed by Starr's performance that day and for the third session on 11 September* he hired session drummer Andy White for the recording.

The easiest way to tell which version is being played is to listen out for the tambourine. If there is a tambourine, then Ringo is playing it and Andy White is on drums. Andy White plays drums on *P.S. I Love You*, accompanied by Ringo on maracas. *Love Me Do* was not released as a single in America until the Tollie version on 27 April* 1964, although it was released by Capitol in Canada on 4 February 1963.

Ironically, the initial UK release of *Love Me Do* had Ringo on drums. The Pete Best version did not see the light of day until the Beatles' *Anthology* collection thirty years later.

Album released today

1968 Muddy Waters *Electric Mud* (US)

When legendary bluesman Muddy Waters ventured into psychedelic blues with *Electric Mud* he generated one his more controversial recordings. The album sold very well but not everyone took to the new sound. The blues purists amongst his fans had much the same response to the album as the folk purists had expressed towards Dylan's infamous electric concert at the Newport Folk Festival on 25 July* 1965.

Birthdays today

1943 Steve Miller guitar and vocals: Goldberg Miller Band, Steve Miller Band

1947 Brian Johnson singer: Geordie, AC/DC

Brian Johnson found commercial success in the early-to-mid-1970s with English glam-rockers Geordie. In 1980 he replaced the recently deceased Bon Scott as AC/DC's frontman.

Events today

1958 Music Milestones British music scene in the 2nd half of the 1950s

Marty Wilde and Nancy Whiskey shared the bill at a concert in Chatham's Empire Theatre in Kent. Not a landmark concert in itself but a snapshot of the British music scene. Marty Wilde was one of the most successful British rock'n'roll stars and Nancy Whiskey, with her original partner Chas McDevitt, were pioneers of skiffle music.

The trad jazz bands of the early 1950s introduced British audiences to skiffle music. Chris Barber and Ken Colyer's bands had interval skiffle groups that, as the name suggests, would play during the break when the jazz musicians were resting between sets. Skiffle exploded onto the UK scene with Lonnie Donegan's cover of Lead Belly's *Rock Island Line*, recorded on 13 July* 1954. British rock'n'roll soon grew from the proliferation of skiffle groups across the country. Tommy Steele was the first British rock'n'roll star, followed by a host of others, including Cliff Richard, Marty Wilde, Billy Fury and lesser known heroes like the colourful characters Wee Willie Harris and Screaming Lord Sutch.

British rock'n'roll then was mostly a pale imitation of its American counterpart. By the end of the decade the golden age of rock'n'roll was over on both sides of the Atlantic. In the UK rock'n'rollers were fading away with the emergence of the beat groups. Tommy Steele became a family entertainer and Cliff Richard reinvented himself as a pop star.

1967 Landmark Events *Death of Hippie* march

The residents of San Francisco's Haight-Ashbury district organized the *Death of Hippie* march to mark the end of an era. The Hippie movement started with high ideals but had become polluted by outsiders. The march was staged as a mock funeral with a coffin for an imaginary character "Hippie", killed off by overexposure and rampant commercialism. The march was to mark the passing of the genuine article and to tell aspiring flower children to stay at home, where they should take the hippie message to their neighbours.

Haight-Ashbury had become the centre of the hippie world. The drug-fuelled hippie philosophy was one of free love, in a sharing, communal society where money was meaningless. This idea had been hijacked by hip-capitalists and the hippie ideals were now big business. At this time Frank Zappa and the Mothers of Invention were recording the final sessions for their album *We're Only in It for the Money*, a parody of the Beatles' *Sgt Pepper*. The phoney hippies found themselves as an integral part of Zappa's satire on American society. The sentiment was also summed up years later by Don Henley in his song *The Boys of Summer*, with the observation of a Deadhead sticker on a Cadillac.

The year of the *Summer of Love* began on 14 January* with *A Gathering of the Tribes*, a meeting of hippie and beat cultures, and ended with the *Death of Hippie* march.

Recording session today

1972 David Bowie *The Jean Genie*

Written during the American leg of the *Ziggy Stardust* tour and inspired by Bo Diddley's *I'm a Man*, David Bowie took time out to record *The Jean Genie* in RCA's New York studios.

The song featured Mick Ronson on guitar. Bowie and the Spiders from Mars played the song for the first time in Chicago the following night.

Single released today

1969 The Beatles *Something* c/w *Come Together* (US)

Events today

7

1955 Allen Ginsberg first reading of *Howl*

This was a landmark day for the Beat Generation. Allen Ginsberg read his poem *Howl* for the first time at a poetry reading at the Six Gallery in San Francisco.

From the opening line, where he talked of the best minds of his generation being destroyed by madness, Ginsberg's seminal beat poem, *Howl*, was set to challenge the establishment. The work was published by City Lights Books the following year. In the summer of 1957 the publisher Lawrence Ferlinghetti was in court facing obscenity charges. In finding the defendant not guilty, Judge Clayton W Horn quoted the motto of the English Order of the Garter, "Evil to him who evil thinks".

Ginsberg's ideas were also in sync with the 1960s and he appeared at a number of San Francisco's landmark events, including the *Trips Festival* on 23 January* 1966 and *A Gathering of the Tribes* on 14 January* 1967. He also appeared briefly in the background of the video for Bob Dylan's *Subterranean Homesick Blues* in 1965 and was a part of Dylan's *Rolling Thunder Review* tour in 1975.

1964 Rock'n'Roll Landmarks — from rock'n'roll to the British Invasion

A concert in England at Sheffield's City Hall depicted rock'n'roll's changing times. The show included Bill Haley, Manfred Mann and The Nashville Teens, representing both the beginning of American rock'n'roll and the UK's new dominance of American music.

Bill Haley recorded *Rock Around the Clock* on 12 April* 1954. Rock'n'Roll exploded onto an unsuspecting world after the song was included in the 1955 movie *Blackboard Jungle.* In 1964 the British Invasion groups arrived in America and dominated the music scene. Manfred Mann scored with their cover of the Exciters' *Do-Wah-Diddy* and the Nashville Teens with their cover of John D Loudermilk's self-penned *Tobacco Road.*

American rock'n'roll came to a premature end in the late 1950s when its main protagonists left the stage. Little Richard found God in Australia and renounced rock'n'roll, 12 October* 1957. Elvis joined the US Army, 24 March* 1958. Jerry Lee Lewis's career nosedived after he married his cousin's thirteen-year-old daughter, 22 May* 1958. The last nail in its coffin came when Buddy Holly died in a plane crash on 3 February* 1959.

In the early 1960s American music developed in a number of directions. Berry Gordy Jr formed Motown with doo wop groups like the Four Tops and the Temptations. Dion and the Four Seasons emerged from their doo wop roots. Chubby Checker danced to twist beats and heralded in a host of new dance crazes. Clean-cut teen idols like Bobby Vee and Ricky Nelson became the acceptable face of American rock'n'roll. Phil Spector created his multi-layered "wall of sound". Surf music became the staple West Coast diet. But, all were swept away by the British Invasion, launched on 1 February* 1964.

Died today

1966 Johnny Kidd — second wave British rock'n'roll singer, died aged thirty

Whilst on tour in the north of England, Johnny Kidd died when his Ford Cortina GT was involved in a head-on collision with a Mini, near Radcliffe in Lancashire. Seventeen-year-old Helen Read, a passenger in the other car, also died. On that fateful night they had arrived late for their engagement in Bolton and despite offering to play free of charge the venue manager cancelled the gig. Some time before this when Kidd's career had been in the doldrums *Disc* ran a story about him under the double-deck headline *Johnny Kidd dead keen to come back* – and, yes, the headline, prophetically, "broke" to a second deck after the first three words.

The New Pirates bass player Nick Simper was also injured in the crash. He went on to become a founding member of Deep Purple.

Events today

8

1968 Cass Elliot — disastrous beginning to her solo career

Following the demise of The Mamas & The Papas, Mama Cass gave her debut solo performance at Caesar's Palace in Las Vegas. The concert was a disaster, with an ailing Elliot performing with an under-rehearsed band. The failure of the first night led to the cancellation of the remaining residency.

1976 Sex Pistols — signed to EMI ...and then on to Virgin ...via A&M

After performing their debut gig at London's St Martin's College of Art on 6 November* 1975, the Sex Pistols signed their first, albeit short-lived, record deal with EMI. It earned them £40,000[110] when it was cancelled shortly afterwards.

October

The Sex Pistols were pioneers of the British punk scene. With the principle that anyone could play in a group, punk was an antidote to the excesses of progressive rock. This distaste for corporate rock ushered in a whole new era of independent UK record labels.

The lineup of vocalist Johnny Rotten (born John Lydon), guitarist Steve Jones, drummer Paul Cook and bassist Glen Matlock, came together as the Swankers, managed by Malcolm McLaren. At EMI they released one single on 26 November*, *Anarchy in the UK* c/w *I Wanna Be Me*. On 1 December* they made their infamous TV appearance with Bill Grundy. By the end of December the EMI mandarins realised that the Sex Pistols were far too controversial for the company that gave the world the Beatles. EMI and the Sex Pistols parted company in early January.

The Sex Pistols were without a record deal for two months and in that time they had a change of bass player. Out went Glen Matlock and in came Sid Vicious from the Flowers of Romance. The band signed to A&M in early March but by the middle of the month they were once again without a recording contract. On the upside, the boys were £75,000[110] richer for their two weeks of life at A&M. One single did emerge with an A&M label, *God Save the Queen* c/w *No Feelings*. This single more escaped than was released and the few copies available are now highly prized collector's items.

In mid-May the Sex Pistols finally found recording stability with Richard Branson's Virgin label. The first release on 27 May* was, once again, *God Save the Queen* but this time it was coupled with *Did You No Wrong*.

The Pistols may have found a recording home but the controversy continued.

Album released today

1971 John Lennon *Imagine* (UK)

John Lennon's lyrics for the title track were inspired by poems in Yoko Ono's book *Grapefruit*, published in 1964. He suggested later that Yoko deserved a joint writing credit for the song.

The album featured contributions from George Harrison and saxophonist King Curtis.

Birthdays today

(Good day for Ramones fans!)

1948 Johnny Ramone guitar and vocals: Ramones

Johnny was a founding member of the Ramones in 1974.

1965 CJ Ramone bass: Ramones

CJ replaced founding member Dee Dee Ramone in 1989.

Event today

1971 Vietnam War "combat refusal"

Members of the 1st Air Cavalry Division famously refused to take part in a ground patrol by expressing "a desire not to go". This was one of a number of "combat refusals" by American ground forces.

By 1971 the morale of American troops was extremely low. As well as "combat refusals", incidents of "fragging" were also widespread. "Fragging" was the practice of enlisted men killing unpopular officers or NCOs, usually by shooting them or by despatching them with a grenade.

Births and deaths today

1940 John Lennon road to the Beatles

John Lennon's mother and father split up when he was only four years old, resulting in him being brought up by his auntie Mimi at *Mendips*, 251 Menlove Avenue, Liverpool. When he was in his mid-teens John started to re-establish the relationship with his mother, Julia. Sadly, this new relationship was destined to be short-lived: on 15 July 1958 she was killed by an off-duty policeman whilst crossing the road.

With his best friend Pete Shotton, Lennon formed his first skiffle group, The Black Jacks, in 1956. They changed the name shortly afterwards to "The Quarry Men". He met Paul McCartney on 6 July* 1957, Paul's friend George Harrison joined them shortly afterwards. The Quarry Men had a number of drummers before Pete Best became sticksman on the eve of their first trip to Hamburg, opening there on 17 August* 1960. For the trip to Hamburg they changed their name for the last time – to "The Beatles".

1944 John Entwistle bass: The Detours, The High Numbers, The Who; solo

John Entwistle originally teamed up with future Who guitarist Pete Townshend in 1959, when they both played trad jazz in the Confederates. They were together again in the Scorpions, until Entwistle left in mid-1961 to join Roger Daltrey in the Detours.

1948 Jackson Browne musician, singer and songwriter

When he was in his late teens Jackson Brown had a short stint in the Nitty Gritty Dirt Band. Shortly afterwards he signed as a songwriter to Nina Music, a branch of Elektra Records. Since then he has achieved considerable success as both a songwriter and performer. His songs have been recorded by a host of rock luminaries, including Nico, The Byrds, Eagles and Gregg Allman.

1967 Che Guevara death of a 1960s revolutionary icon, aged thirty-nine

Argentinean born Che Guevara became the iconic revolutionary figure for a generation of 1960s college students. He came to prominence in the Cuban Revolution, joining Fidel Castro in the overthrow of the Batista regime. The revolutionary forces took power in early 1959 and Guevara took his place in the new Cuban Government. In 1960 he wrote the book *Guerrilla Warfare*. By the mid-1960s Guevara was preaching revolution in Africa, before finding his way to Bolivia. It was there that he was finally hunted down by the Bolivian Army and America's CIA. He was captured and executed.

Guevara went on to become one of the 20th Century's most iconic figures, named by *Time* magazine as one of *The Time 100: The Most Important People of the Century*. The photograph of Guevara by Alberto Korda has emblazoned 'a million' T-shirts.

Events today

1963 Gerry and the Pacemakers first three singles entered the UK charts at #1

When *You'll Never Walk Alone* entered the British charts by going straight in at #1, Gerry and the Pacemakers became the first act in the UK to have their first three singles enter at the #1 spot. It started with *How Do You Do It* on 14 March* and was followed by *I Like it* on 30 May. Their third #1, *You'll Never Walk Alone*, was written by Rodgers and Hammerstein for their 1945 musical *Carousel*.

It would be twenty years before this feat was achieved again. Frankie Goes to Hollywood charted the first of three #1s with the controversial *Relax* in November 1983.

1965 Lenny Bruce lodged a harassment complaint with the FBI

After five years of arrests and court appearances on obscenity and drugs charges, iconoclastic comedian Lenny Bruce lodged a complaint with the San Francisco office of the FBI. He claimed that the New York and Californian courts were conspiring to violate his rights.

Bruce's nightclub performances as a stand-up comedian constantly brought him into conflict with the authorities. His anti-establishment material was often peppered with words considered to be obscene and since the early 1960s his performances had resulted in repeated arrests on obscenity charges. He was also arrested a number of times on drug related charges. Eventually he found himself banned from entering Australia and Britain. Some of his American concerts were also stopped by local State authorities. By October 1965, illness, crippling legal costs and difficulty in staging appearances added up to bankruptcy for Bruce. He died of a morphine overdose on 3 August* 1966.

The FBI took no action after the complaint in 1965 but in 2003 New York Governor George E Pataki took the unprecedented step of pardoning Bruce for an obscenity conviction he had received in 1964, after a performance at the Café au Go Go.

Recording session today

1966 The 13th Floor Elevators *The Psychedelic Sounds of the 13th Floor Elevators*

Seminal psychedelic group the 13th Floor Elevators spent their penultimate day in the studio, recording their debut album.

The 13th Floor Elevators' *Psychedelic Sounds* was one of the earliest albums of the emerging psychedelic scene. It featured *You're Gonna Miss Me*, released as the band's debut single. Guitarist Roky Erickson wrote the song and originally released it when he was with his previous band, the Spades.

In the summer of 1966 the Dallas-based 13th Floor Elevators invited Janis Joplin to join their ranks but she chose to relocate to San Francisco and become the vocalist for Big Brother and the Holding Company.

Album released today

1969 King Crimson *In the Court of the Crimson King* (UK)

King Crimson released their groundbreaking debut album.

The band had recently morphed from Giles, Giles and Fripp. The trio was initially augmented by multi-instrumentalist Ian McDonald and Fairport Convention's vocalist Judy Dyble. Dyble's stay was very short, before she left to form Trader Horne. Bassist Peter Giles left, to be replaced by Greg Lake. Drummer Mike Giles remained, lyricist Pete Sinfield entered the scene – and they became King Crimson.

Events today

1966 Landmark Magazines Britain's first underground newspaper

Britain's first underground newspaper the *International Times*, better known as *it*, was launched with a party at London's Roundhouse. The gig featured performances from those doyens of the underground scene, Pink Floyd and Soft Machine.

The era of the beat groups was fading away as rock music became far more sophisticated. Cream made their debut on 31 July*. Underground bands like Pink Floyd and Soft Machine were emerging, with performances that incorporated light shows and movie clips. The war in Vietnam had escalated dramatically and was encountering considerable student opposition across America. With its mixture of politics and music the new counterculture *it* newspaper captured this growing mood of the mid-1960s.

The following February the Australian counterculture magazine *OZ* printed its first edition in Britain. OZ later gained notoriety in 1970 with its *School Kids Issue.*

1967 The Move lawsuit from Britain's Prime Minister

The libel lawsuit brought by Prime Minister Harold Wilson against the Move was settled.

As part of the promotional materials for their third single, *Flowers in the Rain*, a postcard was produced and distributed depicting a cartoon of Harold Wilson in a romantic liaison. Wilson took a dim view of the postcard and served a libel action on the group and its associates. The defendants all apologised for the content on the postcard and agreed that all the proceeds from *Flowers in the Rain* would go to charity, in perpetuity. The two charities selected by Wilson were the Spastics Society and Stoke Mandeville Hospital.

As well as giving the Move a libel action and their third British hit single, *Flowers in the Rain* had also been used as the opening song when Britain's first legal pop music station, Radio 1, was launched a couple of weeks earlier on 30 September*.

1969 Vietnam War *Days of Rage* protest

Known as the *Days of Rage*, the Weathermen's four days of protest in Chicago came to an end. It was supported by posters bearing the slogan "Bring the WAR Home".

Protests had become commonplace throughout 1960s America, many were peaceful but some used violence to make their point. The first half of the 1960s was dominated by civil rights protests but by the end of the decade the focus of protest had turned to the extremely unpopular Vietnam War. Violence at the 1968 Democratic Party Convention in Chicago started on 25 August* and escalated throughout the week. In 1969 a group of left-wing radicals split from the SDS, Students for a Democratic Society, and formed themselves into the notorious Weathermen. They believed in direct action rather than peaceful protest. The Chicago *Days of Rage* was partly a protest against the *Chicago 8* arrests, following the Democratic Party Convention and their indictment on 20 March*. The protest did not become the revolutionary focal point that the Weathermen had anticipated. Hundreds rather than thousands of people turned up for the protests. The Weathermen continued to wreak havoc well into the 1970s, with demonstrations that included bombings of American government buildings.

The Weathermen's name was inspired by Bob Dylan's song *Subterranean Homesick Blues*, which suggested that it was not necessary to have a professional meteorologist to determine the direction of the prevailing wind.

Events today

1957 Little Richard end of the line

On his Australian tour Little Richard found God and renounced rock'n'roll. Billed as the *Big Show, Rock'n'Roll*, Little Richard was supported by Gene Vincent, Eddie Cochran and Australia's first rock'n'roll band Johnny O'Keefe and the Dee Jays. Partway through the tour he played in Sydney and is reputed to have said to the audience "If you want to live for the Lord, you can't take rock'n'roll too. God doesn't like it." Sources vary as to the details but the date of the announcement is most frequently given as 12 October.

Shortly after this he threw his jewellery into the Hunter River, or maybe Sydney Harbour. Sources vary as to the location of the watery grave he consigned his worldly goods to. Some suggest the epiphany was due to a sputnik passing overhead and signifying the end of the world, others a traumatic plane journey with the engines on fire.

Whatever the reasons and sequence of events, rock'n'roll was much the poorer when Little Richard returned to America. He recorded one final session for Speciality and enrolled to become a Seventh Day Adventist preacher at Oakwood Theological College in Huntsville, Alabama. Following his conversion he only performed gospel songs until his return to rock'n'roll in 1962...

1962 Little Richard ...returned to rock'n'roll

A week after opening his first British concert, Little Richard played at New Brighton's Tower Ballroom in Merseyside. His backing band included keyboard player Billy Preston and one of the support bands was the Beatles. Their career was just about to take off, having released their debut single, *Love Me Do*, a week earlier on 5 October*.

Billed as *The Night of Nights*, the concert was promoted by the Beatles' manager Brian Epstein. The night's entertainment also featured Rory Storm and the Hurricanes, which Ringo Starr left to join the Beatles on 18 August*. Starr replaced Pete Best in the Beatles and he was also there that night in his new group, Lee Curtis and the All Stars.

Births and deaths today

1948 Rick Parfitt guitar and vocals: The Highlights, Traffic Jam, Status Quo

1971 Gene Vincent seminal rock'n'roll singer, died at the age of thirty-six

One of America's first wave of rock'n'roll singers, Gene Vincent died of internal haemorrhaging.

1978 Nancy Spungen Sid Vicious's girlfriend, died at the age of twenty

Sid Vicious's girlfriend Nancy Spungen was found dead in their hotel bathroom at the Chelsea Hotel in New York. She had been stabbed once with a knife.

Sex Pistols' bass player Sid Vicious and Spungen had been together since she moved to London nearly two years earlier. Following the Sex Pistols' disintegration after their last concert in San Francisco on 14 January*, Vicious and Spungen stayed on in America. Their tempestuous, drug-fuelled relationship came to an abrupt end when Spungen died in very hazy circumstances. Spungen had bought the knife that killed her as a present for Vicious. The police arrested Vicious shortly afterwards but he claimed to have no recollection of the events leading up to her death. The matter never reached court. Sid Vicious was the only suspect but he died of a drug overdose before the trial was set to begin.

Events today

1962 The Everly Brothers British tour by just one Brother

On the eve of their British tour, Don Everly collapsed on stage during a rehearsal at London's Prince of Wales Theatre. He immediately returned to America, leaving his elder brother Phil to continue the tour alone.

Support acts included Ketty Lester, Frank Ifield and The Vernons Girls.

1964 The Pretty Things the early days

The Pretty Things played one of their regular Tuesday night spots at London's 100 Club on Oxford Street; support that night came from Blues By Six.

The Pretty Things was formed by guitarist Dick Taylor and vocalist Phil May at Sidcup Art College in late 1963. They were joined by rhythm guitarist Brian Pendleton and bassist John Stax. The lineup went through a couple of drummers before Viv Prince joined from Carter Lewis and the Southerners, which also boasted future Led Zeppelin guitarist Jimmy Page amongst its ranks.

Before co-founding the Pretty Things, Taylor had been the bass player for the original Rollin' Stones. He started out as the guitarist in Mick Jagger and Keith Richard's group Little Boy Blue and the Blue Boys. All three of them joined Brian Jones's second lineup and became the Rollin' Stones, playing their first gig to bear that name on 12 July* 1962.

Before leaving to form Blues By Six, Brian Knight had also been a member of Brian Jones's first lineup, along with original Stones pianist Ian Stewart. The Rolling Stones connection does not end there. Future Stones drummer Charlie Watts left Alexis Korner's Blues Incorporated to join Knight in his new venture, Blues By Six.

The group took their name from Bo Diddley's song *Pretty Thing*.

1966 Jimi Hendrix Experience formed in London

The Jimi Hendrix Experience played their first-ever gig at the Novelty Cinema in Evreux, near Paris. The short tour ended at the Paris Olympia five days later.

When Jimi Hendrix arrived in London his new manager Chas Chandler quickly set about forming a new band around his protégé. First to join was Noel Redding, who moved from guitar to bass for his new role. The power trio was completed by drummer Mitch Mitchell, recently departed from Georgie Fame and the Blue Flames. French rock star Johnny Hallyday had seen Hendrix sit in with Brian Auger at Blaises Club in London and invited the newly formed Jimi Hendrix Experience to open for him on his upcoming four concert dates in France.

Birthdays today

1925 Lenny Bruce iconoclastic American comedian

Two of the rock world's luminaries were involved with Lenny Bruce. Phil Spector helped Bruce in his constant battle with the establishment and in late 1965 produced the album *Lenny Bruce Is Out Again*. When Frank Zappa set up his own Bizarre record label in 1969, the first release was Lenny Bruce's *The Berkeley Concert*, recorded in December 1965. On 24* and 25 June 1966, the Mothers opened for Bruce when he gave his final performances at San Francisco's Fillmore Auditorium.

1940 Chris Farlowe singer: CF and Thunderbirds, Colosseum, Atomic Rooster

1947 Sammy Hagar guitar and vocals: Montrose, Van Halen; solo

Events today

1966 Pink Floyd early 'underground' gig

Those doyens of British counterculture, Pink Floyd, gave one of their earliest 'underground' performance at the All Saints Hall, in London's Powis Gardens. This was the original lineup – guitarist, singer and songwriter Syd Barrett, bassist Roger Waters, drummer Nick Mason and keyboardist Richard Wright. The evening's entertainment was an early experimentation with psychedelic effects and mixed media.

Waters, Mason and Wright had met whilst studying architecture at Regent Street Poly. They formed Sigma 6 and played R&B covers. They also performed as "The Meggadeaths", "The Abdabs", sometimes "The Screaming Abdabs" or "Architectural Abdabs", and "The Tea Set". The lineup evolved and Waters, Mason and Wright were joined by jazz guitarist Bob Klose (sometimes spelt Close) and Syd Barrett. The name evolved to "The Pink Floyd Sound", chosen by Barrett after bluesmen Pink Anderson and Floyd Council. The gestation was complete when Klose left and the name was shortened to "Pink Floyd".

1977 Johnny Thunders and the Heartbreakers British tour

Johnny Thunders and the Heartbreakers had originally toured the UK in late 1976, when they were a support act for the Sex Pistols' notorious *Anarchy in the UK* tour. Now they were back and appearing in Edinburgh to promote their debut album, *L.A.M.F.*

The group formed as a trio in mid-1975. Guitarist Johnny Thunders and drummer Jerry Nolan left the New York Dolls and were joined by bassist Richard Hell, who had recently parted company with Television. Hell left the group in mid-1976 to form his own group.

This current lineup decided to call it a day at the end of the tour.

Single released today

1958 Ritchie Valens *Donna* c/w *La Bamba* (US)

Ritchie Valens released his second and final single in his lifetime. The A-side was the self-penned *Donna*, written as a love song for his high school sweetheart, Donna Ludwig-Fox. This was coupled with *La Bamba*, reworked by Valens from a Mexican folk song.

Tragically, he died shortly afterwards in the plane crash on 3 February* that also killed Buddy Holly and the Big Bopper.

Birthdays today

1939 Brian Knight guitar: pre-Rollin' Stones lineup, Blues By Six

One of the unsung heroes of the early British blues scene. Brian Knight was a member of Brian Jones's first lineup, before Jones was joined by Mick Jagger and Keith Richard and they became the Rollin' Stones. Knight moved on to form Blues By Six and poached future Rolling Stones drummer Charlie Watts from Alexis Korner's Blues Incorporated.

1940 Cliff Richard singer and actor: 1950s British rock'n'roll star

Cliff Richard was a phenomenal success in Britain but achieved only minimal recognition in America. With his backing band the Drifters, who renamed to "The Shadows", he was one of the original British rock'n'roll stars, scoring his first hit with *Move It!* in 1958. In the early 1960s he gravitated to pop music and movies. Since then he has continued to have hit records and has sold over 21 million singles in the UK.

1946 Justin Hayward guitar and vocals: The Moody Blues; solo

Events today

15

1965 Jimi Hendrix signed a deal with Ed Chalpin

After leaving the Army in mid-1962 Jimi Hendrix played with a number of bands, including the King Casuals with Billy Cox, and Bobby Taylor and the Vancouvers, in a lineup with guitarist Tommy Chong of hippie duo Cheech and Chong fame. He also joined touring bands for various artists, including Sam Cooke, Jackie Wilson and Little Richard, plus work as a session guitarist, including the Isley Brothers' *Testify*.

Hendrix met R&B bandleader Curtis Knight in New York and was invited to become the new lead guitarist with his group the Squires. Knight also introduced him to his manager Ed Chalpin, who signed Hendrix to a three-year exclusive recording agreement. Knight had just written *How Would You Feel*, a seminal black rock protest song. On the single he is credited as arranger, Jimmy Hendrix.

That contract with Chalpin, signed on 15 October 1965, came back to haunt Hendrix. After he parted company with Knight and Chalpin, Hendrix met Chas Chandler, became the Jimi Hendrix Experience and found international fame. When Chalpin noticed Hendrix's new-found success he invoked the contract and claimed his share of the royalties. The initial settlement included 100 per cent of the royalties from Hendrix's fourth album, *Band of Gypsys*. The legal wrangling continued long after Hendrix's death.

1969 Vietnam War Hanoi acknowledged the US anti-war movement

The National Moratorium was a series of anti-war demonstrations held across America, with more than a million people participating in the events. North Vietnam's Prime Minister Pham Van Dong sent a letter to the demonstration's organisers acknowledging the American anti-war movement and wishing them success in their endeavours.

Recording sessions today

1956 Little Richard *Good Golly, Miss Molly*

Little Richard recorded *Good Golly, Miss Molly* at J&M Studio in New Orleans, on the first of a two-day session with co-writer and producer Bumps Blackwell. By the time that it was released in January 1958, Little Richard had found God and renounced rock'n'roll.

The single's B-side was the Little Richard composition *Hey-Hey-Hey-Hey*. In live performances he would often sing it as a medley with Leiber and Stoller's *Kansas City*. The Beatles were obviously inspired by this when they spent two weeks sharing the bill with Little Richard at the Star-Club, on their fourth trip to Hamburg. When the Beatles recorded *Kansas City* they also opted for the medley with *Hey-Hey-Hey-Hey*.

Little Richard was born Richard Wayne Penniman and it was his surname that he used for songwriting credits.

1960 The Beatles recorded together for the first time

During their first trip to Hamburg, John, Paul, George and Ringo made their first recording together.

With Walter Eymond, stage name "Lu Walters" and known as "Wally", they made a recording at the small Akustik Studio in Hamburg. Eymond was the bass player and singer with another Liverpool group Rory Storm and the Hurricanes, who were also appearing in Hamburg at the time. The Hurricanes' drummer was Ringo Starr. The lineup making that recording of Gershwin's *Summertime*, from *Porgy and Bess*, was Wally and Ringo from the Hurricanes and John, Paul and George from the Beatles.

Events today

1951 Little Richard from talent show to recording studio

Little Richard gained the opportunity to record for RCA as the result of winning a talent competition. He cut four tracks at his first-ever session, including *Taxi Blues* and *Every Hour*. These two songs were coupled for his debut single.

This was not yet Little Richard's time and the single gave him little more than local success. He released another three RCA singles and a couple on Peacock, before he took the rock'n'roll world by storm in 1955 with his first single on Speciality, *Tutti-Frutti*.

1965 Family Dog first concert

The first Family Dog concert and dance was held at the Longshoreman's Hall near San Francisco's Fisherman's Warf. Billed as a rock'n'roll dance concert and tribute to the *Marvel Comics'* hero Dr Strange, concertgoers were treated to performances from Jefferson Airplane, The Charlatans, The Marbles and The Great Society.

The Family Dog was a loose ensemble of people which later included legendary San Francisco promoter Chet Helms, often called the "Father of the Summer of Love".

1966 Jefferson Airplane Grace Slick's debut concert

Shortly after leaving the Great Society, Grace Slick made her debut at the Fillmore as Jefferson Airplane's new vocalist. She replaced original singer Signe Toly Anderson.

The Fillmore was a two-night gig. Anderson provided lead vocals for the last time on the 15th and Slick stepped into her shoes and gave her debut performance on 16th.

The classic Jefferson Airplane lineup was now in place: vocals from Grace Slick and Marty Balin, guitarists Jorma Kaukonen and Paul Kantner, bassist Jack Casady and drummer Spencer Dryden, who had replaced Skip Spence when he left to form Moby Grape after the band's debut album, *Takes Off*.

1973 Vietnam War Nobel Peace Prizes for Kissinger and Le Duc Tho

The Nobel Peace Prize for 1973 was awarded jointly to America's Henry Kissinger and North Vietnam's Le Duc Tho.

Henry Kissinger accepted the Prize but was not present at the awards ceremony. His speech was read out by Thomas Byrne, the American Ambassador to Norway.

In contrast, Le Duc Tho rejected the award because in his view the war was not over. The 'peace' was simply America's withdrawal from the war on 27 January* 1973. Fighting continued and the war ended in victory for North Vietnam on 30 April* 1975.

Single released today

1954 Richard Berry *The Big Break* c/w *What You Do to Me* (US)

Richard Berry wrote and recorded his own prison opus after appearing, uncredited, as lead singer on the Leiber and Stoller penned Robins' song *Riot in Cell Block #9.*

The Robins later morphed into the Coasters.

Birthdays today

1938 Nico singer and actress: The Velvet Underground; solo

1943 Fred Turner bass and singer: Brave Belt, Bachman-Turner Overdrive

1947 Bob Weir guitar and vocals: Warlocks, Grateful Dead; solo

Events today

17

1962 Landmark Events *Cuban Missile Crisis*

The world polarised after the Second World War into the communist East and capitalist West, with the USSR (led by Russia) championing the former and America the latter. The nuclear arms race was gathering speed when Russia gained agreement from communist leader Fidel Castro to site Russian nuclear missiles on Cuban soil, just a hundred miles from the coast of Florida. In mid-October 1962 the world stood on the edge of nuclear war. Tension between the two countries was increasing when, on 17 October an American U2 spy-plane flew over the Cuban missile site and took clear photographs of the first nuclear missile installation being constructed.

On 22 October President Kennedy appeared on television to warn the American public that the USSR was building a nuclear missile base in Cuba, rendering America vulnerable to a nuclear attack. In order to prevent this, he was establishing a naval 'quarantine' around Cuba to stop any more Russian ships from delivering their cargos of weapons and materials to the Cuban missile site.

The 'quarantine' was established but the Russian ships continued on their course for Cuba. America set its military war-footing to DEFCON-2 (DEFence CONdition). The crisis reached its peak on the 27 October when Major Rudolph Anderson was shot down and killed by a SAM missile as he flew his U-2 spy-plane over Cuba. Negotiations with the USSR's Premier Khrushchev continued and an agreement was reached the following day. The Russian ships turned around and a nuclear holocaust was averted.

1967 Landmark Theatre *Hair* opened off-Broadway

The "American Tribal Love-Rock Musical" *Hair* opened off-Broadway, as the first production at Joseph Papp's New York Shakespeare Festival Public Theater.

After six weeks it moved to the Cheetah discotheque in Manhattan. The show was staged early in the evening before the disco crowds arrived for the dancing. After a short run the show went back into rehearsal with new songs and a new script before opening on Broadway at the Biltmore Theatre on 29 April 1968. It ran until 1972.

Rock singer Meat Loaf appeared in the cast during its run at the Biltmore.

1975 New York Dolls post-Johnny Thunders era

The New York Dolls' best days were behind them when Mercury issued a press release on 7 October, saying that they were not renewing the Dolls' recording contract.

By the autumn of 1976 the band's fortunes were waning. They had fallen out with their management, bassist Arthur Kane had left, and guitarist Johnny Thunders and drummer Jerry Nolan had moved on to form Johnny Thunders and the Heartbreakers. Future Sex Pistols Svengali Malcolm McLaren, stepped in and took over the Dolls' management but they did little more than limp on until the end of 1976 when they split up.

Album released today

1977 Lynyrd Skynyrd *Street Survivors* (US)

Lynyrd Skynyrd released the album *Street Survivors* just three days before the fatal plane crash on 20 October* that killed three band members.

The original album cover showed the band standing amid burning buildings. After the crash their record company, MCA, withdrew the album and replaced the cover with a new picture of the band. This time they were standing against a plain black background.

Events today

1957 The Quarry Men Paul McCartney's debut performance

Paul McCartney gave his debut performance with the Quarry Men at the Conservative Club's New Clubmoor Hall, in Liverpool's Norris Green. Paul played lead guitar but was overcome by stage fright when it came to his guitar solo in *Guitar Boogie*. George Harrison joined shortly afterwards and took over the mantle of lead guitarist.

Although McCartney was a Quarry Man at the time, he missed his opportunity to debut at the Cavern Club on 7 August* because he'd been away at a Boy Scout camp.

1967 John Lennon *How I Won the War* opened

Dick Lester's *How I Won the War* opened in London. John Lennon had a starring role in the movie for this, his first solo project away from the Beatles. It was a black comedy set in the Second World War, centring on a hapless group of soldiers whose mission was to set up an advanced cricket pitch behind enemy lines. The movie also featured Roy Kinnear and Michael Crawford as their inept officer.

John Lennon released a single, *How I Won the War* c/w *Aftermath*, as his movie character Musketeer Gripweed and the Third Troop.

1976 Throbbing Gristle *Prostitution* gig at the ICA

Originally formed as COUM Transmissions in Hull in 1969. The performance art group then moved to London, changed its name to "Throbbing Gristle" and performed the notorious *Prostitution* gig at London's Institute of Contemporary Arts.

Throbbing Gristle was contemporaneous with the emerging British punk scene but was a far darker Dadaist performance group, looking to shock and disturb its audience.

Recording session today

1957 Little Richard final rock'n'roll recording session of the 1950s

Little Richard with his band the Upsetters entered Master Recorders studio in Los Angeles to record rock'n'roll songs for the last time in the 1950s. A number of songs were recorded that day, including *I'll Never Let You Go*, issued as the B-side to *Baby Face*; *She Knows How to Rock* and *Early One Morning*, coupled as the follow-up single to *Baby Face*.

Richard had recently returned from his Australian tour, where he experienced an epiphany and announced to his audience on 12 October* that he had found God and was renouncing rock'n'roll. This last session was necessary to fulfil his recording contract with Speciality. He then withdrew from rock'n'roll and on 27 January* enrolled into a theological college to become a Seventh Day Adventist minister. After this recording session he only performed religious and gospel music. In 1962 he returned to rock'n'roll with a tour of the UK. At a gig on 12 October* he was supported by the Beatles, going on to share billing with the Fab Four for two weeks at Hamburg's Star-Club in Germany.

Birthday today

1926 Chuck Berry singer, guitarist and songwriter

John Lennon famously said that if you tried to give rock'n'roll another name you might call it "Chuck Berry". A guitarist, singer, songwriter and duck-walker, covers of his songs were the staple diet of 1960s rockers, including the Beatles cover of *Roll Over Beethoven* and Jimi Hendrix's *Johnny B Goode*. In 1954 Chuck Berry made his first recoding, *Oh Maria*, as a part of Joe Alexander and the Cubans.

Events today

19

1961 The Beatmakers for one night only

Two of Liverpool's top groups, the Beatles and Gerry and the Pacemakers, joined forces for a one-time-only performance and created Liverpool's first supergroup, the Beatmakers. They were playing a mid-week gig at Liverpool's Litherland Town Hall when they decided to join forces and perform as a single unit.

The lineup comprised guitarists George on lead and Paul on rhythm, John with vocals and piano, Pete Best and Freddy Marsden sharing the drumming stool, Les McGuire on saxophone, Les Chadwick with bass and Gerry Marsden brought additional lead guitar and vocals. Another Liverpool group Karl Terry and the Cruisers were also on the bill and Karl added more vocals to complete the Beatmakers' lineup.

Gerry and the Pacemakers was one of the most successful of the British Invasion groups, notching up seven *Billboard Top 40* hits between 1964 and 1966. In the UK they were one of the top Merseybeat groups, with nine Top 30 hits including three #1s.

Karl Terry and the Cruisers were popular in Liverpool but never managed to achieve a wider commercial success.

1963 The Yardbirds Top Topham's final gig as lead guitarist

Original lead guitarist Top Topham played his farewell concert with the Yardbirds at the Crawdaddy, Richmond's popular R&B club in south-west London.

Topham was just sixteen, when growing local fame for the Yardbirds meant that the group was turning professional. The other band members were all several years older than Topham and his parents were against him becoming a professional musician. He quit the group to continue with his studies. Eric Clapton took over as lead guitarist.

Alongside Clapton, the lineup consisted of: lead singer and harp player Keith Relf, rhythm guitarist Chris Dreja, bassist Paul Samwell-Smith and drummer Jim McCarty.

Eric Clapton was previously with the Roosters, and Casey Jones and the Engineers.

Recording session today

1958 Brenda Lee *Rockin' Around the Christmas Tree*

This Christmas classic failed to chart when it was first released in 1958 and success eluded it for a second time with its 1959 re-release. It was only after Brenda Lee made her chart breakthrough with *Sweet Nothin's* in 1960, that *Rockin' Around the Christmas Tree* showed that it was third time lucky for the song, when it made the best-seller lists that festive season.

In Britain, *Sweet Nothin's* charted in 1960, with *Rockin' Around the Christmas Tree* finding chart success two years later in 1962.

Album released today

1979 Tom Petty and the Heartbreakers *Damn the Torpedoes* (US)

This third album was recorded during very trying times for Tom Petty and his band. He was embroiled in a bitter legal battle with his record company, before they came together and released the album to great critical acclaim. The song titles and lyrics hinted at the problems endured during the recording process. The title says it all.

The album's title was inspired by the famous order given by Admiral David Farragut at the battle of Mobile Bay during the American Civil War, usually paraphrased as, "Damn the torpedoes, full steam ahead!"

Events today

1960 British Legislation end of literary censorship in Britain

Under the *Obscene Publications Act 1959*, the trial of English writer DH Lawrence's novel *Lady Chatterley's Lover* opened at London's Old Bailey courtrooms.

The novel was originally published in Italy in 1928. In 1960 Penguin Books published the book in Britain. Two weeks after the trial began the verdict went in favour of the publisher, effectively marking the end of literary censorship in Britain.

It would be another six years before America threw off the shackles of literary censorship, with the decision by the Massachusetts Supreme Court that William Burroughs' epic beat novel *Naked Lunch* was not obscene.

1969 The Who *Tommy* at the Fillmore

The Who began a six-night run performing *Tommy* at New York's Fillmore East.

The album is often cited as the first "rock opera" but some argue that the Pretty Things beat them to it with their album *SF Sorrow*, released in the UK in 1968.

1976 Led Zeppelin premiere of *The Song Remains the Same*

Led Zeppelin's movie *The Song Remains the Same* opened in New York.

The movie featured a fantasy sequence from each member of the group. Guitarist Jimmy Page chose a location near his home at *Boleskine House*, situated on the shores of Loch Ness in Scotland. Page had become fascinated in the occult and particularly in the doctrines of Satanist Aleister Crowley. *Boleskine House* was bought by Page in 1971 and had been a former home of Crowley. A further connection with Led Zeppelin can be seen with the Crowley quote "Do what thou wilt", written into the run-out section of their second album, released on 23 October* 1970.

1977 Lynyrd Skynyrd fatal plane crash

Southern rock band Lynyrd Skynyrd came to a tragic end when their tour plane crashed, killing lead vocalist Ronnie Van Zant, guitarist Steve Gaines and his sister and vocalist Cassie Gaines. Other band members were also seriously injured.

The crash followed their concert at the Greenville Memorial Auditorium, South Carolina. Tragedy struck when the band was flying on to their next gig at Louisiana University in Baton Rouge. Their chartered tour plane apparently ran out of fuel and crashed in a forest near Gillsburg, Mississippi. As well as the three band members, road manager Dean Kilpatrick and the two pilots were also killed.

The tour was promoting their recently released album *Street Survivors*. After the crash MCA withdrew the album and changed the front cover artwork. The original album showed the band standing amid flames in a burning street scene. The new cover was a simple shot of the band standing and contrasted against a black background.

Birthday today

1950 Tom Petty guitar, vocals: TP and the Heartbreakers, Wilburys; solo

As well as achieving fame with his own band the Heartbreakers, Tom Petty teamed up with Bob Dylan, George Harrison, Roy Orbison and Jeff Lynne in the late 1980s to form the Traveling Wilburys. He was "Charlie T Wilbury Jnr" on the first album and "Muddy Wilbury" on the second album, strangely titled *Volume 3*. The musicians originally came together in 1988 to play on a George Harrison B-side, *Handle with Care*.

Events today

1967 Vietnam War — anti-war march to levitate the Pentagon

In an anti-war demonstration led by Jerry Ruben over 50,000 protestors marched on the Pentagon. Abbie Hoffman announced that the plan was to exorcise the evil spirits, by encircling the Pentagon and levitating it. Poets and rock band the Fugs were amongst the crowd chanting, "out, demons out". The protestors were met by a strong force of soldiers and police, resulting in more than 600 arrests.

1976 The Who — Keith Moon's final concert appearance

Toronto's Maple Leaf Gardens was the final night of the Who's North American tour and the last-ever concert performance with drummer Keith Moon.

Moon did perform with the Who again, twice but both times were for closed audiences during filming for the movie *The Kids Are Alright*. His final performance came on 25 May* 1978.

Recording session today

1958 Buddy Holly — final recording session

Buddy Holly's final studio recording session took place in the Pythian Temple Studios in New York. He famously used a string accompaniment to record four songs: *It Doesn't Matter Any More*, *Moondreams*, *Raining in My Heart* and *True Love Ways*. His final recordings were made at home in December.

Shortly after this session he parted company with his manager Norman Petty. The Crickets opted to stay with Petty, leaving Holly to become a solo artist.

Album released today

1977 Meat Loaf — *Bat Out of Hell* (US)

Almost ten years after releasing his first single as Popcorn Blizzard's singer, *Once Upon a Time* c/w *Hello*, Meat Loaf released one of the best-selling albums of all time.

Births and deaths today

1940 Manfred Mann — keyboards: Manfred Mann, Earth Band

1941 Steve Cropper — guitarist and songwriter: Booker T and the MGs

Throughout the 1960s Steve Cropper was a member of the Stax house band, Booker T and the MGs. As well as playing on many of the Stax hits, he was also a prolific songwriter and producer.

1942 Elvin Bishop — guitar: Paul Butterfield Blues Band; solo

Elvin Bishop was initially the lead guitarist with the Paul Butterfield Blues Band but moved to rhythm guitar when Mike Bloomfield joined. The title of the Blues Band's 1967 album, *The Resurrection of Pigboy Crabshaw*, was taken from Elvin Bishop's nickname.

1965 Bill Black — Elvis's bass player, died at the age of thirty-nine

Bass player Bill Black died of a brain tumour.

Black worked with Elvis Presley in his pre-Army days and received a performer credit on all five of Elvis's Sun singles, Elvis Presley, Scotty and Bill. When Elvis came out of the Army Black opted for a solo career with his own group, the Bill Black Combo.

Events today

1966 Chain Reaction — supported the Yardbirds

A fledgling Chain Reaction supported the Yardbirds at Staples High School in Westport, Connecticut, with a lineup which included future Aerosmith front man Stephen Tyler.

1967 Bruce Springsteen — Bart Haynes was killed in Vietnam

In mid-1965 when Bruce Springsteen joined his first band, the New Jersey based Castiles, Bart Haynes was already the group's drummer. Shortly afterwards, Haynes split from the band to join the United States Marine Corps. This was at the time when America was escalating its involvement in the Vietnam War. The turning point in the war came a few months after Haynes's death, when the North launched their *Tet Offensive* on 31 January*. By then there were half a million American troops serving in Vietnam. Haynes was a nineteen-year-old Lance Corporal when he was killed by mortar fire in the Quang Tri Province.

The band continued after Haynes's departure in 1965 and on 18 May 1966 they made a demo recording at Mr Music studio in New Jersey. This was Springsteen's first-ever recording session. They recorded two songs that day, *That's What You Get* and *Baby I*, both co-written by the Boss.

The Castiles finally called it a day in the summer of 1968. Springsteen continued in a number of different groups, until the summer of 1971 when he gathered together the musicians who would become the E Street Band. He released his first album in January 1973. Jon Landau famously saw "rock'n'roll future" at a gig on 9 May* 1974. But it took the Boss's *Born to Run* album in the summer of 1975 to elevate Bruce Springsteen to the ranks of rock royalty.

Single released today

1976 The Damned — *New Rose* c/w *Help* (UK)

Written by guitarist Brian James, *New Rose* was the first single to be released by a British punk band. The B-side was an express train cover version of the Beatles' *Help*.

Birthdays today

1920 Timothy Leary — psychologist, author and advocate of LSD

A legion of 1960s hippies heeded psychologist and writer Timothy Leary's counterculture advice to, "turn on, tune in, drop out".

1942 Bobby Fuller — singer and guitarist: Bobby Fuller Four

Bobby Fuller Four's 1966 hit *I Fought the Law* was a Sonny Curtis penned song that was originally released on the 1960 album *In Style with the Crickets*.

1945 Leslie West guitar: The Vagrants, Mountain

In 1971 Leslie West worked in the studio with Pete Townshend to record a number of songs for Townshend's 'lost' album *Lifehouse*.

1946 Eddie Brigati singer: Joey Dee and the Starliters, Young Rascals

Before co-founding the Young Rascals, Eddie Brigati had replaced his brother David as a vocalist with peppermint twisters Joey Dee and the Starliters. Other members of the Starliters included Felix Cavaliere and Gene Cornish. In 1965 all three quit to form the Young Rascals.

Events today

1956 Landmark Events Hungarian uprising

The Hungarian uprising began when a huge crowd of protestors marched on the Budapest radio station to read out a list of their desired reforms.

The confrontation with their Russian masters came about, not as the result of a carefully planned revolution but as a spontaneous uprising uniting workers and intellectuals. The events in Budapest inspired other areas and the revolution soon spread to locations across Hungary. Sadly, the initial successes were not a sign of things to come and the rebellion was crushed by Soviet troops just two weeks later.

When the Second World War ended in 1945 Hungary remained under the control of its liberator, Russia. It became a satellite state of the Soviet Union and was under Russian occupation until the collapse of communism in 1990.

1978 Police played to an audience of three people

The Police's concert at the Last Chance Saloon in Poughkeepsie, New York was rated by *Rolling Stone* magazine as one of its *Twenty Concerts That Changed Rock & Roll.*[53]

Although the tour provided a springboard for future Police success, the Last Chance Saloon gig was not witnessed by too many people. Reputedly, Sting and the boys played to just three people. Three very lucky people indeed!

Recording session today

1966 Jimi Hendrix Experience first recording session

The Jimi Hendrix Experience had recently returned from a short tour of France where they gave their debut performance opening for Johnny Hallyday. In London's De Lane Lea Studios they recorded *Hey Joe* and *Stone Free*, which were coupled and released as their debut British single.

This first British Hendrix single was issued on the Polydor label. By the time that their second single, *Purple Haze*, was released, they had moved to Kit Lambert and Chris Stamp's newly formed Track Records label.

Album released today

1970 Led Zeppelin *Led Zeppelin III* (UK)

Jimmy Page's interest in the occult and the doctrines of Aleister Crowley led to the words "Do what thou wilt" and "So mete it be" being written into the run-out groove of the early albums.

"Do what thou wilt ..." was taken from a line in verse 40, Chapter 1, of Aleister Crowley's book, *The Book of the Law*.

The last track on the album, *Hats Off to (Roy) Harper*, was a tribute to the British folk singer. Harper was a friend of the band and sometimes opened for them. John Bonham and Jimmy Page returned the compliment by performing in Harper's backing group, Intergalactic Elephant Band, at his Rainbow Theatre concert on 14 February* 1974. Listed as "S Flavius Mercurius", Page also appeared on Harper's 1971 album *Stormcock*.

Birthday today

1947 Greg Ridley bass: The VIPs, Art, Spooky Tooth, Humble Pie

Greg Ridley joined the VIPs in 1964, before the band morphed into Art and finally Spooky Tooth. In 1970 he left to join Steve Marriott and Peter Frampton in Humble Pie.

Events today

24

1968 Joe Cocker Beatles song ...but Cocker classic

Shortly after releasing the Lennon and McCartney penned *With a Little Help from My Friends*, Joe Cocker appeared on the British TV show *Top of the Pops* to promote this new single.

With a Little Help from My Friends originally appeared on the Beatles' iconic *Sgt Pepper* album in 1967. Cocker's recording became a rare example of a song originally recorded by the Fab Four being overshadowed by the cover version. This was in fact the second Beatles song that Cocker had recorded. In 1964, after abandoning his stage name of "Vance Arnold" and his backing group the Avengers, he released *I'll Cry Instead* as a single. Sadly, it sank without trace.

1968 Landmark Events LSD became illegal in America

The mind-altering hippie drug of choice LSD (acid) became illegal in America after the passing of the Staggers-Dodd Bill.

Lysergic Acid Diethylamide (LSD-25) was synthesized by the Swiss chemist Albert Hofmann in 1938. In the 1950s, long before hippies discovered LSD's mind bending effects, America's Secret Service, the CIA, experimented with it to study the effects of psychoactive drugs. In 1959 beat icon Ken Kesey, author of *One Flew Over the Cuckoo's Nest* and leader of the Merry Pranksters, took part in the CIA funded LSD experimental programme MKULTRA at the Menlo Park Veterans Hospital. In the 1960s Kesey organised the infamous "Acid Tests" at a number of festivals and gatherings, the first of which was held on 27 November* 1965. Timothy Leary was another well-known champion of acid, enticing people to "turn on, tune in, drop out".

In October 1966 California became the first American state to make the drug illegal.

Birthdays today

1930 Big Bopper DJ turned singer and songwriter

Jiles Perry Richardson started his career as a disk jockey on radio KTRM in Beaumont, Texas. It was there that he created his alter ego "Big Bopper", inspired by watching a new dance craze, the bop. From spinning platters, he extended his skills to songwriting and performing. As a writer he had chart success with country legend George Jones's hit *White Lightning* and a #1 on both sides of the Atlantic with Johnny Preston's *Running Bear*. In 1958 he scored his own hit record with *Chantilly Lace*. This brought him the offer of a place on Buddy Holly's ill-fated *Winter Dance Party* tour. Tragically, he died along with Holly and Ritchie Valens when their plane crashed on 3 February* 1959.

1936 Bill Wyman bass: Cliftons, Rolling Stones, Rhythm Kings

Bill Wyman came to the Rolling Stones via a different route to the others guys. They had all performed in various lineups of Alexis Korner's Blues Incorporated. Wyman played with the Cliftons before joining the Stones in December 1962. It was there that he adopted the stage name "Lee Wyman", modified to Bill Wyman after borrowing the name of a friend from his National Service days. In the early 1980s he ventured out into a solo career and formed his own bands, including Willie and the Poor Boys and the Rhythm Kings. By the early 1990s he had left the Stones for good and was replaced by Darryl Jones.

Event today

25

1966 The Jimi Hendrix Experience British debut gig

Recently returned from France after giving their first-ever performance opening for Johnny Hallyday on 13 October*, the Jimi Hendrix Experience made its British debut at London's Scotch of St James club.

Albums released today

1968 Jethro Tull *This Was* (UK)

Jethro Tull released their first album, *This Was*. The title was an indication that the band was moving away from its blues-rock roots.

Jethro Tull evolved from the blues-based John Evan Band. The lineup that became Jethro Tull was: flautist and singer Ian Anderson, bassist Glen Cornick, guitarist and vocalist Mick Abrahams and drummer Clive Bunker.

Shortly after their debut album was released Mick Abrahams left to form Blodwyn Pig. Before guitarist Martin Barre was recruited, in time for Tull's second album *Stand Up*, two other guitarists briefly filled Abrahams's shoes. Future Black Sabbath's Tony Iommi was with the band just long enough to appear on the Rolling Stones' *Rock'n'Roll Circus*, recorded on 11 December* 1968. He was followed briefly by ex-Nice axeman David O'List.

The band took their inspiration for a name from the 18th-century agriculturist who invented the seed drill.

1968 The Jimi Hendrix Experience *Electric Ladyland* (UK)

Their third album, *Electric Ladyland*, marked the end of the Jimi Hendrix Experience and Hendrix's relationship with Chas Chandler. The frustration of constant re-takes during the recording sessions resulted in Chandler relinquishing his management of Hendrix and bassist Noel Redding forming his own band Fat Mattress.

Unlike the first two albums, *Are You Experienced* and *Axis: Bold as Love*, which were simply the Jimi Hendrix Experience trio of Hendrix, Redding and drummer Mitch Mitchell, *Electric Ladyland* featured a host of rock luminaries. Those adding their skills to the project included: Steve Winwood, Al Kooper, Traffic founding member Dave Mason and future Band of Gypsys drummer Buddy Miles. The double album's release in Britain sported a sleeve adorned with a bevy of naked ladies.

Noel Redding switched to guitar and vocals for his new band. Fat Mattress opened for the Jimi Hendrix Experience on the upcoming US tour. Redding played in both bands.

1969 Pink Floyd *Ummagumma* (UK)

Pink Floyd released their fourth British album, *Ummagumma*. This was the band's first double album and comprised two studio and two live sides. For the studio recordings each of the four members of the band contributed one composition. The live tracks were recorded in 1969 at three different venues, Bromley Technical College in Kent on 26 April, Birmingham's Mothers on 27 April and Manchester's College of Commerce on 2 May.

The album's title was reputedly a local Cambridge slang word for sex.

Birthday today

1944 Jon Anderson singer: The Warriors, Mabel Greer's Toyshop, Yes; solo

Morphing from Mabel Greer's Toyshop in 1968, Yes's original vocalist Jon Anderson left the band in 1980, although he did return a couple of years later.

Events today

26

1958 Bill Haley rock'n'roll makes youth ripe for atomic war

Bill Haley and His Comets sparked a riot when they played, what is often referred to as Germany's first-ever rock'n'roll concert, at West Berlin's Sportpalast.

Haley was rock'n'roll's first superstar and also the first American act to tour Europe. Their 1958 European tour was blighted by riots and cancellations. It even brought a comment from East Germany's Defence Minister Willi Stoph, who reputedly proclaimed that rock'n'roll was "a means of seduction to make youth ripe for atomic war."

1958 Muddy Waters first British tour

Muddy Waters recorded his performance at Manchester's Free Trade Hall.

This was a seminal moment in the development of British rock'n'roll. Jazz band leader Chris Barber invited Muddy Waters over for his first British tour. Accompanied by pianist Otis Spann and sometimes Barber's own jazz band, Waters introduced British audiences to American blues and also to the new sound of his amplified electric guitar.

1959 Johnny and the Moondogs on TV's *Star Search*

The Carroll Levis television talent show *Star Search* began a week of local finals at Liverpool's Empire Theatre.

At this time the Beatles were calling themselves "Johnny and the Moondogs". They didn't win this regional heat, an accolade taken away by the Connaughts, although they did qualify for the finals, to be held in Manchester in mid-November.

This was just before bassist Stuart Sutcliffe joined their ranks and they were still without a regular drummer.

1973 Fleetwood Mac — faux Fleetwood Mac

Guitarist Bob Weston was sacked from Fleetwood Mac. Weston's departure led to one of rock'n'roll's strangest episodes, when a completely bogus band embarked on an American tour in early 1974 under the name of "Fleetwood Mac".

Weston was hired to fill the void left when Danny Kirwan moved on. He featured on just two Fleetwood Mac albums, *Penguin* and *Mystery to Me*. Relationships in the band were already fraught when Weston began a relationship with drummer and founding member Mick Fleetwood's wife – Jenny, sister of Pattie Boyd. The band was on an American tour when it all became too much for Fleetwood. Weston was sacked and the remaining tour dates were cancelled. The band's manager, Clifford Davis, believed that he owned the rights to the band's name. He put together a faux band to go on the road as "Fleetwood Mac" and complete the tour commitments. This band consisted of guitarist and singer Elmer Gantry, guitarist Kirby Gregory, bassist Paul Martinez, keyboard player John Wilkinson and drummer Craig Collinge.

The bogus Fleetwood Mac embarked on an American tour in January 1974 but it soon ground to a premature end with negative fan reaction and injunctions from the real Fleetwood Mac. Lawsuits followed to wrest the ownership of the band's name away from Davis and back to the group.

The bogus group returned to Britain and changed their name to "Stretch".

Birthday today

1911 Mahalia Jackson — hugely influential gospel singer

Events today

1955 James Dean — *Rebel Without a Cause*

James Dean's second movie, *Rebel Without a Cause*, opened in America less than a month after his tragic death in a car crash on 30 September*. In the movie Dean played angst-ridden teenager Jim Stark, at odds with his parents and trying to find friends in a hostile world. This classic tale of teenage torment was directed by Nicholas Ray and featured Natalie Wood, Sal Mineo and Dennis Hopper.

The movie marked the beginning of the new phenomenon of "teenagers". Before the baby boomers, adolescents were simply smaller versions of their parents. This was the first generation of teenagers to have their own fashions, music and culture.

1958 Tommy Steele — appeared on *This Is Your Life*

British rock'n'roll became establishment the night Tommy Steele, Britain's first rock'n'roll star, appeared on the British version of the TV show *This Is Your Life*.

Recording sessions today

1953 Guitar Slim *The Things That I Used to Do*

The Things That I Used to Do is generally considered to be one of the blues songs that had a considerable influence on early rock'n'roll.

The session featured Ray Charles on piano.

1962 The Rolling Stones first-ever recording session

The Rolling Stones (although it might have been spelt Rollin') went into Curly Clayton's Studios in London's Highgate for their first recording session. The lineup was not yet the classic five but consisted of: vocalist Mick Jagger, guitarists Brian Jones and Keith Richard, pianist Ian Stewart and drummer Tony Chapman. Sources are split as to whether or not bassist Dick Taylor played on the session; he left the group around this time. They recorded Muddy Waters' *Soon Forgotten*, Jimmy Reed's *Close Together* and Bo Diddley's *You Can't Judge a Book By the Cover.*

The recording was made in order to produce a demo tape that could be hawked around London's record companies in search of a deal. Unbelievably, there were no takers. You could say that, like the Beatles, the Rolling Stones failed their first audition.

Chapman was previously with the Cliftons, the group that would also provide bassist Bill Wyman in the not-too-distant future. Charlie Watts was still with Blues By Six. It would be another three months before Bill and Charlie joined in.

Births and deaths today

1927 Bonnie Lou one of the first female rock'n'roll stars

1933 Floyd Cramer piano: one of the architects of "The Nashville Sound"

1951 KK Downing guitar: Judas Priest

1980 Steve Peregrin Took half of Tyrannosaurus Rex, died aged thirty-one

Steve Peregrine Took, the original bongo playing half of the 1960s hippie duo Tyrannosaurus Rex, died when he choked to death on a cocktail cherry.

Born Stephen Ross Porter, he took his stage name "Peregrin Took" from the Hobbit character also known as Pippin in Tolkien's epic story of the *Lord of the Rings*.

Events today

1958 Buddy Holly final TV appearance with the Crickets

Buddy Holly and the Crickets made one of their last appearances together on the TV show *American Bandstand*, where they performed *Heartbeat* and *It's So Easy*.

Holly parted company shortly afterwards with his manager Norman Petty and his backing group, the Crickets. Three months later, on 23 January*, Holly embarked on his ill-fated *Winter Dance Party* tour which ended with the plane crash on 3 February*, killing Holly, the Big Bopper and Ritchie Valens.

1961 The Beatles Brian Epstein was asked for a copy of *My Bonnie*

It might well have been apocryphal but as the story goes...Raymond Jones walked into Brian Epstein's NEMS record store in Liverpool and asked him for a copy of the Beatles' *My Bonnie*. It was actually by Tony Sheridan and the Beat Brothers and only released in Germany. More requests followed, prompting Epstein to check out this much sought after group. Then, in a life-changing decision, he become the Beatles' manager.

The Beatles had backed Tony Sheridan on *My Bonnie* but were credited as "The Beat Brothers" because "Beatles" sounded like "peedles", a German slang word for penis.

1973 The Who debut performance of *Quadrophenia*

The Who played *Quadrophenia* for the first time, at Trentham Garden in Stoke-on-Trent. The premiere did not go well. There were problems with the backing tracks and the band was under-rehearsed.

In an attempt to improve matters, three songs were removed from the set.

Album released today

1977 Sex Pistols *Never Mind the Bollocks Here's the Sex Pistols* (UK)

This was to be the only album officially released by the Sex Pistols in the band's lifetime.

The Sex Pistols were not the first British punk band to release an album: the Damned's debut appeared on 18 February*, followed by the Clash on 8 April*.

Birthdays today

1937 Graham Bond sax, keyboards and vocals: Graham Bond Organisation

Graham Bond was one of the founding fathers of British R&B. His band the Graham Bond Organisation was one of the platforms for up and coming British musicians. Various lineups included: Ginger Baker, Jon Hiseman, Jack Bruce and John McLaughlin. In late 1962 Bond replaced Cyril Davies in Alexis Korner's Blues Incorporated.

1941 Hank Marvin guitar: The Vipers, The Drifters, The Shadows

Hank Marvin was one of the earliest British guitar heroes.

1945 Elton Dean saxophone: Bluesology, Soft Machine

Elton Dean and Reg Dwight were together in Bluesology in the mid-1960s. Dean's first name, Elton, was taken by Dwight to create half of his stage name "Elton John".

1945 Wayne Fontana singer: Wayne Fontana and Mindbenders; solo

The inspiration[69] for his stage name came from the name of Elvis Presley's drummer, DJ Fontana, rather than from his record label, the Philips subsidiary Fontana.

Events today

1955 Sam Phillips opened the first all-female radio station

Three weeks before Sun Records' boss Sam Phillips signed over his protégé Elvis Presley to RCA on 20 November*, he started broadcasting from his new radio station WHER. Based at the local Memphis Holiday Inn motel, this was the first all-female radio station. It captivated its audience with the slogan, "1,000 beautiful watts".

1973 The Who *Quadrophenia* tour lumbered on

The second night of the ill-fated *Quadrophenia* tour played Wolverhampton's Civic Hall.

The opening night on 28 October* had suffered a number of problems and in an attempt to tighten up the show three songs were removed from the set: *The Dirty Jobs, Is It in My Head* and *I've Had Enough.* The rest of the British tour fared little better. Guitarist Pete Townshend stormed off the stage at Newcastle on 5 November* and cramped conditions at the final UK gigs in London's Lyceum attracted yet more complaints from the fans.

The opening night of the North American tour on 20 November* started ominously with Keith Moon collapsing on stage. Their trip over the border for the Montreal gig on 2 December* nearly resulted in the band and entourage failing to turn up for the Boston concert. They had missed their flight after being arrested for a spot of hotel wrecking.

Pub-rockers Kilburn and the High Roads opened for some of the British tour and southern-rockers Lynyrd Skynyrd did the honours for the American leg.

Recording session today

1976 Elvis Presley final recording session

Elvis began his last-ever recording session, at his Graceland mansion in Memphis.

Amongst the songs he recorded over those three days were *It's Easy for You*, written by Andrew Lloyd Webber and Tim Rice; *Way Down*, the last single to be released in his lifetime; his cover of Johnny Ace's *Pledging My Love*, a hit for Ace in early 1955 shortly after he killed himself playing Russian roulette on 25 December*; and the last song Elvis ever recorded, *He'll Have to Go*, an international hit for Jim Reeves in early 1960.

Single released today

1965 The Who *My Generation* c/w *Shout and Shimmy* (UK)

In the US, the Pete Townshend penned *My Generation* was coupled with *Out in the Street*.

Births and deaths today

1944 Denny Laine guitar and vocals: The Moody Blues, Airforce, Wings

Denny Laine sang the lead vocal on the Moody Blues' debut hit *Go Now!*, a cover of the American R&B hit for Bessie Banks.

1946 Peter Green guitar, vocals: John Mayall, Fleetwood Mac

Peter Green was one of the most respected British blues guitarists of his generation.

1971 Duane Allman Allman Brothers' guitarist, died at the age of twenty-four

Duane Allman was killed in a motorcycle accident in Macon, Georgia when he swerved to avoid a tractor-trailer.

In a bizarre twist of fate, Allman Brothers' bassist Berry Oakley died in a motorcycle crash thirteen months later, just a few blocks away from where Allman had been killed.

Events today

30

1962 The Beatles fourth Hamburg trip

The Beatles flew to Hamburg to begin a two-week residency at the Star Club, sharing the billing with Little Richard. Billy Preston was the keyboardist in Little Richard's backing band and he was later invited by the Beatles to join them in the *Get Back* project.

1967 The Rolling Stones Brian Jones and the drug charges

Brian Jones pleaded guilty to charges of drug possession, dating from a police raid on his home earlier in the year.

Jones's nine-month prison sentence was commuted on appeal to three years on probation and a £1,000 fine. Despite this, it gave him a real problem in obtaining a visa to work in America and contributed to his departure from the Stones in 1969.

1970 The Doors Jim Morrison's Miami concert incident

The Doors' frontman, Jim Morrison, was sentenced to six months' hard labour and a $500 fine, for charges brought about after his notorious concert at Miami's Dinner Key Auditorium on 2 March* 1969.

The charges at his trial in August included: lewd and lascivious behaviour, profanity, drunkenness and indecent exposure. Morrison's legal team immediately lodged an appeal and he was freed on a $50,000 bond. Before his appeal could be heard, Morrison died in Paris on 3 July* 1971.

This Miami incident proved to be disastrous for the Doors. Radio stations shunned their records and promoters cancelled tour dates.

1975 Bob Dylan *Rolling Thunder Review* tour opened

Bob Dylan's *Rolling Thunder Review* tour kicked off with its first port of call at the Plymouth Memorial Auditorium in Massachusetts. The *Review* included Joan Baez, Ramblin' Jack Elliott, Roger McGuinn, Mick Ronson, Joni Mitchell and Allen Ginsberg.

Tour highlights were captured along the way for the movie *Renaldo and Clara*. It ended with *The Night of the Hurricane* at New York's Madison Square Garden on 9 December*.

Live album recorded today

1968 MC5 *Kick Out the Jams*

The first of two concerts at Detroit's Grande Ballroom was recorded for what would become MC5's explosive debut album.

Birthdays today

1939 Grace Slick singer: The Great Society, Jefferson Airplane/Starship

Grace Slick replaced the original Jefferson Airplane singer Signe Anderson in 1966.

1941 Otis Williams singer: The Siberians, The Distants, The Temptations

Otis Williams was the driving force behind the Temptations. His group the Distants secured an audition for Motown and he invited members of the disbanded Primes to join him. They auditioned as the Elgins but changed their name to "The Temptations". The group went through many changes but Williams remained the one constant member.

1947 Timothy B Schmit bass, vocals: replaced Randy Meisner in Poco and Eagles

Events today

1962 Joni Mitchell first paid gig

Canadian folk singer Joni Mitchell gave her first paid performance at the Louis Riel coffee house in Saskatoon, Canada.

She released her debut album, *Song to a Seagull*, in the spring of 1968 and went on to become one of the most respected singer-songwriters of the late 1960s and '70s.

1963 The Beatles Ed Sullivan experienced Beatlemania

The Fab Four were returning from their first foreign tour, a hectic week of radio, TV and live performances in Sweden. They flew back into the UK at London's Heathrow airport and were greeted by hundreds of screaming fans. By sheer coincidence, American TV host Ed Sullivan was passing through the airport at the same time and witnessed the excitement caused by the Beatles. This personal introduction to Beatlemania influenced his decision to have the Fab Four on his show four months later.

1968 Vietnam War President Johnson ended the bombing

President Johnson gave his *Address to the Nation* in a televised broadcast announcing his decision to halt the bombing of North Vietnam. "Now, as a result of all of these developments [in the Paris peace talks], I have now ordered that all air, naval, and artillery bombardment of North Vietnam cease as of 8 a.m., Washington time, Friday morning. ...I have reached [my decision] in the belief that this action can lead to progress toward a peaceful settlement of the Vietnamese war".[87] Thus ended the bombing campaign *Operation Rolling Thunder*, which had begun on 2 March* 1965.

This was one of President Johnson's final acts of the Vietnam War. Richard Nixon was elected President of the United States of America a week later.

Singles released today

1969 The Beatles *Something* c/w *Come Together* (UK)

Something was George Harrison's only song to be issued as a Beatles A-side. It also became the Beatles' second most covered song after *Yesterday* and was the only time in the UK that album tracks were used as a single, both sides originated on *Abbey Road.*

Chuck Berry's publisher, Morris Levy, sued John Lennon for plagiarism because *Come Together* utilised lyrics from Berry's *You Can't Catch Me*. The situation was resolved by the inclusion of two Berry penned songs on Lennon's 1975 album *Rock'n'Roll*.

1975 Queen *Bohemian Rhapsody c/w I Love My Car* (UK)

Bohemian Rhapsody still regularly tops the polls to find "the best single of all time".

Album released today

1969 Led Zeppelin *Led Zeppelin II* (UK)

This second album found Led Zeppelin in publishing disputes over three of the tracks. Initially they only credited the band members as the writers. Legal actions followed from two blues legends and the authorship of the songs was suitably amended.

Willie Dixon was added to the writing credits for *Whole Lotta Love*, after identifying links to his song *You Need Love*. Dixon was also subsequently acknowledged for *Bring It on Home*. Howlin' Wolf (Chester Burnett) received his recognition for *The Lemon Song*, owing to the similarity with his blues standard, *Killing Floor*.

November

Events today

1964 Vietnam War — Viet Cong attack

One of the earliest Viet Cong attacks against the Americans occurred at Bien Hoa airbase, just twenty miles from Saigon. This night mortar attack killed four US personnel and destroyed or damaged a number of B57 bombers.

1965 Small Faces — Ian McLagan completed the classic lineup

At the invitation of manager Don Arden, keyboard player Ian McLagan joined the Small Faces to replace Jimmy Winston. The group had already achieved limited success in Britain with their first single, *Whatcha Gonna Do About It*.

The classic lineup of Steve Marriott, Ronnie Lane, Kenny Jones and now Ian McLagan released their first single *Sha-La-La-La-Lee* in January 1966. It went Top five and established the Small Faces as one of Britain's premier Mod bands.

1969 The Masked Marauders — *Rolling Stone* magazine's hoax album

In issue #45 *Rolling Stone* magazine continued with its Masked Marauders hoax album story, by reporting that there was a proposed date set for a Christmas release.[58]

In the previous issue, published on 18 October, the magazine had run a faux review of a double album purporting to be by supergroup the Masked Marauders, featuring Bob Dylan, Mick Jagger, John Lennon, Paul McCartney and George Harrison, and produced by Al Kooper. Despite obvious jokes in the review, the release was taken seriously enough for *Rolling Stone* to actually issue an album of songs mentioned in the review.

Single released today

1963 The Rolling Stones — *I Wanna Be Your Man* c/w *Stoned* (UK)

Written by Lennon and McCartney and released before the Beatles' version. The song was included on the UK album *With the Beatles* and *Meet the Beatles* in America.

This coupling was released in America three months later as the Stones' US debut but was quickly withdrawn and is now a much sought after collector's item.

Album released today

1968 George Harrison — *Wonderwall Music* (UK)

The first solo release by a Beatle was the soundtrack album *Wonderwall Music* by George Harrison. This was also the first album released on the Beatles' new Apple label. Harrison produced the album but surprisingly does not play on it, although he did elicit guest performances from Eddie Clayton and Richie Snare, otherwise known as Eric Clapton and Ringo Starr respectively. It also featured music from the Remo Four.

Birthdays today

1946 Rick Grech — bass: Family, Blind Faith, Ginger Baker's Airforce, Traffic

Born Richard Roman Grechko, Rick Grech was in Eric Clapton's band for old Slowhand's comeback concert on 13 January* 1973. He also worked with many of rock's luminaries including Graham Bond, Gram Parsons and The Crickets.

1963 Rick Allen — drums: Def Leppard

Rick Allen joined Def Leppard in late 1978. He lost his left arm in an automobile accident on 31 December* 1984.

Events today

2

1974 George Harrison — opened his North American tour

George Harrison kicked off his North American *Dark Horse* tour in Canada, at Vancouver's Pacific Coliseum.

He was the first Beatle to undertake a solo tour but it didn't go as well as he would have hoped. His voice was hoarse and the performances from support act Ravi Shankar were poorly received.

1959 Cliff Richard and the Drifters — first American hit

Cliff Richard was one of the first British rock'n'roll superstars but this was his first appearance on the American charts. In Britain *Living Doll* was his sixth Top 30 hit and gave him his first #1.

This was to be the last record issued by Cliff Richard and the Drifters. His backing group changed their name to "The Shadows" in order to prevent confusion with the American vocal group.

Despite achieving considerable success in Britain, he never quite managed to replicate that acclaim across the Atlantic. He only managed to achieve a handful of chart appearances in America, mostly in the early 1980s. It was such a different picture in the UK. By the end of 1982 he had scored over eighty chart appearances including ten #1s. In fact, in the *Virgin Book of British Hit Singles* published in 2010, Cliff is positioned at the top of its *Top 40 Acts by Singles Sales*, with sales exceeding twenty-one million singles, beating both Elvis and the Beatles.[29]

Album released today

1973 The Who — *Quadrophenia* — (UK)

Pete Townshend's tale of rock'n'roll angst was actually released in late October but pressing problems delayed its arrival in the record shops until after the tour had started.

The album captured the mid-1960s clashes between scooter-riding Mods and leather-clad Rockers. The first confrontation between them broke out on the beaches of Margate over the weekend of 28 March* 1964. The battles were repeated in other seaside towns up and down the country for several more summers to come.

The 1979 movie of *Quadrophenia* set the Who's music against a backdrop of mid-1960s Brighton.

Birthdays today

1937 Earl "Speedo" Carroll — singer: The Carnations, The Cadillacs, The Coasters

Earl Carroll was one of the founding members of the Cadillacs when the New York doo wop group changed their name from "The Carnations" in the mid-1950s. In 1956 they recorded the doo wop classic *Speedoo*. Carroll went on to replace singer Cornell Gunter in the Coasters in 1961.

1938 Jay Black — singer: Jay and the Americans

Jay Black replaced original lead singer Jay Traynor after their first hit, *She Cried*, in 1962.

1944 Keith Emerson — vocals, keyboards: The Nice, Emerson, Lake & Palmer

Keith Emerson had a penchant for enhancing his solos by stabbing his keyboard with a knife to hold down the keys.

Event today

1960 Elvis Presley — first act ever to have five #1s in Britain

Elvis joined the record books with *It's Now or Never,* by becoming the first act ever to have five #1s in the UK. The others were: *All Shook Up*, *Jailhouse Rock*, and both sides of *One Night c/w I Got Stung* and a *Fool Such as I c/w I Need Your Love Tonight*.

Recording sessions today

1965 Grateful Dead — first recording session

Just before changing their name to "Grateful Dead", the Warlocks made a demo recording at San Francisco's Golden Gate Studios. Using the name "The Emergency Crew", they recorded six songs: *Can't Come Down*, *Mindbender*, *The Only Time Is Now*, *Caution (Do Not Stop on the Tracks)*, *I Know You Rider* and *Early Morning Rain.*

The band comprised guitarist and vocalist Jerry Garcia, second guitarist and vocalist Bob Weir, harmonica, keyboardist and vocalist Ron "Pigpen" McKernan, bassist and vocalist Phil Lesh, and drummer Bill Kreutzmann. Still calling themselves "Warlocks" they played at Ken Kesey's first Acid Test on 27 November*, before performing as "Grateful Dead" for the first time on 10 December*.

1966 Jefferson Airplane — *White Rabbit*

This Grace Slick penned psychedelic classic was recorded for inclusion on Jefferson Airplane's second album, *Surrealistic Pillow.*

The album also contained another classic, *Somebody to Love*, written by Grace Slick's brother-in-law Darby Slick. Both songs were also on the album *Conspicuous Only in Its Absence*, recorded live at San Francisco's Matrix Club in 1966 by Grace Slick's previous band the Great Society but not released until 1968.

Single released today

1957 Jerry Lee Lewis — *Great Balls of Fire c/w You Win Again* (US)

Jerry Lee Lewis scored his second and biggest hit on both sides of the Atlantic with the Otis Blackwood penned *Great Balls of Fire*.

This was Lewis's chance to become the King of Rock'n'Roll. Two weeks earlier, on 12 October*, Little Richard had found God and renounced rock'n'roll. A week later, on 10 November*, Elvis gave his last performance before joining the US Army. But it was not to be... Lewis married his cousin's thirteen-year-old daughter, Myra Gale, a month later. He had one more Top 10 hit with another Blackwell penned song, *Breathless* but the end was nigh. When he arrived in England on 22 May* 1958, the news of his marriage became public and he had to pull out of his own headlining tour. He returned to America, sales of *High School Confidential* stalled and for Lewis, the rock'n'roll good times were over.

Birthdays today

1933 John Barry — bandleader and film score composer: John Barry Seven

He was an early British rock'n'roll band-leader but is best known for writing the film scores for eleven of the *James Bond* movies.

1945 Nick Simper — bass: Johnny Kidd and the New Pirates, Deep Purple

Nick Simper survived the car crash that killed Johnny Kidd in 1966. He went on to become a founding member of Deep Purple.

Events today

1961 Bob Dylan — first paid-attendance gig

Bob Dylan arrived in New York in January 1961 and was a regular performer around the Greenwich Village coffee houses. He moved up a gear with this first concert where people actually paid to see him perform. Held in Carnegie Hall's Chapter Hall with an entrance fee of $2, it was only attended by fifty or so people but Dylan was on his way.

1963 The Beatles — *Royal Command Performance*

In 1963 the prestigious *Royal Command Performance* was held at London's Prince of Wales Theatre, in front of The Queen Mother and Princess Margaret. The highlight of the Beatles' performance that night was *Twist and Shout*. In his introduction to the song John Lennon famously suggested that "... those in the cheaper seats clap your hands and the rest of you just rattle your jewellery".

1966 The Incredible String Band — first gig outside Scotland

Psychedelic-folk duo the Incredible String Band, in the form of Robin Williamson and Mike Heron, played their first gig outside Scotland at London's Royal Albert Hall. The duo performed as a support act for fellow Elektra folk artists Tom Paxton and Judy Collins.

Robin Williamson and Clive Palmer started performing together as a folk duo in the mid-1960s. They were joined by guitarist Mike Heron and became the Incredible String Band. The trio released an eponymous album in mid-1966 and promptly split up. The producer of the album, Joe Boyd, was also their manager and a representative for Elektra. He arranged the support slot with Tom Paxton and in mid-1967, augmented by others, they released their second album, *The 5,000 Spirits or the Layers of the Onion*.

1967 Pink Floyd American concert debut

Pink Floyd kicked off their disastrous debut tour of America with a concert at San Francisco's Winterland Ballroom. They shared the bill with Richie Havens and headliners Big Brother and the Holding Company.

Due to visa problems the tour was late starting, resulting in the cancellation of a number of concert dates. To make matters worse, Syd Barrett's behaviour was becoming increasingly erratic. During their infamous appearance on TV's *Pat Boone Show*, Barrett stared silently at Boone during the interview and remained motionless when they gave a mimed performance of their latest single, *See Emily Play*.

1968 Cream final American concert

Cream played their final American concert at the Rhode Island Auditorium in Providence, Rhode Island. Terry Reid was their support act. He had famously turned down the opportunity to become the vocalist for the recently formed Led Zeppelin.

1971 The Who London's Rainbow Theatre opened

The Who started a three-day run at the grand opening of London's Rainbow Theatre.

Birthday today

1940 Delbert McClinton harmonica player, singer and songwriter

Delbert Clinton played harmonica on Bruce Channel's 1962 #1 *Hey! Baby* and reputedly inspired John Lennon's harmonica work on *Love Me Do*.

Events today

1973 The Who Pete Townshend stormed off the stage

The Who's ill-fated *Quadrophenia* tour reached a new low point at Newcastle's Odeon cinema in the north of England.

The tour opened on 28 October*, had songs cut the following night on the 29th* and was still experiencing problems with the backing tapes when the Who reached Newcastle. Pete Townshend's frustration turned to rage when he hauled the hapless soundman, Bob Pridden, onto the stage. In a fit of anger he smashed his guitar and sound equipment before storming off. The others followed. They returned shortly afterwards but abandoned *Quadrophenia* in favour of playing old favourites.

Even the *Quadrophenia* album seemed doomed. It was due for release at the end of October but pressing problems caused delays in distribution and it did not reach the shops until November 2*, after the tour had started.

1988 The Beach Boys twenty-two years between American #1s

After a gap of twenty-two years, the Beach Boys once again scored a #1 on the American charts with *Kokomo*. The song was written for the Tom Cruise film *Cocktail* and received a Grammy nomination for "Best song written specifically for a Motion Picture or Television". It lost out to Phil Collins' *Two Hearts*, from the movie *Buster*. The Beach Boys' previous American #1 was way back in 1966 with *Good Vibrations*.

In a bizarre twist of fate, the Beach Boys lost out to Phil Collins for the Grammy but took their revenge by knocking Collins' *Groovy Kind Of Love* off the #1 spot with *Kokomo*.

Single released today

1958 Buddy Holly *Heartbeat* c/w *Well....All Right* (US)

By the time that this final Buddy Holly and the Crickets single was released, Holly had parted company with both his manager Norman Petty and the Crickets.

Births and deaths today

1931 Ike Turner piano, guitar: Kings of Rhythm, Ike and Tina Turner Revue

On 5 March* 1951 Ike's band the Kings of Rhythm recorded *Rocket 88*, generally considered to be the first rock'n'roll record. It was cut at Sun studios with Sam Phillips at the controls and released as "Jackie Brenston and His Delta Cats".

1946 Gram Parsons guitar and vocals: The Byrds, The Flying Burrito Brothers

After the departure of David Crosby and Michael Clarke from the Byrds, Gram Parsons joined for *Sweetheart of the Rodeo*, his only album with the band. He went on to form the Flying Burrito Brothers with former Byrds founding member Chris Hillman.

1960 Johnny Horton eerie similarity with Hank Williams's death

Johnny Horton's death had a spooky series of coincidences with that of country legend Hank Williams. Both performers had just made what would be their final appearances, at the Skyline Club in Austin, Texas. Both men left the same widow, Billy Jean, whom Horton had married after Hank Williams's death. Both singers died in their cars. Williams passed away peacefully on the back seat of his chauffeur-driven limo, whilst Horton was the victim of a collision with a drunk driver. In a way, booze killed both men.

Events today

1954 Elvis Presley radio commercial

The only radio commercial that the King of Rock'n'Roll ever made aired on the Shreveport concert show *Louisiana Hayride*.

It was for Southern Maid Donuts and the jingle enticed the locals not only to buy them but to "get 'em piping hot".

1965 Eric Clapton ill-fated trip to Greece with the Glands

Eric Clapton rejoined John Mayall's Bluesbreakers after his trip to Greece. The gig was at, or near, London's Heathrow airport but details are sketchy.

In August Clapton formed the Glands, a loose collection of musicians which included pianist Ben Palmer. The plan was to play their way across Europe and Australia but they only managed to get as far as Greece. There they were blackmailed by a club owner for working without permits. They made their escape but Clapton lost his amp.

When he rejoined the Bluesbreakers he replaced guitarist Peter Green, who had only joined a week earlier. He also played alongside bassist Jack Bruce for the first time.

1968 The Monkees world premiere of *Head*

The Monkees controversial movie *Head* premiered in New York. It was co-written by Jack Nicholson and featured an unlikely appearance from Frank Zappa.

1970 Aerosmith debut concert

Everyone has to start somewhere and Aerosmith started with their debut concert in the Nipmuc Regional High School gymnasium in Mendon, Massachusetts.

Four of the classic lineup performed that day: guitarist Joe Perry, vocalist Steven Tyler, bassist Tom Hamilton and drummer Joey Kramer. Ray Tabano played the second guitar but he soon gave way to Brad Whitford, to complete the classic Aerosmith lineup.

1975 Sex Pistols first gig

The Sex Pistols made their debut at St Martin's College of Art in London. It was a short affair, with the organisers pulling the plug mid-performance. The show may have had a rather ignominious end but they still went on to become the poster boys of British punk.

Births and deaths today

1938 PJ Proby singer: The Moon Dogs, Jett Powers; solo

1947 George Young guitar: The Easybeats; producer: AC/DC

George Young was a founding member of the Easybeats and co-writer of their 1967 hit *Friday on My Mind*. He also produced the early albums for AC/DC, keeping it in the family with his guitar playing brothers Angus and Malcolm.

1948 Glen Frey guitar, vocals and songwriter: Eagles; solo

1972 Billy Murcia original New York Dolls drummer, died aged twenty-one

Whilst in London on their first British tour, New York Dolls' original drummer Billy Murcia passed out in his hotel room after a combination of drugs and alcohol. Attempts to revive him with a cold bath and coffee failed and he reputedly choked to death.

Event today

1969 Rolling Stones American tour kicked off

With their first American concert for three years, the Rolling Stones opened their historic 1969 American tour with a gig in Fort Collins, at the Colorado State University.

The support acts varied across the tour but included Ike and Tina Turner, blues legend BB King, Chuck Berry and the man who turned down the job as Led Zeppelin's lead singer, Terry Reid.

This tour included their triumphant performances at New York's Madison Square Garden, where they opened on 27 November*. At the other end of the spectrum, their American experience ended with the notorious free concert at Altamont on 6 December*. The Hells Angels were hired to handle security at the concert. Tragedy struck when one of the Angels killed a member of the audience during the Rolling Stones' set.

The Rolling Stones had not performed in America since their 1966 tour, when Brian Jones gave his American swan song performance at the International Sports Centre in Honolulu on 28 July*.

Single released today

1969 Led Zeppelin *Whole Lotta Love* c/w *Living Loving Maid* (US)

Willie Dixon successfully sued Led Zeppelin for not giving him a writing credit, after adapting his song *You Need Love* for their *Whole Lotta Love.*

This single was also due for a British release but was withdrawn due to their policy of not releasing singles in their homeland. The withdrawn UK Atlantic Records release number 584309 originally given to *Whole Lotta Love*, was reused and given to Clarence Carter's *Take It Off Him and Put It On Me.*

Alexis Korner's big-band version of *Whole Lotta Love* with CCS (Collective Consciousness Society) made the British charts in 1970. This big-band arrangement was also recorded by BBC TV's *Top of the Pops'* musical director, Johnny Pearson, and used as the show's theme music for much of the 1970s.

It must be one of rock'n'roll's most beautiful ironies that one of Led Zeppelin's most popular songs was used as the theme tune on for a singles-based TV show, when they themselves derided the 45-rpm format.

Album released today

1969 John Lennon *Wedding Album* (UK)

Two weeks after the album was released in America and seven and a half months after their marriage, John Lennon and Yoko Ono released *Wedding Album* in the UK.

John Lennon married his second wife, Yoko Ono, in Gibraltar less than two weeks after Paul McCartney's marriage to Linda Eastman. Following a brief stay in Gibraltar the Lennons headed off to Canada for their honeymoon, a bed-in at Montreal's Queen Elizabeth Hotel.

Birthdays today

1942 Johnny Rivers guitarist, singer, songwriter and producer

Achieved success across the 1950s, '60s and '70s.

1943 Joni Mitchell Canadian singer-songwriter

Events today

1957 Elvis Presley end of his rock'n'roll years

Three weeks after its premiere in Memphis, Elvis Presley's third movie, *Jailhouse Rock*, opened for general release across America.

Elvis was inducted into the US Army on 24 March* 1958. His last concert before entering the service of his nation was on 10 November*, just two days after *Jailhouse Rock* opened. To all intents and purposes this marked the end of Elvis the rock'n'roller. His record company, RCA, kept the fans happy with a steady flow of singles throughout 1958 and '59, until the King released his first post-Army single *Stuck on You* on 23 March* 1960. It was a very different Elvis who returned from the Army. After releasing the album *Pot Luck* on 5 June* 1962, new rock and pop material was a thing of the past. After that, the only record releases available were those taken from his movie soundtrack recordings. He also bade a fond farewell to live performances, making his last live appearance for seven years on 25 March* 1961.

Elvis's induction into the US Army was delayed so that he could finish work on his fourth movie *King Creole*. That was to be the last glimpse the world would have of Elvis the dramatic actor. When he returned from the Army he starred in twenty-seven more movies throughout the 1960s but this was a new fluffy Elvis, light years away from his 1950s rock'n'roll persona.

1972 Norman Pilcher arrested

One of the most infamous policemen of the era, Detective Sergeant Norman Pilcher was arrested and charged with conspiracy to pervert the course of justice. He was ultimately sentenced to four years in prison.

Pilcher became notorious for his zealous pursuit of rock stars, in a quest to bust them for drugs related offences. At various times he famously arrested Donovan, Mick Jagger, Keith Richard, George Harrison and John Lennon. "Semolina pilchard" in John Lennon's song *I Am the Walrus* is reputed to be a reference to Pilcher.

1974 Connie Francis raped in her hotel room

Seminal rock'n'roll singer Connie Francis was raped in her hotel room at the Howard Johnson Motor Lodge in New York.

Francis had only recently returned to performing when she undertook a series of appearances at the Westbury Music Fair, starting on 6 November. She had returned to the hotel after her concert in Westbury, when a man forced his way in through one of the sliding glass doors and raped her. She subsequently won a lawsuit against the hotel for not providing adequate security.

The rapist was never caught. More personal tragedy was to follow when her brother was murdered in 1981.

Album released today

1969 The Allman Brothers Band *The Allman Brothers Band* 1st album (US)

Birthday today

1946 Roy Wood singer and multi-instrumentalist: The Move, ELO, Wizzard

Roy Wood left Mike Sheridan's Lot in early 1966 to form the Move. In the early 1970s he morphed the Move into the Electric Light Orchestra, a new venture that he hoped would achieve his vision of picking up where the Beatles' *Sgt Pepper* left off.

9

Events today

1961 The Beatles — Brian Epstein's first glimpse of the Beatles

After being asked for a copy of the Beatles' *My Bonnie* on 28 October*, Brian Epstein visited the Cavern's lunchtime session to hear the Beatles for himself. He became their manager shortly afterwards and accompanied them to their audition with Decca on 1 January*.

1967 Landmark Magazines — first issue of *Rolling Stone*

The first issue of *Rolling Stone* magazine hit the news-stands. The front cover sported a photo of John Lennon in World War II battle fatigues, taken from his role as Private Gripweed in Dick Lester's new movie *How I Won the War*. The twenty-four page inaugural issue, costing just 25c, carried articles on the Grateful Dead's recent drugs bust, David Crosby's sacking from the Byrds, a review of Arlo Guthrie's album *Alice's Restaurant* along with the first-ever *Rolling Stone Interview*, with Donovan.

The magazine's philosophy was outlined in a *Letter from the Editor*. It was not just about rock'n'roll but also "things and attitudes that the music embraces".[64] To reflect the changing times, the name came from the old saying, "A rolling stone gathers no moss".

1968 Led Zeppelin — first concert as "Led Zeppelin"

Led Zeppelin performed their first gig under the new name of "Led Zeppelin" at London's Roundhouse club. On the poster[88] they were billed as the "YARDBIRDS now known as LED ZEPPELIN". The all-night gig also featured blues from John Lee Hooker.

With the demise of the old Yardbirds, Jimmy Page had reinvented the band with new members: singer Robert Plant, drummer John Bonham and bassist John Paul Jones. They had just returned from a short tour of Denmark and Sweden where, for contractual reasons, they had still been billed as "The Yardbirds". Following their return to England they played a couple of gigs still billed as "The Yardbirds" or "New Yardbirds" but it was the Roundhouse which witnessed the first Led Zeppelin concert.

Their first gig as "Led Zeppelin" is sometimes quoted as the previous gig at the University of Surrey on 25 October. The poster[24] for that concert billed them as the "New Yardbirds featuring Jimmy Page".

The band's name came courtesy of the Who's Keith Moon and John Entwistle, who liked to refer to disastrous gigs as going down like a "lead Zeppelin". Page and his cohorts liked the name, dropped the "a" – and a legend was born.

Recording session today

1967 Spirit — *Spirit*

Spirit were in the studio recording tracks for their eponymous debut album, an eclectic fusion of jazz, blues, psychedelic rock and whatever-else came to hand.

The band was formed by guitarist Randy California and drummer Ed Cassidy.

Birthdays today

1944 Phil May — singer: Pretty Things

The Pretty Things' 1968 album *SF Sorrow* is often referred to as the first "concept album". It predated the Who's *Tommy*, which was released in the UK on 23 May* 1969.

1941 Tom Fogerty vocals, guitar: Golliwogs, Creedence Clearwater Revival

Events today

1957 Elvis Presley goodbye to live performances

The opening phase of the King of Rock'n'Roll's career came to an end with the first of two days of concerts in Hawaii. These were to be his last live performances before being inducted into the US Army on 24 March*.

This was goodbye to Elvis the rock'n'roll singer – and hello to Elvis the Hollywood movie star. When he came out of the Army he had a complete change of direction and limited his appearances to the big screen, with twenty-seven non-concert movies across the 1960s. With the exception of a rare personal appearance when he first came out of the Army, his next live concert would not be until 31 July* 1969, when he opened in Las Vegas. This heralded the third and final stage of his career – Elvis the cabaret performer.

Interspersed with his Las Vegas performances he did tour America but never again ventured outside his native borders. In fact, during his whole career the only non-USA appearances he ever made were a handful of gigs in neighbouring Canada in 1957.

1969 Elvis Presley goodbye to Elvis the movie star

Change of Habit opened in America, Elvis Presley's 31st and final movie as an actor.

Elvis played the part of Dr Carpenter, who was busy cleaning up the ghetto when he fell in love with Mary Tyler Moore, not realising that she was a nun. The only movie song to make it onto a single was *Rubberneckin'*, on the B-side of *Don't Cry Daddy*.

1999 Landmark Events RIAA's *Artists of the Century*

The RIAA, who certify "Gold" and "Platinum" discs, announced their *Artists of the Century*.

The Eagles' album *Greatest Hits 1971-1975* was the first Platinum album ever certified and with twenty-six million sales, became the best-selling album of all time. It passed Michael Jackson's *Thriller*, which had held the record since 1984 but Jackson's album remained the best-selling studio album by a solo artist.

Elvis remained the performer with the most Gold and Platinum albums and singles, with more than seventy-seven million albums sold in America alone.

The Beatles was the only act in history with five Diamond albums – American sales of 10 million copies or more: *Sgt Pepper's Lonely Hearts Club Band*, *The Beatles* (White Album), *Abbey Road*, and two 1973 compilations, *The Beatles* 1962 – 1966 and *The Beatles* 1967 – 1970.

Album released today

1978 The Clash *Give 'Em Enough Rope* (UK)

Give 'Em Enough Rope was the Clash's second album in the UK but their debut release in America. This was the first album to feature drummer Topper Headon.

With some variation on the track listing, their eponymous UK debut album became their second American release, featuring both Tory Crimes and Topper Headon on drums.

Birthday today

1947 Greg Lake bass and vocals: The Gods, King Crimson, ELP; solo

Greg Lake was a founding member of both King Crimson, and Emerson, Lake & Palmer.

Events today

1965 The Velvet Underground first gig

The Velvet Underground played their first gig, opening for the Myddle Class at a high school dance at Summit High School, New Jersey. The Myddle Class lineup featured future Steely Dan vocalist David Palmer.

The band's name was inspired by the title of Michael Leigh's book about the sexual twilight zone that existed in early 1960s America.

1967 Van Morrison first solo appearance on *American Bandstand*

When Van Morrison made his first solo appearance on *American Bandstand*, he performed two songs, *Brown Eyed Girl* and *Ro Ro Rosy*.

Van Morrison had come to fame with Belfast's R&B giants Them. The relationship ended when singer and band parted company in mid-1966. Them recruited a new vocalist and carried on in the R&B mould. Morrison signed to Bert Berns's Bang label and embarked on a solo career that traded-in his old R&B style for a new direction concentrating on his own material.

1969 The Doors Jim Morrison arrested

On his way to a Rolling Stones concert, Doors frontman Jim Morrison was arrested in Phoenix after becoming drunk and obnoxious on a flight from Los Angeles.

Recording session today

1958 Hank Ballard and the Midnighters *The Twist*

The twist dance craze started out as the B-side to *Teardrops on Your Letter*. DJs flipped the record and the coupling gave Hank Ballard and the Midnighters a double-sided R&B hit in the spring of 1959.

The real success for the Hank Ballard penned song came with Chubby Checker's American #1 cover version in the late summer of 1960. The twist had arrived and heralded a host of other 1960s dance crazes.

Births and deaths today

1927 Mose Allison jazz and blues pianist, singer and songwriter

Mose Allison was a rare example of a white blues and jazz hero from the Mississippi Delta. The Who covered *Blues* as *Young Man* on their 1970 album *Live at Leeds* and John Mayall covered the classic *Parchman Farm* as a single in 1966, both penned by Allison. In 1996 Van Morrison recorded the tribute album *Tell Me Something: The Songs of Mose Allison*.

1945 Chris Dreja guitar and bass: Metropolis Blues Quartet, The Yardbirds

Chris Dreja was with the London-based Metropolis Blues Quartet when they morphed into the Yardbirds. He moved across from rhythm guitar to bass when Jimmy Page joined the lineup, giving the Yardbirds the phenomenal talents of both Jimmy Page and Jeff Beck as dual lead guitarists.

1972 Berry Oakley Allman Brothers' bassist, died at the age of twenty-four

Allman Brothers bass guitarist Berry Oakley died in a motorcycle accident. In a bizarre coincidence, he died in Macon, Georgia, only a few blocks away from the spot where Duane Allman had also been killed when his motorcycle crashed a year earlier.

Events today

1965 Marc Bolan first TV performance

Marc Bolan performed his first single, *The Wizard*, on UK TV's *Ready Steady Go!*

Bolan previously called himself "Toby Tyler" and in 1964 made an acetate recording of *The Road I'm On* and a cover of Bob Dylan's *Blowin' in the Wind*. By the time that he made this TV debut he had changed his name to "Marc Bolan". Two more unsuccessful singles followed, before he joined John's Children in early 1967. Success finally came after he formed Tyrannosaurus Rex in mid-1967 and released *Debora* in 1968.

1970 Jim Morrison last performance with the Doors

Singer Jim Morrison's swan song performance with the Doors came at the Warehouse in New Orleans. At this last gig Morrison's increasingly erratic behaviour culminated in him smashing a hole through the stage with the mike stand. The concert was stopped and the group decided that this would mark an end to their live performances.

1979 Marty Balin *Rock Justice* opened

Jefferson Airplane's Marty Balin opened a four-day run of his new rock opera, *Rock Justice*, at the Old Waldorf in San Francisco.

The story line told of a rock musician on trial for not having a hit record.

Recording session today

1953 The Drifters *Such a Night*

When the Drifters' second single, *Such a Night*, was released it was coupled with *Lucille*, a song that had been recorded at the Drifters first-ever recording session.

After that first session, founder and lead singer Clyde McPhatter fired the rest of the group and recruited a completely new lineup for the second recording session on 9 August*. This new lineup was also the one that recorded *Such a Night*. These changes meant that McPhatter was with a different set of Drifters on each side of the single.

Elvis recorded the song shortly after he left the US Army, for inclusion on his first post-military album *Elvis Is Back!*, released in the spring of 1960. In 1964 it was released as a single, one of only a few singles at the time not to be taken from his movie soundtracks.

Album released today

1971 Led Zeppelin untitled (aka *Led Zeppelin IV*) (UK)

This untitled album is also known as "*Led Zeppelin IV*", "*Four Symbols*", "*Zoso*" and "*Runes*". It contained two rock classics: *When the Levee Breaks*, one of the most sampled drum rhythms ever and *Stairway to Heaven*, one of the most played songs on FM radio.

Birthdays today

1934 Charles Manson serial killer, friend of Dennis Wilson

The notorious killer Charles Manson had a number of links with the world of rock'n'roll. He was friendly with the Beach Boys' drummer Dennis Wilson, who allowed Manson to cut some tracks at his brother Brian's home studio. The Beach Boys also recorded one of Manson's songs, *Cease to Exist*. They renamed it *Never Learn Not to Love* and it appeared as the B-side of their 1968 single *Bluebirds Over the Mountain.*

1945 Neil Young guitar, singer, songwriter: Buffalo Springfield, CSNY; solo

Events today

1963 Vance Arnold and the Avengers early outing for Joe Cocker

Joe Cocker, using his original stage name "Vance Arnold" and with his backing group the Avengers, supported the Rolling Stones in *The R&B Show* at Sheffield's City Hall. Alongside the Sheffield born Cocker, a number of other local hopefuls made up the bill alongside Liverpool bands The Big Three, and Wayne Fontana and the Mindbenders.

Cocker parted company with the Avengers in 1964, after he was offered the opportunity by Decca Records to record the Lennon and McCartney song *I'll Cry Instead*. The single sank without trace. In 1966 he formed a new backing group, the Grease Band. This took his career in the right direction and in late 1968 he secured his place in rock'n'roll history, when he released his tour de force with another Lennon and McCartney song, *With a Little Help from My Friends.*

1968 The Beatles *Yellow Submarine* opened

The Beatles animated movie *Yellow Submarine* opened in America.

The song *Hey Bulldog* was cut from the movie for the American release because it was felt that the movie was too long.

1974 Richie Blackmore problems with an imposter

An imposter posing as Deep Purple's Richie Blackmore borrowed a Porsche in Iowa City and promptly wrecked it.

Before totalling the Porsche he had already conned food and shelter out of some other hapless Deep Purple fans. Blackmore was in America at the time of the subterfuge but he was with the band in San Francisco. The imposter was apprehended and charged with misrepresentation.

Singles released today

1964 The Moody Blues *Go Now! c/w It's Easy Child* (UK)

Go Now! was a cover of a blues song originally released in America by Bessie Banks. It featured future Wings sideman Denny Laine on guitar and lead vocal, and was produced by their co-manager Alex Murray, aka Alex Wharton.

Murray had previously been half of the Most Brothers with producer Mickie Most. He also produced a video promo for the song, one of rock's first promotional videos.

1964 The Rolling Stones *Little Red Rooster c/w Off the Hook* (UK)

This reworking to *Little Red Rooster* gave the Stones their second British #1.

Willie Dixon's song *The Red Rooster* was originally recorded by Howlin' Wolf in 1961 and featured Dixon on bass and drummer Sam Lay.

Birthday today

1949 Terry Reid vocals and guitar: Peter Jay and the Jaywalkers; solo

The man who was nearly Led Zeppelin's vocalist. There might be one decision in Terry Reid's life that he now regrets. After the original Yardbirds folded, Jimmy Page asked Reid to be the new vocalist. Reid turned him down but suggested that Robert Plant might be interested. The Yardbirds became Led Zeppelin and Plant became one of rock'n'roll's best known singers.

Events today

1952 Landmark Events first British singles chart

The *New Musical Express* (NME) published Britain's first singles chart, with Al Martino's *Here in My Heart* as the first UK #1. This first chart listed the Top 12 singles and was based on sales from a couple of dozen record shops in the London area.

The first Top 20 appeared two years later on 1 October 1954.

1967 Pink Floyd Syd Barrett's time was nigh

Jimi Hendrix's first British headlining tour kicked off with a gig at London's Royal Albert Hall. Hendrix was supported by an array of groups, including The Move, Pink Floyd, Amen Corner, and The Nice.

This tour marked the end for Syd Barrett, the Pink Floyd's mercurial leading light. His behaviour had become increasingly erratic and his absence from some performances resulted in his place on stage being filled by the Nice's guitarist David O'List.

At the *Christmas on Earth Continued* concert, held at London's Olympia on 22 December*, Barrett could only stand on the stage staring at the audience. Around this time guitarist Dave Gilmour was asked to join the band, making them briefly a five-piece outfit. The end came for Barrett with a press release on 6 April* 1968, announcing that he was no longer a member of Pink Floyd.

1969 Faces from Small Faces ...to Faces ...and beyond

Faces played a gig in Basel, halfway through their short tour of Switzerland. Small Faces had undergone some personnel changes and this was one of the first concerts with the new lineup, although they were still sometimes billed as "Small Faces".

Small Faces lead singer Steve Marriott had moved on and formed Humble Pie with guitarist Peter Frampton. Marriott was replaced by singer Rod Stewart and guitarist Ron Wood, both refugees from the Jeff Beck Group. Wood had been in a late incarnation of another Mod band, the Creation. Stewart and Wood joined Small Faces' founding members, bassist Ronnie Lane and drummer Kenny Jones, with keyboard player Ian McLagan who had replaced founding member Jimmy Winston in 1965.

Rod Stewart progressively eclipsed the rest of the band and in 1975 took off for a solo career. Drummer Kenny Jones went on to replace Keith Moon in the Who and guitarist Ron Wood later filled Mick Taylor's shoes in the Rolling Stones.

1969 Skid Row early gig as a power trio

Guitarist Gary Moore, drummer Noel Bridgeman and bassist Brush Shiels performed one of their early gigs as a power trio at Dublin's Ierne Club.

After they released the single *New Places Old Faces*, original vocalist Phil Lynott left the group to form Orphanage. Shiels took over the vocal duties and the band became a power trio. Lynott found fame after forming Thin Lizzy in 1970. Moore and Lynott were reunited when Moore joined Thin Lizzy on a permanent basis in 1978.

Birthdays today

1936 Freddie Garrity lead singer: Freddie and the Dreamers; solo

He was well known for his manic dance performances. Freddie and the Dreamers covered a number of R&B classics, including James Ray's 1961 hit *If You Gotta Make a Fool of Somebody* and *I Understand*, a hit in 1954 for the Four Tunes and 1961 for the G-Clefs.

Events today

15

1956 Elvis Presley first movie

The first Hollywood venture for Elvis Presley, *Love Me Tender*, opened at New York's Paramount cinema in Times Square.

Originally called *The Reno Brothers*, the movie's name was changed to cash in on Elvis's growing popularity. This was to be the only occasion where Elvis's character died and he did not receive top billing.

Elvis also starred in *Loving You*, *Jailhouse Rock* and *King Creole*, before being inducted into the United States Army on 24 March* 1958. When Elvis returned from his military service the only access his fans had to him was through his, much maligned, 1960s cinema appearances. Excluding the concert documentaries Elvis made 31 movies, drawing to an end with *Change of Habit* released on 10 November* 1969.

1969 Vietnam War largest-ever anti-war demonstration

The three-day *March Against Death* ended with a mass rally at the White House. With estimates of as many as 500,000 people taking part, it was the biggest anti-war protest in American history. The demonstrators sang John Lennon's *Give Peace a Chance* outside the White House. Speeches were delivered by a number of speakers, including two Senators opposed to the war, George McGovern and Eugene McCarthy. Protest songs were provided by Peter Paul and Mary, Pete Seeger and Arlo Guthrie.

Singles released today

1974 Elton John *Lucy in the Sky with Diamonds* c/w *One Day at a Time* (UK)

Elton John released his cover of the Beatles' *Lucy in the Sky with Diamonds* as "Elton John featuring the Reggae guitars of Dr Winston O'Boogie", aka John Lennon.

When Lennon agreed to perform on Elton's cover version, the flamboyant singer reciprocated by lending a hand on Lennon's *Whatever Gets You Thru the Night*. The ex-Beatle also agreed that if *Whatever Gets You Thru the Night* topped the American charts, he would appear on stage with Elton John and perform the song. This indeed happened and Lennon took to the stage to join Elton on 28 November* 1974. This was to be Lennon's only #1 in his lifetime.

When the Beatles originally released *Lucy in the Sky with Diamonds* on their groundbreaking *Sgt Pepper* album, it was believed that the song was paying homage to the hallucinogenic drug LSD. This notion came from the prominence of the letters "L", "S" and "D" in the song's title. Lennon denied this, suggesting that the inspiration came from a painting by his son, Julian, of his nursery school friend Lucy O'Donnell. Julian had painted his friend surrounded by stars and told his father that it was called "Lucy in the Sky with Diamonds".

1974 Faces/Rod Stewart *You Can Make...* c/w *As Long as You Tell Him* (UK)

The Faces released their final single giving it one of the longest titles in rock'n'roll history, *You Can Make Me Dance, Sing or Anything (Even Take the Dog for a Walk, Mend a Fuse, Fold Away the Ironing Board, or Any Other Domestic Shortcomings)*.

Birthday today

1932 Clyde McPhatter lead singer: Ques, The Dominoes, The Drifters; solo

Clyde McPhatter was a founding member of both the Dominoes and the Drifters.

Event today

1969 Janis Joplin arrested at a gig

Janis Joplin was arrested for "vulgar and indecent language", after shouting obscenities at the police who were trying to control an unruly crowd at a gig in Tampa's Curtis Hixon Hall in Florida. BB King was on the same bill that night.

Joplin finished the concert before being arrested backstage. She was later released on a bond of $504. The experience concluded the following March with a fine of $200.

Recording session today

1956 Conway Twitty failed his audition at Sun Records

Harold Jenkins made his second visit to Sun Studios and recorded three songs with owner Sam Phillips at the controls: *Crazy Dreams*, *Give Me Some Love* and *I Need Your Lovin'*. Phillips, the man who discovered Elvis Presley, Jerry Lee Lewis and Carl Perkins, failed to see any potential in Jenkins's recordings and they were unissued at the time.

Failing to gain a record contract at Sun, Jenkins changed his name to Conway Twitty and became one of America's most successful country artists of all time. In 1957 he signed to Mercury and released the self-penned *I Need Your Lovin'* as his first single. Success finally came in 1958 when he signed to MGM. His first release on the new label, *It's Only Make Believe*, made #1 on both sides of the Atlantic. More pop hits followed, before Twitty settled into a lifelong run of country hits. His recording output was staggering, with 110[97] albums and fifty-five[97] #1 records.

In 1964 British rock'n'roll singer Billy Fury garnered a Top 10 hit with his cover of *It's Only Make Believe*, written by Twitty and his drummer Jack Nance.

Born Harold Jenkins, Conway Twitty took his stage name from two American towns, Conway in Arkansas and Twitty in Texas.

Single released today

1968 Cliff Richard and the Shadows *Don't Forget to Catch Me* (UK)

Cliff Richard and The Shadows released their final single together. Taken from the album *Established 1958*, it marked the end of more than a decade of working side by side. The B-side was just Cliff on his own with *What's More (I Don't Need Her)*.

Cliff Richard and the Drifters released *Move It!* as their first single, on 29 August* 1958. The Drifters' lineup evolved from that debut single and by the summer of 1960 they had changed their name to "The Shadows". With their second single and first hit *Apache*, they established themselves as Britain's premier instrumental combo.

The end came after a short residency at the London Palladium. The Shadows who supported Cliff that night were guitarists Hank Marvin and Bruce Welch from the original lineup, with drummer Brian Bennett and bassist John Rostill.

Various musicians came and went from the Shadows' lineup but to the fans' delight Cliff Richard and The Shadows occasionally teamed up to perform together again.

Birthday today

1933 Garnet Mimms singer: Gainors, Garnet Mimms and the Enchanters; solo

Garnet Mimms started his singing career in church choirs and after a stint in the Army formed the doo wop group the Gainors, before finding success with the Enchanters.

Mimms' 1963 hit *Cry Baby* was covered by Janis Joplin on her final album, *Pearl*.

Event today

1959 Johnny and the Moondogs Stuart Sutcliffe financed his bass guitar

The prestigious John Moores Exhibition opened in Liverpool's Walker Art Gallery. Included in the exhibits was Stuart Sutcliffe's abstract expressionist piece, *The Summer Painting*.

At the end of the exhibition in mid-January, John Moores purchased the painting for £65. Sutcliffe bought a Hofner President bass guitar and joined his art college friend John Lennon in Johnny and the Moondogs, soon to rename to "The Silver Beetles".

Recording session today

1971 Bob Dylan and Allen Ginsberg recording session together

Bob Dylan and beat poet Allen Ginsberg recorded together in New York's Record Plant studios. In this and other sessions they cut a number of songs, including *The Tyger* and *Vomit Express*. These recordings were released piecemeal over the next twenty years. Some of the songs were composed by Dylan and Ginsberg. Others were based on the works of 18/19th century British poet, writer and illustrator William Blake.

This was one of a number of Dylan's collaborations with Ginsberg. The poet can be seen in the background of Dylan's promotional video for *Subterranean Homesick Blues*. He was also one of the entourage with Dylan's touring company for the *Rolling Thunder Review* in 1975. In early 1982 they once again recorded together, producing *Airplane Blues* and *Do the Meditation Rock*.

Album released today

1980 John Lennon *Double Fantasy* (US)

John Lennon's final album was released just three weeks before he was murdered.

Births and deaths today

1942 Bob Gaudio keyboards, singer, songwriter, producer: Four Seasons

Bob Gaudio first found fame with the Royal Teens in the second half of the 1950s. After that he hooked up with Frankie Valli and his group the Four Lovers, just before they became the Four Seasons.

1944 Gene Clark singer: New Christy Minstrels, Jet Set, Beefeaters, Byrds

Founding member and main songwriter, Gene Clark parted amicably from the Byrds in March 1966 after their third album *Fifth Dimension*.

1946 Martin Barre guitar: Gethsemane, Jethro Tull

When original guitarist Mick Abrahams left Jethro Tull after their first album, his shoes were briefly filled by Tony Iommi. He soon returned to his Black Sabbath chums and ex-Nice guitarist David O'List had a short stay before Martin Barre took on the role.

1979 John Glascock Jethro Tull's bass guitarist, died at the age of twenty-eight

Bassist John Glascock died after major heart surgery to replace a faulty heart valve.

At the time of his death he was with Jethro Tull, having joined the band in 1975. In the early 1970s he played in Stan Webb's British blues band Chicken Shack. He was also one of the original members of the Gods in the mid-1960s, alongside future Rolling Stones guitarist Mick Taylor and Uriah Heep's Ken Hensley.

Events today

1975 Bruce Springsteen European debut

Bruce Springsteen kicked off his first European tour at London's Hammersmith Odeon.

The hype surrounding the *Born to Run* tour was massive, with claims of the new Bob Dylan and posters announcing that "FINALLY The world is ready for Bruce Springsteen". Difficult to imagine it now, but his debut was greeted with very mixed reviews.

1994 The Rolling Stones first live internet broadcast

A tad ironic that a 1960s band, The Rolling Stones, was to become the first major band to have a segment of their gig broadcast live on the internet. Fans were treated to twenty minutes of their *Voodoo Lounge* concert at Dallas' Fair Park in Texas.

Single released today

1967 Pink Floyd *Apples and Oranges* (UK)

This was Pink Floyd's third single, the last one penned by Syd Barrett and the first one to fail to make an impact on the British charts.

The group had opened their debut American tour on 4 November* and returned to the UK to open their British tour on 14 November*. By this time Barrett was succumbing to his drug problems. America saw his disastrous appearance on the *Pat Boone Show* and he was regularly replaced by David O'List on the British tour. Barrett was nearing the end of his days with the band and by 6 April* he was out.

Births and deaths today

1927 Hank Ballard singer, songwriter: Royals, The Midnighters

Hank Ballard joined the seminal Detroit R&B vocal group the Royals, before they changed their name to "The Midnighters" and released the 1954 rock'n'roll classic *Work With Me Annie*, a controversial song with racy lyrics.

Ballard wrote *The Twist* and released it as the B-side to *Teardrops on Your Letter*. As Hank Ballard and the Midnighters it gave them a minor hit in 1959 but Chubby Checker was catapulted to international fame when he covered *The Twist* in 1960.

1950 Graham Parker singer: Graham Parker and the Rumour; solo

Graham Parker came together with the Rumour in mid-1975. This was the tail end of pub rock, with punk rock just about to burst on the scene. The Rumour was formed by musicians from several pub-rock bands and included guitarist Brinsley Schwarz.

1972 Danny Whitten guitarist, died at the age of twenty-nine

Crazy Horse guitarist Danny Whitten died after a drug overdose.

He was best remembered for his work with Neil Young and Crazy Horse. His drug addiction became a problem for the band and he was fired shortly after their debut album *Crazy Horse* was released in early 1971. In the autumn of 1972 Young, believing that Whitten was off the drugs, contacted him to join his touring band. Whitten had replaced heroin with alcohol and it became evident that the guitarist could not function effectively in the band. He was sacked. On 18 November Whitten returned to Los Angeles, where he was found dead later that evening.

Neil Young's song *The Needle and the Damage Done* was a cautionary tale of Whitten's premature death from drug abuse.

Events today

1949 Jerry Lee Lewis first public performance

The career of rock'n'roll wild man Jerry Lee Lewis began with his first public performance, given at a Ford dealership in his Ferriday hometown in Louisiana. The fourteen-year-old Lewis performed *Drinking Wine Spo-Dee-O-Dee*.

Stick McGhee and His Buddies' re-recorded *Drinking Wine Spo-Dee-O-Dee* in 1949 and gave Ahmet Ertegun's fledgling Atlantic label its first real hit. Stick McGhee and His Buddy had originally released the song on the Harlem Records label in 1947.

1965 David Bowie with The Lower Third early appearance as "David Bowie"

Having recently changed his name from "David Jones" to "David Bowie", he appeared at London's Marquee club, as "David Bowie with The Lower Third".

Two months earlier, on 16 September*, Bowie announced that he had changed his name from "Davie Jones". He had already made his first recording with the Konrads, performed with the Manish Boys and the King Bees but he was still four years away from his first real taste of success, with *Space Oddity* in 1969.

1965 The Who Roger Daltrey stormed off stage

The Who performed live on *Ready Steady Go!* before rushing across London to the 10,000-seater Wembley Empire Pool to appear at the *Glad Rag Ball*.

There were around 3,000 people in the hall when the Who took to the stage and using the hall's own PA equipment started their performance. Daltrey was so disgusted with the quality of the sound that he stormed off the stage. The Who's road crew hurriedly began the task of setting up the band's own equipment whilst the other three band members played on. Once the sound system was in place Daltrey returned to the stage and continued with the concert.

1979 Chuck Berry released from prison (again!)

Chuck Berry was released from California's Lompoc Prison after serving his sentence for tax evasion.

This was Berry's third stay in prison. The first time was in the 1940s for armed robbery and then again in the early 1960s for violation of the *Mann Act*, taking a minor over the state line for naughty purposes.

1995 The Beatles *The Beatles Anthology* arrived

Part 1 of *The Beatles Anthology* series was first shown on ABC TV in America.

The premiere of the promotional video for *Free as a Bird*, the Beatles first new song for twenty-five years, was screened after this first *Beatles Anthology* episode.

Births and deaths today

1943 Fred Lipsius sax: Blood, Sweat & Tears; played with many jazz greats

Fred Lipsius was the original sax player with Blood, Sweat & Tears and also acted as their conductor and arranger. He was a member of the band from 1967 to 1971.

1983 Tom Evans — Badfinger bassist and songwriter, died aged thirty-six

Tom Evans took his own life by hanging himself from a tree in his garden, eight years after his Badfinger band mate Pete Ham had committed suicide on 24 April* 1975.

Events today

1955 Elvis Presley — from Sun to RCA

Elvis spent his last day on the Sun Records roster. His new manager, Colonel Tom Parker, had negotiated a contract for Elvis with RCA Records, with an official contract signing ceremony arranged for the following day at Sun Records in Memphis.

Sun Records' owner Sam Phillips sold his Elvis Presley contract to RCA for $35,000 with an additional $5,000 payment to Elvis for outstanding royalties on his Sun records. The deal included released and unreleased songs recorded by Presley at Sun.

1955 Bo Diddley — appeared on the *Ed Sullivan Show*

As his first appearance on national TV, Bo Diddley gave his only performance on the *Ed Sullivan Show*. Diddley had been due to sing Tennessee Ernie Ford's hit *Sixteen Tons* but instead performed his own song *Bo Diddley*. He was never invited back.

1973 The Who — Keith Moon collapsed on stage

The North American leg of the Who's ill-fated *Quadrophenia* tour started badly when drummer Keith Moon collapsed on stage, twice, at San Francisco's Cow Palace. After the second time, Pete Townshend called to the audience for a substitute stricksman. For nineteen-year-old fan Scott Halpin, from Muscatine, Iowa, this was his wildest dream come true. He took to the stage and for the remaining three numbers he was the Who's drummer. They were supported that night by southern-rockers Lynyrd Skynyrd.

Legend has it that Moon's backstage drink had been spiked with a horse tranquiliser.

Recording session today

1961 Bob Dylan — first recording session for his own album

Three weeks after signing to Columbia, Bob Dylan was in the studio with John Hammond recording tracks that would soon appear on his eponymous debut album. The remaining tracks were recorded at a second session two days later.

This was not Dylan's first appearance in the recording studio, on 30 September* he had played harmonica at a Carolyn Hester session.

Birthdays today

1944 Mike Vernon — producer and founder of Blue Horizon

Mike Vernon was one of the prime movers of the British blues movement. As well as producing albums for some of the premier British blues bands, he also founded the record label Blue Horizon. One of Vernon's first production gigs was with the Yardbirds, which included Eric Clapton, when they cut a demo recording in February 1964.

Blue Horizon included releases by Peter Green's Fleetwood Mac, Chicken Shack and Aynsley Dunbar's Retaliation.

1946 Duane Allman guitar: Allman Joys, Hour Glass, Allman Brothers Band

Rolling Stone magazine rated Duane Allman as #2 in its list of *The 100 Greatest Guitarists of All Time*, second only to Jimi Hendrix.[23]

1947 Joe Walsh guitar and vocals: James Gang, Eagles; solo

Joe Walsh's first taste of success came with the James Gang. He joined the Eagles in late 1975, in time to perform on their epic *Hotel California*.

Events today

1959 Alan Freed payola scandal

Iconic American disc jockey Alan Freed, accredited with coining the phrase "rock'n'roll", was sacked by ABC. He refused to sign an affidavit stating that he had never promoted any artists' recordings in return for payment.

The practice of taking payment for pushing new recordings or particular artists was known as "payola" and was widespread amongst radio and television DJs in the 1950s. As well as payments being in the form of money or gifts, a more subtle payment vehicle was to include the DJ's name on the writing credit of a song. Freed was one of the highest profile DJs that the House of Representatives subcommittee took action against when it turned its attention to payola in late 1959. In May 1960 Freed was arrested for receiving payments of over $30,000 from a number of record companies.

In December 1962 he pleaded guilty and received a fine of $300 with a six month suspended sentence. The experience broke Freed. His career was over. At the time of his alcohol related death on 20 January* 1965, he was penniless and facing tax-evasion charges.

1968 Iggy Pop from the Iguanas to the Stooges

Having shortened their name from the "Psychedelic Stooges" to simply "The Stooges", they supported Tim Buckley and Blue Cheer at Detroit's Grande Ballroom.

Iggy Pop started out as a drummer with his first group, the Iguanas, in the early 1960s. He also played with other groups in the Ann Arbor area of Michigan and even had a stint drumming with blues musicians in Chicago. In late 1967 he formed the Psychedelic Stooges. The group built up a strong reputation and after dropping the "Psychedelic" element of their name secured a recording contract with Elektra in the summer of 1968. Their eponymous debut album was produced by the Velvet Underground's John Cale.

Iggy Pop went on to a successful solo career and became a major inspiration for many of the mid-1970s punk rockers.

Birthdays today

1907 Buck Ram songwriter, arranger and Platters' manager

Buck Ram was one of the powerhouses behind early 1950s R&B music. He managed both the Penguins and the Platters. Mercury was keen to sign the Penguins after their smash hit *Earth Angel* and Ram persuaded the record label to take the Platters as well in a two-for-one deal. Ironically, the Penguins never managed to repeat their earlier achievements but the Platters become one of the era's most successful vocal groups. Ram was also a talented arranger and songwriter, writing many of the Platters greatest songs, including *Only You (And You Alone)* and *The Great Pretender*. His many activities also included the ownership of his own record label, Antler Records

1940 Dr John keyboards and vocals: solo; sessions

Dr John, also known as "The Night Tripper", was born and brought up in New Orleans, where he developed a highly theatrical style and a keen interest in voodoo. He started his musical career as a guitarist playing with many of New Orleans' luminaries, including Professor Longhair. A gunshot injury to his hand ended his guitar days. Undaunted, he moved to bass and then keyboards, where he found great success as a performer and a much sought-after session musician.

Events today

1957 Simon & Garfunkel Tom & Jerry on *American Bandstand*

Three months after *American Bandstand* went national on 5 August*, Dick Clark introduced Tom & Jerry singing their debut single, the self-penned *Hey, Schoolgirl*.

This was the first taste of chart success, albeit only a titbit, for future international stars Paul Simon and Art Garfunkel. In 1957, as Tom & Jerry, they shared the American charts with Elvis Presley at #1 with *Jailhouse Rock*, Jerry Lee Lewis's first hit *Whole Lot of Shakin' Going On*, and Little Richard's *Keep a Knockin'*. It would be the middle of the next decade before they experienced any real chart success themselves and that was as "Simon & Garfunkel", with their 1965 masterpiece *The Sounds of Silence*.

1963 President John F Kennedy assassinated

America's President Kennedy was assassinated in Texas, whilst travelling in a motorcade from the airport to a civil reception in downtown Dallas.

Lee Harvey Oswald had secured employment at the Texas School Book Depositary building in advance of the assassination. On the day of the shooting he allegedly positioned himself on the sixth floor and just after 12.30pm shot and fatally wounded President Kennedy. As well as the President and his wife Jacqueline, Governor John Connally and his wife were also in the open-topped Presidential limousine. Connally was seriously wounded but survived the attack. The President was taken to Parkland Memorial Hospital where he was pronounced dead half an hour later.

As an employee of the building, Oswald was able to make good his escape. He left the rifle on the sixth floor and exited the building. Little more than an hour after shooting the President, Oswald shot and killed Dallas police officer JD Tippit. Police traced the assailant to the *Texas* movie theatre where he was arrested.

Oswald never stood trial because two days later, as he was being escorted from the police station, he was gunned down by local nightclub owner Jack Ruby.

Vice-President Johnson became the new President of the United States of America.

Albums released today

1963 The Beatles *With the Beatles* (UK)

This was the first album to contain a George Harrison composition, *Don't Bother Me*. It was also the first British album to sell more than a million copies in the UK.

The first UK million-seller was the soundtrack to the movie *South Pacific*.

1968 The Beatles *The Beatles* (aka *The White Album*) (UK)

1968 The Kinks *The Kinks Are the Village Green Preservation Society* (UK)

When the album was originally pressed up for release it contained twelve tracks. By the time of its UK release that had extended to fifteen tracks, with some of the original songs being reworked. The original twelve track version of the album was released in Europe.

This was the last Kinks album to feature original bassist Pete Quaife.

Birthday today

1950 Stevie Van Zant guitar: E Street Band; solo

Events today

23

1963 The Rolling Stones Jagger and Richard's first hit song

The Rolling Stones and Gene Pitney both appeared on the British TV pop-music show *Thank Your Lucky Stars*. A backstage discussion gave Jagger and Richard their first taste of songwriting success.

A couple of days earlier the Stones had recorded a batch of songs. When Gene Pitney heard the Jagger and Richard penned *My Only Girl* he agreed to record it. He liked the lyrics but changed the melody. The song was renamed *That Girl Belongs to Yesterday* and it gave the fledgling songwriting team of Jagger and Richard their first hit record. It made Top 10 in Britain and achieved a minor impact on the American charts.

The Stones never released their version of the song.

1968 John and Yoko naked on the cover of *Rolling Stone*

Having appeared on the cover of the inaugural issue of *Rolling Stone* magazine, John Lennon was back. But for issue #22 it was a naked John and Yoko that adorned the cover page. The picture was the back view from the artwork for their *Two Virgins* album. The full-frontal picture was shown inside the magazine.

1976 Jerry Lee Lewis arrested outside Graceland

Jerry Lee Lewis was arrested outside Elvis's Memphis home, Graceland. He was waving a gun around and demanding to see Elvis, reputedly asking a security guard to tell Elvis that "the Killer's here to see him". Rather than inform Elvis, the guard called the police and Lewis was arrested.

Recording session today

1936 Robert Johnson first recording session ...San Antonio

Blues legend Robert Johnson recorded a total of twenty-nine songs over two recording sessions. This first session was in San Antonio's Gunter Hotel in Texas. He used hotel room 414, with his engineer operating from the adjoining room 413. This first day of recording was followed by two more, on the 26th and 27th. He recorded sixteen of his own songs:

Kind Hearted Woman Blues – I Believe I'll Dust My Broom – Last Fair Deal Gone Down – Sweet Home Chicago If I Had Possession Over Judgment Day – Cross Road Blues – Rambling on My Mind – Dead Shrimp Blues They're Red Hot – Preaching Blues – Walking Blues – When You Got a Good Friend – 32-20 Blues Terraplane Blues – Phonograph Blues – Come on in My Kitchen

The second, two-day, session took place in Dallas, starting on 19 June* 1937.

Cream covered *Cross Road Blues*, as *Crossroads* on their 1968 album *Wheels of Fire* and Elmore James's reworked version of *Dust My Broom* became a 1960s standard.

Single released today

1964 The Beatles *I Feel Fine* c/w *She's a Woman* (US)

The distinctive feedback at the beginning of *I Feel Fine* was one of the Beatles' first experiments and became a familiar sound with bands such as Hendrix and the Who.

Album released today

1964 The Beatles *The Beatles Story* (US)

Capitol's fourth Beatles release was a double album of words and music.

Events today

1961 Howlin' Wolf first British tour

American blues legend Howlin Wolf arrived in Britain for his first UK tour.

Wolf was one of the most influential bluesmen of his generation and in 1971 recorded *The London Sessions* with: Eric Clapton, Stevie Winwood, Charlie Watts and Bill Wyman.

1964 The Who from the Detours ...to the Who

On 1 February Pye recording act Johnny Devlin and the Detours appeared on TV's *Thank Your Lucky Stars*, galvanising Pete Townshend, Roger Daltrey and John Entwistle to rethink their own use of "The Detours" moniker. Townshend's art college friend Richard Barnes suggested "The Who".

At this time the drumming stool was occupied by Doug Sandom, who had been with the group since the early days. On 9 April*, as "The Who", they unsuccessfully auditioned for Fontana. Sandom was identified as the problem and left the group shortly afterwards. Session drummer Dave Golding filled the gap whilst auditions continued, including a young Mitch Mitchell who went on to find fame with the Jimi Hendrix Experience.

Keith Moon had been playing with surf-rock band the Beachcombers, before completing the Who's classic lineup in early May 1964. Around this time publicist Peter Meaden came onto the scene and helped mould their new Mod image, including a name change to "The High Numbers". He was an ex-colleague of Rolling Stones' image maker Andrew Loog Oldham. The newly branded group released one single on 3 July*, *I'm the Face* c/w *Zoot Suit*. In the summer of 1964 they signed a management contract with Chris Stamp and Keith Lambert, who secured a recording deal with producer Shel Talmy.

By the time that they opened their groundbreaking Tuesday night residency at London's Marquee club on 24 November, they were back to being called "The Who".

Recording session today

1966 The Beatles *Strawberry Fields Forever*

The Beatles were back in the studio again to begin work on their new album. The first song recorded was *Strawberry Fields Forever*, released as a single before the *Sgt Pepper* album was completed.

Strawberry Field was a Salvation Army children's home in Liverpool, near to John's childhood home in Menlove Avenue.

Single released today

1967 The Beatles *Hello Goodbye c/w I Am the Walrus* (UK)

John Lennon reputedly decided to make the lyrics for *I Am the Walrus* confusing, in order to confound interpretation and also to have a pop at various people, including Bob Dylan, the corrupt drug-busting policeman Norman Pilcher and beat poet Allen Ginsberg for his constant chanting of Hare Krishna.

Birthdays today

1941 Pete Best drums: Beatles' drummer, replaced by Ringo Starr in 1962

Joined the band just as they changed their name to "The Beatles" on 17 August* 1960.

1941 Donald "Duck" Dunn bass: The Mar-Keys, Booker T and the MGs; sessions

1947 Dave Sinclair keyboards: Wilde Flowers, Caravan, Matching Mole

Events today

25

1957 Ray Charles first cross-over hit

Ray Charles scored his first crossover hit with *Swanee River Rock*, albeit only just a hit!

Chart success first came in 1949 with the R&B hit *Confession Blues*. His 1959 classic *What'd I Say*, recorded on 18 February*, also provided chart successes for Jerry Lee Lewis, Bobby Darin and Elvis Presley. Charles's hits continued throughout the 1960s.

1961 The Everly Brothers inducted into the US Marine Corps

The Everlys followed Elvis into the nation's armed forces. They were sworn into the US Marine Corps Reserves in Nashville and then inducted at San Diego's Camp Pendleton.

1966 Jimi Hendrix Experience introduced to the British press

Chas Chandler introduced the Jimi Hendrix Experience to the British press with a gig at London's Bag O'Nails club.

Ex-Animals bass player turned artist manager had discovered Hendrix in New York and brought him to Britain in late September to form his own group.

1966 Moby Grape first major gig

Keeping it in the family, the newly formed Moby Grape played their first major gig supporting Jefferson Airplane at the Fillmore West.

Skip Spence had been with Jefferson Airplane long enough to appear on their debut album, *Takes Off*. He then opted to leave his Airplane drumsticks behind, switch to guitar and form Moby Grape. The Grape and Spence were together for the band's first two albums. The parting of the ways came shortly after his last performance with them on 31 May* 1968, following an incident with an axe and a hotel door.

1976 The Band *The Last Waltz*

The Band's legendary final concert, *The Last Waltz*, was held at San Francisco's Winterland Ballroom on Thanksgiving Day.

Martin Scorsese captured the event on film. A host of superstars made guest appearances, including Bob Dylan, Ronnie Hawkins, Eric Clapton, Neil Young, Muddy Waters, Van Morrison, Ringo Starr, Ron Wood, Dr John and Paul Butterfield.

Albums released today

1963 The Beatles *Beatlemania! With The Beatles* (Canada)

The first Capitol Records album to be released in North America was not in the USA but in Canada, by the Canadian arm of Capitol Records. *Beatlemania! With the Beatles* had the same track listing as the second British album *With the Beatles*, a concept not followed by American Capitol Records until *Sgt Pepper*.

1968 The Beatles *The Beatles* (aka *White Album*) (US)

By the time of the *White Album*, the Beatles were falling apart. Ringo had temporarily quit the group during the recording sessions in August. John caused a fatal division in the Fab Four when he introduced business manager Allen Klein into the Beatles' lives. This initiated a bitter feud between Paul and the rest of the group.

Several songs from the album were cited by Charles Manson as containing messages pertaining to his notorious murder spree on 10 August* 1969.

Events today

1968 Cream farewell concert

Cream played its two legendary *Farewell Concerts* at London's Royal Albert Hall, supported by Yes and Taste.

Guitarist Eric Clapton and drummer Ginger Baker went on to form the short-lived Blind Faith. Bassist Jack Bruce opted to go it alone and released his first solo album *Songs for a Taylor* on 29 August* 1969.

1979 Bill Haley last-ever British appearance

Bill Haley made his final appearance in Britain. It was an auspicious exit in front of the Queen at the prestigious *Royal Variety Performance*.

Recording sessions today

1958 Billy Fury *Maybe Tomorrow*

Having signed up with Larry Parnes and scoring a recording contract with Decca, Billy Fury went into the studios for the first time, to cut the self-penned *Maybe Tomorrow*.

The song was coupled with *Gonna Type a Letter* and released as his first single. It made the British Top 20 and began a run of hit singles that lasted until the mid-1960s.

1962 The Beatles first 'true' Beatles recording session

The fourth session at Abbey Road produced the first 'true' Beatles recordings. At last, music made by the Fab Four without the aid of any session musicians. They recorded *Please Please Me* and *Ask Me Why*, released in Britain as their second single.

Please Please Me had originally been recorded as a Roy Orbison-esque ballad at the 11 September* session, with Andy White on drums. Producer George Martin felt that the song was a little dreary and was unhappy with the results. Sadly, outtakes of the song were not kept at the time and this version has been lost to posterity.

A third Lennon and McCartney offering, *Tip of My Tongue*, was also recorded at this session but it was abandoned as unsatisfactory. The song was later given to another Brian Epstein act, Tommy Quickly but his recording sank without trace.

Single released today

1976 Sex Pistols *Anarchy in the UK* c/w *I Wanna Be Me* (UK)

This Sex Pistols debut single was to be the only one released on EMI. They had a very turbulent journey after signing to EMI on 8 October*, including one single with A&M, before settling down at Virgin.

This was the only single to feature bass player Glen Matlock. He was replaced by Sid Vicious in February 1977, between the Pistols leaving EMI and signing to A&M.

Birthdays today

1945 John McVie bass: John Mayall and the Bluesbreakers, Fleetwood Mac

Before forming Fleetwood Mac in 1967, John McVie was bass player with the seminal British blues band John Mayall and the Bluesbreakers.

The band's name was taken from a combination of his and drummer Mick Fleetwood's names, although the band was originally called "Peter Green's Fleetwood Mac".

1939 Tina Turner singer: Ike Turner Review, solo

Events today

27

1965 Grateful Dead birth of psychedelic rock

Ken Kesey and His Merry Pranksters held the first of their public LSD laced *Acid Tests*. This event is often referred to as the birth of psychedelic rock.

The Warlocks played at this *Acid Test*, just before changing their name to "Grateful Dead". They were regular performers at other Ken Kesey organised *Acid Tests*.

1969 The Rolling Stones Madison Square Garden concerts

The Rolling Stones opened for the first of two nights at New York's Madison Square Garden, with supporting acts BB King, and The Ike and Tina Turner Review. One of the show's highlights came when Janis Joplin joined Tina Turner on stage for a duet.

Nine of the ten tracks on their 1970 live album *Get Yer Ya-Ya's Out!* were recorded at these shows.

1978 Def Leppard one of the bands heralding in the post-punk era

Rick Allen joined Def Leppard to replace original drummer Tony Kenning.

Formed in Sheffield in late 1977, Kenning had been responsible for renaming the band from "Deaf Leopard" to "Def Leppard". As the result of an automobile accident on 31 December* 1984, Allen became rock'n'roll's first one-armed drummer.

By this time punk had had its day and was morphing into new wave. Def Leppard was one of a number of new bands ushering in other new musical styles.

Singles released today

1964 The Beatles *I Feel Fine* c/w *She's a Woman* (UK)

1967 The Beatles *Hello Goodbye* c/w *I Am the Walrus* (US)

Albums released today

1957 Buddy Holly and the Crickets *The Chirping Crickets* (US)

Their first album was released on Brunswick and credited to "The Crickets".

The second and final Holly album to be released in his lifetime was *Buddy Holly*, credited to "Buddy Holly" and released in March 1958 on the Coral label. In April 1958 his first record label Decca released the album *That'll Be the Day*, using material that Holly had recorded before he joined Coral/Brunswick on 16 May* 1957.

1967 The Beatles *Magical Mystery Tour* (US)

This soundtrack to the Beatles' Christmas TV Special was released in the UK in an elaborately packaged, six-track, double EP format. Side one of this American album contained these six EP tracks, side two simply regurgitated existing A and B-sides.

1970 George Harrison *All Things Must Pass* (UK)

Harrison's debut album featured guitarist Eric Clapton and keyboardist Gary Wright.

Birthday today

1942 Jimi Hendrix — guitarist: Jimi Hendrix Experience, Band of Gypsys

Hendrix acquired his first acoustic guitar in 1958. Shortly afterwards, he joined his first group the Velvetones. He moved to electric guitar and later joined the Rocking Kings. The Army enrolled him into its ranks on 31 May* 1961.

Events today

1957 Chris Barber — unsung hero of British blues and rock'n'roll

The Chris Barber Jazz Band and American gospel singer Sister Rosetta Tharpe played a concert at Cardiff's Sophia Gardens. The tour programme[68] showed this to be the fifth of a twenty-date British tour, winding up at London's Coliseum on 15 December.

Trombonist and jazz band leader Chris Barber was one of the unsung heroes of British blues and rock'n'roll. His trad-jazz band was one of the pioneers of British skiffle. A separate interval band played skiffle, whilst the jazz band musicians relaxed between sets. His interval band was the Lonnie Donegan Skiffle Group, who sowed the seeds for British rock'n'roll with their cover of Lead Belly's *Rock Island Line*, recorded on 13 July* 1954 and released as a single in November 1955.

Barber was also responsible for bringing American blues giants to Britain, including Sonny Terry and Brownie McGhee, Big Bill Broonzy, and Muddy Waters.

In 1962 he organised another interval band. This time he wanted a blues group to accompany his wife and vocalist Ottilie Patterson. His new interval band included guitarist Alexis Korner and harmonica player Cyril Davies. They went on to form Alexis Korner's Blues Incorporated, often referred to as Britain's first blues band.

1974 John Lennon — last concert appearance

John Lennon made his final appearance on stage when he joined Elton John at New York's Madison Square Garden. They performed three songs together: *Whatever Gets You Thru the Night*, *Lucy in the Sky with Diamonds* and *I Saw Her Standing There*.

The stage appearance came about after Elton appeared on Lennon's single *Whatever Gets You Thru the Night*. Lennon had agreed to perform with Elton, if his single ever made #1. As for the other songs, the ex-Beatle had appeared on Elton's *Lucy in the Sky with Diamonds* as "Dr Winston O'Boogie" and *I Saw Her Standing There* was a treat for Beatles fans because Paul had always sung it when it was performed by the Fab Four.

As well as being Lennon's swan song performance, it also marked another turning point in his life. Eighteen months earlier he and Yoko had gone their separate ways. He met Yoko backstage that night and it marked the beginning of their reconciliation and an end of the period in his life that he called his "lost weekend".

1975 Rod Stewart and the Faces — end of the road

London Weekend Television aired a Rod Stewart and the Faces concert which had been recorded the previous December at Kilburn's State Gaumont Theatre; Keith Richard joined the lineup that night. A month later the group announced that they were splitting up.

The Faces had started out as the Mod group Small Faces in 1965 and morphed into Faces in late 1969, when vocalist Steve Marriott left the band to form Humble Pie. Marriott was replaced by singer Rod Stewart and guitarist Ron Wood.

By the time of this gig, original Faces bassist Ronnie Lane had left to form his own band, Slim Chance. He had been replaced by Tetsu Yamauchi, previously with Free.

Birthday today

1929 Berry Gordy Jr songwriter and founder of the Motown record company

Berry Gordy Jr's break as a songwriter came in 1957 with Jackie Wilson's *Reet Petite*. In 1959 he launched his Motown empire with Marv Johnson's *Come to Me*, written by Gordy and Johnson, and released as the first record on his Tamla label, Tamla 101.

Event today

1967 Vietnam War Robert McNamara resigned

President Johnson announced that Robert McNamara was resigning to become President of the World Bank. He had served as the US Secretary of Defense since 1961 but had become increasingly critical of Johnson's strategy for the Vietnam War.

American public opinion against the war was hardening. Johnson was still talking up the war but this changed after the *Tet Offensive*, launched by the North on 31 January* 1968. After that, America spent the next five years trying to extricate itself from the war.

Single released today

1963 The Beatles *I Want to Hold Your Hand c/w This Boy* (UK)

This was the first-ever single in Britain to notch up more than a million advance orders.

Album released today

1968 John and Yoko *Unfinished Music No.1: Two Virgins* (UK)

John Lennon's debut solo album, *Unfinished Music No.1: Two Virgins*, was released in Britain two weeks after it reached American fans. This experimental recording was made by John and Yoko at his Weybridge home six months earlier. The album was adorned with the infamous nude sleeve.

Birthdays today

1933 John Mayall keyboards, guitar, harmonica and vocals: Bluesbreakers

John Mayall grew up listening to jazz and blues, and taught himself to play piano, guitar and harmonica. In 1956 he formed his first part-time group, the Powerhouse Four. He then moved on to another semi-pro band the Blues Syndicate, which included drummer Hughie Flint. In early 1963 Mayall moved to London and formed the Bluesbreakers.

Along with Alexis Korner, John Mayall was one of the fathers of British blues. His Bluesbreakers band was a breeding ground for British blues and rock musicians. At various times the Bluesbreakers' lineups have included Eric Clapton, Jack Bruce, Aynsley Dunbar, Mick Fleetwood, John McVie and Peter Green.

Hughie Flint played on the 1966 album *Bluesbreakers with Eric Clapton*.

1944 Felix Cavaliere keyboards and vocals: The Starliters, The Young Rascals

Felix Cavalier, along with percussionist Eddie Brigati and guitarist Gene Cornish, left Joey Dee and the Starliters to form the Young Rascals, with jazz drummer Dino Danelli. The group started out as "The Rascals" but when they were signed by Atlantic the name was extended to "The Young Rascals", to avoid possible litigation with an existing group called "The Harmonica Rascals". In 1968 they reverted to "The Rascals".

1944 Twink drums: Fairies, Tomorrow, Pretty Things, Pink Fairies; solo

Twink was one of the most respected drummers of the psychedelic era. In mid-1967, as a member of Tomorrow, he played on the psychedelic classic *My White Bicycle*. After a short stint with Ron Wood and Jon Lord in Santa Barbara Machine Head, he was with the Pretty Things long enough to perform on their album *SF Sorrow*. One of his shortest-lived bands was Stars, a trio that played a handful of gigs in the Cambridge area around February 1972. Stars' lineup included ex-Pink Floyd guitarist and guiding light Syd Barrett, in his last band before fading into a drug-induced solitude.

Events today

30

1963 The Kingsmen *Louie Louie* hit the charts

The iconic rock song *Louie Louie* moved out of the garage when the Kingsmen's version made the American Top 20 and then went on to become an international phenomenon.

The song was written and originally recorded by Richard Berry and the Pharaohs, and released on Flip in April 1957. His version made the local charts but he sold the song for few dollars in order to embark on married life. In the early 1960s the song took on a life of its own and it took him thirty years to win back the rights to the writing credit.

The *Louie Louie* story started in the Pacific North West in March 1961, when Rockin' Robin Roberts released the first garage version of the song. This became a local hit in the Seattle area and the song was regularly included in local repertoires. It was in the spring of 1963 that the song's momentum really started to build up. Two bands from the area, The Kingsmen, and Paul Revere and the Raiders, both recorded the song. The Kingsmen's version won out and a legend was born.

The Kingsmen's version attracted an FBI investigation to determine if the lyrics were obscene. A lengthy investigation and a 118-page report[98] later – they decided they were not!

Radio stations have devoted entire days to playing it. *Louie Louie* college parties have rocked to the one song all night long. It has been covered over 2,000[99] times. As well as straight rock versions by the Kinks and many others, there have been ironic covers from Frank Zappa and stranger versions from the Rice University Marching Owl Band.

1969 The Monkees from a quartet ...to a duo

The Monkees were nearing the end of their 1969 tour, with this penultimate concert at the Oakland Coliseum in California. Their final gig was set for 6 December, the same day as the Rolling Stones ill-fated Altamont concert. The 1960s was truly over.

This was a three-Monkee tour as Peter Tork had already left the group at the end of 1968. Mike Nesmith departed at the end of this tour. The Monkees became a duo.

Birthdays today

1929 Dick Clark — long-time host of *American Bandstand*

Dick Clark became the host of the TV show in mid-1956, when it was still simply called *Bandstand*. The name change came when ABC-TV took the show national and renamed it *American Bandstand* on 5 August* 1957.

1937 Frank Ifield — pop singer ...but very sought out by Beatles fans

Frank Ifield has one of the most collectable commercially released albums of all time. In 1962 the Beatles were only available on Vee-Jay in America and on the back of Ifield's hit on Vee-Jay, the label created an album with tracks from both artists, *The Beatles & Frank Ifield on Stage*. Although neither of them was actually recorded "on stage", the stereo/portrait sleeve version has sold for more than $20,000 – and the price is rising.

1943 Leo Lyons — bass: The Jaybirds, Ten Years After

In 1962 as "The Jaybirds", Leo Lyons and guitarist Alvin Lee followed in the Beatles' footsteps with a residency in Hamburg. By 1967 they had morphed into Ten Years After.

1945 Roger Glover — bass: Episode Six, Deep Purple, Rainbow

1955 Billy Idol — guitar: Chelsea; vocals: Generation X; solo

December

Events today

1955 Civil Rights Movement Rosa Parks was arrested

The modern Civil Rights Movement started in Montgomery, Alabama, when seamstress Rosa Parks was arrested for refusing to give up her seat on a bus for a white passenger.

Parks was fined for her defiant stance, initiating a bus boycott by the black citizens of Montgomery. The campaign was led by a young Martin Luther King Jr, who was to become a pivotal figure in the Civil Rights Movement.

The *Montgomery Bus Boycott* lasted for 381 days and resulted in the Supreme Court declaring that segregation on transportation was unconstitutional.

1960 The Beatles McCartney and Best were deported from Germany

The Beatles' first trip to Hamburg ended ignominiously, when two more of the Liverpool lads arrived back in England after being deported from Germany. This time it was Paul McCartney and Pete Best for suspected arson.

George Harrison had been deported a week earlier for working underage.

1968 Big Brother and the Holding Company last gig with Janis Joplin

At San Francisco's Avalon Ballroom, Big Brother and Janis Joplin took the stage together for the last time. Joplin left to form her own Kozmic Blues Band.

1976 Sex Pistols notorious TV appearance

The Sex Pistols' notorious appearance on the *Today* show brought shock and horror to its TV audience.

The show was a live early evening news-magazine programme hosted by presenter Bill Grundy. The Sex Pistols were in the vanguard of the new British punk rock phenomenon. With an entourage that included Siouxsie Sioux, they were being interviewed to promote their debut single, *Anarchy in the UK*. At the end of the interview Grundy goaded them into being controversial and suggested that they should say something "outrageous". Steve Jones could not resist and said, "...you dirty fucker. What a fuckin' rotter".

The fallout from the show was immediate. Veteran broadcaster Bill Grundy was sacked, 80 per cent of the gigs on the upcoming Pistols UK tour were cancelled and they were dropped by their record company EMI. But the Sex Pistols were now national news – and British punk rock was well and truly on the map.

Single released today

1956 Jerry Lee Lewis *Crazy Arms c/w End of the Road* (US)

Jerry Lee Lewis released his debut single, on the Sun label. It was a cover of Ray Price's massive country hit from the previous April.

Birthdays today

1938 Sandy Nelson — drums: session drummer and solo performer

Sandy Nelson was the first rock'n'roll drummer to have hits in his own right, with *Teen Beat* and *Let There Be Drums*. He also played on the Teddy Bears' single *To Know Him, Is to Love Him*. In 1963 his lower right leg was amputated after a motorcycle accident but rather than quitting, he adapted his style and continued to play.

1944 John Densmore — drums: Psychedelic Rangers, The Doors, Butts Band

Events today

2

1961 Billy Fury — on tour with the Blue Flames

Billy Fury was appearing at Salisbury's Gaumont in Wiltshire, halfway through his British package tour. He was co-headlining the show along with singer Eden Kane, with support acts that included: skiffle legend Chas McDevitt, Peter Jay and the Jaywalkers, and The Karl Denver Trio.

Billy Fury was one of the pioneers of British rock'n'roll and developed a very successful career as a solo singer. Shortly before the tour started, his manager Larry Parnes had decided that it was time for him to have his own backing band and selected four musicians to form Billy Fury and the Blue Flames. The group's piano player was another Parnes protégé, Georgie Fame, and the drummer was Clem Cattini.

After just six months Parnes felt that the group was becoming too jazz orientated and replaced them with the Tornados, who would later find their own success with *Telstar*. As for the Blue Flames, Georgie Fame took over as front man and they too went on to success as "Georgie Fame and the Blue Flames".

1963 The Beatles — appearance on TV's *Morecambe and Wise Show*

The Beatles recorded their appearance on TV's highly rated *Morecambe and Wise Show*. Paul and Eric famously exchanged good-hearted banter about "fat hairy legs".

1964 Frank Zappa — nearly the first-ever rock opera

Frank Zappa's outline for his rock opera, *I Was a Teen-age Malt Shop*, was turned down by Joseph Landis of KNXT, a division of CBS Television.

As well as the title song, Zappa recorded *The Birth of Captain Beefheart*. Musicians working with Zappa included Don Van Vliet, soon to adopt the name "Captain Beefheart" and future Mother of Invention Jim Sherwood. If Zappa's proposals had been accepted by the TV executive this would have been rock's first opera, preceding the Who's *Tommy* by nearly five years.

1969 George Harrison — joined Delaney & Bonnie on stage

George Harrison had seen Delaney & Bonnie the previous night at their British debut concert at London's Royal Albert Hall. He enjoyed their performance so much that he joined them on stage in Bristol.

Standing unobtrusively at the back of the stage, he performed with them for the remainder of the tour, rounding off with a gig in Copenhagen on 12 December.

1973 The Who arrested in Montreal for wrecking a hotel suite

The Who, along with members of their entourage, ended up behind bars for trashing a suite in the Bonaventure Hotel in Montreal, following a show at the Forum.

Their record company had arranged an after-show press party, which resulted in high jinks and the obligatory TV-in-the-swimming-pool rock'n'roll fun.

Birthday today

1941 Tom McGuinness guitar and bass: The Roosters, Manfred Mann

In his early days, Tom McGuinness played guitar alongside Eric Clapton in Slowhand's first two groups, the Roosters, and Casey Jones and the Engineers. He then joined Manfred Mann and moved over to bass, returning to guitar when Jack Bruce joined.

Events today

1966 The Monkees first-ever concert

Less than three months after the first episode of their TV show aired on 12 September*, the Monkees made their live debut at the International Centre Arena in Honolulu.

1968 Elvis Presley TV *Comeback Special*

NBC-TV broadcasted a leather suited Elvis in his Singer Company sponsored *Comeback Special*. He was accompanied by guitarist Scotty Moore and drummer DJ Fontana, in their swan song performances with the King of Rock'n'Roll.

This TV show was a landmark for Elvis in that it marked his return to live performance. His 1960s persona as a Hollywood movie star was drawing to close. He made three more movies in 1969, finishing with *Change of Habit* released on 10 November*.

1969 John Lennon offer to play Jesus Christ

Tim Rice and Andrew Lloyd Webber reputedly offered John Lennon the opportunity to play the role of Jesus Christ in their new musical *Jesus Christ Superstar*.

1976 Pink Floyd pigs on the wing

Pink Floyd took a 40-foot inflatable pig to London's Battersea Power Station to fly it above the iconic four-chimney building. The plan was to capture the image and use it on the cover of their new album, *Animals*. Unfortunately, the pig broke free from its mooring and floated dangerously into the flight paths around Heathrow Airport.

1979 The Who eleven fans died at a concert

Six months after Kenny Jones took up the role of drummer, tragedy struck the Who at the Riverfront Coliseum concert in Cincinnati. When the doors opened, eleven people were crushed to death in a stampede to be the first to reach the unreserved seats.

The use of festival seating, the practice of first-come-first-seated, was reviewed at rock venues in the wake of this tragedy.

Single released today

1965 The Beatles *We Can Work it Out c/w Day Tripper* (UK)

The Beatles' new single and album were released on the first day of their final British tour. They gave their last-ever UK concert performance in Cardiff on 12 December*.

Album released today

1965 The Beatles *Rubber Soul* (UK)

This was the Beatles' first non-movie album to contain all original songs. The songwriting was maturing and the recording techniques were beginning to manipulate the music. It was the last album to feature Norman "Hurricane" Smith as the engineer.

Birthdays today

1942 Ken Lewis singer and songwriter: Ivy League

Carter Lewis and the Southerners briefly featured both Jimmy Page and Viv Prince.

1948 Ozzy Osbourne singer: Polka Tulk Blues Band, Earth, Black Sabbath; solo

Ozzy Osbourne, along with Geezer Butler, came to Polka Tulk from Rare Breed in 1968.

Event today

1971 Frank Zappa Deep Purple's *Smoke on the Water*

Frank Zappa and the Mothers of Invention were playing at the Montreux Casino in Switzerland, when a flare gun fired by a fan ignited the building's ceiling. The resulting fire razed the Casino to the ground and Zappa lost equipment worth $50,000.[100]

Deep Purple were due to record their next album at the Casino and some of the band were in the audience when the fire broke out. They decided that the better part of valour was discression and watched the fire from the safety of their hotel on the other side of Lake Geneva. The sight of the smoke billowing across the lake inspired the song *Smoke on the Water*.

Recording session today

1956 Sam Phillips Million Dollar Quartet

Four music legends, Elvis Presley, Jerry Lee Lewis, Carl Perkins and Johnny Cash jammed at Sun Studios in Memphis, in what has come to be known as the "Million Dollar Quartet".

Carl Perkins was in Sun Studios to record *Matchbox*, with the recently signed Jerry Lee Lewis backing him on piano. Elvis, who by now was with RCA, and Johnny Cash just happened to drop by. Sam Phillips kept the tape running to record the ensuing jam session but it was several decades before the recordings saw the light of day.

Johnny Cash left the studio shortly after posing for the famous photograph of the four of them, with Elvis seated at the piano. The jury is still out as to whether or not Cash was involved in the actual recording.

Album released today

1964 The Beatles *Beatles for Sale* (UK)

The Fab Four's cover of Little Willie John's *Leave My Kitten Alone* was recorded for this album but remained as an outtake, until its inclusion on the *Anthology* album in 1995.

Births and deaths today

1934 Chas McDevitt British skiffle pioneer

Chas McDevitt was one of the leading lights of the British skiffle boom in the mid-1950s. McDevitt's skiffle group replaced Jerry Lee Lewis on his notorious 1958 UK tour, when it transpired that the lady accompanying Lewis was Myra Gale. British fans were outraged to discover that she was his cousin's thirteen-year-old daughter and also Lewis's wife.

1944 Chris Hillman guitar, bass, vocals: Byrds, Flying Burrito Brothers; solo

1944 Dennis Wilson drums and vocals: The Pendletones, The Beach Boys

1951 Gary Rossington guitar: My Backyard, Noble Five, Lynyrd Skynyrd

Lynyrd Skynyrd founding member and guitarist Gary Rossington survived the plane crash of 20 October* 1977 which killed three of his band mates. He was seriously injured in the crash but recovered and returned to the stage in 1980 with the Rossington Collins Band, before eventually returning with a reunited Lynyrd Skynyrd.

1976 Tommy Bolin guitarist, died at the age of twenty-five

Ex-James Gang and Deep Purple guitarist Tommy Bolin died of a drug overdose whilst on tour in support of his solo album *Private Eyes*.

Event today

1970 Eric Clapton beginning of his self-imposed seclusion

Derek and the Dominos gave their penultimate concert performance at Portchester's Capitol Theatre in New York. This swan song tour ended in New York the following night at Selden's Suffolk Community College. After a fruitless attempt at a second album Clapton descended into a drug-fuelled seclusion.

The quantity of drugs consumed on their final tour resulted in lacklustre performances. In April the band went into the studio to record their second album. By now the magic accompanying the *Layla* recordings was long gone and in May the sessions fell apart. After the Dominos imploded, Clapton retreated to the seclusion of Hurtwood Edge, his home in Surrey, where he sank deeper into his drugs induced solitude.

Clapton's demise seemed almost inevitable. He found the adulation of Cream difficult to cope with. Blind Faith never really made it out of third gear and his attempt at being just a regular band member with Delaney & Bonnie never quite worked. All this, coupled with his unrequited love for George Harrison's wife, Pattie Boyd and the deaths of his grandfather and friend Jimi Hendrix, all served to drag him deeper into the abyss.

This self-induced exile lasted for two years, punctuated by the occasional appearance at events such as at George Harrison's *Concert for Bangladesh* on 1 August* 1971. The Who's Pete Townshend finally enticed Clapton out of his seclusion for a comeback concert at London's Rainbow Theatre on 13 January* 1973.

Recording sessions today

1955 The Teenagers featuring Frankie Lymon *Why Do Fools Fall in Love*

The group's first recording session produced a smash hit on both sides of the Atlantic with *Why Do Fools Fall in Love*. The authorship of the song was co-credited to Lymon but this has since been disputed. The single catapulted the group's thirteen-year-old lead singer to fame as the first black teenage idol.

1966 Buffalo Springfield *For What It's Worth (Stop, Hey What's That Sound)*

Steven Stills's protest anthem was inspired by the Sunset Strip riots in Los Angeles during the summer of 1965.

The song was not included on the track listing of the original version of their eponymous debut album but with the song's success as a single, the album was withdrawn and reissued with *For What it's Worth* replacing *Baby Don't Scold Me*.

Album released today

1960 The Crickets *In Style with the Crickets* (US)

This was the first Crickets album to be released after Buddy Holly's death.

Birthdays today

1932 Little Richard iconic rock'n'roll singer

Little Richard discovered God on 12 October* 1957 and renounced rock'n'roll.

1947 Jim Messina bass, guitar: Buffalo Springfield, Poco, Loggins & Messina

Having worked as an engineer on Buffalo Springfield's second album, *Buffalo Springfield Again*, Jim Messina was asked to replace bass guitarist Bruce Palmer, when he was deported to his Canadian homeland following a drugs bust. With the demise of Buffalo Springfield, Messina and guitarist Richie Furay stayed together to form Poco.

Events today

6

1965 The Who Viv Prince substituted for Keith Moon

Viv Prince's first performance with the Who was at Eltham Baths in south-east London.

Illness forced Keith Moon to take a break from live performances. His place for the next ten days was taken by drummer Viv Prince, who had recently been sacked from the Pretty Things.

1969 The Rolling Stones ill-fated Altamont concert ...end of the 1960s

The free concert and final show on the Rolling Stones 1969 American tour was originally planned to be staged at San Francisco's Golden Gate Park but was relocated to Livermore's Altamont Raceway in northern California.

Following the use of Hells Angels as security at the free concert in London's Hyde Park on 5 July*, they were employed once again for Altamont but this time with disastrous results. Violence escalated throughout the day, with Jefferson Airplane's Marty Balin being knocked out by one of the Angels. During the Rolling Stones' performance, audience member Meredith Hunter was standing near the front of the stage when he pulled out a gun. One of the Hells Angels, Alan Passaro, tackled him and stabbed him to death. Passaro was charged with murder but acquitted later. The incident was caught on film in the concert documentary *Gimme Shelter*.

The rest of the bill that day comprised: Santana, Jefferson Airplane, The Flying Burrito Brothers and, Crosby, Stills, Nash & Young. The Grateful Dead were also due to play but pulled out because of the escalating violence.

Altamont is often cited as the spiritual end of the 1960s, heralding the end of the baby boomers' 1960's dream of an optimistic future.

1976 Sex Pistols infamous *Anarchy in the UK* tour kicked off

Following the Sex Pistols' notorious TV appearance on the 1 December* edition of *Today*, the public outrage at their behaviour was immediate. The *Anarchy in the UK* tour was set to start in Norwich on 3 December and finish on the 26th at London's Roxy Theatre. The two-dozen appearances lined up to span England, Scotland and Wales were suddenly plagued with cancellations. The first of just half a dozen gigs to survive was staged at Leeds Polytechnic on 6 December.

The Clash, The Damned and, Johnny Thunders and the Heartbreakers provided the support. The Clash's drummer, Terry Chimes, aka Tory Crimes, was replaced on the tour by Rob Harper. Chimes remained with the band until March when he was permanently replaced by Topper Headon, although he did return in the early 1980s.

Single released today

1965 The Beatles *We Can Work it Out c/w Day Tripper* (US)

Album released today

1965 The Beatles *Rubber Soul* (US)

This was the Beatles' first American non-movie album to bear the same title as its British counterpart. It might have borne the same title but the track listings were different. The American album contained songs from both the British *Rubber Soul* and *Help* albums. Meanwhile, some of the tracks on the British version of *Rubber Soul* ended up on the next American album, *Yesterday...and Today*.

Events today

1962 The Rolling Stones Bill Wyman's audition

Previously with the Cliftons, Bill Wyman auditioned for the Rolling Stones at the Wetherby Arms in London's trendy Chelsea. The Stones were particularly impressed with Wyman's gear, a pair of Vox AC30 amplifiers and an echo unit, described by Wyman as, "my enormous wardrobe size cabinet with the 18 inch speaker".[85] A week later he played his first gig as the Stones' new bassist at Windsor's Ricky Tick Club.

Despite having played with the prestigious Alexis Korner's Blues Incorporated and Blues By Six, drummer Charlie Watts still had a day job. He finally quit his position as a graphic designer with a

London Advertising Agency to accept an offer to join the Rolling Stones. By early February the classic lineup was in place, albeit still a sextet with pianist Ian Stewart.

1963 The Beatles all appeared on *Juke Box Jury*

The panel of the TV show *Juke Box Jury* comprised of all four Beatles, in front of an audience of 2,500 members of the Beatles Northern Area Fan Club.

After fulfilling their jury duties of voting ten songs a "hit" or "miss", the Fab Four performed live for the audience, before crossing Liverpool to continue their British tour.

1968 Eric Burdon bade a fond farewell to the music business

Eric Burdon announced that he was quitting the music business to become a movie star. The planned vehicle for this new venture was based on his idea for a psychedelic racial western called *Jim Crow*.

The final lineup of the New Animals had fallen apart a few months earlier after recording the *Love Is* album. Burdon's Hollywood plans were all set to start after a charity reunion concert with the original Animals, due to be held in their Newcastle hometown on 22 December.

In America the "Jim Crow" laws came into effect after the Civil War in the mid-19th century. They propounded "separate but equal" treatment for black Americans. This continued until the Civil Rights laws were passed in the mid-1960s.

Live album recorded today

1969 Eric Clapton and George Harrison in the same lineup

Delaney & Bonnie recorded the final concert of their British tour, at Croydon's Fairfield Hall in south London.

The album was released as *Delaney & Bonnie & Friends: On Tour with Eric Clapton*, George Harrison appeared under the nom de plume "L'Angelo Mysterioso".

Birthdays today

1924 Boyd Bennett rockabilly singer and songwriter

He wrote specifically for the teenage market. Boyd Bennett and His Rockets are best remembered for their biggest hit *Seventeen* in 1955, the first song to be written specifically for teenage girls. He also co-wrote *My Boy Flat Top*, aimed at teenage boys.

1949 Tom Waits pianist, singer and songwriter:

Californian singer-songwriter Tom Waits had a distinctive bourbon and cigarettes voice and wrote songs that reflected the low-life underbelly of American culture.

Events today

1968 The Hollies Graham Nash moved on

Graham Nash left the Hollies to form Crosby, Stills & Nash, following a charity gig at the London Palladium. He was replaced by Terry Sylvester from the Swinging Blue Jeans.

1969 Jimi Hendrix found not guilty of drug possession in Canada

Jimi Hendrix went on trial in Toronto, for drug possession.

Three days later, after eight hours deliberation, the jury found him not guilty. During the trial Hendrix told the judge that he had "outgrown" drugs.

1975 Bob Dylan *Night of the Hurricane* concert

Bob Dylan's *Rolling Thunder Review* rolled into New York's Madison Square Garden and finished the first leg of the tour with the *Night of the Hurricane* concert.

The gig was to raise awareness of the boxer Rubin "Hurricane" Carter's plight. He was arrested, with John Artis, for the murder of three people at the Lafayette Grill in Peterson, New Jersey on 17 June 1966. In mid-1967 they were convicted. Another trial and appeals followed, until February 1988 when the 1966 indictments were dismissed.

Live album recorded today

1963 The Yardbirds recorded with Sonny Boy Williamson (II)

The Yardbirds backed blues legend Sonny Boy Williamson (II) on the second night of a two-night stint at the Crawdaddy Club.

The Yardbirds had recently taken over from the Rolling Stones as the house band at the Crawdaddy Club in Richmond in Surrey. Manager Giorgio Gomelsky taped the gig and it was released a couple of years later as *Sonny Boy Williamson and The Yardbirds*. This early 1960s gem provides fans with some of the Yardbirds' earliest recordings.

A young Eric Clapton played lead guitar, having joined the band six weeks earlier.

EP released today

1967 The Beatles *Magical Mystery Tour* double-EP (UK)

Album released today

1976 Eagles *Hotel California* (US)

After replacing original guitarist Bernie Leadon, this was Joe Walsh's first Eagles album.

Births and deaths today

1943 Jim Morrison singer: Rick & the Ravens, The Doors

1947 Gregg Allman keyboards and vocals: Hour Glass, Allman Brothers Band

1980 John Lennon murdered, at the age of forty

That morning Annie Leibovitz had photographed John and Yoko inside their apartment on the seventh floor of the Dakota. At about 4.30pm they arrived at the Hit Factory for what would be their last recording session together. They worked on a Yoko composition *Walking on Thin Ice*, planned for release as a single. At around 10.30pm they left and headed home, arriving back at their apartment half an hour later. John was approached outside the Dakota building and shot dead by Mark Chapman.

9

Events today

1961 The Beatles first gig in the south of England

Still with drummer Pete Best, the Beatles played their first gig in the south of England at Aldershot's Palais Ballroom.

It was promoted as a "Battle of the Bands, Liverpool v London: Liverpool's No. '1' Rock Outfit The Beatles versus One of London's Top 'Beat' Groups Ivor Jay & the Jaywalkers". Unfortunately the concert was poorly advertised and only 18[101] people turned up to witness the Beatles' southern debut.

After the gig they headed off to Soho's Blue Gardenia club in London, managed by their old Scouse mate Brian Casser. There, they surprised the punters with an impromptu set.

1967 The Doors Jim Morrison arrested on stage at New Haven

The Doors frontman, Jim Morrison, was arrested on stage at the New Haven Arena in Connecticut.

In an earlier incident backstage, a policeman had seen the Lizard King with a female companion in the shower stall. The cop confronted Morrison. He became aggressive and the officer sprayed him with mace. The concert went on but halfway through the set Morrison regaled the audience with his expletive-ridden version of events. The police took a dim view of this and dragged the singer off stage, stopping the concert in mid-flow. The sudden end to the show caused a riot. The fighting between fans and police spilled out onto the streets of New Haven. The Dade County Sheriff's Office charged Morrison with indecent exhibition and resisting arrest.

The incident was referred to in the song *Peace Frog* on the album *Morrison Hotel*.

1970 Jerry Lee Lewis divorced Myra Gale

Rock'n'roll legend Jerry Lee Lewis divorced his third wife Myra Gale (née Brown).

Lewis married his cousin's thirteen-year-old daughter in December 1957. News of the event broke on 22 May* 1958 when he arrived for his UK tour. The public was outraged, his fans on both sides of the Atlantic deserted him and his rock'n'roll career was over.

1972 The Who orchestral performance of *Tommy*

Tommy was performed at London's Rainbow Theatre with a full orchestra and guest artists. There were two performances in aid of the Stars Organisation for Spastics. The London Symphony Orchestra was supported by actor Peter Sellers and a host of rock luminaries, including Richie Havens, Steve Winwood, Rod Stewart and Ron Wood.

The concerts were originally intended to be held at the Royal Albert Hall but were cancelled by the Hall when it was discovered that the Who were involved. At a concert on 5 July 1969 the Who had appeared there with Chuck Berry and there was a near riot.

Albums released today

1966 The Beatles *A Collection of Beatles Oldies* (UK)

The inclusion of *Bad Boy*, the only new song on the album, meant that for the first time ever, all of the Beatles' tracks had been released on both sides of the Atlantic.

1967 The Rolling Stones *Their Satanic Majesties Request* (US)

Released in America the day after its British release, this was the first Rolling Stones album to attract a mixed reception from fans and critics alike.

Events today

1961 Cliff Richard Cliff became an entertainer

Cliff Richard's third movie, *The Young Ones*, had its premiere in London.

The early 1960s marked Cliff's transition from British rock'n'roll star to pop star. He was one of only a handful of 1950s performers who managed to reinvent themselves for the 1960s; another notable transformation came from Tommy Steele. With the emergence of beat music in the early 1960s most of the big 1950s stars faded away. They often departed with rather prophetic song titles: Tommy Steele's *Writing on the Wall* in 1961; Marty Wilde with *Ever Since You Said Goodbye* in 1962; and the man who started it all, Lonnie Donegan, with his penultimate chart appearance, *The Party's Over* in 1962.

Cliff's backing group, The Shadows, were also building their own separate identity. The previous summer they had scored their own chart success with *Apache*. Cliff and the Shadows continued to perform together and separately, until 16 November* 1968.

1965 Grateful Dead debut gig as "Grateful Dead"

The Warlocks changed their name to "Grateful Dead" and gave their first concert at San Francisco's Fillmore West. The gig was at the second *San Francisco Mime Troupe Appeal Party*. The concert also featured Jefferson Airplane and the Great Society.

1971 Frank Zappa pushed off the stage

December 1971 was not one of Frank Zappa's best months. On 4 December* he lost all of his equipment in Switzerland, in the *Smoke on the Water* casino fire. A week later at London's Rainbow Theatre, he was seriously injured when he was pushed off the stage by an irate fan. The push came just as he was announcing his encore, the unlikely *I Want to Hold Your Hand*. The resulting fall of ten feet into the orchestra pit below seriously injured the rock hero, bringing him weeks in a hospital and months in a wheelchair.

The culprit, Trevor Howell, was arrested and sentenced to a year in jail.

2007 Led Zeppelin first concert since the death of John Bonham

Led Zeppelin played their first concert in twenty-seven years at London's O2 Stadium. The vacant drum stool was filled by Jason Bonham, John Bonham's son.

The original group's last gig was in Berlin's Eissporthalle on 7 July* 1980, at the end of their last European tour. *Whole Lotta Love* was to be their swan song.

Recording session today

1949 Fats Domino *The Fat Man*

Fats Domino recorded eight tracks at Cosimo Matassa's J&M Studios in New Orleans. One of the tracks, *The Fat Man*, gave him his first R&B hit two months later.

The Fat Man is often referred to as a contender the title of "first rock'n'roll record". The main contender, Jackie Brenston's *Rocket 88*, was not recorded until eighteen months later.

Birthdays today

1926 Guitar Slim — influential blues singer and guitarist

He was one of the first artists to develop a flamboyant stage show, wearing colourful suits and dyeing his hair to match. He was a major influence on Jimi Hendrix.

1946 Chris Kefford — bass: Carl Wayne and the Vikings, The Move

Events today

1968 The Rolling Stones — *Rock and Roll Circus*

Rock and Roll Circus was a TV-special extravaganza filmed in front of an invited audience.

Resplendent in top hat, red jacket, boots and holding a whip, Mick Jagger acted as ringmaster and introduced some of rock'n'roll's finest, including Taj Mahal, The Who, Jethro Tull (including future Black Sabbath guitarist Tony Iommi), The Dirty Mac and Marianne Faithful.

John Lennon introduced himself as Winston Legthigh; his Dirty Mac band comprised guitarist Eric Clapton, Keith Richard on bass and Jimi Hendrix's drummer Mitch Mitchell. They performed *Yer Blues* before being joined on stage by violinist Ivry Gitlis and Yoko Ono, who provided vocals on the blues jam *Whole Lotta Yoko*. Lennon was still with the Beatles at the time and this was his first performance outside the Fab Four.

Sadly, this proved to be Brian Jones's final live performance with the Stones. Urban legend has it that Mick Jagger felt that the Stones had been eclipsed by the Who and the recording was not shown at the time. It was given a DVD release in 1996.

1972 Genesis — American concert debut

Genesis gave their first American concert performance at Brandeis University in Waltham, Massachusetts.

They were on tour to promote their new album *Foxtrot*, with a lineup consisting of Peter Gabriel, Phil Collins, Steve Hackett, Mike Rutherford and Tony Banks.

1978 Black Sabbath — Ozzy Osbourne's final performance

Ozzy Osbourne's curtain call as front man for Black Sabbath came in Albuquerque's Tingley Coliseum at the end of their *Never Say Die* tour.

Recording session today

1958 The Coasters — *Charlie Brown*

Written and produced by Leiber and Stoller, with King Curtis on tenor saxophone.

Albums released today

1970 John Lennon *Plastic Ono Band* (UK)

This was John Lennon's fifth album but his first 'real' solo album, not a John-and-Yoko or live album. It also featured Ringo Starr and bassist Klaus Voormann.

1970 T.Rex *T.Rex* (UK)

Mark Bolan progressed from a psychedelic duo to a glam-rock band.

Births and deaths today

1944 Brenda Lee singer: the original "Little Miss Dynamite"

1961 Darryl Jones bass: replaced Bill Wyman in the Stones in late 1993

1964 Sam Cooke singer, died at the age of thirty-three

Sam Cooke was shot dead by Bertha Franklin, the manager at the Hacienda Motel in Los Angeles. The facts surrounding Cooke's death are hazy. Franklin claimed that the shooting occurred after Cooke attacked his female companion, Elisa Boyer and then tried to assault her. The coroner returned a verdict of justifiable homicide.

Events today

1965 The Beatles final British concert performance

The Beatles opened their UK tour in Glasgow on 3 December. That was the first of nine concerts that ended in Cardiff's Capitol Theatre with what would prove to be their final British concert performance. This was not planned to be the Fab Four's last tour, it just turned out that way.

The support acts included Liverpudlian singer Beryl Marsden, The Moody Blues with future Wings singer Denny Laine, and The Paramounts who morphed into Procol Harum.

1974 The Rolling Stones Mick Taylor moved on

After a stint of over five years as the Rolling Stones' guitarist, Mick Taylor left to join the Jack Bruce Band.

Taylor joined the Stones a few weeks before founder Brian Jones's death, in time to contribute to the *Let It Bleed* album. This was followed by the live album *Get Yer Ya-Ya's Out!* and the classic albums *Sticky Fingers* and *Exile on Main Street*. His final album with the Stones was the unspectacular *It's Only Rock'n'Roll*. Several guitarists were in the frame to replace Taylor, before the Stones settled on the Faces' Ron Wood.

1976 Elvis Presley end of the Las Vegas era

Elvis gave his last-ever performance in Las Vegas, at the Las Vegas Hilton Hotel.

Recording session today

1955 Bill Haley and His Comets *See You Later Alligator*

Bill Haley recorded his iconic hit *Rock Around the Clock* on 12 April* 1954 but it took the movie *Blackboard Jungle* before the song entered the charts in May 1955. Haley's cover of Bobby Charles's *Later Alligator* was his last American Top 10 appearance.

The song was written and originally released by Charles as his debut single on the Chess label in 1955. The writing credit on Haley's single was given as Robert Guidry, Bobby Charles's real name.

The expression "see you later alligator" was used by teenagers in the 1950s as a parting idiom, often eliciting the reply, "in a while crocodile".

Births and deaths today

1938 Connie Francis seminal female rock'n'roll singer

1944 Rob Tyner singer and harmonica: MC5

1985 Ian Stewart the 6th Rolling Stone, died at the age of forty-seven

Original Rolling Stones pianist Ian Stewart died of a heart attack, whilst sitting in his doctor's waiting room awaiting his appointment.

Ian Stewart was the first of the Rolling Stones to join Brian Jones's band. He played at the first Rollin' Stones gig at London's Marquee club on 12 July* 1962. When the classic Rolling Stones lineup was assembled it was a sextet, with Brian, Mick, Keith, Bill, Charlie and pianist Ian Stewart. Andrew Loog Oldham became the Stones manager shortly after seeing them in action on 28 April* 1963. He felt that Stewart did not have the right image for the group. The Stones became a quintet and Stewart was relegated to road manager. However, he did continue to provide keyboards on many of the band's recordings and unobtrusively at some concert performances.

Events today

1963 Cleo's Mood formation of a typical 1960s semi-pro group

Derek Shelmerdine (that's me, at that time aged fifteen), then known as "Shelley", gave a lifelong love of music a practical outlet, forming a beat group with my best mate "Bone".

After a very brief flirtation with the bass guitar I opted for drums. Bone took the role of lead guitarist. We were soon joined by "Bunz" on bass. "Cleo's Mood" was eventually settled on as the band's moniker, taken from a Junior Walker album track. We mostly played as a trio, a mixture of R&B covers, Atlantic soul, and Who and Stones numbers. My philosophy as a drummer was to hit everything as hard as I could as fast as I could as often as I could. I left in mid-1967 to get an education, Cleo's Mood morphed into Fairground and turned professional. Bunz became a full-time musician and played a stint with legendary Liverpool band the Undertakers. It was a GREAT time!

1971 John Sinclair freed from prison

Poet and political activist John Sinclair was released from prison, after being sentenced in July 1967 to ten years for the possession of two marijuana cigarettes.

Sinclair was arrested in January 1967 after a sting operation by the Detroit Police Department. Six months later he was sentenced to ten years imprisonment for the possession of two marijuana joints. Protests against this draconian sentence followed, including a passionate appeal by Abbie Hoffman from the Woodstock stage in 1969. He jumped on stage and interrupted the Who's performance but when he started to protest against Sinclair's incarceration he was given short shrift by guitarist Pete Townshend. On 10 December a host of rock and counterculture luminaries appeared at the *John Sinclair Freedom Rally* at Ann Arbor's Crisler Arena in Michigan. Those taking part that day included John Lennon, Yoko One, Stevie Wonder, Bob Seger, Commander Cody, protest singer Phil Ochs, poet Allen Ginsberg, poet and ex-Fug Ed Sanders, and political activists Jerry Rubin and Bobby Seale. Sinclair was freed by the courts just three days later.

As well as being a poet, Sinclair was also a leading counterculture figure, having formed the White Panthers in late 1968. This was a far-left anti-racist organisation which endorsed and complimented Bobby Seale's Black Panthers. Sinclair's activities even extended into the world of rock'n'roll, where he managed Detroit's MC5.

Birthdays today

1948 David O'List — guitar: The Attack, The Nice, Jethro Tull, Roxy Music

Guitarist David O'List came to fame as a member of early prog-rockers the Nice. They were on the British Jimi Hendrix tour that kicked off on 14 November* 1967. During the latter part of the tour he stood in for Pink Floyd's guitarist Syd Barrett after he became too detached from reality to play. Following his departure from the Nice, O'List had a very brief spell with Jethro Tull between their first and second albums. He also had a brief sojourn with the early Roxy Music but left before the band recorded their debut album.

1949 Tom Verlaine — guitar and vocals: Neon Boys, Television; solo

Tom Verlaine formed the Neon Boys with bassist Richard Hell in the early 1970s. By the end of 1973 they had morphed into Television. Verlaine's songwriting skills soon established Television as one of the leading lights in New York's emerging new wave scene.

The inspiration for his stage name came from French symbolist poet Paul Verlaine.

Events today

1959 Berry Gordy Jr — Motown came into existence

Berry Gordy Jr formed the highly successful Motown record company.

Based in Detroit, Michigan and operating out of its aptly named recording studios *Hitsville U.S.A.*, it became one of the most influential recording companies of the 1960s with a family of record labels that included Motown, Tamla, Gordy and Soul. The doo wop vocal groups of the 1950s were one of rock'n'roll's roots and Motown transformed some of the best of these into successful 1960s vocal groups, such as the Miracles, the Four Tops and the Temptations.

The first release on the Motown label was a limited edition of the Miracles' *Bad Girl*, the main release for the single was on licence through Chess Records. The first full release on Tamla, with the number 1,000, was *My Beloved* by the Satintones.

1963 The Beatles knocked themselves off the UK #1 spot

The Beatles' *I Want to Hold Your Hand*, with advance orders of over 1,000,000 units, went to #1 in Britain and knocked the Fab Four's own *She Loves You* off the top spot.

This was the first time in the UK that a band had replaced itself at #1.

1972 Marc Bolan *Born to Boogie* opened

Directed by Ringo Starr, the Marc Bolan/T.Rex movie *Born to Boogie* premiered in London.

1999 Paul McCartney played the Cavern

After a gap of thirty-six years (3 August* 1963) Paul McCartney performed live for 300 people at Liverpool's Cavern Club. Ably assisting the ex-Beatle were Pink Floyd's guitarist David Gilmour and Deep Purple's drummer Ian Paice.

Single released today

1962 Bob Dylan *Mixed-Up Confusion c/w Corrina Corrina* (US)

Bob Dylan's debut single, *Mixed-Up Confusion*, was recorded with an electric backing band. Produced by John Hammond, it was withdrawn by Columbia shortly after release.

Mixed-Up Confusion was recorded during the sessions for Dylan's second album, *The Freewheelin' Bob Dylan* but was not included on the acoustic-only final track listing. Maybe the audience at the *Newport Folk Festival* on 25 July* 1965 would not have been quite so surprised by Dylan's electric set if they had heard this outtake recorded over two years earlier.

Album released today

1979 The Clash *London Calling* (UK)

Released in America at the beginning of 1980, the Clash's *London Calling* was voted by *Rolling Stone* magazine as #1 in its poll *The 100 Best Albums of the Eighties.*[89]

Birthday today

1943 Frank Allen bass and vocals: Cliff Bennett, The Searchers

Frank Allen was one of the founding members of Cliff Bennett and the Rebel Rousers in the late 1950s. He left them in mid-1964 to replace Tony Jackson in the Searchers.

Events today

15

1956 Elvis Presley "Elvis has left the building"

At the end of Elvis's final performance on the *Louisiana Hayride*, Horace Logan uttered the famous phrase "Elvis has left the building", in an attempt to settle down the rowdy crowd and encourage them to listen to the remaining acts on the show.

Louisiana Hayride was a country show syndicated on radio stations across much of the South and West. It provided Elvis with his first exposure to a wider audience.

1969 John Lennon *War is Over* campaign

John and Yoko launched their international peace campaign with posters proclaiming "War is over! ...If you want it ...Happy Christmas from John & Yoko".

It kicked off with a *Peace for Christmas* benefit concert by the Plastic Ono Band at London's Lyceum Ballroom. This was the band's British debut and was the first time that Lennon and George Harrison had shared a stage since 1966. The lineup included Harrison, Eric Clapton, Keith Moon, Delaney and Bonnie, Klaus Voormann and Billy Preston. They played extended versions of just two songs *Cold Turkey and Don't Worry Kyoko*. The performance was included on Lennon's album *Sometime in New York City*.

Album released today

1964 The Beatles *Beatles '65* (US)

The fifth Capitol album contained seven original Lennon and McCartney songs and four covers. *Rock and Roll Music* was their second cover version of a Chuck Berry song. Piano Red recorded *Mister Moonlight* in 1962 as "Dr. Feelgood and the Interns", using it as the B-side of *Doctor Feel-Good*. The second Carl Perkins song to be covered by the Beatles *Honey Don't*, was the B-side of *Blue Suede Shoes*. *Everybody's Trying to Be My Baby* is often attributed to Carl Perkins but he only adapted the song, which was written and originally recorded by Rex Griffin in 1936. Carl Perkins released his version, and took the writing credit, on his 1957 Sun album, *Dance Album of ...Carl Perkins*.

Birthdays today

1921 Alan Freed disc jockey, promoter: coined the phrase "rock'n'roll"

Alan Freed was one of the most influential of the non-performing rock'n'roll pioneers, accredited with coining the term "rock'n'roll". He was a pioneering DJ who brought black R&B music to a white teenage audience. As well as his radio work, he hosted TV shows, promoted rock'n'roll concerts and appeared in rock'n'roll movies. His world started to collapse around him in 1960 when he was accused of payola, taking money or rewards for playing particular records on his radio shows. His radio and TV work dried up and his life went downhill, until he died a bankrupt and broken man in 1965.

1942 Dave Clark drums and vocals: The Dave Clark Five

1946 Carmine Appice drums: Vanilla Fudge, Cactus, Beck, Bogert & Appice

A founding member of Vanilla Fudge and Cactus, Carmine Appice went on to Beck, Bogert & Appice, and the supergroup KGB, with Mike Bloomfield and Rick Grech.

1955 Paul Simonon bass: London SS, The Clash

Event today

1960 Cass and the Cassanovas end of the road

Cass and the Cassanovas played at the *Mardi Gras Arts Ball* in St George's Hall shortly before breaking up. Leader Brian Casser headed off to try his luck in London. Guitarist Adrian Barber, bassist Johnny

Gustafson and drummer Johnny Hutchinson remained in Liverpool, changed their name to "The Big Three" and became one of the early 1960s most respected groups.

Singer and guitarist Brian Casser formed Cass and the Cassanovas in mid-1959 and it became one of the most popular groups on the early Liverpool scene. On 10 May* 1960 both the Beatles and Cass and the Cassanovas were auditioning to back singer Billy Fury on his upcoming British tour. The Silver Beetles, as they were known at that time, had a problem when their drummer Tommy Moore was late but the Cassanovas' drummer Johnny Hutchinson filled in for the early part of the audition. Neither band secured the gig but the audition did result in the Beatles backing Johnny Gentle and the Cassanovas backing Duffy Power.

In late 1957, before forming the Cassanovas, Casser teamed up with future-Rolling Stone Bill Wyman to form a skiffle group. After the demise of Cass and the Cassanovas, Casser relocated to London where he became the manager of the Blue Gardenia club in Soho. On 9 December* 1961 his old friends the Beatles dropped in to see him after playing their first gig in the south of England. It was a disastrous affair with a reputed audience of 18. Casser went on to form Casey Jones and the Engineers and for seven gigs in late 1963 his guitarist was Eric Clapton, before he left to join the Yardbirds.

The Big Three went on to become one of Liverpool's most popular bands but never quite managed to transfer the raw energy from their stage performances to vinyl recordings.

Single released today

1966 The Jimi Hendrix Experience *Hey Joe c/w Stone Free* (UK)

Jimi Hendrix released *Hey Joe* in Britain, his first single in his own right.

Hendrix was honourably discharged from the American Army in the summer of 1962. Following this, he performed and recorded with a host of well-known American acts, including Little Richard and the Isley Brothers. But he did not find international fame until he was discovered by ex-Animals bass player Chas Chandler. He brought Hendrix to the UK and recruited a British band, bass player Noel Redding and drummer Mitch Mitchell. This debut single was released and Hendrix became one of rock'n'roll's icons.

When *Hey Joe* was released in America six months later, the B-side was changed to 51st *Anniversary*. This American release was just six weeks before the Jimi Hendrix Experience made their legendary concert debut at the *Monterey Pop Festival*.

Hey Joe was copyrighted by American folk singer Billy Roberts in 1962. On this original Polydor release, Hendrix took the songwriting credit as "Trad. arr. Hendrix" but later releases accredited Billy Roberts. The origins of the song have aroused much discussion about its influences and possible beginnings as a traditional folk song. The Roberts song was popularised by the Leaves but it was Tim Rose's slower arrangement in 1966 that influenced the Hendrix version. The 1965 Leaves version, on the Mira label, credited Dino Valenti as the writer.

Birthday today

1949 Billy Gibbons guitar and vocals: The Moving Sidewalks, ZZ Top

Events today

1960 The Beatles — Chas Newby covered on bass guitar

Chas Newby played the first of four gigs with the Beatles at the Casbah Coffee Club, a popular Liverpool venue run by Pete Best's mother, Mona.

John, Paul, George and drummer Pete Best were back from Hamburg but with Stuart Sutcliffe staying on in Germany the group was missing a bass player. Chas Newby had been a member of Pete Best's old group the Blackjacks. He was in Liverpool on Christmas vacation from his college course and was amenable to temporarily filling the gap left by Sutcliffe. His final performance on 31 December, also at the Casbah, left the Beatles with only half of their rhythm section.

This need for a bass player led to Paul's permanent move to the instrument. Although the Beatles would return to Hamburg and be reunited with Sutcliffe, this effectively marked the end of his time in the group.

1969 Tiny Tim — married on TV's *Johnny Carson Show*

Eccentric singer and ukulele player Tiny Tim, born Herbert Buckingham Khaury, married his seventeen-year-old girlfriend Victoria Budinger, known as Miss Vicki, live on the *Tonight Show Starring Johnny Carson*. The event attracted a TV audience of 40 million viewers.

They divorced eight years later but not before bringing a daughter, aptly named "Tulip", into the world. In 1968 he famously recorded a falsetto rendition of *Tip-Toe Thru' The Tulips with Me*. He was also an unlikely performer at the 1970 Isle of Wight festival, which included one of Jimi Hendrix's final gigs.

The name "Tiny Tim" was inspired by a character in Charles Dickens's heart-warming novel *A Christmas Carol*, a Victorian tale of greed, selfishness and redemption.

Birthdays today

1936 Tommy Steele — singer: Britain's first rock'n'roll star

1938 Carlo Little — drums: Screaming Lord Sutch, Cyril Davies, Neil Christian

Carlo Little was one of the most respected drummers of the early British skiffle and rock'n'roll era. As well as playing with Screaming Lord Sutch's Savages and Cyril Davies's Rhythm and Blues All Stars, he also filled in as drummer for the Rolling Stones before Charlie Watts became their permanent sticksman. At a Screaming Lord Sutch gig on 25 June* 1962 a young, pre-Who Keith Moon tentatively made his way backstage and asked Little if he would give him some drumming lessons.

1942 Paul Butterfield — harmonica: Paul Butterfield Blues Band

In the mid-1960s seminal white blues harmonica player Paul Butterfield formed one of the first mixed race blues bands. The Butterfield Blues Band's original lineup consisted of: Butterfield, guitarist Elvin Bishop, drummer Sam Lay and bassist Jerome Arnold, the rhythm section from Howlin' Wolf's band. Their first recording deal, with Elektra, was achieved after they were joined by guitarist Mike Bloomfield.

1949 Paul Rodgers singer: Free, Bad Company, The Firm, Queen

As well as being lead vocalist and a founding member of both Free and Bad Company, Paul Rodgers teamed up with ex-Led Zeppelin guitarist Jimmy Page in 1984 to form the Firm and stood in for Freddie Mercury as the front man for Queen in the mid-2000s.

Events today

1966 The Yardbirds dual lead guitarists

Directed by Michelangelo Antonioni, the movie *Blow-Up* opened in America. It featured a performance of *Stroll On* by the Yardbirds. This was a rare recording from the brief period when the band featured the dual lead guitars of Jeff Beck and Jimmy Page.

1972 Vietnam War *Christmas Bombings* of Hanoi began

With the failure of the Paris peace talks in mid-December, President Nixon launched *Operation Linebacker II.*

This intensive eleven-day bombing campaign of Hanoi became known as the *Christmas Bombings*. Nixon's aim was to bomb Hanoi back to the negotiating table but it was widely denounced in America and across the world. On 26 December Hanoi agreed to resume peace negotiations. Nixon terminated the bombing on 29 December.

Birthdays today

1931 Allen Klein music industry accountant, executive and manager

Accountant Allen Klein was one of the first businessmen to see a role in managing an artist's interests when dealing with a record company. In the late 1950s he reputedly earned Bobby Darin $100,000 by studiously studying the singer's accounts and entitlements. Klein went on to handle Sam Cooke's business affairs before taking over the Rolling Stones from Andrew Loog Oldham. After Brian Epstein died the Beatles were split over who should run their affairs. Paul McCartney wanted his future father-in-law Lee Eastman but John Lennon persuaded the others that Klein was their man.

1938 Chas Chandler bass: The Animals; manager: Jimi Hendrix, Slade

Chas Chandler was the bass player with British R&B combo the Animals. After the band split up he turned his hand to artist management. He saw Jimi Hendrix playing in New York, became his manager and persuaded him to move to London. After parting company with Hendrix in 1968, Chandler went on to manage Slade's career throughout the 1970s.

1941 Sam Andrew guitar: Big Brother Holding Company, Kozmic Blues Band

Sam Andrew was one of the founding members of Big Brother and the Holding Company. Janis Joplin joined slightly later as lead singer. Andrew and Joplin left in December 1968 to form the Kozmic Blues Band.

1943 Keith Richard guitarist and songwriter: The Rolling Stones

Keith Richard and Mick Jagger had been friends in junior school before losing touch when they went to different secondary schools. A chance encounter on Dartford railway station in late 1961 brought them back together. Their mutual love of the blues inspired them to form their first band, Little Boy Blue and the Blue Boys, which also boasted future Pretty Things founder Dick Taylor as guitarist. Richard also performed occasionally with seminal British blues band, Alexis Korner's Blues Incorporated. Jagger, Richard and Taylor went on to join Brian Jones's group and as "The Rollin' Stones", they stood in for Blues Incorporated at London's Marquee club on 12 July* 1962.

Born Keith Richards, in the early 1960s he dropped the "s" from his name, reverting to the original spelling in the late 1970s.

Recording session today

1955 Carl Perkins three covers by the Beatles

In a recording session at Sun Records, with Sam Phillips at the controls, Carl Perkins recorded two of his own songs, *Blue Suede Shoes* and *Honey Don't.*

The Beatles chose to cover three songs associated with Carl Perkins. The first, *Honey Don't* was a true Carl Perkins song, written and originally recorded by him. In Britain it appeared on the *Beatles for Sale* album, in America it graced *Beatles '65.*

The other two covers were not quite so authentically Carl Perkins originals. *Matchbox* was based on *Match Box Blues*, recorded by folk-blues singer Blind Lemon Jefferson in 1927, which itself was inspired by Ma Rainey's 1924 song *Lost Wandering Blues.* For the Beatles the song was exceptional in both live performance and recording terms. In pre-Ringo days it was a rare opportunity to hear drummer Pete Best taking the lead vocal. It was also a rare example of a Beatles song that did not find a UK release on either a single or an album. British fans had to buy the EP *Long Tall Sally* in order to add the song to their collections. American fans had two opportunities to acquire the song, as a single and also on the album *Something New.*

The third song had its roots in country music. *Everybody's Trying to Be My Baby* was adapted by Perkins from the song of the same name, written and originally recorded by Rex Griffin in 1936. British Beatles enthusiasts discovered this as the second Perkins song on *Beatles for Sale*, likewise for American fans on the *Beatles '65* album.

All three tracks appeared on *Dance Album Of ...Carl Perkins*, released around 1958. Maybe one of the Fab Four had this LP in his own record collection.

Birthdays today

1940 Phil Ochs folk protest singer and songwriter

Along with Bob Dylan and Tom Paxton, Phil Ochs was one of the foremost 1960s folk protest singers and songwriters. Like Dylan, he started out singing around the coffee-houses of New York's Greenwich Village. He became a vocal supporter of Civil Rights and an opponent of the Vietnam War, writing songs such as *Here's to the State of Mississippi* and *Love Me, I'm a Liberal.* He protested at the notorious Democratic Party Convention in Chicago on 15 August* 1968 and gave evidence at the subsequent *Chicago Seven* trial. This event marked a turning point for Ochs. His next and penultimate studio album, *Rehearsals for Retirement*, depicted Ochs's tombstone on the album cover, inscribed "Died: Chicago, Illinois 1968". His final studio album came in early 1970, ironically titled *Greatest Hits* but containing all new songs. The final track on the album was the prophetic *No More Songs.* For the tour to promote his *Greatest Hits* album he famously wore a gold lamé suit. The parody was lost on some of his audience and he received a mixed reception at his Carnegie Hall concert on 27 March 1970. This performance was captured for posterity and released in 1975 as his final album, *Gunfight at Carnegie Hall*. He died by his own hand in 1976.

1944 Alvin Lee guitar and vocals: Jaybirds, Ten Years After; solo

Alvin Lee was a founding member of Ten Years After and one of the premier British blues guitarists of the 1960s and '70s.

1944 Zal Yanovsky guitar and vocals: The Mugwumps, The Lovin' Spoonful

Zal Yanovsky was in the Mugwumps with future Mama Cass and Papa Denny Doherty.

Events today

1967 Joan Baez increasing opposition to the Vietnam War

Singer Joan Baez was sentenced to a prison term of forty-five days, following her arrest at an anti-Vietnam War demonstration at Oakland Induction Centre the previous October.

1967 represented a watershed in America's involvement in the Vietnam War. The American military and administration were still talking up the war but the public protests were escalating. Joan Baez's husband, David Harris, formed a group called "The Resistance" to actively protest against the war. Around the same time that the Resistance was formed, Martin Luther King Jr made his *Beyond Vietnam* speech, on 4 April* and Muhammad Ali was arrested for refusing to be drafted, on 28 April*. Protests continued throughout 1967, including the march led by Jerry Ruben and Abbie Hoffman to levitate the Pentagon, on 21 October*.

On 31 January* 1968 everything changed when North Vietnam launched their *Tet Offensive*. Even though it was crushed, American public opinion across the board turned firmly against the war and it was the beginning of the end for America in Vietnam.

1975 Cat Stevens last British performance

Although nobody knew at the time, this performance at London's Hammersmith Odeon by singer and songwriter Cat Stevens was to be his British swan song.

In 1976 Stevens had a near-death experience when he nearly drowned whilst swimming off the Californian coast at Malibu. He found himself in difficulties and called out to God for help. The tide turned and he swam back to shore with ease. After this experience he converted to Islam and turned his back on the music industry.

Stevens had his first taste of success with the single *I Love My Dog* in late 1966. In 1968 he was diagnosed with tuberculosis. By the time that he returned in 1970 he had acquired a new manager and changed his record label to Island. His interest in religions reflected a more contemplative approach to his music. His growing disdain for the music industry was combined with an increasing interest in religion, philosophy and numerology. These influences were reflected in his album titles, *Buddha and the Chocolate Box* in 1974 and the 1975 concept album, *Numbers: A Pythagorean Theory Tale*. By the time that his final album, *Back to Earth*, was released in 1978, he had already converted to Islam.

Born Steven Demetre Georgiou, he adopted the stage name when a girlfriend told him that he had cat-like eyes. After he turned his back on the music industry and embraced Islam, he took the new name "Yusuf Islam".

Birthday today

1938 Terry Dene seminal British rock'n'roll singer

Terry Dene was one of Britain's earliest rock'n'roll singers. He made regular appearances on Britain's first rock'n'roll TV show the *Six-Five Special* and scored a handful of hit singles in the late 1950s. In 1958 he married fellow pop singer Edna Savage. That summer he was conscripted into the British Army in a blaze of publicity, reminiscent of Elvis Presley's entry into the US Army. Sadly, unlike Presley Dene's career went into a downward spiral. He was discharged from the Army shortly after joining, reputedly due to psychological ill-health. His marriage proved to be equally short-lived.

He was managed by Larry Parnes, one of the most successful of the early rock'n'roll managers, whose roster of artists included Tommy Steele, Marty Wilde and Billy Fury.

Events today

1970 Elvis Presley became a drugs enforcement officer

The King of Rock'n'Roll met the President of the United States of America, Richard Nixon, at the White House in Washington DC. Elvis was particularly keen to receive a BNDD (Bureau of Narcotics and Dangerous Drugs) badge and become an official drugs enforcement officer.

Elvis had initiated the meeting by sending President Nixon a hand-written letter, on American Airlines notepaper. In it he outlined his concerns for "our country", which included "The Drug Culture, The Hippie Elements" and went on to request that he might be "made a Federal agent at Large". He finished off his six-page letter by requesting a meeting "just to say hello if you're not to [sic] Busy"[46]. After the meeting Nixon sent Elvis a thank you letter and expressed his gratitude for the commemorative World War II Colt 45 that Elvis had presented to him at their meeting.

Nixon agreed to Elvis's request for an official BNDD badge, a possession that Elvis was extremely proud of.

1976 Generation X Roxy Club opened

London's first punk-rock venue, the Roxy Club, opened in Covent Garden with performances from Generation X and Siouxsie and the Banshees.

Billy Idol and most of the group had parted company with the short-lived band Chelsea a month earlier and formed Generation X. (Singer Gene October rebuilt the second incarnation of Chelsea with new band members.) Generation X explored a more commercial edge to the punk genre and achieved a number of hit singles before their demise in 1981. Billy Idol moved on to a successful solo career.

The band's name was inspired by the 1964 book *Generation X*, by Charles Hamblett and Jane Deverson. The term "Generation X" refers to the generation born after the "Baby Boomers", i.e. the people born from the early 1960s to the early 1980s.

The Roxy Club was opened by Generation X's manager Andy Czezowski and was London's first venue exclusively given over to performances by punk bands. It closed its doors in early 1978.

Birthdays today

1940 Frank Zappa guitar, vocals and composer: Mothers of Invention; solo

Frank Zappa was one of rock'n'roll's true geniuses. Before founding the groundbreaking Mothers of Invention, he had already owned his own recording studio, Studio Z in Cucamonga and performed his

Concerto for Two Bicycles on television, on 27 March* 1963. Always controversial, on 26 March* 1965 he was arrested on pornography charges. Zappa had a great interest in classical music, particularly that of Stravinsky and Edgard Varése. His early recordings were issued on Verve, before he founded his own labels, Bizarre and Straight. The final recording released in his lifetime was *The Yellow Shark*, an orchestral work taken from performances by the Ensemble Modern in 1992.

1946 Carl Wilson guitar and vocals: The Pendletones, The Beach Boys; solo

Lead guitarist and singer, Carl was the youngest of the three Wilson brothers who co-founded the Beach Boys. In the early 1980s he was dissatisfied with the direction the other Beach Boys were taking and opted out of the band to pursue a solo career. His sabbatical lasted just over a year.

Events today

1963 The Detours Townshend's swinging arm motion was born

Before they became the Who, the Detours opened for the Rolling Stones at St Mary's Hall in Putney, an affluent suburb of London.

Urban legend has it that this was where Pete Townshend saw Keith Richard stretch his arm high above his head just as the curtains were about to open. Townshend's trademark swinging arm motion was born that night.

The Detours on stage that night were singer Roger Daltrey, bassist John Entwistle, guitarist Pete Townshend and drummer Doug Sandom. It would be another four months before Keith Moon auditioned for the group on 13 April*.

1967 Landmark Concerts *Christmas on Earth Continued*

The last major British hippie event following the *Summer of Love* came with the *Christmas on Earth Continued* concert at London's Olympia. It was advertised as an "all night Christmas dream party" and featured performances from a galaxy of acts, including Pink Floyd, The Jimi Hendrix Experience, Eric Burdon and the Animals, The Move, Tomorrow, The Graham Bond Organisation and Soft Machine.

The show proved to be the end of the road for Pink Floyd's main songwriter and guiding light, Syd Barrett. This was his last major 'performance' with the group but, sadly, it consisted mostly of a motionless appearance on stage. By the time of this concert the writing was already on the wall for Barrett. On 14 November* Jimi Hendrix opened a package tour of the UK, which included Pink Floyd and the Nice. During the tour Barrett's performances became increasing erratic and the Nice's guitarist David O'List substituted for the Floyd's errant leader when he was unable to take to the stage.

1967 Vietnam War end of the positive spin

After travelling to Australia to attend the late Prime Minister Harold Holt's funeral, America's President Johnson travelled to Vietnam to visit military personnel.

Johnson was still very bullish about the way that the war was going and in a speech delivered the following day he told the assembled troops that "The enemy cannot win, now, in Vietnam." His upbeat assessment continued with the view that "All the challenges have been met. The enemy is not beaten but he knows that he has met his master in the field ...he is trying to buy time".[90]

How things were to change in a very short space of time. Just five weeks later, on 31 January*, the North Vietnamese launched their devastating *Tet Offensive*. By early March the attackers had been pushed back but this marked the beginning of the end for America in Vietnam. The world no longer heard the victory rhetoric of people like General Westmoreland and President Johnson.

Shortly after the offensive was contained, General Westmorland was replaced by General Creighton W Abrams. Westmorland returned to America to be appointed Chief of Staff to the United States Army. On 31 March* 1968 President Johnson announced that he would not be seeking reappointment in the upcoming Presidential elections.

Birthday today

1946 Rick Nielsen guitar, vocals and songwriter: Fuse, Cheap Trick

Cheap Trick's roots were in Fuse, formed by Rick Nielsen in the late 1960s. It became Sick Man of Europe, before morphing into Cheap Trick in 1973.

Events today

1964 The Beach Boys Brian Wilson's nervous breakdown

The pressures of writing, producing and touring took their toll on Brian Wilson. On a flight to Houston the Beach Boys' guiding light suffered a nervous breakdown.

This marked the end of Brian Wilson's live appearances with the band. Instead, he stayed at home to concentrate on the creative side of writing, arranging and production. His place on tour was taken by Glen Campbell, who filled the gap for a few months until he was replaced by Bruce Johnston.

1966 Landmark TV end of the road for *Ready Steady Go!*

After opening on 9 August* 1963 for a run of three and a half years, *Ready Steady Go!* took its final bow. The last "weekend to start here" featured a host of stars, including: Mick Jagger, The Who, Paul Jones, Eric Burdon, Cat Stevens and Small Faces. Some performed, others were simply there to bid a fond farewell to the best rock music show on British television.

Drummer Dave Clark, of The Dave Clark Five fame, made the astute decision to buy the rights to this iconic TV show.

1972 Grand Funk Railroad ex-manager seized the band's equipment

On the afternoon of their charity concert at New York's Carnegie Hall, Grand Funk Railroad's ex-manager, Terry Knight, turned up at the sound check with two deputy sheriffs and a court order to seize the band's equipment.

Earlier in the year the band had sacked Knight, resulting in a flurry of legal actions. The show was in aid of the Phoenix House drug rehab programme and the band had pledged all their money from the show to the charity. Fearful of a riot if the concert was cancelled at such short notice, negotiations ensued and it was agreed to allow the concert to go ahead. Knight then impounded the equipment at the end of the show.

1985 Judas Priest lawsuit following fans' suicide pact

After a session of listening to Judas Priest's album *Stained Glass*, two American boys, Raymond Belknap and James Vance, made a suicide pact to kill themselves with a shotgun. Belknap succeeded but Vance only managed to blow away the bottom half of his face, leaving him severely disfigured.

The parents of the two boys blamed Judas Priest and their record company CBS for the use of subliminal messages in triggering the suicide pact. They took the group and record label to court in Reno, Nevada to claim for damages. The track on the *Stained Glass* album singled out as the catalyst for the boys' actions was Priest's cover of the Spooky Tooth song *Better By You, Better Than Me*, written by Gary Wright. It was this track that was alleged to contain the subliminal message to, "do it, do it".

It would be nearly five years before the case was settled in the band's favour.

Birthdays today

1935 Johnny Kidd singer: Johnny Kidd and the Pirates

1940 Jorma Kaukonen guitar and vocals: Jefferson Airplane, Hot Tuna

Jorma Kaukonen co-founded Hot Tuna towards the end of Jefferson Airplane's lifetime.

Events today

1955 The Weavers reunion concert after communist blacklisting

The four Weavers, Pete Seeger, Lee Hays, Fred Hellerman and Ronnie Gilbert reunited for their famous reunion concert at New York's Carnegie Hall.

Pete Seeger was one of America's seminal protest singers. In the early 1940s he formed the Almanac Singers. They were an itinerant folk-protest group that travelled across America supporting union meetings and civil rights assemblies, singing songs of solidarity and equal rights for all. Its loose ensemble of members at times included Bob Dylan's hero, Woody Guthrie. In 1948 Seeger formed the Weavers, who continued in the same vein of folk and protest songs. In mid-1950 the Weavers achieved considerable success with their cover of Lead Belly's *Goodnight Irene*. This was a full five years before Lonnie Donegan ignited the British skiffle movement with another Lead Belly cover, *Rock Island Line*.

In the early 1950s, America was paranoid about communist infiltration of all areas of its society. Senator Joe McCarthy and the House Un-American Activities Committee pursued politicians, movie people and musicians with all the gusto of a 16th-century European witch-hunter. The Weavers fell foul of the Committee and were blacklisted as communist sympathisers. DJs stopped playing their records, promoters no longer booked concerts and they famously lost a regular TV booking because the programme's sponsor, Van Camp's Pork & Beans, pulled out of the deal. By the end of 1952 the Weavers had parted company and moved on to their own individual pastures green.

The Weavers' Carnegie Hall concert was a stand against anti-communist zealots. It heralded the folk revival and paved the way for the 1960s protest singers such as Bob Dylan, Joan Baez and Phil Ochs.

1974 Elvis Presley abandoned his karate movie

Elvis conceived the idea of making another movie but this time it would be his love of the martial art of karate that would be the centre of his attention. Work started in the spring of 1974 but by Christmas Eve it was all over. Author Peter Guralnick, in his excellent book *Careless Love: The Unmaking of Elvis*

Presley, succinctly described the film's demise. "The karate movie was ingloriously shut down on December 24 ...with no other explanation than 'health problems'."[39]

Presley's interest in karate had been stimulated during his Army days in Germany. His dedication to the sport had grown to the extent that he had become a black belt exponent of the art. He often included karate demonstrations in his stage shows, sometimes lasting as long as fifteen minutes. In early 1974 he felt that it was time to make another movie, this time with a karate theme. The original idea was that Elvis would be a karate fighting hero but that concept was abandoned in favour of a serious documentary approach, with Presley introducing karate to the world. Presley's karate instructor Ed Parker and producer George Waite set about filming demonstrations and tournaments but the project was destined not to be completed in Presley's lifetime.

The film did finally see the light of day as a DVD in 2002, *Gladiators: The 1974 Elvis Karate Legacy Project*.

Birthday today

1945 Lemmy — vocals and bass: Hawkwind, Motörhead

Before joining Hawkwind, Lemmy was a roadie for Jimi Hendrix.

Events today

25

1964 The Zombies — British Invasion was in full swing

The Zombies kicked off the first of ten days in *Murray the K's Christmas Show*, at New York's Brooklyn Fox Theatre. In the show they played one or two songs for seven performances a day.

The group was formed in the early 1960s by vocalist Colin Blunstone and pianist Rod Argent. Their current hit, *She's Not There*, fared better in America than it did in their UK homeland.

1970 Little Feat — debut concert

Little Feat gave their debut performance in Ohio at Cincinnati's Reflections Club.

Lowell George formed Little Feat after leaving Frank Zappa's band. George had joined Zappa in late 1968 and played guitar on three Zappa albums: *Hot Rats*, *Burnt Weeny Sandwich* and *Weasel's Ripped My Flesh*. To form Little Feat he enlisted ex-Mothers of Invention bassist Roy Estrada, along with ex-Fraternity of Man drummer Richie Hayward and highly respected keyboards player Bill Payne.

The band's name came about after a comment from Zappa's drummer Jimmy Carl Black, regarding George's shoe size. The "ea" was a Beatlesque twist on the spelling.

Births and deaths today

1940 Pete Brown — poet, lyricist and singer: Battered Ornaments, Piblokto

Pete Brown collaborated with Jack Bruce on the writing of many of the songs recorded by Cream. He formed Battered Ornaments but suffered the ignominy of being thrown out of his own band the day before the Rolling Stones Hyde Park concert on 5 July* 1969. He then formed a new group, Piblokto.

1944 Henry Vestine — guitar: Mothers of Invention, Canned Heat

An enthusiastic blues guitarist, Henry Vestine played in a very early lineup of Frank Zappa's Mothers of Invention. He joined in late 1965 but left just before they recorded their first album. He left Zappa because that was not a blues band but Vestine's next venture Canned Heat certainly ticked that box. As lead guitarist, he joined Canned Heat in time for their eponymous debut album and played in the classic lineup until internal tensions led to him moving on at the end of the decade, although he did return later.

1945 Noel Redding bass: Jimi Hendrix Experience; guitar/vocals: Fat Mattress

Noel Redding switched from guitar to bass when he joined the Jimi Hendrix Experience in the autumn of 1966. Both Redding and manager Chas Chandler became increasingly frustrated with Hendrix during the *Electric Ladyland* recording sessions. Chandler left but Redding stayed on for the 1969 American tour. At that time he moved back to playing the guitar and put together his own band Fat Mattress. Redding's band supported Hendrix on the American tour, giving Redding a bass spot with the Experience and a switch to guitar and vocals for Fat Mattress.

1954 Johnny Ace seminal R&B singer, died at the age of twenty-five

Johnny Ace was a rising R&B star who became one of rock'n'roll's first casualties. He died when a game of Russian roulette went tragically wrong, during a backstage break at a Christmas gig with Big Mama Thornton at the City Auditorium in Houston, Texas.

Events today

1964 The Rolling Stones tongue-in-cheek Christmas greeting to hairdressers

The Rolling Stones placed an ad in the British music paper New Musical Express wishing starving hairdressers and their families a Happy Christmas.

The Beatles started this trend for long hair amongst young men, after being inspired by the Exis during their early trips to Hamburg; it began on a trip to Paris, 1 October* 1961.

1967 The Beatles *Magical Mystery Tour* premiere

The UK premiere of the Beatles made-for-TV movie *Magical Mystery Tour* received a thorough panning from the critics. Despite being a colour production, it was shown on BBC-1 in black and white on Boxing Day, in the primetime Christmas evening schedule.

At that time BBC-1 was not capable of showing colour productions. Fans had to wait for the repeat on BBC-2 on 5 January to see the movie in all its colour glory.

The soundtrack was originally released in Britain on a six-track double EP.

1968 Led Zeppelin American concert debut

Led Zeppelin made their American concert debut at Denver's Auditorium Arena, supporting Vanilla Fudge and Spirit. As the opening act, they were not always billed.

This short American tour started before the band had even released their debut album. Manager Peter Grant's gamble paid off and Led Zeppelin were on their way to stardom.

Single released today

1963 The Beatles *I Want to Hold Your Hand c/w I Saw Her Standing There* (US)

The Beatles' breakthrough in America came with their fourth single. Following the release of two singles on Vee-Jay and one on Swan, Capitol Records finally decided that the Beatles were worthy of a shot at the American charts.

In an interview with *Beat Instrumental*, Paul McCartney suggested that the bass line for *I Saw Her Standing There* was inspired by Chuck Berry's *I'm Talking About You.*[102]

Birthday today

1939 Phil Spector writer and producer: creator of the "wall of sound"

Phil Spector was one of the best known record producers of his time, famous for multi-layering instruments to obtain his trademark "wall of sound". Tragically his father committed suicide when Spector was nine years old. He later wrote, produced and recorded his first hit as the Teddy Bears, by changing the tense of the inscription on his father's headstone, "To Know Him Was To Love Him". In his early career he worked as a producer at Atlantic Records, where he produced the Top Notes' original version of the Beatles favourite, *Twist and Shout*.

In 1961 he set up his own record label, Philles, with Lester Sill. This era was Spector's golden age. He created his "wall of sound" with artists such as The Crystals, Darlene Love, The Ronettes and The Righteous Brothers. It effectively came to an end in 1966 when Ike and Tina Turner's *River Deep–Mountain High* failed to make an impact on the US charts. On 23 March* 1970 he started work with the Beatles to transform the ailing *Get Back* project into their swan song album *Let it Be*. After that he produced a number of albums for a range of artists, including: John Lennon's *Rock'n'Roll* (1975), Leonard Cohen's *Death of a Ladies' Man* (1977) and the Ramones' *End of the Century* (1980).

Event today

1958 Landmark TV last episode of *Six-Five Special*

The BBC's first-ever pop-music programme, *Six-Five Special*, came to an end after a run of nearly two years. The debut show aired on 16 February* 1957.

The original presenters, Pete Murray and Jo Douglas, were later joined by other hosts, including boxer Freddie Mills and pop singer Jim Dale. The programme showcased skiffle music and promoted home-grown rock'n'rollers like Marty Wilde, Tommy Steele and Adam Faith. In November 1957 a live episode of the *Six-Five Special* featuring Wee Willie Harris, was broadcast from the legendary 2i's coffee bar in London's Soho.

Albums released today

1967 Leonard Cohen *Songs of Leonard Cohen* (US)

Leonard Cohen released his debut album *Songs of Leonard Cohen*. The opening song *Suzanne* had already been recorded by Judy Collins on her 1966 album *In My Life*.

Before finding fame in the music world, Cohen had established himself as a poet. In 1964 he published a collection of poems under the title of *Flowers for Hitler*. His lyrics, such as *Bird on the Wire*, tended to have a much darker tone than the political protest of previous singer-songwriters such as Bob Dylan. Like Dylan, Cohen was signed to Columbia by John Hammond. In 1970 he appeared at the British *Isle of Wight Festival* alongside a host of rock luminaries, including Jimi Hendrix, The Who and The Doors. An unlikely collaboration in 1977 with "wall of sound" producer Phil Spector delivered the album *Death of a Ladies Man*, with most of the writing credits going to both men.

1967 Bob Dylan *John Wesley Harding* (US)

This was Dylan's first album release since his motorcycle accident in July 1966.

Birthdays today

1931 Scotty Moore guitar: Starlite Wranglers, Blue Moon Boys, Elvis Presley

Before finding fame with Elvis Presley, guitarist Scotty Moore was already working with bass player Bill Black at Sam Phillips's Sun Records in Memphis. In May 1954 they released *Now She Cares No More*, as members of Doug Poindexter's Starlite Wranglers. When Phillips brought Elvis into Sun studios for the first time, he invited Moore and Black to accompany him. Elvis's first single, *That's All Right*, was released on 19 July* 1954 and credited to Elvis Presley, Scotty and Bill. Each of Elvis's four subsequent Sun releases received a similar credit. Moore and Black parted company with the Starlite Wranglers after meeting Elvis and formed the Blue Moon Boys, to back the soon-to-be King of Rock'n'Roll at his early live performances. By the time that Elvis had signed to RCA they had been augmented by drummer DJ Fontana. Moore worked with Elvis throughout the 1960s. Their swan song together came with Elvis's return to live performances, at his TV *Comeback Special* on 3 December* 1968.

1941 Mike Pinder keyboards and vocals: Krew Cats, The Moody Blues; solo

Mike Pinder, along with Ray Thomas, was with the Krew Cats before they became founding members of the Moody Blues. Pinder was one of the pioneers of the Mellotron.

1944 Tracy Nelson singer: Mother Earth; solo

1946 Lenny Kaye guitar: Patti Smith Group; solo

Recording sessions today

1947 Wynonie Harris *Good Rockin' Tonight*

Written and released by Roy Brown in mid-1947, *Good Rockin' Tonight* was a major R&B hit for Wynonie Harris on King Records in 1948.

Jackie Brenston's *Rocket 88*, recorded at Sun Records on 5 March* 1951, is often cited as the first rock'n'roll record but Wynonie Harris's *Good Rockin' Tonight* preceded this by over three years.

In 1954 Elvis Presley released *Good Rockin' Tonight* as his second single for Sun Records. Harris's version is often cited as the inspiration behind Elvis's cover.

1976 Buzzcocks *Spiral Scratch*

Manchester group Buzzcocks used their own money to finance their first recording, the EP *Spiral Scratch*.

The Buzzcocks was formed by guitarist Pete Shelley and singer Howard Devoto in early 1976. The group gave their debut performance supporting the Sex Pistols at Manchester's Lesser Free Trade Hall on 26 July and also appeared at the 100 Club's first punk festival a month later.

The *Spiral Scratch* EP was recorded at Manchester's Indigo Sound Studio. The group released the EP a month later on their own New Hormones record label. Shortly afterwards Devoto moved on to form Magazine.

This was one of the earliest punk records to be released on an independent label.

Births and deaths today

1921 Johnny Otis drums, bandleader, talent scout, producer and club owner

Johnny Otis was a pivotal figure in the development of R&B. In 1948 he opened the Barrelhouse Club in Los Angeles, a venue accredited with being the first club to be dedicated solely to R&B. As a performer he started out as a drummer, before developing his own band, the Johnny Otis Show. With the Johnny Otis Show he recorded one of his own compositions *Willie and the Hand Jive* in 1958. In music's backroom he was a gifted talent scout, discovering Etta James and Jackie Wilson. His production credits included early Little Richard recordings and Big Mama Thornton's original version of *Hound Dog*. All this and he even found time to operate his own record label, Dig Records, formerly Ultra Records.

When two of Britain's blues pioneers Cyril Davies and Alexis Korner came together in the late 1950s, Davis was running the Thursday night London Skiffle Club at the Roundhouse. Davies and Korner formed a partnership to focus more on blues based music. Inspired by Otis's LA club, they changed the name of the weekly skiffle gathering to the "London Blues and Barrelhouse Club".

1950 Alex Chilton vocals and guitar: The Box Tops, Big Star

Alex Chilton was a founding member of both the Box Tops and Big Star.

1983 Dennis Wilson Beach Boys drummer, died at the age of thirty-nine

Dennis Wilson was a founding member of the Beach Boys and played with them until his death. He drowned whilst swimming off his boat in Marina Del Ray, Los Angeles.

With special dispensation from the White House, Wilson's body was buried at sea.

Events today

29

1956 Elvis Presley held 10 slots on *Billboard's Top 100*

Elvis had ten entries on *Billboard's Top 100*, a phenomenal achievement considering that he had only recorded his first single for RCA, *Heartbreak Hotel*, on 10 January*.

Two of the songs, *Love Me Tender* and *Poor Boy* were from the soundtrack of Elvis's first movie *Love Me Tender*, released on 15 November*. Five of the songs on the chart listing were covers. *Hound Dog* was written by Leiber and Stoller and recorded by Big Mama Thornton on 13 August* 1952. *Blue Moon* was written by Rodgers and Hart and performed by Shirley Ross as *The Bad in Every Man* in the 1934 movie *Manhattan Melodrama*. *Old Shep* was written and recorded by Red Foley in 1935, this was the first song that Elvis ever performed in public, at a talent show in Tupelo on 3 October 1945.

1968 Poco early gig as "Pogo"

Pogo played the last gig of a four-night stint at San Francisco's Fillmore West, opening for Sly and the Family Stone and Steve Miller Band.

Still calling themselves "Pogo", this first incarnation of Poco consisted of: guitarists Richie Furay and Jim Messina from Buffalo Springfield, pedal steel guitarist Rusty Young and drummer George Grantham from the Colorado group Boenzee Cryque, and bassist Randy Meisner from the Poor. Meisner soon became disenchanted with Poco and moved on after their first album, *Pickin' Up the Pieces*. He joined Rick Nelson's Stone Canyon Band, before becoming a founding member of the Eagles.

The group had taken their name "Pogo" from the popular Walt Kelly cartoon character. With the threat of legal action looming, the name was changed shortly after the Fillmore gig to the similar sounding "Poco".

Recording session today

1953 Jimmy Reed *You Don't Have to Go*

Jimmy Reed scored one of his early successes on the Vee-Jay label with his own composition, *You Don't Have to Go*.

Reed and the Spaniels were the first acts to record for the newly formed Vee-Jay label. The Spaniels had the first recording session on 5 May* when they recorded *Baby It's You* (not to be confused with the song of the same name made famous by the Shirelles and covered by the Beatles). Although, Reed's *High and Lonesome* was the first Vee-Jay single, released as VJ100.

Reed was one of the most influential of the bluesmen and many of his songs were later covered by 1960s R&B groups. The Rolling Stones covered Reed's self-penned 1957 single *Honest I Do* on their eponymous 1964 debut album. The Animals included Reed's 1961 composition *Bright Lights Big City* on the British version of their second album, *Animal Tracks* released in 1965. Even the King of Rock'n'Roll, Elvis Presley, had a hit in 1967 with a cover of Reed's 1961 R&B hit *Big Boss Man*.

Birthdays today

1943 Rick Danko bass, vocals: Ronnie Hawkins and the Hawks, The Band

After splitting from rockabilly star Ronnie Hawkins, the Hawks backed Bob Dylan on his ground breaking electric tour of 1965/1966.

1947 Cozy Powell drums: Jeff Beck Group, Rainbow; sessions; solo

Events today

1953 Landmark Movies *The Wild One*

Over a year before *Blackboard Jungle* opened on 25 March* 1955 and James Dean's tale of teenage angst, *Rebel Without A Cause*, screened six months later on 27 October*, Marlon Brando's motorcycle gang movie, *The Wild One*, opened in New York.

In one of movies' truly classic moments, the motorcycle gang were dancing with some of the local girls when one of them asked what the letters B-R-M-C on the back of the gang's leather jackets stood for. When she was told *Black Rebels Motorcycle Club*, she turned to the gang's leader and asked, "Hey Johnny what are you rebelling against?" To which Brando replied, "What've you got?"[28]

Lee Marvin's motorcycle gang in the movie was called "The Beetles". Beatles mythology has this as one of the potential origins of the group's name. The movie was banned in the UK until 1968, maybe it was, maybe...

1968 Popcorn Blizzard Meat Loaf supported the Fugs

Popcorn Blizzard supported the Fugs at Detroit's Grande Ballroom.

Blizzard's front man, Meat Loaf, later found fame as a solo artist, recording one of the best-selling albums of all time, *Bat Out of Hell*. Around this time Popcorn Blizzard recorded their only single *Once Upon a Time* c/w *Hello*, Meat Loaf's first-ever recording.

The Fugs were counterculture favourites, with roots in the beat (literature) movement. The Fugs debuted on 24 February 1965. Founding members Tuli Kupferberg and Ed Sanders, with drummer Ken Weaver, were joined shortly afterwards by Peter Stampfel and Steve Weber, after the duo had recorded two albums as the Holy Modal Rounders. The band was at its journey's end, Kupferberg, Sanders and Weaver were still mainstays but the Fugs played their swan song gig in Austin, Texas, two months later on 22 February*.

Recording session today

1950 The Dominoes *Sixty Minute Man*

This was one of the first R&B songs to become a crossover hit and is often quoted as a contender for the accolade of first rock'n'roll record. The lineup included Billy Ward and had lead vocals from future Drifters founder Clyde McPhatter.

Birthdays today

1928 Bo Diddley pioneering rock'n'roll writer, singer and guitarist

Bo Diddley was born Ellas Bates in McComb, Mississippi and raised by his mother's cousin Gussie McDaniel, whose surname he took for his own. He used Ellas McDaniel for his writing credits. His very distinctive rhythm was known as "shave 'n' a haircut, two bits". This pioneering sound found its way into the fabric of rock'n'roll and was used to great effect by the Rolling Stones on their cover of Buddy Holly's *Not Fade Away*.

1934 Del Shannon second wave rock'n'roll singer

1946 Patti Smith poet and singer: Patti Smith Group; solo

1947 Jeff Lynne singer and multi-instrument: Idle Race, The Move, ELO

Monkees' birthdays

1942 Mike Nesmith guitarist, singer and songwriter: The Monkees; solo

1945 Davy Jones singer: The Monkees; solo; actor

Events today

1961 The Beach Boys — early gig as "The Beach Boys"

Having recently changed their name from "The Pendletones" and released their debut single *Surfin*, the Beach Boys played one of their earliest gigs, the *Ritchie Valens Memorial Concert* at the Long Beach Municipal Auditorium, California.

The original lineup consisted of the three Wilson brothers Brian, Dennis and Carl, their cousin Mike Love and friend Al Jardine.

1968 Small Faces — Steve Marriott stormed off stage

The end for the quintessential Mod group Small Faces came when lead singer Steve Marriott stormed off stage during a New Year's Eve gig at London's Alexandra Palace. This was not the last Small Faces gig but the writing was on the wall.

Marriott then teamed up with ex-Herd guitarist Peter Frampton and ex-Spooky Tooth bassist Greg Ridley to form Humble Pie.

The Small Faces replaced Marriott with guitarist Ron Wood and vocalist Rod Stewart. They went on to release one final album as "Small Faces", before shortening the name to "Faces". Success followed, until Rod Stewart eclipsed the group as a solo act.

1973 AC/DC — first-ever performance

AC/DC gave their first official concert at Chequers club in Sydney, Australia, with a lineup consisting of lead guitarist Angus Young, rhythm guitarist Malcolm Young, bassist Larry Van Kriedt, drummer Colin Burgess and vocalist Dave Evans.

Dave Evans provided the vocals on the first AC/DC single, *Can I Sit Next To You Girl c/w Rocking in the Parlour*, before being replaced by Bon Scott. The single was released in Australia and New Zealand in mid-1974.

New Year's Eve swan song gigs

1972 MC5 — at Detroit's Grande Ballroom (also the venue's last gig)

1978 The Runaways — at San Francisco's Cow Palace

1984 Def Leppard — Rick Allen lost his arm in a car crash

On New Year's Eve Def Leppard's drummer Rick Allen was driving along the A57 near Sheffield in the north of England when tragedy struck and he was involved in a car accident which resulted in the loss of his left arm.

The band stood by him and by the summer of 1986 he was back on stage with a custom-built electronic drum kit.

Live album recorded today

1984 Aerosmith — *Classic Live II*

The majority of the tracks were recorded at the Orpheum Theatre in their Boston hometown.

The *Back in the Saddle* tour marked the reunion of the original members of Aerosmith. This recording preceded the studio album *Done With Mirrors*.

Birthdays today

1942	Andy Summers	guitar: Big Roll Band, Dantalian's Chariot, Police
1951	Tom Hamilton	bass: The Jam Band, Aerosmith

PART THREE

Pocket Histories

The People, Bands and Events in What Happened Today?

Pocket Histories cross-references the people, bands and events found in Part 2: *What Happened Today?*

People and bands are listed alphabetically.

EVENTS are included under the following headings:

CIVIL RIGHTS MOVEMENT
CONCERTS AND FESTIVALS
FAILED AUDITIONS AND 'LOST' ALBUMS
MOVIES, THEATRE, LITERATURE, TV AND RADIO
PLAGIARISM, LITIGATION, MURDER AND SUICIDE
ROCK'N'ROLL – HIGH JINKS AND MAYHEM
ROCK'N'ROLL – LANDMARKS
27 *CLUB* – MEMBERSHIP LIST
VIETNAM WAR
WHAT'S GOING ON – AROUND THE WORLD
WHAT'S GOING ON – UK
WHAT'S GOING ON – USA

Record Releases

(UK) British record release (US) American record release

In most cases UK release dates have been chosen for British artists and US release dates for American artists.

The Beatles

The only act to have a complete listing for British, and American (Capitol/Apple) singles and albums. American singles released on Vee-Jay, Swan and Tollie are included but only the first Vee-Jay album and its reissue are listed. Subsequent Vee-Jay album releases, although highly regarded collector's items, simply repackaged the same recordings.

AC/DC

		Inducted into the Rock and Roll Hall of Fame in 2003
1946	Jul 9	Bon Scott: singer, born in Kirriemuir, Scotland... ...member of the Valentines in the late 1960s and Fraternity in the early 1970s
1947	Oct 5	Brian Johnson: singer, born in Dunston, Gateshead... ...previously with Geordie
	Nov 6	George Young: guitarist and producer, born in Glasgow, Scotland... ...founding member of the Easybeats and producer of early AC/DC albums
1953	Jan 6	Malcolm Young: rhythm guitarist, born in Glasgow, Scotland
1955	Mar 31	Angus Young: lead guitarist, born in Glasgow, Scotland

1973	Dec 31	1st official concert...
		...AC/DC:
		Angus Young: lead guitar Malcolm Young: rhythm guitar Larry Van Kriedt: bass – left shortly afterwards Colin Burgess: drums – left in early 1974 Dave Evans: vocals – left in late 1974 – replaced by Bon Scott
1974	Jul 22	debut single *Can I Sit Next to You Girl* released in Australia and New Zealand...
		...Bon Scott replaced vocalist Dave Evans shortly afterwards
1979	Aug 3	issued breakthrough album *Highway to Hell* (US), with the track *Night Prowler*...
		...cited by Richard "Night Stalker" Ramirez as inspiration for his serial killings
1980	Feb 19	Bon Scott died of alcoholic poisoning at the age of 33
1980	Jul 25	released *Back in Black* (US) – 1st album with new vocalist Brian Johnson...
		...with a degree of gallows humour, it included the track *Have a Drink on Me*

Johnny Ace

1954	Dec 25	singer, died when a backstage game of Russian roulette went wrong: aged 25...
		...probably rock'n'roll's first casualty ...he was supported that night by Willie Mae "Big Mama" Thornton
1977	Jun 6	Elvis released *Pledging My Love* as the B-side of his last single – Ace hit in 1955

Aerosmith

		Inducted into the Rock and Roll Hall of Fame in 2001
1948	Mar 26	Steven Tyler: singer and songwriter, born in Yonkers, New York
1950	Sep 10	Joe Perry: guitarist and songwriter, born in Lawrence, Massachusetts
1951	Dec 31	Tom Hamilton: bassist, born in Colorado Springs, Colorado

Before Aerosmith

1966	Oct 22	Chain Reaction, with Steven Tyler, supported Yardbirds in Westport, Connecticut
1970	Nov 6	debut concert...
		...Aerosmith:
		Steven Tyler: vocals – from Chain Reaction Joe Perry: lead guitar – from the Jam Band Tom Hamilton: bass – from the Jam Band Joey Kramer: drums – from the Turnpikes Ray Tabano: guitar – left mid-1971 – replaced by Brad Whitford... ...returned to a backstage role c.1974
1973	Jan 13	released their debut album, *Aerosmith* (US)
1984	Jun 22	classic lineup was reunited for the *Back in the Saddle* tour...
		...Aerosmith:
		Tyler – Perry – Hamilton – Kramer – Whitford

...Jimmy Crespo: guitar – replaced Joe Perry in 1979 – left before this reunion
...Rick Dufay: guitar – replaced Brad Whitford in 1981 – left before reunion

1984 Dec 31 *Classic Live II* recorded live (mostly) in Boston

Alice Cooper

Inducted into the Rock and Roll Hall of Fame in 2011

1948 Feb 4 Alice Cooper: singer, born Vincent Damon Furnier, in Detroit, Michigan

Started as the Earwigs (early 1964), morphed into the Spiders, then Nazz...
...and finally Alice Cooper (the band).

The Earwigs – The Spiders – Nazz – Alice Cooper: constant band members:

Glen Buxton: guitar

Vincent Furnier (Alice Cooper): singer

The group's singer, Vincent Furnier, adopted the band's name as his own.

1969 May 19 released 1st single *Reflected* (US) – "Alice Cooper", still the name of the band...
...group credit for writing and production
...1st single on Frank Zappa's Straight label

Jul 26 played the *Seattle Pop Festival*

Sep 13 notorious *Chicken Incident* at the *Toronto Rock and Roll Revival* festival

1970 Aug 7 performed at the *Goose Lake International Music Festival*

Mose Allison

1927 Nov 11 jazz and blues pianist, singer and songwriter, born in Tippo, Mississippi...
...recorded *Parchman Farm* in 1957 – single from John Mayall in 1966

1957 Mar 7 recorded the self-penned *Blues* – released on his album *Back Country Suite*...
...famously covered by the Who as *Young Man* on *Live at Leeds* in 1970

The Allman Brothers Band

Inducted into the Rock and Roll Hall of Fame in 1995

1946 Nov 20 Duane Allman: guitarist, born in Nashville, Tennessee

1947 Dec 8 Gregg Allman: keyboardist and singer, born in Nashville, Tennessee...
...Duane and Gregg Allman were both founding members of:

Allman Joys – Hour Glass

1969 Mar 30 1st gig – but without keyboard player Gregg Allman...
...The Allman Brothers Band:

Duane Allman: dual lead guitar – died in 1971
Dickey Betts: dual lead guitar
Berry Oakley: bass – died in 1972
Jai Johanny "Jaimoe" Johanson: drums
Butch Trucks: drums
Reese Wynans: keyboards – stood in for Gregg Allman at this 1st gig

Nov 8 released their eponymous debut album (US)

1970	Sep 9	Duane Allman recorded *Layla* with Derek and the Dominos
1971	Mar 11	opened historic performance at the Fillmore East – caught on the live album...
		...*The Allman Brothers at Fillmore East* – produced by Tom Dowd ...album included *Whipping Post* – written by Gregg Allman
	May 6	Fillmore closures announced – performed at final Fillmore East concerts in June
	Oct 29	Duane Allman died in a motorcycle accident: 24 years old
1972	Feb 12	released *Eat a Peach* (US)...
		...album title taken from a Duane Allman quote
	Nov 11	Berry Oakley died in a motorcycle accident: 24 years old...
		...died just a few blocks away from where Duane Allman died
1973	Jul 28	played to 600,000 people at the *Summer Jam* at Watkins Glen Raceway
1976	May 4	last gig before their acrimonious split...
		...The Allman Brothers Band:
		Gregg Allman – Dickey Betts – Butch Trucks – Jaimoe Chuck Leavell: keyboards – joined in mid-1972 – 2nd keyboardist Lamar Williams: bass – joined in late 1972, replaced Berry Oakley
		...Scooter Herring: road manager – instrumental in the band splitting up

The Almanac Singers

1941	Jul 7	recorded the album *Sod Buster Ballads*...
		...The Almanac Singers:
		Pete Seeger: banjo, singer, songwriter and founding member Woody Guthrie: guitar, singer and songwriter Lee Hays: singer, songwriter and founding member Millard Lampell: singer, songwriter and founding member Peter Hawes: singer
		...Seeger and Hays went on to form the Weavers
1964	May 18	Animals recorded *House of the Rising Sun*...
		...*Sod Buster Ballads* included the song *House of the Rising Sun*

Amazing Blondel

1970	Sep 19	performed at the 1st Glastonbury festival
1971	Jan 19	supported Mott the Hoople at the Marquee club...
		...band's name taken from the 12th-century minstrel Blondel de Nesle

The Animals

		Inducted into the Rock and Roll Hall of Fame in 1994
1938	Dec 18	Chas Chandler: bassist, born in Heaton, Newcastle upon Tyne
1941	May 11	Eric Burdon: singer, born in Walker, Newcastle upon Tyne
	Jul 7	Almanac Singers recorded *House of the Rising Sun* – covered in 1964
1942	Apr 19	Alan Price: keyboards, born in Fatfield, County Durham

Jul 17 Zoot Money: keyboards, born in Bournemouth, Dorset...
...joined Eric Burdon's New Animals in early 1968

Dec 31 Andy Summers: guitar, born Andrew Somers, in Poulton-le-Fylde, Lancashire...
...previously with Zoot Money's bands and joined the New Animals with him
...later in the Police

1953 Dec 29 bluesman Jimmy Reed recorded *You Don't Have to Go*...
...*Bright Lights Big City* was a Reed single in '61 – covered by the Animals '65

Alan Price Rhythm and Blues Combo

1963 Sep 7 1st performance of the lineup that became the Animals...
...Alan Price Rhythm and Blues Combo:

Alan Price: keyboards – left in mid-1965 and formed the Alan Price Set
John Steel: drums – left in early 1966
Chas Chandler: bass – became Jimi Hendrix's manager in mid-1966
Hilton Valentine: guitar – stayed until the end of the 1st incarnation
Eric Burdon: singer – continued with New Animals after the band folded

The Animals

1963 Sep 15 1st-ever recording session, at Graphic Sound Studios in Newcastle...
...covers included:

Big Boss Man – 1961 single from Jimmy Reed
Boom Boom – John Lee Hooker single in 1962
Pretty Thing – Bo Diddley single in 1955
I Just Wanna Make Love to You – Muddy Waters single in 1954

1964 May 9 support act for Chuck Berry when he toured the UK for the 1st time

May 18 recorded *House of the Rising Sun*...
...Alan Price was the only Animal to receive a writing credit

1966 Jul 4 Frank Zappa arranged two of the songs on their American *Animalism* album

Sep 5 final performance – just three original members remained...
Eric Burdon – Chas Chandler – Hilton Valentine
...Eric Burdon continued as Eric Burdon and the New Animals

Eric Burdon and the New Animals

1966 Dec 23 Eric Burdon featured in the final *Ready Steady Go!* TV show

1967 Dec 22 performed at the *Christmas on Earth Continued* concert

1968 Dec 7 Eric Burdon said goodbye to the music world – New Animals folded just before

By the turn of the decade Eric Burdon was back, and teamed up with War.

1970 Sep 12 performed at Hyde Park...
...last-ever Jimi Hendrix gig was with Eric Burdon and War on 16 September

1971 Jan 30 collapsed on stage – parted company with War – troubled times for Eric Burdon

2008 Feb 27 Burdon's 'lost' *Mirage* album finally released (US) – recorded in 1973 and '74...
...included lyrics written by Jimi Hendrix on the night that he died

Paul Anka

1941 Jul 30 singer and songwriter, Canada's 1st rock'n'roll star, born in Ottawa, Canada...

...prolific songwriter, with credits including:

Diana – international hit for Paul Anka in 1957
(You're) Having My Baby – Paul Anka single in 1974
My Way – Frank Sinatra single in 1969 – English lyrics from Paul Anka

1959 Jan 5 Buddy Holly released *It Doesn't Matter Anymore* – written by Paul Anka

The Artwoods

1941 Jun 9 Jon Lord: keyboardist, born in Leicester, Leicestershire...

...one of Jon Lord's earliest bands was the Don Wilson Combo in 1963:

he was with them when they combined with the Art Wood Combo

...amongst other things:

he was a session musician,
in Santa Barbara Machine Head and the Flower Pot Men touring band,
before leaving for Roundabout, which morphed into Deep Purple

...he joined Whitesnake in the late 1970s

1944 Mar 8 Keef Hartley: drummer, born in Preston, Lancashire...

...previously with Ringo's old group, Rory Storm and the Hurricanes
...later with John Mayall's Bluesbreakers and the Keef Hartley Band

Art Wood formed the Art Wood Combo after he left Alexis Korner's Blues Incorporated.
This became the New Art Wood Combo after amalgamating with the Don Wilson Combo.
The New Art Wood Combo morphed into the Artwoods in the early 1960s.
Before the Artwoods

1962 Mar 17 Alexis Korner's Blues Incorporated played their debut gig – with singer Art Wood

Aug 18 Ringo Starr's 1st gig with the Beatles – Hartley joined Rory Storm in mid-1963

1964 Aug 4 Kinks released *You Really Got Me* – Jon Lord was the session keyboardist

The Artwoods

1965 Apr 2 appeared on the 1st live edition of *Ready Steady Go!*...

...lineup included:

Art Wood: singer
Jon Lord: keyboards – went on to be founding member of Deep Purple
Keef Hartley: drums – next stop was John Mayall's Bluesbreakers

...performed *Sweet Mary* – recorded by Lead Belly in 1944

Chet Atkins

Inducted into the Rock and Roll Hall of Fame in 2002

1924 Jun 20 "Mr Guitar", guitarist, architect of "Nashville sound", born in Luttrell, Tennessee

1947 Aug 11 1st recording session for RCA

1956 Jan 10 played on Elvis Presley's *Heartbreak Hotel*

	Feb 6	Everly Brothers released 1st single – Everlys introduced to Columbia by Atkins
1958	Mar 24	Elvis was inducted into the US Army – recording session with Elvis in June 1958

Atomic Rooster

1940 Oct 13 Chris Farlowe: singer, born John Henry Deighton, in Islington, London...
...joined in 1972

1950 Mar 20 Carl Palmer: drummer and founding member, born in Birmingham, England

The Crazy World of Arthur Brown

1967 Apr 29 performed at the *14-Hour Technicolor Dream*...
...with founding member Vincent Crane, formed '66 – Carl Palmer joined '68
...*Fire* – Crazy World of Arthur Brown single '68 – written by Crane and Brown

Atomic Rooster

1969 Jun 13 Crane and Palmer conceived idea for the band after leaving the Crazy World...
...Atomic Rooster:
Carl Palmer: drums – left in mid-'70 to form Emerson, Lake & Palmer
Vincent Crane: keyboards
Nick Graham: vocals and bass

1989 Feb 14 Vincent Crane died after taking an overdose of painkillers: 45 years old

Meher Baba

1969 May 23 Who released *Tommy* – Baba was a major inspiration for the writing of *Tommy*

1972 Sep 29 Pete Townshend released *Who Came First* – dedicated to Meher Baba

Bad Company

1974 Mar 8 debut gig...
...Bad Company:
Paul Rodgers: singer – from Free
Simon Kirke: drums – from Free
Mick Ralphs: guitar – from Mott the Hoople
Boz Burrell: bass – from Snape, previously with King Crimson
...Peter Grant: manager – also Led Zeppelin's manager
...band's name came from title of Robert Benton's American Civil War movie

Badfinger

1971 Aug 1 performed at the *Concert for Bangladesh*

1974 Mar 8 released *Apple of My Eye* (UK) – last single to be released on the Apple label...
...written by Pete Ham

1975 Apr 24 Pete Ham: singer and founding member, committed suicide: 27 years old

1983 Nov 19 Tom Evans: bassist and founding member, committed suicide: 36 years old

Joan Baez

1963 Aug 28 Martin Luther King Jr delivered his *I Have a Dream* speech – performed at event
1967 Dec 20 received a 45-day jail sentence for anti-Vietnam War activities
1970 Aug 28 performed at the *Isle of Wight Festival*
1975 May 11 performed *There but for Fortune* at the *War Is Over* rally...
...written and released by Phil Ochs in 1964 – UK hit for Baez in 1965
1975 Oct 30 support act: Bob Dylan's *Rolling Thunder Review* tour opened

Hank Ballard and the Midnighters

Hank Ballard

Inducted into the Rock and Roll Hall of Fame in 1990
singer: The Royals – The Midnighters – Hank Ballard and the Midnighters
1927 Nov 18 singer and songwriter, born John Henry Kendricks, in Detroit, Michigan

The Midnighters

Inducted into the Rock and Roll Hall of Fame in 2012
1954 Apr 10 released *Work with Me Annie* (US) – written by Hank Ballard
Apr 24 *Work with Me Annie* entered the R&B charts...
...originally called "The Royals", their first major hit was *Get It in* 1953:
written by Hank Ballard and the Royals' Alonzo Tucker
...name change to avoid confusion with the Five Royals

Hank Ballard and the Midnighters

1958 Nov 11 recorded The Twist – released as the B-side of *Teardrops on Your Letter...*
...Hank Ballard wrote *The Twist*
1960 Aug 1 Chubby Checker released *The Twist* and ignited the dance sensation

The Band

Inducted into the Rock and Roll Hall of Fame in 1994
1935 Jan 10 Ronnie Hawkins: rockabilly singer, born in Huntsville, Arkansas...
...but found fame in Canada
1937 Aug 2 Garth Hudson: keyboards and horns, born in Windsor, Ontario, Canada
1940 May 26 Levon Helm: drummer, mandolin player and singer, born in Elaine, Arkansas
1943 Apr 3 Richard Manuel: keyboards, drums, singer, born in Stratford, Ontario, Canada
Jul 5 Robbie Robertson: guitarist, born Jamie Robert Klegerman, in Toronto, Canada
1943 Dec 29 Rick Danko: bassist and singer, born in Simcoe, Ontario, Canada
The Band were all previously members of Ronnie Hawkins's backing band, the Hawks.
1962 Feb 2 Ronnie Hawkins recording session – with all five future members of the Band...
...session produced by Jerry Leiber and Mike Stoller
Hawks broke away from Ronnie Hawkins in 1965 and as "The Hawks", backed Bob Dylan.
1966 Feb 4 backed Dylan on his infamous electric tour – minus drummer Levon Helm...
...Mickey Jones: drums

1966 May 17 backed Dylan on *Live at the Albert Hall* bootleg album – drummer Mickey Jones

The Hawks changed their name to "The Band" in 1967.

1968 Jul 1 released their debut album, *Music from the Big Pink* (US)

1969 Apr 17 debut concert as "The Band"...

...The Band:

Garth Hudson: keyboards and horns
Levon Helm: drums, mandolin and singer – the only non-Canadian
Richard Manuel: keyboards, drums and vocals
Robbie Robertson: guitar
Rick Danko: bass and vocals

Aug 15 performed at the *Woodstock* festival

1970 Jun 28 performed at the *Festival Express* event in Toronto

1973 Jul 28 played to 600,000 people at the *Summer Jam* at Watkins Glen Raceway

1975 Jun 26 Bob Dylan's *Basement Tapes* was finally released – backed by the Hawks

1976 Nov 25 Band's swan song concert, *The Last Waltz*...

...guest appearances included: Ronnie Hawkins, Bob Dylan, Eric Clapton, Neil Young, Muddy Waters, Van Morrison, Ringo Starr, Ron Wood, Dr John and Paul Butterfield

1986 Mar 4 Richard Manuel committed suicide: 42 years old...

...at a Band reunion in 1983, guitarist Earl Cate replaced Robbie Robertson

Chris Barber

trombone and band-leader: Chris Barber's Jazz Band – Ken Colyer's Jazzmen
Chris Barber's Jazz Band

1930 Apr 17 skiffle and blues pioneer, born in Welwyn Garden City, Hertfordshire

1953 Sep 2 Ken Colyer's Jazzmen recorded *New Orleans to London*

Chris Barber's Jazz Band

1954 Jul 13 recorded *New Orleans Joys* – included Lonnie Donegan's *Rock Island Line*...

...Chris Barber's Jazz Band included:

Chris Barber: trombone – formed in the late 1940s
Lonnie Donegan: banjo

...skiffle songs recorded as "The Lonnie Donegan Skiffle Group":

Chris Barber: bass
Lonnie Donegan: vocals and guitar
Beryl Bryden: washboard

...Lonnie Donegan's *Rock Island Line* was released as UK single in Nov 1955

1957 Nov 28 concert with American gospel singer Sister Rosetta Tharpe...

...Barber brought blues legends to the UK – unsung hero of UK rock'n'roll

1958 Oct 26 brought Muddy Waters over for his historic debut tour of the UK

1962 Apr 6 Alexis Korner played the Marquee as Chris Barber's Jazz Band's interval group...

...Chris Barber's R&B interval act included:

Alexis Korner: guitar
Cyril Davies: guitar and harmonica
Ottilie Patterson: singer

John Barry

1933 Nov 3 early British rock'n'roll bandleader and composer, born in York, North Yorkshire

1957 Oct 4 John Barry and the Seven recorded *Zip Zip* – released as his 1st UK single

1958 Oct 1 Billy Fury spot at a Marty Wilde concert – John Barry Seven were a support act

Dave Bartholomew

Inducted into the Rock and Roll Hall of Fame in 1991

producer: Fats Domino – Lloyd Price

1928 Feb 26 Fats Domino: singer, pianist and songwriter, born in New Orleans, Louisiana...

...song collaborations: Dave Bartholomew and Fats Domino included:

The Fat Man – Fats Domino single '50 – contender, 1st rock'n'roll record
Ain't It a Shame – Fats Domino single in 1955:

covered by Pat Boone in mid-1955

1952 Mar 13 producer: Lloyd Price recorded *Lawdy Miss Clawdy*

1955 May 23 writer: Smiley Lewis recorded *I Hear You Knocking*

1957 Apr 10 Ricky Nelson performed *I'm Walkin'* on TV – co-written with Fats Domino

Battered Ornaments

1940 Dec 25 Pete Brown: lyricist, singer and founding member, born in Ashtead, Surrey...

...formed Piblokto after he was sacked from Battered Ornaments
...Cream lyricist, in collaboration with Jack Bruce

1944 Jun 17 Chris Spedding: guitarist, born Peter Robinson, in Staveley, Derbyshire...

...founding member, took over lead vocals after Pete Brown left

1969 Jan 4 Jimi Hendrix performed *Sunshine of Your Love* on Lulu's TV show...

...written by Jack Bruce, Pete Brown and Eric Clapton

Battered Ornaments (without Pete Brown)

1969 Jul 5 supported the Rolling Stones at the free concert in London's Hyde Park...

...Pete Brown was sacked by the band the day before the gig

The Beach Boys

Inducted into the Rock and Roll Hall of Fame in 1988

1941 Mar 15 Mike Love: saxophonist, singer and songwriter, born in Los Angeles, California

1942 Jun 20 Brian Wilson: creative genius behind the band, born in Inglewood, California

Sep 3 Al Jardine: guitarist and singer, born in Lima, Ohio

1944 Dec 4 Dennis Wilson: drummer and singer, born in Hawthorn, California

1946 Dec 21 Carl Wilson: guitarist and singer, born in Hawthorn, California

1958 Mar 28 Eddie Cochran recorded *Summertime Blues* – covered on their 1st album in 1962

The final lineup of the Pendletones became the Beach Boys.

1961 Oct 3 recorded *Surfin* at their 1st-ever recording session

Dec 31 early Beach Boys gig...

...The Beach Boys:

Brian Wilson: bass, keyboards and vocals – band's guiding light
Dennis Wilson: drums and vocals
Carl Wilson: lead guitar and vocals
Mike Love: singer and saxophone – Wilson brothers' cousin
Al Jardine: guitar – Wilson brothers' friend

1962 Jun 4 released *Surfin' Safari* (US) – 1st Capitol single...

...David Marks: guitar and vocals – replaced Jardine, early 1962 to late '63
...written by Brian Wilson and Mike Love

1963 Jan 31 recorded *Surfin' USA* – Brian Wilson later sued by Chuck Berry for plagiarism

1964 Dec 23 Brian Wilson had a nervous breakdown – replaced on stage by Glen Campbell

1965 Apr 9 Bruce Johnston's debut performance...

...Glen Campbell: bass and vocals – replaced Brian Wilson in early 1965
...Bruce Johnston: vocals and bass – replaced Glen Campbell

1966 Feb 17 recording started on the epic *Good Vibrations* – written by Brian and Mike Love

Apr 12 Jan Berry was hurt in a car crash near Dead Man's Curve...

...*Dead Man's Curve* was a Jan and Dean single in 1964:

songwriters included Brian Wilson and Jan Berry

May 16 released *Pet Sounds* (US)...

...with Wrecking Crew's drummer Hal Blaine and saxophonist Steve Douglas

1967 May 2 Brian Wilson abandoned his magnum opus, *Smile*

Sep 11 released *Smiley Smile* (US) – 1st album released on their Brother label...

...this marked the end of the era of Brian's domination of the Beach Boys

1969 Jan 27 released *20/20* (US) – contained a song written by Charles Manson...

...Dennis had previously befriended Charles Manson

1971 Apr 27 performed together with the Grateful Dead at the Fillmore East...

...covers performed together:

Johnny B Goode – Chuck Berry single in 1958
Okie From Muskogee – Merle Haggard single in 1969
Riot in Cell Block #9 – Robins single in 1954
Searchin' – Coasters single in 1957

May 6 announcement of the end of the Fillmores...

...performed at the final Fillmore East concert in June

Aug 30 released *Surf's Up* album (US)...

...title song was written by Brian and Van Dyke Parks, and destined for *Smile*

1980 Mar 17 released *Keepin' the Summer Alive* (US) – last album with all three Wilsons...
...Carl left for a solo career shortly afterwards
1983 Dec 28 drumming brother Dennis drowned: at the age of 39
1988 Nov 5 22 years between US #1s – *Good Vibrations* in 1966 and *Kokomo* in 1988
2004 Sep 28 Brian Wilson finally released his 'lost' 1960s album, *Smile* (US)

The Beatles

Inducted into the Rock and Roll Hall of Fame in 1988 (3rd year)...
+...John in 1994 ...Paul in 1999 ...George in 2004 ...Ringo in 2015
+...George Martin in 1999 +...Brian Epstein in 2014

Beatles and Associates

1923 Feb 22 Norman "Hurricane" Smith: engineer and producer, born in Edmonton, London...
...engineer for all of their recordings up to and including *Rubber Soul*
1926 Jan 3 George Martin: producer, born in Holloway, London...
...signed the band to Parlophone and produced most of their recordings
1931 Dec 18 Allen Klein: accountant and business manager, born in Newark, New Jersey...
...managed the Beatles' business affairs after Brian Epstein died
1933 Feb 18 Yoko Ono: artist, born in Tokyo, Japan...
...John Lennon's 2nd wife and collaborator
1934 Sep 19 Brian Epstein: manager and promoter, born in Liverpool, England...
...managed the band from late 1961 until his death on 27 August* 1967
1939 Dec 26 Phil Spector: musician, songwriter and producer, born in New York...
...transformed the album *Get Back* into *Let It Be*
1940 Jun 23 Stuart Sutcliffe: bassist, born in Edinburgh, Scotland...
...artist and original bass player – joined late 1959, died 10 April* 1962
Jul 7 Ringo Starr: drummer, born Richard Starkey, in Liverpool, England...
...stage name derived from: penchant for wearing rings + surname Starkey
Jul 18 Johnny Hutchinson: drummer and singer, born in Malta...
...stood in for Tommy Moore at the failed Billy Fury audition
...occupied the empty drum stool between Pete Best and Ringo
Oct 9 John Lennon, rhythm guitarist and singer, born in Liverpool, England
1941 Nov 24 Pete Best: drummer, born in Madras, India...
...joined the band in August 1960 – replaced by Ringo in 1962
1942 Feb 15 Glyn Johns: record producer and engineer, born in Epsom, Surrey...
...led the *Get Back* sessions and produced the 'lost' *Get Back* album
Jun 18 Paul McCartney: bassist and singer, born in Liverpool, England
1943 Feb 24 George Harrison: lead guitarist, born in Liverpool, England...
...it all started with: *Raunchy* – Bill Justis single in 1957:
George used it for his Quarry Men audition in early 1958

1951 May 19 Joey Ramone was born Jeffrey Hyman, in Forest Hills, New York...

...band's name, "Ramones", was inspired by an early McCartney stage name

...stage names used by the Beatles in their early days:

Paul McCartney – Paul Ramon
John Lennon – Long John
George Harrison – Carl Harrison

Covers: The Beatles – Fab Four (after Ringo joined)

1952 Mar 13 Lloyd Price recorded *Lawdy Miss Clawdy* – covered in 1970

Aug 18 Little Willie Littlefield recorded *KC Loving*...

...rewritten by Leiber & Stoller as *Kansas City* – covered, 1964 UK & 1965 US

...covered as a medley of *Kansas City* and *Hey-Hey-Hey-Hey*:

Kansas City – US #1 for Wilbert Harrison in 1959
Hey-Hey-Hey-Hey – Little Richard B-side in 1958

1955 Dec 19 Carl Perkins recorded *Honey Don't* – covered in 1964...

...Beatles covered two other Carl Perkins songs:

Matchbox – Carl Perkins single in 1957 – covered in 1964...

...based on Ma Rainey's *Lost Wandering Blues*, 1924
...and Blind Lemon Jefferson's *Match Box Blues*, 1927

Everybody's Trying to Be My Baby – Carl Perkins 1957 – covered 1964...

...originally by Rex Griffin in 1936

1958 Feb 19 Larry Williams recorded *Dizzy Miss Lizzy* – covered in 1965

...Beatles covered two other Larry Williams songs:

Slow Down – Larry Williams B-side in 1958 – covered in 1964
Bad Boy – Larry Williams single 1959 – covered in 1965 US and '66 UK

1961 Feb 23 Top Notes recorded *Twist and Shout* – covered in 1963...

...co-produced by Phil Spector

...famously covered by the Isley Brothers in mid-1962

1961 Aug 21 Marvelettes released *Please Mr. Postman* – covered 1963 UK and 1964 US

These covers appeared on various singles and albums, including:

1964 Jan 20 *Meet the Beatles*: 1st US album from Capitol Records

Till There Was You – taken from the 1957 musical *The Music Man*

Jan 27 *Introducing the Beatles* reissued by Vee-Jay (US):

Baby It's You – American hit for the Shirelles in 1962
Boys – B-side of the Shirelles' *Will You Love Me Tomorrow* in 1960
Chains – American hit for the Cookies in 1962 – written by Goffin and King
Anna (Go to Him) – written and released by Arthur Alexander in 1962
Taste of Honey – originally an instrumental – Lenny Welch vocal version, '62

Apr 10 *The Beatles' Second Album* (US):

Roll Over Beethoven – written by Chuck Berry and released as a single 1956

You Really Got a Hold on Me – Miracles 1962 – written by Smokey Robinson
Devil in Her Heart – released by the Donays as *The Devil in His Heart* in 1962
Money – R&B hit for Barrett Strong in 1960 – co-written by Berry Gordy Jr
Long Tall Sally – recorded by Little Richard in 1956 – covered in 1964...
...written by Little Richard, Bumps Blackwell and Enortis Johnson

Dec 4 *Beatles for Sale* (UK):

Leave My Kitten Alone – recorded for this album but not released until 1995...
...cover of a 1959 Little Willie John single

Dec 15 *Beatles '65* (US):

Rock and Roll Music – written and released as a single by Chuck Berry 1957

Mr. Moonlight – single from Dr Feelgood and the Interns in 1962

1965 Jun 14 *Beatles VI* (US):

Words of Love – 1st Coral single credited to "Buddy Holly", 1957 – Holly penned

1965 Sep 13 B-side of American single *Yesterday*:

Act Naturally – country #1 for Buck Owens in 1963

Road to the Beatles

1956 Aug 22 *The Girl Can't Help It* opened, it included Eddie Cochran's *Twenty Flight Rock*...
...Paul used the song for his Quarry Men audition in 1957

The Black Jacks was formed by John and Pete Shotton in 1957 – renamed to "The Quarry Men".

Road to the Beatles began when Paul joined John's group, the Quarry Men.

1957 Jul 6 John Lennon met Paul McCartney at St Peter's Church fete in Woolton...
...Paul was introduced to John by Ivan Vaughan

Aug 7 John Lennon's Cavern Club debut

1957 Oct 18 Paul McCartney's debut performance in the Quarry Men

George Harrison joined the Quarry Men in early 1958, after the Rebels.

The Rebels lineup included:

George Harrison: guitar
Peter Harrison – George's brother
Arthur Kelly

Other members of the Quarry Men are mentioned in *23 June 1962*

Colin Hanton: drums – played on the Quarry Men recording of 14 July 1958
John Lowe: piano – played on the Quarry Men recording of 14 July 1958
Ken Brown: guitar – last version of the Q.Men late 1959 + John, Paul and George
Percy Phillips – owned the studio where the Quarry Men made their recording

Ringo Starr was the only Beatle not to follow the Quarry Men route.

He was a member of Rory Storm and the Hurricanes.

1959 Sep 26 Ringo appeared at Lathom Hall

Quarry Men became the trio Johnny and the Moondogs, with John, Paul and George.

1959 Oct 26 qualified for the final of the talent contest, *Carroll Levis Search for a Star*...
...the heat was won by the Connaughts

Stuart Sutcliffe joined as bassist and the Moondogs became the Silver Beetles.

They used a range of names around this time including the Beatals and the Silver Beats.

1959 Nov 17 Stuart Sutcliffe financed his bass guitar

1960 May 10 failed their audition to become Billy Fury's backing band...
...The Silver Beetles:
John – Paul – George – Stuart Sutcliffe
Tommy Moore: drums, mid-1960 – late for the audition
Johnny Hutchinson: drums – stood in for Tommy Moore...
...from Cass and the Cassanovas – also auditioned that day
...audition arranged by Allan Williams, their 1st manager/booking agent

Ringo was still with Rory Storm and the Hurricanes.

1960 May 25 Ringo played at the Cavern Club's 1st "Beat Night"

Drummer Tommy Moore left, replaced briefly by Norman Chapman. *SEE 23 June 1962*
Pete Best, from the Blackjacks, replaced Norman Chapman.
They became "The Beatles" and headed off to Hamburg.
"The Beatles" name is variously accredited to:
Buddy Holly's Crickets or the Beetles gang in Brando's movie The Wild One...
...although, The Wild One *was banned in the UK until 1968.*
"Beetles" to "Beatles" is attributed to beat poet Royston Ellis.

THE BEATLES

The Beatles were: John, Paul, George, Stuart Sutcliffe and Pete Best.

1960 Aug 17 opening night of their 1st Hamburg trip...
...1st time that they called themselves "The Beatles"
...1st gig with their new drummer Pete Best
...Allan Williams organised the gig

John, Paul, George and Ringo

1960 Oct 15 John, Paul, George and Ringo recorded together for the 1st time...
...with bassist Lu "Wally" Walters from Rory Storm and the Hurricanes:
Ringo was with Rory Storm and the Hurricanes
...they recorded *Summertime* – from Gershwin's *Porgy and Bess*
...Walters was born Walter Eymond

The Beatles

1960 Dec 1 Paul and Pete Best deported from Germany – George had already been expelled

Dec 17 1st of four gigs with Chas Newby, as the Beatles' temporary bass player...

...Stuart Sutcliffe had stayed on in Hamburg

1961 Jan 5 Paul's debut as bass guitarist

1961 Feb 9 1st Cavern appearance as "The Beatles" – also George's Cavern debut

Tony Sheridan and the Beat Brothers

1961 Jun 22 recording session in Hamburg – John, Paul, George and Pete Best...

...original German single released as Tony Sheridan and the Beat Brothers

My Bonnie c/w *The Saints* – traditional, arranged by Tony Sheridan

..."Beatles" was too close to the German word "peedles", slang for penis

...plus two recordings without Sheridan:

Ain't She Sweet – standard, written in 1927
Cry for a Shadow – instrumental written by George and John

...produced by Bert Kaempfert

John and Stuart Sutcliffe in the Dissenters

1961 Jul 21 Jimmy Page backed beat poet Royston Ellis in a fusion of music and poetry...

...John and Stuart had backed Ellis in June 1960.

The Beatles

1961 Oct 1 iconic Beatles hairstyle arrived...

...Sutcliffe's girlfriend Astrid Kirchherr introduced them to the famous cut

The Beatmakers

1961 Oct 19 Beatles combined with Gerry and the Pacemakers to form the Beatmakers...

...The Beatmakers:

John: piano – Paul: rhythm guitar – George: lead guitar – Pete Best: drums
Gerry Marsden: lead guitar and vocals – Gerry and the Pacemakers
Freddy Marsden: drums – Gerry and the Pacemakers
Les McGuire: saxophone – Gerry and the Pacemakers
Les Chadwick: bass – Gerry and the Pacemakers
Karl Terry: vocals – Karl Terry and the Cruisers

The Beatles

1961 Oct 28 Brian Epstein was asked for a copy of *My Bonnie*

Nov 9 Brian Epstein visited the Cavern to see the Beatles for the 1st time

Dec 9 1st Beatles gig in the south of England

1962 Jan 1 failed their audition for a Decca recording contract...

...covers included:

To Know Her is to Love Her – Teddy Bears single 1958 (SEE 20 May)

Money – Barrett Strong single in 1959

...plus three Lennon and McCartney compositions:

Hello Little Girl – Fourmost single in 1963
Love of the Loved – Cilla Black single in 1963
Like Dreamers Do – Applejacks single in 1964

Tony Sheridan and the Beatles

1962 Jan 5 released *My Bonnie* (UK) – 1st UK recording as "The Beatles"

The Beatles

1962 Apr 10 original bassist Stuart Sutcliffe died of a brain haemorrhage: 21 years old

Tony Sheridan and the Beat Brothers

1962 Apr 23 *My Bonnie* was released on Decca in America – 1st US release

The Beatles

1962 Jun 6 1st *Love Me Do* recording session at Abbey Road – with drummer Pete Best...

...also recorded, *Besame Mucho* – writer Consuelo Velazquez, early 1940s:

Jet Harris released *Besame Mucho* as a single in 1962

...Pete Best was sacked shortly after this recording session

1962 Jun 23 Brian Epstein formed NEMS Enterprises Ltd

THE BEATLES – THE FAB FOUR

Ringo joined, having already recorded and performed with John, Paul and George.

Ringo's route to the Beatles was unique and included:

The Eddie Clayton Skiffle Group
Darktown Skiffle Group
The Raving Texans
Rory Storm and the Hurricanes

The Beatles were now the "Fab Four": John, Paul, George and Ringo.

1962 Aug 18 Ringo's 1st gig as an official Beatle – he left Rory Storm and the Hurricanes...

...Johnny Hutchinson: drums – between Pete Best leaving and Ringo joining

Sep 4 2nd *Love Me Do* recording session – with drummer Ringo Starr...

...also recorded *How Do You Do It* as a possible debut single:

this song gave Gerry and the Pacemakers their 1st UK #1 in 1963

Sep 11 3rd *Love Me Do* recording session – Andy White drums and Ringo tambourine

1962 Oct 5 released their UK debut single, *Love Me Do c/w P.S. I Love You* (UK-1)...

...vinyl history of *Love Me Do*:

1962	June 6	1st recording session at Abbey Road – drummer Pete Best
	Sep 4	2nd Abbey Road recording session – drummer Ringo Starr
	Sep 11	3rd Abbey Road recording session – Andy White drums and Ringo tambourine
	Oct 5	UK single released – original copies (red label) with Ringo on drums
1963		released by Capitol in Canada – with Ringo on drums
	Mar 22	UK album, *Please Please Me* released – Andy White version
1963		UK Parlophone changed singles' label from red to black – also to Andy White
	Jul 22	US album, *Introducing the Beatles* released on Vee-Jay – Andy White...
		...track was replaced by *Please Please Me* on the reissued album
1964	Apr 27	US single released on the Tollie label – Andy White
1965	Mar 22	1st release in America from Capitol, *The Early Beatles* – Andy White
1995	Nov 21	Pete Best's version was finally made legally available on *Anthology 1*
		...listen for a tambourine to determine which version you are listening to!

1962	Oct 12	supported Little Richard on his UK rock'n'roll comeback tour – met Billy Preston
	Oct 30	4th Hamburg trip – same bill as Little Richard
	Nov 26	recorded *Please Please Me* – 1st 'true' Beatles recording session...
		...also recorded *Tip of My Tongue* – Tommy Quickly single in mid-1963
1963	Jan 11	released *Please Please Me* c/w *Ask Me Why* (UK-2) – only #1 on some charts
	Jan 26	supported by Wayne Fontana and the Jets in Macclesfield
	Feb 2	opening night of their 1st UK package tour – supporting Helen Shapiro
	Feb 20	Duffy Power recorded *I Saw Her Standing There* – released by the Beatles 1963
	Feb 25	released 1st US single *Please Please Me* c/w *Ask Me Why* (US-1)...
		...Capitol Records were not interested so Vee-Jay picked them up
		...this started a string of releases on Vee-Jay, Swan and Tollie
	Mar 22	released UK debut album *Please Please Me* (UK-1)
	Apr 11	released *From Me to You* c/w *Thank You Girl* (UK-3) – 1st UK #1
	Apr 14	Beatles met the Rolling Stones for the 1st time
	Apr 18	Del Shannon supported them and decided to record *From Me to You*...
		...this gave Lennon and McCartney their 1st American hit record
	May 27	released *From Me to You* c/w *Thank You Girl* (US-2) – 2nd Vee-Jay single
	Jul 22	Vee-Jay released 1st American album, *Introducing the Beatles* (US-1)
	Jul 26	Billy J Kramer released *I Call Your Name* (UK B-side) – released by Beatles 1964
	Aug 3	last appearance at the Cavern Club
	Aug 23	released *She Loves You* c/w *I'll Get You* (UK-4) – 1st British million-seller
	Aug 30	Fourmost released *Hello Little Girl* (UK) – not released by the Beatles until 1995
	Sep 16	released *She Loves You* c/w *I'll Get You* (US-3) – on Swan, charted February 1964
	Oct 31	Ed Sullivan experienced Beatlemania

	Nov 1	Rolling Stones released *I Wanna Be Your Man* (UK) – before the Beatles' version
	Nov 4	appeared on the *Royal Command Performance* TV show
	Nov 22	released *With the Beatles* (UK-2) – 1st British album to sell more than 1m copies
	Nov 25	Capitol's 1st North American release, *Beatlemania! With The Beatles* – in Canada
	Nov 29	released *I Want to Hold Your Hand* c/w *This Boy* (UK-5) – 1st 1m advance orders
	Dec 2	appeared on UK TV's *Morecambe and Wise Show*
	Dec 7	all four Beatles appeared on *Juke Box Jury*
	Dec 14	*I Want to Hold Your Hand* knocked *She Loves You* off the UK #1 spot
	Dec 26	1st Capitol 45, *I Want to Hold Your Hand* c/w *I Saw Her Standing There* (US-4)
1964	Jan 20	Capitol released 1st album in the US, *Meet the Beatles* (US-2)
	Jan 27	Vee-Jay reissued the album *Introducing the Beatles* (US-1)... ...*Love Me Do, P.S. I Love You* replaced by *Please Please Me, Ask Me Why*
	Jan 30	Vee-Jay released their 3rd single, *Please Please Me* c/w *From Me to You* (US-5)
	Feb 1	1st US #1, *I Want to Hold Your Hand* – beginning of the British Invasion
	Feb 9	1st appearance on the *Ed Sullivan Show*
	Feb 11	American concert debut – but fans had to wait until August for the 1st US tour
	Mar 2	released *Twist and Shout* c/w *There's a Place* (US-6) – 1st single on Tollie
	Mar 16	released *Can't Buy Me Love* c/w *You Can't Do That* (US-7) – Capitol's 2nd single
	Mar 20	released *Can't Buy Me Love* c/w *You Can't Do That* (UK-6)
	Mar 23	released 4th and last V-J 45, *Do You Want...Secret* c/w *Thank You Girl* (US-8)... ...Billy J Kramer's 1st UK hit single, 1963
	Apr 4	dominated the American charts with 12 songs in the Top 100
	Apr 10	released *The Beatles' Second Album* (US-3)
	Apr 27	2nd Tollie single *Love Me Do* c/w *PS I Love You* (US-9) – Andy White on drums
	May 21	released *Sie Liebt Dich* c/w *I'll Get You* (US-10) – 2nd Swan single
	Jun 4	Jimmy Nicol stood in for Ringo for a week on their 1st world tour... ...in 1964 he formed his own group, Jimmy Nicol and the Shubdubs
	Jun 26	released movie soundtrack album *A Hard Day's Night* (US-4)
	Jul 10	released *A Hard Day's Night* c/w *Things We Said Today* (UK-7)... ...and *A Hard Day's Night* movie soundtrack album (UK-3): included *I'll Cry Instead* – Joe Cocker single in 1964 SEE 13 Nov 1963
	Jul 13	released *A Hard Day's Night* c/w *I Should Have Known Better* (US-11)... ...3rd Capitol single – from here, all the US releases were on Capitol or Apple
	Jul 20	released: *Something New* (US-5) – well, half the tracks were new... ...and *I'll Cry Instead* c/w *I'm Happy Just to Dance with You* (US-12) ...and, *And I Love Her* c/w *If I Fell* (US-13)
	Aug 16	Beatles concert – supported by the High Numbers and the Kinks
	Aug 19	opened their 1st American tour
	Aug 24	released *Matchbox* c/w *Slowdown* (US-14)

	Aug 28	Bob Dylan introduced them to pot – halfway through their 1st American tour
	Nov 23	released *I Feel Fine* c/w *She's a Woman* (US-15)...
		...and *The Beatles' Story* (US-6)
	Nov 27	released *I Feel Fine* c/w *She's a Woman* (UK-8)
	Dec 4	released *Beatles for Sale* (UK-4)...
		...*Leave My Kitten Alone* was recorded for the album but was not included:
		original version was a Little Willie John single in mid-1959
	Dec 15	released *Beatles '65* (US-7)
1965	Feb 15	released *Eight Days a Week* c/w *I Don't Want to Spoil the Party* (US-16)
	Mar 22	Capitol issued *The Early Beatles* (US-8) – similar content to the Vee-Jay album
	Apr 9	released *Ticket to Ride* c/w *Yes It Is* (UK-9)
	Apr 19	released *Ticket to Ride* c/w *Yes It Is* (US-17)
	Jun 14	released *Beatles VI* (US-9)
	Jul 19	released *Help* c/w *I'm Down* (US-18)
	Jul 23	released *Help* c/w *I'm Down* (UK-10)
	Aug 6	released *Help* (UK-5)
	Aug 13	released *Help* (US-10) – different track listing to the UK version
	Aug 15	legendary Shea Stadium concert – 1st-ever rock concert held in a stadium
	Aug 27	met their rock'n'roll idol Elvis Presley
	Sep 13	released *Yesterday* c/w *Act Naturally* (US-19)...
		...*Yesterday* was originally offered to Billy J Kramer
	Dec 3	released *We Can Work it Out* c/w *Day Tripper* (UK-11)...
		...and *Rubber Soul* (UK-6) – 1st album with all original material
	Dec 6	released *We Can Work it Out* c/w *Day Tripper* (US-20)...
		...and *Rubber Soul* (US-11)
	Dec 12	last-ever UK concert
1966	Feb 21	released *Nowhere Man* c/w *What Goes On* (US-21)...
		...B-side gave Ringo his 1st writing credit
	Mar 4	JOHN: original "more popular than Jesus" Maureen Cleave interview published
	May 30	released *Paperback Writer* c/w *Rain* (US-22)
	Jun 10	released *Paperback Writer* c/w *Rain* (UK-12) – *Writer* inspired by Royston Ellis
	Jun 20	released *Yesterday...And Today* (US-12) – notorious "butcher" cover
	Jun 24	final world tour opened – from Germany to Japan, the Philippines and the USA
	Aug 5	released *Yellow Submarine* c/w *Eleanor Rigby* (UK-13)...
		...and *Revolver* (UK-7):
		included *Got to Get You Into My Life* – Cliff Bennett cover in 1966
		Revolver sleeve designed by Klaus Voormann
	Aug 8	released *Eleanor Rigby* c/w *Yellow Submarine* (US-23)
		...and *Revolver* (US-13)

	Aug 8	from the Brill Building to song-writing bands – transition led by the Beatles
	Aug 29	gave their last-ever concert performance, at San Francisco's Candlestick Park
	Nov 24	recorded *Strawberry Fields Forever* – originally destined for *Sgt Pepper*
	Dec 9	released *A Collection of Beatles Oldies* (UK-8) – *Bad Boy* was the only new song
1967	Jan 6	PAUL: issued *The Family Way* soundtrack album (UK) – 1st solo Beatle project...
		...collaboration with George Martin
	Jan 7	denial by *Beatles Monthly* magazine that Paul McCartney was dead
	Feb 13	released *Strawberry Fields Forever* c/w *Penny Lane* (US-24)
	Feb 17	released *Strawberry Fields Forever* c/w *Penny Lane* (UK-14)
	Apr 8	Engelbert Humperdinck's *Release Me* broke Beatles' run of 11 consecutive #1s
	Apr 29	Yoko Ono performed at the 14-*Hour Technicolor Dream*
	Jun 1	released *Sgt Pepper's Lonely Hearts Club Band* (UK-9)...
		...Peter Blake designed sleeve
		...topped "best albums of all-time" charts for decades to come
	Jun 2	released *Sgt Pepper* (US-14) – 1st US album to be the same as in UK
	Jun 25	appeared on the *Our World* live global TV broadcast – to 400 million viewers
	Jul 7	released *All You Need Is Love* c/w *Baby You're a Rich Man* (UK-15)
	Jul 17	released *All You Need Is Love* c/w *Baby You're a Rich Man* (US-25)
	Jul 24	ad in *The Times* to legalise marijuana – signed by the Beatles and Brian Epstein
	Aug 18	JOHN and PAUL: backing vocals: Rolling Stones released *We Love You*
	Aug 27	manager Brian Epstein died – the Beatles were with Maharishi Mahesh Yogi
	Oct 18	JOHN: *How I Won the War* movie premiered in London...
		...spawned a single as Musketeer Gripweed and the Third Troop
	Nov 9	JOHN: featured on the front cover of the 1st issue of *Rolling Stone* magazine
	Nov 24	released *Hello Goodbye* c/w *I Am the Walrus* (UK-16)
	Nov 27	released *Hello Goodbye* c/w *I Am the Walrus* (US-26)...
		...and *Magical Mystery Tour*, on an album format in America (US-15)
	Dec 8	released *Magical Mystery Tour* on a double-EP format in the UK
	Dec 26	UK TV premiere of *Magical Mystery Tour* – it was panned by the critics
1968	Mar 15	released *Lady Madonna* c/w *The Inner Light* (UK-17)...
		...*The Inner Light* was Harrison's 1st composition on a single
	Mar 18	released *Lady Madonna* c/w *The Inner Light* (US-27)
	Jun 11	recording session for *Revolution 9* – song became linked to Charles Manson
	Jul 30	end of Apple Boutique...
		...ex-Quarry Man, Pete Shotton was initially manager of the project
	Aug 26	released *Hey Jude* c/w *Revolution* (US-28)...
		...*Hey Jude* was written by Paul for John's son, Julian
	Aug 30	released *Hey Jude* c/w *Revolution* (UK-18)
	Sep 6	Eric Clapton recorded the guitar solo for *While My Guitar Gently Weeps*

	Oct 24	Joe Cocker performed *With a Little Help from My Friends* on *Top of the Pops*... ...from *Sgt Pepper* – a rare example of a cover being better than the original
	Nov 1	GEORGE: released *Wonderwall Music* (UK) – 1st solo album by a Beatle... ...RINGO: performed on the album as "Richie Snare"
	Nov 13	animated movie *Yellow Submarine* opened (US)
	Nov 22	released *The Beatles* (aka *The White Album*) (UK-10)
	Nov 23	JOHN: John and Yoko appeared naked on the cover of *Rolling Stone* magazine
	Nov 25	released *The Beatles* (aka *The White Album*) (US-16)
	Nov 29	JOHN: released his debut solo album, *Unfinished Music No.1: Two Virgins* (UK)
	Dec 11	JOHN: Dirty Mac performed on the Stones' TV special, *Rock and Roll Circus*... ...Dirty Mac: Winston Legthigh, aka John Lennon: guitar and vocals Keith Richard: bass – from the Rolling Stones Eric Clapton: guitar – from the recently disbanded Cream Mitch Mitchell: drums – from the Jimi Hendrix Experience Ivry Gitlis: violin Yoko Ono: vocals
1969	Jan 2	work started on the ill-fated *Get Back* project
	Jan 13	released *Yellow Submarine* (US-17)
	Jan 17	released *Yellow Submarine* (UK-11)
	Jan 18	settled the lawsuit issued against the Beatles by ex-drummer Pete Best
	Jan 30	final performance – given on the rooftop of their Apple building in London... ...with keyboardist Billy Preston
	Mar 1	GEORGE: Cream released *Goodbye* – was L'Angelo Misterioso on *Badge*... ...he also wrote *Badge* with Eric Clapton
	Apr 11	released *Get Back* c/w *Don't Let Me Down* (UK-19) – early lyrics deemed racist
	May 5	released *Get Back* c/w *Don't Let Me Down* (US-29)
	May 30	released *Ballad of John and Yoko* c/w *Old Brown Shoe* (UK-20) – last UK #1... ...no involvement from George and Ringo on *Ballad*
	Jun 4	released *The Ballad of John and Yoko* c/w *Old Brown Shoe* (US-30)... ...*Old Brown Shoe* was George's 2nd and final Beatles B-side
	Aug 10	Charles Manson murders – cited Beatles songs from *White Album* as inspiration
	Aug 20	final recording session with all four Beatles
	Aug 22	GEORGE: producer: Radha Krishna Temple released *Hare Krishna Mantra* (US)
	Aug 29	GEORGE: "L'Angelo Misterioso" on Jack Bruce's solo album *Songs for a Tailor*
	Sep 13	JOHN: Plastic Ono Band's debut gig at the *Toronto Rock and Roll Revival*... ...Plastic Ono Band: John Lennon: vocals and guitar Yoko Ono: vocals Eric Clapton: guitar

Klaus Voormann: bass – friend of the Beatles from the Hamburg days
Alan White: drums – future Yes drummer

	Sep 26	released *Abbey Road* (UK-12) – recorded after *Let It Be*...
		...*Maxwell's Silver Hammer* – Format cover in 1969 SEE 1 March 1961
	Oct 1	released *Abbey Road* (US-18)
	Oct 6	released *Something* c/w *Come Together* (US-31)
	Oct 31	released *Something* c/w *Come Together* (UK-21) – 1st Harrison A-side
	Nov 1	JOHN, PAUL and GEORGE: named in *Rolling Stone*'s Masked Marauders hoax
	Nov 7	JOHN: released *Wedding Album* (UK)
	Dec 2	GEORGE: joined Delaney and Bonnie on stage in Bristol – continued on the tour
	Dec 3	JOHN: asked by Tim Rice and Andrew Lloyd Webber to play Jesus Christ
	Dec 7	GEORGE: recorded *Delaney & Bonnie & Friends: On Tour with Eric Clapton*...
		...credited as "L'Angelo Misterioso"
	Dec 15	JOHN: start of the international peace campaign, *War is Over*...
		...Plastic Ono Band:
		John Lennon – Yoko Ono – Klaus Voormann – Eric Clapton GEORGE: guitar – 1st time on stage with JOHN since 1966 Keith Moon: drums – from the Who Billy Preston: keyboards – met the Beatles in Hamburg Delaney and Bonnie...
		...fresh from their European tour, with guests Harrison and Clapton
1970	Jan 27	JOHN: wrote and recorded *Instant Karma*...
		...Plastic Ono Band:
		John Lennon – Yoko Ono – Klaus Voormann – Alan White Billy Preston – GEORGE
		...1st collaboration with producer Phil Spector
	Feb 26	released the album *Hey Jude* (US-19) – not released in the UK
	Mar 6	released their final UK single *Let It Be* c/w *You Know My Name*...(UK-22)
	Mar 11	released *Let It Be* c/w *You Know My Name* (*Look up the Number*) (US-32)
	Mar 23	Phil Spector started work on the project to turn *Get Back* into the *Let It Be* album
	Apr 10	*Daily Mirror* (UK) headline "Paul Is Quitting The Beatles"
	Apr 17	PAUL: released his debut album, *McCartney* (UK)
	Apr 24	RINGO: issued debut album, *Sentimental Journey* (US) – last of the solo albums
	May 8	released *Let It Be* (UK-13) – produced by Phil Spector...
		...started out as the *Get Back* project in January 1969
	May 11	released *Long and Winding Road* c/w *For You Blue* (US-33)
	May 18	released *Let It Be* (US-20)
1970	May 20	*Let It Be* movie premiered in Britain – none of the Beatles attended
		END OF THE BEATLES

1970	Nov 27	GEORGE: released *All Things Must Pass* (UK)...
		...featured guitarist Eric Clapton and keyboardist Gary Wright
	Dec 11	JOHN: released his 1st 'true' solo album, *Plastic Ono Band* (UK)...
		...featured RINGO and bassist Klaus Voormann
1971	Feb 10	GEORGE: received a plagiarism lawsuit for *My Sweet Lord*
	Jun 6	JOHN: and Yoko jammed with Frank Zappa at the Fillmore East...
		...released as the bonus live album with *Some Time in New York City*
	Jul 16	JOHN: co-writer and co-producer: Electric Oz Band released *God Save Us*...
		...co-produced with Phil Spector and ex-Beatles roadie Mal Evans
		...co-written with Yoko Ono
		...single in support of OZ magazine's obscenity trial of their *School Kids Issue*
	Aug 1	GEORGE: *Concert for Bangladesh* – organised with Ravi Shankar...
		...RINGO: played at the concert
	Oct 8	JOHN: released his *Imagine* album – featured GEORGE...
		...lyrics for the title track were inspired by Yoko Ono's book *Grapefruit*
	Dec 13	John Sinclair freed from jail – JOHN and Yoko performed at the *Freedom Rally*
1972	Feb 25	PAUL: Wings released the protest single, *Give Ireland Back to the Irish* (UK)...
		...lineup included:
		Paul McCartney
		Linda McCartney: keyboards and vocals
		Denny Laine: guitar, vocals and founding member – 1971 to '81
		Henry McCullough: guitar – joined in early 1972, from the Grease Band
	Nov 8	GEORGE and JOHN: Detective Sergeant Norman Pilcher arrested for perjury...
		...he had previously bust George and John for drugs
	Dec 14	RINGO: director: London premiere of Mark Bolan's movie *Born to Boogie*
1974	Mar 12	JOHN: ejected from the Troubadour – halfway through his "lost weekend"...
		...thrown out for heckling the Smothers Brothers
		...John's "lost weekend", cut two albums *Walls and Bridges*, and *Rock'n'Roll*
		...he also turned his hand to the role of producer:
		Pussy Cats – Harry Nilsson album released in 1974
		Too Many Cooks (Spoil the Soup) – Mick Jagger recording in late 1973
	Mar 31	JOHN and PAUL: last time that they ever played together...
		...jam session musicians with John and Paul:
		Stevie Wonder – Harry Nilsson – Jesse Ed Davies – Bobby Keys
		...captured on the bootleg album *A Toot and a Snore in '74*
	Sep 20	GEORGE: Splinter issued *The Place I Love* – 1st album on Dark Horse Records
	Nov 2	GEORGE: opened his ill-fated tour – 1st Beatle to undertake a solo tour
	Nov 15	Elton John released *Lucy in the Sky with Diamonds* – from *Sgt Pepper*, 1967...
		...JOHN: featured as "Dr Winston O'Boogie"
		...song's title referred to John's son Julian's friend, Lucy O'Donnell

	Nov 28	JOHN: last concert appearance, with Elton John – end of his "lost weekend"...
		...included the Lennon penned duet, *Whatever Gets You Thru the Night*
1975	Jan 9	formal end of the road – the dissolution of "The Beatles"
	Feb 21	JOHN: issued *Rock'n'Roll* (UK) – problems with Phil Spector and Chuck Berry...
		...included covers of two Chuck Berry penned songs:
		Sweet Little Sixteen – Chuck Berry single in 1958
		You Can't Catch Me – Chuck Berry single in 1956
1976	Jan 5	ex-road manager Mal Evans was shot dead by Los Angeles police: 40 years old
	Jan 19	offered $30m by promoter Bill Sargent for a single Beatles reunion concert
	Oct 22	Damned released 1st single *New Rose*, with B-side *Help* – Beatles single in 1965
	Nov 25	RINGO: guest appearance at the Band's swan song concert, *The Last Waltz*
1979	Mar 27	Eric Clapton married GEORGE's ex-wife, Pattie Boyd
1980	Nov 17	JOHN: released his final album, *Double Fantasy* (US)
	Dec 8	JOHN: shot dead outside his New York apartment: 40 years old
1988	Jan 20	The Beatles was 1st British act to be inducted into the Rock and Roll Hall of Fame
1995	Nov 19	*The Beatles Anthology* arrived – with 1st new single for 25 years, *Free as a Bird*
1999	Nov 10	RIAA's *Artists of the Century* – only act ever, with five Diamond albums
1999	Dec 14	PAUL: appeared at the Cavern – backed by David Gilmour and Ian Paice

Jeff Beck

Inducted into the Rock and Roll Hall of Fame in 2009...
+...as a member of The Yardbirds in 1992

guitar: The Yardbirds – Jeff Beck Group – Jeff Beck Group (Version 2) – Beck, Bogert & Appice

1944	Jun 24	Jeff Beck was born in Wallington, Surrey

Jeff Beck Group

1945	Jan 10	Rod Stewart: singer, born in Highgate, London – 1st lineup
1946	Jan 10	Aynsley Dunbar: drummer, born in Liverpool, England – 1st lineup
1947	Jun 1	Ron Wood: guitarist and bassist, born in Hillingdon, London – 1st lineup
1947	Dec 29	Cosy Powell: drummer, born Colin Flooks, in Cirencester, Gloucestershire...
		...2nd lineup – went on to join Rainbow

Jeff Beck

1965	Mar 3	Eric Clapton's final gig with the Yardbirds – Jeff Beck replaced him soon after
1966	May 16	recorded *Beck's Bolero* with Keith Moon and Jimmy Page
1966	Dec 18	*Blow-Up* movie opened – Yardbirds dual lead guitars of Beck and Jimmy Page

Jeff Beck Group

1967	Mar 3	newly formed Jeff Beck Group supported Roy Orbison on his UK tour...
		...lineup included:
		Jeff Beck: guitar – formed the group in early 1967 – ended in mid-1969
		Rod Stewart: singer – went on to join the Faces

Ron Wood: guitar then bass – went on to join the Faces

...other musicians in various lineups included:

Viv Prince: drums – brief stay in an early Jeff Beck Group lineup
Jet Harris: bass – brief stay in an early Jeff Beck Group lineup
Aynsley Dunbar: drums – from mid-1967

Sep 29 performed at the final gig held at London's 1st psychedelic club, the UFO

1968 Jun 15 performed at New York's Fillmore East – where they upstaged Grateful Dead...

...Jeff Beck Group:

Jeff Beck – Rod Stewart – Ron Wood
Mickey Waller: drums – joined in mid-1967 – replaced Aynsley Dunbar

1969 Aug 15 performed at the *Woodstock* festival

1st version of the Jeff Beck Group folded in the summer of 1969.

Jeff Beck

1969 Sep 29 G.T.O.'s released *Circular Circulation* – Beck played on *Permanent Damage*

1970 May 16 Cactus's debut gig – Beck's accident delayed band with Appice and Bogert

2nd version of the Jeff Beck Group was formed in the spring of 1971.

Jeff Beck finally came together as, Beck, Bogert & Appice in mid-1972.

1974 Jan 26 live performance recorded shortly before splitting up...

Jeff Beck: guitar
Tim Bogert: bass – from Cactus
Carmine Appice: drums – from Cactus

Jeff Beck

1983 Sep 20 performed at the ARMS charity concert with Eric Clapton and Jimmy Page

Jesse Belvin

singer: The Shields

1960 Feb 6 R&B singer and songwriter, died in an automobile crash: 27 years old...

...songwriting credits included:

Earth Angel – Penguins single in 1954

...member of late '50s vocal group the Shields – with Johnny "Guitar" Watson

Boyd Bennett

1924 Dec 7 pioneering rockabilly singer and songwriter, born in Muscle Shoals, Alabama...

...songwriting credits included:

Seventeen – mid-1955 single from Boyd Bennett and His Rockets...

...co-written with John Young and Carl Gorman

My Boy Flat Top – single from Boyd Bennett and His Rockets in 1955...

...co-written with John Young

Cliff Bennett

singer: Cliff Bennett and the Rebel Rousers – Toe Fat

1940 Jun 4 pioneering British R&B singer, born in Slough, Berkshire...
...formed the British R&B Band, the Rebel Rousers, in the late 1950s

Cliff Bennett and the Rebel Rousers

1943 Dec 14 Frank Allen: bass, singer, born Francis Renaud McNeice, in Hayes, Middlesex...
...founding member of the Rebel Rousers – left to join the Searchers in 1964

1944 Feb 24 Nicky Hopkins: keyboardist, born in Perivale, London...
...band member in the early 1960s

1962 Jun 25 Screaming Lord Sutch gig – Nicky Hopkins left Sutch just before, to join Bennett

1966 Aug 5 Beatles issued *Revolver*, incl. *Got to Get You into My Life* – Bennett single in 1966

Emile Berliner

1955 Feb 26 45s outsold 78s for 1st time in America – Berliner created the 1st 'disc' in 1890s

Bert Berns

record label owner: Bang producer: Van Morrison

1944 Jan 9 Jimmy Page: guitarist, born in Heston, Middlesex...
...session guitarist on Them's 1965 *Here Comes the Night* – written by Berns

1961 Feb 23 Top Notes recorded *Twist and Shout*...
...written by Bert Berns and co-produced by Phil Spector

1964 May 21 Drifters recorded *Under the Boardwalk* – produced by Berns

1967 Mar 28 1st day of recording for Van Morison's 1st solo album, *Blowin' Your Mind*

1970 Oct 3 Janis Joplin's last session for *Pearl* – the album included *Cry Baby*...
...written by Bert Berns and Jerry Ragovoy

Chuck Berry

Inducted into the Rock and Roll Hall of Fame in 1986 (inaugural year)

guitar: Joe Alexander and the Cubans

1926 Oct 18 singer, guitarist and songwriter, born in St Louis, Missouri

1954 Aug 13 1st-ever recording session – as a member of Joe Alexander and the Cubans

1955 May 21 recorded *Maybellene* – 1st recording session at Chess...
...based on Bob Wills's 1938 recording of *Ida Red*

Sep 15 Alan Freed concert – Berry's "duck-walk" came into existence around this time

1958 Feb 28 recorded *Johnny B Goode* and *Around and Around*:

Around and Around was coupled as B-side of *Johnny B Goode*
Johnny B Goode – covered by Jimi Hendrix in 1972

...two more Chuck Berry songs featured the character Johnny B Goode:

Bye Bye Johnny – Chuck Berry single in 1960
Go-Go-Go – 1961 B-side of *Come On*

...all four songs were written by Chuck Berry

	Mar 28	tour opened – featured the piano burning antics of Jerry Lee Lewis
	May 3	performed at Alan Freed's *Big Beat* show – ended in the infamous "Boston Riot"
1961	Jul 29	recorded *Come On* and *Go-Go-Go* – both songs written by Berry...
		...Rolling Stones covered *Come On*, as their UK debut single in 1963
1962	Jan 1	Beatles recorded *Memphis Tennessee* at Decca audition – Berry single in 1959
	Feb 19	started a three-year jail stretch for violating the *Mann Act*
1963	Jan 31	Beach Boys recorded *Surfin' USA*...
		...Berry later sued for plagiarism – *Sweet Little Sixteen*, single in 1958
	Dec 26	Beatles released *I Saw Her Standing There* as a US B-side...
		...bass line borrowed from *I'm Talking About You* – Berry single in 1961
1964	Apr 10	Beatles released *The Beatles Second Album*, included *Roll Over Beethoven*...
		...written by Berry and a single from him in 1956
	May 9	opened his 1st UK tour
	Dec 15	Beatles released *Beatles '65*, included *Rock and Roll Music*...
		...written by Berry and a single from him in 1957
1969	Jul 26	played the *Seattle Pop Festival*
	Sep 13	appeared at the *Toronto Rock and Roll Revival* festival
	Oct 31	Beatles released *Come Together* as the B-side of *Something*...
		...Berry sued over lyrics from *You Can't Catch Me* – Berry single in 1956
	Nov 7	supported the Rolling Stones on their US tour
1971	Apr 16	Rolling Stones released *Let It Rock* as a UK B-side...
		...written by Berry, as "E Anderson", and a B-side from him in 1960
		..."E Anderson" – taken from his full name Chuck Edward Anderson Berry
1975	Feb 21	John Lennon released his album *Rock'n'Roll*...
		...this settled a plagiarism charge for the Beatles' *Come Together*
		...Lennon agreed to include Chuck Berry penned songs on his album:
		You Can't Catch Me – Berry single in 1956
		Sweet Little Sixteen – Berry single in 1958
1979	Nov 19	released from prison (again! – for the 3rd time)

Richard Berry

singer: The Flamingos – The Debonairs – The Flairs

1935	Apr 11	Richard Berry: singer and songwriter, born in Extension, Louisiana...
		...member of the Flamingos in early '50s – Los Angeles, not the famous one
		...left Flamingos to join the Debonairs – then founding member of the Flairs
1938	Jan 25	Etta James: blues singer, born Jamesetta Hawkins, in Los Angeles, California...
		...*The Wallflower* aka *Roll With Me Henry* – Etta James single in 1955: featured vocals from Richard Berry
1954	Oct 16	released *The Big Break* (US) – written by Berry...
		...Berry was uncredited as lead singer on the Robins' '54 *Riot in Cell Block #9*

1963	Nov 30	*Louie Louie* became an international hit for the Kingsmen – a legend was born... ...written by Berry and a single from him in 1957

Pete Best

drums: The Blackjacks – The Beatles –The Beatmakers – Tony Sheridan and the Beat Brothers
The Beatles – Lee Curtis and the All Stars – The Pete Best Four – The Pete Best Combo

1941	Nov 24	born in Madras, India
1960	Aug 17	debut as the Beatles' drummer, opening night of their 1st visit to Hamburg... ...joined from his own band the Blackjacks ...Blackjacks also included future Beatles stand-in bassist Chas Newby
	Dec 1	Paul and Best deported from Germany – George had already been expelled
1961	Feb 9	1st Cavern appearance as "The Beatles"
	Jun 22	recorded *My Bonnie* – released as Tony Sheridan and the Beat Brothers
	Oct 19	Beatles and Gerry and the Pacemakers formed the Beatmakers
1962	Apr 23	Beatles' 1st US single released – as Tony Sheridan and the Beat Brothers
	Jun 6	Beatles' 1st recording session at Abbey Road – Best was fired shortly afterwards
	Oct 12	with Lee Curtis and the All Stars – supported Little Richard... ...Best joined in mid-1962, after he was sacked from the Beatles
1966	Jul 23	Pete Best Combo performed at the reopening of Liverpool's Cavern Club
1969	Jan 18	Pete Best won his lawsuit against the Beatles

Big Bopper

1930	Oct 24	DJ, singer and songwriter, born Jiles Perry Richardson, in Sabine Pass, Texas... ...songwriting credits included: *Chantilly Lace* – Big Bopper hit on both sides of the Atlantic in 1958 *White Lightning* – George Jones country hit in 1959 *Running Bear* – Johnny Preston hit on both sides of the Atlantic in 1960
1959	Feb 3	died in the same plane crash as Buddy Holly: 28 years old
1959	Feb 5	Eddie Cochran recorded the tribute song *Three Stars* – Bopper, Holly and Valens

Big Maybelle

1955	Mar 21	Big Maybelle recorded the original version of *Whole Lotta Shakin' Goin' On*... ...written by Roy Hall, as "Sunny David", and Dave Williams ...released by Roy Hall in 1955 – after Big Maybelle ...definitive Jerry Lee Lewis version in 1957

The Big Three

1940	Jul 18	Johnny Hutchinson: drummer, born in Malta... ...stood in with the Beatles, twice
1960	Dec 16	end of the road for Cass and the Cassanovas... ...after Brian Casser left they became the Big Three:

Johnny Hutchinson: drums and vocals
Adrian Barber: guitar
Johnny Gustafson: bass and vocals

1963 Nov 13 supported the Rolling Stones in the *R&B Show* at Sheffield's City Hall

Ronnie Biggs

1965 Jul 8 Ronnie Biggs escaped from prison – he was one of the "Great Train Robbers"...
...recorded with ex-Sex Pistols' Jones, Cook and manager McLaren in 1978

Acker Bilk

clarinet: Ken Colyer's Jazzmen

1954 Sep 10 Ken Colyer's Jazzmen recorded *Back to the Delta*

1962 Aug 16 Tornados released *Telstar* – Tornados were 1st British group with a US #1...
...Bilk was the 1st UK artist with a US #1, *Stranger on the Shore* in 1962

The Birds

1947 Jun 1 Ron Wood: guitarist, born in Hillingdon, London...
...later with the Faces and the Rolling Stones

1965 Aug 2 The Birds issued The Byrds with a writ for using a similar sounding name...
...Thunderbirds formed in 1963, morphed into the Birds by mid-1964
...original Thunderbirds lineup included:
Ron Wood: guitar
Kim Gardner: bass

Cilla Black

1934 Sep 19 Brian Epstein: manager, born in Liverpool, England...
...Cilla Black was the 3rd act he signed up, after the Beatles and Pacemakers

1962 Jan 1 Beatles recorded *Love of the Loved* at failed Decca audition – Cilla single in '63...
...Lennon and McCartney song recorded by Beatles but not released by them

1965 Jan 29 co-headlined with PJ Proby on the infamous trouser-splitting UK tour

Black Sabbath

Inducted into the Rock and Roll Hall of Fame in 2006

1942 Jul 10 Ronnie Dio: singer, born Ronald James Padavona, in Portsmouth, New Jersey...
...previously with Rainbow

1945 Jan 25 Dave Walker: singer, born in Walsall, Staffordshire...
...very brief stint with the band in late 1977 to early 1978
...Walker came with an impressive pedigree that included:
Redcaps, Idle Race, Savoy Brown and Fleetwood Mac

Aug 19 Ian Gillan: ex-Deep Purple singer, born in Hounslow, Middlesex...
...replaced Dio in 1983 – stayed for one year

1948 Feb 19 Tony Iommi: guitarist, born in Birmingham, England

May 5 Bill Ward: drummer, born in Aston, London...
...with Mythology prior to joining Polka Tulk Blues Band

Dec 3 Ozzy Osbourne: singer, born in Aston, Birmingham...
...with Rare Breed prior to joining Polka Tulk Blues Band

1949 Jul 17 Terry "Geezer" Butler: bassist, born in Aston, Birmingham...
...with Rare Breed prior to joining Polka Tulk Blues Band

Black Sabbath morphed out of the earlier bands, Polka Tulk Blues Band and Earth.

Earth

1968 Dec 11 Tony Iommi was with Jethro Tull for the Stones' TV special, *Rock and Roll Circus*

1969 Jan 3 as Earth they supported Colosseum at the Marquee

Black Sabbath

1969 Sep 27 1st date as "Black Sabbath"...
...Black Sabbath:
Tony Iommi: guitar
Bill Ward: drums
Ozzy Osbourne: singer
Terry "Geezer" Butler: bass
...all previously members of the Polka Tulk Blues Band and Earth
...band's name was inspired by the title of a 1963 Boris Karloff movie

1970 Feb 13 released their debut album, *Black Sabbath* (UK)

Sep 18 released *Paranoid* (UK)

1978 Jan 6 rare appearance with Dave Walker – Ozzy Osbourne rejoined soon afterwards...
...they performed an early version *of Junior's Eyes* – written by the band

Oct 1 released *Never Say Die* (UK) – last album with vocalist Ozzy Osbourne

Dec 11 Ozzy Osbourne's final performance with Black Sabbath – replaced by Ronnie Dio

1980 Apr 5 Ozzy Osbourne recording session for the *Blizzard of Ozz*...
...Ozzy Osbourne's band included:
Randy Rhoads: guitar, founding member – previously with Quiet Riot...
...died 19 March* 1982 in an air crash: 25 years old
Bob Daisley: bass – previously with Rainbow
...a suicide in 1984 led to a lawsuit citing the track *Suicide Solution*:
Suicide Solution was written by Osbourne, Rhoads and Daisley

Apr 17 singer Ronnie James Dio's debut performance

1982 Jan 20 Ozzy Osbourne famously bit off a bat's head during a concert in Iowa

Chris Blackwell

Inducted into the Rock and Roll Hall of Fame in 2001

manager: The Spencer Davis Group record label owner: Island Records

1937 Jun 22 artist manager and founder of Island Records, born in London, England...
...Alec Waugh's novel *Island in the Sun* inspired the name of his record label

1967 Mar 13 final Spencer Davis Group tour with Steve and Muff Winwood

Otis Blackwell

Inducted into the Rock and Roll Hall of Fame in 2010

Songwriting credits:

1957 Jan 6 Elvis Presley performed *Don't Be Cruel*

Nov 3 Jerry Lee Lewis released *Great Balls of Fire*...

...his next single, *Breathless*, was his last big hit – both Blackwell penned

...title for *Great Balls of Fire* was conceived by Jack Hammer

1965 May 28 co-writer: Elvis's *Tickle Me* opened, included *(Such An) Easy Question*

Hal Blaine

Inducted into the Rock and Roll Hall of Fame in 2000

session drummer: The Wrecking Crew

1929 Feb 5 born Harold Simon Belsky, in Holyoke, Massachusetts

1962 Jun 5 Elvis Presley released *Pot Luck with Elvis*

Jul 13 Darlene Love recorded *He's a Rebel* – early Blaine association with Phil Spector

1965 Apr 12 Byrds released debut single, *Mr. Tambourine Man* – nearly all session musicians

1966 May 16 Beach Boys released *Pet Sounds*

Blind Faith

1939 Aug 19 Ginger Baker: drummer, born in Lewisham, London

1945 Mar 30 Eric Clapton: guitarist, born in Ripley, Surrey

1946 Nov 1 Rick Grech: bassist, born Richard Roman Grechko, in Bordeaux, France...

...formed KGB in '75 with Mike Bloomfield and Carmine Appice – folded in '76

1948 May 12 Steve Winwood: keyboards and vocals, born in Birmingham, England

1969 Jun 7 debut performance at a free concert in London's Hyde Park...

...Blind Faith:

Ginger Baker: drums – from Cream – formed Airforce
Eric Clapton: guitar – from Cream – joined Delaney and Bonnie
Rick Grech: bass – from Family – joined Airforce
Steve Winwood: keyboards and vocals – from Traffic – joined Airforce

1969 Aug 24 Hawaii, the final concert

Blondie

Inducted into the Rock and Roll Hall of Fame in 2006

1945 Jul 1 Debbie Harry: singer and songwriter, born in Miami, Florida...

...1st studio album was with Wind in the Willows, recorded in 1968

1975 Jul 16 appeared at CBGB's *Top 40 New York Unrecorded Rock Bands* festival

1977 May 22 began their 1st tour of the UK – as support for Television...

...lineup included:

Debbie Harry joined Stillettos late '73 – left in mid-'74 to form Blondie

Blood, Sweat & Tears

1941 Sep 13 David Clayton-Thomas: singer, born David Henry Thomsett, in Surrey, UK...
...moved to Canada in the mid-1940s

1943 Nov 19 Fred Lipsius: saxophone, born in the Bronx, New York City...
...founding member, also acted as the band's conductor and arranger

1944 Feb 5 Al Kooper: keyboards and vocals, born in Brooklyn, New York

1945 May 9 Steve Katz: guitarist, born in Brooklyn, New York

Al Kooper and Steve Katz were previously founding members of the Blues Project.

1967 Mar 25 Blues Project on Murray the "K"'s *Live in Person...*package show in New York

They left in 1967 to form Blood, Sweat & Tears.

1968 Apr 11 four-day stint opened in New York...
...lineup included:
Al Kooper – left after this gig, on 14 April
Steve Katz – left in mid-1973
Dick Halligan: trombone...
...moved to keyboards when Al Kooper left
...David Clayton-Thomas: lead singer – replaced Al Kooper:
formed David Clayton-Thomas and the Fabulous Shays in the mid-1960s
...band's name inspired by Kooper's experience of a blood-stained keyboard

Mike Bloomfield

guitar: Paul Butterfield Blues Band – Electric Flag – KGB

1943 Jul 28 seminal guitar hero, born in Chicago, Illinois...
...formed KGB in 1975 with Rick Grech and Carmine Appice – folded in 1976

1965 Jun 15 recorded *Like a Rolling Stone* with Bob Dylan

Jul 25 backed Dylan for his infamous electric set at the *Newport Folk Festival*

Jul 29 Bob Dylan recording session for *Highway 61 Revisited*

1967 Jun 16 Electric Flag's debut performance at the *Monterey Pop Festival*

1968 Apr 3 Moby Grape released *Wow/Grape Jam* – Bloomfield featured on *Grape Jam*

May 28 recorded the album *Supersession*

1981 Feb 15 died of a drugs overdose: 37 years old

The Blue Flames (Billy Fury's backing band)

1937 Aug 28 Clem Cattini: drummer, born in London, England – member in the late 1950s...
...later with Johnny Kidd, Colin Hicks and the Cabin Boys, and the Tornados

1940 Apr 17 Billy Fury: singer, born Ron Wycherley, in Liverpool, England

1943 Jun 26 Georgie Fame: keyboardist, born Clive Powell, in Leigh, Lancashire...
...after Billy Fury they became Georgie Fame and the Blue Flames

Larry Parnes's house band, the Beat Boys, became the Blue Flames.

1960 Jul 27 Beat Boys were the house band on Larry Parnes's *Meet the Beat* summer show

1961 Dec 2 Billy Fury was on tour with the Blue Flames...
...became Fury's backing band in 1961
...Blue Flames were replaced as Parnes's house band by the Tornados in '62
...keyboardist Georgie Fame became band-leader after the split from Fury

The Blue Flames (they became Georgie Fame's backing band)

1942 Jan 4 John McLaughlin: guitarist, born in Yorkshire, England...
...joined in mid-1962 – left in early 1963

1943 Jun 26 Georgie Fame: keyboards, born Clive Powell, in Leigh, Lancashire...
...his manager Larry Parnes gave his artists descriptive stage names

1944 Jun 21 Jon Hiseman: drummer, born in Woolwich, London...
...joined in mid-1967 – went on to form Colosseum and Tempest

1947 Jul 9 Mitch Mitchell: drummer, born in Ealing, London...
...joined in mid-1965 – left to join Jimi Hendrix in 1966

Larry Parnes ditched the Blue Flames in favour of the Tornados.

Georgie Fame took over the band and they became "Georgie Fame and the Blue Flames".

Georgie Fame

1960 Jan 24 Georgie Fame supported Eddie Cochran on his last UK tour

1961 Dec 2 Billy Fury was on tour with the Blue Flames – including pianist Georgie Fame...
...split with Billy Fury shortly after – became Georgie Fame and the Blue Flames

1964 Jun 4 Jimmy Nicol stood in for Ringo Starr for a week on the Beatles' 1st world tour...
...drummer: brief stint with the Blue Flames in mid-'64, just before the Beatles

1966 Jul 31 Georgie Fame played the 6th *National Jazz and Blues Festival* at Windsor

Bluesology

1941 Jan 12 Long John Baldry: singer, born in East Haddon, Northamptonshire...
...formed in the early 1960s, it became Baldry's backing band in 1966
...Baldry left in 1968

1945 Oct 28 Elton Dean: saxophone, born in Nottingham, England – band member mid-1960s

1947 Mar 25 Elton John: piano, born Reginald Kenneth Dwight, in Pinner, Middlesex...
...Elton John took his stage name from Elton Dean and Long John Baldry

Marc Bolan

guitar and vocals: Susie and the Hula Hoops – John's Children – Tyrannosaurus Rex – T.Rex

1947 Sep 30 musician and songwriter, born Mark Feld, aka Toby Tyler, in Hackney, London

1949 Jul 28 Steve Peregrin Took: bongos, born Stephen Ross Porter, in Eltham, London

1961 Jan 16 Helen Shapiro's 1st single – Bolan had been in a school band with Shapiro...
...Susie and the Hula Hoops in the late 1950s

1965 Nov 12 1st TV performance, *Ready Steady Go!* – performed his 1st single, *The Wizard*...
...had previously recorded Dylan's *Blowing in the Wind* as Toby Tyler in 1964

John's Children

1967 Apr 12 guitarist: end of John's Children's infamous German tour supporting the Who

Apr 29 performed at the *14-Hour Technicolor Dream*

May 24 released *Desdemona* – Bolan penned, 1st single with John's Children

1967 Jul 14 released *Come and Play with Me In the Garden* (UK)...

...Bolan wrote the original withdrawn A-side, *Midsummer Night's Scene*

Marc Bolan formed the duo Tyrannosaurus Rex.

1968 Apr 19 released *Debora* (UK) – Bolan penned, 1st single as Tyrannosaurus Rex...

...Tyrannosaurus Rex:

Marc Bolan: guitar and vocals – formed in mid-1967
Steve Peregrin Took: percussion – left in mid-1969...

...replaced by Mickey Finn

1970 Apr 21 Elton John's debut solo concert performance – as Marc Bolan's support act

The duo became the rock band T.Rex.

1970 Sep 19 performed at the 1st Glastonbury festival

Oct 2 released their debut single, *Ride a White Swan* (UK) – written by Marc Bolan...

...with B-side *Summertime Blues* – Eddie Cochran single in 1958

Dec 11 released their debut album, *T.Rex* (UK)

1971 Sep 17 released *Electric Warrior* (UK)

1972 Dec 14 London premiere of the movie *Born to Boogie* – directed by Ringo Starr

1977 Mar 10 supported by the Damned on his last UK tour

Sep 16 Marc Bolan died in a car crash: 29 years old

1980 Oct 27 Steve Peregrin Took choked to death on a cocktail cherry: 31 years old...

...stage name inspired by a character in JRR Tolkien's *Lord of the Rings*

Graham Bond

saxophone, keyboards and vocals: Alexis Korner's Blues Incorporated – Graham Bond Trio
Graham Bond Quartet – Graham Bond Organisation

1934 Sep 26 Dick Heckstall-Smith: saxophone, born Richard Malden, in Ludlow, Shropshire...

...joined in 1963 – left in 1967

1937 Oct 28 Graham Bond was born in Romford, Essex

1939 Aug 19 Ginger Baker: drummer, born in Lewisham, London

1942 Jan 4 John McLaughlin: guitarist, born in Yorkshire, England

1943 May 14 Jack Bruce: bassist, born in Bishopbriggs, Lanarkshire, Scotland

1944 Jun 21 Jon Hiseman: drummer, born in Woolwich, London...

...replaced Ginger Baker in 1966
...later with Georgie Fame and John Mayall: formed Colosseum and Tempest

1946 Nov 1 Rick Grech: bassist, born Richard Roman Grechko, in Bordeaux, France...

...featured on Bond's 1970 album, *Holy Magick*

Graham Bond Quartet

1963 Feb 20 backed Duffy Power on his recording of *I Saw Her Standing There...*

...Graham Bond Quartet:

Graham Bond: organ and vocals
Ginger Baker: drums – left Bond in 1966 to form Cream
Jack Bruce: bass – left Bond in late 1965 to join John Mayall
John McLaughlin: guitar – augmented GB Trio to become the Quartet

...Bond left Alexis Korner in early '63 with Baker and Bruce to form GB Trio

Graham Bond Organisation

1966 Mar 14 they were "The Who Orchestra" on *Waltz for a Pig*, B-side of the *Substitute...*

...*Waltz for a Pig* was written by drummer Ginger Baker

1967 Apr 29 performed at the *14-Hour Technicolor Dream*

1967 Dec 22 performed at the *Christmas on Earth Continued* concert

Graham Bond

1974 May 8 died under the wheels of a train at a London tube (metro) station: 36 years old

Booker T and the MGs

Inducted into the Rock and Roll Hall of Fame in 1992

Stax Records' house band: musicians included:

1941 Oct 21 Steve Cropper: guitarist and songwriter, born in Willow Springs, Missouri

1941 Nov 24 Donald "Duck" Dunn: bass, born in Memphis, Tennessee...

...founding member of the Mar-Keys in the late 1950s

Pat Boone

1957 Oct 3 1st episode of his own TV show aired...

...Boone established his career with R&B covers, including:

Two Hearts – 1954 single from the Charms – Pat Boone cover in 1955
Ain't It a Shame – 1955 single from Fats Domino – cover in 1955
Gee Whittakers – 1955 single from the Five Keys – cover in 1955
I'll Be Home – 1956 single from the Flamingos – cover in 1956
Long Tall Sally – Little Richard single in early 1956 – cover in 1956
Tutti-Frutti – 1955 single from Little Richard – cover in 1956
Chains of Love – 1951 single from Big Joe Turner – cover in 1956
I'm Waiting Just for You – 1951 single from Lucky Millinder – cover 1957

1967 Nov 4 Floyd's US debut gig – Barrett made legendary appearance on Boone's TV show

David Bowie

Inducted into the Rock and Roll Hall of Fame in 1996

saxophone and vocals: Davie Jones with The King Bees – The Manish Boys
David Bowie with The Lower Third – David Bowie and the Buzz – The Riot Squad – Turquoise Feathers – Ziggy Stardust and the Spiders from Mars

1939 Jul 14 Vince Taylor: singer, born Brian Maurice Holden, in Isleworth, Middlesex...
...Taylor was David Bowie's inspiration for his character Ziggy Stardust

1946 May 26 Mick Ronson: guitar, born in Hull, Yorkshire – member of Spiders from Mars...
...later in Mott the Hoople and the Hunter-Ronson Band

1947 Jan 8 David Bowie: musician, producer, singer and songwriter...
...born David Robert Jones, in Brixton, London
...Riot Squad: lead vocal, guitar and harmonica – brief stint in the spring of '67

David Bowie's career started out as David Jones, in the Konrads.

1963 Aug 30 Bowie's 1st-ever recording session – recorded *I Never Dreamed*...
...vocals and sax: joined the Konrads in mid-1962 – left at the end of 1963

Davie Jones with The King Bees

1964 Jun 5 released *Liza Jane* c/w *Louie, Louie Go Home* (UK) – Bowie's 1st-ever single...
...based on *Li'l Liza Jane* from the 1916 comedy *Come Out of the Kitchen*
...B-side, *Louie, Louie Go Home* – Paul Revere single in 1964

The Manish Boys

1965 Mar 8 UK TV debut – performed their (only) single, *I Pity the Fool*...
...cover of Bobby "Blue" Bland's 1961 single

Changed his name from "David Jones" to "David Bowie".

1965 Sep 16 announced his name-change...
..."David Bowie", inspired by the American frontiersman, Jim Bowie

David Bowie with The Lower Third

1965 Nov 19 early appearance as "David Bowie"

1966 Jan 14 released *Can't Help Thinking about Me* (UK) – written by David Bowie

Solo Career: David Bowie

1966 Apr 1 released 1st solo single, *Do Anything You Say* (UK) – written by David Bowie

1967 Jun 1 released his eponymous debut album (UK)

1969 Jul 11 released his break-through single, *Space Oddity* (UK)

1972 Mar 24 rescued a disillusioned Mott the Hoople from splitting up

May 14 writer and producer: Mott the Hoople recorded *All the Young Dudes*...
...Bowie had previously offered them *Suffragette City* but they turned it down

Jun 6 released *The Rise and Fall of Ziggy Stardust and the Spiders from Mars* (UK)...
...Spiders from Mars:
Mick Ronson: guitar – joined Bowie in 1970
Trevor Bolder: bass – replaced Tony Visconti in 1971
Mick Woodmansey: drums

Sep 22 1st concert appearance in America

Oct 6 recorded *The Jean Genie*

1973 Apr 13 released *Aladdin Sane* (UK) – play on the words "a lad insane"

	Jul 3	last outing for Ziggy Stardust and the Spiders from Mars...
		...Spiders from Mars:
		Mick Ronson – Trevor Bolder Mick Woodmansey – replaced in Bowie's band by Aynsley Dunbar
1975	Oct 30	Bob Dylan's *Rolling Thunder Review* tour opened – with guitarist Mick Ronson
1977	Mar 18	producer and musician: Iggy Pop released his debut solo album, *The Idiot*

Joe Boyd

manager: The Incredible String Band   venue owner: UFO

producer: The Incredible String Band – Pink Floyd

1966	Nov 4	arranged for the Incredible String Band to support Tom Paxton
1967	Feb 27	producer: Pink Floyd recorded their debut single, *Arnold Layne*
1967	Sep 29	final gig at London's 1st psychedelic club, the UFO...
		...co-founded by Boyd in December 1966

Richard Branson

record label owner: Virgin

1973	May 25	Mike Oldfield's *Tubular Bells* was the 1st release on Branson's new Virgin label
1976	Oct 8	Sex Pistols signed to EMI – seven months later they signed to Virgin

Jackie Brenston

saxophone and singer: Ike Turner and His Kings of Rhythm – Jackie Brenston and His Delta Cats
Lowell Fulson's band

1930	Aug 15	born in Clarksdale, Mississippi...
		...joined Lowell Fulson's backing band in the mid-1950s

Jackie Brenston and His Delta Cats

1951	Mar 5	recorded *Rocket 88* at Sam Phillips's studio in Memphis – released on Chess...
		...often cited as the 1st rock'n'roll record
		...lineup included:
		Jackie Brenston: saxophone and vocals – also wrote the song Ike Turner: piano Willie Kizart: guitar...
		...early example of deliberately distorted guitar sound
		...song was covered by Bill Haley and His Saddlemen in mid-1951

Brinsley Schwarz (band)

1947	Mar 25	Brinsley Schwarz: guitarist and singer, born in Woodbridge, Suffolk...
		...founding member of the Rumour in mid-1975
1949	Mar 24	Nick Lowe: bassist and singer, born in Walton-on-Thames, Surrey...
		...formed Rockpile in 1976

Kippington Lodge morphed into Brinsley Schwartz.

1970 Apr 3 over-hyped concert – the band flew UK rock journalists to a gig in America...
...lineup included (both musicians previously in Kippington Lodge):
Brinsley Schwarz: guitar and vocals
Nick Lowe: bass and vocals
...headlined by Quicksilver Messenger Service:
with Tom Paxton and Van Morrison

1972 Feb 13 recorded *Greasy Truckers Party* live album at London's Roundhouse
Apr 28 released *Greasy Truckers Party* (UK) – early days of pub rock

1976 Aug 14 Nick Lowe released *So It Goes* c/w *Heart of the City*...
...1st-ever single released on Stiff Records

Jackson Browne

Inducted into the Rock and Roll Hall of Fame in 2004

guitar and vocals: The Nitty Gritty Dirt Band

1948 Oct 9 guitarist, singer and songwriter, born in Heidelberg, Germany...
...short stint with the Nitty Gritty Dirt Band in mid-1966

James Brown and The Famous Flames

James Brown

Inducted into the Rock and Roll Hall of Fame in 1986 (inaugural year)

1933 May 3 singer and songwriter, aka "Godfather of Soul", born in Barnwell, South Carolina

The Famous Flames

Inducted into the Rock and Roll Hall of Fame in 2012

James Brown with The Famous Flames

1956 Mar 3 released their debut single, *Please, Please, Please* (US)...
...written by James Brown and Johnny Terry of the Famous Flames

James Brown

1968 May 26 Little Willie John died – Brown tribute album, *Thinking about Little Willie John*

Joe Brown

guitar and vocals: The Spacemen – Joe Brown and the Bruvvers

1940 Mar 11 Bobby Graham: drummer, born Robert Francis Neate, in Edmonton, London...
...joined from the Outlaws – went on to become a top session drummer

1941 May 13 Joe Brown was born in Swarby, Lincolnshire...
...formed the Spacemen c.1956 – morphed into the Bruvvers in the late 1950s

1960 Jan 24 Joe Brown and the Bruvvers supported Eddie Cochran on his last UK tour

1960 May 21 guitarist: Billy Fury released his debut album, *The Sound of Fury* (UK)

Lenny Bruce

1925 Oct 13 iconoclastic US comedian, born Leonard Alfred Schneider, in Mineola, New York
1965 Oct 10 lodged a harassment complaint with the FBI
1966 Jun 24 opened what were to be his last concerts – supported by the Mothers
1966 Aug 3 died of a drug overdose: 40 years old

Beryl Bryden

washboard: Lonnie Donegan Skiffle Group – Beryl Bryden's Backroom Skiffle Group

1954 Jul 13 Lonnie Donegan recorded *Rock Island Line* – Bryden played washboard
1957 Feb 13 Alexis Korner's Breakdown Group recorded Blues from the Roundhouse...
...Beryl Bryden's Backroom Skiffle Group: musicians included:
Alexis Korner: guitar – recordings in 1956
Cyril Davies: guitar and harmonica – recordings in 1956

Buffalo Springfield

Inducted into the Rock and Roll Hall of Fame in 1997

1944 May 9 Richie Furay: guitarist and singer, born in Yellow Springs, Ohio
1945 Jan 3 Stephen Stills: guitarist and singer, born in Dallas, Texas
Nov 12 Neil Young: guitarist and singer, born in Ontario, Canada
1946 Sep 9 Bruce Palmer: bassist, born in Liverpool, Nova Scotia
1947 Dec 5 Jim Messina: bassist and producer, born in Maywood, California

Before Buffalo Springfield

1965 Jul 23 Neil Young's 1st-ever recording – with the Squires...
...met Bruce Palmer shortly afterwards, when Palmer was swapped from Jack London and the Sparrows, and into the Mynah Birds

Buffalo Springfield

1966 Apr 6 chance encounter led to the band's formation...
...Buffalo Springfield:
Richie Furay: guitar and vocals – from the Au Go-Go Singers
Stephen Stills: guitar and vocals – from the Au Go-Go Singers
Neil Young: guitar and vocals – from the Mynah Birds...
...previously in the Squires
Bruce Palmer: bass – from the Mynah Birds – replaced by Jim Messina
Dewey Martin: drums
...band's name: steam-roller manufacturer, Buffalo-Springfield Roller Company
Dec 5 recorded the protest anthem *For What It's Worth*
1967 Jan 9 recording session for the 'lost' 2nd album, *Stampede*...
...recorded Furay's *My Kind of Love* – Young's *Mr. Soul* – Stills's *We'll See*
...bassist Bruce Palmer was deported back to Canada around this time
Mar 6 1st album, *Buffalo Springfield*, was re-released with track changes

	Jun 16	David Crosby stood in for an absent Neil Young at the *Monterey Pop Festival*
1968	May 5	last concert:

Neil Young – opted for a solo career
Jim Messina and Richie Furay – formed Poco
Stephen Stills – joined up with David Crosby and Graham Nash
Dewey Martin – tried his luck with a New Buffalo Springfield

Johnny Burnette

singer: Johnny Burnette Rock'n Roll Trio

1934 Mar 25 seminal rockabilly singer, born in Memphis, Tennessee

1956 Jul 2 Johnny Burnette Trio recorded *The Train Kept A-Rollin'*...

...for inclusion on their debut album and as a single

...The Johnny Burnette Trio:

Johnny Burnette: singer – formed the trio c.1954 – disbanded in 1957
Dorsey Burnette: upright bass
Paul Burlison: guitar

...rockabilly version of Tiny Bradshaw's 1951 single

...inspired covers by the Yardbirds and Screaming Lord Sutch

...B-side *Honey Hush* was also a cover – Big Joe Turner single in 1953

1964 Aug 14 drowned in a fishing accident: 30 years old

Paul Butterfield Blues Band

Inducted into the Rock and Roll Hall of Fame in 2015

1942 Oct 21 Elvin Bishop, aka Pigboy Crabshaw: guitarist, born in Glendale, California

Dec 17 Paul Butterfield: seminal white harmonica player, born in Chicago, Illinois...

...in 1963 he formed the Paul Butterfield Blues Band:

Paul Butterfield: harmonica
Elvin Bishop: guitar – moved to rhythm when Mike Bloomfield joined
Jerome Arnold: bass – from Howlin' Wolf's backing band
Sam Lay: drums – from Howlin' Wolf's backing band

...Mike Bloomfield: guitarist, joined in early 1965

1943 Jul 28 Mike Bloomfield: guitarist, born in Chicago, Illinois

1965 Jul 25 Butterfield's band backed Dylan for his electric set at the *Newport Folk Festival*

1966 Jun 1 various artists album *What's Shakin'* was released

1967 Jun 16 played the *Monterey Pop Festival*

1969 Aug 15 performed at the *Woodstock* festival

1976 Nov 25 Butterfield made a guest appearance at the Band's last concert, *The Last Waltz*

Buzzcocks

1976 Sep 20 appeared at the 1st punk festival, held at London's 100 Cub

Dec 28 recorded the EP *Spinal Scratch*...

...lineup included:

Pete Shelley: guitar, vocals and founding member – formed in 1976
Howard Devoto: vocals, founding member – left in early '77 after EP...
...formed Magazine after he left the Buzzcocks

1977 May 1 Clash's *White Riot* tour opened – Buzzcocks supported at the Rainbow riot

The Byrds

Inducted into the Rock and Roll Hall of Fame in 1991

1941 Aug 14 David Crosby: guitarist and singer, born in Los Angeles, California

1942 Jul 13 Jim McGuinn: guitarist and singer, born in Chicago, Illinois...
...Indonesian guru recommended a name change, "Jim" to "Roger", 1967

1944 Nov 17 Gene Clark: singer, born in Tipton, Missouri...
...member of the New Christy Minstrels before he joined Jet Set

Dec 4 Chris Hillman: guitar, bass, mandolin, vocals, born in Los Angeles, California...
...joined Gram Parsons as an original member of the Flying Burrito Brothers

1946 Jun 3 Michael Clarke: drummer, born Michael James Dick, in Spokane, Washington...
...went on to join Gram Parsons in the Flying Burrito Brothers

1946 Nov 5 Gram Parsons was born Ingram Cecil Connor, in Winter Haven, Florida...
...guitarist and singer: his only Byrds album was *Sweetheart of the Rodeo*

Started as Jet Set, formed in 1964.

David Crosby – Jim (later Roger) McGuinn – Gene Clark

Morphed into the Beefeaters and finally the Byrds.

David Crosby – Jim (later Roger) McGuinn – Gene Clark – Michael Clarke

The Byrds

1965 Apr 12 released *Mr. Tambourine Man* (US)...
...The Byrds:

Jim (later Roger) McGuinn: guitar and vocals...
...McGuinn was the only constant band member

David Crosby: guitar and vocals – left in late 1967
Gene Clark: vocals and main songwriter – left in early 1966
Chris Hillman: bass and vocals – left in late 1968
Michael Clarke: drums – left at the end of 1967

...Roger McGuinn was the only Byrd to play – accompanied by session guys
...written and originally released by Bob Dylan

Aug 2 The Birds, issued The Byrds with a writ for using a similar sounding name...
...Byrds released cover of Dylan's *All I Really Want to Do* shortly afterwards

1966 Jul 1 Mama Michelle was replaced by Mama Jill in the Mamas & The Papas...
...following Michelle's affair with Gene Clark

1967 Jun 10 played the *Fantasy Fair and Magic Mountain Music Festival*

	Jun 16	played the *Monterey Pop Festival*
	Nov 9	Crosby's sacking from the Byrds featured in the inaugural issue of *Rolling Stone*
1968	Jan 3	released *The Notorious Byrd Brothers* (US)...
		...David Crosby and Michael Clarke left shortly afterwards
	Jul 8	Gram Parsons left – formed the Flying Burrito Brothers...
		...Chris Hillman left after the Byrds' South African tour – to join the Burritos
1969	Jul 26	played the *Seattle Pop Festival*
1973	Feb 24	final concert...
		...The Byrds:
		Roger McGuinn – Chris Hillman Clarence White: guitar, mandolin and vocals – joined in late 1968 Joe Lala: drums – had previously played with Manassas
		...other musicians who had moved on before the final gig:
		Gene Parsons: drums – joined in late 1968 Skip Battin: bass – joined in late 1969
		...Roger McGuinn was the only constant band member across the years
1975	Oct 30	Roger McGuinn, support act: Bob Dylan's *Rolling Thunder Review* tour opened

Canned Heat

1944	Dec 25	Henry Vestine: guitarist, born in Takoma Park, Maryland...
		...in an early Zappa lineup, left just before the 1st album to join Canned Heat ...with Canned Heat from their 1st album to 1969 – left just before Woodstock
1945	Mar 11	Harvey Mandel: guitarist, aka "The Snake", born in Detroit, Michigan...
		...replaced Henry Vestine in 1969 ...Mandel left with bassist Larry Taylor in 1970 to join John Mayall
1967	Jun 10	played the *Fantasy Fair and Magic Mountain Music Festival*
1969	Aug 15	performed at the *Woodstock* festival
1970	Sep 3	Alan "Blind Owl" Wilson died of a drug overdose: 27 years old...
		...Canned Heat was formed in 1966 by:
		Alan "Blind Owl" Wilson: guitar, harmonica and vocals Bob Hite: vocals
1970	Sep 12	appeared at the Hyde Park concert in London

Captain Beefheart

multi-instrumentalist and vocalist: Captain Beefheart and His Magic Band

1941	Jan 15	born Don Glen Vliet, in Glendale, California...
		...Don Glen Vliet – then Don Van Vliet – then Captain Beefheart ...name from Zappa collaboration, *Captain Beefheart vs The Grunt People*
1943	Apr 17	Roy Estrada: bassist, born in Santa Ana, California...
		...left Little Feet and joined Beefheart in 1972

Captain Beefheart

1964 Aug 1 Frank Zappa opened Studio Z – Beefheart was a regular collaborator

1964 Dec 2 collaborated with Frank Zappa on *I Was a Teen-age Malt Shop*

Captain Beefheart and His Magic Band

1967 Jun 10 played the *Fantasy Fair and Magic Mountain Music Festival*

1969 Jun 16 released *Trout Mask Replica* (US)

Caravan

1947 Jan 21 Pye Hastings: guitarist and singer, born in Taminavoulin, Banffshire, Scotland...
...co-founder of Caravan formed in early 1968

Nov 24 Dave Sinclair: keyboardist and founding member, born in Herne Bay, Kent...
...left in mid-1971 – went on to join Robert Wyatt in Matching Mole

1970 Jul 11 played at the *Tivoli Pop Festival* in Germany

Earl "Speedo" Carroll

singer: The Carnations – The Cadillacs – The Coasters

The Carnations morphed into the Cadillacs:

1937 Nov 2 born in New York City, New York

1964 May 31 Hollies concert – in 1963 they had a hit single with *(Ain't That) Just Like Me*...
...this was a Coasters single in 1961 – written by Carroll and Billy Guy

Carter Lewis and the Southerners

1942 Dec 3 Ken Lewis: born Kenneth James Hawker, in Small Heath, Birmingham...
...songwriting partnership with John Carter

1963 May 11 appeared on BBC Radio's *Saturday Club*...
...lineup included:

John Carter: guitar and vocals – the band formed in 1961 – ended in 1964
Ken Lewis: keyboards, vocals
Jimmy Page: guitar – group member in 1963 – before the Yardbirds
Viv Prince: drums – group member in 1963 – later with the Pretty Things

...Page and Prince were in the band in mid-1963 and were probably at this gig

...Carter and Lewis reinvented themselves in 1964 as the Ivy League:

Funny How Love Can Be – Ivy League 1965 – written by Carter and Lewis

1965 Jan 15 Who released *I Can't Explain* – Ivy League sang background vocals

Howie Casey and the Seniors

1959 Sep 26 early Liverpool Scene – 1st Liverpool group to release an album, early 1962

Johnny Cash

Inducted into the Rock and Roll Hall of Fame in 1992

1932 Feb 26 country and rockabilly singer and songwriter, born in Kingsland, Arkansas

1956 Dec 4 *Million Dollar Quartet* recording session with Cash, Presley, Lewis and Perkins

Cass and the Cassanovas

1940 Jul 18 Johnny Hutchinson: drummer and singer, born in Malta

1960 May 10 Silver Beetles failed audition to back Billy Fury – they also auditioned that day

Dec 16 end of the road – Cass and the Cassanovas became the Big Three...

...Cass and the Cassanovas:

Brian Casser: guitar and vocals – formed by Casser in mid-1959
Johnny Hutchinson: drums and vocals – formed the Big Three
Adrian Barber: guitar – formed the Big Three
Johnny Gustafson: bass and vocals – formed the Big Three

...Brian Casser relocated to London:

formed Casey Jones and the Engineers in 1963:
lineup included a handful of gigs with Eric Clapton

1961 Dec 9 Beatles' 1st gig in the south of England – visited Casser at the Blue Gardenia

Cynthia Plaster Caster

1947 May 24 groupie, artist and politician, born Cynthia Albritton, in Chicago, Illinois

1968 Feb 25 Jimi Hendrix had a stimulating encounter with the *Plaster Casters of Chicago...*

...Hendrix's plaster-cast, 00004, is currently valued at $2,000

...other contributors to Cynthia's collection included:

Eddie Brigati: Young Rascals singer, 00018
Harvey Mandel: Canned Heat's guitarist, 00020
Zal Yanovsky: Lovin' Spoonful's guitarist, 00028

Clem Cattini

drums: The Beat Boys (became) The Blue Flames – Johnny Kidd and the Pirates
Colin Hicks and the Cabin Boys – The Tornados

1937 Aug 28 born in London, England...

...session drummer: reputedly played on over 40 British #1 singles

1960 May 13 Johnny Kidd and the Pirates recorded *Shakin' All Over* – joined shortly before

1969 Apr 8 session drummer: PJ Proby released *Three Week Hero*

The Champs

1958 Jan 15 released *Tequila* as the B-side of *Train to Nowhere* (US)...

...band's name inspired by cowboy Gene Autry's horse's name, Champion

Chas Chandler

Inducted into the Rock and Roll Hall of Fame in 1994 – The Animals

bass: Alan Price Rhythm and Blues Combo – The Animals
manager: The Jimi Hendrix Experience – Ambrose Slade – Slade

1938 Dec 18 born in Heaton, Newcastle upon Tyne

1963 Sep 7 1st performance of the lineup that became the Animals

1965 Oct 15 Jimmy Hendrix signed by Ed Chalpin...

...Chandler became Hendrix's manager in late '66 but Chalpin still had a claim

1966	Sep 5	Animals' final gig before splitting up
	Oct 1	Jimi Hendrix jammed on stage with Cream – became his manager just before
	Oct 13	debut performance of the Jimi Hendrix Experience
1968	Oct 25	*Electric Ladyland* released – end of his time as Jimi Hendrix's manager
1969	May 2	took over management of Slade – managed them throughout the 1970s

The Charlatans

1965	Jun 21	played at the opening night of the Red Dog Saloon – 1st house band
1965	Oct 16	performed at the 1st Family Dog dance concert at Longshoreman's Hall

Ray Charles

Inducted into the Rock and Roll Hall of Fame in 1986 (inaugural year)

piano and vocals: Lowell Fulson's backing band

1930	Sep 23	singer and pianist, born in Albany, Georgia
1952	Sep 8	1st recording session for Atlantic Records... ...pianist for Lowell Fulson's backing band before moving to Atlantic
1953	Oct 27	session pianist: Guitar Slim recorded *The Things That I Used to Do*
1956	Jan 28	Elvis Presley TV performance, *I've Got a Woman*... ...written by Ray Charles and a single from him in 1954
1957	Nov 25	scored his 1st crossover hit with *Swanee River Rock*
1958	May 30	on the same Apollo bill as the Drifters when the whole group was fired
1959	Feb 18	recorded his breakthrough crossover hit, *What'd I Say*... ...covers of the song included: UK and US hit for Jerry Lee Lewis in 1961; US hit for Bobby Darin in 1962; US hit for Elvis in 1964 – taken from the movie *Viva Las Vegas*

Chubby Checker

1941	Oct 3	singer, king of the *Twist*, born Ernest Evans, in Spring Gulley, South Carolina... ...his stage name was a tip of the cap to Fats Domino
1958	Nov 11	Hank Ballard and the Midnighters recorded *The Twist* – written by Hank Ballard
1960	Aug 1	released his cover of *The Twist* (US) – start of the dance sensation

Leonard Chess

Inducted into the Rock and Roll Hall of Fame in 1987

record label owner: Chess

1917	Mar 12	born Lejzor Czyz, in Motal, Poland
1950	Jun 3	took control of the Aristocrat label and renamed it to "Chess Records"

Chicago Transit Authority/Chicago

Chicago Transit Authority

1969 Sep 13 appeared at the *Toronto Rock and Roll Revival* festival

Chicago

1970 Aug 7 performed at the *Goose Lake International Music Festival*

1978 Jan 23 Terry Kath died, accidentally shot himself: 31 years old...
...guitarist, vocalist and founding member

The Chiffons

1964 Feb 11 supported the Beatles at their 1st American concert

1971 Feb 10 *My Sweet Lord* plagiarism lawsuit filed for similarity with *He's So Fine*

The Chords

1954 Mar 15 recorded the doo-wop classic *Sh-Boom*...
...B-side was a cover of Patti Page's *Cross Over the Bridge*

Neil Christian and the Crusaders

1938 Dec 17 Carlo Little: drummer, born in Sudbury, London – brief stint in mid-1965...
...previously with Screaming Lord Sutch, Cyril Davies and the Rolling Stones

1943 Apr 7 Mick Abrahams: guitarist, born in Luton, Bedfordshire...
...later founding member of Jethro Tull and Blodwyn Pig

1944 Jan 9 Jimmy Page: guitarist, born in Heston, Middlesex...
...later in Yardbirds and Led Zeppelin

1945 Apr 14 Ritchie Blackmore: guitarist, born in Weston-super-Mare, Somerset...
...later founding member of Deep Purple and Rainbow

1961 Jul 21 Jimmy Page was in the band when he accompanied beat poet Royston Ellis

1966 Apr 25 gig with Ritchie Blackmore – lead guitarist until the band folded in mid-1967...
...previous lead guitarists included:

Jimmy Page: original guitarist – formed in 1960 – left in late 1962
Albert Lee: replaced Jimmy Page – went on to Chris Farlowe in mid-'64
Mick Abrahams: band member in 1965 – went on to form Jethro Tull

CIVIL RIGHTS MOVEMENT

1929 Jan 15 Martin Luther King Jr: iconic Civil Rights leader, born in Atlanta, Georgia

President Eisenhower – US President: 1953 Jan 20 to 1961 Jan 20: Republican Party

1954 May 17 *Brown v Board of Education* – dawn of the modern Civil Rights Movement

1955 Dec 1 Rosa Parks was arrested for refusing to give up her seat on the bus...
...Martin Luther King Jr led the subsequent *Montgomery Bus Boycott*
...it resulted in the end of segregation on transportation

1956 Jan 24 *The Shocking Story of Approved Killing in Mississippi*...
...*Look* magazine's article about the murder of Emmett Till
...immortalised in Bob Dylan's song *The Ballad of Emmett Till*

1957 Feb 19 dynamite thrown at the stage during a Louis Armstrong concert

1957 Sep 25 *Little Rock Nine* attended school...

...protected by the 101st Airborne, with bayonets fixed

President Kennedy – US President: 1961 Jan 20 to 1963 Nov 22: Democratic Party

1961 May 4 1st *Freedom Riders* set out from Washington DC

1963 Jan 14 George Wallace's inaugural speech as Governor – "segregation forever"

Jun 11 George Wallace's *Schoolhouse Door* stand, at the University of Alabama...

...President Kennedy announced that he was introducing a *Civil Rights Bill*

Jun 12 Medgar Evers was murdered in Jackson, Mississippi...

...inspiration for Bob Dylan's song *Only a Pawn in Their Game*

Aug 28 Martin Luther King Jr delivered his famous *I Have a Dream* speech...

...performers included: Peter Paul & Mary, Bob Dylan, Odetta and Joan Baez

1963 Sep 15 four young girls murdered by the Ku Klux Klan in a church bombing in Alabama

President Johnson – US President: 1963 Nov 22 to 1969 Jan 20: Republican Party

1964 Jul 2 *Civil Rights Act* became law – initiated by Kennedy but passed by Johnson

1965 Mar 15 Civil Rights march from Selma to Montgomery, Alabama...

...heavily opposed by Alabama's governor George Wallace
...Johnson addressed Congress with his *Right to Vote* speech
...*Voting Rights Act* became law in August – just before the Watts riots

Aug 11 1st day of the Watts riots...

...began after a white policemen stopped and arrested a black motorist

1967 Apr4 Martin Luther King Jr delivered his anti-war speech, *Beyond Vietnam*

1968 Apr 4 Martin Luther King Jr was assassinated in Memphis, Tennessee: 39 years old

Eric Clapton

Inducted into the Rock and Roll Hall of Fame in 2000...

+...as a member of The Yardbirds in 1992
+...as a member of Cream in 1993

guitar and vocals: The Roosters – Casey Jones and the Engineers – The Yardbirds
John Mayall's Bluesbreakers – The Glands – John Mayall's Bluesbreakers
Eric Clapton and the Powerhouse – Cream – Dirty Mac – Blind Faith – Plastic Ono Band
Delaney & Bonnie – Derek and the Dominos – Eric and the Palpitations

1937 Feb 8 Ben Palmer: pianist and roadie, born in Berkshire, England...

...with Clapton in the Roosters and the Glands, and as a Cream roadie

1945 Mar 30 Eric Clapton: iconic British guitarist, singer and songwriter, born in Ripley, Surrey

1958 Apr 3 Johnny Otis recorded *Willie and the Hand Jive* – Clapton single in 1974

1963 Oct 19 Top Topham's final gig as the Yardbirds' lead guitarist – replaced by Clapton...

...Eric Clapton had previously been with:

The Roosters: lineup included:

Eric Clapton: guitar – 1st band, 1963

Ben Palmer: piano – later in the Glands and a Cream roadie
Tom McGuinness: guitar

Casey Jones and the Engineers: lineup included:

Eric Clapton: guitar – played seven gigs, c.September 1963
Brian Casser: vocals and founding member – formed in 1963...
...previously with Liverpool's Cass and the Cassanovas

Tom McGuinness: guitar – joined Manfred Mann in 1964

1965 Mar 3 final gig with the Yardbirds – he moved on to join John Mayall's Bluesbreakers

Mar 5 Yardbirds released *For Your Love* (UK)...
...B-side, *Got to Hurry*, was Clapton's 1st recorded composition

Nov 6 back with John Mayall after his summer Greek jaunt with the Glands...
...The Glands lineup included:

Eric Clapton: guitar
Ben Palmer: piano – previously with Clapton in the Roosters

1966 Jun 1 Eric Clapton and the Powerhouse released three tracks on *What's Shakin'* (US):

Steppin' Out – Memphis Slim single in 1959
Crossroads – written and recorded by Robert Johnson in 1936
I Want to Know – writing credit to "S Macleod"...
...Paul Jones was married to Sheila MacLeod at the time

Eric Clapton and the Powerhouse:

Ben Palmer: piano – was with Clapton in the Roosters and the Glands
Paul Jones: harmonica – with Manfred Mann
Jack Bruce: bass – with Manfred Mann
Eric Clapton: guitar – with John Mayall's Bluesbreakers
Steve Winwood, as "Steve Anglo": vocals – with Spencer Davis Group
Pete York: drums – with the Spencer Davis Group

Jul 22 John Mayall released *Bluesbreakers with Eric Clapton* (UK)

Jul 31 Cream's official debut gig

Oct 1 Cream concert in London – jammed on stage with Jimi Hendrix

1967 Jun 25 sang along with the Beatles on the *Our World* live global TV broadcast

1968 Sep 6 recorded the guitar solo for George Harrison's *While My Guitar Gently Weeps*

Nov 1 performed as "Eddie Clayton" on George Harrison's album *Wonderwall Music*

Nov 26 Cream's farewell concert at the Royal Albert Hall

Dec 11 guitarist in Dirty Mac, on the Rolling Stones' TV special *Rock and Roll Circus*

1969 Jan 4 Jimi Hendrix performed *Sunshine of Your Love* on Lulu's TV show...
...Cream song from 1967 – co-written with Jack Bruce and Pete Brown

Mar 1 Cream released *Goodbye*...
...contained the song *Badge*, written by Clapton and George Harrison

Jun 7 Blind Faith's debut performance at a free concert in London's Hyde Park

Aug 24 Hawaii, the final Blind Faith concert

	Sep 13	appeared with the Plastic Ono Band at the *Toronto Rock and Roll Revival*
	Dec 7	recorded the album, *Delaney & Bonnie & Friends: On Tour with Eric Clapton*
	Dec 15	Plastic Ono Band concert for the start of John Lennon's *War is Over* campaign
1970	Jun 14	Derek and the Dominos' debut concert...

...Derek and the Dominos:

Eric Clapton: guitar and vocals – formed after Delaney & Bonnie
Bobby Whitlock: keyboards – from Delaney & Bonnie & Friends
Carl Randle: bass – from Delaney & Bonnie & Friends
Jim Gordon: drums – from Delaney & Bonnie & Friends
Dave Mason: guitar – from Delaney & Bonnie & Friends – a short stay

	Sep 9	recorded *Layla* – his ode to Pattie Boyd...

...Bobby Whitlock – Carl Randle – Jim Gordon
...guitarist Duane Allman made a guest appearance

	Nov 27	George Harrison released *All Things Must Pass* – featured Eric Clapton
	Dec 5	Derek and the Dominos' penultimate gig – Clapton became a recluse after this
1971	Aug 1	performed at the *Concert for Bangladesh*
1973	Jan 13	Rainbow Theatre comeback concert – arranged by Pete Townshend...

...Eric and the Palpitations:

Eric Clapton: guitar
Pete Townshend: guitar – from the Who – arranged the concert
Ron Wood: guitar – from the Faces
Jim Capaldi: drums – from Traffic
Jimmy Karstein: drums – session musician
Rick Grech: bass – formally with Family, Blind Faith and Traffic

1974	Jun 19	opened his *461 Ocean Boulevard* tour – old Slowhand was back
1976	Nov 25	made a guest appearance at the Band's swan song, *The Last Waltz*
1979	Mar 27	his dreams came true when he married George Harrison's ex-wife Pattie Boyd...
		...as well as *Layla* he also wrote *Wonderful Tonight* for Boyd
1983	Sep 20	performed at the ARMS charity concert – with Jeff Beck and Jimmy Page
1987	Jan 6	opening night of the 1st Royal Albert Hall residency
2000	Mar 6	inducted into the Rock and Roll Hall of Fame – for the 3rd time

The Dave Clark Five

Inducted into the Rock and Roll Hall of Fame in 2008

1942	Dec 15	Dave Clark: drummer and singer, born in Tottenham, London...
		...formed the Dave Clark Five in 1958
1962	Jun 29	Contours released *Do You Love Me* – Dave Clark Five's cover was 1st hit, 1963
	Sep 5	BBC Radio audition Mark Twain and the Strangers, with a pre-Who Keith Moon
		...lost out to the Dave Clark Five
1964	Jan 1	performed on the 1st edition of UK TV's *Top of the Pops*
	Feb 1	in the vanguard of the British Invasion

	Feb 21	performed *Bits and Pieces* – but was it Clark or Bobby Graham on the singles?
	Mar 8	performed *Glad All Over* on the *Ed Sullivan Show*...
		...written by Dave Clark and Mike Smith
	May 24	arrived in the US for their 1st tour – 1st US tour by a British Invasion group
1966	Dec 23	final edition of *Ready Steady Go!* – Dave Clark bought the rights to the show

The Clash

		Inducted into the Rock and Roll Hall of Fame in 2003
1952	Aug 21	Joe Strummer: guitarist, singer, born John Graham Mellor, in Ankara, Turkey...
		...previously with Vultures, El Huaso and the 101 All Stars, and the 101'ers
		...Vultures: guitar, vocals, founding member – Newport, Wales 1973 and '74
1955	Jun 26	Mick Jones: guitarist and singer, born in Brixton, London...
		...previously with the Delinquents and London SS
1955	Dec 15	Paul Simonon: bassist, born in Brixton, London...
		...previously with London SS

London SS spawned two of Britain's major punk bands:

The Clash

Mick Jones: guitar and vocals – Paul Simonon: singer

The Damned

Rat Scabies: drums – Brian James: guitar

Clash cover versions included:

1959	May 18	Crickets recorded *I Fought the Law* – on the Clash's 1979 EP *Cost of Living*

Before the Clash

1974	Sep 7	1st gig, calling themselves "El Huaso and the 101 All Stars"...
		...lineup included:
		Joe Strummer: guitar and vocals – left to form the Clash in mid-1976
		...band's name was inspired by its squat address at 101 Walterton Road, W9
		...the name was shortened to "The 101'ers"

The Clash

1976	Jul 4	debut gig, opened for the Sex Pistols...
		...The Clash:
		Joe Strummer: guitar and vocals – from the 101'ers
		Mick Jones: guitar and vocals – from London SS
		Paul Simonon: bass – from London SS
		Terry Chimes, aka "Tory Crimes": drums – left after the 1st album
		Keith Levine: guitar – left after a handful of gigs...
		...moved on to join Flowers of Romance:
		Flowers of Romance included a pre-Sex Pistols Sid Vicious
	Sep 20	appeared at the 1st punk festival, held at London's 100 Cub

	Dec 6	supported Sex Pistols on the *Anarchy in the UK* tour – with drummer Rob Harper
1977	Mar 18	released UK debut single, *White Riot* – written by Joe Strummer and Mick Jones
	Apr 8	released debut album, *The Clash* (UK)
	May 1	British *White Riot* tour opened...
		...Chimes left: Topper Headon joined as permanent drummer shortly before
1978	Nov 10	released *Give 'Em Enough Rope* (UK) – 1st album with Topper Headon
1979	May 11	released *The Cost Of Living* EP (UK) – contained the track *I Fought the Law*
	Dec 14	released *London Calling* (UK)
1981	May 28	opened a 15-day residency in New York – guest appearance from Allen Ginsberg
1982	May 29	opened the US leg of their *Casbah Club* tour...
		...Terry Chimes returned to replace Topper Headon shortly before

Cleanliness and Godliness Skiffle Band

1971 Apr 15 the 'real' Masked Marauders in the audacious *Rolling Stone* album hoax

Cleo's Mood

1963 Dec 13 semi-pro group formed by Shelley and Bone, joined shortly afterwards by Bunz...
...band's name taken from a Jr Walker album track
...Shelley wrote this book

The Clovers

1959 Jun 8 Clovers recorded *Love Potion #9*...
...written and produced by Jerry Leiber and Mike Stoller
...staple for 1960s R&B groups – provided the Searchers with a US hit in 1964

The Coasters

Inducted into the Rock and Roll Hall of Fame in 1987

1928	Apr 29	Carl Gardner: lead singer of the Robins and the Coasters, born in Tyler, Texas
1937	Nov 2	Earl "Speedo" Carroll, singer, born in New York City, New York...
		...replaced Cornell Gunter in 1961 – previously with the Cadillacs
1956	Jan 11	1st recording session...
		...The Coasters:
		Carl Gardner: lead singer – from the Robins Bobby Nunn: singer – from the Robins Leon Hughes: singer Billy Guy: singer
1958	Mar 17	recorded *Yakety Yak* – featuring the sax solo from King Curtis
	Dec 11	recorded *Charlie Brown* – with session saxophonist King Curtis
1959	Jul 16	recorded *Poison Ivy* – covered by the Stones and the Paramounts in 1963...
		...17 July, recorded *I'm a Hog for You* – Screaming Lord Sutch single in 1963
1971	Apr 27	Beach Boys and the Grateful Dead on stage together at the Fillmore East...

...performed covers of:

Riot in Cell Block #9 – Robins single in 1954
Searchin' – Coasters single in 1957

Eddie Cochran

Inducted into the Rock and Roll Hall of Fame in 1987

1938 Oct 3 singer, guitarist and songwriter, born in Albert Lea, Minnesota

1956 Aug 22 appeared in the movie *The Girl Can't Help It*...

...sang his own composition, *Twenty Flight Rock*
...Paul McCartney used the song as his audition for the Quarry Men

1957 Oct 12 on the tour in Australia when Little Richard found God and renounced rock'n'roll

1958 Mar 28 recorded *Summertime Blues*...

...covered by the Beach Boys in 1962 – T.Rex in 1970 – the Who in 1970

1959 Feb 5 recorded Buddy Holly tribute song *Three Stars* – not released until 1966 in UK...

...written by Tommy Dee and a hit for him in mid-1959

1960 Jan 8 final recording session

Jan 24 fateful last tour opened in the UK

1960 Apr 17 died in an automobile accident: 21 years old

Joe Cocker

singer: Vance Arnold and the Avengers – Joe Cocker's Big Blues – Grease Band

1944 May 20 aka Vance Arnold, born in Sheffield, Yorkshire...

...Grease Band formed as Cocker's backing band in 1966 – he left in 1969
...Grease Band included Henry McCullough, who left in 1972 to join Wings

1963 Nov 13 supported the Stones when he was with Vance Arnold and the Avengers...

...*I'll Cry Instead*, Cocker single in '64 – from Beatles' *Hard Day's Night*, '64

1968 Jul 8 supported the Byrds at London's Royal Albert Hall the previous day

Oct 24 promoted *With a Little Help from My Friends* on *Top of the Pops*...

...cover of a Beatles song, 1st released on *Sgt Pepper* in 1967

1969 Aug 15 performed at the *Woodstock* festival

1970 Mar 27 recorded *Mad Dogs & Englishmen*, live at the Fillmore East

Aug 7 performed at the *Goose Lake International Music Festival*

1983 Sep 20 UK ARMS concerts – Cocker performed at the American ARMS concerts

Leonard Cohen

Inducted into the Rock and Roll Hall of Fame in 2008

1934 Sep 21 singer-songwriter, born in Montreal, Canada

1967 Dec 27 released his debut album, *Songs of Leonard Cohen* (US)...

...*Suzanne* had previously been released by Judy Collins in 1966

1970 Aug 28 performed at the *Isle of Wight Festival*

Phil Collins

Inducted into the Rock and Roll Hall of Fame in 2010 – Genesis

drums and vocals: The Freehold – Hickory – Flaming Youth – Genesis – Brand X

1951 Jan 30 musician and songwriter, born in Chiswick, London...

...Brand X was a mid-1970s jazz-rock side project

1970 Feb 4 Flaming Youth gig...

...songwriting credits included:

Lying Crying Dying – recorded by Freehold in 1968 – recording debut
Green Light – Hickory single released in 1969 – 1st-ever Collins single

1972 Dec 11 Genesis's US concert debut

1976 Mar 26 1st gig as vocalist for Genesis

1987 Jan 6 Eric Clapton's 1st residency at the Albert Hall – Collins performed at some shows

1988 Nov 5 *Groovy Kind of Love* knocked off US #1 spot by Beach Boys' 1st #1 in 22 years

Colosseum

1934 Sep 26 Dick Heckstall-Smith: saxophone, born Richard Malden, in Ludlow, Shropshire...

...previously with Alexis Korner, Graham Bond and John Mayall

1940 Oct 13 Chris Farlowe: singer, born John Henry Deighton, in Islington, London...

...went on to join Atomic Rooster

1943 Jan 18 Dave Greenslade: keyboards, born in Woking, Surrey...

...from Chris Farlowe's Thunderbirds and Gino Washington's Ram Jam Band

1944 Jun 21 Jon Hiseman: drummer, born in Woolwich, London...

...previously with Graham Bond, Georgie Fame and John Mayall

1949 Sep 5 Dave "Clem" Clempson: guitarist, born in Tamworth, Staffordshire...

...founding member of Bakerloo – formed 1967 – left 1969
...replaced Peter Frampton in Humble Pie in 1971

Colosseum II

1952 Apr 4 Gary Moore: guitarist and founding member, born in Belfast, Northern Ireland

Colosseum

1969 Jan 3 early gig...

...Colosseum:

Jon Hiseman: drums and leader – formed mid-1968 – from John Mayall
Dick Heckstall-Smith: saxophone – from John Mayall's Bluesbreakers
Tony Reeves: bass – from John Mayall's Bluesbreakers
Dave Greenslade: keyboards – from Geno Washington
Jim Roach: guitar – very short tenure with the band

...James Litherland: guitar – replaced Jim Roach before the 1st album

Jun 18 recording session for the 2nd album, *Valentyne Suite*...

...by the time that they came to record the 3rd album, *Daughter of Time*:

Dave "Clem" Clempson had replaced guitarist James Litherland:

Clempson joined in 1969 – left in 1971 to join Humble Pie
Litherland formed his own band, it morphed into Mogul Thrash

Mark Clarke had replaced bassist Tony Reeves

Chris Farlowe: singer, had joined the band

1971 Mar 18 concert recorded for the *Live* album – group split up at the end of the year...

...Colosseum:

Jon Hiseman – formed Tempest
Dick Heckstall-Smith – opted for a solo career
Mark Clarke – short stint in Uriah Heep and then joined Tempest
Dave Greenslade – formed Greenslade with bassist Tony Reeves
Dave "Clem" Clempson – replaced Peter Frampton in Humble Pie

After Tempest folded, Jon Hiseman formed Colosseum II in 1975.

Ken Colyer

trumpet and band leader: Crane River Jazz Band – Ken Colyer's Jazzmen – Ken Colyer's Skiffle Group

1928 Apr 18 born in Great Yarmouth, Norfolk

Ken Colyer's Jazzmen/Skiffle Group

1953 Sep 2 recorded *New Orleans to London* – classic Ken Colyer and Chris Barber lineup...

...Ken Colyer's Jazzmen: musicians included:

Ken Colyer: trumpet
Chris Barber: trombone
Tony (Lonnie) Donegan: banjo

...the band was formed after Colyer's return from America in 1953

1954 Sep 10 recorded *Back to the Delta* – new lineup after Barber left to form his own band...

...Ken Colyer's Jazzmen: musicians included:

Bernard (Acker) Bilk: clarinet

...Ken Colyer's Skiffle Group: musicians included:

Alexis Korner: guitar and mandolin

CONCERTS AND FESTIVALS

1952 Mar 21 Alan Freed organised the 1st-ever rock'n'roll concert – ended in a near-riot

1964 Oct 7 rock'n'roll's changing times – concert that included Bill Haley and Manfred Mann

1965 Aug 15 Beatles' Shea Stadium concert – 1st-ever rock'n'roll gig in a stadium

Oct 16 1st Family Dog dance concert at Longshoreman's Hall

1966 Jan 22 psychedelic multimedia *Trips Festival* in San Francisco

1967 Jan 14 *A Gathering of the Tribes for a Human Be-In* – a prelude to the *Summer of Love*

Apr 29 *14-Hour Technicolor Dream* at London's Alexandra Palace

Jun 10 *Fantasy Fair and Magic Mountain Music Festival*, San Francisco...

...1st rock festival

Jun 16 *1st Monterey International Pop Festival...*
...organised by Lou Adler, Alan Pariser and John Phillips
Dec 22 *Christmas on Earth Continued* concert in London
1969 Jul 26 *Seattle Pop Festival* held in Woodinville's Gold Creek Park
Aug 15 the most famous festival of them all – *Woodstock, "3 Days of Peace & Music"*
Sep 13 *Toronto Rock and Roll Revival* – Plastic Ono Band's debut
Dec 6 notorious Altamont festival – spiritual end of the 1960s
1970 Jun 28 *Festival Express* played Toronto
Aug 7 start of the three-day *Goose Lake International Music Festival* in Michigan
Aug 28 *Isle of Wight Festival* – 500,000 people saw Hendrix, Who, Doors, ELP, et al
Sep 19 1st Glastonbury *Pop Folk & Blues* festival
1971 Aug 1 *Concert for Bangladesh* – organised by George Harrison and Ravi Shankar
1973 Jun 28 *British Re-Invasion Show* at New York's Madison Square Garden
Jul 28 *Summer Jam* at Watkins Glen Raceway, New York – bigger than Woodstock
1975 Jul 16 *Top 40 New York Unrecorded Rock Bands* opened in New York's CBGB club
1976 Sep 20 1st British punk festival – held at London's 100 Cub
1983 Sep 20 ARMS charity concert – featured Clapton, Beck and Page on stage together

The Contours

1962 Jun 29 released *Do You Love Me...*
...UK hit for the Dave Clark Five in 1963
...UK #1 for Brian Poole and the Tremeloes in 1963

Robert Convey

1958 Jan 20 Radio KWK station manager who decided that "rock'n'roll had to go"

Sam Cooke

Inducted into the Rock and Roll Hall of Fame in 1986 (inaugural year)...
+...as a member of The Soul Stirrers in 1989

singer: The Singing Children – Highway QC's – The Soul Stirrers

1918 May 23 Bumps Blackwell: producer, songwriter, arranger, born in Seattle, Washington
1931 Jan 22 Sam Cooke: singer and songwriter, born Sam Cook, in Clarksdale, Mississippi...
...member of the family gospel group the Singing Children in the early 1940s
...with the Highway QC's before joining the Soul Stirrers
...replaced Robert Harris as lead singer of the Soul Stirrers in 1951
...recorded as "Dale Cook" – early recording name for his secular songs
1960 Jan 25 recorded *Chain Gang* during his 1st recording session at RCA...
...credited as co-written with Charles Cooke
1964 Sep 16 performed on the 1st edition of *Shindig!*
Dec 11 shot dead in a Los Angeles motel: 33 years old
1965 Oct 15 Jimmy (Jimi) Hendrix signed a management deal with Ed Chalpin...
...Hendrix had previously played with Cooke's touring band

Elvis Costello and the Attractions

		Inducted into the Rock and Roll Hall of Fame in 2003
1977	Aug 2	early Elvis Costello and the Attractions concert...
		...in 1972 Elvis Costello and Allan Mayes formed the folk duo Rusty
		...by the mid-1970s Costello was in the group Flip City

Country Joe and the Fish

1942	Jan 1	Country Joe McDonald: singer, born in Washington, DC...
		...name taken from the USSR's leader Joe Stalin's nickname, "Country Joe"
		...Country Joe's songwriting credits included:
		Super Bird – from the 1967 album *Electric Music for Mind and Body*
		Feel Like I'm Fixin' to Die Rag – from '67 LP *I Feel Like I'm Fixin' to Die*
		...founding member when the band formed in 1965
1967	Jun 10	played the *Fantasy Fair and Magic Mountain Music Festival*
	Jun 16	played the *Monterey Pop Festival*
1969	Aug 15	performed at the *Woodstock* festival
1971	May 6	Country Joe McDonald performed at the final Fillmore East concert in June

Floyd Cramer

		Inducted into the Rock and Roll Hall of Fame in 2003
1933	Oct 27	pianist, one of the architects of "The Nashville Sound", born in Samti, Louisiana
1956	Jan 10	played on Elvis Presley's *Heartbreak Hotel*
1958	Mar 24	Elvis inducted into the US Army – recording session with Elvis in June 1958
1960	Mar 20	Elvis Presley's 1st recording session since leaving the Army
	Aug 8	Roy Orbison recorded *Blue Angel*
1962	Jun 5	played on Elvis Presley's album *Pot Luck with Elvis*
1966	May 25	played on Elvis Presley's album *How Great Thou Art*

Crazy Horse

1945	Nov 12	Neil Young: musician, singer and songwriter, born in Ontario, Canada...
		...Crazy Horse formed from the Rockets in late '60s, as Young's backing band
1972	Nov 18	Danny Whitten: guitarist, died of a drug overdose: 29 years old...
		...founding member of the Rockets

Cream

		Inducted into the Rock and Roll Hall of Fame in 1993
1936	Nov 23	Robert Johnson recorded *Cross Road Blues* – covered by Cream in 1968
1937	Feb 8	Ben Palmer: roadie, born in Berkshire, England...
		...pianist, previously in the Roosters with Eric Clapton
1939	Aug 19	Ginger Baker: drummer, born in Lewisham, London
1940	Dec 25	Pete Brown: lyricist, in collaboration with Jack Bruce, born in Ashtead, Surrey

1943 May 14 Jack Bruce: bassist and singer, born in Bishopbriggs, Lanarkshire, Scotland

1945 Mar 30 Eric Clapton: guitarist, born in Ripley, Surrey

Road to Cream

Alexis Korner's Blues Incorporated:

Ginger Baker and Jack Bruce

Both left with Graham Bond to form the Graham Bond Trio in early 1963.

Became the Graham Bond Quartet and Graham Bond Organisation.

Ginger Baker and Jack Bruce

The Roosters – Casey Jones and the Engineers – The Yardbirds

John Mayall's Bluesbreakers – The Glands:

Eric Clapton

John Mayall's Bluesbreakers:

Jack Bruce
Eric Clapton

Manfred Mann:

Jack Bruce

Before Cream

1963 Feb 20 Graham Bond Quartet backed Duffy Power on *I Saw Her Standing There...*
...featured Jack Bruce and Ginger Baker

Oct 19 Top Topham's final gig as the Yardbirds' lead guitarist – replaced by Eric Clapton

1965 Mar 3 Clapton's final gig with the Yardbirds – he moved on to join John Mayall

Mar 5 Yardbirds released *For Your Love* (UK)...
...B-side, *Got to Hurry*, was Clapton's 1st recorded composition

Nov 6 1st time Bruce played alongside Clapton – in John Mayall's Bluesbreakers...
...Clapton was back from his summer stint in Greece with the Glands
...Glands included Ben Palmer: piano – previously with Clapton in Roosters

1966 Mar 14 Baker wrote and performed on *Waltz for a Pig* – B-side of the *Who's Substitute...*
...Graham Bond Organisation was credited as "The Who Orchestra"

Apr 15 Manfred Mann released *Pretty Flamingo* – with bassist Jack Bruce

Jun 1 Eric Clapton and the Powerhouse issued the compilation album *What's Shakin'...*
...featured Eric Clapton, Jack Bruce and pianist Ben Palmer

1966 Jul 22 John Mayall released *Bluesbreakers with Eric Clapton* (UK)

Cream

1966 Jul 31 official debut concert...
...Cream:

Ginger Baker: drums – from the Graham Bond Organisation
Jack Bruce: bass and vocals – from Manfred Mann
Eric Clapton: guitar – from John Mayall's Bluesbreakers

	Aug 6	early gig at Torquay's Town Hall – post-beat rock became more sophisticated
	Oct 1	Jimi Hendrix joined them on stage for a jam – shortly after he arrived in London...
		...played *Killing Floor* – Howlin' Wolf single in 1965
1967	Mar 25	American concert debut on Murray the "K"'s *Live in Person*...package show
	Apr 3	began recording *Disraeli Gears* – produced by Felix Pappalardi
1968	Mar 7	recorded Baker's epic drum solo, *Toad* – for the live part of *Wheels of Fire*
	Nov 4	final concert in America
	Nov 26	farewell concert at London's Royal Albert Hall
1969	Jan 4	legendary Hendrix performance of *Sunshine of Your Love* on Lulu's TV show...
		...taken from Cream's 1967 album *Disraeli Gears*
		...written by Jack Bruce, Pete Brown and Eric Clapton
1969	Mar 1	released *Goodbye* (UK)

After Cream

Eric Clapton

(John Lennon's) Dirty Mac, Blind Faith, Plastic Ono Band, Delaney & Bonnie, and Derek and the Dominos ...and on to a legendary solo career

SEE Eric Clapton

Jack Bruce

Went on to a solo career...

1969	May 12	Jeannie "Genie the Tailor" Franklin died – the "Tailor" in *Songs for a Tailor*
	Aug 29	released the solo album *Songs for a Tailor* (UK)...
		...musicians included:

Chris Spedding: guitar
Jon Hiseman: drums
Dick Heckstall-Smith: saxophone
Felix Pappalardi: guitar, percussion and vocals – Cream's producer
George Harrison: guitar – as "L'Angelo Misterioso"

1974	Dec 12	Mick Taylor left the Rolling Stones to join the Jack Bruce Band

Ginger Baker

initially Blind Faith, then Ginger Baker's Airforce
other projects included a brief stint with Hawkwind in 1980

1969	Jun 7	Blind Faith's debut performance at a free concert in London's Hyde Park
1969	Aug 24	Hawaii, the final Blind Faith concert – formed Airforce in early 1970...
		...Ginger Baker's Airforce: lineup included:

Denny Laine: guitar and vocals – ex-Moody Blues
Rick Grech: bass and violin – from Blind Faith
Steve Winwood: keyboards and vocals – from Blind Faith

The Creation

The Mark Four and The Creation both included:

1942 Aug 15 Eddie Phillips: guitarist, born in London, England...
...1st guitarist to play his guitar with a violin bow

1942 Sep 3 Kenny Pickett: singer, aka Kenny Lee, born in Ware, Hertfordshire...
...Grandad – Clive Dunn single in 1970 – co-writer with Herbie Flowers
...went on to become a roadie with Led Zeppelin

Mark Four formed in 1963: Eddie Phillips and Kenny Pickett were both founding members.

1943 May 21 John Dalton: bassist, born in Enfield, London – left in mid-1966 to join the Kinks

In mid-1966 the Mark Four morphed into the Mod group, the Creation.

1947 Jun 1 Ron Wood: guitarist, born in Hillingdon, London...
...band member for the 1st half of 1968, whilst still in the Jeff Beck Group

1965 Aug 2 The Birds issued The Byrds with a writ for using a similar sounding name...
...bassist Kim Gardner joined the Creation in 1967:
went on to form Ashton Gardner and Dyke in 1968

1967 Apr 29 performed at the 14-Hour Technicolor Dream

Creedence Clearwater Revival

Inducted into the Rock and Roll Hall of Fame in 1993

1941 Nov 9 Tom Fogerty: guitarist and singer, born in Berkeley, California

1945 May 28 John Fogerty: guitarist, singer and songwriter, born in Berkeley, California

Started as the Blue Velvets before morphing into the Golliwogs and finally Creedence.

1969 Aug 15 performed at the *Woodstock* festival

1972 May 22 end of the road, with a final concert in Denver – just the one brother, John...
...Tom Fogerty had already left the band in 1971

1985 Jan 7 John Fogerty released Centerfield (US)...
...sued over the track *Old Man Down the Road*

Crosby, Stills & Nash

Inducted into the Rock and Roll Hall of Fame in 1997

1941 Aug 14 David Crosby: guitarist, singer and songwriter, born in Los Angeles, California

1942 Feb 2 Graham Nash: guitarist, singer and songwriter, born in Blackpool, Lancashire

1945 Jan 3 Stephen Stills: guitarist, singer and songwriter, born in Dallas, Texas

1945 Nov 12 Neil Young: guitarist, singer and songwriter, born in Ontario, Canada

Before Crosby, Stills & Nash

1967 Jun 16 Crosby stood in for Neil Young with Buffalo Springfield at *Monterey Pop Festival*

Nov 9 Crosby's sacking from the Byrds featured in the inaugural issue of *Rolling Stone*

1968 May 5 Buffalo Springfields' final concert

Aug 25 riots at the Democratic Party Convention in Chicago – inspired the song *Chicago*

1968 Dec 8 Graham Nash left the Hollies to form Crosby, Stills & Nash

Crosby, Stills & Nash

1969 Jul 25 gave their debut performance at New York's Fillmore East...

...Crosby, Stills & Nash:

David Crosby – recently sacked from the Byrds
Graham Nash – from the Hollies
Stephen Stills – joined after Buffalo Springfield imploded

...Young joined them on stage at the end of the gig – later became a quartet:

Neil Young was also with Buffalo Springfield

...by now they had already released their 1st album – contained two singles:

Marrakesh Express: 1st single, written by Graham Nash
Suite: Judy Blue Eyes: written by Stephen Stills

1969 Aug 15 performed at the Woodstock festival – Neil Young joined them on stage

Crosby, Stills, Nash & Young

1969 Dec 6 performed at the ill-fated Altamont festival

1970 May 1 killings at Kent State University – inspired the song *Ohio*, released in June...

...written by Neil Young

Aleister Crowley

1970 Oct 23 Led Zeppelin released *Led Zeppelin III* – quotes from Crowley cut into the run-out

1976 Oct 20 premiere of Zeppelin's movie *The Song Remains the Same* – homage to Crowley

The Crows

1953 Feb 10 recorded *Gee* – one of the contenders for the accolade of 1st rock'n'roll record

Dick Dale

1937 May 4 "King of the Surf Guitar", born Richard Monsour, in Boston, Massachusetts

1961 Aug 23 Dick Dale and the Del-Tones recorded the surf classic, *Let's Go Trippin'*...

...written by Dale and often cited as the 1st surf-rock record

The Damned

1954 Apr 24 Captain Sensible: bassist, born Raymond Burns, in Balham, London...

...previously with Oasis

1957 Jul 30 Rat Scabies: drummer, born Chris Millar, in Kingston-upon-Thames, London

London SS spawned two of Britain's major punk bands:

The Damned

Rat Scabies: drums – Brian James: guitar

The Clash

Mick Jones: guitar and vocals – Paul Simonon: singer

The Damned

1976 Sep 20 appeared at the 1st punk festival, held at London's 100 Cub

Oct 22 released *New Rose* – 1st single to be released by a UK punk band...

...with the B-side *Help* – Beatles song from 1965

...*New Rose* was written by Brian James

Dec 6 supported the Sex Pistols on the ill-fated *Anarchy in the UK* tour

1977 Feb 18 released their debut album, *Damned Damned Damned* (UK)...

...1st album from a British punk band

Mar 10 supported Marc Bolan on his last-ever UK tour – 1st major tour by UK punk band

1977 Apr 7 opened at New York's CBGB club – 1st British punk band to play in America...

...The Damned:

Captain Sensible: bass – previously in Johnny Moped
Rat Scabies: drums – previously in London SS
Brian James: guitar – previously in London SS
David Vanian: vocalist – 1st band

Cyril Davies

SEE Alexis Korner

Miles Davis

Inducted into the Rock and Roll Hall of Fame in 2006

1949 Jan 21 1st recording session for the album *Birth of the Cool* – released in 1957

1969 Aug 19 recording started on the seminal jazz-rock album, *Bitches Brew*...

...lineup included:

John McLaughlin: guitar – later formed the Mahavishnu Orchestra
Billy Cobham: drums – later formed the Mahavishnu Orchestra
Wayne Shorter: saxophone – later formed Weather Report
Joe Zawinul: piano – later formed Weather Report
Chick Corea: piano – later formed Return to Forever

1970 Aug 28 performed at the *Isle of Wight Festival*

The Spencer Davis Group

1937 Jun 22 Chris Blackwell, manager, founder of Island Records, born in London, England

1948 May 12 Steve Winwood: keyboardist and singer, born in Birmingham, England

Rhythm and Blues Quartet morphed into the Spencer Davis Group in 1964.

1967 Mar 13 final tour with Steve and Muff Winwood...

...The Spencer Davis Group:

Spencer Davis: guitar and vocals
Pete York: drums
Steve Winwood: vocals and keyboards – left in 1967 to form Traffic
Muff Winwood: bass – left in 1967 and became an A&R man for Island

...Chris Blackwell: manager – changed their name to "Spencer Davis Group"

...the Winwoods were replaced by:

Eddie Hardin: keyboards
Phil Sawyer: guitar

...roadie Dave Mason, shortly to find fame as a founding member of Traffic

1967 Apr 2 Steve Winwood left to form Traffic

James Dean

1955 Sep 30 actor, died in an automobile accident: 24 years old

1955 Oct 27 *Rebel Without a Cause* opened in America – 2nd of three James Dean movies

Joey Dee

singer: Joey Dee and the Starliters

1940 Jun 11 born Joseph DiNicola, in Passaic, New Jersey

Joey Dee and the Starliters

...Joey Dee and the Starliters: musicians included:

Joey Dee: singer and leader – the band evolved in the late 1950s
Veronica Bennett: backing singer – later the Ronettes' lead singer
Estelle Bennett: backing singer – later in the Ronettes
Nedra Talley: backing singer – later in the Ronettes
Jimmy James (Jimi Hendrix): guitar – brief stay in late 1965

...other musicians: left in 1965 to form the (Young) Rascals:

Felix Cavalier: keyboards
Eddie Brigati: singer
Gene Cornish: guitar

Tommy Dee with Carol Kay and the Teen-Aires

1959 Feb 5 Eddie Cochran recorded Three Stars – but it was not released until later...

...written by Tommy Dee and a US hit for him in mid-1959
...tribute to the deaths of Buddy Holly, Ritchie Valens and the Big Bopper

Deep Purple

1941 Jun 9 Jon Lord: keyboardist, born in Leicester, Leicestershire...

...one of Jon Lord's earliest bands was the Don Wilson Combo in 1963:

he was with the band when they combined with the Art Wood Combo
they became the New Art Wood Combo and morphed into the Artwoods

...amongst other things:

he was a session musician
a member of Santa Barbara Machine Head and the Flower Pot Men touring band, before leaving to join Roundabout

...he joined Whitesnake in the late 1970s

Aug 26 Chris Curtis: drummer, singer, born Chris Crummey, in Oldham, Lancashire...

...member of Johnny Sandon and the Searchers – became the Searchers
...he originally started to form Roundabout but left before it came to fruition

1945	Apr 14	Ritchie Blackmore: guitarist, born in Weston-super-Mare, Somerset...
		...previously a member of various bands, including: Screaming Lord Sutch and the Savages, the Outlaws, and Neil Christian and the Crusaders
		...left Deep Purple in 1975 and formed Rainbow soon afterwards
	Aug 19	Ian Gillan: singer, born in Hounslow, Middlesex...
		...member of Episode Six, when he left to replace Rod Evans ...left in 1973 and formed the Ian Gillan Band ...member of Black Sabbath in the early 1980s
	Nov 3	Nick Simper: bassist, born in Norwood Green, Middlesex...
		...member of Johnny Kidd and the New Pirates, (and the Pirates after Johnny Kidd's death); member of the Flower Pot Men touring band before leaving to join Roundabout
	Nov 30	Roger Glover: bassist, born in Brecon, South Wales...
		...member of Episode Six, when he left to replace Nick Simper ...joined Rainbow in 1979
1948	Jun 29	Ian Paice: drummer, born in Nottingham, Nottinghamshire...
		...with the Maze before joining Roundabout
1951	Aug 1	Tommy Bolin: guitarist, born in Sioux City, Iowa...
		...joined in 1975 to replace Ritchie Blackmore ...previously with Zephyr and the James Gang
1951	Sep 22	David Coverdale: singer, born in Saltburn-by-the-Sea, Cleveland...
		...joined in 1973 to replace Ian Gillan ...formed Whitesnake after Deep Purple folded

On the way to Deep Purple

1962	Jun 25	Ritchie Blackmore: was with Screaming Lord Sutch from May until October
1963	Feb 27	Chris Curtis: drummer, when the Searchers supported Gene Vincent in Hamburg
1964	Aug 4	Jon Lord: session keyboardist: Kinks released *You Really Got Me*
1965	Apr 2	Jon Lord: Artwoods appeared on the 1st live edition of *Ready Steady Go!*
1966	Apr 25	Neil Christian and the Crusaders gig – Blackmore lead guitar from early '66 to '67
1966	Oct 7	Nick Simper: New Pirates – injured in the car crash that killed Johnny Kidd

Final Roundabout lineup became Deep Purple.

1968	Apr 20	debut gig...
		...as "Roundabout":
		Jon Lord: keyboards – stayed until the end of the band in 1976 Nick Simper: bass – left in mid-1969 Ritchie Blackmore: guitar – left in mid-1975 Rod Evans: vocals – from Maze – left in mid-1969 Ian Paice: drums – from Maze – stayed until the end of the band in 1976
1969	Jun 4	Jon Lord and Ritchie Blackmore went to an Episode Six gig...
		...Episode Six's lineup included:

		Roger Glover: bass – founding member in 1963
		Ian Gillan: vocals – joined in 1965
		Mick Underwood: drummer...
		...formed Quatermass after the demise of Episode Six
		...he had previously played with Blackmore in the Outlaws
		...Ian Gillan and Roger Glover left Episode Six shortly afterwards:
		Deep Purple became:
		Ritchie Blackmore – Ian Paice – Jon Lord
		Ian Gillan: vocals – replaced Rod Evans – left in 1973
		Roger Glover: bass – replaced Nick Simper – left in 1973
	Sep 24	recorded *Concerto for Group and Orchestra...*
		...composed by Jon Lord with lyrics from Ian Gillan
		...Rod Evans and Nick Simper left shortly before this album was recorded
		...1st album with Ian Gillan and Roger Glover
1970	Jun 3	released *In Rock* (UK) – 1st rock album with the classic lineup
	Jul 11	played at the *Tivoli Pop Festival* in Germany
1971	May 9	end of their Australian tour – support act Free split up shortly afterwards
	Dec 4	fire at Frank Zappa's Montreux Casino concert – inspired *Smoke on the Water*
1974	Nov 13	Blackmore imposter wrecked a Porsche and conned fans for food and shelter
1975	Apr 7	last gig with original guitarist Ritchie Blackmore...
		...Deep Purple:
		Ritchie Blackmore – Ian Paice – Jon Lord
		David Coverdale: vocals – replaced Ian Gillan in mid-1973
		Glenn Hughes: bass and vocals – replaced Roger Glover in mid-1973
		...Ritchie Blackmore was replaced by Tommy Bolin
1976	Mar 15	final gig:
		Jon Lord – Ian Paice – Glenn Hughes – Tommy Bolin – David Coverdale
	Dec 4	Tommy Bolin died of a drug overdose: 25 years old
1984	Apr 27	announcement that Deep Purple was back:
		Jon Lord – Ian Paice – Roger Glover – Ritchie Blackmore – Ian Gillan
1999	Dec 14	Paul McCartney gig at the Cavern – backed by Ian Paice and David Gilmour

Def Leppard

1963	Nov 1	Rick Allen: drummer, born in Dronfield, Derbyshire
1978	Nov 27	Rick Allen replaced original drummer Tony Kenning
1984	Dec 31	Rick Allen lost his arm in a car crash
1987	Aug 3	released Hysteria (UK) – 1st album recorded after Rick Allen lost his arm

Delaney & Bonnie

1969	Aug 24	support act: final Blind Faith concert – Eric Clapton joined D&B on tour soon after
	Dec 7	recorded live album *Delaney & Bonnie & Friends: On Tour with Eric Clapton*

1969 Dec 15 members of the Plastic Ono Band at the concert for the *War is Over* campaign

Some of Delaney & Bonnie's 'Friends' went on to join Derek and the Dominos.

1970 Jun 14 Derek and the Dominos debut gig...

...ex-Delaney & Bonnie Friends included:

Eric Clapton: guitar
Bobby Whitlock: keyboards
Carl Randle: bass
Jim Gordon: drums
Dave Mason: guitar – his stay with the Dominos was very brief

1970 Jun 28 performed at the *Festival Express* event in Toronto

Terry Dene

1938 Dec 20 singer, born Terrence Williams, in Elephant and Castle, London...

...managed by Larry Parnes

1956 Apr 22 London's 2i's coffee bar opened – Dene was a regular at this iconic skiffle venue

1958 Feb 18 arrested for being drunk and disorderly – the beginning of the end of his career

The Diamonds

1957 Feb 8 Diamonds released *Little Darlin'* (US) – one in a long line of cover versions...

...cover of a Gladiolas single – written by Maurice Williams

Bo Diddley

Inducted into the Rock and Roll Hall of Fame in 1987

1928 Dec 30 writer, singer and guitarist, born Ellas Bates, in McComb, Mississippi...

...used the name "Ellas McDaniel" for his songwriting credits

1955 Mar 2 recorded *Bo Diddley and I'm a Man* – released as his 1st single...

...wrote both songs – *I'm a Man* was recorded by the Yardbirds in 1965

Nov 20 performed *Bo Diddley* on the *Ed Sullivan Show* – he was never invited back

1962 Oct 27 Rolling Stones recorded *You Can't Judge a Book by the Cover*...

...Bo Diddley single in mid-1962 – written by Willie Dixon

1963 Mar 11 Rolling Stones recording session...

...recorded two Bo Diddley penned songs:

Diddley Daddy – Bo Diddley single in 1955
Road Runner – Bo Diddley single in 1960

Sep 15 Animals recorded *Pretty Thing* – Bo Diddley single in 1955...

...co-written with Willie Dixon

1964 Apr 30 Keith Moon's audition as drummer for the Who...

...he played *Road Runner* – penned by Bo Diddley

Oct 13 early Pretty Things gig – British R&B band...

...named themselves after Bo Diddley's 1955 single *Pretty Thing*

1969 Jul 26 played the *Seattle Pop Festival*

1969 Sep 13 appeared at the *Toronto Rock and Roll Revival* festival

Dion (DiMucci)

Inducted into the Rock and Roll Hall of Fame in 1989

singer: Dion and the Belmonts

1939 Jul 18 born in the Bronx, New York

1959 Feb 3 supported Buddy Holly on his ill-fated *Winter Dance Party* tour

Dire Straits

Morphed from Café Racers

1949 Aug 12 Mark Knopfler: guitarist and singer, born in Glasgow, Scotland

1977 Aug 2 early gig...

...Dire Straits:

Mark Knopfler: guitar, vocals – previously in Café Racers
David Knopfler: guitar – previously in Café Racers
John Illsley: bass
Pick Withers: drums – previously with Mark Knopfler in Brewers Droop

1987 Jan 6 performed with Eric Clapton at his 1st Royal Albert Hall residency

Willie Dixon

Inducted into the Rock and Roll Hall of Fame in 1994

bass: Muddy Waters' band

1915 Jul 1 iconic blues songwriter, born in Vicksburg, Mississippi...

...wrote *Spoonful*, recorded by Howlin' Wolf in 1960 and covered by Cream

1954 Jan 7 bassist and writer: Muddy Waters recorded *(I'm Your) Hoochie Coochie Man*

1955 Jan 25 bassist and writer: Little Walter recorded *My Babe*

Aug 12 bassist: Sonny Boy Williamson (II) recorded *Don't Start Me Talkin'*

1958 Feb 28 bassist: Chuck Berry recorded *Johnny B Goode*

1962 Jun 27 Muddy Waters recorded *You Shook Me* – covered by Led Zeppelin on 1st LP...

...Earl Hooker recorded the instrumental *Blue Guitar* in 1961:

Dixon added lyrics and Muddy Waters released it as *You Shook Me*

Oct 27 writer: Rolling Stones recorded *You Can't Judge a Book by the Cover*

1963 Jun 7 writer: Rolling Stones released *I Want to Be Loved* as B-side of 1st UK single

Sep 15 Animals recording session – recorded two Willie Dixon penned songs:

I Just Wanna Make Love to You – Muddy Waters single in 1954
Pretty Thing – co-written with Bo Diddley and a single from him in 1955

1964 Nov 13 writer: Stones released *Little Red Rooster* – Howlin' Wolf's *The Red Rooster*, '61

1969 Oct 31 Led Zeppelin released *Led Zeppelin II* – Dixon credit later for *Bring It on Home...*

...Sonny Boy Williamson (II) had recorded *Bring It on Home* in 1963

Nov 7 Led Zeppelin released *Whole Lotta Love* – Dixon sued over *You Need Love*

1974 Mar 12 writer: Mick Jagger recorded *Too Many Cooks (Spoil the Soup)* in 1973

Dr Hook and the Medicine Show

1937 Feb 1 Ray Sawyer: singer, guitarist, the one with eye-patch, born Chickasaw, Alabama

1949 Jun 13 Dennis Locorriere: singer and guitarist, born in Jersey City, New Jersey

1973 Mar 29 a dream come true – they made the cover of issue 131 of *Rolling Stone*...

...the three cover-boys were:

Ray Sawyer: singer and founding member
Dennis Locorriere: vocals, guitar and founding member
Bill Francis: keyboards and founding member

Dr John

Inducted into the Rock and Roll Hall of Fame in 2011

1940 Nov 21 guitar, keyboards, born Malcolm John Rebennack, in New Orleans, Louisiana...

...aka "The Night Tripper"

1972 Jul 21 support act on the Doors' last-ever tour

1976 Nov 25 made a guest appearance at the Band's swan song, *The Last Waltz*

Fats Domino

Inducted into the Rock and Roll Hall of Fame in 1986 (inaugural year)

1928 Feb 26 seminal rock'n'roll singer, born in New Orleans, Louisiana

1949 Dec 10 recorded *The Fat Man* – one of the contenders for the 1st rock'n'roll record...

...written by Fats Domino and Dave Bartholomew

1952 Mar 13 pianist: Lloyd Price recorded *Lawdy Miss Clawdy*

1956 Aug 22 appeared in the movie *The Girl Can't Help It*

1957 Apr 10 Ricky Nelson performed *I'm Walkin'* on his family's TV show – Domino hit in '57...

...written by Fats Domino and Dave Bartholomew

1957 Oct 3 Pat Boone had his own TV show – he built his career on sanitised R&B covers...

...he released a simultaneous cover of Domino's *Ain't It a Shame* in 1955:

Ain't It a Shame was written by Fats Domino and Dave Bartholomew

The Dominoes/Billy Ward and His Dominoes

1932 Nov 15 Clyde McPhatter: singer and founder of the group, born in North Carolina

1934 Jun 9 Jackie Wilson: singer, aka "Mr Excitement", born in Detroit, Michigan

Ques morphed into the Dominoes in 1950.

1950 Dec 30 recorded *Sixty Minute Man* – one of the contenders for the 1st rock'n'roll record...

...The Dominoes included:

Clyde McPhatter: lead singer and founding member...

...left in 1953 to form the Drifters

Billy Ward – founding member of the original Ques

1952 Mar 21 appeared at the 1st-ever rock'n'roll concert – organised by Alan Freed

1957 Sep 8 Jackie Wilson released 1st solo single *Reet Petite* – left Dominoes just before...

...Wilson replaced Clyde McPhatter as lead singer in 1953

Lonnie Donegan

guitar, banjo and vocals: Tony Donegan Jazz band – Chris Barber's Jazz Band – Ken Colyer's Jazzmen
Chris Barber's Jazz Band/interval skiffle group – The Lonnie Donegan Skiffle Group

1931 Apr 29 British skiffle pioneer, born Tony Donegan, in Glasgow, Scotland...
...“Lonnie”, after the MC confused his introduction with Lonnie Johnson

1953 Sep 2 banjo: Ken Colyer's Jazzmen recorded *New Orleans to London*

1954 Jul 13 recorded *Rock Island Line* and *John Henry* – issued as a single in November '55:
Rock Island Line was recorded by Lead Belly in 1937
John Henry was recorded by Lead Belly in 1943

1961 Dec 10 premiere of Cliff's *The Young Ones* – Donegan's last chart outing was mid-1962

Donovan

Inducted into the Rock and Roll Hall of Fame in 2012

1938 Jun 20 Mickie Most: producer, born Michael Hayes, in Aldershot, Hampshire...
...Donovan's *Mellow Yellow* single in '67 was credited to “Donovan Leitch”

1965 Feb 12 career started with three consecutive appearances on *Ready Steady Go!*...
...writing credits included:
Catch the Wind – debut single in 1965
Sunshine Superman – single in '66 – 1st single produced by Mickie Most

Apr 2 appeared on the 1st live edition of *Ready Steady Go!*

1967 Nov 9 1st *Rolling Stone Interview*, featured in the inaugural issue of the magazine

1969 Jun 7 supported Blind Faith at their debut concert

1972 Nov 8 DS Norman Pilcher arrested for perjury – Pilcher had bust Donovan for drugs

The Doors

Inducted into the Rock and Roll Hall of Fame in 1993

1939 Feb 12 Ray Manzarek: keyboardist and singer, born in Chicago, Illinois

1943 Dec 8 Jim Morrison: aka “The Lizard King”, singer, born in Melbourne, Florida

1944 Dec 1 John Densmore: drummer, born in Los Angeles, California

1946 Jan 8 Robbie Krieger: guitarist, born in Los Angeles, California

Psychedelic Rangers *SEE 2 September 1965*

John Densmore: drums
Robbie Krieger: guitar

Rick & the Ravens

1965 Sep 2 Rick & the Ravens demo recording session...
...Rick & the Ravens:
Rick Manczarek – Ray's brother – left soon after this recording session
Jim Manczarek – Ray's brother – left soon after this recording session
Ray Manzarek: keyboards – went on to form the Doors
Jim Morrison: singer – went on to form the Doors

John Densmore: drums – went on to form the Doors

...Jim Morrison's 1st time in the studio

...Robbie Krieger: guitar – joined shortly after this demo recording

Rick & the Ravens morphed into the Doors.

1966 May 9 Doors auditioned at LA's Whisky a Go Go club...

...The Doors:

Ray Manzarek: keyboards and vocals
Jim Morrison: singer – aka "The Lizard King"
John Densmore: drums
Robbie Krieger: guitar

...name inspired by Aldous Huxley and William Blake – "doors of perception"

Aug 18 signed to Elektra

1967 Jan 4 released their 1st album, *The Doors* (US)...

...also released debut single, *Break on Through (to the Other Side)* (US)

...following songs co-written by the band:

Break on Through (To the Other Side) – Light My Fire – The End

Jun 10 played the *Fantasy Fair and Magic Mountain Music Festival*

Sep 17 refused to change the lyrics to *Light My Fire* on the *Ed Sullivan Show*

Dec 9 Jim Morrison was arrested on stage at New Haven

1969 Mar 2 Jim Morrison faced obscenity charges after a concert in Miami

Jul 26 played the *Seattle Pop Festival*

Sep 13 headlined at the *Toronto Rock and Roll Revival* festival

Nov 11 Jim Morrison arrested for being drunk on an aeroplane

1970 Aug 28 performed at the *Isle of Wight Festival*

Oct 30 Morrison was sentenced following the notorious Miami concert on 2 March 1969

Nov 12 Jim Morrison's last performance with the Doors

1971 Jul 3 Jim Morrison died in Paris: at the age of 27

1972 Jul 21 1st gig of the last-ever Doors tour...

...Ray Manzarek took over lead vocals after Morrison's death

The Doors was history.

Ray Manzarek opted for a solo career.

John Densmore and Robbie Krieger went to England ...and formed the Butts Band.

1974 Jun 16 Butts Band supported the Kinks – it was nearing the end of its 1st incarnation...

...formed in early 1973, the lineup included:

John Densmore: drums
Robbie Krieger: guitar
Jess Roden: singer – left shortly after this gig...

...previously with the Alan Bown Set and Bronco

...band's name was inspired by a British street name in Kidderminster

...the trip to England was made to find a singer to replace Jim Morrison:
ex-Audience singer Howard Werth auditioned ...but it never happened

The Drifters

Inducted into the Rock and Roll Hall of Fame in 1988

1932 Nov 15 Clyde McPhatter: singer and founder of the group, born in North Carolina...
...previously lead singer with the Dominos – recorded *Sixty Minute Man*

1936 Aug 23 Rudy Lewis: singer, born Charles Rudolf Harrell, in Philadelphia, Pennsylvania

1938 Sep 28 Ben E King: singer, born Benjamin Earl Nelson, in Henderson, North Carolina...
...previously in the Five Crowns and the Crowns

For the story of the road to two Drifters groups, "The Drifters" and "Original Drifters"...
...SEE 7 May 1953

Clyde McPhatter founded the Drifters with members of Mount Lebanon Gospel Singers.

1953 May 7 Ahmet Ertegun signed Clyde McPhatter to Atlantic Records...
...George Treadwell – Drifters' manager
...band's name was inspired by a bird called "the drifter"
...after a weak recording session McPhatter disbanded that lineup

Clyde McPhatter recruited a new lineup.

1953 Aug 9 recorded their 1st R&B hit, *Money Honey*...
...The Drifters:
Clyde McPhatter: lead singer – left to join the Army in 1954
Bill Pinkney
Andrew Thrasher
Gerhart Thrasher
Willie Ferbie

Nov 12 recorded *Such a Night* – lead singer Clyde McPhatter...
...covered by Elvis on a 1960 album and a 1964 single

After McPhatter left in 1954, the Drifters had a number of different lead singers...
...Drifters' lead singers included: *SEE 7 May 1953*
David Baughan – replaced Clyde McPhatter in 1954
Johnny Moore – replaced David Baughan in mid-1955
Bobby Hendricks – replaced Johnny Moore in 1957...
...Hendricks left just before the sackings on 30 May 1958

1958 May 30 whole group was sacked at the end of their week at Harlem's Apollo...
...sacked group was replaced by the Crowns but renamed "The Drifters":
Benjamin Earl Nelson (Ben E King) – lead singer
Charlie Thomas
Dock Green
Elsbeary Hobbs

After the sackings on 30 May 1958, the unofficial "Original Drifters" was formed...
...unofficial "Original Drifters" lineup: *SEE 7 May 1953*

Bill Pinkney – formed this unofficial group
David Baughan: lead singer
Andrew Thrasher
Gerhart Thrasher

...there were now two different groups: "The Drifters" and "Original Drifters"

The official "The Drifters" group continued.

1959 Mar 6 new Drifters lineup recorded *There Goes My Baby* – Ben E King era began...
...written by King, George Treadwell and Lover Patterson

1964 May 20 Rudy Lewis died on the eve of the *Under the Boardwalk* recording session...
...Lewis replaced Ben E King as lead singer in 1960

May 21 recorded *Under the Boardwalk* – lead singer Johnny Moore

1972 Jun 13 Clyde McPhatter died of heart-failure: 39 years old

Aynsley Dunbar

drums: Stu James and the Mojos – John Mayall's Bluesbreakers – Jeff Beck Group
Aynsley Dunbar's Retaliation – Frank Zappa – David Bowie's backing band – Journey

1946 Jan 10 born in Liverpool, England...
...with Stu James and the Mojos: from late 1964 to autumn 1966
...band's name "Aynsley Dunbar Retaliation" reputedly a response to:
failing an audition for the Jimi Hendrix Experience

1967 Mar 3 recently formed Jeff Beck Group supported Roy Orbison...
...Dunbar joined shortly afterwards and stayed for about six months

1968 Feb 23 Band of Joy gig at the Marquee – Aynsley Dunbar Retaliation also on the bill

1970 May 15 orchestral premiere of Frank Zappa's *200 Motels*

1973 Jul 3 Ziggy Stardust & Spiders from Mars' last gig – Dunbar joined Bowie shortly after

Bob Dylan

Inducted into the Rock and Roll Hall of Fame in 1988

guitar, harmonica and vocals: Traveling Wilburys

1926 May 21 Albert Grossman: manager, born in Chicago, Illinois

1941 May 24 Dylan: singer, songwriter, born Robert Allen Zimmerman, in Duluth, Minnesota

1956 Jan 24 *Look* magazine article about the murder of 14-year-old Emmett Till...
...immortalised in Dylan's *The Ballad of Emmett Till*:
recorded using the pseudonym "Blind Boy Grunt"

1961 Apr 11 played his 1st major gig – at Gerde's Folk City in New York's Greenwich Village

Sep 30 1st-ever studio recording session – provided harmonica for Carolyn Hester

Nov 4 1st paid-attendance gig

Nov 20 1st recording session for one of his own recordings – 1st album, *Bob Dylan*

1962 Feb 2 recorded harmonica for Harry Belafonte's version of *The Midnight Special*

Mar 19 released his debut album, *Bob Dylan* (US) – contained two original songs:
Talkin' New York – Song to Woody

Dec 14 released 1st single, *Mixed-Up Confusion* (US) – withdrawn shortly afterwards

1963 Jan 13 1st UK visit – for an appearance in BBC TV's *The Madhouse on Castle Street*...
...1st broadcast performance of *Blowing in the Wind*

May 12 pulled out of the *Ed Sullivan Show* because of censorship issues

May 27 released 2nd album, *The Freewheelin' Bob Dylan* (US)...
...*Talkin' John Birch Society Blues* was removed from the original album:
song's inspiration came from the right-wing John Birch Society

Jun 12 Civil Rights leader Medgar Evers killed – subject of *Only a Pawn in Their Game*

Aug 28 Martin Luther King Jr's *I Have a Dream* speech – performed as "Blind Boy Grunt"

1964 Jan 13 released 3rd LP, *The Times They Are A-Changin'* (US) – 1st with all original songs

May 17 1st formal concert in the UK

Jun 9 recorded 4th album, *Another Side of Bob Dylan* – last completely acoustic album

Aug 28 Bob Dylan met the Beatles for the 1st time – he introduced them to pot

1965 Jan 15 recorded *If You Gotta Go, Go Now* – released in Benelux as a single in 1967...
...released by the Liverpool Five in the US in July 1965
...released by Manfred Mann in the UK in September 1965

Mar 22 released *Bringing It All Back Home* (US) – 1st album with electric songs

Apr 12 Byrds released *Mr. Tambourine Man*...
...cover taken from Dylan's 1965 album, *Bringing It All Back Home*

Jun 15 recorded *Like a Rolling Stone*

Jul 25 played his infamous electric set at the *Newport Folk Festival*...
...backing band:
Mike Bloomfield: guitar
Al Kooper: keyboards
Barry Goldberg: keyboards
Jerome Arnold: bass
Sam Lay: drums

Jul 29 recording session for *Highway 61 Revisited*...
...backing musicians included:
Mike Bloomfield: guitar
Al Kooper: keyboards

Aug 2 Byrds shortly to release their cover of *All I Really Want to Do* in the UK...
...taken from Dylan's 1964 album, *Another Side of Bob Dylan*

Nov 12 Marc Bolan performed his 1st single on TV...
...in 1964 Toby Tyler (Marc Bolan) recorded a demo of *Blowing in the Wind*:
taken from Dylan's 1963 album, *The Freewheelin' Bob Dylan*

1966 Feb 4 infamous electric world tour opened in Kentucky – backed by the Hawks...
...The Hawks:
Robbie Robertson: guitar
Rick Danko: bass

		Richard Manuel: piano
		Garth Hudson: organ
		Mickey Jones: drums – filling in for regular Hawks drummer Levon Helm
	May 16	released *Blonde on Blonde* (US)
	May 17	(not-quite-at-the) *Royal Albert Hall* bootleg album recorded
	Jul 29	motorcycle accident
1967	Nov 24	Beatles released *I Am the Walrus* – reputedly a pop at Dylan, amongst others
	Dec 27	released *John Wesley Harding* (US) – 1st album since his motorcycle accident
1969	Oct 11	Weathermen protest – radicals' name inspired by *Subterranean Homesick Blues*
	Nov 1	mentioned by *Rolling Stone* magazine as part of Masked Marauders hoax album
1971	Aug 1	performed at the *Concert for Bangladesh*
	Nov 17	recording session with beat poet Allen Ginsberg
1975	Jun 26	finally released *The Basement Tapes* (US) – it had been recorded back in 1967
	Oct 30	*Rolling Thunder Review* tour opened
	Dec 8	*Night of the Hurricane* concert
1976	Nov 25	made a guest appearance at the Band's swan song, *The Last Waltz*
1987	Jul 4	Dylan and the Grateful Dead tour opened – to very mixed reviews

Vince Eager

1958	Oct 1	support act: Billy Fury made an impromptu appearance at a Marty Wilde concert
1960	Jan 24	supported Eddie Cochran on his last UK tour
	Jul 27	performed at Larry Parnes's *Meet the Beat* show – Parnes was his manager...
		...born Rod Taylor, Parnes gave him a stage name to reflect his personality
1962	Apr 29	support act: opening night of Jerry Lee Lewis's 1st UK tour since the 1958 fiasco

Eagles

		Inducted into the Rock and Roll Hall of Fame in 1998
1946	Mar 8	Randy Meisner: bassist and singer, born in Scottsbluff, Nebraska...
		...previously with the Poor, Poco and the Stone Canyon Band
1947	Jul 19	Bernie Leadon: guitar, banjo and singer, born in Minneapolis, Minnesota...
		...previously in Dillard and Clark, and the Flying Burrito Brothers
	Jul 22	Don Henley: drummer and singer, born in Gilmer, Texas...
		...previously with Felicity, which morphed into Shiloh
	Oct 30	Timothy B Schmit: bassist and singer, born in Oakland, California...
		...previously with Poco
	Nov 20	Joe Walsh: guitarist and singer, born in Wichita, Kansas...
		...previously with the James Gang – joined in 1969 – left in 1971
1948	Nov 6	Glen Frey: guitarist and singer, born in Detroit, Michigan...
		...previously with Longbranch Pennywhistle – late 1960s duo with JD Souther:
		JD Souther went on to co-write many of the Eagles' songs

Before the Eagles

1971 Jul 12 1st time the 'Eagles' played together – as Linda Ronstadt's backing band:
Randy Meisner – Glen Frey – Bernie Leadon – Don Henley

Eagles

1972 Jun 1 released their 1st album, *Eagles* (US)
Jun 14 early gig, supporting Jethro Tull...
...Eagles:
Randy Meisner: bass and vocals – left in mid-1977
Glenn Frey: guitar, vocals and songwriter
Bernie Leadon: guitar and vocals – left at the end of 1975
Don Henley: drums, vocals and songwriter
1976 Dec 8 released *Hotel California* (US) – 1st album to feature guitarist Joe Walsh
1977 Sep 3 end of *Hotel California* tour – Timothy B Schmit replaced Randy Meisner...
...relationships were strained, Frey fist fight with Meisner earlier in the tour
1980 Jul 30 day before their notorious Long Beach gig – and the end of the band...
...Eagles:
Glen Frey – Don Henley
Don Felder: guitar and vocals – joined in 1974...
...with Felder, the original Eagles became a quintet
Joe Walsh: guitar and vocals – replaced Bernie Leaden in late 1975
Timothy B Schmit: bass, vocals
1994 May 26 day before the two-year *Hell Freezes Over* tour opened...
...Eagles:
Glen Frey – Don Henley – Don Felder – Joe Walsh – Timothy B Schmit
1999 Nov 10 *Greatest Hits 1971-1975* accredited with being the best-selling album of all time

Michael Eavis

1970 Sep 19 farmer and organiser of the 1st (and subsequent) Glastonbury festivals

Duane Eddy

Inducted into the Rock and Roll Hall of Fame in 1994
1938 Apr 26 "King of the Twang Guitar", born in Corning, New York

Thomas Edison

1955 Feb 26 45s outsold 78s for the 1st time in America – Edison started it all in 1877

The Electric Flag

1938 Oct 2 Nick Gravenites: singer, born in Chicago, Illinois...
...member of the original lineup – later in the re-formed Big Brother in 1969
1943 Jul 28 Mike Bloomfield: guitarist, born in Chicago, Illinois...
...left the Paul Butterfield Blues band to form the Electric Flag

1947 Sep 5 Buddy Miles: drummer, born in Omaha, Nebraska...
...member of the original lineup – later with Jimi Hendrix's Band of Gypsys
1967 Jun 16 Electric Flag made their debut at the *Monterey Pop Festival*
1969 Aug 19 Miles Davies recording session for Bitches Brew...
...bassist Harvey Brooks had been in the original Electric Flag lineup

Bill Elliot

vocals: Half Breed – Electric Oz Band – Splinter
1971 Jul 16 Electric Oz Band released *God Save Us* – single in support of the *OZ* trial
1974 Sep 20 Splinter, formed by Elliot, released their debut album, *The Place I Love* (UK)...
...1st album on George Harrison's Dark Horse

"Mama" Cass Elliot

Inducted into the Rock and Roll Hall of Fame in 1998 – Mamas & The Papas
singer: The Big Three – The Mugwumps – The Journeymen – The Mamas & The Papas
1941 Sep 19 born Ellen Naomi Cohen, in Baltimore, Maryland
1964 Feb 9 Elliot's links to the Mugwumps and the Lovin' Spoonful
1966 Jul 1 Mamas & The Papas sacked Michelle Phillips, replaced her with Jill Gibson
1967 Jun 16 Mamas & The Papas played the *Monterey Pop Festival*
1968 Oct 8 disastrous beginning to her solo career
1974 Jul 29 died of a heart attack: 32 years old

Royston Ellis

1961 Jul 21 beat poet: accompanied by Jimmy Page in a fusion of music and poetry...
...around this time he was also backed by several Beatles, and Shadows
1966 Jun 10 Beatles released *Paperback Writer*...
...he was an inspiration for this song and also *Polythene Pam*

Emerson, Lake & Palmer

1944 Nov 2 Keith Emerson: keyboards and singer, born in Todmorden, West Yorkshire
1947 Nov 10 Greg Lake: bassist and singer, born in Bournemouth, Dorset
1950 Mar 20 Carl Palmer: drummer, born in Birmingham, England
1970 Aug 25 debut gig...
...Emerson, Lake & Palmer:
Keith Emerson: keyboards – from the Nice
Greg Lake: bass and vocals – from King Crimson
Carl Palmer: drums – from Atomic Rooster
Aug 28 performed at the *Isle of Wight Festival*
1971 Mar 26 recorded *Pictures at an Exhibition*, live in concert

Emil and the Detectives

1949 Apr 3 Richard Thompson: guitarist and singer, born in Notting Hill, London

1949 Aug 28 Hugh Cornwell: bassist and singer born in Tufnell Park, North London...

...1964 schoolboy band, formed by Thompson and Cornwell
...band's name was inspired by the title of a 1929 book by Erich Kästner

Brian Epstein

Inducted into the Rock and Roll Hall of Fame in 2014

manager: The Beatles – Gerry and the Pacemakers – Cilla Black – The Fourmost
Billy J Kramer with The Dakotas – Tommy Quickly – The Remo Four
Cliff Bennett and the Rebel Rousers – Sounds Incorporated – The Cyrkle – PJ Proby
The Paramounts – The Moody Blues

1934 Sep 19 Beatles' manager, born in Liverpool, England – also managed other acts

1961 Mar 1 Fourmost's Cavern Club debut, as "The Four Jays" – signed to Epstein mid-1963

Oct 28 he was asked for a copy of *My Bonnie* in his NEMS record store

Nov 9 visited the Cavern's lunchtime session to see the Beatles for the 1st time

1962 Jun 6 Beatles' 1st recording session at Abbey Road

Jun 23 set up NEMS Enterprises Ltd

Oct 12 promoted Little Richard's UK rock'n'roll comeback tour – supported by Beatles

1965 Jan 29 co-promoter of PJ Proby's trouser splitting UK tour with Cilla Black

1967 Aug 27 died of an accidental overdose: 32 years old

Ahmet Ertegun

Inducted into the Rock and Roll Hall of Fame in 1987

record label owner: Atlantic – Bang

1923 Jul 31 born in Istanbul, Turkey...

...co-founded Atlantic Records in 1947
...used the name "Nugetre" for songwriting credits – Ertegun spelt backwards

1949 Nov 19 Jerry Lee Lewis performed *Drinking Wine Spo-Dee-o-Dee*...

...Stick McGhee and His Buddies 1949 single gave Atlantic an early hit

1952 Sep 8 Ray Charles's 1st recording session for Atlantic

1954 May 7 Clyde McPhatter signed to Atlantic – the birth of the Drifters

1968 Sep 27 Led Zeppelin's 1st recording session – signed to Atlantic two months later

Bob Evans and the Five Shillings

1959 Sep 26 the early Liverpool Scene – the Five Shillings morphed into the Undertakers

Everly Brothers

Inducted into the Rock and Roll Hall of Fame in 1986 (inaugural year)

1937 Feb 1 Don Everly was born in Brownie, Kentucky

1939 Jan 19 Phil Everly was born in Chicago, Illinois

1956 Feb 6 released *Keep A' Lovin' Me* (US) – recording debut, a brief spell with Columbia...

...written by Don and Phil

1957	Apr 20	released *Bye Bye Love* (US) – 1st single on Cadence and beginning of success...
		...written by Felice and Boudleaux Bryant – regular writers for the Everlys
1960	Mar 18	recorded *Cathy's Clown* – $1m deal from Warner Brothers...
		...written by Don and Phil
1961	Nov 25	Don and Phil joined the US Marine Corps
1962	Oct 13	single brother UK Everly Brothers tour – only Phil, Don had to return home
1964	Sep 16	performed on the 1st edition of *Shindig!*
1973	Jul 14	on stage bust up – parting of the ways for the two brothers

Fabian

1943	Feb 6	teen-idol, born Fabiano Anthony Forte, in Philadelphia, Pennsylvania
1959	Feb 3	replacement act to complete the ill-fated Buddy Holly tour after the plane crash

FAILED AUDITIONS AND 'LOST' ALBUMS

1946	Jan 10	Aynsley Dunbar: drummer, born in Liverpool, England...
		...lost out on the flip of a coin to become Jimi Hendrix's drummer
	Aug 23	Keith Moon: drummer, born in Wembley, London...
		...lost out to Bobby Elliott to become Shane Fenton's drummer
1956	Nov 16	Harold Jenkins (aka Conway Twitty) failed his audition at Sun Records
1960	May 10	Silver Beetles failed their audition to be Billy Fury's backing band
1962	Jan 1	Beatles failed their Decca audition – lost out to Brian Poole and the Tremeloes
	Sep 5	Keith Moon's band Mark Twain and the Strangers failed their BBC Radio audition
1963	Apr 21	Four Tops' 'lost' album, *Breaking Through*: recorded mid-1963, released in 1999
1964	Apr 9	Who failed their audition for Fontana and BBC Radio on the same day
	May 5	classic Who lineup was in place...
		...drummers Mitch Mitchell and Brian Redman lost out to Keith Moon
	Dec 2	Frank Zappa nearly laid claim to the 1st rock opera, *I was a Teen-age Malt Shop*
1965	Sep 8	Monkees might have been a very different group...
		...people who tried out unsuccessfully to become Monkees included:
		Danny Hutton – Harry Nilsson – Van Dyke Parks – Stephen Stills
1966	Apr 15	Rolling Stones' 'lost' album *Could YOU Walk on Water* surfaced as *Aftermath*
	Jun 10	Janis Joplin's 1st concert with Big Brother and the Holding Company...
		...after turning down the offer of lead singer for the 13th Floor Elevators
1967	Jan 9	Buffalo Springfield's 'lost' album *Stampede* would have been their 2nd album
	Mar 13	end of the road for the original lineup of the Spencer Davis Group...
		...Elton John failed his audition to replace Steve Winwood
	May 2	Beach Boys' 'lost' album *Smile* was abandoned – finally released in 2004
1968	Mar 9	Love's 'lost' album, *Gethsemane*: nearly the 4th album but original band imploded
	May 29	Who's 'lost' album, *Who's for Tennis*: planned as follow-up to *The Who Sell Out*

	Sep 7	Terry Reid turned down the offer to become Led Zeppelin's vocalist
1969	Jan 2	Beatles' 'lost' album, *Get Back*: produced by Glyn Johns, morphed into *Let It Be*
1971	Apr 26	Who's 'lost' album, *Lifehouse*: Pete Townshend's ambitious 2nd rock opera
1972	Feb 17	Floyd's *Dark Side of the Moon* started as *Eclipse (A Piece for Assorted Lunatics)*
1973	Oct 4	Pink Floyd's 'lost' album *Household Objects*: household objects as instruments
1974	Jun 16	end was nigh for the 1st incarnation of the Butts Band...
		...Doors nearly restarted with a new singer, ex-Audience's Howard Werth: this was not to be – Densmore and Krieger formed the Butts Band
2008	Feb 27	Eric Burdon's 'lost' album, *Mirage*: recorded in the early 1970s, released in 2008

Fairport Convention

1941	Apr 5	Dave Swarbrick: violin, born in New Malden, Surrey...
		...seminal folk-rock fiddle player, previously with Ian Campbell Folk Group ...joined Fairport Convention in 1969
1947	Jan 6	Sandy Denny: folk-rock singer and songwriter, born in Wimbledon, London...
		...duet with Robert Plant on *The Battle of Evermore*, Led Zeppelin's 4th album
1949	Apr 3	Richard Thompson: musician and songwriter, born in Notting Hill, London...
		...in Emil and the Detectives, a mid-'60s school band with Hugh Cornwell
1969	May 12	Martin Lamble died, group's van crashed returning from a gig: aged 19...
		...Thompson's girlfriend, Jeannie Franklyn, also died in the crash ...Ashley Hutchings was seriously injured
	Sep 24	Albert Hall concert to promote their forthcoming album, *Liege & Lief*...
		...singer Sandy Denny left shortly afterwards to form Fotheringay
1971	Feb 6	Richard Thompson left to pursue a solo career...
		...Fairport Convention was formed in mid-1967 with the original lineup:
		Richard Thompson: guitar, vocals and songwriter
		Shaun Frater: drums – replaced by Martin Lamble after just one gig... ...Lamble was replaced by Dave Mattacks in mid-1969
		Martin Lamble: drums– died returning from a gig in mid-1969
		Judy Dibble: singer – left in mid-1968 – replaced by Sandy Denny
		Iain Matthews: singer – left in '69 – formed Matthews' Southern Comfort
		Ashley Hutchings: bass – left in late 1969 – formed Steeleye Span... ...replaced by Dave Pegg
		Simon Nicol: guitar – left in late 1971 – formed the Albion Country Band
1978	Apr 21	Sandy Denny died from a brain haemorrhage following a fall: 31 years old

Adam Faith

singer: The Worried Men

1956	Apr 22	2i's coffee bar opened – Adam Faith played there with the Worried Men...
		...left the Worried Men for a solo career in late 1957 ...decided that he needed a stage name and changed from Terry Nelhams

1964 May 31 topped a star-studded bill at Wembley – included the Rolling Stones
1965 Mar 14 top-of-the-bill on a package tour with Sandie Shaw

Marianne Faithful

1966 Feb 4 Rolling Stones released *As Tears Go By* – 1964 hit for Faithful in the UK and US
1968 Dec 11 performed on the Rolling Stones' TV special, *Rock and Roll Circus*

Family

1942 Apr 8 Roger Chapman: singer, born in Leicester, Leicestershire...
...joined the Farinas in 1966: formed Streetwalkers after Family folded in 1973
1946 Nov 1 Rick Grech: bassist, born Richard Roman Grechko, in Bordeaux, France...
...joined the Farinas in 1965: left Family in 1969 to form Blind Faith

The Farinas morphed into Family.

1969 Jul 5 supported the Rolling Stones at the free concert in London's Hyde Park

Chris Farlowe

singer: John Henry Skiffle Group – Chris Farlowe and the Thunderbirds – Colosseum
Atomic Rooster

Chris Farlowe and the Thunderbirds, morphed from John Henry Skiffle Group in late 1950s

1940 Oct 13 Chris Farlowe was born John Henry Deighton, in Islington, London...
...disbanded the Thunderbirds in the late 1960s
1943 Jan 18 Dave Greenslade: keyboards, born in Woking, Surrey...
...member of the Thunderbirds from 1964 to '67
...went on to Gino Washington's Ram Jam Band, Colosseum and Greenslade
1950 Mar 20 Carl Palmer: drummer, born in Birmingham, England...
...member of the Thunderbirds, joined in 1966 – left in '68 to join Arthur Brown
...went on to Atomic Rooster, and Emerson, Lake & Palmer
1966 Apr 25 Neil Christian and the Crusaders gig – with guitarist Albert Lee...
...Lee was with the Crusaders when he left in 1964 to join the Thunderbirds

Chris Farlowe

1969 Jun 18 recording for Colosseum's *Valentyne Suite* – Farlowe joined before next album
1971 Mar 18 concert recorded for Colosseum *Live* LP – went on to join Atomic Rooster in '72

Leo Fender

Inducted into the Rock and Roll Hall of Fame in 1992

1909 Aug 10 guitar innovator, born near Anaheim, California

Fleetwood Mac

Inducted into the Rock and Roll Hall of Fame in 1998

1943 Jun 29 Bob Brunning: original bassist, born in Bournemouth, Dorset...
...later with Savoy Brown and his own Brunning Sunflower Blues Band

1945 Jan 25 Dave Walker: singer, born in Walsall, Staffordshire...

...joined in 1972, played on the *Penguin* and *Mystery to Me* albums
...previously with the Redcaps, Beckett, Idle Race and Savoy Brown
...made a brief appearance in Black Sabbath in 1978

Nov 26 John McVie: bassist, born in Ealing, West London...

...band's name derived from Mick Fleetwood and John McVie's names

1946 Oct 29 Peter Green: guitarist, born Peter Allen Greenbaum, in Bethnal Green, London

1967 Aug 13 debut gig – as "Peter Green's Fleetwood Mac"...

...Peter Green's Fleetwood Mac:

Peter Green: guitar – previously with John Mayall's Bluesbreakers
Mick Fleetwood: drums – previously Bo Street Runners and John Mayall
Jeremy Spencer: guitar – left in early 1971
Bob Brunning: bass

...Bob Brunning was replaced shortly afterwards by John McVie:

McVie was previously with John Mayall's Bluesbreakers

1970 May 28 original guitarist Peter Green's final gig

Sep 18 released *Kiln House* (US)...

...Fleetwood Mac:

Mick Fleetwood – John McVie
Jeremy Spencer: his last album with the band
Danny Kirwan: guitar – joined in mid-1968 – left in mid-1972
Christine McVie: vocals – joined the band in mid-1970...
...aka Christine Perfect – previously with Chicken Shack

...this was the 1st album following the departure of Peter Green

1971 Feb 15 Jeremy Spencer found God and quit the band midway through their US tour...

...Peter Green rejoined the band temporarily to complete the tour

1973 Oct 26 Bob Weston was sacked – bogus Fleetwood Mac created shortly afterwards...

...Fleetwood Mac included:

Bob Weston: guitar – replaced Danny Kirwan in 1972 – left in late 1973
Clifford Davis: manager – from the beginning until the law suit in 1974
Mick Fleetwood – friction after Weston's affair with his wife

...Bogus Fleetwood Mac: very brief lifespan in early 1974:

Elmer Gantry: vocals and guitar
Kirby Gregory: guitar
Paul Martinez: bass
John Wilkinson: keyboards
Craig Collinge: drums

...renamed afterwards to "Stretch"

1977 Jan 26 Peter Green was institutionalised for threatening his accountant with an air rifle

Herbie Flowers

bass: Blue Mink – Sky

1938 May 19 musician and songwriter, born in Isleworth, Middlesex...

...songwriter:

Grandad – Clive Dunn single in 1970 – co-written with Kenny Pickett

...session musician:

Walk on the Wild Side – signature bass riff on Lou Reed's 1973 single

...founding member of bands:

Blue Mink – formed in 1969
Sky – formed in the late 1970s – with classical guitarist John Williams

The Flying Burrito Brothers

1944 Dec 4 Chris Hillman: guitar, bass, mandolin, vocals, born in Los Angeles, California...

...previously with the Byrds

1946 Jun 3 Michael Clarke: drummer, born Michael James Dick, in Spokane, Washington...

...previously with the Byrds – joined in early 1969

Nov 5 Gram Parsons: guitar, singer, born Ingram Cecil Connor in Winter Haven, Florida

1947 Jul 19 Bernie Leadon: guitarist and singer, born in Minneapolis, Minnesota...

...joined in late 1969 – went on to become a founding member of the Eagles

Mk 1 of the Flying Burrito Brothers morphed out of the International Submarine Band in 1967.

In mid-1968 the Flying Burrito Brothers Mk 1 moved to the East Coast.

Gram Parsons left the Byrds and formed the Flying Burrito Brothers Mk 2 in mid-1968.

Two different bands, both using the same name.

1968 Jul 8 Gram Parsons left the Byrds – formed Flying Burrito Brothers shortly afterwards

1969 Jul 26 Mk 2 version of the Flying Burrito Brothers played the *Seattle Pop Festival*...

...Mk 1 lineup included:

Ian Dunlop: bass and founding member – formed in the spring of 1967
Mickey Gauvin: drums and founding member
Gram Parsons: guitar, vocals and occasional Burrito Mk 1 member...
...stayed on in the Submarine Band after Dunlop and Gauvin left

...Mk 2 lineup included:

Gram Parsons: guitar, vocals and founding member
Chris Hillman: guitar, bass, mandolin, singer and founding member
Sneaky Pete Kleinow: steel guitar and founding member

Dec 6 performed at the ill-fated Altamont festival

1970 Jun 28 performed at the *Festival Express* event in Toronto

Aug 7 performed at the *Goose Lake International Music Festival*

1973 Sep 19 Gram Parsons died of a drug overdose: 26 years old...

...roadie Phil Kaufman famously stole the body and set fire to it in the desert

Red Foley

1956 Mar 31 eleven-year-old Brenda Lee's 1st national TV appearance, Foley's *Ozark Jubilee*

1956 Dec 29 *Old Shep* charted for Elvis Presley – written and recorded by Red Foley in 1935

Wayne Fontana

singer: Wayne Fontana and the Jets – Wayne Fontana and the Mindbenders

1945 Jan 20 Eric Stewart: Mindbenders' guitarist and singer, born in Manchester, England...
...later in the post-Wayne Fontana Mindbenders and 10cc

1945 Oct 28 Wayne Fontana: singer, born Glyn Geoffrey Ellis, in Manchester, England...
...name inspired by Elvis Presley's drummer's name, DJ Fontana
...split from the Mindbenders in 1965

Wayne Fontana and the Jets

1963 Jan 26 supported the Beatles in Macclesfield...

With a change of lineup they became Wayne Fontana and the Mindbenders.

...Mindbenders: lineup included:

Eric Stewart: guitar, vocals and founding member – left in 1966
Ric Rothwell: drums and founding member

...band's name inspired by the 1963 movie title *The Mind Benders*

1963 Nov 13 supported the Rolling Stones in *The R&B Show* at Sheffield's City Hall

1964 May 31 appeared on a star-studded bill at Wembley – with Adam Faith top of the bill

1973 Jun 28 performed at the *British Re-Invasion Show* at Madison Square Garden

The Four Seasons

Inducted into the Rock and Roll Hall of Fame in 1990

The Four Lovers developed in the mid-1950s.

Bob Gaudio joined the Four Lovers just before they morphed into the Four Seasons in 1960.

1934 May 3 Frankie Valli: lead singer, born Francis Castelluccio, in Newark, New Jersey

1942 Nov 17 Bob Gaudio: keyboards, singer and songwriter, born in the Bronx, New York...
...previously a founding member of the Royal Teens

The Four Tops

Inducted into the Rock and Roll Hall of Fame in 1990

1936 Jun 6 Levi Stubbs: singer, born Levi Stubbles, in Detroit, Michigan

Came together as the Four Aims in 1954.

Renamed from "The Four Aims" to avoid confusion with the Ames Brothers.

1963 Apr 21 recording session for the 'lost' *Breaking Through* album – released in 1999

1964 Jul 10 released *Baby I Need Your Loving* – Motown debut...

...The Four Tops:

Levi Stubbs: lead singer
Abdul "Duke" Fakir

Lawrence Payton
Renaldo "Obie" Benson

...*Baby I Need Your Loving* was written by Holland – Dozier – Holland:
this trio of songwriters gave Motown many of their hit records

...Billy Davis wrote the Four Tops' 1st-ever single *Could It Be You*:
released on the Chess label in 1956

1997 Jun 20 Lawrence Payton's death brought an end to the original lineup...
...formed in 1954, this was the longest career lineup in rock'n'roll history

The Fourmost

1934 Sep 19 Brian Epstein: manager, born in Liverpool, England

Started out as the Blue Jays, became the Four Jays and morphed into the Fourmost.

Brian O'Hara: guitarist and singer...
...formed the Blue Jays in the late 1950s

Brian Redman: drummer...
...joined as the Four Jays – left in 1962

Mike Millward: guitarist and singer...
...joined the Fourmost – from the Undertakers

1961 Mar 1 as the Four Jays, debuted at Liverpool's Cavern Club

1962 Jan 1 Beatles cut *Hello Little Girl* at failed Decca audition – Fourmost single in 1963...
...Lennon and McCartney song: recorded by the Beatles but not released

1963 Aug 30 released their 1st single, *Hello Little Girl* (UK)

1964 May 5 Who's 2nd audition for Fontana...
...Brian Redman lost out to Keith Moon as the Who's new drummer

1965 Jan 29 performed on PJ Proby's infamous trouser-splitting UK tour

1966 Mar 7 Mike Millward died of leukaemia: 23 years old

1999 Jun 27 Brian O'Hara found hanged in his home: 57 years old

Peter Frampton

guitar and vocals: The Herd – Humble Pie

1950 Apr 22 born in Beckenham, Kent...
...member of the Herd from the mid-1960s to the end of the 1960s

1968 Dec 31 Small Faces gig – Frampton and Steve Marriott formed Humble Pie soon after

1976 Feb 13 released *Frampton Comes Alive!* (UK) – one of best-selling live albums of all time

Connie Francis

1938 Dec 12 singer, born Concetta Maria Franconero, in Newark, New Jersey

1957 Oct 2 recorded her 1st international hit *Who's Sorry Now*...
...released by Bob Thompson in 1923

1958 Jun 18 recorded *Stupid Cupid* – co-written by Neil Sedaka – 1st hit for Aldon Music

1974 Nov 8 raped in her hotel room

Jeannie Franklyn

1969 May 12 designer, aka "Genie the Tailor": died when Fairport Convention's van crashed

1969 Aug 29 Jack Bruce released *Songs for a Tailor* – Franklyn was the "Tailor"

Freddie and the Dreamers

1936 Nov 14 Freddie Garrity: manic lead singer, born in Manchester, England...
...covered a number of R&B classics including:
If You Gotta Make a Fool of Somebody – James Ray hit in 1961
I Understand – 1954 hit for the Four Tunes – 1961 hit for the G-Clefs

Free

1949 Dec 17 Paul Rodgers: singer, born in Middlesbrough, North of England...
...relationship with Queen started in 2004

1950 Sep 14 Paul Kossoff: guitarist, born in London, England...
...formed Back Street Crawler when Free folded in mid-1973:
band's name taken from the title of Paul Kossoff's 1973 solo album

1968 Apr 19 debut gig...
...Free:
Paul Rodgers: singer – from Brown Sugar
Paul Kossoff: guitar – from Black Cat Bones...
...band took its name from the Hoodoo good-luck charm
Simon Kirke: drums – from Black Cat Bones
Andy Fraser: bass – from John Mayall's Bluesbreakers
...band's name suggested by Alexis Korner:
taken from the name of one of his previous bands, "Free at Last"

1969 Sep 25 Alexis Korner's New Church recording session for *Both Sides*...
...included Paul Rodgers and Andy Fraser

1970 Jan 11 recorded *All Right Now* – written by Paul Rodgers and Andy Fraser

Jul 11 played at the *Tivoli Pop Festival* in Germany

1971 May 9 supported Deep Purple in Australia – Free split up for 1st time shortly afterwards

1974 Mar 8 Bad Company's debut gig – formed by Rodgers and Kirke after Free folded

1975 Nov 28 end of the road for Rod Stewart and the Faces – with bassist Tetsu Yamauchi...
...he joined Free in mid-1972 – joined the Faces in mid-'73 when Free folded

1976 Mar 19 Paul Kossoff died of drug related heart problems: 25 years old

1983 Sep 20 Ronnie Lane's UK ARMS gig – Paul Rodgers performed at US ARMS concerts

Alan Freed

Inducted into the Rock and Roll Hall of Fame in 1986 (inaugural year)

1916 May 26 New York street performer Louis Thomas Hardin, born in Marysville, Kansas...
...called himself "Moondog" – sued Freed when he started to use the name

1921 Dec 15 coined the phrase "rock'n'roll", DJ, promoter, born in Johnstown, Pennsylvania

1951	Jul 11	as "Moondog" he opened his R&B show on Radio WJW in Cleveland
1952	Mar 21	organised the 1st-ever rock'n'roll concert – ended in a near-riot
1955	May 21	*Maybellene* – recorded by Chuck Berry – co-writing credit originally with Freed
	Sep 15	*Alan Freed and his Rock'n Roll First Anniversary* gig at Brooklyn's Paramount
1956	Mar 21	appeared in the 1st rock'n'roll movie *Rock Around the Clock*
1957	Jul 19	outrage when Frankie Lymon danced with a white girl on *The Big Beat* TV show
1958	Mar 28	promoter: tour opened which featured the piano burning antics of Jerry Lee Lewis
	May 3	charged with incitement to riot after the Boston *Big Beat* show
1959	Jun 12	Moonglows concert appearance – Moonglows were discovered by Freed in '52... ...*I Just Can't Tell No Lie* – Moonglows single in 1953 – credited to Al Lance ...Al Lance: name used by Freed for writing credits – from children's names
	Nov 21	sacked by ABC – the payola scandal took hold
1965	Jan 20	died of natural causes: 43 years old

Fripp and Eno

1946	May 16	Robert Fripp: guitarist, born in Wimborne Minster, Dorset... ...previously with Giles, Giles and Fripp, founding member of King Crimson
1948	May 15	Brian Eno: keyboardist, born in Woodbridge, Suffolk... ...previously a founding member of Roxy Music
1973	Aug 4	recording session, *No Pussyfooting* album – early example of "ambient music"

The Fugs

1923	Sep 28	Tuli Kupferberg: poet and performer, born in New York, New York... ...immortalized in Allen Ginsberg's 1955 poem *Howl*
1967	Oct 21	took part in the anti-war protest that sought to levitate the Pentagon
1968	Dec 30	supported by Popcorn Blizzard in Detroit – Blizzard's lead singer was Meat Loaf
1969	Feb 22	final gig – re-formed in 1984... ...lineup included: Tuli Kupferberg: poet, vocals and founding member Ed Sanders: poet, vocals and founding member Ken Weaver: drums and founding member ...name taken from euphemism in Norman Mailer's *The Naked and the Dead* ...earlier lineups had included: Peter Stampfel: violin, vocals – joined from the Holy Modal Rounders Steve Webber: guitar, vocals – joined from the Holy Modal Rounders
	Aug 22	Radha Krishna Temple released *Hare Krishna Mantra*... ...the song was included on the Fugs' album *Tenderness Junction* in early '68
1971	Dec 13	John Sinclair freed from prison – Ed Sanders performed at the *Freedom Rally*

Bobby Fuller

vocals and guitar: Bobby Fuller Four

1942 Oct 22 born in Baytown, Texas

1959 May 18 Crickets recorded *I Fought the Law* – covered by the Bobby Fuller Four in 1966

1966 Jul 18 died in strange circumstances: 23 years old

Billy Fury

1940 Apr 17 singer, born Ron Wycherley, in Liverpool, England

1956 Nov 16 Harold Jenkins (aka Conway Twitty) failed his audition at Sun Records...

...Twitty's 1958 smash hit *It's Only Make Believe* was covered by Fury in '64

1958 Oct 1 impromptu appearance at a Marty Wilde concert

Nov 26 recorded his 1st single, *Maybe Tomorrow* – written by Billy Fury

1960 Jan 24 supported Eddie Cochran on his last UK tour

May 10 Silver Beetles failed their audition to back Billy Fury on his upcoming UK tour

May 21 released his debut album, *The Sound of Fury* (UK)...

...lineup included Andy White – played on Beatles recording of *Love Me Do*

Jul 27 headlined Larry Parnes's *Meet the Beat* summer show...

...Parnes was his manager, gave his artists descriptive stage names

1961 Apr 3 released *Halfway to Paradise* (UK) – originally by Tony Orlando

Billy Fury was originally backed by the Blue Flames and then the Tornados.

1961 Dec 2 on tour as Billy Fury and the Blue Flames...

...lineup included:

Clem Cattini: drums
Georgie Fame: keyboards

1963 Apr 30 recorded the 'live' album *We Want Billy*, with the Tornados

Aug 9 performed on UK TV's *Ready Steady Go!* debut

1983 Jan 28 died of natural causes: 42 years old

The Gamblers

1964 Apr 14 the Gamblers (Belfast) morphed into Them...

There were two other well-known bands called "The Gamblers".

The Gamblers (Los Angeles)

...in 1960 the Gamblers released their surf classic, *Moon Dawg* c/w *LSD-25*...

...lineup included:

Derry Weaver: lead guitar – wrote *Moon Dawg*
Elliot Ingber: rhythm guitar – later in the Mothers of Invention
Larry Taylor: bass – later in Canned Heat
Bruce Johnston: piano – later in the Beach Boys

...Sandy Nelson – 1st rock'n'roll drum hero but did not play on this

The Gamblers (Newcastle)

...replaced the Tornados as Billy Fury's backing group in early 1964

Marvin Gaye

Inducted into the Rock and Roll Hall of Fame in 1987

drums and vocals: The Marquees – The Moonglows

1939 Apr 2 singer and songwriter, born Marvin Pentz Gay Jr, in Washington, DC

1959 Jun 12 Moonglows concert appearance – with a new lineup including Marvin Gay...

...added the "e" to his surname when he started his solo career

1961 Aug 21 drummer: Marvelettes released their debut single, *Please Mr. Postman*

1962 Aug 16 drummer: Stevie Wonder released his 1st single, *I Call It Pretty Music*

1966 Aug 6 Miracles recorded *I Heard It Through the Grapevine* – Marvin Gaye single in '68

David Geffen

Inducted into the Rock and Roll Hall of Fame in 2010

record label owner: Asylum – Geffen

1943 Feb 21 music executive, born in Brooklyn, New York

1983 Jul 27 Neil Young issued *Everybody's Rockin'* – Geffen sued him, lack of commerciality

Generation X

1955 Nov 30 Billy Idol: guitarist and singer, born William Michael Albert Broad...

...in Stanmore, Middlesex

1976 Dec 21 played at the new Roxy Club – shortly after breaking away from Chelsea...

...lineup included:

Billy Idol: singer and founding member

...band's name from title of a book by Charles Hamblett and Jane Deverson
...both the club and the band were managed by Andy Czezowski
...Gene October: singer – formed a new version of Chelsea after Billy Idol left

Genesis

Inducted into the Rock and Roll Hall of Fame in 2010

1949 May 17 Bill Bruford: drummer, born in Sevenoaks, Kent

1950 Feb 13 Peter Gabriel: flautist and original lead singer, born in Surrey, England

Oct 2 Mike Rutherford: bassist, born in Guildford, Surrey

1951 Jan 30 Phil Collins: drummer then lead singer, born in Chiswick, London

1968 Feb 22 released their debut single, *The Silent Sun* (UK)...

...Genesis:

Chris Stewart: drums – left before the 1st album
Anthony Phillips: guitar – left in mid-1970
Peter Gabriel: lead singer and songwriter – left in 1975
Tony Banks: keyboards – long-term band member
Mike Rutherford: bass – long-term band member

...*The Silent Sun* was written by Peter Gabriel and Tony Banks

...Jonathan King signed them to Decca; produced early singles and 1st album

1969 Mar 7 released their debut album, *From Genesis to Revelation* (UK)...

...by the 1st album, drummer Chris Stewart had been replaced by John Silver
...by the 2nd album Silver had been replaced by John Mayhew
...Phil Collins brought stability to the drum stool in 1970

1972 Dec 11 American concert debut...

...Genesis:

Peter Gabriel – Tony Banks – Mike Rutherford – Phil Collins
Steve Hackett: guitar – joined late 1970 – previously with Quiet World

1976 Mar 26 Phil Collins' 1st gig as vocalist...

...touring band was augmented by drummer Bill Bruford
...Peter Gabriel left after the *Lamb Lies Down on Broadway* tour

Johnny Gentle

1960 May 10 Silver Beetles failed audition to back Billy Fury – backed singer Gentle instead

1960 Jul 27 performed on Larry Parnes's *Meet the Beat* summer show...

...Larry Parnes was also his manager
...born John Askew, Parnes liked his artists to have descriptive stage names

Lowell George

guitar and vocals: The Factory – Frank Zappa's band – Little Feet

1943 Apr 17 Roy Estrada: bassist, born in Santa Ana, California

1945 Apr 13 Lowell George was born in Hollywood, California...

...with the Factory in the mid-1960s

1969 Sep 29 producer: G.T.O.'s released their single *Circular Circulation*

1970 Dec 25 Little Feat's debut concert...

...Little Feat:

Lowell George: guitar and vocals – from Frank Zappa's band
Roy Estrada: bass and vocals – from Frank Zappa's band
Richie Hayward: drums – previously with Fraternity of Man
Bill Payne: keyboards

...band's name was inspired by a reference to Lowell George's shoe size

1979 Jun 29 died of a heart attack: 34 years old

Gerry and the Pacemakers

1934 Sep 19 Brian Epstein: manager, born in Liverpool, England...

...2nd act to be signed up, after the Beatles

1942 Sep 24 Gerry Marsden: singer and guitarist, born in Liverpool, England

1961 Oct 19 for one night only, they combined with the Beatles to form the Beatmakers...

...Gerry and the Pacemakers lineup:

Gerry Marsden: vocals and guitar
Freddy Marsden: drums – early musical association with his brother
Les McGuire: piano – joined in 1961 – played sax in the Beatmakers
Les Chadwick: bass – early association with Gerry Marsden

...Gerry Marsden started out with skiffle bands in the late 1950s

1963 Mar 14 their 1st single, *How Do You Do It*, went straight into the UK charts at #1

Aug 30 Fourmost released *Hello Little Girl* – recorded by G&P as a possible 3rd single

Oct 10 1st act in the UK to have their 1st three singles enter the charts at #1...

...3rd UK #1, *You'll Never Walk Alone*, originally in the 1945 musical *Carousel*

1973 Jun 28 performed at the *British Re-Invasion Show* at Madison Square Garden

Allen Ginsberg

1926 Jun 3 iconic beat poet, born in Newark, New Jersey

1955 Oct 7 gave the 1st reading of his beat poem *Howl*

1966 Jan 22 performed at the psychedelic multimedia *Trips Festival* in San Francisco

1967 Jan 14 participated in *A Gathering of the Tribes for a Human Be-In*

Nov 24 Beatles released *I Am the Walrus* – reputed to be a pop at Ginsberg

1969 Aug 22 Radha Krishna Temple released their single of the *Hare Krishna Mantra*...

...Ginsberg was famed for reciting the mantra since the mid-1960s

1971 Nov 17 recording session with Bob Dylan

Dec 13 John Sinclair freed from prison – Ginsberg performed at the *Freedom Rally*

1975 Oct 30 performer: Bob Dylan's *Rolling Thunder Review* tour opened

1981 May 28 Clash opened in New York – Ginsberg joined them on stage on 10 June

The Gods

1945 Aug 24 Ken Hensley: keyboardist and singer, born in Plumstead, London...

...founding member – formed in 1965 – later founding member of Uriah Heep

1947 Nov 10 Greg Lake: bassist and singer, born in Bournemouth, Dorset...

...replaced John Glascock in 1967
...later with King Crimson, and Emerson, Lake & Palmer

1948 Jan 17 Mick Taylor: guitarist, born in Barnet, Hertfordshire...

...founding member of the Gods – later with John Mayall and Rolling Stones

1979 Nov 17 John Glascock: bassist, died after major heart surgery: at the age of 28...

...founding member of the Gods – later with Chicken Shack and Jethro Tull

Gerry Goffin and Carole King

Inducted into the Rock and Roll Hall of Fame in 1990

Husband and wife songwriting team – songwriting credits included the following songs:

1936 Aug 23 Rudy Lewis: one of Drifters' lead singers, born in Philadelphia, Pennsylvania...

...*Some Kind of Wonderful* – Drifters single in 1961

1939	Feb 11	Gerry Goffin: songwriter, born in Brooklyn, New York:
		Up on the Roof – Drifters single in 1962
		Loco-Motion – Little Eva single in 1962
		Pleasant Valley Sunday – Monkees single in 1967
1942	Feb 9	Carole King: songwriter and singer, born in Brooklyn, New York
1961	Apr 3	Billy Fury released *Halfway to Paradise* as a single
1962	Jul 21	*Billboard* review for the Crystals' *He Hit Me (And it Felt Like a Kiss)*
1964	Jan 27	Vee-Jay reissued *Introducing the Beatles*, included *Chains*

Giorgio Gomelsky

manager: The Rolling Stones – The Yardbirds venue owner: Crawdaddy Club
producer: The Yardbirds – John McLaughlin record label owner: Marmalade

1934	Feb 28	manager early-Rolling Stones and Yardbirds, born in Georgia, Russia
1963	Apr 14	Beatles met the Stones for the 1st time – Gomelsky was the Stones' 1st manager
	Apr 28	Andrew Loog Oldham met the Stones – replaced Gomelsky shortly afterwards
	Jun 30	Crawdaddy Club moved to a new location – Rolling Stones were the house band
	Dec 8	recorded the Yardbirds live with Sonny Boy Williamson (II) at the Crawdaddy
1965	Mar 5	producer: Yardbirds released *For Your Love*
1969	Jan 18	producer: John McLaughlin recorded his debut album, *Extrapolation*...
		...released on Gomelsky's Marmalade Records label

Jack Good

TV producer: *Six-Five Special – Oh Boy! – Shindig!*

1957	Feb 16	produced the 1st edition of the UK's 1st pop music TV show, *Six-Five Special*
1958	Aug 29	Cliff issued *Schoolboy Crush* – Good focused on promoting the B-side, *Move It!*
1964	Sep 16	produced the 1st edition of *Shindig!*
1968	Mar 5	theatre producer of *Catch My Soul* – featuring Jerry Lee Lewis as Iago

Berry Gordy Jr

Inducted into the Rock and Roll Hall of Fame in 1988

record label owner: Tamla – Motown – Workshop Jazz

1929	Nov 28	songwriter and founder of the Motown record company, born in Detroit, Michigan
1957	Sep 8	Jackie Wilson released *Reet Petite* – written by Gordy and Billy Davis
1959	Jan 12	formed his 1st record label, Tamla...
		...1st single, Marv Johnson's *Come to Me* – written by Gordy and Johnson
	Dec 14	founded the Motown recording company
1961	Jul 24	Temptations released debut single *Oh, Mother of Mine* – signed up shortly before
1962	Jun 29	Contours released *Do You Love Me* – written by Gordy
1964	Apr 10	*Beatles' Second Album* issued, with *Money* – writers, Gordy and Janie Bradford
1966	Aug 6	decided not to release Miracles recording of *I Heard It Through the Grapevine*

Bill Graham

Inducted into the Rock and Roll Hall of Fame in 1992

venue owner: Fillmore East – Fillmore West

1931 Jan 8 concert promoter and venue owner, born Wolfgang Grajonca, in Berlin, Germany

1966 Jun 24 promoted Lenny Bruce's last-ever concerts – held at the Fillmore Auditorium

1967 Jun 21 *Summer of Love* began – a phrase later trademarked by Bill Graham

1968 Mar 8 opened the Fillmore East in New York

Mar 16 ill-fated Carousel Ballroom venture – became the Fillmore West soon afterwards

1971 May 6 announced that he was closing the Fillmore East and Fillmore West

Bobby Graham

drums: Joe Brown and the Bruvvers – The Outlaws

session drummer: claims to have played on over 15,000 titles

1940 Mar 11 born Robert Francis Neate, in Edmonton, London

1964 Feb 21 Dave Clark Five appeared on TV – but did Graham play drums on their singles?

1964 Aug 4 Kinks released *You Really Got Me* – session drummer

Grand Funk Railroad

1948 Sep 29 Mark Farner: guitarist and singer, born in Flint, Michigan...

...previously in the Pack

The Pack morphed into Grand Funk Railroad in 1969.

1972 Dec 23 ex-manager Terry Knight seized the band's equipment at a concert...

...Knight was singer with Terry Knight and the Pack – then manager for GFR

1976 Aug 9 released *Good Singin' Good Playin'* – band re-formed to work with Frank Zappa

Grateful Dead

Inducted into the Rock and Roll Hall of Fame in 1994

venue owner: Carousel Ballroom (with Jefferson Airplane)

1942 Aug 1 Jerry Garcia: Grateful Dead's guiding light, born in San Francisco, California

1947 Oct 16 Bob Weir: guitarist and singer, born in San Francisco, California

Warlocks

1965 Nov 3 1st-ever Grateful Dead recording session – as "The Emergency Crew"...

...Warlocks: lineup that became the Grateful Dead:

Jerry Garcia: guitar and vocals
Bob Weir: guitar and vocals
Pigpen McKernan: keyboards, harmonica and vocals – died early 1973
Phil Lesh: bass and vocals
Bill Kreutzmann: drums

1965 Nov 27 performed at the 1st of Ken Kesey's *Acid Tests*

Warlocks changed their name to "Grateful Dead".

1965 Dec 10 Warlocks debuted as the "Grateful Dead"

1966 Jan 22 performed at the psychedelic multimedia *Trips Festival* in San Francisco

May 19 Avalon concert bootlegged – Grateful Dead encouraged fans to record gigs

1967 Jan 14 performed at *A Gathering of the Tribes for a Human Be-In*

Jun 16 played the *Monterey Pop Festival* – refused to be on the album or in the movie

Nov 9 recent drugs bust featured in the inaugural issue of *Rolling Stone* magazine

1968 Mar 16 ill-fated Carousel Ballroom venture with Jefferson Airplane

Jun 15 upstaged by the Jeff Beck Group at New York's Fillmore East

Jul 18 Grateful Dead released 2nd LP, *Anthem of the Sun*...

...1st album with 2nd drummer, Mickey Hart

1969 Feb 27 opened four nights at the Fillmore West – recordings used for *Live Dead*...

...included two songs from lyricist Robert Hunter:

Dark Star – Grateful Dead 1968 – co-written with Jerry Garcia
St Stephen – Grateful Dead 1969 – co-written with Garcia and Phil Lesh

Aug 15 performed at the *Woodstock* festival

Dec 6 due to play at Altamont – declined because of the escalating violence

1970 May 16 supported the Jimi Hendrix Experience in Philadelphia

Jun 28 performed at the *Festival Express* event in Toronto

1971 Apr 27 performed together with the Beach Boys at the Fillmore East...

...songs performed together:

Johnny B Goode – Chuck Berry single in 1958
Okie From Muskogee – Merle Haggard single in 1969
Riot in Cell Block #9 – Robins single in 1954
Searchin' – Coasters single in 1957

...Grateful Dead:

Jerry Garcia – Bob Weir – Pigpen McKernan – Phil Lesh – Bill Kreutzmann

May 6 performed during the final concerts at the Fillmore West

1973 Jul 28 played to 600,000 people at the *Summer Jam* at Watkins Glen Raceway

1987 Jul 4 Bob Dylan and the Grateful Dead tour opened – to very mixed reviews...

...Grateful Dead:

Jerry Garcia – Bob Weir – Phil Lesh – Bill Kreutzmann
Mickey Hart: drums – joined in mid-1967 as the second drummer
Brent Mydland: keyboards – joined in 1979 – replaced Keith Godchaux

...tour resulted in the album *Dylan and the Dead*

1995 Jul 9 last-ever concert...

...Grateful Dead: a very robust lineup:

Jerry Garcia – Bob Weir – Phil Lesh – Bill Kreutzmann – Mickey Hart
Garcia – Weir – Lesh – Kreutzmann – were all members of Warlocks
Mickey Hart joined in 1967
Vince Welnick: keyboards – joined in 1990...
...Welnick was a founder of the Tubes in the early 1970s

...gig ended with two songs from lyricist Robert Hunter:

Black Muddy River – Grateful Dead 1987 – co-written with Jerry Garcia
Box of Rain – Grateful Dead 1970 – co-written with Phil Lesh
Robert Hunter: lyricist since the late 1960s

The Great Society

1965 Oct 16 performed at the 1st Family Dog dance concert at Longshoreman's Hall

Dec 10 support act when Warlocks debuted as "Grateful Dead"

1966 Oct 16 vocalist Grace Slick's debut with Jefferson Airplane – recently left Great Society

1966 Nov 3 Jefferson Airplane recorded *White Rabbit* – recorded by the Great Society in '66

G.T.O.'s

Started as Cherry Sisters, became Laurel Canyon Ballet Company and finally G.T.O.'s.

1969 Sep 29 groupies turned singers: released their single, *Circular Circulation* (US)...

...lineup included:

Pamela Des Barres: groupie, performer and founding member

...Girls Together Outrageously – formed in the late 1960s:

G.T.O.'s: where the "O" tended to stand for different things

Ernesto "Che" Guevara

1967 Oct 9 executed by the Bolivian Army – iconic hero of the Cuban Revolution...

...Guevara's image was to adorn 'a million' T-shirts for decades to come

Guitar Slim

1926 Dec 10 flamboyant blues singer, guitarist, born Eddie Jones, in Greenwood, Mississippi

1953 Oct 27 recorded *The Things That I Used to Do* – writing credit to his birth name, E Jones

1959 Feb 7 died of pneumonia: 32 years old

Arlo Guthrie

1967 Nov 9 *Alice's Restaurant* album reviewed in the 1st issue of *Rolling Stone* magazine

1969 Nov 15 sang protest songs at the anti-war *March Against Death* rally in Washington

Woody Guthrie

Inducted into the Rock and Roll Hall of Fame in 1988

guitarist, singer and songwriter: The Almanac Singers

1912 Jul 14 iconic folk singer and songwriter, born in Okemah, Oklahoma...

...prolific songwriter, with songs including:

Pretty Boy Floyd written in 1939
This Land Is Your Land written in 1940

1941 Jul 7 Almanac Singers recorded the album *Sod Buster Ballads*

1962 Mar 19 Bob Dylan released his debut album – contained the tribute, *Song to Woody*

1964 May 18 Animals recorded *House of the Rising Sun*...

...song included on the Almanac Singers' 1941 album *Sod Buster Ballads*

Bill Haley

Inducted into the Rock and Roll Hall of Fame in 1987

guitar and vocals: Bill Haley and the Saddlemen – Bill Haley and His Comets

1925 Jul 6 1st rock'n'roll superstar, born in Highland Park, Michigan

1951 Jun 14 Bill Haley and the Saddlemen recorded their cover version of *Rocket 88*...
...originally recorded by Jackie Brenston a few months earlier

1954 Apr 12 Bill Haley and His Comets recorded *(We're Gonna) Rock Around the Clock*...
...originally recorded by Sonny Dae and the Knights

Jul 10 released *Shake, Rattle and Roll* (US) – 1st hit single...
...cover of Big Joe Turner's 1954 single

1955 Mar 25 *Blackboard Jungle* movie released – opening credits had *Rock Around the Clock*

Dec 12 recorded *See You Later Alligator* – last US Top 10 hit...
...cover of Bobby Charles's self-penned 1955 single:
used his birth name for songwriting credits, Robert Charles Guidry

1956 Mar 21 appeared in the 1st rock'n'roll movie, *Rock Around the Clock*

1957 Jan 31 *Rock Around the Clock* became the UK's 1st million selling single

Feb 5 arrived in the UK for the 1st tour by an American rock'n'roll star...
...supported by the Vic Lewis Orchestra – featuring drummer Andy White:
White famously performed on the Beatles' recording of *Love Me Do*

1958 Oct 26 riot at the 1st rock'n'roll gig in Germany

1964 Oct 7 appeared in Sheffield with Manfred Mann and the Nashville Teens

1979 Nov 26 last-ever British appearance

Johnny Hallyday

1943 Jun 15 French rock'n'roll singer, born Jean-Philippe Smet, in Paris, France...
...his album *Rivière ...Ouvre ton Lit*: (released in France in 1969) featured:
Small Faces – playing together in the studio for the last time
Peter Frampton: guitar – just before setting up Humble Pie
Mick Jones: guitar – went on to form Foreigner in 1976
Glyn Johns: producer

1966 Oct 13 Jimmy Hendrix Experience's debut performance – backing Hallyday in France

John Hammond

Inducted into the Rock and Roll Hall of Fame in 1986 (inaugural year)

producer: Carolyn Hester – Bob Dylan

1961 Sep 30 producer: Bob Dylan's 1st-ever recording session, for Carolyn Hester's album

Nov 20 producer: Bob Dylan's 1st recording session for one of his own recordings

1962 Mar 19 Bob Dylan released his debut album – it became known as "Hammond's folly"

Dec 14 producer: Bob Dylan released his 1st single, *Mixed-Up Confusion*

1967 Dec 27 Leonard Cohen released his 1st album – Hammond signed Cohen to Columbia

Roy Harper

1941 Jun 12 guitarist, singer and songwriter, born in Manchester, England

1969 Jul 5 supported the Rolling Stones at the free concert in London's Hyde Park

1970 Oct 23 Led Zeppelin released *Led Zeppelin III* – with the track *Hats Off to (Roy) Harper*

1974 Feb 14 concert at the Rainbow – backed by the Intergalactic Elephant Band...

...Intergalactic Elephant Band:

Keith Moon: drums – from the Who
Jimmy Page: guitar – from Led Zeppelin
John Bonham: drums – from Led Zeppelin
Ronnie Lane: bass – ex-Small Faces/Faces
Max Middleton: keyboards – ex-Jeff Beck Group

1975 Sep 15 sang lead vocal on *Have a Cigar*, on Pink Floyd's *Wish You Were Here* album

Wee Willie Harris

1933 Mar 25 seminal British rock'n'roll singer, born in Bermondsey, London

1956 Apr 22 2i's coffee bar opened – he was a regular performer at this iconic skiffle venue

1958 Dec 27 last outing for the *Six-Five Special* – Harris was on the live 2i's special in 1957

1960 Jan 24 supported Gene Vincent just before the Eddie Cochran leg of Vincent's UK tour

Wynonie Harris

1947 Dec 28 Wynonie Harris recorded *Good Rockin' Tonight*...

...written by Roy Brown and a single from him in mid-1947

1954 Sep 22 Elvis Presley released *Good Rockin' Tonight* as his 2nd Sun single...

...influenced by Harris's version

Mike Harrison

1976 Aug 27 early Boston gig...

...disc jockey Mike Harrison coined the phrase "album oriented rock" (AOR)

Richie Havens

1941 Jan 21 singer, guitarist and songwriter, born in Brooklyn, New York

1967 Nov 4 supported by Pink Floyd – who were making their US concert debut

1969 Jun 7 supported Blind Faith at their debut concert

1972 Dec 9 performed in the orchestral performance of *Tommy* at the Rainbow

1975 May 11 performed at the *War Is Over* rally in New York's Central Park

Hawkwind

1939 Aug 19 Ginger Baker: drummer, born in Lewisham, London...

...brief stint with the band in 1980 to record the album *Levitation*

1945 Dec 24 Lemmy: bassist and singer: born Ian Kilmister, in Burslem, Stoke-on-Trent...

...previously a roadie with the Jimi Hendrix Experience

1969 Aug 29 calling themselves "Group X", Hawkwind played their 1st gig

1970 Aug 14 released their 1st album, *Hawkwind* (UK)...
...lineup included:
Dave Brock: guitar, vocals and founding member – formed mid-1969
...album produced by ex-Pretty Thing Dick Taylor

1972 Feb 13 recorded *Greasy Truckers Party* – *Silver Machine* vocals by Robert Calvert...
...Calvert: poet, lyricist and musician – with the band intermittently in the '70s

Apr 28 released *Greasy Truckers Party*

1975 May 18 Lemmy was sacked after a drugs bust on the Canadian border...
...formed his own band Motörhead shortly afterwards
...Lemmy had joined Hawkwind in mid-1971

Jimi Hendrix

Jimi Hendrix Experience inducted into the Rock and Roll Hall of Fame in 1992

guitar and vocals: The Velvetones – The Rocking Kings – The King Casuals
Bobby Taylor and the Vancouvers – Joey Dee and the Starliters – Curtis Knight and the Squires
Jimmy James and the Blue Flames – The Jimi Hendrix Experience – Gypsy Sun and Rainbows
Band of Gypsys – The Jimi Hendrix Experience (2nd incarnation)

1938 Dec 18 Chas Chandler: manager, born in Heaton, Newcastle upon Tyne...
...previously the Animals' bass player – went on to manage Slade

1942 Nov 27 Jimi Hendrix: guitarist, singer and songwriter, born in Seattle, Washington...
...Velvetones – his 1st group in 1958
...Rocking Kings – joined in 1959

1945 Dec 24 Lemmy: roadie, born Ian Kilmister, in Burslem, Stoke-on-Trent...
...roadie in 1967 – later with Hawkwind and founder of Motörhead

Dec 25 Noel Redding: bassist, born in Folkestone, Kent...
...when he formed Fat Mattress he switched back to guitar and vocals

1947 Jul 9 Mitch Mitchell: drummer, born in Ealing, London...
...founding member of the Riot Squad in the mid-1960s

Sep 5 Buddy Miles: drummer, born in Omaha, Nebraska...
...previously a founding member of the Electric Flag

1951 Feb 20 Randy California: guitar and vocals...
...born Randy Craig Wolfe, in Los Angeles, California
...nickname coined by Hendrix, in Jimmy James and the Blue Flames:
"California" taken from his home state, two Randys in the band

Before the Experience

1961 May 31 Hendrix enlisted into the US Army...
...met bassist Billy Cox and formed the King Casuals

1964 May 5 Who's 2nd Fontana audition – Mitch Mitchell tried out for drummer shortly before

1965 Apr 2 Artwoods appeared on TV – Mitchell unsuccessfully auditioned for them in 1964

Oct 15 Hendrix signed a management deal with Ed Chalpin...
...lead guitarist for Curtis Knight and the Squires at the time: formed c.1963:

Hendrix joined the Squires in 1965

...he had also played with numerous prestigious artists, including:

Jackie Wilson, Sam Cooke and Little Richard's touring bands
Tommy Chong in Bobby Taylor and the Vancouvers – brief stint c.1963
Isley Brothers' 1964 single *Testify* – session guitarist
Joey Dee and the Starliters – brief stint in 1965

1966 Apr 22 Troggs issued *Wild Thing* – Jimi set fire to his guitar playing it at Monterey in '67

The Animals had just finished their final American tour.

Hendrix had formed his own group, Jimmy James and the Blue Flames in 1966.

Chandler saw Hendrix playing in a club – became his manager and they flew to London.

1966 Oct 1 jammed on stage with Cream – shortly after arriving in London...

...played *Killing Floor* – Howlin' Wolf single in 1965
...Chas Chandler became Hendrix's manager shortly before this

The Jimi Hendrix Experience was formed.

1966 Oct 13 1st performance, supporting Johnny Hallyday in France...

...The Jimi Hendrix Experience:

Jimi Hendrix: guitar, vocals – recently relocated to the UK from the US
Noel Redding: bass – moved to bass, previously a guitarist
Mitch Mitchell: drums – from Georgie Fame and the Blue Flames

Oct 23 1st recording session

Oct 25 UK debut concert at London's Scotch of St James club

Nov 25 introduced to the UK press at the Bag O' Nails club

Dec 16 released his 1st single, *Hey Joe* (UK)...

...*Hey Joe* had history:

Billy Roberts copyrighted the song in 1962
Leaves single in late 1965
Tim Rose's 1966 version influenced Hendrix's arrangement

1967 Mar 17 released his 2nd single, *Purple Haze* (UK)...

...1st single on Kit Lambert and Chris Stamp's Track Records

Mar 31 1st time that Hendrix set fire to his guitar on stage

May 12 released his 1st album, *Are You Experienced* (UK)

Jun 16 US debut performance at the *International Monterey Pop Festival*

Jul 8 joined the Monkees' American tour as the opening act

Dec 22 performed at the *Christmas on Earth Continued* concert

1968 Feb 25 had a stimulating encounter with legendary groupie Cynthia Plaster Caster

Oct 25 released his 3rd album, *Electric Ladyland* (UK) – end of an era...

...manager Chas Chandler parted company with Hendrix

...bassist Noel Redding formed his own band, Fat Mattress:

Redding continued to play in the Experience and Fat Mattress...

...in Fat Mattress he moved back to playing guitar

...guest appearances on the album included:

Steve Winwood – Al Kooper – Dave Mason – Buddy Miles

Dec 11 Mitch Mitchell was the drummer in John Lennon's Dirty Mac...

...on the Rolling Stones' TV special, *Rock and Roll Circus*

1969 Jan 4 legendary performance of *Sunshine of Your Love* on Lulu's TV show...

...song was originally on Cream's 1967 album, *Disraeli Gears*

Jun 29 final concert for the classic lineup – Noel Redding left shortly afterwards

Aug 15 performed at the *Woodstock* festival as "Gypsy Sun and Rainbows"

1969 Dec 8 found not guilty of drug possession in Canada

Band of Gypsys

1970 Jan 28 demise of the short-lived Band of Gypsys...

...Band of Gypsys:

Jimi Hendrix: guitar and vocals
Buddy Miles: drums
Billy Cox: bass

...royalties from Hendrix's *Band of Gypsys* album went to Ed Chalpin

Hendrix re-formed the Jimi Hendrix Experience.

1970 Apr 25 opened his last US tour – then on to his final concerts...

...Jimi Hendrix Experience (2nd incarnation):

Jimi Hendrix: guitar and vocals
Billy Cox: bass
Mitch Mitchell: drums

May 16 headlined at the Temple Stadium in Philadelphia – Cactus's debut gig

1970 Aug 28 performed at the *Isle of Wight Festival*

Jimi Hendrix, the final days:

1970 Sep 12 Eric Burdon and War concert in London's Hyde Park...

...Hendrix's last performance was four days later – jamming with Eric Burdon

Sep 18 died, "inhalation of vomit ...open verdict": 27 years old

2008 Feb 27 Hendrix's song *The Story of Life*, reworked by Eric Burdon as *Mirage*...

...lyrics written on the night that Hendrix died

Herman's Hermits

1964 Feb 1 in the vanguard of the British Invasion

1973 Jun 28 performed at the *British Re-Invasion Show* at Madison Square Garden

Colin Hicks and the Cabin Boys

1937 Aug 28 Clem Cattini: drummer, born in London, England

1960 May 13 Johnny Kidd and the Pirates recorded Shakin' All Over...

...in mid-1961 the Pirates decamped to join Colin Hicks:

Alan Caddy: guitar

Brian Gregg: bass
Clem Cattini: drums

...Colin Hicks: vocals – he was Tommy Steele's brother

1964 Jun 4 drummer Jimmy Nicol stood in for the Beatles' Ringo Starr...
...member of the Cabin Boys in 1957 and '58

Abbie Hoffman

1967 Oct 21 one of the organisers of the anti-war demonstration to levitate the Pentagon
1968 Jul 15 Yippies applied for a youth festival permit for the Chicago Democratic Convention
Aug 25 arrested following the violence at the Democratic Party Convention in Chicago
1969 Mar 20 one of *Chicago 8* indicted after the riots at the 1968 Democratic Convention
1971 Dec 13 John Sinclair was freed from prison – Hoffman famously protested at Woodstock

Albert Hofmann

1968 Oct 24 LSD became illegal in America – LSD originally synthesized by Hofmann in 1938

The Hollies

Inducted into the Rock and Roll Hall of Fame in 2010

1942 Feb 2 Graham Nash: guitarist and singer, born in Blackpool, Lancashire
Apr 5 Allan Clarke: singer, born in Salford, Greater Manchester
1943 Aug 18 Carl Wayne: singer, born Colin Tooley, in Birmingham, England...
...replaced Allan Clarke in the Hollies in early 2000
...with the Move in the mid-1960s – then on to a solo career

Road to the Hollies *SEE 31 May 1964*

Started with a mid-1950s duo.

The Two Teens:

Graham Nash: guitar and vocals
Allan Clarke: singer

Nash and Clarke eventually joined Eric Haydock in the Deltas.

The Deltas' lineup included:

Allan Clarke – Graham Nash
Eric Haydock: bass

The Deltas morphed into the Hollies.

1964 Jan 1 performed on the 1st edition of UK TV's *Top of the Pops*
May 31 appeared on a star-studded bill at Wembley – with Adam Faith top of the bill...
...lineup included:

Eric Haydock: bass – left in early 1966
Graham Nash: guitar, vocals – left in late 1968
Allan Clarke: lead singer

1967 Mar 13 UK package tour with the Spencer Davis Group
1968 Dec 8 Graham Nash left to form Crosby, Stills & Nash...

...Nash was replaced by Terry Sylvester from the Swinging Blue Jeans

1969 Jun 4 Episode Six gig – in '66 Episode Six issued the single *Put Yourself in My Place...*

...written by "L Ransford" – pseudonym for the Hollies' songwriting team:

Graham Nash – Allan Clarke – Tony Hicks

1969 Sep 1 released *He Ain't Heavy....He's My Brother* (UK) – featured Elton John on piano

Buddy Holly and The Crickets

Buddy Holly

Inducted into the Rock and Roll Hall of Fame in 1986 (inaugural year)

vocals and guitar: Buddy and Bob – Buddy Holly and the Crickets

1936 Sep 7 musician and songwriter, born Charles Hardin Holley, in Lubbock, Texas...

...Holly often used the name "Charles Hardin" for his writing credits

The Crickets

Inducted into the Rock and Roll Hall of Fame in 2012

1937 May 9 Sonny Curtis: guitarist, born in Meadow, Texas

1939 Aug 31 Jerry Ivan Allison: drummer, aka Ivan, born in Hillsboro, Texas

1940 Jul 8 Joe B Mauldin: bassist, born in Lubbock, Texas

1946 Nov 1 Rick Grech: bassist, born Richard Roman Grechko, in Bordeaux, France...

...played with the Crickets in the early 1970s

Buddy Holly

1955 Feb 13 Buddy (Holley) and Bob (Montgomery) opened for Elvis in Lubbock, Texas

1956 Jan 26 Buddy Holley's 1st recording session, at Decca...

...lineup included:

Sonny Curtis: guitar – early-Holly and post-Holly Crickets
Don Guess: bass

Feb 8 Buddy Holley signed his 1st record deal with Decca – and became Buddy Holly

1956 Apr 16 Buddy Holly released his 1st single, *Blue Days - Black Nights* (US)

Buddy Holly and the Crickets

1957 Feb 25 recorded *That'll Be the Day...*

...The Crickets:

Jerry Allison: drums – Holly and post-Holly Crickets
Niki Sullivan: guitar – from the beginning to the end of 1957
Larry Welborn: bass – replaced by Mauldin after *That'll Be the Day*

...written by Buddy Holly and Jerry Allison

...recorded in Norman Petty's studios...

...Joe B Mauldin: bass – Holly and post-Holly Crickets – replaced Welborn

May 16 Buddy Holly signed to Coral – records released on both Brunswick and Coral...

...Norman Petty was now the manager of both Buddy Holly, and The Crickets

May 27 released *That'll Be the Day* – on Brunswick as "The Crickets" (US)

May 29 drummer Jerry Allison used his knees rather than his drum kit for *Everyday*...
...written by Buddy Holly

Aug 12 Decca released Buddy Holly's earlier solo version of *That'll Be the Day* (US)

Sep 20 released *Peggy Sue* on Coral – 1st single to be credited to "Buddy Holly" (US)...
...Peggy Sue was Jerry Allison's girlfriend

Nov 27 released their 1st album, *The Chirping Crickets* – credited to "The Crickets" (US)

1958 Mar 1 opening night of their UK tour – as a trio of Holly, Allison and Mauldin

Mar 28 US tour opened – featured the piano burning antics of Jerry Lee Lewis

May 3 performed on Alan Freed's *Big Beat* show – ended in the infamous "Boston Riot"

Jul 5 Johnny O'Keefe released *The Wild One*...
...covered by Jerry Allison, as "Ivan", in 1958

Jul 22 Jerry Allison married Peggy Sue

Oct 21 Buddy Holly's final session in the recording studio – famous string recordings

Oct 28 made one of their last appearances together, on TV's *American Bandstand*...
...Holly split with Norman Petty shortly afterwards
...Crickets stayed with Petty – Holly became a solo act

1958 Nov 5 released *Heartbeat* – final Buddy Holly and the Crickets single (US)

Buddy Holly, after parting with the Crickets.

1959 Jan 5 issued *It Doesn't Matter Anymore* (US) – 1st single after parting with the Crickets

Jan 23 Buddy Holly's ill-fated *Winter Dance Party* tour opened in Milwaukee...
...Buddy Holly's backing group:

Tommy Allsup: guitar
Waylon Jennings: bass
Carl Bunch: drums – hospitalised with frostbite, missed the plane crash

Feb 3 Buddy Holly died in a plane crash: 22 years old...
...Tommy Allsup gave up his seat on the plane for Ritchie Valens
...Waylon Jennings gave up his seat on the plane for the Big Bopper

1959 Feb 5 Eddie Cochran recorded his tribute, *Three Stars* – Holly, Valens and Big Bopper

The Crickets, after Buddy Holly.

1959 May 18 recorded *I Fought the Law*...
...The Crickets:

Sonny Curtis: lead guitar
Joe B Mauldin: bass
Jerry Allison: drums
Earl Sinks: rhythm guitar and vocals

...written by Sonny Curtis
...covered by:

Bobby Fuller single in 1964
Bobby Fuller Four single in 1966
Clash in 1979 – on *The Cost of Living* EP

1960 Jan 8 Jerry Allison and Sonny Curtis played at Eddie Cochran's final recording session

Dec 5 released their 1st post-Holly album, *In Style with the Crickets*

1964 Feb 21 Rolling Stones released the Buddy Holly penned *Not Fade Away* as a single...

...B-side of *Oh Boy* in 1957

1965 Jun 14 Beatles released *Beatles VI*, included the Buddy Holly penned *Words of Love*...

...single from Holly in 1957

The Holy Modal Rounders

1964 Jan 17 2nd and last recording session for their debut album, *The Holy Modal Rounders*...

...The Holy Modal Rounders:

Peter Stampfel: violin and vocals – duo formed in the early 1960s
Steve Weber: guitar and vocals – duo teamed up with the Fugs in 1965

John Lee Hooker

Inducted into the Rock and Roll Hall of Fame in 1991

1917 Aug 22 blues guitarist, singer and songwriter, born near Clarksdale, Mississippi...

...pseudonyms used for recording included:

"Delta John" – "John Lee Booker" – "John Lee Cooker" – "Texas Slim"
"Birmingham Sam" – "Johnny Lee" – "Little Pork Chops" and many more

...Hooker penned songs much favoured by blues revival groups in the 1960s:

Boogie Chillun – released as a single by Hooker in 1948 and 1959
Crawlin Kingsnake – Hooker single in 1949 and 1959

1961 Apr 11 Bob Dylan played his 1st major gig – as the supporting act for Hooker

1963 Sep 15 *Boom Boom* – recorded by the Animals...

...written by Hooker and a single from him in mid-1962

1968 Nov 9 same bill as Led Zeppelin – who were using that name for the 1st time

John "Hoppy" Hopkins

venue owner: UFO

1967 Jul 24 ad in *Times* newspaper calling for pot to be legal – following jailing of Hopkins

1967 Sep 29 final gig at London's 1st psychedelic club, UFO – co-founded by Hopkins in 1966

Nicky Hopkins

keyboards: Screaming Lord Sutch and the Savages – Cliff Bennett and the Rebel Rousers
Cyril Davies's Rhythm and Blues All Stars – The Rolling Stones (touring and studio)

1944 Feb 24 keyboard player and session musician, born in Perivale, London...

...session work included:

Truth – album from the Jeff Beck Group in 1968
Beck-Ola – album from the Jeff Beck Group in 1969
Their Satanic Majesties Request – 1967 Rolling Stones album
Let It Bleed – 1969 Rolling Stones album
My Generation – debut album from the Who in 1965

1962	Jun 25	Screaming Lord Sutch gig – left a month earlier to join Cliff Bennett's band
1963	Jan 16	early Cyril Davies gig – original pianist with Davies's R&B All Stars
1966	May 16	Jeff Beck recorded *Beck's Bolero*
1969	Sep 29	G.T.O.'s released *Circular Circulation* – played on the album *Permanent Damage*
1971	Mar 4	Rolling Stones' *Goodbye to Great Britain* tour opened
1972	May 12	Rolling Stones released *Exile on Main Street*

Johnny Horton

1960 Nov 5 died in an automobile accident: 35 years old...
...eerie similarities with Hank Williams's death

Howlin' Wolf

Inducted into the Rock and Roll Hall of Fame in 1991

1910 Jun 10 blues guitarist, singer, born Chester Arthur Burnett, in West Point, Mississippi...
...songwriting credits included:
Smokestack Lightning – single in 1956
Back Door Man – single in 1961
Killing Floor – single in 1965

1961 Nov 24 arrived in the UK for his 1st British tour

Howlin' Wolf songs covered by others included:

1964 Nov 13 Rolling Stones released *Little Red Rooster* as a single...
...written by Willie Dixon – Howlin' Wolf single, *The Red Rooster* in 1961

1969 Oct 31 Led Zeppelin released *The Lemon Song* on their album *Led Zeppelin II*...
...Howlin' Wolf sued for similarity with his song, *Killing Floor*

Humble Pie

1947 Jan 30 Steve Marriott: singer and guitarist, born in Bow, London...
...founding member – from Small Faces

Oct 23 Greg Ridley: bassist, born in Carlisle, England...
...founding member – from Spooky Tooth

1949 Sep 5 Dave "Clem" Clempson: guitarist, born in Tamworth, Staffordshire...
...replaced Peter Frampton in 1971 – from Colosseum

1950 Apr 22 Peter Frampton: guitarist and singer, born in Beckenham, Kent...
...founding member – from the Herd

1968 Dec 31 Steve Marriott stormed off during Small Faces gig – Pie formed soon afterwards

Engelbert Humperdinck

1967 Mar 31 1st time that Hendrix set fire to his guitar on stage – also on the bill that night

1967 Apr 8 6th week at #1 for *Release Me*...
...broke the Beatles' run of 11 consecutive UK #1s...
...cover of Jimmy Heap's 1954 country hit and Ester Phillips's 1962 hit
...Gerry Dorsey took his stage name from the 19th-century German composer

Dave Hunt R&B Band

1941 Jun 2 Charlie Watts: drummer, born in London, England...
...occasional drummer in 1962 – later in the Rolling Stones

1944 Jun 21 Ray Davies: guitarist, born in Muswell Hill, London...
...brief spell as guitarist in early 1963 – later in the Kinks

1963 Jun 30 Crawdaddy Club reopened – with the Rolling Stones as the house band...
...Dave Hunt R&B Band was the house band before the Stones

Idle Race

1945 Jan 25 Dave Walker: singer, born in Walsall, Staffordshire...
...replaced Jeff Lynne in 1970

1947 Dec 30 Jeff Lynne: guitarist and singer, born in Birmingham, England...
...joined the Nightriders after the name changed from "Mike Sheridan's Lot"

1966 Jan 17 Move formed from three Birmingham bands...
...Roy Wood had been in Mike Sheridan and the Nightriders:
the remaining Nightriders morphed into Idle Race: including...
...Jeff Lynne: guitar and vocals:
left the Idle Race in 1970 to join the Move

Frank Ifield

1937 Nov 30 pop singer, but very sought out by Beatles fans, born in Coventry, West Midlands

1962 Oct 13 support act on the single brother UK Everly Brothers tour

The Incredible String Band

1966 Nov 4 1st gig outside of Scotland – support act for Tom Paxton and Judy Collins...
...the band started out as a folk duo:
Robin Williamson
Clive Palmer
...became a trio: The Incredible String Band:
Robin Williamson
Clive Palmer – left after their eponymous debut album
Mike Heron
...The Incredible String Band: duo, before developing into a full band:
Robin Williamson – with the band until it folded in 1974
Mike Heron – with the band until it folded in 1974

Iron Butterfly

1968 Jun 14 released the album, *In-A-Gadda-Da-Vida* (US)...
...title track written by keyboardist Doug Ingle – accredited with deriving the title

1969 Aug 15 performed at the *Woodstock* festival

The Isley Brothers

		Inducted into the Rock and Roll Hall of Fame in 1992
1961	Feb 23	Top Notes recorded *Twist and Shout* – hit for the Isley Brothers in 1962
1965	Oct 15	Jimi Hendrix signed a management deal with Ed Chalpin...
		...Jimi Hendrix had previously played on their 1964 single *Testify*

The Jam

1958	May 25	Paul Weller, singer, guitarist and songwriter, born in Woking, Surrey
1977	May 1	Clash's UK *White Riot* tour opened – Jam left the tour after the gig on 9 May
1977	May 6	released their 1st album, *In the City* (UK)...
		...The Jam:
		Paul Weller: guitar and vocals – formed in 1972 Bruce Foxton: bass Rick Buckler: drums
		...Paul Weller wrote most of the material on the album

Elmore James

		Inducted into the Rock and Roll Hall of Fame in 1992
1918	Jan 27	blues guitarist, singer, songwriter, born Elmore Brooks, in Richland, Mississippi
1936	Nov 23	Robert Johnson recorded *I Believe I'll Dust My Broom* – James single in 1951
1951	Aug 5	recorded *Dust My Broom* – as Elmo James
1962	Apr 7	Brian Jones met Mick and Keith – played *Dust My Blues*, James single in 1955

Etta James

		Inducted into the Rock and Roll Hall of Fame in 1993
1938	Jan 25	blues singer, born Jamesetta Hawkins, in Los Angeles, California
1954	Apr 10	Midnighters released *Work with Me Annie*...
		...written by Etta James and Johnny Otis ...*The Wallflower* was Etta James's 1955 answer song to *Work with Me Annie*

Jan and Dean

1940	Mar 10	Dean Torrence was born in Los Angeles, California...
		...with Jan Berry, they were the highly successful surf-duo Jan and Dean
		...Jan and Dean's backing musicians variously included:
		Sandy Nelson: drums – in an early Jan and Dean backing band
		Bruce Johnston – went on to join the Beach Boys
1966	Apr 12	Jan was badly injured when he crashed his Stingray near Dead Man's Curve...
		...*Dead Man's Curve* was a Jan and Dean single in 1964:
		songwriters included Jan Berry and the Beach Boys' Brian Wilson

Jay and the Americans

1938	Nov 2	Jay Black: lead singer, born David Blatt, in New York...
		...replaced Jay Traynor, who left in 1962 after their 1st hit, *She Cried*

1964 Feb 11 supported the Beatles at their 1st American concert

Jefferson Airplane

Inducted into the Rock and Roll Hall of Fame in 1996

venue owners: Carousel Ballroom (with the Grateful Dead)

1939 Oct 30 Grace Slick: singer, born Grace Barnett Wing, in Chicago, Illinois...
...previously with the Great Society

1940 Dec 23 Jorma Kaukonen: guitarist and singer, born in Washington, DC

1941 Mar 17 Paul Kantner: guitarist, born in San Francisco, California

1942 Jan 30 Marty Balin: singer, born Martyn Buchwald, in Cincinnati, Ohio...
...joined Jefferson Starship on a permanent basis in 1975

1944 Apr 13 Jack Casady: bassist, born in Washington, DC

1946 Apr 18 Skip Spence: drummer, born in Windsor, Ontario, Canada...
...left after the 1st album, moved to guitar and formed Moby Grape

1965 Aug 13 debut gig
...Jefferson Airplane:

Bob Harvey: bass – replaced shortly afterwards by Jack Casady
Jerry Peloquin: drums – replaced shortly afterwards by Skip Spence
Marty Balin: vocals – left in early 1971
Signe Anderson: vocals – left in late 1966 – replaced by Grace Slick
Jorma Kaukonen: guitar – formed Hot Tuna with Casady in 1969
Paul Kantner: guitar and vocals – founded Jefferson Starship

...Jack Casady: bass – joined shortly after this debut gig – formed Hot Tuna
...Skip Spence: drums – joined soon after gig – left after 1st album, *Takes Off*

Oct 16 performed at the 1st Family Dog dance concert at Longshoreman's Hall

Dec 10 support act when Warlocks debuted as "Grateful Dead"

1966 Oct 16 Grace Slick replaced Signe Toly Anderson as vocalist...
...drummer was Spencer Dryden – replaced Skip Spence – left in early 1970

Nov 3 recorded *White Rabbit* for their 2nd album, *Surrealistic Pillow*...
...written by Grace Slick, she originally recorded it with the Great Society 1966

Nov 25 Moby Grape's 1st gig, supporting Jefferson Airplane...
...Skip Spence had recently left Jefferson Airplane to form Moby Grape

1967 Jan 14 performed at *A Gathering of the Tribes for a Human Be-In*

Jun 10 played the *Fantasy Fair and Magic Mountain Music Festival*

Jun 16 played the *Monterey Pop Festival*

1968 Mar 16 ill-fated Carousel Ballroom venture with Grateful Dead

1969 Aug 15 performed at the *Woodstock* festival

Dec 6 performed at the ill-fated Altamont festival...
...Marty Balin was knocked out by a Hells Angel

1971 May 6 performed during the final concerts at Fillmore West – Hot Tuna also there...

...Hot Tuna was formed by Kaukonen and Casady in mid-1969:

they played in both bands – continued with Tuna after Airplane folded

1972 Aug 21 riot at their concert in Akron, Ohio – Grace Slick was arrested

1972 Sep 21 final performances, the 1st of two nights at San Francisco's Winterland...

...Jefferson Airplane:

Jorma Kaukonen – Paul Kantner – Jack Casady – Grace Slick
Papa John Creach: violin – joined in late 1970
John Barbata: drums – ex-Turtles, joined in 1972
David Freiberg: vocals – ex-Quicksilver Messenger Service, joined 1972

Jorma Kaukonen and Jack Casady continued with Hot Tuna.

The others re-formed, as the more mainstream Jefferson Starship.

1974 Mar 19 debut gig with the new "Jefferson Starship" name...

...Jefferson Starship:

Grace Slick: singer – from Jefferson Airplane
Paul Kantner: guitar and vocals – from Jefferson Airplane
John Barbata: drums – from the late Jefferson Airplane lineup
David Freiberg: vocals and keyboards – from the late Airplane lineup
Papa John Creach: violin – joined Jefferson Airplane in late 1970
Craig Chaquico: guitar
Peter Kaukonen: bass

1979 Nov 12 Marty Balin's rock opera, *Rock Justice*, opened

Jethro Tull

1943 Apr 7 Mick Abrahams: guitarist and singer, born in Luton, Bedfordshire

1946 Nov 17 Martin Barre: guitarist, born in Birmingham, England...

...left Gethsemane to replace Mick Abrahams in late 1968

1947 Aug 10 Ian Anderson: musician and songwriter, born in Dunfermline, Scotland

1948 Feb 19 Tony Iommi: guitarist, born in Birmingham, England...

...had a brief stay with Jethro Tull before Martin Barre joined

1948 Dec 13 David O'List: guitarist, born in Chiswick, London...

...played with Tull between their 1st and 2nd albums

Final lineup of the John Evan Band became Jethro Tull.

1968 Oct 25 released their debut album, *This Was*...

...Jethro Tull:

Mick Abrahams: guitar and vocals...

...left after the 1st album to form Blodwyn Pig

Glen Cornick: bass – left in late 1970 and formed Wild Turkey
Clive Bunker: drums – left in mid-1971 and formed Jude
Ian Anderson: singer and multi-instrumentalist – long-term member

...band's name inspired by the 18th-century agriculturist

Dec 11 performed on the Rolling Stones' TV special, *Rock and Roll Circus*...
...featured guitarist Tony Iommi, in a brief stint away from Earth

1970 Aug 7 performed at the *Goose Lake International Music Festival*

Aug 28 performed at the *Isle of Wight Festival*

Sep 19 Ian Anderson performed at the 1st Glastonbury festival

1972 Jun 14 supported by the Eagles in Oklahoma City

1979 Nov 17 bassist John Glascock died after major heart surgery: at the age of 28...
...previously with the Gods and Chicken Shack
...joined Tull in 1975 – replaced by Dave Pegg

Elton John

Inducted into the Rock and Roll Hall of Fame in 1994

singer and pianist: Bluesology

1947 Mar 25 singer and composer, born Reginald Kenneth Dwight, in Pinner, Middlesex...
...stage name derived from:
Bluesology guys: saxophonist Elton Dean and singer Long John Baldry

1967 Mar 13 failed an audition to replace Steve Winwood in the Spencer Davis Group

Jun 17 met Bernie Taupin through an ad in the *New Musical Express*

1969 Sep 1 session pianist: Hollies released *He Ain't Heavy....He's My Brother*

1970 Apr 21 debut solo concert performance – supporting T.Rex

1974 Nov 15 released *Lucy in the Sky with Diamonds* (UK) – featured John Lennon...
...cover of a Beatles song from the 1967 album, *Sgt Pepper*

1974 Nov 28 John Lennon's final concert appearance – on stage with Elton John

Little Willie John

Inducted into the Rock and Roll Hall of Fame in 1996

1968 May 26 R&B singer, died in prison: 30 years old...
...songwriting credits included *Leave My Kitten Alone*:
Little Willie John single in 1959
written by Little Willie John, Titus Turner and James McDougal
Beatles' version finally available on *Anthology 1* in 1995
...songs covered by others included *Fever*:
Little Willie John single in 1956
Peggy Lee's cover was an international hit in 1958

John's Children

1947 Sep 30 Marc Bolan: guitarist, born Mark Feld, aka Toby Tyler, in Hackney, London

1967 Apr 12 end of their infamous German tour supporting the Who...
...lineup included:
Chris Townson: drums – founding member of the Silence
Marc Bolan: guitar – left to form Tyrannosaurus Rex in late 1967

	Apr 29	performed at the 14-Hour *Technicolor Dream*
	May 24	released *Desdemona* (UK) – 1st single to feature guitarist Marc Bolan
1967	Jul 14	released *Come and Play with Me in the Garden* (UK) – Bolan left shortly after

Glyn Johns

Inducted into the Rock and Roll Hall of Fame in 2012

engineer and producer: The Rolling Stones – Led Zeppelin – Eagles – The Who – The Beatles
Eric Clapton

1942	Feb 15	record producer and engineer, born in Epsom, Surrey
1963	Mar 11	producer: Rolling Stones demo recording session at IBC Studios
1968	Sep 27	engineer: Led Zeppelin's 1st recording session
1969	Jan 2	work started on the Beatles' *Get Back* – Johns produced the original album
1970	Mar 23	Phil Spector began work on *Get Back*, to turn it into the *Let It Be* album

Robert Johnson

Inducted into the Rock and Roll Hall of Fame in 1986 (inaugural year)

1911	May 8	iconic blues guitarist, singer and songwriter, born in Hazlehurst, Mississippi

Only had two recording sessions, San Antonio and Dallas.

1936	Nov 23	1st day of the three-day San Antonio recording sessions – total songs recorded:
		Kind Hearted Woman Blues – I Believe I'll Dust My Broom – Walking Blues
		Last Fair Deal Gone Down – Sweet Home Chicago – Terraplane Blues
		If I Had Possession Over Judgment Day – Cross Road Blues
		Rambling on My Mind – Dead Shrimp Blues – They're Red Hot
		Preaching Blues – When You Got a Good Friend – 32-20 Blues
		Phonograph Blues – Come on In My Kitchen
1937	Jun 19	1st day of the two-day Dallas recording sessions – total songs recorded:
		Stones in My Passway – I'm a Steady Rollin' Man – From Four Till Late
		Malted Milk – Little Queen of Spades – Me and the Devil Blues
		Traveling Riverside Blues – Honeymoon Blues – Love in Vain
		Milkcow's Calf Blues – Hellhound on My Trail – Drunken Hearted Man
		Stop Breakin' Down Blues
1938	Aug 16	died, supposedly poisoned by a jealous husband: 27 years old...
		...an early member of the "27 Club"

Bruce Johnston

piano and vocals: Jan and Dean's backing band – The Gamblers – The Beach Boys

1959	Jul 15	session pianist: Sandy Nelson recorded his 1st single, *Teen Beat*
1964	Apr 14	played piano on the Gamblers' 1960 single, *Moon Dawg c/w LSD-25*
1965	Apr 9	replaced Glen Campbell in Beach Boys – then became a full member of the band
1971	Apr 27	Beach Boys performed together with Grateful Dead at the Fillmore East

Paul Jones

vocals and harmonica: Thunder Odin and the Big Secret – Alexis Korner's Blues Incorporated
Manfred Mann – Eric Clapton and the Powerhouse – The Blues Band

1942 Feb 24 born Paul Pond, in Portsmouth, Hampshire...
...in Thunder Odin and the Big Secret, with future Rolling Stone Brian Jones
...formed the Blues Band in 1979

1962 Apr 7 Ealing Club gig, as the singer with Alexis Korner's Blues Incorporated

1963 Jan 11 Rolling Stones: Stones that kept right on rolling

1964 Jan 10 Manfred Mann issued *5-4-3-2-1* – co-written with Manfred Mann and Mike Hugg

1966 Apr 15 Manfred Mann released *Pretty Flamingo* – last single to feature Jones

Jun 1 played harmonica with Eric Clapton and the Powerhouse on *What's Shakin'*...
...included the song, *I Want to Know* – writing credit to "S MacLeod":
Paul Jones was married to Sheila MacLeod at the time

Dec 23 appeared on the final *Ready Steady Go!* TV show

1967 Mar 13 UK package tour with the Spencer Davis Group

1968 Jan 31 end of the ill-fated tour of Australia and New Zealand, supporting the Who

Janis Joplin

Inducted into the Rock and Roll Hall of Fame in 1995

singer: The Waller Creek Boys – Big Brother and the Holding Company – Kozmic Blues Band

1926 May 21 Albert Grossman: manager, born in Chicago, Illinois

1937 Sep 26 Bessie Smith: blues singer, died in a car crash: 43 years old...
...in 1970 Joplin funded a headstone for Smith's unmarked grave

Big Brother and the Holding Company: lineup included:

1938 Oct 2 Nick Gravenites: singer and songwriter, born in Chicago, Illinois...
...joined the re-formed band in 1969 – previously in the Electric Flag

1941 Dec 18 Sam Andrew: guitarist and founding member, born in Taft, California...
...left with Janis Joplin in 1968 to form the Kozmic Blues Band

1943 Jan 19 Janis Joplin was born in Port Arthur, Texas...
...Waller Creek Boys: Austin, Texas based group, Joplin was their singer '62

Big Brother and the Holding Company

1965 Jun 21 Red Dog Saloon opened – Big Brother became the club's house band in 1966

1966 Jan 22 performed at the psychedelic multimedia *Trips Festival* in San Francisco

Feb 10 13th Floor Elevators gig – Joplin turned down their offer of lead singer soon after

Jun 10 Janis Joplin's 1st gig as lead vocalist with Big Brother and the Holding Company

1967 Jun 16 played the *Monterey Pop Festival* – called back for a repeat performance

Nov 4 supported by Pink Floyd – who were making their American concert debut

1968 Mar 8 performed on the opening night at New York's Fillmore East

1968 Dec 1 Joplin's last performance with Big Brother and the Holding Company...

...Joplin formed the Kozmic Blues Band shortly afterwards: lineup included:
Sam Andrew: guitar – left Big Brother with Joplin

Janis Joplin

1969 Aug 15 performed at the *Woodstock* festival
Nov 16 arrested at a gig for using "vulgar and indecent language"
Nov 27 duet with Tina Turner at the Rolling Stones' Madison Square Garden gig
1970 Jun 28 performed at the *Festival Express* event in Toronto
Oct 3 Joplin's final recording session for *Pearl*...
...included *Cry Baby*, cover of Garnet Mimms and the Enchanters' 1963 hit
...Joplin died before recording the lyrics for *Buried Alive in the Blues*:
written by Nick Gravenites
1970 Oct 4 died of a heroin overdose: 27 years old

Judas Priest

1951 Aug 25 Rob Halford: singer, born in the West Midlands, England...
...previously with Hiroshima before joining Judas Priest in 1973
Oct 27 KK Downing: guitarist, born in West Bromwich, England...
...founding member when Judas Priest was formed in 1970
1978 Feb 10 released the album *Stained Glass* (UK) – subject of a suicide lawsuit in 1985
1985 Dec 23 lawsuit following fans' suicide pact, citing Priest's *Stained Glass* album...
...specifically the song, *Better By You, Better Than Me*:
originally on Spooky Tooth's 1969 album *Spooky Two*

Ken Kesey

1935 Sep 17 writer, created the Merry Pranksters and "acid tests", born in La Junta, Colorado

Ken Kesey and His Merry Pranksters

1965 Nov 27 held the 1st of his *Acid Test* events
1966 Jan 22 *Acid Test* at the psychedelic multimedia *Trips Festival* in San Francisco

KGB

Formed in 1975, folded in 1976

1943 Jul 28 Mike Bloomfield: guitarist, born in Chicago, Illinois...
...previously with Paul Butterfield Blues Band and Electric Flag
1946 Nov 1 Rick Grech: bassist, born Richard Roman Grechko, in Bordeaux, France...
...previously with Family and Blind Faith
1946 Dec 15 Carmine Appice: drums and vocals, born in Staten Island, New York...
...founding member of Vanilla Fudge, Cactus, and Beck, Bogert & Appice

Johnny Kidd

singer: The Five Nutters – Johnny Kidd and the Pirates – Johnny Kidd and the New Pirates

1935 Dec 23 Johnny Kidd was born Frederick Heath, in Willesden, London

1937 Aug 28 Clem Cattini: drummer, born in London, England...
...previously with Larry Parnes's Beat Boys/Blue Flames

1945 Nov 3 Nick Simper: bassist, born in Norwood Green, Middlesex...
...joined the New Pirates in mid-1966 – went on to form Deep Purple

Johnny Kidd's group the Five Nutters morphed into Johnny Kidd and the Pirates.

1959 Apr 18 1st recording session, recorded *Please Don't Touch* and *Growl*...
...both written by Johnny Kidd and coupled as his 1st single
...*Please Don't Touch* was released as a single by the Bachelors in early 1959
(The Bachelors: the English duo, not the Irish trio)

1960 May 13 recorded *Shakin' All Over* – written by Johnny Kidd...
...lineup included:
Johnny Kidd: lead singer – morphed from his groups in the late 1950s
Alan Caddy: guitar – left mid-1961 to join Colin Hicks and the Cabin Boys
Brian Gregg: bass – left mid-1961 to join Colin Hicks and the Cabin Boys
Clem Cattini: drums – left mid-1961 for Colin Hicks and the Cabin Boys
...Mike West: guitar – left before the recording of *Shakin' All Over*
...covered by the Who on their legendary 1970 album, *Live at Leeds*

1962 Apr 29 support act: opening night of Jerry Lee Lewis's 1st UK tour since the 1958 fiasco

Johnny Kidd and the New Pirates

1966 Oct 7 Johnny Kidd died in an automobile accident: 30 years old...
...Nick Simper was also injured in the crash

The band continued as "The Pirates" after Johnny Kidd's death.

BB King

Inducted into the Rock and Roll Hall of Fame in 1987

1925 Sep 16 influential blues guitarist and singer, born in Itta Bena, Mississippi

1969 Nov 7 supported the Rolling Stones on their US tour

Nov 16 support act: Janis Joplin arrested at gig for using "vulgar and indecent language"

1969 Nov 27 support act: Rolling Stones' Madison Square Garden gig

King Crimson

1946 May 16 Robert Fripp: guitarist, born in Wimborne Minster, Dorset

1947 Nov 10 Greg Lake: bassist and singer, born in Bournemouth, Dorset...
...previously with the Gods

1949 May 17 Bill Bruford: drummer, born in Sevenoaks, Kent

Giles, Giles and Fripp extended their lineup, before morphing into King Crimson.

...Giles, Giles and Fripp:
Peter Giles: bass – joined Crimson by 2nd LP, *In the Wake of Poseidon*
Mike Giles: drums and vocals – original King Crimson lineup
Robert Fripp: guitar – original King Crimson lineup

...Giles, Giles and Fripp lineup was extended to include:

Greg Lake: bass and vocals – replaced Peter Giles in expanded lineup
Ian McDonald: multi-instrumentalist – original King Crimson lineup
Judy Dyble: singer – short stay – left to form Trader Horne

King Crimson

1969 Jul 5 supported the Rolling Stones at the free concert in London's Hyde Park

Oct 10 released their 1st album, *In the Court of the Crimson King* (UK)...

...King Crimson: after morphing from the extended Giles, Giles and Fripp:

Robert Fripp: guitar and keyboards – long-term member
Mike Giles: drums – left after the 2nd album
Ian McDonald: multi-instrumentalist – left after the 1st album
Greg Lake: bass and vocals – left mid-1970 to form ELP
Pete Sinfield: lyricist

...Peter Giles: bass – replaced Greg Lake, joined before the 2nd album

1972 Feb 11 opened their US tour...

...lineup included: Robert Fripp and:

Mel Collins: saxophone
Ian Wallace: drums
Boz Burrell: bass and vocals

...at the tour's end these three members left to join Alexis Korner's Snape

...this lineup was responsible for the 4th album, *Islands*:

this was the last album to feature the work of lyricist Pete Sinfield

...American tour was captured on the live album *Earthbound*

1973 Mar 23 released *Larks' Tongues in Aspic* (UK) – Robert Fripp plus a new lineup...

...lineup included:

John Wetton: bass and vocals – from Family, replaced Boz Burrell
Bill Bruford: drums – from Yes, replaced Ian Wallace
Richard Palmer-James: lyricist – replaced Pete Sinfield

1973 Aug 4 Fripp and Eno recording session for the *No Pussyfooting* album...

...early example of "ambient music"

King Curtis

Inducted into the Rock and Roll Hall of Fame in 2000

1934 Feb 7 legendary session saxophonist, born Curtis Ousley, in Fort Worth, Texas...

...session recordings included:

Reminiscing – posthumous Buddy Holly single in '62 – written by Curtis
Live at the Harlem Square Club 1963 – Sam Cooke album

...own recordings included the self-penned:

Soul Twist – US hit for King Curtis and the Noble Knights in 1962

1958 Mar 17 session saxophonist: Coasters recorded *Yakety Yak*

Dec 11 session saxophonist: Coasters recorded *Charlie Brown*

1965	Aug 15	King Curtis Band supported the Beatles at their Shea Stadium concert
1971	Aug 13	knifed to death by a junkie: 37 years old
1971	Oct 8	John Lennon released his album *Imagine* – featured Curtis

The Kingsmen

1963	Nov 30	*Louie Louie* became an international hit for the Kingsmen – a legend was born...
		...written by Richard Berry and a single from him in 1957

The Kingston Trio

1958	Jun 2	released eponymous debut album – American folk revival music came of age...
		...lineup included:
		Dave Guard: guitar, banjo, vocals and founding member

The Kinks

		Inducted into the Rock and Roll Hall of Fame in 1990
1943	May 21	John Dalton: bassist, born in Enfield, London...
		...replaced Pete Quaife, became permanent band member in 1969
1944	Jun 21	Ray Davies: musician, songwriter and founder 1963, born in Muswell Hill, London
Before the Kinks		
1962	Jul 12	Rollin' Stones debut gig – lineup did not feature Mick Avory...
		...Mick Avory: drummer and Kinks founding member – left in 1984
1963	Jun 30	Crawdaddy gig – Ray Davies with original house band, Dave Hunt R&B Band
1963	Nov 30	Kingsmen's version of *Louie Louie* entered the US charts...
		...covered by the Kinks on their 1964 EP, *Kinksize Session*
The Kinks		
1964	Aug 4	released *You Really Got Me* (UK) – featured Jon Lord – written by Ray Davies
	Aug 16	supported the Beatles in concert – High Numbers were also on the bill
1965	Apr 2	appeared on the 1st live edition of *Ready Steady Go!*
	Jun 19	opened the ill-fated US debut tour – Ray Davies reputedly thumped union-man...
		...did not perform in America again until 1969
1968	Nov 22	released *Village Green Preservation Society* (UK)...
		...last album with bassist Pete Quaife – replaced by John Dalton
1974	Jun 16	supported by the Butts Band at the London Palladium

Don Kirshner

		Inducted into the Rock and Roll Hall of Fame in 2012
1958	Jun 18	Connie Francis recorded *Stupid Cupid* – 1st hit for Kirshner's Aldon Music...
		...a time of the Brill Building and songwriting factories
1967	Jan 21	*A Little Bit Me, A Little Bit You* led to his downfall as Monkees' musical director

Kiss

Inducted into the Rock and Roll Hall of Fame in 2014

1947 May 24 Cynthia Plaster Caster: notorious artist, born Cynthia Albritton, Chicago, Illinois...
...Gene Simmons wrote *Plaster Casters* – on the 1977 Kiss album *Love Gun*

1949 Aug 25 Gene Simmons: bassist and singer, born Chaim Witz, in Haifa, Israel

1951 Apr 27 Ace Frehley: guitarist, born in the Bronx, New York

1952 Jan 20 Paul Stanley: guitarist and singer, born Stanley Harvey Eisen, in New York

Kiss was formed after Gene Simmons and Paul Stanley left Wicked Lester.

1973 Jan 30 debut gig...
...Kiss:
Gene Simmons: aka "Demon": bass and vocals
Paul Stanley: aka "Starchild": guitar and vocals
Peter Criss: aka "The Catman": drums – left in 1980
Ace Frehley: aka "Spaceman" or "Space Ace": lead guitar – left in 1982

Allen Klein

manager: Sam Cooke – The Rolling Stones – The Beatles – John Lennon – George Harrison
Ringo Starr

1931 Dec 18 accountant and business manager, born in Newark, New Jersey

1965 Feb 26 Rolling Stones released *The Last Time* – Klein sued the group Verve 30 years on

1971 Sep 1 Rolling Stones issued a lawsuit against their ex-manager, Allen Klein

1975 Jan 9 dissolution of the Beatles – in mid-'69 Klein represented John, George and Ringo

Brian Knight

guitar, harmonica and vocals: Brian Jones's group (1st lineup) – Blues By Six

1939 Oct 14 unsung hero of the early British blues scene, born in Perivale, Middlesex

1963 Jan 11 Rolling Stones: Stones that kept right on rolling

1964 Oct 13 Blues By Six played London's 100 Club – Knight was the founding member

Al Kooper

keyboards, guitar and vocals: Royal Teens – The Blues Project – Blood, Sweat & Tears
producer: Lynyrd Skynyrd

1944 Feb 5 musician and producer, born in Brooklyn, New York...
...career started in 1958 as the 14-year-old guitarist with the Royal Teens
...songwriting: Gary Lewis and the Playboys' 1964 single *This Diamond Ring*

1965 Jun 15 Bob Dylan cut *Like a Rolling Stone* – Kooper provided the Hammond organ riff

Jul 25 backed Dylan for his infamous electric set at the *Newport Folk Festival*

Jul 29 keyboards: Bob Dylan recording session for *Highway 61 Revisited*

1966 Jun 1 various artists album *What's Shakin'* was issued – included tracks from Kooper

1968 Apr 3 Moby Grape released *Wow/Grape Jam* – Kooper featured on *Grape Jam*

Apr 11 left Blood, Sweat & Tears after a four-night stint in New York

May 28 keyboards, guitar and vocals: recorded the album *Supersession*

	Oct 25	keyboards: Jimi Hendrix Experience released *Electric Ladyland*
1969	Nov 1	mentioned by *Rolling Stone* magazine as part of Masked Marauders hoax album
1971	Apr 26	live recording for Pete Townshend's 'lost' *Lifehouse* album...
		...Kooper played keyboards on studio tracks destined for the album
1974	Jun 24	producer: Lynyrd Skynyrd released *Sweet Home Alabama*

Alexis Korner (and Cyril Davies)

Alexis Korner: guitar and vocals: Chris Barber's Jazz Band – Ken Colyer's Skiffle Group
Beryl Bryden's Backroom Skiffle Group – Alexis Korner's Breakdown Group
Chris Barber's Jazz Band/interval R&B group – Alexis Korner's Blues Incorporated
Alexis Korner's New Church – CCS – Snape

Cyril Davies: guitar, harmonica and vocals: Beryl Bryden's Backroom Skiffle Group
Alexis Korner's Breakdown Group – Chris Barber's Jazz Band/interval R&B group
Alexis Korner's Blues Incorporate – Cyril Davies and His Rhythm and Blues All Stars

1921	Dec 28	Johnny Otis: R&B pioneer, bandleader and producer, born in Vallejo, California...
		...Otis's Barrelhouse Club inspired the name of Korner and Davies's club
1928	Apr 19	Alexis Korner: godfather of British blues, guitar and vocals, born in Paris, France
1932	Jan 23	Cyril Davies: harmonica, guitar and vocals, born in Denham, Buckinghamshire...
		...his collaboration with Korner lasted from the mid-'50s until he left in late '62
		...as well as Korner's bands, they were together in Beryl Bryden's Backroom Skiffle Group and Chris Barber's Jazz Band's blues-based interval group

Musicians in Blues Incorporated included:

1934	Sep 26	Dick Heckstall-Smith: saxophone, born Richard Malden, in Ludlow, Shropshire...
		...later played with Graham Bond, John Mayall and Colosseum
1937	Oct 28	Graham Bond: saxophone and keyboards, born in Romford, Essex...
		...joined in late 1962 – left with Jack Bruce and Ginger Baker in early 1963
1939	Aug 19	Ginger Baker: drummer, born in Lewisham, London...
		...replaced Charlie Watts in the summer of 1962
		...left with Jack Bruce and Graham Bond – later in Cream
1941	Jan 12	Long John Baldry: singer, born in East Haddon, Northamptonshire...
		...he was in Blues Incorporated before leaving for the Horace Silver Quintet
		...when Davies split from Korner he opted to join Davies's group
		...took over Davies's band after he died, renamed it "Hoochie Coochie Men"
	Jun 2	Charlie Watts: drummer, born in London, England...
		...left in mid-1962 to join Blues By Six – later in the Rolling Stones
	Sep 9	Duffy Power: singer, born Ray Howard, in Fulham, London...
		..."guest vocalist" sleeve credit on the 1966 album *Sky High*
1942	Feb 24	Paul Jones: singer, born Paul Pond, in Portsmouth, Hampshire...
		...later in Manfred Mann
	Feb 28	Brian Jones: guitarist, born in Cheltenham, Gloucestershire...
		...went on to form the Rolling Stones

	Jul 17	Zoot Money: keyboards, born in Bournemouth, Dorset...
		...brief tenure in 1963
1943	May 14	Jack Bruce: bassist, born in Bishopbriggs, Lanarkshire, Scotland...
		...regular bassist mid-1962 to early 1963 ...left with Graham Bond and Ginger Baker – later in Cream
	Jul 26	Mick Jagger: singer, born in Dartford, Kent...
		...later in the Rolling Stones
1943	Dec 18	Keith Richard: guitarist, born in Dartford, Kent...
		...later in the Rolling Stones

Musicians in Cyril Davies and His Rhythm and Blues All Stars included:

1938	Dec 17	Carlo Little: drummer, born in Sudbury, London...
		...previously a founding member of Lord Sutch's Savages ...later an occasional drummer with the Rolling Stones
1941	Jan 12	Long John Baldry: singer, born in East Haddon, Northamptonshire...
		...previously with Alexis Korner's Blues Incorporated
1944	Jan 9	Jimmy Page: guitarist, born in Heston, Middlesex...
		...later with the Yardbirds and founding member of Led Zeppelin
1944	Feb 24	Nicky Hopkins: keyboardist, born in Perivale, London...
		...previously with Screaming Lord Sutch and the Savages, and Cliff Bennett ...later a sought after session musician

Ken Colyer's Skiffle Group

1954	Sep 10	Alexis Korner: mandolin and vocals in the skiffle section for *Back to the Delta*

Alexis Korner's Breakdown Group featuring Cyril Davies

1957	Feb 13	recorded the seminal British blues album, *Blues from the Roundhouse*

Alexis Korner's Blues Incorporated

1962	Mar 17	debut at the Ealing Club...
		...lineup included: Alexis Korner: guitar and vocals – formed the band in early 1962 Cyril Davies: harmonica and guitar – left in late '62 to form his own band Charlie Watts: drummer – left in mid-1962 to join Blues By Six Art Wood: singer – went on to form the Artwoods Dick Heckstall-Smith: sax – later with Graham Bond and John Mayall
	Apr 6	Korner and Davies gig at the Marquee, Chris Barber's Jazz Band's interval group
	Apr 7	gig the Ealing Club – night that Brian Jones met Mick Jagger and Keith Richard...
		...lineup included: Alexis Korner – Cyril Davies – Charlie Watts Brian Jones: guitar – used the stage name "Elmo Lewis"... ...Jones left soon afterwards and formed his own group: Jones's group eventually became the Rolling Stones

Paul Pond: singer and harmonica – occasional singer in 1962...
...Pond became "Paul Jones" and co-founded Manfred Mann
...Mick Jagger: became a regular singer soon after this gig:
left in mid-1962 to join Brian Jones's group
...Keith Richard: became an occasional guitarist in 1962:
joined Jones's group with Mick Jagger

Jun 8 recorded *R&B from the Marquee* – actually recorded in Decca's studios...
...lineup included:
Alexis Korner – Cyril Davies – Dick Heckstall-Smith
Long John Baldry: singer – joined in 1962 – left in late 1962

1962 Jul 12 Rollin' Stones debut gig – they deputised for Blues Incorporated at the Marquee

Cyril Davies left Blues Incorporated in Nov 1962, formed His Rhythm and Blues All Stars.

1963 Jan 16 Cyril Davies and His Rhythm and Blues All Stars gig...
...lineup included:
Long John Baldry: singer – joined shortly before this gig
Ricky Fenson: bass – from Screaming Lord Sutch's Savages
Carlo Little: drums – from Screaming Lord Sutch's Savages...
...replaced by Mickey Waller in mid-1963
Nicky Hopkins: keyboards – from Screaming Lord Sutch's Savages
Jimmy Page: guitar – original guitarist but short tenure
...Bernie Watson: guitar – replaced Jimmy Page – from Lord Sutch's Savages

1964 Jan 2 Cyril Davies's last Marquee residency performance with the R&B All Stars

1964 Jan 7 Cyril Davies died of natural causes: 31 years old...
...Long John Baldry took over leadership of the Rhythm and Blues All Stars:
Baldry renamed the group "The Hoochie Coochie Men"...
...taken from Muddy Waters' *(I'm Your) Hoochie Coochie Man*, 1954
...Rod Stewart joined the Hoochie Coochie Men in 1964 and left in 1965
...Long John Baldry went on to join Bluesology

Alexis Korner

1967 Apr 29 performed at the *14-Hour Technicolor Dream*

1968 Feb 23 (future Zeppelin singer Robert Plant's) Band of Joy gig – band folded soon after...
...Plant performed and recorded with Korner in 1968

1968 Apr 19 Free's 1st gig – Korner assisted in the formation of band and suggested the name

Alexis Korner's New Church

1969 Jul 5 made their debut at the Rolling Stones' free concert in London's Hyde Park

1969 Sep 25 recording session for the studio portion of the *Both Sides* album...
...lineup included:
Alexis Korner
Peter Thorup: vocals, guitar, harmonica – joined Korner after Blues Inc.

Paul Rodgers: vocals – in Free at the time
Andy Fraser: bass – in Free at the time

...ex-Rolling Stone Brian Jones was keen to join Korner in New Church

CCS

1969 Nov 7 Led Zeppelin released *Whole Lotta Love*...

...covered as a single by Korner with his CCS big-band in 1970
...CCS version was the basis for Johnny Pearson's theme for *Top of the Pops*
...CCS = Collective Consciousness Society

Snape

1972 Feb 11 King Crimson musicians decamped to join Snape at the end of their US tour...

...Snape lineup included:

Alexis Korner: guitar and vocals
Peter Thorup: guitar and vocals
Mel Collins: saxophone – left King Crimson to join Snape
Ian Wallace: drums – left King Crimson to join Snape
Boz Burrell: vocals and bass – left King Crimson to join Snape

...Snape = Something Nasty 'Appens Practically Everyday

Kraftwerk

Kraftwerk was formed after Organisation folded.

1970 Jul 11 early Kraftwerk concert, at the *Tivoli* festival in Germany...

...lineup included:

Ralf Hütter: multi-instrumentalist and founding member
Florian Schneider: multi-instrumentalist and founding member

...both had been in Organisation when it was formed in 1968

Billy J Kramer

singer: Billy Kramer and the Coasters – Billy J Kramer with The Dakotas

1934 Sep 19 Brian Epstein: manager, born in Liverpool, England

1943 Aug 19 Billy J Kramer: singer, born William Ashton, in Bootle, Liverpool...

...after meeting Brian Epstein, he split with the Coasters for the Dakotas:
and added the "J" to his name

...singer Chick Graham replaced Kramer as the Coasters' front man

1963 Feb 27 Dakotas supported Gene Vincent in Hamburg...

...they later became Billy J Kramer's backing group

As well as being Billy J's backing group, they were an independent instrumental combo.

Billy J Kramer with The Dakotas

1963 Jul 26 issued *Bad to Me* (UK) – 1st #1 Lennon and McCartney song, not by the Beatles

1964 Jan 27 *Do You Want to Know a Secret* – released on *Introducing the Beatles*...

...originally on the Beatles' UK debut album and Kramer's 1st hit in 1963

	Jul 17	released *From a Window* (UK) – last of four Lennon/McCartney penned singles...
		...only one of their 1st five singles was written by somebody else:
		Little Children was written by Mort Shuman and Leslie McFarland
1965	Sep 13	Beatles released *Yesterday* – offered to Kramer but he turned it down
1973	Jun 28	Kramer performed at the *British Re-Invasion Show* at Madison Square Garden

Art Laboe

1959 Jul 15 *Teen Beat* – recorded by Sandy Nelson...
...written by Sandy Nelson and Art Laboe:
Laboe was the DJ credited with the phrase "Oldies but Goodies"

Lead Belly

Inducted into the Rock and Roll Hall of Fame in 1988

1954 Jul 13 Lonnie Donegan recorded *Rock Island Line* – recorded by Lead Belly in 1937...
...also recorded *John Henry* – recorded by Lead Belly in 1943

1962 Feb 2 Dylan and Harry Belafonte recorded *The Midnight Special* – cut by Lead Belly '34

1965 Apr 2 Artwoods performed *Sweet Mary* – recorded by Lead Belly in 1944

Timothy Leary

1920 Oct 22 psychologist, writer and LSD advocate, born in Springfield, Massachusetts...
...famously proclaimed, "turn on, tune in, drop out"

1967 Jan 14 participated in *A Gathering of the Tribes for a Human Be-In*

The Leaves

1943 Mar 14 Jim Pons: bassist and singer, born in Santa Monica, California...
...founding member of the Leaves – left in 1967 to join the Turtles
...later a member of Frank Zappa's band

1966 Dec 16 Jimi Hendrix Experience released *Hey Joe* – Leaves single in 1965...
...copyrighted by Billy Roberts in 1962

Led Zeppelin

Inducted into the Rock and Roll Hall of Fame in 1995

1942 Sep 3 Kenny Pickett: roadie, born in Ware, Hertfordshire...
...previously the Creation's lead singer

1944 Jan 9 Jimmy Page: guitarist, born in Heston, Middlesex...
...before Led Zeppelin Page made numerous session appearances, including:
Tobacco Road – Nashville Teens single in 1964
Here Comes the Night – Them single in 1965
You Really Got Me – Kinks single in 1964 (maybe!)
...in 1984 Page formed the Firm with ex-Free singer Paul Rodgers

1946 Jan 3 John Paul Jones: bassist and arranger, born John Baldwin, in Sidcup, Kent...
...stage name inspired by the American revolutionary hero

1947 Jan 6 Sandy Denny: singer, born in Wimbledon, London...
...duet with Plant on *The Battle of Evermore*, on the Led Zeppelin 4 album

1948 May 31 John Bonham: drummer, born in Redditch, Worcestershire

1948 Aug 20 Robert Plant: singer, born in West Bromwich, Staffordshire

Road to Led Zeppelin *SEE 23 February 1968*

Robert Plant and John Bonham:

Crawling King Snakes

Plant and Bonham went their separate ways but came back together in Band of Joy.

Robert Plant: singer and founding member
John Bonham: drums – joined Plant in his re-formed Band of Joy

Band of Joy split up, Plant and Bonham once again went their separate ways.

Robert Plant recorded with Alexis Korner before joining Hobbstweedle
John Bonham accepted the offer to join Tim Rose's touring band

John Paul Jones worked with:

Jet Harris and Tony Meehan
Andrew Loog Oldham and copious other session work:

Before the Yardbirds, Jimmy Page was a member of:

Red E Lewis and the Red Caps – late 1950s
Neil Christian and the Crusaders, morphed from Red E Lewis and the Red Caps
Cyril Davies and His Rhythm and Blues All Stars – original guitarist
Carter Lewis and the Southerners
Page was also in great demand as a session guitarist

Lineup when the Yardbirds imploded:

Jimmy Page	guitar
Keith Relf	vocals and harmonica
Chris Dreja	bass
Jim McCarty	drums
Peter Grant	manager

Relf and McCarty left and formed Together, which morphed into Renaissance.

Dreja quit the music business to become a photographer.

Manager Peter Grant and guitarist Jimmy Page set out to build a new band.

They recruited Plant, on came Bonham and Jones ...and Led Zeppelin was born.

Before Led Zeppelin

1961 Jul 21 Page accompanied beat poet Royston Ellis in a fusion of music and poetry...
...he was in Neil Christian and the Crusaders at the time

1962 Jun 27 Muddy Waters recorded *You Shook Me* – covered on Zeppelin's 1st album

1963 Jan 16 Cyril Davies gig – Page was the original guitarist with Davies's R&B All Stars

May 11 Carter Lewis and the Southerners performed live on British radio...
...Jimmy Page joined the group around this time

	Jun 30	John Paul Jones backed Jet Harris and Tony Meehan on a package tour... ...Jimmy Page performed as a session guitarist on their 1st single, *Diamonds*
1964	Sep 10	Rod Stewart recorded his 1st single, *Good Morning Little Schoolgirl*... ...John Paul Jones was a session musician
1965	Jan 15	Who released *I Can't Explain* – jury is out as to whether or not Page performed
	Aug 20	Fifth Avenue released *The Bells of Rhymney* on Immediate – produced by Page
1966	May 16	Jeff Beck recorded *Beck's Bolero* – whilst he was still in the Yardbirds... ...writing credit on early releases went to Jeff Beck – later releases, J. Page ...John Paul Jones played bass
	Jun 21	Jimmy Page's 1st gig with the Yardbirds... ...joined as bassist before changing to (duel) lead guitar with Jeff Beck
	Dec 18	*Blow-Up* movie opened – Yardbirds dual lead guitars of Page and Jeff Beck
1968	Feb 23	Band of Joy gig – near the end of the band's lifespan... ...Band of Joy lineup included: Robert Plant: vocals – went on to record with Alexis Korner John Bonham: drums – joined Tim Rose's touring band ...Page morphed the Yardbirds into Led Zeppelin Terry Reid – rejected an offer to become Led Zeppelin's singer Peter Grant – Yardbirds' manager continued with Led Zeppelin ...Band of Joy boasted assorted rock'n'roll luminaries amongst its members: Kevyn Gammond: guitar – joined Jess Roden in Bronco Pete Robinson: drums – joined Jess Roden in Bronco Noddy Holder: roadie – founding member of Slade Dave Pegg: went on to join Fairport Convention and Jethro Tull
1968	Jul 7	final gig for the Yardbirds – Page morphed the group into Led Zeppelin

Led Zeppelin

1968	Sep 7	Led Zeppelin lineup's debut gig – but billed as "The Yardbirds"... ...Led Zeppelin: Jimmy Page: guitar John Paul Jones: bass and arranger John Bonham: drums Robert Plant: singer Peter Grant: manager
	Sep 27	1st recording session
	Nov 9	1st concert as "Led Zeppelin" – name was inspired by... ...Keith Moon and John Entwistle's reference to a "lead Zeppelin"
	Dec 26	concert debut in America
1969	Jan 12	debut album *Led Zeppelin* released in America – ten weeks before the UK... ...Peter Grant closed the Atlantic deal in November
	Mar 10	released their 1st single, *Good Times Bad Times* (US)... ...written by Jimmy Page John Paul Jones and John Bonham

	Mar 28	released their debut album *Led Zeppelin* in the UK
	Apr 8	PJ Proby released *Three Week Hero* – 1st time "Led Zeppelin" recorded together
	Jul 26	played the *Seattle Pop Festival*
	Jul 28	notorious *Edgewater Inn Mud Shark Incident*
	Oct 31	released *Led Zeppelin II* (UK)...
		...album attracted three claims of plagiarism:
		The Lemon Song – Howlin' Wolf's song, *Killing Floor*
		Whole Lotta Love – Willie Dixon's song, *You Need Love*
		Bring it on Home – Willie Dixon received another belated writing credit
	Nov 7	released *Whole Lotta Love* (US)...
		...song was also released as a single in the UK but was quickly withdrawn
		...notable cover versions:
		Alexis Korner had a rare UK hit as CCS in 1970
		Johnny Pearson's version was used as the theme for *Top of the Pops*
1970	Feb 28	performed in Denmark, billed as "The Nobs"
	Oct 23	released *Led Zeppelin III* (UK)...
		...Aleister Crowley quotes cut into the run-out groove
		...included the track, *Hats off to Roy Harper*:
		Page played on Harper's '71 album *Stormcock*, as "S Flavius Mercurius"
1971	Mar 5	debut performance of *Stairway to Heaven* – written by Page and Plant
	Jul 5	riot at a Led Zeppelin concert in Italy
	Nov 12	released their untitled 4th album (UK) – included *Stairway to Heaven*
1974	Feb 14	Roy Harper concert at the Rainbow...
		...backed by Page and Bonham, with Plant as the evening's MC
		...performed as the Intergalactic Elephant Band
	Mar 8	Bad Company's debut gig – Peter Grant managed the band
1976	Oct 20	premiere of their movie *The Song Remains the Same*...
		...Jimmy Page's segment was a homage to Aleister Crowley
1977	Apr 1	ill-fated 11th American tour opened – it proved to be their last outing in the US...
		...Chicago show was halted due to Page's food poisoning
		...Bonham and Grant were arrested in Oakland
	Jun 23	Who's drummer Keith Moon joined them on stage
	Jul 24	last-ever American concert...
		...tour cut short after Plant received news of his son's illness
1980	Jun 27	John Bonham collapsed on stage in Germany
	Jul 7	end of the European tour and the final performance with John Bonham...
		...set finished with *Whole Lotta Love* – written by the band in 1969
	Sep 25	John Bonham died after a heavy drinking session: at the age of 32
1983	Sep 20	Page performed at the ARMS charity concert with Eric Clapton and Jeff Beck
2007	Dec 10	1st Led Zeppelin gig in 27 years – with John Bonham's son, Jason, as drummer

Brenda Lee

Inducted into the Rock and Roll Hall of Fame in 2002

1944 Dec 11 seminal female rock'n'roll singer, born Brenda Mae Tarpley, in Atlanta, Georgia...
...the original "Little Miss Dynamite"

1956 Mar 31 eleven-year-old Brenda Lee made her 1st national TV appearance

Sep 17 released debut single, *Jambalaya* (US) – country hit for Hank Williams in 1952

1958 Oct 19 recorded *Rockin' Around the Christmas Tree* – it did not chart until 1960

Jerry Leiber and Mike Stoller

Inducted into the Rock and Roll Hall of Fame in 1987

producers: The Coasters – Ronnie Hawkins record label owners: Spark

Leiber and Stoller were titans amongst rock'n'roll songwriters.

Their songwriting credits included:

1933 Mar 13 Mike Stoller: producer and songwriter, born in Queens, New York:
Smokey Joe's Cafe – Robins single in 1955

Apr 25 Jerry Leiber: producer and songwriter, was born in Baltimore, Maryland:
King Creole – title track from Elvis's 4th movie, made in 1958
Spanish Harlem – Ben E King single in '60 – co-written with Phil Spector
Some Other Guy – Richie Barrett single in 1962 – co-written with Barrett

1952 Aug 13 Big Mama Thornton recorded *Hound Dog*...
...original release gave a writing credit to Johnny Otis
...produced by Johnny Otis

Aug 18 writers and producers: Little Willie Littlefield recorded *KC Loving*...
...*KC Loving* was rewritten as *Kansas City* in 1959

1954 Oct 16 Richard Berry released his self-penned single *The Big Break*...
...Leiber/Stoller wrote and produced *Riot in Cell Block #9* - Robins single '54

1956 Jan 11 produced the Coasters 1st recording session – generated their 1st two singles...
...Coasters recorded three Leiber and Stoller penned songs:
Down in Mexico – released as their 1st single
Turtle Dovin' – released as their 1st B-side
One Kiss Led to Another – 2nd A-side
...also wrote their 3rd single, *Searchin'*, a Coasters single in 1957

1958 Jan 24 Elvis's *Jailhouse Rock* was the 1st single to enter the UK charts at #1...
...A-Side, and B-Side *Treat Me Nice*, both written by Leiber and Stoller

Mar 17 writers and producers: Coasters recorded *Yakety Yak*

May 30 whole Drifters group were sacked and replaced by a new "Drifters" group...
...last hit before the cull was *Fools Fall in Love*, in 1957

Dec 11 writers and producers: Coasters recorded *Charlie Brown*

1959 Jun 8 writers and producers: Clovers recorded *Love Potion #9*

Jul 16 writers and producers: Coasters recorded *Poison Ivy*...
...writers and producers: Coasters recorded *I'm a Hog for You* on 17 July

1965 Jun 14 writers: Beatles released *Kansas City* in America – released in the UK in 1964

Morris Levy

1969 Oct 31 Beatles released *Come Together*...
...Levy sued over lyrics lifted from Chuck Berry's *You Can't Catch Me*

1975 Feb 21 released then withdrawn, *Roots: John Lennon Sings the Great Rock & Roll Hits*

Jerry Lee Lewis

Inducted into the Rock and Roll Hall of Fame in 1986 (inaugural year)

1935 Sep 29 seminal rock'n'roll pianist and singer, aka "The Killer", born in Ferriday, Louisiana

1949 Nov 19 1st public performance, sang *Drinking Wine Spo-Dee-O-Dee*...
...originally a single from Stick McGhee and His Buddy in 1947

1950 Sep 1 enrolled in a theological college in Texas

1955 Mar 21 Big Maybelle recorded *Whole Lotta Shakin' Goin' On* – Lewis single in 1957...
...single from Roy Hall in late 1955 (after Big Maybelle's version)
...written by Hall as "Sunny David", and Dave Williams

1956 Dec 1 released his 1st Sun single, *Crazy Arms* (US) – country hit for Ray Price in 1956

Dec 4 *Million Dollar Quartet* recording session – with Lewis, Presley, Perkins and Cash

1957 Jan 23 two rock'n'roll classics released by Sun – with session piano from Lewis:
Matchbox from Carl Perkins
Flyin' Saucers Rock & Roll from Billy Riley and His Little Green Men

Mar 15 released *Whole Lot of Shakin' Going On* (US) – Lewis's 1st hit single

Nov 3 released *Great Balls of Fire* (US)

1958 Mar 28 tour opened which featured Lewis's piano burning rivalry with Chuck Berry

Apr 9 released his last rock'n'roll hit, *High School Confidential* (US)

May 3 performed at Alan Freed's *Big Beat* show – ended in the infamous "Boston Riot"

May 17 *Jerry Lee Lewis Day* in Ferriday – marked the high point of his career

May 22 arrived in London for ill-fated British tour – abandoned it after only three gigs...
...career imploded after news broke that his wife Myra Gale was only 13

May 30 recorded *The Return of Jerry Lee* – 1st attempt at damage limitation

Jun 7 Cliff Richard recorded *Breathless* – last major rock'n'roll hit for Lewis, 1958

Jun 9 open letter in *Billboard* magazine – more damage limitation after the UK tour

Jul 5 Johnny O'Keefe with The Dee Jays issued *The Wild One* – cut by Lewis in 1958

Aug 10 released *Break Up* (US) – very poor sales following his disastrous British tour

1959 Feb 18 Ray Charles recorded *What'd I Say* – hit for Lewis in mid-1961

1962 Apr 29 opening night of the 1st UK tour since his disastrous 1958 tour

1963 Aug 23 final Sun recording session

Sep 6 recording contract expired at Sun Records – moved on to Smash

1965 Mar 15 released his final Sun single, *Carry Me Back to Old Virginia* (US)

1968 Mar 5 appeared as Iago in *Catch My Soul* – musical version of Shakespeare's *Othello*

1969 Sep 13 appeared at the *Toronto Rock and Roll Revival* festival
1970 Dec 9 divorced his 3rd wife, Myra Gale – Gale was 13 years old when they married
1973 Jan 20 finally made his debut at Nashville's *Grand Ole Opry*
1976 Sep 29 accidentally shot his bass player in the chest
1976 Nov 23 arrested for brandishing a gun outside Elvis's Graceland home

Little Richard

Inducted into the Rock and Roll Hall of Fame in 1986 (inaugural year)
1918 May 23 Bumps Blackwell: producer, songwriter, arranger, born in Seattle, Washington...
...*Long Tall Sally* – Richard single in '56 – written by Blackwell and Richard:
original idea for the song was brought to Blackwell by Enortis Johnson
1932 Dec 5 Little Richard: singer and songwriter, born in Macon, Georgia...
...often used birth name (Richard Wayne) R Penniman for songwriting credits
1942 Nov 27 Jimmy (later Jimi) Hendrix: guitarist, born in Seattle, Washington...
...played with Little Richard's touring band in 1963
1951 Oct 16 1st-ever recording session – gave him his 1st single for RCA
1952 Mar 13 Lloyd Price recorded *Lawdy Miss Clawdy* – album track from Richard in 1964
1955 Sep 14 recorded *Tutti-Frutti* – 1st single on Speciality...
...co-written with Dorothy LaBostrie – produced by Bumps Blackwell
1956 Aug 22 appeared in the movie *The Girl Can't Help It*
Oct 15 recorded *Good Golly, Miss Molly*...
...written by Bumps Blackwell and John Marascalco – produced by Blackwell
1957 Oct 12 whilst on tour in Australia Little Richard found God and renounced rock'n'roll
Oct 18 final rock'n'roll recording session of the 1950s
Nov 22 *Keep a Knockin'* was a US hit for Richard – originally by James Wiggins in 1928
1962 Oct 12 supported by the Beatles in New Brighton – British rock'n'roll comeback tour...
...Little Richard's backing band included:
Billy Preston: keyboards – Preston later worked with the Beatles
Oct 30 shared the stage with the Beatles for a two-week residency in Hamburg
1965 Jun 14 Beatles released *Beatles VI*, included *Hey-Hey-Hey-Hey*...
...written by Little Richard and a B-side from him in 1958
Oct 15 Jimmy (Jimi) Hendrix signed a management deal with Ed Chalpin...
...had played with Little Richard's touring band in 1963
1969 Sep 13 appeared at the *Toronto Rock and Roll Revival* festival

Little Walter

Inducted into the Rock and Roll Hall of Fame in 2008
harmonica: Muddy Waters' band
1930 May 1 influential blues harpist, born Marion Walter Jacobs, in Marksville, Louisiana...
...wrote the harmonica classic *Juke*, released as a single in 1952

1954 Jan 7 Muddy Waters recorded *(I'm Your) Hoochie Coochie Man*

1955 Jan 25 recorded *My Babe*...

...based on *This Train*, recorded by Sister Rosetta Tharpe in 1939

1968 Feb 15 died from injuries sustained in a street fight in Chicago: 37 years old

Little Willie Littlefield

1952 Aug 18 Little Willie Littlefield recorded *KC Loving*...

...writers Leiber and Stoller rewrote it as *Kansas City* for Wilbert Harrison:

million seller and US #1 for Harrison in 1959

1965 Jun 14 *Beatles VI* released, included *Kansas City*

Horace Logan

1956 Dec 15 1st person to announce that "Elvis has left the building"

Johnny London

1952 Mar 1 recorded *Drivin' Slow* – 1st single to be released on Sun Records...

...A-side and B-side, *Flat Tyre*, written by Johnny London

Jerry Lordan

1962 Apr 13 Shadows received the 1st Gold Disc for a British group – 1960 single *Apache*...

...written by Jerry Lordan
...originally recorded by Britain's 1st guitar hero Bert Weedon
...Lordan also wrote *Diamonds* – Jet Harris and Tony Meehan single in 1963

Bonnie Lou

1924 Oct 27 one of the 1st female rock'n'roll stars, born in Towanda, Illinois

Love

1966 Aug 18 Doors signed to Elektra – introduced to the label by Love's guitarist Arthur Lee

1968 Mar 9 on tour to support *Forever Changes*...

...Love:

Arthur Lee: guitar, vocals and founding member – leader
Brian MacLean: guitar, vocals and founding member
John Echols: guitar and founding member
Ken Forssi: bass and founding member
Michael Stuart: drums – joined before 2nd album *Da Capo*

...'lost' album *Gethsemane* started before this lineup imploded:

band recorded one single before splitting up...

...*Your Mind and We Belong Together* c/w *Laughing Stock*:

both sides written by Arthur Lee

...Arthur Lee sacked the band at the end of the tour

The Lovin' Spoonful

Inducted into the Rock and Roll Hall of Fame in 2000

1944 Mar 17 John Sebastian: guitarist, singer and songwriter, born in New York City

Dec 19 Zal Yanovsky: guitarist and singer, born in Toronto, Canada

1964 Feb 9 John Sebastian met Zal Yanovsky – the road to the Lovin' Spoonful began...

...The Lovin' Spoonful: original lineup:

John Sebastian: guitar and vocals – from the Even Dozen Jug Band
Zal Yanovsky: guitar and vocals – from the Mugwumps...

...previously with the Halifax Three

Steve Boone: bass – from the (Long Island) Kingsmen
Joe Butler: drums – from the (Long Island) Kingsmen

...band's name from a reference in Mississippi John Hurt's song, *Coffee Blues*

1966 Jun 1 released various artists album, *What's Shakin'*

1968 Feb 25 Jimi Hendrix had a stimulating meeting with Cynthia Plaster Caster...

...Zal Yanovsky had a similar encounter and became plaster-cast 00028

John Sebastian, solo performances

1970 Aug 7 performed at the *Goose Lake International Music Festival*

Aug 28 performed at the *Isle of Wight Festival...*

...Yanovsky was in the audience and joined Sebastian on stage

1970 Sep 12 appeared at the Hyde Park concert in London

Lulu

1964 Feb 1 British Invasion began – end of Invasion marked by the last #1 by Lulu, in 1967

1969 Jan 4 Hendrix's unscheduled *Sunshine of Your Love* on *Happening for Lulu* TV show

Frankie Lymon and the Teenagers

Inducted into the Rock and Roll Hall of Fame in 1993

1942 Sep 30 Frankie Lymon, the 1st black teenage idol, was born in Harlem, New York

1955 Dec 5 Teenagers featuring Frankie Lymon recorded *Why Do Fools Fall in Love...*

...co-writing credit to Lymon but the song's authorship has been disputed

1957 Jul 19 Lymon outraged public decency by dancing with a white girl on live TV

1958 Mar 28 tour opened which featured the piano burning Jerry Lee Lewis

Lynyrd Skynyrd

Inducted into the Rock and Roll Hall of Fame in 2006

1948 Jan 15 Ronnie Van Zant: singer, born in Jacksonville, Florida...

...the band's name was inspired by their gym teacher, Leonard Skinner

1949 Sep 14 Ed King: bassist and guitarist, born in Glendale, California...

...guitarist and founder of Strawberry Alarm Clock – left in '72 to join Skynyrd

Sep 14 Steve Gains: guitarist, born in Miami, Oklahoma

1951 Dec 4 Gary Rossington: guitarist, born in Jacksonville, Florida

1952 Jul 19 Allen Collins: guitarist, born in Jacksonville, Florida

Lynyrd Skynyrd morphed from My Backyard and Noble Five: both lineups included:

Ronnie Van Zant – Gary Rossington – Allen Collins

Lynyrd Skynyrd

1971 Jun 30 recording session at Muscle Shoals – intended 1st album but not released...

...lineup varied but included:

Ronnie Van Zant – Gary Rossington – Allen Collins

Billy Powell: keyboards – survived the plane crash...

...joined as a roadie before becoming the keyboardist

1973 Aug 13 released debut album, *(pronounced 'lĕh-'nérd 'skin-'nérd)* (US)

Oct 29 supported the Who on the US leg of the *Quadrophenia* tour

Nov 20 support act the night that the Who's drummer Keith Moon collapsed on stage

1974 Jun 24 released *Sweet Home Alabama* (US)...

...written by Ronnie Van Zant, Garry Rossington and Ed King
...produced by Al Kooper
...written as an answer to Neil Young's songs *Southern Man* and *Alabama*
...Ed King: guitar – joined as bass in 1972, moved to guitar – left before crash

1977 Oct 17 released *Street Survivors* (US) – cover design changed after fatal plane crash

Oct 20 plane crash that killed three band members:

Ronnie Van Zant – Steve Gains – Cassie Gains (backing singer)...

...Steve Gains had replaced Ed King in 1976

...two of the founding members survived:

Garry Rossington – Allen Collins

1987 Sep 23 the tribute tour opened – Lynyrd Skynyrd was back...

...car crash injuries stopped Allen Collins performing, was musical director

...Rossington Collins Band was formed in the early 1980s:

lineup included:

Gary Rossington: guitar
Allen Collins: guitar
Leon Wilkeson: bass
Billy Powell: keyboards

The Mamas & The Papas

Inducted into the Rock and Roll Hall of Fame in 1998

1935 Aug 30 Papa John (Phillips), singer, songwriter, born in Parris Island, South Carolina...

...formed the Journeymen in 1961 – early 1960s folk trio

1941 Sep 19 Mama Cass (Elliot): singer, born Ellen Naomi Cohen, in Baltimore, Maryland

1964 Feb 9 links to the Mugwumps and the Lovin' Spoonful...

...Mugwumps lineup included the future Mama and Papa:

Cass Elliott – previously with the Big Three

Denny Doherty – previously with the Halifax Three

...Mugwumps lineup included the future Lovin' Spoonful members:

Zal Yanovsky – with the Halifax Three and the Big Three
John Sebastian – occasional member of the band

...Denny and then Elliot, teamed up with John Phillips in the New Journeymen

...New Journeymen became The Mamas & The Papas in 1965

1966 Jul 1 goodbye Mama Michelle and hello Mama Jill – a short-lived new lineup

1967 Jun 16 played the *Monterey Pop Festival* – John Phillips co-organised the gig

Man

1972 Feb 13 recorded the live album *Greasy Truckers Party*, at London's Roundhouse

1972 Apr 28 released *Greasy Truckers Party* (UK)

Manfred Mann

1940 Oct 21 Manfred Mann: keyboards, born Manfred Lubowitz...

...in Johannesburg, South Africa

1941 Dec 2 Tom McGuinness: bass then guitar, born in Wimbledon, London...

...previously with the Roosters, and Casey Jones and the Engineers

1942 Feb 24 Paul Jones: original singer, born Paul Pond, in Portsmouth, Hampshire...

...previously with Brian Jones in Thunder Odin and the Big Secret
...also performed with Brian Jones in Alexis Korner's Blues Incorporated

Aug 11 Mike Hugg: drums then keyboards, born Mike Hug, in Andover, Hampshire

1943 May 14 Jack Bruce: bassist, born in Bishopbriggs, Lanarkshire, Scotland...

...previously with Alexis Korner, Graham Bond and John Mayall

1944 Mar 1 Mike d'Abo: singer and songwriter, born in Betchworth, Surrey...

...previously with A Band of Angels

...songwriting credits included:

Handbags and Gladrags – Chris Farlowe 1967 and Rod Stewart 1970

Manfred Mann (band) started out as the Mann-Hugg Blues Band. *SEE 11 August 1942*

...Mann-Hugg Blues Band: lineup included:

Manfred Mann: keyboards
Mike Hugg: drums
Paul Jones: harmonica and vocals

Mann-Hugg Blues Band changed its name to Manfred Mann in mid-1963.

Manfred Mann

1964 Jan 10 released 5-4-3-2-1 (UK) – became the theme tune for *Ready Steady Go!*...

...lineup included:

Manfred Mann: keyboards
Paul Jones: harmonica and vocals – left in 1966 to go solo
Mike Hugg: drums – also in Chapter Three

...written by Manfred Mann, Mike Hugg and Paul Jones

...Tom McGuinness: bass and guitar – joined early '64 – switched to guitar '65

Oct 7 appeared in Sheffield with Bill Haley and His Comets

1965 Jan 15 Bob Dylan recorded *If You Gotta Go, Go Now* – Mann UK single in late 1965...
...released in America in July, by the British Invasion group the Liverpool Five

Apr 2 appeared on the 1st live edition of *Ready Steady Go!*

1966 Apr 15 released *Pretty Flamingo* (UK)...
...Paul Jones's last single before leaving for a solo career
...Mike D'Abo replaced Jones
...Jack Bruce: bass – joined in late 1965 – left in mid-1966 to form Cream
...Tom McGuinness switched to guitar when Jack Bruce joined

Manfred Mann became Manfred Mann Chapter Three in 1969. *SEE 11 August 1942*

...Manfred Mann Chapter Three: lineup included:
Manfred Mann: keyboards
Mike Hugg: moved from drums to keyboards

1971 May 9 end of the Australian tour supporting Deep Purple

Chapter Three became Manfred Mann's Earth Band in 1971.

1973 Jan 5 Springsteen issued 1st album, with *Blinded by the Light* – Earth Band hit in '76...
...Earth Band lineup included:
Manfred Mann: keyboards

Charles Manson

1934 Nov 12 born Charles Milles Maddox, in Cincinnati, Ohio...
...cult leader, serial killer, song-writer and wannabe rock star

1965 Sep 8 contrary to the urban myth, Manson did not audition to become a Monkee

1968 Jun 11 Beatles recording session for *Revolution 9* – became linked to Manson's murders

1969 Jan 27 Beach Boys released *20/20* – contained a song written by Manson...
...*Cease to Exist* – reworked by the Beach Boys as *Learn Not to Love*

1969 Aug 10 infamous murders of Leno and Rosemary LaBianca, and Sharon Tate

The Marvelettes

1961 Aug 21 released their 1st single, *Please Mr. Postman* (US) – 1st Motown #1...
...lineup included:
Gladys Horton: singer – lead singer until 1965 – left in 1967
...covered by the Beatles: 1963 in the UK and 1964 in America

The Masked Marauders

1969 Nov 1 *Rolling Stone* magazine hoax album review – which led to a spoof album...
...supposed lineup: Dylan, Jagger, Lennon, McCartney and Harrison

1971 Apr 15 dropped from Warner Brothers' catalogue – the hoax was over

John Mayall

keyboards, guitar and vocals: The Powerhouse Four – The Blues Syndicate
John Mayall's Bluesbreakers

1927 Nov 11 Mose Allison: jazz and blues pianist, singer and songwriter...
...born in Tippo, Mississippi:
recorded *Parchman Farm* in 1957 – single from Mayall in 1966

1933 Nov 29 John Mayall was born in Macclesfield, Cheshire...
...in 1956 he was the pianist and founding member of the Powerhouse Four
...he joined the Blues Syndicate in 1962: piano, guitar, harmonica and vocals:
drummer Hughie Flint was also a member of the Blues Syndicate...
...he joined the Bluesbreakers from 1964 to '66

Bluesbreakers included:

1934 Sep 26 Dick Heckstall-Smith: saxophone, born Richard Malden, in Ludlow, Shropshire...
...joined in 1967 – left mid-1968 to form Colosseum

1943 May 14 Jack Bruce: bassist, born in Bishopbriggs, Lanarkshire, Scotland...
...short stay in late '65 – following stints with Alexis Korner and Graham Bond

1944 Mar 8 Keef Hartley: drummer, born in Preston, Lancashire...
...from mid-1967 to mid-1968 – back again in the 1970s...
...formed the Keef Hartley Band in 1968

Jun 21 Jon Hiseman: drummer, born in Woolwich, London...
...replaced Keef Hartley – left shortly afterwards to form Colosseum

1945 Mar 11 Harvey Mandel: guitarist, aka "The Snake", born in Detroit, Michigan...
...joined the 1st all-American lineup in 1970 – after leaving Canned Heat:
bassist Larry Taylor left Canned Heat with Mandel to join Mayall

Mar 30 Eric Clapton: guitarist, born in Ripley, Surrey...
...joined in early 1965 from the Yardbirds

Nov 26 John McVie: bassist, born in Ealing, West London...
...delayed joining the original Fleetwood Mac to stay with Mayall

1946 Jan 10 Aynsley Dunbar: drummer, born in Liverpool, England...
...from autumn 1966 to spring 1967

Oct 29 Peter Green: guitarist, born Peter Allen Greenbaum, in Bethnal Green, London...
...replaced Eric Clapton in July 1966, when Clapton left to form Cream

1948 Jan 17 Mick Taylor: guitarist, born in Barnet, Hertfordshire...
...replaced Peter Green in mid-'67 – left in 1969 and joined the Rolling Stones

John Mayall's Bluesbreakers

1965 Mar 5 Yardbirds released *For Your Love* – Eric Clapton joined Mayall shortly afterwards

Nov 6 Eric Clapton rejoined Bluesbreakers after a brief trip to Greece with the Glands...
...replaced Peter Green, he had only joined the Bluesbreakers a week earlier

1966 Jul 22 released *Bluesbreakers with Eric Clapton* (UK)...
...The Bluesbreakers:

John Mayall: keyboards and vocals – formed the Bluesbreakers in 1963
John McVie: bass – left in late 1967 to join Fleetwood Mac
Hughie Flint: drums – joined in early 1964 – left in mid-1966
Eric Clapton: guitar – joined in early '65 – left in mid-'66 to form Cream

	Jul 31	Cream's official debut concert – Clapton left the Bluesbreakers shortly before...
		...he was replaced by Peter Green
1967	Aug 13	Peter Green's Fleetwood Mac's debut gig – featuring guitarist Peter Green...
		...Green was replaced in the Bluesbreakers by Terry Edmonds in June:
		future Rolling Stone, Mick Taylor replaced Edmonds in late June
		...drummer Mick Fleetwood had a very brief tenure with Mayall in mid-1967
1968	Apr 19	Free's debut gig...
		...bassist Andy Fraser joined in early '68 – left a few weeks later to form Free
1968	Jun 15	Jeff Beck Group gig at the Fillmore East...
		...drummer Mickey Waller: brief spell in early '67 – replaced Aynsley Dunbar

Delbert McClinton

1940	Nov 4	harmonica player, born in Lubbock, Texas...
		...provided the harmonica on Bruce Channel's 1962 #1, *Hey Baby*
		...reputedly inspired John Lennon's harmonica rendition on *Love Me Do*

Chas McDevitt

1934	Dec 4	British skiffle pioneer, born in Glasgow, Scotland
1958	May 22	replaced Jerry Lee Lewis when he was forced to abandon his British tour
1961	Dec 2	UK tour as a support act with Billy Fury and the Blue Flames

MC5

1944	Dec 12	Rob Tyner: vocals and harmonica, born Robert Derminer, in Detroit, Michigan...
		...Tyner and Smith were founding members when Motor City 5 formed in '64
1949	Sep 13	Fred "Sonic" Smith: guitar and vocals, born in West Virginia...
		...Smith formed Sonic's Rendezvous Band in the mid-1970s
1968	Jul 15	Yippie permit application – MC5 was only band to play at Democratic Convention
	Oct 30	debut album *Kick Out the Jams* was recorded live in Detroit
1969	Apr 16	dropped by Elektra after running ads deemed to be offensive
1971	Dec 13	John Sinclair freed from prison – ten years for possession of two joints...
		...dropped by the band as manager in mid-1969, just before sentencing
1972	Dec 31	last-ever gig – also the last gig ever at the venue Detroit's Grande Ballroom

John McLaughlin

guitar: Georgie Fame's Blue Flames – Graham Bond Quartet – Mahavishnu Orchestra

1942	Jan 4	jazz-rock guitarist, born in Yorkshire, England
1963	Feb 20	Graham Bond Quartet backed Duffy Power on *I Saw Her Standing There*

1969 Jan 18 recorded his debut solo album, *Extrapolation*

1969 Aug 19 recording started on Miles Davis's seminal jazz rock album, *Bitches Brew*...

...lineup included the future Mahavishnu Orchestra members:

John McLaughlin: guitar and founding member – band formed in 1971
Billy Cobham: drums and founding member

Meat Loaf

singer: Meat Loaf Soul – Popcorn Blizzard

1947 Sep 27 singer and actor, born Marvin Lee Aday, in Dallas, Texas...

...Meat Loaf was a founding member of Meat Loaf Soul, formed in 1967:

Meat Loaf Soul morphed into Popcorn Blizzard – lead singer, Meat Loaf

1967 Oct 17 the musical *Hair* opened off-Broadway – he appeared in a later Broadway cast

1968 Dec 30 Popcorn Blizzard supported the Fugs in Detroit

1977 Oct 21 released *Bat Out of Hell* (US)

Joe Meek

producer: Carter Lewis and the Southerners – The Outlaws – John Leyton – The Tornados
Heinz – Cliff Bennett and the Rebel Rousers – Screaming Lord Sutch and the Savages
record label owner: Triumph

1929 Apr 5 groundbreaking British independent producer, born in Newent, Gloucestershire

1956 Jul 2 Johnny Burnette recorded *The Train Kept A-Rollin'*; and *Honey Hush* on 3 July...

...both sides covered by Screaming Lord Sutch in 1965, produced by Meek

1959 Jul 16 Coasters recorded *Poison Ivy* – they recorded *I'm a Hog for You* the next day...

...Joe Meek produced Screaming Lord Sutch's 1963 cover of *Hog*

1962 Aug 17 writer, producer: Tornados released *Telstar* (UK) – 1st US #1 by a British group

1964 May 27 Lord Sutch's pirate radio station opened with the Meek-produced *Jack the Ripper*

1967 Feb 3 committed suicide: 37 years old

Steve Miller

guitar and vocals: The Marksmen – Goldberg Miller Blues Band – Miller Blues Band
Steve Miller Band

1943 Oct 5 born in Milwaukee, Wisconsin

Steve Miller Band

1967 Sep 1 1st Steve Miller Band appearance with Boz Scaggs...

...lineup included:

Steve Miller: guitar and vocals – band formed in late 1966...

...previously with the Goldberg Miller Blues Band

Boz Scaggs: guitar – joined mid-1967 – left mid-1968 for a solo career

...Miller and Scaggs had been together in the late 1950s in the Marksmen

1968 Dec 29 early Poco gig at the Fillmore West – Steve Miller Band were top of the bill

1970 May 16 supported the Jimi Hendrix Experience in Philadelphia

Million Dollar Quartet

1956	Dec 4	legendary Sun Records jam session: Elvis, Cash, Perkins and Jerry Lee Lewis

Garnet Mimms

1933	Nov 16	singer, born in Ashland, West Virginia
1970	Oct 3	Janis Joplin covered *Cry Baby* on her album *Pearl* – 1963 hit for the Enchanters

Joni Mitchell

Inducted into the Rock and Roll Hall of Fame in 1997

1943	Nov 7	singer-songwriter, born Roberta Joan Anderson...
		...in Fort McLeod, Alberta, Canada
1962	Oct 31	1st paid gig
1975	Oct 30	support act: Bob Dylan's *Rolling Thunder Review* tour opened

Moby Grape

1946	Apr 18	Skip Spence: guitarist, singer, founding member...
		...born in Windsor, Ontario, Canada
1966	Nov 25	1st major gig...
		...Skip Spence had previously been Jefferson Airplane's drummer
1967	May 29	released their eponymous debut album (US)
	Jun 10	played the *Fantasy Fair and Magic Mountain Music Festival*
1968	Mar 29	a fake Moby Grape played a gig in Santa Monica
	Apr 3	released *Wow/Grape Jam* (US) – Skip Spence's final album
1968	May 31	final performances with Skip Spence – the axe and hotel door beckoned

Zoot Money

keyboards and vocals: Zoot Money's Big Roll Band – Alexis Korner's Blues Incorporated
Dantalian's Chariot – Eric Burdon and the Animals

Zoot Money's Big Roll Band was formed in 1961.

1942	Jul 17	Zoot Money was born in Bournemouth, Dorset
1942	Dec 31	Andy Summers: guitar, born Andrew Somers, in Poulton-le-Fylde, Lancashire...
		...joined in the mid-1960s – his 1st professional gig:
		went on to join the Police

Zoot Money's Big Roll Band morphed into Dantalian's Chariot in 1967.

They both joined Eric Burdon's New Animals in 1968.

The Monkees

1942	Feb 13	Peter Tork: musician, singer, born Peter Halsten Thorkelson, in Washington, DC
	Dec 30	Mike Nesmith: guitarist, singer and songwriter, born in Houston, Texas
1945	Mar 8	Micky Dolenz: drummer and singer, born in Los Angeles, California...
		...previously a child star in the TV show *Circus Boy*

	Dec 30	Davy Jones: singer, born in Manchester, England...
		...previously appeared in *Coronation Street* as Ena Sharples' grandson
1964	Feb 9	Beatles' 1st appearance on the *Ed Sullivan Show* – Jones was also on the show
1965	Sep 8	casting ads appeared looking for "4 insane boys"...
		...wannabe Monkees who auditioned included:
		Van Dyke Parks: future Beach Boys collaborator Danny Hutton: future Three Dog Night singer Paul Williams: songwriter Harry Nilsson: John Lennon collaborator and singer-songwriter Steven Stills: later in Buffalo Springfield, and Crosby, Stills & Nash
1966	Sep 12	1st *Monkees* TV show aired in America...
		...The Monkees:
		Peter Tork: vocals, bass, keyboards and other instruments Mike Nesmith: vocals, guitar and songwriter Micky Dolenz: vocals and drums Davy Jones: vocals
	Dec 3	1st-ever concert performance
1967	Jan 21	recorded *A Little Bit Me, A Little Bit You* – led to the end of Don Kirshner...
		...original release was withdrawn for a new B-side:
		Mike Nesmith's *The Girl I Knew Somewhere* was the new coupling
	Jan 22	last gig on the 1st American tour
	Jun 16	Monkees saw Jimi Hendrix at *Monterey* – invited him to join their US tour
	Jul 8	Jimi Hendrix Experience joined the Monkees' American tour as the opening act
1968	Nov 6	world premiere of their movie, *Head* – co-written by Jack Nicholson
1969	Nov 30	penultimate concert of the 1969 three-Monkee tour – on from there as a duo...
		...Mike Nesmith left after the tour

The Moody Blues

1934	Sep 19	Brian Epstein: manager, born in Liverpool, England...
		...managed the group after they had their hit record *Go Now!*
1941	Dec 27	Mike Pinder: keyboardist and singer, born in Birmingham, England...
		...before the Krew Kats, he was with El Riot and the Rebels ...he was later one of the pioneers of the mellotron
1944	Oct 29	Denny Laine: guitarist and singer, born Brian Hines, in Jersey, Channel Isles
1946	Oct 14	Justin Hayward: guitarist and singer, born in Swindon, Wiltshire...
		...joined in late 1966, replaced Denny Laine
1958	Oct 5	Alex Murray performed as one half of the Most Brothers – with Mickie Most...
		...Murray was the band's early manager and produced their single *Go Now!*

Road to the Moody Blues, all from other Midlands bands. *SEE 2 May 1962*

Denny Laine	Denny Laine and the Diplomats
Clint Warwick	Danny King and the Dukes

Mike Pinder and Ray Thomas — Krew Cats
Graeme Edge — Gerry Levine and the Avengers

1964 May 2 1st gig
...The Moody Blues:
Denny Laine: guitar and vocals – left in late 1966...
...left to form Denny Laine's Electric String Band
...later with Ginger Baker's Airforce and Wings
Clint Warwick: bass and vocals – left in late 1966
Mike Pinder: keyboards and vocals – left in 1974
Ray Thomas: flute and vocals...
...previously with El Riot and the Rebels, and the Krew Cats
Graeme Edge: drums
...the band's name was inspired by the Midlands brewery M&B
Nov 13 released 1st single, *Go Now!* (UK) – Bessie Bank's R&B hit in early 1964...
...lead vocals from Denny Laine
1965 Jun 19 Kinks opened their 1st US tour – Moodies due to tour with them but visa issues
Dec 12 support act for the Beatles' last-ever UK concert – with singer Denny Laine
1970 Aug 28 performed at the *Isle of Wight Festival*
1972 Feb 25 Denny Laine was with Wings when they released *Give Ireland Back to the Irish*
1974 Jul 17 opened their own recording studio – one of the 1st with quadraphonic capabilities

Moondog

1916 May 26 New York street performer, born Louis Thomas Hardin, in Marysville, Kansas...
...name inspired from time spent with his pet dog, howling at the moon together
1951 Jul 11 Alan Freed called himself "Moondog" on his radio show – later sued by Moondog

The Moonglows

Inducted into the Rock and Roll Hall of Fame in 2000
1929 Jul 27 Harvey Fuqua: singer and early Motown executive, born in Louisville, Kentucky
1939 Apr 2 Marvin Gaye: singer, born Marvin Pentz Gay Jr, in Washington, DC
1959 Jun 12 concert appearance with a new lineup that included Marvin Gaye...
...lineup included:
Harvey Fuqua: founding member – moved on to the new Motown label
Marvin Gay – Fuqua later signed Gay to Motown (became Gaye)...
...Gay's group, the Marquees, became 'new' Moonglows in mid-1959
...Moonglows were called "The Crazy Sounds" but renamed by Alan Freed

Van Morrison

Inducted into the Rock and Roll Hall of Fame in 1993
saxophone and vocals: Deanie Sands and the Javelins – The Monarchs – Manhattan Showband
The Golden Eagles – The Gamblers – Them
1945 Aug 31 singer and songwriter, born in Belfast, Northern Ireland...

...Deanie Sands and the Javelins: guitar and vocals – skiffle group c.1959
...Monarchs: singer and saxophonist – early 1960s
...Manhattan Showband: saxophone – short stay, c. early 1964
...Golden Eagles: vocals and saxophone – early '64, left to join the Gamblers
...Gamblers: singer – became "Them" soon after Van Morrison joined:
band took its name from the 1954 sci-fi movie *Them*

Them

1964 Apr 14 birth of Them
Jul 5 Them's 1st recording session for Decca...
...included songs written by Van Morrison:
Gloria – B-side of Them's *Baby Please Don't Go*
One Two Brown Eyes – B-side of *Don't Start Crying Now*
...covers recorded included:
Baby Please Don't Go – Big Joe Williams single in 1935
Don't Start Crying Now – Slim Harpo single in 1961...
...written by Slim Harpo (as James Moore)

Van Morrison

1967 Mar 28 1st day of recording for *Blowin' Your Mind!* – recently split from Them...
...included his 1st single, the Morrison penned *Brown Eyed Girl*
Nov 11 1st solo appearance on *American Bandstand*
1970 Apr 3 over-hyped Brinsley Schwarz gig at the Fillmore East – Morrison also on the bill
1976 Nov 25 made a guest appearance at the Band's swan song concert, *The Last Waltz*

Mickie Most

singer: The Most Brothers – Mickie Most and the Gear record label owner: RAK
producer: The Animals – Donovan – Jeff Beck

1938 Jun 20 singer and producer, born Michael Hayes, in Aldershot, Hampshire...
...in the mid-1960s he was a singer with Mickie Most and the Gear
1958 Oct 5 on tour with the Kalin Twins and Cliff Richard, as one-half of the Most Brothers...
...The Most Brothers:
Mickie Most: singer – went on to become a renowned record producer
Alex Murray: singer – went on to manage the Moody Blues
1964 May 18 produced the Animals recording of *House of the Rising Sun*
1965 Feb 12 Donovan's career was just starting out – Most became his producer in late 1966

Mother Earth

1944 Dec 27 Tracy Nelson: singer, born in French Camp, California
1967 Sep 1 supported the Steve Miller Band for their 1st appearance with Boz Scaggs...
...Mother Earth lineup included:
Tracy Nelson: singer and founding member – formed in the late 1960s

Motörhead

1945 Dec 24 Lemmy: bassist and singer, born Ian Kilmister, in Burslem, Stoke-on-Trent...
...he formed the band after he was sacked from Hawkwind
...previously a roadie with the Jimi Hendrix Experience

1975 May 18 Lemmy was sacked from Hawkwind after a drugs bust on the Canadian border

1975 Jul 20 debut gig...
...Motörhead: a trio, originally called "Bastard":
Lemmy: bass and vocals
Lucas Fox: drums – left '76 after recording unreleased 1st album for UA
Larry Wallis: guitar – joined from the Pink Fairies – left shortly after Fox
...band's name was inspired by the American slang word for "speed freak"
...*Motorhead* was a Hawkwind B-side in '75 – last song he wrote with them

Mott the Hoople

1939 Jun 3 Ian Hunter: keyboards and vocals, born Ian Hunter Patterson...
...in Oswestry, Shropshire:
formed Hunter-Ronson Band in early '75, after Mott the Hoople folded

1944 Mar 31 Mick Ralphs: guitarist, born in Hereford, Herefordshire...
...with Buddies before the Doc Thomas Group, c.1964

1946 May 26 Mick Ronson: guitarist, born in Hull, Yorkshire...
...joined in 1974, shortly before the band folded
...formed the Hunter-Ronson Band in early 1975

1947 Mar 11 Blue Weaver: keyboardist, born in Cardiff, South Wales...
...joined in 1973 – previously with Amen Corner and the Strawbs

The Doc Thomas Group morphed into Silence and became Mott the Hoople.

1969 Sep 5 early gig as Mott the Hoople:
...Silence:
Dale Griffin: drums – from the Doc Thomas Group
Overend Watts: bass – from the Doc Thomas Group
Mick Ralphs: guitar – from the Doc Thomas Group
Verden Allen: keyboards – from the Shakedown Sound
Ian Hunter: vocals and piano – replaced original singer Stan Tippins
...Stan Tippins: roadie – ex-Doc Thomas lead singer, displaced by Hunter
...Mott the Hoople:
Dale Griffin: drums – formed Mott when Mott the Hoople folded
Overend Watts: bass – formed Mott when Mott the Hoople folded
Mick Ralphs: guitar – left in mid-1973 to form Bad Company
Verden Allen: keyboards – left in early 1973
Ian Hunter: vocals and piano – formed Hunter-Ronson when MtH folded
...band's name taken from the title of a 1966 Willard Manus novel

1971 Jan 19 supported by Amazing Blondel at the Marquee club

1972	Mar 24	David Bowie rescued a disillusioned Mott the Hoople from splitting up...
		...Swiss gig inspired the band to write *Ballad of Mott (March 26th '72, Zurich)*
	May 14	recorded *All the Young Dudes*
1974	Mar 8	Bad Company's debut gig – formed by Mick Ralphs after he left Mott the Hoople

Mountain

1945	Oct 22	Leslie West: guitarist, born Leslie Weinstein, in New York, New York...
		...previously with the Vagrants – mid-1960s band ...formed Mountain in 1969
1970	Jun 28	performed at the *Festival Express* event in Toronto
	Aug 7	performed at the *Goose Lake International Music Festival*
1971	Apr 26	West played on studio recordings for Pete Townshend's 'lost' album, *Lifehouse*
	May 6	Fillmore closures announced – performed at final Fillmore East concerts in June
1983	Apr 17	Felix Pappalardi was shot dead by his wife: 43 years old...
		...bassist, keyboardist, singer and founding member of Mountain ...previously Cream's producer

The Move

1940	Sep 23	Mike Sheridan: born in Sparkbrook, Birmingham...
		...Mike Sheridan's Nightriders became Mike Sheridan's Lot
		...Sheridan then left the band and they reverted to the Nightriders, before morphing into Idle Race
1943	Aug 18	Carl Wayne: singer, born Colin Tooley, in Birmingham, England
1946	Nov 8	Roy Wood: multi-instrumentalist and songwriter, born in Kitts Green, Birmingham
	Dec 10	Chris "Ace" Kefford: bass, aka "Ace the Face"...
		...born in Yardley Wood, Birmingham
1947	Dec 30	Jeff Lynne: keyboards, guitar and vocals, born in Birmingham, England

The Move formed from three other Birmingham bands.

1966	Jan 17	five musicians met and decided to form a band...
		...musicians:
		Bev Bevan, Chris Kefford, Carl Wayne – Carl Wayne and the Vikings Trevor Burton – Danny King and the Mayfair Set Roy Wood – Mike Sheridan's Lot
		...they called the new band "The Move":
		Roy Wood: multi-instrumentalist and singer...
		...morphed the Move into the Electric Light Orchestra (ELO) in 1971
		Bev Bevan: drummer...
		...co-founded ELO with Roy Wood
		Chris "Ace" Kefford: bassist...
		...left in 1968 for an ill-fated solo career

Carl Wayne: singer...
...left in early 1970 for a solo career – fronted the Hollies in 2000
Trevor Burton: guitarist...
...left in 1969: played with Balls and the Steve Gibbons Band
...Jeff Lynne: keyboards, guitar and vocals...
...replaced Carl Wayne in 1970 – founding member of ELO
...previously with Mike Sheridan's Nightriders:
which morphed into Idle Race
...later with the Traveling Wilburys

1967 Apr 29 performed at the *14-Hour Technicolor Dream*
Sep 30 UK's 1st legal pop radio station, Radio 1 opened – 1st song, *Flowers in the Rain*
Oct 11 *Flowers in the Rain* libel suit with Harold Wilson was settled
Nov 14 UK tour opened, with the Move supporting headliner Jimi Hendrix
Dec 22 performed at the *Christmas on Earth Continued* concert
1968 Jul 8 supported the Byrds at London's Royal Albert Hall the previous day
1972 Apr 16 1st gig as the Electric Light Orchestra – in the transition from the Move to ELO...
...lineup included:
Roy Wood: multi-instrumentalist and vocals
Jeff Lynne: guitar and vocals
Bev Bevan: drums
...Roy Wood left ELO after the 1st album, to form Wizzard

MOVIES, THEATRE, LITERATURE TV AND RADIO

1901 Sep 28 Ed Sullivan: presenter of *The Ed Sullivan Show*, born in Harlem, New York...
...introduced America to Elvis Presley and the Beatles
...censored the Rolling Stones but failed to censor the Doors
1929 Nov 30 Dick Clark, host of *American Bandstand*, born in Mount Vernon, New York
1953 Dec 30 Marlon Brando's movie *The Wild One* opened in New York
1955 Mar 25 *Blackboard Jungle* released – opening credits featured *Rock Around the Clock*...
...the movie that kick-started rock'n'roll
Oct 7 Allen Ginsberg gave the 1st reading of his beat poem, *Howl*
Oct 27 *Rebel Without a Cause* – heralded the 1st generation of teenagers...
...James Dean's 2nd movie, released less than a month after his death
...co-starred Dennis Hopper, who later made the 1960s classic *Easy Rider*
Oct 29 Sam Phillips opened the 1st American all-female radio station, WHER
1956 Mar 21 *Rock Around the Clock* opened in America – 1st rock'n'roll movie
Aug 22 *The Girl Can't Help It* opened – seminal rock'n'roll movie
Sep 9 Elvis Presley's 1st appearance on the *Ed Sullivan Show*
Nov 15 *Love Me Tender* opened in New York – Elvis Presley's 1st movie
1957 Jan 6 Elvis Presley's censored "no hips" performance on his final *Ed Sullivan Show*

	Feb 16	1st episode of *Six-Five Special* – the UK's 1st pop music TV show
	May 3	*The Tommy Steele Story* premiered in London – Britain's 1st rock'n'roll movie
	Jul 19	Frankie Lymon outraged public decency by dancing with a white girl on live TV...
		...incident resulted in Alan Freed's *The Big Beat* being taken off air
	Aug 5	national TV debut of *American Bandstand* – Dick Clark was the show's host
1958	Jan 20	Radio KWK's "Record Breaking Week" – smashed rock'n'roll records on air
	Sep 11	Lloyd Price recorded *Stagger Lee* – re-recorded for *American Bandstand*
	Dec 27	last episode of UK TV's 1st pop music show, *Six-Five Special*
1960	Oct 20	*Lady Chatterley's Lover* trial in the UK – end of literary censorship...
		...in America, the end came with William Burroughs' *Naked Lunch* in 1966
1963	May 12	Bob Dylan pulled out of the *Ed Sullivan Show* – because of censorship issues
	Aug 9	*Ready Steady Go!* TV show opened in the UK
1964	Jan 1	debut of UK TV's *Top of the Pops*
	Jan 10	Manfred Mann's *5-4-3-2-1* replaced Surfaris's *Wipe Out* on *Ready Steady Go!*
	Feb 9	Beatles' 1st appearance on the *Ed Sullivan Show*...
		...Sullivan experienced Beatlemania at Heathrow airport on 31 October
	Mar 29	Radio Caroline made the 1st-ever pirate radio broadcast to the UK
	May 27	Screaming Lord Sutch launched his own pirate radio station, Radio Sutch
	Sep 16	*Shindig!* debuted on US TV
1965	Apr 2	1st live edition of UK TV's *Ready Steady Go!*, as "*Ready Steady Goes Live!*"
1966	Sep 12	1st *Monkees* TV show aired in America
	Oct 11	launch party at the Roundhouse for Britain's 1st counterculture newspaper, *it*
	Dec 23	final episode of the British TV show *Ready Steady Go!*
1967	Jan 15	Stones censored on the *Ed Sullivan Show* – not to spend "the night" together
	Jan 22	Stones refused to wave from revolving stage at the end of Palladium TV show...
		...maybe an attempt to regain street credibility after the *Ed Sullivan Show*
	Jun 25	1st global TV broadcast, *Our World* – with Beatles singing *All You Need Is Love*
	Sep 10	Pete Seeger's *Waist Deep in the Big Muddy* censored on the *Smothers Brothers*
	Sep 17	Doors refused to censor *Light My Fire* on the *Ed Sullivan Show*
	Sep 21	1st *John Peel Sessions* programme on BBC Radio – with music from Tomorrow
	Sep 30	Radio 1 started broadcasting – 1st official pop and rock radio station in the UK
	Oct 17	hippie musical *Hair* opened off-Broadway
	Nov 9	1st issue of *Rolling Stone* magazine hit the streets
1968	Sep 27	*Hair* opened in London...
		...marked the end of formal censorship in live British theatre
	Dec 11	Stones recorded their TV special *Rock and Roll Circus* – not seen until 1996
1969	Jan 4	Hendrix's unscheduled performance of *Sunshine of Your Love* on Lulu's TV show
	May 8	premiere of *Easy Rider* at the Cannes Film Festival:
		Peter Fonda: co-wrote, starred and produced the movie

Dennis Hopper: co-wrote, starred and directed
Jack Nicholson: Oscar nomination for *Best Supporting Actor*
Terry Southern: co-wrote the Oscar nominated screenplay
Phil Spector: cameo appearance as a drug dealer

	Nov 10	Elvis Presley's *Change of Habit* opened (US) – 31st and final movie as an actor
	Dec 17	Tiny Tim married Miss Vicki live on TV's *Johnny Carson Show*
1970	May 20	*Let It Be* movie premiered in Britain – none of the Beatles attended
1971	Jan 18	Canada introduced a minimum radio playlist quota of 30% of home-grown music
	Sep 21	1st edition of the British rock based TV show, *The Old Grey Whistle Test*
1976	Dec 1	Sex Pistols' notorious TV appearance on Bill Grundy's *Today* show
1979	Nov 12	Marty Balin's rock opera, *Rock Justice*, opened at San Francisco's Old Waldorf
1995	Nov 19	*The Beatles Anthology* premiered in America on ABC TV

Moon Mullican

1909 Mar 29 country and rockabilly singer, songwriter, piano player, born in Corrigan, Texas
1956 Sep 17 Brenda Lee released *Jambalaya*...
...Mullican reputedly co-wrote it with Hank Williams but was not credited

Mitch Murray

1963 Mar 14 Gerry and the Pacemakers' single *How Do You Do It* went straight in at UK #1...
...written by Mitch Murray
1963 May 11 Carter Lewis and the Southerners radio performance...
...Murray wrote Carter Lewis's 1963 single *Your Momma's Out of Town*

Murray the K

1964 Dec 25 *Murray the K's Christmas Show* opened – included Zombies' 1st US appearance
1967 Mar 25 Cream's US concert debut – at Murray the K's *Live in Person*...package show

Charlie Musselwhite

1944 Jan 31 blues harmonica player, born in Kosciusko, Mississippi
Charlie Musselwhite (band) included:
1945 Mar 11 Harvey Mandel: guitarist, aka "The Snake", born in Detroit, Michigan...
...lead guitarist in the mid-1960s – later with Canned Heat and John Mayall

Rick(y) Nelson

Inducted into the Rock and Roll Hall of Fame in 1987
guitar and vocals: The Stone Canyon Band
1939 Aug 21 James Burton: guitarist, born in Dubberly, Louisiana, but grew up in Shreveport...
...member of Nelson's backing band c.1958 to c.1967
1940 May 8 Rick Nelson: teenage idol, musician, songwriter, born in Teaneck, New Jersey
1946 Mar 8 Randy Meisner: bassist and singer, born in Scottsbluff, Nebraska...
...member of the Stone Canyon Band – later founding member of the Eagles

1957 Apr 10 sang *I'm Walkin'* on the family's TV show, *The Adventures of Ozzie and Harriet...*
...a hit on both sides of the Atlantic for Fats Domino in early 1957

Sandy Nelson

drums: Jan and Dean's backing band – The Gamblers

1938 Dec 1 rock'n'roll's 1st drum hero, born in Santa Monica, California...
...continued to play after he lost his right leg in a motorcycle accident in 1963

1959 Jul 15 recorded his 1st single, *Teen Beat* – joint writing credit with Art Laboe

New York Dolls

1952 Jul 15 Johnny Thunders: guitarist and singer, born John Anthony Genzale...
...in Queens, New York

New York Dolls came together as Actress in late 1971.

1972 Aug 22 early New York Dolls gig...
...Actress:

Johnny Thunders: guitar and vocals
Billy Murcia: drums
Arthur Kane: bass
Rick Rivets: guitar – left before they became the New York Dolls

Actress morphed into the New York Dolls.

...New York Dolls:

Johnny Thunders: guitar, vocals – left 1975, formed the Heartbreakers
Billy Murcia: drums – died 6 November* 1972 – replaced by Jerry Nolan
Arthur Kane: bass – left mid-1975 – on to a number of short-lived bands
David Johansen: vocals – stayed until the end, in late 1976
Sylvain Sylvain: guitar – stayed until the end

Nov 6 original drummer Billy Murcia died during their 1st UK tour: 21 years old

1975 Oct 17 post-Johnny Thunders era, no record contract...
...Johnny Thunders and Jerry Nolan had left to form the Heartbreakers
...Malcolm McLaren: manager – took over the ailing band in mid-1975

The Nice

1944 Nov 2 Keith Emerson: keyboards, singer and co-founder...
...born in Todmorden, West Yorkshire

1948 Dec 13 David O'List: guitarist and founding member, born in Chiswick, London...
...founding member of the Attack – left in early 1967 to join the Nice
...after Nice he had very short stints with Jethro Tull and Roxy Music

1967 Nov 14 guitarist David O'List covered on stage for Syd Barrett on Jimi Hendrix's UK tour

1968 Jun 26 banned for life from the Albert Hall after a flag-burning performance of *America*

1970 Aug 25 Emerson, Lake & Palmer's debut gig – shortly after the Nice folded

Harry Nilsson

1941 Jun 15 singer and songwriter, born in Brooklyn, New York
1965 Sep 8 auditioned unsuccessfully to become a Monkee – but later wrote songs for them
1974 Mar 12 ejected from the Troubadour club with John Lennon – Lennon's "lost weekend"...
...Lennon produced Nilsson's album *Pussy Cats* around this time
Mar 31 was at the jam session the last time that Lennon and McCartney played together
Jul 29 Mama Cass Elliott died in Nilsson's London apartment
1978 Sep 7 Keith Moon died in Nilsson's London apartment – the same one as Mama Cass

Jack Nitzsche

1937 Apr 22 musician, arranger, producer and songwriter, born in Chicago, Illinois...
...wrote *Needles and Pins* with Sonny Bono – Jackie DeShannon single 1963
1962 Jul 13 arranger for Phil Spector's *He's a Rebel* – 1st recording with Spector
1965 Feb 26 Rolling Stones released *Play with Fire* – Nitzsche played harpsichord

Phil Ochs

1940 Dec 19 folk protest singer and songwriter, born in El Paso, Texas
1971 Dec 13 John Sinclair freed from jail – Ochs performed at the *Freedom Rally*
1975 May 11 performed at the *War Is Over* rally in New York's Central Park...
...sang *There but for Fortune* as a duet with Joan Baez:
Ochs album track in 1964 – UK hit for Joan Baez in 1965
1976 Apr 9 committed suicide by hanging himself: 35 years old

Johnny O'Keefe

1935 Jan 19 singer, songwriter and Australia's 1st rock'n'roll star, born in Sydney, Australia
Johnny O'Keefe and the Dee Jays
1957 Oct 12 supported Little Richard on his fateful Australian tour
1958 Jul 5 released *The Wild One* – gave birth to Australian rock'n'roll...
...notable covers included:
recorded by Jerry Lee Lewis in 1958
Jerry Allison, as "Ivan", single in 1958
Jet Harris EP track in 1962
Iggy Pop album track in 1986

Mike Oldfield

bass and guitar: The Sallyangie – Kevin Ayres and the Whole World
1953 May 15 composer and multi-instrumentalist, born in Reading, Berkshire...
...Sallyangie: his first band was a folk duo with his sister Sally, late 1960s
...in 1969 he joined Kevin Ayres and the Whole World
1973 May 25 Virgin released *Tubular Bells* as its inaugural album release (UK)

Roy Orbison

Inducted into the Rock and Roll Hall of Fame in 1987

guitar and vocals: The Teen Kings – Traveling Wilburys

1936 Apr 23 singer and songwriter, born in Vernon, Texas

1956 Mar 27 re-recorded *Ooby Dooby* at Sun Records

...he had recorded the song with the Teen Kings three weeks earlier:

at Norman Petty's studio – it was released on Je-Wel

...Orbison wrote the B-side, *Go! Go! Go!*

1960 Aug 8 recorded *Blue Angel* as his follow-up to *Only the Lonely (Know How I Feel)*...

...both songs were written by Orbison and Joe Melson

1966 Jun 6 his wife died in a motorcycle accident – two of his children died two years later...

...*Claudette* – 1958 Everly Brothers B-side – Orbison's ode to his wife

1967 Mar 3 UK tour kicked off – supported by Jeff Beck Group and Small Faces

The Orioles

Inducted into the Rock and Roll Hall of Fame in 1995

1928 Aug 18 Sonny Til: singer, born Earlington Carl Tilghman, in Baltimore, Maryland

Morphed from the Vibranaires in the late 1940s.

1948 Sep 4 review of their 1st single, *It's Too Soon to Know* – dawn of the doo wop era...

...lineup included:

Sonny Til: lead singer and founding member

Johnny Otis

Inducted into the Rock and Roll Hall of Fame in 1994

club owner: The Barrelhouse Club (Los Angeles) record label owner: Dig

1921 Dec 28 R&B pioneer, bandleader, producer and talent scout, born in Vallejo, California...

...his Barrelhouse Club was an inspiration for Alexis Korner and Cyril Davies

1938 Jan 25 Etta James: blues singer, born Jamesetta Hawkins, in Los Angeles, California...

...co-wrote *The Wallflower* with Etta James – Etta James single in 1955:

The Wallflower was an answer song to Midnighters' *Work with Me Annie*

1952 Aug 13 with Otis's backing band, Big Mama Thornton recorded *Hound Dog*...

...written by Leiber and Stoller

...produced by Johnny Otis – original releases also gave him a writing credit

1954 Apr 24 Midnighters charted with *Work with Me Annie* – discovered by Otis in 1951

1958 Apr 3 recorded *Willie and the Hand Jive* – as the Johnny Otis Show...

...covered by Cliff Richard in 1960 and Eric Clapton in 1974

The Outlaws

Renamed from "The Stormers" in late 1960, Joe Meek's house band.

1929 Apr 5 Joe Meek: independent producer, born in Newent, Gloucestershire

1940	Mar 11	Bobby Graham: drummer, born Robert Francis Neate, in Edmonton, London...
		...original member of the Outlaws – left in 1961 to join Joe Brown's Bruvvers
1962	Jun 25	Screaming Lord Sutch and the Savages gig – with guitarist Ritchie Blackmore...
		...Blackmore left to join the Outlaws in Oct 1962 – left the Outlaws in 1964
1969	Jun 4	Jon Lord and Ritchie Blackmore went to an Episode Six gig...
		...Episode Six's lineup included: drummer Mick Underwood: he left the Outlaws in mid-1965 to join the Herd

Jimmy Page

SEE Led Zeppelin

Graham Parker and the Rumour

1947	Mar 25	Brinsley Schwarz: guitarist and singer, born in Woodbridge, Suffolk...
		...founding member of the Rumour in mid-1975
1950	Nov 18	Graham Parker: singer and guitarist, born in London, England...
		...teamed up with the Rumour in mid-1975

Van Dyke Parks

1965	Sep 8	auditioned unsuccessfully to become a Monkee
1967	May 2	*Smile* was abandoned – collaboration between Brian Wilson and Parks
1971	Aug 30	Beach Boys released *Surf's Up*...
		...Parks and Brian Wilson wrote the title track
2004	Sep 28	co-writer: Brian Wilson finally released his 'lost' 1960s album, *Smile* (US)

Larry Parnes

manager: Tommy Steele – Marty Wilde – Billy Fury – Vince Eager – Dickie Pride – Johnny Gentle
Duffy Power – Terry Dene – Georgie Fame – Joe Brown – The Beat Boys (became) The Blue Flames

1956	Sep 24	Tommy Steele recorded the 1st UK rock'n'roll hit, *Rock With the Caveman*
1958	Oct 1	promoter: invited Billy Fury to make an impromptu concert appearance
	Nov 26	Billy Fury recorded 1st single – recently signed a management deal with Parnes
1960	Jan 24	promoter: Eddie Cochran's last tour opened in Ipswich, England
	May 10	Silver Beetles failed their audition to become Billy Fury's backing band
	Jul 27	promoted the *Meet the Beat* show...
		...Parnes gave his performers expressive stage names
1961	Dec 2	Billy Fury toured the UK with his backing band, the newly-formed Blue Flames

Les Paul

		Inducted into the Rock and Roll Hall of Fame in 1988
1915	Jun 9	born Lester William Polsfuss, in Waukesha, Wisconsin...
		...electric guitar pioneer and recording innovator

Pavlov's Dog

1977 May 31 final concert...

...lineup included original members:

David Surkamp: vocals – formed in 1972
Siegfried Carver: violin
Steve Scorfina: guitar
Rick Stockton: bass
Doug Rayburn: keyboards

John Peel

record label owner: Dandelion

1939 Aug 30 influential British DJ, born John Robert Parker Ravenscroft, in Heswall, Wirral

1967 Sep 21 Tomorrow appeared on the 1st *John Peel Sessions* on BBC Radio

1968 Apr 19 Tyrannosaurus Rex released *Debora* – Peel was a major champion of the band

The Penguins

1907 Nov 21 Buck Ram: songwriter, arranger and manager, born in Chicago, Illinois

1963 Feb 20 issued *Memories of El Monte* (US) – co-written and produced by Frank Zappa...

...lineup included:

Cleveland Duncan: singer – lead singer on their classic *Earth Angel*
Walter Saulsberry: singer – member of the 2nd incarnation of the group

Carl Perkins

Inducted into the Rock and Roll Hall of Fame in 1987

1932 Apr 9 guitarist, singer and songwriter, born in Tiptonville, Tennessee...

...toured with Johnny Cash in the mid-1960s – wrote *Daddy Sang Bass*

1955 Mar 19 released his self-penned 1st single, *Movie Magg* – on Sam Phillips's Flip label

Aug 1 released his self-penned 1st single on Sun, *Let the Juke Box Keep on Playing*

Dec 19 recorded two of his own compositions, *Honey Don't* and *Blue Suede Shoes*...

...*Honey Don't* was one of three Carl Perkins songs covered by the Beatles:

Honey Don't – Everybody's Trying to Be My Baby – Matchbox

1956 Jan 1 released *Blue Suede Shoes* c/w *Honey Don't* (US)...

...*Blue Suede Shoes* became a rock'n'roll classic with Elvis's single in 1956

Mar 22 near-fatal car accident

Dec 4 *Million Dollar Quartet* recording session with Perkins, Presley, Lewis, and Cash...

...also a Perkins recording session for *Matchbox* – Jerry Lee Lewis on piano

1957 Jan 23 released *Matchbox* on Sun (US) – covered by the Beatles in 1964...

...the song's roots lay in:

Ma Rainey's *Lost Wandering Blues*, recorded in 1924
Blind Lemon Jefferson's *Match Box Blues*, recorded in 1927

...although, on his single Perkins claimed authorship of the song

1964	May 9	he was a support act for Chuck Berry, when Berry toured the UK for the 1st time
1964	Dec 15	Beatles released *Beatles '65*, included *Everybody's Trying to Be My Baby*...
		...original by Rex Griffin in 1936
		...Perkins claimed the writing credit on his 1957 *Dance Album*

Tom Petty and the Heartbreakers

		Inducted into the Rock and Roll Hall of Fame in 2002
1950	Oct 20	Tom Petty: singer and guitarist, born in Gainesville, Florida...
		...later with Traveling Wilburys
1979	Oct 19	released *Damn the Torpedoes* (US)...
		...lineup included:
		Tom Petty: guitar and vocals – band formed in 1975
		...Admiral David Farragut was accredited with the quotation:
		"Damn the Torpedoes, full steam ahead!"

Dewey "Daddy-O" Phillips

1950	Aug 30	poor record sales on It's The Phillips label – launched with Sam Phillips
1954	Jul 19	Elvis released 1st single, *That's All Right* – he was the 1st DJ to play the record

Sam Phillips

Inducted into the Rock and Roll Hall of Fame in 1986 (inaugural year)

producer: Joe Hill Louis – Jackie Brenston and His Delta Cats – Ike Turner and His Kings of Rhythm
Johnny London – Elvis Presley – Carl Perkins – Johnny Cash – Roy Orbison – Jerry Lee Lewis
The Yardbirds
record label owner: It's The Phillips – Flip – Sun

1923	Jan 5	producer and founder of Sun Records, born in Florence, Alabama
1950	Aug 30	poor record sales for the only release on short-lived record label, It's The Phillips
1951	Mar 5	recorded *Rocket 88* with Jackie Brenston and Ike Turner – released on Chess
1952	Mar 1	recorded Johnny London's *Drivin' Slow* – 1st single released on Sun
1953	Jul 18	Elvis Presley's 1st visit to Sam Phillips's Memphis Recording Service
1954	Jan 4	Elvis Presley's 2nd visit to Sam Phillips's Memphis Recording Service
	Jul 19	Elvis Presley released his 1st Sun single, *That's All Right*
	Sep 22	Elvis Presley released his 2nd Sun single, *Good Rockin' Tonight*
1955	Jan 8	Elvis Presley released *Milkcow Blues Boogie* as his 3rd Sun single
	Mar 19	Carl Perkins released his 1st single, *Movie Magg* on the Flip label
	Apr 25	Elvis Presley released his 4th Sun single, *Baby Let's Play House*
	Aug 1	Elvis Presley released his 5th and final Sun single, *Mystery Train*...
		...Jr Parker's version in 1953 had the writing credit "Parker"
		...Sam Phillips's name was added as a writing credit for Elvis's version
	Aug 1	Carl Perkins released his 1st single on Sun, *Let the Juke Box Keep on Playing*
	Oct 29	Sam Phillips opened the 1st all-female radio station

	Nov 20	Elvis Presley left Sun and signed with RCA the following day
	Dec 19	Carl Perkins recorded *Honey Don't* – one of three songs covered by the Beatles
1956	Jan 1	Carl Perkins released *Blue Suede Shoes c/w Honey Don't*
	Mar 22	despite his car crash, Perkins's *Blue Suede Shoes* was Sun's 1st million-seller
	Mar 27	Roy Orbison and the Teen Kings re-recorded *Ooby Dooby*
	Nov 16	Harold Jenkins (later Conway Twitty) failed his audition at Sun Records
	Dec 1	Jerry Lee Lewis released his 1st Sun single, *Crazy Arms*
	Dec 4	*Million Dollar Quartet* recording session, with Presley, Lewis, Perkins and Cash
1957	Jan 23	Billy Riley and His Little Green Men released *Flyin' Saucers Rock & Roll*
	Jan 23	Carl Perkins released *Matchbox* – with Jerry Lee Lewis on piano
	Mar 15	Jerry Lee Lewis released *Whole Lot of Shakin' Going On*
	Nov 3	Jerry Lee Lewis released *Great Balls of Fire*
1958	Apr 9	Jerry Lee Lewis released his last rock'n'roll hit, *High School Confidential*
	May 30	Jerry Lee Lewis recorded *The Return of Jerry Lee* – attempt at damage limitation
	Aug 10	Jerry Lee Lewis released *Break Up* – poor sales following his UK tour revelations
1963	Aug 23	final Jerry Lee Lewis Sun recording session
	Sep 6	Jerry Lee Lewis was the last rock'n'roll star to move on from Sun Records
1965	Mar 15	Jerry Lee Lewis released his last Sun single, *Take Me Back to Old Virginia*
	Sep 12	produced the Yardbirds recording of *The Train Kept A-Rollin'*, at Sun studios
1969	Jul 1	sold the Sun Records label and back catalogue to Shelby Singleton

Norman Pilcher

1967	Nov 24	Beatles released *I Am the Walrus* – reputed to be a pop at Pilcher
1972	Nov 8	drug-busting Detective Sergeant Norman Pilcher was arrested for perjury

Pink Floyd

		Inducted into the Rock and Roll Hall of Fame in 1996
1943	Jul 28	Rick Wright: keyboardist, born in Hatch End, London... ...formed Zee in 1984
	Sep 6	Roger Waters: bassist, singer and songwriter, born in Great Bookham, Surrey... ...after an acrimonious split with the band he followed a solo career
1944	Jan 27	Nick Mason: drummer, born in Birmingham, England
1946	Jan 6	Syd Barrett: guitarist, singer and songwriter, born in Cambridge, England... ...after leaving the band for a solo career he formed the short-lived Stars
1946	Mar 6	David Gilmour: guitarist and singer, born in Cambridge, Cambridgeshire... ...replaced Syd Barrett in 1968

Road to Pink Floyd *SEE 14 October 1966*

Sigma 6

Rick Wright – Roger Waters – Nick Mason

Meggadeaths

Rick Wright – Roger Waters – Nick Mason

The Abdabs: sometimes, The Screaming Abdabs or The Architectural Abdabs

Rick Wright – Roger Waters – Nick Mason – Bob Klose – Syd Barrett

Bob Klose probably played in some or all incarnations of the Abdabs

Syd Barrett probably joined during the latter days of the Abdabs...

...name changed frequently, before settling on "The Tea Set"

The Tea Set

Rick Wright – Roger Waters – Nick Mason – Bob Klose – Syd Barrett

The Pink Floyd Sound

Rick Wright – Roger Waters – Nick Mason – Bob Klose – Syd Barrett...
...Bob Klose: lead guitar
...when Bob Klose left, Syd Barrett took over lead guitar

Pink Floyd, original lineup:

Rick Wright: keyboards – sacked during the recording of *The Wall*
Roger Waters: bass, vocals and songwriter
Nick Mason: drums
Syd Barrett: original guitarist, singer and main songwriter

...name inspired by two bluesmen, Pink Anderson and Floyd Council
...Syd Barrett was replaced by David Gilmour in early 1968
...Roger Waters became the main songwriter after Barrett left

David Gilmour followed a different route into Pink Floyd, bands included:

Jokers Wild – Flowers – Bullitt

Pink Floyd

1966	Oct 11	performed at the *it* launch party at the Roundhouse
	Oct 14	early 'underground' concert
1967	Feb 27	recorded *Arnold Layne* – released as their 1st single – written by Syd Barrett
	Apr 29	performed at the *14-Hour Technicolor Dream*
	May 23	recorded their 2nd single, *See Emily Play* – written by Syd Barrett
	Aug 5	released 1st album, *Piper at the Gates of Dawn* (UK) – mostly written by Barrett...
		...*Take Up Thy Stethoscope and Walk* was the only Waters penned song
	Nov 4	concert debut to open their disastrous 1st American tour...
		...Syd Barrett's behaviour was becoming increasingly erratic
	Nov 14	UK tour supporting Jimi Hendrix...
		...Syd Barrett replaced on stage at times by Nice's David O'List
	Nov 18	released their 3rd and last Barrett penned single, *Apples and Oranges* (UK)
	Dec 22	performed at the *Christmas on Earth Continued* concert – last major gig with Syd
1968	Apr 6	goodbye Syd Barrett – hello David Gilmour...
		...leadership and songwriting moved from Syd Barrett to Roger Waters

	Jun 29	released *A Saucerful of Secrets* (UK) – input from Syd Barrett and Dave Gilmour
1969	Oct 25	released their 4th album, *Ummagumma* (UK) – an album side from each musician
1970	Jan 3	Syd Barrett released his 1st solo album, *The Madcap Laughs* (UK)...
		...featured Roger Waters and David Gilmour
	Jul 11	played at the *Tivoli Pop Festival* in Germany
1972	Feb 17	press debut concert of *Dark Side of the Moon* – a year before album's release
1973	Mar 24	released *Dark Side of the Moon* (UK) – 1st album with all tracks by Roger Waters
	Oct 4	recording session for the aborted album *Household Objects*
1975	Jun 5	recording session for *Shine on You Crazy Diamond* – last contact with Barrett
	Sep 15	released *Wish You Were Here* (UK)...
		...guest appearance from Roy Harper on the vocals for *Have a Cigar*
1976	Dec 3	pigs on the wing over Battersea Power Station
1977	Jul 6	Roger Waters spat in a fan's face at a gig in Montreal – and *The Wall* was born
1980	Feb 7	1st concert performance of *The Wall*...
		...Surrogate Band included:
		Snowy White: guitar – 1980 concerts
		Andy Bown: bass – 1980 and 1981 concerts
		Andy Roberts: guitar – 1981 concerts
		...Richard Wright had been sacked from the band and was now on the payroll
1981	Jun 17	last performance of *The Wall* – Roger Waters' last concert with Pink Floyd
1983	Mar 21	released *The Final Cut* (UK) – last album to include Roger Waters...
		...Rick Wright was not involved in the project
1999	Dec 14	Paul McCartney appeared at the Cavern – backed by Gilmour and Ian Paice
2005	Jul 2	Pigs did fly! Pink Floyd and Roger Waters reunited on stage – 1st time in 24 years

Gene Pitney

		Inducted into the Rock and Roll Hall of Fame in 2002
1940	Feb 17	singer and songwriter, born in Hartford, Connecticut
1960	Aug 8	Roy Orbison recorded Pitney penned *Today's Teardrops* – B-side of *Blue Angel*
1962	Jul 13	recording session for the Pitney penned, *He's a Rebel* – not a Crystal in sight!
1963	Nov 23	recorded a Jagger/Richard song after meeting the Stones on a UK TV show...
		...*That Girl Belongs to Yesterday* – based on Jagger/Richard's *My Only Girl*

PLAGIARISM, LITIGATION, MURDER AND SUICIDE

1963	Jan 31	Beach Boys recorded *Surfin' USA*...
		...sued by Chuck Berry for its similarity to *Sweet Little Sixteen* (1958)
1965	Feb 26	Rolling Stones released *The Last Time*...
		...the Andrew Oldham Orchestra version later attracted a lawsuit:
		Allen Klein sued the Verve's *Bitter Sweet Symphony* (1997)
1969	Aug 10	Sharon Tate murders...

		...Charles Manson cited songs on the Beatles' *White Album* as inspiration
	Oct 31	*Led Zeppelin II* album released – it attracted three claims of plagiarism:
		Whole Lotta Love
		Willie Dixon's *You Need Love* – recorded by Muddy Waters in 1962
		Bring It on Home
		Willie Dixon song – recorded by Sonny Boy Williamson (II) in 1963
		The Lemon Song
		Howlin' Wolf's *Killing Floor* – written by Wolf and recorded in 1964
1971	Feb 10	George Harrison's *My Sweet Lord* attracted a lawsuit for plagiarism...
		...too similar to the Chiffons' hit *He's So Fine* (1963)
1973	Oct 26	Fleetwood Mac's manager Clifford Davis formed a bogus Fleetwood Mac in '74...
		...the band sued him in order to regain ownership of the band's name
1975	Feb 21	John Lennon released his *Rock'n'Roll* album...
		...*Come Together* used lyrics from Chuck Berry's *You Can't Catch Me* (1956)
		...Lennon placated the situation by including two Berry songs on the album
		...Morris Levy prematurely released some of the tracks as:
		Roots: John Lennon Sings the Great Rock & Roll Hits
1979	Aug 3	AC/DC released *Highway to Hell*...
		...Richard "Night Stalker" Ramirez cited *Night Prowler* as inspiration to murder
1980	Apr 5	Ozzy Osbourne recording session for *Blizzard of Ozz*...
		...*Suicide Solution* later attracted a lawsuit for inspiration to suicide
1983	Jul 27	Neil Young released *Everybody's Rockin'*...
		...David Geffen sued Young for not trying hard enough on the album
1985	Jan 7	John Fogerty issued the album *Centerfield* – included *Old Man Down the River*...
		...Fogerty was charged with plagiarism of his own song:
		Creedence Clearwater Revival's *Run Through the Jungle* (1970)
	Dec 23	suicide pact made by two youths after listening to Judas Priest...
		...Priest's *Stained Glass* included the track *Better By You, Better Than Me*
2003	Feb 3	actress Lana Clarkson was found shot dead in Phil Spector's mansion...
		...Spector was eventually convicted of her murder

The Platters

		Inducted into the Rock and Roll Hall of Fame in 1990
1907	Nov 21	Buck Ram: songwriter, arranger and manager, born in Chicago, Illinois...
		...owner of the Antler record label
		...wrote many of the Platters' hits, including *The Great Pretender*, 1955
1928	Apr 5	Tony Williams: lead singer in the 1950s, born in Elizabeth, New Jersey
	Aug 7	Herb Reed: bass singer and founding member, born in Kansas City, Missouri
1955	May 6	released the re-recorded Mercury version of *Only You (And You Alone)* (US)...
		...written by Buck Ram

1956 Mar 21 appeared in the 1st rock'n'roll movie, *Rock Around the Clock*

1959 Aug 10 all four male singers were arrested in Cincinnati for lewd behaviour:

Tony Williams: lead singer and founding member – formed '53 – left '59
David Lynch: founding member
Paul Robi – replaced founding member Alex Hodge in 1954
Herb Reed: founding member – long-term member

Poco

1944 May 9 Richie Furay: guitarist and singer, born in Yellow Springs, Ohio

1946 Mar 8 Randy Meisner: bassist and singer, born in Scottsbluff, Nebraska

1947 Oct 30 Timothy B Schmit: bassist and singer, born in Oakland, California...
...joined in late 1969 – left in mid-1977

Dec 5 Jim Messina: guitarist and singer, born in Maywood, California

1968 Dec 29 early gig, still calling themselves "Pogo" – changed to "Poco" shortly afterwards...
...Pogo: lineup that became Poco:

Richie Furay: guitar and vocals – from Buffalo Springfield
Jim Messina: guitar and vocals – from Buffalo Springfield...
...successful duo in the early 1970s with Loggins and Messina
Rusty Young: pedal steel guitar – from Boenzee Cryque
George Grantham: drums – from Boenzee Cryque
Randy Meisner: bass and vocals – from the Poor – left in mid-1969...
...later a founding member of the Eagles

...originally called "Pogo" after the cartoon character, modified to avoid lawsuit

The Police

Inducted into the Rock and Roll Hall of Fame in 2003

1942 Dec 31 Andy Summers: guitar, born Andrew Somers, in Poulton-le-Fylde, Lancashire...
...previously with Zoot Money's Big Roll Band, Dantalian's Chariot,
Soft Machine, and Eric Burdon and the New Animals

1951 Oct 2 Sting: bassist and singer, born Gordon Sumner, in Wallsend, Tyne and Wear...
...nickname from wearing a black and yellow sweater in the Phoenix Jazzmen
...left Last Exit in early 1977 to form the Police

1952 Jul 16 Stuart Copeland: drummer, born in Alexandria, Virginia...
...previously in Curved Air – joined as a roadie, then became drummer

1977 Feb 12 recorded their debut single, *Fall Out* – with original guitarist Henri Padovani...
...written by Stuart Copeland:

B-side, *Nothing Achieved*, co-written with his brother Ian

Mar 12 early Police gig, supporting Cherry Vanilla...
...Sting and Stuart Copeland were Cherry Vanilla's rhythm section that night
...The Police:

Sting – Stuart Copeland

Henri Padovani: guitar – left in mid-1977

...classic lineup completed when Andy Summers joined in mid-1977:

there was a brief period when the Police had two guitarists

...the band Strontium 90 ran in parallel to the Police: lineup:

Andy Summers: guitar – soon to replace Henri Padovani in the Police
Sting: singer – member of the Police
Stuart Copeland: drums – member of the Police

1978 Oct 23 played to an audience of just three people on their American tour

Brian Poole and the Tremeloes

1962 Jan 1 passed audition for a Decca recording contract – Beatles failed on the same day

May 19 promoted their debut single *Twist Little Sister*, on TV's *Thank Your Lucky Stars*

Jun 29 Contours released *Do You Love Me* – Brian Poole UK #1 single in 1963

1963 Aug 9 performed on the UK TV debut of *Ready Steady Go!*

Jimmy Powell

vocals: The Rockin' Berries – Jimmy Powell and the Five Dimensions

1963 Oct 4 Jimmy Powell and the Five Dimensions gig at London's Studio 51...

...lineup included:

Rod Stewart: vocals and harmonica – 1st group, joined in 1963...

...joined before Powell, when the band was "The Dimensions"

Jimmy Powell: vocals...

...previously released the 1st Brum Beat single, in 1962

...was the Rockin' Berries' singer – joined in 1961 – left in 1962:

recorded a handful of singles with them...

...went on to join Rod Stewart in the Dimensions

Duffy Power

1941 Sep 9 British R&B singer, born Ray Howard, in Fulham, London...

...stage name from his manager, Larry Parnes

1963 Feb 20 recorded *I Saw Her Standing There* – backed by the Graham Bond Quartet...

...cover of a Lennon and McCartney song from the Beatles' 1st album

Elvis Presley

Inducted into the Rock and Roll Hall of Fame in 1986 (inaugural year)

1909 Jun 26 Col. Tom Parker: born Andreas Cornelis van Kuijk, in Breda, The Netherlands...

...took over Elvis's management from Bob Neal
...responsible for Elvis's unique career strategy
...managed Hank Snow and Eddy Arnold before taking on Elvis Presley

1935 Jan 8 Elvis Presley: aka "King of Rock'n'Roll", born in Tupelo, Mississippi

Elvis's regular backing musicians:

1931 Dec 27 Scotty Moore: guitarist, born near Gadsden, Tennessee...

...member of Starlite Wranglers: formed the Blue Moon Boys to back Elvis:

Bill Black: bassist – was in these two bands with Moore
DJ Fontana: drummer – joined them in the Blue Moon Boys

...all five Sun singles were credited to "Elvis, Scotty and Bill"
...DJ Fontana came on board in time for the 1st RCA recording session
...Bill Black was with Elvis up until the King joined the US Army
...Scotty and DJ's swan song came with the 1968 TV *Comeback Special*

1939 Aug 21 James Burton: guitarist, born in Dubberly, Louisiana, but grew up in Shreveport...

...backed Elvis in the 1970s

...previously: Dale Hawkins, Ricky Nelson's backing band, and the Shindogs:

reputedly wrote music, uncredited, Dale Hawkins' 1957 single *Susie-Q*
Ricky Nelson's backing band: lead guitar c.1958 to c.1967

Shindogs were the house band for the TV show *Shindig!*...

...guitarist from 1965 until the show ended in January 1966

Elvis covers included:

1947 Dec 28 Wynonie Harris recorded *Good Rockin' Tonight* – Elvis's 2nd Sun single, 1954

1952 Mar 13 Lloyd Price recorded *Lawdy Miss Clawdy* – Elvis single in 1956

1952 Aug 13 Big Mama Thornton recorded *Hound Dog* – Elvis single in 1956

Elvis Presley

1953 Jul 18 1st private recording session at Sam Phillips's Memphis Recording Service

Nov 12 Drifters recorded *Such a Night* – Elvis cover, on a 1960 album and 1964 single

Dec 29 Jimmy Reed recorded *You Don't Have to Go*...

...in 1967 Elvis covered Jimmy Reed's 1961 single *Big Boss Man*

1954 Jan 4 2nd private recording at Sam Phillips's Memphis Recording Service

Jul 19 released his 1st Sun single, *That's All Right* c/w *Blue Moon of Kentucky*:

A-side: written by Arthur Crudup and a single from him in 1946
B-side: Bill Monroe single in 1947

...all five Sun singles were credited to Elvis Presley, Scotty and Bill

Sep 22 2nd Sun single, *Good Rockin' Tonight* c/w *I Don't Care if the Sun Don't Shine*...

...*Good Rockin' Tonight* written by Roy Brown and a single from him in 1947:

definitive version of *Good Rockin' Tonight* from Wynonie Harris in 1948

...*I Don't Care if the Sun Don't Shine* – Patti Page single in 1950

Oct 2 Elvis's only performance at the Grand Ole Opry – he did not go down well

Nov 6 The King's only radio commercial was aired on the *Louisiana Hayride*

1955 Jan 8 3rd Sun single, *Milkcow Blues Boogie* c/w *You're a Heartbreaker*...

...*Milkcow Blues Boogie* – recorded by Kokomo Arnold in 1934

Feb 13 Buddy (Holly) and Bob opened for Elvis in Lubbock, Texas

	Apr 25	4th Sun single, *Baby Let's Play House c/w I'm Left, You're Right, She's Gone...*
		...*Baby Let's Play House* – single from Arthur Gunter in 1954
	Aug 1	5th and last Sun single, *I Forgot to Remember to Forget c/w Mystery Train...*
		...*Mystery Train* – Little Junior's Blue Flames' single in '53 – written by Jr Parker:
		Sam Phillips's name was added as a writing credit for Elvis's version
	Aug 15	signed with Colonel Tom Parker – Elvis had two managers, Bob Neal and Parker
	Nov 20	last day at Sun – signed with RCA the following day
1956	Jan 1	Carl Perkins released *Blue Suede Shoes* – Elvis single in early 1956
	Jan 10	recorded *Heartbreak Hotel* at his 1st recording session for RCA...
		...backing musicians included:
		Scotty Moore – Bill Black
		DJ Fontana: drums – regular drummer since late 1955
		Chet Atkins: guitar – regular session guitarist with Elvis
		Floyd Cramer: piano – regular session pianist with Elvis
		...written by Mae Boren Axton and Tommy Durden
	Jan 28	1st appearance on national TV – performed:
		I've Got a Woman – single from Ray Charles in late 1954
		Shake, Rattle and Roll – Big Joe Turner single in 1954
		Flip Flop and Fly – Big Joe Turner single in 1955
		...backed by: Scotty Moore – Bill Black – DJ Fontana
	Mar 23	released his debut album, *Elvis Presley* (US)
	Apr 23	1st concert performance in Las Vegas...
		...backed by: Scotty Moore – Bill Black – DJ Fontana
	Sep 9	1st appearance on *The Ed Sullivan Show*
	Nov 15	*Love Me Tender* opened in New York – 1st movie
	Dec 4	Million Dollar Quartet recording session – with Elvis, Lewis, Perkins and Cash
	Dec 15	"Elvis has left the building" announced for the very 1st time
	Dec 29	ten singles on the *Billboard Top 100* – including the covers:
		Blue Moon – from the 1934 film *Manhattan Melodrama*
		Old Shep – recorded by Red Foley in 1935
1957	Jan 6	censored "no hips" performance on his 3rd and final *Ed Sullivan Show*
	Aug 31	Elvis's last gig outside the USA (in neighbouring Canada)...
		...with the Jordanaires: vocal backing group – regulars, 1956 to Vegas
		...Bill Black was also on the bill with his Bill Black Combo
	Nov 8	3rd movie *Jailhouse Rock* opened in America – end of Elvis's rock'n'roll years
	Nov 10	final concert appearances before joining the Army
	Nov 22	at #1 in America with *Jailhouse Rock*
1958	Jan 24	*Jailhouse Rock* was the 1st single to enter the UK charts at #1
	Mar 24	inducted into the US Army
1959	Feb 18	Ray Charles recorded *What'd I Say* – Elvis hit in 1964, from *Viva Las Vegas*

1960	Mar 3	stopped off in Scotland, the only time he set foot on British soil (officially!)
	Mar 20	1st recording session since leaving the Army...
		...backed by: Scotty Moore – DJ Fontana – The Jordanaires
		...and session musicians: Floyd Cramer – "Boots" Randolph
	Mar 23	released *Stuck on You* (US) – 1st single since leaving the Army
	Apr 8	released *Elvis Is Back!* (US) – 1st album since returning from the Army
	Nov 3	with *Now or Never*, Elvis became the 1st act ever to have five #1s in the UK
1961	Mar 25	last live performance for seven years
1962	Jun 5	released *Pot Luck* (US) – last album of new rock material for seven years...
		...backed by: Scotty Moore – DJ Fontana – the Jordanaires
		...and session musicians: Floyd Cramer – "Boots" Randolph – Hal Blaine
1963	Sep 15	Animals recorded *Big Boss Man* – Jimmy Reed single 1961 – Elvis hit in 1967
1964	Aug 19	Beatles opened their 1st American tour – supported by the Bill Black Combo
1965	May 28	18th movie *Tickle Me* premiered in US – soundtrack of previously released songs:
		(It's a) Long Lonely Highway was a bonus track on *Kissin' Cousins*...
		...written by Doc Pomus and Mort Shuman
		Slowly but Surely was a bonus track on Fun in Acapulco
	Aug 27	Elvis met the Beatles at his Bel Air home
	Oct 21	Bill Black died of a brain tumour: 39 years old
1966	May 25	1st recording session to produce a non-movie-soundtrack album since *Pot Luck*...
		...majority of the recordings were for the album *How Great Thou Art*
		...backed by: Scotty Moore – DJ Fontana – Floyd Cramer – "Boots" Randolph
		...and vocal groups: the Jordanaires – the Imperials with Jake Hess
1968	Dec 3	TV *Comeback Special* – last performance with Scotty Moore and DJ Fontana
1969	Jun 17	released *From Elvis in Memphis* (US) – 1st new rock material since 1962
	Jul 31	1st performance at Las Vegas International Hotel – heralded his cabaret years
	Aug 26	released *Suspicious Minds* (US) – last American chart topper...
		...Mark James single in 1968
	Nov 10	*Change of Habit* opened (US) – 31st and final movie as an actor
1970	Jan 26	wore a jumpsuit on stage for the 1st time
	Sep 14	back on the road again for the 1st time since 1957...
		...backing group included: (all three were with Elvis throughout the 1970s):
		James Burton: guitar
		Ronnie Tutt: drums
		Joe Guercio: musical director
	Dec 21	met President Nixon at the White House – became a drugs enforcement officer
1971	Jul 20	1st stage entrance to *Also Sprach Zarathustra*
1973	Jan 14	*Aloha from Hawaii* concert played to over a billion people
1974	Dec 24	abandoned his karate movie
1976	Apr 29	Bruce Springsteen was ejected from Graceland after climbing over the wall

	Oct 29	final studio recording session, at Graceland...
		...included *He'll Have to Go* – Jim Reeves hit in 1960
	Nov 23	Jerry Lee Lewis arrested for brandishing a gun outside Elvis's Graceland home
	Dec 12	last-ever Las Vegas performance
1977	Jun 6	released *Way Down* c/w *Pledging My Love* (US) – last single in his lifetime...
		...*Pledging My Love* was a Johnny Ace single in 1955
	Jun 26	last-ever concert performance – given in Indianapolis
	Jul 19	released *Moody Blue* (US) – last album to be released in Elvis's lifetime
	Aug 16	"King of Rock'n'Roll" died of heart failure: 42 years old
1999	Nov 10	cited as the performer with the most Gold and Platinum albums and singles
2008	Apr 21	it was revealed that Tommy Steele showed Elvis around London in 1958

Billy Preston

keyboards: Little Richard's backing band – The Beatles (label credit) – Plastic Ono Band

1962	Oct 12	keyboard player in Little Richard's backing band on UK rock'n'roll comeback tour
	Oct 30	keyboards in Little Richard's backing band for a two week residency in Hamburg
1969	Jan 2	work started on the Beatles' ill-fated *Get Back* project
	Jan 30	performed with the Beatles on their swan song rooftop performance
	Apr 11	Beatles released *Get Back* – Billy Preston received a recording credit
	Dec 15	Plastic Ono Band member at the concert for start of the *War is Over* campaign
1970	Jan 27	John Lennon recorded *Instant Karma*
1971	Aug 1	performed at the *Concert for Bangladesh*
1972	May 12	Rolling Stones released *Exile on Main Street*

The Pretty Things

1943	Jan 28	Dick Taylor: guitarist, born in Dartford, Kent...
		...(guitar) with Mick Jagger/Keith Richard in Little Boy Blue and the Blue Boys ...moved to bass in Brian Jones's Rollin' Stones, with Jagger and Richard
1944	Nov 9	Phil May: singer, born Phillip Arthur Dennis Wadey, in Dartford, Kent
1944	Nov 29	Twink: drummer, born John Charles Alder, in Colchester, Essex...
		...member of the Fairies in the mid-1960s – left to join the In Crowd/Tomorrow ...in 1967 he joined Jon Lord and Ron Wood in Santa Barbara Machine Head ...formed the Pink Fairies in 1969 ...in 1972 he teamed up with ex-Pink Floyd guiding light, Syd Barrett in Stars

Before the Pretty Things

1962	Jul 12	Dick Taylor played bass for the Rollin' Stones debut at the Marquee...
		...he left shortly after this gig – formed the Pretty Things in late 1963
	Oct 27	1st Rolling Stones recording session – Dick Taylor probably left just before this
1963	May 11	Carter Lewis and the Southerners gig – Viv Prince joined around this time

The Pretty Things

1964	Oct 13	played London's 100 Club...

...The Pretty Things:

Dick Taylor: lead guitar – from the embryonic Rollin' Stones
Phil May: lead singer – left in 1976 for a solo career
Brian Pendleton: rhythm guitar – left end '66 – replaced by John Povey
John Stax: bass – left in early 1977 – replaced by Wally Allen
Viv Prince: drums – joined early 1964, after a couple of other drummers

...band's name was inspired by Bo Diddley's song *Pretty Thing*

1965 Dec 6 Viv Prince began a ten-day stint in the Who, as substitute for Keith Moon...
...he was sacked from the Pretty Things shortly before

1967 Mar 3 Jeff Beck Group gig – Viv Prince had brief stay in an early lineup shortly before
Apr 29 performed at the *14-Hour Technicolor Dream*
Sep 21 Twink appeared with Tomorrow on the 1st *John Peel Sessions* on BBC Radio...
...joined the Pretty Things in time to perform on *SF Sorrow* – left in 1969

1969 May 23 Who released *Tommy* – often claimed to be the 1st rock opera...
...Pretty Things released their rock opera *SF Sorrow* in late 1968 in the UK

1970 Aug 14 Hawkwind's 1st LP released – produced by Dick Taylor, recently left Pretty Things

Lloyd Price

Inducted into the Rock and Roll Hall of Fame in 1998

record label owner: Kent – Double-L

1933 Mar 9 seminal R&B singer and songwriter, born in Kenner, Louisiana...
...his nickname, "Mr Personality", was taken from his song *Personality*

1952 Mar 13 recorded *Lawdy Miss Clawdy* – became his 1st single...
...much covered song, versions by Elvis, Cliff, the Beatles and many others

1958 Sep 11 recorded *Stagger Lee* for the 1st time...
...based on Mississippi John Hurt's *Stack O'Lee Blues* recorded in 1927
...recorded by Ma Rainey in 1925
...he was required to re-record a sanitised version for *American Bandstand*

PJ Proby

singer: Moon Dogs

1938 Nov 6 aka "Jett Powers", singer, born James Marcus Smith, in Houston, Texas...
...singer in the short-lived Moon Dogs, late 1950s

1965 Jan 29 notorious trouser-splitting British tour with Cilla Black

1969 Apr 8 released *Three Week Hero* (UK)...
...1st time that "Led Zeppelin" recorded together
...session musicians included drummer Clem Cattini
...back in 1957, as Jet Powers, he released his 1st single, *Go, Girl, Go*:
written by Proby and Ray Gilbert

Procol Harum

1934 Sep 19 Brian Epstein: Paramounts manager, born in Liverpool, England...
...took over their management in early 1965

1945 Mar 9 Robin Trower: guitarist, born in Catford, London...
...founding member of the short-lived Jude, formed in 1971

May 29 Gary Brooker: keyboards and vocals, born in Hackney, London

1959 Jul 16 Coasters recorded *Poison Ivy* – Paramounts single in 1963

At the beginning of the 1960s the Paramounts were one of the UK's premier R&B bands.

By the mid-1960s they were Sandie Shaw's backing band.

1965 Mar 14 gig as Sandie Shaw's backing band – from Sandie Shaw to Procol Harum...
...Paramounts musicians in the original Procol Harum lineup:

Robin Trower: guitar and founding member – formed in the early 1960s
Gary Brooker: vocals, piano and founding member
BJ Wilson: drums – joined in 1962

1965 Dec 12 Paramounts supported the Beatles at their last-ever UK concert

The Paramounts morphed into Procol Harum.

1967 May 12 released *A Whiter Shade of Pale* (UK)...
...Keith Reid: lyricist – teamed up with Brooker as they became Procol Harum
...formed early '67, lineup changed after recording *A Whiter Shade of Pale*:

Gary Brooker: vocals, piano and founding member
Robin Trower: guitar – joined after *A Whiter Shade of Pale*
BJ Wilson: drums – joined after *A Whiter Shade of Pale*

...Matthew Fisher sued 40 years later for a co-credit on the music

1969 Jul 6 performance with the Stratford Festival Orchestra and Chorus

1970 Jan 17 recorded *Ain't Nothing to Get Excited About* – as "Liquorice John Death"...
...lineup were all ex-members of the Paramounts

Queen

Inducted into the Rock and Roll Hall of Fame in 2001

1946 Sep 5 Freddy Mercury: singer, born Farrokh Bulsara, in Zanzibar, Tanzania...
...member of Wreckage, previously Ibex
...joined Sour Milk Sea in early 1970 – left to join Smile

1947 Jul 19 Brian May: guitarist, born in Twickenham, Middlesex

1949 Dec 17 Paul Rodgers: singer, born in Middlesbrough, North of England...
...Free and Bad Company's lead singer, relationship with Queen started in '04

1969 Sep 9 1st time Mercury, Brian May and Roger Taylor played together – at an Ibex gig...
...Mercury was in Ibex – Brian May and Roger Taylor were in Smile

Smile morphed into Queen.

1970 Jun 27 Queen's debut concert – billed as "Smile"...
...Queen: (lineup that morphed from Smile)

Freddie Mercury: singer
Brian May: guitar
Roger Taylor: drums
Mike Grose: bass – replaced by John Deacon in mid-1971

1971 Jul 2 debut concert by the classic Queen lineup...
...Queen:
Freddie Mercury – Brian May – Roger Taylor
John Deacon: bass – replaced Mike Grose

1973 Jul 13 released eponymous debut album (UK)

1975 Oct 31 released *Bohemian Rhapsody* (UK) – often voted as "best single of all time"

Tommy Quickly

singer: Tommy Quickly and the Remo Four

1962 Nov 26 Beatles recorded *Tip of My Tongue* – Tommy Quickly single in 1963...
...Quickly was managed by the Beatles' manager, Brian Epstein

1963 Feb 27 Searchers gig in Hamburg – original singer Johnny Sandon had moved on...
...he went to the Remo Four – Quickly replaced him in the Remo Four in 1963

1965 Jan 29 performed on PJ Proby's infamous trouser-splitting UK tour

Quicksilver Messenger Service

1943 Aug 24 John Cipollina: guitarist, born in Berkeley, California...
...founding member, formed late 1964 – left in late 1970, formed Copperhead

1946 Apr 18 Skip Spence: guitarist, born in Windsor, Ontario, Canada...
...in an early lineup in 1965 – left to become Jefferson Airplane's drummer

1967 Jan 14 performed at *A Gathering of the Tribes for a Human Be-In*

Jun 16 played the *Monterey Pop Festival*

1970 Apr 3 over-hyped Brinsley Schwarz gig at the Fillmore East – QMS headlined the bill

1971 May 6 Fillmores came to the end of the line – played at final Fillmore West gigs

1972 Sep 21 David Freiberg performed with Jefferson Airplane at their swan song gig...
...founding member of Quicksilver Messenger Service – left in mid-1971

Rainbow

1945 Apr 14 Ritchie Blackmore: guitarist, born in Weston-super-Mare, Somerset...
...founded Rainbow after leaving Deep Purple in 1975

Nov 30 Roger Glover: bassist, born in Brecon, South Wales...
...previously with Deep Purple – joined in 1979

1947 Dec 29 Cosy Powell: drummer, born Colin Flooks, in Cirencester, Gloucestershire...
...previously in the 2nd lineup of the Jeff Beck Group – joined Rainbow mid-'75

1980 Apr 17 Ronnie James Dio's final appearance with Black Sabbath...
...singer and founding member of Rainbow – left in late '78 for Black Sabbath

Ramones

		Inducted into the Rock and Roll Hall of Fame in 2002
1948	Oct 8	Johnny Ramone: guitarist, born John Cummings, in Long Island, New York
1951	May 19	Joey Ramone: drums then vocals...
		...born Jeffrey Hyman, in Forest Hills, New York:
		band's name inspired by early McCartney stage name, Paul Ramon
1965	Oct 8	CJ Ramone: bassist, born Christopher Joseph Ward, in Queens, New York
1974	Mar 30	debut performance, as a trio...
		...Ramones:
		Joey Ramone: drums – moved from drums to lead vocals shortly after
		Johnny Ramone: guitar
		Dee Dee Ramone: bass – replaced by CJ Ramone in 1989
		...Tom Erdelyi: manager:
		became drummer Tommy Ramone, when Joey moved to vocals
1975	Jun 8	played at CBGB – supported by Talking Heads making their concert debut
	Jul 16	appeared at CBGB's *Top 40 New York Unrecorded Rock Bands* festival
1976	Apr 16	released debut album, *Ramones* (US)
	Jul 4	UK debut concert – a seminal moment in British punk rock
1979	May 1	recording sessions began with Phil Spector for the album *End of the Century*

Boots Randolph

session saxophonist:

1958	Sep 8	recorded *Yakety Sax* – co-written with James "Spider" Rich
1960	Mar 20	Elvis Presley's 1st recording session since leaving the Army
	Aug 8	Roy Orbison recorded *Blue Angel*
1962	Jun 5	played on Elvis Presley's album, *Pot Luck with Elvis*
1966	May 25	played on Elvis Presley's album, *How Great Thou Art*

Jimmy Reed

		Inducted into the Rock and Roll Hall of Fame in 1991
1953	Dec 29	recorded *You Don't Have to Go* – written by Reed...
		...other Jimmy Reed penned songs included:
		Honest I Do – Reed single in 1957 – covered by the Stones in 1964
1962	Oct 27	Rolling Stones recorded *Close Together*...
		...written by Reed and a single from him in 1961
1963	Mar 11	Rolling Stones recording session – recorded two Reed penned songs:
		Baby What's Wrong – Reed single in 1962
		Bright Lights Big City – Reed single in 1961
1963	Sep 15	Animals recorded *Big Boss Man* – Reed single in 1961

Terry Reid

vocals and guitar: Peter Jay and the Jaywalkers – (nearly Led Zeppelin)

1949 Nov 13 born in Huntingdon, Cambridgeshire...

...in the mid-1960s he replaced Pete Miller in Peter Jay and the Jaywalkers

1968 Feb 23 Band of Joy gig – Reid rejected an offer to join Led Zeppelin as lead singer

Nov 4 supported Cream at their final concert in America

1969 Nov 7 supported the Rolling Stones on their American tour

The Remo Four

1963 Feb 27 Searchers gig in Hamburg...

...lead singer Johnny Sandon left the Searchers in 1962 to front Remo Four:

Tommy Quickly replaced Sandon as Remo Four's lead singer in 1963

1965 Jan 29 performed on PJ Proby's infamous trouser-splitting UK tour

1968 Nov 1 George Harrison released the movie soundtrack for *Wonderwall Music*

Renaissance

When the Yardbirds split up:

Keith Relf and Jim McCarty formed the acoustic duo, Together

Together extended its ranks to become Renaissance.

1968 Jul 7 Yardbirds last gig...

...Renaissance: (morphed from the duo Together in 1969):

Keith Relf: guitar and vocals – from Together
Jim McCarty: drums – from Together
John Hawken: piano – previously founding member of Nashville Teens
Louis Cennamo: bass – previously with the Herd
Jane Relf: vocals – Keith Relf's sister, 1st job as a professional singer

Paul Revere and the Raiders

1938 Jan 7 Paul Revere: keyboardist, born Paul Revere Dick, in Harvard, Nebraska

The Downbeats started in 1958 and morphed into Paul Revere and the Raiders.

1963 Nov 30 Kingsmen hit the US charts with *Louie Louie* – classic cover by the Raiders '63...

...written by Richard Berry and a single from him in 1957

1964 Jun 5 David Bowie released *Louie, Louie Go Home* as a B-side...

...Raiders single in 1964 – written by Paul Revere and Mark Lindsay

Cliff Richard and the Drifters

1936 Jul 6 Jet Harris: bassist, born in Kingsbury, London...

...member of the Vipers in the early days of British skiffle

1940 Oct 14 Cliff Richard: singer, born Harry Webb, in Lucknow, India...

...UK superstar but never quite cracked America

1941 Oct 28 Hank Marvin: guitar, born Brian Robson Rankin, in Newcastle upon Tyne...

...in the vanguard of British guitar heroes

1956 Apr 22 2i's coffee bar opened – Cliff and various Drifters/Shadows performed there

Jul 14 Vipers Skiffle Group played at the 2i's for the 1st time...

...three of the original Shadows played in various Vipers lineups:

Hank Marvin – Jet Harris – Tony Meehan

1958 Apr 3 Johnny Otis recorded *Willie and the Hand Jive* – covered as a B-side in 1960...

...A-side was the Ian Samwell penned *Fall in Love with You*

Cliff Richard and the Drifters

1958 Jun 7 1st recording session – to make a private demo recording...

...recorded two covers:

Breathless – Jerry Lee Lewis's last rock'n'roll hit, 1958
Lawdy Miss Clawdy – Lloyd Price's 1st single, 1952

...Norrie Paramour heard it and signed them to Columbia

Jul 5 Johnny O'Keefe released *The Wild One* – covered by Jet Harris on an EP in '62

Aug 29 released their 1st single, *Schoolboy Crush* c/w *Move It!* (UK)...

...lineup included:

Cliff Richard: vocals
Ian Samwell: guitar and songwriter
Terry Smart: drums

...*Move It!* was written by Ian Samwell and was originally the B-side

...*Schoolboy Crush* was a cover of a 1958 Bobby Helms single

...produced by Norrie Paramour

Oct 5 Kalin Twins' tour opened – supported by Cliff Richard and the Drifters...

...The Drifters:

Ian Samwell: had now moved from guitar to bass
Terry Smart: drums – replaced by Tony Meehan in early 1959
Hank Marvin: lead guitar – debut performance with the Drifters
Bruce Welch: rhythm guitar – debut performance with the Drifters

...bassist Jet Harris was also on the tour, backing the Most Brothers

...Samwell left at the end of the tour and was replaced by Jet Harris

1959 Jan 9 Drifters recorded their 1st single without Cliff, *Feelin' Fine* – not an instrumental...

...written by Ian Samwell

Jan 10 debut of the lineup that became the Shadows:

Hank Marvin: lead guitar
Bruce Welch: rhythm guitar
Jet Harris: bass – replaced Ian Samwell – left in 1962
Tony Meehan: drums – replaced Terry Smart – left in 1961

Feb 9 1st of two days of recording for their debut album, *Cliff*

May 14 Cliff's 1st movie, *Serious Charge*, opened in London – music from the Drifters...

...included *Living Doll*, Richard's 1st UK #1 – written by Lionel Bart

1959 Nov 2 1st appearance on the US charts, with *Living Doll*

Cliff Richard and the Shadows

The Drifters changed their name to "The Shadows" in the autumn of 1959 to avoid confusion with the US vocal group.

1960 Jan 24 Marty Wilde's Wildcats backed Eddie Cochran on his last UK tour...

...lineup included future Shadows:

Brian Bennett: drums
Brian "Licorice" Locking: bass...

...Bennett and Locking were with Vince Taylor and the Playboys

1961 Jul 21 beat poet Royston Ellis was accompanied by Jimmy Page...

...Hank Marvin, Jet Harris and Tony Meehan also accompanied Ellis, c.1961

Dec 10 London premiere of *The Young Ones* – Cliff transitioned into an entertainer

1962 Apr 13 Shadows were the 1st British group to be awarded a Gold Disc – for *Apache*

Jet Harris and Tony Meehan left the Shadows and reunited as a duo in late 1962.

1963 Jun 30 Jet Harris and Tony Meehan package tour gig – supported by Shane Fenton:

Jet Harris: bass – left the Shadows in early 1962
Tony Meehan: drums – left the Shadows in late 1961

...Jet Harris and Tony Meehan backing musicians included:

Jimmy Page – session guitarist on *Diamonds* – later in Led Zeppelin
John Paul Jones – played in their backing band – later in Led Zeppelin

...Jet Harris and Tony Meehan had been replaced in the Shadows by:

Brian Bennett: drums
Brian "Licorice" Locking: bass

...Shane Fenton later reinvented himself as Alvin Stardust

1965 Aug 6 Small Faces released *Whatcha Gonna Do About It*...

...produced and co-written by the Drifters' original guitarist, Ian Samwell

1967 Mar 3 Jeff Beck Group gig – Harris had a brief stay in an early lineup shortly before

1968 Nov 16 released *Don't Forget to Catch Me* (UK) – end of the road together...

...The Shadows:

Hank Marvin – Bruce Welch – Brian Bennett
John Rostill: bass – replaced Brian Locking in late 1963

1977 Jul 19 Elvis released his last album *Moody Blue*...

...it included the track *Let Me Be There*, written by John Rostill

The Righteous Brothers

Inducted into the Rock and Roll Hall of Fame in 2003

1940 Aug 10 Bobby Hatfield: singer, born in Beaver Dam, Wisconsin...

...member of the Variations and the Paramours before the Righteous Brothers

1940 Sep 19 Bill Medley: singer and the taller half of the duo, born in Santa Ana, California...

...member of the Paramours before the Righteous Brothers

Duo met in the Paramours in 1962 and become the Righteous Brothers in 1963.

1964	Feb 11	supported the Beatles at their 1st American concert
	Aug 19	support act when the Beatles opened their 1st American tour
1964	Sep 16	performed on the 1st edition of *Shindig!*

Billy Riley and His Little Green Men

1957 Jan 23 released *Flyin' Saucers Rock & Roll* (US) – Jerry Lee Lewis played piano

1962 Feb 2 Ronnie Hawkins recorded *Mojo Man* – written by Billy Riley

Rising Sons

1947 Mar 15 Ry Cooder: musician and songwriter, born in Los Angeles, California

1965 Jul 11 early gig, at the Ash Grove in Los Angeles...

...Rising Sons:

Ry Cooder: musician and songwriter – became a successful solo artist
Taj Mahal: guitar – went on to a successful solo career
Ed Cassidy: drums – went on to form Spirit
Garry Marker: bass – went on to work with Captain Beefheart
Jesse Lee Kincaid: guitar

...Kevin Kelly: drums – replaced Ed Cassidy soon after – later with the Byrds

Johnny Rivers

1942 Nov 7 guitarist, singer and songwriter, born John Henry Ramistella, in New York

Smokey Robinson and the Miracles

Smokey Robinson

Inducted into the Rock'n'Roll Hall of Fame in 1987

The Miracles

Inducted into the Rock'n'Roll Hall of Fame in 2012

1959 Dec 14 Motown founded – Miracles' *Bad Girl* was the 1st (limited) release on the label

1961 Jul 24 Temptations released their debut single – written and produced by Robinson

1964 Apr 10 Beatles' *Second Album* included *Really Got a Hold on Me* – Miracles single in '62

1966 Aug 6 Miracles recorded the original version of *I Heard It Through the Grapevine*...

...but not released by the Miracles at the time:

Gladys Knight and the Pips hit in late 1967
definitive version, a hit for Marvin Gaye in 1968

...written by Norman Whitfield and Barrett Strong

1967 Mar 25 billed on Murray the "K"'s *Live in Person*...package show in New York

ROCK'N'ROLL – HIGH JINKS AND MAYHEM

1952 Mar 21 Alan Freed organised the 1st-ever rock'n'roll concert – it nearly ended in a riot

1958 Mar 28 Jerry Lee Lewis set fire to his piano, to upstage Chuck Berry who was on next

May 3 Alan Freed was charged with incitement to riot after the Boston *Big Beat* show

Oct 26 riot at 1st Bill Haley gig in Germany – rock'n'roll made youth "ripe for atomic war"

1965	Jan 29	PJ Proby's notorious trouser-splitting UK tour with Cilla Black
	Mar 18	call of nature had Jagger, Jones and Wyman charged with "insulting behaviour"
	Jun 19	Kinks' ill-fated US tour opened – Ray Davies reputedly thumped a union-man
	Sep 15	a goose-stepping Mick Jagger caused a riot at a Rolling Stones concert in Berlin
1967	Dec 9	Jim Morrison was arrested on stage at New Haven for indecent exhibition
1968	May 31	Skip Spence took an axe and went looking for Moby Grape's drummer
	Jun 26	Nice banned from the Albert Hall after a flag-burning performance of *America*
1969	Mar 2	Doors frontman Jim Morrison faced obscenity charges after a concert in Miami
	Apr 16	MC5's infamous "Fuck Hudson's!" campaign
	Jul 28	Led Zeppelin participated in the legendary *Edgewater Inn Mud Shark Incident*
	Sep 13	Alice Cooper's *Chicken Incident* at the *Toronto Rock and Roll Revival*
	Dec 6	Rolling Stones headlined the notorious Altamont Festival
1970	Oct 30	Jim Morrison was sentenced, following events at the Doors' Miami concert in '69
1971	Dec 4	fire at Zappa's Montreux concert inspired Deep Purple's *Smoke on the Water*... ...fire started after a fan fired a flare gun into the casino's ceiling
1972	Jun 3	Stones opened their legendary US tour – riots, bombs, arrests and Hugh Heffner
	Dec 23	Grand Funk Railroad's ex-manager, Terry Knight, seized their gear at a concert
1973	Nov 5	in a rage, Pete Townshend pulled the sound-man onto the stage
	Nov 20	Keith Moon collapsed on stage – replaced by audience member Scott Halpin
	Dec 2	Who were arrested for hotel-wrecking high jinks after a concert in Montreal
1976	Sep 29	Jerry Lee Lewis accidentally shot his bass player, Norman Owens, in the chest
	Dec 1	Sex Pistols' foul-mouthed appearance on Bill Grundy's UK TV show, *Today*
	Dec 3	Pink Floyd with pigs on the wing over Battersea Power Station
1977	Jan 26	Peter Green was institutionalised for threatening his accountant with an air rifle
	Apr 1	Led Zeppelin's ill-fated 11th and final US tour opened, beset by riots and arrests
	Sep 3	Eagles' relationships were deteriorating, even a fist-fight with Meisner and Frey
	Nov 19	Chuck Berry was released from prison – again! for the 3rd time
	Dec 3	eleven fans died in a rush for seating at a Who concert
1982	Jan 20	Ozzy Osbourne bit off a bat's head during a concert in Iowa

ROCK'N'ROLL – LANDMARKS

1938	Aug 16	Robert Johnson died – an early member of the macabre 27 *Club*
1941	Jul 7	American folk music revival underway with Almanac Singers' *Sod Buster Ballads*
1948	Jan 1	Petrillo recording ban came into effect – musicians boycotted recording sessions
	Sep 4	birth of doo wop – pioneered by the Ravens and the Orioles in the late 1940s
1949	Jun 25	*Billboard* magazine started to refer to "Rhythm & Blues"... ...changed the name of its "Race Music" charts to "Rhythm & Blues"
1951	Mar 5	Jackie Brenston recorded *Rocket 88* – generally considered 1st rock'n'roll record
1952	Nov 14	1st UK singles chart was published in the *New Musical Express* – Al Martino at #1

1953	Sep 2	skiffle's roots in trad jazz
1954	Sep 22	some contenders for the accolade of being the 1st rock'n'roll record
1955	Feb 26	in America 45s outsold 78s for the 1st time
1956	Apr 22	2i's coffee bar opened – London's most famous skiffle venue
1957	Jan 16	Liverpool's Cavern Club opened – as a jazz club
1958	Feb 22	1st stereo single to make an impact on the American charts
	Jun 18	Aldon Music joined the Brill Building
	Oct 6	British music scene in the second half of the1950s
1959	Feb 29	end of the golden age of rock'n'roll
	Sep 26	Liverpool music scene before the Beatles
	Nov 21	payola scandal took hold in America
1960	May 25	1st "Beat Night" at Liverpool's Cavern Club
	Jul 9	dawn of the British beat groups
1963	Aug 7	British beat groups rekindled interest in the American blues and R&B masters
1964	Feb 1	beginning of the British Invasion
	Mar 28	Mods and Rockers chose Margate to battle it out for the 1st time
	Oct 7	from rock'n'roll to the British Invasion
1965	Jun 21	Red Dog Saloon opened in Virginia City, Nevada – early psychedelic venue... ...Charlatans were the house band
1966	Aug 6	from beat music to virtuoso prog rock
	Aug 8	from professional "Brill Building" songwriters to songwriting bands
1967	Jun 21	*Summer of Love* dawned in Haight-Ashbury
	Sep 29	final gig at London's 1st psychedelic club, UFO – opened 23 December 1966
	Oct 6	*Death of Hippie* march in Haight-Ashbury, San Francisco
1968	Mar 8	Fillmore East opened in New York
	Mar 16	Jefferson Airplane and Grateful Dead's Carousel Ballroom venture... ...became the Fillmore West six months later
1969	Sep 24	dawn of British folk rock
1971	May 6	Bill Graham announced the end of the Fillmore East and Fillmore West
	Sep 17	dawn of British glam rock
	Nov 4	London's Rainbow Theatre opened, with a performance from the Who
1972	Dec 31	last-ever gig at Detroit's Grande Ballroom – also MC5's swan song
1974	Jul 17	Moody Blues opened one of the 1st quadraphonic recording studios
1975	Jul 16	New York's CBGB club hosted the *Top 40 New York Unrecorded Rock Bands...* ...name derived from the planned music – country, bluegrass and blues ...dawn of US punk and new wave
1976	Sep 20	1st British punk festival – held at London's 100 Club
	Dec 21	London's Roxy Club opened – 1st UK venue specifically for punk bands
1977	Apr 26	Club 54 discotheque opened in New York

1986 Jan 23 inaugural inductions into America's Rock and Roll Hall of Fame

1999 Nov 10 RIAA announced its *Artists of the Century*

Jimmie Rodgers

Inducted into the Rock and Roll Hall of Fame in 1986 (inaugural year)

1897 Sep 8 born in Meridian, Mississippi...

...aka the "Father of Country Music" and the "Singing Brakeman"

1927 Aug 4 1st recording session...

...recorded *The Soldier's Sweetheart* and *Sleep Baby Sleep*
...wrote *Blue Yodel #1*, aka *T for Texas* – recorded in late November

The Rolling Stones

Inducted into the Rock and Roll Hall of Fame in 1989

1931 Dec 18 Allen Klein: accountant and business manager, born in Newark, New Jersey...

...the Stones' 3rd manager – took over from Andrew Loog Oldham

1934 Feb 28 Giorgio Gomelsky: manager, club and label owner, born in Georgia, Russia...

...the Stones' 1st manager

1936 Oct 24 Bill Wyman: bassist, born William Perks, in Sydenham, South London...

...stage name was inspired by a friend's name from his National Service days
...later formed Willie and the Poor Boys and Bill Wyman's Rhythm Kings

1938 Jul 18 Ian Stewart: pianist then roadie, born in Pittenweem, Fife, Scotland...

...sidelined from the stage to the road crew in mid-1963

Dec 17 Carlo Little: drummer, born in Sudbury, London

1939 Oct 14 Brian Knight: harmonica player and vocalist, born in Perivale, Middlesex

1941 Jun 2 Charlie Watts: drummer, born in London, England

1942 Feb 24 Paul Jones: singer, born Paul Pond, in Portsmouth, Hampshire

Feb 28 Lewis Brian Hopkin Jones: guitarist, born in Cheltenham, Gloucestershire...

...Brian sometimes used the pseudonym Elmo Lewis:

from bluesman Elmore (sometimes Elmo) James + his own first name

...the lineup of Brian Jones's 2nd band morphed into the Rolling Stones

1943 Jan 28 Dick Taylor: guitarist and bassist, born in Dartford, Kent

Jul 26 Mick Jagger: singer and songwriter, born in Dartford, Kent

Dec 18 Kieth Richard: guitarist and songwriter, born Keith Richards, in Dartford, Kent...

...dropped the "s" and was "Keith Richard" from the early '60s to the late '70s

1944 Jan 29 Andrew Loog Oldham: manager and entrepreneur, born in Paddington, London...

...the Stones' 2nd manager – took over from Giorgio Gomelsky

1947 Jun 1 Ron Wood: guitarist, born in Hillingdon, London

1948 Jan 17 Mick Taylor: guitarist, born in Barnet, Hertfordshire

1961 Dec 11 Darryl Jones: bassist, born in Chicago, Illinois...

...replaced Bill Wyman in late 1993

Road to the Rolling Stones *SEE 11 January 1963*

Brian Jones started out playing saxophone with jazz bands in his native Cheltenham. He then played alongside Paul Jones in Thunder Odin and the Big Secret.

Brian Jones: guitar
Paul Pond (Paul Jones): singer – founding member of Manfred Mann

Brian set the ball rolling for the band that became the Rolling Stones.

...Brian Jones's group, 1st lineup: musicians included:

Brian Jones: guitar
Ian Stewart: piano – 1st Rolling Stone to team up with Brian
Brian Knight: vocals and harmonica – left to form Blues By Six
Geoff Bradford: guitar – left to join Blues By Six

Mick Jagger and Keith Richard had their own group, Little Boy Blue and the Blue Boys.

Mick Jagger: singer – joined Brian Jones's 2nd lineup
Keith Richard: guitar – joined Brian Jones's 2nd lineup
Dick Taylor: guitar – moved to bass in Brian Jones's 2nd lineup

Brian Jones and Charlie Watts were playing with Alexis Korner's Blues Incorporated the night that they first met Mick Jagger and Keith Richard.

Mick and Keith also became guest members of Blues Incorporated.

Mick Jagger and Keith Richard joined Brian Jones's group's 2nd lineup, Rollin' Stones.

Brian Jones: guitar
Ian Stewart: piano
Mick Jagger: vocals
Keith Richard: guitar
Dick Taylor: bass – went on to form the Pretty Things
Tony Chapman: drums – from the Cliftons...
...regular drummer before Charlie Watts
Carlo Little: drums – with Screaming Lord Sutch and the Savages...
...occasional drummer before Charlie Watts
Tony Fenson: regular bassist before Bill Wyman

Bill Wyman joined, from the Cliftons.

Bill Wyman joined in late 1962

Charlie Watts joined in January 1963, previously with:

Dave Hunt R&B Band – Alexis Korner's Blues Incorporated – Blues By Six

By early 1963 the Rolling Stones was a sextet:

Brian – Mick – Keith – Bill – Charlie + pianist Ian Stewart

The Stones met Andrew Loog Oldham in April 1963

Oldham moved pianist Ian Stewart from the stage to the road crew

And the band became a quintet:

Brian Jones – Mick Jagger – Keith Richard – Bill Wyman – Charlie Watts

Post-Brian Jones

Guitarist Mick Taylor joined, previously with:

The Gods – John Mayall's Bluesbreakers...

...joined in mid-1969 and stayed until the end of 1974

Guitarist Ron Wood joined, previously with:

The Birds – Jeff Beck Group – Faces...

...joined for the US tour in early 1975 – become the 2nd guitarist in 1976

Origins of band names and pseudonyms:

Little Boy Blue and the Blue Boys

1955 Aug 12 Sonny Boy Williamson performed as "Little Boy Blue" in his early days

The Rolling Stones

1950 Jun 3 Muddy Waters' *Rollin' Stone* – Chess Records' 2nd release

Phelge

1964 Feb 21 Phelge was a pseudonym used when the song was written by the whole band...

...taken from Mick, Keith and Brian's flatmate, James Phelge

Songs covered by the Rolling Stones included:

1953 Dec 29 Jimmy Reed recorded *You Don't Have to Go...*

...Stones covered Reed's 1957 single *Honest I Do* on their 1st album in 1964

1959 Jul 16 Coasters recorded *Poison Ivy* – B-side of withdrawn 2nd UK single in 1963

1961 Jul 29 Chuck Berry recorded *Come On* – Stones' 1st UK single in 1963

The Rolling Stones

1962 Apr 7 Mick Jagger and Keith Richard, met Brian Jones and Charlie Watts...

...Brian and Charlie were with Alexis Korner's Blues Incorporated:

they performed *Dust My Blues* – Elmore James single in 1955

Jul 12 1st-ever gig as the "Rollin' Stones", at London's Marquee club...

...Rollin' Stones:

Brian Jones – Mick Jagger – Keith Richard
Ian Stewart: piano
Tony Chapman: drums (not the future Kinks drummer Mick Avory)...

...Chapman joined the Stones from the Cliftons

Dick Taylor: bass – went on to form the Pretty Things

...substituted for Alexis Korner's Blues Incorporated

Oct 27 1st-ever recording session – demo recorded at Curly Clayton's studio...

...songs recorded included:

Close Together – Jimmy Reed single in 1961
Soon Forgotten – Muddy Waters' set at *Newport Festival* in 1960
You Can't Judge a Book by the Cover – Bo Diddley single in 1962

...lineup included:

Brian – Mick – Keith – Ian Stewart – Tony Chapman

Dec 7 Bill Wyman auditioned as bass player – previously with the Cliftons

1963 Jan 11 last outing with drummer Tony Chapman – replaced by Charley Watts

Jan 16 supported Cyril Davies and His R&B All Stars at their Marquee residency

Feb 2 debut of the classic five members – plus pianist Ian Stewart

Mar 11 demo recording session at IBC Studios...

...songs recorded included:

Bright Lights Big City – Jimmy Reed single in 1961
Baby What's Wrong – Jimmy Reed single in 1962
Diddley Daddy – Bo Diddley single in 1955
Road Runner – Bo Diddley single in 1960

...Rolling Stones:

Brian – Mick – Keith – Bill – Charlie and Ian Stewart

Apr 14 Stones met the Beatles for the 1st time

Apr 28 manager Andrew Loog Oldham met the Stones – birth of the Rolling Stones...

...Ian Stewart took a back seat and the classic lineup was in place

Jun 7 released their 1st UK single – cover of Chuck Berry's *Come On*...

...B-side, *I Want to Be Loved* – Muddy Waters single in 1955
...both sides produced by Andrew Loog Oldham

Jun 30 house band at the Crawdaddy Club, played at the 1st gig following its relocation...

...the club was managed by Giorgio Gomelsky – also the Stones' 1st manager
...Andrew Loog Oldham took over as their new manager around this time
...original house band was the Dave Hunt R&B Band, with Charlie Watts

Jul 9 recorded *Fortune Teller* – released as their 2nd UK single but was withdrawn...

...Benny Spellman's 1962 B-side of *Lipstick Traces (On a Cigarette)*

Aug 7 performed at Eel Pie Island

Nov 1 released Lennon and McCartney's *I Wanna Be Your Man* as 2nd official UK single

Nov 13 supported by Joe Cocker – when he was with Vance Arnold and the Avengers

Nov 23 Stones met Gene Pitney on a TV show...

...Pitney later recorded *That Girl Belongs to Yesterday* – 1st Jagger/Richard hit

Dec 8 Yardbirds recorded at the Crawdaddy – recently replaced Stones as house band

Dec 22 Detours opened for the Stones – birth of Townshend's swinging arm playing style

1964 Jan 1 opened the 1st broadcast of UK TV's *Top of the Pops* with *I Wanna Be Your Man*

Feb 1 in the vanguard of the British Invasion

Feb 21 released *Not Fade Away* as their 3rd UK single – Buddy Holly B-side in 1957...

...Stones' B-side *Little By Little*, writing credit to Phelge and Phil Spector

Mar 29 Caroline made the 1st pirate radio broadcast – 1st song played, *Not Fade Away*

Apr 17 released their 1st album, *The Rolling Stones* (UK)

May 31 appeared on a star-studded bill at Wembley – with Adam Faith top of the bill

Jun 20 last night of their 1st American tour

	Jun 26	released their 4th UK single, *It's All Over Now* – 1st UK #1...
		...written by Bobby and Shirley Womack – 1964 R&B hit for the Valentinos
	Jul 25	released *It's All Over Now* as their 4th American single...
		...3rd single, Jagger/Richard's *Tell Me (You're Coming Back)* was 1st US hit
	Nov 13	released Willie Dixon's *Little Red Rooster* – gave them their 2nd UK #1...
		...Howlin' Wolf single as *The Red Rooster* in 1961
	Dec 26	tongue-in-cheek Christmas greeting to British hairdressers
1965	Feb 26	released *The Last Time* (UK) – 1st Jagger and Richard A-side in the UK...
		...Verve were sued 30 years later over the Andrew Oldham Orchestra version
	Mar 18	Jagger, Jones and Wyman were charged with "insulting behaviour"
	Aug 20	released *(I Can't Get No) Satisfaction* (UK)...
		...different B-side in the US – 1st Jagger and Richard penned US #1
	Aug 20	Andrew Oldham launched his Immediate record label – with three singles
	Sep 15	a goose-stepping Mick Jagger caused a riot at a Stones concert in Berlin
1966	Feb 4	released *19th Nervous Breakdown* c/w *As Tears Go By* (UK)...
		...Jagger and Richard's *As Tears Go By* was a hit for Marianne Faithfull in '64
	Apr 15	released *Aftermath* (UK) – album almost called *"Could YOU Walk on Water"*...
		...4th album but 1st to contain all Jagger and Richard songs
	Jul 28	Brian Jones played his last concert in America
1967	Jan 13	released *Let's Spend the Night Together* (UK)...
		...B-side *Ruby Tuesday* was a UK hit for Melanie in 1970
		...both sides were written by Jagger and Richard
	Jan 15	censorship on the *Ed Sullivan Show* for *Let's Spend the Night Together*
	Jan 22	refused to wave from the revolving stage at the end of the Palladium TV show
	Jun 28	Who recorded *The Last Time* and *Under My Thumb* – solidarity for drugs bust:
		The Last Time was a hit for the Stones in 1965
		Under My Thumb was originally on the 1966 album *Aftermath*
		...both sides were written by Jagger and Richard
	Jul 31	Appeals Court victory against drugs convictions for Jagger and Richard
	Aug 18	released *We Love You* (UK) – inspired by Jagger and Richard's spell in jail...
		...last Stones single to be produced by Andrew Loog Oldham
	Oct 30	Brian Jones pleaded guilty to drugs offences
	Dec 9	released *Their Satanic Majesties Request* (US) – it received mixed reviews
1968	May 24	released *Jumping Jack Flash* (UK) – 1st of their singles produced by Jimmy Miller
	Dec 11	recorded the TV special *Rock and Roll Circus* – not seen until 1996...
		...Brian Jones's final live performance with the Stones
		...Mick Jagger acted as the ringmaster
		...Keith Richard played bass in John Lennon's band, Dirty Mac
1969	June 8	Brian Jones left the Rolling Stones

Jul 3 Brian Jones died: drowned in his own swimming pool at the age of 27
Jul 4 released *Honky Tonk Women* (UK) – 1st single to feature Mick Taylor
Jul 5 free concert in London's Hyde Park – 1st gig with guitarist Mick Taylor...
...Mick Jagger read out an elegy for Brian Jones
Sep 25 Alexis Korner's New Church recording session...
...after leaving the Stones, Brian Jones had been keen to hook up with Korner
Nov 1 Jagger named as one of the Masked Marauders, in *Rolling Stone*'s hoax album
Nov 7 opened their 1st American tour for three years
Nov 27 Madison Square Garden gig – recorded their live album *Get Yer Ya-Ya's Out!*
Dec 6 headlined the ill-fated Altamont festival

1970 Mar 6 Beatles released *Let It Be* c/w *You Know My Name* – Jones played sax on B-side
Aug 3 Mick Jagger's 1st movie, *Performance*, was released...
...Jagger's single *Memo from Turner* was taken from the movie:
written by Jagger and Richard

1971 Mar 4 opened the *Goodbye to Great Britain* tour – before becoming tax exiles...
...lineup included:
Nicky Hopkins: keyboards
Apr 16 released *Brown Sugar* (UK) – 1st single on their Rolling Stones Records label...
...B-side *Let it Rock* was a Chuck Berry B-side in 1960
Apr 23 released *Sticky Fingers* (UK)...
...the album's zipper cover was designed by Pop artist Andy Warhol
Sep 1 issued a lawsuit against their ex-manager Allen Klein

1972 May 12 released *Exile on Main Street* (US) – Ian Stewart performed on the album
Jun 3 start of the fabled North American *Exile on Main Street* tour
Nov 8 Detective Sergeant Norman Pilcher was arrested for perjury...
...Pilcher had previously bust Jagger and other rock stars, for drugs

1974 Mar 12 John Lennon's "lost week-end"...
...Lennon produced Jagger's *Too Many Cooks (Spoil the Soup)* in 1973
Dec 12 Mick Taylor left and joined the Jack Bruce Band

1975 Apr 14 Ron Wood joined for the US tour – stayed on to become the 2nd guitarist
Nov 28 Keith Richard appeared with Rod Stewart and the Faces

1976 Apr 23 released *Black and Blue* (UK) – featured Ron Wood and Harvey Mandel...
...both guitarists auditioned to replace Mick Taylor

1983 Sep 20 Bill Wyman and Charlie Watts played at the ARMS charity concert...
...with Eric Clapton and Jimmy Page

1985 Dec 12 original pianist and latterly road manager, Ian Stewart died at the age of 47

1994 Nov 18 1st live internet broadcast of a concert by a major band

Fred Rose

1954 Jan 4 Elvis's 2nd visit to Sam Phillips's studio – recorded two Fred Rose songs:

I'll Never Stand in Your Way – co-written with Hy Heath
It Wouldn't Be the Same Without You – co-written with Jimmy Wakely

...Rose set up *Acuff-Rose* publishing in 1942

Tim Rose

singer: The Big Three

1941 Sep 19 Cass Elliot: singer, born Ellen Naomi Cohen, in Baltimore, Maryland...

...Rose, with Elliot, was a founding member of the Big Three – he left in 1964

1966 Dec 16 Jimi Hendrix Experience released *Hey Joe*...

...copyrighted version by Billy Roberts in 1962
...Tim Rose's 1966 version influenced Jimi Hendrix's recording

1968 Feb 23 Band of Joy gig at the Marquee – Tim Rose headlined the night...

...Band of Joy lineup included:

John Bonham: drums – joined Rose's touring band after Band of Joy

Dick Rowe

1962 Jan 1 Beatles failed Decca audition – Rowe was the man who turned down the Beatles

Roxy Music

1945 Sep 26 Brian Ferry: singer, born in Washington, County Durham...

...previously with the Gas Board – mid-1960s band at Newcastle University

1948 May 15 Brian Eno: keyboardist, born in Woodbridge, Suffolk

Dec 13 David O'List: guitarist, born in Chiswick, London...

...very short stint with Roxy music – previously a founding member of Nice

1972 Feb 18 1st gig for the lineup that recorded the 1st album...

...Roxy Music:

Brian Ferry: vocals
Graham Simpson: bass
Andy MacKay: saxophone and oboe
Brian Eno: keyboards – left in mid-1973
Paul Thompson: drums
Phil Manzanera: guitar – band's soundman but became guitarist

...original guitarist Roger Bunn was replaced by David O'List:

O'List left and was replaced by Phil Manzanera...

...soundman Philip Targett-Adams: name change to Phil Manzanera

...original drummer Dexter Lloyd had been replaced by Paul Thompson

Jun 16 released their debut album *Roxy Music* (UK)

1973 Aug 4 Brian Eno: recording session for *No Pussyfooting* album...

...collaboration with Robert Fripp

Royal Teens

1942 Nov 17 Bob Gaudio: pianist, singer and songwriter, born in the Bronx, New York...
...founding member in the mid-1950s – left in 1960 for the Four Seasons

1944 Feb 5 Al Kooper: guitarist, born in Brooklyn, New York...
...career started here when he joined the band in 1958, he was 14 years old

Jerry Rubin

1938 Jul 14 political activist, born in Cincinnati, Ohio

1967 Jan 14 participated in *A Gathering of the Tribes for a Human Be-In*

Oct 21 organiser of the anti-war march to levitate the Pentagon

1968 Jul 15 Yippies applied for a youth festival permit for the Chicago Democratic Convention

Aug 25 arrested following the violence at the Democratic Party Convention in Chicago

1969 Mar 20 one of *Chicago 8*, indicted because of the riots at 1968 Democratic Convention

1971 Dec 13 John Sinclair freed from prison – Rubin appeared at the *Freedom Rally*

The Runaways

1959 Jul 10 Sandy West: drummer, born in Long Beach, California

1975 Sep 12 1st gig, a private party at rock writer Phast Phreddie Patterson's home...
...The Runaways: originally a trio:

Sandy West: drums
Joan Jett: guitar
Micki Steele: bass – left before the band recorded their 1st album

...Kim Fowley: manager – instrumental in forming the band

1976 Jun 1 released their eponymous debut album (US)...
...The Runaways:

Sandy West – Joan Jett
Jackie Fox: bass – replaced Micki Steele
Lita Ford: lead guitar
Cherie Currie: vocals

1978 Dec 31 final performance

Todd Rundgren

guitar and vocals: The Nazz – Utopia

1948 Jun 22 musician and songwriter, born in Upper Darby, Pennsylvania...
...formed the Nazz in Philadelphia in mid-1967, and Utopia in the mid-1970s

Rush

Inducted into the Rock and Roll Hall of Fame in 2013

1953 Aug 27 Alex Lifeson: guitarist and founding member, born Aleksander Živojinović...
...in Fernie, British Columbia, Canada

The Projection, formed in Toronto in early 1968. *SEE 26 August 1974*

John Rutsey – Alex Lifeson

The Projection morphed into Rush.

1968 Sep 18 1st paid gig...

...Rush:

Alex Lifeson: guitar
John Rutsey: drums
Jeff Jones: bass – left shortly after the 1st gig

...in 1969 they used the name "Hadrian", before returning to "Rush"

1974 Aug 26 Agora Ballroom gig – classic trio was in place...

...Rush:

Alex Lifeson: guitar
Geddy Lee: bass and vocals – replaced Jeff Jones shortly after 1st gig
Neil Peart: drums – replaced ailing John Rutsey shortly before this gig

...In 1973 Rush released a cover of Buddy Holly's *Not Fade Away*, in Canada

1977 Aug 17 *A Farewell to Kings* tour opened – dawn of Rush's international success

Leon Russell

Inducted into the Rock and Roll Hall of Fame in 2011

keyboards, session musician: The Wrecking Crew record label owner: Shelter

1942 Apr 2 musician, producer, songwriter, born Claude Russell Bridges, Lawton, Oklahoma

1962 Jul 13 session musician: Darlene Love cut *He's a Rebel* – released as "The Crystals"

1965 Apr 12 session musician: Byrds released their debut single, *Mr. Tambourine Man*

1970 Mar 27 musical director: *Mad Dogs & Englishmen* was recorded live at the Fillmore East

1971 Aug 1 performed at the *Concert for Bangladesh*

Santa Barbara Machine Head

Short-lived band in 1967.

1941 Jun 9 Jon Lord: keyboardist, born in Leicester, Leicestershire...

...later in Deep Purple

1944 Nov 29 Twink: drummer, born John Charles Alder, in Colchester, Essex...

...founding member of Tomorrow and the Pink Fairies
...in 1972 he teamed up with ex-Pink Floyd guiding light Syd Barrett in Stars

1947 Jun 1 Ron Wood: guitarist, born in Hillingdon, London...

...later in Small Faces/Faces and the Rolling Stones

Santana

Inducted into the Rock and Roll Hall of Fame in 1998

1947 Jul 20 Carlos Santana: rock-fusion guitarist, born in Autlan de Navarra, Mexico...

...formed Santana in 1966

1969 Jul 26 played the *Seattle Pop Festival*

Aug 15 performed at the *Woodstock* festival

	Dec 6	performed at the ill-fated Altamont festival
1971	May 6	performed during the final concerts at the Fillmore West

The Satintones

1959	Dec 14	Motown was founded – *My Beloved* was the 1st full release on the label

Savoy Brown

1943	Jun 29	Bob Brunning: bassist, born in Bournemouth, Dorset...
		...joined in late 1967, after leaving Fleetwood Mac
1945	Jan 25	Dave Walker: singer, born in Walsall, Staffordshire...
		...joined in 1971 for three albums – went on to join Fleetwood Mac
1970	Aug 7	performed at the *Goose Lake International Music Festival*

Ronnie Scott

saxophonist and venue owner: Ronnie Scott's Jazz Club

1956	Sep 24	saxophone: Tommy Steele recorded *Rock with the Caveman*
1968	Mar 15	saxophone: Beatles released *Lady Madonna*
1970	Apr 25	Jimi Hendrix's last-ever gig was a jam with War at Scott's club

Bobby Seale

1968	Aug 25	arrested following the violence at the Democratic Party Convention in Chicago
1969	Mar 20	one of *Chicago 8*, indicted because of the riots at 1968 Democratic Convention
1971	Dec 13	John Sinclair freed from prison – Seale participated at the *Freedom Rally*

The Searchers

1941	Aug 26	Chris Curtis: drummer, born Chris Crummey, in Oldham, Lancashire...
		...later started the process to form Roundabout – which became Deep Purple
1942	Mar 3	Mike Pender: guitar, singer, born Michael Prendergast, Liverpool, Lancashire...
		...member of Johnny Sandon and the Searchers
1943	Dec 14	Frank Allen: bass, singer, born Francis Renaud McNeice, in Hayes, Middlesex...
		...left Cliff Bennett and the Rebel Rousers to join the Searchers in 1964
1959	Jun 8	Clovers recorded *Love Potion #9* – US hit single for the Searchers in 1964
1963	Feb 27	supported Gene Vincent in Hamburg...
		...The Searchers:
		Tony Jackson: bass and vocals – left in mid-1964 to form the Vibrations
		Chris Curtis: drums and vocals – left in mid-1966...
		...formed Roundabout, which morphed into Deep Purple in 1968
		Mike Pender: guitar and vocals...
		...broke away and formed Mike Pender's Searchers in 1985
		John McNally: guitar – long-time member of the group
		...band's name was inspired by the John Wayne movie, *The Searchers*
		...early '60s were Johnny Sandon & Searchers: Sandon left to join Remo 4

1968 Apr 20 Deep Purple played their 1st gig, they were still called "Roundabout"...
...Chris Curtis initiated the formation of Roundabout but left before it matured
1973 Jun 28 performed in the *British Re-Invasion Show* at Madison Square Garden

Pete Seeger

Inducted into the Rock and Roll Hall of Fame in 1996
banjo and vocals: The Almanac Singers – The Weavers
1919 May 3 influential banjo player, folk singer and songwriter, born in New York City...
...songwriting credits included:
Where Have All the Flowers Gone – written in 1955...
...inspired by *And Quiet Flows the Don* by Mikhail Sholokhov
We Shall Overcome – traditional, augmented by Seeger
1941 Jul 7 Almanac Singers recorded the album *Sod Buster Ballads*
1955 Dec 24 Weavers reunion concert at Carnegie Hall
1957 Mar 26 indicted for Contempt of Congress, after refusing to disclose his political views
1962 Jan 2 Weavers were banned from performing on US TV's *Jack Parr Show*
1964 May 18 Animals recorded *House of the Rising Sun*...
...song included on the Almanac Singers' 1941 album *Sod Buster Ballads*
1965 Aug 20 co-writer: Fifth Avenue released *Bells of Rhymney*...
...based on a 1938 poem by Idris Davies
1967 Sep 10 *Waist Deep in the Big Muddy* censored on the Smothers Brothers TV show
1969 Nov 15 sang protest songs at the anti-war *March Against Death* rally in Washington
1975 May 11 performed at the *War Is Over* rally in New York's Central Park

Bob Seger

Inducted into the Rock and Roll Hall of Fame in 2004
guitar and vocals: The Bob Seger System – Bob Seger and the Silver Bullet Band
1970 Aug 7 performed at the *Goose Lake International Music Festival*
1971 Dec 13 John Sinclair freed from prison – Seger performed at the *Freedom Rally*
1975 Sep 4 1st day of recording for the album *Live Bullet* – with the Silver Bullet Band

Sex Pistols

Inducted into the Rock and Roll Hall of Fame in 2006
1955 Sep 3 Steve Jones: guitarist, born in London, England
1956 Jan 31 Johnny Rotten: singer, born John Lydon, in Finsbury Park, London...
...later with Public Image Ltd (PIL):
reverted to his birth name, John Lydon, when he formed PIL in 1978
Jul 20 Paul Cook: drummer, born in London, England
Aug 27 Glen Matlock: bassist, born in London, England...
...later with Rich Kids and Iggy Pop:
Rich Kids featured Midge Ure, who went on to join Ultravox in late 1979

1957 May 10 Sid Vicious: bassist and singer, born John Simon Ritchie, in London, England...
...previously with Siouxsie and the Banshees, and Flowers of Romance
1965 Jul 8 Ronnie Biggs escaped from prison...
...recorded with Malcolm McLaren, Steve Jones and Paul Cook in 1978
1975 Oct 17 New York Dolls lost their record contract...
...Malcolm McLaren became their manager in early 1975

The band came together as the Swankers. *SEE 8 October 1976*

Paul Cook: drums
Steve Jones: singer – then moved to guitarist
Glen Matlock: bass
Johnny Rotten: singer – joined after McLaren became the manager
Malcolm McLaren: manager

Swankers became the Sex Pistols.

Nov 6 debut gig
1976 Sep 20 Sex Pistols and Sid Vicious – same gig but different bands...
...when they appeared at the 1st punk festival, held at London's 100 Cub
...Sid Vicious was Siouxsie and the Banshees' drummer
Oct 8 signed their 1st record deal, with EMI – then on to A&M and finally Virgin...
...Sex Pistols:

Steve Jones: guitar
Johnny Rotten: singer
Paul Cook: drums
Glen Matlock: bass – left after the 1st single – formed Rich Kids

...Malcolm McLaren: manager
Nov 26 released their debut single, *Anarchy in the UK*, on the EMI label (UK)...
...only single to feature bassist Glen Matlock:
replaced by Sid Vicious in February 1977
Dec 1 notorious appearance on the UK TV show, *Today*...
...Steve Jones said the f-word – resulted in the sacking of host Bill Grundy
Dec 6 what was left of the *Anarchy in the UK* tour opened in Leeds
1977 May 27 released *God Save the Queen* (UK) – 1st single on Virgin, written by the band
Oct 28 released their only album, *Never Mind the Bollocks Here's the Sex Pistols* (UK)
1978 Jan 14 final concert
Oct 12 Sid Vicious's girlfriend Nancy Spungen died – he was charged with her murder
1979 Feb 2 Sid Vicious died from a drug overdose

Ravi Shankar

1967 Jun 16 appeared at the *Monterey Pop Festival*
1971 Aug 1 organised and performed at the *Concert for Bangladesh*
1974 Nov 2 George Harrison opened his ill-fated solo tour – supported by Shankar

Del Shannon

Inducted into the Rock and Roll Hall of Fame in 1999

1934 Dec 30 singer, born Charles Weedon Westover, in Grand Rapids, Michigan

1961 Jan 24 recorded his 1st single, *Runaway* – written with his keyboard player, Max Crook

1963 Apr 18 supported the Beatles – Shannon decided to record *From Me to You*...
...1st US hit penned by Lennon and McCartney

1990 Feb 8 committed suicide by shooting himself: 55 years old

Helen Shapiro

singer: Susie and the Hula Hoops

1961 Jan 16 recorded her 1st single, *Don't Treat Me Like a Child*...
...in school band, Susie and the Hula Hoops, with Marc Bolan in the late '50s

1963 Feb 2 opening night of her UK package tour – with the Beatles as a supporting act

Sharon Sheeley

1940 Apr 4 songwriter, born in Los Angeles, California...
...songwriting credits included:
Poor Little Fool – Ricky Nelson single in 1958
Somethin' Else – Eddie Cochran single 1959...
...co-written with Eddie's brother, Bob

1960 Jan 8 writer: Eddie Cochran recorded *Cherished Memories*

1960 Apr 17 survived the car crash that killed her boyfriend, Eddie Cochran

Tony Sheridan

guitar and vocals: Vince Taylor and the Playboys – Tony Sheridan Trio – Tony Sheridan and the Jets
Tony Sheridan and the Beat Brothers – Tony Sheridan and the Beatles

1940 May 21 born Anthony Esmond Sheridan McGinnity, in Norwich, Norfolk

1960 Jan 24 Tony Sheridan Trio supported Eddie Cochran on his last UK tour

Jul 9 Tony Sheridan and the Jets opened at Hamburg's Top Ten Club

1961 Jun 22 recorded *My Bonnie* with Lennon, McCartney, Harrison and drummer Pete Best

1962 Jan 5 Tony Sheridan and the Beatles released *My Bonnie* (UK)

1962 Apr 23 Tony Sheridan and the Beat Brothers released *My Bonnie* on Decca (US)...
...Beat Brothers were actually the Beatles

The Shirelles

Inducted into the Rock and Roll Hall of Fame in 1996

1940 Jan 22 Addie "Micki" Harris: founding member, born in Passaic, New Jersey

1964 Jan 27 Beatles released *Introducing the Beatles*...
...included the Shirelles covers:
Baby It's You – Shirelles single in 1961
Boys – B-side of *Will You Love Me Tomorrow* in 1960

Simon & Garfunkel

Inducted into the Rock and Roll Hall of Fame in 1990

Tom & Jerry

1957 Nov 22 performed their debut single, *Hey, Schoolgirl*, on *American Bandstand*...
...writing credit: Tommy Graph (Art Garfunkel) and Jerry Landis (Paul Simon)

Simon & Garfunkel

1964 Mar 10 recorded their original acoustic version of *The Sounds of Silence*...
...written by Paul Simon

Paul Simon

1975 May 11 Paul Simon performed at the *War Is Over* rally in New York's Central Park

John Sinclair

manager: MC5

1971 Dec 13 freed from prison – given a ten-year sentence for possession of two joints...
...*John Sinclair Freedom Rally* on 10 December featured performances from:
John Lennon and Yoko Ono – Stevie Wonder – Bob Seger – Phil Ochs
Commander Cody – Allen Ginsberg – Ed Sanders
and appearances from political activists Jerry Rubin and Bobby Seal

Siouxsie and the Banshees

1957 May 27 Siouxsie Sioux, born Susan Janet Ballion, in Chislehurst, Kent
1976 Sep 20 appeared at the 1st punk festival, held at London's 100 Cub...
...lineup included:
Siouxsie Sioux: singer and founding member
Sid Vicious: drums – before he moved to bass guitar in the Sex Pistols
Dec 1 Sioux's notorious appearance with the Sex Pistols on the UK TV show, *Today*
1976 Dec 21 played at the opening of the Roxy Club

Slade

1938 Dec 18 Chas Chandler: manager, born in Heaton, Newcastle upon Tyne...
...previously the Animals' bassist and then Jimi Hendrix's manager
1946 Jun 15 Noddy Holder: singer, born in Walsall, West Midlands...
...previously a roadie in Robert Plant's group, Band of Joy
1966 Apr 1 Noddy Holder joined the 'N Betweens...
...future Slade lineup was then in place:
Noddy Holder: vocals
Dave Hill: guitar
Don Powell: drums
Jim Lea: bass

'N Betweens became Ambrose Slade and finally Slade.

1969 May 2 Ambrose Slade released their only single, *Genesis* c/w *Roach Daddy* (UK)...
...both sides written by the band members
...Chas Chandler: manager – from Ambrose Slade to the end of the 1970s

PF Sloan

1945 Sep 18 singer, songwriter and producer, born Philip Gary Schlein, in New York...
...wrote the 1960s anthem, *Eve of Destruction*

Small Faces (and Faces)

Inducted into the Rock'n'Roll Hall of Fame in 2012

Small Faces

1946 Apr 1 Ronnie "Plonk" Lane: bassist, born in Plaistow, London – also in Faces
1947 Jan 30 Steve Marriott: singer and guitarist, born in Bow, London
1948 Sep 16 Kenney Jones: drummer, born in Stepney, East London – also in Faces

Faces also included:

1945 Jan 10 Rod Stewart: singer, born in Highgate, London
1947 Jun 1 Ron Wood: guitarist, born in Hillingdon, London

Small Faces

1965 Aug 6 released their debut single, *Whatcha Gonna Do About It* (UK)...
...featured original organist, Jimmy Winston – left late 1965
...produced/co-written by the Drifters (Cliff's) original guitarist, Ian Samwell

Nov 1 keyboardist Ian McLagan joined the band – classic lineup was then in place...
...Small Faces:
Ronnie "Plonk" Lane: bass – went on to form Faces
Kenney Jones: drums – went on to form Faces
Steve Marriott: lead singer – left to form Humble Pie
Ian McLagan: keyboards – replaced Jimmy Winston – went on to Faces
...Don Arden: manager – went on to manage ELO and Black Sabbath

1966 Jan 28 released *Sha-La-La-La-Lee* (UK) – 1st single with Ian McLagan

Dec 23 appeared on the final *Ready Steady Go!* TV show

1967 Mar 3 Roy Orbison tour – with Small Faces and Jeff Beck Group...
...Jeff Beck Group included Rod Stewart and Ron Wood

Jun 2 released their 1st single on Immediate, *Here Comes the Nice* (UK)...
...A-side, and B-side *Talk to You*, written by Ronnie Lane and Steve Marriott

Jun 2 Decca also released the album *From the Beginning* on the same day (UK)...
...despite the fact that the band had already left Decca for Immediate
...this Decca album and their 1st Immediate album both contained the songs:
(Tell Me) Have You Ever Seen Me – *My Way of Giving*...
...both songs were written by Ronnie Lane and Steve Marriott

1968 Jan 31 end of the ill-fated tour of Australia and New Zealand supporting the Who

May 24 released *Ogden's Nut Gone Flake* (UK)

1968 Dec 31 Steve Marriott stormed off stage – he formed Humble Pie shortly afterwards

Small Faces changed their name to "Faces" in late 1969.

Faces

1969 Nov 14 early Faces gig...

...Faces:

Ronnie Lane: bass – ex-Small Faces – left in 1973 to form Slim Chance
Kenney Jones: drums – ex-Small Faces – went on to join the Who
Ian McLagan: keyboards – ex-Small Faces
Rod Stewart: singer – ex-Jeff Beck Group – went on to a solo career
Ron Wood: guitar – ex-Jeff Beck Group – went on to join the Stones

1972 Aug 22 early New York Dolls gig – on UK tour supporting Faces and the Groundhogs

Sep 29 Pete Townshend released his 1st solo album, *Who Came First* – Lane contributed

1974 Feb 14 Ronnie Lane backed Roy Harper at his Rainbow Theatre concert...

...as a member of the Intergalactic Elephant Band

Faces eventually became Rod Stewart and the Faces.

1974 Nov 15 released their final single as "Faces/Rod Stewart": 28-word title:

You Can Make Me Dance, Sing or Anything (even take the dog for a walk, mend a fuse, fold away the ironing board, or any other domestic shortcomings) (UK)

1975 Apr 14 Ron Wood joined the Stones' US tour – Wood was 'on loan' from the Faces

Nov 28 end of the road...

...lineup now included bassist Tetsu Yamauchi – replaced Lane in 1973

1983 Sep 20 Lane performed at the ARMS charity concert with Eric Clapton and Jimmy Page

1991 Apr 20 Steve Marriott died in a fire at his home: 44 years old

George "Harmonica" Smith

harmonica: Muddy Waters' band – Bacon Fat

1924 Apr 22 pioneer of the amplified harmonica, born in Helena, Arkansas...

...formed Bacon Fat in the late 1960s, as a dual harp band with Rod Piazza

Huey "Piano" Smith

1934 Jan 26 influential R&B pianist, born in New Orleans, Louisiana...

...formed Huey Lewis and the Clowns in 1957

1955 May 23 Smiley Lewis recorded *I Hear You Knocking* – session piano from Smith

1955 Sep 14 Little Richard recorded *Tutti-Frutti* – session piano from Smith

Norman "Hurricane" Smith

engineer and producer: The Beatles – Pink Floyd – The Pretty Things

1923 Feb 22 Beatles engineer, Pink Floyd producer and hit singer, born in Edmonton, London

1965 Dec 3 Beatles released *Rubber Soul* – last Beatles album with Smith as the engineer

1967 May 23 producer: Pink Floyd released their 2nd single, *See Emily Play*

1967 Aug 5 producer: Pink Floyd released their debut album, *Piper at the Gates of Dawn*...
...Smith's talents also extended to singer-songwriting:
Oh Babe, What Would You Say – single from Hurricane Smith in 1972

Patti Smith

Inducted into the Rock'n'Roll Hall of Fame in 2007

1946 Dec 27 Lenny Kaye: guitarist, born in Manhattan, New York...
...member of the Patti Smith Group

Dec 30 Patti Smith: poet and singer, born in Chicago, Illinois

1971 Feb 10 Patti Smith's 1st performance with guitarist Lenny Kaye

1975 May 11 performed at the *War Is Over* rally in New York's Central Park

Soft Machine

1938 Jan 13 Daevid Allen: guitarist, born in Melbourne, Australia

1944 Aug 16 Kevin Ayres: guitarist and singer, born in Herne Bay, Kent...
...formed Kevin Ayres and the Whole World in the late 1960s: included:
Mike Oldfield: bass and guitar, joined in 1969

1945 Jan 28 Robert Wyatt: drummer and singer, born in Bristol, England...
...after Soft Machine, Wyatt formed Matching Mole in 1971: included:
Dave Sinclair: keyboardist – after Caravan

1945 Oct 28 Elton Dean: saxophone, born Nottingham, England – the "Elton" in Elton John...
...band member in late 1969 to mid-1972

Road to Soft Machine *SEE 24 August 1967*

Daevid Allen Trio

Daevid Allen: guitar – formed in 1963
Robert Wyatt: drums, vocals – Wilde Flowers and on to Soft Machine
Hugh Hopper: bass – Wilde Flowers – joined Soft Machine in 1968

Mister Head was formed in mid-1966, morphed into Soft Machine shortly afterwards.

...Mister Head lineup that morphed into Soft Machine:

Daevid Allen: guitar
Kevin Ayers: guitar and vocals – previously with Wilde Flowers
Robert Wyatt: drums and vocals – previously with Wilde Flowers
Mike Ratledge: keyboards – sometime member of the Daevid Allen Trio
Larry Nolan: guitar – American guitarist who left after a brief stay

...band's name inspired by William S Burroughs' 1961 novel, *Soft Machine*

1966 Oct 11 performed at the *it* launch party at the Roundhouse

1967 Feb 17 released their debut single, *Love Makes Sweet Music* (UK)...
...Soft Machine:

Daevid Allen: guitar – left after the 1st single, formed Gong
Kevin Ayers: guitar and vocals – left 1968, formed the Whole World
Robert Wyatt: drums and vocals – left in 1971, formed Matching Mole

Mike Ratledge: keyboards – left in 1976

...written by Kevin Ayres

Apr 29 performed at the *14-Hour Technicolor Dream*

Aug 24 Daevid Allen left – end of the band's 1st era...

...Allen formed Gong shortly afterwards
...the band continued as a trio
...Kevin Ayres left Soft Machine in 1968 – replaced by Hugh Hopper

Dec 22 performed at the *Christmas on Earth Continued* concert

1977 Mar 12 Police gig – with a pre-Andy Summers lineup...

...guitarist Andy Summers had a brief stint with Soft Machine in mid-1968

Sonny & Cher

Sonny Bono

singer: The Wrecking Crew – Caesar & Cleo – Sonny & Cher

1935 Feb 16 singer, songwriter and politician, born in Detroit, Michigan...

...songwriting credits included:

Needles and Pins – Jackie DeShannon 1963, co-writer Jack Nitzsche
Laugh at Me – Sony Bono single in 1965
The Revolution Kind – Sony Bono single in 1965

Sonny & Cher, originally called Caesar & Cleo. *SEE 16 February 1935*

Sonny Bono – went on to become the mayor of Palm Springs, California

Cher – went on to international success as a solo singer

Otis Spann

piano: Muddy Waters' band

1954 Jan 7 Muddy Waters recorded *(I'm Your) Hoochie Coochie Man*

1955 Mar 2 Bo Diddley recording session, *Bo Diddley* and *I'm a Man*

Aug 12 Sonny Boy Williamson (II) recorded *Don't Start Me Talkin'*

1958 Oct 26 piano accompaniment for Muddy Waters on his historic 1st UK tour

The Spaniels

1953 May 5 1st recording session – also the birth of Vee-Jay Records...

...recorded *Baby, It's You** and *Bounce* – written by the Spaniels

*not the same song as the one with the same title recorded by the Shirelles

1953 Sep 23 recorded the doo wop classic *Goodnite Sweetheart Goodnite*

Phil Spector

Inducted into the Rock and Roll Hall of Fame in 1989

producer: The Top Notes – The Crystals – The Ronettes – Bob B Soxx and the Blue Jeans
Darlene Love – The Righteous Brothers – Ike and Tina Turner – John Lennon –The Beatles
Leonard Cohen – Ramones
record label owner: Philles guitarist and singer: The Teddy Bears

1939 Dec 26 Phil Spector: musician, songwriter, "wall of sound" producer, born in New York

"Wall of Sound" singers included:

1941 Jul 26 Darlene Love: born Darlene Wright, in Los Angeles, California...

...performed solo and also as a member of Bob B Soxx and the Blue Jeans
...came to fame with the Blossoms – replaced Nannette Williams in 1957

1943 Aug 10 Veronica Bennett: Ronettes lead singer, born in Spanish Harlem, New York...

...previously with Joey Dee and the Starliters
...married Phil Spector

The Wrecking Crew: musicians associated with the "Wall of Sound" included:

1929 Feb 5 Hal Blaine: drums, born Harold Simon Belsky, in Holyoke, Massachusetts

1935 Feb 16 Sonny Bono: singer, percussion and general assistant, born in Detroit, Michigan

1937 Apr 22 Jack Nitzsche: musician, arranger, producer, songwriter, born in Chicago, Illinois

1938 Sep 24 Steve Douglas: saxophone, born in Los Angeles, California

1942 Apr 2 Leon Russell: keyboards, born Claude Russell Bridges, Lawton, Oklahoma

Phil Spector

1949 Apr 20 Phil Spector's father committed suicide

1958 May 20 1st-ever recording session, *Don't You Worry My Little Pet* – written by Spector...

...with *To Know Him, Is to Love Him* for his 1st single, as "The Teddy Bears"

1961 Feb 23 co-producer: Top Notes cut the original version of *Twist and Shout* at Atlantic

1962 Jan 1 Beatles recorded *To Know Her Is to Love Her* at their failed Decca Audition

Jul 13 Spector's 1st #1, *He's a Rebel* – written by Gene Pitney...

...recorded by Darlene Love but released as a Crystals single

Jul 21 *Billboard Music Week* review of the Crystals' *He Hit Me (And It Felt Like a Kiss)*...

...written by Goffin and King
...withdrawn shortly afterwards and replaced by *He's a Rebel*

1964 Feb 21 Rolling Stones released *Not Fade Away* c/w *Little By Little*...

...B-side written by Spector and Phelge (Rolling Stones)

1965 Feb 26 played tuned-down guitar on the Rolling Stones' *Play with Fire*

1966 Mar 7 Tina Turner recording session for *River Deep–Mountain High*...

...written by Jeff Barry and Ellie Greenwich, and Spector
...end of the "wall of sound" era

1968 Mar 5 Darlene Love appeared with Jerry Lee Lewis in the show *Catch My Soul*

1969 Jan 2 work started on the Beatles' *Get Back* project – Spector turned it into *Let It Be*

May 8 premiere of the movie *Easy Rider* – cameo appearance as a drug dealer

1970 Jan 27 producer: John Lennon recorded *Instant Karma*

Mar 23 began work on the Beatles' *Get Back* album – turned it into *Let It Be*

May 8 producer: Beatles released their *Let It Be* album

1971 Jul 16 co-producer: Electric Oz Band released *God Save Us*

1975 Feb 21 part produced John Lennon's *Rock'n'Roll album* – last time they worked together

1979 May 1 recording sessions began with the Ramones on the album *End of the Century*

2003 Feb 3 actress Lana Clarkson was found dead in Spector's mansion...
...after two trials Spector was found guilty of her murder

Benny Spellman

Fortune Teller: B-side of Lipstick Traces (On a Cigarette), 1962 single (US) Written by Allen Toussaint.

1963 Jul 9 Rolling Stones recorded *Fortune Teller* – withdrawn 2nd UK single

1968 May 29 Who recorded *Fortune Teller* – destined for the 'lost' album *Who's for Tennis*

Barbara Spencer

1979 Jan 29 went on a shooting spree, justified by saying "I don't like Mondays"...
...immortalised in the Boomtown Rats' hit single

Spirit

1951 Feb 20 Randy California: guitar and vocals, born Randy Craig Wolfe, in LA, California...
...nickname came from Hendrix in Jimmy James and the Blue Flames:
"California" taken from his home state – two Randys in the band

1967 Nov 9 recording session for their eponymous debut album...
...lineup included:
Randy California: guitar, vocals and founding member – left in 1972
Ed Cassidy – drums and founding member – from the Rising Sons

1968 Dec 26 Led Zeppelin's debut concert in America – Spirit was also on the bill

1969 Jul 26 played the *Seattle Pop Festival*

Spooky Tooth

1942 Sep 22 Mike Patto: singer, born Michael McCarthy, in Cirencester, Gloucestershire...
...previously with Bo Street Runners, Timebox and Patto
...replaced Gary Wright in Spooky Tooth in 1974

1943 Apr 26 Gary Wright: keyboards, singer and songwriter, born in Cresskill, New Jersey

1947 Oct 23 Greg Ridley: bassist, born in Carlisle, England...
...joined the VIPs in 1964, they became Art

The VIPs morphed into Art – Art became Spooky Tooth when Gary Wright joined in 1967.

1968 Dec 31 Steve Marriott walked off stage during a Small Faces gig...
...he formed Humble Pie soon after – Ridley left Spooky Tooth to join him

1970 Apr 21 supported T.Rex – this was also Elton John's debut solo concert performance

Nov 27 George Harrison released *All Things Must Pass* – album featured Gary Wright

1978 Feb 10 Judas Priest released *Stained Glass* with *Better By You, Better Than Me*...
...track was a cover of a song from their 1969 album *Spooky Two*

1985 Dec 23 lawsuit, after suicide citing Judas Priest's *Better By You, Better Than Me*...
...written by Gary Wright

Dusty Springfield

Inducted into the Rock and Roll Hall of Fame in 1999

singer: The Springfields

1939 Apr 16 singer, born Mary O'Brien, in Hampstead, London...

...co-founded the folk trio, the Springfields, in 1960

1964 Jan 1 performed *I Only Want to Be with You* on the 1st-ever *Top of the Pops*

Bruce Springsteen

Inducted into the Rock and Roll Hall of Fame in 1999

guitar and vocals: The Castiles – Bruce Springsteen and the E Street Band

1949 Sep 23 guitarist, singer and songwriter, aka "The Boss", born in Freehold, New Jersey

The E Street Band

Inducted into the Rock and Roll Hall of Fame in 2014

1950 Nov 22 Stevie Van Zant, guitarist, born Steven Lento, in Winthrop, Massachusetts...

...aka "Little Steven" and "Miami Steve"

...member of Springsteen's backing band, E Street Band, formed early 1970s

1967 Oct 22 Bart Haynes: the Castiles' drummer, killed in action in Vietnam...

...Springsteen's 1st band, mid-1965 to '68

1973 Jan 5 released his debut album, *Greetings from Asbury Park N.J.* (US)...

...Springsteen penned *Blinded by the Light*, covered by the Earth Band in '76

1974 May 9 Jon Landau's premonition when he saw Springsteen as "rock'n'roll future"

1975 Aug 17 gig at New York's Bottom Line club – Springsteen went from hype to legend

Aug 25 released his breakthrough 3rd album, *Born to Run* (US)

Nov 18 opened his 1st European tour – to mixed reviews

1976 Apr 29 removed from Graceland after climbing over the wall in an attempt to meet Elvis

Viv Stanshall

multi-instrumentalist and singer: Bonzo Dog Doo-Dah Band

1971 May 14 percussion on John Entwistle's solo album, *Smash Your Head Against the Wall*

1973 May 25 acted as Master of Ceremonies on Mike Oldfield's album *Tubular Bells*

1995 Mar 5 died in a house fire: 51 years old...

...founding member and frontman for Bonzo Dog Doo-Dah Band – formed '62

Tommy Steele

guitar and vocals: The Vipers Skiffle Group – The Cavemen – Tommy Steele and the Steelmen

1936 Dec 17 Britain's 1st rock'n'roll star, born Tommy Hicks, in Bermondsey, South London

1956 Apr 22 2i's opened – Steele was a regular performer there with the Vipers Skiffle Group

Sep 24 1st recording session, *Rock with the Caveman* – 1st British rock'n'roll hit...

...Tommy Steele and the Steelmen:

Tommy Steele – previously Tommy Hicks in the Cavemen

Mike Pratt – previously with the Cavemen

Lionel Bart – previously with the Cavemen
Ronnie Scott – legendary jazz musician and club owner
+ other session musicians

...written by the "Cavemen": Steele, Lionel Bart and Mike Pratt

1957 May 3 Britain's 1st rock'n'roll movie, *The Tommy Steele Story*, premiered in London...
...songs written by various combinations of Steele, Lionel Bart and Mike Pratt

1958 Oct 27 appeared on the British TV show *This Is Your Life*

1960 Mar 3 Elvis's only official UK visit – Steele reputedly showed him around London in '58

Jul 27 Larry Parnes's end-of-the-pier summer show in Great Yarmouth...
...one of the most important managers of the time – Steele was his 1st artist

1961 Dec 10 premiere of Cliff's *The Young Ones* – Steele's last chart showing was mid-1961...
...the two ex-rock'n'rollers both became family entertainers

2008 Apr 21 revelation that Tommy Steele showed Elvis Presley around London in 1958

Steely Dan

Inducted into the Rock and Roll Hall of Fame in 2001

1965 Nov 11 Velvet Underground's debut gig – supporting Myddle Class...
...Myddle Class featured Steely Dan's original lead singer David Palmer:
Palmer left after the 2nd album, *Countdown to Ecstasy*

1974 Jul 4 final concert – Steely Dan went on from there to become a studio band...
...lineup included:

Donald Fagan: keyboards, vocals and founding member
Walter Becker: bass, vocals and founding member

...band's name taken from a reference in William Burroughs' *Naked Lunch*

...Jeff "Skunk" Baxter: guitar – left to join the Doobie Brothers

Steppenwolf

Jack London and the Sparrows became The Sparrows and then Steppenwolf.

Jack London and the Sparrows included:

Mars Bonfire: guitarist and founding member
Bruce Palmer: bass – then Mynah Birds and Buffalo Springfield
John Kay: joined after they became the Sparrows...
...formed Steppenwolf after the Sparrows folded

1944 Apr 12 John Kay: guitarist and singer, born in Tilsit, Germany – formed the band in 1967

1968 Jan 25 early gig – recorded *Born to Be Wild* around this time...
...band's name inspired by the title of a Herman Hesse novel
...*Born to Be Wild* was written by Mars Bonfire
...song accredited with coining the phrase "heavy metal"

Cat Stevens

Inducted into the Rock and Roll Hall of Fame in 2014

1966 Jul 10 recorded *I Love My Dog* – 1st British hit single...

...used a melody from Yusef Lateef's *The Plum Blossom*, recorded in 1961

Dec 23 appeared on the final *Ready Steady Go!* TV show

1967 Mar 31 1st time that Hendrix set fire to his guitar on stage – he was on the bill that night

1975 Dec 20 final British concert performance...

...born Steven Demetre Georgiou – girlfriend told him he had eyes like a cat

Rod Stewart

Inducted into the Rock and Roll Hall of Fame in 1994...

+...as a member of the Faces in 2012

singer: The Dimensions – Jimmy Powell and the Five Dimension
Long John Baldry's Hoochie Coochie Men – Jeff Beck Group (1st incarnation) – Faces

1945 Jan 10 born in Highgate, London

1963 Oct 4 gig with his 1st band, Jimmy Powell and the Five Dimensions

1964 Sep 10 recorded his 1st solo single, *Good Morning Little Schoolgirl*...

...written and recorded by Sonny Boy Williamson (I) in 1937
...1st UK hit, not until 1971 – cover of *Reason to Believe* – on *Tim Hardin* 1, '66

1967 Mar 3 Roy Orbison tour opened – Stewart was singer in newly formed Jeff Beck Group

1968 Jun 15 Jeff Beck Group performed at New York's Fillmore East

Dec 31 Steve Marriott stormed off stage during a Small Faces gig...

...end of the road for Small Faces – Stewart joined and they became Faces

1969 Sep 29 G.T.O.'s released *Circular Circulation* – Stewart on album *Permanent Damage*

1972 Dec 9 orchestral performance of *Tommy* at the Rainbow

1974 Nov 15 released his final single with the Faces, *You Can Make Me Dance*...

1975 Nov 28 end of the road for Rod Stewart and the Faces

Stephen Stills

Inducted into the Rock and Roll Hall of Fame...

...in 1997 as a member of Buffalo Springfield

...also in 1997 as a member of Crosby, Stills & Nash

guitar and vocals: Au Go-Go Singers – Buffalo Springfield – Crosby, Stills & Nash
Crosby, Stills, Nash & Young

1945 Jan 3 musician and songwriter, born in Dallas, Texas

1965 Jul 23 met Neil Young in Canada around this time

Sep 8 auditioned unsuccessfully to become a Monkee

1966 Apr 6 chance encounter led to the formation of Buffalo Springfield

Dec 5 Buffalo Springfield recorded *For What It's Worth* – written by Stills

1967 Jan 9 Stills's *We'll See* was recorded for the 'lost' Buffalo Springfield album *Stampede*

Mar 6 *Baby Don't Scold Me* was replaced on the 1st album by *For What It's Worth*

1968 May 5 end of the road for Buffalo Springfield

	May 28	replaced Mike Bloomfield to complete the recording of the album *Supersession*
1969	Jul 25	Crosby, Stills & Nash gave their debut performance at the Fillmore East
	Aug 15	Crosby, Stills & Nash performed at the *Woodstock Festival*
1969	Dec 6	Crosby, Stills, Nash & Young performed at the ill-fated Altamont festival

Jesse Stone

Songwriting credits included:

1953	Aug 9	Drifters recorded *Money Honey* – their 1st R&B hit
1954	Feb 15	Big Joe Turner recorded *Shake, Rattle and Roll* – also Bill Haley's 1st hit
1956	Jan 28	Elvis Presley performed *Flip Flop and Fly* – Big Joe Turner single in 1955
1958	Feb 22	*Don't Let Go* was a US hit for Roy Hamilton – one of the 1st stereo singles

Stone the Crows

1972	May 3	Les Harvey: guitarist and founding member – died on stage in Swansea: aged 25

The Stooges

		Inducted into the Rock and Roll Hall of Fame in 2010
1947	Apr 21	Iggy Pop: singer, punk icon, born James Osterberg, in Muskegon, Michigan...
		...started out as the drummer with the Iguanas in the early 1960s ...formed Psychedelic Stooges, as vocalist after his flirtation with drumming ...Psychedelic Stooges morphed into the Stooges
1956	Aug 27	ex-Sex Pistol Glen Matlock: bassist, born in London, England...
		...joined Iggy Pop in 1979, after the Rich Kids folded
1958	Jul 5	Johnny O'Keefe issued *The Wild One* – covered by Iggy Pop on an album in '86
1968	Nov 21	Stooges concert – formed in 1967 – debut album released in mid-1969
1970	Aug 7	performed at the *Goose Lake International Music Festival...*
		...lineup included:
		Iggy Pop: singer Dave Alexander: bass – left after this gig
1974	Aug 11	Iggy Pop's infamous chest-slashing gig – performance of *Murder of the Virgin...*
		...backed by James Williamson: guitar – joined the Stooges at the end of '70
1977	Mar 18	Iggy Pop released his debut solo album, *The Idiot* (US)
1978	Jan 14	Sex Pistols final concert – ended with *No Fun...*
		...penned by the Stooges: from their 1st album in 1969 – Pistols B-side in '77

Willi Stoph

1958	Oct 26	East German Defence Minister: said rock'n'roll made youth "ripe for atomic war"

Rory Storm and the Hurricanes

1940	Jul 7	Ringo Starr: drummer, born Richard Starkey, in Liverpool, England...
		...left in August 1962 to join the Beatles
1944	Mar 8	Keef Hartley: drummer, born in Preston, Lancashire...

...joined in mid-1963
...later went on to: the Artwoods, John Mayall, and the Keef Hartley Band

Rory Storm and the Hurricanes started out as the Raving Texans in 1957.

1959 Sep 26 appeared at Lathom Hall...
...lineup included:
Rory Storm: vocals – born Alan Caldwell
Ringo Starr: drums – joined the Raving Texans in 1959

1960 May 25 headlined at the Cavern Club's 1st "Beat Night"
Oct 15 bassist Wally Walters and drummer Ringo recorded with John, Paul and George

1962 Aug 18 Ringo Starr's 1st gig with the Beatles, having just left the Hurricanes
Oct 12 played at New Brighton on Little Richard's UK rock'n'roll comeback tour

1972 Sep 28 lead singer Rory Storm died from an overdose of sleeping tablets: 33 years old

The Stranglers

1949 Aug 28 Hugh Cornwell: guitarist and singer, born in Tufnell Park, North London...
...previously in Emil and the Detectives, and Johnny Sox:
Emil and the Detectives, mid-'60s school band with Richard Thompson
Johnny Sox was formed in Sweden in 1972: lineup included:
Hugh Cornwell: guitar and founding member
Hans Wärmling: guitar and keyboards
...Jet Black: drums – joined Johnny Sox after the band relocated to England

Johnny Sox morphed into the Guildford Strangles and then the Stranglers.

1974 Sep 11 formed in Guildford, Surrey, as "The Guildford Stranglers"

1976 Feb 29 beginning of their rise to fame...
...Guildford Strangles – shortened to "The Stranglers":
Hugh Cornwell: guitar and vocals
Jet Black: drums
Hans Wärmling: guitar and keyboards – left in mid-1975
Jean Jacques Burnel: bass
...The Stranglers:
Dave Greenfield: keyboards – replaced Hans Wärmling in mid-1975

1977 Apr 15 released their 1st album, *IV Rattus Norvegicus* (UK)

Strawbs

1945 Jan 7 Dave Cousins: born David Joseph Hindson, in Hounslow, Middlesex...
...guitar, vocals and founding member
...started out as the Strawberry Hill Boys in 1967 – morphed into Strawbs

1947 Jan 6 Sandy Denny: singer, born in Wimbledon, London...
...band member from mid-1967 to mid-1968
Mar 11 Blue Weaver: keyboardist, born in Cardiff, South Wales...
...founding member of Amen Corner – with the band from 1966 to '69

...replaced Rick Wakeman in the Strawbs in mid-1971
...later in Mott the Hoople

1949 May 18 Rick Wakeman: keyboardist, born in Northolt, London...
...joined in 1970 – left in mid-1971 for Yes

Big Jim Sullivan

guitar: Marty Wilde and the Wildcats

1941 Feb 14 session guitarist, born in Uxbridge, Middlesex

1960 Jan 24 Wildcats backed Eddie Cochran on his last fateful UK tour

1962 Jun 8 recorded *R&B from the Marquee*, with Alexis Korner's Blues Incorporated

1963 Feb 20 Duffy Power recorded *I Saw Her Standing There* – backed by Graham Bond...
...Sullivan replaced John McLaughlin for the re-recording a month later

The Surfaris

1963 Aug 9 *Wipe Out* was used as the opening music on *Ready Steady Go!*'s TV debut...
...Surfaris' *Wipe Out* album was mostly recorded by the Challengers

1964 Jan 10 Manfred Mann's *5-4-3-2-1* replaced *Wipe Out* as theme for *Ready Steady Go!*

Susie and the Hula Hoops

1961 Jan 16 Helen Shapiro recorded her 1st single, *Don't Treat Me Like a Child...*
...previously in Susie and the Hula Hoops – school-band in the late 1950s:
Helen Shapiro: singer
Mark Feld (Marc Bolan): guitar and vocals

Screaming Lord Sutch and the Savages

1932 Jan 23 Cyril Davies: harmonica and guitarist, born in Denham, Buckinghamshire...
...when he formed his R&B All Stars in 1962, they were mostly ex-Savages

1938 Dec 17 Carlo Little: drummer, born in Sudbury, London...
...regular drummer with the Rolling Stones, before Charlie Watts

1944 Feb 24 Nicky Hopkins: keyboardist, born in Perivale, London...
...went on to become a very successful session musician

1945 Apr 14 Ritchie Blackmore: guitarist, born in Weston-super-Mare, Somerset...
...went on to become a founding member of Deep Purple

1956 Jul 2 Johnny Burnette recorded *The Train Kept A-Rollin'*; and *Honey Hush* on 3 July...
...Sutch covered both sides on a 1965 single – produced by Joe Meek

1959 Jul 16 Coasters recorded *Poison Ivy...*
...they recorded *I'm a Hog for You* next day – Joe Meek produced cover '63

Screaming Lord Sutch and the Savages

1962 Jun 25 Sutch and the Savages gig – Keith Moon asked Carlo Little for drum lessons...
...lineup included:

Screaming Lord Sutch: vocals and founding member – formed in 1960
Carlo Little: original drummer – left to join Cyril Davies at the end of '62
Ritchie Blackmore: guitar – May to Oct 1962 – left to join the Outlaws
...Nicky Hopkins: keyboards and founding member – left just before this gig

Screaming Lord Sutch

1964 May 27 launched his own pirate radio station, Radio Sutch...
...sold out to his manager, Reg Calvert, who renamed it "Radio City"
1966 Jun 21 his manager Reg Calvert was shot dead
1969 Sep 13 appeared at the *Toronto Rock and Roll Revival* festival
1983 Feb 24 1st election as the candidate for the Official Monster Raving Loony Party
1999 Jun 16 committed suicide: 58 years old

The Swinging Blue Jeans

1964 Jan 1 performed on the 1st edition of UK TV's *Top of the Pops*
May 9 support act for Chuck Berry when he toured the UK for the 1st time
May 31 appeared on a star-studded bill at Wembley – with Adam Faith top of the bill
1968 Dec 8 Graham Nash left the Hollies to form Crosby, Stills & Nash...
...Nash was replaced by Terry Sylvester from the Swinging Blue Jeans

Alan Sytner

venue owner: Cavern Club

1957 Jan 16 Liverpool's Cavern Club opened – as a jazz club
1957 Aug 7 admonished John Lennon for playing rock'n'roll at the Cavern

Talking Heads

Inducted into the Rock and Roll Hall of Fame in 2002
1975 Jun 8 debut concert – at CBGB supporting the Ramones...
...Talking Heads:
David Byrne: guitar and vocals
Chris Franz: drums
Tina Weymouth: bass
...Jerry Harrison: guitar and keyboards – joined late '76, completed the quartet
1975 Jul 16 appeared at CBGB's *Top 40 New York Unrecorded Rock Bands* festival

Taste

1948 Mar 2 Rory Gallagher, guitarist, born in Ballyshannon, County Donegal, Ireland...
...member of the Impact before becoming a founding member of Taste in '66
1968 Nov 26 supported Cream at their farewell concert at London's Royal Albert Hall
1970 Jul 11 played at the *Tivoli Pop Festival* in Germany

Vince Taylor

singer: Vince Taylor and the Playboys

1939 Jul 14 born Brian Maurice Holden, in Isleworth, Middlesex...

...Taylor was David Bowie's inspiration for his character Ziggy Stardust

Vince Taylor and the Playboys

1939 Jul 14 Vince Taylor: singer and founding member – formed in mid-1958

1940 May 21 Tony Sheridan: born Anthony Esmond Sheridan McGinnity, in Norwich, Norfolk...

...Playboys included:

Tony Sheridan: guitar – later backed by the Beatles
Brian Bennett: drums – later in the Shadows
Brian "Licorice" Locking: bass – later in the Shadows

Television

1949 Dec 13 Tom Verlaine: guitarist, singer, born Thomas Miller, Morristown, New Jersey...

...stage name inspired by the French symbolist poet Paul Verlaine

1975 Jul 16 appeared at CBGB's *Top 40 New York Unrecorded Rock Bands* festival

1977 May 22 began their 1st tour of the UK – supported by Blondie...

...lineup included:

Tom Verlaine: guitar, vocals, songwriter and founding member

...Richard Hell: bass, singer and founding member – left Television in mid-'75

...Verlaine and Hell formed the Neon Boys in '72 – it morphed into Television

The Temptations

Inducted into the Rock and Roll Hall of Fame in 1989

1941 Jan 18 David Ruffin was born in Whynot, Mississippi...

...previously with the Soul Stirrers

1941 Oct 30 Otis Williams was born Otis Miles, in Texarkarna, Texas...

...formed Otis Williams and the Siberians, which morphed into the Distants

Road to the Temptations *SEE 24 July 1961*

Temptations grew out of two vocal groups, the Distants and the Primes...

...The Distants: included:

Otis Williams
Elbridge "Al" Bryant
Melvin Franklin

...The Primes: included:

Eddie Kendricks
Paul Williams

The Distants and the Primes combined to form the Elgins.

...The Elgins became the Temptations:

Otis Williams – one of the so-called "Classic Five" – 1964 to '68

Melvin Franklin – one of the so-called "Classic Five"
Eddie Kendricks – one of the so-called "Classic Five"
Paul Williams – one of the so-called "Classic Five"
Elbridge "Al" Bryant – replaced by David Ruffin in 1964

...David Ruffin, lead singer, one of the so-called "Classic Five" – joined 1964

1961 Jul 24 released their debut single, *Oh, Mother of Mine* (US)...
...written by Otis Williams and Mickey Stevenson

Ten Years After

Jaybirds had its roots in the early 1960s, morphed into Ten Years After in 1967.
Musicians in both bands included:

1943 Nov 30 Leo Lyons: bassist, born in Mansfield, Nottinghamshire

1944 Dec 19 Alvin Lee: guitarist, singer, born Graham Barnes, in Nottingham, Nottinghamshire

Ten Years After

1967 Sep 29 performed at the final gig held at London's 1st psychedelic club, the UFO

1969 Jul 26 played the *Seattle Pop Festival*

Aug 15 performed at the *Woodstock* festival

1970 Jun 28 performed at the *Festival Express* event in Toronto

Aug 7 performed at the *Goose Lake International Music Festival*

1970 Aug 28 performed at the *Isle of Wight Festival*

Thin Lizzy

1949 Aug 20 Phil Lynott: singer and bassist, born in West Bromwich, West Midlands...
...founding member – formed in 1970

1952 Apr 4 Gary Moore: guitarist, born in Belfast, Northern Ireland...
...joined in 1978 – replaced Brian Robertson
...previously with Colosseum II

Phil Lynott was with Skid Row when they were a quartet.

1969 Nov 14 early outing for Skid Row as a power trio...
...Skid Row:

Noel Bridgeman: drums and founding member
Brush Shiels: bass and founding member
Gary Moore: guitar – 1st band of note, joined in 1968

...became a trio after singer Phil Lynott left and formed Orphanage

Phil Lynott left Orphanage in 1970 and formed Thin Lizzy.

1980 Feb 7 Pink Floyd's 1st concert performance of *The Wall* – with guitarist Snowy White...
...White joined Thin Lizzy after completing *The Wall* concerts

The 13th Floor Elevators

1947 Jul 15 Roky Erickson: guitarist, singer and songwriter, born in Dallas, Texas...
...aka Emil Schwartze

...previously in the Spades
...formed Bleib Alien in 1974 – band's name "Bleib" is an anagram of "Bible"

1966 Feb 10 one of the earliest concerts to be reviewed as "Psychedelic Rock"

Jun 10 Janis Joplin's 1st gig with Big Brother...
...Joplin had previously turned down a lead singer offer from the Elevators

Oct 10 penultimate recording session for the album *The Psychedelic Sounds of the...*
...lineup included:
Roky Erickson – in 1969 he pleaded insanity to avoid a jail sentence

1967 Jun 10 played the *Fantasy Fair and Magic Mountain Music Festival*

Willie Mae "Big Mama" Thornton

1952 Aug 13 recorded the original version of *Hound Dog...*
...hit for Elvis Presley in 1956
...early composition from Leiber and Stoller
...original release gave a writing credit to producer Johnny Otis

Johnny Thunders and the Heartbreakers

1952 Jul 15 Johnny Thunders: guitar, singer, born John Anthony Genzale, Queens, New York

1975 Jul 16 appeared at CBGB's *Top 40 New York Unrecorded Rock Bands* festival

Oct 17 New York Dolls lost their record contract – Thunders left the band shortly before

1976 Dec 6 supported the Sex Pistols on their infamous *Anarchy in the UK* tour

1977 Mar 12 gig with Cherry Vanilla and a recently formed Police

1977 Oct 14 UK tour to promote their debut album, *L.A.M.F.* – split up at the end of the tour...
...original trio:
Johnny Thunders: guitar and vocals
Jerry Nolan: drums
Richard Hell: bass – from Television – left the Heartbreakers in mid-'76
...formed in mid-1975 after Thunders and Nolan left the New York Dolls

Tiny Tim

1969 Dec 17 married Miss Vicki live on TV's *Johnny Carson Show...*
...born Herbert Buckingham Khaury – stage name from a Dickens character

1970 Aug 28 performed at the *Isle of Wight Festival*

Toe Fat

1940 Jun 4 Cliff Bennett: singer, born in Slough, Berkshire...
...founding member – Toe Fat formed in mid-1969
...formed the British R&B Band, the Rebel Rousers, in the late 1950s

1945 Aug 24 Ken Hensley: keyboards, singer, founding member, born in Plumstead, London...
...founding member of Uriah Heep

Top Notes

1961 Feb 23 Top Notes recorded the original version of *Twist and Shout*...
...co-produced by Phil Spector
...famously covered by the Isley Brothers in 1962 and the Beatles in 1963

Tomorrow

1944 Nov 29 Twink: drummer, born John Charles Alder, in Colchester, Essex

1947 Apr 8 Steve Howe: guitarist, born in Holloway, North London

Final lineup of the In Crowd became Tomorrow.

1967 Sep 21 appeared on the 1st *John Peel Sessions* on BBC Radio...
...final lineup of The In Crowd:
Keith West: vocals – In Crowd morphed from Four + One
John Wood: rhythm guitar – also from Four + One
Steve Howe: guitar – joined in 1965 from the Syndicats
Twink: drums – joined from the Fairies
...Tomorrow:
Steve Howe: guitar – went on to join Yes
Keith West: vocals – solo career started in parallel with Tomorrow
John Wood: rhythm guitar
Twink: drums – joined the Pretty Things and recorded *SF Sorrow*

1967 Dec 22 performed at the *Christmas on Earth Continued* concert

The Tornados

1929 Apr 5 Joe Meek: producer, born in Newent, Gloucestershire

1937 Aug 28 Clem Cattini: drummer, born in London, England...
...previously with Larry Parnes's house band, the Beat Boys/Blue Flames:
Tornados replaced the Blues Flames as his house band in early 1962
...left in 1965

1960 May 13 Johnny Kidd and the Pirates recorded *Shakin' All Over*...
...two of those Pirates went on to become Tornados:
Alan Caddy: guitarist – founding member – left in 1964
Brian Gregg: bassist – replaced Heinz in 1963

1962 Aug 17 released *Telstar* (UK) – in December, this was the 1st US #1 by a British group

1963 Apr 30 recorded 'live' album *We Want Billy*, with Billy Fury...
...Billy Fury's backing band, early 1962 to late 1963

1967 Feb 3 Joe Meek committed suicide: 37 years old – the gun was owned by Heinz...
...Heinz: bassist and founding member – left in 1963 to become a solo singer

Traffic

Inducted into the Rock and Roll Hall of Fame in 2004

1944 Aug 2 Jim Capaldi: drummer, born in Evesham, Worcestershire

1946 Nov 1 Rick Grech: bassist, born Richard Roman Grechko, in Bordeaux, France...
...joined the re-formed lineup in 1970 – left at the end of 1971

1948 May 12 Steve Winwood: keyboards and vocals, born in Birmingham, England

1967 Apr 2 Steve Winwood left the Spencer Davis Group to form Traffic...
...original Traffic lineup:

Steve Winwood: keyboards and vocals – from the Spencer Davis Group
Dave Mason: guitar and vocals – previously a Spencer Davis roadie...
...late of the Hellions

Jim Capaldi: drums – founding member of the Hellions, 1963
Chris Wood: saxophone and flute – previously with Locomotive

...*Paper Sun* – Traffic single in 1967 – original writing credit to the whole band:

later issues only credited Winwood and Capaldi
produced by Jimmy Miller

1970 Jun 28 performed at the *Festival Express* event in Toronto

1973 Jan 13 Jim Capaldi performed at Eric Clapton's Rainbow Theatre comeback concert

Traveling Wilburys

1950 Oct 20 Tom Petty: singer and guitarist, born in Gainesville, Florida...
...Traveling Wilburys started out in 1988 to play on a George Harrison B-side:

George Harrison: guitar and vocals
Tom Petty: guitar and vocals
Bob Dylan: guitar and vocals
Jeff Lynne: guitar and vocals
Roy Orbison: guitar and vocals – died before 2nd album was recorded

The Troggs

1966 Apr 22 released *Wild Thing* (UK) – originally released by the Wild Ones in late 1965...
...Troggs' 2nd single – written by Chip Taylor
...lead singer Reg Presley also took some of the writing credits:

Lost Girl – Troggs' 1st single, 1966 – in his birth name Reginald Ball
I Can't Control Myself – Troggs single in 1966

Big Joe Turner

1954 Feb 15 recorded *Shake, Rattle and Roll*

Jul 10 Bill Haley released his cover version of *Shake, Rattle and Roll*

1956 Jul 2 Johnny Burnette Trio recorded *Honey Hush* on 3 July...
...released as a single by Turner in 1953

Ike and Tina Turner

Inducted into the Rock and Roll Hall of Fame in 1991

1931 Nov 5 Ike Turner: pianist, guitarist and singer, born in Clarksdale, Mississippi...
...formed: Ike Turner and His Kings of Rhythm
Ike and Tina Turner Review

1939 Nov 26 Tina Turner: singer, born Anna Mae Bullock, in Brownsville, Tennessee

Ike Turner and His Kings of Rhythm

1951 Mar 5 Jackie Brenston recorded *Rocket 88*...

...the band was Ike Turner's Kings of Rhythm: lineup included:

Ike Turner: piano and vocals
Jackie Brenston: saxophone and vocals
Willie Kizart: guitar

Ike and Tina Turner

1966 Mar 7 recording session for *River Deep–Mountain High*

1969 Jul 26 played the *Seattle Pop Festival*

Nov 7 supported the Rolling Stones on their American tour

1969 Nov 27 Tina Turner duet with Janis Joplin at Stones' Madison Square Garden gig

The Turtles

1943 Mar 14 Jim Pons: bassist and singer, born in Santa Monica, California...

...joined in early 1967 – stayed until the band split up in late 1970
...previously with the Leaves – later with Frank Zappa

1947 Apr 19 Mark Volman: singer, born in Los Angeles, California...

...formed the band in mid-1965 – later with Frank Zappa and, Flo & Eddie

Jun 22 Howard Kaylan: singer, born Howard Kaplan, in New York City, New York...

...Turtles co-founder with Volman – later with Frank Zappa and, Flo & Eddie

1971 Sep 17 T.Rex released *Electric Warrior* – Volman and Kaylan provided backing vocals

1972 Jul 21 Flo & Eddie was the support act on the Doors' last-ever tour...

...Flo & Eddie was formed by Mark Volman and Howard Kaylan in early '72

Sep 21 Jefferson Airplane's final gig – lineup included drummer John Barbata...

...joined the Turtles in 1966 – left 1969, joined Crosby, Stills, Nash & Young

1974 Mar 19 John Barbata played with Jefferson Starship at their debut gig

27 *CLUB* – MEMBERSHIP LIST

1938 Aug 16 Robert Johnson died at the age of 27 – an early member of the *27 Club*...

...reputedly sold his soul to the devil (at the crossroads) for fame and virtuosity

Artists who died at the age of 27 included:

1938	Aug 16	Robert Johnson	blues icon	murdered – poisoned
1960	Feb 6	Jesse Belvin	singer	automobile accident
1964	May 20	Rudy Lewis	singer	various causes cited
1969	Jul 3	Brian Jones	guitarist	drowned in his swimming pool
1970	Sep 3	Alan "Blind Owl" Wilson	guitarist	drug overdose
	Sep 18	Jimi Hendrix	guitarist	inhalation of vomit, open verdict
	Oct 4	Janis Joplin	singer	heroin overdose

1971	Jul 3	Jim Morrison	singer	heart failure
1975	Apr 24	Pete Ham	singer	suicide – hanged

Conway Twitty

1956 Nov 16 failed his audition with Sam Phillips at Sun Records...
...born Harold Jenkins
...stage name from two US towns, Conway in Arkansas and Twitty in Texas
...songwriting credits included:
I Need Your Lovin' – his 1st Mercury single, 1957...
...co-written with James Paulman
It's Only Make Believe – Twitty single in 1958 – Billy Fury single in '64...
...written by Conway Twitty and Jack Nance

The Undertakers

1959 Sep 26 early Liverpool Scene – Undertakers began as Bob Evans and the Five Shillings
1966 Mar 7 Mike Millward: singer – died of leukaemia – left in late 1961 to join the Fourmost

Uriah Heep

Spice: musicians included:
1945 Aug 24 Ken Hensley: keyboardist, guitarist and singer, born in Plumstead, London...
...previously with Toe Fat and the Gods
1947 Jan 29 David Byron: singer, born David Garrick, in Epping, Essex...
...formed Rough Diamond after leaving Uriah Heep
Spice morphed into Uriah Heep in 1970. Other musicians in Uriah Heep included:
1971 Mar 18 Colosseum gig recorded for *Live* album – lineup included bass Mark Clarke...
...Clarke had a brief tenure with Uriah Heep in late 1971 and early 1972

Ritchie Valens

Inducted into the Rock and Roll Hall of Fame in 2001
guitar and vocals: The Silhouettes
1941 May 13 musician, songwriter, born Richard Steven Valenzuela, Pacoima, Los Angeles...
...before going solo he was a member of the local band Silhouettes
1958 Jun 9 released his 1st single, *Come on, Let's Go* (US) – written by Valens
Oct 14 issued 2nd and final single, *Donna* c/w *La Bamba* (US) – *Donna* written by Valens
1959 Feb 3 died in the plane crash that killed Buddy Holly: 17 years old
1959 Feb 5 Eddie Cochran recorded the tribute song *Three Stars* – Valens, Holly, Big Bopper

Van Halen

Inducted into the Rock and Roll Hall of Fame in 2007
1947 Oct 13 guitarist and singer, Sammy Hagar was born in Monterey, California...
...with Montrose before he joined Van Halen

1955 Jan 26 guitarist, Eddie Van Halen was born in Nijmegen, The Netherlands

1974 Apr 5 early Van Halen gig – recently renamed from "Mammoth"...

...Mammoth lineup that became Van Halen:

Eddie Van Halen: guitar
Alex Van Halen: drums
David Lee Roth: vocals – replaced by Sammy Hagar in 1985
Michael Anthony: bass

Vanilla Fudge

Vanilla Fudge morphed from the Pigeons in 1967.

1944 Aug 27 Tim Bogert: bassist and founding member, born in New York City...

...later in Cactus, and Beck, Bogert & Appice

1946 Dec 15 Carmine Appice: drums, singer and founder, born in Staten Island, New York...

...later in Cactus; Beck, Bogert & Appice, and KGB
...formed KGB in 1975 with Rick Grech and Mike Bloomfield – folded in 1976

1968 Dec 26 Led Zeppelin's debut concert in America – Vanilla Fudge was the headlining act

1969 Jul 26 played the *Seattle Pop Festival*

1969 Jul 28 Led Zeppelin's notorious *Mud Shark Incident* – allegedly filmed by Vanilla Fudge

Vanilla Fudge folded in the spring of 1970.

Bogert and Appice wanted to hook up with Jeff Beck but that was not to be.

Instead, they formed Cactus.

1970 May 16 Cactus's debut gig...

...in mid-1972 the trio concept came to pass, with Beck, Bogert & Appice

Bobby Vee

1959 Feb 3 substituted for Buddy Holly at the Moorhead gig on evening after plane crash...

...performed with his group, the Shadows

The Velvet Underground

Inducted into the Rock and Roll Hall of Fame in 1996

1938 May 19 Herbie Flowers: bassist, born in Isleworth, Middlesex...

...bass riff on Reed's self-penned 1973 single *Walk on the Wild Side*

Oct 16 Nico: singer, born Christa Päffgen, in Cologne, Germany

1942 Mar 2 Lou Reed: guitarist, singer and songwriter, born in Brooklyn, New York...

...previously with the Primitives

1942 Mar 9 John Cale: multi-instrumentalist and singer, born in Garnant, Wales

Original Velvet Underground lineup:

Lou Reed: guitar, vocals and songwriter
John Cale: viola, bass, keyboards and vocals – left in mid-1968
Sterling Morrison: guitar – became a tugboat captain after the VU folded
Maureen Tucker: drums – retired temporarily after the VU folded

The Velvet Underground

1965 Aug 20 Nico released the single, *I'm Not Sayin...*

...this was one of the 1st three singles released on Immediate (UK)

Nov 11 1st Velvet Underground gig...

...opened for Myddle Class, with singer David Palmer – later in Steely Dan
...band's name inspired by the title of a book by Michael Leigh

1966 Jan 13 1st gig with vocalist Nico

1967 Mar 12 released their debut album, *The Velvet Underground and Nico* (US)...

...famous banana cover, designed by Pop artist Andy Warhol

1970 Aug 23 last concert with Lou Reed...

...The Velvet Underground:

Lou Reed and Sterling Morrison: original members
Doug Yule: bass – replaced John Cale in 1968
Bill Yule: drums – stood in for a pregnant Maureen Tucker

The Ventures

Inducted into the Rock and Roll Hall of Fame in 2008

1933 Feb 10 Don Wilson: guitarist, born in Tacoma, Washington

1934 Jan 16 Bob Bogle: bassist and guitarist, born in Wagoner, Oklahoma

1960 Mar 22 recorded the original Blue Horizon version of *Walk–Don't Run...*

...The Ventures:

Don Wilson: guitar
Bob Bogle: bass and guitar
George Babbitt: drums

...1st single for Blue Horizon was *The Real McCoy* c/w *Cookies and Cream*:

both songs written by Don Wilson and Bob Bogle

B-side lyrics credited to Jo Wilson

Mike Vernon

producer: The Yardbirds record label owner: Blue Horizon

1944 Nov 20 producer and founder of Blue Horizon record label, born in Harrow, London

VIETNAM WAR

President Eisenhower – US President: 1953 Jan 20 to 1961 Jan 20: Republican Party

1954 May 7 French were defeated at Dien Bien Phu – America's war in Vietnam began...

...the Vietnamese forces were led by Ho Chi Minh
...he was a war hero from World War II – to the whole population of Vietnam

1959 Jul 9 1st Americans killed – Major Dale Buis along with Master Sgt Chester Ovnand

President Kennedy – US President: 1961 Jan 20 to 1963 Nov 22: Democratic Party

1961 Mar 23 Kennedy was concerned about "domino effect" of communism in Southeast Asia

1962 Jan 12 1st direct participation of US forces in combat

President Johnson: US President: 1963 Nov 22 to 1969 Jan 20: Democratic Party

1964	Aug 4	*Gulf of Tonkin Incident* – US military operations without a declaration of war
	Aug 5	1st American bombing raid
	Nov 1	one of the earliest Viet Cong attacks on an American military base
1965	Mar 2	*Operation Rolling Thunder* bombing campaign began – it lasted until late 1968
	Mar 8	1st US combat troops arrived in Vietnam
	Apr 7	President Johnson delivered his *Peace Without Conquest* speech
	Jun 29	General Westmorland launched the 1st "search and destroy" offensive
	Aug 31	legislation was passed in America to criminalize the burning of draft cards
1967	Jan 8	*Operation Cedar Falls* began – the largest ground operation of the war...
		...1st use of "tunnel rats"
	Apr 4	Martin Luther King Jr delivered his anti-war speech *Beyond Vietnam*
	Apr 28	boxer Mohammad Ali was arrested for refusing to join the US Army
	Sep 10	Pete Seeger's anti-war song *Waist Deep in the Big Muddy* was censored on TV
	Oct 21	anti-war demonstration to levitate the Pentagon
	Nov 29	Robert McNamara resigned as Secretary of Defense
	Dec 20	Joan Baez received a 45-day jail sentence for anti-Vietnam War activities
	Dec 22	last days of positive spin by American politicians and senior military personnel...
		...following the *Tet Offensive*, General Westmorland was replaced in June '68
1968	Jan 21	siege of Khe Sanh began...
		...*Operation Pegasus* relieved the siege on 8 April
	Jan 31	*Tet Offensive* began – beginning of the end for America in Vietnam
	Mar 16	infamous My Lai Massacre...
		...investigation into the atrocity was instigated by General Westmorland
		...First Platoon Leader Lt William Calley was the only person convicted
		...Captain Ernest Medina led the assault on the Vietnamese hamlet
		...President Nixon was personally involved in managing the outcome
	Mar 17	violent anti-war demonstration in London
	Mar 31	President Johnson announced his policy of "Vietnamization"...
		...and the fact that he would not be seeking re-election as President
	May 10	Paris Peace Talks began...
		...Henry Kissinger also conducted secret talks in parallel with the official talks
	Jul 15	Yippies applied for a youth festival permit for the Chicago Democratic Convention
	Aug 25	anti-Vietnam War riots at the Democratic Party Convention in Chicago
1968	Oct 31	President Johnson terminated the *Operation Rolling Thunder* bombing campaign

President Nixon: US President: 1969 Jan 20 to 1974 Aug 9: Republican Party

1969	Jan 22	beginning of *Operation Dewey Canyon*...
		...one of the last of the major operations by US Marines
	Mar 20	*Chicago 8* indicted as a result of the riots at the 1968 Democratic Convention

May 15 battle for Hill 937, *Hamburger Hill* – Operation *Apache Snow*, 10-20 May...
...military strategy changed from "maximum pressure" to "protective reaction"

Jun 8 Nixon announced the 1st American troop withdrawals

Sep 3 announcement of the death of Ho Chi Minh – he actually died on 2 September

Oct 11 Weathermen's *Days of Rage* protest in Chicago...
...radical political group, name from Dylan's *Subterranean Homesick Blues*

Oct 15 North Vietnam's Pham Van Dong sent encouragement to US anti-war protestors

Nov 15 three-day *March Against Death* ended – one of the biggest anti-war protests...
...performances included Peter Paul and Mary, Pete Seeger and Arlo Guthrie

1970 May 1 1st day of the Kent University protests – four students were shot dead on 4 May

Sep 5 last major engagement to use American ground forces

1971 Jun 13 1st publication of the damning *Pentagon Papers*...
...Nixon famously used "Plumbers" to stop the leaks

Jun 27 last US Marine combat unit left Vietnam

Oct 9 "combat refusal" by the 1st Air Cavalry Division

1972 Mar 30 *Easter Offensive* began – full-scale attack by Northern forces on the South

Jun 17 *Watergate* scandal began – indirectly sealed the fate of South Vietnam

Dec 18 Nixon initiated the *Christmas Bombing* of Hanoi – finished on 29 December

1973 Jan 23 President Nixon's *Peace with Honor* speech

Jan 27 *Paris Peace Accords* were signed – America's war in Vietnam was over...
...Statistics:

Peak troop strength in Vietnam (30 April 1969)	543,482
Troops on active duty during the Vietnam era	9,078,000
Deaths	58,272

Feb 12 *Operation Homecoming* began – repatriation of American prisoners of war

1973 Oct 16 *Nobel Peace Prizes* for Henry Kissinger and Le Duc Tho...
...Henry Kissinger accepted his award – for brokering 'peace' in Vietnam
...Le Duc Tho refused his award – he believed that the war was not over

President Ford: US President: 1974 Aug 9 to 1977 Jan 20: Republican Party

1975 Mar 10 final invasion of South Vietnam began...
...speech at Tulane University 23 April, Ford distanced the US from the war

Apr 30 last Americans left Vietnam – THE VIETNAM WAR WAS OVER

1975 May 11 *War Is Over* rally in New York's Central Park

Gene Vincent

Inducted into the Rock and Roll Hall of Fame in 1998

1935 Feb 11 singer, born Vincent Eugene Craddock, in Norfolk, Virginia

1956 May 4 recorded *Be-Bop-A-Lula* at his 1st recording session for Capitol records...
...co-written with his manager, Sheriff Tex Davis

Aug 22 appeared in the movie *The Girl Can't Help It*

1957 Oct 12 support act: Australian tour, Little Richard found God and renounced rock'n'roll
1960 Jan 24 co-headlined with Eddie Cochran on Cochran's last UK tour
Apr 17 injured in the car crash that killed Eddie Cochran
1963 Feb 27 supported by the Searchers in Hamburg
1969 Sep 13 appeared at the *Toronto Rock and Roll Revival* festival
1971 Oct 12 died from natural causes: 36 years old

The Vipers Skiffle Group/later shortened to The Vipers

1956 Jul 14 played at the 2i's coffee bar for the 1st time...
...various lineups included:
Wally Whyton: guitar, vocals and founding member – formed in early '56
Tommy Steele: guitar and vocals – made guest appearances in mid-'56
Jet Harris: bass – member of one of the later lineups, c.1958
Hank Marvin: guitar – member of one of the later lineups, c.1958
Tony Meehan: drums – member of one of the later lineups, c.1958

Rick Wakeman

keyboards: Spinning Wheel – Strawbs – Yes

1949 May 18 flamboyant keyboards player and composer, born in Northolt, London...
...joined Spinning Wheel in 1969 – left to join the Strawbs
1969 Jul 11 session musician: David Bowie released his breakthrough single, *Space Oddity*

Dave Walker

singer: The Redcaps – Beckett – Idle Race – Savoy Brown – Fleetwood Mac – Black Sabbath

1945 Jan 25 born in Walsall, Staffordshire...
...Walkers pedigree included:
The Redcaps: lead vocals, guitarist and founding member – early 1960s
Beckett: mid-to-late 1960s
Idle Race: replaced Jeff Lynne in 1970
Savoy Brown: joined in 1971 for three albums
Fleetwood Mac: joined 1972, on *Penguin* and *Mystery to Me* albums
1978 Jan 6 rare appearance with Black Sabbath – Ozzy Osbourne rejoined soon afterwards

Andy Warhol

1966 Jan 13 Exploding Plastic Inevitable, Nico sang for the 1st time with Velvet Underground
1967 Mar 12 *The Velvet Underground and Nico* album released – Warhol designed the sleeve
1971 Apr 23 Rolling Stones released *Sticky Fingers* – Warhol designed the zipper cover

Muddy Waters

Inducted into the Rock and Roll Hall of Fame in 1987

1915 Apr 4 born McKinley Morganfield, in Rolling Fork, Mississippi
1950 Jun 3 Waters' *Rollin' Stone* was the 2nd release on the new Chess Records label...
...song title was the inspiration for the name of the Rolling Stones

1954 Jan 7 recorded *(I'm Your) Hoochie Coochie Man...*

...backed by some of his regular musicians:

Willie Dixon: bass
Little Walter: harmonica
Otis Span: piano
Jimmy Rogers: guitar
Fred Bellow: drums

...Long John Baldry took the song title as his band's name

1955 May 21 Chuck Berry's 1st recording session at Chess – introduced to Chess by Waters

Aug 12 session guitarist: Sonny Boy Williamson (II) recorded *Don't Start Me Talkin'*

1958 Oct 26 recorded his performance in Manchester during his historic 1st UK tour

1962 Jun 27 recorded the lyrics to Earl Hooker's *Blue Guitar*, to produce *You Shook Me...*

...*Blue Guitar* – recorded by Hooker as an instrumental in 1961:

Willie Dixon added lyrics and Waters released it as *You Shook Me*

...covered by Led Zeppelin on their eponymous 1st album

Oct 27 Rolling Stones recorded *Soon Forgotten...*

...song was a part of Waters' set at the *Newport Festival* in 1960

1963 Jun 7 Stones released *I Want to Be Loved*, B-side 1st UK single – Waters single in '55

Sep 15 Animals recorded *I Just Wanna Make Love to You* – Waters single in 1954

1968 Oct 5 released his psychedelic blues album, *Electric Mud* (US)

1969 Nov 7 Zeppelin released *Whole Lotta Love* – based on Waters' *You Need Love*, 1962

1976 Nov 25 made a guest appearance at the Band's swan song concert, *The Last Waltz*

Johnny "Guitar" Watson

guitar and vocals: The Shields – guest appearances with Frank Zappa

1935 Feb 3 innovative guitarist, born in Houston, Texas...

...member of the late 1950s vocal group the Shields – with Jessie Belvin

1954 Feb 1 recorded the self-penned *Space Guitar* – with pioneering feedback and reverb

Weather Report

1969 Aug 19 Joe Zawinul and Wayne Shorter recorded with Miles Davis on *Bitches Brew*

1971 Feb 16 recording started on their eponymous debut album...

...lineup included:

Wayne Shorter: saxophone and founding member
Joe Zawinul: keyboards and founding member

...Jaco Pastorius: bass – joined in 1976

The Weathermen

1969 Oct 11 organised the anti-Vietnam War demonstration in Chicago, *Days of Rage...*

...radical group's name inspired by Dylan's *Subterranean Homesick Blues*

The Weavers

1955 Dec 24 reunion concert at Carnegie Hall...

...The Weavers:

Pete Seeger: banjo and singer
Lee Hays: singer
Fred Hellerman: guitar and singer
Ronnie Gilbert: singer

1962 Jan 2 Weavers were banned from performing on US TV's *The Jack Parr Show*

Bert Weedon

1920 May 10 Britain's 1st guitar hero, born in West Ham, London...

...his book *Play in a Day* inspired a generation of British axemen

1962 Apr 13 Shadows received the 1st Gold Disc for a British group – 1960 single *Apache*...

...originally recorded by Weedon

WHAT'S GOING ON – AROUND THE WORLD

1948 Jun 25 Berlin Airlift began – dawning of the Cold War...

...Bernard Baruch coined the expression "Cold War" in 1947
...Winston Churchill referred to the "Iron Curtain" in a speech on 5 March '47

1956 Oct 23 Hungarian uprising began

1961 Apr 15 President Kennedy launched the ill-fated *Bay of Pigs* invasion of Cuba...

...Kennedy was continuing Eisenhower's policy to overthrow President Castro

1962 Oct 17 1st missile site photographed in the *Cuban Missile Crisis*...

...standoff between America's JFK and the USSR's Nikita Khrushchev:
took the world to the brink of World War III

...Major Rudolph Anderson was the U-2 pilot shot down over Cuba

1967 Oct 9 Che Guevara was executed in Bolivia

WHAT'S GOING ON – UK

Prime Minister: Harold Wilson: 1964 – 1970: Labour

1967 Jul 24 call for legalisation of marijuana in an ad placed in the UK newspaper *The Times*

Jul 27 *Sexual Offences Act 1967* decriminalised homosexuality in England and Wales

1968 Apr 20 Enoch Powell delivered his infamous "rivers of blood" speech...

...Powel was Conservative Member of Parliament for Wolverhampton South

WHAT'S GOING ON – USA

President Truman – US President: 1945 Apr 12 to 1953 Jan 20: Democratic Party

1950 Feb 20 McCarthy's six-hour speech to the Senate about communist infiltration...

...dawning of the communist witch hunt era – led by Senator Joe McCarthy

President Eisenhower – US President: 1953 Jan 20 to 1961 Jan 20: Republican Party

1957 Mar 26 Pete Seeger indicted for Contempt of Congress...

...for failing to disclose his political views

President Kennedy – US President: 1961 Jan 20 to 1963 Nov 22: Democratic Party

1961 Mar 23 concerned about the "domino effect" of communism in Southeast Asia

1962 Jan 2 Weavers were banned from performing on American TV's *The Jack Parr Show*...

...they had been blacklisted as communists

1963 Nov 22 President Kennedy was assassinated in Dallas, Texas...

...Lyndon Baines Johnson became America's new president
...police officer JD Tippit was shot dead by Oswald after the assassination
...Lee Harvey Oswald was arrested for the assassination
...Jack Ruby shot dead Lee Harvey Oswald

President Johnson: US President: 1963 Nov 22 to 1969 Jan 20: Democratic Party

1968 Apr 4 Martin Luther King Jr was assassinated in Memphis, Tennessee...

...James Earl Ray was convicted of his murder

Jun 5 Robert Kennedy was assassinated in Los Angeles...

...Sirhan Sirhan was found guilty of his murder

1968 Oct 24 LSD (Acid) became an illegal substance in America

President Nixon: US President: 1969 Jan 20 to 1974 Aug 9: Republican Party

1969 Aug 10 Charles Manson "Family" murdered Sharon Tate

1971 Jun 13 1st publication of the *Pentagon Papers*...

...Robert McNamara commissioned the *Papers*
...Daniel Ellsberg was responsible for the leaks

1972 Jun 17 Watergate scandal began – resulted in Nixon's resignation in August 1974

Whitesnake

1941 Jun 9 Jon Lord: keyboardist, born in Leicester, Leicestershire...

...joined in the late 1970s

1951 Sep 22 David Coverdale: singer and founder, born in Saltburn-by-the-Sea, Cleveland...

...band's name taken from Coverdale's 1977 solo album

The Who

Inducted into the Rock and Roll Hall of Fame in 1990

1944 Mar 1 Roger Daltrey: singer, born in Shepherds Bush, London

Oct 9 John Entwistle: bassist, born in Chiswick, London

1945 May 19 Pete Townshend: guitarist, singer and songwriter, born in Chiswick, London

1946 Aug 23 Keith Moon: drummer, born in Wembley, London

1948 Sep 16 Kenny Jones, drummer, born in Stepney, East London...

...replaced Keith Moon, who died on 7 September 1978

Road to the Who

Before the Detours: Pete Townshend and John Entwistle:

...The Confederates – trad jazz band c.1959:

John Entwistle: French horn and trumpet
Pete Townshend: banjo

...The Scorpions:

John Entwistle: bass – left in mid-1961 to join Daltrey in the Detours
Pete Townshend: guitar – left in 1962 to join the Detours

The Detours

Daltrey was in the Detours before the others joined – by late 1963 the band was:

Roger Daltrey: guitar and vocals
John Entwistle: bass – joined in mid-1961
Pete Townshend: guitar – joined in 1962
Doug Sandom: drums – joined in mid-1962

The Detours changed their name to "The Who"

Sandom played a handful of gigs as "The Who" before being replaced by Keith Moon.

Keith Moon

Pre-Who bands included: Mark Twain and the Strangers
The Beachcombers

The band become the "High Numbers" for one single, before finally settling on "The Who".

Pre-Who Keith Moon

1962 Jun 25 asked Screaming Lord Sutch's drummer, Carlo Little, for drumming lessons

1962 Sep 5 auditioned for BBC Radio with Mark Twain and the Strangers – failed...
...went on to join the Beachcombers:
left to replace Doug Sandom in the Who in early May 1964

The Detours

1963 Dec 22 opened for the Rolling Stones...
Daltrey – Entwistle – Townshend – and drummer Doug Sandom
...Townshend's swinging-arm style reputedly started here

The Who

1964 Apr 9 less than successful auditions for Fontana and BBC Radio...
...Fontana audition with Chris Parmenter – he was unimpressed by Sandom

Apr 13 drummer Doug Sandom's last gig

Apr 30 Keith Moon's audition as drummer...
...he played *Road Runner* – penned by Bo Diddley and a single in 1960

1964 May 5 2nd audition for Fontana – once again with Chris Parmenter...
...Keith Moon was established as the new drummer

The High Numbers

1964 Jul 3 released *Zoot Suit* (UK) – only High Numbers single and the 1st by 'The Who'...
...Kit Lambert and Chris Stamp became their managers shortly afterwards

1964 Aug 16 opened the 2nd half of a Beatles concert

The Who

1964	Nov 24	opened their historic residency at London's Marquee club
1965	Jan 15	released their 1st single, *I Can't Explain* (UK) – written by Pete Townshend...
		...Ivy League provided background vocals
	Oct 29	released *My Generation* c/w *Shout and Shimmy* (UK)...
		...Townshend-penned *My Generation* became a baby-boomer anthem
	Nov 19	Roger Daltrey stormed off the stage during the *Glad Rag Ball* at Wembley
	Dec 6	Viv Prince began a ten-day stint as substitute drummer for Keith Moon
1966	Mar 14	released the 3rd version of *Substitute* – with *Waltz for a Pig* on the B-side...
		...*Substitute* was released with three different B-sides
		...Townshend wrote the A-side and two B-sides, *Instant Party* and *Circles*
		...he also wrote *A Legal Matter*:
		Matter was Shel Talmy's A-side for Brunswick's release of *Instant Party*
		...*Waltz for a Pig* was credited to "The Who Orchestra":
		Who Orchestra was actually the Graham Bond Organisation
	May 16	Jeff Beck recorded *Beck's Bolero* – with Keith Moon and Jimmy Page
	May 20	Keith Moon and John Entwistle temporarily quit, after an on stage altercation
	Dec 23	appeared on the final *Ready Steady Go!* TV show
1967	Mar 25	performed in New York on Murray the "K"'s *Live in Person...*package show
	Apr 12	tour of Germany – end of the line for the support band, John's Children
	May 29	owing to an injury Keith Moon was substituted by Julian Covey...
		...Covey was in Brian Auger's Trinity in the early 1960s
		...he formed Julian Covey and the Machine in the mid-1960s
	Jun 10	Chris Townson deputised for an incapacitated Keith Moon
	Jun 16	played the *Monterey Pop Festival*
	Jun 28	recorded *The Last Time* and *Under My Thumb* – without John Entwistle:
		The Last Time – hit for the Rolling Stones in 1965
		Under My Thumb – originally on the Stones' 1966 album *Aftermath*
	Aug 14	traumatic plane flight – inspired Townshend to write *Glow Girl* and led to *Tommy*
	Sep 17	exploding bass drum performance on the *Smothers Brothers Comedy Hour*
1968	Jan 31	end of ill-fated antipodean tour – Townshend vowed never to play Australia again
	May 29	recording session for what might have been on 'lost' album *Who's for Tennis...*
		...included *Fortune Teller* – Benny Spellman B-side in 1962
	Nov 9	Led Zeppelin's 1st gig with that moniker – name inspired by Moon and Entwistle
	Dec 11	stole the show on the Rolling Stones' TV special, *Rock and Roll Circus*
1969	May 23	released Tommy (UK)
	Aug 15	performed at the *Woodstock* festival
	Oct 20	1st of six nights at the Fillmore East performing *Tommy*
	Dec 15	Moon performed with the Plastic Ono Band, start of the *War is Over* campaign

1970	Feb 14	legendary *Live at Leeds* concert performance...
		...included the covers:
		Young Man – recorded by Mose Allison as *Blues* in 1957
		Summertime Blues – Eddie Cochran single in 1958
		Shakin' All Over – Johnny Kidd and the Pirates single in 1960
	Jun 7	*Tommy* took a bow at New York's Metropolitan Opera House...
		...Townshend admonished the crowd for booing at the end of the gig
	Aug 28	performed at the *Isle of Wight Festival*
1971	Apr 26	recorded a performance of *Lifehouse* – Townshend's lost magnum opus
	May 14	John Entwistle issued 1st solo album, *Smash Your Head Against the* Wall (UK)...
		...Moon played percussion
	Aug 27	released *Who's Next* (UK) – some tracks salvaged from the *Lifehouse* project
	Nov 4	performed on the opening night of London's Rainbow Theatre
1972	Sep 29	Pete Townshend released his debut solo album, *Who Came First* (UK)...
		...he dedicated it to Meher Baba
	Dec 9	orchestral performance of *Tommy* at the Rainbow
1973	Jan 13	Townshend organised and played at Clapton's Rainbow Theatre comeback gig...
		...they performed as Eric and the Palpitations
	Oct 28	shambolic debut performance of *Quadrophenia*
	Oct 29	*Quadrophenia* tour lumbered on
	Nov 2	released *Quadrophenia* (UK) – released end of October but only just available
	Nov 5	Pete Townshend stormed off stage during a performance of *Quadrophenia*...
		...in a fit of rage he pulled the soundman, Bob Pridden, onto the stage
	Nov 20	Keith Moon collapsed on stage – replaced by an audience member, Scott Halpin
	Dec 2	arrested for hotel-wrecking high jinks after a concert in Montreal
1974	Feb 14	Keith Moon backed Roy Harper at his Rainbow Theatre concert...
		...they performed as the Intergalactic Elephant Band
1976	Oct 21	Keith Moon's last-ever concert performance, in Toronto
1977	Jun 23	Keith Moon joined Led Zeppelin on stage and played alongside John Bonham
1978	May 25	Keith Moon's final performance
	Aug 18	released *Who Are You* (UK)...
		...cover photo: Moon sitting on a chair inscribed "not to be taken away"
	Sep 7	Keith Moon died: at the age of 32
1979	May 13	new era dawned – with drummer Kenny Jones...
		...Jones gave his debut performance on 2 May
	Dec 3	11 fans died in a rush for seating at a Who concert
1983	Sep 20	Kenny Jones played at ARMS charity concert with Eric Clapton and Jimmy Page

Marty Wilde

1939 Apr 15 seminal British rock'n'roll singer, born Reginald Smith, in Blackheath, London...
...stage name provided by his manager Larry Parnes

1958 Oct 1 invited Billy Fury to make an impromptu concert appearance

Oct 6 appeared with Nancy Whiskey at a gig in Kent

1960 Jan 24 Marty Wilde's Wildcats backed Eddie Cochran on his last UK tour...
...lineup included:

Big Jim Sullivan: guitar – later a much sought after session musician
Brian Bennett: drums – later with the Shadows
Brian "Licorice" Locking: bass – later with the Shadows...
...Bennett and Locking had been with Vince Taylor and the Playboys

1961 Dec 10 premiere of Cliff's *The Young Ones* – Wilde's last chart appearance was late '62

Wilde Flowers

Stalwarts of the Canterbury Scene, morphed into Caravan in 1968.

1944 Aug 16 Kevin Ayres: singer and founding member, born in Herne Bay, Kent...
...went on to become a founding member of Soft Machine

1945 Jan 28 Robert Wyatt: drummer and singer, born in Bristol, England...
...went on to become a founding member of Soft Machine

1947 Jan 21 Pye Hastings: guitarist and singer, born in Taminavoulin, Banffshire, Scotland...
...went on to become a founding member of Caravan

Nov 24 Dave Sinclair: keyboardist, born in Herne Bay, Kent...
...joined in early 1967 – went on to become a founding member of Caravan

1967 Aug 24 Daevid Allen left Soft Machine – end of the band's 1st era...
...bassist Hugh Hopper formed Wilde Flowers with Robert Wyatt, mid-'60s

Hank Williams

Inducted into the Rock and Roll Hall of Fame in 1987

1923 Sep 17 enormously influential singer, guitarist, songwriter, born in Georgiana, Alabama

1953 Jan 1 died on the way to a gig: 29 years old

1956 Sep 17 Brenda Lee released *Jambalaya* – country hit for Hank Williams in 1952

Larry Williams

1935 May 10 seminal rock'n'roll singer and songwriter, born in New Orleans, Louisiana

1958 Feb 19 recorded *Dizzy Miss Lizzy* – covered by the Beatles in 1965...
...other Beatles covers penned by Larry Williams:

Slow Down – B-side of Williams's *Dizzy Miss Lizzy* – Beatles cover '64
Bad Boy – Williams single in 1959 – Beatles cover in US '65 and UK '66

1958 Mar 28 support act: package tour opened, featured a piano burning Jerry Lee Lewis

Sonny Boy Williamson (I) (John Lee)

1948 Jun 1 blues harmonica player, murdered during a street robbery: 34 years old

1964 Sep 10 Rod Stewart recorded *Good Morning Little Schoolgirl*...

...written and recorded by Sonny Boy Williamson in 1937

When John Lee died in 1948, Rice Miller adopted the name "Sonny Boy Williamson".

Sonny Boy Williamson (II) (Rice Miller)

1951 Aug 5 session harmonica: Elmore James recorded *Dust My Broom*

1955 Aug 12 recorded the self-penned *Don't Start Me Talkin'*...

...featured guitarist Jimmy Rogers

...Alex "Rice" Miller – copied the name "Sonny Boy Williamson":

aka "Little Boy Blue" in his early days

1963 Dec 8 recorded the live album *Sonny Boy Williamson and The Yardbirds*

Harold Wilson

(UK Prime Minister: 1964 to '70 and 1974 to '76)

1966 Jul 23 Liverpool's Cavern Club reopened – officially opened by Wilson

1967 Oct 11 Move's *Flowers in the Rain* libel suit with Wilson settled

Jackie Wilson

Inducted into the Rock and Roll Hall of Fame in 1987

singer: Billy Ward and His Dominoes

1934 Jun 9 aka "Mr Excitement", singer, born in Detroit, Michigan

1957 Sep 8 released his debut solo single, *Reet Petite* (US)...

...written by Berry Gordy Jr and Billy Davis

1965 Oct 15 Jimmy (Jimi) Hendrix signed a management deal with Ed Chalpin...

...had previously played with Wilson's touring band

1984 Jan 21 died after being semi-comatose since collapsing on stage in 1975: 49 years old

Steve Winwood

Inducted into the Rock and Roll Hall of Fame in 2004 – Traffic

keyboards and vocals: Rhythm and Blues Quartet – The Spencer Davis Group
Eric Clapton and the Powerhouse – Traffic – Blind Faith – Ginger Baker's Airforce

1948 May 12 aka "Steve Anglo", born in Birmingham, England

1966 Jun 1 vocalist (Steve Anglo) with Eric Clapton and the Powerhouse on *What's Shakin'*

1967 Mar 13 final tour with the Spencer Davis Group

Apr 2 left the Spencer Davis Group to form Traffic

1968 Oct 25 performed on the Jimi Hendrix Experience's *Electric Ladyland*

1969 Jun 7 Blind Faith's debut performance at a free concert in London's Hyde Park

Aug 24 final Blind Faith concert – joined Ginger Baker's Airforce in January 1970

1972 Dec 9 performed in the orchestral performance of *Tommy* at the Rainbow

1973 Jan 13 keyboardist at Eric Clapton's Rainbow Theatre comeback concert
1983 Sep 20 performed at the ARMS charity concert with Eric Clapton and Jimmy Page

Wolfman Jack

1938 Jan 21 legendary gravel-voiced DJ, born Robert Weston Smith, in Brooklyn, New York...
...as a DJ, he also went by the name of "Daddy Jules"

Stevie Wonder

Inducted into the Rock and Roll Hall of Fame in 1989
1962 Aug 16 released 1st single, *I Call It Pretty Music (But Old People Call It the Blues)* (US)
1971 Dec 13 John Sinclair freed from prison – Wonder performed at the *Freedom Rally*
1972 Jun 3 start of the Stones' American *Exile on Main Street* tour – he was the opening act
1974 Mar 31 at the jam session when Lennon and McCartney played together for the last time

Ron Wood

Inducted into the Rock and Roll Hall of Fame in 1989 – The Rolling Stones...
+...as a member of the Faces in 2012

guitar and bass: The Thunderbirds – The Birds – Santa Barbara Machine Head
Jeff Beck Group (1st incarnation) – The Creation – Faces – Eric and the Palpitations
The Rolling Stones

1947 Jun 1 born in Hillingdon, London
1965 Aug 2 guitar: the Birds issued the Byrds with a writ for using a similar sounding name
1967 Mar 3 bass: newly formed Jeff Beck Group were support act on Roy Orbison's UK tour
1968 Jun 15 bass: Jeff Beck Group performed at New York's Fillmore East
Dec 31 Steve Marriott stormed off stage during a Small Faces gig...
...Marriott left: Wood and Rod Stewart joined and it became Faces
1969 Nov 14 guitar: early Faces gig – recently joined from the Jeff Beck Group
1972 Dec 9 performed in the orchestral version of *Tommy* at the Rainbow
1973 Jan 13 guitar: performed at Eric Clapton's Rainbow Theatre comeback concert
1975 Apr 14 joined the Rolling Stones US tour – stayed on to become their 2nd guitarist
Nov 28 end of the road for Rod Stewart and the Faces
1976 Apr 23 Rolling Stones album *Black and Blue* was released – featured Wood
1976 Nov 25 made a guest appearance at the Band's swan song concert, *The Last Waltz*

Link Wray

1929 May 2 early guitar hero and father of the power chord, born in Dunn, North Carolina...
...1958 single *Rumble* – co-writing credit for disk jockey Milt Grant

The Wrecking Crew

An association of session musicians including:
1929 Feb 5 Hal Blaine: drums
1935 Feb 16 Sonny Bono: percussion – found fame as Sonny & Cher

1938	Sep 24	Steve Douglas: saxophonist
1942	Apr 2	Leon Russell: keyboards
1962	Jul 13	Barney Kessel: guitar

Jimmy Yancey

		Inducted into the Rock and Roll Hall of Fame in 1986 (inaugural year)
1898	Feb 20	seminal boogie-woogie piano player, born in Chicago, Illinois

The Yardbirds

		Inducted into the Rock and Roll Hall of Fame in 1992
1934	Feb 28	Giorgio Gomelsky: manager, born in Georgia, Russia...
		...replaced by Peter Grant towards the end of the band's career
1943	Mar 22	Keith Relf: singer and harmonica player, born in Richmond, Surrey
1944	Jan 9	Jimmy Page: 4th lead guitarist, born in Heston, Middlesex
	Jun 24	Jeff Beck: 3rd lead guitarist, born in Wallington, Surrey
1945	Mar 30	Eric Clapton: 2nd lead guitarist, born in Ripley, Surrey
	Nov 11	Chris Dreja: rhythm guitarist, moved to bass, born in Surbiton, London
1947	Jul 3	Anthony "Top" Topham: 1st lead guitarist, born in Southall, Middlesex

Road to the Yardbirds

Country Gentlemen *SEE 3 July 1947*

Paul Samwell-Smith: guitar – teamed up with the Metropolis Blues Quartet

Jim McCarty: drums – teamed up with the Metropolis Blues Quartet

Metropolis Blues Quartet *SEE 19 October 1963*

(Sometimes referred to as the "Metropolitan Blues Quartet".)

Metropolis Blues Quartet: lineup that morphed into the Yardbirds:

Keith Relf: vocals and harmonica
Chris Dreja: rhythm guitar
Top Topham: lead guitar – replaced by Eric Clapton in late 1963
Jim McCarty: drums – joined from the Country Gentlemen
Paul Samwell-Smith – Country Gentlemen guitarist – moved to bass

Before the Yardbirds

1955	Mar 2	Bo Diddley recorded *I'm a Man* – recorded by the Yardbirds in 1965
1956	Jul 2	Johnny Burnette recorded *The Train Kept A-Rollin'* – covered in late 1965
1963	Jun 30	Rolling Stones gig as house band at the Crawdaddy Club...
		...Yardbirds replaced the Stones as the house band in September

The Yardbirds

1963	Oct 19	Top Topham's final gig as lead guitarist – replaced by Eric Clapton
	Dec 8	recorded live with Sonny Boy Williamson (II) at the Crawdaddy Club...
		...recorded by their manager Giorgio Gomelsky – who also owned the Club
1964	Sep 10	Rod Stewart recorded *Good Morning Little Schoolgirl* – just before Yardbirds...

...written and originally released by Sonny Boy Williamson (I) in 1937

1965 Mar 3 Eric Clapton's final gig – he was replaced by Jeff Beck

Mar 5 released *For Your Love* (UK) – final single with Eric Clapton

Sep 12 recorded *The Train Kept A-Rollin'* at Sun studios – with Jeff Beck

1966 Jun 21 Jimmy Page's 1st gig – started out on bass, before moving to dual lead guitar...

...replaced bassist Paul Samwell-Smith

...Chris Dreja moved to bass and Page became (dual) lead guitarist

Oct 22 supported by Chain Reaction in Westport, Connecticut

Dec 18 *Blow-Up* opened (US) – featured dual lead guitarists Jeff Beck and Jimmy Page

1967 Mar 3 Jeff Beck Group supported Roy Orbison on his UK tour...

...Beck had recently moved on from the Yardbirds

1968 Feb 23 Band of Joy gig – Roger Plant and John Bonham...

...Page and manager Peter Grant jointly formed Led Zeppelin soon afterwards

Jul 7 Yardbirds final gig:

Jimmy Page: formed Led Zeppelin – along with manager Peter Grant

Keith Relf and Jim McCarty: formed the duo Together...

...which extended to become Renaissance

Chris Dreja: became a professional photographer

Sep 7 Led Zeppelin lineup's debut gig – billed as "The Yardbirds"

1976 May 14 Keith Relf died: electrocuted whilst playing his guitar at home: 33 years old

Yes

1944 Oct 25 Jon Anderson: singer, born in Accrington, Lancashire...

...previously with the Warriors – 1962 to '67

1947 Apr 8 Steve Howe: guitarist, born in Holloway, North London...

...replaced original guitarist Peter Banks in early 1970

1949 May 17 Bill Bruford: drummer, born in Sevenoaks, Kent

1949 May 18 Rick Wakeman: flamboyant keyboardist, born in Northolt, London...

...joined in mid-1971, to replace Tony Kaye

Mabel Greer's Toyshop morphed into Yes.

1968 Aug 4 debut performance from Yes...

...Mabel Greer's Toyshop: lineup that became Yes:

Jon Anderson: vocals – previously in the Warriors

Peter Banks: guitar – previously with the Syn

Chris Squire: bass – previously with the Syn

Bill Bruford: drums – from a very short stint in Savoy Brown Blues Band

Tony Kaye: keyboards – previously: the Federals and Winston's Fumbs

...Yes:

Jon Anderson: vocals

Peter Banks: guitar – left in early 1970 – formed Flash

Chris Squire: bass
Bill Bruford: drums – left in mid-1972 to join King Crimson
Tony Kaye: keyboards – left in mid-1971, joined Flash

	Nov 26	supported Cream at their farewell concert at London's Royal Albert Hall
1969	Sep 13	drummer Alan White performed with the Plastic Ono Band in Toronto...
		...joined Yes in mid-1972, to replace Bill Bruford

Neil Young

Inducted into the Rock and Roll Hall of Fame in 1995...
+...as a member of Buffalo Springfield in 1997

guitar and vocals: The Squires – Mynah Birds – Buffalo Springfield – Crosby, Stills, Nash & Young

1945	Nov 12	musician and songwriter, born in Ontario, Canada
1965	Jul 23	1st-ever recording – with the Squires – recorded their only single, *The Sultan*...
		...went on to join the Mynah Birds
1966	Apr 6	chance encounter led to the formation of Buffalo Springfield
1967	Jan 9	recording session for the 'lost' 2nd album, *Stampede* – recorded Young's *Mr. Soul*
1968	May 5	end of the road for Buffalo Springfield – Young started his solo career
1969	Jul 25	joined Crosby, Stills & Nash on stage at their debut performance
	Aug 15	performed with Crosby, Stills & Nash at the *Woodstock* festival
1970	May 1	wrote *Ohio* in response to the killing of four students at Kent State University
1973	Jan 23	Nixon's "Peace With Honor" speech...
		...Young was in concert and announced on stage that "peace has come"
1974	Jun 24	Lynyrd Skynyrd released *Sweet Home Alabama*...
		...in response to two Neil Young songs:
		Southern Man – track on the1970 album *After the Gold Rush*
		Alabama – track on the 1972 album *Harvest*
1976	Nov 25	made a guest appearance at the Band's swan song concert, *The Last Waltz*
1983	Jul 27	released *Everybody's Rockin'* (US) – it attracted a lawsuit from Geffen

The Young Rascals

Inducted into the Rock and Roll Hall of Fame in 1997

1944	Nov 29	Felix Cavaliere: keyboardist and singer, born in Pelham, New York
1946	Oct 22	Eddie Brigati: singer and songwriter, born in Garfield, New Jersey

Originally called "The Rascals", they changed it to "The Young Rascals" to avoid possible litigation with the Harmonica Rascals. Changed back to "The Rascals" in early 1968.

1968	Feb 25	Jimi Hendrix had a stimulating encounter with Cynthia Plaster Caster...
		...Eddie Brigati had a similar experience and became plaster-cast 00018

The Rascals

1968	Mar 6	recorded *A Beautiful Morning* – written by Eddie Brigati and Felix Cavaliere...
		...The (Young) Rascals: still the original lineup:

Felix Cavaliere: keyboards, vocals – from Joey Dee and the Starliters
Eddie Brigati: singer, percussionist – from Joey Dee and the Starliters
Gene Cornish: guitar and vocals – from Joey Dee and the Starliters
Dino Danelli: drums

...written by Felix Cavaliere and Eddie Brigati

1969 Feb 1 announced that they would only perform if 50% of the artists were black

Frank Zappa

Inducted into the Rock and Roll Hall of Fame in 1995

guitar and vocals: The Soul Giants – The Mothers – The Mothers of Invention
record label owner: Bizarre – Straight

1935 Feb 3 Johnny "Guitar" Watson: pioneering guitarist, born in Houston, Texas...
...one of Zappa's heroes, made guest appearances on albums and at shows

1940 Dec 21 Frank Zappa: musician and songwriter, born in Baltimore, Maryland

1941 Jan 15 Captain Beefheart: singer, born Don Glen Vliet, in Glendale, California...
...name from Zappa collaboration, *Captain Beefheart vs The Grunt People*
...many collaborations with Zappa, from before the days of the Mothers

1943 Mar 14 Jim Pons: bassist, born in Santa Monica, California...
...joined Zappa in late 1970 – previously with the Leaves and the Turtles

Apr 17 Roy Estrada: bassist, born in Santa Ana, California...
...one of the Soul Giants – later with Little Feet and Captain Beefheart

May 14 Jack Bruce: bassist, born in Bishopbriggs, Lanarkshire, Scotland...
...appeared on Zappa's 1974 album *Apostrophe'*

1944 Dec 25 Henry Vestine: guitarist, born in Takoma Park, Maryland...
...in an early lineup but left just before the 1st album – joined Canned Heat

1945 Apr 13 Lowell George: singer and guitarist, born in Hollywood, California...
...joined Zappa in late 1968 – left in 1969 to form Little Feat

1946 Jan 10 Aynsley Dunbar: drummer, born in Liverpool, England...
...with Zappa from early 1970 to mid-1972

1947 Apr 19 Mark Volman: singer, born in Los Angeles, California...
...with Zappa from early 1970 to '72 – then formed Flo & Eddie

1947 Jun 22 Howard Kaylan: singer, born Howard Kaplan, in New York City, New York...
...with Zappa from early 1970 to '72 – then formed Flo & Eddie

Before the Mothers

1963 Feb 20 Penguins released *Memories of El Monte*...
...Zappa produced, and co-wrote the song with Ray Collins

Mar 27 performed his *Concerto for Two Bicycles* on TV's *The Steve Allen Show*

Nov 30 Kingsmen scored a hit with *Louie Louie* – covered ironically many times...
...*Plastic People* on the 1967 album *Absolutely Free*, used the famous riff

1964 Aug 1 opened his Studio Z in Cucamonga – purchased the studio from Paul Buff...
...Zappa was a regular collaborator with Ray Collins at this time:

Collins's songwriting credits included:

Deseri – released by Frank Zappa in 1968 – co-written with Paul Buff
Love of My Life – released by Frank Zappa '68 – co-written with Zappa

...saxophonist Jim "Motorhead" Sherwood also regularly worked with Zappa

1964 Dec 2 *I Was a Teen-age Malt Shop* was nearly the 1st-ever rock opera...

...saxophonist Jim "Motorhead" Sherwood worked with Zappa on this project

1965 Mar 26 arrested in Cucamonga on pornography charges

The Mothers

1965 May 10 Soul Giants became the Mothers and moved to original (Zappa) material...

...Soul Giants lineup that became the Mothers:

Frank Zappa: guitar
Roy Estrada: bass
Ray Collins: vocals
Jimmy Carl Black: drums

Aug 11 1st day of the Watts riots – immortalised in Zappa's song *Trouble Every Day*

1966 Jun 24 support act for Lenny Bruce at his last-ever concerts...

...Mothers' lineup now included guitarist Elliott Ingber

..."The Mothers" was a tad too risqué for their record company, MGM

MGM insisted that the Mothers changed their name to "The Mothers of Invention".

1966 Jun 27 released their debut album, *Freak Out* (US)...

...The Mothers of Invention:

Frank Zappa – Ray Collins – Jimmy Carl Black – Roy Estrada
Elliott Ingber: guitar – left after the 1st album, for the Fraternity of Man

Frank Zappa

1966 Jul 4 arranged two of the songs on the Animals' US album *Animalism*

1968 Nov 6 world premiere of the Monkees' movie *Head* – appearance from Zappa

1969 May 19 Alice Cooper released their 1st single, *Reflected* – 1st single on the Straight label

Jun 16 Captain Beefheart released *Trout Mask Replica* – produced by Zappa

Jul 28 Led Zeppelin's notorious *Edgewater Inn Mud Shark Incident*...

...immortalised in Zappa's song, *The Mud Shark*

Aug 20 disbanded the original Mothers of Invention

Sep 13 offered advice to Alice Cooper after the notorious *Chicken Incident*

Sep 29 G.T.O.'s issued *Circular Circulation* on Straight label – Zappa mentored them...

...G.T.O.'s backed by Mothers of Invention musicians:

Roy Estrada – Jimmy Carl Black – Ian Underwood – Don Preston

1970 May 15 orchestral premiere of *200 Motels* – with the LA Philharmonic Orchestra...

...lineup included:

Ray Collins: vocals – from the Soul Giants and original Mothers
Don Preston: keyboards – Mothers of Invention regular

Motorhead Sherwood: saxophone – Mothers of Invention regular
Billy Mundi: drums – Mothers of Invention regular
Ian Underwood: multi-instrumentalist – 1967 to 1973
Jeff Simmons: bass, guitar and vocals – early 1970s
Aynsley Dunbar: drums – from early 1970 to mid-1972

	Dec 25	Little Feat's debut concert – Lowell George left Zappa in '69 to form Little Feat...
		...lineup included:
		Roy Estrada: bass – from Zappa's original Soul Giants and Mothers
		...band's name inspired by Jimmy Carl Black's comment about George's feet
1971	Mar 11	*Whipping Post* performed by the Allman Brothers – recorded by Zappa in 1984
	Jun 6	jammed with John Lennon and Yoko Ono at the Fillmore East
	Dec 4	fire at Montreux Casino concert – inspired Deep Purple's *Smoke on the Water*
	Dec 10	pushed off the stage and seriously injured
1976	Aug 9	producer and performer: Grand Funk Railroad issued *Good Singin' Good Playin'*
1985	Sep 19	addressed Congress and spoke out against censorship in music

Warren Zevon

1947	Jan 24	keyboardist, guitarist, singer and songwriter, born in Chicago, Illinois

The Zombies

1964	Dec 25	1st US concert appearance, on *Murray the K's Christmas Show*...
		...lineup included:
		Rod Argent: keyboardist, founding member – formed in the early '60s
		Colin Blunstone: vocals and founding member

ZZ Top

		Inducted into the Rock and Roll Hall of Fame in 2004
1949	Dec 16	Billy Gibbons: guitarist and singer, born in Houston, Texas...
		...previously founding member of the Moving Sidewalks, 1966 to '69
1970	Feb 10	debut gig – but international success eluded them until the next decade

References and Sources

References

Where the reference is for a quotation, it is provided with the kind permission of the stated source. Other references give the provenance of factual information.

1. May 29 Keith Moon put himself out of action
   Book: *Dear Boy: The Life of Keith Moon* page 186

2. May 15 President Nixon commenting on his Vietnam War strategy
   Website: *The American Presidency Project*
   248 – The President's News Conference
   www.presidency.ucsb.edu/ws/index.php?pid=2106#axzz1lsnjvTY4 (9 Feb 2012)

3. Feb 25 cast of Jimi Hendrix's stimulating encounter with Cynthia Plaster Caster
   Website: *Cynthia P Caster Foundation*
   www.cynthiapcaster.org/casts/_dicks/casts_hendrix_page/hendrix_page.htm (6 Feb 2012)

4. Apr 8 Engelbert Humperdinck spent six weeks at #1 with *Release Me*
   Book: *20 Years of British Records Charts 1955-1975* page 122

5. Sep 27 poster advertising a Led Zeppelin concert
   Surrey University poster, 25 October
   Website: *Led Zeppelin*
   www.ledzeppelin.com/show/october-25-1968 (13 Jul 2013)

6. Jun 6 Frank Zappa performance with John Lennon
   Book: *Frank Zappa* page 214

7. Mar 24 *Dark Side Of The Moon* album chart duration
   Website: *Billboard*
   www.billboard.com/bbcom/news/article_display.jsp?vnu_content_id=1002463719#/bbcom/news/article_display.jsp?vnu_content_id=1002463719 (3 Nov 2012)

8. Oct 2 Elvis Presley's appearance at the Grand Ole Opry
   Book: *Sun King: The Life and Times of Sam Phillips: The Man Behind Sun Records* page 82

9. Apr 8 Engelbert Humperdinck spent 56 weeks on the charts with *Release Me*
   Book: *British Hit Singles: Edition 6* page 122

10. Sep 27 poster advertising a Led Zeppelin concert
Middle Earth at the Roundhouse poster, 9 November
Website: *Led Zeppelin*
www.ledzeppelin.com/show/november-9-1968 (13 Jul 2013)

11. Jul 3 Jim Morrison, cause of death
Website: *Find a Death*
www.findadeath.com/Deceased/m/Jim%20Morrison/Morrison%20DC%20English.JPG
(27 Jan 2012)

12. Sep 5 early Keith Moon audition for BBC Radio
Book: *Anyway Anyhow Anywhere: The Complete Chronicle of the Who 1958 – 1978* page 11

13. Mar 31 President Johnson announced that he was stepping down
Website: *The American Presidency Project*
170 – The President's Address to the Nation Announcing Steps To Limit the War in Vietnam and Reporting His Decision Not To Seek Reelection
www.presidency.ucsb.edu/ws/index.php?pid=28772&st=&st1=#axzz10KzmFEGY (6 Mar 2012)

14. Aug 30 Sam Phillips's first record label, It's The Phillips
Book: *Sun King: The Life and Times of Sam Phillips: The Man Behind Sun Records* page 26

15. Feb 13 sales of *Frampton Comes Alive!* album
Website: *Peter Frampton*
www.frampton.com/70.html (11 Feb 2012)

16. Feb 24 results for the 1983 Bermondsey by-election
Website: *Richard Kimber's Political Science Resources*
www.politicsresources.net/area/uk/ge66/i11.htm (12 Feb 2012)

17. Mar 19 Carl Perkins's description of rockabilly music
Book: *Good Rockin' Tonight: Sun Records and the Birth of Rock'n'Roll* page 128

18. Jul 18 Bobby Fuller, cause of death
Website: *Find a Death*
www.findadeath.com/Deceased/F/Bobby%20Fuller/dc.jpg (1 Feb 2012)

19. Mar 10 President Ford's speech at Tulane University
Website: *The American Presidency Project*
208 – Address at a Tulane University Convocation
www.presidency.ucsb.edu/ws/index.php?pid=4859&st=&st1=#axzz1mSgqrpFI (3 Nov 2012)

20. Jan 6 Elvis censored on *The Ed Sullivan Show*
Website: *The Official Ed Sullivan Site*
www.edsullivan.com/artists/elvis-presley (1 Feb 2012)

21. Jan 20 Radio Station KWK's "Record Breaking Week"
Website: *FM106 KWK AM13.8: The Rockin' Best!*
www.kwk106.com/history.htm (1 Feb 2012)

22. Mar 11 Bobby Graham's 15,000 recordings
Website: *The Legendary Bobby Graham*
www.bobbygraham.co.uk/bobbygraham/discography.htm (3 Nov 2012)

23. Nov 20 Duane Allman #2 in the list of *The 100 Greatest Guitarists of All Time*
Magazine: *Rolling Stone:* issue #931: 18 Sep 2003 page 61

24. Nov 9 Poster for Led Zeppelin concert at Surry University, 25 Oct 1968
Website: *Led Zeppelin*
www.ledzeppelin.com/show/october-25-1968 (25 Mar 2013)

25. Jun 7 Pete Townshend's retort to a *Tommy* audience
Book: *Anyway Anyhow Anywhere: The Complete Chronicle of the Who 1958 – 1978* page 183

26. Mar 15 President Johnson, *Special Message to the Congress on the Right To Vote*
Website: *The American Presidency Project*
108 – Special Message to the Congress on the Right To Vote
www.presidency.ucsb.edu/ws/index.php?pid=26806&st=&st1#axzz1n5hoTu5C (28 Feb 2012)

27. Mar 17 Blues Incorporated, billed as the "First British R&B Band"
Advertisement: in *Jazz News* 14 Mar 1962

28. Dec 30 Marlon Brando quote from the movie *The Wild One*

29. Nov 2 Cliff Richard UK singles sales
Book: *The Virgin Book of British Hit Singles: Volume 2:*
Complete UK Chart Data from 1952-2010 page 395

30. Aug 31 Elvis Presley concert in Vancouver, 31 Aug 1957
Newspaper: *Vancouver Province*

31. Aug 3 Def Leppard's *Hysteria* album certified as 12xPlatinum, 17 Aug 1998
Website: *RIAA website* (5 Feb 2013)
http://riaa.com/goldandplatinumdata.php?content_selector=gold-platinum-searchable-database

32. May 10 Soul Giants became The Mothers
Book: *Frank Zappa* page 68

33. Aug 3 *Performance* theatrical trailer
Warner Bros Entertainment Inc. 1970

34. Jan 8 Elvis Presley bought his first guitar
Tupelo Hardware Company Inc.
Letter from Mr Forrest L Bobo, who served Elvis that day, recalling the occasion.
www.tupelohardware.com/guitar.php (3 Nov 2012)

35. Aug 3 Lenny Bruce's Death Certificate
Website: *Find a Death*
www.findadeath.com/Deceased/b/lenny/dc.jpg (4 Feb 2013)

36. Mar 23 President Kennedy's concerns about the "domino effect" of communism
Website: *The American Presidency Project*
92 – *The President's News Conference*
www.presidency.ucsb.edu/ws/index.php?pid=8547#axzz1neZovy4S (28 Feb 2012)

37. Jan 1 Carl Perkins made the top-3 on all three *Billboard* Charts
Top 40 Hits made #2 page 487
Book: *The Billboard Book of Top 40 Hits:* 8th Edition
Top 40 Country Hits made #1 page 266
Book: *The Billboard Book of Top 40 Country Hits:* Second Edition
Top 40 R&B Hits made #2 page 451
Book: *The Billboard Book of Top 40 R&B Hits:* 1st Edition

38. Mar 18 John Hiseman interview with Dmitry M Epstein
Website: *DME – Let It Rock*
http://dmme.net/interviews/hiseman1.html (2 Feb 2012)

39. Dec 24 Elvis Presley's proposed karate movie
Book: *Careless Love: The Unmaking of Elvis Presley* page 552

40. Feb 21 Bobby Graham, session drummer
Website: *The Legendary Bobby Graham*
www.bobbygraham.co.uk/bobbygraham/hits.htm (2 Feb 2012)

41. Apr 7 President Johnson's *Peace Without Conquest* speech
Website: *The American Presidency Project*
172 – *Address at Johns Hopkins University: "Peace Without Conquest"*
www.presidency.ucsb.edu/ws/index.php?pid=26877&st=&st1=#axzz1otpVHUME (12 Mar 2012)

42. Sep 9 Elvis's first appearance on *The Ed Sullivan Show*
Website: *The Official Ed Sullivan Site*
www.edsullivan.com/artists/elvis-presley (3 Feb 2012)

43. Jul 1 letter sacking Michelle Phillips from The Mamas & The Papas
Website: *Dream a Little Dream*
www.dennydoherty.com/dream/dream13.html (4 Aug 2011)

44. Feb 27 Eric Burdon's description of the *Mirage* project
Eric Burdon interview with Peter Doggett
Magazine: *Record Collector:* #209 January 1997 page 109

45. Jan 14 Elvis Presley's *Aloha From Hawaii* seen by 50% of the US TV audience
Website: *IMDb*
www.imdb.com/title/tt0167923/ (20 Mar 2012)

46. Dec 21 Elvis Presley's letter to President Nixon
Website: *The National Security Archive: The George Washington University*
www.gwu.edu/~nsarchiv/nsa/elvis/docs/doc1.pdf (4 Feb 2012)

47. Apr 30 Keith Moon's audition for the Who
Website: *The Who: the official home of The Who online*
www.thewho.com/tour/date/220 (2 Mar 2012)

48. Sep 18 Jimi Hendrix's death certificate
Website: *Find a Death*
www.findadeath.com/Deceased/h/Jimi%20Hendrix/jimidc.jpg (21 Sep 2011)

49. Mar 5 Jerry Lee Lewis review for *Catch My Soul*
Magazine: *Billboard:* 30 Mar 1968 page 28

50. Jul 3 Brian Jones's death certificate
Website: *Find a Death*
www.findadeath.com/Deceased/j/Brian%20Jones/dc.jpg (23 Sep 2011)

51. Oct 4 Janis Joplin's certificate of death
Website: *Find a Death*
www.findadeath.com/Deceased/j/Janis%20%20Joplin/Joplin%20DC.JPG (23 Sep 2011)

52. Feb 2 debut performance of the five Rolling Stones in the classic lineup
Website: *The Ultimate Guide to the Rolling Stones*
http://aeppli.ch/TUG08/CD1962-1965Up.pdf (25 Sep 2011)

53. Oct 23 Police concert attended by three people
Magazine: *Rolling Stone:* issue #501: 4 Jun 1987 page 103

54. Jan 14 Elvis Presley's *Aloha from Hawaii* seen by over 1 billion people
Website: *Elvis Presley: Official Site of the King of Rock'n'Roll*
www.elvis.com/news/detail.aspx?id=2081 (20 Mar 2012)

55. Jul 25 AC/DC album *Back in Black* certified 22xMulti-Platinum on 13 Dec 2007
Website: *RIAA* (30 Jan 2013)
www.riaa.com/goldandplatinumdata.php?content_selector=gold-platinum-searchable-database

56. Feb 1 Young Rascals announced that they would only perform when half of the acts were black
Magazine: *Rolling Stone:* issue #26: 1 Feb 1969 page 8

57. May 26 origin of Moondog's name
Website: *Moondog's Corner*
www.moondogscorner.de/frame.html (12 Oct 2011)

58. Nov 1 *Rolling Stone* magazine's Masked Marauders hoax
Magazine: *Rolling Stone:* issue #45: 1 Nov 1969 page 44

59. Jan 27 Vietnam Veterans Memorial Wall
Website: *The Vietnam Veterans Memorial*
thewall-usa.com/information.asp (21 Mar 2012)

60. Jan 18 requirement to play Canadian music on Canadian radio
Website: *Canadian Radio-television and Telecommunications Commission*
www.crtc.gc.ca/eng/info_sht/r1.htm (23 Nov 2011)

61. Apr 15 *Rolling Stone* magazine's Masked Marauders hoax
Magazine: *Rolling Stone:* issue #80: 15 Apr 1971 page 4

62. Jun 15 Jeff Beck Group at the Fillmore East
Magazine: *Rolling Stone:* issue #117: 14 Sep 1972 page 48

63. Jan 4 Elvis Presley's second private recording
Website: *Master and Session: Elvis Presley Studio Recordings*
www.elvisrecordings.com (5 Nov 2011)

64. Nov 9 *Rolling Stone* magazine hit the streets
Magazine: *Rolling Stone:* issue #1: 9 Nov 1967 page 2

65. Jan 30 Kiss record sales of over 100 million
Website: *Kiss*
www.kissonline.com/history (21 Mar 2012)

66. Feb 5 Hal Blaine's track record
Website: *Hal Blaine*
www.halblaine.com/discography (21 Mar 2012)

67. Feb 9 73 million people watched the Beatles on the *Ed Sullivan Show*
Website: *The Official Ed Sullivan Site*
www.edsullivan.com/the-beatles-on-the-ed-sullivan-show-on-february-9-1964 (21 Mar 2012)

68. Nov 28 Chris Barber's Jazz Band and Sister Rosetta Tharpe, tour programme
Website: *Chris Barber*
www.chrisbarber.net/tours4/tharpe-1957-03.htm (23 Nov 2011)

69. Oct 28 origin of Wayne Fontana's stage name
Website: *Wayne Fontana*
www.waynefontanauk.com (24 Nov 2011)

70. Jul 12 drummer Mick Avory never played a gig with the Rollin' Stones
Website: *The Kast Off Kinks*
http://kastoffkinks.co.uk/Mick%20Avory%20interview%20part%201.htm (6 Feb 2012)

71. Jul 12 drummer Mick Avory played with the Rollin' Stones at their debut in 1962
Website: *The Rolling Stones*
www.rollingstones.com/release/12th-july-1962/ (21 Sep 2013)

72. Feb 14 recordings by session guitarist Big Jim Sullivan
Website: *Big Jim Sullivan*
www.bigjimsullivan.com/History.html (22 Mar 2012)

73. Feb 17 cost of recording the Beach Boys' *Good Vibrations*
Website: *1,000 Recordings to Hear Before You Die*
www.1000recordings.com/music/good-vibrations (22 Mar 2012)

74. Feb 12 Allman Brothers album *Eat A Peach*
Magazine: Ellen Mandel in *Good Times:* 1971
Reprinted in *Guitar World:* November 1991

75. Feb 13 Alexis Corner's *Blues from the Roundhouse* album, limited edition of 99
Book: *Record Collector Rare Record Price Guide 2008:* page 667

76. Feb 26 Fats Domino sold over 65 million records
Website: *Rolling Stone*
www.rollingstone.com/music/artists/fats-domino/biography (3 Nov 2012)

77. Feb 26 sales of 45s exceeded that of 78s
Magazine: *Billboard:* 26 Feb 1955: page 27

78. Apr 20 Enoch Powel's "rivers of blood" speech
Website: *Enoch Powell: Life and Views*
www.enochpowell.net/fr-79.html (28 Mar 2012)

79. Apr 12 sales of *Rock Around The Clock* exceeded 25 million
Website: *Rockabilly Hall of Fame*
www.rockabillyhall.com/RockClockTribute.html (28 Mar 2012)

80. Mar 4 Maureen Cleave's original interview with John Lennon
How Does A Beatle Live? John Lennon Lives Like This: an article by Maureen Cleave
Newspaper: *London Evening Standard:* 4 Mar 1966

81. Apr 15 $53m of aid from America to Cuba after the *Bay of Pigs* invasion of Cuba
Website: *John F Kennedy: Presidential Library and Museum*
www.jfklibrary.org/JFK/JFK-in-History/The-Bay-of-Pigs.aspx (29 Mar 2012)

82. Apr 16 Ramones debut album cost $6,000 to make
Website: *1,000 Recordings to Hear Before You Die*
www.1000recordings.com/music/ramones/ (3 Nov 2012)

83. May 26 Eagles were the first band to charge more than $100 for a concert ticket
Newspaper: *U-T San Diego*
www.signonsandiego.com/uniontrib/20081214/news_1a14tickets.html (10 Apr 2012)

84. Jun 8 President Nixon announced the first US troop withdrawals from Vietnam
Website: *The American Presidency Project*
231- Remarks Following Initial Meeting With President Thieu at Midway Island
www.presidency.ucsb.edu/ws/index.php?pid=2088&st=&st1=#axzz1s1ChoijD (14 Apr 2012)

85. Dec 7 Bill Wyman's audition for the Rolling Stones
Book: *Bill Wyman's Blues Odyssey:* page 321

86. Jun 11 President Kennedy announced that he would introduce a *Civil Rights Bill*
Website: *The American Presidency Project*
237 – Radio and Television Report to the American People on Civil Rights
www.presidency.ucsb.edu/ws/index.php?pid=9271&st=&st1=#axzz1s7CKqshj (15 Apr 2012)

87. Oct 31 President Johnson announced an end to the bombing of North Vietnam
Website: *The American Presidency Project*
572 – The President's Address to the Nation
www.presidency.ucsb.edu/ws/index.php?pid=29218&st=&st1= (3 Nov 2012)

88. Nov 9 Led Zeppelin's Roundhouse concert poster for 9 Nov 1968
Website: *Led Zeppelin*
www.ledzeppelin.com/show/november-9-1968 (25 Mar 2013)

89. Dec 14 *The 100 Best Albums of the Eighties*
Magazine: *Rolling Stone:* issue #565: 16 Nov 1989 page 54

90. Dec 22 end of the American positive rhetoric about winning the Vietnam War
Website: *The American Presidency Project*
567 – Remarks to Service Personnel and Award of Distinguished Service Medal and Medal of Freedom to Military and Civilian Leaders, Cam Ranh Bay, Vietnam
www.presidency.ucsb.edu/ws/index.php?pid=28635 (12 Nov 2012)

91. Jun 25 statistics for the Berlin Airlift
Website: *Stars and Stripes*
http://www.stripes.com/blogs/archive-photo-of-the-day/archive-photo-of-the-day-1.9717/first-berlin-airlift-crash-1948-1.170156 (15 Feb 2013)

92. Jun 9 Jerry Lee Lewis's *Open Letter to the Industry*
Magazine: *The Billboard:* 9 Jun 1958 page 11

93. Jul 22 first release of the album *Introducing the Beatles*
Book: *The Complete Beatles Recording Sessions* page 201

94. Mar 28 Eddie Cochran's hit singles
Website: *Remember Eddie Cochran*
www.eddiecochran.info/Biography/Biography.htm (8 Feb 2013)

95. Aug 25 riots in Chicago, 1968
Website: *Chicago History Museum*
www.chicagohs.org/history/politics/1968.html (12 Feb 2013)

96. Sep 3 Ho Chi Minh's *Testament*, 10 May 1969
Website: *Communist Party of Vietnam Online Newspaper* (15 Feb 2013)
http://dangcongsan.vn/cpv/Modules/News_English/News_Detail_E.aspx?CN_ID=89253&CO_ID=30036

97. Nov 16 Conway Twitty albums recorded and #1 hits
Website: *Conway Twitty*
http://conwaytwitty.com (28 Mar 2013)

98. Nov 30 FBI report from the investigation into *Louie Louie*
Website: *The FBI Federal Bureau of Investigation*
http://vault.fbi.gov/louie-louie-the-song/louie-louie-the-song/view (5 Apr 2013)

99. Nov 30 cover versions of *Louie Louie*
Website: *Louie Louie.Net*
www.louielouie.net (5 Apr 2013)

100. Dec 4 Frank Zappa lost $50,000 worth of equipment in the *Smoke on the Water* fire
Book: *Frank Zappa* page 221

101. Dec 9 Beatles concert attended by just 18 people
Book: *The Beatles Diary: An Intimate Day by Day History* page 41

102. Dec 26 Paul McCartney borrowed a baseline from Chuck Berry
Book: *The Beatles: The Story Behind the Songs 1962 -1966* page 18

103. Feb 25 stimulating encounters with The Plaster Casters of Chicago
Website: *Cynthia P Caster Foundation*
www.cynthiaplastercaster.com/flash/home.html (16 May 2013)

104. Aug 17 "Beetles" to "Beatles" inspired by Royston Ellis
Website: *Royston Ellis, the British Beat Poet* (4 Jun 2013)
http://roystonellisbeatpoet.blogspot.ae/2009/04/royston-ellis-beatles-june-1960-then.html

105. Jan 27 Vietnam War statistics
Website: *The American Legion*
www.alpost66.org/misc/vietnam-vet.htm (15 Jun 2013)

106. May 12 *A Whiter Shade of Pale* was the most played song
Website: *BBC*
http://news.bbc.co.uk/2/hi/entertainment/7996979.stm (3 Jul 2013)

107. Aug 11 statistics resulting from the Watts Riots
Website: *USC: University of Southern California*
www.usc.edu/libraries/archives/cityinstress/mccone/part4.html (10 Sep 2013)

108. Jan 23 Richard Nixon "Peace With Honor" speech
Website: *The American Presidency Project*
12 – Address to the Nation Announcing Conclusion of an Agreement on Ending the War and Restoring Peace in Vietnam
www.presidency.ucsb.edu/ws/index.php?pid=3808#axzz1fXsCrQ30 (4 Dec 2011)

109. Jul 29 "Mama Cass" Elliot, cause of death
Website: *Find a Death*
www.findadeath.com/Deceased/e/Cass%20Elliot/DC.JPG (6 Apr 2014)

110. Oct 8 Sex Pistols: contracts with EMI and A&M
Magazine: *Record Collector:* #87 November 1986 page 31

Books Referenced

Reference #

1 *Dear Boy: The Life of Keith Moon*
Tony Fletcher, 2005: Omnibus Press

4 *20 Years of British Records Charts 1955-1975*
Edited by Tony Jasper, 1976: London, Queen Anne Press Limited

6 – 32 – 100 *Frank Zappa*
Barry Miles, 2004: Great Britain, Atlantic Books

8 – 14 *Sun King: The Life and Times of Sam Phillips: The Man Behind Sun Records*
Kevin and Tanja Crouch, 2009: Great Britain, Piatkus

9 *British Hit Singles: Edition 6*
Paul Gambaccini, Tim Rice and Jo Rice, Edition 6, 1987: Great Britain, GRR Publications Ltd. and Guinness Superlatives Ltd 1987

12 – 25 *Anyway Anyhow Anywhere: The Complete Chronicle of the Who 1958 – 1978*
Andy Neill & Matt Kent, 2005: New York, Sterling Publishing Co. Inc.

17 *Good Rockin' Tonight: Sun Records and the Birth of Rock'n'Roll*
Colin Escott with Martin Hawkins, 1991: New York, St. Martin's Press

29 *The Virgin Book of British Hit Singles: Volume 2: Complete UK Chart Data from 1952-2010*
Entry Biographies by Dave McAleer, Andy Gregory and Matthew White, 2010: Virgin Books / Random House Group Company

37 *The Billboard Book of Top 40 Hits:* 8th Edition
Joel Whitburn, 2004: New York, Billboard Books

37 *The Billboard Book of Top 40 Country Hits*: Second Edition
Joel Whitburn 2006: New York, Billboard Books

37 *The Billboard Book of Top 40 R&B Hits:* 1st Edition
Joel Whitburn, 2006: New York, Billboard Books

39 *Careless Love: The Unmaking of Elvis Presley*
Peter Guralnick, 2000: USA, Little, Brown and Company

75 *Record Collector Rare Record Price Guide 2008*
Editor Ian Shirley, 2006: United Kingdom, Diamond Publishing Ltd

85 *Bill Wyman's Blues Odyssey*
Bill Wyman with Richard Havers, 2001: London, Dorling Kindersley Limited

93 *The Complete Beatles Recording Sessions*
Mark Lewisohn, 2004: Great Britain, Hamlyn

101 *The Beatles Diary: An Intimate Day by Day History*
Barry Miles, 2007: East Bridgwater, MA, World Publications Group Inc.

102 *The Beatles: The Story Behind the Songs 1962 – 1966*
Steve Turner, 2009: Carlton Books Limited

Magazines Referenced

Reference

23 – 53 – 56 *Rolling Stone* (US)

58 – 61 – 62 *Rolling Stone Cover To Cover* 4xDVD, 1967 to 2007

64 – 89 Also the website www.rollingstone.com

44 – 75 – 110 *Record Collector* (UK)

Personal collection (almost all copies) from: July 1980 to #281 January 2003

49 – 77 – 92 *Billboard* (US)

The magazines were accessed online at:
http://books.google.com/books?id=HA4EAAAAMBAJ&dq=Audrey+Schulz&ie=ISO-8859-1&source=gbs_gdata

Other books frequently used for background research included:

The Beatles and Some Other Guys: Rock Family Trees of the Early Sixties
Pete Frame, 1977: Great Britain, Omnibus Press

The Beatles Anthology
The Beatles, 2000: United Kingdom, Cassell & Co

The Complete Beatles Chronicle
Mark Lewisohn, 2003: London, Hamlyn

Doo Wop the Music, the Times, the Era
"Cousin Brucie" Morrow with Rich Maloof, First Edition, 2007: New York, Sterling Publishing Co. Inc.

Bob Dylan
Anthony Scaduto, 1972: Great Britain, WH Allen & Co. Ltd.

The Elvis Encyclopedia
Adam Victor, 2008: Australia, Murdoch Books

Elvis: The Ultimate Guide to Elvis Presley's British Record Releases 1956 – 86
John Townson, Gordon Minto & George Richardson, 1987: Poole, Dorset, Blandford Press

Goldmine Record Album Price Guide: 4th Edition
Tim Neely, 2005: USA, KP Books

Goldmine Price Guide to 45rpm Records: 5th Edition
Tim Neely, 2005: USA, KP Books

Hammer of the Gods
Stephen Davis, 2008: London, Pan Macmillan Publishers Ltd

Legacy of Ashes: The History of the CIA
Tim Weiner, 2008: USA, First Anchor Books Edition 2008

London Live
Tony Bacon, 1999: San Francisco, Miller Freeman Books

The Record Producers
John Tobler & Stuart Grundy, 1982: London, British Broadcasting Corporation

Rock Family Trees
Pete Frame, 1980: Great Britain, Omnibus Press

Survivor: The Authorised Biography of Eric Clapton
Ray Coleman, 1985: Great Britain, Sidgwick and Jackson Limited

Tearing Down the Wall of Sound: The Rise and Fall of Phil Spector
Mick Brown, 2007: Great Britain, Bloomsbury Publishing Plc.

Web Sites

During my research I accessed literally thousands of websites, sadly, a great deal of the information available on the internet is contradictory and inaccurate. In order to be as rigorous as possible the facts have been comprehensively cross-referenced, with specialist web sites used wherever possible.

Other web sites frequently accessed for background research included:

The Beatles	www.beatlesagain.com
	www.beatlesbible.com
	www.dmbeatles.com
	www.jpgr.co.uk
The Byrds	www.ebni.com/byrds
Deep Purple	www.deep-purple.net
Bob Dylan	www.bjorner.com/bob.htm
	www.searchingforagem.com
Jimi Hendrix	www.earlyhendrix.com

Elvis Presley	www.elvispresleymusic.com.au
	www.keithflynn.com
The Rolling Stones	www.nzentgraf.de
	www.timeisonourside.com
Frank Zappa	http://globalia.net/donlope/fz/
Background (Music)	http://albumlinernotes.com
	www.allmusic.com
	http://thebritishsound.blogspot.com
	www.uncamarvy.com
Concerts & Venues	www.bradfordtimeline.co.uk/music.htm
	www.chromeoxide.com/sitemap.htm
Discographies	www.boija.com
	www.discogs.com
	www.45cat.com
	www.softshoe-slim.com
	www.wirz.de/music/howlwfrm.htm
Recording Sessions	http://members.home.nl/henk.gorter/ltcindex.html
	www.706unionavenue.nl/64258499
Rock and Roll Hall of Fame	http://rockhall.com
Television & Radio	www.tv.com
	http://epguides.com